W9-BAS-155

A12703 286554

AN ENCYCLOPEDIA OF
BRITISH WOMEN WRITERS

GARLAND REFERENCE LIBRARY
OF THE HUMANITIES
(*Vol. 818*)

AN ENCYCLOPEDIA OF

British
Women
Writers

edited by

Paul Schlueter
June Schlueter

BRADLEY UNIVERSITY LIBRARY

Garland Publishing, Inc.
NEW YORK & LONDON   1988

© 1988 Paul Schlueter and June Schlueter

All rights reserved

Library of Congress Cataloging-in-Publication Data

Schlueter, Paul, 1933–
  Encyclopedia of British women writers / Paul Schlueter, June
Schlueter.
      p.   cm. — (Garland reference library of the humanities ; vol.
818)
  Includes index.
  ISBN 0-8240-8449-7 (alk. paper)
  1. English literature—Women authors—Dictionaries. 2. Women
authors. English—Biography—Dictionaries. 3. English literrture—
Women authors—Bibliography. I. Schlueter, June. II. Title.
III. Series.
PR111.S34 1988
820′.9′9287—dc19   88-21393
                                                             CIP

Printed on acid-free, 250-year-life paper

MANUFACTURED IN THE UNITED STATES OF AMERICA

Ref
PR
111
.E54
1988

TO
Frederick Ungar
Publisher and Friend

When the column of light on the waters is glassed,
As blent in one glow seem the shine and the stream;
But wave after wave through the glory has passed,
Just catches, and flies as it catches, the beam:
So honors but mirror on mortals their light;
Not the man but the place that he passes is bright.

—Schiller

MAY   2 1990

CONTENTS

PREFACE

An Encyclopedia of British Women Writers was originally intended as a companion to the four-volume *American Women Writers*, ed. Lina Mainiero (Ungar, 1979), which contained entries for 1,000 writers, and its two-volume abridgement, ed. Langdon Faust (Ungar, 1983). For a variety of reasons, the book changed focus as work on it progressed, and changed publishers as well. But the book still owes its stimulus and direction to Frederick Ungar, to whom it is dedicated.

Not the least of the problems that had to be resolved with this *Encyclopedia* was the thorny and somewhat arbitrary one of what constitutes a *British* woman writer. True, this problem also exists with a work devoted to American writers, but not nearly to the same extent. We found we couldn't depend upon place of birth as a criterion, since so much trans-Atlantic migration (in both directions) has occurred. Hence we do not include, for example, Anne Bradstreet or Denise Levertov, both of whom were born in the United Kingdom; both are usually considered American writers and as such are normally catalogued in works on American literature. Contrarily, Sylvia Plath, though born in the United States, moved to England, where she lived and died. She too is usually considered American. But Anne Stevenson, also an American by birth (to American parents residing in Great Britain) but long resident in England, seems more appropriately British than American.

It is also difficult to know how long a writer must live in a country to fit within one category or the other. For example, several writers included in this work—Frances Wright, Ann Raney Thomas Coleman, Mina Loy, Jan Struther, several others—lived in the United States for major portions of their mature lives, and while some of these writers are also included in reference works devoted to American writers, it is legitimate to include them in a work on British literature.

Even more problematic, perhaps, is the distinction between a *British* writer and an *English* one. We deliberately chose the former, more inclusive term because a number of significant writers have come from parts of the British Isles other than England. And even though Ireland has been independent since 1922, we have also drawn freely from among Irish writers born before independence and have selectively included some since that date, especially because some of these (e.g., Julia O'Faolain, Edna O'Brien) have long been resident in Great Britain. Similarly, writers from various parts of the British Commonwealth are also included if a major portion of their lives and careers was spent in Great Britain. For example, several writers from Oceania are included, such as Mary Golding Bright (George Egerton), Katherine Mansfield, Christina Stead, and Ngaio Marsh, even though Marsh re-emigrated to her native New Zealand before she died.

There is no way any single reference work such as this could include every writer who might qualify. For one thing, some early figures are so shadowy or elusive that little more than a name exists; these could include the possibly apocryphal Nossis (fl. 3rd c. B.C.), Liadain (fl. 7th c.), and Gormlaith (d. 947 or 948). Clearly nothing could be gained by attempting to include such writers. We have tried, however, to include as many medieval and Renaissance women as possible, even though usually little is known of their lives, and their writing, given the circumstances under which they lived, usually consists only of journals or letters. The majority of the nearly 400 entries in this *Encyclopedia* are necessarily from the eighteenth century or later. Since there are reference works that have a selection of women writers from the eighteenth and nineteenth centuries, we have tried to include as many twentieth-century writers as possible, including some found in very few other reference books.

Our procedure in preparing this book is simple in the telling, though much more complicated in the effort. Each contributor provided as complete a set of biographical data as possible; in the cases of some contemporary figures the writers were contacted directly to clear up omissions and ambiguities. Hence the entries on Christine Brooke-Rose, Anne Stevenson, and Fay Weldon, among others, are as authoritative as possible since the authors shared information with us and our contributors that corrects data found in other reference works. In some cases, however, even with writers still living, there is simply no way of tracking down dates of birth, for example, or dates of marriage, or even places of birth or death. We have retrieved as much information as possible, so an omission simply indicates that the data aren't available. Until Olivia Manning died, for instance, no reference work even included a guess as to her year of birth; since her death in 1980, however, one now finds either 1911 or 1915 (both with a

	Waller (Cambridge: Cambridge University Press, 1907–1933)
CLC	*Contemporary Literary Critics*, ed. Elmer Borklund (New York: St. Martin's, 1977, 1982)
CN	*Contemporary Novelists*, ed. James Vinson (New York: St. Martin's, 1972, 1976, 1982)
ConSFA	*Contemporary Science Fiction Authors*, ed. Robert Reginald (New York: Arno, 1975; previously published as *Stella Nova: Contemporary Science Fiction Authors* [Los Angeles: Unicorn & Son, 1970])
CP	*Contemporary Poets*, ed. James Vinson (New York: St. Martin's, 1970, 1975, 1980, 1985)
Cromek	*Select Scottish Songs, Ancient and Modern*, ed. R. H. Cromek (Edinburgh: Cadell and Davies, 1810)
DAB	*Dictionary of American Biography*, ed. American Council of Learned Societies (New York: Scribner, 1928–)
DBPP	*Dictionary of Biography, Past and Present*, ed. Benjamin Vincent (London: Ward, Lock, 1877; Detroit: Gale, 1974)
DIB	*Dictionary of Irish Biography*, ed. Henry Boylan (Dublin: Gill and Macmillan; New York: Barnes & Noble, 1978)
DIL	*Dictionary of Irish Literature*, ed. Robert Hogan (Westport, Conn.: Greenwood, 1979)
DLB	*Dictionary of Literary Biography* (Detroit: Gale, 1978–)
DLEL	*Dictionary of Literature in the English Language from 1940 to 1970*, ed. Robin Myers (Oxford: Pergamon, 1978)
DNB	*Dictionary of National Biography* (London: Macmillan, 1885–)
ELB	*Everyman's Dictionary of Literary Biography, English and American*, ed. D. C. Browning (New York: Dutton, 1960)
EMD	*Encyclopedia of Mystery and Detection*, ed. Cris Steinbrunner and Otto Penzler (New York: McGraw-Hill, 1976)
Europa	*Europa Biographical Dictionary of British Women*, ed. Anne Crawford and others (London: Europa, 1983)
EWLTC	*Encyclopedia of World Literature in the 20th Century*, rev. ed., ed. Leonard Klein (New York: Ungar, 1981)
IDWB	*International Dictionary of Women's Biography*, ed. Jennifer Uglow (New York: Continuum, 1982) (also published as *Macmillan Dictionary of Women's Biography*; London: Macmillan, 1982)
Junior Bk of Authors	*Junior Book of Authors*, ed. Stanley J. Kunitz

and Howard Haycraft (New York: Wilson, 1934, 1951)

LLC   *Library of Literary Criticism*, ed. Ruth Z. Temple and Martin Tucker (New York: Ungar, 1966)

Longman   *Longman Companion to Twentieth Century Literature*, ed. A. C. Ward (London: Longman, 1970; 2nd ed. [ed. Christopher Gillie], London: Longman, 1977)

MBL   *Modern British Literature*, ed. Ruth Z. Temple and Martin Tucker (New York: Ungar, 1966)

MBL SUP   *Modern British Literature Supplement*, ed. Martin Tucker and Rita Stein (New York: Ungar, 1975)

MCL   *Modern Commonwealth Literature*, ed. John H. Ferres and Martin Tucker (New York: Ungar, 1977)

Modern World Theatre   *Modern World Theatre: A Guide to Productions in Europe and the United States Since 1945*, ed. Siegfried Kienzle, trans. Alexander and Elizabeth Henderson (New York: Ungar, 1970)

Moulton   *Moulton's Library of Literary Criticism of English and American Authors through the Beginning of the 20th Century*, ed. Martin Tucker (New York: Ungar, 1966)

MWD   *Modern World Drama: An Encyclopedia*, ed. Myron Matlaw (New York: Dutton, 1972)

NCBEL   *New Cambridge Bibliography of English Literature*, ed. George Watson (Cambridge: Cambridge University Press, 1969)

NCHEL   *New Century Handbook of English Literature*, rev. ed., ed. C. L. Barnhart and William D. Halsey (New York: Appleton-Century-Crofts, 1967)

NCLC   *Nineteenth Century Literary Criticism*, ed. L. L. Harry and others (Detroit: Gale, 1981–)

OCCL   *Oxford Companion to Children's Literature*, ed. Humphrey Carpenter and Mari Pritchard (New York: Oxford University Press, 1984)

OCEL   *Oxford Companion to English Literature*, rev. ed., ed. Margaret Drabble (New York: Oxford University Press, 1985)

RE   *Reader's Encyclopedia*, ed. W. R. Benet (New York: Crowell, 1948, 1965; London: Black, 1987)

Roberton   *The Novel Reader's Handbook: A Brief Guide to Recent Novels and Novelists*, ed. William Roberton (Birmingham: Holland, 1899)

SATA   *Something About the Author*, ed. Anne Commire (Detroit: Gale, 1971–)

SF&FL   *Science Fiction and Fantasy Literature*, ed. Robert Reginald (Detroit: Gale, 1979)

Todd   *A Dictionary of British and American*

	ture and Language)	*WSCL*	*Wisconsin Studies in Contemporary Literature* (now *Contemporary Literature*)
VS	*Victorian Studies*		
WL	*Women and Literature*		
WLT	*World Literature Today*	*WVPP*	*West Virginia University Philological Papers*
WLWE	*World Literature Written in English*		
		ZAA	*Zeitschrift für Anglistik und Amerikanistik*
WS	*Women's Studies*		

The Encyclopedia

Jean Adam(s)

BORN: 1710, Crawfordsdyke in Renfrewshire, Scotland.
DIED: 3 April 1765.
WROTE UNDER: Mrs. Jane Adams.

The daughter of a shipmaster, A. became a poet, schoolmistress, and nursery governess. A.'s career began with opportunity and support. Orphaned young and employed as nursery governess and housemaid to a Mr. Turner, a minister, A. educated herself in the library of her employer. Here she wrote poems which were collected by a Mrs. Drummond of Greenock, who published *Miscellany Poems, by Mrs. Jane Adams, in Crawfordsdyke*, in Glasgow in 1734. A. dedicated the collection to Thomas Crawford of Crawfordburn. Among the 154 subscribers to the indexed volume of religious poetry were ministers, merchants, and gentry.

Except for Archibald Crawford, who wrote the preface, critics have shown no interest in A.'s poetry in general. Her published poetry, mostly didactic and religious in tone, shows A.'s loving scrutiny of human nature. Of the power of refined and directed passion, she laments that anger might be directed at good instead of evil: "Why should a Virtue make it self a Lust?" Nor should grief be wasted: "It is a shame below our Kind to stoop,/More Glory 'tis to imitate the Top." The attribution of "There's nae Luck aboot the House" or "Song of the Mariner's Wife," however, has at times been of interest. A.'s associates attributed this lyric poem, said to have been heard on the streets by Robert Burns, to her.

In the girls' school she founded at the quay head at Crawford's bridge, she was known for her emotive readings of Shakespeare. In spite of her pedagogical pyrotechnics, even swooning while reading *Othello*, A. closed her school for six weeks to walk to London to visit Samuel Richardson whose *Clarissa* she admired.

Meanwhile, her poetry brought little profit; many copies, sent to Boston for distribution, have never been discovered. Finally, then, unable to depend on sales of her poetry, she closed the school and survived as a peddlar for years. She died in the poorhouse in Glasgow in 1765.

WORKS: Miscellany Poems, by Mrs. Jane Adams, in Crawfordsdyke (1734). Chalmers, A., ed. The Works of the English Poets (1810). "Song of the Mariner's Wife" in Select Scottish Songs, Ancient and Modern, ed. R.H. Cromek (1810). Chambers, R., ed. Songs of Scotland Prior to Burns (1825). Cunningham, A., ed. Songs of Scotland (1825).

BIBLIOGRAPHY: Keddie, H. [pseud. Sarah Tytler] and J.L. Watson. Songstresses of Scotland (1871). N&Q (1866, 1869).
    For articles in reference works, see: Chambers, Chalmers. DNB. ELB. NCHEL. Todd.

Mary S. Comfort

Cecilia Mary Ady

BORN: 28 November 1881, Edgcote, Northamptonshire.
DIED: 27 March 1958, Oxford.
DAUGHTER OF: Henry Ady and Julia Cartwright.

A. was a scholar and historian of the Italian Renaissance, following in the steps of her mother, Julia Cartwright, the renowned writer of many popular books on the art and history of the Italian Renaissance. In 1881, the year in which A. was born, her mother's first book on art, *Mantegna and Francia*, was published. As a young child A. was taught her alphabet with the letter D representing the Italian writer Dante, and in 1903, the year in which she took her first class honors degree in History at Oxford University, her mother's most successful book, *Isabella d'Este*, the biography of a Renaissance princess, was published.

Julia Cartwright had decided much earlier to earn enough money from her writing to pay for the formal education she envisaged for A., who was finally to gain a place at what was then known as St. Hugh's Hall, Oxford. The 1880's had seen a new statute for women's exams passed at Oxford. Lady Margaret Hall had been founded in 1878 and St. Hugh's in 1886. Her mother's aspirations for the intellectual development of her daughter were realized, and A. obtained her M.A. and a D.Lit., but she never married nor had children. She became an academic and as such she was one of the first women to be awarded her degree at Oxford University. Her work concentrated on the study of the Renaissance in Italy, and her main interest lay in the signorial families and their influence on politics and society during the fifteenth century. She thus depicted the Sforza, the Medici, the Bentivoglio, and the ascent of a Piccolomini to the papacy.

Her first book, which appeared in 1907, was *History of Milan under the Sforza*. Her tutor, the historian Edward Armstrong, was then general editor of a series, *The States of Italy*, and encouraged her in this project. This book was followed in 1913 by *Pius II: The Humanist Pope*. Both these books remain of lasting value to scholars. In 1937 she published her most substantial book, *The Bentivoglio of Bologna*, and in 1955 she contributed *Lorenzo dei Medici and Renaissance Italy* to the *Teach Yourself History* series edited by A.L. Rowse. She also wrote sections for general history books such as *Italy, Mediaeval and Modern* (1917) and was invited to write a chapter in Volume VIII of the *Cambridge Modern History* (1930). Only one year prior to her death she contributed a chapter entitled "The Invasions of Italy" to the *New Cambridge Modern History*, Vol. I.

A. had a fine reputation not only as a scholar but as a teacher. She was tutor in modern history from 1909 to 1923 at St. Hugh's, but her involvement in the problems at the college arising from the psychical experience recounted anonymously (1911) in *An Adventure* by the then Principal, Miss Moberly, and the Vice-Principal, Miss Jourdain, led A. to leave her position. She then became tutor to the Society of Home Studies and only returned to her own college in 1929 as a Research Fellow, where on her retirement in 1951 she was elected to an Honorary Fellowship. She continued throughout her life to exert an influence on Italian studies, writing many articles as well as her books, and giving many papers at conferences all over the world. Her paper on the "Manners and Morals of the Quattrocento" was delivered in the midst of the war as the Annual Lecture of the British Academy.

English students of Renaissance Italy invariably came under her influence, for she wrote reviews of most of the books published on her subject. Her style was admired for its clarity and precision. She enjoyed teaching, and her orderly yet humorous approach was of great benefit to her students. Both her parents were pious people, her father a rector. She remained throughout her life a devoted churchwoman and wrote a booklet, "The Role of Women in the Church" (1948). As a moderate Anglo-Catholic believing in the spiritual independence of the Church of England, she showed a great respect for English local custom, tempered always with her breadth of historical outlook. It was the latter quality for which she was particularly respected, and at her death the volume *Italian Renaissance Studies*, ed. E.F. Jacob, was dedicated to her memory.

WORKS: *A History of Milan under the Sforza* (1907). *Pius II (Aeneas Silvius Piccolomini): The Humanist Pope* (1913). *The Contribution of Women to History in Some Aspects of the Woman's Movement* (1915). *Italy, Mediaeval and Modern: A History* (1915). *Outlines of European History*, Part 4: From 1494 to 1684 (1926). (trans.) *A History of Italy, 1871-1915* by B. Croce (1929). *The Bentivoglio of Bologna* (1937). *Morals and Manners of the Quattrocento* (1942). *Lorenzo dei Medici and Renaissance Italy* (1955).

See also *Italian Renaissance Studies*, ed., E.F. Jacob (1960).

Angela Emanuel

Grace Aguilar

BORN: 2 June 1816, Hackney, London.
DIED: 16 September 1847, Frankfurt, Germany.
DAUGHTER OF: Emanuel Aguilar and Sarah Dias Fernandes.

In the thirty-one brief years of her life, A. wrote twelve books (seven published posthumously) and a large volume of poetry, essays, and articles in journals in England and America. Her literary reputation was so widespread that many of her works were translated into foreign languages. But today almost no one has heard of her or of her works, and the only public reminder of her existence is the 110th Street Branch of The New York Public Library, one of five branches of the defunct Aguilar Free Library Society, which provided free books to immigrants to help them become assimilated in America.

Certainly it was most appropriate to honor A. in this manner because the earliest recognition given her work was as the popularizer of an alien culture. In a review of A.'s posthumous novel, *The Days of Bruce*, an historical romance, *Sharpe's Magazine* noted that while the book was "full of interest and the characters are well drawn . . . it is not equal to those productions of her pen, in which she is unrivalled because they illustrate a 'peculiar people.'" It was as a representative of that people that A. had first become known. Her religious writings were her first major works to be published, but her reputation grew with the publication of her novels.

A. was the first woman to write in English

about Judaism, her religion and the faith of her ancestors; her maternal great-grandfather, Benjamin Dias Fernandes, wrote religious polemics, but A.'s religious writings were not polemical but rather explanatory. It was her desire to dispel prejudice and the mistrust of her people by providing accurate depictions of Judaic beliefs and practices to the English reading public. She was particularly eager to provide this material in an era when Catholicism was becoming more acceptable in England following Catholic Emancipation in 1830. Her fears of Catholicism and Catholic influence on fiction were informed by the legacy of suppression and the secret practice of Judaism handed down to her from the Marranos, Spanish and Portuguese Jews forced by the Inquisition to relinquish their faith or risk being burnt alive. Heiress to this colonial tradition, she was doubly marginalized by being a Jew in a Christian world and a woman in a world dominated by patriarchal ideology.

Her most popular domestic novels, *Home Influence* (1847) and its sequel, *The Mother's Recompense* (1851), promulgated the Victorian ideals of motherhood and the limited freedom of women. The details of her own life contain both this tradition of suppression of women's identities and the strong religious involvement which helped to promote this suppression.

A.'s early life was spent in London, where her father was a merchant and an important figure in the Sephardic Jewish community and her mother ran a small private school for young boys with A.'s help. Since both parents were plagued by ill health, the family spent many of A.'s early years away from London in Devonshire, where A. first became acquainted with British Protestantism by attending services in churches of many denominations. This was one of the few elements of her education that occurred outside the home, since both parents tutored her in the classics and history. The level of her erudition is astonishing in the light of what Charles Dudley Warner characterized as "her peculiar sheltered training."

Even when she had attained a wide literary reputation, she was not allowed to travel outside the family circle. Her father's death in 1845 made

it necessary for the family to depend on her literary earnings for some of its support, while her two younger brothers, for whom she had written prayer books and whom she tutored, were permitted to seek careers away from the home; one of her brothers was a musician and composer and was educated abroad, and the other had a career in the British Navy. An archive of her letters in the Southern History Collection, University of North Carolina (available on microfilm through the American Jewish Archives), provides painful evidence of the confines within which she lived. Some of her mother's letters, also in this archive, show Sarah as the dominant influence on A.'s life. Like Mrs. Hamilton, the mother in *Home Influence* and *The Mother's Recompense*, Sarah Aguilar controlled her children's lives, the only socially acceptable use of power for women in the Victorian era.

A.'s final months were spent in Germany, where her mother had taken her to seek medical attention since she was always in frail health after having had the measles when she was 21. At the end she suffered violent spasms and lost all power of speech, but continued to communicate by using her fingers, with her last words being: "Though He may slay me, yet I will trust in Him."

WORKS: *The Magic Wreath* (anon., 1835). *The Spirit of Judaism* (1842). *Records of Israel* (1844). *Women of Israel* (1845). *The Jewish Faith* (1846). *History of the Jews in England* (1847). *Home Influence* (1847). *The Vale of Cedars* (1850). *The Mother's Recompense* (1851). *The Days of Bruce* (1852). *Women's Friendship* (1853). *Home Scenes and Heart Studies* (1853). *Sabbath Thoughts and Sacred Communings* (1853).

BIBLIOGRAPHY: Abrahams, B.-Z. *Transactions of the Jewish Historical Society of England* (1948). Hall, S.C. *Art Union Journal* (1852). Zeitlin, L.G., *The Nineteenth Century Anglo-Jewish Novel* (1981).

For articles in reference works, see: *BA19C.* *DNB.*

Gail Kraidman

Margery Allingham

BORN: 20 May 1904, London.
DIED: 30 June 1966, Colchester, Essex.
DAUGHTER OF: Herbert John and Emily Jane Hughes Allingham.
MARRIED: Philip Youngman Caret, 1927.

Although A. attended the Perse High School for Girls and the Polytechnic of Speech Training,

her real education occurred at home. Since her father was a serial writer and hack journalist as were many of his friends who continually visited the house, A. took writing as a profession for granted. Under her father's tutelage, A. began writing at seven and produced her first published novel at sixteen. That hack work and serial writing could be vehicles for serious expression as well as a means of livelihood she also learned at an early age. Her father's friend, G.R.M. Hearne, who wrote both Robin Hood and Sexton Blake adventures, gave her the following axiom: "They never mind you putting all you've got into this sort of stuff. They never pay you any more for it, but they don't stop you."

A.'s books before 1930 are strictly in the thriller genre, in which she said the plot must contain "as many colorful, exciting or ingenious inventions . . . [and] incidents . . . as one [can] lay hands on," and must contain "a surprise every tenth page and a shock every twentieth." For most of her writing career her protagonist is mild-mannered Albert Campion, a character in the Robin Hood mode of the hero-outlaw. Like Sayers and Christie (q.v.), A. transcends the sentimental nostalgia adhering to such a hero by the use of comedy: irony, wit, whimsy, puns, jokes, absurdities, burlesques, slapstick, and zany Wodehouseian repartee. Her mastermind criminals, for example, have names like Simister and Ali Fergusson Barber. Campion himself carries a water pistol rather than a gun; has a pet mouse named Haig; is always described as having an "idiotic" or "inane" expression; and permits his manservant, the ineffable and lugubrious Magersfontein Lugg, to answer the phone by announcing, "Aphrodite Glue Works."

With Police at the Funeral, A. left the thriller behind and entered the world of the detective novel proper, which she continued to explore in her novels of the 30s, moving from international intrigue and mastermind criminals to domestic crime in mansions full of brooding atmosphere; from picaresque construction to Arthur Conan Doyle plots, replete with disguised clues; and leaving behind the exotic and the supernatural. The early humor remains, but it is muted and understated.

Toward the end of the decade, A. finally engaged the theme she had been avoiding, love, thus moving away from both the thriller and the detective tale toward the components of the serious novel: character, description, and analysis. With Fashion in Shrouds, A.'s fiction reached maturity by achieving a meld of the thriller, the detective story, and the psychological novel. After the war, during which she was engaged in war work, including a non-fiction work, The Oaken Heart, she returned to this fusion in a series of delightful and considerable works of which the best is the Dickensian and ominous Tiger in the Smoke. Elegant writing coupled with wit, invention, and a sense of fun, in addition to serious interest in character and interpersonal relations, help A.'s work transcend its genres and endure.

WORKS: Blackkerchief Dick (1923). The White Cottage Mystery (1928). The Black Dudley Murder (1929; published in England as Crime at Black Dudley, 1929). Mystery Mile (1930). Police at the Funeral (1931). The Gyrth Chalice Mystery (1931; published in England as Look to the Lady 1931). Kingdom of Death (1933; published in England as Sweet Danger, 1933). Death of a Ghost (1934). Flower for the Judge (1936). The Case of the Late Pig (1937). Mr. Campion, Criminologist (1937). Dancers in Mourning (1937; published as Who Killed Chloe? 1943). The Fashion in Shrouds (1938). Black Plumes (1940). Traitor's Purse (1941). The Oaken Heart (1941). The Galantrys (1943; published in England as Dance of the Years, 1943). Pearls Before Swine (1945; published in England as Coroner's Pidgin, 1945). The Case Book of Mr. Campion (1947). Deadly Duo (1949; published in England as Take Two at Bedtime, 1950). More Work for the Undertaker (1949). The Tiger in the Smoke (1952). No Love Lost: Two Stories of Suspense (1954). The Estate of the Beckoning Lady (1955; published in England as The Beckoning Lady, 1955). Tether's End (1958). Hide My Eyes (1958). Crime and Mr. Campion (contains Death of a Ghost, Flowers for the Judge and Dancers in Mourning) (1959). Three Cases for Mr. Campion (1961). The China Governess (1962). The Mysterious Mr. Campion (omnibus) (1963). The Mind Readers (1965). Mr. Campion's Lady (omnibus) (1965). Mr. Campion's Clowns (anthology) (1966). The Mysterious Mr. Campion (anthology) (1966). Cargo of Eagles (1967). Mr. Campion and Others (1967). The Allingham Case-Book (1969). The Allingham Minibus (1973). The Fear Sign (1976). Also author of Water in a Sieve: A Fantasy in One Act.

BIBLIOGRAPHY: For articles in reference works, see: CA. Encyclopedia of Mystery and Detection, ed. C. Steinbrunner and O. Penzler (1976).

Other references: Armchair Detective (Winter 1982). Craig, P., and M. Cadogan, The Lady Investigates (1981). Gaskill, R. W. And Then There Were Nine: More Women of Mystery, ed. J.S. Bakerman (1985). Mann, J. Deadlier Than the Male (1981). Panek, L.L. Watteau's Shepherds: The Detective Novel in Britain, 1914-1940 (1979). Pike, B.A. Campion's Career: A Study of the Novels of Margery Allingham (1987).

Carey Kaplan

Jane Anger

FL.: 1589.

We know nothing for certain about this elusive Elizabethan personality apart from the contents of *Jane Anger, her protection for women*, a pamphlet published in London in 1589 by Richard Iones and Thomas Orwin and written, says the title, by one Ia. Anger, Gent. In fact, the latter identity raises more questions than it answers, for "Gent." was usually employed as an abbreviation for "gentleman." Indeed, this epithet, plus the evidence in the pamphlet of a knowledge of Latin, the bold tone of the title and Anger's two prefatory letters, and the open avowal of authorship (practically unheard of for a woman in Elizabethan England) cast some doubt on the identity of the author.

The possibility cannot be eliminated that Jane Anger was a pseudonym used by a male writer, for it was not uncommon for male writers to compose heated defenses of the opposite sex. The position of women in relation to their male counterparts formed a recurrent theme in the popular literature of the sixteenth and seventeenth centuries, with pamphlets arguing pro and con appearing till the late 1600s.

A.'s pamphlet was one such work. If she is a woman, and there is no hard evidence to refute positively her own claim that she is female, it is the first occurrence in English prose of a woman defending her own sex, and *Protection* is the earliest example of a feminist pamphlet written by a woman. A. claims to have written her book in answer to another pamphlet containing the "Scandalous reportes of a Late Surfeiting Louer." There are several candidates for this book, among them John Lyly's *Eupheus his Censure to Philautus*; however, in all probability A. is referring to *Boke, his Surfeyt in love*, entered in the Stationer's Register for November 1588. Unfortunately, copies of the pamphlet are no longer extant.

In answer to the lover, A. claims that men "have been so daintely fed with our good natures that like iades (their stomackes are grown so queasey), they surfeit of our kindnesse." Her protection, in the main, advises fellow women to beware of men's sexual trickery. "A goose," she writes, "standing before a rauenous fox is in as good case as the woman that trusted to a mans fidelitie." But also, interestingly, she advises her readers to distrust men who speak slightingly of their sex. For A., as she makes clear in the prefatory letter, argues that men are the moral inferiors of women.

Despite such claims, however, A. also lays many censures at the door of her fellow women, blaming their vulnerability on their own silliness, credulity, bashfulness, garrulity, and weakness of wit. In many instances, despite the tone of her opening letters and her claims of feminine superiority, she accepts the stereotyped accusations leveled at her sex by the hostile male pamphleteers of the period.

Just as the contents of A.'s book mix angry feminism with a curious acceptance of stereotype, so her style exhibits a strange melange of erudition and folk wisdom. The text is sprinkled with Latin quotations, indicating a possible familiarity with the language and a degree of education unusual for a middle-class Elizabethan woman. A. also cites examples of famous women from classical and Biblical traditions in support of her arguments, a further clue to her erudition. There are three poems in the tract, playful puns on the "surfeiting lover" throughout, and an admission by A. herself that the lover's book came to hand because "as well women as men are desirous of nouelities."

On the other hand, the pamphlet is also strewn with numerous indications of a popular tradition. Proverbs, references to creatures from folk stories (the fox, for example), and at least one anecdote (the story of the wise man), a cross between a joke and a parable, point to the middle-class audience for which the tract was published. The odd mixture again raises questions about A.'s social status, but most critics are agreed that A., if a woman, was of middle- or lower-class birth. There is no record of any Elizabethan woman of noble or even gentle birth penning a set piece in defense of her sex.

While A.'s pamphlet was the first of its kind to be written by a woman, two other women followed suit in the 1600s as the debate on the woman question intensified under the rule of James I (who was in favor of the suppression of women). Of these two, Racheal Speght and Esther Sowerman, only Speght used her own name. A.'s pamphlet, in its bold tone, its vigorous defense, and spirited attacks, thus marks a landmark in the history of women writers in England. Its appearance in the Elizabethan popular press also gives witness to the new interest in woman as a social factor and to the seriousness with which London burghers were considering the practical implications of change in her social condition.

WORKS: Jane Anger her protection for women. To defend them against Scandalous Reportes of a late Surfeiting Louer, and all other Venerians that complaine so to bee ouercloyed with womens kindnesse. (1589).

BIBLIOGRAPHY: Travitsky, B. *The Paradise of Women* (1983). Warnicke, R. *Women of the English Renaissance and Reformation* (1983). Wright, L.B. *Middle Class Culture in Elizabethan England* (1935).

Other references: *MLQ* (1947).

Glenda Wall

"Ariadne"

FL.: 1696.

"A." is the pseudonym of a playwright whose only known work is *She Ventures and He Wins*, a comedy staged at "the New Theatre in Little Lincoln's-Inn Fields" in September 1695 and published the following year. This "Young Lady," as she identifies herself on the title page, was the first woman to publish plays after Aphra Behn. The preface and prologue indicate that Behn's talent was both inspiring and confining for this self-deprecating woman. Very conscious of literary succession and of the harsh criticism that she could draw because she was female, "A." comments in the preface, "The best Apology I can make for my Self and Play, is, that 'tis the Error of a weak Woman's Pen, one altogether unlearn'd, ignorant of any, but her Mother-Tongue, and very far from being a perfect mistress of that too." It is this fear of criticism, Motteux writes in the epilogue, that forces "A." to hide her true identity. The epilogue concludes by suggesting that a good reception for this play might encourage the playwright to reveal her identity.

A conventional comedy of the late seventeenth century, *She Ventures and He Wins* weaves together two relatively unrelated love plots. In the main plot, which starred Mrs. Bracegirdle as Charlot in 1695, a young woman disguises herself as a man in order to study potential husbands. Knowing that men often flatter women and lie to them, she wants to observe men as they talk more naturally among themselves. Rather than treating the audience to an extended exploration of male duplicity, "A." allows her heroine to find a suitable man very soon. Having identified Lovewell as loving and faithful, Charlot tests him by sending other women to flirt with him and by pretending to arrest him for debts that she has incurred in his name. When he passes all these tests, she marries him. The subplot involves a bumbling would-be philanderer, whose exploits are revealed to his ever-forgiving wife. The plots are linked only by their common concern for disguise, yet somehow all the characters end up in the same tavern at the end of the play. *She Ventures and He Wins* is more interesting for its portrayal of wise and powerful women than for clever dialogue or plotting. Although we have no record of how it was received by contemporary audiences at Lincoln's Inn Fields, certainly it did not earn enough praise to warrant the playwright's revealing her identity.

No other plays can be attributed to "A." with any real assurance; it has been suggested that she also wrote *The Unnatural Mother*, staged at Lincoln's Inn Fields in 1697 and published in 1698, both anonymously.

WORK: *She Ventures and He Wins* (1696).

BIBLIOGRAPHY:
For articles in reference works, see: Todd.

Tori Haring-Smith

Anne Askew (Kyme)

BORN: 1521, Lincolnshire (presumably).
DIED: 16 July 1546, London.
DAUGHTER OF: Sir William Askew (Ayskough), of Kelsey, Lincolnshire; mother's name unknown.
MARRIED: Thomas Kyme, n.d.

Had A. (as she is generally known) been born fifty years after her actual date of birth, she would most probably have lived a quietly pious and uneventful life. However, as events did transpire, she fell victim to two current trends: the commonplace insensitivity of many sixteenth-century parents to their children's preferences in a marriage partner, and the atmosphere of hysteria concerning deviations from the doctrines of the Henrician church.

Substituted by her callous father for her deceased older sister, who had been promised, on profitable terms, as the bride of Thomas Kyme, A. reportedly comported herself as a dutiful wife, bearing Kyme two children. However, her rejection of Catholicism for Protestantism led to her husband's rejection of her and her eviction from their home. In London, where she settled herself, apparently to obtain a divorce, A. was brought up for questioning before Edmund Bonner in 1545, possibly at the instigation of her in-laws, and possibly for the purpose of entrapping Catherine Parr and her sympathizers at court. She outwitted her examiners with apparent ease and was released (*First examinacyon . . .*, 1546).

Unhappily, the outcome of a second round of interrogation, detailed in *The lattre examinacyon . . .* (1547), was brutal and final. In 1546, she was rearrested, questioned twice, convicted as a heretic, and condemned to death. Heroically, she refused to recant her beliefs, even when, in her words, "my lorde Chancellor and master Ryche, toke paynes to racke me their own handes, tyll I was nygh dead." When she was burnt to death, on 16 July, she had to be brought to the stake in a chair and strapped to the stake for support because of the condition she had been brought to. Since the torture of a noblewoman was unheard of, as was the torture of an already condemned person, this mistreatment supports the idea that A.'s interrogators were attempting to implicate Catherine Parr and her coterie in heresy. A. was apparently caught in a net set for her superiors.

On the evidence of her *Examinacyons*, A.'s offenses seem to have arisen from her independent reading and interpretations of Scripture, which, by her own testimony, were disapproved of by the priests in her native Lincolnshire. A. left her husband, who had evicted her from their home, on the basis of 1 Cor. 7: "If a faythfull woman have an unbelevynge husbande, whych wyll not tarrye with her she may leave hym." However poignant her plight, these grounds were not accepted by the Henrician church; Henry's annulment of his first marriage had been based on a claim of consanguinity. Finally, A. denied the doctrine of transubstantiation. These independent positions were perceived as inherently subversive to both the political and social fabric of Henrician England. It is unlikely that they alone would have earned A. the crown of martyrdom if she had not been joined, as seems probable from both her own and Foxe's accounts, to the coterie of reformist women surrounding Catherine Parr, Henry's sixth and surviving queen.

After A.'s death, John Bale, the Bishop of Ossory, printed the records which she had composed of her examinations. Included with the second examination were a letter composed during her imprisonment, a confession of her faith, and a vivid ballad attacking the injustice and hypocrisy of her tormentors and affirming her beliefs ("The Balade whych Anne Askewe Made and Sange Whan She Was in Newgate"). These verses illustrate A.'s courage, intellect, and independence, as the following excerpt demonstrates: "Fayth is that weapon strong/Whych wyll not fayle at nede/My foes therfor amonge/Therwith wyll I procede.// . . .Faythe in the fathers olde/Obtayned ryghtooysnesse/Whych makes me verye bolde/To feare no worldes distresse."

WORKS: *The first examimacyon of Anne Askewe, lately martyred in Smythefelde, by the Romysh popes upholders, with the Elucydacyon of Johan Bale.* (1546). *The lattre examinacyon of Anne Askewe, lately martyred in Smythefelde, by the wycked Synagogue of Antichrist, with the Elucydacyon of Johan Bale.* (1547).

BIBLIOGRAPHY: Ballard, G. *Memoirs of Severall Ladies of Great Britain . . .* (1752). Beilin, E. In *Silent but for the Word . . . .* Ed. M.P. Hannay. (1985). Foxe, J. *Actes and monuments . . .* (1563). Hays, M. *Female Biography . . .* (1807). Hogrefe, P. *Tudor Women . . .* (1975). Levin, C. *International Journal of Women's Studies* (1980). Smith, L.B. *Henry VIII: The Mask of Royalty* (1971). Travitsky, B., ed. *Paradise of Women . . .* (1981). Warnicke, R.M. *Women of the English Renaissance and Reformation* (1983). Webb, M.L. *The Fells of Swarthmoor . . . with an Account of Their Ancestor Anne Askewe, the Martyr* (1865). Williams, J. *Literary Women of England . . .* (1861). *Writings of Edward VI, William Hugh, Queen Catherine Parr, Anne Askew, Lady Jane Grey, Hamilton and Balnaves* (1842).

For articles in reference works, see: *DNB*.

Betty Travitsky

Mary Astell

BORN: 12 November 1666, Newcastle-on-Tyne.
DIED: 9 May 1731, Chelsea, London.
DAUGHTER OF: Peter Astell and Mary Errington Astell.

An ardent feminist, A. wrote prodigiously concerning the education of women, religion, and politics. She was the daughter of a provincial middle-class family which was loyal to the Church of England and the monarch. Though A. was not formally educated, she did read widely on her own, and she knew a little French. A clergyman uncle may have taught her Latin, but her knowledge of it, along with Greek and Hebrew, was certainly not extensive, a fact of which she was painfully aware. She says in *The Christian Religion as Professed by a Daughter of the Church of England* (1705): "My ignorance in the sacred languages, besides all other disadvantages makes me incapable of expounding scripture with the learned."

Two years after her mother's death in 1684, A., aged 20, went to Chelsea. Once there, she held court as the central focus of a group of progressive upper-class women, naturally assuming the role of teacher. Her friends included Lady Catherine Jones (to whom she dedicated some of her works), Lady Elizabeth Hastings, and most famous of all, Lady Mary Wortley Montagu. A. carried on a lengthy correspondence with Lady Elizabeth, but unfortunately all manuscripts were destroyed by Lady Elizabeth prior to her death. To A., Lady Mary Wortley Montagu was an exemplar of the brilliant woman envisioned in her writings, but this did not prevent A. from exhorting her to reject the vanities of upper-class life and attempting to persuade her of the truth of the immortality of the soul.

A.'s distinguished and often tempestuous career in controversial writing began in 1694 with the publication of *A Serious Proposal to the Ladies*. This work advanced the idea that a "monastery" or "religious retirement" should be established for women. In this sequestered institution, they would receive a program of religious and secular training, with the heaviest emphasis on religious study, because A. felt that religion was the primary aim of life. But A. also felt that women could only fulfill their duty to God by developing their full intellectual potential; therefore, secular training was crucial. In contrast to most of her contemporaries, who believed a woman's religious duty was always to obey her husband, being only a mere adjunct to him, A. believed that God intended women to develop their highest potential. They could not achieve this goal by remaining extensions of men. Through knowledge, women could also benefit society. Indeed, it was their express obligation to do so. A. felt strongly that the conventional upbringing of women served only to blunt their minds and make them dull company for themselves and others. In *A Serious Proposal to the Ladies: Part II* (1697), A. elaborated on her arguments in the first part.

The publication of *A Serious Proposal to the Ladies* provoked immediate attention, some of it favorable. Daniel Defoe approved of the program set forth by A. for her institution, but he had one reservation. He suggested that the emphasis should favor secular rather than religious training, thereby avoiding a dangerous resemblance to a Roman Catholic convent. A. also attracted the response of John Evelyn, who included her in his *Numismata* among women he felt should be known to fame. Unfortunately, most of A.'s contemporaries believed that she was advocating a return to Roman Catholicism; her "monastery" reminded them far too much of popery. Even feminist sympathizers, like Defoe, felt that the needs of women could not justify the establishment of such an institution; hence public support for A.'s ideas was not forthcoming.

In *Letters Concerning the Love of God* (1695), "by the author of the Proposal to the Ladies," A. set forth her position that mankind could best achieve an understanding of God through love. Though study and speculation have some relevance, we can only truly understand God through love, and when we love God, then we love one another. It is no wonder that A. vehemently rejected Deism, which injected too much reason into the understanding of God and asserted that He was indifferent to the affairs of humanity.

With the publication of *Some Reflections upon Marriage Occasioned by the Duke and Duchess of Mazarine's Case* (1700), A. turned back to the subject of women. The acidity of A.'s tone might cause some to conclude that she was against marriage in general. A. was only against unwise marriage, and this she defined as obedience without love: "And if a woman can neither love nor honour, she does ill in promising to obey, since she is like to have a crooked rule to regulate her actions. A mere obedience, such as is paid only to authority, and not out of love and a sense of the justice and reasonableness of the command, will be of uncertain tenure." Again, unlike most of her contemporaries, A. was aware of the unhappy consequences of unwise marriage and the fact that women had no hope of remedying such a situation: "If therefore it be a woman's hard fate to meet with a disagreeable temper, and of all others the haughty, imperious, and self-conceited are the most so, she is as unhappy as anything in this world can make her. For when a wife's temper does not please, if she makes her husband uneasy, he can find entertainments abroad; he has a hundred ways of relieving himself; but neither prudence nor duty will allow a woman to fly out: her business and entertainment are at home; and though he makes it ever so uneasy to her, she must be content and make her best on't." A. realized it was virtually impossible for women to escape their tenuous position in society, for "what poor woman is ever taught that she should have a higher design than to get her a husband?"

With the publication of *Moderation Truly Stated, A Fair Way with the Dissenters and Their Patrons*, and *An Impartial Enquiry into the Causes of Rebellion and Civil War in This Kingdom* (all 1704), A. became embroiled in political controversy. In these works, the loyalty to church and state which she was brought up with is evident. In *Moderation Truly Stated*, A. strongly contends that the true statesman must maintain loyalty to his monarch and not oppress his fellow subjects. He must be vigilant in the suppression of vice while encouraging "true religion." A. unequivocally states in *An Impartial Enquiry . . .* that those who dare to rebel turn "religion into rebellion" and "faith into faction." A king could only succumb to tyranny if he was seduced into it by ambitious courtiers, so A. effectively removed all blame for oppression from the monarch. In *A Fair Way with the Dissenters and Their Patrons*, she forcefully attacked Defoe.

The Christian Religion as Professed by a Daughter of the Church of England summarized A.'s religious and educational theories (1705), and she continued her political involvement by opposing Shaftesbury in *Bart'lemy Fair or an Enquiry After Wit* (1709). From that date, A. was also involved in writing new prefaces to her works. She remained active in polemics by writing a letter to Henry Dodwell concerning the non-juror debate and helped Dr. John Walker collect material for his work, *The Sufferings of the Clergy.* During this time, A. led a contemplative life and enjoyed religious meditation, but she was not the severe recluse tradition would have us believe.

At the end of her life, A. very much wanted to establish the "monastery" for women made famous in *A Serious Proposal to the Ladies*, but since there was no public support for this, she instead formulated a plan for a charity school for the girls of Chelsea. Though Bishop Burnet dissuaded a prominent lady from donating ten thousand pounds to the school, A. at least had the satisfaction of realizing that her plans would be carried out. The charity school was established in 1729, two years before A.'s death, by her old friends, Lady Catherine Jones, Lady Elizabeth Hastings, Lady Ann Coventry, and others.

Because of A.'s strong beliefs, which never wavered throughout her life, she experienced the isolation that the pioneer inevitably suffers, but it was precisely through her radical views that her readers could come to a better understanding of the social and educational problems facing women. Today, when the religious and political controversies of the eighteenth century have lost their potency, A. is mainly remembered for *A Serious Proposal to the Ladies* and *Some Reflections upon Marriage, Occasioned by the Duke and Duchess of Mazarine's Case.* It would be a mistake, however, to discount or separate religion from the corpus of her work, for religion was for A. the paramount direction of her life.

WORKS: *A Serious Proposal to the Ladies for the Advancement of Their True and Greatest Interest* (1694). *Letters Concerning the Love of God* (1695). *A Serious Proposal to the Ladies: Part II* (1697). *Some Reflections upon Marriage, Occasioned by the Duke and Duchess of Mazarine's Case* (1700). *Moderation Truly Stated* (1704). *A Fair Way with the Dissenters and Their Patrons* (1704). *An Impartial Enquiry into the Causes of Rebellion and Civil War in This Kingdom* (1704). *The Christian Religion as Professed by a Daughter of the Church of England* (1705). *Bart'lemy Fair or an Enquiry After Wit* (1709). *The First English Feminist: "Reflections on Marriage" and Other Writings*, ed. B. Hill (1986).

BIBLIOGRAPHY: Perry, R. *The Celebrated Mary Astell: An Early English Feminist* (1986). Perry, R. *Women and the Enlightenment*, ed. M. Hunt and others (1984). Rogers, K.M. *Before Their Time: Six Women Writers of the Eighteenth Century* (1979). Smith, F.M. *Mary Astell* (1916). Wallace, A. *Before the Bluestockings* (1929).

For articles in reference works, see: Chalmers. DNB.

Anne Prescott

Jane Austen

BORN: 16 December 1775, Steventon, Hampshire.
DIED: 18 July 1817, Winchester, Hampshire.
DAUGHTER OF: the Reverend George and Cassandra Leigh Austen.

A "small square two inches of ivory" is the way A. once described her own work. Yet this same work, apparently being lightly dismissed, is among the most enduring and most popular literature of the nineteenth century. Categorized as novels of manners, the careful detail given to both setting and character in A.'s works has captivated readers for over a century.

Born in 1775, A. was the seventh of eight children born to the rector of Steventon, Hampshire. A. began writing at about age eleven. Her notebooks containing "novels," chiefly parodies of eighteenth-century sentimental novels, were passed around her family for their entertainment. A. and her family were, as she said, "great Novel-readers and not ashamed of being so."

A.'s writing and publishing history is somewhat confusing. Her writing falls into two groups of three novels with a "silent" decade between, yet her publishing history does not reflect this division.

The following chronology shows the dates of composition, revision, and publication of A.'s novels:

c. 1790-1793: *Love and Freindship* [sic]; *Volume the First*; juvenilia.

Before 1796: *Elinor and Marianne* (not extant); recast, 1797-1799, as *Sense and Sensibility*; further revision, 1809-1810; published 1811.

1792-1796(?): *Lady Susan*; survives in a fair copy of c. 1805 or later; first published in *Memoir* (Austen-Leigh), 2nd ed., 1871.

1796-1797: *First Impressions* (not extant); rewritten, c. 1812, as *Pride and Prejudice*; published 1813.

1797-1798: *Susan* (not extant); recast and much expanded as *Northanger Abbey*, 1805; posthumously published 1818.

1803: *The Watsons* (a fragment); first published in *Memoir* (Austen-Leigh), 1871.

1811-1813: *Mansfield Park*; published 1814.

1814-1815: *Emma*; published late 1815 or, more probably, early 1816.

1815–1816:   *Persuasion*; published posthumously 1818.

1817:   *Sanditon* (a fragment, given title by
Austen family); first published,
from ms., 1925.

Many scholars believe that A.'s silent period was caused by discouragement after *First Impressions* was rejected unread and *Northanger Abbey* was picked up by a publisher in 1803 for a pittance but never issued, after which A. bought back the manuscript in 1816. Although she probably made some minor revisions, *Northanger Abbey* appears to be the earliest example of A.'s work. It is, however, a mistake to differentiate too sharply between the novels of the two periods. For the three of the first group were being revised while A. was writing the three of the second group. The most obvious influence occurs in the change of genre in *Sense and Sensibility* and *Pride and Prejudice*; in their original forms, *Elinor and Marianne* and *First Impressions* were both epistolary novels, a technique A. dropped in revision and never again employed.

According to A., "three or four Families in a Country Village is [the] very thing to work upon." She concentrated on a limited part of English society, provincial gentry and the aligning of the rural upper-middle class with the aristocracy. A. wrote about that with which she was familiar; and when her niece sought her advice about a novel, A. advised her to "stick to Bath" where she was "quite at home."

A. herself resisted the temptation to stray from familiar ground, even when nudged by royalty. When the domestic chaplain to the Prince of Wales suggested that in her next novel she might delineate the character of a clergyman, A. realized that the hints he supplied were based on his own experiences. A. replied, somewhat mischievously, that she might be able to do "the comic parts of the characters" but "not the good, the enthusiastic, the literary."

Such an answer, with its somewhat stinging implications, was typical of A. Her satirical treatment of social standards and literary expectations in her novels and her acidic comments in her letters have earned A. a reputation for a sharp tongue. After A.'s death in 1817 her sister, Cassandra, burned many of A.'s letters, implying to some critics that the worst, the sharpest, of the letters were destroyed. But it is more likely that the more personal letters, the ones most likely to show the gentler side, were destroyed to protect A.'s privacy even after death. For it is important to realize how fiercely A. and her family guarded her privacy. All her novels were published anonymously and their authorship was a well-kept secret.

Nevertheless, much of A.'s personality, tastes, and interests can be discerned through her novels. In *Northanger Abbey*, for example, A. satirizes gothic romantic mysteries (Radcliffe's *Mysteries of Udolpho* in particular) and presents what was to become a recurrent theme: feminine self-delusion. A. picks up the latter theme again in *Sense and Sensibility* and *Pride and Prejudice* but demonstrates its pitfalls by contrasting the actions and reactions of two sisters. In *Sense and Sensibility* the two sisters, Elinor and Marianne Dashwood, represent "sense" and "sensibility," respectively. Each is deserted by the young man from whom she has been led to expect a matrimonial offer. Reacting with sense, Elinor eventually untangles the complications surrounding her lover and they become engaged; Marianne, on the other hand, reacts with sensibility and impetuosity. She gradually comes to realize the foolishness of her love and see her real affection for another, a quieter and more serious lover. In *Pride and Prejudice* the contrast between sisters is more subtle and further complicated by a parallel male paring, Bingley and Darcy. One of the most popular of Austen's novels, *Pride and Prejudice* introduces many of the stylistic devices commonly associated with A.'s work: witty, cutting dialogue between couples; strong-willed heroines without a strong role model (her mother is either weak and ineffectual, or dead); settings that reveal the underlying character of the male protagonist (in this instance, Pemberley); and an ironic undertone, often established in the opening lines of the novel ("It is a truth universally acknowledged that a single man in possession of a good fortune must be in want of a wife.")

Mansfield Park marks a slight diversion from the pattern established in A.'s earlier novels, for here the heroine is an orphan adopted into her rich uncle's family. Despite being condescendingly treated as a poor relation, Fanny's honesty and modest disposition gradually make her an indispensable part of the household, particularly when her uncle is away on business for an extended period and the family's sense of discipline is relaxed. In this novel it is the male characters, particularly Edmund Bertram and Henry Crawford, who represent contrasting personalities, and it is Edmund who is self-deluded and eventually comes to see Fanny's virtues. To many critics *Mansfield Park* is one of A.'s lesser novels, perhaps because of her reversal of her usual male and female portrayals, a reversal she did not repeat.

In contrast, the novels which followed—*Emma* and *Persuasion*—are considered by many to be her best works. The heroine in *Emma* is again virtually alone in the world: her mother is dead, her father is absentminded and ineffectual, and her governess-companion has left to be married. But unlike Fanny in *Mansfield Park*, Emma is not especially wise. In this novel A. again deals with the theme of feminine self-delusion, but the focus on a single, strong-willed character makes the impact stronger than in previous works. In *Persuasion* A. returns to the contrasting of sisters but focuses primarily on the second of three (Anne Elliot). Anne is pretty, intelligent, amiable, but also malleable. She is persuaded by a trusted friend, Lady Russell, to break off a long-standing engagement despite her feelings for her lover. During the resulting confusion both lovers become entangled in other relationships but eventually realize that their affection for each other still exists. In this, A.'s last complete work, the satire and ridicule take a milder form, the tone is graver and tenderer, the interest lies in a more subtle interplay of characters. A. herself apparently recognized the difference in tone, for she wrote of Anne: "She is almost too good for me."

Although well received, A. was not immediately successful; few of her works reached a second edition during her lifetime. In fact, the collected edition of 1833 supplied the market until 1882. Attention began to increase during the 1890s as indicated by the appearance of biographies and critical pieces. Today, almost 175 years later, all of her books are in print and A. is one of the top-selling authors. No doubt much of her popularity is due to a desire to escape to a better place and time. Yet because much of her work depends on character analysis, many readers still identify with much of her work. Others are captivated by her style, her careful construction and use of the dramatic method where characters are introduced through dialogue before putting in an appearance. To some she is one of the greatest ironists who ever lived. And to most she is a challenge. As A. herself put it, "I do not write for dull elves who cannot think for themselves."

WORKS: *Sense and Sensibility* (1811). *Pride and Prejudice* (1813). *Mansfield Park* (1814). *Emma* (1815). *Northanger Abbey* (1818). *Persuasion* (1818). *Lady Susan* (1871). *The Watsons* (1871). Austen-Leigh, W., and R.A. Austen-Leigh, *Jane Austen: Her Life and Letters, a Family Record* (1913). *The Novels of Jane Austen*, ed. R.W. Chapman (1923). *Sanditon* (1925). *The Letters of Jane Austen*, ed. R.W. Chapman (1923). *Minor Works*, ed. R.W. Chapman (1954). *Letters 1796–1817*, ed. R.W. Chapman (1955). *Love and Freindship* [sic], *and Other Early Works* (1978).

BIBLIOGRAPHY: Austen-Leigh, J.E. *A Memoir of Jane Austen* (1871). Austen-Leigh, W., and R.A. Austen-Leigh, ed. *Jane Austen: Her Life and Letters, a Family Record* (1913). Babb, H.S. *Jane Austen's Novels: The Fabric of Dialogue* (1962). Burrows, J.F. *Computation into Criticism: A Study of Jane Austen's Novels and An Experiment in Method* (1987). Cecil, D. *Jane Austen* (1935). Chapman, R.W. *Jane Austen: A Critical Biography* (1953). Chapman, R.W. *Jane Austen, Facts and Problems* (1948). Craik, W.A. *Jane Austen: The Six Novels* (1965). Firkins, D.W. *Jane Austen* (1920). Gilson, D. *A Bibliography of Jane Austen* (1982). Halperin, J. *The Life of Jane Austen* (1984). Honan, P. *Jane Austen: Her Life* (1987). Jenkins, E. *Jane Austen* (1949). Lascelles, M. *Jane Austen and Her Art* (1939). Liddell, R. *The Novels of Jane Austen* (1963). Litz, A.W. *Jane Austen: A Study of Her Artistic Development* (1965). Mudrick, M. *Jane Austen: Irony as Defense and Discovery* (1952). Southam, B.C. *Jane Austen's Literary Manuscripts* (1964). Southam, B.C. ed. *Jane Austen: The Critical Heritage* (1968). Tanner, T. *Jane Austen* (1987). Williams, M. *Jane Austen: Ten Novels and Their Methods* (1986). Wright, A. *Jane Austen's Novels: A Study in Structure* (1953).

For articles in reference works, see: *Allibone. BA19C. Chambers. DLB. DNB. Moulton.*

Other references: Adams, T.D. *Studies in the Novel* (1982). Auerbach, N. *Women and Literature* (1983). Booth, W.C. *Nineteenth-Century Fiction* (1961). Booth, W.C. *Persuasions* (December 1983). Cohen, L.D. *Nineteenth-Century Fiction* (1953). Duckworth, A.M. *Women and Literature* (1983). Duffy, J.M., Jr. *ELH* (1954). Elsbree, L. *Nineteenth-Century Fiction* (1960). Forster, E.M. *Abinger Harvest* (1936). Greene, D.J. *PMLA* (1953). Griffin, C. *ELH* (1963). Halperin, J. *MLQ* (1983). Harding, D.W. *Scrutiny* (1940). Karl, F.R. *Age of Fiction: The Nineteenth Century British Novel* (1964). Kelly, G. *English Studies in Canada* (June 1984). Leavis, Q.D. *Scrutiny* (1941, 1942). McCann, C.J. *Nineteenth-Century Fiction* (1964). Millard, M. *Persuasions* (December 1980). Schorer, M. *Kenyon* (1956). Shannon, E.F., Jr. *PMLA* (1956). Woolf, V. *The Common Reader* (1925).

Lynn M. Alexander

Lady Ann Bacon

BORN: 1528, Gidea Hall, Essex.
DIED: August 1610 at Gorhambury, Hertford-
shire.
DAUGHTER OF: Sir Anthony and Ann Fitz-
william Cooke.
MARRIED: Sir Nicholas Bacon, 1556–1557(?).
WROTE UNDER: A.C., Lady Ann Bacon.

As a classicist, B. was unusual for her learning and influence. Typically a well-to-do Renaissance woman had a limited number of interests,
with her household, her family, and her faith most
important. Unlike such notable women as Bess of
Hardwick or Lady Anne Clifford, whose lasting
accomplishments center on their administration
of large households, B. achieved her reputation
because her writing reflects her concern for her
religion and for her two sons. Her translations
and personal letters have survived; the translations are the more substantial achievement, while
the letters are more human.

B. was able to translate from several languages
because of her unusually thorough education. Although her mother, Ann Fitzwilliam Cooke, objected, her father, Sir Anthony Cooke, gave all five of
his daughters the advanced training that had been
advocated by some Tudor humanists, enabling his
children to study Latin, Hebrew, Greek, Italian, and
French. Despite maternal opposition to her education, B. dedicated her first published work to her
mother: a translation into English of fourteen Italian sermons by Bernardino Ochino, a friar who had
left the Roman Catholic Church and taken refuge in
Canterbury. Published around 1550, Ochino's sermons enjoyed a fair success, and an enlarged edition
was published in 1570.

B.'s major achievement was her English version of Bishop John Jewel's *Apologia pro Ecclesia
Anglicana* (1562), which she translated as *An
Apologie or aunswer in defence of the Church of
England* (1564). Jewel's great work describes the
Church of England's doctrine, defends it from
Roman Catholic charges of heresy, and attacks the
doctrine of papal supremacy; today it remains a
central document of the Anglican Church. After B.
read Jewel's Latin text, she was so moved by what
he said that she immediately essayed a translation,
which she sent to the Archbishop of Canterbury,

Matthew Parker, as well as to Bishop Jewel. Both
men approved her work, so Parker sent it into
print without changes and without her knowledge, fearing her modesty would forbid its publication. It was popular, being issued again in 1600
and after her death. The quality of her work is
high: her translation is concise, her diction is
exact, and her style is close to the vernacular so
that the work does not sound forced or foreign. As
C. S. Lewis remarks, "If quality without bulk were
enough, Lady Bacon might be put forward as the
best of all sixteenth-century translators."

In addition to her scholarly work, a number of
B.'s letters survive. Most of these are to her sons,
Francis and Anthony, though others are to such
noted men as Robert Devereaux, Earl of Essex, and
to her brother-in-law, William Cecil, Lord Burgh-
ley. These letters offer a clearer view of her character. Her intense piety, her concern for her sons, and
her dislike of Anthony's servant Lawson are topics
that recur. Given the exalted reputation of Francis
Bacon, one is amused to read a letter from B.
scolding him for drinking at bedtime or the way he
treats his tenants and sending him a basket of
pigeons as a special treat. Irritable and loving in the
same breath, she seems always convinced that both
her sons are behaving injudiciously in London. Such
letters provide welcome insight into the private life
of a remarkable woman.

WORKS: *Fourteene Sermons of Barnardine Ochyne*
(1550?, STC 18766). *Sermons Concerning the Pre-
destinacion and Election of God* (1570?, STC 18768).
*An Apologie or aunswer in defence of the Church of
England* (1562, STC 14590). For B.'s letters, James
Spedding, et al., eds., *The Works of Francis Bacon*,
VIII (1862), passim.

BIBLIOGRAPHY: Barnes, S. *Essex Review*,
(1912). Hogrefe, P. *Women of Action in Tudor England* (1977). Hughey, R. *RES* (1934). Lewis, C.S.
*English Literature in the Sixteenth Century, Exclud-
ing Drama* (1954).

For articles in reference works, see: *DNB*.
Palmer, A. and V. *Who's Who in Shakespeare's England* (1981).

Frances Teague

Enid Bagnold

BORN: 27 October 1889, Borstal Cottage,
Rochester.
DIED: 31 March 1981, London.
DAUGHTER OF: Col. Arthur Bagnold and
Ethel Alger.
MARRIED: Sir Roderick Jones, 1919.

As the spirited eldest child of a well-to-do
officer in the Royal Engineers, B. travelled extensively during her childhood and began writing
poetry nightly at the age of nine while living in
Jamaica, a habit she preserved throughout her
youth. When the family returned to England in

1902, her father enrolled B. in an exclusive school administered by Mrs. Leonard Huxley (the mother of Aldous and Julian, the niece of Matthew Arnold, and the sister of Mrs. Humphrey Ward), where B.'s performance was unremarkable except for her poetic talent. At this time, B. recalls in her *Autobiography*, Yeats advised her: ". . . never interest yourself in politics, welfare, or the conditions in which people live. Only in their aspect, their hearts and minds, and *what they are.*" Although B. made frequent literary forays into the world of political commentary, her best and most popular work was indeed produced when she heeded Yeats's advice.

From 1912 to 1919, B. lived in Chelsea, where her friends included Lovat Fraser, Gaudier-Brzeska, Katherine Mansfield, John Middleton Murry, Shaw, Max Beerbohm, Desmond Mac-Carthy, Bertrand Russell, and the Bibesco princes among many others. B.'s first literary employment came from her first lover, Frank Harris, who hired her as a journalist for his new *Hearth and Home* magazine, and when that folded, for *Modern Society*, a glorified scandal sheet. B. became a shameless and self-confessed plagiarist for the magazine, often translating Maupassant stories and passing them off as her own. Although her work at this time was of poor quality, she did learn valuable skills such as editing, writing to deadlines, and researching, all of which provided a solid foundation for future projects.

During World War I, B. trained and worked as a nurse in London, keeping a journal of her experiences which became her first published book, *A Diary Without Dates* (1918). Her journalistic training enabled her to compose a detailed and vivid impression, based on her close observation, of the horror and necessary cold-heartedness of a hospital system that was hopelessly unprepared for and overwhelmed by the casualties from France. Her descriptions of limbs piled in buckets and family members of the dying given callous treatment moved H.G. Wells to review the book favorably but also moved the hospital to fire her. Perhaps to balance the grotesqueness of her medical experience, B. also published her only volume of poems, *The Sailing Ships and Other Poems*, during the same year.

After the war, B. married into the working aristocracy in the person of Sir Roderick Jones, owner and head of Reuters, the news service. After her marriage, B. moved into high society, forming friendships with diplomats, peers, and such important literary figures as Vita Sackville-West, the Woolfs, Kipling, Maurice Baring, and Rebecca West. The conversations, anecdotes, personalities, and intrigues of this circle would provide models and materials for her writing to come.

From journalism and poetry, B., now Lady Jones, turned to the novel, publishing three be-

tween 1920 and 1930, the most popular of which was *Serena Blandish: or the Difficulty of Getting Married*, which S.N. Behrman adapted as a play in 1929. In 1933 B. once again demonstrated the lack of political acumen that had gotten her into trouble with *A Diary Without Dates* by travelling to Nazi Germany and describing it somewhat favorably in an article for the *Times* of London, for which she was severely attacked even by her friends. Two years later she had retreated into the safer and more familiar world of steeplechasing, producing her best-known work, *National Velvet*, for which B. drew from her own experiences. Characters were modeled closely on her servants and friends and plot situations upon her own daughter's love for horses and avid competitiveness.

Although she continued to write novels, B. became more and more drawn to the drama from the 1940s on, and it is perhaps as a playwright that she earned the greatest popularity and professional recognition. *Poor Judas*, a symbolic play that concerns a failed English writer who perseveres despite his lack of financial and popular success, won the Arts Theatre Prize in 1951. B.'s most famous play, *The Chalk Garden*, which received the Award of Merit for Drama from the American Academy of Arts and Letters in 1964, has as its protagonist Miss Madrigal, a woman with a questionable past who becomes governess to the spoiled pyromaniacal granddaughter of a selfish old dowager, and who manages to introduce sanity, forgiveness, and love into the emotionally sterile household. Kenneth Tynan, reviewing the play for *The Observer*, called it ". . .the finest artificial comedy to have flowed from an English (as opposed to an Irish) pen since the death of Congreve. . . ." B. continued to write successful plays until 1976, when *A Matter of Gravity* was published, taking time from drama to write her *Autobiography* in 1969. Written in B.'s typically light and flippant style, the *Autobiography* is a rather stream-of-consciousness reminiscence, lacking in facts and figures but rich in impressions and ideas. It is chiefly valuable for B.'s anecdotes of famous people and for the letters and drawings she reproduces.

B. felt that Henry James was a strong influence on her style, and many of her novels concern the same characters and ideas that James found fascinating. B., like James, is concerned with the shadings and gradations of truth and illusion as perceived from subjective individual perspectives, and consequently her work, in particular her plays, turn toward the symbolic, peopled with headstrong eccentrics who enact barbaric confrontations in exceedingly civilized syntax. Since most of her work is set in the ironic tone, it tends, paradoxically, to be highly comic while treating serious philosophical themes such as truth and illusion,

main characters; despite an elaborate, careful production, it failed to capture the public in its eleven-night run. Undeterred by adverse criticism, B. issued a second volume of *Plays on the Passions*, which included a comedy on hatred, a two-part tragedy on ambition, and a comedy on ambition. The comedy on hatred was produced at the English Opera House, but its tragic companion was considered too unwieldy for stage production. Shortly after the volume appeared, B., her sister, and her mother moved to Hampstead, where the mother died in 1806 and where the sisters lived till their deaths "in retirement" and B. later in life "in strict seclusion." This did not preclude their receiving visitors, including many friends eminent in letters, science, art, and society, such as Siddons, Scott, and their closest friend, Laetitia Barbauld.

In 1804 B. published *Miscellaneous Plays*, which included two tragedies, *Raynor* and *Constantine Paleologus*, constructed on traditional lines. The latter work, based on Gibbon's account of the Turkish siege of Constantinople, was produced at the Surrey Theatre as a melodrama and also in Liverpool, Dublin, and Edinburgh, in each case to large houses. In 1810 she produced *Family Legend*, based on a Highland feud; Scott wrote a prologue and sponsored its production in Edinburgh, and Henry Mackenzie, author of *The Man of Feeling*, wrote an epilogue. Its success led to a revival of *De Monfort*. In 1812, the third series of *Plays on the Passions* appeared; it contained two tragedies and a comedy on fear and a musical drama on hope. *Metrical Legends* appeared in 1821, a collection of poems suggested by her stay in Scotland with Scott the previous year. Sir William Wallace is the principal character in one poem, and Grizell Baillie in another, and the volume also included dramatic ballads cast in "the ancient mould."

Poetic Miscellanies was edited by B. in 1823; contributors included Scott, Catherine Fanshawe, Felicia Hemens, herself, and others. *Martyr*, a drama, appeared in 1826, though it had been written earlier; this play presents the martyrdom of Cordenius Maro, an officer in Nero's imperial guard, who had converted to Christianity. B.'s Unitarian view of Jesus led to the publication when she was seventy of *A View of the General Tenor of the New Testament Regarding the Nature and Dignity of Jesus Christ*. In 1836 she published three volumes of *Miscellaneous Plays*, including a tragedy and comedy on jealousy and a tragedy on remorse. Some of the poems in *Fugitive Verses* were written when she was nearly eighty.

B.'s inventiveness is great, and her blank verse possesses a notable dignity and sonorousness that cause her works to be ranked among English classical dramas, though they will never again be popular. Her minor works have beauty and delicacy, and some of her songs will doubtless live on. Her status currently is that of a virtual unknown, but renewed interest in literature written by women should reveal her to be an innovator whose efforts inspired both Scott and other Romantics to redefine the type of drama to appear on the English stage.

WORKS: *Fugitive Verses* (1790). *Plays on the Passions* (1798; second series, 1802; third series, 1812). *Miscellaneous Plays* (1804). *The Family Legend: A Tragedy* (1810). *The Beacon: A Serious Musical Drama in Two Acts* (1812). *Metrical Legends of Exalted Characters* (1821). *A Collection of Poems* (1823). *Martyr* (1826). *Complete Poetical Works* (1832). *A View of the General Tenor of the New Testament Regarding the Nature and Dignity of Jesus Christ* (1832). *Miscellaneous Plays* (1836). *Ahalya Bace: A Poem* (1849). *Dramatic and Poetical Works* (1851).

BIBLIOGRAPHY:

For articles in reference works, see: *Allibone*. *BA19C. DNB. Todd.*

Other references: Keddie, H. [pseud. Sarah Tytler] and J.L. Watson. *Songstresses of Scotland* (1871).

Priscilla Dorr

Beryl (Margaret) Bainbridge

BORN: 21 November 1933, Liverpool.
DAUGHTER OF: Richard and Winifred Baines Bainbridge.
MARRIED: Austin Davies, 1954.

B. is a prolific novelist whose books derive from her childhood in working-class Liverpool; her many novels evoke a dull, unhappy world of lower-middle-class people whose lives are generally unrelieved by joy or hope. But these drab, dreary characters and their limited worlds are presented with such grotesque wit and savage irony, such skill in narrative and characterization, that B. has established a deserved reputation as an original writer.

Raised on the coast near Liverpool, B. was obsessed with writing from an early age. Her father, a sometime (but unsuccessful) salesman, and her mother, self-consciously aware of the family's low status and her own higher origins in a Britain obsessed with class differences, together stimulated B. to write of her own world. Her father opened the world of Dickens to B., and her mother, the world of the theatre. B. began tap dancing in public at six, studied ballet while quite young, appeared on radio at ten, and acted with a repertory company at fifteen, continuing on stage till she was nearly forty. She briefly became a Roman Catholic in order to marry Austin Davies, a painter, and began writing during her children's early lives until her divorce in 1959.

B.'s first novels are explicitly based on her family memories. Though she had begun to write while only twelve (a melange of Dickens and Stevenson's *Treasure Island*), her first completed novel was submitted when she was barely seventeen and quickly rejected because of its "indecency." This first work was eventually published as B.'s third novel, *Harriet Said . . .* (1972). Two schoolgirls, one the chubby thirteen-year-old narrator, the other the domineering Harriet, spy on a middle-age man (including Oedipally observing his lovemaking) and write lurid diary entries about him. After the narrator seduces him, she kills his wife (at Harriet's urging). Though some critics praised the book as a good specimen of the "corrupt childhood" novel and compared its grim psychological effects to those of Poe, its incoherence and sensationalism struck others as reflective of its author's age at the time of writing.

Her first two books to be published, *A Weekend with Claud* (1967) and *Another Part of the Wood* (1968; revised 1979), differ considerably. The first is explicitly experimental: a photo prompts three stream-of-consciousness narratives about Claud's weekend a year previously with the unappealing, sloppy Maggie, her roomer, Norman, and a bag-lady, Shebah, ending with Claud's own recollections. Maggie's disorderly life constitutes the book's plotline, including Shebah's wounding and the various men in her life. Claud, though, is a type B. often writes about in later books, the man who ruthlessly takes advantage of and abuses women. The book was poorly received, and B. considers it a failure. The second novel, by contrast, derives from (and seems similar to) events at the end of her marriage: a divorced man takes several friends, as well as his lover and son, on a routine but awful vacation in the country, with the son's death resulting from his father's excessive expectations and cruelty. (B. subsequently revised the novel and republished it once she was able to gain a better perspective on her married life.)

The Dressmaker (1973; published in the United States as *The Secret Glass*) reverts to B.'s Liverpool life and is especially noted for its desperate working-class atmosphere and accuracy. Young Rita, living drearily with her two aunts, lusts after (and competes with one aunt for) a disgusting G.I. stationed nearby. After the other aunt kills the soldier, both aunts wrap up the body

to keep Rita from noticing it. B.'s brief job in a bottling factory working with immigrants resulted in *The Bottle Factory Outing* (1974), an excellent novel, skillfully balancing humor and horror, about another pair of contrasting English women and their various relationships with Italian workers, both male and female, in such a factory. One woman, Freda, is brusque and gregarious compared to Brenda, and the book moves inexorably from a funeral before the picnic to Freda's own death, following a series of morbid but comic incidents culminating in Brenda's disposing of the body by putting it in a barrel in the ocean.

In these first books, as in her numerous subsequent ones, B. is concerned with the common distinction between people's naive expectations and the harshness of reality, between belief and truth. B. has been repeatedly criticized for a seemingly indifferent, even cruel attitude toward her often pathetic characters. Despite her skill at capturing proletarian people and surroundings, B.'s tone is admittedly narrowly focused and limited.

Sweet William (1975) did little to alter such conclusions, though it was commonly agreed that B.'s skill at characterization was superb. William, a charming though amoral male opportunist, woos Ann through his power of persuasion even though she is engaged to Gerald, only slightly William's better. Gerald beds Ann the night before he leaves for the United States, and her mother—another of B.'s string of such women—asserts her convictions about social propriety. William completely manipulates her life, seduces others in the building, and Ann, pregnant and amazingly unaware of his inadequacies, moves away. When the child is born, it resembles Gerald, not William, with B.'s point being that none of her unlikable (though admittedly well-developed) characters really understands much about the nature of love.

A Quiet Life (1976) is explicitly autobiographical and also concerns a family with various emotional, even tragic, conflicts. B.'s male narrator is a man who meets his sister to divide a small inheritance and who reflects on their unhappy childhood, along with touches of macabre humor in which death, for example, is described in the same passage and tone as locating clean bedding. Though B. often writes about such claustrophobic families, her control of her material and subtle characterization make this one of her best works. In *Injury Time* (1977), B. uses various narrative voices to offer alternative views of distinguishing truth from illusion. Though the forty-year-old Binny has a lover, Edward, the two only dimly understand each other, and when she persuades him to invite his friends for dinner, chaos, both real and imagined, results as assorted unsavory neighbors invade the dinner and escaping bank robbers try to take the group hostage. Small wonder that Binny thinks she is watching a television drama, so unreal is all of this for her.

B. visited Israel after writing *Injury Time* and, after reflecting on the Holocaust and reading a biography of Hitler, wrote *Young Adolf* (1978). Based on the premise of Hitler's secretly having visited Liverpool in 1910 to see his brother, this comic/prophetic novel features a deluded protagonist who, critics noted, sometimes seemed like Charlie Chaplin's *The Great Dictator*.

Winter Garden (1980) also combines wild comedy with earnest characterization. Based on B.'s visit to the U.S.S.R. as part of an exchange group, the novel focuses on Douglas Ashburner who has also made such a visit and who plans an outing with his lover while telling his wife that he is going fishing. The inevitable confusion and complications occur: after both his luggage and lover mysteriously disappear and he is confused with both his lover's husband (a noted physician) and another man (an artist), Ashburner falls prey to B.'s complex plot, which satirizes both Soviet bureaucratic thinking and English conventionality, and the novel's bleak, predictable conclusion offers little comedy or comfort.

Watson's Apology (1984), unlike most of B.'s works, is set in the past, specifically in 1872: an elderly retired headmaster pistol-whipped his wife to death and died in prison twelve years later, during which years he produced several impenetrable scholarly works as well as a curious, ambiguous note in Latin about the killing: "Often heretofore constant love has been injurious to the lover." B.'s novel recreates courtship correspondence between Watson and his wife as well as scenes from their marriage; her instability contrasts with his genius and discipline. B.'s comic sense is somewhat daunted by this scenario, but it never flags; indeed, as with other books by B., one is never sure whether to laugh or cry, so effective is her character study.

In almost all of her fiction, her brilliant wit and imagination focuses on luckless misfits from the post-World War II Liverpool she has known so well—people not quite tragic, certainly not intrinsically comic, but all, even the suicides and those doomed to continue living without hope, are seen with a clear, unsentimental eye and a highly original comic sense. B. has also written nonfiction (*English Journey, or, The Road to Milton Keynes*, 1984, a travel book based on J.B. Priestley's work with a similar title, and *Forever En-*

gland North and South, 1987, a study of social life and customs) in which the same sharp skill of observation is found, as well as other fiction (*Mum and Mr. Armitage: Selected Stories*, 1985, and another novel, *Filthy Lucre, or, The Tragedy of Ernest Ledwhistle and Richard Soleway*, 1986); thus far, though, her major talent has received relatively little substantial criticism.

WORKS: *A Weekend with Claud* (1967). *Another Part of the Wood* (1968, 1979). *Harriet Said . . .* (1972). *The Dressmaker* (1973; in the U.S. as *The Secret Glass*, 1974). *The Bottle Factory Outing* (1975). *Sweet William* (1975). *A Quiet Life* (1976). *Injury Time* (1977). *Young Adolf* (1978). *Winter Garden* (1980). *English Journey, or, The Road to Milton Keynes* (1984). *Watson's Apology* (1984). *Mum and Mr. Armitage: Selected Stories of Beryl Bainbridge* (1985). *Filthy Lucre, or, The Tragedy of Ernest Ledwhistle and Richard Soleway* (1986). *Forever England North and South* (1987).

BIBLIOGRAPHY: Pickering, J. *Albion* (1979). Yakovleva, V. *Soviet Literature* (1984).

For articles in reference works, see: *CA. CLC. CN. DLB. EWL20C. WA.*

Other references: *Altantic* (March 1979). *Books and Bookmen* (January 1974, December 1977, November 1978, February 1980, May 1984, August 1985, April 1987). *Encounter* (February 1975, February 1976, February 1985, May 1986). *Hudson Review* (Winter 1977-1978). *Listener* (13 December 1979, 20 November 1980, 5 December 1985). *London Magazine* (January 1978, April-May 1979). *LRB* (20 November to 3 December 1980). *New Leader* (2 September 1974, 5 May 1980). *New Statesman* (1 November 1974, 10 November 1978, 21 and 28 December 1979, 7 November 1980, 11 September 1981, 13 April 1984, 29 November 1985). *Newsweek* (12 August 1974). *NR* (28 September 1974, 24 May 1975, 25 March 1978). *NYRB* (16 May 1974, 15 July 1976, 5 April 1979, 17 July 1980, 25 October 1984). *NYTBR* (15 September 1974, 8 June 1975, 20 March 1977, 13 April 1980, 1 March 1981, 21 March 1982, 23 September 1984, 20 October 1985). *Spectator* (2 November 1974, 9 October 1976, 8 December 1979, 1 November 1980, 28 April 1984, 3 November 1984). *TLS* (28 September 1973, 1 December 1978, 29 February 1980, 31 October 1980, 11 September 1981, 5 October 1984, 20 December 1985, 17 October 1986, 24 April 1987). *Yale Review* (Winter 1978).

Paul Schlueter

Isabella Varley Banks

BORN: 25 March 1821, Manchester.
DIED: 5 May 1897, Dalston.
DAUGHTER OF: James Varley and Amelia Daniels.
MARRIED: George Linnaeus Banks, 1846.
WROTE UNDER: Isabella Varley; Mrs. G. Linnaeus Banks.

A poet, journalist, and novelist, B. was the daughter of a Manchester chemist, smallware dealer, and amateur artist. She took charge of a school at Cheetham (near Manchester) when she was a teenager and taught for nine years. At the age of twenty-five she married George Linnaeus Banks, a poet, journalist, editor, and orator from Birmingham. Despite her many pregnancies—she bore eight children, losing five of them—and ill health, she assisted her husband with his work and contributed to the periodicals he edited.

Her first published work, a poem entitled "A Dying Girl to Her Mother," was printed in the *Manchester Guardian* when B. was sixteen. B. continued to write poetry throughout her life, but she published only three books of poems: *Ivy Leaves* (1844); *Daisies in the Grass* (with her husband, 1865), and *Ripples and Breakers* (1878, 1893). These works are typical of the "popular" mediocre verse of the time.

B. evidenced an avid interest in social issues, e.g., corporal punishment, flogging, the status of women, treatment of servants, education of girls, etc. She publicized her views in writing and speaking, once lecturing on "Woman—as She Was, as She Is, and as She May Be" at the Harrogate Mechanics' Institute. Skilled as a designer, she created and published original fancy-work patterns every month for 45 years. B. lived a difficult, sad life, moving frequently to follow her husband's work, enduring the deaths of five of her eight children, living with a drunken, raving husband threatening suicide, and suffering personal ill health. She died at Dalston on 5 May 1897.

B. turned from the pleasure of writing poetry to the serious task of writing prose as a practical necessity in 1863. Her husband was ill, and she needed money for food and education for her children. *God's Providence House* (1865) was the first of the many novels that she would write throughout her life. Called "meritorious" and obviously successful (a second edition was printed), the book is typical of B.'s novels, her style being relatively consistent. The characters, based on real persons, appear under their own names or in thinly disguised forms; incidents of family history within the framework are actual places of the late eighteenth century. B's style is almost cluttered with detail, making scenes and characters vivid and concrete. The emphasis in her works is on character rather than action; intelligence is subordinated to the heart and soul as the means for realizing happiness and success. Principal characters are reminiscent of the "Horatio Alger" type, and nearly all her works have a message of moral or social import, some almost to the point of didacticism. The terms "old-fashioned," "homey," "well-cooked," and "lovingly written" were often attributed to her style.

B. had to take on the male role of breadwinner even before the death of her husband, and her books present decided views about the prevailing attitudes toward women in her time. B. took responsibility, as did the characters Isobel Raines, Caroline Booth, Alice Latham, Edith, and Rosanna in her writings. She also deals with the unpopular theme of the illegitimate child and unwed mother in *Father and Daughter* and *Stung to the Quick*. Many stories focus on discrimination against women by individuals, law, and society.

B. was a constant contributor to magazines and Christmas annuals; she wrote many short stories and poems. Acknowledged as a minor nineteenth-century writer, commanding respect and interest, Banks was often called the "Lancashire novelist" because of her frequent use of the Manchester area as setting. Her best-known work is *The Manchester Man*, published in 1876. Its primary significance lies in the realistic depiction of social and industrial life in Manchester during the first quarter of the nineteenth century, including the riots of 1819. The conversational tone and profusion of literary detail are reminiscent of Defoe. It clearly exemplifies B.'s consummate interest as expressed in a letter to John Harland in December 1865, an interest in the "habits, customs, manners and daily life of the ancestors who have made us what we are. . . ."

WORKS: *Ivy Leaves: A Collection of Poems* (1844). *Daisies in the Grass: Songs and Poems* (with her husband, 1865). *God's Providence House* (1865). *Stung to the Quick* (1867). *The Manchester Man* (1876). *Glory: A Wiltshire Story* (1877). *Ripples and Breakers* (1878). *Caleb Booth's Clerk* (1878). *Wooers and Winners: Under the Scars* (1880). *More Than Coronets* (1881). *Through the Night: Short Stories* (1882). *The Watchmaker's Daughter: Short Stories* (1883). *Forbidden to Marry* (1883, under title *Forbidden to Wed*, 1885). *Sibylla, and Other Stories* (1884). *In His Own Hand* (1885). *Geoffrey Ollivant's Folly* (1886). *A Rough Road* (1892). *Bondslaves* (1893). *The Slowly Grinding Mills* (1893). *The Bridge of Beauty* (1894).

BIBLIOGRAPHY: *Athenaeum* (9 May 1896). *Biograph* (1879). Burney, E.L. *Mrs. G. Linnaeus Banks* (1969). *Daily Graphic* (7 May 1896). Dorland, W. A. N. *The Sum of Feminine Achievement* (1917). *Manchester Faces and Places* (December 1892). *Manchester Guardian* (6 May 1897). *The Manchester Man* (1876). *Men and Women of the Time*, 14th ed., ed. V.G. Plarr (1895). *Times* (London) (6 May 1897).

For articles in reference works, see: *Allibone*. *DNB*. *NCHEL*.

Phyllis J. Scherle

Anna Laetitia Barbauld

BORN: 20 June 1743, Kibworth-Harcourt.
DIED: 9 March 1825, Stoke-Newington.
DAUGHTER OF: John Aikin and Jane Jennings Aiken.
MARRIED: Rochemont Barbauld, 1774.

B., poet, editor, essayist, and writer for children, was one of four women to be cited (lines from two of her poems, "The Invitation" and "A Summer Evening Meditation") in the first edition of *Bartlett's Familiar Quotations* (1851). This honor most likely stems from B.'s popularity based on her widely known inspirational books for children. B.'s literary output, however, was not limited to children's books. She was active in the political and social circles of her day in spite of the problems she encountered in an unfortunate marriage.

At an early age B. showed an uncanny talent and desire for learning. It was said that by the age of three she could read a book as well as any woman and that as a child she was acquainted with the best in English literature. She also mastered French and Italian very early, and through the special pleading of her mother, she was allowed to expand her knowledge of languages by studying Greek and Latin even though her father discouraged such study.

B.'s life changed for the better, however, when her father was appointed tutor in 1758 at the newly opened Warrington Academy, established to give dissenters, who were shut out from Oxford and Cambridge, the benefits of a university education. B.'s brother, John Aikin, a physician with decidedly literary interests, encouraged her to publish, in 1773, her first volume of poems, which included "The Invitation," quoted by Bartlett, and "Corsica," a poem greatly admired by Mary Wortley Montagu. The book was an immediate success and went through four editions in the first year.

In the same year B. also published, with her brother, *Miscellaneous Pieces in Prose*, also reprinted several times. Exact attribution of the essays is difficult since the authors did not sign all of their respective pieces, but B.'s known contributions include some of her best essays, notably on "Inconsistency in Our Expectations" and "On Romances." "On Romances" represents B.'s imitation of Samuel Johnson's style and method of reasoning, this type of imitation a frequent pastime of aspiring neoclassical writers. Of this essay Johnson observed: "The imitators of my style have not hit it. Miss Aikin has done it the best, for she has imitated the sentiment as well as the diction."

In the midst of these literary successes, B. married the Rev. Rochemont Barbauld, a student of the academy at Warrington, with whom she established a successful boys' school at Palgrave. While at Palgrave B. wrote her best-known work, *Hymns in Prose for Children* (1781), which went through many editions and was translated into several European languages. She also wrote her *Early Lessons for Children* (1781), which also went through a number of editions and was translated into French. Her *Devotional Pieces, Composed from the Psalms and the Book of Job* (1775) was received respectfully by the literary community. B.'s literary fame and her devotion to the academy soon brought it celebrity and success, and her home became an important gathering place for dissenters who aspired to prove themselves as intellectual, broad-minded, and skilled in the graces and amenities of social life as their Church of England contemporaries.

In 1785, due to her husband's declining mental condition, they closed the school and spent a year travelling abroad, settling a year later at Hampstead, where B. became close friends with Joanna Baillie and her sister. This new literary milieu inspired B. to write essays of a different kind. In 1790 B. wrote "A Poetical Epistle to Mr. Wilberforce, on the Rejection of the Bill for Abolishing the Slave Trade." In 1792 she published "Remarks on Gilbert Wakefield's Inquiry into the Expediency and Propriety of Public and Social Worship." B., like many women of her time, was concerned with the social injustices and controversies of her days; her essays prefigure the kind of feminine social consciousness that was to blossom in the mid-nineteenth century into the novel of social reform. Also in 1792 B., in collaboration with her brother, published the first of six volumes of their best-known work, *Evenings at Home*. The book contributed to B.'s popularity and provided evening entertainment when read aloud for many British families, including the family of novelist Maria Edgeworth. B. is said to have contributed "fifteen papers" to this work though the major part of the writing was done by her brother.

In 1804 she published *Selections from the Spectator, Tatler, Guardian, and Freeholder*, a work which reflected the interests of British readers who preferred serious books on religion and morality, essays of the *Spectator* and *Tatler* type. In the same year she contributed a *Life of Samuel Richardson* to his *Correspondence*, which she edited. But her literary career was interrupted when her husband's mental health deteriorated to the point that he was forced to give up his pastoral work and eventually to be institutionalized. He died, insane, in London in 1808. Shortly after her husband's death, B. undertook an edition in fifty volumes of the best English novelists to which she prefixed a lengthy essay on the "Origin and Progress of Novel Writing," and she introduced the works of each author by short but complete biographical notices.

In 1811 B. "prepared for the use of young ladies, a selection, formerly well known and popular, of the best passages from English poets and prose writers," called *The Female Speaker*. Her greatest notoriety came from her criticism in this work of Coleridge's "The Rime of the Ancient Mariner." B. did not approve of this poem. She acknowledged its "queer, wizard-like quality," but she complained, characteristically, that it had no moral. Since the B. household was known not to be receptive to the romantic notions of progress and the emphasis on the imagination, a movement away from reason presented for B. and her circle an inadequacy in art. The same year she wrote a poem which again embroiled her in literary controversy, "Eighteen Hundred and Eleven." Written at a time of the deepest national gloom, it was considered eloquent but too despondent. B. incurred much reproach by writing it because it prophesied that in some future day a visitor to London would be able to contemplate the ruin of St. Paul's from a broken arch of Blackfriars Bridge. The poem evoked "a very coarse review" in *The Quarterly* by Robert Southey, who said later that he regretted the harshness of his review.

Though this was the last of B.'s published works, she continued to write both letters and minor pieces published after her death. Her letters show that "though her life was habitually retired she greatly enjoyed society." They record friendships formed or casual acquaintance made with Montagu, Hannah More, Joseph Priestley, Maria Edgeworth, Hester Chapone, Gilbert Wakefield, Walter Scott, Joanna Baillie, H. Crab

Robinson, William Roscoe, Wordsworth, W.E. Channing, Samuel Rogers, and Sir James Mackintosh, among others. All her work is characterized by a grace of style and lofty but not Puritanical principles.

WORKS: *Corsica: An Ode* (1768). *Poems* (1773). (with J. Aikin) *Miscellaneous Pieces in Prose* (1773). *Devotional Pieces, Composed from the Psalms and the Book of Job* (1775). *Hymns in Prose for Children* (1781). *Early Lessons for Children* (1781). *Lessons for Children, from Two to Three Years Old* (1788). *Lessons for Children, from Four to Five Years Old* (1788). *Lessons for Children of Four Years Old* (Part 2) (1788). *An Address to the Opposers of the Repeal of the Corporation and Test Acts* (1790). *Epistle to Mr. Wilberforce on the Rejection of the Bill for Abolishing the Slave Trade* (1791). *Letter to John Bull* (1792). *Remarks on Mr. Gilbert Wakefield's Enquiry into the Expediency and Propriety of Public or Social Worship* (1792). (with J. Aikin) *Evenings at Home, or, The Juvenile Budget Opened: Consisting of a Variety of Miscellaneous Pieces for the Instruction and Amusement of Young Persons* (6 vol., 1792-1795). *Civic Sermons to the People* (1793). *Sins of the Government, Sins of the Nation; or, A Discourse for the Fast, Appointed on April 19, 1793* (1793). *Essay on Akenside's Pleasures of the Imagination* (1795). *Essay on the Odes of Collins* (1797). *Gothic Stories* (1797). *Lessons for Children* (1798). *Poetic Gift; Containing Mrs. Barbauld's Hymns, in Verse* (1800). (with J. Aikin) *The Art of Life* (1802). *Eighteen Hundred and Eleven* (1812). *Lessons for Children* (1818). *Works*, ed. L. Aikin (1825). *Mrs. Barbauld's Little Stories for Children*, ed. J. Stephens (1830). *Things By Their Right Names, and Other Stories, Fables, and Moral Pieces, in Prose and Verse*, ed. S.J. Hale (1840). *A Memoir, Letters, and a Selection from the Writings of Anna Laetitia Barbauld*, ed. G.A.E. (Little) Oliver (1874). *Letters of Maria Edgeworth and Anna Laetitia Barbauld*, ed. W.S. Scott (1953).

BIBLIOGRAPHY: Le Breton, A.L. *A Memoir of Mrs. Barbauld* (1874). Oliver, G.A.L. *A Memoir, Letters, and a Selection from the Writings of Anna Laetitia Barbauld* (1874).

For articles in reference works, see: *Allibone. BA19C. DNB. Todd.*

Other references: Brodribb, C.W. *Contemporary Review* (1935). Darton, F.J.H. *Children's Books in English* (1932). Kramnick, M. "Preface" to *Hymns in Prose for Children* (1977). Moore, C.E. *Fetter'd or Free? British Women Novelists, 1670-1815*, ed. M.A. Schofield and C. Macheski (1986). O'Shea, M.V., ed. *Eyes and No Eyes* (1900). Thackeray, A.R., *A Book of Sibyls* (1883). Whiting, M.B. *London Mercury* (September 1932).

Priscilla Dorr

Audrey Lilian Barker

BORN: 13 April 1918, Kent.
DAUGHTER OF: Harry and Elsie A. Dutton
Barker.
WRITES UNDER: A.L. Barker.

B.'s best received works are her short stories. Although all her fiction has some commitment to plot, that is, to tell a story, the primary impression of a B. story or novel is its surreal, detached aura of fiction itself. Critics have searched for traces of autobiographical threads in B.'s works, but they are reduced to such statements as "does not reveal herself" and "reticent."

When *Life Stories,* a collection of loosely connected narratives, appeared in 1981, critics searched for—and finally found—some authorial intrusions. But, as Francis King noted, some of the "stories" were actual reminiscences and those "life stories" were fiction. The whole narrative, then, is a series of fables, or extended metaphors, "concerned with the jarring impact caused by a collision between innocence and experience" (*Spectator*, 26 Sept. 1981). B.'s persona recalls the time she became aware of the role of experience in her imagination. In a section that describes her stay in France in 1947, B. is Wordsworthian in her analysis: ". . . I realised that the net value of any experience fluctuates, depending not on its quality, or nature, or on whether it is first- or second-hand, but on who has digested it. Because after something has happened, it has to be broken down to manageable proportions. I saw that people took only what they could manage, what they could use, from any one sequence of events" (*Life Stories*).

B.'s works do not spring from a highly specialized, formal education. She attended a county secondary school, which she left at 16. B. found secretarial jobs in London offices and later as a sub-editor in the Amalgamated Press. After World War II she wrote for the British Broadcasting Corp. and free-lanced. She has written some screen adaptations of her stories.

The characters and plots of a B. story or novel seem to be everyday, but soon the situations become Kafkaesque. It is "as though we were continually being shown banal scenes but told original and disturbing things about them by some voice 'off camera'" (*Books and Bookmen*, May 1985). In *A Source of Embarrassment* (1974), for example, the novel's main character Edith is supposedly dying of a brain tumor. Ironically, her inability to communicate with her sister, daughter, and husband is the theme. It is left unclear whether the "source" of the embarrassment is Edith's bizarre actions that may be tumor induced or the lack of compassionate sympathy from those around her.

B.'s characters come from all age groups and classes although a common environ is middle or upper-middle class. A frequent theme in her works is the exploration of the difference "between adult and adolescent visions of the world" (*TLS*, 3 Aug. 1984). B.'s works parade a collection of all kinds of unexceptional characters who nevertheless have some quirky element to their personalities and experiences that makes the reader contrast reality and fiction. In one story, a 48-year-old mother is seduced by an ageless and androgynous youth, only to realize that all he wanted from her was her seat in the family car returning from a vacation at the beach ("Belle Amie," *No Word of Love*). In "A Communications Failure" a priest convinces the impoverished mother of a paralyzed deaf-mute girl to immure her daughter in the church basement. The priest, who sees this as an opportunity to be recognized and "ascend," never recognizes in himself the terror he inflicts on the girl, who dies trying to escape her crypt (*No Word of Love*).

B. has found higher praise for her short stories than for her novels. Her collections have won awards: Atlantic Award in Literature (1946), Somerset Maugham Award for *Innocents* (1947), Cheltenham Festival Literary Award (1962), and the Katherine Mansfield Short Story Prize (1984).

B.'s short stories are frequently organized around a thematic concept. The collections are: *Innocents: Variations on a Theme* (1947), *Novelette, with Other Stories* (1951), *The Joy-Ride and After* (1963), *Lost upon the Roundabouts* (1964), *Femina Real* (1971), *Life Stories* (1981), and *No Word of Love* (1985). *Femina Real*, for example, is a collection of stories exploring the psychology and sociology of women as daughters, students, singles, wives, mothers, and friends of men as well as women. The situations range from an Austen variation on arranged marriage ("La Matière") to tourists in provincial Italy ("Almost an International Incident") to the power of a "frail" woman ("Useless If Dropped"). *No Word of Love* (1985) keeps its promise by tracing relationships between people that are not only devoid of compassionate love but silent as well. While the tone is primarily "abrasive and comfortless" (*TLS*, 21 June 1985), there are some less harsh points, especially in "His Wonders to Perform," in which the dying priest rejects the meaningless ritualistic words of comfort of his young visitor. Instead he finds consolation in the rough and unsympathetic approach of Sister Annunciata, who has waged a bet with the nurses that the failing father would not eat his soup. When the sister is denounced for not "showing any love," he replies: "At my time of life—" he amended, still with that secret relish—"of death—love changes out of all recognition. And all degree."

B.'s works have been termed off-beat, highly individual, precise, and controlled. She shows a concern and commitment to language, just as Flaubert toiled in trying to keep a detached control of his words: "Searching for the exact word I sometimes came round full circle to a thumping cliché. It was as if all the best things had already been said, and written. Still, as a writer, I could sit down and explore and go farther than many other people had time or inclination for. For practical purposes there was simply no knowing. To me that was good news, freedom news. . . . Out of infinite combinations I was free to choose, within my own constitutional limits. . . . Truth was relative as it related to me" (*Life Stories*).

WORKS: *Innocents: Variations on a Theme* (1947). *Apology for a Hero* (1950). *Novelette, with Other Stories* (1951). *The Joy-Ride and After* (1963). *Lost upon the Roundabouts* (1964). *A Case Examined* (1965). *The Middling: Chapters in the Life of Ellie Toms* (1967). *John Brown's Body* (1969). *Femina Real* (1971). *A Source of Embarrassment* (1974). *A Heavy Feather* (1978). *Life Stories* (1981). *Relative Successes* (1984). *No Word of Love* (1985). *The Gooseboy* (1987).

BIBLIOGRAPHY: For articles in reference works, see: *CA. DLB. TCA SUP. 20th CAISM* (1955).

Other references: *Books and Bookmen* (September 1984, May 1985). *Brit. Book News* (February 1982, October 1984). *Guardian Weekly* (16 September 1984). *Listener* (5 November 1981, 4 October 1984). *New Statesman* (2 October 1981, 10 August 1984, 31 May 1985). *Spectator* (26 September 1981, 10 August 1984). *TLS* (22 March 1974, 19 April 1974, 25 September 1981, 3 August 1984, 21 June 1985).

Marilynn J. Smith

Jane Barker

BAPTIZED: 17 May 1652, Blatherwicke, Northamptonshire.
DIED: c. 1727 (France?).
DAUGHTER OF: Thomas Barker and Anne Connock.
WROTE UNDER: Mrs. Jane Barker, "A Young Lady," "Galesia," "Fidelia."

B. was an artist who accepted the outward forms of convention without allowing them to restrict the originality of her work or its honest depiction of the life of an educated, unmarried woman in seventeenth-century England. In both her personal life and her writing, B. upheld the ideal of chastity that was urged upon all women of her time, but she was never easy with society's enforced separation of female sexuality and female intellect. Drawing upon her own experience, B. dramatized the conflict between a woman's conventional "public" role—that of a wife—and the "public" nature of writing. In all of B.'s novels, women are forced to choose between marriage and their intellectual pursuits, but B. rarely romanticizes the results of these choices and often denies her heroines the typical romance ending of a happy marriage. Yet she was unconventional not only in her willingness to depict the harsh demands that society placed on educated women but also in her innovative use of poetic and autobiographical techniques to shape the form of the novel itself.

Born in rural Northamptonshire to a Royalist family, B. was baptized into the Church of England on 17 May 1652. Her mother, Anne Connock, came from a Cornish family who were staunch supporters of the Stuarts, while her father, Thomas Barker, had taken up arms in defense of Charles I. B. spent most of her childhood in Wilsthorp, a tiny Lincolnshire village where her father was a tenant farmer of the Earl of Essex. Despite the relative seclusion of her early years, B. secured the advantages of a good education through her brother, Edward, who assisted her in her studies of Latin and medicine. Nor was she denied access to the higher ranks of society. Years later in the dedication she wrote to the Countess of Exeter for her novel, *Exilius*, B. recalled that it was "Burleigh-house, with its Park, Shades, and Walks" that first inspired the bucolic setting of her romance.

In her later writing, B. makes it clear that her early poems received the approbation of her brother and his circle of friends at St. John's College, Oxford. B. recalled these years with nostalgia, and she portrayed them as a period of intellectual and emotional felicity when she was courted by young men and compared favorably with the acclaimed poet, Katherine Phillips, known as the "Matchless Orinda." Yet B.'s early happiness and her contentment with her rural surroundings proved shortlived. In the late 1670s, both her father and her beloved brother died, leaving her alone with her mother. The two women then moved to London where B. describes her sense of loneliness and estrangement through her semi-autobiographical character, "Galesia": "This was a new Life to me, and very little fitted the Shape of my Rural Fancy . . . I was like a Wild Ass in a

Forest, and liv'd alone in the midst of this great Multitude, even the great and populous City of London."

After the death of her mother in 1685, B. remained a spinster, living on the income of the tenancy she had inherited from her father. The loss of so many family ties effectively left her independent, but her mature years were often lonely and filled with hardship. By this time, B. had either converted to the Catholic faith or had ceased to conceal her family's Catholicism; as a penalty for her admission of her faith, she had to pay double tax, and her strong sympathies for the Catholic Stuart, James II, prompted her to follow his court-in-exile to France. She finally returned to England and began publishing her novels in 1713. In later years, B. suffered from cataracts, which she claims to have treated herself with some success, but her letters and manuscripts of unpublished poems offer little other information about her personal life. A letter from a relative refers to her serious illness in 1726; another letter mentions a projected trip to France in 1727. After that date nothing is known of B., nor of the circumstances of her death.

In fact, the best sources of information about B.'s personal life and literary ambitions consist of her largely autobiographical poems and novels. Through the persona of "Galesia," the "author" and heroine of many of her poems and novels, B. created an alter ego whose adventures cast her own experiences in a fictive setting. Several poems in *Poetical Recreations* (1688) that were written by B.'s admirers address her as "the incomparable Galesia" as well as the "ingenious Mrs. Barker," indicating that this was a long-standing pseudonym. By choosing to publish *Poetical Recreations* first, B. defined herself as primarily a poet, yet the collection also traces an autobiographical outline of her career, and these same poems would eventually form the "fabric" of her novel, *A Patch-work Screen*, in which they were interspersed with tales and commentary.

By 1688, B. had evidently begun writing a novel, for her *Poetical Recreations* excerpts a poem from her novel, *Exilius, or the Banish'd Roman*, which remained unpublished until 1715. Although its repetitive form and complex interweaving of plots may weary the reader, *Exilius* contains some of B.'s most imaginative episodes and exhibits an intriguing, often comic imposition of seventeenth-century sensibility upon the uninhibited, pagan world of Greek romance. In *Love Intrigues* (1713), B. begins her history of the semi-autobiographical "Galesia," recounting her unhappy love for her cousin, Bosvil, and her uneasy devotion to the Muses. B.'s title is an ironic one, for the novel offers little intrigue and its heroine appears to be betrayed not so much by love as by her own adherence to the Muses. The

ending of the novel is unsettling since it offers no resolution of the heroine's troubles, while B.'s portrayal of Galesia's anguish and confusion demonstrate a rare psychological acuity by hinting at the rage and self-destructiveness that underlie Galesia's apparent passivity.

A Patch-work Screen (1723) and *The Lining of the Patch-work Screen* (1726) continue Galesia's history after her return from a sojourn in France. Galesia is by now a much older woman, and the tone of these novels becomes progressively darker as she not only abandons her hopes of a happy marriage but also her poetic aspirations. In another dream sequence, Galesia attends the coronation of the "Matchless Orinda," her literary idol, yet in this vision, she is merely a spectator and not the "Heiress of that Ladies Muse" as she had once claimed to be. Yet despite this shift in the narrator's tone, B.'s late novels are her most colorful and original works. By choosing the "patch-work screen" as a metaphor for her method of composition, B. defined the novel as a peculiarly feminine pursuit and justified the unusual form of her work by noting that "whenever one sees a Set of Ladies together, their *Sentiments* are as differently mix'd as the *Patches* in their Work."

B.'s refusal to observe the usual boundaries of form and genre has drawn criticism from literary historians, who disparage her novels as "weak" and "incoherent." Yet her experimental combinations of poetry, autobiography, and social commentary in her narratives serve as a reminder that the "novel" as we know it was still taking shape in the seventeenth century; they do not suggest a lack of stylistic control so much as B.'s determination to give the novel a peculiarly "feminine" form. By blending fact and fiction, B. consciously constructed an identity through her alter ego, Galesia, that was neither a fictive "character" nor a historical "person" but a self designed to communicate a wide range of female experience and to explore the conflict she faced between her sexual and intellectual desires.

WORKS: *Poetical Recreations: Consisting of Original Poems, Songs, Odes &c. With Several New Translations* (1688). "Poems on Several Occasions in three parts" (Oxford, Magdalen MS. 343, c. 1701). "A Collection of Poems refering to the times" (British Library MS. ADD. 21, 621). *Love Intrigues, or, The History of the Amours of Bosvil and Galesia: as Related to Lucasia, in St. Germains Garden* (1713, revised 1719). *Exilius, or, The Banish'd Roman: A New Romance: In Two Parts, Written after the Manner of Telemachus* (1715). *The Christian Pilgrimage* (1718). *The Entertaining Novels of Mrs. Jane Barker* (1719). *A Patch-work Screen for the Ladies: or, Love and Virtue Recommended* (1723). *The Lining of the Patch-work Screen: Design'd for the Farther Entertainment of the Ladies* (1726).

BIBLIOGRAPHY: Horner, J. *The English Women Novelists and Their Connection with the Feminist Movement 1688-1797* (1929). MacCarthy, B. *Women Writers: Their Contribution to the English Novel 1621-1744* (1944). Morgan, C. *The Rise of the Novel of Manners* (1911). Reynolds, M. *The Learned Lady in England 1650-1760* (1920). Richetti, J. *Popular Fiction Before Richardson: Narrative Patterns 1700-1739* (1969). Spacks, P.M. *Imagining a Self: Autobiography and Novel in Eighteenth-Century England* (1976). Spencer, J. *The Rise of the Woman Novelist: From Aphra Behn to Jane Austen* (1986).

For articles in reference works, see: *DLB*. Todd. Other references: Backscheider, P. *Studies in the Novel* (Spring 1979). Doody, M.A. *Genre* (Winter 1977). Gibbons, G.S. *N & Q* series 12 (1922). McBurney, W.H. *P Q* (1958). Spencer, J. *Tulsa Studies in Women's Literature* (Fall 1983).

Elizabeth Wahl

Mary Bateson

BORN: 12 September 1865, Ings House, Robin Hood's Bay, near Whitby.
DIED: 30 November 1906, Cambridge.
DAUGHTER OF: William Henry Bateson and Anna Aikin.

As the daughter of the Master of St. John's College, Cambridge, B. lived in an atmosphere of committed liberalism. She was educated at the Misses Thornton's School, Cambridge; the Institut Friedlander, Baden (1880-81), and the Perse School, Cambridge. In 1884, B. enrolled in Newnham College, Cambridge, a recently established college for women. Mandell Creighton, professor of ecclesiastical history at Cambridge, suggested that B. pursue a career as a professional historian. Her dissertation, "Monastic Civilisation in the Fens," won the college's historical essay prize. In 1888, after winning a first class in the historical tripos, she began a lifelong association with Newnham as teacher, member of the council, and liberal financial supporter. In 1903 she accepted a three-year research fellowship at Newnham.

As a protégé of Creighton, B. began her career as a student of medieval monasticism. In 1889 her first publication appeared, an edition of *The Register of Crabhouse Nunnery*; the next year she published a lengthy essay on the Pilgrimage of Grace in the *English Historical Review*, and she continued to publish articles and contributed numerous reviews, especially on medieval German urban history, in this journal. Her final contribution to monastic history was her important study "Origin and Early History of Double Monasteries" (1899).

Working closely with the great legal historian F.W. Maitland, Downing Professor at Cambridge, B. became a recognized authority in medieval English municipal history. She worked extensively in local history, publishing records on Cambridge as well as her monumental edition of sources on the Corporation of Leicester from the eleventh through the seventeenth centuries. Her painstaking editing brought to publication documents from many periods, including records of the Privy Council of the sixteenth century, letters of the Duke of Newcastle from the eighteenth century, a monastic library catalogue, and the poems of the fifteenth-century English writer George Ashby. Her finest achievement as editor came at the end of her life with the publication of her two-volume *Borough Customs* for the Selden Society.

B. demonstrated her capacity for historical popularization with her delightful *Mediaeval England, 1066-1350* (1903), a volume in the Story of Nations series and the first extensive social history of medieval England. Her flair for narrative enlivens her essay on the French in America written for the *Cambridge Modern History* (1903). By 1900, B. had contributed more than one hundred entries on medieval figures to the *Dictionary of National Biography*. Her scholarly stature earned her, in 1906, appointment as one of the three editors of the projected *Cambridge Mediaeval History*. Her greatness as an historian (as opposed to an editor) is best demonstrated in her papers on "The Laws of Breteuil," where she proves convincingly that a large number of English towns based their institutions on the little Norman town of Breteuil, not on Bristol as previously thought.

B. died in Cambridge at the age of 41 after a short illness. Her indefatigable labors in English urban history were matched only by her early interest and continuing activity for women's suffrage and women's emancipation. According to contemporaries, B. was generous, steady, hard-working, cheerful and completely without pretense. She was, at the same time, according to Mrs. Creighton, writing in 1906, "one of the best, if not the best, women historical students that England has ever produced."

WORKS: Ed. *The Register of Crabhouse Nunnery*. Ed. *A Collection of Original Letters from the Bishops to the Privy Council, 1564.* (1893). Ed. Thomas Pelham-Holes, 1st Duke of Newcastle. *A Narra-*

tive of the *Changes in the Ministry, 1765–1767* (1898). Ed. *Catalogue of the Library of Synon Monastery* (1898). Ed. *George Ashby's Poem*, EETS, extra ser. 76 (1899). "Origin and Early History of Double Monasteries," *Transactions of the Royal Historical Society*, n. ser. 13 (1899). Ed. *Records of the Borough of Leicester* (vol. I, 1899; vol. II, 1901; vol. III, 1905). "The Laws of Breteuil," *English Historical Review* 15 (1900), 16 (1901). "The French in America," *Cambridge Modern History* (1903).

Ed. *Cambridge Guild Records* (1903). *Mediaeval England, 1066–1350* (1903). "The Scottish King's Household and Other Fragments," *Scottish History Society Miscellany* 2 (1904). Ed. *Borough Customs*, Selden Society, 18, 21 (vol. I, 1904; vol. II, 1906).

BIBLIOGRAPHY: DNB. Maitland, F.W. *Collected Papers* Vol. 3 (1911). Poole, R.L. *English Historical Review* (1907).

Judith C. Kohl

Nina Bawden (Kark)

BORN: 19 January 1925, London.
DAUGHTER: Charles Mabey and Ellalaine Ursula May Cushing.
MARRIED: H.W. Bawden, 1946; Austen Steven Kark, 1954.

A prolific author, producing thirty novels in thirty-five years, B. was raised in London, attended Somerville College, Oxford (from which she received both bachelor's and master's degrees), and also studied American studies in Salzburg. Besides her writing, B. has worked as an assistant for a town-and-country planning firm and as a justice of the peace for eight years. She has written in various fictional genres, including murder mysteries (*Who Calls the Tune*, 1953, published in the U.S. as *Eyes of Green*; *The Odd Flamingo*, 1954; and *Change Here for Babylon*, 1955), a gothic romance (*The Solitary Child*, 1956), horror stories, and the *Bildungsroman*, as well as the satiric, psychologically probing explorations into middle-class life for which she is best known. She has won several awards for her fiction, notably her children's books.

Her novels for adults are for the most part domestic moral comedies, highlighting the fine shadings and repercussions of seemingly small, everyday actions and decisions, and her talent as an effective ironist enables her to probe into potentially tragic situations, as in *Devil by the Sea* (1957), about the murder of children, without undue reliance on bizarre characterization or plotting. In particular, her books since *Just Like a Lady* (1960; published in the U.S. as *Glass Slippers Always Pinch*) focus on her "social comedies with modern themes and settings," as she has called them. Her subtlety in satirizing her characters, especially her adults, enables her to focus on issues that in heavier hands would be oppressive, for example, implied incest and a man's midlife crisis in *George Beneath a Paper Moon* (1974) and a character's discovery of her true father in *Familiar Passions* (1979). *Afternoon of a Good Woman*

(1976) examines the antecedents and reverberations of one afternoon's activities in the life of the "good woman" of the title, a married justice of the peace who is considering leaving her husband. *Walking Naked* (1981) applies a similar sort of scrutiny to the novel-writing process itself, revealing the process whereby the fiction writer orders and makes meaning out of random events and limited choices. *The Ice House* (1983) focuses on two women who have been friends for some thirty years. The death of one woman's husband enables a long-hidden secret to be revealed, which, in turn, forces both to reexamine their entire lives.

B. began writing children's books in 1962 and has produced well over a dozen to date, with most of these dramatized for British television. Her juvenile novels, like her books for adults, are conventionally structured, but her extraordinarily sensitive prose style and delicate imagery allow the situations she depicts to transcend stock fictional formulas. Indeed, many of B.'s children's books may be read with equal pleasure by adults as well. *Tortoise by Candlelight* (1963), like other books by B. (e.g., *In Honour Bound*, 1961), is told from a child's point of view, in this case by a fourteen-year-old girl who necessarily has to be responsible for her family, including an older sister. *Squib* (1971), with its subtly nuanced characterizations, also deals with a young person's responsibility for others, in this case about a battered boy (Squib) being taken care of by other children; in *Anna Apparent* (1972), a novel for adults, B. wrote about a battered girl, suggesting her continuing interest in such social issues.

B. has been criticized for skimming too lightly over the issues of morality that she raises in her fiction. Her novels, however, are intended less as critiques of wrong or right behavior than as studies of introspective minds at work. The sophisticated, introspective characters B. delineates—like the novelist herself—illuminate for the reader the attempt to find a believable morality out of daily life by constructing small patterns of cause and effect and assigning symbolic value in otherwise fragmented experience.

WORKS: Who Calls the Tune (1953; in the U.S. as Eyes of Green). The Odd Flamingo (1954). Change Here for Babylon (1955). The Solitary Child (1956). Devil by the Sea (1957). Just like a Lady (1960; in the U.S. as Glass Slippers Always Pinch). In Honour Bound (1961). Tortoise by Candlelight (1963). Secret Passage (1963; in the U.S. as The House of Secrets, 1964). Under the Skin (1964). On the Run (1964; in the U.S. as Three on the Run, 1965). The White Horse Gang (1966). The Witch's Daughter (1966). A Little Love, A Little Learning (1966). A Woman of My Age (1967). A Handful of Thieves (1967). The Grain of Truth (1968). The Runaway Summer (1969). The Birds on the Trees (1970). Squib (1971).

Anna Apparent (1972). Carrie's War (1973). George Beneath a Paper Moon (1974). The Peppermint Pig (1975). Afternoon of a Good Woman (1976). Rebel on a Rock (1978). The Robbers (1979). Familiar Passions (1979). William Tell (1981). Walking Naked (1981). Kept in the Dark (1982). St. Francis of Assisi (1983). The Ice House (1983). The Finding (1985). Princess Alice (1986). Circles of Deceit (1987).

BIBLIOGRAPHY: For articles in reference works, see: CA. Children's Literature Review (1976). CN. DLB. TCCW. TCC& MW.

Other references: NYTBR (3 June 1973). TLS (17 April 1981, 22 July 1983).

Jane Weiss

Ada Ellen Bayly

BORN: 25 March 1857, Brighton.
DIED: 8 February 1903, Eastbourne.
DAUGHTER OF: Robert Bayly and Mary Winter.
WROTE UNDER: Ada Ellen Bayly, Edna Lyall.

Youngest in a family of three daughters and one son, B. was left fatherless at age eleven and an orphan at fourteen. A delicate child, she was first educated at home, then later in the house of her guardian and uncle T.B. Winter, and finally in Brighton private schools. She describes her youth in The Burgess Letters (1902). After her education, she lived successively with her married sisters, both wives of clergymen. Until 1880 she lived in Lincoln with her older sister; from 1880 until her death she lived with her younger sister in London in 1881, in Lincoln from 1881 to 1884, and after 1884 in Eastbourne, where she became very involved in religious and charitable activities. She was an active supporter of the women's suffrage movement and the Women's Liberal Association.

By transposing the letters of her name, B. invented the pseudonym Edna Lyall under which she wrote her first book, Won by Waiting (1879), a girls' story that was not well received. Her second novel, Donovan, A Modern Englishman (1882), received much attention, in particular from Gladstone, with whom she began correspondence. The novel deals with the religious crisis of Donovan Farrant, a physician who becomes a Member of Parliament and his conversion from atheism to Christianity. The novel also led to her

correspondence with Charles Bradlaugh, with whom she shared many political beliefs. Although she did not agree with his atheism, her liberal views led her to campaign against his exclusion from the House of Commons. After Bradlaugh's death, B. based her next novel, We Two, on his experiences. The book details the extraordinary relationship between the secularist Luke Raeburn and his daughter Erica who eventually converts to Christianity. B. expounds open-mindedness and attacks Christians for their intolerance toward religious unorthodoxy, though she was criticized by the Church Quarterly for being unfair, an absurd accusation since she was advocating what she considered basic Christianity.

B.'s first popular book was the novel In Golden Days, a well-written historical work on the seventeenth century and the last work read to Ruskin on his deathbed. Her popularity prompted false gossip about her which she describes in Autobiography of a Slander. In subsequent novels she espoused her liberal support of the Irish cause and denounced the Boer War.

B.'s plots are always well-constructed; her best characterizations are of women and young girls. Her prose is easy to read and is sprinkled liberally with quotations from Longfellow, Whittier, and Plato. In the long run, however, the militancy expressed in her novels far outweighs any esthetic quality they may contain. Her reputation rests on Donovan, We Two, and In Golden Days.

WORKS: Won by Waiting (1879). Donovan: A Modern Englishman (1882). In Golden Days (1885).

Autobiography of a Slander (1887). Knight Errant (1887). Their Happiest Christmas (1889). Derrick Vaughn, Novelist (1889). A Hardy Norseman (1890). Max Hereford's Dream: A Tale (1891). To Right the Wrong (1894). Doreen: the Story of a Singer (1894). How the Children Raised the Wind (1896). Autobiography of a Truth (1896). Wayfaring Men (1897). Hope the Hermit (1897). In Spite of All (1901). Burgess Letters: A Record of Child Life in the 60's (1902). The Hinderers (1902).

BIBLIOGRAPHY: Escreet, J.M. Life of Edna Lyall (1904). Payne, G.A. Edna Lyall (1903).
For articles in reference works, see: Allibone. DNB.

Carole M. Shaffer-Koros

Sybille Bedford

BORN: 16 March 1911, Charlottenburg, Germany.
DAUGHTER OF: Maximillian von Schönebeck and Elizabeth Bernard.
MARRIED: Walter Bedford, 1935.

B. has published novels, biographies, and various works of reportage and memoirs, and she has been praised by Nancy Mitford, Evelyn Waugh, Aldous Huxley (she wrote a well-received biography of Huxley), Janet Flanner (Genêt), and Christopher Sykes, among others, for her incisive, sharply defined fictional character portraits. Born in Germany, she left that country while still quite young and was subsequently privately educated in France, Italy, and England, all countries in which—in addition to the United States—she has lived. Though she considered both the Sorbonne and Oxford for her university education and also considered studying law, she turned instead at age sixteen to writing, producing literary essays and several novels that were never published.

B. has also written widely for many British and American magazines on such topics as food, travel, and the law. She has written extensively about such trials as those of Jack Ruby in Dallas, Stephen Ward in London, the Auschwitz trials in Frankfurt, and the obscenity trials of D.H. Lawrence's Lady Chatterley's Lover. Her An Account of the Trial of John Bodkin Adams (1958; published in the United States as The Trial of Dr. Adams) has been praised as "an exposition of human justice at its careful best" and "a masterpiece of objective yet sensitive reporting." The Faces of Justice (1961) is a detailed analysis of criminal court procedures in England and four Continental countries; it was praised for being both objective and compassionate, winning special praise from British critics, who found its comparative approach helpful in understanding legal systems other than their own.

B.'s long, carefully researched authorized Aldous Huxley: A Biography (1973) received less consistently favorable reception because of its "deficiencies of critical perception," as Diana Trilling called them, not its "affectionate compendiousness." She was able to bring Huxley's complex life and changing commitments into sharp focus, though she said little about his writing. As a longtime friend of Huxley's, she could hardly avoid suggestions of a lack of objectivity, though she did openly discuss Huxley's experiments with drugs; rather, the biography was criticized because of its faults in organization and style and, more importantly, for its lack of coherent judgment regarding her assessment of Huxley's life and accomplishments.

B.'s fiction has also received a mixed reception. A Legacy (1956), her first novel, tells of two wealthy families in pre-World War I Germany, one Roman Catholic, one Jewish, who reflect an entire era with all its conflicts. The book is witty, elegantly stylish in language, and vividly realized in its astonishing understanding of a society B. only dimly recalled, even though the book begins with the narrator describing a childhood in Charlottenburg. A Favourite of the Gods (1963), B.'s second novel, is a study of three women in Italian society in the late 1920s, one a rich American who married an Italian prince, her Italian daughter, and her English granddaughter. Also based on B.'s early life, the novel leisurely and sensitively explores B.'s nostalgic concern with a world of privilege and the role of free will in decision-making. A Compass Error (1968), to complete the range of settings from B.'s early life, is set in a French town and concerns a shy, intellectual young woman who is lured into a lesbian relationship and eventually turns on her family and friends.

Though critics have been generous in praising B.'s precise descriptions, complex characterization, clear, graceful style, and knowledgeable detail, they have also been consistent in citing the brittle, superficial worlds of the anachronistic European aristocracy about which she writes, the irrelevant activities in which they are involved, and the contrived handling of such themes as sexual jealousy and betrayals. Her ability to link personal and political history is admittedly effective, but her sometimes self-conscious detail about food and wine, family intrigues and villas, and her stylized, contrived, witty plot manipulations increasingly strike critics as superficial and trivial.

WORKS: *The Sudden View: A Mexican Journey* (1953, 1963; also publ. as *A Visit to Don Otavio: A Traveller's Tale from Mexico*). *A Legacy* (1956). *The Best We Can Do: The Trial of John Bodkin Adams* (1958; in the U.S. as *The Trial of Dr. Adams*, 1959). *The Faces of Justice: A Traveller's Report* (1961). *A Favourite of the Gods* (1963). *A Compass Error* (1968). *Aldous Huxley: A Biography* (1973).

BIBLIOGRAPHY: For articles in reference works, see *The Author Speaks. CA. CN. MBL. WA.*

Other references: Davenport, J. *New Statesman* (28 March 1953). Evans, R.O. *Studies in the Literary Imagination* (1978). Marcus, L. *TLS* (1 June 1984). Matthews, T.S. *NYT* (1 March 1959). *Nation* (4 May 1963). *New Statesman* (11 January 1963). *NYRB* (24 April 1969). Olney, J. *South Atlantic Quarterly* (1975). Sale, R. *Hudson Review* (1975). *SR* (9 February 1957). Sykes, C. *Encounter* (June 1956). *TLS* (24 October 1968). Waugh, E. *Spectator* (13 April 1956).

Paul Schlueter

Isabella Mary Mayson Beeton

BORN: 14 March 1836, London.
DIED: 6 February 1865, Grandhithe, Kent.
DAUGHTER OF: Benjamin and Elizabeth Jerram Mayson.
MARRIED: Samuel Orchart Beeton, 1856.

B.'s name is a household word literally as well as metaphorically, for she wrote *Mrs. Beeton's Book of Household Management*, a pioneering work in cookery and housewifery (1861) whose latest edition, a reprint of the original, appeared in 1984. More than any other woman in the nineteenth century, B. changed the nature of women's work in the home.

Married at twenty to Samuel Orchart Beeton, the nineteenth century's most famous writer of Christmas Annuals and a prolific publisher, B. intended no more than the usual wifely care of an active, demanding, and sickly husband. But her determination to learn cookery and household management in order to make life harmonious for him resulted in the famous *Book of Household Management* in 1861 and *Mrs. Beeton's Cookery Book* (1862).

The Athenaeum called *Household Management* "the most imposing work of all" advice-books for wives (19 July 1862). Embellished with colored plates printed by a new process that obviated hand-coloring, it contained 46 chapters covering (in addition to recipes) legal issues, the care of children and treatment of childhood diseases and injuries, anecdotes and homilies about food, quotations from Homer, Pinney, Linnaeus, Sir Humphry Davy, Erasmus, Darwin, and others, information on sanitation, reasonable wages for servants, etiquette, homemade cleansers and polishes, invalid cookery, and just about everything else a woman was likely to encounter in her daily life. Its helpful hints for housewives included "A place for everything, and everything in its place," and "Clear as you go," two immortal pieces of modern kitchen lore. B.'s direct, clear style and her chatty, almost personal tone

make *Household Management* as readable today as it was in 1861.

The cookery sections of both books were innovative in a number of respects. They offered an index and a cross-referencing system that made it easy to locate recipes, menus, and information. Within each section, recipes were listed alphabetically. Although by no means the first to write a cookbook (a popular one appeared in the early eighteenth century), B. was the first to list ingredients at the top of a recipe so the cook could easily assemble them; she was also the first regularly to indicate the amount of preparation and cooking time. Finally, B. believed in economical household management, and to this end she listed the approximate cost of each dish and indicated ways to utilize every sort of leftover. Herself a poor cook and unenthusiastic housewife, B. included in her books all the items she had been uncertain about in her early married life, thus making them accessible to the novice and the uneducated. In these books B. established the modern cookbook format.

B. is also noted for setting up, with her husband, the first mail-order system for buying dress patterns from a pattern-book; she herself devised the dress pattern format we use today.

B.'s various adaptations of *Household Management* served to elevate the housewife into an important family manager and placed the information and skills she needed at her fingertips for the first time. *Household Management* was reprinted in parts in the 1920s and has gone through fourteen complete editions. Its lively style, its timeless information, and its adaptability to a variety of formats have made "Mrs. Beeton" a household word for over 125 years.

WORKS: *Mrs. Beeton's Book of Household Management* (1861). *Mrs. Beeton's Cookery Book* (1862). *Dictionary of Everyday Cookery* (1865). *Mrs. Beeton's House and Home Books* (1866-67). *Mrs. Beeton's All About Cookery* (1871). *Mrs. Beeton's*

How to Manage House, Servants, and Children (1871). Beeton's Every-Day Cookery and House-keeping Book (1872). Mrs. Beeton's Cookery Book and Household Guide (1890).

BIBLIOGRAPHY: Freeman, S. Isabella and Sam: The Story of Mrs. Beeton (1977). Hyde, H. Mr. and Mrs. Beeton (1951). Spain, N. Mrs. Beeton and Her Husband (1948).

For articles in reference works, see: Allibone SUP.

Loralee MacPike

Aphra Behn

BORN: 1640, Harbledown, Kent (?).
DIED: 16 April 1689, London.
DAUGHTER OF: Bartholomew and Elizabeth Denham Johnson (?).
MARRIED: Mr. Behn, 1665 (?).
WROTE UNDER: Astrea.

B.'s origins are uncertain, but recent evidence suggests that she was the Aphra Johnson christened in 1640 in Harbledown, Kent, although the yeoman status of her supposed father does not accord with her education, which is that of a gentlewoman. According to her novel Oronooko, she traveled to Surinam in 1663–64 when she was a young woman. Tradition has it that upon her return to London she married a merchant named Behn, of Dutch extraction, who perhaps died of the plague in 1665; however, she never once refers to such a person. The earliest indisputable external evidence about her life is a series of letters documenting her employment in 1666 as a secret agent for the English government. She was sent to Antwerp to get information about exiled Cromwellians and to relay Dutch military plans. She used Astrea as her code name as a spy, later as her literary name. In the Netherlands she ran into debt, and in 1667 when she returned home, went briefly to debtor's prison. She was noted among a wide circle of friends and fellow writers for her beauty, wit, and generosity; Sir Peter Lely and Mary Beale painted portraits of her. Her strong Tory sentiments and personal loyalty to the royal family led to a political outspokenness that earned her enemies among some powerful Whigs. She satirized the Earl of Shaftesbury, the Whig leader, in The City Heiress (1682) but offended the king in the same year when she attacked the Duke of Monmouth in an epilogue, for which she was arrested. During her life she was forced to fend off not only political and personal attacks but also attacks on her as a woman who wrote with the same freedoms as a man. In her last years she suffered from poverty and a painful crippling disease, and her political hopes were crushed by the Revolution of 1688.

B. first achieved literary celebrity as a playwright, entering the theater in 1670 and producing seventeen extant plays; two more plays have been lost—Like Father, Like Son (1682) and The Wavering Nymph (1684). Four anonymous plays have been attributed to her—The Woman Turned Bully (1675), The Debauchee (1677), The Counterfeit Bridegroom (1677), and The Revenge (1680); these, however, may have been written by Thomas Betterton. B.'s dramatic specialty was the "Spanish" comedy of intrigue written in brisk, colloquial prose. Typically she manipulates several sources into a complexly and wittily plotted play of expert stage craftsmanship. A number of couples—eluding the unwanted marriages arranged for them—meet, bed and/or wed after innumerable intrigues, mistaken identities, duels, disguises, and practical jokes. Her plays abound in bedroom farce and scenes of comic lowlife with delightful portrayals of landladies, bawds, buffoons, and prostitutes. She provides spectacle in masquing, costuming, and dance and uses stage machinery and other technical resources to create special effects.

The best of B.'s intrigue comedies is The Rover; or, The Banished Cavaliers (1677), set at carnival time in Naples, where impoverished English cavaliers-in-exile become entangled with Spanish ladies and win their persons and fortunes. B.'s rover, Willmore, is her distinctive version of a favorite Restoration character, the wild gallant. The Rover stayed in the repertory until the middle of the eighteenth century, the role of the witty heroine being taken by such famous actresses as Elizabeth Barry, Anne Bracegirdle, Anne Oldfield, and Peg Woffington. Also among B.'s best plays is Sir Patient Fancy (1678), an amusing tangle of the amours of two neighboring London families. Her Emperor of the Moon was an instant success in 1687. A gay and extravagant combination of commedia dell' arte, operatic spectacle, sumptuous costuming, dance, song, satire, intrigue, and a bit of manners comedy, the play was performed for nearly a hundred years.

A number of her plays deal centrally with her most distinctive theme, her attack on forced marriage. She titled her first play The Forced Marriage (1670) and went on to write The Town Fop (1676) and The Lucky Chance (1686), respectively a sentimental and a harder treatment of the same subject. While New Comedy in general depicts the witty stratagems of young lovers who outwit their elders in order to marry according to their own choice, Behn goes beyond this to attack the arranged marriage as an institution. In doing so, she uses in distinctive ways two stock characters, the courtesan and the amazon. In *The Rover*, Parts I and II (1677, 1681), and *The Feigned Courtesans* (1679), B. uses the courtesan to suggest that marriage for money is a form of prostitution. In *The Young King* (1679) and *The Widow Ranter* (1689) the woman warrior in both romantic and comic versions provides a visual metaphor for the battle of the sexes and suggests the compatibility of lovers who are equals in wit and war.

B. was a versatile and sometimes distinguished poet. She wrote topical and witty prologues and epilogues for the theater. Her elegies and panegyrics in baroque pindarics for members of the royal family and the nobility were usually published in folio or quarto to celebrate a state occasion. Her elegies for the Earl of Rochester and the Duke of Buckingham display her personal affection and admiration for these two fellow wits. B. had a fine lyric gift; her elegant and sophisticated songs appeared both in her plays and in contemporary collections. Her best known song, "Love in Fantastic Triumph Sat," appeared in her one tragedy, *Abdelazer* (1676), and has often been reprinted.

B. made a number of miscellaneous translations from Latin and French in the latter part of her career, apparently for the money. She had no Latin and worked from a prose paraphrase of Ovid and Cowley; her French, however, was fluent, and she produced able, sometimes improved, versions of Tallament, La Rochefoucauld, Bonnecorse, Aesop, and de Fontenelle.

In the last years of her life she also wrote fiction, producing more than a dozen novels, some of which were published posthumously. Her novels achieved great popularity: two were dramatized, and collections of her novels appeared throughout the eighteenth century; some continue to be reprinted. In her fictions B. pioneered in the transition from romance to novel by providing extensive circumstantial detail. Her two best tales—*The Fair Jilt* and *Oronooko*—are based on events she herself witnessed. *Oronooko*, the story of an African prince enslaved in Surinam, displays great originality in theme and structure and is perhaps her best-known work.

B. wrote ably in a number of genres. She is significant not only as an artist but also as the first professional woman writer and the first woman whose writing won her burial in Westminster Abbey. On her tombstone are these verses: "Here lies a proof that wit can never be/ Defence enough against mortality."

WORKS: *The Forced Marriage* (1670). *The Amorous Prince* (1671). *The Dutch Lover* (1673).*Abdelazer* (1676). *The Town Fop* (1676). *The Rover* (1677; edited by F. Link, 1967). *Sir Patient Fancy* (1678). *The Feigned Courtesans* (1679). *The Young King* (1679). *The Second Part of the Rover* (1681). *The False Count* (1681). *The Roundheads* (1681). *Like Father, Like Son* (1682). *The City Heiress* (1682). *Poems upon Several Occasions* (1684). *Love Letters between a Nobleman and His Sister* (1684). *The Wavering Nymph* (1684). *A Pindaric on the Death of Our Late Sovereign* (1685). *A Poem to Catherine Queen Dowager* (1685). *A Pindaric Poem on the Happy Coronation* (1685). *The Lucky Chance* (1686). *The Emperor of the Moon* (1687; edited by L. Hughes, *Ten English Farces*, 1948). *To Christopher, Duke of Albemarle* (1687). *To the Memory of George, Duke of Buckingham* (1687). *The Amours of Philander and Sylvia* (1687). *A Congratulatory Poem to Her Most Sacred Majesty* (1688). *The Fair Jilt* (1688). *A Congratulatory Poem on the Happy Birth of the Prince of Wales* (1688). *Oronooko* (1688). *Agnes de Castro* (1688). *A Poem to Sir Roger L'Estrange* (1688). *To Poet Bavius* (1688). *A Congratulatory Poem to Queen Mary* (1689). *The History of the Nun* (1689). *The Lucky Mistake* (1689). *A Pindaric Poem to the Reverend Dr. Burnet* (1689). *The Widow Ranter* (1689). *The Younger Brother* (1696). *The Adventure of the Black Lady* (1698). *The Court of the King of Bantam* (1698). *The Nun* (1698). *The Unfortunate Happy Lady* (1698). *The Wandering Beauty* (1698). *The Dumb Virgin* (1700). *The Unhappy Mistake* (1700). *Works*, 6 vols., ed. M. Summers (1915). *Love Letters Between a Nobleman and His Sister* (1684-1687; modern ed. 1987).

BIBLIOGRAPHY: Cameron, W.J. *New Light on Aphra Behn* (1961). Cotton, N. *Women Playwrights in England c. 1363-1750* (1980). Duffy, M. *The Passionate Shepherdess* (1977). Goreau, A. *Reconstructing Aphra* (1980). Guffey, G. *Two English Novelists* (1975). Link, F. *Aphra Behn* (1968). Loftis, J. *The Spanish Plays of Neoclassical England* (1973). O'Donnell, M.A. *Aphra Behn: An Annotated Bibliography of Primary and Secondary Sources* (1906). Sackville-West, V. *Aphra Behn* (1928). Woodcock, G. *The Incomparable Aphra* (1948).

Other references: Campbell, E. *Kunapipi* (1985). Day, R.A. *Fetter'd or Free? British Women Novelists, 1670-1815*, ed. M.A. Schofield and C. Macheski (1986). DeRitter, J. *Restoration* (1986). Houston, B. *Literature & Psychology* (1986). *MLQ* (1946, 1951). *N&Q* (1960, 1962, 1976, 1979). *PLL* (1978). *PMLA* (1913, 1934, 1936, 1960). *SB* (1969). *SP* (1962). *WL* (1977). *WS* (1980).

Nancy Cotton

George Anne Bellamy

BORN: 1731 (?), Fingal, Ireland (?).
DIED: 16 February 1788, London.
DAUGHTER OF: Mrs. Bellamy (née Seal) and her lover, John O'Hara, second Baron of Tyrawley.
MARRIED: West Digges, 1763, but since he was a bigamist, the marrige was illegal.

B. was a popular eighteenth-century actress who claimed to have written *An Apology for the Life of George Anne Bellamy* (1785). In truth, this highly idealized "autobiography" was probably written by Alexander Bicknell, a historian, from material provided by B.; most reference works now list Bicknell as the editor for these volumes. Regardless of the details of its authorship, this six-volume work offers valuable insights into eighteenth-century England and its theatre.

Like her mother, B. was an actress who experienced one unhappy love affair after another and bore one illegitimate child after another. At the age of eleven or so, she defied her father, in whose custody she was living, and went to live with her mother. This relationship soon gave her access to the stage where she played several small parts in the early 1740s and was introduced to the great actors and actresses of the day. Success came when she was playing Andromache in an informal staging of *The Distrest Mother*. John Rich was apparently enchanted with her and convinced James Quin, the manager of Covent Garden, to allow her a starring role in 1744. From that time until her last season in 1770, she was quite popular on the London, Dublin, and Edinburgh stages.

This popularity brought her the attentions of several men. She lived with but did not marry George Metham, John Calcraft, and West Digges, and she bore children to Metham and Calcraft. Although she went through a wedding ceremony with Digges, the ceremony was illegal since Digges had another wife still living. The only man with whom she seems to have lived happily was the great actor, Henry Woodward. Their relationship, which she claimed was platonic, lasted from 1767 until his death ten years later. Woodward was the only one of her many lovers to leave her large amounts of money in his will, a significant gesture because her taste for luxury left her continually in debt. But because she was unable to claim all of her inheritance from Woodward, her debts grew steadily worse after his death until she died in 1788.

An Apology for the Life of George Anne Bellamy provides a mild and quite moralistic picture of her life, conveyed through letters written to the anonymous "Hon. Miss—." The preface explains that she wrote the book in order to recover her reputation and to provide a morally instructive tale for young girls. In fact, the *Apology* omits many details from Bellamy's early stage career and glosses over others in order to dramatize and tidy up her life. Although these volumes may today seem stilted and didactic, they were popular enough to be translated into French in 1799. Appended to the *Apology* is an angry letter to John Calcraft that she had intended to publish in 1767. Even though this letter did not appear until twelve years after Calcraft's death, certain portions of it were softened in order to protect his reputation and hers. In addition to the *Apology*, Bellamy is credited with writing a single-volume narrative autobiography, *Memoirs of a Celebrated Actress* (1785?).

WORKS: *An Apology for the Life of George Anne Bellamy* (1785). *Memoirs of a Celebrated Actress* (1785?).

BIBLIOGRAPHY: Doran, J. *Annals of the English Stage from T. Betterton to E. Kean* (1888). Genest, J. *Some Account of the English Stage, 1660–1830* (1832). Hartmann, C. *Enchanting Bellamy* (1956). Wilkinson, T. *The Wandering Patentee* (1795).

For articles in reference works, see: *DNB*. Highfill, P., et al. *A Biographical Dictionary of Actors . . .* (1973). Todd.

Tori Haring-Smith

Stella Benson

BORN: 6 January 1892, Shropshire.
DIED: 6 December 1933, China.
DAUGHTER OF: Ralph Beaumont and Caroline Essex Cholmondeley Benson.
MARRIED: James O'Gorman Anderson, 1921.

B. wrote essays, short stories, poetry, and the novels for which she is best known. In her first three novels, especially, her personality as a writer shines through and her unique perception of the world is displayed with an imagination and a sympathy which can only be called humane. She satirizes her own British society, wherever she may find it—in London, in the West Indies, in China—with a voice that never forgets its own bent to occasional folly. She demonstrates a remarkable knack for combining reality and fantasy, criticism and compassion. Fanciful characters symbolize her feelings about serious social problems such as women's suffrage, imperial colonization, and World War I. She achieved popular success with her fifth novel, *The Far-Away Bride* (1930; published in Great Britain as *Tobit Transplanted*, 1931), for which she won the Femina Vie Heureuse Prize and the A.C. Benson silver medal of the Royal Society of Literature in 1932.

B. was educated at home and in France, Germany, and Switzerland, and she continued to travel widely despite the fact that she suffered from weak lungs and was often plagued by ill health. She visited the West Indies, accumulating material for her first book. Home from the voyage, she worked from 1913 to 1917 in the East End of London, first serving in the Charity Organization Society and then, disillusioned with their methods, helping the poor in her own way by opening a small store. She was active as a suffragette during this time, and, drawing on all her recent experiences, she wrote her first two novels. *I Pose* (1915) is a light-hearted feminist manifesto in which B. deals with woman's suffrage as an emotional, political, and economic concern. The novel centers on an unnamed suffragette whose adventures on the exotic Trinity Island and in the Brown Borrough of London illustrate the disheartening and sometimes fatal consequences of living in a world where "Oh, my dear, too killing" is the motto for women. *This Is the End* (1917) is also set in Brown Borrough and features a young woman, Jay, who has disowned her wealth, taken a job as a bus conductor, and escaped into the world of her own imagination. Jay's secret world is destroyed with the news that her brother and confidant, Kew, has been killed in France. The novel presents a cross section of attitudes toward World War I, ranging from the condescension of a pretentious Brown Borrough social worker, to the logic of a pacifist Quaker, to Kew's own nonchalance about his possible death.

B. lived in the United States from June 1918 to January 1920, supporting herself with various odd jobs while she wrote her third novel, *Living Alone* (1919). The setting is once again the Brown Borrough of London during World War I and draws on B.'s experiences with the Charity Organization Society. This novel, written—as B. herself said— for "the magically-inclined minority," criticizes a society which does not temper charity with common sense. In January 1920, B. set out on an eighteen-month voyage to England by way of India and China. This journey included another series of various occupations. In China, she met James O'Gorman Anderson, a customs officer; they were married in London in September 1921, and their honeymoon was a trip to America, crossing the continent from east to west in a Ford.

Many of her experiences in the United States and in the Far East are captured in *The Little World* (1925), a collection of essays, and in *The Poor Man* (1922), her fourth novel. Except for occasional trips, the remainder of B.'s life, until her death from pneumonia in a hospital at Honkai, Tonkin, in December 1933, was spent in various regions of China where her husband was stationed. One of these places was Manchuria, the setting for her last-completed and best-known novel, *The Far-Away Bride* (1930). This unusual novel follows the outline of the legend of Tobit in the Old Testament Apocrypha, replacing the exiled families of ancient Israel with two families of White Russian refugees in Manchuria and Korea during the 1920s. Despite the novel's allegorical aspects, B. creates a realistic environment in which a complex and realistic tale of love and family conflicts is enacted. In *The Far-Away Bride* and *The Poor Man*, psychological characterization replaces the fanciful, humorous mode of B.'s earlier novels.

B.'s last novel, *Mundos* (published posthumously in 1935), is unfinished: thirteen chapters were completed and revised; four, perhaps five, chapters remained unwritten. For this novel, B. creates an island, Mundos, which is somewhat like the Trinity Island of her first novel. Surprisingly, in the descriptions of both these island worlds, B. falls prey to instances of what the contemporary reader would regard as blatant stereotyping and racial prejudice. Despite the way in which these unfortunate remarks date the novels, B.'s thought is still progressive and her goal is to observe the attendant ills and conflicts of what she terms, ironically, "liberal imperialistic thought."

In 1923, Joseph Collins wrote of B. in conjunction with Virginia Woolf, naming them as two of the most promising women writers in England at the time. B. visited Woolf on 16 July 1932, and Woolf wrote in her diary that B. talked of "making money by stories . . . in a sensible matter of fact way, like a working class woman." When Woolf heard of B.'s death the following year, she wrote, "I did not know her, but have a sense of those fine patient eyes: the weak voice; the cough; the sense of oppression. She sat on the terrace with me at Rodmell. And now, so quickly, it is gone, what might have been a friendship. . . . A very fine steady mind: much suffering; suppressed."

Though her life and literary career were cut short, both were characterized by a remarkable energy and love for life. Marked by her fresh, original, and irrefutable wit, her novels and essays convey the fine sensitivity noted by Woolf. B. achieves a careful balance between honest detachment from and empathetic involvement with her characters and her readers, thus making her work a superb study of human identity, motive, instinct, and behavior.

WORKS: *I Pose* (1915). *This Is the End* (1917). *Twenty* (1918). *Living Alone* (1919). *Kwan-yin* (1922). *The Poor Man* (1922). *Pipers and a Dancer* (1924). *The Awakening, A Fantasy* (1925). *The Little World* (1925). *Goodbye, Stranger* (1926). *The Man Who Missed the Bus* (1928). *Worlds Within Worlds* (1928). *The Far-Away Bride* (1930). *Hope Against Hope and Other Stories* (1931). *Christmas Formula and Other Stories* (1932). *Pull Devil, Pull Baker* (1933). *Mundos* (1935). *Poems* (1935). *Collected Short Stories* (1936).

BIBLIOGRAPHY: Collins, J. *The Doctor Looks at Literature* (1923). Grant, J. *Stella Benson: A Biography* (1987). Mais, S.P.B. *Some Modern Authors* (1923). Roberts, R. E. *Portrait of Stella Benson* (1939).

For articles in reference works, see: *DLB. DNB. TCA.*

Kitti Carriker

Phyllis Bentley

BORN: 19 November 1894, Halifax, Yorkshire.
DIED: 27 June 1977, Halifax, Yorkshire.
DAUGHTER OF: Joseph Edwin and Eleanor Bentley.

One of four children, only daughter of a textile manufacturer, B. was educated at Cheltenham Ladies College and obtained an external degree from London University. She began her career teaching in a boys' grammar school, but, unsuccessful at this, she remained at home. B.'s autobiography *O Dreams, O Destinations* (1962) tells of the dilemma of the educated woman living in the parental home in the early years of the twentieth century without income or independence. World War I provided the opportunity for B. to go to London to work as a clerk in the Ministry of Munitions, and when the war was over she returned to Yorkshire. After a librarian taught B. the Dewey Decimal System, she spent six years cataloguing books in local libraries and working on a series of short stories and her first novel, *Environment* (1922).

B. wrote primarily about her native West Riding and of the lives of men and women working in the textile trade. With *Inheritance* (1932), the story of the coming of the industrial revolution to Yorkshire, she came to prominence in Great Britain and the United States. The novel is a chronicle of a mill-owning family, the Oldroyds, in which B. delineated the rise and decline of the textile trade from the Luddite riots to the 1926 slump, and many of the events were based on the experiences of her own family. B. returned to the story of the Oldroyds in *The Rise of Henry Morcar* (1946) and ended their saga in *A Man of His Time* (1966).

Befriended by Winifred Holtby and by Vera Brittain, who invited B. to stay with her in London, B. was introduced to the British literary world. From then on her horizons and opportunities expanded. Invited to the United States where her reputation as a regional novelist grew, she made two lecture tours in the 1930s.

B.'s only novel set outside Yorkshire, *Freedom Farewell* (1936), was not a success. Describing the fall of the Roman republic, it was written as a protest against the rise of Hitler and Mussolini. B. was bitter that no one understood why she had written it.

B. continued to live at home in Yorkshire and helped to finance the family textile business during the Depression. World War II found her back in London working for the American Division of the Ministry of Information. In January 1941, braving the perils of submarines, B. crossed the Atlantic to lecture on wartime Britain. On her return she wrote *Here Is America* (1942), a booklet explaining America to the British. She returned to the United States in 1943, by air, to work with the British Information Services in New York. Her Atlantic wartime crossings and the rocket attacks on London provided material for *The Rise of Henry Morcar* (1946).

Following the war, B. nursed her mother devotedly for five years during which time she was unable to write. Following her mother's death in 1949 she worked prodigiously producing articles, reviews, broadcasts, books, and TV scripts. When the novel *Crescendo* (1958) was not a success, B. realized that her popularity was over as a result of changing times. The "angry young men," mostly Yorkshiremen, had taken over and the working-class had replaced the middle-class as material for novels.

An essay, *Yorkshire and the Novelist* (1968), discusses the phenomenon that so many English writers come from Yorkshire. B. believed that although the Yorkshire character had defects—little charm or grace—it had much humor and solidity. *The English Regional Novel* (1941) with special emphasis on Charlotte Brontë, George Eliot, Thomas Hardy and Arnold Bennett, is a survey of English regional fiction that flowered between 1840 to 1940.

B. never married and believed she was unattractive to the opposite sex. This may explain why Henry Morcar was described by a *New York*

Times reviewer as "A stilted lover who sounds as if his sentiments had been strained through the British Ministry of Information." She lived a restricted home life dominated by her mother, a beautiful woman in revolt against the sordidness of life. B. was thirty before she dared to use lipstick or smoke cigarettes. A solitary child and an inveterate daydreamer, she had difficulty with close relationships outside her family. The brotherhood of man became her creed. She believed that if she could present human beings in all their facets she could promote better understanding between them.

B. wished to write a great novel but knew she had not succeeded. A *Manchester Guardian* reviewer described her as "a gifted and skilled practitioner in the art of fiction," and B. accepted this verdict on her work. She was awarded an honorary degree by the University of Leeds in 1949 and the Order of the British Empire in 1970.

WORKS: *Pedagomania: Or, the Gentle Art of Teaching* (1918). *The World's Bane and other Stories* (1918). *Environment* (1922). *Cat-in-the-Manger* (1923). *The Partnership* (1928). *The Spinner of the Years* (1928). *Sounding Brass: a Play in One Act* (1930). *Trio* (1930). *Inheritance* (1932). *A Modern Tragedy* (1934). *The Whole of the Story* (1935). *Freedom, Farewell* (1936). *Sleep in Peace* (1938). *The Power and the Glory* (1940). *Take Courage* (1940). *Manhold* (1941). *The English Regional Novel* (1941). *Here Is America* (1942). *The Rise of Henry Morcar* (1946). *Some Observations on the Art of Narrative* (1946). *Colne Valley Cloth from*

the Earliest Times to the Present Day (1947). *Life Story* (1948). *The Brontës* (1950). *Quorum* (1950). *Panorama: Tales of the West Riding* (1952). *The House of Moreys* (1953). *Chain of Witnesses* (1954). *Noble in Reason* (1955). *Love and Money: Seven Tales of the West Riding* (1957). *Crescendo* (1959). *The New Apprentice* (1959). *Kith and Kin: Nine Tales of Family Life* (1960). *The Young Brontës* (1960). *A Mid-Summer's Night Crime* (1961). *Committees* (1962). *O Dreams, O Destinations* (1962). *Miss Phipps Discovers America* (1963). *Public Speaking* (1964). *Enjoy Books and Reading* (1964). *The Adventures of Tom Leigh* (1964). *Tales of the West Riding* (1965). *A Man of His Time* (1966). *Ned Carver in Danger* (1967). *Gold Pieces* (1968). *Ring in the New* (1969). *The Brontës and Their World* (1969). *Sheep May Safely Graze* (1972). *The New Venturers* (1973). *More Tales of the West Riding* (1974). *Haworth of the Brontës* (with John Ogden) (1977).

BIBLIOGRAPHY: For articles in reference works, see: *CA. Encyclopedia of Mystery and Detection*, ed. C. Steinbrunner and O. Penzler (1975). *Longman. MBL. TCA & Sup. TCC & MW.*

Other references: *Christian Science Monitor* (16 April 1932, 28 November 1969). *Kenyon Review* (1968). *New Yorker* (28 December 1946). *NYHTBR* (13 May 1962). *NYTBR* (18 September 1932, 15 December 1946, 22 December 1946). *TLS* (7 April 1932, 25 May 1946, 13 April 1962, 10 March 1966, 25 May 1967).

Joan Ambrose Cooper

Anne Beresford

BORN: 10 September 1919, Redhill, Surrey.
DAUGHTER OF: Richard and Margaret (Kent) Beresford.
MARRIED: Michael Hamburger, 1951; remarried Hamburger, 1974.

B.'s poems are filled with literary allusions; for example, some titles are "Miranda," "Persephone," "Nicodemus," and "Eurydice and Andromeda." Yet her poetry is often based on daily life. She writes of the countryside, particularly the wild Suffolk landscape near her home. The nature she depicts is often threatening, as in these lines from "Leiston Abbey" describing a rabbit:

This is its sanctuary.
Nothing makes sense
with the heavy clouds spitting rain
onto the rabbit, its eyes obliterated
by the large swellings of diseased flesh.

One also gets frequent references to the past. Two repeated words in her volume *The Curving Shore* are "distance" and "mirror." These words suggest B.'s emphasis on the past and the reflective yet somehow detached nature of her poetry. "Passing Moment," for instance, begins,

As she brushed her hair
she'd looked in the mirror
and the strange woman peered back
curiously. Peering back
from a distance.

Her first volume of verse, the sixteen-page *Walking Without Moving*, is marked by a curious repetition throughout, as in "Against Hope": "I am willingly dragged / gladly brick on brick / pile up press down / just breath breath." A common theme is bittersweet love affairs ("The Falling," "Crows," "Autumn at Four," "Phrase Unanswered"). The conclusion of "Phrase Unanswered" serves as an example:

> Why love
> webbed in barbed wire?
> A pineapple holds no more promises
> Marzipan is not a luxury.
> There is not love, nothing
> but chrysanthemums.

B.'s poems can seem simple on first reading and occasionally sentimental, but her best work often is filled with drama and grotesque irony. As William Cookson states, B.'s "imagination is connected with humor and satire. Her irony succeeds because it is not obvious." This irony is demonstrated in "The Atlantic from a Liner." Here, as the passengers watch "legless birds" and "fried chickens," the speaker realizes that she, too, is "a legless bird / flying nowhere." The grim irony and stark landscapes help foster a generally melancholy mood in B.'s poetry.

In addition to her writing, B. has worked as a broadcaster for the BBC, a drama and poetry teacher, a musician, and an actress. She gives moving readings of her poetry. A sense of her busy life can be gleaned by reading *A Mug's Game*, memoirs by her husband, poet Michael Hamburger (even though she is rarely mentioned specifically).

WORKS: *Struck by Apollo*, with M. Hamburger (1965). *Walking Without Moving* (1967). *The Lair* (1968). *The Villa* (1968). *Footsteps in Snow* (1972). *Modern Fairy Tale* (1972). *The Courtship* (1972). *Alexandros: Selected Poems*, by Vera Lungu (trans.) (1974). *The Curving Shore* (1975). *Words*, with M. Hamburger (1977). *Unholy Giving* (1977). *The Songs of Almut from God's Country* (1980). *Songs a Thracian Taught Me* (1980).

BIBLIOGRAPHY: Levenson, C. *Queen's Quarterly* (Kingston, Ontario), (1971).

For articles in reference works, see: *CA. CP. DLB.*

Other references: *TLS* (13 October 1972, 9 July 1976).

Louis J. Parascandola

Mary Berry

BORN: 16 March 1763, Kirkbridge, Yorkshire.
DIED: 20 November 1852, London.
DAUGHTER OF: Robert Berry and Elizabeth Seaton Berry.

Editor, letter writer, and cultural historian, B. was best known in her youth as the dear companion of the aged Horace Walpole and in her old age as the gifted hostess of her intellectual salons. Her unique place in the London scene during the first half of the nineteenth century is reflected in these words written by Harriet Martineau shortly after B.'s death at the age of eighty-nine: "She was not only the woman of letters of the last century, carried far into our own—she was not only the Woman of Fashion who was familiar with the gaieties of life before the fair daughters of George III were seen abroad, and who had her own will and way with society up to last Saturday night: she was the repository of the whole literary history of four-score years; and when she was pleased to throw open the folding-doors of her memory, they were found to be mirrors of literature, from the mournful Cowper to Tennyson the Laureate."

B.'s origins hardly suggest the central role she was to play in London society. Her father, son of a tailor, took employment with his wealthy uncle, Robert Ferguson, a Scottish merchant. In 1762, when the youth married Elizabeth Seaton, a young lady with no dowry, Ferguson disinherited the newlyweds in favor of William Berry, the younger brother. A year after B.'s birth, a second daughter, Agnes, was born; three years later, Elizabeth Berry died in childbirth and the child also died. B. and her sister were then raised by her maternal grandmother. During these years both girls read widely and their lively, acquisitive minds more than compensated for their lack of formal education.

From her reading, B. developed a longing "to see that world of which [she] had been picking up all sorts of accounts." When her Uncle William, now possessed of Ferguson's fortune, provided the Berrys with an income of £1000 a year, her longing became reality; and she, her father, and her sister traveled to Rotterdam in 1783. After three weeks in Holland, B. celebrated the experience in her journal: "I have always looked back to those three weeks as the most enjoyable and the most enjoyed of my existence, in which I received the greatest number of new ideas, and felt my mind, my understanding, and my judgment increase everyday, while at the same time my imagination was delighted with the charm of novelty in everything I saw or heard." As travel opened her mind, it also influenced her attitudes towards the future. For example, on arriving in Florence she wrote, "I began to feel my situation, and how entirely dependent I was on my resources for my conduct, respectability, and success." Recognizing her role in her small family, she stated "that I must be a protecting mother, instead of a gay companion, to my sister; and to my father a guide and monitor, instead of finding in him a tutor and protector."

In 1788, B. completely captured the affections of the seventy-one-year-old bachelor, Horace Walpole, the brilliant letter writer, art collector, and proud owner of Strawberry Hill in Twickenham. In a letter to Lady Ossory, Walpole described the sisters as "the best-informed and the most perfect creatures I ever saw of their age. They are exceedingly sensible, entirely natural and unaffected, frank, and, being qualified to talk on any subject, nothing is so easy and agreeable as their conversation." Although he referred to the sisters as his "twin wives," he seemed to feel a deeper affection for B. Not surprisingly, the more than four decade age difference excited some humorous response in social circles, but Walpole never wavered in his devotion. In fact, shortly after their meeting he was inspired by the sisters to write one of his most charming books, *Reminiscences, Written by Mr. Horace Walpole in 1788, for the Amusement of Miss Mary and Miss Agnes Berry*. Rumors that he had proposed marriage to B. circulated from time to time, but no evidence exists to support this claim.

Yet there were problems. In 1796 B. became engaged to General Charles O'Hara, but when he was ordered to Gibraltar, she found reasons to delay their marriage and remain in England. Although they corresponded, the engagement ended in April 1797 and B. packed the O'Hara letters away. Forty-eight years later she reopened them and wrote, "This packet of letters relates to the six happiest months of my long and insignificant existence." She believed their problems could have been resolved "had we ever met for twenty-four hours." Another problem had arisen earlier, in 1791, when the Berrys made an extended European tour. Walpole was deeply distressed, especially when the family arrived in Paris, where they were exposed to the dangers of the Revolution. His letters, full of concern, followed them wherever they went.

Yet, on the whole, the relationship was the source of satisfaction to them all. The sisters were Walpole's constant friends and companions, and he responded by contributing to their material security in the form of a charming house called Little Strawberry Hill. Finally, when he died in 1797, in addition to the house, he provided each the interest from £4000, relieving them completely from financial worries. Most important was a wooden box containing "my own literary works as have been heretofore published or have been printed or still remain in manuscript." Although these were directed to Mr. Berry, it was B. who became Walpole's literary executor and published or republished his works.

The fifty-five years left to the sisters would center more in London than in Twickenham. Eventually, settled at 8 Curzon Street, they became the key figures in salons that attracted the most distinguished people in London. Byron, Francis Jeffrey, Sydney Smith, Samuel Rogers, Macaulay, Malthus, Dickens, and Thackeray all dined and conversed under the watchful direction of the Berry sisters. The internationally famous Madame de Staël was a frequent visitor who believed B. was "*by far* the cleverest woman in England." The great actress Fanny Kemble was a favorite visitor during their last years.

B. did however leave behind a literary legacy; yet, aside from her correspondence, it receives little attention today. In 1798, she edited *The Works of Horatio Walpole* in five volumes, an edition that did not carry her name, and in 1810, she edited the letters of the Marquise du Deffand, part of the Walpole legacy. Nine years later, in 1819, B. published *The Life of Rachel, Lady Russell*, a biography consisting of letters and transitional remarks. Joanna Baillie described it as an "edifying example to the young women of the day, who consider religion as too exclusively connected with mystery."

Considered by her contemporaries to be her best work, *A Comparative View of Social Life in England and France* was published in two parts in 1828 and 1831. In 1844, the two parts were published together in her collected works. Her success in managing such a broad topic is reflected in the unreserved praise of the critic for *The Quarterly Review*, who wrote, "she has presented us with a sketch of great power, the result of various and accurate learning, instinct with deep and sober reflection, ever exhibiting a love of justice and virtue, nor deformed by affectation any more than it is tinged with unworthy prejudice."

Yet, for today's reader, *Extracts of the Journal and Correspondence of Miss Berry from the Year 1793 to 1852* has the greatest appeal. The seven decades, often recorded in considerable detail, of a life that touched so many important people during those many evenings in Richmond and London and during the many European tours provide a remarkable picture of English intellectual life in the first half of the nineteenth century; and then there are the memorable scenes when the sisters were received by royalty at home and by Napoleon in France. These experiences and more are mirrored for the reader in the three volumes edited by Lady Teresa Lewis.

B. has vanished from the pages of most literary accounts. Yet for more than half a century she was the center of intellectual life in London. Thackeray, a friend of her old age, wrote of her with affection: "I often thought, as I took my kind old friend's hand, how with it I held on to the old society of wits and men of the world."

WORKS: *The Works of Horatio Walpole, Earl of Orford*, ed. M. Berry (1798). *The Fashionable Friends: A Comedy* (1802). *Letters of the Marquise du Deffand*, ed. M. Berry (1810). *Some Account of Rachel Wriothesley, Lady Russell, by the Editor of Madam Du Deffand's Letters. Followed by a Series of Letters of Mary Russell to Her Husband. . .* , ed. M. Berry (1819). *A Comparative View of the Social Life in England and France.* (1828, 1831). *England and France: a Comparative View of the Social Conditions of Both Countries, from the Restoration of Charles the Second to the Present Time. To which are now first added: Remarks on Lord Orford's Letters, the Life of the Marquise du Deffand, the Life of Rachel Lady Russell, Fashionable Friends, a Comedy.* (1844). *Extracts from the Journal and Correspondence of Miss Berry, from the Year 1783 to 1852*, ed. T. Lewis (1865).

BIBLIOGRAPHY: Byron, G.G. *Byron's Letters and Journals.* Ed. L.A. Marchant (1973-1982). Chorley, H.F. *Recollections* (1873). Ketton-Cremer, R.W. *Horace Walpole* (1940). Kimble, F.A. *Records of a Later Life* (1884). Martineau, H. *Biographical Sketches* (1885). Melville, L. [pseud. L.S. Benjamin]. The Berry Papers: 1763-1852 (1914). Melville, L. [pseud. L.S. Benjamin]. *Regency Ladies* (1926). Moers, E. *Literary Women* (1976). Strachey, L. *Portraits in Miniature* (1931). Thackeray, W.M. *The Letters and Private Papers.* Ed. G.N. Ray (1946). Walpole, H. *Horace Walpole's Correspondence with Mary and Agnes Berry. . .* , in *The Yale Edition of Horace Walpole's Correspondence* (1944). Walpole, H. *Memoirs of Horace Walpole and His Contemporaries.* Ed. E. Warburton (1852).

Other references: *Edinburgh Review* (October 1865). *N&Q* (August 1983). *Quarterly Review* (March 1845). *The Times* [London] (23 November 1852). Stenton D.M. *The English Women in History* (1957).

For articles in reference works, see: Adams, W.D. *Dictionary of English Literature* (n.d.). *BA19C. DNB.* Harlice, P.P. *Index to Literary Biography* (1975). Todd.

Philip Bordinat

Isabella Lucy Bird Bishop

BORN: 15 October 1831, Yorkshire.
DIED: 7 October 1904, Edinburgh.
DAUGHTER OF: Dora Lawson Bird and the Reverend Edward Bird.
MARRIED: John F. Bishop, 1881.
WROTE UNDER: Isabella L. Bird, Isabella Bird Bishop, Isabella L. Bishop, Mrs. J.F. Bishop.

B. was one of the most popular and prolific of the late nineteenth-century Victorian lady travellers. Throughout her early travels, which were motivated by a search for good health, she wrote to her sister Henrietta, and these letters formed the basis for her first books. After the death of her sister in 1880 and of her husband in 1886, her travels centered on visits to missionaries and plans to endow various hospitals in memory of these relatives. The popularity of her travel books earned her membership in the Royal Scottish Geographical Society and later in the Royal Geographical Society. In addition to her eight major books, she wrote articles and pamphlets for British journals and religious societies, and she delivered several lectures.

B. was born in 1831 into a strongly religious family headed by the Reverend Edward Bird. Though troubled by chronic spinal problems, B. learned early to ride horses and walk long distances in the fresh air. Her first travels, which took her in 1854 to Prince Edward Island and then on to continental Canada and the United States, were recorded in *The Englishwoman in America* (1856). She returned to North America in 1857-58, where she studied the current religious revivals and described them in essays for *The Patriot*, later collected as *The Aspects of Religion in the United States of America* (1859).

After another trip to New York and the Mediterranean in 1871, B. embarked in 1872 on the first of her long, challenging expeditions. She was directed to Australia and New Zealand for her health, but these countries soon bored her, and she boarded a rickety steamer for the Sandwich Islands, now Hawaii. As always, she travelled without concern for the comforts of civilization, camping on the edge of volcanoes, riding horseback for hours on end, and sleeping and eating in the only accommodations available—frequently filthy, wet, and insect-ridden rattraps. She did not travel the well-worn routes of British aristocrats and colonists. This rustic existence did not bother her strong digestion, and she frequently withstood the rigors of travel better than her occasional travelling companions.

After leaving the Sandwich Islands, she sailed to California, the start of a lengthy tour in the Rocky Mountains. In the Rockies, she met Jim Nugent, known as "Rocky Mountain Jim," a seasoned trapper and frontiersman with a violent history. She spent a month or so near him and grew very fond of him. Although this rough man frequently recounted for her his unsavory past, he was also very solicitous, showing her the land around Estes Park, Colorado. When he proposed to her, however, she realized, "He is a man any woman might love, but no sane woman would marry." At the conclusion of this eighteen-month trip, B. returned to England, where she published *The Hawaiian Archipelago* (1875) and *A Lady's Life in the Rocky Mountains* (1879). Her next trips took her to Japan, the Malay Peninsula, and Egypt in 1878–79 and resulted in the publication of *Unbeaten Tracks in Japan* (1880) and *The Golden Chersonese and the Way Thither* (1883).

Soon after she returned to England from these travels, B. suffered the first major personal tragedy of her life: the death of her sister Henrietta. Henrietta had served as her lodestar and her audience during all of her travels. Writing to Henrietta, she tried to make the scenery and people around her come alive with vivid description. Her later books have scattered passages that recall this style, but they are more didactic and dryly informative.

After Henrietta's death, B. married John F. Bishop, a physician who had proposed to her two years earlier. This marriage lasted only five years, however, until John's death in 1886. During her marriage, B. remained in England, was active in charity work, and studied nursing and first aid.

When her husband died, B. turned again to her travels, moving now almost compulsively around the globe on tours that defied both man and nature. In 1889–90, she travelled to India, Kashmir, and Tibet before crossing Asia to the Black Sea. This journey produced *Among the Tibetans* (1894) and *Journeys in Persia and Kurdistan* (1891). Four years later, she undertook a three-year jaunt through Canada, Japan, Korea, and China, writing her longest books, *Korea and her Neighbors* (1898) and *The Yangtze Valley and Beyond* (1899). These two books are of greater interest than her earlier works because of their subject matter, but their vivid descriptions of nature are frequently interrupted by statistics and moral reflections.

By this point, she was travelling more often by carrying chair than on horseback, but she frequently alighted for long walks in the fresh air. It is, however, extraordinary that at this age she was able to travel alone for fifteen months at a time across 8000 miles of China. Her travels were also becoming emotionally more arduous. In her early

letters and books, she repeatedly assured her reader that it was safe for a lady to travel alone. But in her last trip to China, she suffered anti-foreign riots for the first time that forced her to reconsider this opinion. These experiences also led her to revise her earlier, Rousseauistic picture of the savage as noble.

When she returned to England after this lengthy expedition, she was restless and moved about a good deal, setting up one house only in time to pack and move on to a different one. Her last trip took her on horseback through Morocco at the age of 70, but her growing illness restricted her to recording this travel only in articles. She died two years later in Edinburgh, still hoping for one more trip to China.

As well as being a valuable and accurate record of life in America and Asia in the late nineteenth century, B.'s work is a fascinating study of the late Victorian mind. Although she slept in filthy stables and ate maggotty food, B. insisted on retaining certain Victorian proprieties. She considered trousers unacceptable, for example, and asked her friend and publisher John Murray to defend her publicly when *The Times* reported that she wore "male habiliments" in the Rockies. Although she was not troubled by often being the only woman in a caravan, she always rode in an uncomfortable sidesaddle position when passing through inhabited areas. Her excellent memory and her love of nature that give life to her vivid narratives brought her well-deserved fame in her lifetime. As *The Spectator* said of *A Lady's Life in the Rocky Mountains*, "There never was anybody who had adventures so well as Miss Bird."

WORKS: *The Englishwoman in America* (1856). *The Aspects of Religion in the United States of America* (1859). *The Hawaiian Archipelago* (1875). *A Lady's Life in the Rocky Mountains* (1879). *Unbeaten Tracks in Japan* (1880). *The Golden Chersonese and the Way Thither* (1883). *Journeys in Persia and Kurdistan* (1891). *Among the Tibetans* (1894). *Korea and Her Neighbors* (1898). *The Yangtze Valley and Beyond* (1899). *Chinese Pictures* (1900).

BIBLIOGRAPHY: Campbell, J. *Women of Worth* (1908). Middleton, D. *Victorian Lady Travellers* (1965). Stoddart, A.M. *The Life of Isabella Bird* (1906). Williams, C. *The Story of Isabella Bird Bishop* (1909).

For articles in reference works, see: *BA19C. DNB.*

Tori Haring-Smith

Susanna Blamire

BORN: 1747 near Carlisle, Cumberland County.
DIED: 1794, Carlisle.
DAUGHTER OF: William Blamire.

B. was a poet and songwriter. "Highly esteemed in her own day," B. was known as the "Muse of Cumberland." She never married and lived a secluded life with relatives in Cumberland. She died at the age of forty-seven from "complications" of rheumatism.

B. received what little formal education she had at Raughton Head, the village school, and during her youth gave herself "completely up to her studies." She began early on to write poetry in imitation of her favorite authors. Her earliest known poem, "Written in a Churchyard, on seeing a number of cattle grazing in it," is written in imitation of Gray's "Elegy."

Her sister's marriage to a Colonel Graham of Gartmore (author of a popular song, "Oh tell me how to woo thee") allowed B. access to a circle of educated persons with literary tastes similar to her own, and, with her sister, B. made frequent trips to Scotland. Asked by a new acquaintance, Lord Tankerville, to write a poem about her rustic life, B. composed, in dialect, "Why, Ned, man, thou luiks sae down-hearted":

> Wey, Ned, Man! thou luiks sae down-hearted,
> Yen wad swear aw thy kindred were dead,
> For sixpence, thy Jean and thee's parted,
> What then, man ne're bodder thy head!
> There's lasses enow, I'll uphod te,
> And thou may be suin as weel match'd
> Tou knows there's still fish in the river
> As guid as has ever been catch'd.

Frederic Rowton, who included two of B.'s songs, "What ails this heart o' mine?" and "The Silver Crown," in his anthology *The Female Poets of Great Britain* (1853), described the characteristics of B.'s poetry as "considerable tenderness of feeling, very gracefully expressed, and a refined delicacy of imagination, which, whilst it never

thrills, always pleases." Her songs, Rowton says, "though not without marks of elaboration, display great simplicity and force of feeling." B.'s most popular poem, "The Nabob" or "The Traveller's Return," is the poignant story of an Indian traveller's return home to his native village. Rowton refers to this poem as a "very affecting and delightful production," and, indeed, it is.

In modern terms, the value of B.'s poetry is that it recreates, sympathetically as well as accurately, the language and customs of a remote section of eighteenth-century England. B.'s poem "Stoklewath, or the Cumbrian Village," written in imitation of Goldsmith's "The Deserted Village," gives a fascinating account of the daily lives of the rustic villagers who were B.'s neighbors. B. captures "the peculiar humor of the Cumbrian folk with admirable truth, and depicts it faithfully so far as was consistent with her own refinement."

B. wrote her songs and poems hastily, without plans for publication, although she did publish, anonymously, several poems in magazines. Unfortunately, none of her correspondence has survived. Nearly fifty years after her death, Patrick Maxwell, an Englishman living in India, began collecting B.'s work. In 1842, Maxwell and Henry Lonsdale, a physician from Carlisle, published an anthology of B.'s poems entitled *The Poetical Works of Miss Susanna Blamire,* "*The Muse of Cumberland,*" *Now for the First Time Collected by Henry Lonsdale,* M.D., *with a Preface, Memoir, and Notes by Patrick Maxwell.*

WORKS: The Poetical Works of Susanna Blamire, ed. H. Lonsdale and P. Maxwell (1842). *Songs By Miss Blamire, together with Songs by Her Friend Miss Gilpin,* ed. S. Gilpin (1866).

BIBLIOGRAPHY: The Female Poets of Great Britain, ed. Frederic Rowton (1853, rpt. 1981).

For articles in reference works, see: *DNB.* Keddie, H. [Sarah Tytler, pseud.] and J.L. Watson, ed. *Songstresses of Scotland* (1871).

Kate Beaird Meyers

Margaret (Marguerite) Blessington

BORN: 1 September 1789, Knockbrit, Tipperary, Ireland.
DIED: 4 June 1849, Paris.
DAUGHTER OF: Edmund and Ellen Sheehy Power.
MARRIED: Maurice St. Leger Farmer, 1804; Charles John Gardiner, First Earl of Blessington, 1818.

WROTE UNDER: Anonymously, Author of *The Magic Lantern,* Author of *Sketches and Fragments,* Countess of Blessington.

When B. was 14, her father forced her to marry a brutal man. After three months, she left her husband and returned home. A few years thereafter, she began living with Captain Thomas

Jenkins, and when she and the Earl of Blessington became interested in each other, the Earl paid Jenkins to release her. B. was able to marry the Earl when her husband died, at which time she changed her name from Margaret to Marguerite. As the Countess of Blessington, she became an important hostess to influential men. Their wives rebuffed her, though, because of her past. After the Earl died, B. lived with Count D'Orsay, the son-in-law of her second husband. They may have been lovers, or she may have assumed a maternal role. Whatever the relationship, London was outraged that they lived together. She spent her last years writing to support herself and the Count. She died bankrupt in Paris.

B.'s most important literary contribution is *Conversations of Lord Byron* (1834). She wrote that when she met Byron in Genoa in 1823, she found him to be less heroic-looking than she had imagined. She was also surprised to find him flippant rather than haughty. According to B., Byron loved to ridicule people, especially the English for their cant and hypocrisy. The book is unnecessarily long and self-serving at times, but it is an accurate account of Lord Byron.

B.'s other works are hastily constructed in a desperate effort to make enough money to pay her bills. These works include nonfiction as well as poetry and fiction. She is remembered primarily, though, as a victim of a patriarchal society and for writing a sustained account of one of the most important Romantic poets.

WORKS: *Journal of a Tour through the Netherlands to Paris* (1822). *The Magic Lantern* (1822). *Sketches and Fragments* (1822). *Rambles in Waltham Forest* (1827). *Ella Stratford* (1830). *The Repealers* (1833). *Conversations of Lord Byron with the Countess of Blessington* (1834). *Two Friends* (1835). *The Confessions of an Elderly Gentleman* (1936). *Galeria* (1836). *Gems of Beauty* (1836). *The Honeymoon* (1837). *The Victims of Society* (1837). *The Works of Lady Blessington* (1838). *The Confessions of an Elderly Lady* (1838). *Desultory Thoughts and Reflections* (1839). *The Idler in Italy* (1839). *The Governess* (1839). *The Belle of a Season* (1840). *The Idler in France* (1841). *Veronica of Castille* (1842). *The Lottery of Life* (1842). *Meredith* (1843). *Strathern* (1844). *Etiquette of Courtship and Marriage* (1844). *The Memoirs of a Femme de Chambre* (1846). *Marmaduke Herbert* (1847). *The Book of Beauty or Regal Gallery* (1849). *Country Quarters* (1850). *Journal of the Correspondence and Conversations between Lord Byron and the Countess of Blessington* (1851). *One Hundred Valuable Receipts for the Young Lady of the Period* (1878). *The Blessington Papers* (1895). *Lady Blessington at Naples* (edited by E. Clay, 1979).

BIBLIOGRAPHY: Connely, W. *Count D'Orsay, the Dandy of Dandies* (1952). Hickok, K. *Representations of Women: Nineteenth-Century British Women's Poetry* (1984). Lovell, E.J. *Lady Blessington's Conversations of Lord Byron* (1969). Madden, R.R. *The Literary Life and Correspondence of the Countess of Blessington* (1855). Sadleir, M. *The Strange Life of Lady Blessington* (1933).

For articles in reference works, see: *Allibone, BA19C. Cassell. NCHEL.*

Margaret Ann Baker

Mathilde Blind

BORN: 21 March 1841, Mannheim, Germany.
DIED: 26 November 1896, London.
DAUGHTER OF: Cohen and Friederike Ettlinger, adoptive father Karl Blind.
WROTE UNDER: Claude Lake, Mathilde Blind.

A free thinker and a feminist, B. sought, in her writings, to combine Shelleyean romanticism with Victorian political and scientific concerns.

With a stepfather who was a well-known political writer, exiled from Germany for his revolutionary activities in the Baden insurrection of 1848, B. grew up in an environment that encouraged radical thinking. Her brother, Ferdinand, attempted an attack on Bismarck in 1866 and subsequently committed suicide in prison. In 1848, the family moved to England where their home became a meeting place for political refugees. There

B. met Garibaldi, in 1864, and Mazzini, whom she particularly admired. Her upbringing, combining both the European and the English, led B. to be extremely independent. She travelled by herself in Switzerland at age eighteen. At thirty, she moved out of her parents' house and lived on her own, travelling throughout England, Europe, and even to Egypt.

B. admired the romantic poets. Her first known work was an "Ode to Schiller" (1859). And she was later to write introductions to editions of both Shelley (1872) and Byron (1886). Her own work, after an initial book, *Poems by Claude Lake* (1867), was kindled by a trip to Scotland, which led to two books, *The Prophecy of St. Oran* (1881) and *The Heather on Fire* (1886), both noted for their descriptions of Scottish scenery, the second including a denunciation of indiscriminate highland evictions. Her only novel, *Tarantella* (1885), an imaginative romance, was unsuccessful, perhaps because it did not suit the tastes of the time. Her most ambitious work, *The Ascent of Man* (1889), is a romantic epic based on Darwin's theory of evolution, a combination she had attempted earlier, in a public lecture entitled "Shelley's View of Nature Contrasted with Darwin's" (1886). She later wrote a series of poems based on her travels, *Birds of Passage: Songs of the Orient and Occident* (1896), and finally, during her stay at Stratford, a book of sonnets inspired by Shakespeare.

B.'s interest in feminism and women writers led her to translate "The Journal of Marie Bashkirsteff" (1892) and to write biographies of George Eliot (1883) and Madame Roland (1889) for the "Eminent Woman Series." B. was particularly motivated to write the second biography because it allowed her to return to her early Republican thinking and to Carlyle's *French Revolution*. At her death, B. arranged to have the bulk of her money, a legacy from a stepbrother, given to Newnham College, Cambridge, in support of women's education.

B. is interesting as a figure because her concerns so closely parallel George Eliot's. B. even translated a work of Strauss's early in her career. B.'s contemporaries viewed her as more successful at getting her ideas across in conversation than in writing, but Vita Sackville-West has asserted that B.'s poetic gifts and vision of nature have been underestimated by critics.

WORKS: *Poems by Claude Lake* (1867). (trans.) *The Old Faith and the New* by David Friedrich Strauss (1873). *The Prophecy of St. Oran* (1881). *George Eliot* (1883). *Tarantella: a Romance* (1885). *The Heather on Fire* (1886). *Madame Roland* (1886). *The Ascent of Man* (1889). *Dramas in Miniature* (1891). (trans.) *A Study of Marie Bashkirtseff* (1892). *Songs and Sonnets* (1893). *Birds of Passage: Songs of the Orient and Occident* (1896). *A Selection from the Poems of Mathilde Blind* (ed. by A. Symons, 1897). *Poetical Works of Mathilde Blind* (ed. with a memoir by A. Symons, 1900). *Romola* by George Eliot (with a life of George Eliot by B., 1900). *Shakespeare Sonnets* (1900).

BIBLIOGRAPHY: Hickok, K. *Representations of Women: Nineteenth Century British Women's Poetry* (1984). Kaplan, C. *Salt and Bitter and Good: Three Centuries of English Women Poets* (1975).

For articles in reference works, see: *DNB*, Sup. I., Sup. II (under Karl Blind).

Elsie B. Michie

Barbara Bodichon

BORN: 18 April 1827, London.
DIED: 11 June 1891, at Scalands, near Robertsbridge, Sussex.
DAUGHTER OF: Anne Longden and Benjamin Leigh Smith.
MARRIED: Eugene Bodichon, 1857.
WROTE UNDER: Barbara Leigh Smith, Barbara Bodichon.

B., a leader of the Victorian feminist movement and the daughter and granddaughter of abolitionist members of Parliament, felt the stigma of illegitimacy: her father, a Unitarian minister, had not married her mother, Anne Longden, a milliner's apprentice. At the age of twenty-one, B. received an annual income of £300; the resulting independence greatly shaped her life. In 1857, she married Eugene Bodichon, a radical humanitarian doctor who lived in Algeria. Thereafter she divided her time between Algeria and England until the last decade of her life when, partially paralyzed from a stroke, she remained in England.

B. was a painter throughout her life. She also established a progressive school in London for children of both sexes and different classes. In the 1850s she wrote a diary of a trip to America that was not published until 1972. An intimate friend of George Eliot, she guessed the identity of the author of *Adam Bede* simply from quotations in book reviews. In 1854, B. published a pamphlet titled *A Brief Summary in Plain Language of the Most Important Laws Concerning Women*. She organized a campaign to change the law preventing married women from owning property in their name, but the fight was not completely won until 1893, two years after her death. She argued that all professions be opened to women in the pamphlet *Women and Work* (1857). She also wrote articles on education for the *Englishwoman's Review*. In the 1860s she supported the fledgling movement for equality in two ways: by writing and by philanthropy. Her pamphlets on suffrage were widely circulated, and, with Emily Davies, she became a founder of Girton College.

In an 1866 pamphlet titled *Reasons for the Enfranchisement of Women*, Bodichon argued that the status of non-voter contributed to the low self-esteem of women. She connected external barriers to a full life with the psychological harm caused by women's acceptance of those barriers. In another pamphlet the same year, *Objections to the Enfranchisement of Women Considered*, she challenged the powerful Victorian myth that gave women's influence in the home an almost mystical significance by noting that women at different times and in different places have assumed a variety of roles. More radically, she dismissed the notion that women should be moral guardians who could exert indirect influence on men and politics.

American Diary, a series of letters to B.'s family in England, was based on a year of travel in 1857 and 1858. The work is valuable for its observations on slavery and women's rights and equally valuable for its self-portrait of an emancipated Victorian woman. In Boston at the end of her trip, B. met many women's rights activists, and the sketch she gives of this circle anticipates the portrait drawn thirty years later by Henry James in *The Bostonians*.

One of the deepest expressions of B.'s feminism was her loving friendship with George Eliot. The many letters these women exchanged show a rare spiritual affinity. Apart from the light they shed on a particular friendship, their letters are valuable for all they reveal about the private lives of two public figures. Such friendships were especially important in the Victorian period, when intellectual or creative work by women was seen as odd and even unnatural. Each woman had felt the sting of ostracism: B. had been John Chapman's mistress before she married, and Eliot lived for twenty-five years with a man to whom she was not married.

Few women have been as successful as B. in work as varied as painting, politics, philanthropy, and writing. She was equally successful in her private life, living happily with her husband and happily away from him. One of the greatest writ-

ers of her time was her devoted friend for thirty-five years. She described herself as "one of the cracked people of the world," adding that she was "never happy in an English genteel family life. I try to do it like other people, but I long always to be off on some wild adventure, or long to lecture on a tub in St. Giles, or go to see the Mormons, or ride off into the interior on horseback alone and leave the world for a month." B.'s complexity is revealed here: the wealthy woman attempting to be like others of her class; the artist needing isolation; and the reformer seeking a platform. Both B.'s fighting spirit and her independence are shown in her cartoon "Ye Newe Generation." Four women form a tableau on a mountain top. They hold a spear, a palette, a petition, and a pen.

WORKS: *A Brief Summary in Plain Language of the Most Important Laws Concerning Women* (1854). *Women and Work* (1857). *Reasons for the Enfranchisement of Women* (1866). *Objections to the Enfranchisement of Women* (1866). *Barbara Leigh Smith Bodichon, An American Diary 1857-1858*, ed. J. Reed (1972).

BIBLIOGRAPHY: Burton, H. *Barbara Bodichon 1827-1891* (1949). Haight, G. ed., *The George Eliot Letters* (1954-1955). Herstein, S.R. *A Mid-Victorian Feminist: Barbara Leigh Smith Bodichon* (1986). Lacy, C.A., ed. *Barbara Leigh Smith and the Langham Place Group* (1987). Reed, J., ed. and intro. *Barbara Leigh Smith Bodichon, An American Diary 1857-1858* (1972). Spender, D. *Women of Ideas* (1982).

Margaret Cruikshank

Amy Maud Bodkin

BORN: 30 March 1875, Chelmsford, Essex.
DIED: 1967, England.
DAUGHTER OF: William and Mrs. Bodkin.
WROTE UNDER: A.M. Bodkin, Maud Bodkin.

B.'s major work, *Archetypal Patterns in Poetry* (1934) is arguably one of the most important early uses of psychoanalysis in literary criticism. Her use of Freud and Jung for analysis of poetry's emotional depths is also historically important given the growing interest, from the 1960s into the 1980s, in the theories of French psychoanalyst Jacques Lacan and the *école freudienne*. In his 1947 study of the most important British and American literary critics, *The Armed Vision*, Stanley Edgar Hyman devotes an entire chapter to B. and psychological criticism because, he claims, her *Archetypal Patterns* is "probably

the best use to date of psychoanalysis in literary criticism."

B. was the daughter of a physician, William Bodkin, and of a woman devoted to charity causes sponsored by the Congregational Church. Since his intellectual interests were very extensive, William Bodkin spent all his leisure time reading philosophy. His interest in abstract questions of meaning was the major influence in B.'s life: "I have thought lately, turning the much marked and many times re-read pages of my father's copy of William James' *Varieties of Religious Experience*, that my life's quest has been, perhaps, a continuation of his" (*Twentieth Century Authors*). Along with Plato's *Dialogues*, B. believed that James's study was the most decisive influence on her career in teaching and psychology.

In 1901 she attended the University College

43

of Wales, Aberystwyth, where she earned a B.A. and later an M.A. After leaving the university she began an eleven-year career as a lecturer in educational theory at a training college in Cambridge, where she concentrated on the pedagogical problems of communicating the perspectives of psychology to her students. During this time she spent a year in the United States to study methods of teaching educational psychology. She was dissatisfied with institutional answers to the problem of bringing psychology into the work of the schools and decided soon afterwards, influenced partly by health problems, to retire and study literary and philosophical questions on her own.

For several years during the 1920s Bodkin studied Carl Jung's theories and attended one of his seminars for non-professional students of analytical psychology. He became the most important influence on her first book, *Archetypal Patterns in Poetry*. In this, her most influential work, B. draws on the definition of "archetypes" that Jung gives in his 1928 article "On the Relation of Analytical Psychology to Poetic Art." Jung argues that our emotional response in reading poetry can be attributed to primordial symbols or archetypes. These images result from numberless experiences that occurred not to the individual but to his ancestors, and that were inherited in the structure of the brain. Such a group of stories forms a "collective unconscious" that generates mythic heroes, fantasies, and recurring symbolism. In *Archetypes*, B. claims that such patterns and images are present in poetry and may be discovered there by "reflective analysis."

From the publication of *Archetypes* in the mid-thirties to her death in 1967, B. continued to write and lecture on the patterns and meaning of poetry. An article on the "philosophical novel," E.M. Forster's *A Passage to India*, appeared in *The Wind and the Rain* for 1942. B. praises Forster's novel for its concern with the human relationships of love and understanding and with the impediments, what she calls the "goblin elements," that distort human communication between individuals and cultures. In *A Passage to India* the Marabar Caves represent the frustrations and misunderstandings that can occur between two people or two groups of people.

B.'s second book, *The Quest for Salvation in an Ancient and a Modern Play* (1941), compares the pattern of redemption in Aeschylus's *Eumenides* with the pattern of personal salvation in T. S. Eliot's *Family Reunion*. In both plays the Furies are represented as ministers of revenge and primitive justice. The theme of both plays, Bodkin argues, is that wisdom and salvation come through suffering. B.'s last work, *Studies of Type-Images in Poetry, Religion, and Philosophy* (1951), investigates types and patterns of thought which she regards as "God-given" and "clues to life's meaning" (*Twentieth Century Authors*). In

this study she extends the argument of *Archetypes* by indicating that if collective patterns are operative in poetry, they may also be found in religious and philosophical writings concerning the origin and meaning of the human condition. B. argues that the true nature of God is not an omnipotent being but one of infinite wisdom. Human perversity does not originate in him but in humans themselves. God urges us beyond limited outlooks to the wisest courses. In her conclusion Bodkin says that those who cannot believe in divine revelation must do without certainty but not without image-symbols, which give meaning to life and spiritual energy to our experience.

Although *Type-Images* was B.'s last book, she continued to write articles for the *British Journal of Medical Psychology*, the *British Journal of Psychology*, the *Hibbert Journal*, *Philosophy*, and *The Wind and the Rain*. Despite these substantial contributions to the role of psychology in literary criticism, B. is not well known either in Britain or the United States. *Archetypal Patterns in Poetry* received condescending reviews or was completely ignored until Hyman rehabilitated its reputation in the late 1940s. The reasons for B.'s obscurity are unclear, unless the lack of an academic degree in literature or professional training in psychoanalysis lessened her credibility for those who admired the recent increase in specialization. Possibly, her reliance on Jung brought her trouble since she did not challenge his ideas far enough. She did not, for example, explain the inadequacy of Jung's belief in archetypal patterns that are inherited biologically rather than culturally. Neither did she emphasize, although she herself avoided, the dangers that Jung posed for a mindless "glorification of the irrational." B. avoided all these questions about Jung by arguing in her later work for a faith in God as a kind of "ideal Statesman persuading men to the wisest course, in the interest of the whole, that their conflicting self-interests and limited outlooks suffer them to accept" (*Type-Images*). Toward the end of her career, B. seemed to become a moral and theistic critic who moved away from psychoanalytic approaches to literature.

Although critics like Stanley Edgar Hyman criticized B.'s moral and religious interests as outside the purview of the literary critic, her work deserves reconsideration in the 1980s as an important forerunner of the new school of literary critics who are once again using psychoanalysis as a heuristic device in looking at the literary canon. B. never made the mistake of seeing only patterns in literature; rather, she used Jungian psychology as one very innovative and creative perspective on literature.

WORKS: Archetypal Patterns in Poetry: Psychological Studies of Imagination (1934; with additional preface 1963). The Quest for Salvation in an Ancient and a Modern Play (1941). *Studies of Type-Images in Poetry, Religion, and Philosophy* (1951).

BIBLIOGRAPHY: Lewis, C. Day. *The Poetic Image* (1947). Hyman, S.E. *The Armed Vision: A Study in the Methods of Modern Literary Criticism* (1947). Knight, J. *The Wind and the Rain* (Autumn 1942).

For articles in reference works, see: *CA. CLC. NCBEL. TCA SUP.*
        Other references: *Folk-Lore* (June 1935). *The Hibbert Journal* (January 1952). *Life and Letters* (January 1935). *Theology* (December 1951).

Laura Niesen de Abruña

Phyllis Bottome

BORN: 31 May 1884, Rochester, Kent.
DIED: 22 August 1963, Hampstead.
DAUGHTER OF: William Macdonald and Mary Leatham Bottome.
MARRIED: A.E. Forbes-Dennis, 1917.

B. was a lecturer and a novelist known primarily for her romances—love affairs conducted against a backdrop of war and intrigue—and for her perceptive insight into the psychological motivations of her characters.

B.'s father was an American clergyman from New York; her mother was a wealthy Englishwoman from Leatham, Yorkshire. Between the ages of nine and sixteen, B. lived in Jamaica, New York, where her father was minister of Grace Church. In 1901 the family returned to England, and B. entered an acting school. A few months later, a severe case of tuberculosis ended B.'s hopes for a career in the theatre, and she turned to writing. Her first novel, *Raw Material* (1905), was completed when B. was only seventeen. During World War I (1914–1915), B. was a relief worker in Belgium. In 1916 she was hired by the British Ministry of Munitions as a writer of special public relations articles.

B. married A.E. Forbes-Dennis in 1917. When her husband was appointed Intelligence Officer at Marseilles and, later, Passport Control Officer in Vienna, B. traveled with him. In Vienna, B. became involved in post-war relief efforts and helped organize "food depots" for starving refugees. She lived in Austria until the Nazi occupation of that country made it necessary for her to return to England.

B. remained a life-long enemy of fascism. *The Mortal Storm* (1937), published shortly after B.'s return to England, is often credited with alerting the rest of the world to the "menace of Nazism." In 1938, B. wrote a pamphlet entitled "J'Accuse," modeled after Emile Zola's famous broadside, in which she accused the English government of ignoring the threat of fascism. Unable to find anyone in England who was willing to print the pamphlet, B., taking advantage of *The Mortal Storm's* popularity, began giving public lectures on the subject.

After World War II began, B. was made a lecturer for the British Ministry of Information and published several "patriotic" novels of love and war, including *The Mansion House of Liberty* (1941) and *London Pride* (1941). *Mansion House* is dedicated "To all those who love human beings better than they love power," and the Foreword contains one of B.'s strongest anti-fascist statements:

> We must never forget that we are not only fighting against "Principalities and Powers" but against a Swastika—an empty cross with hooks, rather than a cross with a Human figure on it drawing us not by force but by love. . . . the crux of what we are fighting for is the human spirit. Should the Nazis win, there would be a world without human spirits; a world of conscienceless State slaves. . . . it is equally our duty now, and in the future, to give the utmost protection and fair play to those who are the victims of such force.

While living in Austria, B. developed a deep interest in psychiatry—and in the lives of psychiatrists. In the 1920s both B. and her husband became disciples of Alfred Adler, a Viennese psychiatrist who was president of the "Freudian circle" and editor of its *Psychoanalytical Journal*, and B. studied with Adler until he moved to New York City in 1934. Shortly after Adler's death in 1937, B. published a highly complimentary biography, *Alfred Adler: Apostle of Freedom* (1939).

In *Within the Cup* (1943) B. tells the "true" story of Rudi von Ritterhaus, a Viennese psychiatrist and surgeon who was exiled to London in 1939. The book is particularly interesting in that, rather than simply telling the "life" of von Ritterhaus, B. tells the story through the doctor's "journal," in which he records his observations of English wartime living and contemplates the meanings of individual reactions to it.

Search for a Soul (1947) is the first of B.'s two autobiographical works. In *Search*, she describes in detail the first eighteen years of her life, carefully psychoanalyzing herself according to Adlerian principles. The message of the work is that life rarely turns out as we, when we are young, assume that it will. B. concludes that "Our first choice of a self, since it is made in the dark spaces of early childhood . . . cannot be a very successful one and it is not perhaps surprising that we hardly like to be reminded of it." B.'s self-analysis continues in *The Challenge* (1953), her second autobiographical volume.

In 1944, B. moved to St. Ives, Cornwall. Her late work consists mainly of short-story collections such as the unusual *Man and Beast* (1954), in which the turning point of each "psychological tale" depends on the relationship between a human being and an animal.

WORKS: *Raw Material* (1905). *Broken Music* (1907). *The Dark Tower* (1909). *The Crystal Heart* (1911). *Old Wine* (1920). *Belated Reckoning* (1925). *Plain Case* (1928). *Strange Fruit* (1928). *Windlestraws* (1929). *Tatter'd Loving* (1929). *Wind in His Fists* (1931). *Devil's Due* (1931). *The Ad-*vances of *Harriet* (1933). *Private Worlds* (1934). *Innocence and Experience* (1935). *Level Crossing* (1936). *The Mortal Storm* (1937). *Danger Signal* (1939; in America: *Murder in The Bud*). *Alfred Adler: Apostle of Freedom* (1939; in America: *Alfred Adler*). *The Heart of a Child* (1940). *Masks and Faces* (1940). *The Mansion House of Liberty* (1941). *London Pride* (1941). *Within the Cup* (1943; in America: *Survival*). *From the Life* (1944). *The Life Line* (1946). *Search for a Soul* (1947). *Under the Skin* (1950). *Fortune's Finger* (1950). *The Challenge* (1953). *Man and Beast* (1954).

BIBLIOGRAPHY: For articles in reference works, see: *Biographical Index CA. TCA* and *sup.*

Other references: *NYT* (23 August 1963, 24 August 1963). *Publishers Weekly*, 184 (9 September 1963). *Time*, 82 (28 August 1963).

                                            Kate Beaird Meyers

Elizabeth (Dorothea Cole) Bowen

BORN: 7 June 1899, Dublin.
DIED: 22 February 1973, London.
DAUGHTER OF: Henry and Florence Colley Bowen.
MARRIED: Alan Cameron, 1923.

Like two scissors blades working against one another, B.'s identification with the Anglo-Irish gentry and her sense of being an outsider to English culture sharpen her perception of social change during the twentieth century. Her characters fascinate and engage readers' imaginations, but her plots are sometimes improbable. Her elegant prose encompasses both the distortions of her characters' observations and the cold-eyed judgment of an authorial intelligence. Influenced by Marcel Proust, Henry James, and Jane Austen, B. utilized their technical narrative devices, but her fiction, rarely solemn, succeeds by exploiting the witty, satirical insights of moral comedy.

At the age of seven, B. was moved from Dublin to Folkestone, on the coast of Kent, and B. credits that split between her Irish heredity and her English childhood with making her a novelist. B. was raised by her mother alone after B.'s father certified himself insane. At the age of thirteen, B. lost her mother to cancer (B. herself later died of lung cancer), and B.'s aunt assumed responsibility for her niece's education and social training. B. transformed some of her schoolgirl experiences in *The Little Girls* (1964), and she set down her impressions of the Kentish resort town "Seale-on-Sea" in several of her novels. In 1917, B. left school to live with her recovered father, in Ire-land, occupied by the British army since 1916. The Bowens, as members of the Anglo-Irish gentry, entertained the British officers, and B. was briefly engaged to a British lieutenant. Without a clear sense of vocation, B. attended a London school of art for two terms, quit, and began her literary career by showing some short stories to the established novelist Rose Macaulay, who offered both encouragement and introductions to the London literary circles. B.'s first collection of stories, *Encounters*, was published in 1923. That year also, B. married a British World War I veteran, Alan Cameron, with whom she lived until his death in 1952. The couple resided where his work as educational administrator took them, first to Northamptonshire, then to Oxford in 1925, to London in 1935, and, after spending World War II in London, they chose to retire in County Cork at Bowen's Court.

As the only child of an Anglo-Irish landowner, B. inherited Bowen's Court in 1930, and, as long as she was financially able, spent part of each year writing and entertaining at her Irish country estate. During 1921, B. had feared Bowen's Court would be burned down by Irish rebels; her nightmares prompted by that fear are recorded in her novel, *The Last September* (1929). B. often retreated to Bowen's Court to write in solitude. Her love for the great house and her sense of being rooted there may be seen in the family history she wrote, *Bowen's Court* (1942).

B.'s first novel, *The Hotel* (1927) succeeds as a satirical comedy of a young woman, Sydney, attracted too suddenly to the sexuality of an older man. In the character of Mrs. Kerr, B. creates the first of many overly protective aunts and mothers who break off the young heroines' precipitous love affairs.

The Last September (1929), set during the Irish civil war, depicts the conflicting loyalties and hostilities felt by the Anglo-Irish gentry for their Irish tenants and their English guests. Lois, the heroine, loves the Irish great house which closely resembles Bowen's Court, but she also loves an English soldier stationed in Ireland. In a lightly comic style, B. depicts the nineteen-year-old Lois's inexperience: "She could not remember, though she had read so many books, who spoke first after a kiss had been, not exchanged but—administered." Her aunt, Lady Naylor, discourages Lois's lover by suggesting, first, that Lois is too young, and, then, that the young man is too far below her class. Suddenly shifting to tragedy, B. has the English soldier killed and has Lady Naylor's great house burned by the Irish rebels.

B.'s third novel, *Friends and Relations* (1931), is a competent light comedy. B.'s sharply-focused comic vision produced Elfrida's entrance: "Down the long shop, narrow and cumbered like the past, with its dull mirrors, she came very tall, *distraite*, balancing nervously in her speed like a ship just launched." *To the North* (1932) is a better novel, because B. makes her readers believe the naive, humorless character of Emmeline, slow to make connections. When Markie almost apologizes for not wanting to marry her, saying, "Sorry. . . . But you knew I was always out for what I could get," Emmeline does begin to see, but, nevertheless, she compliantly continues their relationship. In an unconvincing and melodramatic conclusion, Emmeline drives with reckless speed, as if trying to escape the past, though Markie is her passenger in the car; as they crash, her final word to him is "Sorry."

In her next novel, *The House in Paris* (1935), B. explores the divided personality of Karen, who becomes a deceiver in order to carry on an illicit affair with Max. Less impressively, B. characterizes Max as a French Jew, treating his rootlessness unsympathetically, and she ridicules his nervous fiancée, Naomi, because her eyes "start out of her head." In this history, "fate . . . creeps like a rat."

B's two finest novels, *The Death of the Heart* (1938) and *The Heat of the Day* (1949), depict characters who respond to contemporary moral problems. *The Death of the Heart* explores the cultural and psychological aftermath of World War I through the overly sensitive perceptions of an adolescent orphan, Portia, who has come to live in London with her brother, Thomas, and her sister-in-law, Anna. *The Heat of the Day* explores the psychological and moral problems of loyalty in the context of the wearing years of World War II.

B.'s lyrical, allusive descriptions of Regent's Park are an unmatched achievement in British fiction. While walking in Regent's Park, Anna, in *The Death of the Heart*, gradually thaws her frozen feelings and begins, painfully, to allow compassion a role in her life. In *The Heat of the Day*, the Londoners in wartime Regent's Park take refuge from and, paradoxically, wrestle with their moral choices. B.'s visual and psychological images make the locale emblematic of changes suffered by individuals caught in a particular historical moment.

Written as if history did not matter, *A World of Love* (1955) juxtaposes the passionate dreams of the adolescent Jane with the unsatisfied dreams of the adults around her in a shabby Irish great house. *The Little Girls* (1964) depicts three old women excavating their own childhood secrets. *Eva Trout* (1968) is a broad social comedy dominated by the wealthy, clumsy, troublemaking Eva, who is killed by her adopted child. These last three novels won public acclaim, but they are not as finely written as B.'s *The Death of the Heart* and *The Heat of the Day*.

B.'s development as a fiction writer is reflected in her short stories. *Encounters* (1923) and *Ann Lee's* (1926) offer mannered observations that are, as B. herself acknowledged, "a blend of precocity and naiveté." In her stories of wartime London, collected in *The Demon Lover* (1945), B. skillfully captures the eeriness, the trauma, and the intensity she experienced during the blitz. The melodramatic turns of plot that sometimes mar her novels succeed in the tighter shape of her short stories.

In her novels, B. sometimes failed to create credible plots, which proceed inevitably from actions taken by her characters. It does not seem possible that Stella, the sensible, self-controlled heroine of *The Heat of the Day*, would carry on an affair for months without knowing much about her lover, without suspecting that he feels no patriotic loyalty, and without having any information to verify or deny a charge that he is a traitor selling secrets to the Nazis. Nor is B.'s explanation for the lover's behavior very credible: Robert betrays his country as part of his rebellion against a grasping, middle-class family who lacks a gentrified attachment to the land. Max, whom Karen loves in *The House in Paris*, hardly seems capable of fathering Karen's child or of committing suicide. Markie, in *To the North*, is such a complete cad that his desire for Emmeline cannot be comprehended. B. succeeds brilliantly, however, in her portrait of Portia's adolescent sensibility in *The Death of the Heart*, so that her disturbing behavior precipitates action.

B.'s reputation as a fiction writer rests on her creation of memorable characters, on her imaginative evocation of the atmosphere of a particular locale at a precise moment, and on her brilliant, mannered English prose.

WORKS: *Encounters* (1923). *Ann Lee's and Other Stories* (1926). *The Hotel* (1927). *The Last September* (1929). *Joining Charles* (1929). *Friends and Relations* (1931). *To the North* (1932). *The Cat Jumps* (1934). *The House in Paris* (1935). *The Death of the Heart* (1938). *Look at All Those Roses* (1941). *Seven Winters* (1942). *Bowen's Court* (1942). *English Novelists* (1942). *The Demon Lover* (1945; American ed., *Ivy Gripped the Steps and Other Stories*, 1946). *The Heat of the Day* (1949). *Collected Impressions* (1950). *The Shelbourne* (1951). *The Early Stories* (1951). *A World of Love* (1955). *Stories by Elizabeth Bowen* (1959). *A Time in Rome* (1960). *Afterthought* (1962; American ed., *Seven Winters and Afterthoughts*, 1962). *The Little Girls* (1964). *The Good Tiger* (1965). *A Day in the Dark and Other Stories* (1965). *Eva Trout* (1968). *Pictures and Conversations* (1975). *Collected Stories* (1981). *The Mulberry Tree: Writings of Elizabeth Bowen*, ed. H. Lee (1987).

BIBLIOGRAPHY: Austin, A. *Elizabeth Bowen* (1971). Blodgett, H. *Patterns of Reality: Elizabeth Bowen's Novels* (1975). Brooke, J. *Elizabeth Bowen* (1952). Glendinning, V. *Elizabeth Bowen* (1978). Heath, W. *Elizabeth Bowen: An Introduction to Her Novels* (1961). Kenney, E. *Elizabeth Bowen* (1974). O'Toole, B. *Across a Roaring Hill: The Protestant Imagination in Modern Ireland, Essays in Honour of John Hewitt*, ed. G. Daure and E. Longley (1985). Sellery, J. *Elizabeth Bowen: A Descriptive Bibliography* (1981). Lee, H. *Elizabeth Bowen: An Estimation* (1981).

For articles in reference works, see: *CA. CLC. DIL. DLB. EWLTC. Longman. MBL* and *sup. TCA.* & *sup. TCW.*

Other references: Drabble, M. *The Listener* (13 February 1969). Hall, J. *The Lunatic in the Drawing Room: The British and American Novel Since 1930* (1968). Hardwick, E. "Elizabeth Bowen's Fiction." *Partisan Review* (November 1949). Kershner, R.B., Jr. *TSLL* (1986). Lassner, P. *Eire* (1986). Moss, H. *NYTBR* (8 April 1973). Partridge, A.C. *Irish Writers and Society at Large*, ed. M. Sekine (1985).

Judith L. Johnston

Mary Elizabeth Braddon (Maxwell)

BORN: 4 October 1835, London.
DIED: 4 February 1915, Richmond.
DAUGHTER OF: Henry and Fanny White Braddon.
MARRIED: John Maxwell, 1874.
WROTE UNDER: Babington White, Aunt Belinda.

A prolific, controversial, and best-selling novelist, B. also wrote poetry, plays, and short fiction. She also edited several magazines owned by her husband, the publisher John Maxwell, including *Belgravia* and *The Mistletoe Bough*, and contributed to *Punch, The World*, and *Figaro*.

B.'s life was in ways as sensational as the fiction that became her trademark. Her father deserted the family while B. was still a child. To help support the family, she went on the stage at age nineteen under the name Mary Seyton. The financial support of an admiring Yorkshire squire named Gilby allowed her to leave the stage and finish *Garibaldi and Other Poems* (1861), "The Loves of Arcadia" (a comedietta produced at the Strand Theatre in 1860), and her first novel, *Three Times Dead* (1860), revised and released by Maxwell as *The Trail of the Serpent* (1861). By mid-1861 B. was living with Maxwell, whose actual wife, Mary Anne, remained in a Dublin insane asylum until her death in 1874. Only then did B. and Maxwell marry legally, after she had already borne him five children and helped raise the five from his first marriage. Maxwell's attempts to present B. as his lawful wife before 1874 were publicly refuted by his in-laws, leaving his and B.'s standing in society painfully ambiguous.

B.'s sufferings at the hands of smug Victorian respectability are reflected in the subtle undermining of social conventions that marks her most interesting novels. B. became adept at manipulating the intricately plotted suspense in everyday settings that had been popularized by Wilkie Collins' *Woman in White*. In *Lady Audley's Secret* (1862), the spectacular best-seller that defined the "sensation novel" of the 1860s, the blue-eyed, flaxen haired "angel in the house" turns bigamist in order to marry well and murders in order to protect her position; the insanity that constitutes her deepest secret metaphorically underlines her subversion of feminine stereotypes. The heroines of *Aurora Floyd* (1863) and *John Marchmont's Legacy* (1863) similarly confound convention by combining all the traits of the model woman with heinous villainy. In *The Lady's Mile* (1866) B. uses the circular bridal path in Hyde Park to represent the constriction of respectable female lives and the moral and social wilderness beyond it. Despite the fact that *Lady Audley* had made her rich, B. never slackened her pace. Several of her novels during this period began as bloodthirsty serials turned out for magazines like *The Halfpenny Journal* and *Belgravia*, some under the pen name "Babington White." B. herself maintained a wry distance from such work, joking in her frequent letters to Edward Bulwer-Lytton about "the amount of crime, treachery, murder, slow poisoning, and general infamy required by the halfpenny reader." Some of her experience as a potboiling journalist colors the portrait of Sigismund Smith in *The Doctor's Wife* (1864), B.'s English version of *Madame Bovary*. *Birds of Prey* (1867) and its sequel, *Charlotte's Inheritance* (1868), offer the best examples of what B. referred to as writing of "the Balzac-morbid-anatomy-school."

B.'s early novels came under attack for their "immorality" and "sensuality"—criticism that often carried innuendoes about her private life with Maxwell. B. learned to be more skillful in appearing to satisfy middle-class ideals while subtly satirizing them. In *Strangers and Pilgrims* (1873) and *Lost for Love* (1874) evangelical cant is her target. *Joshua Haggard's Daughter* (1876) was the first of many novels criticizing the irresponsibility and conspicuous consumption of the idle rich, among them *Vixen* (1879), *Just As I Am* (1880), *One Thing Needful* (1886), *Gerard* (1891), and *Rough Justice* (1898). B.'s interest in Zola is reflected in the settings and detail of works like "Under the Red Flag" (1883), *Ishmael* (1884), and *Like and Unlike* (1887). She returned to the sensation novel with spectacular success in *The Fatal Three* (1888). B.'s contemporaries often appeared in fictional guise in her works: Gladstone in *The One Thing Needful*, Gerard de Nerval in *Ishmael*, Wilde in *The Rose of Life* (1905). During the 80s and 90s B. also produced condensations of Scott's novels for the penny press, children's stories, short sentimental fiction, and several plays. *Dead Love Has Chains* (1907), like several novels in her final years, offers penetrating psychological studies of the sexual ambivalence of the nineties and beyond.

Although she may have tried out of deference to the advice of Bulwer-Lytton and Charles Reade to make her work more "serious" and "artistic," B. remained an unabashed popularizer. As she herself admitted, she was too often struck by the ridiculous side of things to be swayed much by the sentimental; she always maintained an ironic distance from the very stereotypes she was exploiting. Notwithstanding the unevenness of her work, B. stands out as a shrewd and skillful manipulator of plot, convention, and detail who earned the admiration of writers like Thackeray, Bulwer-Lytton, Charles Reade, Robert Louis Stevenson, George Moore, Henry James, and others. Her tremendous success sprang from her ability to satisfy popular tastes, but her lasting interest derives from the skill with which she questioned and unsettled popular values.

WORKS: *Loves of Aracadia* (1860, unpublished).
Three Times Dead (1860; republished as *Trail of the Serpent*, 1861). *The Black Band* (1861). *Garibaldi* (1861). *The Lady Lisle* (1862). *Lady Audley's Secret* (1862). *Captain of the Vulture* (1863). *Aurora Floyd* (1863). *Eleanor's Victory* (1863). *John Marchmont's Legacy* (1863). *Henry Dunbar* (1864). *The Doctor's Wife* (1864). *Only a Clod* (1865). *Sir Jasper's Tenant* (1865). *The Lady's Mile* (1866). *Ralph the Bailiff and Other Tales* (1867). *Circe* (1867, by "Babington White"). *Rupert Godwin* (1867). *Birds of Prey* (1867). *Charlotte's Inheritance* (1868). *Run to Earth* (1868). *Dead Sea Fruit* (1868). *Fenton's Quest* (1871). *The Lovels of Arden* (1871). *Robert Ainsleigh* (1872). *To the Bitter End* (1872). *Milly Darrell* (1873). *Griselda* (1873, unpublished). *Strangers and Pilgrims* (1873). *Lucius Davoren* (1873). *Taken at the Flood* (1874). *Lost for Love* (1874). *A Strange World* (1875). *Hostages to Fortune* (1875). *Dead Men's Shoes* (1876). *Joshua Haggard's Daughter* (1876). *Weavers and Weft and Other Stories* (1877). *An Open Verdict* (1878). *Vixen* (1879). *The Cloven Foot* (1879). *Aladdin and Other Stories* (1880). *The Missing Witness* (1880). *The Story of Barbara* (1880). *Just as I Am* (1880). *Asphodel* (1881). *Mount Royal* (1882). *Flower and Weed* (1883). *The Golden Calf* (1883). *Phantom Fortune* (1883). *Ishmael* (1884). *Wyllard's Weird* (1885). *The Good Hermione* (1886, by "Aunt Belinda"). *One Thing Needful* (1886). *Under the Red Flag and Other Stories* (1886). *Cut by the County* (1886). *Mohawks* (1886). *Like and Unlike* (1887). *The Fatal Three* (1888). *The Day Will Come* (1889). *One Life, One Love* (1890). *Gerard* (1891). *The Venetians* (1892). *A Life Interest* (1893, unpublished). *All Along the River* (1893). *The Christmas Hirelings* (1894). *Thou Art the Man* (1894). *Sons of Fire* (1895). *London Pride* (1896). *Under Love's Rule* (1897). *In High Places* (1898). *Rough Justice* (1898). *His Darling Sin* (1899). *The Infidel* (1900). *The Conflict* (1903). *A Lost Eden* (1904). *The Rose of Life* (1905). *The White House* (1906). *Dead Love Has Chains* (1907). *Her Convict* (1907). *During Her Majesty's Pleasure* (1908). *Our Adversary* (1909). *Beyond These Voices* (1910). *The Green Curtain* (1911). *Miranda* (1913). *Mary* (1916).

BIBLIOGRAPHY: Hughes, W. *The Maniac in the Cellar* (1980). James, H. *Notes and Reviews* (1921). Sadleir, M. *Things Past* (1944). Showalter, E. *A Literature of Their Own* (1977). Wolff, R.L. *Sensational Victorian* (1979).

For articles in reference works, see: BA19C. DLB. DNB. Hays, F. *Women of the Day* (1885). Plarr, V. *Men and Women of the Time* (1899). DLB.

Other references: *The World* (25 April 1905). *The Bookman* (July 1912). *New York Evening Post* (1915).

Rosemary Jann

Mrs. Anna Eliza (Kempe) Bray

BORN: 25 December 1790, Newington, Surrey.
DIED: 21 January 1883, London.
DAUGHTER OF: John Kempe and Ann Arrow.
MARRIED: Charles Alfred Stothard, 1818; the Rev. Edward Atkyns Bray, about 1823.

B. was a prolific, diversified writer; she published historical romances, children's tales, folklore, biographies, and travel accounts. As a child she had a fondness for art, and an early drawing, "Madonna and Child," served as the means for meeting the artist Thomas Stothard; later, she planned to be an actress and was scheduled to appear at the Bath Theatre on 27 May 1815. Becoming ill, she did not perform; circumstances did not provide another opportunity in the theatre.

At 28 she married the artist Charles Alfred Stothard (son of Thomas), who devoted his talents to illustrating the sculptured monuments of England. After a journey to France with her husband, she published her first work, *Letters Written during a Tour through Normandy, Britanny and Other Parts of France*, in 1818. After her husband was killed on 28 May 1821, while making drawings of a stained-glass window for his book *The Monumental Effigies of Great Britain*, she decided, with the aid of her brother, Alfred John Kempe, to complete her husband's work. She published the work and a memoir to her late husband as well in 1823. This same early period of B.'s life provided information for a book about her father-in-law, *The Life of Thomas Stothard; with Personal Reminiscences* (1851).

A year or two after Stothard's death, B. married the Rev. Edward Atkyns Bray, vicar of Tavistock. During the following fifty years, she published more than a dozen novels. With the publication of one of them, *The Talba, or the Moor of Portugal*, she became acquainted with Robert Southey, whom she idolized throughout her life. Some of B.'s many novels dealt with foreign life, but the most popular ones were based on the history of the principal families of the counties of Devon and Cornwall. These writings were issued as a ten-volume set by Longmans in 1845–46 and reprinted in 1884 (12 volumes) by Chapman and Hall, indisputable testimony to B.'s success as a writer.

After the death of her second husband, B. moved to London, where she edited some of his poetry and sermons before returning to her own original writing, focusing most of her efforts on historical subjects. B.'s final years were embittered by a report that she had stolen a piece of tapestry at Bayeaux in 1816. Ultimately, however, evidence on the subject presented through correspondence and articles in the *Times* cleared her name. B. died at the age of 93.

B.'s most notable work is *The Borders of the Tamar and Tavy*. It is a series of letters written to Robert Southey on the legends and superstitions relating to the rivers Tamar and Tavy in the geographical area of Tavistock. Southey suggested the plan of the work, which contains anecdotes about the common people, describing their traditions and beliefs.

During her lifetime B. was renowned as a writer of historical novels, contemporary critics citing her great powers of description, her ability to depict simple rural life and grandiose baronial halls as well as men and women of all classes. She was also highly commended for her ability to inspire moral purity indirectly through her novels, which could be recommended to sons and daughters with fullest confidence for entertainment and instruction in knowledge, men, and manners. Compared favorably with Shakespeare in her ability to present human experience and emotions and with Daniel Defoe in her delineations of nature, she was also sometimes called "the female Walter Scott."

B. was an accomplished, versatile, and kindly woman; she was proud of her literary efforts. Her *Life of Thomas Stothard, R.A.,* remains a beautiful book, recording the artistry of Thomas Stothard through prints of his principal works and personal reminiscences of his life and art. A travel book, *The Mountains and Lakes of Switzerland, with Notes on the Route There and Back* (1841), was apparently recognized as valuable at the time of publication when the country was not fully explored. Similarly insignificant are three books of French History: *The Good St. Louis and His Times* (1870), *The Revolt of the Protestants of the Cevennes* (1870), and *Joan of Arc* (1874), which suffer for lack of scholarly research.

WORKS: *Letters Written During a Tour Through Normandy, Brittany and Other Parts of France* (1818). *Memoirs, Including Original Journals, Letters, Papers and Antiquarian Tracts of the Late C. A. Stothard; and Some Account of a Journey in the Netherlands* (1823). *De Foix, or Sketches of the Manners and Customs of the Fourteenth Century* (1826). *The White Hoods* (1828). *The Protestant: A Tale of the Reign of Queen Mary,* (1828, 1833). *Fitz of Fitz-ford: A Legend of Devon,* (1830). *The Talba, or Moor of Portugal,* (1830). *Trials of Domestic Life,* (1823, 1848). *Warleigh, or The Fatal Oak: A Legend of Devon,* (1834). *A Description of the Part of Devonshire Bordering on the Tamar and the Tavy in a Series of Letters to Robert Southey, Esq.,* (1836, 1838; as *Traditions, Legends, Superstitions and Sketches of Devonshire*; 1879; as *The Borders of the*

Tamar and the Tavy). Trelawney of Trelawne, or The Prophecy: A Legend of Cornwall (1837, 1845). Trials of the Heart (1839). The Mountains and Lakes of Switzerland; with Descriptive Sketches of Other Parts of the Continent (1841). Henry de Pomeroy, or The Eve of St. John: A Legend of Cornwall and Devon (1842, with The White Rose: A Domestic Tale, 1846). Courtenay of Walreddon: A Romance of the West (1844). The Father's Curse and the Daughter's Sacrifice: Two Tales (1848). The Life of Thomas Stothard; with Personal Reminiscences (1851). A Peep at the Pixies: or Legends of the West (1854). Handel: His Life, Personal and Professional, with Thoughts on Sacred Music (1857): The Good St. Louis and His Times (1870). The Revolt of the Protestants of the Cevennes; with Some Account of the Huguenots in the Seventeenth Century (1870). Hartland Forest: A Legend of North Devon (1871). Roseteague: or The Heir of Treville Crewse (1874). Joan of Arc and the Times of Charles VII, King of France (1874). Silver Linings: or Light and Shade (1880). Autobiography of Anna Eliza Bray, to 1843 (1884).

BIBLIOGRAPHY: Boas, G.C. Library Chronicle (1884). Bray, A.E. Autobiography (1884). Maclean, J. Parochial and Family History of the Deanery of Trigg Minor in the County of Cornwall (1873). Southey, R. Life and Correspondence (1849–50). Spectator (1884).

For articles in reference works, see: CBEL. Chambers. DNB. NCBEL.

Phyllis J. Scherle

Mary Golding Bright

BORN: 14 December 1857, Melbourne, Australia.
DIED: 12 August 1945, Ifield Park, Crawley.
DAUGHTER OF: Captain John J. Dunne and Isabel George Bynon.
MARRIED: H.H.W. Melville, 1888; Egerton Clairmonte, 1891; Reginald Golding Bright, 1901.
WROTE UNDER: Mary Chavelita Dunne, Mary Golding Bright, George Egerton.

Writing under the name George Egerton, B. is best remembered for a series of short stories she wrote in the 1890s, the theme of which is the difficulty in maintaining loving relationships between the sexes. Her style and substance shocked Victorian sensibilities; her technique and theme foreshadow twentieth-century concerns, and she is seen as a pioneering figure in both the refinement of the British short story and in her portrayal of female characters.

Born the daughter of an Australian sea captain, she was educated privately. She wanted to be an artist, before turning her attention to writing. In 1888, she eloped with her father's friend, H.H.W. Melville, a bigamist. They travelled widely together, but within two years, he died, leaving her stranded in Norway. It is at this time that she had an affair with Knut Hamsun. In 1891, she married Egerton Clairmonte, a penniless writer, and she turned to writing initially to support them both.

Keynotes (1893), her first work, created an immediate sensation, and Punch parodied the work as "She-Notes." The six stories are a study of female sexuality, much of which is autobiographical in nature. Included in the volume were the stories "A Cross-Line," which draws on her experiences in rural living with Clairmonte, "Now Spring Has Come," which has its genesis in her relationship with Hamsun, and "Under Northern Sky," which draws on her relationship with Melville in Norway. Although much of her fiction is personal and autobiographical, critics have noted that it does reflect the historical direction that English fiction was moving in and the literary climate of the 1890s.

Her second book of short stories, Discords (1894), continued similar themes. Two of the women depicted are alcoholics, and the story "Virgin Soil" protests the naiveté with which women approach marriage. The work did much to shatter Victorian conceptions of femininity. Two other collections of short stories, Symphonies (1897) and Fantasias (1898), are deemed less successful because she experimented with allegory and symbolism, whereas her talent was for psychological realism. This realism was learned from her knowledge of Scandinavian literature; she had already begun work on translating Hamsun's Hunger before Keynotes, and had read Ibsen, Strindberg, and other Scandinavian writers. Critics concede that from them she learned how to depict moments of private thought; in "A Lost Masterpiece" she depicts the way the scenes of a morning ride through London register on a woman's mind, and in "A Psychological Moment at Three Periods" she depicts the stoicism of her protagonist at three key periods in her life.

Critics have claimed that part of the originality of her technique is that she provides very few details about a character's past; her style is stark. Her stories are often made up of distinct episodes with no direct links. She sees characters and relationships in a constant state of transition and flux; she does not provide a sense of permanence or closure, a staple of Victorian fiction. Her presentation of the sexuality of adolescents predates Freud and garnered the wrath of contemporary reviewers.

With *The Wheel of God* (1898), B. began to use the novel form, yet her talent was for the shorter form; one can see this novel as three related short stories concerning a young woman at three stages of her life: a young idealistic woman, a disillusioned woman who has her ideals shattered through two marriages, and finally as a middle-aged woman dedicating herself to the lives of other women. She concludes: "The men we women today need, or who need us, are not of our time—it lies in the mothers to rear them for the women who follow us." In general, however, her stories never became propagandistic and her characters are not mere mouthpieces for her feminism; instead, her writing is introspective and psychologically astute.

In 1901, Clairmonte died, leaving her widowed again. She married Reginald Golding Bright, a journalist and theatrical agent fifteen years her junior. He persuaded her to shift her attention from fiction to drama and acted as her literary agent. It is now generally recognized that she had no natural talent for the theatre, either as a writer or in recognizing talent. She thought that Shaw had ruined the drama in England; Shaw, for his part, felt that "many sought to meet her once, but not twice." Her theatrical activity brought her into the center of London's theatre circle, and she numbered James Barrie, Somerset Maugham, and Ellen Terry among her acquaintances. Her knowledge of several languages and dialects served her well as she undertook a series of translations in her later life, outliving her much younger husband. In addition, she was interested in genealogy and was a founding member of the Irish Genealogical Research Society.

WORKS: *Keynotes* (1893). *Discords* (1894). *Young Olaf's Ditties* (1895). *The Africander: A Plain Tale of Colonial Life* (1896). *Symphonies* (1897). *Fantasias* (1898). *The Wheel of God* (1898). *Rosa Amorosa: The Love Letters of a Woman* (1901). *Flies in Amber* (1905). *His Wife's Family* (1908). *The Backsliders* (1910). (trans.) *La Rafale* (1911). (trans.) *Camilla States Her Case* (1925). *Daughter of Heaven* (1912). (trans.) *The Attack* (1912). *Wild Thyme, Fleurs et Caillavet* (1914). (trans.) *Hunger* (1926).

BIBLIOGRAPHY: Fernando, L. *"New Women" in the Late Victorian Novel* (1977). Harris. W.V. *Victorian Newsletter* (1968).

For articles in reference works, see: *Europa. Guide to the Best Fiction in English*, ed. E. Baker (1913).

Other references: *TLS* (31 October 1958). *Toward a Feminist Tradition*, ed. D. Daims and J. Grimes (1982).

Tony Giffone

Vera Brittain

BORN: 29 December 1893, Newcastle-under-Lyme, Staffordshire.
DIED: 29 March 1970, London.
DAUGHTER OF: Thomas Arthur and Edith Mary Bervon Brittain.
MARRIED: George E.G. Catlin, 1925.

An ardent pacifist and feminist, B. wrote over twenty-five books, which range from poetry to history and which discuss women's contribution to politics around the world. B. said that she wrote both of her famous autobiographies—*Testament of Youth* (1933) and *Testament of Experience* (1957)—to work through personal pain and to interpret history in terms of personal events. Her haunting and relentless spiritual self-evaluation has been compared to one of her major influences, the nonconformist John Bunyan, especially his *Grace Abounding to the Chief of Sinners* (1666).

The only daughter of a leisured provincial family, B. claimed that her life was molded by feminism and by her experience of World War I. While attending St. Monica's boarding school, B. read Olive Schreiner's *Woman and Labour* (1911), which made her a feminist, and convinced her reluctant parents to let her go up to Somerville College, Oxford, in 1914. After a year at Oxford, she became a Voluntary Aid Detachment nurse and went abroad to help the British effort in World War I. In *Testament of Youth*, B. describes the personal and sexual liberation involved in caring for wounded soldiers and prisoners of war. She says that she became a pacifist when she realized the absurdity of struggling to save the same soldiers her brother and his friends were trying to kill farther north. Through the deaths of her brother, her fiancé, and her closest friends, B. came to realize the way an entire society, particularly women, bears the emotional shock of war.

Returning from abroad, B. and other women who had served the war effort fought to gain degree status for women students at Oxford. B.

also helped to edit a volume of *Oxford Poetry* (1920) that launched the careers of many students who would become prominent writers, including Robert Graves and Winifred Holtby. B. met Holtby in 1920 and they remained close friends, encouraging one another's political and creative writings, until Holtby's death in 1935. Using Elizabeth Gaskell's biography of Charlotte Brontë as its model, *Testament of Friendship* (1940) discusses the relationship between Holtby's family background and her writings, particularly the constant struggle faced by a woman who believes in numerous causes but who also requires time alone in order to write well. This struggle was B.'s as well.

After graduating from Oxford, B. settled in London with Holtby and committed her career to social and political change. She became a lecturer for the League of Nations Union in 1922, giving as many as four speeches a week, while contributing regularly to the *Manchester Guardian*, the *Nation*, and the feminist journal *Time and Tide* and completing her first published novel, *The Dark Tide* (1923).

While B.'s novels are more traditional in structure and tone than those of "modern" writers like Virginia Woolf and May Sinclair, the smooth nap of B.'s prose consistently explores those themes we have come to call feminist. From the frank discussion of women students and teachers at Oxford in *The Dark Tide* to the attempted rape in *Born 1925* (1948), B. builds her novels around the vastly different constraints and expectations that shape men's and women's lives. As with her friend Radclyffe Hall's *Well of Loneliness* (1928), B.'s *Honourable Estate* (1936) shows both the power of male and female homoerotic relationships and the ways in which those relationships are crippled by socially imposed distance and silence. *Honourable Estate*'s exposure of the need for more open attitudes toward homosexuality and abortion, as well as its portrayal of both old- and new-style marriages, are part of B.'s lifelong plea for the removal of double standards of sexual morality.

Between the wars, B.'s political energies were focused on feminist concerns. In the 1920s she was closely aligned with Lady Margaret Rhondda and the women writers who centered around *Time and Tide* and the Six Point Group. The group's goals—vast changes in human attitudes, a new concept of marriage, women's advancement to political and economic equality, improved social services for women, radical changes in sexual morality, and a new understanding of women's potential—formed the basis of her theoretical writing in *Women's Work in Modern England* (1928), *Halcyon* (1929), and *Lady into Woman* (1953). *Women's Work* encourages women to pursue their own careers as it exposes the legal obstacles

that have prevented them from doing so in the past. B. was perhaps most original in *Halcyon*'s ideal of "semi-detached" marriage, a call for women's freedom to travel and to development of both emotional equality and independent careers. *Lady into Woman* brings feminist achievements from around the world to bear on the specific political situation of contemporary English women. During World War II, B. became vice-president of the Women's International League for Peace and Freedom, and she campaigned for improved Anglo-Indian relations.

Testament of Experience (1957) traces B.'s commitment to pacifism through the Peace Pledge Union and World War II. On behalf of world peace, B. wrote numerous pamphlets and contributed to hundreds of periodicals internationally. *Seed of Chaos, or What Mass Bombing Really Means* (1944) was the most widely known and scathing of these critiques. B.'s unpopular advocacy of peace made her an enemy of both the Home Office and the Gestapo during the war, and it obliterated the sale of her books in the United States. In the novel *Born 1925*, B.'s experience of two wars is spread out among the three major characters.

B.'s marriage to political philosopher George Catlin was much like the ideal she described in *Halcyon* and *Lady into Woman*. She traveled internationally on behalf of peace and feminism and remained devoted to her women friends, particularly Winifred Holtby, who lived with B. most of her married life. B. had two children, John Edward and Shirley (Williams), who was a Member of Parliament when her mother died in 1970. True to her diverse sympathies, B. was still participating in demonstrations and sit-ins and working on several books, including the final *Testament of Time*, when she died.

WORKS: *Verses of a V.A.D.* (1918). *The Dark Tide* (1923). *Good Citizenship and the League* (1924). *Not Without Honour* (1924). *Women's Work in Modern England* (1928). *Halcyon, or the Future of Monogamy* (1929). *Testament of Youth* (1933). *Poems of the War and After* (1934). *Honourable Estate* (1936). *Thrice a Stranger* (1938). *Testament of Friendship, the Story of Winifred Holtby* (1940). *War-Time Letters to Peace Lovers* (1940). *England's Hour* (1941). *Humiliation with Honour* (1942). *Law Versus War* (1944). *Seed of Chaos* (1944, U.S. title *Massacre by Bombing*). *Account Rendered* (1945). *Conscription or Cooperation?* (1946). *On Becoming a Writer* (1947, U.S. title *On Being an Author*, 1948). *Born 1925: A Novel of Youth* (1948). *Vera Brittain Writes on How Shall the Christian Church Prepare for the New World Order?* (194?). *In the Steps of John Bunyan* (1950, U.S. title *Valiant Pilgrim*). *The Story of St. Martin's: An Epic of London* (1951). *Search After Sunrise: A Traveller's Story*

(1951). *Lady into Woman: A History of Women from Victoria to Elizabeth II* (1953). *Testament of Experience* (1957). *Long Shadows* (with G.E.W. Sizer, 1958). *The Women at Oxford: A Fragment of History* (1960). *The Pictorial History of St. Martin-in-the-Fields* (1962). *Pethick-Lawrence: A Portrait* (1963). *The Rebel Passion: A Short History of Some Pioneer Peace-Makers* (1964). *Envoy Extraordinary: A Study of Vijaya Lakshmi Pandit and Her Contribution to Modern India* (1965). *Radclyffe Hall: A Case of Obscenity?* (1968). *Chronicle of Youth* (1981).

BIBLIOGRAPHY: Bailey, H. *Vera Brittain* (1987). Berry, P. Intro. to *Testament of Experience* (1979). Bishop, A., ed. *Chronicle of Youth* (1981). Brittain, V., and G. Handley-Taylor, eds. *Selected Letters of Winifred Holtby and Vera Brittain (1920–1935)* (1960). Catlin, J. *Family Quartet: Vera Brittain and Her Family* (1987). *McMaster University Library Research News* (November 1977 and December 1978). Mellown, M. Pickering, J. *Women's Studies* (1986). *Feminist Theorists* ed. D. Spender (1983).

For articles in reference works see: *Biography and Genealogy Master Index. CA. CLC. Longman. TCA* and *sup. TCW.*

Other references: *Contemporary Statesman* (6 February 1960). *NR* (7 October 1957). *NYTBR* (2 March 1952). *SP* (24 August 1957).

Carol L. Barash

Anne Brontë

BORN: 17 January 1820, Thornton.
DIED: 28 May 1842, Scarborough.
DAUGHTER OF: Patrick and Maria Branwell Brontë.
WROTE UNDER: Acton Bell, Anne Brontë.

The youngest of the famous Brontë Sisters, B. is often regarded as the least talented and therefore overlooked. Whether she deserves this reputation has become the subject of much debate. Her novels, *Agnes Grey: An Autobiography* and *The Tenant of Wildfell Hall*, for which she is best known, demonstrate her eye for detail and talent for storytelling, in addition to an unmistakably Brontëan taste for the unconventional. Although she wrote a great deal of poetry, it has, for the most part, been neglected.

B. escaped attending the Clergy Daughters' School at Cowan Bridge with her sisters because of her age. After the deaths of the two elder girls, Maria and Elizabeth, Charlotte and Emily returned home. During much of their childhood the four remaining Brontë children were allowed to roam and play freely in the Yorkshire moors. Such play encouraged extensive development of their imaginations.

The children created the Glass Town Confederacy—stories of twelve toy soldiers involving conquest, civil war, personal jealousies, loyalties, and loves. In 1831 Charlotte left for Miss Wooler's School at Roe Head, and at this point Emily and B. began chronicling the happenings of their own imaginary kingdom of Gondal. Gondal is the setting for a series of poems characterized by romantic characters and language. Though Emily continued to be absorbed by this fantasy world, B.

apparently lost interest during her late teens and early twenties, contributing Gondal poetry only under Emily's influence.

B. was initially educated at home by Charlotte and then spent two years as a student at Roe Head. In the spring of 1841 she was forced by economic need to find employment as a governess, as was Charlotte. Her experience at Blake Hall was brief and unhappy, and she soon returned home. B. then assumed a position at Thorpe Green, securing a job for her brother as well, but becoming shocked by Branwell's growing obsession with the mistress of the house. Ashamed of Branwell's behavior and unable to endure the separation from her sisters, B. quit her position and returned home. Branwell's subsequent decline into madness is reflected in the writings of all his sisters but particularly in B.'s *The Tenant of Wildfell Hall*. In 1844 the Brontë sisters attempted to start their own school. The endeavor was not successful; they did not receive a single application.

Poems by Currer, Ellis and Acton Bell, a slim volume containing sixty-one poems, was published in May 1846. The Brontës selected male pseudonyms partly to protect themselves from prejudice against women writers and partly to meet Emily's demands for anonymity. Even before all the publication details had been completed, the sisters began working on novels, perhaps inspired by the ease with which their initial dreams of publication had become a reality. But publication did not mean success; by mid-July only two copies of their poems had been sold, despite several complimentary reviews.

By the end of June 1846, the Brontë sisters

had each finished a novel—Charlotte, *The Professor*; Emily, *Wuthering Heights*; and B. *Agnes Grey*—and were trying to locate a publisher who would offer the three novels as a triple decker. In July 1847 Thomas Cautley Newby accepted *Wuthering Heights* and *Agnes Grey* but refused *The Professor. Agnes Grey* appeared with *Wuthering Heights* in December 1847.

Newby promised early sheets of *The Tenant of Wildfell Hall* to an American publisher with the statement that it was his belief that it was by the author of *Jane Eyre*. The resulting publicity caused problems with Charlotte's publishers who had promised her next novel to another American publisher. To straighten out the confusion and prove that the novels were the work of two authors, Charlotte and B. traveled to London to visit Messrs. Smith and Elder, Charlotte's publisher. Upon arriving in London the sisters were caught in a severe storm and B. developed a respiratory infection. When they returned home Charlotte and B. were faced with a series of domestic trials. Branwell died of consumption in September. Emily's health then showed symptoms of collapse, and not until shortly before her death in December 1848 would she agree to see a doctor. After Emily's death B., who had never completely recovered from the illness caused by her soaking in London, quickly sickened. Consumption was soon obvious. On 24 May 1842 she left Haworth for Scarborough, dying there four days later. The poem "I hoped that with the brave and strong" was her last composition.

Most critics find B.'s work more conventional, and therefore less interesting, than that of her sisters. Still, more than her sisters, B. sought a realistic approach to fiction without sentimentalizing or romanticizing her characters. Charlotte's Jane Eyre marries far above her station, while B.'s Agnes Grey is allotted a thoroughly respectable though unglamorous clergyman. B. believed that her duty as a writer was to teach rather than entertain or fantasize.

As the last surviving Brontë, Charlotte greatly influenced the literary reputations of her sisters. Unfortunately, her condescending and apologetic attitude toward B.'s literary talent has set a precedent for much subsequent criticism. Some critics, however, have objected to Charlotte's picture of "gentle Anne." Indeed, the vigor with which B. approached her subjects does not substantiate Charlotte's opinion. Many critics find merit in the presentation of the evils and fallacies of the double standard exercised in child-rearing in *Agnes Grey*. Her approach is similarly forthright in *The Tenant of Wildfell Hall* where the heroine leaves her husband. These novels, with their feminist overtones, were considered immoral and sensational when originally published.

Still, B.'s work does have weaknesses. Critics note that her attempt to portray the tedium of a governess's life in *Agnes Grey* results in many tedious passages. *The Tenant of Wildfell Hall* is often criticized for its weak structure, since the main body of the story is told through the protagonist's diary rather than by the character herself. In spite of her flaws, many critics feel that B. is a talented writer who deserves separate and careful consideration.

WORKS: *Poems by Currer, Ellis and Acton Bell* (as Acton Bell) (1846). *Agnes Grey: an Autobiography* (as Acton Bell) (1847). *The Tenant of Wildfell Hall* (as Acton Bell) (1848). *The Brontës' Life and Letters* (1908). *The Complete Poems of Anne Brontë*. (1920).

BIBLIOGRAPHY: Allott, M. *The Brontës: The Critical Heritage* (1974). Bentley, P. *The Brontës* (1947). Bentley, P. *The Brontës and Their World* (1969). Chadwick, E.A. *In the Footsteps of the Brontës* (1914). Craig Bell, A. *Anne Brontë: The Tenant of Wildfell Hall, A Study and Reappraisal* (1974). Craik, W.A. *The Brontë Novels* (1968). Ewbank, I.-A. *Their Proper Sphere: A Study of the Brontë Sisters as Early-Victorian Female Novelists* (1966). Gerin, W. *Anne Brontë* (1959, 1975). Hale, W.T. *Anne Brontë: Her Life and Writings* (1929). Hanson, L., and E.M. Hanson. *The Four Brontës* (1949, 1967). Harrison, A., and D. Stanford. *Anne Brontë: Her Life and Work* (1959). Prentis, B. *The Brontë Sisters and George Eliot* (1987). Ratchford, F.E. *The Brontës' Web of Childhood* (1941). Sinclair, M. *The Three Brontës* (1912). Stevenson, W.E. *Anne and Emily Brontë* (1968). Wills, I.C. *The Brontës* (1933). Winnifrith, T. *The Brontës* (1977). Wroot, H.E. *The Persons and Places in the Brontë Novels* (1935).

For articles in reference works, see: *BA19C. Cassell. CBEL. Chambers. DEL. DLB. DLEL. Longman. NCLC. OCEL.*

Other references: Bentley, P. "Introduction" to *The Tenant of Wildfell Hall and Agnes Gray*, by Anne Brontë (1954). Brontë, C. "Introduction" to *The Complete Poems of Anne Brontë*, ed. C. Shorter (1920). Brooke, S. *Brontë Society Transactions* (1959). Gordon, J.B. *ELH* (1984). Hargreaves, G.D. *Brontë Society Transactions* (1972). Kunert, J. *Research Studies, Washington State University* (December 1978). Schofield, G. *Brontë Society Transactions* (1971). Visick, M. *Brontë Society Transactions* (1959).

Lynn M. Alexander

Charlotte Brontë

BORN: 21 April 1816, Thornton, Yorkshire.
DIED: 31 March 1855, Haworth, Yorkshire.
DAUGHTER OF: Patrick and Maria Branwell Brontë.
MARRIED: Arthur Bell Nicholls, 1854.
WROTE UNDER: Currer Bell, Charlotte Brontë.

B. is recognized by literary historians for her contributions to the development of the novel. Her fame and influence rests on four novels and contributions to a single volume of poetry. Although much of her reputation is based upon the immediate success of *Jane Eyre* (1847) and the romantic appeal of her personal history, especially as presented by Elizabeth Gaskell (whose biography of B. is preeminent in its genre), B.'s real contribution was in the fictional exploration of emotional repression and of the female psyche. B.'s work introduced new depth and intensity to character development and the portrayal of emotion in fiction.

In 1824 her father, a Church of England clergyman, sent his two eldest daughters, Maria and Elizabeth, to the Clergy Daughters' School at Cowan Bridge, and in August of the following year he sent B. to join them. According to Brontë, "typhus fever decimated the school periodically, and consumption and scrofula in every variety of form, [which] bad air and water, and bad insufficient diet can generate, preyed on the ill-fated pupils." Both of B.'s sisters fell victim to consumption and returned home to die. B. was particularly close to Maria and later eulogized her in the portrait of Helen Burns in *Jane Eyre*.

After the deaths of his two eldest daughters, Mr. Brontë decided to educate his children at home. The children read Shakespeare, Milton, Bunyan, Dryden, Scott, Wordsworth, Byron, the *Arabian Nights*, and journals such as *Blackwood's Edinburgh Magazine*. Thrown upon their own resources, the children invented two kingdoms inhabited by twelve soldiers given to Branwell by Mr. Brontë: B. and Branwell created the kingdom of Angria, Emily and Anne the kingdom of Gondal, and the children wrote the histories and adventures of the characters inhabiting their kingdoms. In 1845 Emily and Anne were still devising plots for Gondal, but in 1839 B. consciously rejected Angria in order to free herself from what she felt to be an unhealthy obsession.

In January 1831 B. attended Roe Head, a small private school near Mirfield, where she stayed for a year and a half and returned in 1835 as an assistant teacher. Here B. made two lifelong friendships: Ellen Nussey and Mary Taylor. The three women corresponded for over twenty years, and B.'s periodic visits provided her with scenes and impressions upon which to draw when writing. In December 1837 B. returned to Haworth; however, financial circumstances soon forced her to seek employment once again, and in May 1839 she became a governess for three months and again in March 1841 for nine months, after which B. traveled to Brussels with Emily. The three Brontë sisters wished to open their own school, and in order to strengthen their credentials Emily and B. wished to spend a half-year in school on the Continent improving their foreign languages.

B. and Emily arrived at the Pensionnat Heger on 15 February 1842, but returned at the end of October when their aunt died. B. returned to Brussels towards the end of January 1843 and formed a passionate, but unrequited, attachment to Constantin Heger, her married instructor. Portraits of her relationship and feelings for Heger can be seen in *The Professor* (1857) and *Villette* (1853), and many scholars believe that Heger inspired the character of Fairfax Rochester in *Jane Eyre*. But by the end of the year, B.'s loneliness and homesickness became too much for her and she left Brussels on 1 January 1844. The sisters' plan to open a school proved to be fruitless; not one prospective pupil applied and by the close of the year the plan was abandoned.

Upon her return from Belgium, B. discovered that Emily and Anne, like herself, had been writing poetry. The three published, at their own expense, *Poems by Currer, Ellis, and Acton Bell*, assuming male pseudonyms to preserve secrecy and to avoid the patronizing treatment they believed critics accorded women. The book received few reviews and sold only two copies.

Their lack of success, however, did not deter the sisters; even before the appearance of the *Poems* they began working on fiction. Each wrote a short novel—*Wuthering Heights* by Emily, *Agnes Grey* by Anne, and *The Professor* by B.— intended to be one volume of a triple decker. Publication, however, proved to be elusive. The novels were rejected by half a dozen publishers before Thomas Cautley Newby agreed, in July 1847, to publish *Wuthering Heights* and *Agnes Grey* if the authors contributed fifty pounds toward production costs. But Newby refused to include *The Professor*. The sisters agreed and B. continued, unsuccessfully, her search for a publisher for *The Professor*. When one publishing house agreed instead to consider a lengthier, more exciting novel, B. immediately completed and submitted *Jane Eyre*, which she had begun several months earlier. The work, which appeared before that of her sisters, was an immediate success.

B.'s publisher, George Smith, was eager to

follow up the success of *Jane Eyre* with another work, and in early 1848 she began working on what was to become *Shirley*. The composition of the novel was arrested half way through by a series of tragedies: B.'s brother and two sisters fell ill with tuberculosis, and all died within the space of nine months. At thirty-three, B. was the sole survivor of the six Brontë children. Although grief-stricken, B. found solace in writing and pressed on with *Shirley*, completing it in August 1848. Although many scholars cite the subdued tone of the ending as a major weakness, *Shirley* nevertheless provides readers with one of B.'s most charming heroines: Caroline Helstone. Even though a somewhat passive victim, Caroline did make a plea for opportunities for women that was both novel and rousing: "I believe single women could have more to do—better chances of interesting and profitable occupations than they do now possess. . . . The brothers of these girls are every one in business or in professions; they have something to do; their sisters have no earthly employment, but household work or sewing; no earthly pleasure but an unprofitable visiting; and no hope, in all their life to come, of anything better. This stagnant state of things makes them decline in health. . . . The great wish—the sole aim of every-one of them—is to be married, but the majority will never marry; they will die as they now live." The protagonist of the novel, Shirley Keeldar, is an idealized portrait of Emily Brontë, but, B.'s desire to eulogize her sister resulted in a character so saintly that she lacks substance. The plot of *Shirley* deals with the hardships of the Yorkshire unemployed and the bitter confrontations of masters and men. And it is by interweaving the stories of Caroline and Shirley with the theme of industrial conflict that B. can explore the failure of Victorian society to give women the opportunity to develop their abilities, realize their potential, and control their lives.

The publication of *Shirley* brought B. the friendship of Elizabeth Gaskell, Harriet Martineau, Thackeray, and other writers. And it was mainly at Gaskell's home that she wrote *Villette*, a novel which some critics feel is her richest and most completely integrated work, in the three years following *Shirley*. With *Villette* B. returned to the autobiographical mode which had given *Jane Eyre* much of its coherence and conviction. But this time, unlike *The Professor*, she avoided an uncritical identification with her protagonist. Although Lucy Snowe embodies much of B.'s own experience and is in many respects a projection of her inner self, she is not simply an enactment of B.'s secret dreams and fantasies or a fictionalized expression of personal feelings. With *Villette* B. comes full circle, returning to the fictionalized presentation of her experiences in Brussels first discussed in *The Professor*. But unlike the earlier portrayal, in *Villette* B. is able to distance herself from the character and present a stronger, more mature exploration of the experience.

In the year following the publication of *Villette*, B. married her father's curate. B. found married life congenial and satisfying, and her husband daily revealed qualities which won her respect and increased her attachment to him. But her happiness was short-lived. In January 1855 she discovered she was pregnant. She suffered from extreme nausea and vomiting, conditions which her constitution, already weakened by incipient tuberculosis, was unable to bear. She died on 31 March 1855, ten months after her marriage, one month before her fortieth birthday.

WORKS: *Poems by Currer, Ellis and Acton Bell* (1846) ("Edited by Currer Bell"). (as Currer Bell) *Jane Eyre: An Autobiography* (1847). (as Currer Bell). *Shirley: A Tale* (1849). (as Currer Bell) *Villette* (1853). *The Professor: A Tale* (1857). *The Twelve Adventurers and Other Stories*, ed. C.K. Shorter and C.W. Hatfield (1925). *Legends of Angria: Compiled from the Early Writings of Charlotte Brontë*, ed. F.E. Ratchford and W.C. de Vane (1933). *Five Novelettes*, ed. W. Gérin (1971). *Complete Edition of the Early Writings of Charlotte Brontë, 1826-32.* Vol. 1: *The Glass Town Saga*, ed. C. Alexander (1987).

BIBLIOGRAPHY: Alexander, C. *The Early Writings of Charlotte Brontë* (1983). Allott, M., ed. *The Brontës: The Critical Heritage* (1974). Bentley, P. *The Brontës* (1947). Bentley, P. *The Brontës and Their World* (1969). Burkhart, C. *Charlotte Brontë: A Psychosexual Study of Her Novels* (1973). Chadwick, E.A., *In the Footsteps of the Brontës* (1914). Craik, W.A. *The Brontë Novels* (1968). Crump, R.W. *Charlotte and Emily Brontë, 1846-1913: A Reference Guide* (1982). Dry, F.S. *The Sources of Jane Eyre* (1940). Duthie, E.L. *The Foreign Vision of Charlotte Brontë* (1975). Eagleton, T. *Myths of Power: A Marxist Study of the Brontës* (1975). Ewbank, I.-S. *Their Proper Sphere: A Study of the Brontë Sisters as Early Victorian Novelists* (1966). Gaskell, E.C. *The Life of Charlotte Brontë* (1857). Gérin, W., *Charlotte Brontë: The Evolution of Genius* (1966). Hanson, L., and E.M. Hanson, *The Four Brontës* (1949). Knies, E.A. *The Art of Charlotte Brontë* (1969). Martin, R.B. *The Accents of Persuasion: Charlotte Brontë's Novels* (1966). Myer, V.G. *Charlotte Brontë: Truculent Spirit* (1987). Nestor, P. *Charlotte Brontë* (1987). Peters, M. *Charlotte Brontë: Style in the Novel* (1973). Peters, M. *Unquiet Soul: A Biography of Charlotte Brontë* (1986). Prentis, B. *The Brontë Sisters and George Eliot* (1987). Ratchford, F.E. *The Brontës' Web of Childhood* (1941). Shorter, C.K. *Charlotte Brontë and her Sisters* (1905). Tillotson, K. *Novels of the Eighteen-Forties* (1954). Winnifrith, T. *The Brontës and Their Background: Romance and Reality* (1973).

Wise, T.J., and J.A. Symington, ed. *The Brontës: Their Lives, Friendships, and Correspondence* (1932). Yablon, G.A., and J.R. Turner, *A Brontë Bibliography* (1978).

For articles in reference works, see: *Allibone. BA19C. Chambers. DLB. DNB. Moulton.*

Other references: Cecil, D. *Early Victorian Novelists* (1934). Chase, R. *Kenyon* (1947). Freeman, J.H. *Studies in English Literature* (1984). Heilman, R.B. *From Jane Austen to Joseph Conrad*, ed. R.C. Rathburn and M. Steinmann, Jr. (1958). Heilman, R.B. *Nineteenth-Century Fiction* (1959). Heilman, R.B. *Studies in the Novel* (1982). Homans, M. *The Female Gothic*, ed. J.E. Fleenor (1983). Hunt, L. *Colby Library Quarterly* (March 1983). Kestner, J. *PLL* (1984). Scargill, M.H. *University of Toronto Quarterly* (1950). Woolf, V. *The Common Reader* (1926).

Lynn M. Alexander

Emily Brontë

BORN: 30 July 1818, Thornton.
DIED: 19 December 1848, Haworth.
DAUGHTER OF: Patrick and Maria Branwell Brontë.
WROTE UNDER: Ellis Bell, Emily Brontë.

B.'s actual development as a writer began in 1831 when her sister Charlotte left for school at Roe Head. At this time B. and her sister Anne began to record the saga of Gondal. Previously they had helped with the Glasstown Confederacy, but Charlotte and Branwell were the leaders in those creations.

Another factor in B.'s creative development was the freedom she and her siblings were allowed. Free to roam and play upon the moors as they wished, the girls expanded their imaginations beyond normal boundaries. Also contributing to their mental stimulation was the free access they had of their father's library, where they found histories, biographies, and poetry—including the complete works of Byron. B.'s writing shows the influence of the moors and the romanticism of writers such as Byron and Scott: the poetry of Gondal depends on landscape for its major effects and is filled with the reckless actions of outlaws and rebels fleeing from justice or from pursuing armies and sheltering in the hollows of rocks or down in the glens where their secret haunts were located.

On the eve of B.'s seventeenth birthday, she and Charlotte left for Roe Head School; Charlotte was to teach and B.'s acceptance as a pupil was partial payment of Charlotte's salary. B.'s stay lasted only three months, as she sickened physically and mentally pining for the moors. Many years later, when preparing a memoir for B.'s publisher, Charlotte tried to explain her sister's strong reaction to the strictures of boarding school: "Liberty was the breath of Emily's nostrils; without it, she perished. The change from her own home to a school, and from her own very noiseless, very secluded, but unrestricted and inartificial mode of life, to one of disciplined routine (though under the kindliest auspices) was what she failed in enduring. Her nature proved here too strong for her fortitude. Every morning when she woke, the vision of home and the moors rushed on her and darkened and saddened the day that lay before her. Nobody knew what ailed her but me— I knew only too well. In this struggle her health was quickly broken; her white face, attenuated form, and failing strength threatened rapid decline. I felt in my heart she would die, if she did not go home, and with this conviction obtained her recall."

Anne was sent to Roe Head in her place, leaving B. without the companionship at home that she craved. At this same time Branwell returned home from his unsuccessful attempt to establish himself in London. Because both felt their attempts to confront the outside world to be steeped in failure, a new bond developed between Branwell and B. This period of close association lasted for two years, and it was during this time that her preoccupation with the themes of guilt and failure began to root.

Abruptly, in the autumn of 1837, B. took a position as a teacher in a large school near Halifax. Exact details as to how and why are not known, but it is generally assumed that, while the position was secured by Charlotte, a desire to be near Branwell, who went as an usher at a boys' school that autumn, was behind the decision. Although B. did not particularly enjoy her stay at Law Hill School—she once told a classroom of unruly girls that the only individual she liked in the whole establishment was the house dog—it was to have a lasting effect on her, for much of the salient features of the history of Law Hill found their way into *Wuthering Heights*. The evidence as to the length of B.'s stay at Law Hill is conflicting, but the recent discovery that a letter from Charlotte, complaining of the harsh conditions under which B. worked, dated by most biographers 2 October 1837, is clearly postmarked 2 October 1838, would seem to fix B.'s stay in the winter of 1838 to 1839.

Scholars regard B.'s stay at Law House as important because a nearby house, High Southerland Hall, is believed to be the model for the house known as Wuthering Heights, and it has been suggested that the kernel of the Heathcliff story was found in the recollections of a local Halifax man, Jack Sharp. However, the parallels are not exact, and there is another credible possibility for a model—Top Withens, near Haworth.

B. returned to Haworth in 1839 and remained there until February 1842 when she and Charlotte left for Brussels in order to study foreign languages and equip themselves to open their own school. Forced to return home by the death of their aunt in November 1842, B. decided to remain at Haworth when Charlotte returned to Brussels. It was at this time that B. wrote much of her poetry. By 1844 the three sisters' plan to start a school had foundered through lack of response, and the sisters found themselves in low spirits, trying to conceive of earning their livings in a congenial manner.

It was at this point that Charlotte discovered a notebook of B.'s poetry, which she thought to be quite good. Anne soon admitted that she, too, had been writing poetry, as had Charlotte. Together the sisters published *Poems by Currer, Ellis and Acton Bell.* The male pseudonyms were used at the insistance of Emily to maintain anonymity and protect their privacy. Not even the publishers knew the actual identities of the authors.

The three sisters, perhaps inspired by the ease with which they were able to publish their poems, quickly decided to try their hand at writing fiction. By July 1846 each had written a novel— Charlotte, *The Professor*; Anne, *Agnes Grey*; and B., *Wuthering Heights.* The sisters wished to publish the three works as a triple decker, and after some searching a publisher, Thomas Newby, was found who would publish *Agnes Grey* and *Wuthering Heights*, but not *The Professor.* Charlotte wrote *Jane Eyre* in the interval and quickly found a publisher of her own. *Wuthering Heights* was published in two volumes and *Agnes Grey* in one volume in December 1847. Reviewers were baffled and shocked by *Wuthering Heights*, though some expressed admiration for its strange power. Even modern critics have difficulty dealing with the novel, tending either towards eccentricity or concentration on very small sections.

Setting the tone with the Yorkshire word, "wuthering," an adjective referring to turbulent weather, B. created a novel of such intensity that it is the standard by which subsequent gothic novels are measured. Heathcliff's violent obsession for Catherine and the almost incestuous nature of their relationship has fascinated critics and scholars since the novel's publication. The narrative itself is a stylistic challenge with its multiple narrators and the two Catherines, mother and daughter. The passionate tone of the novel was so shocking to Victorian readers that when it was revealed that the author was a woman, there was immediate speculation that Patrick Branwell Brontë, B.'s brother, had written it. However, comparisons with extant juvenilia and poetry leave no doubt that B. wrote *Wuthering Heights.*

It is not known what B. did after finishing *Wuthering Heights.* A letter from Newby, fitting an envelope addressed to Ellis Bell and referring to another novel, has been found; but Newby tended to confuse the sisters and the novel mentioned could be Anne's *The Tenant of Wildfell Hall* (published June 1848). It has also been suggested that B.'s time was taken up with expanding *Wuthering Heights* from one to two volumes. Whatever work B. might have done in the two years between the finishing of *Wuthering Heights* and her death, however, remains conjecture.

Branwell, who had been declining mentally and physically ever since he returned home in disgrace, died of consumption on 24 September 1848. His physical and spiritual welfare caused anxiety for all three sisters; and there are stories of B., the largest of the three, bearing the brunt of looking after him and carrying him about. Soon after his death B. was reported to have a cough and a cold, which quickly developed into consumption. B. struggled to continue her everyday tasks until almost the day of her death, refusing, according to most biographers, all medical assistance. She died suddenly on 19 December 1848.

B. remains enigmatic because so little is known about her, and what is known is often contradictory. Her life seems one of self-isolation and conformity; her writings seem designed to shock and outrage. B.'s defiance of rigid categories and her refusal to divide characters into obvious categories—good and bad, saints and sinners, aristocracy and servants—is very un-Victorian, but does not seem out of keeping with her temperament.

WORKS: *Poems by Currer, Ellis and Acton Bell* (1848). (as Ellis Bell) *Wuthering Heights* (1848). *The Life and Works of Charlotte Brontë and Her Sisters* (1899-1900). *Poems of Emily Brontë* (1906). *The Complete Works of Emily Jane Brontë* (1906). *The Complete Poems of Emily Jane Brontë* (1924). "An Unpublished Verse by Emily Jane Brontë" (1934). *Two Poems: Love's Rebuke, Remembrance* (1934). *The Gondal Saga* (1934). *Gondal Poems, Now First Published from the Manuscript in the British Museum* (1938). *The Complete Poems* (1941). *Five Essays Written in French by Emily Jane Brontë* (1948). *The Complete Poems* (1951). *A Diary Paper* (1951). *Gondal's Queen: a Novel in Verse* (1955).

BIBLIOGRAPHY: Brown, H. MLR (1939). Chitham, E. *A Life of Emily Brontë* (1987). Dodds, M.G.

MLR (1923). Dry, F.S. *The Sources of Wuthering Heights* (1937). Gerin, Winifred. *Emily Brontë* (1971). Homans, M. *Women Writers and Poetic Identity: Dorothy Wordsworth, Emily Brontë, and Emily Dickinson* (1987). Hewish, J. *Emily Brontë* (1969). Law, A. *Altham* (1925). Paden, W.D. *An Investigation of Gondal* (1958). Petit, J.F., ed. *Emily Brontë* (1973). Prentis, B. *The Brontë Sisters and George Eliot* (1987). Ratchford, F.E. *The Brontës' Web of Childhood* (1941). Shorter, C.K. *The Brontës: Life and Letters* (1908). Simpson, C. *Emily Brontë* (1929). Smith, J.C. *Essays and Studies* (1914). Sinclair, M. *The Three Brontës* (1914). Spark, M., and D. Stanford, *Emily Brontë: Her Life and Work* (1953). Wallace, R.K. *Emily Brontë and Beethoven: Romantic Equilibrium in Fiction and Music* (1986). Williams, M.H. *A Strange Way of Killing: The Poetic Structure of "Wuthering Heights"* (1987). Winnifrith, T. *The Brontës* (1977). Woolf, V. *The Common Reader* (1925).

For articles in reference works, see: *Allibone. BA19C. Chambers. DLB. DNB. Moulton.*

Lynn M. Alexander

Charlotte Brooke

BORN: 1740, Rantavan (Co. Cavan), Ireland.
DIED: 29 March 1793, Longford.
DAUGHTER OF: Henry Brooke.

This neglected writer gets only four lines in Brady and Cleeve's *Biographical Dictionary of Irish Writers* (1985) but may soon, as a subject of at least one doctoral dissertation and as a woman attractive to feminist critics, receive more of the attention she deserves, both as contributor to literature and representative of a kind of literary lady in the eighteenth century. Long ago a critic said she "did an acceptable service to her country in rescuing from oblivion a few of the interesting remains of its ancient genius," for while her tragedy of *Belasarius* never saw print she did manage to collect, translate, and print some of the old Irish poetry which still survived, among the last of the wandering minstrels, in her time. All who value Ireland's literary heritage must honor her and wish there had been earlier and as dedicated persons in that field.

One of 22 children of the poet and playwright Henry Brooke (1703?-1783), who was famous in his day as the author of the novel published in five volumes (1766-1770) as *The Fool of Quality*, B. was brought up in a busy literary household. Her father's work was various. He wrote in addition to the novels some plays (*Gustavas Vasa* was banned in England but produced with great success on the Dublin stage as *The Patriot*), many political tracts (one of which was *The Interests of Ireland* of 1759 and another *The Tryal of the Roman Catholics* of 1761), some poetry (Pope was said to have assisted him on his *Universal Beauty*, 1735), and miscellaneous publications of great charm for both children and adults. It was the father whose work came first in the household, the father who was so occupied with his literary efforts that his children were left more or less to their mother's care, and the father for whom B. (who never married) stayed home and cared for after the death of his wife and the

dispersal of the rest of the family. Henry Brooke lived to be 80; his daughter devoted her life to his care and turned to writing not only because of his example but because it was one of the few occupations that a woman in her circumstances could adopt to give some exercise to her lively mind.

When her mother died (1772), her father took the loss very hard. He had married his cousin when she was only 14 and he only 20 and they had been very close all their lives, so the death of his wife was crushing and there was even more need for B. to become "the child of his old age" in still another sense, taking care of him. Nonetheless he published three volumes of *Juliet Grenville; or, The History of the Human Heart* (1774) with her support. Then he sank into senility, sitting (as B. confessed to her great friend Maria Edgeworth) staring at vacancy. She had to be full-time nurse and part-time writer.

The death of her father freed her from one burden but she had others, including loneliness and want. Her dashing cousin Captain Robert Brooke had long supported Henry Brooke's large family, but now his vast cotton mills were failing; he could no longer prevent her from becoming a pitiful "gentlewoman living in reduced circumstances." She was forced to try to get some pension from her late father's political friends or some advice from his literary ones. She begged from Bishop Thomas Percy, compiler of *Reliques of Ancient Poetry* (1765).

Bishop Percy may have given her something more than a little cash—the idea of saving some of Ireland's ancient literary treasures. In 1786 an anonymous translation by her of an Old Gaelic poem appeared in *Historical Memoirs of Irish Bards*. She rendered into English a poem ascribed to Turlogh (Terence) O'Carolan (1670-1738), one of the last of the romantic breed of blind, itinerant, harp-playing singers of the old songs. "Ossian"'s *Fragments of Ancient Poetry Translated from the Gaelic* (1760) and the epics *Fingal* (1762) and *Temora* (1763) may also have inspired her and helped to create a market. In 1789 she published for subscribers her own translations of heroic poems, odes, elegies, and lyrics, along with her "Thoughts on Irish Song" and an original "Irish Tale." She was encouraged by William Hayley (1745-1820), Blake's patron, a man of whom Poet Laureate Robert Southey said: "Everything about that man is good except his poetry." For her *Reliques* she went much farther back than Carolan, to "remotest antiquity." She sensed that Irish politics and Irish pride were intimately connected with Ireland as the center of Western Culture in remote times; she put her finger on what Douglas Hyde (speaking to the Irish National Literary Society in 1892) called the "de-Anglicising of Ireland," culturally and eventually politically, by stress on ancient glories and the Gaelic heritage.

In her day Gaelic poetry was still being written. It was soon to fade. Had her *Reliques of Irish Poetry* not appeared and given impetus to other attempts to save the legacy, the older materials might have disappeared altogether. Her translations were generally adequate although never inspired, but she was very instrumental in keeping alive the old literature until the philologists got around to studying Old Irish (before the tenth century) in the middle of the nineteenth century and until the scholars and patriots such as Standish O'Grady and a host of others saw the practical use of revitalizing the myths and legends of ancient Ireland, creating an Irish Literary Renaissance and, in the long run, an Irish Republic.

Like so many of those who exalted the Irish past (and worked for political freedom for Roman Catholics and Protestants alike in Ireland), B. was Protestant, indeed the daughter of a clergyman of the Church of Ireland. Her work, however, was for all the Irish, as was (for example) the ballad collecting by Sir Charles Gavan Duffy (*The Ballad Poetry of Ireland*). Her *Reliques of Irish Poetry* became one of Ireland's minor national treasures.

Where her father in his poem *Conrade*, which pretended to be a fragment of ancient Celtic saga, was fully in tune with "the poetic revival of Irish poetry exemplified by the Ossian controversy" but engaging in mere imitation, in *Reliques of Irish Poetry* B. translated and transmitted the "reliques" of the real thing. Her translations and other literary works were the "children" of this spinster.

WORKS: *Reliques of Irish Poetry* (1789, reprinted Scholars' Facsimiles & Reprints, with an introduction by Leonard R.N. Ashley and a memoir of the life of Charlotte Brooke, 1970). *Belisarius* (a tragedy, lost). "A Collection of Choice Irish Songs" in the periodical *Bolg an Tsoháir; or, The Gaelic Magazine* (1795). Edited her father's works (1792).

BIBLIOGRAPHY: Included in memoirs and biographical works on her father by Charles Henry Wilson (*Brookiana*, anecdotes 1804), mentioned in editions of his works such as those by Chalmers (1810) and Baker (1906). *A Memoir of Miss Brooke* by Aaron Crossley Hobart Seymour (1806) included in L.R.N. Ashley's edition of *Reliques of Irish Poetry* (SF&R, 1970), which adds to her translations of old Irish verse her own "Mäon: An Irish Tale." Ashley is also the author of an article on B., "From Foul Oblivion Snatch'd," *Études Irlandais*, 1979.

For articles in reference works, see: Brady, A.M., and B. Cleeve. *A Biographical Dictionary of Irish Writers* (1986). Crone, J.H. *Concise Dictionary of Irish Biography* (1928). *DNB*. Warburton, J., et al. *History of the City of Dublin* (1818).

Leonard R.N. Ashley

Christine Brooke-Rose

BORN: 16 January 1923, Geneva, Switzerland.
DAUGHTER OF: Alfred Northbrook Rose and Evelyn Blanche Brooke.
MARRIED: Jerzy Peterkiewicz, 1953.

A novelist, poet and critic, B. is Professor of English Language and Literature at the University of Paris VIII. First appointed as lecturer at Vincennes in 1969 after she gave up free-lance reviewing and journalism in London, B. is regarded as a "European intellectual." Daughter of an English father and a half-Swiss, half-American mother, B. was raised in Brussels and educated at Somerville College, Oxford (B.A. 1949; M.A. 1953) and University College, London (Ph.D.

1954). Her doctoral thesis laid the foundation for her first important publication, *A Grammar of Metaphor* (1958), a study of metaphoric language in fifteen English poets from Chaucer to Dylan Thomas. Prior to her severe illness in 1962, B.'s fiction was light-hearted and witty. *The Languages of Love* (1957), her first novel, satirizes philologists, and B. has described *The Sycamore Tree* (1958), *The Dear Deceit* (1960) and *The Middlemen* (1960) as novels of "love-affairs, class-distinctions and one-upmanships or portraits of society." Dissatisfied with this early fiction and influenced by Sarraute, Beckett, and Robbe-Grillet, she has carried her linguistic interest into her more recent fiction. Heavily influenced by scientific writing, her new style incorporates chemical imagery in *Out* (1964), modeled after Robbe-Grillet's *La Jalousie* and set in Africa in the aftermath of nuclear war where the color problem has reversed itself, and astrophysics in *Such* (1966), a narrative that covers the three minutes before Lazarus, an astronomer, is revived from death. *Between* (1968) describes the life of a female simultaneous translator in terms of language, and *Thru* (1975), again using linguistics and combining the theories of Barthes, Greimas, and Kristeva, is a *nouveau roman* which "progressively destroys itself" as B. plays "with the reader's habit of trusting the reliable narrator."

B.'s passionate concern with language influences her literary criticism. *A ZBC of Ezra Pound* (1971), written as an introductory text for students, explains Pound's technique of "repetition and echoes"; she acknowledges her debt to Pound's "attempt to make everything cohere through juxtaposition," a technical method she uses in *Thru*, and to his mixture of languages (B. herself speaks French, German, Spanish, and a little Polish, Portuguese, and Italian). B.'s *A Structural Analysis of Pound's Usura Canto* (1976), an application of Roman Jakobson's structuralist method to "Canto 45," has sparked critical discussion in *Paideuma*, the Pound journal on whose board she serves as the associate for France. *A Rhetoric of the Unreal* (1981), a collection of essays, investigates the interaction of narrative techniques in the science fiction of Henry James, Tolkien, Vonnegut, and Joseph McElroy. In this collection B. continues her integration of narrative writing with critical theories, particularly of Barthes, Todorov, and Lodge.

B. has contributed to *London Magazine, The Observer, The Times Literary Supplement, Modern Fiction Studies, Revue des Lettres Modernes* and *The Quarterly Review of Literature*, among others. She won the 1965 Society of Authors Travelling Prize for *Out* and the 1969 Arts Council Translation prize for her translation of Robbe-Grillet's *Dans le Labyrinthe. Such* shared the 1967 James Tait Black Memorial Prize.

WORKS: *Gold* (1955). *The Languages of Love* (1957). *The Sycamore Tree* (1958). *A Grammar of Metaphor* (1958); Trans. of Goytisolo. *Children of Chaos* (1959). *The Dear Deceit* (1961). Trans. of Sauvy, *Fertility and Survival: Population Problems from Malthus to Mao Tse Tung* (1960). *The Middlemen* (1961). *Out* (1964). *Such* (1966). Trans. of Robbe-Grillet, *In the Labyrinth* (1968). *Between* (1968). *Go When You See the Green Man Walking* (1970). *A ZBC of Ezra Pound* (1971). *Thru* (1975). *A Structural Analysis of Pound's Usura Canto* (1976). *A Rhetoric of the Unreal: Studies in Narrative and Structure, Especially of the Fantastic* (1981). *Amalgamemnon* (1985). *Xorandor* (1986).

BIBLIOGRAPHY: Hayman, D., and K. Cohen *CL.* (1976). Wolfe, G.K. *SFS* (1982).

For articles in reference works, see: CA. DLB. EWLTC. TCW. WA.

Judith C. Kohl

Anita Brookner

BORN: 16 July 1938, London.
DAUGHTER OF: Newson and Maude Brookner.

B. was educated at James Allen's Girls' School, King's College, University of London, the Courtauld Institute, and in Paris. A visiting lecturer at the University of Reading from 1959 to 1964, she was Slade Professor of Fine Arts at Cambridge, the first woman to hold the position. A Fellow of New Hall, Cambridge, she currently teaches at the Courtauld Institute. An internationally respected authority on eighteenth- and nineteenth-century French art, B. is the author of four specialized studies in the field: *Watteau* (1968); *The Genius of the Future* (1971); *Greuze* (1972); and *Jacques-Louis David* (1980). In addition, she is the author of six novels: *The Debut* (1981); *Providence* (1982); *Look at Me* (1983); *Hotel du Lac* (1984); *Family and Friends* (1985); and *A Misalliance* (1986).

B.'s work in art history has earned her the respect of colleagues, critics, and students. Her scholarly articles and texts are characterized by meticulous research, fluent expression, and extraordinary erudition. Her lectures give evidence of the same careful attention to logic, detail, and style; B. is known as one of the Courtauld's finest tutors.

B. has also demonstrated skill as a novelist. *The Debut* (published as *A Start in Life* in the U.K.) tells the story of Dr. Ruth Weiss, a quiet scholar devoted to the study of Balzac. At the age of 40, Dr. Weiss decides that literature has ruined her life: Balzac was right—the virtuous are passive victims doomed to unsatisfying lives. Temporarily freeing herself from clinging parents who are little more than spoiled, overgrown adolescents, she goes to Paris in search of a great romantic affair. Inevitably disappointed, she returns to London and ends up caring for her invalid, widowed father and is consumed anew by her study of virtue and vice in the fiction of Balzac.

Providence is the story of Kitty Maule, daughter of a long-deceased British army colonel and his French wife. A university lecturer who specializes in the Romantic tradition, Kitty delivers a series of presentations on Benjamin Constant's *Adolphe*, a short novel about failure. She lives in two worlds, one of her doting but demanding French grandparents, the other of British academe. Her perceptions clouded by fantasies, Kitty misreads the meaning of an affair with a colleague and retreats to a life of disappointment, unable to change, an intelligent heroine defeated.

B.'s third novel, *Look at Me*, is a work of metafiction. Frances Hinton, cataloguer in an art library devoted to pictorial representations of medical illness, seems to crave companionship; living with an ancient housekeeper in a tomb-like flat, she catalogues and observes rather than experiences the people she meets. As an outsider with sensibilities too fine to allow her to develop the attributes she needs to survive in a social world, she returns, disappointed, to the bed in which her mother died in order to write the novel we read. Initially described as a "beggar at the feast," Frances ends up taking revenge, consuming her enemies while making literature a substitute for life.

Edith Hope, the protagonist of *Hotel du Lac*, is a writer of romantic fiction sent into temporary exile after an "unfortunate lapse"; her scandalous behavior has caused her friends to banish her to Switzerland. At the elegant Hotel du Lac, she spends her time in genteel fashion, joining in the rituals of hotel residence with a number of interesting, eccentric characters, writing undelivered letters to her lover, and working on sections of a new novel. Edith achieves some insight into her own predicament but chooses to reject a life of practical, pragmatic arrangements in favor of returning to London and a life of romantic fictions.

In these four novels B. presents several consistent concerns while demonstrating considerable technical advance. From *The Debut* through *Hotel du Lac*, B. portrays a woman of early middle age, often an exile or orphan, bound to, if not oppressed by, traditions, whether intellectual or social, and alienated. Lonely and inhibited, she nonetheless ventures, albeit timidly, into a love affair that will follow a preordained course: infatuation, disappointment, and failure, followed by accentuated isolation, with the whole experience transmuted to artistic creation of one sort or another.

Typically, the B. heroine has yearnings for the romantic and the impossible, a desire for courtly love in Chelsea, as it were. Though she is perceptive and intelligent, she appears incapable of recognizing the impossibility of translating romantic fantasy into quotidian existence; when she does achieve some insight, as in the case of Edith Hope, she ignores it and returns to her customary

life, incapable, or perhaps just unwilling, to change.

B.'s mastery of technical elements has increased. The earlier novels showed a rather tentative hand outlining a plot perhaps more suited to a short story, a voice neither fully modulated nor smoothly inflected. In *Providence* and, to a greater extent, in *Hotel du Lac*, B. creates a developed plot of substance and breadth with events well-paced; sure wit and irony enrich a repertory of voices. Particularly in the case of the latter, the prose is controlled, graceful, and richly evocative. B.'s style, accurately described as "hyperliterate" and distinguished by references to Dickens, Balzac, Colette, and Henry James, holds a decided appeal for an audience both literate and literary. In a world rather carefully circumscribed, B. succeeds, particularly in *Providence* and *Hotel du Lac*, in depicting the plight of a twentieth-century woman with a comic richness deeply suggestive of more serious concerns.

Yet little in any of these novels prepared readers for B.'s 1985 novel, *Family and Friends*, a striking departure and an answer to those critics who have claimed that B.'s fiction is essentially autobiographical. *Family and Friends* chronicles the affairs of a wealthy Jewish family, the Dorns, during the late 1930s and 1940s. The story of a powerful matriarch, Sophia (Sofka), and her four children, Frederick, Alfred, Mimi, and Betty, this novel embraces not only a larger cast of characters but also a wider geography than the previous four. Transplanted to London in the hectic days preceding the outbreak of World War II, the family continues to prosper without their recently-deceased patriarch. Sofka assumes his place and dominates the life of the clan, openly favoring Frederick and Betty. B. traces the Dorn family story from London to Paris and the Riviera to Hollywood, integrating new relations and acquaintances as she creates a rather densely populated narrative. *Family and Friends* is rich and robust, full-bodied and sparkling. The greater narrative breadth of this novel has enabled B. to portray characters of far greater complexity and range than in her previous novels; they are so finely modelled, with such carefully limned sensibilities (and hungers), that these wonderful black-and-white family photographs described a half-dozen times in the novel actually come to life as full-color cinema. With *Family and Friends*, B. has given a significant demonstration of extended range and power as a writer of fiction; she has created a vital, engaging tale of absorbing interest, characteristically fluent articulation, and emotional resonance.

WORKS: *Watteau* (1968). *The Genius of the Future* (1971). *Greuze* (1972). *Jacques-Louis David* (1980). *The Debut* (1981). *Providence* (1982). *Look at Me* (1983). *Hotel du Lac* (1984). *Family and*

Friends (1985). A Misalliance (1986). A Friend from England (1987).

BIBLIOGRAPHY: For articles in reference works, see: CLC.

    Other references: Boston Review (April/May 1985). Harper's (April 1981, February 1984). Library Journal (17 March 1981, January 1984). NR (26 March 1984). NYRB (31 January 1985). NYT (22 January 1985). NYTBR (22 May 1983, 18 March 1984, 3 February 1985). TLS (28 May 1982, 25 March 1983). Vogue (February 1985).

                        Robert E. Hosmer, Jr.

Brigid Brophy

BORN: 12 June 1929, London.
DAUGHTER OF: John Brophy and Charis (Grundy) Brophy.
MARRIED: Michael Levey, 1954.

    Outspoken and often irreverent novelist and critic, B. embodied the values and even the hijinks of the sixties to perfection. She has made life and literature nearly inseparable, capturing the high excitability of a youth-driven era and giving expression to its iconoclasm. Her improprieties were decidedly indelicate and won her the pugnacious image she sought. A penchant for the bipolar—instinct and reason, eros and thanatos—the bedeviling dialectic of thrust and parry has come to define her analytic framework. Fluent, sardonic, self-taught, B. is heir to a half-century of modernism and to such self-acknowledged masters as Freud, Joyce, and Shaw, whose disturbing discoveries laid bare the compelling forces of life. Her sharp eye for the absurd, the pompous, and the second-rate has oftentimes made her a perfect antidote to the self-intoxicated cant of the age.

    Daughter of John Brophy, author of two novels, The Bitter End (1928) and The Waterfront (1934), B. appears to have inherited her instinct for nonconformity from her mother, the Chicago-born daughter of Liverpool's Irvingite bishop. B.'s education at St. Paul's Girls' School was interrupted during the war years, encouraging an autodidacticism that has stood her in good stead. In 1947 she won a Jubilee Scholarship to St. Hugh's College, Oxford, to read classics, but boisterous behavior—drinking in chapel—ended in her expulsion. After several years as a short-hand typist for a distributor of pornographic books among others, she published The Crown Princess and Other Stories (1953), an apprentice work marred by didacticism. Her first novel, Hackenfeller's Ape (1953), published to critical acclaim, is a piquant melange of science fiction, fable, and fantasia in which an animal acquires a disconcerting set of human inhibitions. In 1954 she was awarded the Cheltenham Literary Festival prize for a first novel. Hackenfeller's Ape, originally planned as a narrative poem, is B.'s favorite work, exemplifying her contrapuntal style of composition. The King of a Rainy Country (1956), a witty and pointed naturalistic portrait of a bohemian girl, typifies B.'s fascination with the erotic and the comic anti-romance. Examination of this polymorphous theme is extended in Flesh (1963), a sharply satirical fable of London life, in which a diffident and retiring young man is transformed into a hedonistic dynamo. Going even a step further is Finishing Touch (1963), a mordant seriocomedy of a girl's boarding school on the French Riviera, which critics have conceded is a posthumous monument to Ronald Firbank. Writing at a rapid clip, B. sharpened her seriocomic touch in The Snow Ball (1964), a black comedy of manners that attempts to transcribe in literature the erotic angles and the marmoreal effects of a baroque tomb. This carefully contrived novella was dramatized on BBC television in April 1964.

    B.'s prolific criticism has met with considerable ambivalence. A Freudian, she has come in for the usual drubbing psychoanalysis has received at the hands of literary critics. Black Ship to Hell (1962) decries the suppression of instinct and imagination attendant upon the rise of reason. A longish meditation on the repercussions of a hypertrophied rationality, it has been compared to Norman O. Brown's Life Against Death. Her love of the high speculative mode and her restless lurching for effect can tire the reader. Despite what has been called the "magazinish naturalism" of her prose and her penchant for erudite self-indulgence in miscellaneous arcana, her writing is never drearily slack.

    Mozart the Dramatist (1964) lauds the classical composer for the perfection of design and the audacity of his plans. Arguing that Mozart's operas lifted "his genius to the highest and most sustained pitch," B. debunks the myth of his presumed serenity and imperturbability. Rather, she views him as a trailblazing psychologist sorting out the internal conflicts of an age renowned for its conservative exclusiveness. Her considerable erudition serves to undo the "bogus, long-posthumous, idolatrous image of Beethoven" and replace it with the limpidity of Mozart.

    In 1967 B. collaborated with husband Michael Levey, the art historian and administrator, and

Charles Osborne on a saucy dismissal of many of the revered classics entitled *Fifty Works of English and American Literature We Could Do Without.* Such puzzling and wrongheaded asseverations as "Melville is not a novelist: he is an annotator," "Hopkins' poetry is the poetry of a mental cripple," and "Whitman's so-called poetry ranges from a simpleton's idea of Shakespeare and the purpler passages of the Bible to sheer semi-literate sludge" have been widely dismissed for their obvious archness and tartness of tone and for an exasperatingly insistent need to be controversial and cute—a very sixtyish posture.

An admirer of the *fin de siècle* and its preciosity, B. has written books on several of its most characteristic writers and artists. *Black and White: The World of Beardsley* (1968) is a detailed photographic essay on the artist whose hypertrophied decorativeness received popular acclaim. *Prancing Novelist: A Defence of Fiction in the Form of a Critical Biography in Praise of Ronald Firbank* (1972) demonstrates an exhaustive knowledge of the English novelist known as the "Beardsley in prose." B. articulates the precise contrapuntal nature of Firbank's mature style—his archness and his dismissal of the conventional novel's discursive and descriptive *longueurs*—with an intense and concentrated zeal. B. takes vigorous exception to those who have dismissed the author of *Valmouth* as the "reductio ad absurdum of aestheticism."

B. has also come to be known as a television personality, appearing on "Not So Much a Pro-

gramme, More a Way of Life" in 1964 and 1965 and "The Book Programme" in 1974 and 1976. In 1969 she collaborated with the novelist Maureen Duffy on the preparation of a Pop-Art exhibition, consisting of polystyrene wigheads adorned with plastic carrots, toy drums, and masks.

B., who has also tried her hand at drama, has published *The Burglar* (1967), an account of a puritanical thief put out by the depravity of his social superiors, and a radio play, *The Waste Disposal Unit* (1964), a satirical portrayal of American life and language.

WORKS: *The Crown Princess* (1953). *Hackenfeller's Ape* (1953). *The King of a Rainy Country* (1956). *Flesh* (1962). *Black Ship to Hell* (1962). *The Finishing Touch* (1963). *The Snow Ball* (1964). *Mozart the Dramatist* (1964). *Don't Never Forget: Collected Views and Reviews* (1966). (with Michael Levey and Charles Osborne) *Fifty Works of English and American Literature We Could Do Without* (1967). *The Burglar* (1968). *Black and White: a Portrait of Aubrey Beardsley* (1968). *In Transit* (1969). *Prancing Novelist: A Defence of Fiction in the Form of a Critical Biography of Ronald Firbank* (1973). *Baroque 'n' Roll and Other Essays* (1987).

BIBLIOGRAPHY:
For articles in reference works, see: *CA. CLC. CN. DLB, EWLTC. MBL. WA.*
Other references: *Atlantic* (February 1970). *SR* (12 June 1954, 24 January 1970).

Michael Skakun

Rhoda Broughton

BORN: 20 November 1840, near Denbigh, North Wales.
DIED: 5 June 1920, near Oxford.
DAUGHTER OF: Delves and Jane Bennett Broughton.

B. was the author of almost thirty novels satirizing the mercenary marriages and idle young women of aristocratic England. She never married but passed her life first with her father in Staffordshire and, after his death in 1863, at Oxford with other relatives. One of four daughters of a Church of England clergyman who reportedly forbade her to read her own books, she was also the niece of Sheridan Le Fanu, the well-known Irish writer of suspenseful and supernatural tales. It was he who helped her begin her career when he serialized her first two novels, *Not Wisely, But Too Well* (1867) and *Cometh up As a Flower* (1867), in the *Dublin University Magazine*, which he owned. He also introduced her to the London

publisher Richard Bentley, the beginning of a mutually profitable relationship.

B. combined social satire with a toned-down version of the sensation novel (a form popular in the 1860s that often featured an adventuress anti-heroine, mysterious secrets, and shocking deeds). Her work was immediately successful and was considered as audacious as it was readable. (Gladstone was once seen in Mudie's Circulating Library absorbed in a B. novel.) During her more than fifty years as an author she wrote with wit, wry humor, and a keen eye for the absurd social codes of the upper classes and their social-climbing relatives. In widely-read works like *Belinda* (1883) and *A Waif's Progress* (1905), B. featured an engaging young woman who pays lip service to the ladylike ideal but is in reality mercenary and amoral. The spirited namesake of *Belinda*, for example, wearied in three days of a marriage of convenience to a pedantic Oxford don, Professor Forth, is ready to fly off with the romantic David

Rivers. After lamentations about the boredom and drudgery of a proper marriage (complaints which must have echoed the sentiments of many female readers), Belinda is rescued from her own imprudence by a providential event: Professor Forth dies and she is free to wed again. Typically, B. both satirizes the high-minded ideal of feminine chastity and saves her flighty heroine's reputation.

In *A Waif's Progress*, the machinations of Bonnybell Ransome, a spiritual cousin of Mary Elizabeth Braddon's sensation heroine Lady Audley (*Lady Audley's Secret*, 1862), are the subject of B.'s satire on feminine duplicity and masculine gullibility. Bonnybell schemes to marry any wealthy man who will have her, a project in which, after some setbacks, she exuberantly succeeds. Almost wholly uneducated, Bonnybell is only skilled in prevarication, but she is more likable than the various prigs who attempt so unsuccessfully to control her.

George Bernard Shaw approvingly saw B.'s novels as trenchant comment on the miseducation of the English girl. There were other B. targets as well. Again in *A Waif's Progress*, B. lampoons the self-advertising piety of Bonnybell's "protector," the wealthy Mrs. Tancred, and the obsequiousness and materialism of her repressed young husband, Edward Tancred. The novel *Second Thoughts* (1880) includes a comic criticism of a fashionable young aesthete's maudlin poetry and narcissistic sensitivity. *Lavinia* (1902) has a hero who commits the double sin of opposing the Boer War and cultivating an interest in old lace.

B.'s books were considered improper reading for the young lady so often invoked as the ideal audience of light fiction, and B. may have suffered for this reputation. Oxford Mathematics don C.L. Dodgson (Lewis Carroll), for one, refused to dine out where he knew she had been invited. At one time she was friendly with Mark Pattison, Rector of Lincoln College, yet the friendship soured and she was ostracized for her caricature of him as Forth, the Professor of Etruscan in *Belinda*. Yet—a woman of intellect—she had enduring friendships with Henry James and Matthew Arnold.

B.'s reputation for "immoral" books all but disappeared as the twentieth century arrived, and recent critics have seen her work as little more than the tail end of sensation fiction. Her antiheroines, tame compared to the tigresses of Wilkie Collins, usually salvage their reputations, especially in her early novels. The enduring value of B.'s work is her indictment of the emotional dishonesty of the upper classes. "How I hate shams!" remarks the narrator of *Not Wisely, But Too Well*, a credo to which B. remained faithful.

WORKS: *Not Wisely, But Too Well* (1867). *Cometh Up as a Flower* (1867). *Red as a Rose Is She* (1870). *"Goodbye, Sweetheart": A Tale* (1872). *Nancy: Novel* (1873). *Tales for Christmas Eve* (1873). *Joan: A Tale* (1876). *Second Thoughts* (1880). *Belinda* (1883). *Doctor Cupid* (1886). *Alas!* (1890). *A Widower Indeed* (with E. Bisland) (1891). *Mrs. Bligh* (1892). *A Beginner* (1894). *Scylla or Charybdis?* (1895). *Dear Faustina* (1897). *The Game and the Candle* (1899). *Foes in Law* (1900). *Lavinia* (1902). *A Waif's Progress* (1905). *Mamma* (1908). *The Devil and the Deep Sea* (1910). *Between Two Stools* (1912). *Concerning a Vow* (1914). *A Thorn in the Flesh* (1917). *A Fool in Her Folly* (1920).

BIBLIOGRAPHY:
For articles in reference works, see: *CBEL*.
Other references: *American Quarterly* (Spring 1976). *Encounter* (April 1971). *Fortnightly Review* (August 1920). Sadleir, M. *Things Past* (1944). Showalter, E. *A Literature of Their Own* (1977). *TLS* (November 30, 1940).

Laura Hapke

Elizabeth Barrett Browning

BORN: 6 March 1806, Durham.
DIED: 30 June 1861, Florence, Italy.
DAUGHTER OF: Edward Barrett Moulton-Barrett and Mary Graham Clarke Moulton-Barrett.
MARRIED: Robert Browning, 1846.
WROTE UNDER: Elizabeth Barrett Barrett, Elizabeth Barrett Browning.

A celebrated nineteenth-century poet whose work has recently enjoyed an important feminist critical revaluation, B. was the oldest of twelve children. Educated at home by tutors, B. was endowed with a profound desire for knowledge and engaged herself in a remarkable curriculum of languages, classics, literature, and philosophy. Late in 1820 her father suffered financial losses, and shortly thereafter B. was stricken with her first serious illness for which opium, which became a lifetime habit, was prescribed. Mrs. Barrett died in 1828, and in 1832 the Barretts left their beloved Hope End estate, settling first in Sidmouth, then London.

By 1838 B. had published three volumes of poetry but had not yet earned any real critical attention. She moved that year with her favorite brother, Samuel, to the gentler climate of Torquay for her health, but returned to London two years

later when he drowned, for B. a terrible and traumatic loss. Although *Poems* (1844) gained her a
wide and admiring reading public, she lived a
circumscribed life until her elopement with
Browning in 1846.

The courtship of B. and Robert Browning,
which resulted in volumes of letters and the
famous *Sonnets from the Portuguese,* began with
Browning's 1845 letter to the famous poetess in
which he declared: "I do . . . love these books with
all my heart—and I love you too." B. concealed the
romance from her father, who opposed the marriage of any of his children. In September 1846 the
couple was secretly married and shortly after left
for the Continent, settling ultimately in Florence.
The change of climate and mode of living vastly
improved B.'s health, and in 1849 she gave birth
to a son, Robert Wiedman Barrett-Browning
(Pen). During the years 1850–1859 the Brownings travelled a great deal, passing summers in
England but always returning to Florence as their
home. She never communicated with her father,
who had disowned her upon her marriage, and in
1857 Mr. Browning died, never reconciled to his
favorite daughter. In 1861 B. died and was buried
in Florence. B.'s life, particularly her marriage to
Robert Browning, has been the subject of many
critical and romantic biographies. The last few
years have witnessed several important studies
that explore the influence of B. and Robert
Browning on each other's work.

Today her early poetry is neither widely read
nor highly regarded; nonetheless, these volumes
reveal her erudition and her passionate commitment to poetry. *The Battle of Marathon* (1820)
and *An Essay on Mind* (1826) are long, didactic,
neoclassical poems in heroic couplets. *The Battle
of Marathon* narrates the 490 B.C. battle between
the Greeks and the Persians. *An Essay on Mind* is
a metaphysical and epistemological enquiry that
asserts the primary value of the imagination and
poetry. Her earlier works also include a translation of Aeschylus' *Prometheus Bound* (1833) and
The Seraphim and Other Poems (1838), a diverse
collection of poems marked by a religious preoccupation and a certain morbidity.

Poems (1844) was B.'s first volume to draw
wide attention. Although "Lady Geraldine's Courtship" was a favorite, she considered "A Drama of
Exile" the best poem in the volume. "The Cry of
the Children" is noteworthy, for it marks B.'s commitment to political and social issues, in this case
the child labor system. B. became increasingly convinced that women writers must devote themselves
and their work to pressing contemporary issues and
injustices, a conviction that shapes her later poetry.
Only in the last twenty years have critics addressed
B.'s political commitment.

B.'s next major work was *Sonnets from the
Portuguese,* published with *Poems* in 1850 but

written several years earlier for Browning during
their courtship. Because of their highly personal
nature, she titled them to suggest a translation.
Sonnets, which enjoyed enormous popularity, is a
sequence of forty-four poems that traces the call of
love, the attendant fears, doubts, and insecurities,
and the final triumph of love. Several of these
poems are considered masterful executions in the
genre of amatory verse. Greater critical attention
has recently been paid to *Sonnets,* a result of
feminist revaluation of B.'s work and its place in
the tradition of women's writing.

It is mainly B.'s later poetry, largely concerned with political and social issues, that has
been the subject of feminist reconsideration. In
1851 she published *Casa Guidi Windows,* a well-
crafted poem, which moves from optimism and
hopefulness for the cause of Italian liberty to disillusionment. B.'s passionate commitment to Italian
politics, which is just beginning to receive critical
consideration, is also reflected in many of the
poems in *Poems Before Congress* (1860). However, one poem in this volume, "A Curse for a
Nation," is a condemnation of slavery in America.
The poem embodies B.'s convictions about the
power and responsibility of women to raise their
voices in protest against injustice, claiming that
"A curse from the depths of womanhood / Is very
salt, and bitter and good."

Aurora Leigh (1857), a long epic poem, remains the most widely discussed poem of B.'s later
years. In the narration of the trials, travels, and
career of an independent woman poet, she explores
feminist, political, and aesthetic issues. *Aurora
Leigh,* which B. prefaced as the work "into which
my highest convictions of work and art have entered," was admired by Swinburne, Ruskin, and the
Rossetti brothers, but received mixed, often highly
critical reviews and was largely forgotten until Virginia Woolf urged reconsideration of the "stimulating and boring, ungainly and eloquent, monstrous
and exquisite" poem that "commands our interest
and inspires our respect" (*Second Common
Reader*). The critical interest in the poem initiated
by feminist criticism continues to produce fascinating and important psychoanalytic and feminist
work on the poem. Recent criticism emphasizes the
subversions and anger and gender conflicts in her
poetry and relocates B. in a women's literary tradition. As a result, a greater degree of seriousness has
become attached to her work, and a fuller portrait
of this Victorian woman poet of deeply-held convictions has emerged.

WORKS: *The Battle of Marathon: a Poem* (1820).
Essay on Mind, with Other Poems (1826). *Prometheus Bound, Translated from the Greek of Aeschylus, and Miscellaneous Poems* (1833). *The Seraphim and Other Poems* (1838). *Queen Annelida and
False Arcite, in The Poems of Chaucer Modernized*

(1841). (with R.H. Horne) *A New Spirit of the Age* (1844). *Poems* (1844). *Poems: New Edition*, (1850). *Sonnets* [or] *Sonnets from the Portuguese*, in *Poems* (1850). *Casa Guidi Windows: a Poem* (1851). *The Cry of the Children*, in *Two Poems* (1854). *Aurora Leigh* (1857). *Poems Before Congress* (1860). *Last Poems* (1862). *Poetical Works*, (1866). *Letters Addressed to R. Hengist Horn*, ed. S.R. Townshend Mayer (1877). *Poetical Works from 1826 to 1844*, ed. J.H. Ingram (1887). Kenyon, F.G., ed. *Letters of Elizabeth Barrett Browning* (1897). *Letters of Robert Browning and Elizabeth Barrett Browning 1845-1846* (1899). *Complete Works*, ed. C. Porter and H. Clarke (1900). *Poetical works* (1904). Meynell, A. ed., *The Art of Scansion: Letters of E.B. Browning to Uvedale Price* (1916). Wise, T.J., ed. *Letters of Elizabeth Barrett Browning to Robert Browning and Other Correspondents* (1916). Huxley, L., ed. *Letters to Her Sister 1846-59* (1929). *Twenty-two Unpublished Letters of Elizabeth Barrett Browning and Robert Browning (to Her Sisters)* (1935). Benet, W.R., ed. *From Robert and Elizabeth Browning: A Further Selection* (1936). Shackford, M.H., ed. *Letters to B.R. Haydon* (1939). Harrod, H., ed. "Correspondence of Harriet Beecher Stowe and Elizabeth Barrett Browning," *SE* (1948). Weaver, B., ed. "Twenty Unpublished Letters of Elizabeth Barrett to H.S. Boyd." *PMLA*, 65 (1950). McAleer, E.C., ed. "New Letters from Mrs. Browning to Isa Blagden." *PMLA*, 66 (1951). Miller, B., ed. *Elizabeth Barrett to Miss Mitford: Unpublished* (1954). Musgrove, S., ed. "Unpublished Letters of Thomas de Quincey and E.B. Browning." *Auckland University College Bulletin*, 44 (1954). McCarthy, B.P., ed. *Elizabeth Barrett to Mr. Boyd: Unpublished Letters* (1955). Landis, P., and R.E. Freeman, eds. *Letters of the Brownings to George Barrett* (1958). Kelley, P., and R. Hudson, eds. *Diary of E.B.B.: The Unpublished Diary of Elizabeth Barrett Browning, 1831-1832* (1969). Heydon, P., and P. Kelley, eds. *Elizabeth Barrett Browning's Letters to Mrs. David Ogilvy, 1849-1861* (1974). Kelley, P., and R. Hudson, eds. *The Brownings' Correspondence*, vols. I and II (1984); vol. III (1985). Kelley, P. and B. Coley, eds. *The Browning Collections: A Reconstruction with Other Memorabilia* (1984).

BIBLIOGRAPHY: Barnes, W.A. *Bibliography of Elizabeth Barrett Browning* (1967). Cooper, H. *Shakespeare's Sisters*, eds. S. Gilbert and S. Gubar (1979). David, D. *Intellectual Women and Victorian Patriarchy: Harriet Martineau, Elizabeth Barrett Browning, and George Eliot* (1987). Erickson, L. *Robert Browning: His Poetry and His Audiences* (1894). Gilbert, S., and S. Gubar, *The Madwoman in the Attic: The Woman Writer and the Nineteenth-Century Literary Imagination* (1979). Grylls, R. *Mrs. Browning: The Story of Elizabeth Barrett* (1980). Hayter, A. *Elizabeth Barrett Browning* (1965). Hayter, A. *Mrs. Browning: A Poet's Work in Its Setting* (1962). Hewlitt, D. *Elizabeth Barrett Browning* (1953). Hudson, G.W. *An Elizabeth Barrett Browning Concordance* (1973). Karlin, D. *The Courtship of Robert Browning and Elizabeth Barrett* (1985). Lubbock, P. *Elizabeth Barrett Browning in Her Letters* (1906). Lupton, M. *Elizabeth Barrett Browning* (1972). Moers, E. *Literary Women* (1976). Radley, V. *Elizabeth Barrett Browning* (1972). Mermin, D. "The Domestic Economy of Art: Elizabeth Barrett and Robert Browning." *Mothering the Mind: Twelve Studies of Writers and their Silent Partners*, eds. R. Perry and B.M. Watson (1984). Taplin, G. *The Life of Elizabeth Barrett Browning* (1958). Tomkins, J.M.S. *Aurora Leigh* (1962). Ward, M. *Robert Browning and His World: The Private Face* (1967). Woolf, V. *The Second Common Reader* (1932).

For articles in reference works, see: *DLB. DNB. NCBEL. NCLC.*

Other references: Blake, K. *Victorian Poetry* (1986). *Browning Institute Studies*, (1985). *Browning Society Notes* (1977). *Durham University Journal* (1972). *ELH.* (1981). Friedman, S.S. *Tulsa Studies in Women's Literature* (1986). Gilbert, S. *Textual Analysis: Some Readers Reading*, ed. M.A. Caws (1986). Mermin, D. *Critical Inquiry* (1986). Mermin, D. *Studies in English Literature* (1986). *PMLA* (1984). *Signs* (1978). *Studies in Browning and His Circle* (1979). *Studies in Browning and His Circle* (1981). *Victorian Poetry* (1983). *Victorian Poetry* (1984). *Victorian Studies* (1983).

Patricia A. O'Hara

Mary Balfour Brunton

BORN: 1 November 1778, Island of Burra, Orkney.
DIED: 19 December 1818, Edinburgh.
DAUGHTER OF: Colonel Thomas and Francis Ligonier Balfour.
MARRIED: the Rev. Alexander Brunton, 1798(?).

B.'s life was essentially quiet, varied by travel, frequent socializing (especially after the author-ship of *Self-Control* was revealed), and many philanthropic endeavors. She died shortly after giving birth to her stillborn child. B. wrote two novels: *Self-Control* (1811) and *Discipline* (1814). She left a third, *Emmeline*, unfinished when she died. B. also projected a series of moral tales, but these were never written. In 1819 her husband attached *Emmeline* to his *Memoir* of her life, along with some of B.'s religious musings, verse, and extracts from her letters and journals. Her husband comments in the *Memoir* that B.'s books "rose very fast into popularity, and their popularity seems to have as quickly sunk away." Nonetheless, Robert Colby notes that the popularity of *Self-Control*, at least, "appears to have been sustained well into the Victorian period to judge from its continuous appearance on Mudie's lists through 1884." The 1974 reprint may signal a revived interest in Brunton's works.

B., who is usually classed with the Scottish moral novelists, attempted in her writing to provide pleasantly couched moral lessons. *Self-Control* was written "to shew the power of the religious principle in bestowing self-command; and to bear testimony against a maxim as immoral as indelicate, that a reformed rake makes the best husband." *Discipline*, a companion piece to *Self-Control*, was "to shew the means through which, when Self-Control has been neglected the mind must be trained for suffering ere it can hope for usefulness or for true enjoyment." *Emmeline's* text was "how little chance there is of happiness when the divorced wife marries her seducer." These central themes are explored within the context of a number of other concerns. As Margaret Bruce notes, she "drew on her experience as a minister's wife to comment on such subjects as poverty, philanthropy, and the treatment of the insane, while her interest in the situation of her own sex encouraged her to comment on love and marriage, the appropriate role for women, women's education, and the plight of the single woman."

Despite her avowed didacticism, B.'s novels have a freshness and a power that make them still quite readable. *Self-Control* was begun in secret, then continued under her husband's guidance. The heroine, Laura Montreville, rich in religious training but a novice in worldly matters, unwarily falls in love with the glib rake, Col. Hargrave (probably named after a character in Richardson's *Sir Charles Grandison*). Shocked at Hargrave's attempt to seduce her, Laura conquers her love for him and eventually comes to love and marry Montague De Courcy, a Grandisonian paradigm. Before this, however, Hargrave has pursued Laura and abducted her repeatedly. Transported by him to America, she escapes in a canoe and manages to find her way back to Scotland. Hargrave, believing her dead, exonerates her and kills himself. This extravagant plot is redeemed somewhat by pungent character studies—most notably of the querulous and selfish Lady Pelham—and (albeit unintentionally) by the deliciously absurd portrayal of the New World. The novel drew gentle fire from Austen, who describes it as "an excellently meant, elegantly written Work, without anything of Nature or Probability in it . . ."

Discipline, although even more earnest in its moral intent, is a better, tighter, and wittier novel.

In an 1810 letter, B. wrote: "If ever I undertake another lady, I will manage her in a different manner. Laura is so decently kerchiefed . . . that to dress her is a work of time and pains. Her younger sister, if she ever have one, shall wear loose, floating easy robes, that will slip on in a minute." Ellen Percy, this more credible younger sister, is spoiled as a child, then painfully schooled by the loss of fortune, friends, protection, and even, for a time, liberty itself. The Christian fortitude and charity that she ultimately attains earn her the hand of Henry Graham (alias Maitland), who has loved her from the beginning. The vigor and verisimilitude of the early part of *Discipline* suggests that it may well be autobiographical. The *Memoir* of B. hints that she, like Ellen, had been overly indulged as a child and given, at best, a fashionable and desultory education.

Whereas *Self-Control* reflects a Richardsonian model, *Discipline* recalls Burney's *Camilla*. The heroine's pride, strong feelings, imprudence, and reluctance to inflict pain on herself or on others lead her into one indiscretion after another until she becomes thoroughly entangled with the unscrupulous Lord Frederick de Burgh. Ironically, the ruin of her father's fortune and his subsequent suicide prevent her from eloping with Lord Frederick. Impoverished and driven abroad, Ellen weathers despair, illness, poverty, and repeated humiliation. Her mother's friend, Miss Mortimer, teaches her the principles of religion and guides her painful and gradual reformation. Ellen eventually recovers some of her fortune, meets Charlotte Graham, and accompanies her to the Highlands where she again encounters Henry.

In *Discipline*, Ellen tells her own story. The first retrospective, conjoined with the vivid portrayal of a young child, anticipates the Victorian novel and gives the work a richer flavor and stronger appeal than *Self-Control*. The London and Edinburgh sections of the novel, written in the Fanny Burney style, are enlivened with some very effective satirical figures. Best are the designing Julia Arnold (Ellen's fair-weather friend) and the jealous and indolent Mrs. Boswell, who hires Ellen as a governess. The novel is graced with wit, especially in the early pages: "My father . . . gave no instructions in regard to [my education], except that expense should not be spared on it; and he certainly never found reason to complain that this injunction was neglected." The Highlands section, however, freighted with long explanatory footnotes, is excessively sentimental. (There is, for instance, no such thing as adultery among the Highlanders.) B. notes with honest admiration and, perhaps, some chagrin, the inferiority of her Highland portraits to those of *Waverley* which was published just as she was finishing *Discipline*.

B.'s novels bear clear evidence of her attempt—not always fully successful—to adhere to her own formula for an effective novelist: "Irish humour, Scotch prudence, and English sincerity,— the first, that his work may be read; the second, that it may be read without injury to himself; the third, that the perusal of it may be profitable to others."

WORKS: (Anonymous) *Self-Control* (1811). *Discipline* (1814). (Anonymous) *Emmeline, with Some Other Pieces* (1819). *Self-Control* (1832).

BIBLIOGRAPHY: Alexander, B. *Memoir* (attached to the 1819 edition of *Emmeline* and the 1832 and 1849 edition of *Discipline*). Bruce, M.H. *Journal of Women's Studies in Literature*, Vol. 1 (1979).

Elwood, Mrs. A.K. *Memoirs of the Literary Ladies of England* (1843).

For articles in reference works, see: Allibone. *BA19C. CHEL.* Ward, W.S. *Literary Reviews in British Periodicals, 1798-1820* (1973).

Other references: Baker, E. *The History of the English Novel* (1929, rpt., 1967). Colby, R. *Fiction with a Purpose* (1967). Moers, E. *Literary Women* (1976). Moler, K. *Jane Austen's Art of Allusion* (1968). Utter, R. and Needham, G. *Pamela's Daughters* (1936).

Kathleen Fowler

Bryher (pseudonym of Annie Winifred Ellerman)

BORN: 2 September 1894, London.
DIED: 28 January 1983, Vevey, Switzerland.
DAUGHTER OF: Sir John Reeves Ellerman and Hannah Glover Ellerman.
MARRIED: Robert McAlmon, 1921; Kenneth Macpherson, 1927.

Born Annie Winifred Ellerman, first child of a shipping magnate, one of England's richest men, B. thoroughly rebelled against Victorian restrictions on women which thwarted her childhood desires— to go to sea as a cabin boy and then to inherit and operate her father's business and maritime empire. Her lifelong love of the sea, coasts, islands, and dangerous adventures began very early in her life, when, instead of being sent to school, she traveled abroad with her family. For her travel was far more educational. It formed her artistic tastes and independent character as well as arousing the "geographical emotions," as she later described them, which motivate and permeate her historical novels, the writing for which she is best known.

With her parents, she wintered in Italy from 1901 to 1907 and in the south of France in 1908 and 1909. In that time she also went twice to Egypt, once to Sicily, and spent long periods in Paris. She taught herself to read at the age of four, spoke French well—and a bit of Arabic—by the age of seven, and, resisting British insularity, had, even before adolescence, formed the sense of herself as European, a feeling she never lost. Through travel she developed a large sense of time and space, and, having met all kinds of people, viewed all races and religions as worthy of respect. She considered as essential to her writing the fact that she had early been close to "poverty, fire, and death." Thus she developed a deep identification with the life of ordinary people in the stark milieux of ancient times, leading critics to feel in her work a vivid sense that the author was "somehow there," present at the events she recounts.

An experience decisive for B.'s literary future occurred when she was three years old: a nursery-maid read her *The Swiss Family Robinson*. Other important early literary influences were Shakespeare in E. Nesbit's retelling and Homer in W.C. Perry's *The Boy's Iliad*, which she read after a visit to the Colosseum in Rome in 1903 fired her interest in the Graeco-Roman world. This interest grew as she read first G.A. Henty's *The Young Carthaginian*, then Flaubert's *Salammbo*, and later the Loeb Greek and Roman historians. When she was sixteen B. took art lessons and wanted to be an artist; to prevent her, her family finally sent her to Queenwood School in Eastbourne, Sussex. School was "a violation of the spirit," she later said, but it strengthened rather than weakened her independence and intellectual bent. She pursued her own love of history, archaeology, and poetry and began to write. In 1914 she published *Region of Lutany and Other Poems* and in 1918 two books—a translation of Bion's *The Lament of Adonis* and *Amy Lowell: A Critical Appreciation*.

B.'s love of poetry brought about the most crucial event of her life. Early in 1919 she met the American poet H.D. (Hilda Doolittle) who was then pregnant, critically ill with pneumonia, and not expected to survive the birth of her child. Bryher saved H.D.'s life by providing personal support and medical care. After a daughter, Perdita, was safely born, the two women traveled together to the Scilly Isles, the name of one of which inspired the pseudonym "Bryher" when a year later B. published her first novel, *Development* (1920). Thus began a deep lifetime friendship which richly fed both literary careers. B., admiring H.D.'s work, committed herself to creating an environment in which her friend's poetic genius could flourish. However, after the unexpected success of *Development*, a candid reflection of her school days at Queenwood, B. was also able to think of herself as a professional writer. *Development* has a sequel in *Two Selves* (1923).

Late in 1920 B., H.D., and Perdita went to America, which B. hated, except for their meeting the American poet Marianne Moore, who from then on continually wrote to, praised, and encouraged Bryher as a writer. B.'s impressions of America, which she later modified, are recorded in *West* (1925). In New York B. also met Robert McAlmon, with whom she felt strong intellectual affinities, and in 1921 they married. They moved to Paris, with H.D. nearby, and B. financed The Contact Press under McAlmon's editorship, publishing almost all of the modernist writers active in Europe between the wars, including James Joyce, Mina Loy, Gertrude Stein, Djuna Barnes, Ezra Pound, F.M. Ford, Ernest Hemingway, and Dorothy Richardson, whose work B. admired and promoted all her life. In this period B. also subsidized The Egoist Press which published McAlmon and H.D. among others.

Early in 1927 B. and McAlmon were divorced. In September 1927 she married Kenneth Macpherson, whose interest in filmmaking stimulated her to found Pool Productions, a film company which also put out the magazine *Close Up* from 1927 until 1933. With B.'s help Macpherson made a film, *Foothills*, in 1927, starring H.D., and in 1931 the remarkable film *Borderline*, starring Paul Robeson, Robeson's wife, and H.D. B.'s interest in film took her to Vienna and Berlin, where in 1927 she met Dr. Hans Sachs, the psychoanalyst, and began the psychoanalysis which was key to the release of her literary creativity. Her book *Film Problems of Soviet Russia* (1929) shows her to be a fine film critic, but she never wrote on film again.

In 1930 B. made Switzerland her permanent residence, and she lived primarily at Kenwin, the home she built near Vevey—now a Bauhaus landmark—until the end of her life, although she and H.D. also shared an apartment in London from 1934 to 1946. In England from 1935 to 1950 she published the influential literary review *Life and Letters Today* and worked to rescue European intellectuals who were victims of Nazi persecution. She wrote little in the thirties but continued her research and from 1940 to 1966 had a period of high productivity in which she wrote ten novels and two volumes of autobiography, *The Heart to Artemis* (1962) and *The Days of Mars* (1972).

The first of the novels, *Beowulf*, depicting her London neighborhood during the bombings, appeared in France in 1948 but was not translated into English until 1956. Next she wrote *The Fourteenth of October* (1952), about the battle of Hastings, and *This January Tale* (1966) on the Norman Conquest. *Roman Wall* (1954) documents life in 298 A.D. on the borders of the Roman Empire as Germanic tribes invaded what is now Switzerland. *Ruan* takes place in B.'s beloved Cornwall as Christianity is infiltrating pagan Britain around 315 A.D. The events of *The Coin of Carthage* (1964) occur at the end of the Punic Wars (218-202 B.C.) at the time of Hannibal's death.

B.'s typical heroes are homeless young men or itinerant traders. Friendship and loyalty among men are dominant themes; sexual love and marriage are seldom mentioned. Although B. was an ardent feminist, her female characters are usually peripheral although an exception is the Greek priestess Harmonia, heroine of *Gate to the Sea* (1958), whose courage saves her companions' lives in 326 B.C. when Poseidonia fell to Italian tribes after the death of Alexander.

While B.'s primary aim is to recreate the texture of ordinary lives of long ago, her themes also inevitably reflect the concerns of her contemporary world. She writes about past periods of social breakdown and upheaval, analogues of the chaos she saw created in Europe by two world wars. Her characters, itinerant and in danger, are prevented from establishing lasting human relations. Separations and deaths usually end her novels on a note of isolation and *tristesse*, yet often with meditative consolation. Valerius in *Roman Wall* says: "Things ended, and yet were continuous. . . . Creation sprang from eternity, but it also was transient; no second experience was exactly like the first." In times of cultural change and dissolution she believed the old, true values could survive if individuals took the responsibility to incorporate, maintain, and carry them through war and destruction.

The strengths of B.'s writing are masterly documentation of historical fact, sensuous evocation of place, clarity of verbal description, and warmth of feeling for others. One critic called her "that very gifted, very human writer." She unremittingly upheld her belief in friendship and loyalty as primary virtues in human life. These virtues informed B.'s dual literary career as recreator of history and as generous supporter of avant-garde arts, activities for which she remains important to this day.

WORKS: *Region of Lutany and Other Poems* (1914). *Amy Lowell: A Critical Appreciation* (1918). *The Lament for Adonis*, translated from the Greek of Bion of Smyrna (1918). *Development, A Novel* (1920). *Arrow Music*, with others (1922). *Two Selves* (1923). *West* (1925). *A Picture Geography for Little Children: Asia* (1925). *Civilians* (1927). *Film Problems of Soviet Russia* (1929). *The Lighthearted Student*, with T. Weiss (1930). *Cinema Survey*, with R. Herring and D. Bower (1937). *The Fourteenth of October* (1952). *The Player's Boy, A Novel* (1953). *Roman Wall* (1954). *Beowulf, A Novel* (1948; 1956). *Gate to the Sea* (1958). *Ruan* (1960). *The Heart to Artemis: A Wri-*

ter's *Memoirs* (1962). *The Coin of Carthage* (1964). *Visa for Avalon* (1965). *This January Tale* (1966). *The Colors of Vaud* (1969). *The Days of Mars: A Memoir 1940–1946* (1972).

BIBLIOGRAPHY: Beach, S. *Shakespeare and Company* (1956). Ford, H. *Published in Paris: American and British Writers, Printers and Publishers in Paris 1920-1939* (1975). Guest, B. *Herself Defined: The Poet H.D. and her World* (1984). McAlmon, R., and K. Boyle *Being Geniuses Together 1920-1930* (1968). For articles in reference works, see: *CA. CN.*

Other references: *Book Week* (6 November 1966). *Commonweal* (30 May 1952, 20 August 1954, 12 October 1956, 10 October 1958, 2 December 1960). *NYTBR* (2 June 1963, 25 April 1965, 27 November 1966, 8 February 1970). *Observer Review* (7 January 1968). *Poetry* (February 1959). *San Francisco Chronicle* (10 June 1952). *SR* (1 September 1956, 12 November 1960). *Time* (21 June 1963).

Jane Augustine

Elizabeth Burnet

BORN: 8 November 1661, Earontoun, Hampshire.
DIED: 3 February 1709, London.
DAUGHTER OF: Sir Richard Blake and Elizabeth Bathurst Blake.
MARRIED: Robert Berkeley, 1678; Bishop Gilbert Burnet, c. 1700.

B., devotional writer and benefactress, was born into a well-connected Hampshire family. At seventeen, through the good offices of Dr. Fell, Bishop of Oxford, she met and married Robert Berkeley. Deeply religious, her convictions were soon tested by her mother-in-law, a devout Roman Catholic. To offset this powerful influence, B. became a determined student of her own religion. She finally journeyed to Holland with her husband to escape the pressures to renounce her faith. On her return to her husband's home in Spetchley in Worchestershire, she devoted her life to religious studies and charitable works.

During the years of her marriage until her husband's death in 1693, she gave freely of her time and money for the welfare of others. She attended the sick and dying, provided food and books for the clergy, and established schools for the children of the poor. At a time when education was available to only the privileged few, she paid for schooling for more than a hundred children. When her husband died, she implemented plans, liberally supported by his bequest, for a hospital for the poor in Worcester.

During the seven years following the death of her husband until she remarried, she continued her charitable work. Unlike many widows of the times, she was left wealthy by her husband, a blessing she shared freely with others less fortunate than herself. The practice she followed was to keep one-fifth of her income for herself and use the remainder for others. Though she gave liberally, she had the rare quality of not humiliating the recipients of her kindness. She was loved for her saintly ways by those who knew her.

In c. 1700, she married Gilbert Burnet, Bishop of Salisbury, who is remembered for his *History of the Reformation* (1674-1714) and his *History of My Own Times* (1724-34). She took in hand the Bishop's children from a previous marriage and raised them as her own. With the full support of her husband, she continued her charitable work for the remainder of her life. In 1707, she traveled to Spa for her health. Somewhat recovered, she returned to England, but she again became ill and died in 1709 of pleuritic fever.

B.'s literary reputation depends on a single work of devotions, written for her own use during her seven years of widowhood. Reflecting the importance she placed on religion as a part of everyday experience, *A Method of Devotion* was designed, according to her preface, to achieve "The great End of all Religions and Devotions . . . to restore the depraved Nature of Men to its original Perfection" and to assist "weak young and ignorant Persons . . . to Purify their Hearts and Lives by Duties of Religion." She emphasizes that avoidance of "scandalous Vices" and repetition of prayers are not sufficient to achieve these goals. She apologizes for the repetitions which are explained by "Part . . . [having been] drawn up many years ago, and enlarged at several times." Adroitly, she turns weakness to advantage when she writes, "it is not thought worth while to correct those Repetitions, which might serve better to fix necessary truths in the Memory of young and ignorant Persons."

The work of nearly four hundred pages is divided into two parts. The first part involves rules for living; the second, rules for worship. Part I provides schedules for prayer and directions for dealing with daily problems like eating, dressing, and working. Of principal importance is a concern for others, as the following directions on dress reveal: "Let your Cloathing be with a decent Frugality, the better to enable you to cloath the Poor." For B., the Bible was a practical guide in everyday affairs. For example, the Golden Rule is apparent in these directions regarding dealings with others: "In all your Transactions with your Neighbours, be it Friend or Enemy, do as you would be done to," or regarding employees, "Exact no more work of any than their Strength and Health enable them to Perform." Part II focuses on "Some Rules Relating to the Devotions" and surveys in its chapters a variety of subjects including days of fasting, humiliation, retirement, and contemplation. *A Method of Devotion*, with its clear, unaffected language, reflects in both style and content the saintly qualities of its author.

George Ballard recognized the unique nature of these qualities when he wrote of B., "Her design, indeed, was to render a strictness in religion as agreeable to all companies as was possible, and to show that it did not take off from that easiness and freedom which is the life of conversation; and few ever succeeded better in recommending it thus to the world than she did."

WORKS: *A Method of Devotion: or, Rules for Holy & Devout Living, with Prayers on Several Occasions, And Advices & Devotions For the Holy Sacrament. In Two Parts* (1708).

BIBLIOGRAPHY: Ballard, G. *Memoirs of Several Ladies of Great Britain* (1752; ed. Ruth Perry, 1985). *Biographica Britannica; Or, The Lives of the most Eminent Persons who have Flourished in Great Britain and Ireland*, 2nd ed., ed. A. Kippis (1778-93). Goodwyn, Archdeacon T. *Memorials and Characters of Two Hundred Eminent and Worthy Persons . . . of Great Britain* (1744) (rpt. of "Some Account of Her Life," which accompanied the Second and Third Editions of *A Method of Devotion*, 1709 and 1713). Nichols, J. *Illustrations of the Literary History of the Eighteenth Century, Consisting of Authentic Memoirs and Original Letters* (1817-58).

For articles in reference works, see: *DNB. Fifty Famous Women; Their Virtues and Failings, and the Lessons of their Lives* (n.d.). Ireland, N. O. *Index to Women of the World* (1970). Todd.

Philip Bordinat

Frances (Fanny) Burney

BORN: 13 June 1752, King's Lynn, Norfolk.
DIED: 6 January 1840, London.
DAUGHTER OF: Charles and Esther Sleepe Burney.
MARRIED: Alexandre Gabriel Jean-Baptiste Piochard d'Arblay, 1793.

B. was the daughter of a music-master and organist later to gain renown as a historian of music and member of Samuel Johnson's circle. She was a shy and seemingly backward child but displayed an early talent for mimicry and a remarkably retentive memory. B.'s mother died in 1762, and five years later her father married Elizabeth Allen, a widow with a keen interest in literature. B. became a voracious reader and began an extensive experimentation with writing. In 1767 her stepmother concluded that B. and her sister Susan were taking their writing too seriously, and the girls dutifully consigned their "scribblings"—including the draft of a novel by B., "Carolyn Evelyn"—to a bonfire.

In 1768 B. began keeping a detailed diary, and in 1778 her first novel, *Evelina, or a Young Lady's Entrance into the World*, was published. The novel was published anonymously, but the secret of its authorship quickly leaked out and B. found herself the center of a whirlwind of adulation. Samuel Johnson, Hester Thrale, Sir Joshua Reynolds, Richard Brinsley Sheridan, and others of the "best" people were effusive in their praise. B. quickly became the darling of the Streatham set and the special pet of Johnson.

B. next tried writing a comedy for the stage, but the project was dropped at the urging of her father and Samuel "Daddy" Crisp, an old family friend. They apparently feared the play's sharp satire on female "wits" would offend the influential "bluestockings." Another novel, *Cecilia*, appeared in 1782. In 1784 B. lost three close and important friends. "Daddy" Crisp died that April. Then, that summer, the widowed Mrs. Thrale announced she would marry an Italian singing master. Her family and friends reacted with shocked disapproval, and she turned to B. for support. The very conservative and socially punctilious B. responded coldly, and the friendship ended. In December, Johnson died.

In 1785 B. was presented to George III and Queen Charlotte and was soon offered the post of second keeper of the robes for Queen Charlotte, entering the royal service in July. She soon found the restrictive nature of her post disagreeable, and she resented the petty tyrannies of her immediate superior. In 1790 she voiced her discontent to her father, but he was reluctant to allow her to resign. The next year, though, her health began to fail, and she left the post in July 1791 with a pension of £100 a year. In January 1793 B. visited a friend at Norbury Park in Surrey and was introduced to a colony of French refugees who had rented nearby Juniper Hall. Among them was a former army officer, Alexandre d'Arblay, who had been adjutant general to the Marquis de Lafayette and accompanied Lafayette when he fled to Austria. A romance blossomed, and B. and d'Arblay were married on 28 July 1793. Their only child, Alexandre, was born on 18 December 1794.

Shortly after her marriage, B. wrote *Brief Reflections Relative to the Emigrant French Clergy*, a pamphlet encouraging charity toward Catholic priests who had fled revolutionary France. March 1795 saw a performance at Drury Lane of *Edwy and Elgiva*, a tragedy written during her years at court. It was a dismal failure, withdrawn after one performance. *Camilla*, B.'s third novel, was published in 1796. A successful subscription sale made the novel a strong moneymaker, but critical reaction was mixed. In 1801 General d'Arblay returned to France to try to reclaim the property he had lost during the revolution, and B. joined him in 1802, intending to stay only a few months. But war broke out again, trapping her in France until 1812. B.'s last novel, *The Wanderer, or Female Difficulties*, appeared in 1814. It sold well, but it was a pitiful example of the deterioration of a once-skilled writer's abilities. B. was surprised and hurt by the harsh criticism it received.

B. returned to France after the fall of Napoleon and was present there during the "Hundred Days." The d'Arblays returned to England in 1815 and settled in Bath, where the general died in 1818. B. moved to London and spent a quiet and retired old age. In 1832 she published the *Memoirs of Doctor Burney*, based on manuscript notes left by her father and fleshed out with her own anecdotes and recollections. The public found the work entertaining, but the critics condemned it roundly. B. became a recluse and died quietly at the age of eighty-seven.

B.'s fame as a novelist depends almost entirely on her first published work, *Evelina*. It is an epistolary novel, written in an easy and still-readable style, and the first important example of the domestic novel of manners. It combined a good-humored but sometimes biting social satire with a sentimentality much more appreciated in her age than in our own. Its sentimentality and occasionally heavy-handed moralizing discomfit the modern reader, but these were important plusses in B.'s day. In fact, the completely moral tone of B.'s works has been cited as an important influence in the establishment of the novel as a respectable literary genre.

In her second novel, *Camilla*, discerning readers noted a disturbing change in B.'s style: a movement toward use of "elevated," more elegant language. This was so marked that there was widespread but unfounded speculation that Samuel Johnson had a hand in the novel's composition. B. had begun to lose her touch, and her style continued to decline into a stilted, pompous verbosity that makes *Camilla* tedious and *The Wanderer* almost unreadable.

Many factors have been advanced as the cause of this decline: a desire to imitate Johnson's style, a striving to enhance the respectability of her novels by elevating their tone, a loss of familiarity with the rhythms of English prose during her absence in France, loss of spirit occasioned by the need to write for money rather than as purely creative expression, and a simple drying up of the creative juices. Most probably, each of these elements had its effect.

Although *Evelina* is the only one of Burney's novels to claim lasting readership, B. was not a "one-shot novelist." *Cecilia* and *Camilla*, too, were widely read and admired in their day. B. did much to make the novel a respectable literary form and novel-writing an acceptable occupation for women. The influence of her works on Jane Austen has long been acknowledged, and traces of B.'s influence have been discerned in the works of Maria Edgeworth, Charlotte Smith, and others.

B. was by no means a pioneer. Other women had written novels before her. B. simply happened to write quite a good novel on her first attempt, and circumstances (particularly her involvement with Johnson and the Streatham set) caused it to get perhaps more attention than it deserved. Nor was B. an innovator in matters of style and technique. In *Evelina* she used proven novelistic techniques, and her later works show no real stylistic inventiveness. What was fresh and engaging about *Evelina* was B.'s choice of her young heroine as the *persona* from whose viewpoint we observe the events of the plot—and her exceptional talent for depicting manners, social behavior, and conversation.

Several modern scholars have suggested the presence of a nascent feminism in B.'s novels. These suggestions should be taken with extreme caution. B. was an almost unswervingly conservative and conventional lady, and it would certainly be surprising to find any progressive social notions in her works. B.'s heroines struggled to improve their lot, but they strove only to regain their proper place in the social order. In B.'s novels, the appropriate reward for a woman's perseverance through adversity is a comfortable marriage to a socially acceptable gentleman.

With the first publication of her journals and correspondence two years after her death, B.'s position of importance in literary history was assured. When she produced her *Memoirs of Doctor Burney*, the volumes provided fascinating glimpses of famous figures of the previous century—unfortunately smothered in turgid and tortuous prose. In her diaries and letters, though, the characters of her life stand out clearly and vividly.

B. rivals Boswell as a recorder of conversation, and her descriptions of people are considerably more lifelike. B., keenly attuned to the externals of character and behavior, provides portraits that are often superficial but also detailed and animated. B. is an excellent storyteller, and she had plenty of good stories to tell—especially about Johnson and the members of his circle, her days at Court, and her time in France during the Napoleonic Wars.

WORKS: *Evelina* (1778). *Cecilia* (1782). *Brief Reflections Relative to the Emigrant French Clergy* (1793). *Edwy and Elgiva* (staged 1795; ed. M.J. Benkovitz, 1957). *Camilla* (1796). *The Wanderer* (1814). *Memoirs of Doctor Burney* (1832). *Diary and Letters of Madame d'Arblay*, ed. C. Barrett (1842–46). *Selected Letters and Journals*, ed. J. Hemlow (1987).

BIBLIOGRAPHY: Adelstein, M.E. *Fanny Burney* (1968). Dobson, A. *Fanny Burney* (1903). Grau, J.A. *Fanny Burney: An Annotated Bibliography* (1981). Hahn, E. *A Degree of Prudery* (1950). Hemlow, J. *The History of Fanny Burney* (1958). Kilpatrick, S. *Fanny Burney* (1980). Lloyd, C. *Fanny Burney* (1936). Overman, A.A. *An Investigation into the Character of Fanny Burney* (1933). Simons, J. *Fanny Burney* (1987). Straub, K. *Divided Fictions: Fanny Burney and Feminine Strategy* (1987). Tourtellot, A.B. *Be Loved No More* (1938). White, E. *Fanny Burney, Novelist* (1960).

Other references: Brown, M.G., *Fetter'd or Free? British Women Novelists, 1670–1815*, ed. M.A. Schofield and C. Macheski (1986). Epstein, J.L. *Eighteenth Century* (1986). Epstein, J. *Representations* (1986). Henlow, J. *PMLA* (1950). Straub, K. *Eighteenth Century* (1986).

Joseph A. Grau

Sarah Harriet Burney

BORN: 29 August 1772, King's Lynn, Norfolk.
DIED: 8 February 1844, Cheltenham, Gloucester.
DAUGHTER OF: Charles and Elizabeth Allen Burney.

B. was the youngest daughter of Charles Burney, musician and member of the Johnson circle. She was his only daughter by his second wife, Elizabeth Allen, and was thus the half-sister of the noted novelist and diarist Fanny Burney (Madame d'Arblay). To be honest, this is probably her greatest claim to a place in literary history.

B. is described during her early years as an ill-tempered and bad-mannered girl, suffering from what her half-sister's biographer, Joyce Hemlow, terms "personality problems." She was not physically attractive and seems to have been pretty much a homebody, though her housekeeping skills—according to her father—were minimal. On the other hand, she is reported to have been quick-witted and intelligent, fluent in both French and Italian.

B. never married, living with her parents until her mother's death in 1796, then remaining with her father at his lodgings in Chelsea College. In September 1798 she eloped with her half-brother, Captain James Burney, who had for some time been estranged from his wife. B.'s siblings were scandalized but tried to put a good public face on the situation and made efforts to intercede in the matter. B.'s father, though, having been suspicious for some time of the "uncommon intimacy" between the two, was horribly wounded by the affair and soon refused even to speak of it. B. and James lived together for five years in a succession of rather shabby dwellings before their affair burned itself out. Although their cohabitation ended after five years, they continued fast friends until James' death in 1821. In 1807 B. returned to Chelsea as her father's housekeeper, remaining with him until his death in 1814.

B. had the advantage of her family's movement in the best circles of English society, having been presented to the royal family by her half-sister, Fanny. In 1821 she was offered a post as governess to the grandchildren of Lord Crewe, a position which offered her welcome financial security. The rest of her life was passed in rather quiet circumstances, punctuated by long travels in Italy. She spent her last years as an invalid, dying in 1844.

B.'s four novels and two books of tales are thoroughly conventional and pedestrian works. They were reasonably successful in their day. *Traits of Nature*, for example, brought its author a respectable £100 a volume. But they have since been decidedly and deservedly forgotten.

WORKS: *Clarentine* (1796). *Geraldine Fauconberg* (1808). *Traits of Nature* (1812). *Tales of Fancy* (1815). *Country Neighbours* (1820). *Romance of Private Life* (1839).

BIBLIOGRAPHY: *DNB*. Hemlow, J. *The History of Fanny Burney* (1958). Kilpatrick, S. *Fanny Burney* (1980).

Joseph A. Grau

Antonia Susan Drabble Byatt

BORN: 24 August 1936, Sheffield.
DAUGHTER OF: John Frederick and Kathleen Marie (Bloor) Drabble.
MARRIED: Ian Charles Rayner Byatt, 1959; Peter John Duffy, 1969.
WRITES UNDER: A.S. Byatt.

B. is a novelist, literary critic, editor, script writer, and university lecturer. She was awarded her B.A. (first class honors) from Newnham College, Cambridge, in 1957, and pursued graduate work at Bryn Mawr College (1957-58) and at Somerville College, Oxford (1958-59). Since 1972, she has been a full-time lecturer in English and American literature at University College, London.

B.'s first novel, *The Shadow of a Sun* (1964), is the story of a young girl who has grown up in the shadow of her famous novelist father. When she falls in love and gets pregnant, her parents are unable to deal with the situation. A student who loves her offers marriage, but she refuses, coming to her own independent insights. *The Game* (1967) is about sisters, one an Oxford don and the other a famous novelist, whose rivalry is rekindled when the person they both loved in their youth re-enters their lives. *The Virgin in the Garden* (1978), the first novel of a tetralogy, takes place in 1953, the year of Elizabeth II's coronation. It is a story about the coming of age of three main characters during preparations for a pageant honoring Elizabeth I. *Still Life* (1980) is the second novel in the tetralogy, and B. is working on the third.

As a critic, B. has published *Degrees of Freedom: The Novels of Iris Murdoch* (1965), and *Wordsworth and Coleridge in Their Time* (1970), six essays on aspects of early nineteenth-century English life. She has also edited and written an introduction to *The Mill on the Floss*, by George Eliot (1979); written prefaces to fiction by Elizabeth Bowen, Grace Paley, and Willa Cather; and contributed to collections, journals, and newspapers.

Perhaps because she has written a book of criticism on Iris Murdoch, B. is often compared with her. Indeed, faith in the power of the intellect is important to her vision; in *The Virgin in the Garden*, for instance, Elizabeth I is perceived as a ruler who prevailed because she used her intelligence, unlike her relative, Mary, Queen of Scots. However, although this work established B. as a writer of depth, it is also "donnish," carrying a great weight of literary and historical allusion. Like her sister, novelist Margaret Drabble, B. often creates characters with literary or academic connections, as in *The Game*. One of the questions raised in this work about sister-rivals concerns the ethics of using real people as characters in fiction.

WORKS: *The Shadow of a Sun* (1964). *Degrees of Freedom: The Novels of Iris Murdoch* (1965). *The Game* (1967). *Wordsworth and Coleridge in Their Time* (1970). *The Virgin in the Garden* (1978). *Still Life* (1980). *Sugar and Other Stories* (1987).

BIBLIOGRAPHY

For articles in reference works, see: *British Novelists Since 1960* (1983). *CLC. DLB.*

Other references: *Books and Bookmen* (4 January 1979). *Critique* (Fall 1982). *Encounter* (July 1968). *Ms.* (June 1979). *New Statesman* (3 November 1978). *NYTBR* (26 July 1964, 17 March 1968, 1 April 1979). *Times* (London) (6 June 1981). *TLS* (2 January 1964, 19 January 1967, 3 November 1968, 9 March 1984).

ANGELA G. DORENKAMP

Alice Mona Caird

BORN: 1858, Ryde, Isle of Wight.
DIED: 4 February 1932.
DAUGHTER OF: Hector (?); mother's name not known.
MARRIED: A. Henryson-Caird, 1877.
WROTE UNDER: Mona Alison Caird, G. Noel Hatton.

Little is known of the life of this women's rights advocate, novelist, and anti-vivisectionist except that she was the daughter of an inventor named Hector, became the wife of A. Henryson-Caird in 1877, and was rather unhappy in her marriage to him.

She published her earlier novels, *Whom Nature Leadeth* (1883) and *One That Wins* (1887), under the pseudonym G. Noel Hatton. In their day her novels were popular and controversial, but she is now chiefly remembered for her essays on marriage, the family, and women's relations to class and economic structure. She achieved notice when she published two articles, "Marriage" and "Ideal Marriage," in the August and November 1888 issues of the *Westminster Review*. The pieces created such controversy that she wrote further essays for the *Daily Telegraph*, collectively entitled "Is Marriage a Failure?" All of these essays were later included in her book *The Morality of Marriage* (1891).

The Morality of Marriage also took on one of the best-known conservative writers of the day, Mrs. Lynn Linton, who called suffragists "the Shrieking Sisterhood" and feminists in general "social insurgents" and "wild women." C. rebutted Linton by denying that nature intended women only for motherhood and scorned Linton for everything from her inability to imagine female heroes to her pettiness in ridiculing the appearance of independent women whose views she disliked.

With such chapter headings as "The Lot of Women Under the Rule of Man," "Motherhood Under Conditions of Dependence," and "Suppression of Variant Types," *The Morality of Marriage* set forth the theory of adverse feminine social conditioning and the difficulties besetting the woman who rebels. C. praises Ibsen's Nora "who dared the terrors of the social torture-chamber" by bearing her children. C. also felt that woman's inequality was directly linked to the marriage state and the subordinate role of the wife. She argued that the way in which society defined marriage— and motherhood—as woman's "proper spheres" fixated women on these goals and imprisoned them in thankless domestic routine, views that earned C. the reputation of an outspoken defender of the New Woman.

Her novel *A Romance of the Moors* (1891) was an exploration of these themes, using the story of a young woman who risks "losing her character" rather than submit to forcing a man to marry her and compromising her desire for an independent life. But it was in *The Daughters of Danaus* (1894) that C. truly harnessed the novel to her feminist aims. (The title is an allusion to the mythical Greek legend of the punishment of Danaus' fifty daughters, who unwillingly wed their suitors in a mass marriage, killed their husbands, and were forced in return to draw water from a sieve for eternity.)

The novel tells the story of Hadria Temperley, whose unhappy marriage to a conventional man illustrates C.'s theory of the limitations of wedlock. After an attempted rebellion and trip to Paris, where she tries to study music, Hadria bows to pressure and returns to England to the life of a middle-class matron. Rebelling again, she has an affair with another man that proves as unsatisfactory as her marriage. Ultimately, despite her belief in the power of ideas and her rather vacillating feminism, she is unable to find her way to a life of principle. The novel closes with her defeat as a lesson in the sacrifice of Talent to Convention.

C. was as passionate about injustice to animals as to women and was an early member of the anti-vivisectionist movement. Her works, with titles like *Legalized Torture* (n.d.) and *The Savagery of Vivisection* (1894–1895), expressed her outrage. Only her travel books (she voyaged frequently on the Continent) seem without the spirit of polemic that characterized her other work. C. ceased writing a number of years before her death but remained active on behalf of the causes that appeared to be the ruling passions of her life.

WORKS: *Whom Nature Leadeth* (1883). *One That Wins* (1887). *For Money or for Love* (1889). *The Wing of Azreal* (1889). *A Romance of the Moors* (1891). *The Morality of Marriage and Other Essays* (1891). *The Daughters of Danaus* (1894). *Some Truths About Vivisection* (1894). *The Savagery of Vivisection* (1894–1895). *Beyond the Pale* (1896). *The Pathway of the Gods* (1898). *A Sentimental View of Vivisection* (189?). *The Proposed Pasteur Institute at Chelsea Bridge* (189?). *The Stones of Sacrifice* (1915). *Legalized Torture* (n.d.). *Sacrifice, Noble and Ignoble* (n.d.).

BIBLIOGRAPHY: Calder, J. *Women and Marriage in Victorian Fiction* (1978). Cunningham, G. *The New Woman and the Victorian Novel* (1978). Showalter, E. *A Literature of Their Own* (1977).

For articles in reference works, see: *BA19C. Bibliophile Dictionary. Chambers.*

Laura Hapke

Margaret Steuart Calderwood

BORN: 1715.
DIED: 1774.
DAUGHTER OF: Sir James Steuart and Anne Dalrymple.
MARRIED: Thomas Calderwood, 1735.

In 1756 C. travelled with her husband, sons, and servants to join her brother, Sir James Steuart, residing abroad because of his part in the Rebel-

lion of 1745. During her journey through England, Holland, and what is now Belgium, C. sent a stream of letters back to Scotland. Settled briefly in Brussels, she revised and organized her writings into a continuous narrative, which circulated privately among her friends. C.'s "Volumes" are typical of eighteenth-century travel journals: she loads her account with facts about each place she visits, and some of the funniest passages of her account describe the mockery her continual petty questions incite. Her Scottishisms enliven violent attacks on the "papaists," carefully copied recipes and manufacturing details, and comic accounts of persons met along the way. C. criticizes the English heavily; at their best, they are not so "uptaking" as the Scots, and in Brussels, the British women "are mostly what I call adventuresses."

The woman portrayed in the journals is forceful, energetic, and commonsensical. Despite her lack of French, C. slogged tenaciously about Brussels by herself until she managed to rent a house and place her sons in school. Back in Britain in December of 1756, she assumed the management of her husband's estates with great success. She tried her hand at novel writing although *Fanny Roberts* never appeared in print, and she continued to write vigorous letters to her daughter and friends. The persona presented in her journal in many ways prefigures the "splenetic" traveller Smollett was to create and Sterne to label, as when C. regrets that the "old Duchess of Aremberg is a-dying," since "on such occasions the bells ring so that you cannot hear what you are saying." Her journal balances two common forms of travel account, the guidebook and the more anecdotal narrative.

WORKS: Letters and journals in *Coltness Collections* (1842). *The Adventures of Fanny Roberts* (unpublished). *Journal* concerning the management of the Calderwood estates (unpublished). Letters (unpublished).

BIBLIOGRAPHY: *Letters and Journals of Mrs. Calderwood of Polton*, ed. A. Fergusson (1884). For articles in reference works, see: *DNB*.

Marie E. McAllister

(Janet) Taylor Caldwell

BORN: 7 September 1900, Preswich, Manchester.
DIED: 30 August 1985, Greenwich, Conn.
DAUGHTER OF: Arthur Francis and Anna M. Caldwell.
MARRIED: William Fairfax Combs, 1919; Marcus Reback, 1931; William E. Stancell, 1972; William Robert Prestie, 1978.

C. is one of the world's most prolific and best-selling novelists; the Fawcett Publishing Company alone has published 25 million paperback editions of twenty-five novels. Most of her novels reached the best-selling lists, and several have been adapted for films. In addition, C. wrote essays, many of which were collected in one volume. Her last novel, *Answer as a Man* (1981), was her thirty-fifth. Shortly after she completed the manuscript in 1980, C. had a stroke that left her paralyzed and speechless. She had also been deaf for several years before her death in 1985.

C.'s parents left England and moved to Buffalo, N.Y., when she was six. They were never financially comfortable, and C. was required not only to do heavy chores around the house but also to quit school at fifteen and work in a factory. She later finished high school at night, and she worked her way through college, graduating from the University of Buffalo in 1931.

Although her first published novel, *Dynasty of Death*, did not appear until 1938, C. had been writing and receiving rejections for twenty years. After the favorable reception of *Dynasty*, novels appeared nearly annually. She claimed, however, that her novels took her three to five years to write; *This Side of Innocence*, for instance, though published in 1946, was begun in 1927 and not finished until four years later.

C.'s novels are long, complicated historical tales, in which, as Richard Freedman said in 1981, "she loftily pretends the 20th century—at least in fiction—never happened." Her plots are complicated by several mysteries and mysterious characters, who often spend many agonizing moments debating with themselves both sides of an imposing social or moral issue. Martin Levin, for example, found *Captains and Kings* (1972) to be "a jungle of a novel" in which secrets "grow like fungi." The fact is, the "literary establishment," as C. called academic and New York critics, dismissed her (in 1981) as a "shining exemplar of Grey Power." Nevertheless, C. had signed a $3.9 million contract for *Answer as a Man* and another yet-to-be-written novel in 1980 with Putnam.

The author of those "very long, very melodramatic" novels expressed such conservative and religious opinions in her novels that she received numerous awards for them. The John Birch Society gave her a plaque in 1975 for being a "great American Patriot and Scholar." Other honors were bestowed upon her by the Daughters of the American Revolution (1956), Marquette University (1964), and the Wisdom Society.

While critics fault her novels as overwhelmingly verbose, C.'s essays are refreshingly charming and witty. Her accounts of people and events in her life are alive and endearing. The essays display the human contradictions of saying one thing and doing another. C. said, for example, that she was no "women's libber" in her collection *On Growing Up*

Tough (1971), and yet she divorced her third husband in 1973 a few months after their marriage, because he thought a "woman was sort of a serf." In 1955, C. said, "I am not, and never was, a housewife. . . . I do not 'keep house.'" C.'s ideas about "manly men" and the "noisy and stupid Liberation Ladies" are the topics of two essays, "What Happened to American Men" and "Women's Lib." Her objections to polyester blends and food substitutes in "Plastic People" anticipate the later all-cotton, natural-food movement. In many ways dated, *On Growing Up Tough* recalls the dissensions of the late 1960s and early 1970s. Speaking in her own voice in this book, C. gives the most intriguing portrait of her colorful personality. In "T.L.C.—Keep Your Paws Off Me!" C. goes from the medical world to "practically every area of my life, with the exception of my family, of course." "As I am an enthusiastic hypochondriac, I had, a few years ago, worn to the very bone the local physicians and their catalogs of diagnoses. So, armed with brand-new symptoms, I went to another city which has a famous clinic, and entered its hospital for tests. I wasn't ill; I was simply curious to know what I had *this* time and if my own diagnosis would pay off to the discomfiture of my home doctors who had declared I was remarkably healthy."

Virtually no serious criticism, outside of reviews and interviews, has been written of C.'s works. The only possible exception is Jess Stearn's account of numerous hypnotic trances in which C. divulged the existence of thirty-seven separate former entities. Stearns was convinced that the medical knowledge displayed in *Dear and Glorious Physician* (1959) had to have come from practical experience that C. did not have. C. added her disclaimer to his book, but she left an element of acceptance: "I am a novelist, and . . . perhaps some or most of the material had lain fallow in my subconscious. . . . I still heartily reject the idea of reincarnation." The two most interesting characters she dealt with were George Eliot's scullery maid and Mary Magdalene's mother. In her life and in her works C. has been entertaining.

WORKS: *Dynasty of Death* (1938, abr. paper, 1957). *The Eagles Gather* (1940). *The Earth is the Lord's: A Tale of the Rise of Genghis Khan* (1941). (as Max Reiner) *Time No Longer* (1941). *The Strong City* (1942). *The Arm and the Darkness* (1943). *The Turnbulls* (1943). *The Final Hour* (1944). *The Wide House* (1945). *This Side of Innocence* (1946). *There Was a Time* (1947). *Melissa* (1948). *Let Love Come Last* (1949). *The Balance Wheel* (1951). *The Devil's Advocate* (1952). *Maggie, Her Marriage* (1953). *Never Victorious, Never Defeated* (1954). *Tender Victory* (1956). *The Sound of Thunder* (1957). *Your Sins and Mine* (1959). *Dear and Glorious Physician* (1959). *The Listener* (1960). *The Man Who Listens* (1961). *A Prologue to Love* (1961). *Grandmother and the Priests* (1963). *To See the Glory* (1963). *The Late Clara Beame* (1963). *A Pillar of Iron* (1965). *Wicked Angel* (1965). *No One Hears But Him* (1966). *Dialogues with the Devil* (1967). *Testimony of Two Men* (1968). *Great Lion of God* (1970). *On Growing Up Tough* (1971). *Captains and the Kings* (1972). *To Look and Pass* (1973). *Glory and the Lightning* (1974). *The Romance of Atlantis* (1975). *Ceremony of the Innocent* (1976). *I, Judas* (1977). *Bright Flows the River* (1978). *Answer As a Man* (1981).

BIBLIOGRAPHY: Stearn, J. *The Search for a Soul: Taylor Caldwell's Psychic Lives* (1973).

For articles in reference works, see: *CA. CLC. TCA SUP.*

Other references: *American Novelists of Today*, ed. H. Warfel (1951). *Life* (6 April 1959). *Newsweek* (9 March 1959). *NYTBR* (28 April 1946, 10 April, 1949, 14 July 1963, 4 May 1972, 15 December 1974, 31 October 1976, 9 October 1977, 11 January 1981, 1 March 1981). *PW* (5 October 1976, 6 November 1981).

Marilynn J. Smith

Mrs. Patrick Campbell
(Beatrice Stella Tanner Campbell Cornwallis-West)

BORN: 9 February 1865, Kensington.
DIED: 9 April 1940, Pau, France.
DAUGHTER OF: John Tanner and Maria Luigia Giovanna Romanini.
MARRIED: Patrick Campbell, 1884; George Cornwallis-West, 1914.

Although C., known as Stella or Mrs. Pat to her friends, was one of the most popular and successful actresses of the Victorian age, theatre historians and critics still disagree about whether she was a genius or a charlatan. Reviews and eyewitness accounts indicate that her stage presence and acting talents were indeed formidable but also show that her performances were notoriously inconsistent. Her temperamental nature made her such a horror and pleasure to work with that Shaw once suggested she title her autobiography "Why, Though I Was a Wonderful Actress, No Manager or Author Would Ever Engage Me Twice If He Could Possibly Help It."

If C. was indeed the genius that Shaw, Yeats,

Barrie, Pinero, Bernhardt, and many others thought her, the talent sprang from her own native intuition and instinct rather than from extensive theatrical training. Raised in poor gentility by her loving but profligate parents, C. was destined for a respectable career as a concert pianist but gave up a scholarship to the Leipzig Conservatoire to marry Patrick Campbell, who was, like her father, utterly unable to earn a living. In 1887 Patrick Campbell set off gold hunting in South Africa, and C., frail of health, broke, and with two young children to support, turned to the professional stage after some success in amateur productions.

Not until 1893 did C. establish herself undeniably as a major star, with the role of Paula Tanqueray in Pinero's *The Second Mrs. Tanqueray*. Capitalizing on her dark, sensuous beauty and rich contralto voice, C. became famous for her ability to sensitively play the "modern" heroine, a reformed woman with a shadowy past, rather than the helpless sentimental victim of the melodramatic stage. Although C. attempted Shakespeare's tragic heroines, she had not the vocal dexterity or technique to act the roles as Ellen Terry could and wisely chose to forge her own style and make her mark with the contemporary English and continental authors. Her most famous roles included Pinero's *Notorious Mrs. Ebbsmith* (1895); Sardou's *Fedora* (which prompted Shaw's devastating review "Sardoodledom," 1895); Sudermann's *Magda* (1896); Maeterlinck's *Mélisande* (1898; in 1904 with Sarah Bernhardt as her leading man); Bjørnson's *Beyond Human Power* (1900); *Hedda Gabler* (1907); Yeats' *Deirdre* (1908); and Eliza Doolittle (1914). Shaw, Pinero, Barrie, and Yeats wrote plays for her, and she prided herself on her early recognition and frequent presentation of Ibsen's dramatic talents.

C. was partnered in her roles by some of the most famous actors of her age, including George Alexander, Herbert Beerbohm Tree, and Johnston Forbes-Robertson. Unfortunately, few actor-managers could either control her or put up with her inconsistencies in performance or in rehearsal. Consequently, she never became part of an acting team, as Ellen Terry and Henry Irving had been, and was never able to form a long-term stylistic or personal relationship. This was, perhaps, fortunate for C. in the long run, for she became one of the first actress-managers, producing her own choice of plays, directing her own repertory company, and almost mismanaging herself into bankruptcy.

It is difficult to explain precisely what quality made C. so overwhelmingly attractive to audiences on stage and off, but C.'s writings provide evidence of her humor, warmth, and intellect. The most significant of these were her memoirs, *My Life and Some Letters* (1922) and the unfinished and unpublished *Chance Medley*, originally titled *Random Reminiscences* (1935) in the Shaw collection at Cornell University. These works contain invaluable anecdotes about the Victorian theatrical scene and the society in which C. moved, which included Wilde, Yeats, Burne-Jones, Gilbert Murray, Sarah Bernhardt, and most of the literary and artistic luminaries of the late-nineteenth century. Combined with her annotated acting scripts (most at the Museum of London), C.'s memoirs demonstrate that she was not just a talented amateur; in spite of her reputation for impulsiveness, C. did in fact carefully consider her roles and devoted a great deal of thought to her technique. Two lecture tours, "Lectures on Diction and Dramatic Art" (London, 1927), and "Beautiful Speech and the Art of Acting" (America, 1930), reinforce this conclusion. She also wrote three unproduced scenarios for films during her years in Hollywood from 1933–40.

It is for her voluminous letters, however, that C. is chiefly remembered. Her most famous correspondence was with George Bernard Shaw, who was platonically (?) in love with her for 30 years. Although she considered herself a mere "footnote" to his life, C. does not emerge the victim in the wit-battle of their letters. Shaw called her a "monster of illiteracy," and she called him a "literary tradesman" when he dared criticize her style, which was indeed fluid and impulsive. Her own comment that his "carnival of words" outshone her "poor whining beggars" is belied by the content of the correspondence. Shaw sent her galleys of his *Quintessence of Ibsenism* and incorporated C.'s critique in the final draft. He shared thoughts for and about his plays and discussed their work on *Pygmalion*. The letters range from pedestrian details to deep emotion, from adoration to anger on both sides, and are themselves entertaining and dramatic enough to have formed the play *Dear Liar*, compiled by Jerome Kilty in 1960.

Toward the end of her life, following an embarrassing failure in Hollywood, what had been artistic temperament dwindled into eccentricity and poverty, which caused her estrangement from her family, friends, and home. Her marriage to George Cornwallis-West (Patrick Campbell had died at war in 1900) had been brief and unhappy as well as financially ruinous. She fought bitterly with Shaw over the publication of their letters— he feeling that their intimate nature would hurt his wife, she desperately needing the notoriety and money they would bring. Unable to return to England because she refused to put her pet dog Moonbeam in quarantine, she died practically penniless in southern France at the age of seventy-five. As a final insult, Cornwallis-West remarried on the day of her memorial service.

The pathos of C.'s final years cannot, however, diminish the brightness of her earlier days as the darling of the English and American stage. She cannot have been talentless, for she was counted with Ellen Terry as one of the two finest actresses of her era, responsible for bringing many new works of realism from the continent to the English theatre. In spite of her reputation for being difficult to work with, she was in continuous demand and received glowing reviews. Her writing, ungrammatical, unpunctuated, and misspelled though it may be, reveals a keen intelligence, an exuberant wit, and a sensitivity that made her both a great actress and a woman of infinite variety.

WORKS: *My Life and Some Letters* (1922). *Chance Medley* (unpublished). *Bernard Shaw and Mrs. Patrick Campbell: Their Correspondence*, ed. Alan Dent (1952).

BIBLIOGRAPHY: Cornwallis-West, G. *Edwardian Hey-Days* (1931). Dent, A. *Mrs. Patrick Campbell* (1961). Peters, M. *Mrs. Pat: The Life of Mrs. Patrick Campbell* (1984). Shaw, G.B. *Our Theatre in the Nineties* (1931).

Suzanne Westfall

Rosa Nouchette Carey

BORN: 24 September 1840, Stratford-le-Bow, London.
DIED: 19 July 1909, Sandilands, Keswick Road, London.
DAUGHTER OF: William Henry Carey and Maria Jane Wooddill Carey.

C. was the eighth child (fourth daughter) of a shipbroker. She spent her early years at Hackney, being educated first at home and then at the Ladies' Institute, St. John's Wood. She was a "delicate" child, but wrote little plays which her brothers and sisters performed. She also wrote poems and told stories to her siblings, especially one sister as she worked needlework; thus the whole of *Nellie's Memories*, her first novel, she originated and told verbally, not writing it down until seven years later (published in 1868). This first novel brought fame, for it was very popular and was reissued in many editions. Although C. wrote 39 novels during her lifetime, she first tried to quench her longing to write, believing it was impossible to combine her joy, i.e., writing, with a useful domestic life. She continued to take her traditional role seriously throughout life, assuming the sole care of nieces and a nephew at a brother's death, even at the expense of her own writing. As Helen Marion Burnside, contemporary writer of children's tales, related, "I do not think that I have known any author who has to make her writing—the real work of her life—so secondary a matter as has Rosa Carey. She has so consistently *lived* her religion, so to speak, that family duty and devotion to its many members

have always come first" (Black, *Notable Women Authors*, pp. 155, 156). Of her objectives in writing, C. stated, "My ambition has been to try to do good and not harm by my works, and to write books which any mother can give a girl to read" (Black, p. 154). Orthodox and conventional, C. for years had a class for young girls and servants over fifteen years of age, formed in connection with the Fulham Sunday School. She wrote fine descriptions, but her style lacks distinction, her plots being similar, microcosms of a conventional society now obsolete.

C. was on the staff of the *Girl's Own Paper* and published several short stories in it. Many other short stories were published by the Religious Tract Society; a volume of brief biographies, *Twelve Notable Good Women of the Nineteenth Century*, appeared in 1899.

C. resided for about thirty-nine years at Hampstead, moving to Putney, where she resided for almost twenty years. She died on 19 July 1909 at Sandilands, Keswick Road, and was buried in the West Hampstead cemetery.

WORKS: *Nellie's Memories* (1868). *Wee Wifie* (1869). *Wooed and Married* (1875). *Not Like Other Girls* (1884). *Uncle Max* (1887). *Only the Governess* (1888). *The Sunny Side of the Hill* (1908).

BIBLIOGRAPHY: Black, H.C., *Notable Women Authors of the Day* (1893). Pratt, A.T.C. *People of the Period* (1897). *Times* (London) (20 July 1909).
For articles in reference works, see: *DNB*, *Longman*.

Phyllis J. Scherle

Jane Welsh Carlyle

BORN: 14 July 1801, Haddington, Scotland.
DIED: 21 April 1866, Chelsea, London.
DAUGHTER OF: John and Grace Baillie Welsh.
MARRIED: Thomas Carlyle, 1826.

The only child of a respected country doctor, C. displayed a powerful intellect at an early age and distinguished herself at local schools. By the age of thirteen she had written a novel, a five-act tragedy, and had convinced her parents that "like a boy" she ought to learn Latin. Edward Irving, a young clergyman and friend of Thomas Carlyle, was appointed C.'s tutor. C.'s father, to whom she was extremely devoted, died when she was eighteen, leaving her the estate of Craiggenputtock and a substantial income. Shortly later, she was introduced to Carlyle, who became not only her friend but her mentor.

C.'s intelligence and wit were complemented by a distinctive appearance; according to one description, she was "bright and beautiful with a certain star-like radiance and grace." She did not lack for suitors, many of whom are satirized in her letters, but only Irving, Carlyle, and the sculptor George Rennie appear to have been viewed seriously by her. C.'s meeting with Carlyle in 1821 was the beginning of a deep intellectual relationship with very little romance. In spite of the affectionate tone that develops in their correspondence until their marriage in 1826, there is very little passion. Later, the biographer J.A. Froude was to characterize their union as a "partnership not marriage," reflecting, among other things, the asexual element of their married life.

After spending two years in Edinburgh, the Carlyles moved to the remote estate of Craiggenputtock where Carlyle labored over *Sartor Resartus*. The six years spent there were among the worst of C.'s life; without society, C. had no outlet for her conversation and wit, and what is worse, she had to contend with her husband's very changeable moods. In 1834 the Carlyles set up permanent residence at No. 5 Cheyne Row in Chelsea, London. Carlyle had emerged as an important literary figure and their home became something of a cultural center. Regular visitors at the Carlyles' evenings at home included Macaulay, Dickens, Ruskin, and Tennyson. Geraldine Jewsbury, who originally visited Cheyne Row to meet Carlyle, eventually became C.'s closest friend and regular correspondent.

C. was extremely attentive to the domestic concerns of Cheyne Row and supervised frequent renovations and redecorations, including the construction of the "quiet place," a room where Carlyle could work without having his fragile disposition disturbed. Insulating Carlyle from the daily activities of the world occupied much of C.'s time, and these efforts form the subject of many of her letters. Carlyle, she tells one correspondent, "dislikes nothing in the world so much as going into a shop to buy anything, even his own trowsers and coats; so that, to the consternation of cockney tailors, I am obliged to go about them." Elsewhere, in the journal she kept in 1855, C. provides a witty and biting description of the Tax Commissioners whom she sees on Carlyle's behalf (21 November 1855). As much as her writing sparkles when she writes of her domestic tasks, it is clear that they wore her down, particularly as she began to feel neglected by Carlyle.

C. was encouraged both by Carlyle and by friends to write a novel, and while she may have started one, nothing of it remains. What emerges in her letters is a clear and simple style that draws strength from her canny sense of detail and her cynical wit. Occasionally her writing is much more subdued, and a tone of sadness and fatigue emerges. C. complained of a weak constitution and severe headaches throughout her life and was often depressed about Carlyle's inattention to her. Only after C.'s death, which though sudden appeared to be of natural causes, did Carlyle (after reading her letters) fully appreciate the stress she bore for his sake. Exactly how great a drain Carlyle was on C.'s spirit is not clear; by her own admission, she had recognized genius in Carlyle, had "married for ambition," and was prepared "to take the consequences."

WORKS: *The Collected Letters of Thomas and Jane Welsh Carlyle* (1970-).

BIBLIOGRAPHY: Blunt, R. *The Carlyles' Chelsea Home* (1895). Carlyle, A. *New Letters and Memorials of Jane Welsh Carlyle* (1903). Carlyle, A., ed. *The Love Letters of Thomas Carlyle and Jane Welsh* (1909). Drew, E. *Jane Welsh and Jane Carlyle* (1928). Froude, J.A., *Letters and Memorials of Jane Welsh Carlyle* (1883). Hanson, L. and E. *Necessary Evil: The Life of Jane Welsh Carlyle* (1952). Rose, P. *Parallel Lives: Five Victorian Marriages* (1983). Simpson, A. and M. McQueen. *I Too Am Here: Selected Letters of Jane Welsh Carlyle* (1977). Woolf, V. "Geraldine and Jane." *The Second Common Reader* (1932). Surtees, V. *Jane Welsh Carlyle* (1986).

BIBLIOGRAPHY:

For articles in reference works, see: *Allibone Sup.*

Other References: *British Quarterly Review* (July 1881). *Carlyle Newsletter* (1979). *Contemporary Review* (May 1883). *Cornhill Magazine* (March, 1920). *Frontiers* (1979). *Prose Studies* (2 September 1982).

Alan Rauch

Angela Carter

BORN: 7 May 1940, London.
DAUGHTER OF: Hugh and Olive Stalker.
MARRIED: Paul Carter, 1960.

In C.'s novels, history and fantasy intersect, while economic determinants collide with the unconscious. In her best-known work, *The Bloody Chamber and Other Adult Fairy Tales*, she juxtaposes various versions of Beauty and the Beast, Little Red Riding Hood, and Bluebeard, hoping to strip away the artifice and return us to our animal natures. But characters who escape their literary roles must still contend with social realities: the handsome bridegroom is not killed by the Countess Nosferatu; instead he dies in World War I. C.'s primary subject is human sexuality as it is structured by social, economic, and cultural forces. She acknowledges "the unarguable fact of sexual differentiation," but would separate it from "the behavioural modes of masculine and feminine, which are culturally defined variables translated in the language of common usage to the status of universals." In *The Sadeian Woman*, she calls for a moral pornographer, a "terrorist of the imagination, a sexual guerrilla" who would use pornography to overturn our most basic notions of the relations between the sexes. Convinced that we are the makers of history, not its slaves, C. maintains that art can either intensify the constraints of convention and myth or shatter them.

C. grew up in London, daughter of a journalist from Scotland and a mother from a Yorkshire mining district. She took a degree in English literature at Bristol University, but it is clear that the sources of her imagination are French: Perrault's fairy tales, Sade's pornography, Balzac's novels. ("The minute I read Racine," she said in an interview, "I knew that it moved me much more savagely than Shakespeare.") Her two-year residency in Japan, the influence of which is especially obvious in *Fireworks*, took her farther away from the realistic tradition of the English novel. The recipient of numerous literary prizes, C. has been a fellow in creative writing at Sheffield University (1976–1978) and a visiting professor at Brown (1980–1981). Although she is best known for her fiction, she writes poetry, reviews, journalistic essays, radio scripts, and texts for children's books, such as *Martin Leman's Comic and Curious Cats* and *Moonshadow*. C. did the screenplay for *The Company of Wolves*, an erotic and uncanny film based on *The Bloody Chamber*.

C. did not set out to describe the strange and fantastic world of dancing tigers and rational centaurs. Indeed, much of C.'s early work is set in the urban milieu of the 1960s. "I thought I was a social realist," she said in speaking of her first three novels. Her rootless bohemian characters are as recognizable and as shabby as the pubs they inhabit. *Shadow Dance*, her first novel, becomes surreal in its imagery of filth and decay, and in the protagonist's bland acceptance of sexual violence—qualities which intensify in the dystopian vision of *Heroes and Villains*. C.'s rejection of realism is evident in *The Infernal Desire Machines of Doctor Hoffman*, which she described as "an inventory of imaginary cities." Desiderio, the narrator, has restored order to his city by killing the diabolical Dr. Hoffman, inventor of reality-altering machines that would have set the unconscious free. Preferring the "barren yet harmonious calm" to the "fertile yet cacophonous tempest," he killed the lover who offered him an eternity of sexual pleasure. Having reinstituted the reality principle and recovered time, he is hailed as a hero. But he writes his autobiography with "insatiable tears" and "that insatiable regret with which we acknowledge that the impossible is, *per se*, impossible."

The Passion of New Eve exposes the systems of representation that define sexual difference. Evelyn, the English protagonist, travels across America in pursuit of a glamorous movie idol. After abandoning Leilah, his black lover, to a botched abortion, he encounters Mother, a ponderous old black woman who rapes him, and then performs psychosurgery to make him into a woman. As Evelyn becomes Eve, he/she experiences shame and dislocation. The movie goddess turns out to be a transvestite, but he and Eve manage to conceive a child before war erupts. Leilah, now a guerrilla fighter named Lilith, rescues Eve and urges her to forsake myth for history. Yet the pregnant Eve can neither accept the old archetypes nor immerse herself in war.

Like Virginia Woolf's *Orlando*, *Nights at the Circus* is a fantastic and wonderfully comic treatment of sex and history. Set in 1899, the novel describes the adventures of Sophia Fevvers, a tall and enormously successful aerialiste, part woman and part swan. Posing first as Cupid, then as Nelson's Winged Victory, she comes to represent the New Woman—"the pure child of the century that just now is waiting in the wings, the New Age in which no women will be bound down to the ground." In the midst of economic and racial oppression, Carter depicts characters who know how to use the power of the word: prostitutes save their lives by telling stories, a black servant rendered speechless by a deformity writes notes to rescue others, while a fiesty group of post-Darwinian performing monkeys learn to rewrite, and eventually to reject, their contract with the circus owner. Sexual violence endures in the MP who plans to murder Fevvers, in the Ape-Man who

83

rapes Mignon, in the troop of dwarfs who abuse their leading lady. But its effects are somewhat mitigated by the women's kindness to one another and by the metamorphosis of Jack Walser, the American journalist who pursues Fevvers into Russia. Fevvers has a friend, an old woman who performs magic, helps her save assorted waifs, and corresponds with Karl Marx. Moreover, when Fevvers is reunited with her New Man, now living in Siberia, she finds that they are not "mutilated by history." During the sexual encounter at the end of the novel—the terms of which are something of a surprise—animosities and anxieties dissolve in laughter.

WORKS: *Shadow Dance* (1966—republished as *Honeybuzzard*). *The Magic Toyshop* (1967). *Several Perceptions* (1968). *Heroes and Villains* (1969). *Love* (1971; rev. 1987). *The Infernal Desire Machines of Doctor Hoffman* (1972—republished as *The War of Dreams*). *Fireworks* (1974; rev. 1987). *The Passion of New Eve* (1977). *The Fairy Tales of Charles Perrault* (1979). *The Sadeian Woman and the Ideology of Pornography* (1979). *The Bloody Chamber* (1979). *Nights at the Circus* (1984). *Black Venus* (1985). *Come Unto These Yellow Sands* (1985). *Saints and Strangers* (1986).

BIBLIOGRAPHY: Haffenden, J. *Novelists in Interview* (1985). Landon, B. *Erotic Universe*, ed. D. Palumbo (1986). Punter, D. *Critique*, (1984). Punter, D. *The Literature of Terror* (1980). Rose, E.C. *The Voyage In*, ed. E. Abel, M. Hirsch, and E. Langland (1983). Sage, L. *New Review*, (1977).

For articles in reference works, see: *CA. CD. CLC. CN. DLB. TCSFW.*

Robin Sheets

Elizabeth Carter

BORN: 16 December 1717, Deal, Kent.
DIED: 19 February 1806, London.
DAUGHTER OF: The Rev. Nicholas Carter and Margaret (Swayne) Carter.
WROTE UNDER: "Eliza."

C. was the most learned lady in England during the eighteenth century. A poet, scholar, essayist, and translator, she achieved her erudition by remaining unmarried and devoting her life to scholarly and literary pursuits. A prominent member of the Bluestocking circle, Carter's friends included Samuel Johnson, Samuel Richardson, Sir Joshua Reynolds, Edmund Burke, and Horace Walpole. Her published letters present vivid and witty accounts of the eighteenth-century literary world and down-to-earth perceptions of women's lives. Her correspondents included Catherine Talbot, Elizabeth Vesey, and Elizabeth Montagu.

C.'s father was a schoolmaster, and she had a desire for learning from an early age. A frequently cited anecdote reveals that she spent many hours in serious study: "She read both late at night and early in the morning, taking snuff, chewing green tea, and using other means to keep herself awake. Beginning with Latin and Greek, she afterwards learned Hebrew, French, Italian, Spanish, and German. Later in life she taught herself Portuguese and Arabic." In addition to languages, C. was interested in historical and scientific matters, such as ancient and modern history and ancient geography. As an eighteenth-century woman, she was expected to be accomplished in the "feminine" learnings: she played both the spinet and German flute and sang, although by her own admission she did not sing well. She was an excellent needlewoman and a good cook. Johnson, one of her dearest friends, gave her this famous two-pronged compliment that exemplifies the position of women in eighteenth-century society and indicates the high quality of Carter's achievements. Upon hearing a lady commended for her learning, Johnson said, "A man is in general better pleased when he has a good dinner upon his table, than when his wife talks Greek. My old friend, Mrs. Carter," he added, "could make a pudding as well as translate Epictetus from the Greek; and work a handkerchief as well as compose a poem."

C.'s father was a friend of Edward Cave, the founder and publisher of the *Gentlemen's Magazine*. In 1734 in his magazine C. published her first poem, an epigram, which was, following the conventions of her era for women writers, published under a pseudonym, "Eliza." As Eliza, she continued to contribute to the magazine for some years. In April 1738 her epigram caught the attention of Samuel Johnson, who had recently come to London, and he wrote a response to the epigram. At Johnson's request, Cave introduced the two, and they were friends until Johnson's death in 1784. In 1738 "Poems upon particular Occasions," a small pamphlet containing a collection of eight of her poems, was published by Cave. The anonymous publication included a translation of the poet Anacreon.

After meeting Johnson, C. contributed two articles to the *Rambler*, No. 44 being on "Religion and Superstition," and No. 100 on "Modish Pleasures." In 1739 she published two anonymous translations: *Sir Isaac Newton's Philosophy explain'd for the use of ladies, translated from the Italian of Sig. Algarotti*; and *An examination of Mr. Pope's Essay on man, translated from the French of M. Crousaz*. Humble about her literary accomplishments, C. "never willingly referred to" the translations after their publication. Her silence is most interesting when the fact is taken into account that the latter translation was for years misattributed to Johnson, and it was Boswell who finally recognized that Carter, not Johnson, had done the work.

In 1741, C. made the acquaintance of Miss Catherine Talbot, an aristocrat by birth, who lived in the household of Thomas Secker, the future Archbishop of Canterbury. Talbot became C.'s closest friend, and Secker became one of C.'s patrons. It was at their suggestion that C. undertook the translation of Epictetus, the Greek Stoic philosopher and emancipated slave who taught that man should wish for nothing that is not under his control. He advocated a serene life, free from unfulfilled desires and calm in the face of death.

C. began the translation in the summer of 1749, but she did not finish until December 1752. It was not originally intended for publication and was sent in sheets as it was written to Talbot. About the publication of the translation Talbot wrote that it would "do honour to Epictetus, yourself, your country, and womankind." At the suggestion of Secker, C. added an introduction and notes to the manuscript, and in April 1758 it was published by subscription (by Samuel Richardson). It brought C. nearly £1000, with which she purchased her residence at Deal. The translation still is considered the standard one.

In 1762 C. published her second volume of poems, *Poems on Several Occasions*, which went through four editions. Included in this volume was the poem "Ode to Wisdom," which had originally been published as part of Richardson's *Clarissa* in 1747. C.'s poetic style is delicate and restrained, and indicates her strong philosophic nature.

Established as an important member of the Bluestocking circle and a recognized female literary figure, C. spent the last forty years of her life in comfortable circumstances. In 1763 she visited France, Germany, and Holland, an interesting account of the trip being given in her letters to Talbot. From 1768 to 1774, many important friends died: her patron Archbishop Secker, her friend Catherine Talbot, her father. In 1782 she visited Paris for the last time. However, she frequently traveled in England until her death in 1806.

C.'s letters comprise the largest segment of her works. Letters, considered the most appropriate type of expression for women during the eighteenth century, offer the biographer and historian great insight into the lives of these eighteenth-century women whose public presence was restricted by stringent social codes but whose thoughts and ideas could be expressed in epistolary fashion. C.'s intellectual importance only now is beginning to receive critical attention. There is no contemporary biography although her name is always included in women's histories of the time.

WORKS: *Poems Upon Particular Occasions* (1738). (trans.) *Sir Isaac Newton's Philosophy Explain'd for the Use of Ladies: in Six Dialogues on Light and Colours* by Algarotti (1739). (trans.) *An Examination of Mr. Pope's Essay on Man* by Crousaz (1739). (trans.) *All the Work of Epictetus, Which Are Now extant, Consisting of His Discourses, Preserved by Arrian, in Four Books, the Enchiridion, and Fragments* (1752). *Poems on Several Occasions* (1762). *A Series of Letters Between Mrs. Elizabeth Carter and Miss Catherine Talbot, from 1741 to 1770, to Which Are Added Letters from Mrs. Carter to Mrs. Vesey, Between the Years 1763 and 1787*, ed. M. Pennington (1809). *Memoirs of the Life of Mrs. Elizabeth Carter, with a New Edition of Her Poems, Including Some Which Have Never Appeared Before, to Which Are Added, Some Miscellaneous Essays in Prose, Together with Her Notes on the Bible, and Answers*, ed. M. Pennington (1807). *Letters from Mrs. Carter to Mrs. Montagu, Between the Years 1755 and 1800, Chiefly Upon Literary and Moral Subjects* (1817). *Sketches in Biography* (1825). *Bluestocking Letters* (1926).

BIBLIOGRAPHY: Gaussen, A. and C.C. *A Woman of Wit and Wisdom: A Memoir of Elizabeth Carter* (1906). *Memoirs of the Life of Mrs. Elizabeth Carter with a New Edition of Her Poems, Including Some Which Have Never Appeared Before, to Which Are Added, Some Miscellaneous Essays in Prose, Together with Her Notes on the Bible, and Answers*, ed. M. Pennington (1807). Rogers, K.M. *Feminism in Eighteenth-Century England* (1982). Rowton, F. *The Female Poets of Great Britain* (1853).

For articles in reference works, see: *Allibone. BAB1800. DNB.*

Other references: Dobson, A. *Later Essays* (1921). Hampshire, G. *Notes and Queries* (England) (1972). Jones, H.P. *Huntington Library Quarterly* (1978). Martin, R. *Publications of the Arkansas Philological Association* (1985). Sena, J.F. *Yearbook of English Studies* (1971).

Priscilla Dorr

Barbara Cartland

BORN: 9 July 1901.
DAUGHTER OF: Bertram and Mary Hamilton "Polly" Cartland.
MARRIED: Alexander McCorquodale, 1927; Hugh McCorquodale, 1936.
WRITES UNDER: Barbara Cartland, Barbara McCorquodale.

The most prolific romance novelist, according to *The Guinness Book of World Records*, and one of the top five best-selling authors of all time (long past the 100,000,000 copy mark set in 1979), C. has also been a playwright, biographer, journalist, pageant designer, decorator, glider pilot, county councillor, philanthropist, businesswoman, and world traveler.

C. runs her estate at Canfield and has raised three children, a daughter born during C.'s six-year marriage to Alexander McCorquodale, and two sons, born during her twenty-seven year union with Alexander's cousin, Hugh. Each son manages either the financial affairs or the extensive corrections for each book.

C. began her career as a writer after World War I, when she was invited by publisher Lord Beaverbrook to contribute paragraphs of gossip to the *Daily News*. Insisting on anonymity for much of this material, as she "preferred to work behind the scenes," C. expanded the market for her columns to other newspapers: *Daily Mail, Daily Mirror,* and *Tatler*.

Her first novel, *Jigsaw* (1925), described as "Mayfair with the lid off," drew, in part, from C.'s own experiences and echoed the styles of favorite authors: Ethel M. Dell (especially *The Sheik*) and Elinor Glyn. *Jigsaw* has a freshness and charm rarely found in her later novels. It concerns the adventures of Mona Vivien, a "strikingly beautiful" young woman who has graduated from convent school and is ready to enter London society. Despite a brief fling with the mysterious, worldly half-brother of her "true love," a Marquis, Mona recognizes that her source of future happiness depends on making the right decision and eventually accepts the Marquis' proposal. Some criticisms of the novel were favorable as in the statement that the book was "a dramatic conflict of emotions, written with zest," but not all concurred. Others bitingly commented that the writing was "amateurish" and one stated "If this is Mayfair, then let me live in Whitechapel." Critics notwithstanding, C.'s first work was published in six editions and five other languages, setting a precedent that has not ceased.

C.'s fictional formula rarely changes. A chaste heroine, whose name must end with the letter "a," meets the handsome, wealthy hero in an exotic nineteenth-century setting. Love blooms; obstacles are overcome; the couple marries and only then give in to the passion that has beset them throughout the novel. Variations only involve the scene for each romance, as C.'s vast travels have inspired many of her stories. The conclusion of each work is relatively similar; lines or passages from one have even been found in other Cartland works.

C.'s lack of pornographic filigree has earned her over 400,000,000 readers. "I am their escape from the depression and boredom and lack of romance in modern life," she once explained to an interviewer. Each thin volume, usually no more than 60,000 words, is dictated to a series of secretaries. Scorning long paragraphs and complicated subplots, C. avoids lengthy explanations or needless descriptions.

C.'s literary strength is an insistence on thorough research. Attention to factual or epistolary evidence is most visible in several of her historical biographies, as is the added attraction of a "romantic angle." One such example is *Metternich: The Passionate Diplomat*, which required thirty sources, including material from the Viennese Court and State Archives as well as numerous histories and biographies, in addition to C.'s own work on Josephine, Empress of France. The text centers on Metternich's political importance: his influence on the development of the Congress of Vienna and his ability to engage Austria in European affairs during the period of 1815-1848. But the ambivalent nature of the man is also pursued with an exposé of his relationships with three wives and four mistresses: "The loves of . . . Metternich, within the marital state or beyond it, softened the character of someone whose icy intellect produced a figure of superhuman coldness, objectivity, and brilliance," C. concludes in the text.

C. has one film scenario to her credit (*The Flame is Love*), which had twenty-four million viewers when shown in America on NBC.

Because of a serious illness, C. became interested in nutrition, especially proper diet and vitamins, and eventually created a series of books on the importance of good health on individual appearance (among them *Be Vivid, Be Vital*, 1956; *Look Lovely, Be Lovely*, 1958; and *Vitamins for Vitality*, 1959).

C. is known as "The Queen of Romance," an accolade that captures the writer's sincere desire to keep alive the fantasy her readers crave: the Cinderella story that ends "happily ever after." She "keeps the faith" with her Regency novels, and her audience happily and constantly responds by demanding more Cartland.

WORKS (a partial list): Jigsaw (1925). Blood Money (1925). Sawdust (1926). If The Tree Is Saved (1929). For What? (1930). Sweet Punishment (1931). A Virgin in Mayfair (1932). Just Off Piccadilly (1933). Not Love Alone (1933). A Beggar Wished (1934). Touch the Stars (1935). Dangerous Experiment (1936). But Never Free (1937). Broken Barriers (1938). The Gods Forget (1939). Stolen Halo (1940). Now Rough, Now Smooth (1941). Ronald Cartland (1942). The Isthmus Years 1919–1939 (1943). Yet She Follows (1944). The Years of Opportunity, 1939-1945 (1948). A Duel of Hearts (1949). The Knave of Hearts (1950; repub. as The Innocent Heiress, 1975). Love Is an Eagle (1951). Love Is the Enemy (1952). The Passionate Pilgrim (1952). Elizabethan Lover (1953). Desire of the Heart (1954). The Fascinating Forties: A Book for the Over-Forties (1954, 1973). Love Me For Ever (1954). Wings on My Heart (1954). The Kiss of the Devil (1955). Bewitching Women (1955). Marriage for Moderns (1955). Be Vivid, Be Vital (1956). The Coin of Love (1956). The Outrageous Queen (1956). Polly, My Wonderful Mother (1956). The Caged Bird (1957). Love, Life and Sex (1957). The Scandalous Life of King Carol (1957). The Thief of Love (1957). Look Lovely, Be Lovely (1958). The Private Life of Charles II (1958). The Kiss of Silk (1959). The Private Life of Elizabeth, Empress of Austria (1959). Vitamins for Vitality (1959). Love Under Fire (1960). The Price Is Love (1960). Josephine, Empress of France (1961). The Messenger of Love (1961). Diane de Poitiers (1962). The Many Facets of Love (1963). Etiquette for Love and Romance (1964). The Fire of Love (1964). Metternich, The Passionate Diplomat (1964). Sex and the Teenager (1964). A Ghost in Monte Carlo (1965). Living Together (1964). Love Holds the Cards (1965). Love on the Run (1965). Woman—the Enigma (1965). A Virgin in Paris (1966). Danger by the Nile (1967). I Search for the Rainbow: 1946-1966 (1967; as I Search for Rainbows, 1973). The Enchanting Evil (1968). Love Is Contraband (1968). The Youth Secret (1968). A Hazard of Hearts (1969). Love in Hiding (1969). Love is Dangerous (1969). The Unknown Heart (1969). The Unpredictable Bride (1969). Cupid Rides Pillion (1970). The Hidden Evil (1970). The Hidden Heart (1970). The Magic of Honey (1970). The Reluctant Bride (1970). Sweet Adventure (1970). We Danced All Night, 1919–1929 (1970). After the Night (1971). Armour Against Love (1971). The Enchanted Waltz (1971). The Golden Gondola (1971). Health Food Cookery Book (1971). Husbands and Wives (1971). If We Will (1971). The Kiss of Paris (1971). The Little Pretender (1971). Out of Reach (1971). Stars in My Heart (1971). The Black Panther (1972). Book of Beauty and Health (1972). The Dream Within (1972). The Enchanted Moment (1972). Halo for the Devil (1972). The Irresistible Buck (1972). Lines on Life and Love (1972). The Little Adventure (1973). Lost Enchantment (1972). Love is Mine (1972). No Heart Is Free (1972). Audacious Adventurer (1973). Blue Heather (1973). The Coin of Love (1973). The Daring Deception (1973). The Leaping Flame (1973). A Light to the Heart (1973). Lights of Love (1973). Love Forbidden (1973). Men Are Wonderful (1973). The Pretty Horse-Breakers (1973). Where Is Love? (1973). The Wicked Marquis (1973). Against the Stream (1974). The Bored Bridegroom (1974). The Castle of Fear (1974). The Cruel Count (1974). The Dangerous Dandy (1974). The Glittering Lights (1974). Journey to Paradise (1974). Lessons in Love (1974). The Mysterious Maid-Servant (1974). No Darkness for Love (1974). No Time for Love (1974). The Penniless Peer (1974). The Ruthless Rake (1974). An Arrow of Love (1975). As Eagles Fly (1975). Bewitched (1975). Call of the Heart (1975). Desperate Defiance (1975). The Devil in Love (1975). Fire on the Snow (1975). The Flame Is Love (1975). Food for Love (1975). A Frame of Dreams (1975). The Frightened Bride (1975). A Gamble with Hearts (1975). The Impetuous Duchess (1975). The Karma of Love (1975). A Kiss for the King (1975). Love Is Innocent (1975). The Mask of Love (1975). Say Yes, Samantha (1975). The Shadow of Sin (1975). A Sword to the Heart (1975). The Tears of Love (1975). Towards the Stars (1975). A Very Naughty Angel (1975). Where Is Love? (1975). An Angel in Hell (1976). The Blue-Eyed Witch (1976). Conquered by Love (1976). The Disgraceful Duke (1976). The Dream and the Glory (1976). The Elusive Earl (1976). Escape from Passion (1976). The Golden Illusion (1976). The Heart Triumphant (1976). The Husband Hunters (1976). The Magic of Honey Cookbook (1976). Moon Over Eden (1976). Passions in the Sand (1976). The Slaves of Love (1976). Vote for Love (1976). The Wild Cry of Love (1976). A Duel with Destiny (1977). Kiss the Moonlight (1977). Look, Listen and Love (1977). Love and the Loathsome Leopard (1977). Love Locked In (1977). The Love Pirate (1977). The Marquis Who Hated Women (1977). No Escape from Love (1977). Recipes for Lovers (1977). A Rhapsody of Love (1977). The Saint and the Sinner (1977). A Sign of Love (1977). The Temptation of Torilla (1977). A Touch of Love (1977). The Wild Unwilling Wife (1977). Alone in Paris (1978). The Chieftain Without a Heart (1978). Flowers for the God of Love (1978). The Ghost Who Fell in Love (1978). The Irresistible Force (1978). I Seek the Miraculous (1978). The Judgement of Love (1978). The Light of Love: Lines to Live by Day by Day (1978). Love and Lovers (1978). Love, Lords and Ladybirds (1978). Magic or Mirage (1978). The Passion and the Flower (1978). A Princess in Distress (1978). The Problems of Love (1978). The Race for Love (1978). The Twists and Turns of Love (1978). The Captive Heart (1979). The Drums of Love (1979). The Duke and the Preacher's Daughter (1979). The Prince and the Pekingese (1979). Ashes of Desire (1980). *Barbara Cartland* (1980). *Barbara Cartland's Scrapbook* (1980). *Bride to the King* (1980). *The Bridge of Kisses* (1980). *The Broad Highway* (1980). *Charles Rex* (1980). *The Dawn of Love* (1980). *Free from Fear* (1980). *A Gentleman in Love* (1980). *The Goddess and the Gaiety Girl* (1980). *The Great Moment* (1980). *Greatheart* (1980). *A Heart Is Stolen* (1980). *The Horizons of Love* (1980). *Imperial Splendour* (1980). *A Kiss of Silk* (1980). *Little White Doves of Love* (1980). *Lost Laughter* (1980). *Love at the Helm* (1980). *Love for Sale* (1980). *Love Has His Way* (1980). *Love in the Moon* (1980). *Lucifer and the Angel* (1980). *Money, Magic and Marriage* (1980). *My Brother, Ronald* (1980). *The Obstacle Race* (1980). *Ola and the Sea Wolf* (1980). *The Perfection of Love* (1980). *The Power and the Prince* (1980). *The Price of Love* (1980). *The Price of Things* (1980). *Pride and the Poor Princess* (1980). *The Prude and the Prodigal* (1980). *Punished with Love* (1980). *Rainbow in the Spray* (1980). *The Runaway Heart* (1980). *The Sequence* (1980). *Signpost to Love* (1980). *Six Days* (1980). *A Song of Love* (1980). *Son of the Turk* (1980). *The Sons of the Sheik* (1980). *The Sweet Enchantress* (1980). *The Waltz of Hearts* (1980). *Who Can Deny Love?* (1980). *Women Have Hearts* (1980). *Afraid* (1980). *The Amateur Gentleman* (1981). *The Complacent Wife* (1981). *Count the Stars* (1981). *Dollars for the Duke* (1981). *Dreams do Come True* (1981). *Enchanted* (1981). *The Explosion of Love* (1981). *For All Eternity* (1981). *From Hell to Heaven* (1981). *A Gamble with Hearts* (1981). *Gift of the Gods* (1981). *The Heart of the Clan* (1981). *His Official Fiancée* (1981). *In the Arms of Love* (1981). *An Innocent in Russia* (1981). *The Kiss of Life* (1981). *The Lion Tamer* (1981). *The Lioness and the Lily* (1981). *Love at the Helm* (1981). *Love in the Dark* (1981). *Love Wins* (1981). *Lucky in Love* (1981). *A Night of Gaiety* (1981). *A Portrait of Love* (1981). *Pure and Untouched* (1981). *The River of Love* (1981). *Romantic Royal Marriages* (1981). *A Shaft of Sunlight* (1981). *Tetherstones* (1981). *Touch a Star* (1981). *Towards the Stars* (1981). *The Wild, Unwilling Wife* (1981). *Winged Magic* (1981). *The Wings of Ecstasy* (1981). *Wings on My Heart* (1981). *Written with Love: Passionate Love Letters* (1981). *Again This Rapture* (1982). *The Audacious Adventures* (1982). *Barbara Cartland Picture Romances* (1982). *Barbara Cartland's Book of Celebrities* (1982). *The Call of the Highlands* (1982). *Camfield Romances* (1982). *Caught By Love* (1982). *For All Eternity* (1982). *The Frightened Bride* (1982). *From Hate to Love* (1982). *The Incredible Honeymoon* (1982). *Keep Young and Beautiful* (1982). *A King in Love* (1982). *Kneel for Mercy* (1982). *Lies for Love* (1982). *Light of the Gods* (1982). *Looking for Love* (1982). *Love and the Marquis* (1982). *Love at the Helm* (1982). *Love Leaves at Midnight* (1982). *Love on the Wind* (1982). *Love Rules* (1982). *Love to the Rescue* (1982). *Love Wears a Veil* (1982). *A Marriage Made in Heaven* (1982). *A Miracle in Music* (1982). *Mission to Monte Carlo* (1982). *Moments of Love* (1982). *Music from the Heart* (1982). *The Naked Battle* (1982). *The Odious Duke* (1982). *Open Wings* (1982). *The Poor Governess* (1982). *The Power and the Prince* (1982). *The Secret Fear* (1982). *Secret Harbour* (1982). *The Smuggled Heart* (1982). *Touch a Star* (1982). *The Unknown Heart* (1982). *The Vibrations of Love* (1982). *Winged Victory* (1982). *Diona and a Dalmatian* (1983). *The Dragon and the Pearl* (1983). *The Duke Comes Home* (1983). *A Duke in Danger* (1983). *Free from Fear* (1983). *From Hate to Love* (1983). *Gypsy Magic* (1983). *A Heart Is Broken* (1983). *Help from the Heart* (1983). *In the Arms of Love* (1983). *Journey to a Star* (1983). *A King in Love* (1983). *The Kiss of Life* (1983). *Lies for Love* (1983). *Lights, Laughter and a Lady* (1983). *Love and Lucia* (1983). *Love in the Dark* (1983). *Love in the Wind* (1983). *Love to the Rescue* (1983). *The Magic of Honey* (1983). *The Magic of Love* (1983). *A Miracle in Music* (1983). *The Poor Governess* (1983). *Riding to the Moon* (1983). *Tempted to Love* (1983). *The Unbreakable Spell* (1983). *Wish for Love* (1983). *Bride to a Brigand* (1984). *The Call of the Highlands* (1984). *A Dream from the Night* (1984). *The Duke Comes Home* (1984). *Etiquette for Love and Romance* (1984). *Fire in the Blood* (1984). *Getting Older, Growing Younger* (1984). *Help from the Heart* (1984). *Hungry for Love* (1984). *The Island of Love* (1984). *Journey to a Star* (1984). *Light of the Gods* (1984). *Little White Doves of Love* (1984). *Looking for Love* (1984). *Lord Ravenscar's Revenge* (1984). *Love Comes West* (1984). *Miracle for a Madonna* (1984). *Moonlight on the Sphinx* (1984). *The Peril and the Prince* (1984). *Princess to the Rescue* (1984). *A Rebel Princess* (1984). *Revenge of the Heart* (1984). *The Romance of Food* (1984). *The Unbreakable Spell* (1984). *Royal Punishment* (1984). *The Scots Never Forget* (1984). *Secrets* (1984). *The Storms of Love* (1984). *The Taming of Lady Lorinda* (1984). *Theresa and a Tiger* (1984). *The Unbreakable Spell* (1984). *The Unwanted Wedding* (1984). *White Lilac* (1984). *Winged Victory* (1984). *A Witch's Spell* (1984). *Alone and Afraid* (1985). *Barbara Cartland's Book of Health* (1985). *The Castle made for Love* (1985). *The Devilish Deception* (1985). *Escape* (1985). *The Etiquette of Romance* (1985). *A Fugitive from Love* (1985). *Hungry for Love* (1985). *Look with Love* (1985). *Love Is a Gamble* (1985). *Love Is Heaven* (1985). *Love on the Wind* (1985). *Miracle for a Madonna* (1985). *The Outrageous Lady* (1985). *Paradise Found* (1985). *Polly: My Wonderful Mother* (1985). *The Proud Princess* (1985). *Safe at Last* (1985). *Temptation of a Teacher* (1985). *A Very Unusual Wife* (1985). *A Victory for Love* (1985). *An Angel Runs Away* (1986). *Count the Stars* (1986). *Crowned with Love* (1986). *The Devil Defeated* (1986). *A Dream in*

Spain (1986). *A Gentleman in Love* (1986). *The Golden Cage* (1986). *Haunted* (1986). *Helga in Hiding* (1986). *The Hell-Cat and the King* (1986). *Listen to Love* (1986). *Love Casts Out Fear* (1986). *Love Climbs In* (1986). *Love Joins the Clan* (1986). *The Love Trap* (1986). *Never Forget Love* (1986). *The Peril and the Prince* (1986). *The Secret of the Mosque* (1986). *A Serpent of Satan* (1986). *Terror in the Sun* (1986). *Bewildered in Berlin* (1987). *The Curse of the Clan* (1987). *Dancing on a Rainbow* (1987). *The Devilish Deception* (1987). *The Earl Escapes* (1987). *Escape* (1987). *For All Eternity* (1987). *Forced to Marry* (1987). *A Heart Is Stolen* (1987). *Journey to a Star* (1987). *Lies for Love* (1987). *Love and Kisses* (1987). *Love Casts Out Fear* (1987). *Love on the Wind* (1987). *The Love Puzzle* (1987). *Lovers in Paradise* (1987). *Never Laugh at*

Love (1987). *The Perfume of the Gods* (1987). *Punishment of a Vixen* (1987). *A Runaway Star* (1987). *The Secret of the Glen* (1987). *Starlight Over Tunis* (1987). *Wanted: A Wedding Ring* (1987). *A World of Love* (1987).

BIBLIOGRAPHY: Cloud, H. *Barbara Cartland, Crusader in Pink* (1979). Robyns, G. *Barbara Cartland* (1985).

For articles in reference works, see: *CA. CB. TCR&GW.*

Other references: *Fifty Plus* (April 1979). *McCall's* (March 1982). *New Yorker* (9 August 1976, 9 May, 1983). *SR* (March 1981). *Vogue* (August 1984). *Writer's Digest* (June 1979).

Zelda Provenzano

Julia Cartwright

BORN: 7 November 1851, Edgcote, Northamptonshire.
DIED: 24 April 1924, Oxford.
DAUGHTER OF: Richard Aubrey Cartwright and Mary Fremantle.
MARRIED: Henry Ady, 1880.

C. was a Victorian writer whose work was primarily concerned with the art and history of the Italian Renaissance, and as such she made a considerable contribution to furthering the understanding and appreciation of Italian art and history in the mainstream tradition of English Italophilia. It is interesting to perceive her view of women, as a woman historian, in history.

She published twenty-three books of art and history including five major biographies on women. Of these her biographies of the Italian Renaissance sisters Beatrice and Isabella d'Este (1899 and 1903) as well as her biography of Castiglione (1908) remain highly respected by modern scholars. She was a prolific writer and contributed regularly to the art magazines and journals of her time, including the *Art Journal* and the *Magazine of Art*. She also wrote for the English newspaper, the *Manchester Guardian*. In her early days as an aspiring author she published anonymously at least thirteen novels for the Society for the Promoting of Christian Knowledge (S.P.C.K.). For these she was extremely well paid, and she only relinquished this work when she had begun to establish her more formal reputation as a scholar.

C. came from a family of English landed gentry. One of nine children with five sisters and three brothers, she was educated at home by a succession of tutors. She nevertheless knew French, German, and Italian by the age of sixteen

and borrowed the text books of her brothers at Eton and Oxford to teach herself Latin. Extremely well read, it was her love of literature and poetry that above all inspired her life's interest in art.

The period in which she wrote witnessed a change in the taste for Italian art with the emphasis gradually shifting from the medieval period to the Renaissance. A growing number of authors provided new literature for an expanding and eager public. C. and others like her provided serious works of scholarship which were nevertheless of popular interest.

C. was essentially a Victorian in her typically didactic approach. Her aim was educational and her emphasis on culture and learning the underlying thread of all her work. It is this aspect she emphasizes in her biographies of women and also in the two-volume biography of the Renaissance author of *The Courtier*, Baldassare Castiglione. Her own ideals and aspirations and those of many women of her class and background in England prior to the enfranchisement of women were for equal educational possibilities.

In 1880 C. married Henry Ady, the local rector, and in 1881, the year her daughter Cecilia was born, her first book, *Mantegna and Francia*, was published. She continued to work. In the eighties, apart from writing the introduction to a translation of La Motte Fouque's *Undine* (1888), she concentrated on articles and romantic stories like *Christabel* (1880), *The Fortunes of Hassan* (1880), *Una Creighton* (1882), and *Miss Judy* (1883). In 1893 she wrote *The Pilgrim's Way*, an account of the ancient walk from Winchester to Canterbury. The Adys were by then living in Charing in Kent near Canterbury.

Her first successful biography, *Sacharissa*

(1893), was an account of Dorothy Sidney who had been the subject of Edmund Waller's seventeenth-century poem of the same name. With this and with *Madame* (1894), the story of Henrietta, the daughter of King Charles I who became the Duchess of Orleans, she established her reputation.

In 1894 she became friends with the English artist Edward Burne-Jones and wrote a very successful monograph: *Sir Edward Burne-Jones, His Life and Work* (1894). This was followed by a similar study of another living artist entitled *G.F. Watts, Royal Academician, His Life and Work* (1896), as well as a large volume about the recently deceased French painter *Jean François Millet, His Life and Letters* (1896).

In spite of this interest in English and French artists, it was the art of the Renaissance which remained C.'s most fervent love. She published several books on Raphael, on Botticelli, and on the Florentine painters, and established herself as an Italian specialist. During this her most prolific period she frequented the artistic and literary milieux of her time and corresponded with Bernard Berenson, Roger Fry, and many others. With the publication of *Beatrice d'Este* (1899) and *Isabella d'Este* (1903), her reputation was secured and her advice often sought on matters appertaining to Italian art and history.

These two biographies of learned and cultivated women of the Renaissance and their environment of a courtly society were of particular significance in the historiography of the Renaissance. With them she secured for two women their place alongside the better-known names of popes and princesses and introduced into the contemporary consciousness of the Renaissance a new and powerful exponent of politics and diplomacy as well as a great patron of the arts, Isabella d'Este.

C. strove for education and admired learning in others. She was determined to earn enough money to send her own daughter to Oxford and this she did. She became a serious and respected scholar without ever losing her passionate enthusiasm for her subject. She travelled extensively in Italy which remained always for her "My dear land."

WORKS: *The Cathedral Organist* (1873). *The Children of Seelisberg* (1875). *Our Valley* (1877). *Rosebuds* (1878). *Christabel* (1880). *The Fortunes of Hassan* (1880). *King's Marden* (1881). *Una Creighton* (1882). *Miss Judy* (1883). *Nimrod Nunn* (1885). *Swanford Bridge* (1886). *Cecily's Birds* (1887). *Troy Farm* (1890). *The Pilgrim's Way* (1893). *Sacharissa* (1893). *Jules Bastien-Lepage* (1894). *Madame* (1894). *Sir Edward Burne-Jones* (1894). *The Early Works of Raphael* (1895). *Raphael in Rome* (1895). *Jean François Millet* (1896). *G.F. Watts, Royal Academician, His Life and Work* (1896). *Christ and His Mother in Italian Art* (1897). *Beatrice d'Este* (1899). *The Painters of Florence* (1901). *Sandro Botticelli* (1903). *Isabella d'Este* (1903). *Raphael* (1905). *Baldassare Castiglione* (1908). *Hampton Court* (1910). *Christina of Denmark* (1913). *San Bernadino in Art* (1913). *Italian Gardens of the Renaissance* (1914). *The Diaries of Julia Cartwright (1851-1914), Art Critic and Historian of the Italian Renaissance*, ed. A. Emanuel (1988).

BIBLIOGRAPHY: Emanuel, A. *Apollo Magazine*, (October 1984). Emanuel, A. *Bulletin of the Society for Renaissance Studies*, (October 1983). Emanuel, A. *Proceedings of Layard Conference in Venice*, (1983).

Angela Emanuel

Elizabeth Cary, Viscountess Falkland

BORN: 1585 or 1586, Burford, Oxfordshire.
DIED: October 1639, London.
DAUGHTER OF: Lawrence and Elizabeth Symondes Tanfield.
MARRIED: Henry Cary, 1602.

Only child and heiress of a wealthy Oxford lawyer, later Lord Chief Baron of the Exchequer, C. was a startlingly precocious child, teaching herself French, Spanish, Italian, Latin, Hebrew, and Transylvanian. By the age of twelve she had incurred a debt of a hundred pounds to the servants for candles (forbidden by her parents) so that she could read late at night. At fifteen or sixteen she was married to Henry Cary, ten years her senior, who later became a member of the Privy Council,

a viscount, and Lord Chief Deputy of Ireland. They began living together about 1607 after Henry returned from military service abroad. C. lived with her husband twenty years, during which she bore eleven living children, all of whom she nursed herself except her eldest son, Lucius, who was reared by her father. When C. mortgaged her jointure to advance her husband's career, her father disinherited her in favor of her eldest son. In 1626 C. converted to Catholicism, damaging her husband's career as a courtier in a Protestant court. He responded by abandoning her, taking custody of her children, and stripping her house of the necessities of life. Her poverty and suffering caused her to appeal to the court for help. In 1627 the Privy Council ordered Lord Falkland to support his wife, but seven months later he had not complied with the order. In her last years she kidnapped two of her sons and smuggled them to the continent to become Catholics. Three of her daughters became nuns; one of these wrote a detailed biography of her mother emphasizing her sufferings for her faith.

Widely and deeply read in many languages, C. early turned her hand to translation. Between the ages of thirteen and fifteen she translated *Le Miroir de Monde*, an epitome of geography, and dedicated it to her great-uncle, Sir Henry Lee. Later in life she translated the works of Cardinal Du Perron. One of these, *The Reply to the King of Great Britain*, published in 1630, was ordered publicly burned. Near the end of her life she was translating the writings of Blosius, a Flemish Benedictine monk.

She began writing poetry shortly after her marriage while living with her mother-in-law. When Lady Cary, angry at her son's wife for reading constantly, took away her books, C. "set herself to make verses" (*Life*, p. 8). According to her daughter, the best thing C. wrote at this time was a life of Tamburlaine in verse; this and a tragedy set in Sicily are lost. During these same years she also wrote *Mariam, the Fair Queen of Jewry*, A Senecan tragedy based on Josephus's *Antiquities*. The first of many English plays about Herod and Mariamne, *Mariam* is carefully researched and constructed, attentive to historical details; the absence of anachronisms is unusual in the period. In style and dramaturgy the play is competent but conventional, with action discussed rather than dramatized and details of the execution left to a messenger. The play is written in quatrains with occasional couplets and sonnets inserted. For reasons not entirely clear, *Mariam* was published in 1613, some ten years after it was written, and C. thus became the first Englishwoman to publish a full-length original play.

C. began writing again after her separation from her husband. She wrote verse lives of several women saints and verses about the Annunciation. The only surviving creative work from this period, however, is a life of Edward II, written, according to the author, to pass the "weary hours and a deep and sad passion."

Always of an intense and intellectual temperament, C. was phenomenally absent-minded and profoundly eccentric; these characteristics were exacerbated by her painful circumstances. She was nonetheless social and generous, as evidenced by numerous friendships and dedications to her of the *Works* of John Marston, of *England's Helicon*, and of Michael Drayton's *England's Heroicall Epistles*. She was the subject of verses by William Basse and John Davies of Hereford. C. died peacefully of a lung disease and was buried in the chapel of the Catholic queen Henrietta Maria.

WORKS: *The Mirror of the World* (c. 1598-1602), translation of A. Ortellius, *Le Miroir du Monde*. (c. 1602-05; lost). *Mariam* (c. 1602-05), ed. A.C. Dunstan and W.W. Greg (1914). "Life of Tamberlaine" (c. 1602-05; lost). *The History of Edward II* (1627). *The Reply to the King of Great Britain* (1630), translation of Cardinal J. Du Perron. Verse lives of Mary Magdalen, St. Agnes, St. Elizabeth of Portugal (c. 1630; lost). Translation of Blosius (c. 1639; lost).

BIBLIOGRAPHY: Cotton, N. *Women Playwrights in England c. 1363-1750* (1980). Dunstan, A.C. *Examination of Two English Dramas* (1908). Fullerton, G. *Life of Elisabeth, Lady Falkland* (1883). Murdock, K. *The Sun at Noon* (1939). Simpson, R., ed., *The Lady Falkland: Her Life* (1861). Stauffer, D.A. *Essays in Dramatic Literature: The Parrott Presentation Volume*, ed. H. Craig (1935).

Other references: *TSLL* (Winter 1977).

Nancy Cotton

Margaret Cavendish, Duchess of Newcastle

BORN: 1623, St. John's Abbey, Colchester, Essex.
DIED: 15 December 1673, Welbeck Abbey, Nottinghamshire.
DAUGHTER OF: Thomas Lucas and Elizabeth Leighton.
MARRIED: William Cavendish, 1645.

C. was among the most conspicuous and prolific female writers of the seventeenth century and the first to experiment with a broad variety of genres. During her lifetime she wrote and published a dozen books of poetry, fiction, plays, orations, letters, philosophical treatises, biography, and autobiography, earning a reputation for genius and eccentricity that has endured for more than three hundred years.

The youngest child of Thomas Lucas, a wealthy landowner who died soon after her birth, and Elizabeth Leighton, who raised C. to be "virtuous . . . modest . . . civil . . . [and] honorable," C. passed an idyllic childhood in rural Essex learning little more than the traditional accomplishments and otherwise devoting her time to the cultivation of her imagination. Upon the outbreak of the Civil War, she fled with her family to Oxford where in 1643 she became a maid of honor to Queen Henrietta Maria. Despite her painful shyness, she braved the loss of her protective family and the ridicule of the court to follow the Queen into exile in Paris. There she met William Cavendish, Marquis of Newcastle, her brother Charles's commander and a Royalist hero of the siege of York. They were married in 1645 and until the Restoration lived in Paris, Rotterdam, and Antwerp.

Although William was a widower and thirty years older than she, C. never tired of rehearsing her husband's virtues: sometime military hero, sometime poet and playwright, an amateur in philosophy and the natural sciences, William was the definitive romantic cavalier, his most serious work a study of the gentlemanly art of horsemanship. In the face of enormous debt, William maintained luxurious households on the Continent where he entertained the famous philosophers of the time, interpreting for his young wife the matter of their discussions. The father of five children from his first marriage, he apparently submitted to C.'s contempt for "breeding women" and encouraged only the growth of her intellect and imagination; in pride and gratitude for such an "Extraordinary Husband," C. wrote, "I cannot for my Life be so good a Huswife as to quit Writing . . . you are pleased to Peruse my Works and Approve of them so well, as to give me Leave to Publish them, which is a Favour few Husbands would grant their Wives. . . ."

Six years after their marriage, C. returned to England in an unsuccessful attempt to obtain money due on William's sequestered estates. During her eighteen-month stay she composed her first book, *Poems and Fancies*, which was published in London in 1653. C.'s theory that, for her, poetry must be grounded in the rational "distinguishment" she had learned from the philosophers and the imaginative "similizing" retained from her childhood play was already apparent, but so too was her habitual dislike of revision: "there was more pleasure in making than mending," she later wrote, and more than once made the preponderance of thoughts in her head her excuse: "I did many times not peruse the copies that were transcribed, lest they should disturb my following conceptions." *Poems and Fancies* was followed within two months by *Philosophical Fancies*, like the first book an enchanting blend of fantasy and the popularization of current scientific inquiry, but because of its uncontrolled leaps from the rational steps of evidence, division, and order into the realm of the imagination, an object of frequent derision. Aware of her shortcomings, C. had tried to apologize to her critics: "The Reason I write in Verse is Because I thought that Errors might better pass there, than in Prose, since poets write

most Fiction and Fiction is not given for Truth, but for pastime"; failing to convince them of the value of her work, but still encouraged by her husband and confident of her own "native wit," she turned to prose. During her remaining years in exile she published three books, which united her desire for personal fame with a growing feminist awareness.

The World's Olio, a collection of essays compiled upon her return to Antwerp, concludes with a defense against charges of plagiarism, ironic because of the censure C. suffered but a theme already common in women's writing. In the dedication of her next book, *The Philosophical and Physical Opinions*, to the universities of Oxford and Cambridge, C. straightforwardly attacked the customs that shut women out of education and power, using a familiar female image to "similize" her argument: ". . . we are kept like Birds in Cages, to Hop up and down in our Houses, not Suffer'd to fly abroad, to see the several Changes of Fortune and the Various Humors, Ordained and Created by Nature, and wanting the Experience of Nature, we must needs want the Understanding and Knowledge." *Natures Pictures drawn by Fancies Pencil to the Life*, a collection of tales of romantic heroines facing fantastic adversity, presented C.'s ideal woman in fiction, formless by modern standards and obviously the product of her vision of herself. The short autobiography attached to *Natures Pictures*, "A True Relation of my Birth, Breeding, and Life," is, however, charming in its "plain natural style," and like the *Life* of her husband she published twelve years later is as direct a portrait of personal experience as ever came out that dramatic period of English history.

When, after the Restoration, Charles II made William Duke of Newcastle and restored some of his property, C. and her husband retired to Welbeck Abbey. There, isolated from the distractions and criticisms of society, C. continued writing, producing within the next eight years a remarkable quantity and variety of works. The fourteen closet dramas included in her *Plays* were obviously modelled upon William's amateur attempts, but within their chaotic dramatic structures they present extraordinary women, skilled in the art of systematic public debate. "Female Orations," a section of *Orations of Divers Sorts*, C.'s next book, laid bare the customs and prejudices that had brought women to their current state of powerlessness. Even in its forthright feminist polemic, however, it could not escape the hallmarks of her "similizing" imagination: "The truth is, we live like bats or owls, labour like beasts, and die like worms." *CCXI Sociable Letters* and *Philosophical Letters* marked C.'s return to her most successful style, witty, enthusiastic, personal, and supremely confident that whatever she had to say was, for the moment, reasonable and right. *Observations upon Experimental Philosophy* was a return to her interest in science, but almost predictably rescinded her earlier opinions about experimentation; the science fiction story attached to it, *The Description of a new Blazing World*, combined C.'s passion for scientific speculation with her romanticized vision of the new woman. *The Life of the Thrice Noble, High and Puissant Prince William Cavendish* and a new book of *Plays* were the last of her original productions, yet her interest in writing seems never to have flagged. In the last years of her life she probably regretted the haste of her earlier composition; always proud of her work, she must have overseen its new editions and made the revisions she thought necessary to insure her fame.

In 1667 C. was an invited guest at the Royal Academy, honored for her scientific achievements, which were not, after all, very much more implausible than those circulating during the period. Still, with her eccentric dress and her embarrassing habit of publishing her own writing, she was a curiosity for the Londoners who flocked to stare at her carriage. She returned to Welbeck Abbey after her triumphant visit, died in 1673, and was buried in Westminster Abbey. In 1676 William collected and published *Letters and Poems in Honour of the Incomparable Princess, Margaret Duchess of Newcastle*, a volume containing praise from Hobbes but also the sound criticism of Walter Charleton: "Your fancy is too generous to be strained, your invention too nimble to be fettered. . . . Hence it is that you do not always confine your sense to your verse, nor your verses to rhythm, nor your rhythm to the quantity and sounds of syllables." C. was hampered in her writing, surely, by her lack of disciplined intellectual training and in her philosophy by her necessary dependence upon the observations of others. Yet in her work there is an inescapable exuberance that makes Virginia Woolf's judgment, "She has the irresponsibility of a child and the arrogance of a Duchess," seem more tribute than blame.

WORKS: *Poems and Fancies: Written by the Right Honourable, the Lady Margaret Countesse of Newcastle* (1653, 1664, 1668). *Philosophicall Fancies. Written by the Right Honourable, the Lady Newcastle* (1653). *The World's Olio. Written by the Most Excellent Lady the Lady M. of Newcastle* (1655, 1671). *The Philosophical and Physical Opinions, Written by her Excellency, The Lady Marchionesse of Newcastle* (1655, 1663, 1668). *Natures Pictures drawn by Fancies Pencil to the Life. Written by the thrice Noble, Illustrious, and Excellent Princess, the Lady Marchioness of Newcastle. . . .* (1656, 1671). *Playes written by the thrice Noble, Illustrious and Excellent Princess, the Lady Marchioness of Newcastle* (1662). *Orations of Divers Sorts, Accommodated to Divers Places. Written by the thrice Noble. . .* (1662, 1668). *CCXI. Sociable Letters, Written by the thrice Noble. . .* (1664). *Philosophical Letters: or, Modest Reflections upon some Opinions in Natural Philosophy, maintained by several famous and learned Authors of this Age, expressed by way of Letters: By the thrice Noble. . . .* (1664). *Observations upon Experimental Philosophy. To which is added, the Description of a new Blazing World. Written by the thrice Noble. . .* (1666, 1668). *The Life of the thrice Noble, High and Puissant Prince William Cavendishe, Duke, Marquess, and Earl of Newcastle. . .* (1667, 1675). *Playes, never before Printed. Written by the thrice Noble. . .* (1668).

BIBLIOGRAPHY: Bickley, F. *The Cavendish Family* (1914). Cotton, N. *Women Playwrights in England c. 1363-1750* (1980). Ferguson, M. *First Feminists: British Women Writers 1578-1799.* Firth, C.H., ed. *The Life of William Cavendish, Duke of Newcastle* (1906). Gagen, J.E. (1956). Gagen, J.E. *The New Woman. Her Emergence in English Drama, 1600-1730* (1954). Goreau, A. *The Whole Duty of a Woman: Female Writers in Seventeenth-Century England* (1985). Goulding, R.W. *Margaret (Lucas) Duchess of Newcastle* (1925). Grant, D. *Margaret the First: A Biography of Margaret Cavendish, Duchess of Newcastle, 1623-1673.* Grant, D. ed. *The Phanseys of William Cavendish, Marquis of Newcastle, Addressed to Margaret Lucas, and Her Letters in Reply* (1956). Meyer, G.D. *The Scientific Lady in England 1650-1760* (1955). Mintz, S.I. *JEGP* (1952). Pearson, J. *Tulsa Studies in Women's Literature* (1985). Palomo, D. *WS* (1979): Perry, H.T.E. *The First Duchess of Newcastle and Her Husband as Figures in Literary History* (1918). Prasad, K. *Essays Presented to Amy G. Stock*, ed. R.K. Kaul (1951). Reynolds, M. *The Learned Lady in England from 1650 to 1760* (1920). Ross, M.B. *Women in the Middle Ages and the Renaissance: Literary and Historical Perspectives*, ed. M.B. Rose (1986). Smith, H.L. *Reason's Disciples: Seventeenth-Century English Feminists* (1982). Stimpson, D. *Scientists and Amateurs* (1948). Turberville, A.S. *A History of Welbeck Abbey and Its Owners* (1938). Whibley, C. *Essays in Biography* (1913). Woolf, V. *The Common Reader* (1925).

Susan Hastings

Susanna Centlivre

BORN: 1667 (?).
DIED: 1 December 1723, London.
MARRIED: Joseph Centlivre, 1707.
WROTE UNDER: Susanna Carroll.

Accounts of C.'s life before 1700 are conjectural, but her frequent visits to Holbeach, Lincolnshire, support the tradition that she was born there. She first appeared in print in 1700, under the name Susanna Carroll; at this time she was living in London and contributing fashionable correspondence to *Familiar and Courtly Letters* and similar collections. In 1707 she married Joseph Centlivre, a royal cook, and in 1713 the couple moved to Buckingham Court, where they lived the rest of their lives. C. was an ardent Whig, attracting a wide circle of friends among Whig writers; her politics and her anti-Catholicism were the main reasons for Pope's including her in the 1728 *Dunciad*. C. is thought by some critics to be the model for Phoebe Clinket, the female playwright ridiculed by Pope, Gay, and Arbuthnot in *Three Hours After Marriage* (1717). Examination of theatrical satire of the woman dramatist shows, however, that Clinket, while embodying specific hits at the Countess of Winchilsea, is a conventionalized comic figure in the tradition of the *femmes savantes*. C. was buried at St. Paul's, Covent Garden. An edition of her plays was advertised for 1732, but the first collected edition did not appear until 1760; her letters and incidental poems remain scattered in eighteenth-century periodicals and anthologies.

The best comic playwright in the early decades of the eighteenth century, C. wrote sixteen full-length plays and three short pieces. Typically, she writes a farcical comedy of intrigue leading to the marriage of an honest hero (often a soldier) and a sensible heroine. Using a wide variety of sources in French, Spanish, and earlier English drama, her plays focus on fast-paced, witty situations rather than witty dialogue. She is an adroit stage technician who writes for actors rather than for readers. Her four best comedies became stock repertory pieces.

The first of these, *The Gamester* (1705), a topical play about a major eighteenth-century vice, initiated a series of plays about gambling. The hero, Valere, faces ruin because of his addiction to gaming, but the rich and resourceful Angelica reclaims him by disguising herself as a man and winning his money, watch, ring, and finally her own portrait set with diamonds, a love token that he had solemnly sworn never to part with. When Valere is penitent, Angelica forgives and marries

him. Ostensibly writing sentimental reform comedy, C. actually exploits audience interest in gaming. Valere's obsession is more convincingly portrayed than his reformation, and the liveliest scene in the play depicts the sharpers and suckers hot over the gaming table, absorbed in their own colorful jargon.

C.'s next success was *The Busy Body* (1709), a beautifully proportioned intrigue comedy in which two young couples outwit two comic old men. The special ingredient of the comedy is the character of Marplot, the busybody. In his impertinent but good-natured eagerness to discover his friends' secrets, Marplot repeatedly brings the young lovers near to disaster. The plot sets up a clever tension: the audience sympathizes with the lovers and at the same time with the idiotic Marplot. As the lovers must outwit not only their enemies but also their friend, the audience is in a continual state of anxious hilarity.

The Wonder (1714) is a masterpiece of comic theater. The action turns on Violante's promise to protect the secret of Isabella's runaway and romance. Although every event conspires to make Violante appear false, she keeps her friend's secret to the point of passionate quarrels with her beloved Don Felix. Around the central pair of lovers revolve delightful minor comic characters. Plot and dialogue are tightly packed so that a surprising turn occurs every few minutes. The role of Don Felix was one of David Garrick's triumphs, and he chose it for his farewell performance in 1776. C.'s last success, *A Bold Stroke for a Wife* (1718) is similarly fast-paced and ingenious. The plot turns on a single premise. Colonel Fainwell, in order to marry Anne Lovely, must gain the consent of four amusingly different guardians—a beau, a virtuoso, a businessman, and a Quaker. He wins the lady by assuming five successive disguises, the last being an impersonation of the real Simon Pure, adding that expression to the language. There is some social satire of the four types represented by the guardians, who are monomaniacal humor characters, but the tone is genial and lighthearted throughout, as it is always in the best of C.'s comedies.

Of these four comedies the most popular in the eighteenth century was *The Busy Body. The Wonder* and *A Bold Stroke for a Wife* continued to grow in popularity, and, while *The Gamester* was replaced in the repertory by other plays about gambling, C.'s three later successes were performed regularly throughout the nineteenth century not only in England but also in the United States and Australia.

WORKS: *The Perjured Husband* (1700). *The Beau's Duel* (1702). *The Stolen Heiress* (1702). *Love's Contrivance* (1703). *The Gamester* (1705). *The Basset Table* (1705). *Love at a Venture* (1706). *The Platonic Lady* (1706). *The Busy Body* (1709; rpt. 1949, introduction by J. Byrd). *The Man's Bewitched* (1709). *A Bickerstaff's Burying* (1710). *Marplot* (1710). *The Perplexed Lovers* (1712). *The Masquerade* (1713). *The Wonder* (1714). *A Poem Humbly Presented to His Most Sacred Majesty* (1714). *An Epistle to Mrs. Wallup* (1714). *The Gotham Election* (1715). *A Wife Well Managed* (1715). *The Cruel Gift* (1716). *An Epistle to the King of Sweden from a Lady of Great Britain* (1717). *A Bold Stroke for a Wife* (1718; edited by T. Stathas, 1968). *A Woman's Case* (1720). *The Artifice* (1722). *Works* (1760). *The Plays of Susanna Centlivre*, 3 vols. edited by R. Frushell (1982).

BIBLIOGRAPHY: Bateson, F.W. *English Comic Drama 1700-1750* (1929). Boas, F.S. *An Introduction to Eighteenth-Century Drama 1700-1780* (1953). Bowyer, J.W. *The Celebrated Mrs. Centlivre* (1952). Cotton, N. *Women Playwrights in England c. 1363-1750* (1980). Lock, F.P. *Susanna Centlivre* (1979).

Other references: *Book Collector* (1957, 1958, 1961). *MLN* (February 1928, February 1933). *MP* (1926). *N&Q* (September 1953). *PLL* (1986). *PQ* (1937). *RES* (1942).

Nancy Cotton

Mary Chandler

BORN: 1687, Malmsbury, Wiltshire.
DIED: 11 September 1745, Bath.
DAUGHTER OF: Henry Chandler and a Miss Bridgman of Marlborough.

The poet C., daughter of a Dissenting minister, did not receive the formal education given her several brothers. Perhaps because of a childhood accident that left her spine deformed, C.'s father raised her to be self-sufficient instead of to excel in more traditional feminine accomplishments. Rather than follow the customary route of marriage, she opened her own millinery shop in Bath in 1705, which she tended for thirty-five years. To supplement her minimal education she studied the major works of ancient and modern authors.

C.'s Neoclassical verse style shows most strongly the influence of Horace's satires, focusing as it does on commonplace subjects presented in an elegant and simple style. Her writing also shows the influence of the reigning poetic satirist, Alexander Pope, who visited her in Bath and who "approved" of her just published gentle satire, the 322-line *A Description of Bath* (1734).

From Pope, she borrowed the genre of the heroic-couplet epistle to present her comic history and description of the popular resort town and its social milieu. A section of the epistle to Burlington (1731) also forms the model for the final section of *A Description of Bath*, a paean to Ralph Allen, Bath's greatest citizen and the noted developer of the British postal service. C. presents, as Pope does, a description of a house and its garden to show the true attributes of its owner. Timon's mythical villa reveals the worst of taste and humanity; Allen's Prior Park, whose construction

had just begun, figures in C.'s poem as the embodiment of its owner's virtues.

The third edition of the *Description* includes several other of her poems, most of which tackle conventional eighteenth-century topics: the need for the harmony of art and nature, the delights of solitude, and the value of friendship. In general, C.'s verse addresses personal instead of public concerns. She wrote primarily for friends, not for a general audience, several poems being on subjects inspired by conversations or visits with particular friends at their country houses.

Other poems derive from incidents in her life. For example, a wealthy sixty-year-old gentleman in love with her poetry traveled 80 miles to propose marriage to the fifty-four-year-old C. He received a refusal from a woman who found she could not bear "loss of liberty." This episode became immortalized in "A True Tale" and appeared in the 1744 edition of her works. As she grew older and her health declined, undermined by an ill-planned vegetarian diet, her verse became less satiric and more reflective. She left behind an unfinished poem on "the being and attributes of God."

C.'s poetry was relatively popular, running to eight editions and being quoted in other works. She was one of the first to exploit Bath as a literary subject, leading the way for similar epistolary poems by others. Christopher Anstey's successful verse satire, *The New Bath Guide* (1766), for example, derives its inspiration and structure from *A Description of Bath*. Anstey's anapestic romp, however, may have unwittingly led to the social demise of C.'s poem. The last edition of her work (1767) appeared after Anstey's poem appeared. His modern and fashionably scandalous poem displaced her delicate verses in praise of tasteful moderation and self-restraint.

WORKS: *A Description of Bath: A Poem in a Letter to a Friend. Humbly Inscribed to her Royal Highness the Princess Amelia* (1734, 2 editions); with several poems added (1736, 1738, 1741); with "A True Tale" added (1744, 1755, 1767).

BIBLIOGRAPHY: Boyce, B. *The Benevolent Man* (1967). Cibber, T., ed. *Lives of the Poets* (1753). For articles in reference works, see: Todd. Other references: Doughty, O. *RES* (1925).

Linda V. Troost

Vera Chapman

BORN: 7 May 1898, Bournemouth.
DAUGHTER OF: John Frederick and Kate Isabella Veronica (Morse) Fogerty.
MARRIED: Charles Sydney Chapman, 1924.

C. was educated at Lady Margaret Hall, Oxford, where she received a B.A. with second class honors in 1921. A member of the Church of England and resident of London, she served as student welfare officer in Her Majesty's Colonial Office for almost two decades after her two children, a son and a daughter, reached adulthood. In 1963 she left her position to become a full-time writer.

For a person who began her writing career at age sixty-five, C. has been unusually prolific and successful. Her most notable publication is her "Damosel" trilogy based on Arthurian legend, consisting of *The Green Knight* (1975), *The King's Damosel* (1976), and *King Arthur's Daughter* (1978). The trilogy has been translated into Dutch, and *The Green Knight* was made into a noncommercial film by the West Surrey College of Art and Design. As fiction the trilogy is distinguished by its original handling of the legendary matter and by its focus on the point of view of its female protagonists.

The Green Knight is more than a retelling of the medieval tale. C. adds to it an episode at Stonehenge, the figure of Merlin, and the story of the Loathly Lady. Part of the narrative is told by Bertilak's wife, Vivian. The events in *The King's Damosel* are related by Lynette, an appealing character who is developed from her tomboy childhood through her traumatic adolescence, when she is raped, to her later years when she becomes a mystic seeker of the Grail. The final volume, *King Arthur's Daughter*, is narrated by

the title character, Ursulet. In this concluding work C. establishes her feminist perspective by stressing inheritance through the maternal line. The spirit of Britain is carried from mother to daughter, "by the line but not the name, by blood but not bloodshed, by the distaff, not the sword."

The "Damosel" trilogy was followed by an imaginative extrapolation from one of Chaucer's best known characters in her novel *The Wife of Bath* (1978). C. also published the juvenile novel *Judy and Julia* (1979) and *Blaedud the Birdman* (1978). Her most recent work is *Miranty and the Alchemist* (1983), set in Elizabethan times and concerning the adventures of a young girl who, while left in the care of her alchemist uncle, is transported to fantastic realms inhabited by supernatural beings. In addition to her novels, C. has contributed short stories to the magazine *Fantastic Imagination*.

Founder of the Tolkien Society, in which she assumes the name of Belladonna Took, C. is primarily a writer of fantasy and medieval adventure. Her fiction not only fulfills her expressed intention to provide reading pleasure but also achieves added depth through inclusion of myth, philosophy, legend, and mysticism.

WORKS: *The Green Knight* (1975). *The King's Damosel* (1976). *King Arthur's Daughter* (1976). *Judy and Julia* (1977). *The Wife of Bath* (1978). *Blaedud the Birdman* (1978). *Miranty and the Alchemist* (1983).

BIBLIOGRAPHY: For articles in reference works, see: *CA. SATA.*

Charlotte Spivack

Hester Mulso Chapone

BORN: 27 October 1727, Twywell, Northamptonshire.
DIED: 25 December 1801, Hadley, Middlesex.
DAUGHTER OF: Thomas Mulso and a Miss Thomas.
MARRIED: John Chapone, 1760.

WROTE UNDER: Hester Mulso, Hester Chapone.

C. was the only surviving daughter in a family of several children. Her first literary effort, a romance written when she was nine, met with maternal disapproval, possibly caused by jealousy at the child's talent. Only after her mother's death, when C. took over the management of her father's household, could she undertake a program of self-improvement, studying French, Italian, Latin, music, and drawing.

One of the Bluestockings, C. associated with Samuel Johnson, Samuel Richardson, and later in her life, with Frances Burney d'Arblay. Through Richardson, one of her closer friends, she met John Chapone, an attorney, whom she married after a long engagement; unfortunately, he died within nine months of their marriage, just before C. turned thirty-four. In general, her friends regarded her highly, overlooking the "uncommon ugliness" of her facial features and noting her goodness and sense. Richardson used her as a model for some of the genteel characters in *Sir Charles Grandison*, and in 1783, the Earl of Carlisle's friends appealed to her when they needed someone who could cajole Johnson into giving his opinion of the Earl's tragedy.

Her first published work appeared in Johnson's *The Rambler* #10 (1750) and in Hawkesworth's *The Adventurer* #77-79 (1753). During these years she also engaged in an epistolary debate with Samuel Richardson about filial obedience. In these letters C. argues that a daughter should not marry without the consent of the parents but that she could refuse anyone the parents might select. Richardson, on the other hand, claimed that a daughter must obey her parents in all things and accept their choice of a spouse. According to Johnson, the friendship of C. and Richardson cooled because he objected to her allowing her verses to be read too publicly.

She wrote or translated poems on traditional subjects: friendship, the beauties of nature, the delights of solitude. For example, her poem to Susanna Highmore, "To Stella," plays with classical conventions while it discusses the superiority of platonic feminine friendship over heterosexual love. (In his 1755 dictionary, Dr. Johnson quoted from the then unpublished poem to provide an example of a *quatrain*.) C. also composed a Pindaric ode on Epictetus for the preface to Elizabeth Carter's 1758 translation of that philosopher's work.

It was her *Letters on the Improvement of the Mind* (1773), however, that brought C. fame, if not fortune. She originally wrote the educational letters for the benefit of her favorite niece. Elizabeth Montagu advised C. to publish them; as a result, she became the dedicatee. One of the earliest in a long line of such treatises, *Letters* presents a detailed plan for educating girls and includes a list of recommended books. Besides the traditional instruction in French, dancing, and etiquette, C. recommends extensive reading, particularly in the Bible, British and European history, the natural sciences, moral philosophy, selected literary works, geography, and chronology.

When first published, *Letters* sold quickly, and by its final appearance in 1851, it had seen about sixty editions in Great Britain, the United States, and France. As the queen revealed to C. in 1778 (both were visiting C.'s uncle, the Bishop of Winchester at the time), even the Princess Royal's education had been guided by the *Letters*.

In 1775, C. published *Miscellanies in Prose and Verse*, which contained her early poems and essays. Two years later, she published her last work, *A Letter to a New-Married Lady* (1777). After her death in 1801, C.'s relatives brought out a four-volume edition of her works that also reprinted her correspondence with Richardson and Carter. The strong and clear prose of the essays and letters demonstrates concretely her point that women can think and behave rationally if educated and that such an education will make them useful, not weak and ornamental, humans.

WORKS: *Letters on the Improvement of the Mind. Addressed to a Young Lady* (1773). *Miscellanies in Prose and Verse* (1775). *A Letter to a New-Married Lady* (1777). *The Works of Mrs. Chapone: Now First Collected*, adding to the above works her letters to Carter and Richardson, fugitive pieces, and a memoir by her family (1807).

CORRESPONDENCE: Fellowes, E., and E. Pine eds. *The Tenbury Letters* (1943). Gaussen, A. *A Later Pepys* (1904). Johnson, R. *Bluestocking Letters* (1926).

BIBLIOGRAPHY: Cole, J., of Scarborough. *Memoirs of Mrs. Chapone* (1839). Elwood, A. *Memoirs of the Literary Ladies of England* (1843). Wheeler, E. *Famous Blue-Stockings* (1910). Wilson, M. *These Were Muses* (1924).

For articles in reference works, see: Todd. Other references: *PMLA* (1950).

Linda V. Troost

Charlotte Cibber Charke

BORN: 1713.
DIED: 1760.
DAUGHTER OF: Colley and Katherine
    Cibber.
MARRIED: Richard Charke c. 1729; possibly
    later married John Sacheverille.

C. failed at a number of careers (including pastrycook and manager, 1745, of The Theatre-Royal in The Haymarket) but is remembered for an autobiography that tells all. Her father was Colley Cibber, actor, dramatist, manager of The Theatre-Royal in Drury Lane, Poet Laureate. Cibber had 10 children, but not even his obstreperous son Theophilus had a career as flamboyant as C.'s. Her father married her off to a violinist at Drury Lane in an attempt to curb her wildness; that did not work. Her life grew wilder. Her father's autobiography (*An Apology for the Life of Colley Cibber, Comedian*, 1740) shows that his eventful career was placid compared to the lurid reminiscences of her scapegrace life she put together for some much-needed cash as *A Narrative of the Life of Mrs. Charlotte Charke . . . Written by Herself* (1755).

Having returned to London after extravagant adventures with, as she wrote, "'only a single Penny in my pocket," she published her story on 19 April 1755. First she had tried to blackmail her father with the threat of embarrassment. He was adamant and would give her no money. As for her plight, his reply was: "You have made your own bed and therein you must lie," and he sent back her begging letter without any accompanying cash. In fact, it was said that in order to get anything out of her father she had to dress up as a highwayman—she often wore men's clothes—and accost Cibber on the road, forcing him to stand and deliver. When Cibber demanded of the "highwayman" why "he" had turned to a life of crime, "he" responded that "his" father was a tightwad who would not provide "him" with money on which to live.

C. made good use of her penchant for appearing in men's clothes during her theatrical career in London and her "nine Years peregrination" on the road. She was "valet" to a homosexual Irish peer for a while. She played Macheath in *The Beggar's Opera* on stage (as well as making the appearance as a "highwayman" already mentioned). She lived as a man and a farmer in the country. She passed as a doctor and an eligible bachelor. On one occasion there was a scheme to marry her off, as a male, to an heiress and seize the woman's fortune, but at the last minute C. (who had taken a liking to the girl) confessed the truth. The young lady would not believe C.'s con-

fession; C. had, she tells us, to offer "ocular proof," whereupon the young girl fled. When Richard Charke ran off to Jamaica it really made little difference to C., because she had grown accustomed to supporting both herself and her daughter by whatever means were at hand.

Once there was hope C. would be a theatrical luminary. Cibber had made a star of his daughter-in-law, Susannah Maria Arne Cibber (Theophilus' wife), and Theophilus was also more or less successful on the stage; moreover, Cibber had connections. But he could not succeed with C., who made her debut as "a young gentlewoman who had never appeared before on any stage" in *The Provok'd Wife* on 8 April 1730. Characteristically, she had spent the previous day riding around London in a hired coach advertising the great event. By sheer nerve and persistence she came to replace the redoubtable Mary Porter in the next season; Mrs. Porter, famed for tragic roles, was to have appeared in Rowe's *Jane Shore* but fell and broke her leg. C. went on to play in *The Tender Husband*, *Orinooko* by Aphra Behn, *Othello* (as Roderigo), *Pasquin* (as Lord Place), even to create a role in one of the two or three greatest hits of the eighteenth century, *George Barnwell; or, The London Merchant*. In female or male clothes she played many parts under the theatrical management of her brother Theophilus and Cibber's partner Fleetwood. When London failed her she turned to simple provincial tours and even penny gaffs. She acted on London stages (1730–1737) and under the sleaziest provincial auspices, but she kept working. The money she made she spent recklessly on "the most idle and thoughtless extravagance" and in some respects her life resembled that of Defoe's fictional Moll Flanders.

That life ended in penury, though not for want of effort or invention in pennycatching schemes. She even ran a London puppet show. A second marriage her autobiography shrouds in silence; it cannot have lasted long. She got into trouble with creditors and with the police. And her family deserted her.

Near the end Samuel Whyte (a sort of Irish publisher) and one H. Slater, Jr. (described as "a wary haberdasher of literature" in London's Grub Street) found C. in "a wretched hovel where it was usual at that time for the scavengers to deposit the sweepings of the streets." They bought from her a story called *The History of Henry Dumont, Esq.; and Miss Charlotte Evelyn* and gave her £10 for it. It went into a third printing, but that brought no more money to C., to her pet dog Fidele, or to her pet magpie in that hovel. She remained in dire poverty.

She also published *The Mercer; or, Fatal Ex-*

travagance (around 1755) and *The Lover's Treat; or, Unnatural Hatred* (1758), both allegedly true stories. But neither those nor occasional theatre pieces could feed her adequately. She perished in want and obscurity about 1760. The *British Chronicle* in that year published a brief obituary under the date of 16 April and called her "a gentlewoman remarkable for her adventures and misfortunes." Today she is remembered for the somewhat frighteningly indomitable courage she showed, for her dedication to rather riotous living, and for the unusual frankness of her autobiography.

WORKS: *A Narrative of the Life of Mrs. Charlotte Charke (Youngest Daughter of Colley Cibber, Esq.)*

Written by Herself (1755). *The Mercer; or, Fatal Extravagance* (1755). *The Lover's Treat; or, Unnatural Hatred* (1758). *The History of Henry Dumont, Esq.; and Miss Charlotte Evelyn* (1758). Theatre pieces include the farce *The Art of Management* (1735), *The Carnival; or, Harlequin Blunderer* ("intermix'd with songs, written by Mrs. Charke"), *Tit for Tat; or, The Comedy and Tragedy of War* (1743), etc.

BIBLIOGRAPHY: Ashley, L.R.N. *Colley Cibber* (1968). Ashley, L.R.N. "Introduction" to Scholars' Facsimiles & reprint edition of *A Narrative* (1969). Waddell, H. *Spectator*, (4 June 1937).

For articles in reference works, see: *DNB*.

Leonard R.N. Ashley

Maria Charlesworth

BORN: 1 October 1819, Suffolk.
DIED: 18 October 1880, Surrey.
DAUGHTER OF: The Rev. John Charlesworth.

Best known as the author of the children's novel *Ministering Children*, C. was born the daughter of the Rev. John Charlesworth, rector of Flowton, Suffolk, from 1814 to 1844. He was simultaneously rector at Blakenham Parva, near Ipswich, for a brief time where C. was privately educated. From the age of six, she ministered among the poor in her father's parish. Later her father would have a small parish near St. Paul's in London, where C. became ill and would be confined to her room as an invalid. After her parents' death, she sometimes lived with her brother, the Rev. Samuel Charlesworth of Limehouse, though her permanent home was in Nutfield, Surrey, where she lived for the last 16 years of her life. She never married.

Ministering Children is a didactic work whose aim was in "training the sympathies of children by personal intercourse with want and sorrow." It is an episodic series of adventures (some published separately) of good children who minister among the poor. Their actions are seen as admirable, and they are intended as role models. Helping the poor is seen as a necessary step towards spiritual salvation; personal sacrifice—even among the poor towards each other—is seen as an enobling experience. The work is strongly in the evangelical children's book tradition; now seen as stylistically unsubtle in its didacticism and politically and socially ineffective in changing the ultimate plight of the impoverished, the work was widely successful in its day. It sold 170,000 copies in the United Kingdom and was also published in the United States, Sweden, Switzerland, France, and Germany. Its success led to the demand for a sequel, and it was influential in aspects of Ameri-

can prison reform. The popularity of the work in this century has waned, and it has not been in print since 1924.

A survey of C.'s other works reveals similarly didactic purposes. Her first work, *A Female Visitor to the Poor*, draws on her autobiographical experiences administering in her father's parish and in establishing a mission school in London. *Sunday Afternoons in the Nursery* is a retelling of "familiar narratives from the Book of Genesis." And *The Last Command of Jesus Christ* is subtitled "Plain Teaching on the Lord's Supper."

Though ultimately a minor figure, C.'s work sheds light on the mid-Victorian sensibility; her emotional excesses and appeal to religious sentiments are shared by several major figures.

WORKS: *The Female Visitor to the Poor* (1846). *A Book for the Cottage* (1848). *A Letter to a Child* (1849). *A Letter to a Friend Under Affliction* (1849). *The Light of Life* (1850). *Sunday Afternoons in the Nursery* (1853). *Ministering Children* (1854). *The Sabbath Given: The Sabbath Lost* (1856). *Africa's Mountain Valley* (1858). *India and the East* (1860). *England's Yeoman* (1861). *The Cottage and the Visitor* (1861). *The Sailor's Choice* (1862). *Beautiful Home and Other Letters to a Child* (1863). *A Sequel to Ministering Children* (1867). *The Last Command of Jesus Christ* (1869). *Where Dwellest Thou, or the Inner Home* (1871). *Oliver of the Mill: A Tale* (1871). *Eden and Heaven* (1872). *The Blind Man's Child* (1872). *Old Looking Glass* (1878). *Broken Looking Glass* (1880).

BIBLIOGRAPHY: Avery, G. *Childhood's Pattern* (1975). Grylls, D. *Guardians and Angels* (1978).

For articles in reference works, see: *Allibone*. *DEL. DNB. Who's Who of Children's Literature*. Other references: *TLS* (18 July 1980).

Tony Giffone

Mary Cholmondeley

BORN: 8 June 1859, Shropshire.
DIED: 15 July 1925, London.
DAUGHTER OF: The Rev. Richard Hugh and Emily Beaumont Cholmondeley.
WROTE UNDER: "Pax," Mary Cholmondeley.

Although C.'s career covered the years from 1878 to 1921, the themes and execution of her fiction identify her as a nineteenth-century writer. Her novels, set in the closely circumscribed world of drawing rooms, estate houses, and country parsonages, are frequently compared to those of Jane Austen. In *Red Pottage* (1899), her finest novel, C. controls much of the melodrama and didacticism for which her critics have always taken her to task; nonetheless, her satiric wit, her carefully rendered characters, and her genuine affection for the pastoral splendor of the English countryside and for the grace and refinement of the genteel classes are evident in all of her novels.

Born the third of eight children to the rector of Hodnet in Shropshire, C. described herself as "a plain silent country girl, an invalid whom no one cared a straw about." Her mother died when she was sixteen, whereupon she assumed the responsibility of head of the household. The Cholmondeley family was of comfortable means, however, and C.'s youth was neither sheltered nor reclusive. The family journeyed to London and abroad and enjoyed the active social life one would expect for a family of their position in their community. Having achieved some measure of success with the publication of her first three novels, she moved to London with her father and two sisters in 1896. In a memoir, *Mary Cholmondeley: A Sketch from Memory*, Percy Lubbock recalls the Cholmondeley residence in London and the social gatherings there which included such guests as Howard Sturgis, Rhoda Broughton, and Lady Ritchie. The publication of the "scandalous" *Red Pottage* in 1899 made C. a celebrity, an occurrence she viewed with both amusement and bitterness. Her subsequent novels and stories were received with disappointment by her critics, and by the time she died in 1925 she was largely forgotten.

Although C. began writing when she was sixteen and published her first story anonymously when she was nineteen, she did not publish her first novel until she was twenty-eight. The first four novels she published—*The Danvers Jewels* (1887), *Sir Charles Danvers* (1889). *Diana Tempest* (1893) and *A Devotee: An Episode in the Life of a Butterfly* (1897)—were serialized in *Temple Bar*. Of these, *Diana Tempest*, the first novel published under her own name, was the best and most successful. The first two are mystery

romances, marked by fine suspense, melodrama, and unlikely but exciting events. *Diana Tempest* is a tale of intrigue and romance, of guilt and retribution, and characteristically examines the irrevocable consequenes of the actions of individuals. The female protagonist is an intelligent, independent woman, and her relationship with her lover is one of equality. In this novel, as in *Red Pottage*, Cholmondeley condemns the loveless Victorian marriage of economic and social convenience.

Red Pottage, however, is C.'s best and most interesting novel. Published in 1899, the novel was enormously popular (one reviewer called it "the English novel of the year"), and its adultery, suicides, violent emotions, and satire of the country clergyman and his indolent, aristocratic parishioners caused, as Lubbock tells it, "quite a stir." More interesting, though, is the novel's angry protest against the marginalization, suppression, and, ultimately, silencing of the nineteenth-century woman writer, in particular the unmarried woman writer. For *Red Pottage* is a novel with two plots, and the tale of love and betrayal is but half the story. The second plot involves a woman novelist, Hester Gresley, and her struggle to complete her novel while residing with her antagonistic, self-righteous clergyman brother, himself a third-rate writer of religious pamphlets. Indignant about her satire of the clergy and her unorthodox religious views, he burns the completed manuscript, which has been accepted for publication and returned for revisions, in an act of monstrous destruction. Unlike the previous novels, *Red Pottage* presents an essentially tragic social vision. By novel's end, the selfish, powerful characters celebrate the triumphant marriage of one of their own, and Hester and her friend, Rachel, exile themselves to Australia.

After *Red Pottage*, C. published three novels: *Moth and Rust* (1902), *Prisoners* (*Fast Bound in Misery and Iron*) (1906), and *Notwithstanding* (1913); two collections of short stories: *The Lowest Rung* (1908) and *The Romance of His Life* (1921); a family memoir, *Under One Roof* (1918); and several contributions to periodicals. Although none of these is of the quality of *Red Pottage*, *Notwithstanding* offers an interesting examination of sexual mores and attitudes about women.

Many of the stories in C.'s last published work, *The Romance of His Life*, are concerned with the opposition between the values and scenes of the nineteenth century and the face of a modern world scarred by a world war. In one of the stories, "The Goldfish," C. returns to an examination of the fate of the female artist. A woman, a very talented artist, is married to a second-rate painter who rescued her from poverty and offered her the opportunity of advanced training. However, having become jealous of her superior ability, he makes her copy and enlarge his own canvasses. Convinced that she has betrayed her art, she drowns herself. Though flawed, "The Goldfish" remains compelling evidence of C.'s preoccupation with the various forms of violence imposed on women artists.

Today only *Red Pottage* is available in reprint. Although her novels exhibit to varying degrees the flaws that characterize much popular fiction of the nineteenth century, she chronicles with wit and understanding the manners and mores of the Victorian upperclasses. The skillful and devastating protest against the subordination of the woman writer in the nineteenth century in *Red Pottage* render it a novel worthy of consideration.

WORKS: *The Danvers Jewels* (1887). *Sir Charles Danvers* (1889). *Diana Tempest* (1893). *A Devotee: An Episode in the Life of a Butterfly* (1897). *Red Pottage* (1899). *Moth and Rust; Together with Geoffrey's Wife and The Pitfall* (1902). *Prisoners (Fast Bound in Misery and Iron)* (1906). *The Lowest Rung. With The Hand on the Latch, St. Luke's Summer and The Understudy* (1908; American ed., *The Hand on the Latch*, 1909). *Notwithstanding* (1913; American ed., *After all*, 1913). *Under One Roof: A Family Record* (1918). *The Romance of His Life and Other Romances* (1921).

BIBLIOGRAPHY: Crisp, J. *Mary Cholmondeley, 1859-1925: A Bibliography*, Victorian Fiction Research Guides, 6 (n.d.). Lubbock, P. *Mary Cholmondeley: A Sketch from Memory* (1928). Showalter, E. *A Literature of Their Own* (1977). Tindall, D. Introduction to *Red Pottage* (rpt. 1968).

For articles in reference works, see: *DNB. Longman. NCBEL.*

Other references: *Cornhill* (February 1935). *Edinburgh Review* (July 1900). *Essays in Criticism* (April 1970). *National Review* (March 1900).

Patricia A. O'Hara

Agatha Christie

BORN: 15 September 1890, Torquay, Devon.
DIED: 12 January 1976, Wallingford.
DAUGHTER OF: Frederick Alvah Miller and an English mother.
MARRIED: Archibald Christie, 1914; Max Edgar Lucien Mallowan, 1930.
WROTE UNDER: Agatha Christie, Agatha Christie Mallowan, Mary Westmacott.

C.'s career, from *The Mysterious Affair at Styles* (1920), written in response to her sister's demand for a detective story not as easily solved by the reader as the popular fiction then in vogue, to *Curtain* (in which she finally disposed of her famous sleuth Hercule Poirot in 1975) and *Sleeping Murder* (serialized in a popular magazine in the year of her death, 1976), was phenomenal. She wrote some 130 or 140 short stories, more than half that many novels, a score of radio and stage plays, a couple volumes of poetry, a travel book, and an autobiography. A film based on one of her novels (*Murder on the Orient Express*, based on *Murder on the Calais Coach*, one of more than a dozen which brought her work to the screen) made more money than any other British film up to that date. A play (*The Mousetrap*), originating in her story "Three Blind Mice," opened in 1952 and is still running, having long since become the most successful play in the history of the English theatre. Her books have sold hundreds of millions of copies and have been translated into more languages (over 100) than has Shakespeare. "A Christie for Christmas" was for generations a British publishing tradition. Quite simply, she was the most famous British woman writer of her half a century or so of fame and the most commercially successful woman writer of all time.

All this production (she called herself "a perfect sausage machine") and practice did not make her an artistic writer. Her first novel was refused by a number of publishers before John Lane bought it for The Bodley Head. Some of the stories in *Poirot Investigates* (1924) and her very controversial novel *The Murder of Roger Ackroyd* (1926) are among her best work; she did not improve over fifty years, perhaps because she was quite good enough for her readers from the start and also perhaps because she was proud of the fact that "though I have given in to people on every [other] subject under the sun, *I have never given in to anyone over what I write.*"

Her skill was said to lie in ingenious plotting, but real invention was not really needed. She simply rang the inevitable changes on the conventions of the genre. She could not have "nobody did it" (suicide being a solution rejected by readers), but she could and did have "everybody did it," one of the "corpses" did it, the narrator did it—just about everything but Stephen Leacock's crazy suggestion in his spoof on the red herrings and tortuous twists of mystery writing: he has the murder committed by two people who are just barely mentioned in the book—they are, in fact, the publishers, noted only at the bottom of the title page.

Julian Symons in his history of the crime

novel, *Bloody Murder*, adds to the fact that "her skill was not in the tight construction of plot," that she did not often "make assumptions about the scientific and medical knowledge of readers," though her war work in pharmacies gave her a certain pride in the way she brought in poisons, playing (as she said) with "the phial" in her little "domestic murders." Nor were her characters or scenes especially well drawn. She created, actually, a "never-never" world of fiction (as critic Edmund Crispin and others have noted) and seems to have had little interest in the world in which she lived. With characters that are "flat" and a rural English setting that had largely disappeared before she could write much about it, she moved from her early sensational claptrap (*The Seven Dials Mystery*, 1929, has been called "almost embarrassing" in its "bright young things, beautiful Balkan spies, and sinister anarchists") to her very own brand of upper-class twits gathered in the library of some country house (Styles, Chimneys, Nasse House, End House, and on and on) to hear the detective unravel the mystery, exactly the sort of thing that is spoofed at the start of the 1980 film version of her *The Mirror Crack'd*, which begins with the showing of *Murder at Midnight* in the village hall of St. Mary Mead, which all the world knows is the home of her eccentric but lovable Miss Marple (of *Murder at the Vicarage*, *The Body in the Library*, *A Caribbean Mystery*, *Nemesis*, and many more). Her world, like that of her contemporary P.G. Wodehouse, remained firmly that of times long past, before Labour lords with low-class accents, when garden fetes and jumble sales, not socialism and common markets, were topics of discussion. In her novels the action is in the library, not in the bedroom.

"What I'm writing is meant to be entertainment," C. told Francis Wyndham in 1966. As the creator of Tommy and Tuppence Beresford (*Partners in Crime*, etc.), Parker Pyne (*Parker Pyne Investigates*, etc.), Harley Quin (*The Mysterious Mr. Quin*, etc.), Superintendent Battle (*The Secret of Chimneys*, etc.), Col. John Race (*The Man in the Brown Suit*, etc.), Mark Easterbrook (*The Pale Horse*), Arthur Calgary (*Ordeal by Innocence*), Inspector Narracott (*The Sittaford Mystery*), the bases of films such as *Witness for the Prosecution*, *And Then there were None*, and *Death on the Nile* (among others), and—most of all—the great Belgian detective Hercule Poirot, with his dapper little moustache, irritating little mannerisms (C.'s substitute for characterization) and "little grey cells," C. was indubitably a genius at popular entertainment.

In a genre with magnificent milestones ever since Wilkie Collins' *The Moonstone* (1868), with Poe and Conan Doyle and many more (including women such as Dorothy Sayers, Josephine Tey, P.D. James, and others whose work is not nearly as "abominably careless" as the London *Times* found, but truly literary), C. by sheer popularity and persistence carved herself out a lasting place that can be enjoyed as well as respected by everyone except the curmudgeons such as Edmund Wilson, who damned the whole detective fiction genre with the nasty guestion: "Who Cares Who Killed Roger Ackroyd?"

WORKS: *The Mysterious Affair at Styles: A Detective Story* (1920). *The Secret Adversary* (1922). *The Murder on the Links* (1923). *The Man in the Brown Suit* (1924). *Poirot Investigates* (1924; in U.S., 1925). *The Secret of Chimneys* (1925). *The Murder of Roger Ackroyd* (1926). *The Big Four* (1927). *The Mystery of the Blue Train* (1928). *The Seven Dials Mystery* (1929). *Partners in Crime* (1929). *The Underdog* (1929). *The Mysterious Mr. Quin* (1930; also as *The Passing of Mr. Quin*). *The Murder at the Vicarage* (1930). (as Mary Westmacott) *Giants' Bread* (1930). *The Sittaford Mystery* (1931; in U.S. as *The Murder at Hazelmoor*). *Black Coffee* (produced 1931, published 1934). *Peril at End House* (1932). *The Thirteen Problems* (1932; in U.S. as *The Tuesday Club Murders*, 1933; also as *Miss Marple and the Thirteen Problems*). *The Hound of Death and Other Stories* (1933; *Witness for the Prosecution*, produced 1953, published 1956). *Lord Edgware Dies* (1933; in U.S. as *Thirteen at Dinner*). *Why Didn't They Ask Evans?* (1934; in U.S. as *Boomerang Clue*, 1935). *Parker Pyne Investigates* (1934; in U.S. as *Mr. Parker Pyne, Detective*). *The Listerdale Mystery and Other Stories* (1934). *Murder on the Orient Express* (1934; in U.S. as *Murder on the Calais Coach*). *Murder in Three Acts* (1934; in U.S. as *Three Act Tragedy*, 1935). (as Mary Westmacott) *Unfinished Portrait* (1934). *Death in the Clouds* (1935; in U.S. as *Death in the Air*). *The A.B.C. Murders: A New Poirot Mystery* (1936). (with F. Vosper) *Love from a Stranger* (1936; based on story, "Philomel Cottage"). *Cards on the Table* (1936). *Murder in Mesopotamia* (1936). *Death on the Nile* (1937; in U.S. 1938; produced as *Murder on the Nile*, 1946). *Murder in the Mews and Other Stories* (1937; in U.S. as *Dead Man's Mirror and Other Stories*). *Dumb Witness* (1937; in U.S. as *Poirot Loses a Client*; also as *Murder at Littlegreen House* and *Mystery at Littlegreen House*). *Appointment with Death: A Poirot Mystery* (1938; produced and published as play, 1945). *Hercule Poirot's Christmas* (1938; in U.S. as *Murder for Christmas: A Poirot Story*, 1939; also as *A Holiday for Murder*). *The Regatta Mystery and Other Stories* (1939; also as *Poirot and the Regatta Mystery*). *Murder Is Easy* (1939; in U.S. as *Easy to Kill*). *Ten Little Niggers* (1939; in U.S. as *And Then There Were None*, 1940, produced 1943, published 1944; produced in U.S. as *Ten Little Indians*, 1944, published 1946). *One, Two, Buckle My Shoe* (1940; in U.S. as *The Patriotic Murders*, 1941). *Sad Cypress*

(1940). *Evil Under the Sun* (1941). *N or M? The New Mystery* (1941). *The Body in the Library* (1942). *The Moving Finger* (1942; in U.S., 1943). *Five Little Pigs* (1942; in U.S. as *Murder in Retrospect*; produced and published as *Go Back for Murder*, 1960). *Death Comes as the End* (1942; in U.S., 1945). *Towards Zero* (1944; with G. Verner, produced 1956; also as *Come and Be Hanged*). (as Mary Westmacott) *Absent in the Spring* (1944). *Sparkling Cyanide* (1945; in U.S. as *Remembered Death*). *The Hollow: A Hercule Poirot Mystery* (also as *Murder After Hours*) (1946; produced as *The Hollow*, 1951, published 1952). *Come Tell Me How You Live* (1946). *The Labours of Hercules: Short Stories* (1947; in U.S. as *Labors of Hercules: New Adventures in Crime by Hercule Poirot*). *Witness for the Prosecution and Other Stories* (1948). *Taken at the Flood* (1948; in U.S. as *There Is a Tide . . .*). (as Mary Westmacott) *The Rose and the Yew Tree* (1948). *Crooked House* (1949). *The Mousetrap and Other Stories* (1949; in U.S. as *Three Blind Mice and Other Stories*, 1950; title story produced as *The Mousetrap*, 1952, published 1956; as radio play, 1952). *A Murder Is Announced* (1950). *They Came to Baghdad* (1951). *The Under Dog and Other Stories* (1951). *They Do It with Mirrors* (1952; in U.S. as *Murder with Mirrors*). *Blood Will Tell* (1951; in U.S. as *Mrs. McGinty's Dead*, 1952). (as Mary Westmacott) *A Daughter's a Daughter* (1952). *After the Funeral* (1953; in U.S. as *Funerals Are Fatal*; also as *Murder at the Gallop*). *A Pocket Full of Rye* (1953; in U.S., 1954). *The Spider's Web* (produced 1954, published 1957). *Destination Unknown* (1954; in U.S. as *So Many Steps to Death*, 1955). *Hickory, Dickory, Dock* (1955; in U.S. as *Hickory, Dickory, Death*). *Dead Man's Folly* (1956). (as Mary Westmacott) *The Burden* (1956). (with G. Verner) *Towards Zero* (produced 1956, published 1957). *4:50 from Paddington* (1957; in U.S. as *What Mrs. McGillicuddy Saw!*, 1961). *Ordeal by Innocence* (1958). *Verdict* (produced and published 1958). *The Unexpected Guest* (produced and published 1958). *Cat Among the Pigeons* (1959). *The Adventures of the Christmas Pudding, and Selection of Entrées* (1960). *Personal Call* (radio play, 1960). *Double Sin and Other Stories* (1961). *13 for Luck: A Selection of Mystery Stories for Young Readers* (1961; in U.S. as *13 for Luck: A Selection of Mystery Stories*, 1966). *The Pale Horse* (1961; in U.S., 1962). *The Mirror Crack'd from Side to Side* (1962; in U.S. as *The Mirror Crack'd*, 1963). *Rule of Three: Afternoon at the Seaside, The Patient, The Rats* (produced 1962, published 1963). *The Clocks* (1963; in U.S., 1964). *A Caribbean Mystery* (1964; in U.S., 1965). (as A.C. Mallowan) *Star over Bethlehem and Other Stories* (1965). *At Bertram's Hotel* (1965). *Surprize! Surprize!* [sic] *A Collection of Mystery Stories* (1965). *13 Clues for Miss Marple: A Collection of Mystery Stories* (1965). *Third Girl* (1966; in U.S., 1967). *Endless Night* (1967; in U.S., 1968). *By the Pricking of My Thumbs* (1968). *Hallowe'en Party* (1969). *Passenger to Frankfurt* (1970). *Nemesis* (1971). *The Golden Ball and Other Stories* (1971). *Fiddlers Three* (produced 1971). *Elephants Can Remember* (1972). *Akhnaton* (1973). *Postern of Fate* (1973). *Hercule Poirot's Early Cases* (1974). *Curtain: Hercule Poirot's Last Case* (1975). *Sleeping Murder* (1976).

BIBLIOGRAPHY: Bargainner, E.F. *The Gentle Art of Murder: The Detective Fiction of Agatha Christie* (1981). Barnard, R.A. *A Talent to Deceive: An Appreciation of Agatha Christie* (1980). Fitzgibbon, R.H. *An Agatha Christie Companion* (1980). Keating, H.R.F., ed. *Christie: First Lady of Crime* (1977). Maida, P.D. and N.B. Spornick. *Murder She Wrote: A Study of Agatha Christie's Detective Fiction* (1982). Morgan, J. *Agatha Christie: A Biography* (1985). Morselt, B. *An A to Z of the Novels and Short Stories of Agatha Christie* (1986). Osborne, C. *The Life and Crimes of Agatha Christie* (1983). Ramsey, G.C. *Mistress of Mystery* (1946). Riley, D., and P. McAllister, ed. *The Bedside, Bathtub & Armchair Companion to Agatha Christie* (1979); rev. 1987. Robyns, G. *The Mystery of Christie* (1978). Sanders, D., and L. Lovallo. *The Agatha Christie Companion: The Complete Guide to Agatha Christie's Life and Work* (1984). Wynne, N.B. *An Agatha Christie Chronology* (1980).

For articles in reference works, see: *CA. CLC. DLB. Longman. TCA* and *SUP. TCC&MW. TCRGW. TCW.*

Other references: Ashley, L.R.N. *Literary Onomastic Studies* (1984). Culhane, J. *Reader's Digest* (October 1985). Fryxell, D.A. *Horizon* (November 1984). James, P.D. *TV Guide* (16 May 1981). James, P.D. *The Writer* (February 1984).

Leonard R.N. Ashley

Caryl Churchill

BORN: 3 September 1938, London.
DAUGHTER OF: Robert Churchill and his wife (name not available).
MARRIED: David Harter, 1961.

C. is a playwright, among the best now writing, who addresses social and political questions with audacity and wit. The talents of her political cartoonist father and her model-actress-secretary mother are extended in the style and substance of her plays. Born in London, she moved with her family to Canada in 1948 where she attended the Trafalgar School, Montreal. Returning to England in 1956 as a young adult gave her a shocked outsider's view of the class system despite her distant relationship to one of that system's staunchest defenders, Sir Winston Churchill. At Lady Margaret Hall, Oxford, she began to write plays. *Downstairs* and *Having a Wonderful Time* were produced there before she received her B.A. in English in 1960 and the Richard Hillary Memorial Prize in 1961.

After her marriage in 1961, she stayed at home raising three sons and writing more than a dozen plays for radio and television. Feeling isolated at home politicized her so that, although she dislikes labels, she now counts herself as a socialist and a feminist. In theme, her plays connect personal and political oppression, often expressed in conflicts about sexuality, mothering, and violence. In form, they are often Brechtian, using popular devices like song in a dance of ideas that emphasizes social rather than psychological conflicts.

In 1972, Michael Codron commissioned C. to write a play for the Royal Court, the theatre that nurtured John Osborne, David Storey, and David Hare. C.'s play was *Owners*, on property values in mates, rowhouses, butcher's meat, infants, and senile mums. Edith Oliver found its American production promising, but, seconding C.'s own estimate of the influence of her father's cartoons, said that the characters talk like the captions in *Punch* cartoons or horror comics. The style reflects Joe Orton's savage mockery of cozy family life as a patriarchal butcher plans to murder his ambitious wife.

As resident dramatist at the Royal Court (1974-75), C. wrote a science fiction play, now called *Moving Clocks Go Slow*, and *Objections to Sex and Violence*. *Objections*, staged in 1975, puts a middle-class divorcee into a caretaker's job and involves her with terrorists, flashers, and pornography. In *Traps*, the next play she wrote, C. began to experiment with time and illusion. Four men, two women, and an infant explore the possibilities of change in a commune which is like a Möbius strip or an impossible Escher drawing. Their changing relationships form flexible traps like the traps that prevent the audience knowing whether the commune is in the city or the country, whether Syl has a child she doesn't want or wants a child she doesn't have. With one small hope for Utopia, the play ends as the characters bathe serially in an old wash tub, the most violent one bathing last, and smiling, in the deepest, dirtiest water of all. Although it was written early in 1976, *Traps* was first produced at the Royal Court Theatre Upstairs in January 1977.

Through *Traps*, C. had worked alone on plays about contemporary life. She then began to work with fringe theatre workshops, a method that she found exhilarating, exhausting, and fruitful. With Monstrous Regiment, a feminist touring company, she wrote *Vinegar Tom* (1976), a play about witches with no witches in it. The play shows that the witchhunts of the seventeenth century used nonconforming women (old, poor, single, or skilled as healers) as scapegoats in a time of social unrest. Having finished a rough draft of *Vinegar Tom*, C. began work with the Joint Stock Theatre Group and its director, Max Stafford-Clark, on *Light Shining in Buckinghamshire* (1976). Ideas derived from improvisations enriched a play about the attempt of Diggers, Levellers, and Ranters to build a New Jerusalem in England's green and pleasant land in the 1640s. Both plays use a historical perspective to show that change can occur, both set groups of people in a political context, both are ensemble pieces without star roles, and both use short, self-contained scenes, interrupted by songs, to raise questions.

Floorshow (1977) was also worked out with Monstrous Regiment and with co-authors, David Bradford, Bryony Lavery, and Michelene Wandor as sketches and lyrics for a cabaret about women and work. Ac C.'s career took off, some of her earlier radio plays were done as lunchtime plays in fringe theatre. She wrote a television play called the *Legion Hall Bombing* (1978) on the trial without jury of Willie Gallagher in Northern Ireland but withdrew her name when the BBC censored it.

In a workshop on sexual politics with Joint Stock, C. developed *Cloud Nine* (1979), a satirical farce set in an African colony in 1880 and in a London park about 1980. Through music hall devices and cross-sex casting, she connects colonial, sexual, and class oppression. In the first act, Clive, the Victorian patriarch, insists that his family and his Africans must live out his ideas. A male actor plays his wife, Betty, in an exaggerated stereotype of feminine compliance. Because he has assumed white values, a white actor plays African Joshua, for whom the walls of Empire finally come tumbling down. In exuberant farcical action, a white hunter tempts wife, son, and servant, but when he tempts Clive himself, he is forced to marry the lesbian governess.

In the second act of C.'s best-known play, the members of Clive's family are only 25 years older and they are no longer his. With new working-class characters, they meet in the public space of a London park and try out new arrangements in a quieter, tenderer questioning of class, gender, and homophobic oppression. *Cloud Nine* opened at the Royal Court in 1979, and the 1981 New York production, which ran for two years, won three Obie awards.

Three More Sleepless Nights (1980), about two couples trying to change by changing partners, followed *Cloud Nine* but did not achieve its critical acclaim. Then *Top Girls* (1982) led Benedict Nightingale to rank C. as one of the half-dozen best contemporary dramatists. Its brilliant opening brings achieving women from the past millennium to a dinner celebrating Marlene's latest promotion. Of the top girls, only Dull Gret, from a Brueghel painting, has challenged the patriarchal hierarchy. Pope Joan, Lady Nijo, and the others, like Marlene, have sacrificed sexuality, maternity, and self-assertion in order to succeed in a man's world. In more naturalistic scenes in Marlene's employment agency and in her sister's working-class home, we see that nothing has changed at the bottom, although there are some places for women at the top.

Remembering *Top Girls*, several critics referred to C.'s next play as "Bottom Girls." *Fen* (1983) peoples a bleak East Anglia landscape with figures, five women and one man, in twenty-two roles on the potato farms. Designer Annie Smart filled the stage with furrowed earth and built the walls of a room around it so that one set serves for each brief scene. Fog steams from the fen to obscure distinctions between past and present, illusion and reality. If there is a heroine it is Val, torn between lover and children, unable, like the others, to give up and live. C. won the Susan Smith Blackburn prize for *Fen* in 1984.

In 1984, C. wrote a cabaret on crime and punishment called *Softcops*. A man of reason in nineteenth century France tries to control crime with educational placards that explain how each punishment fits its crime. Vidocq, a robber who became a policeman as the chief of police, plays against Lacenaire, a glamorous criminal whose publicity distracts attention from genuine threats to authority. Its provocative structure and the

music of a string quartet pleased some critics but most found the play too highbrow, too dependent on its inspiration in *Discipline and Punish* by French philosopher Michel Foucault.

C. is an intellectual playwright, putting new ideas into new theatrical forms based on popular entertainment. Her most recent effort was *Midday Sun* (1984), a script for a dance group at the Institute of Contemporary Arts. Four British tourists fantasize, experience, and then remember a holiday on a Moroccan beach and an encounter with an Arab beggar. In plays marked by beauty, anger, and generous humor, she continues to seek change and to challenge authority and centralized control.

WORKS: *Downstairs* (1958). *Having a Wonderful Time* (1960). *Easy Death* (1961). *Schreber's Nervous Illness* (1972). *Owners* (1972). *Moving Clocks Go Slow* (1975). *Objections to Sex and Violence* (1975). *Light Shining in Buckinghamshire* (1976). *Vinegar Tom* (1976). *Floorshow* (with others, 1977). *Traps* (1977). *Cloud Nine* (1979). *Three More Sleepless Nights* (1980). *Top Girls* (1982). *Fen* (1983). *Softcops* (1983). *Midday Sun* (1984). *Serious Money* (1987).

BIBLIOGRAPHY: Diamond, E. *Theatre Journal* (October 1985). Itzin, C. *Stages in the Revolution: Political Theatre in Britain Since 1968* (1981). Keyssar, H. *Feminist Theatre*, (1984). Wandor, M. *Carry On, Understudies* (1986). Wandor, M. *Look Back in Gender: Sexuality and the Family in Post-War British Drama* (1987). Wandor, M. *Understudies*, 1981.

For articles in reference works, see: *CA. CD. CLC. DLB.*

Other References: *Vogue*, (August 1983). *NYT* (9 January 1983) (25 February 1984).

Mary R. Davidson

Sarah Jennings Churchill, Duchess of Marlborough

BORN: 29 May 1660, Holywell, near St. Albans.
DIED: 18 October 1744, London.
DAUGHTER OF: Richard Jennings [Jenyns] and Frances Thornhurst.
MARRIED: John Churchill, first Duke of Marlborough, 1678.
WROTE UNDER: Sarah, Duchess of Marlborough.

The last of nine children, C. became one of the most celebrated and notorious women of her time because of her court activities, her marriage, and her published explanation of her relationship with the queen.

C.'s association with Queen Anne began when both were children. James' daughter by

Anne Hyde, Princess Anne was six when she met the ten-year-old C. The future queen's admiration for C. began early, and it was, and continues to be, the subject of much speculation. Fueled by C.'s own statements, the girls' relationship even evoked an explanation from Winston Churchill, who wrote: "Very early . . . in these young lives did those ties of love, kindling into passion on one side and into affection on the other, grow deep and strong. . . . There was a romantic, indeed perfervid element in Anne's love for Sarah to which the elder girl responded warmly several years before she realised the worldly importance of such a relationship." Accused in later years of controlling and manipulating the queen for her own ends, C. wrote in her old age that the queen had "a person and appearance very graceful and something of majesty in her look. She was religious without affectation and certainly meant to do everything that was just" (*Blenheim Papers*). C. blames others, not the queen, for C.'s fall from favor.

That C. was influential with the young princess is clear from her history with the court. C. and her sister were placed in court as maids-of-honor to three future queens: the fifteen-year-old Duchess of York, Mary of Modena; her step-daughter the eight-year-old Anne; and Anne's eleven-year-old sister Mary who would later marry William and become Queen Mary II. Evidence of C.'s close relationship with the princess and the duchess appears early. In 1676, when but sixteen, C. persuaded the duchess to expel Mrs. Jennings, C.'s mother, from the court. Two years later, again with the duchess' help, C. secretly married John Churchill. One year later, C. bore the first of her eight children, only five of whom survived their infancy. During those years from 1679 to 1690, C. sustained a close and confidential relationship with Princess Anne, even using names of commoners so that their relationship would not be distanced by royal custom. To address one another as equals, C. became Mrs. Freeman and Princess Anne, Mrs. Morley. By 1685 C. became the First Lady of the Bedchamber and was at the height of her influence with the princess. C.'s husband's lot also continued to improve. From 1667, when he was commissioned ensign in the footguards to 1688 when he became an earl, John Churchill prospered and enjoyed court favor, too.

In 1702 C.'s influence reached its highest point only to plummet in 1703. C.'s fall from favor came about in part as the result of the activities of Abigail Hill, C.'s cousin, an insignificant member of the court and a poor relation. Nonetheless, Abigail won, ousting C. and leaving C. to her second and enduring career—as writer and apologist. From 1722, after the death of John Churchill on June 16, to the end of her life, C. spent her time in quarrels. She was pugnacious, clever, and, depending upon the occasion, shrewd or wrongheaded. She completed the construction of Blenheim Palace, despite a long and bitter quarrel with its architect, Vanbrugh. She argued with two of her daughters: Henrietta, who was married to the Earl of Godolphin, and Mary, Duchess of Montegu. Among others, she quarreled with Lady Mary Wortley Montagu and Sir Robert Walpole.

In 1742, two years before she died, C. published her memoirs with the help of Nathaniel Hooke, who received £500 for his efforts. Even that task presented problems. When Hooke arrived at Blenheim, C. "caused herself to be lifted up, and continued speaking for six hours. Without the aid of notes she delivered her narrative in a lively and connected manner. Hooke resided in the house until the completion of the work. . . .

During his residence with her she commissioned him to negotiate with [Alexander] Pope for the suppression, in consideration of the payment of three-thousand pounds, of the character of 'Atossa' in his 'Epistles.' . . . the duchess took a sudden dislike to Hooke because, finding her without religion, he attempted to convert her to popery" (Thompson Cooper, "Hooke," *DNB*). That, too, provoked a reply. This time, Henry Fielding defended her.

When she died, C. left a fortune to her heirs, but she also left £20,000 to Lord Chesterfield, £10,000 to William Pitt, and £500 each to two men to write the history of the Duke of Marlborough. Her own explanation of her life and her actions remains for posterity to read and debate. For some, like Sir Leslie Stephen, C. is "not an amiable woman." She is, instead, "spiteful and untrustworthy." Grudgingly, however, he notes that her writing is "frequently vigorous and shrewd" (*DNB*). Concerned about her name and her husband's reputation for future ages, C. wrote and generated even more words from others who attacked her. Among the many were Mary Manley and James Ralph who with wit and venom sought to discredit C. Years later, C. admitted, "Writting of books is looked upon as an Imployment not fit for our Sex: and if some have succeeded well in it, others have exposed themselves by it too much to Encourage a woman to venture on being an Authour: but it will appear more unusual for me to write so copiously, as I fear I may be forced to do, to tell my own Story, especially when it will seem to carry reflexions where one owes respect" (*Blenheim Papers*). In that spirit, C. spent her last years writing to vindicate her name, justify her relationship to the queen, and celebrate her husband's ventures.

Only one work was published in her lifetime; the rest have survived either in others' editions of her works or in the *Blenheim Papers*. To read her words and to read of her impact on others is to learn of an amazing woman who dominated an age.

WORKS: *An Account of the Conduct of the Dowager Duchess of Marlborough, From her first coming to Court, To the Year 1710. In a Letter from Herself to My Lord* (1742). *Authentick memoirs of the life and conduct of Her Grace, Sarah, late dutchess of Marlborough, containing a genuine narrative of Her Grace's conduct, from her first coming to court, to the death of Hr Royal Mistress Queen Anne, and from the demise of the Queen to Her Grace's death. Likewise all Her Grace's letters to the Queen and Her Majesty's answers. To which is prefix'd, the last will and testament of Her Grace, from a true copy of the original, lodg'd in Doctors commons* (1744). *The glorious memory of Queen Anne reviv'd: Exem-*

plify'd in the conduct of her chief favourite the Duchess Dowager of Marlborough, from her first coming to court, to the year 1710. In a letter from herself to my Lord—[Nathaniel Hooke] (1742). *Letters of Sarah, Duchess of Marlborough. Now first Published from the Original Manuscripts at Madresfield Court* (1875). *Private correspondence of Sarah, duchess of Marlborough, illustrative of the court and times of Queen Anne; with her sketches and opinions of her contemporaries, and the select correspondence of her husband, John, duke of Marlborough* (1838). *Some years of the life of the Duke and Duchess of Marlborough, from the first coming of the Duchess of to Court, to the year 1710. Written by herself* (1817). *Letters* (1893).

BIBLIOGRAPHY: Butler, I. *Rule of Three: Sarah, Duchess of Marlborough, and Her Companions in Power* (1967). Campbell, K. *Sarah Duchess of Marlborough* (1932). Cecil, D. *Two Quiet Lives* (1948). Chancellor, F. *Sarah Churchill* (1932). Churchill, W. *Marlborough, His Life and Times* (2 vols., 1947). Dalrymple, D. later Lord Hailes, ed. *The Opinions of Sarah, Duchess-Dowager of Marlborough* (1788). Dobree, B. *Sarah Churchill in Three Eighteenth-Century Figures* (1962). Fielding, H. *A Full Vindication of the Dowager Duchess of Marlborough* (1742). Green, D. *Sarah, Duchess of Marlborough* (1967). King, W., ed., *Memoirs of Sarah, Duchess of Marlborough, Together with Her Characters and Her Contemporaries and Her Opinions* (1930). Kronenberger, L. *Marlborough's Duchess* (1958). Reid, S. *John and Sarah, Duke and Duchess of Marlborough* (1914). Rowse, A.L. *The Early Churchills* (1956). Rowse, A.L. *The Later Churchills* (1958). Thomson, G., ed. *Letters of a Grandmother, 1732-1735; Being the Correspondence of Sarah, Duchess of Marlborough with Her Granddaughter Diana, Duchess of Bedford* (1943).

For articles in reference works, see: Abbot, W.J. *Notable Women in History* (1913). CHEL. DNB. Dorland, W. *The Sum of Feminine Achievement* (1917). *Fifty Famous Women.* Hammerton, J.A. *Concise Universal Biography.* Schmidt, M.M. *400 Outstanding Women of the World, The Authors* (1933). OCEL. Sitwell, E. *English Women* (1932).

Sophia B. Blaydes

Lady Anne Clifford

BORN: 30 January 1590, Skipton Castle, Yorkshire.
DIED: 22 March 1676, Brougham Castle, Westmorland.
DAUGHTER OF: George, third earl of Cumberland, and Lady Margaret Russell.
MARRIED: Richard Sackville, Lord Buckhurst and later third earl of Dorset, 1609; Philip Herbert, fourth earl of Pembroke and Montgomery, 1630.

Only three diaries survive that were kept by women who lived during the reign of Queen Elizabeth I. Of these, C.'s diary is the most interesting historically. Those by Margaret Hoby and Grace Mildmay concentrate on the routine of daily life and on religious faith; C. includes accounts of events such as Queen Elizabeth's death and funeral and talks with Queen Anne and John Donne as well as information about the history of her family. Her diary continues to hold our interest both because she led a remarkable life and because she wrote well, recording telling details. When she writes of her first presentation of King James I, for example, she comments that the fashion at court had certainly changed from Queen Elizabeth's time, for everyone in her party came away bitten by lice.

Her life had three stages. As a child, she was dutiful; as a wife, she was unhappy; as a widow, she came into her own. Her parents' marriage was troubled, and C.'s sympathies were with her mother, whom she adored. From her mother, she inherited a love of literature. C.'s reading ranged from works on religion to Ovid, Chaucer, and Jonson. Lady Margaret Russell was one of Spenser's patrons and employed Samuel Daniel as her daughter's tutor; C., in turn, erected monuments to both of these poets and befriended Donne and George Herbert. From her father, C. inherited troublesome lawsuits, for he willed the family lands to his brother rather than his child, and C. spent years suing to regain her estates.

When she married, C. probably hoped that her husband would help her in these suits, but instead Dorset tried to force her to stop the case because he thought settling it would provide him with ready money and please the king. After Dorset's death, C. re-wed. Like Dorset, Pembroke was unfaithful and a spendthrift; unlike him, he sympathized with his wife's claims. Finally in 1643, she received the property, and six years later she left her husband in London to go to her estates. Soon after she arrived, word came that Pembroke was dead.

The long lawsuit, with its frustration and unhappiness, probably led C. to begin writing. From 1605 until 1643, her time and energy had been engaged in lawsuits, and she wished to leave a careful account of what had happened for her two daughters. This desire, her interest in her family's history, and her pleasure in recording her daily activities led to a number of manuscripts: one in third-person and another in first-person that tell of her life, and others that summarize her family history. (The first-person autobiographical manuscript is referred to as C.'s diary.)

After the death of her second husband, C. spent the rest of her life as the industrious chatelaine of her property. She not only ran her large estates but also built or restored six castles, two almshouses, and seven churches and a chapel. As the *DNB* remarks, "Her passion for bricks and mortar was immense." For nearly thirty years she built, administered, wrote, and pleased herself. Mildly eccentric (she pinned scraps of paper with *sententiae* all around her rooms) and extraordinarily generous, C. was a remarkable woman. Her

diary offers a lively account of the life that the well-to-do led in the seventeenth century.

WORKS: *The Diary of Lady Anne Clifford*, ed. V. Sackville-West (1923). *Lives of Lady Anne Clifford and her Parents*, ed. J.P. Gilson (1916). *Letters of the Sixteenth Century*, ed. A.G. Dickens (1962).

BIBLIOGRAPHY: Costello, L.S. *Memoirs of Eminent Englishwomen*, II (1844). Notestein, W. *Four Worthies* (1957). Sackville-West, V. *Knole and the Sackvilles* (1923). Walpole, H. *The World*, (5 April 1753), *Lady Anne Clifford* (1922). Wilson, V. *Society Women of Shakespeare's Time* (1924).

For articles in reference works, see: *DNB*. Palmer, A. and V. *Who's Who in Shakespeare's England* (1981).

Frances Teague

Lucy Lane Clifford

BORN: 1855? Barbados, West Indies.
DIED: 21 April 1929, London.
DAUGHTER OF: John Lane, a well-known West Indian planter.
MARRIED: William Kingdon Clifford, 1875.

Novelist, dramatist, and children's author, C. was born in Barbados. As an art student in London she met and in 1875 married W.K. Clifford, professor of mathematics and "delicious *enfant terrible*," as William James called him, on the literary and scientific scene. Through her husband, C. became part of a circle which included Leslie Stephen, James Russell Lowell, and Henry and William James. She was one of the few women invited to George Eliot's Sunday afternoon parties at the Priory. When in 1879 C. was left a widow with two small daughters (one of whom, Ethel, later Lady Dilke, became a poet), Eliot helped C. to get a small Civil List pension and gave her the introductions that enabled her to augment it by writing articles for *The Standard*.

W.K. Clifford, who before his death at thirty-four had made several contributions to mathematics, had also developed two philosophical concepts to which he gave the terms "mind-stuff" and the "tribal self" and which can be seen as themes in C.'s novels. The first asserts that the mind is the only reality but defines mind as the elements—much like the atomic particles of physical matter—which form the mind, rather than the complex, conscious mind of common definition. The second, "the tribal self," posits a morality developed by the individual regulating his conduct to assure the "welfare of the tribe." These theories were explored fictionally in C.'s novels and tales.

Anyhow Stories (1882) was her first book and was so successful that an enlarged edition appeared in 1899. The literary fairy tale directed to an audience of all ages was popular in the latter part of the nineteenth century and provided a good vehicle for the exploration of "mind-stuff" and the "tribal self." A tale that has attracted recent critical notice, "Wooden Tony," is a plaintive exemplar of "mind-stuff," but also, Alison Lurie suggests, owes something to voodoo.

In the realm of fiction, *Mrs. Keith's Crime* (1885) explores the "tribal self" of a woman with an incurable, suffering child who decides that euthanasia is the solution. A sensational novel to reviewers and the public, it was much admired by Robert Browning and Thomas Hardy. *Aunt Anne* (1893), considered by some to be her best novel, recounted the process of the title character in establishing herself as the dominant power in a family—the tribe. Henry James, her friend from 1880 to his death in 1916, teasingly called her "Aunt Lucy" in reference to this work and her assertive if warm and friendly personality. They were perhaps closest when undergoing simultaneously the throes of seeing their plays staged. Of her writing, James wrote ". . . you don't *squeeze* your material hard and tight enough . . . this is the fault of all fictive writing now." (*Letters* vol. 4, 617).

WORKS: Of several children's books written in the 1880s, the most notable is *Anyhow Stories* (1882), enlarged ed. (1899). *The Dingy House at Kensington* (1882). *Mrs. Keith's Crime* (1885, new revised ed. 1925). *Love Letters of a Worldly Woman* (1891). *A Woman Alone* (1891, produced as a play 1914).

The Last Touches and Other Stories (1892). *Aunt Anne* (1893). *A Wild Proxy* (1894). *A Flash of Summer; the Story of a Simple Woman's Life* (1895). *The Dominant Note, and Other Stories* (1897). *A Long Duel; A Serious Comedy in Four Acts* (1901). *The Likeness of the Night; a Modern Play in Four Acts* based on "The Last Touches" (1901). *Woodside Farm* (1902; also published as *Margaret Vincent*). *A Honeymoon Tragedy; a Comedy in One Act* (1904). *The Getting Well of Dorothy* (1904). *The Modern Way* (1906). Mrs. Hamilton's Second Marriage; Thomas and the Princess; The Modern Way (1909). *Sir George's Objection* (1910). *The Searchlight; A Play* (1913). *Two Company; A Play* (1915). *The House in Marylebone* (1917). *Miss Fingal* (1919). *Eve's Lover* (1927).

BIBLIOGRAPHY: *American Imago: A Psychoanalytic Journal for Culture, Science, and the Arts* (1978). *Bookman* (1920). *NYRB* (11 December 1975). *TCA*.

Eleanor Langstaff

Elizabeth Knevet Clinton

BORN: 1574(?), Charlton, Wiltshire (presumably).
DIED: 1630(?), Great Grimsby, Lincolnshire (presumably).
DAUGHTER OF: Sir Henry Knevet and Anne Pickering Knevet.
MARRIED: Thomas Clinton [later] eleventh Baron Clinton and third earl of Lincoln, 1584.

Married very young, C. was a dutiful, aristocratic wife who, by her own account, bore her husband eighteen children. After his death in 1618, when she became countess-dowager, she apparently concentrated her maternal attentions on the grandchildren born to her daughter-in-law, Brigit, and her son, Theophilus, who succeeded his father as earl in 1619.

As a token of her esteem for Brigit, the countess-dowager dedicated her 1622 tract on breast-feeding, *The Countesse of Lincolnes Nurserie*, to her daughter-in-law, who, unlike many noblewomen including the countess-dowager, breast-fed her children. Clinton publicly bewailed her own negligence in this matter, contending that putting a child out to nurse is a careless practice that often leads to physical neglect of the child as well as to harmful influences on it. In contrast, she writes, nursing by the child's natural mother is an important religious and maternal duty and privilege, prescribed by Holy Writ and incumbent on every mother who is physically able to suckle. "Think alwaies," the countess-dowager enjoins, "that having the child at your breast, and having it in your armes, you have *Gods blessing* there. For children are Gods blessings. Thinke again how your babe crying for your breast, sucking hartily the milke out of it, and growing by it, is the *Lords owne instruction*, every houre, and every day, that you are suckling it, instructing you to shew that you are his new borne *Babes* by your earnest desire after his word, & the syncere doctrine thereof, and by your daily growing in grace and goodnesse therby, so shall you reape pleasure and profit."

Such thoughts echo the books aimed at Renaissance Englishwomen by both humanist and Protestant religious reformers. Although the countess-dowager styles her book, "the first work of mine that ever came in print," no other works by her survive.

WORKS: *The Countesse of Lincolnes Nurserie*. (1622).

BIBLIOGRAPHY: Ballard, G. *Memoirs of Several Ladies of Great Britain* . . . (1752). Hays, M. *Female Biography* . . . (1807). Mahl, M.R. and H. Koon, eds. *The Female Spectator* . . . (1977). McLaren, D. *Women in English Society 1500–1800*, ed. M. Prior. (1985). Travitsky, B. *Mothers and Daughters in Literature* . . . , ed. C.N. Davidson and E.M. Broner (1979). Travitsky, B., ed. *Paradise of Women* . . . . (1981). Williams, J. *Literary Women of England* . . . . (1861).

Betty Travitsky

Catherine ("Kitty") Clive

BORN: 1711
DIED: 1785.
DAUGHTER OF: William Rafter, a Kilkenny lawyer, and "Mrs. Daniel," an Englishwoman.
MARRIED: George Clive, 1733.

Three of C.'s four afterpiece plays and her one prose polemic consistently allude to her personality and career. A brief sketch of both are, then, in order here. Coming to Drury Lane in 1728 while still in her teens, Kitty Rafter quickly became a favorite of the town by virtue of her operatic singing voice, vivacity, and gift for mimicry. Her voice was good enough to attract the attention of Handel who gave her the part of Delilah in his oratorio *Samson*. But her main vocal triumphs were in *entr'acte* songs and such specialty numbers as the Irish ballad "Elin aroon." Admired first as a singing actress, especially gifted in ballad farces, C. in 1731 showed her talents as a comic actress in the role of Nell in Coffey's *The Devil to Pay*, one of over 200 parts she mastered, including many "Miss Kitty" roles. She was often called for as Flora in *The Wonder*, Lady Bab in *High Life Below Stairs*, Lappet in *The Miser*, Catherine in *Catherine and Petruchio*, Mrs. Heidelberg in *The Clandestine Marriage*, and the Fine Lady in *Lethe*. Polly in *The Beggar's Opera* was also a favorite.

A star in an age of stage stars, C. was popular as comedienne and performer of prologues and epilogues, indicated by the frequency of her performances and long tenure at Drury Lane—she retired on 24 April 1769—and documented by the praise of Fielding (see the preface to his farce *The Intriguing Chambermaid*), Murphy, Churchill, Garrick, Johnson, Goldsmith, Horace Walpole (who gave her his cottage on Strawberry Hill), fellow players, contemporary memoir writers, and audiences who admired—and defended—her. Henry Fielding and, later, James Miller wrote parts for her in their plays. The Prince and Princess of Wales were her patrons.

Johnson gives a balanced, just appraisal of C. the actress in Boswell's *Life of Johnson*: "What Clive did best she did better than Garrick; but could not do half so many things well; she was a better romp than any I ever saw in nature." The half she could not do well was tragedy roles, even though she insisted on playing Zara in *The Mourning Bride* and Ophelia in *Hamlet*. Her often-given burlesque of the role of Portia in *The Merchant of Venice* was never well received by audiences or critics, but the stubborn C. insisted on giving this rendering of Portia for many years. The half she could do well, according to her theater contemporary Thomas Davies, included chambermaid roles and roles of "country girls, romps, hoydens and dowdies, superannuated beauties, viragos, and humourists." She brilliantly satirized opera singers, burlettos, and excessiveness of several sorts. As Davies puts it, "Her mirth was so genuine that whether it was restrained to the arch sneer, the suppressed half-laugh, or extended to the downright honest burst of loud laughter, the audience was sure to accompany her."

Negligible as dramatic literature, C.'s farce afterpieces, written between 1750 and 1765, are, with the exception of the 1760 *Every Woman in Her Humour*, written in terms of her public personality and career. Indeed, topical and personal allusions largely constitute the plays' subject matter. Most performances were in March, for her own "benefit," with C. playing the lead woman's part in all productions. Her first play, written and first performed in 1750 but not printed until 1753, the two-act *Rehearsal; or, Bayes in Petticoats*, is in the "rehearsal" tradition begun by Buckingham's *Rehearsal* (1671). C.'s play, however, only borrows that earlier play's form, not its content. Her main satiric targets are would-be women dramatists (herself) and Italian opera singers (then in the mode), the latter called by her "squalling devils" and "a parcel of Italian bitches." In the play, Mrs. Hazard, who is the Bayes in Petticoats played by C. herself, has written a burletto, which of course never comes off.

The piece is a noteworthy showcase of C.'s public personality, including such pet peeves as playing conditions in the theater, her ill-treatment by Garrick, her penchant for a choice benefit night in March, and would-be women and men of fashion, to name a few. Her primary method of ridicule was to burlesque speech and demeanor, C. being one of the greatest mimics of the century. *The Rehearsal* shows how closely C. identified with Drury Lane theater, its denizens, its exigencies. Stories of her battles with Susanna Maria Anne Cibber, the actors Woodward and Shuter, and especially Peg Woffington have passed into the anecdotal record of the age's theatrical scuffles. Her satire either poked fun at her own habits and limitations in a straightforward way or presented herself opposite to what she really was, thereby making the context ironic. While most of C.'s ripostes are merely good fun and tonally light, she does clearly expose such poseurs as the play's Miss Giggle who enters to disrupt the rehearsal. C. is everywhere serious in her barbs aimed at those who do not take the theater seriously.

In the 1730s and 1740s, C. strenuously defended the acting profession and her own part in it. Although neglected today as such, C. is a significant eighteenth-century feminist, most properly viewed in the company of Aphra Behn and Susanna Centlivre. She was ever vigilant of women's artistic rights and freedom. The best indication of this and her thoroughgoing professionalism is her *The Case of Mrs. Clive Submitted to the Publick*, published in October 1744, by which time C. had established herself not only as first lady of comedy but also as a patriot of the acting profession and the Drury Lane company. In the 1733 theater dispute, C. and Charles Macklin, among the principal players, stayed with John Highmore, the unpopular, ineffective proprietor of Drury Lane, rather than join the players' revolt to the New Haymarket theater. She saw defection as disloyalty to her audiences, who were always her concern in matters of professional consequence.

But when Garrick and his Drury Lane colleagues felt their freedom and rights monumentally infringed in 1743, C. joined them. She published her *Case . . . Submitted to the Publick* to explain the unjust, oppressive situation in the two major London theaters, Drury Lane and Covent Garden, and her personal mistreatment by their managers, Fleetwood and Rich. Their cartel had the actors at its mercy in terms of hiring and salary, both abused against "custom," she charged.

C. was forced to seek a place in the Covent Garden company in the 1743–1745 seasons, her only substantial time away from Drury Lane in her 40-year career, save for engagements in Ireland where she was a great favorite. C. considered her treatment at Covent Garden insulting for an actress of her stature. In the last third of her *Case*, she gives an affecting account of the personal costs of the Stage Licensing Act of 1737, which allowed the monopoly of Drury Lane and Covent Garden as the only two licensed theaters in London. November of the 1745–1746 season, however, finds her back at Drury Lane where she will have remaining to her more than 20 years of triumphs, mostly under the management of her friend, colleague, and sometime antagonist, David Garrick.

C.'s second and most literarily ambitious play, the two-act *Every Woman in Her Humour* (1760), focuses on the ridiculousness of affectation. A "humours" play, *Every Woman* has C., who plays the role of Mrs. Croston, speak through her character only once, the opposite of her method in *The Rehearsal*. The comeuppance of the lying Sir Charles Freelove is the major plot, but central interest in the farce is centered on the low or humorous shenanigans of its women characters. A well-structured farce with some precise character writing, *Every Woman* had only one performance. While it has some correspondences to a mainpiece comedy, it was a failure on stage. Perhaps audiences wanted from C.'s pen a more self-regarding work, and this play is her least autobiographical. Too, C. had no talent for repartee or even the memorable phrase. There was little chance, then, that the piece would survive. Her earlier *Rehearsal*, by "literary" standards a lesser play, had 14 mountings over a 12-year period, surely because audiences wanted C.'s self-satire.

C.'s final plays, both farce afterpieces, are *The Sketch of a Fine Lady's Return from a Rout* (1763), whose title tells all, and *The Faithful Irish Woman* (1765), an enlarged and re-worked version of *The Sketch*. C. returns to the self-regarding technique of *The Rehearsal; or, Bayes in Petticoats*. She plays the lead in both plays: *The Sketch* spoofs would-be fine ladies who love cards (as C. did) and "assemblies"; the final play, written only a few years before her retirement from the stage, allows C. to show her Irish patriotism as well as other facets of her celebrated public personality. Both plays are little more than *petite pièces* wherein she shows herself comically.

A very minor writer by literary standards, C. wrote revealing plays and one animated autobiographical prose piece, all directed to audiences who revered her as a supreme actress and sparkling personality, which included common sense, loyalty, and unusual decency, all of which moved Samuel Johnson to say to his biographer: "Clive, Sir, is a good thing to sit by; she always understands what you say."

WORKS: *The Case of Mrs. Clive Submitted to the Publick* (1744). *The Rehearsal; or, Bayes in Petticoats* (1750). *Every Woman in Her Humour* (1760). *The Sketch of a Fine Lady's Return from a Rout* (1763). *The Faithful Irish Woman* (1765). Two plays, *The London 'Prentice* (1754) and *The Island of Slaves* (1761) are less surely from her hand. For the plight of the woman artist in society as well as glimpses of the C. known by Garrick, Walpole, and Jane Pope, C.'s successor in comedy at Drury Lane, see her letters in Crean, Frushell, and especially *A Biographical Dictionary*, below.

BIBLIOGRAPHY:

For articles in reference works, see: Backscheider, P., F. Nussbaum, and P. Anderson, *An Annotated Bibliography of Twentieth-Century Critical Studies of Women and Literature, 1660–1800* (1977). Link, F.M. *English Drama, 1660–1800: A Guide to Information Sources* (1976).

Other references: Frushell, R.C., ed. *The Case of Mrs. Clive Submitted to the Public*, (1973). Frushell, R.C. *DUJ* (March 1971). Frushell, R.C. *N&Q* (September 1969). Frushnell, R.C. *RECTR* (May 1970). Frushell, R.C. *Theatre Survey* (November 1973). Highfill, P.H., Jr., K.A. Burnim, and E.A. Langhans, *A Biographical Dictionary of Actors, Actresses . . . in London, 1660–1800*, vol. 3 (1975).

Richard C. Frushell

Anne (Alice Andrée) Cluysenaar

BORN: 15 March 1936, Brussels.
DAUGHTER OF: John and Sybil Fitzgerald Cluysenaar.
MARRIED: Walter Freeman Jackson, 1976.

C. is an Irish poet, long resident in Britain, whose lyric verse celebrates the role of communication, in particular the ways discourse enables her to explore her family's heritage and "the boundaries of self and others." She has published verse in a variety of magazines (*Dublin, Poetry Review, Poetry Ireland, Hibernia, Stand, Poetry Nation Review*, and *Aberdeen University Review* among them) and anthologies. In addition, she has published three books of verse and two highly regarded theoretical studies.

After studying at Trinity College, Dublin (where she graduated with honors), and the University of Edinburgh (where she studied general linguistics), C. began a career teaching at the university level. She has taught at various English, Irish, and Scottish universities and in 1987 was principal lecturer in English at Sheffield City Polytechnic, Sheffield.

C. published her first book in 1967, *A Fan of Shadows*, a relatively traditional collection of lyric verse, mostly in rhyme. In addition to the individual poems, often setting up syntheses of opposing forces or states of being, C. included notes in which she explained her intent in the explorations of the human predicament that she called "radiations from an occasionally moving centre." Little variety in subject, images, or words differentiates these poems, and several are little more than hackneyed explorations of the familiar, as with the several poems focused on the sea.

But C. has grown as a poet, and though she still favors landscapes, for example, more than the effects of setting on the poet's consciousness, many of her more recent poems are distinctive. *Double Helix*, written with Sybil Hewat (1982), is her most mature work. In it she mixes poetry with such family records as photographs, memoirs, drawings, and correspondence as a means of recording individual and family experience. She has stated that in this book she wants the focus to be on "communication rather than the language drawing attention to itself for its own sake," and to an extent she has succeeded. Her intent is, as she states, "to relate poetry very closely to life." Consequently, she moves easily from her family to forms of universal evil, politics, government policies, and the horrors of annihilation.

C.'s accomplishments in *Double Helix* relates directly to her formal interest in language. She teaches creative writing and linguistics because she finds aspects of writing that can be learned in group discussion and exercise; the formal study of language, she says, enables a person to approach a poem "with an understanding of language capable of matching that of the writer, both through some experience of practical 'thinking with words' and through theoretical understanding of *how* language works." In 1976 C. published *Introduction to Literary Stylistics: A Discussion of Dominant Structures in Verse and Prose* (published in the United States as *Aspects of Literary Stylistics*). In 1985 she continued this analysis in *Verbal Arts: The Missing Subject*, an outgrowth of a *Critical Quarterly* essay she published in 1984.

In the past few years C. has returned to such traditional verse forms as the sonnet to encompass her commentaries on the future. A child in "Double," for example, serves C. as a means of contrasting simple diction and childish fears with complex social commentary; an infant's scream serves as the elemental parallel to the universal horrors of a possible future world. C.'s emotional range is not wide, nor is she especially well known; yet she commands a forcefulness in conception and sensitivity to language that distinguishes her verse.

WORKS: (trans.) *The Sonnets of Michelangelo* (1961, 1969). (with L. Durrell and R.S. Thomas) *Penguin Modern Poets I* (1962). *Recoveries: Poems* (1964). *Frost* (1964). *Christianity and Poetry* (1965; in the U.S. as *Christian Poetry*). *The Mind Has Mountains* (1966). *The Secret Brother and Other Poems for Children* (1966). *Collected Poems* (1967). *A Fan of Shadows* (1967). *The Animals' Arrival* (1969). *Nodes: Selected Poems, 1960-1968* (1969). *Lucidities* (1970). *Hurt* (1970). (with others) *Folio* (1970). *Relationships* (1972). *Growing-Points: New Poems* (1975). *Seven Men of Vision: An Appreciation* (1976). *Introduction to Literary Stylistics: A Discussion of Dominant Structures in Verse and Prose* (1976; in the U.S. as *Aspects of Literary Stylistics*). *Consequently I Rejoice* (1977). *After the Ark* (1978). *Moments of Grace: New Poems* (1979). *Selected Poems* (1979). *Winter Wind* (1979). *Moments of Grace* (1980). *A Dream of Spring* (1980). *Celebrations and Elegies* (1982). (with S. Hewat) *Double Helix* (1982). *Extending the Territory* (1985). *Verbal Arts: The Missing Subject* (1985). *In Shakespeare's Company* (1985). *Collected Poems, 1953-1985* (1986).

BIBLIOGRAPHY: Allott, K., ed. *Penguin Book of Contemporary Verse* (1962). Byers, M. *British Poetry Since 1960*, ed. M. Schmidt and G. Lindop (1972). Morrison, B. *The Movement: English Poetry and Fiction of the 1950's* (1980). Orr, P., ed. *The*

Poet Speaks (1966). Schmidt, M. *An Introduction to 50 Modern British Poets* (1979). Schofield, M.A. *Notes on Contemporary Literature* (1983). Stürzl, E.Z. *On Poetry and Poets, Fifth Series*, ed. J. Hogg (1983). Wheeler, M. *Hopkins Among the Poets: Studies in Modern Responses to Gerard Manley Hopkins* (1985).

For articles in reference works, see: *CA. CLC. CP. EWL. MBL* and *SUP. TCW. WA.*

Other references: *British Book News* (May 1983). *Choice* (December 1976). *TES* (24 June 1983).

Paul Schlueter

Frances Power Cobbe

BORN: 4 December 1822, Newbridge, near Dublin.
DIED: 5 April 1904, Hengwrt, near Dolgelly, Wales.
DAUGHTER OF: Charles and Frances Cobbe.

A feminist, suffragist, philanthropist, and anti-vivisectionist, a prolific writer of pamphlets, articles, essays, and books on religion, philosophy, and social problems, C. was educated by private governesses at the home of her well-to-do family except for two years in a school at Brighton. Her reading was extensive; her preferences, history, astronomy, architecture, and heraldry. Aware of the inadequacies and waste of the female mind because of discrimination in education—her own father would not permit her brother to teach her Latin at home—C. advocated equal access to formal education for women, recommending the granting of university degrees. C. never married. She was deeply interested in theology during her life, becoming a heretic, a Christian, a theist, and finally a deist. Between 1852 and 1855 she wrote her first book, *The Theory of Intuitive Morals*, which she published anonymously to avoid the disapproval of her father.

After inheriting an income of £200 per year upon her father's death in 1857, C. began the first of many periods of foreign travel to Italy, Greece, Switzerland, and even Baalbec. In 1864 she published the lively and fanciful *Italics: Brief Notes on Politics, People, and Places in Italy*. Between trips she devoted much effort to improving conditions for juvenile delinquents, the destitute, and the sick. She was actively engaged in promoting women's suffrage and helped procure passage of the Married Women's Property Act. She was also an avid anti-vivisectionist. C. earned her livelihood working as a journalist for *The Daily News, Echo*, and *Standard*, publishing in the *Spectator, Economist, Quarterly Review, Fraser's Magazine, Macmillan's Magazine*, and others.

C. had personal contact with most of the major English figures of her day, such as Matthew Arnold, Robert Browning, John Stuart Mill, and Alfred Lord Tennyson (letters included in her autobiography); and several of her voluminous religious writings appeared in response to articles or statements by such writers. *The Hopes of the Human Race* (1874) was an optimistic reply to Mill's "Essay on Religion." Her article "A Faithless World" (in *Nineteenth Century*), was written to counteract a remark by Sir Fitzjames Stephen that "we get on very well without religion" (she concluded that the absence of religion would change everything). C.'s *Darwinism in Morals and Other Essays* (1872), in its primary essay on Darwin, which reviews Darwin's *Descent of Man*, argues that the moral history of mankind gives no support to Darwin's hypothesis that conscience arises from human development. Instead, C. asserts the validity of conscience as a divine transcript, reaffirming faith in a fixed and supreme law embodied in the will of God. *Broken Lights* (1864) also supports Christianity, defining its prospects and emphasizing Christ's power in the world. Its sequel, *Dawning Lights* (1868), focuses on change in form and content in religion, (e.g., the method of theology, the idea of God and Christ, the doctrine of sin and concept of hell, and the approaches to happiness and death).

Although C.'s religious writings were popular, they are not original or profound. Typical of contemporary criticism are these words from the *Spectator* concerning *Of the Hopes of the Human Race, Hereafter and Here* (1874): "rather rhetorical lucubrations on the immortality of the soul, varied by a few not particularly original speculations regarding the conditions of the possible life of the future. . . ."

C. was most aggressive about women's rights. In her autobiography she speculated concerning her grandfather's probable disapproval of her career; personally aware of the discrimination against women, she stated that she hoped to show in that book "how pleasant . . . and not altogether useless a life is open to women." In a similar vein, her most notable works, *Essays on the Pursuits of Women* (1863) and *The Duties of Women* (1881), focus on the roles of women. In *Essays* she criticized the myth of "English domestic felicity," as evidenced by and in divorce courts; she analyzed the dilemma of the single woman; and she ridiculed the "dilettantish and ineffectual manner" of most upper-class women. *The Duties of Women* took immediate cognizance of the changes in society concerning women's attitudes, behavior, and status. Although C. approved of the new freedom of function of women, she noted also the difficulties inherent in contemporary concepts of right and duty. Advising caution, she advocated retention of the "old moral ideal" of motherhood, comparing mother-child love to that of God.

A social reformer, C. was more interested in substance than in literary style. She was an earnest, copious, and effective writer. She also edited the works of Theodore Parker, the American abolitionist and preacher.

WORKS: (anonymous) *The Theory of Intuitive Morals* (1855). *Essays on the Pursuits of Women* (1863). *Thanksgiving* (1863). *Religious Duty* (1864). *Broken Lights: An Inquiry into the Present Conditions and Future Prospects of Religious Faith* (1864). *The Cities of the Past* (1864). *Italics: Brief Notes on Politics, People, and Places in Italy in 1864* (1864). *Hours of Work and Play* (1867). *Dawning Lights, Secular Results of the New Reformation* (1868, 1984). *Darwinism in Morals and Other Essays* (1872). *Essays of Life and Death and the Evolution of Moral Sentiment* (1874). *The Hopes of the Human Race* (1874). *False Beasts and True* (1876). *The Moral Aspects of Vivisection* (1875). *Re-Echoes* (1876). *The Duties of Women* (1881). *The Peak in Darien* (1882, 1894). *The Scientific Spirit of the Age* (1888). *The Friend of Man: and His Friends, the Poets* (1889). *Health and Holiness* (1891). *Life, by Herself* (1894).

BIBLIOGRAPHY: Chappell, J. *Women of Worth* (1908). Cobbe, F.P. *Life of Frances Power Cobbe,* ed. B. Atkinson (1904). Hickok, K. *Representations of Women: Nineteenth-Century British Women's Poetry* (1984).

For articles in reference works, see: *Allibone. BA19C. CBEL. Chambers. DNB.*

Other references: *Athenaeum* (12 October 1872), (28 November 1874). *Men and Women of the Time,* 15th ed., V.G. Plarr (1899). *Spectator* (1874, 1881, 1882). *SR* (1864). (London) *Times* (7 April 1904, 11 April 1904).

Phyllis J. Scherle

Alicia (or Alison) Cockburn

BORN: 8 October 1713, Fairnalee, Selkirkshire, Scotland
DIED: 22 November 1794, Edinburgh.
DAUGHTER OF: Robert Rutherford.
MARRIED: Patrick Cockburn, 1731.

Known primarily during her lifetime for her sparkling wit, verse improvisations, and impromptu parodies, C. is now remembered for a ballad beginning "I've seen the smiling of Fortune beguiling," which shares the title (from the tune) "Flowers of the Forest" with a ballad written by Jean Elliot (1727-1805), who belonged to the Edinburgh legal circle C. joined after her marriage. The date of composition is not known, but it was before 1731, the year of her marriage to Patrick Cockburn of Ormiston, an Edinburgh lawyer.

Beautiful, vivacious, and intelligent, C. was a leader in Edinburgh aristocratic and legal circles for sixty years. Her charm was as legendary as her intelligence. Sir Walter Scott knew her as a relation and his mother's intimate friend; when six years old, he described her as "a virtuoso like myself." David Hume, the philosopher, frequently graced her drawing room as did Lord James Burnett Monboddo, judge, anthropologist, and pre-Darwinian advocate of evolution. A staunch and outspoken Whig, C. lived through the 1745 uprising in Scotland and once was nearly apprehended by the Scottish guards with a comic attack on Prince Charles, "The Pretender's Manifesto," in her pocket.

The occasion for the composition of "Flowers of the Forest" is unclear. Custom has it that it was written to commemorate the financial ruin of neighbors in Selkirkshire; others attach it to the departure of a young man to whom C. was attached. Certainly it was written when C. was eighteen or younger and depicts a poignant sense of personal loss, which accounts for its survival; it has since been used, especially in reference to World War I, to describe the loss of gifted youth in battle, dying at the behest of "fickle Fortune." Scott says it is based on a fragment of an anonymous Border ballad commemorating the Battle of Flodden, which has long stood as a symbol of the weakening of society by destruction of its leading youth.

The authenticity of either the Elliot or the C. ballad was for a time a vexing question. Elliot's version, written in 1756, begins "I've heard them liltin' at the ewe-milkin'" and describes young peasant women, first happy in anticipation of their lovers' return and then grief-stricken at their loss. It is placed in the historical past and makes a direct political statement. C.'s, on the other hand, is a personal statement of individual loss with no overt political message other than that supplied by the melody. Possibly what accounts for the survival of the C. version is its literary quality and its more universal appeal. Comparing the last stanzas suggests the values of each: C.: "O fickle Fortune! / Why this cruel sporting? / O why thus perplex us, poor sons of a day? / Thy frown cannot fear me, / Thy smile cannot cheer me, / Since the Flowers of the Forest are a' wede away." Elliot's: "We'll hear nae mair liltin' at the ewe-milkin'; / Women and bairns are heartless and wae; / Sighin' and moanin' on ilka green loanin'— / The Flowers of the Forest are a' wede away."

WORKS: Three letters in *Letters of Eminent Persons Addressed to David Hume* (1749). "I've Seen the Smiling of Fortune's Beguiling," *The Lark* (1765). *Letters and Memoirs, Felix, and Various Songs,* ed. T. Craig-Brown (1900). "Flowers of the Forest." *Oxford Book of Eighteenth Century Verse* (1926) and *Book of Scottish Verse* (1983). "The Pretender's Manifesto." *Love, Labour and Liberty: The Eighteenth Century Scottish Lyric,* ed. T. Crawford (1979).

BIBLIOGRAPHY: Crawford, T. *Society and the Lyric: A Study of the Song Culture of Eighteenth Century Scotland* (1979). Lockhart, J. *Memoirs of the Life of Sir Walter Scott* (1837-38). Scott, W. *Minstrelsy of the Scottish Border* (1802-1803).

For articles in reference works, see: *BAB1800. DNB. ELB. NCHEL. Oxford Companion to Music.* Todd.

Eleanor Langstaff

Isabel Colegate

BORN: 10 September 1931, London.
DAUGHTER OF: Sir Arthur Colegate and Lady Colegate Worsley.
MARRIED: Michael Briggs, 1953.

Born into an aristocratic family, the daughter of a Member of Parliament, C. has used a shrewd eye and acute ear to record the shifting relationships among the powerful, both titled and untitled, and not so powerful elements of English society at various times during the first half of the twentieth century. In a rather special sense, she is a historical novelist, a chronicler of life in England at critical times.

C., the youngest of four daughters, left school at age sixteen and chose not to go to university but to concentrate on writing. Her efforts resulted in a finished novel within a year. In 1950 she went to work as an assistant to Anthony Blond, a literary agent who turned publisher and printed C.'s first novel, *The Blackmailer,* in 1958. While all of her writing is concerned, to a greater or lesser extent, with the themes of money, class, power, and myth, some distinctions can be made among them. Indeed, they fall into clearly discernible groups: two trilogies (*The Blackmailer, A Man of Power,* and *The Great Occasion,* published separately but reissued as a trilogy by Penguin in 1984; *Orlando King, Orlando at the Brazen Threshold,* and *Agatha,* published separately but reissued as a trilogy by Penguin in 1984) and three novels that chronicle the impact of war on life among the upper classes of English society (*Statues in a Garden, News from the City of the Sun,* and *The Shooting Party*). C.'s most recent work, *A Glimpse of Sion's Glory,* is not a novel at all but a collection of three stories, something of a departure for her.

In her foreword to the Penguin reprint of her first three novels, C. notes that "these three seem to me now to be the ones I wrote instinctively and without difficulty." From the reader's point of view, that estimate is somewhat difficult to accept since narrative predictability, stylistic awkwardness, unimaginative character development, and, particularly in the case of *The Great Occasion,* an obvious and rather intrusive concern for technique create problems and sometimes diminish the pleasures of the text.

In *The Blackmailer,* C. tells the story of Judith Lane and Baldwin Rees. Judith, widow of Korean war hero Anthony Lane, keeps alive the myth of his valor in battle. Rees, who had served under Lane, confronts Judith with the "real" story: Lane had been a coward; now Rees's threat to sell the story to a newspaper causes Judith to pay him off. Not satisfied, Rees returns for more money but soon the relationship changes and the blackmail stops. Rees has fallen in love with Judith, and for a time she is fascinated by him. Though somewhat tentative and afflicted with overwriting, syntactical awkwardness, and rather abrupt, implausible character changes, *The Blackmailer* serves to introduce what will be dominant concerns for C.— money, class, and power.

These same concerns appear in C.'s next novel, *A Man of Power,* a work reminiscent of Henry James's *The Awkward Age,* to which direct reference is made at one point. Here the upper-class young woman being educated is Vanessa, daughter of Lady Essex Cooper, who narrates the story of her mother's involvement with Lewis

Ogden, "the man of power." Ogden divorces his wife in order to marry Essex, but his discovery of her with another lover in his own house terminates the relationship. C.'s use of Vanessa as the first-person narrator makes *A Man of Power* at once more assured and engaging than *The Blackmailer*.

C. regards her third novel, *The Great Occasion*, as her most technically successful effort. It is an ambitious autobiographical work as well, for C. tells the story of the five daughters of Gabriel Dodson, a wealthy but bland financier. Dodson's daughters mature in the England of the 1950s when traditional values and roles were just beginning to shift; within this context, each daughter searches for her own niche. The results are devastating: the eldest sacrifices herself to advance her husband's political career; the next suffers a mental breakdown; the third becomes a sexual athlete of sorts; the fourth abandons her own career as an artist to support her husband's; only the fifth seems, at novel's end, to be independent and functioning. Yet the sheer narrative weight of trying to trace the careers of one man and his five daughters through two decades of turbulent history burdens this novel. Clearly, at this stage of her career, such a task lay beyond the range of C.'s technical powers.

And, indeed, it seems that C. might have recognized this, for her next novel, *Statues in a Garden*, while related thematically to her first three, is a departure in stylistic terms. Here, C. focuses her attention on the Weston family during the fateful summer of 1914. Sir Aylmer Weston, a prominent Liberal politician and member of Anthony Asquith's cabinet, is married to Lady Cynthia, a stylish hostess who is the mother of his two children. They are very much a part of a gracious Edwardian world of power and privilege, but this world collapses when Aylmer's nephew and adopted son, Philip, seduces Cynthia. Aylmer kills himself, and Philip leaves Cynthia, who becomes an aging and pathetic sexual adventuress. Philip, who tried to join Aylmer's world of money and leisure by going to work for a shady financial speculator and acquiring an aristocratic mistress, seems to be a metaphor for those new forces that brought an end to a golden world.

With the three novels of the "Orlando Trilogy," C. returned to the best of her previous novels, combining extraordinarily perceptive character insight with richly atmospheric and identifiable historical context in order to craft a far more satisfying narrative. One critic has put it succinctly, and accurately, by calling the trilogy "Colegate's English Oedipal cycle . . . with Sophocles' Fate in a tweed toga." In *Orlando King*, the twenty-one-year-old protagonist, after a sheltered upbringing on an island off the coast of Brittany, establishes a brilliant business career for himself in the London of the 1930s. When asked, "Coming here as a stranger, did anything in particular strike you as a surprise?" Orlando answers, "The importance of class, I think, and the amount people talk about it," and thereby reveals the dominant concern in all of C.'s fiction. Unwittingly, Orlando marries his father's widow, Judith, whose failed attempt at suicide causes her complete breakdown. Orlando discovers his father's identity; partially blinded in the bombing of London, he forsakes his business and political careers and goes into exile.

C. details the last several months of Orlando's life in *Orlando at the Brazen Threshold*, enriching the narrative with interior monologue, flashback sequences, and precise delineation of diverse characters. Orlando returns to the island on which he had been brought up and penetrates some of the mysterious circumstances of his early life. In the course of the novel he is reunited with his daughter, Agatha, returns to London for a brief visit, and retires to Tuscany where he dies. Like its predecessor, which is set in 1951, *Agatha* has a precise temporal context; unlike it, this novel's plot makes use of significant historical events, here the Guy Burgess case in particular, as essential elements in the plot. Once again, C. places us in the world of money, class, power, and politics as Agatha defends her subsidizing Burgess's escape from prison.

All three novels in this trilogy are marked by a certain tentativeness and ambiguity, which, rather than being flaws, may well be understood as stylistic emblems for the difficulties of perception and determination in the modern world. With the pressures of history quickened by financial expansion and social upheaval, to say nothing of war, how can individuals know the right cause or course? More than the parts of the first trilogy, these three novels must be read together in order to appreciate fully the dynamics of character carefully set in motion by C. as she tells us that an awareness of the complexities of human behavior in the modern situation may be all we can hope for.

C.'s next novel, *News from the City of the Sun*, also explores patterns of human activity within a specific historical context, this time England from 1931 until the early 1970s. Three brothers have established a kind of utopian community on the grounds of an unused abbey, gathering members who are distinctly representative of the times. A young female narrator, though participating in some of the novel's activities, remains essentially detached and clear-sighted in presenting a story of class conflicts and power games played during these particularly volatile decades of English history.

C.'s most technically assured novel to date, *The Shooting Party* (1980), earned her not only the W.H. Smith Literary Award but also a wider audience when it became a movie with John Gielgud and James Mason. C. chronicles one weekend in autumn 1913 on the Oxfordshire estate of Sir Randolph Nettleby, with the guests, drawn from the ranks of the aristocracy and the affluent, assembled for a weekend of shooting, sherry, and sexual intrigue. The accidental shooting of one of the "beaters" changes the mood while providing the occasion for telling responses from each of the guests. Such a novel could easily become a static *Grand Hotel* or *Ship of Fools* piece were it not for C.'s ability to endow the narrative with psychological plausibility, technical finesse, and historical dimension.

C.'s next work, *A Glimpse of Sion's Glory*, a collection of three stories, represents neither consolidation of her powers nor real artistic growth. The stories are of uneven quality. The first, "The Girl Who Lived Among Artists," depicts a *menage à trois* consisting of Nancy, a young bohemian from a well-to-do family, and two laborers, Vere and Carley. Told years after their summer together in a boarding house, this tale of seduction and betrayal has the darkly appealing quality of a fairy tale, which makes it the only successful piece in the collection. With "Distant Cousins," a science fiction tale about a race of four-fingered humanoids, C. has offered a rather too familiar narrative weighted down by the trappings of unsuccessful parable. The title story, a parallel-lives' tale of Alison and Raymond, is an uninspired exercise tracing her youth and marriage and his crazy-quilt adventures after leaving Oxford. Ray-

mond's career, narrated in a letter to Alison, follows the stereotypic "bright promise unfulfilled" scheme. As such, it might well serve as an appropriate metaphor for this collection.

WORKS: *The Blackmailer* (1958). *A Man of Power* (1960). *The Great Occasion* (1962). *Statues in a Garden* (1964). *Orlando King* (1968). *Orlando at the Brazen Threshold* (1971). *Agatha* (1973). *News from the City of the Sun* (1979). *The Shooting Party* (1980). *A Glimpse of Sion's Glory* (1985).

BIBLIOGRAPHY:

For articles in reference works, see: *CA. DLB.*
Other references: *Christian Science Monitor* (5 October 1984). *Harper's* (April 1966, May 1969). *Hudson Review* (Autumn 1984). *LRB* (18 July 1985). *Los Angeles Times Book Review* (27 May 1984). *New Statesman* (21 August 1964, 20 September 1968, 13 July 1979, 12 September 1980). *New Yorker* (25 May 1981). *NYT* (16 May 1981). *NYTBR* (20 March 1966, 25 May 1969, 8 December 1985). *New Yorker* (25 May 1981). *Observer* (1 July 1969, 9 June 1985). *PW* (3 February 1984). *Spectator* (13 September 1980, 8 June 1985). *SR* (May 1981). *Times* (London) (18 February 1980, 12 February 1981). *TLS* (28 October 1964, 19 September 1968, 20 May 1971, 5 October 1973, 4 December 1979, 12 September 1980, 25 April 1985, 21 June 1985). *Village Voice Literary Supplement* (December, 1985). *Virginia Quarterly Review* (Autumn 1981). *Washington Post* (13 July 1981).

Robert Hosmer

Ann Raney Thomas Coleman

BORN: 5 November 1810, Whitehaven, Cumberland.
DIED: March, 1897, Cuero, Texas.
DAUGHTER OF: John Raney; Mother's name not known.
MARRIED: John Thomas, 1833; John Coleman, c. 1848.

C. is known for her single autobiographical work. She was born to a well-to-do family in Whitehaven, Cumberland and her early life was one of privilege. Her father was heir to £50,000 and her mother was the daughter of a rich merchant. C. attended "the best boarding schools" until her father's bankruptcy. Then she, her two brothers, and her sister, went to live with their uncle and aunt who enrolled them in a neighborhood school in Newcastle.

C. and her mother later opened a genteel boarding house in Liverpool, where she became romantically attached to Henry Marks. Since Marks was Jewish, the romance was discouraged by C.'s relatives. However, C. showed the sort of courage that was to stand her in good stead later. She continued her close relationship with Marks until her departure for America, at which time he gave her a ring and "his picture in water colors on ivory."

C.'s father and one brother had emigrated to Texas earlier from Liverpool (her brother died shortly after their arrival). C. and her mother and sister sailed for Texas on the merchant vessel *St. George*. Off the coast of Cuba they were accosted by pirates, who took all the ship's provisions. C. and her family hid in a closet during the raid and thus escaped the pirates' notice. The family arrived in Brazoria, Texas, shortly before the outbreak of the Texas War for Independence.

In 1832 the Battle of Velasco took place near Brazoria, and C. "sat the most of two nights and days moulding bullets and making bullet patches." Apparently C. also delivered the bullets to the combatants because in a letter to Governor Roberts, she says she took the bullets "on my horse 15 miles, to Mr. Bertrand's ranch for our men to come after them. I was pursued by two spies, but had the best horse, and made my excape." The Texans were victorious in this opening skirmish of the Texas War for Independence, a war that was to force C. and her family to leave Texas.

C.'s parents died after the Battle of Velasco, and she married John Thomas in "the first public wedding in Brazoria." A son was born before the family fled Texas in the wake of Houston's retreat. They settled in Louisiana, where two more children were born. C.'s husband and both her sons died, and she subsequently married John Coleman, a local storekeeper. Coleman proved to be "unjust and cruel," and C. was very unhappy with her second marriage. The Colemans left Louisiana and moved back to Texas, settling near Matagorda. Later C. returned to England to reclaim her father's estate, but the attempt failed.

Upon her return to Texas, her husband became even more abusive. C. divorced him in September 1855 and for the rest of her life was self-supporting. She taught school for many years but was reduced to poverty in her old age. She wrote that she did not have the money to pay the expenses of paper and postage in order to send her memoirs to her niece.

Her memoirs are her only extant book though C. does mention three other books that she had written for Mrs. Clara Stanton, who was apparently acting as her literary agent. She also wrote a journal of her first Atlantic crossing, which she sent to Henry Marks. Though marred by phonetic spelling and inadequate punctuation, C.'s autobiography is a lively, and sometimes lyrical, account of the hardships and pleasures of the American frontier; here the women were as hardy and independent as the men.

WORKS: *A Victorian Lady on the Texas Frontier.* Ed. C.R. Kind (1971). *Reminiscence of Ann Raney Thomas Coleman,* typescript at University of Texas, Austin, original manuscript at Duke University.

S.A. Winn

Mary Elizabeth Coleridge

BORN: 23 September 1861, London.
DIED: 25 August 1907, Harrogate.
DAUGHTER OF: Arthur Duke and Mary Anne Coleridge.
WROTE UNDER: Avoos, Anodos, Mary Elizabeth Coleridge.

C., the great-great niece of Samuel Taylor Coleridge, was called "the tail of the comet S.T.C." A somewhat enigmatic person, C. was shy and disliked meeting strangers, preferring to remain in her room and indulge her romantic imagination. Yet she was a close, loyal friend, easily overlooking people's flaws. Despite a sensitive, bookish nature, she had a merry disposition. While being educated at home, she learned Greek, French, Italian, German, and Hebrew. C. was fascinated with the age of chivalry and in her youth eagerly read Scott and Malory. By the age of thirteen she began writing poetry; however, she paid little attention to her writing, instead choosing to concentrate on her painting. Although she enjoyed traveling, especially in Italy, C.'s home was the center of her life. She lived a quiet youth with her father, mother, sister, and aunt. Her father, Clerk of the Assize to the Midland Circuit, entertained such guests as Tennyson, Browning, Ruskin, Trollope, Frances Kemble, Jenny Lind, Henry

Newbolt, Robert Bridges, and William Cory, who became her close friend and teacher.

C. began writing essays for *Monthly Review, Guardian,* and other periodicals when she was twenty. From 1902 until her death she wrote articles for the *Times Literary Supplement.* As a critic, she could be prejudiced and become obsessed with details, but she praised Monet, Renoir, and Ibsen before they became fashionable. She also wrote stories for *Cornhill Magazine.*

In 1893 she published *Seven Sleepers of Ephesus,* which describes seven young men's adventures. The novel, like much of her fiction, begins well but becomes bogged down near the middle. Robert Louis Stevenson was impressed with the book, although admitting halfway through it, "If she does get out, she is devilish ingenious." C.'s fiction is hampered by weak plot construction and improbable happenings; her interest is largely in dramatic action.

Bridges helped arrange the publication of *Fancy's Following* (1896), a thin volume of forty-eight short lyrics. This was followed by another volume of poetry, *Fancy's Guerdon* (1897), which contained many of the poems in *Fancy's Following.* Her poems, now considered to be her greatest achievement, are restrained and dignified. As Bridges notes, they show a "delicate harmony," are "sincere and mysterious," and have a "natural and simple expression." He further states that she "brought to her poetry . . . a great literary appetite, knowledge, and memory—a wide sympathy, tenderness of feeling, and profound spirituality—and a humor which such seriousness and devotion of life as were hers can hardly be made palatable in literature." Walter de la Mare, whom she befriended, said her poems read "as though she hardly called before they answered."

However, it was *The King with Two Faces* (1897), a historical romance based on the life of King Gustav III of Sweden, that established her reputation during her lifetime. She followed this with a collection of essays, *Non Sequitur*, in 1900; a novel, *The Fiery Dawn* (1901); a romance, *The Shadows on the Wall* (1904), concerning the Duchess de Berri; and a novel, *The Lady on the Drawing-Room Floor* in 1906. A biography, *Holman Hunt*, written at the artist's request, was published in 1908, after her death.

Despite claiming, "I hate Philanthropy," C. worked with the poor for several years, influenced by her reading of Tolstoy. From 1895 on she was a teacher at the Working Woman's College. Her dry wit can be seen in a lecture on Queen Elizabeth: "Queen Elizabeth, when first she saw the light of day, was a great disappointment. She was a girl—

she ought to have been a boy." C. died of acute appendicitis in 1907. Her students were so fond of her that they disbanded on her death rather than accept a new teacher.

WORKS: *The Seven Sleepers of Ephesus* (1893). *Fancy's Following* (1896, as Avoos). *The King with Two Faces* (1897). *Fancy's Guerdon* (1897, as Anodos). *Non Sequitur* (1900). *The Fiery Dawn* (1901). *The Shadow on the Wall* (1904). *The Lady on the Drawing-Room Floor* (1906). *Holman Hunt* (1908). *Poems*, ed. H. Newbolt (1908). *Gathered Leaves from the Prose of Mary E. Coleridge*, with a memoir by E. Sichel (1910; includes six unpublished poems). *the Collected Poems of Mary Coleridge*, ed. T. Whistler (1954).

BIBLIOGRAPHY: Bridges, R. *Cornhill Magazine* (November 1907; reprinted in *Collected Essays*, 1931). Evans, B.I. *English Poetry in the Later Nineteenth Century* (1933, 1966). Reilly, J. J. *Of Books and Men* (1942). Sichel, E. Memoir in *Gathered Leaves from the Prose of Mary Elizabeth Coleridge* (1910). Whistler, T. "Introduction" to *The Collected Poems of Mary Coleridge* (1954).

Other references: *Nation* (12 September 1907).

Louis J. Parascandola

Sara Coleridge

BORN: 22 December 1802, Greta Hall near Keswick.
DIED: 3 May 1852, Chester Place, Regent's Park.
DAUGHTER OF: Samuel Taylor Coleridge and Sarah Fricker.
MARRIED: Henry Nelson Coleridge, 1829.

The daughter of the distinguished poet and critic, C. spent her formative years in the presence of such famous literary men as Robert Southey, her uncle, and William Wordsworth, her father's intimate friend. She was celebrated by Wordsworth, along with Dora Wordsworth and Edith Southey, in his poem "The Triad"; she, in turn, dedicated her edition of the *Biographia Literaria* to Wordsworth, calling herself his "child in heart, and faithful friend" in the inscription.

C.'s first literary endeavor was a three-volume translation from the Latin of Martin Dobrizhoffer's *Account of the Abipones, an Equestrian People of Paraguay* (1822), published anonymously and initially conceived as a means of defraying her brother Derwent's college expenses. Her next work, published in 1825, was a translation of the "Loyal Servant's" memoirs of the Che-

valier Bayard. In 1829 she married Henry Nelson Coleridge, her barrister cousin, by whom she had a son and a daughter. After her marriage, she turned briefly to original writing, although the scope of this work was influenced by her new domestic role as a mother. Her first creative production, *Pretty Lessons in Verse for Good Children* (1834), consisted of short pieces of poetry addressed to her children, partly for moral guidance and partly for instruction in Latin and other subjects. The fairy tale *Phantasmion*, her only work of fiction, followed in 1837.

With the death of her husband, C. turned her attention to the work he had begun as her father's literary executor—the collection, annotation, and publication of the literary remains of Samuel Taylor Coleridge. The last ten years of her life were devoted to this editorial enterprise, and the results included the *Biographia Literaria*, *Notes and Lectures Upon Shakespeare and Some of the Old Poets and Dramatists*, and *Essays on His Own Times*. Her learning and her energies were poured into the preparation of notes, prefaces, and appendices rather than into original productions. As her American correspondent and memoirist Henry Reed stated, in this labor dedicated to the memory of a father and a husband, she expended "an amount of original thought and an affluence of learning which, differently and more prominently presented, would have made her famous." The range of C.'s intellect, however, can be judged by a representative letter to Reed. In a 3 July 1850 letter, she discusses her editorial work, her daily domestic life, Ruskin's aesthetic theories, the death of Sir Robert Peel, and the theological dogma of baptismal regeneration.

Although much of her work commemorates her father, C. reveals her remarkable creative powers in *Phantasmion*. The *Quarterly Review* praised it as "pure as a crystal in diction, tinted like an opal with the hues of an everspringing sunlit fancy." The fairy tale relates the adventures of Phantasmion, the young prince of Palmland, who loses his mother Queen Zalia and his father King Dorimant at an early age. The fairy Potentilla, the queen of the insect realm watches over Phantasmion and invests him with a succession of insectlike attributes—from wings to feet with suction power—for his explorations of the hostile neighboring kingdom of Rockland. Potentilla also aids Phantasmion in his pursuit of Iarine, the beautiful daughter of the King of Rockland. She is also loved by Glandreth, a fearless but treacherous warrior, and Karadan, a youth who possesses the charmed vessel that controls her fate. The military and amatory exploits of the mortals are complicated by the intervention of good, evil, and fickle spirits—the water witch Seshelma; Feydeleen, the Spirit of the Flowers; Oloola, the Spirit of the Blast—who exist in a complex web of allegiances, counterallegiances, vows, and betrayals, not only to one another but also to the rival mortals.

Phantasmion reveals C.'s striking prose style. Its lush, luxuriant descriptions are replete with vivid, sensuous details and exotic, fantastical images. C.'s presentation of the water witch Seshelma expresses this combination of particularity and whimsey: "[Phantasmion] perceived a strange woman's form rising out of the waves, and gliding towards the beach: a wreath of living, moving flowers, like sea-anemones, clung round her head, from which the slimy locks of whitish blue hung down till they met the waters." The power and charm of *Phantasmion* lies in the fact that it is very much a fairy tale: it resists moralizing intrusions, and its fancifulness and inventiveness never succumb to allegory.

WORKS: (trans.) *Account of the Abipones, an Equestrian People of Paraguay*, by M. Dobrizhoffer (1822). (trans.) *The Right Joyous and Pleasant History of the Feats, Gests, and Prowesses of the Chevalier Bayard*, by "The Loyal Servant" (1825). *Pretty Lessons in Verse for Good Children* (1834). *Phantasmion* (1837). *Biographia Literaria*, by S.T. Coleridge, prepared in part by H.N. Coleridge and completed by S. Coleridge (1847). *Notes and Lectures Upon Shakespeare and Some of the Old Poets and Dramatists*, by S.T. Coleridge, Ed. S. Coleridge (1849). *Essays on His Own Times*, by S.T. Coleridge, ed. S. Coleridge (1850). *The Poems of Samuel Taylor Coleridge*, ed. D. Coleridge and S. Coleridge (1852).

BIBLIOGRAPHY: Broughton, L.N. *Sarah Coleridge and Henry Reed* (1937). *Memoir and Letters of Sara Coleridge* (ed. by her daughter [E. Coleridge], 2 vols. (1873). Coleridge, Lord. Preface to *Phantasmion* (1874). For articles in reference works, see: *BA19C*.

Eileen Finan

Mary Mitchell Collyer

BORN: 1716/1717.
DIED: December 1762 or January 1763, Islington.
DAUGHTER OF: Parents' names not known.
MARRIED: Joseph Collyer, n.d.

C.'s few books were published anonymously, often "printed for" Joseph Collyer, her compiler/translator husband. From her translations of French and German texts and from the cleverness of her epistolary novel, we can guess that C. was well educated, though nothing is known of her early life.

As a contemporary of Samuel Richardson, C. offers intriguing possibilities of influence. Her first known publication, a translation of Mari-

vaux's *La Vie de Marianne*, which Ronald Paulson dates from 1735, remained a standard English version well into the 1880s. C.'s preface to *The Virtuous Orphan* particularly recommends the novel in "English dress" to female readers, and it was perhaps with this audience in mind that she translated a mere third of Marivaux's text, adding a redemptive conclusion in which a penitent Valville marries Marianne. Richardson's *Pamela*, published five years later, was similarly sentimental, its servant girl also converting her would-be seducer to the respectability of "husband."

No source has been discovered for C.'s second "translation," *Memoirs of the Countess de Bressol* (1743), which may simply be a series of tales she connected with her own moralizing passages. If this is so, its formalistic shortcomings may have prompted her writing of *Felicia to Charlotte*, the first volume of which appeared in 1744.

C. published her epistolary novel three years after Richardson's *Pamela*; realizing there could be no more than one servant girl raised to high life, she chose her characters from polite society, anticipating R.'s practice in *Clarissa* (1748) and *Sir Charles Grandison* (1753). The second volume of *Felicia to Charlotte* (1749) appeared one year after *Clarissa*, and, as Richardson's sequel continues Pamela's story after marriage, so C.'s novel presents the domestic life of her characters.

Quite apart from the teasing question of its relationship to R.'s novels, *Felicia to Charlotte* not only is one of the better minor novels of its time, but it also anticipates the pattern women's fiction was to take for the next several decades. The novel begins with Felicia's promise "to discover all the secret folds" of her heart in correspondence with her friend, Charlotte, who remains in London while Felicia pays a visit to her aunt in the country. The correspondence is largely one-sided, yet it maintains the semblance of a conversation, both in its familiar tone and in its response to the figured letters we do not see. Felicia's history in this first volume—the remove from home, courtship, and marriage—assumes a course many feminocentric novels (e.g., the Harriet Byron portion of *Sir Charles Grandison*) were to follow. The novelist's sensibility, her appreciation of nature, and her benevolent principles also seem precocious in the context of contemporary writers. The sequel, published one year after the birth of C.'s first and only child, may have biographic content, for Julius is "so unfashionably polite, as to con-sider the mother's suckling her own child, as one of the indispensable obligations of nature."

With the exception of a children's book (*The Christmas Box*, 1748-1749) she mentions in *Felicia to Charlotte*, C. seems to have published nothing for the next twelve years. Her dedication to *The Death of Abel* (1761) admits that she translated Salomon Gessner's poem to support her family. The translation was so well received that C. wrote *The Death of Cain* (1762) in imitation. Her last work, a translation of Gottlieb Klopstock's *Messiah* (1763), was completed and published by Joseph Collyer after her death in 1763.

C.'s unwillingness to publish even her small literary corpus under her own name finds many parallels in the period. Yet as an intelligent, gifted writer, whose novel anticipated developing conventions and whose work may have influenced Richardson, C. deserves more critical attention than she has received.

WORKS: Felicia to Charlotte (1744). Letters from Felicia to Charlotte, vol. II (1749). The Christmas Box (1748-1749). The Death of Cain (1762?).

TRANSLATIONS: Pierre Carlet de Chamblain de Marivaux, The Virtuous Orphan; or, the Life of Marianne, Countess of . . . . (1735). The Memoirs of the Countess de Bressol (1743). Gessner, S. The Death of Abel (1761). Klopstock, F.G. The Messiah (1763).

BIBLIOGRAPHY: Paulson, R., ed. C.'s tr. of Marivaux's *The Virtuous Orphan* (1979).

For articles in reference works, see: *DLB*. Todd. Other references: Hughes, H.S., *JEGP* (1916).

Catherine S. Green

Elizabeth Colville

BORN: Late 1500s, Halhil, Scotland.
DIED: in 1600s.
DAUGHTER OF: Sir James Melvill.
MARRIED: John Colville, the third lord of Culross, before 1603.
WROTE UNDER: M[istress]. M[elvill]., Gentelwoman in Culros; Eliz. Melvill, Ladie Culross yonger.

C.'s principal work is a long allegorical poem, "Ane Godlie Dreame," first published in 1603. None of C.'s other work survives, although a contemporary, Alexander Hume, wrote of her "delight in poesie" and claimed that she did "excel any of [her] sex in that art that ever I heard within this nation." Member of a prominent Scots family, C. remains a mystery, although much is known of the men around her: her father Sir James Melvill, her husband John Colville, and her son Alexander Colville were all important figures in public life.

The 1603 version of "Ane Godlie Dreame" consists of 55 stanzas in *ottava rima*. In it the speaker laments the mortal world and, longing for release from life, falls asleep. In a dream, Jesus appears and leads the speaker on a long, dangerous journey to a gold and silver castle. Before entering it, the speaker must accompany Jesus to Hell. In the course of their descent, the speaker seems to fall into the flames, then awakens. The poem's final section relates the speaker's thoughts about the dream and heaven. A later edition adds five extra stanzas in the last section as well as a separate, short religious lyric by Alexander Montgomerie.

C. is known to have been a pious woman to whom Alexander Hume dedicated a book of hymns. Certainly the poem gains strength from its emotional sincerity. Nevertheless, it would be a mistake to regard the work as autobiographical for several reasons: it may be based on a lost medieval dream poem; the first-person speaker in C.'s poem is urged to "Play the man"; its details are more conventional than naturalistic.

The poem is interesting on historical and aesthetic grounds. First of all, it is written in Scots dialect and is one of relatively few works by Re-naissance Scotswomen. Second, the description of the journey, particularly the vision of Hell, uses forceful imagery and includes an interesting refutation of the concept of Purgatory.

WORKS: "Ane Godlie Dreame" (1603, STC 17811).

BIBLIOGRAPHY: Laing, D. *Early Metrical Tales* (1826). *N&Q* (1859).

For articles in reference books, see: *DNB*.

Frances Teague

Ivy Compton-Burnett

BORN: 5 June 1884, Pinner, Middlesex.
DIED: 27 August 1969, London.
DAUGHTER OF: Dr. James and Katherine Reese Compton Burnett.
WROTE UNDER: I. Compton-Burnett.

The eldest child of Dr. Compton Burnett's second wife, Katharine, C-B. was brought up with five older step-brothers and sisters and six younger brothers and sisters in suburban Hove. Her father was a homoeopathic doctor who wrote many books and pamphlets defending his kind of medicine. She received a classical education from the family tutor and took a degree in classics at Royal Holloway College, London, in 1902.

A series of family disasters occurred when C-B. became a young adult. With the first, her father's death in 1901, her mother went into formal mourning. C-B. had a strong attachment to her younger brother Guy, who died of pneumonia in 1905. In 1911 her mother died after a painful, lingering illness. C-B. then took over as overbearing head of the house until her sisters rebelled and the family home was broken up in 1915. In 1916 her brother Noel was killed on the Somme. At the end of the next year, her two youngest sisters, believed to be suicides, died of overdoses of veronal. C-B. herself nearly died in the influenza epidemic of 1918.

The outward turmoil seemed to have ceased when in 1919 C-B. began to share living quarters with Margaret Jourdain, a writer and historian of furniture and other antiques. The two lived together until Jourdain died in 1951. During this time, C-B. wrote the bulk of the novels for which she is famous.

C-B.'s first novel, *Dolores* (1911), with its self-sacrificing heroine, is thought to be immature, written in a crude style. C-B. later deprecated the book, saying that her brother Noel had had too great a hand in it. Her next, *Pastors and Masters* (1925), is the first novel in which C-B. achieved her mature style and the distinctive universe she presents in her fiction.

Critics usually note first the idiosyncrasies of C-B.'s technique. Her novels are set in the English countryside, seemingly sometime between 1880 and 1910. The feeling is late Victorian or Edwardian with the family that is depicted an almost self-enclosed set. C-B. explained her typical time frame by saying that she knew the stable society at the beginning of the century, but that it is very difficult to see the present completely and organically when one is living in the midst of it. Critics also speak of the claustrophobic atmosphere of the novels: no character gets to escape very far for very long, and the reader does not get to follow the fugitive on his journey. C-B. remains closeted with the family, the relatives, the children, the servants, and sometimes a few friends; she said that, universally, family relationships and personal experiences are central to everyone, remarking on the amount of destruction and affection in families. Intelligent and unsentimental, C-B. is said to have crossed Victorian domestic fiction with Greek tragedy.

Another notable technique of C-B.'s fiction is that her novels are predominantly expressed in dialogue with very sketchy descriptions of the characters, with almost no authorial comment and with no exploration of the characters' thoughts as such. C-B. suggests that her sketchy descriptions allow the reader to picture the characters in his own imagination. Her abstaining from authorial comment is a modernist technique, reflecting James Joyce's ideal of the author as God, off paring his fingernails while his world seems to exist in its own right. Her reliance on dialogue functions as a deliberately formal technique, abstracting and elevating the characters and their conflicts. The characters' use of language reveals their moral and intellectual natures. Unlike the villains, C-B.'s good characters do not use clichés or slang, and they tell the truth, sometimes disconcertingly. Nathalie Sarraute has described C-B.'s dialogue as reflecting the fluctuating border between conversation and subconversation, between what is said and what is almost said, what is on the tip of the tongue. Of course, in families much of the subconversation is understood by the members, whether or not it is ever articulated.

Part of the tension of C-B.'s novels derives from the contrast of the polished manners and speech with ruthless clashing of wills and egos. Her typical theme concerns power or domination or egotism. She often uses melodramatic devices—like wills destroyed, significant conversations overheard, or illegitimate children newly claimed—to reveal the secret lives of her characters. Frederick Karl complains that these recognition scenes do not lead to reformation or salvation as in Greek tragedy or Christian comedy; instead, the characters try to hush up the scandal and carry on (in the broadest sense of the term). Other critics bemoan the lack of poetic justice. Some call C-B. amoral because her wicked flourish and her good continue to suffer. C-B., however, is a realist, not an allegorist, and she is depicting family life, where love and hate meet most intensely. After a shocking revelation, families have to ignore or forget it, at least on the surface. The alternative would be to break apart. The family is home, the ground. To lose it would be an unthinkable, primal disaster.

The comedy of C-B.'s writing is another contradiction. Critics find her dialogue witty, brilliant, and epigrammatic. Some name her a creator of great comic characters like the parasites and busybodies, and all find her ironic. But part of the force of her comedy is her black comedy, the laughter in the face of outrageous statements and actions, laughter as an expression of shock like the audience's reaction to the plays of Harold Pinter. As in Freud's theory of the joke, we laugh at the emperor with no clothes, at authority denuded.

Manservant and Maidservant (1947), published in America as *Bullivant and the Lambs*, is thought by many to be C-B.'s best novel. Critics praise the juxtaposition of the servants' world with that of the upstairs family. They appreciate the character of the butler Bullivant and that of the serving boy George, a character who seems too modern to settle down in the world of masters and servants. The conflict between parents and children is particularly pointed and poignant here, with the children skeptical of their father's reforming because the memory of their past suffering remains so painfully real.

In America periods of neglect of C-B.'s fiction alternate with periods of qualified critical interest. In England, her reputation as one of the most original and significant novelists of the twentieth century is stable. C-B.'s books were never bestsellers, but fellow writers acknowledge her importance. A number of contemporary British writers seem to have been influenced by her fictional practices. The modernity of her work caused C-B. to be compared to Cubist painters, to writers of the *nouveau roman*, and to Harold Pinter with his absurdist dramas. C-B. is both an innovator and a classicist.

WORKS: *Dolores* (1911). *Pastors and Masters* (1925). *Brothers and Sisters* (1929). *Men and Wives* (1931). *More Women and Men* (1933). *A House and Its Head* (1935). *Daughters and Sons* (1937). *A Family and a Fortune* (1939). *Parents and Children* (1941). *Elders and Betters* (1944). *Manservant and Maidservant* (1947, in America *Bullivant and the Lambs*). *Two Worlds and Their Ways* (1949). *Darkness and Day* (1951). *The Present and the Past* (1953). *Mother and Son* (1955, James Tait Black Memorial Prize). *A Father and His Fate* (1957). *A Heritage and Its History* (1959, dramatized by Julian Mitchell, 1965). *The Mighty and Their Fall* (1961). *A God and His Gifts* (1963). *The Last and the First* (1971).

BIBLIOGRAPHY: Baldanza, F. *Ivy Compton-Burnett* (1964). Johnson, P.H. *I. Compton-Burnett* (1951). Karl, F. *A Reader's Guide to the Contemporary Novel* (1971). Liddle, R. *The Novels of I. Compton-Burnett* (1956). Nevius, B. *Ivy Compton-Burnett* (1970). Spurling, H. *Ivy: The Life of I. Compton-Burnett* (1984).

For articles in reference works, see: *CLC. DLB. DNB. IDWB.*

Other references: *Criticism* (1960). *WSCL* (1964).

Kate Begnal

Eliza Cook

BORN: 24 December 1818, London.
DIED: 23 September 1889, Wimbledon.

C. was a middle-class Victorian writer whose feminist essays on women and work coexisted with her sentimental verses on domestic themes.

Victorian readers mostly preferred C.'s poetry, while modern readers may find her clear and lively prose more interesting.

Entirely self-educated, C. was the youngest of eleven children who grew up in the country; she thus escaped much of the conventional social-

tional socialization of young women in the nineteenth century. As a result, she defiantly dressed in a way perceived to be masculine, unself-consciously displayed a passionate attachment to the actress Charlotte Cushman, and published essays and poems criticizing the restrictions society placed upon middle-class women's lives.

C. began writing at the age of fifteen and published her first volume of verses, *Lays of a Wild Harp*, at seventeen; favorable reception of the book led her to submit poems to the *Weekly Dispatch*, the *Metropolitan Magazine*, and the *New Monthly Magazine*. Her most famous poem, "The Old Arm Chair," a sentimental tribute to her deceased mother, appeared in the *Dispatch* in 1837. This poem was reproduced in 1930 in *The Stuffed Owl: An Anthology of Bad Verse*, edited by D.B. Wyndham Lewis and Charles Lee. Despite their modern aversion to sentimentalism, however, this and many others of her poems on the subject of her mother's death expressed a genuine grief that contemporary readers were likely to share. *Melaia and Other Poems*, published in 1838, was a great success in both England and the United States. This volume includes some lively satire (including the title poem), along with the simple and homey pieces for which C. was best known.

Despite the popularity of C.'s poetry, her real talent was for journalism. *Eliza Cook's Journal*, which she wrote and edited virtually single-handedly from May 1849 to May 1854, was a miscellany of sketches, reviews, social essays, and verses intended to improve the lives of middle-class women—by entertaining and informing them and by contributing a feminist voice to contemporary debates about women's proper role in society. In the pages of this journal, C. particularly addressed the difficulties and despair of English working women, be they governesses, seamstresses, factory workers, or servants. She attacked the interpreta-

tion of English law that allowed husbands to "discipline" their wives physically, she defended "old maids," and she criticized the superficiality of English girls' education. The journal ceased publication after five years because of C.'s failing health and consequent poor business management, not for lack of an audience. A large portion of the contents of the journal was reissued in 1860 as *Jottings from My Journal*.

In 1863 C. was awarded a Civil List pension of £100 per year. *New Echoes and Other Poems* (1864) was her last book of new poetry; a collection of aphorisms, *Diamond Dust* (1865), was her last book of prose. For the final 25 years of her life, C. was an invalid. She died at the age of seventy-one, having outlived her popularity as a poet but not her reputation as a radical feminist.

WORKS: *Lays of a Wild Harp* (1835). *Melaia and Other Poems* (1838). *Poems, second series* (1845). *Eliza Cook's Journal* (1849–1854). *I'm Afloat: Songs* (1850?). *Jottings from My Journal* (1860). *New Echoes, and Other Poems* (1864). *Diamond Dust* (1865). *Poetical Works* (1870). *The Old Armchair* (1886).

BIBLIOGRAPHY: For articles in reference works, see: *BA19C. DNB. Notable Women of Our Own Times* (1883?). *OCEL. The Poets and the Poetry of the Century*, Ed. A.H. Miles, vol. 7.

Other references: Faderman, L. *Surpassing the Love of Men: Romantic Friendship and Love Between Women from the Renaissance to the Present* (1981). Hickok, K. *Representations of Women: Nineteenth-Century British Women's Poetry* (1984). Mitchell, S. *The Fallen Angel: Chastity, Class and Women's Reading 1835-1880* (1981). Woodring, C. *Victorian Samplers: William and Mary Howitt* (1952).

Kathleen Hickok

Marie Corelli (pseudonym of Mary Mackay)

BORN: 1 May 1855, Perth, Scotland.
DIED: 21 April 1924, Stratford-on-Avon.
DAUGHTER OF: Charles Mackay (?) and Mary Elizabeth Kirtland Mackay (?).
WROTE UNDER: Marie Corelli.

The storytelling of C., world-famous novelist of late Victorian England, extended to her own life. To some she claimed to have been adopted at birth by literary man Charles Mackay, her real parents an Italian father and a Scottish clairvoyant mother. To others she said she was Mackay's stepdaughter, but rumor had it that she was actually his illegitimate daughter. Whether her adoptive,

legitimate, or natural father, Charles Mackay provided the young Mary with a useful model of literary endeavor. He was a lyricist, essayist, poet, war correspondent, editor of the *London Illustrated News*, and author of *Popular Delusions and the Madness of Crowds*. Mackay's literary connections helped his convent-bred, musically-inclined daughter with publication of her early work.

Changing her name to Corelli in her attempt at a concert recital career, she had some initial successes. But with the publication of her first novel, *The Romance of Two Worlds* (1886), when she was only twenty-two, she became a best-selling author. So she remained for the rest of the century and into the next, half of her more than thirty novels selling a then impressive 100,000 copies.

Most literary people concurred with Arnold Bennett that "if Joseph Conrad is one pole [of artistic talent], Marie Corelli is the other." She was the subject of much critical derision, including an unflattering special issue of the *Westminster Review*. Yet she was also the favorite novelist of Queen Victoria and was admired by Gladstone, Asquith, Oscar Wilde, Italian queens, Indian potentates, circulating libraries, and an enthusiastic lower- and middle-class following.

Her immensely popular *The Romance of Two Worlds*, an entertaining and original tale of occultism and clairvoyance, features a heroine of great appeal to Victorian audiences, the neurasthenic girl seeking a meaning to existence. In this novel the heroine is providentially rejuvenated by the Electric Principle of Christianity, the control of magnetic force emanating from a celestial Electric Ring. The novel features a mysterious mesmerist, Dr. Casimir, and his exotic sister Zara, who is thirty-eight but looks sixteen as a result of the blessings of spiritual electricity. Also intriguing are the opulent interiors with secret light sources and herbal opiate-induced visions of angels. The novel obviously catered to Victorian fascination with spiritualism (though C. claimed to scorn the spiritualists of the day) and ingeniously combined pseudo-scientific theory and Christianity.

C. followed up her first success with a number of novels combining romance, religion, and social criticism, notably *Barabbas: A Dream of the World's Tragedy* (1893), her treatment of the Crucifixion, and *The Murder of Delicia* (1896), a novel condemning marital infidelity. However, *The Sorrows of Satan* (1895)—whose initial sale was greater than that of any prior English novel—was her landmark success. It concerns a Faustian pact between one Geoffrey Tempest and the Devil who, in a clever twist of characterization, is weary of sinners and sorrowed at the evil of man. Typically, C. used the novel to criticize the loose morality of wealthy women and aristocratic men-about-town. She urged a return to Christian living, embodied by Mavis Clarke, a young woman novelist who is Geoffrey's savior and bears a marked resemblance to C. herself. Despite C.'s self-promotion, the novel was so popular that it was in its sixtieth edition by the time of her death. It even supplemented the Bible as the text of many sermons. What readers perhaps liked better than its evangelism, however, were its florid descriptions of the haunts and sins of the rich.

A child of her time, C. united a desire for moral uplift—she did passionate battle against what she termed "the evils of nineteenth-century cynicism and general flippancy of thought"—with prodigious industry. In addition to fiction, her almost forty books included verse and social criticism, and she wrote numerous articles for the popular papers of the day. A woman of drive and egotism (she published fan letters in a reissue of *The Romance of Two Worlds*), she railed against the "marriage market" for upper-class women but opposed suffrage because she considered it unladylike.

Though her works are still in print and she has been praised by twentieth-century writers as diverse as Rebecca West, Leonard Woolf, and Henry Miller, some of her own biographers have ridiculed her, accusing her of wooden characterization, purple prose, and endless moralizing. Whether she is guilty of the besetting sins of Victorian fiction is debatable. What is not debatable is her brilliant understanding of the public's need for fictions combining sinful excitement with spiritual exhortation. She was a literary phenomenon created by her own shrewdness and the rise of a mass market, a readership whose opinions continue to enshrine such artists as C. who give imaginative expression to its own longings and beliefs.

WORKS: *A Romance of Two Worlds* (1886). *Vendetta, or the Story of One Forgotten* (1886). *Thelma: A Society Novel* (1887). *Ardath: The Story of a Dead Self* (1889). *My Wonderful Wife: A Study in Smoke* (1889). *Wormwood: A Drama of Paris* (1890). *The Silver Domino* (1892). *The Soul of Lilith* (1892). *Barabbas: A Dream of the World's Tragedy* (1893). *The Sorrows of Satan* (1895). *The Murder of Delicia* (1896). *The Mighty Atom* (1896). *Cameos* (1896). *Zisha: The Problem of a Wicked Soul* (1897). *Jane: A Social Incident* (1897). *Boy: A Sketch* (1900). *The Master Christian* (1900). *A Christmas Greeting of Various Thoughts, Verses and Fancies* (1901). *"Temporal Power": A Study in Supremacy* (1902). *The Vanishing Gift* (1902). *The Plain Truth of the Stratford-on-Avon Controversy* (1903). *God's Good Man: A Simple Love Story* (1904). *The Strange Visitation of Josiah McNason: A Christmas Ghost Story* (1904). *Free Opinions Freely Expressed on Certain Phases of Modern Social Life and Conduct* (1905). *The Treasure of Heaven: A Romance of Riches* (1906). *Woman or Suffragette? A Question of National Choice* (1907). *Holy Orders* (1908). *The Devil's Motor* (1910). *The Life Everlasting: A Reality of Romance* (1911). *Eyes of the Sea* (1917). *The Young Diana: An Experience of the Future* (1918). *My Little Bit* (1919). *The Love of Long Ago* (1920). *The Secret Power* (1921). *Love and the Philosopher* (1923). *Open Confession to a Man from a Woman* (1925). *Poems*, ed. B. Vyver (1925).

BIBLIOGRAPHY: Bigland, E. *Marie Corelli: The Woman and the Legend* (1953). Carr, K. *Miss Marie Corelli* (1901). Kowalczyk, R.L. *JPC* (1974). Kowalczyk, R.L. *MP* (1969). Masters, B. *Now Barabbas Was a Rotter: The Extraordinary Life of Marie Corelli*

(1978). Scott, W.S. *Marie Corelli: The Story of a Friendship* (1953). Vyver, B. *Memoirs of Marie Corelli* (1930). Magalaner, M. *Modern Irish Literature: Essays in Honor of William York Tindall*, ed. R.J. Porter and J.D. Brophy (1972).

Other references: *Bookman* (February 1918). *N&Q* (April 1943). *Strand* (1898). *Westminster Review* (December 1906).

Laura Hapke

Mary Victoria (Novello) Cowden Clarke

BORN: 22 June 1809, London.
DIED: 12 January 1898, Genoa, Italy.
DAUGHTER OF: Vincent and Mary Sabilla Novello.
MARRIED: Charles Cowden Clarke, 1828.

C. is remembered especially as a popularizer of William Shakespeare for nineteenth-century readers by her production of the first concordance to the plays, two editions of the plays, and many appreciations. The daughter of a popular organist, choirmaster, and music teacher, she received a musical as well as a sound general education at home and in France. Her well-read and vivacious mother was the most popular hostess in the Leigh Hunt–Charles Lamb circle and an author in her own right. The family had frequent evening parties attended by, among others, the Shelleys, with the widowed Mary Shelley continuing to visit after her return from Italy. In 1828 C. married Charles Cowden Clarke, a frequenter of these evening parties. He had been educated at his father's school at Enfield and was a staunch friend and beloved teacher of John Keats. Soon after their marriage, her husband, who had ventured into publishing, went bankrupt and began a new career in journalism, writing art, theater, and music reviews. C.'s father and her brother Joseph are known as the first in England to publish church music in popular editions, early English music from manuscript sources at Cambridge, and the first full edition of Henry Purcell, for much of which C. provided translations and notes. C.'s talented family included, among her eight brothers and sisters who lived to adulthood, Clara Anastasia (1818–1908), who had a very successful musical career before marrying an Italian count, and Edward Petre (1813–1834?), a precocious painter who exhibited successfully at the Royal Academy of Art.

At eighteen, C. published her first essays in Hone's *Table Book* (1827) but established her reputation, when, after fifteen years' work, *The Complete Concordance to Shakespeare* was issued in eighteen monthly parts and in complete editions in 1844–1845. In the following years, mostly after their move in 1856 to Nice and then Genoa, C. and her husband were to produce two major editions of Shakespeare's plays and poems and C.

to produce many works of appreciation, thus keeping at fever pitch the Bard's popularity in the nineteenth century. Her *The Girlhood of Shakespeare's Heroines* (1851–1852) provided a lead-in to the plays for generations of readers and is still in print. Charles Dickens cast her as Dame Quickly in his amateur production of *The Merry Wives of Windsor*, which played in London and in the provinces for a season to raise funds for the Shakespeare curator at Stratford. C. produced translations in Novello's theory of music series, a few children's stories, and several novels and volumes of verses. Her most valued work today is the body of reminiscences of the important literary figures with whom she and her husband were associated; most of these were included in *Recollections of Writers* (1878) and her autobiography, *My Long Life: An Autobiographic Sketch* (1896), and they have withstood the modern scholars' tests for accuracy.

Richard Altick describes C.'s writing style, modeled on Leigh Hunt's, as "cockney prose." It is characterized by overuse of compound epithets, of Latinisms, archaisms, and coinages. This style and an overwhelmingly sentimental tone are the reasons that C.'s work is little read today, although several titles are still in print. The style belies her spirited approach to a life, which included cold showers every morning, stiff walks in the mountains above Nice and Genoa, an egalitarian attitude toward her husband and their work, and a clear idea of the heroic woman.

WORKS: *The Complete Concordance to Shakespeare* (1844–1845). *Shakespeare's Proverbs; or The Wise Saws of Our Wisest Poet Collected into a Modern Instance* (1847). *Kit Bam's Adventures, or, The Yarns of an Old Mariner* (1848). *The Girlhood of Shakespeare's Heroines in a Series of Tales* (1850–1852). (trans.) *Treatise on Counterpoint and Fugue*, by Luigi Cherubini (1854). (trans.) *A Treatise upon Modern Instrumentation and Orchestration* by Hector Berlioz, (1855). *The Iron Cousin, or, Mutual Influence* (1854). *The Song of Drop o' Wather. By Harry Wandsworth Shortfellow* (1856). *The Life and Labours of Vincent Novello* (1864). *The Trust and The Remittance: Two Love Stories* (1873). *Recollections of Writers* (1878). *Honey from the*

Weed, Verses (1881). *Verse Waifs: Forming an Appendix to Honey from the Weed* (1883). *A Score of Sonnets to One Object* (1884). *Uncle, Peep, and I; a Child's Novel* (1886). *Centennial Biographic Sketch of Charles Cowden Clarke* (1887). *My Long Life: An Autobiographic Sketch* (1896). *Letters to an Enthusiast: Being a Series of Letters Addressed to Robert Balmanno, Esqu., of New York, 1850-1861*, ed. A.U. Nettleton (1902).

BIBLIOGRAPHY: Altick, R. *The Cowden Clarkes* (1948). Ellis, R. *Notes and Queries* (England) (1984). Gross, G.C. *Victirian Studies* (1972). Law, P. *Sydney Studies in English*(1985-1986).

For articles in reference works, see *DNB. New Century Handbook.*

Eleanor Langstaff

Hannah Parkhouse Cowley

BORN: 1743, Tiverton, Devon.
DIED: 11 March 1809, Tiverton, Devon.
DAUGHTER OF: Philip Parkhouse.
MARRIED: Captain Cowley, c. 1768.

Although not as well-known as Aphra Behn or Susanna Centlivre, playwrights of the late seventeenth and early eighteenth-centuries respectively, C. warrants attention for her thirteen plays written for the patent theaters during the late eighteenth century. She may have been influenced by the fact that her father, Philip Parkhouse, was a bookseller who could trace his heritage to John Gay. At twenty-five, she married Captain Cowley of the East India Company. On visiting the playhouse with her husband, she declared that she could do better than the playwright being staged. This enthusiasm caused her to write her first play, *The Runaway*, which was successfully produced by Garrick at Drury Lane on 15 February 1776. Later she was to write of the play "that it was one of the most profitable Plays, both to the Author and Manager, that appears in the records of the *Treasury books* at either house. . . ."

For eighteen years she wrote plays, chiefly comedies, her most successful being *The Belle's Strategem* (1781), *A Bold Stroke for a Husband* (1783), and *Who's the Dupe?* (1779). She twice ventured into the world of tragedy and twice failed. C.'s first tragedy, *Albina,* produced an unpleasant confrontation with Hannah More, whom she accused of plagiarism. Puzzled at production delays, C. later wrote in her preface to the play, "I learnt with great surprise, that it [More's *The Law of Lombardy*] bore a resemblance to *Albina. . . .*" The argument that followed carried over into an unpleasant exchange of articles in the newspapers, none of which helped the play, which was relegated to unprofitable summer production at the Haymarket. Her other tragedy, *The Fate of Sparta*, which Leigh Hunt described as hackneyed in its sentiments, was not revived after its initial run of eight performances at Drury Lane.

Yet, C. is best remembered for her comedies of manners, which depend on lovely heroines, who through clever intrigues, inspired by the love of virtue and the goal of an ideal marriage, triumph over attractive but superficial males. *The Belle's Strategem* reveals C. at her best. The play opens with Doricourt contracted to marry Letitia Hardy, an English "country cousin," whom he has not met, and who, he is sure, lacks the vitality of "the restless charmers of Italy and France." Beautiful, modest Letitia, realizing that she will be doomed to a loveless marriage, plots to make Doricourt dislike her on the assumption "that it is easier to convert a sentiment to its opposite than to transform indifference to a tender passion." She then alienates Doricourt by becoming a parody of the "country cousin"; later, at a masquerade, she uses all her English charms and conquers him completely. Finally, using the further intrigue of a false marriage, she wins him. The play ends with Doricourt's praising English women, with their innate modesty, above their Continental counterparts.

The effectiveness of *The Belle's Strategem* undoubtedly resides in the character of Letitia Hardy, which was a favorite role of Mrs. Jordan and which was to appeal to fine actresses for the next century including Fanny Davenport, Ada Rehan, and Ellen Terry, who acted the part opposite Henry Irving's Doricourt. In this century, the play was presented at the Royal Court in 1913.

Most of the comedies had limited stage histories of from one to sixteen performances over one to two-year spans. The exceptions were, in addition to *The Belle's Strategem, The Runaway, Which Is the Man?, A Bold Stroke for a Husband,* and *Who's the Dupe?* These were frequently revived during the last two decades of the eighteenth century, and *A Bold Stroke for a Husband* was revived successfully in 1872, at New York's Fifth Avenue Theater, where Fanny Davenport played Donna Olivia. The critic for *The New York Times* paid tribute to the actors and the playwright when he expressed the wish that "modern writers would more frequently strive to catch something of the briskness and rapidity of their dialogue and the fun and contrast of their characters. . . ."

C.'s non-dramatic work includes a number of long, sentimental romances and a poetic correspondence between Anna Matilda (C.) and Della Crusca (Robert Merry), which was attacked by William Gifford in his satire *The Baviad* (1794).

C.'s best plays reflect clever plots, sound characterization, and lively dialogue, qualities that make them good reading today. Her *Works* (1813), published in three volumes, contain eleven plays and most of the poems.

WORKS: *The Runaway* (1776). *Who's the Dupe?* (1779). *Albina, Countess Raymond* (1779). *The School for Eloquence* (In MS; Drury Lane 1780). *The Maid of Arragon; a Tale* (1780). *The Belle's Stratagem* (1781). *The World as It Goes; or a Party at Montpellier* (In MS; Covent Garden 1781; also titled *Second Thoughts Are Best*). *Which Is Man?* (1782). *A Bold Stroke for a Husband* (1783). *More Ways Than One* (1784). *A School for Greybeards, or the Mourning Bride* (1786). *The Scottish Village, or Pitcairne Green* (1786). *The Poetry of Anna Matilda* (1788). *The Fate of Sparta, or the Rival Kings* (1788). *A Day in Turkey: or the Russian Slaves* (1792). *The Town Before You* (1795). *The Siege of Acre: An Epic Poem* (1801). *Works of Mrs. Cowley: Poems and Dramas.* (1813).

BIBLIOGRAPHY: "Life of Mrs. Cowley." In *Works of Mrs. Cowley. . . .* Vol. 1 (1813). Norton, J.E. *Book Collector* (1958). Rhodes, R.C. *R.E.S.* (1929).

For articles in reference works, see: *DNB. Ocel. Oxford Companion to the Theatre* (1983). Todd.

Philip Bordinat

Dinah Maria Mulock Craik

BORN: 20 April 1826, Stroke-on-Trent, Staffordshire.
DIED: 12 October 1887, Shortlands, Kent.
DAUGHTER OF: Thomas and Dinah Mellard Mulock.
MARRIED: George Lillie Craik, 1865.
WROTE UNDER: D.M.M., author of *John Halifax, Gentleman.*

C., a popular and prolific Victorian author, wrote novels, short stories, poetry, and essays. A working woman all her adult life, C. began writing to support herself and her two younger brothers; she continued writing in spite of her husband's objections after she married. C.'s works appeared in such popular periodicals as *Chambers's Edinburgh Journal, Good Words,* and *Harper's Bazaar.*

C. thought a woman was happiest married and raising children. She also believed a woman should be meek, tender, tidy, obedient, patient, and charitable. However, she also believed a husband must respect his wife and her opinions. In *A Woman's Thoughts About Women* (1858), C. states that a woman should learn a vocation in case she does not marry and should remain useful even after marriage. In other essays, C. argues that a married woman should have the legal right to manage her own money as well as the right to seek legal separation from her husband and custody of her children if her spouse is unfit.

At least two of C.'s fictional pieces, both marred by sentimentality and moralizing, reflect the author's life. In *Bread upon the Waters* (1852), a man, like C.'s own father, refuses to support his daughter and two sons. The narrator of this work, the silently suffering daughter, practices fully the Victorian virtue of duty by sacrificing her freedom and youth for her brothers. Although C. accepted duty as a necessary virtue of women and believed women should marry, this tale shows that she also held the romantic notion that a woman should marry only for love. Twice the narrator receives marriage proposals from kind men who would rescue her from a narrow life. Both times she refuses because she does not love them. *King Arthur* (1886) is C.'s novel describing the unfortunate social and legal problems faced in an adoption in nineteenth-century England. C. herself adopted a baby girl a few years after she married.

Better works than *Bread upon the Waters* and *King Arthur* are C.'s fairy tales. In *Alice Learmont* (1852), a girl stolen by fairies painfully learns to set aside selfish irresponsibility. This reworking of a Scottish fairy tale enjoys authentic dialect, a suspenseful plot, and an unobtrusive moral. *The Little Lame Prince and His Travelling Cloak* (1875), an original fairy tale, recounts the adventure of Prince Dolor, who escapes exile with a magic cloak that allows him to see the world without being a part of it.

John Halifax, Gentleman (1856), C.'s most popular work, describes the life of a poor orphan who, through Christian virtue, becomes a loving family man and a prosperous businessman. C. successfully portrays Halifax as being morally earnest but not dull and pompous. The novel includes historical details such as the innovation of small pox inoculation and the emancipation of Catholics; such famous figures as Lady Hamilton and

Lord Byron make brief appearances in the novel. In *Dinah Mulock Craik* (1983), S. Mitchell states that *Will Denbigh, Nobleman* (1877), a novel frequently attributed to C., was written by someone else.

Best known for her novels, C. usually wrote sentimental and didactic fiction that typifies what middle-class readers in the mid-nineteenth century enjoyed reading—domestic stories of virtuous people who eventually find their just rewards in life.

WORKS: *Michael the Miner* (1846). *How to Win Love* (1848). *The Ogilvies* (1849). *Cola Monti* (1849). *Olive* (1850). *The Half-Caste* (1851). *The Head of the Family* (1852). *Bread upon the Waters* (1852). *Alice Learmont* (1852). *A Hero* (1853). *Avillon and Other Tales* (1853). *Agatha's Husband* (1853). *The Little Lychetts* (1855). *John Halifax, Gentleman* (1856). *Nothing New* (1857). *A Woman's Thoughts About Women* (1858). *A Life for a Life* (1859). *Poems* (1859). *Domestic Stories* (1859). *Romantic Tales* (1859). *Our Year* (1860). *Studies from Life* (1861). *Mistress and Maid* (1863). *The Fairy Book* (1863). *Christian's Mistake* (1865). *A New Year's Gift to Sick Children* (1865). *A Noble Life* (1866). *Two Marriages* (1867). *M. de Barante, a Memoir* by F.P.G. Guizot (translated by Craik 1867). *A French Country Family* by H. de Witt (translated by Craik, 1867). *The Woman's Kingdom* (1869). *A Brave Lady* (1870). *The Unkind Word and Other Stories* (1870). *Motherless* by H. de Witt (translated by Craik, 1871). *Fair France* (1871). *Little Sunshine's Holiday* (1871). *Hannah* (1872). *The Adventures of a Brownie* (1872). *My Mother and I* (1874). *Sermons out of Church* (1875). *Songs of Our Youth* (1875). *The Little Lame Prince and His Travelling Cloak* (1875). *The Laurel Bush* (1877). *A Legacy* (1878). *Young Mrs. Jardine* (1879). *Thirty Years* (1880). *His Little Mother and Other Tales and Sketches* (1881). *Children's Poetry* (1881). *Plain Speaking* (1882). *A Christian Woman* by H. de Witt (translated by Craik, 1882). *An Unsentimental Journey through Cornwall* (1884). *Miss Tommy* (1884). *King Arthur* (1886). *About Money and Other Things* (1886). *An Unknown Country* (1887). *Fifty Golden Years* (1887). *Poems* (1888). *Concerning Men and Other Papers* (1888).

BIBLIOGRAPHY: Brantlinger, P. *The Spirit of Reform: British Literature and Politics, 1832-1867* (1977). Hickok, K. *Representations of Women: Nineteenth-Century Women's Poetry* (1984). Mitchell, S. *Dinah Mulock Craik* (1983). Showalter, E. *Feminist Studies* (1975). Showalter, E. *A Literature of Their Own: British Women Novelists from Brontë to Lessing* (1977).

For articles in reference works, see: *BA19C. Great Writers of the English Language: Novelists*, ed. J. Vinson (1979).

Margaret Ann Baker Graham

Elizabeth (Berkeley) Craven, Baroness Craven, afterward Margravine of Anspach (Ansbach)

BORN: 17 December 1750, Spring Gardens, Middlesex.
DIED: 12 January 1828, Naples.
DAUGHTER OF: Augustus, fourth Earl of Berkeley, and Elizabeth (Drax), Countess of Berkeley.
MARRIED: William Craven, 1767; Christian Frederic, Margrave of Anspach (Ansbach), 1791.

C. was a playwright, novelist, translator, librettist, and musician whose learning, alliances, travels, and memoirs earned her an international audience for fifty years. The occasional nature of her most popular writings meant that their vogue did not much outlast their author. C.'s idiosyncrasies led to the jaundiced viewpoint of later biographers, such as George Paston, who wrote a classic hatchet job in *Little Memoirs of the Eighteenth Century*:

Her ladyship, who is said to have been an admirable *raconteur* in society, had a dull and incoherent prose style; and was so engrossed by the contemplation of her own beauty, virtues, and accomplishments, that it is necessary to sift her autobiography and letters very carefully in order to extract a few grains of amusement, or even of truth.

Such criticism misses much that is attractive about C.'s work and life.

Not expected to survive at birth, C. had a delicate childhood. Despite her poor health and negligent mother, C. developed intellectually at an early age. When she married the nephew and heir of Lord Craven at age seventeen, C. had already gained a reputation as a linguist, wit, and beauty. Her social circle came to include Horace Walpole, Samuel Johnson, David Garrick, and Sir Joshua Reynolds. Johnson thought she talked too much;

Reynolds began but never finished a portrait of her. Walpole was an early champion of her work, either because of a toadying impulse or a genuine crush. He had her play *The Sleep-Walker* printed at his own Strawberry Hill Press in 1778.

C. worked comfortably in French, German, Latin, and Italian (by no means unparalleled accomplishments for a woman of her rank), but C. was unusual in the extent to which she used her wide reading in these languages as a basis for stories and plays. Her oeuvre reflects the tastes of the times: private theatricals, light opera, "humors" comedy, and sentimental drama. *The Sleep-Walker* was the first work of Count de Pont de Vesle's to be translated; *The Statue Feast* (1782) was a translation of Molière's *Le Festin de Pierre*; *The Robbers* (1799) was a version of Schiller's *Die Räuber*. Her short novel *Modern Anecdotes of the Ancient Family of the Kinkvervankotdarsprackingatchderns* (1780) was popular enough to see five editions; a play based on it was written by Miles Andrews and performed at the Theatre Royal in Haymarket in 1781. Though C. intended most of her plays as private entertainments, some, like *The Silver Tankard* and *A Miniature Picture*, had public runs.

A pivotal event both in her life and her literary career was C.'s separation from Lord Craven in 1780. He had taken a mistress quite publicly and was surprised to find out that C. knew. She resisted an effort by Craven's family to silence her, and she seems to have triumphed over the standard counter-rumor of her own intrigues with a servant. Her response to the separation was to depart for the Continent and travel through Greece, Turkey, Austria, Russia, and what is now Romania. While in Ansbach she visited and became the mistress of Christian Frederic, Margrave of Ansbach. Their correspondence was published in London in 1786 under the title *Journey through the Crimea to Constantinople*. Partly because of C.'s scandalous reputation, this melange of travel sketches, opinions and reflections on customs became an international success; it was published in France in 1789 and in Vienna in 1800.

In September 1791 Lord Craven died, and a little more than a month later C. and the Margrave were married. They moved to England the next year and purchased Brandenburgh House in Hammersmith and Benham House in Berkshire; both houses became sites of theatricals and feasts for the rest of the decade. C.'s most popular book, her *Memoirs*, appeared in 1826, two years before her death.

Far from being dull, her prose, especially *Journey* and *Memoirs*, bears out her reputation for wit, storytelling, and cattiness (for example, she met and was unimpressed by the Empress Catherine, who had "the remains of a fine skin"). Her

by-the-way opinions are often as interesting as the subject at hand. As for incoherence, she clearly wrote at great speed without looking back—but then, she was neither the first nor the last *memoiriste* with that failing.

For a woman who enjoyed a form of emancipation, she is ambivalent about the place of women. "Through every age and every country we shall find women adored and oppressed," she writes. Further, she defends the adeptness and versatility of the feminine intelligence: "Whenever women are indulged with any freedom, they polish sooner than man." Nevertheless, when actually comparing the roles of women and men, C. reverts to a standard defense of male domination—the idea that biology is destiny:

> Intellectual powers respond to the destination of nature: men have pentration and solid judgment to fit them for governing; women have sufficient understanding to make a respectable figure under good government;—a greater proportion would excite a dangerous rivalship.

Still, C. was very conscious of being both a writer and a woman of rank. Some of the prefaces to her plays plead for the same critical openness accorded to male authors.

C. was much more comfortable with comedy than with serious drama. Of her comedies, *The Sleep-Walker* is quite good, as is *A Miniature Picture*. Moralism and the urge to sentimentalize weigh down action, character, and dialogue in her noncomic plays. The range of her female characterizations reflects the split in her thinking: her female characters are either stereotypes or women who exploit the little freedom they can find within their social niches. Eliza of *The Georgian Princess* (1799), who gains an advantageous marriage through disguise and gender role reversal, ends the play by saying, "Ladies, I trust you will adopt my plan/and only wear the dress to gain the man." The marriage game is itself a form of role playing that the resourceful woman can work to her own advantage.

Her reading, if not always deep, was promiscuous. She preferred contemporary authors to ancient ones (she once censured Johnson for having precisely the opposite taste) and continental authors to her English countrymen. She prescribed Henault, Fontenelle, Buffon, and Montesquieu as the beginnings of any serious library. C. was certainly not averse either to demonstrating her learning or to talking about herself ("My taste for music and my style of imagination in writing . . . were great sources of delight to me"). C.'s literary persona is so open and unself-conscious that her frequent discussions of herself do not seem like mordant conceit, but rather more as Walpole himself recognized:

There is such an integrity and frankness in her consciousness of her own talents, that she speaks of these with a naiveté as if she had no property in them, but only wore them as gifts of the gods.

Walpole, not a faithful friend, revised his opinion later into a sort of bitchy condemnation. C.'s writings, however, present her as a learned, ingenuous, authentically accomplished writer.

WORKS: *A Christmas-Box* (1773). (trans.) *The Sleep-Walker*, by P. deVesle (1778). *Modern Anecdotes of the Ancient Family of Kinkvervankotdarsprackingatchderns. A Tale for Christmas 1799* (1780). *A Fashionable Day* (1780). *A Miniature Picture* (1780). *The Point at Portsmouth, or The Silver Tankard* (1781). *La Folie du Jour* (1781). (trans.) *The Statue Feast*, by Molière (1782). *The Arcadian Pastoral* (1782). *A Journey through the Crimea to Constantinople* (1786). *Le Philosophe Moderne* (1790). *The Yorkshire Ghost* (1799). (trans.) *The Robbers*, by Schiller (1799). *The Georgian Princess* (1799). *Puss in Boots* (1799). *Love Rewarded* (1799). *Nourgad* (1803). *Love in a Convent* (1805). *Memoirs* (1826).

BIBLIOGRAPHY: For articles in reference works, see: *Annual Biography and Obituary* (1828). *Biographica Dramatica* (1812). *DNB*. Genest, J. *History of the Stage* (1832).

Other references: Nicoll, A. *A History of Late Eighteenth Century Drama* (1927). Rodgers, K.M. *Feminism in Eighteenth-Century England* (1982). Symonds, E.M. *Little Memoirs of the Eighteenth Century* (1901). Walpole, H. *Letters* (1857-1859).

John Timpane

Catherine Ann Crowe

BORN: 1800 [?], Borough Green, Kent.
DIED: 1876, Folkestone.
DAUGHTER OF: John Stevens.
MARRIED: Lt. Col. John Crowe, 1822.

Novelist and writer on the supernatural, C. enjoyed wide popular success and the friendship of many prominent people during the mid-nineteenth century. Between 1841 and 1854, she produced five novels, a play, a book of short stories, an anthology of writings on the supernatural, tales for children, an adaptation of *Uncle Tom's Cabin*, and a translation. In Edinburgh, where she had moved after her marriage, she was welcomed in intellectual and artistic circles. Her friends included astronomer John Pringle Nichol, chemist Samuel Brown, painter David Scott, writer Thomas DeQuincey, and the founder of the *Edinburgh Review*, Francis Jeffrey. She met Dickens and Emerson on their visits to Edinburgh, and when she went to London, she called on the Carlyles and dined with Thackeray and Charlotte Brontë. In 1854 she suffered a serious breakdown. According to Dickens, she was seen "walking down her own street in Edinburgh, not only stark mad but stark naked too"—on the instruction of "spirits." After her recovery, she published a Christmas book, a treatise on spiritualism, and more stories for children, but she did not receive serious attention. The last years of her life are obscure.

C.'s fiction gives little evidence of learning or literary self-consciousness; her other writing suggests eclectic reading. *Aristodemus* (1838), her first work, suggests that she had some knowledge of classical tragedy. However, C. used historical legends of the Messenian king not to analyze the end of a dynasty but rather to assert the primacy of domestic virtue: her king falls because he denies his family. C. was fluent enough in German to translate the *Seeress of Prevorst* (1845). In *Spiritualism and the Age We Live in* (1859), she identifies herself as a disciple of Scottish phrenologist George Combe; inspired by his work, she studied phrenology, physiology, and spiritualism. That she was regarded as a person of considerable learning willing to speak boldly on controversial issues can be deduced from the fact that *Vestiges of the Natural History of Creation*, which Robert Chambers published anonymously in 1844, was often attributed to her; that she was overly eager to have the intellectual respect of her contemporaries might be assumed by her reluctance to undeceive them.

C.'s first novel, *Adventures of Susan Hopley; or, Circumstantial Evidence* (1841) is, according to one of the characters, a picture of "real life and human nature," an experiment in disclosing "the exact truth with all its detail." It was followed by four more novels—*Men and Women; or, Manorial Rights* (1843), *The Story of Lilly Dawson* (1847), *Adventures of a Beauty* (1852), and *Linny Lockwood* (1854)—and by stories in such periodicals as *Household Words* and *Chambers's Journal*. *Susan Hopley* became "a great hit" at the circulating libraries, and like many of her later works quickly went into cheap editions. Nineteenth-century readers regarded C. as a realist because she set her novels in ordinary surroundings and chose working people—merchants, lawyers, even servants—for her characters. Susan Hopley is a housekeeper; Lilly Dawson works as a nurse, milliner's assistant, and maid. When Jane Carlyle compared her life to a C. novel—"futile in the extreme, but so full of plot that the *interest . . .* has never been allowed to flag"—she caught the prevailing response of Victorian readers. As one reviewer said, C. liked to cram her novels with "scheming and cross-scheming, ravelling and unravelling, plot and counter plot." Even the *Westminster Review* described C. as a "conjurer who can make a card fly out of the pack into a gentleman's pocket or a lady's reticule, and restore it to its proper place with a wave of his wand." Although the plots are marked by melodrama, lurid intrigue, and violent incidents—what novelist Susan Ferrier called "bad doings and bloody murders"—malefactors are punished in the end; hence C. acquired a reputation for conveying "good moral instruction in an exceedingly pleasing form." Moreover, since her novels upheld the importance of "homely duties, faithful attachment, and domestic happiness," they were regarded as safe reading in the turbulent 1840s. Even in cheap editions, her novels were fit "for the perusal of all classes."

Although C. does not undertake a sustained criticism of English society, her novels do express discontent regarding the status of women. In *Lilly Dawson*, she claims that nature intended woman "to play a noble part in the world's history, if man would but let her play it out, and not treat her like a full-grown baby, to be flattered and spoilt on the one hand, and coerced and restricted on the other, vibrating between royal rule and slavish serfdom." C.'s women frequently find themselves in trouble because their education has not provided them with practical skill or sound judgment. The most interesting characters deviate from conventional literary roles. The brave and stalwart Susan Hopley chooses to remain single. "Husbands and lovers have great power over women, and can not only oblige them to do as they please, but very often can make them see with their eyes, and hear with their ears," she observes. C.'s fallen women are not punished for "sins" which are the result of economic circumstances. Instead of dying, they live to raise their children, help their parents, or

at worst, enter convents. The heroine of *Linny Lockwood* (1854), who has been deserted by her husband, forms a close emotional bond with his mistress and assists at the birth of their illegitimate child, whom she promises to raise.

In her writings about the supernatural, C. was influenced by physician and poet Justinus Kerner, whose study of the somnambulist and clairvoyant Frederike Hauffe she translated as *The Seeress of Prevorst*. C. scorned the rationalism of the eighteenth century and the orthodox religions of the nineteenth. In *The Night Side of Nature; or, Ghosts and Ghost Seers* (1848) she set out to explore "all that class of phenomena which appears to throw some light on our psychical nature, and on the probable state of the soul after death." Drawing heavily on French and German authorities, she filled two volumes with enthusiastic accounts of dreams, trances, presentiments, wraiths, *Doppelgängers*, spectral lights, haunted houses and poltergeists. Despite disorganization and occasional fits of stylistic incoherence, the book was very popular; in 1921 Richard Garnett could still describe *The Night Side of Nature* as "one of the best collections of supernatural stories in our language."

WORKS: *Aristodemus* (1838). *Adventures of Susan Hopley; or, Circumstantial Evidence* (1841). *Men and Women; or, Manorial Rights* (1843). *The Story of Lilly Dawson* (1847). *Pippie's Warning; or, Mind your Temper* (1848). *The Night Side of Nature; or, Ghosts and Ghost Seers* (1848). *Light and Darkness; or, Mysteries of Life* (1850). *Adventures of a Beauty* (1852). *The Cruel Kindness: A Romantic Play* (1853). *Linny Lockwood* (1854). *Ghosts and Family Legends* (1859). *Spiritualism and the Age We Live in* (1859). *The Story of Arthur Hunter and his First Shilling* (1861). *The Adventures of a Monkey* (1862).

BIBLIOGRAPHY: Clapton, G.T. *MLR* (1930). Dalziel, M. *Popular Fiction 100 Years Ago* (1957). Keegan, P.Q. *Victoria Magazine* (1879). Mitchell, S. *The Fallen Angel: Chastity, Class and Women's Reading, 1835-1880* (1981). Sergeant, A. *Women Novelists of Queen Victoria's Reign* (1897).

For articles in reference works, see: *Allibone. BA19C.* Boase. *CBEL. DNB. Europa. NCBEL.*

Robin Sheets

Nancy Cunard

BORN: 10 March 1896, Nevill Holt, Leicestershire.
DIED: 16 March 1965, Paris.
DAUGHTER OF: Sir Bache and Lady Maud Burke Cunard.
MARRIED: Sidney Fairbairne, 1916.

C. was born into the British upper class and spent her childhood at the family estate, Nevill Holt. Her mother, a wealthy American socialite who later changed her name to "Emerald," was a patron of the arts, and C. grew up surrounded by artists, musicians, and writers. One of her closest companions during her formative years was her mother's friend, George Moore. C. was educated at home by a governess until the age of fourteen, when she and her mother moved to London so Lady Cunard could be near her lover, the conductor Sir Thomas Beecham. She then attended private schools in London, Germany, and Paris.

C. preferred the company of her friends, who called themselves the Corrupt Coterie, to the fashionable society world. C., Iris Tree, Diana Manners, Augustus John, Osbert Sitwell, Ezra Pound, and Wyndham Lewis spent their evenings in 1914 at the Cafe Royal or the Eiffel Tower Restaurant discussing politics and poetry. Also during that period, C. began writing poetry, most of which was conventional in theme and style. Her first poems were published in 1915 in the *Eton College Chronicle*, and in 1916 she contributed several poems to the *Wheels* anthology edited by Edith Sitwell.

After World War I C. spent most of her time in Paris, where she became involved in the newest movements in art and literature—Dada, Surrealism, Modernism. She became more dependent on alcohol and also started to experiment with drugs. In 1920 C. began a lengthy affair with Michael Arlen, a novelist who would later use C. as the model for Iris March, the main character in his novel *The Green Hat*. In 1922 C. had a brief liaison with Aldous Huxley. The relationship ended badly, and Huxley made C. the basis for Lucy Tantamount, his ultimate femme fatale, in *Point Counter Point*.

Outlaws, C.'s first volume of poetry, was published in 1921. In general it received kind reviews, even though much of the poetry was melodramatic. *Sublunary*, a volume of mostly autobiographical poetry, appeared in 1923. Although this book, too, received only mediocre reviews, one poem, "To the Eiffel Tower Restaurant," is interesting for its nostalgic view of C.'s past: "Those old nights of drinking,/Furtive adventures, solitary thinking . . ./I think the Tower shall go up to heaven/One night in a flame of fire, about eleven." C.'s best book of pooems, *Parallax*, was published in 1925 by the Hogarth Press of Virginia and Leonard Woolf. It records the thoughts of a young poet as he travels around Europe contemplating youth and ambition, love and friendship. Although the poetry is often imitative of *The Waste Land*, it is introspective and self-revealing: "Think now how friends grow old—/ Their diverse brains, hearts, faces, modify; . . ./ Am I the same?/Or a vagrant, of other breed, gone further, lost. . . ." The reviewer for the *Times Literary Supplement* declared that *Parallax* "seems to be the creation of a resilient mind; it has a complexity and grasp of reality which is so frequently lacking from women's poetry."

In 1927 C. bought an old farmhouse at Reanville, outside Paris, where she set up the Hours Press. Reacting against the conservatism of British publishers who refused to print anything innovative or controversial, C. published works by both new and well-established authors who could not get their material into print elsewhere. C. printed *A Draft of XXX Cantos* by Ezra Pound because it would be "the first printing of all the thirty cantos ready at that date." She was the first person to print work by Samuel Beckett, a long poem called *Whoroscope*. The Hours Press also featured stories, poetry, and essays by George Moore, Norman Douglas, Laura Riding, Roy Campbell, Robert Graves, Brian Howard, and Havelock Ellis.

Hours Press survived for only four years, as C.'s attention was diverted, in 1930, to what she considered a more important cause, the civil rights movement in the United States. C. had been romantically involved since 1928 with Henry Crowder, a black American musician, and had become an avid collector of African art and jewelry. In fact, C. had become so renowned for her collection of ivory bracelets that both Cecil Beaton and Man Ray had photographed her wearing them, her arms covered in ivory bangles. Through Crowder C. learned about America's problems with segregation and racism. Always in favor of the underdog, C. decided to create a record of the history of the American Negro. She spent more than two years collecting poetry, stories, and essays by and about blacks, and many of C.'s friends contributed to the anthology; both Samuel Beckett and William Carlos Williams were very much involved in the project. C. made two trips to New York City to gather work from black writers, but because she stayed in Harlem with a black man, she received hundreds of obscene letters and death threats, many of which she boldly printed in *Negro*. *Negro* was finally published in 1934, at C.'s expense. The book was a failure commercially and was often called "communistic" because of its leftist slant. C. and her co-workers put thousands of hours and thousands of dollars into creating a history of the American black that would stand as a reminder of the evils of hatred and prejudice. *Negro* also enabled writers such as Langston Hughes, Claude McKay, and Zora Neale Hurston to find an outlet for their work.

During the Spanish Civil War C. worked as a free-lance writer/correspondent. She lived most of the years 1936-1939 in Madrid with the poet Pablo Neruda. In 1937 she printed a pamphlet entitled "Poets of the World Defend the Spanish People," which included poems by Neruda, Louis Aragon, Tristan Tzara, García Lorca, Brian Howard, and the first printed version of W.H. Auden's controversial poem "Spain." At the same time, she circulated a questionnaire among several hundred writers in England, Scotland, Ireland, and Wales, asking them: "Are you for, or against, the legal government and the People of Republican Spain? Are you for, or against, Franco and Fascism?" *The Left Review* published the 148 responses in a special issue called *Authors Take Sides on the Spanish War.*

C. spent the last years of World War II in London. In 1944, inspired by Stephen Spender and John Lehmann's *Poems for Spain,* C. put together another anthology, *Poems for France.* The contents were highly diversified in style (both Vita Sackville-West and Hugh MacDiarmid, for example, were included) but were unified in celebrating France and her people. This anthology, combined with C.'s anti-fascist activities in Spain, earned her a place on Hitler's enemies list. When she returned to Reanville in 1945, C. was devastated to find that nearly all her books and personal papers, jewelry, artwork, and furnishings had been stolen or desecrated by the Germans.

C.'s last years were spent traveling, visiting friends, and writing. C. published *Grand Man: Memories of Norman Douglas* in 1954 and *GM: Memories of George Moore* in 1956. Her own memoir, *These Were the Hours,* was published posthumously in 1969. C. died, alone and penniless, in the public ward of a Paris Hospital in 1965.

WORKS: *Outlaws* (1921). *Sublunary* (1923). *Parallax* (1925). *Poems (Two) 1925* (1930). *Black Man and White Ladyship: An Anniversary* (1931). (with G. Padmore) *The White Man's Duty* (1942). *Relève in Manquis* (1944). *Man-Ship-Tank-Gun-Plane* (1944). *Grand Man: Memories of Norman Douglas* (1954). *Thoughts About Ronald Firbank* (1954). *GM: Memories of George Moore* (1956). *These Were the Hours: Memories of My Hours Press, Reanville and Paris, 1928-1931* (1969), ed. H. Ford.

BIBLIOGRAPHY: Burkhart, C. *Herman & Nancy & Ivy: Three Lives in Art* (1977). Chisholm, A. *Nancy Cunard* (1979). Fielding, D. *Emerald and Nancy: Lady Cunard and Her Daughter* (1968). Ford, H. ed. *Nancy Cunard: Brave Poet, Indomitable Rebel, 1896-1965* (1968).

For articles in reference works, see: *Biographical Index.*

Other references: Flanner, J. *London Was Yesterday, 1934-1939* (1975). Ford, H. "Introduction" to *Negro: An Anthology,* ed. N. Cunard (rpt. 1970). Green, M. *Children of the Sun: A Narrative of "Decadence" in England After 1918* (1976).

Kate Beaird Meyers

Clemence Dane *(pseudonym of Winifred Ashton)*

BORN: 1887, Blackheath, London.
DIED: 28 March 1965, London.

Winifred Ashton, born in Blackheath (London), used the pseudonym "Clemence Dane" (suggested by the church of St. Clement's Dane in The Strand) to disguise the sex of the unimportant actress "Diana Portis" when she wrote some popular plays, screen plays, and radio plays. It was more importantly the name under which she turned out a score or more of well-received fictions. A male pseudonym was perhaps understandable in the light of the disdain in critical circles for the title of her first novel, *Regiment of Women* (1917), and the attitudes of the male Establishment toward some women writers. Also, London had a literary jungle; she portrayed it in her third novel, *Legend* (1919). Eventually, she triumphed in it. She made "Clemence Dane," in her time, as famous a pseudonym as "George Eliot" or at least "Acton Bell," and she showed the public that women could write something besides detective fiction, low-brow sentimental novels, and middle-brow historical fiction, at that period

the major products of the many women in the literary marketplace.

Raised in a late-Victorian suburb, she showed some rebelliousness in becoming an art student (at The Slade 1904-1906 and in Dresden 1906-1907), a teacher far from home (in Geneva 1903 and in Ireland 1907-1913), then a mildly successful young actress in London under the name "Diana Portis" (1913-1915). Then she tried her hand at writing.

Her life as a teacher was drawn upon to some extent for her first novel, *Regiment of Women;* it involves a complex but not very sensational relationship between a couple of teachers. Her second novel, *First the Blade* (1918), described in a subtitle as "a comedy of growth," was less autobiographical, but also well received. She returned to her own experience for her third novel, *Legend* (1919), in which the "legend" of the career of a minor novelist is cattily dissected on the night of her death by a few of her friends (or perhaps one ought to say "associates"). The cat-eat-cat (rather than dog-eat-dog) world of backbiting and blatant careerism among types which the British have now come to call *pseuds* is beautifully illustrated in this study of the London writing world just after World War I.

Some of the denizens of London's bohemia in her work might have been even more vividly shown had she drawn on her personal life as a struggling actress and written of the theatre backstage. But she determined to write for the stage, rather than act on it, so maybe she needed not to annoy the powers that were. In 1921 she began as a playwright with *A Bill of Divorcement*, a piece of the sort Sir Arthur Wing Pinero had firmly established, one that asks a question of supposed social importance (but in theatrical terms) and answers it with equal theatricality. The question in *A Bill of Divorcement* may sound odd today: Should a marriage be annulled on grounds of insanity? Still the play is finely crafted and has several effective moments, though *coups de théâtre* is too strong a term for them. The same year saw *The Terror* (a minor effort) and an ingenious short play, *Will Shakespeare* (a charming "invention" concerned with his affair with Anne Hathaway). She was off to a fast start as playwright.

Her dramatic career seldom lagged. She adapted *Legend* for the stage (1923), followed with a couple of "plays for boys" (*Shivering Shocks* of 1923, *Mr. Fox* of 1927), some commercial West End fare (*Naboth's Vineyard*, *Granite*, *Mariners*, *A Traveller Returns*, etc.), some musicals with Richard Addinsell (*Adam's Opera* in 1928, *Come of Age* in 1934), some adaptations (*L'Aiglon* from Rostand, *The Happy Hypocrite* from Sir Max Beerbohm, *Herod and Mariamne* from Hebbel, *Alice's Adventures in Wonderland and Through the Looking-Glass* with music by Addinsell), and many pleasant entertainments for matinées (such as *Gooseberry Fool*, *Wild Decembers*, *Moonlight Is Silver*, *England's Darling*, *Cousin Muriel*, *The Golden Reign of Queen Elizabeth*, *The Lion and the Unicorn*, *Call Home the Heart*, *Eighty in the Shade*, *The Godson*, etc.). In an era when theatre was the ordinary middle-class way of ending or highlighting a day in town after sightseeing or shopping, the West End theatres produced many plays like these. They were not world-shaking nor were they meant to be. They were (by modern standards) inexpensive to mount and to attend. The woman who took her name from a building standing right in the middle of The Strand could just as conspicuously establish herself in London's commercial theatre. She understood playwriting and the theatre market. She was able to supply that market with contemporary drawing-room plays such as *The Way Things Happen* (from *Legend* and life) or costume pieces on familiar subjects (the Brontës in *Wild Decembers*, Alfred in *England's Darling*, Good Queen Bess, etc.) or musical entertainments on

romantic figures (the young son of Napoleon in *L'Aiglon*, the young eighteenth-century poet Thomas Chatterton in *Come of Age*). She could be serious when required, as in *Granite* or *Eighty in the Shade*. Predictably, the "serious" dramas were considered her best work. *Granite* (1926) long endured, a tragedy much appreciated by repertory and amateur players in its day, though for our day, the dialogue is too heavy. The stars of the original *Granite*, Dame Sybil Thorndike and Sir Lewis Casson, also appeared years later in D.'s last work for the stage, *Eighty in the Shade*, a play long since eclipsed by David Storey's powerful play with a similar setting, *Home*.

A critically neglected aspect of D.'s work is her significant contribution to radio, television, and cinema drama. She worked with others on the BBC serial of *The Scoop* (1931) and wrote *The Saviours: Seven Plays on One Theme* for radio (1940–1941), as well as adapting for radio Shakespeare's *Henry VIII* and Schiller's *Don Carlos*. Her last radio play was *Scandal at Coventry* (1958) and that same year *Till Time Shall End* (based on the life of Elizabeth I) was televised. That was included in the first (and only) volume of her *Collected Plays* (1961). Elizabeth I was also the focus (magisterially played by Dame Flora Robson) of the film script *Fire over England* (1936), in which Sir Alexander Korda hoped to repeat the success of *Henry VIII*. D. wrote it with Sergei Nolbandov.

Other film scripts were *The Tunnel* (also called *Transatlantic Tunnel*) and *Anna Karenina* (starring Garbo and Basil Rathbone), both 1935; *The Amateur Gentleman* (from Jeffrey Farnol's novel of the Regency), written with Edward Knoblock; *Farewell Again* (also called *Troopship*), written with Patrick Kirwin (1937); *St. Martin's Lane* (in America called *Sidewalks of London*), 1938; *Salute John Citizen* (written with Elizabeth Baron), 1942; *Perfect Strangers* (in America called *Vacation from Marriage*, written with Anthony Pelissier), 1945; *Bonnie Prince Charlie*, 1948; *Bride of Vengeance* (written with Cyril Hume and Michael Hogan), 1949; and *Angel with a Trumpet* (written with Karl Hartl and Franz Tassie), 1950. Unfortunately, neither Leslie Halliwell nor Ephraim Katz, leading encyclopedists of the movies, think D. is worth a mention. Even the fiction she wrote in collaboration (with Helen Simpson) gets a mention in some places, but film collaborations and original scripts seem quickly forgotten. Actually, her film writing is better than average and *Fire over England* is a classic.

D. was active in the Society of Women Journalists (president in 1941) and was the author of critical studies of literature, a book about gardening, editor of Lord Nelson's letters, and even *The Shelter Book* during the war. She was made a Commander of the Order of the British Empire in 1953.

She was never much of an actress, but we ought to mention acting in any discussion of D. She debuted in H.V. Esmond's best sentimental comedy, *Eliza Comes to Stay* (1913), and probably would have continued in similar light parts had not *A Bill of Divorcement* changed her direction. She was sometimes lucky in the leads for her own plays: Katherine Cornell played in *A Bill of Divorcement*; the casts of *Fire over England* on the screen and *Wild Decembers* on stage were extraordinary (the Brontës were Diana Wynyard, Beatrix Lehmann, and Emlyn Williams). But her own experience as "Diana Portis" onstage and her own observation of theatre permitted her to give to actors as much as she gained from them; her plays are eminently considerate of actors, even generous to them. She deserves a better place in theatre history than she has, if not a bust in the lobby of The Theatre-Royal in Drury Lane, where now is hung her excellent portrait of Ivor Novello, no more important a theatre personality than herself. Her plays may be dated, but they were part of London theatre of her time, if not always as typical of her talent as the novel *The Moon Is Feminine* (1938) and the nine stories of *Fate Cries Out* (1935). The career in fiction that stretched from *Regiment of Women* (1917) to her last novel, *Bonfire* (1981), published posthumously, is notable by any standard though it is as a playwright whose range ran from drawing-room comedy and Lady Godiva (*Scandal at Coventry*) to murder on Lundy Island (*Granite*) and seven generations of an acting family (*Broome Stages*) that D. has the most secure place in history.

WORKS: Fiction: *Regiment of Women* (1917). *First the Blade* (1918). *Legend* (1919). *Wandering Stars, with the Lover* (1924). *The Dearly Beloved of Benjamin Cobb* (1927). *The Baylons: A Family Chronicle* (1928). *Enter Sir John* (with Helen Simpson, 1928). *The King Waits* (1929). *Printer's Devil* (with Helen Simpson, 1930; also as *Author Unknown*). *Broome Stages* (1931). *Re-Enter Sir John* (with Helen Simpson, 1932). *Fate Cries Out: Nine Tales* (1935). *The Moon Is Feminine* (1938). *The Arrogant History of White Ben* (1939). *He Brings Great News* (1944). *The Flower Girls* (1954). *Bonfire* (1981).
Verse: *Trafalgar Day 1940* (1940).
Non-Fiction: *The Woman's Side* (1926). *Tradition and High Walpole* (1929). *Recapture* (1932). *London Has a Garden* (1964).
Plays [date of stage production in brackets] (date of publication in parentheses): *A Bill of Divorcement* [1921] (1921). *The Terror* [1921]. *Will Shakespeare* [1921] (1921). *The Way Things Happen* [from *Legend*, 1923] (1924). *Shivering Shocks; or, The Hiding Place* (1923). *Naboth's Vineyard* (1925). *Granite* [1926] (1927). *Mariners* [1927] (1927). *Mr. Fox* (1927). *A Traveller Returns* (1927). *Adam's Opera* [1928] (1928). *Gooseberry Fool* [1929]. *The Scoop* [radio serial written with others, broadcast 1931]. *Wild Decembers* [1933] (1932). *Come of Age* [1934] (1933). *L'Aiglon* [after Rostand, 1934] (1934). *Moonlight Is Silver* [1934] (1934). *The Happy Hypocrite* [after Sir Max Beerbohm, 1936]. *Herod and Mariamne* [after Hebbel, 1938] (1938). *England's Darling* (1940). *Cousin Muriel* [1940] (1940). *The Saviours: Seven Plays on One Theme* [radio broadcasts, 1940–1941] (1942). *The Golden Reign of Queen Elizabeth* [1941] (1941). *Alice's Adventures in Wonderland and Through the Looking-Glass* [after "Lewis Carroll," 1943] (1948). *The Lion and the Unicorn* (1943). *Call Home the Heart* [1947] (1947). *Henry VIII* [radio broadcast of Shakespearean adaptation, 1954]. *Don Carlos* [radio adaptation of Schiller's play, broadcast 1955]. *Scandal at Coventry* [radio broadcast, 1958] (in *Collected Plays*, 1961). *Eighty in the Shade* [1958] (1959). *Till Time Shall End* [television broadcast, 1958] (in *Collected Plays*, 1961). *Collected Plays* I (1961, only one volume published). *The Godson: A Fantasy* (1964). Screenplays: *The Tunnel* (*Transatlantic Tunnel*), with Kurt Siodmak and L.D. Peach (1935). *Anna Karenina* (1935). *The Amateur Gentleman*, with Edward Knoblock (1936). *Farewell Again* (*Troopship*), with Patrick Kirwan (1937). *Fire over England*, with Sergei Noblandov (1937). *St. Martin's Lane* (*Sidewalks of London*) (1938). *Salute John Citizen*, with Elizabeth Baron (1942). *Perfect Strangers* (*Vacation from Marriage*), with Anthony Pelissier (1945). *Bonnie Prince Charlie* (1948). *Bride of Vengeance*, with Cyril Hume and Michael Hogan (1949). *Angel with a Trumpet*, with Karl Hartl and Franz Tassie (1950).

BIBLIOGRAPHY: "Clemence Dane." *Approaches to Drama* (Oxford University Press, 1960). Mais, S.P.B. *Some Modern Authors* (1923). Sutton, C. *Some Contemporary Dramatists* (1924). Tydeman, W.M. "Clemence Dane." *Great Writers of the English Language: Dramatists* (ed. J. Vinson, 1979). [Winifred Ashton]
For articles in reference works, see: *CA. CMD. DLB. MBL. MWD. TCA. TCC&MW. TCW.* Temple, R. Z. and M. Tucker, eds. *Library of Literary Criticism* (1966).

Leonard R.N. Ashley

Emily Davies

BORN: 22 April 1830, Southampton.
DIED: 13 July 1921, Hampstead.
DAUGHTER OF: the Rev. John and Mary
 Hopkinson Davies.

Feminist, educator, and polemicist, D. founded Girton College in 1869, determined to make it "a college like a man's," with the same curriculum and examination standards as Cambridge. A skillful rhetorician, she wrote in support of the women's issues that occupied her life: women's employment, suffrage, and education.

The fourth of five children, D. was educated at home by her mother and sister. She and her sister had lessons in French, Italian, and music, and she learned "a little Latin" from her brothers' tutor. Her writing skill may be traced to the weekly compositions she wrote under the direction of her father, John Davies, an evangelical clergyman and author. As a young woman, D. was influenced by her brother Llewelyn, a supporter of F.D. Maurice in his efforts to improve the education of governesses at Queen's College.

Friendship with Barbara Bodichon and the women working at Langham Place helped D. to understand her "feeling of resentment at the subjection of women" and to take a leading part in feminist activities of the mid-nineteenth century. The substance and style of D.'s essays are best understood in the context of the reforms she accomplished. She used language for practical purposes, whether she was speaking at the National Association for the Promotion of the Social Sciences, a reform organization open to women; undertaking an extensive letter-writing campaign; or editing the *Englishwoman's Journal* (1862) and *Victoria Magazine* (1864). D. founded an employment society for women and, in her determination to help Elizabeth Garrett Anderson become a doctor, became a strong advocate of medical education for women. She and Anderson delivered the first petition for women's suffrage to John Stuart Mill in 1866; during 1866–1867 she acted as secretary to the first women's suffrage committee.

Her most important achievements were in education. D. persuaded the Schools Inquiry Commission of 1864 to include girls' secondary schools in its epoch-making study. To provide the schools with an external standard of measurement, she campaigned for the admission of girls to the Cambridge Local Examinations. D. founded the London Schoolmistresses' Association in 1866 and served on the London School Board from 1870 to 1873. For more than forty years, she was the practical force behind Girton College, raising money, supervising construction, setting policy. As the first

women's college to follow the university model, Girton provided an opportunity for women to demonstrate their intellectual equality with men.

D.'s educational philosophy is contained in *The Higher Education of Women* (1866), a book praised by Matthew Arnold and Frances Power Cobbe. Unlike many other reformers, D. did not base her argument for higher education on the necessity of providing single women with a way to support themselves. The "education of a lady" ought to be considered irrespective of "any specific uses to which it may afterwards be turned"; education "ought to mean the highest and the finest culture of the time." Thus D. made liberal education a good in itself rather than a solution to a dilemma. Then she did something even more radical: she pronounced the question of its "womanliness" to be irrelevant. According to D., theories of woman's "special" nature were factually unfounded and contrary to religious principle. She built her educational philosophy on the "deep and broad basis of likeness" between the sexes. Rejecting prevailing systems of "womanly" education, she urged her students to pursue classics and mathematics and to compete with men in the demanding university examinations. Eager to see both sexes transcend the conventional limitations of their assigned spheres, she foresaw husbands and wives working together as doctors, ministers, and artists. In the present, she regarded a liberal education "as a means of bringing men and women together, and bridging over the intellectual gulf between them."

In addressing the public, D. found that two issues were especially controversial: the use of examinations and the creation of a residential college. Many Victorians objected to taking women out of the home: novelist Charlotte Yonge warned D. that when girls were brought together they "always hurt one another in manner and tone if in nothing else." D. maintained that a residential college located in the country was necessary to protect women from the demands of domestic routine and social propriety. D. wanted each student to have "a small sitting room to herself where she will be free to study undisturbed, and to enjoy at her discretion the companionship of friends of her own choice." Only a residential college could offer women the unique combination of personal privacy and sympathetic support. While doctors, parents, and professors predicted that testing would cause undue stress and competition among the students, D. argued that university examinations would provide students and teachers with an exciting challenge, a communal goal, and public evidence of their ability.

In the controversial area of women's education, D. carefully anticipates objections to her argument. With well-chosen quotations, she shows her opponents contradicting themselves or finds support in unexpected places. She uses metaphors from nature to undermine society's promised land and is a pragmatic strategist. She can be witty about the inconsistencies in Victorian society, while remaining polite toward her detractors. Her persona is cautious, reasonable, and willing to qualify her assertions ("perhaps" and "probably"). Gestures of sympathy for her opponents are often followed by quietly incontrovertible assertions of her own ("No doubt they honestly believe . . . but the fact is . . ."). Her prose, which might be studied in conjunction with Arnold's and Mill's, is clear, logical, and understated, her voice, controlled. She told Barbara Bodichon, "Men cannot stand indignation, and tho' of course I think it is just, it seems to me better to suppress the manifestation of it." Such tactical accommodations to her audience should not obscure the radical implications of D.'s thought.

WORKS: *The Higher Education of Women* (1866). *Thoughts on Some Questions Relating to Women* (1910). *The Papers of Emily Davies and Barbara Bodichon from Girton College, Cambridge* (1985).

BIBLIOGRAPHY: Bradbrook, M.C. *"That Infidel Place": A Short History of Girton College* (1969). Forster, M. *Significant Sisters: The Grassroots of Active Feminism, 1839-1939* (1984). Murray, J.H. *Strong-Minded Women and Other Lost Voices from Nineteenth-Century England* (1982). McWilliams-Tullberg, R. *Women at Cambridge: A Men's University—Though of a Mixed Type* (1975). Stephen, B. *Emily Davies and Girton College* (1927). Vicinus, M. *Independent Women: Work and Community for Single Women, 1850-1920* (1985).

For articles in reference works, see: *BDBF. DNB. Europa. VB.*

Robin Sheets

Shelagh Delaney

BORN: 25 November 1939, Salford, Lancashire.
DAUGHTER OF: Joseph and Elsie Delaney.

"To talk as we do about popular theatre, about new working class audiences, about plays that will interpret the common experiences of today—all this is one thing, and a good thing, too. But how much better even, how much more exciting, to find such theatre suddenly here, suddenly sprung up under our feet! This was the first joyful thing about Theatre Workshop's performance of *A Taste of Honey.*" So Lindsay Anderson wrote during the summer of 1958 of the first play of a nineteen-year-old girl from a working-class family from the north of England. With the critical and popular success of *A Taste of Honey*, D. was catapulted into prominence as an extraordinarily promising and precocious writer of the New Drama. Although in 1960 she produced a second play, *The Lion in Love*, the hopes of many exuberant early supporters for a bountiful body of writing from her has not been rewarded.

D. was raised in Salford, an industrial suburb of Manchester that serves as background setting for both of her plays. She left school at age seventeen and found employment variously as a salesgirl, a milk depot clerk, and as an usherette at a local cinema. She had an ambition to write, however, and had begun work on a novel at the time she was working as an usherette. The novel was transformed to playscript when, upon going to the theatre one evening and seeing a touring production of Terence Rattigan's bourgeois entertainment, *Variations on a Theme*, she was so disgusted by the febrile character of Rattigan's tea-tinkling conventions that she became convinced she could do better herself. When she completed the script, D. sent a copy to Joan Littlewood, director of the Theatre Workshop at the Theatre Royal Stratford-East, expecting only, perhaps, some helpful criticism. Within two weeks, *A Taste of Honey* was in rehearsal with Miss Littlewood directing.

Set in a "comfortless flat," *A Taste of Honey* examines the misfortunes of Jo, a sensitive and awkward teenager who defends herself with a sometimes caustic tongue and hardened outer shell of indifference to the general squalor of life that surrounds her. The play, written in two acts, progresses by examining Jo's relationships, within the context of a sordid environment she can never fully overcome, with her sluttish mother, a lover, and a new-found friend. In turn, Jo is abandoned by each of them. Her mother agrees to marry a current lover and leaves Jo to fend for herself. Her lover, a black seaman, ships out leaving her with an engagement ring from Woolworth's and a child in her womb. Her friend Geof, a spirited homosexual lad, helps Jo during her pregnancy and, by drawing her away from being overwhelmed by hate and self-pity, introduces her to the joy of simple affection (the taste of honey). Geof proposes marriage to Jo and is refused. He also departs when the prodigal mother returns, her own fling at marriage in ruin, to reclaim rudely the territory.

Audiences and critics alike were impressed by the unaffected honesty of character and relationships. What may have been the material of cliché melodrama came off with such vitality and directness that the pathos of situation was illuminated all the more clearly by the brightness of the ironic humor found in Joan Littlewood's glowing production—performed in a style blending elements of modern naturalism with the presentational openness of the traditional music hall. Indeed, some suggested that director Littlewood (widely known for her success at shaping theatrically effective productions out of unlikely sources) had substantially rewritten the script during the course of rehearsal. However, John Russell Taylor's examination of the original typescript (provided by Littlewood) determined that "The dialogue throughout has been pruned and tightened—rather more, evidently, than is usual in rehearsal—but most of the celebrated lines are already there . . . and the character of Jo, the play's *raison d'être*, is already completely created and unmistakably the same. . . . The play is obviously much superior in the final version, but it is not *so* different, and the only modifications which one might find out of keeping are very minor. . . ."

The *eclat* that accompanied *A Taste of Honey*'s 1958 premiere brought its then nineteen-year-old author international attention. The play was produced in New York in 1960 and received enthusiastic critical acclaim as well as The New York Drama Critics Award for "Best Foreign Play." D.'s screenplay for the 1962 cinema adaptation, written with the film's director Tony Richardson, brought her a British Film Academy Award and the Robert Flaherty Award for "Best Screenplay."

Some observers of the theatre scene, inclined to categorize D. as the "Angry Young Woman" of the new drama, were cautioned in a program note for the original production that because D. "knows what she is angry about," she may well be the antithesis of the so-called "Angry Young Men." Unlike Jimmy Porter, in Osborne's *Look Back in Anger*, Jo does not account for her situation in terms of bitter denunciations directed against the government of socioeconomic injustice. In dramatic situations where she might be moved to anger, Jo's commentary is colored by statements like, "I hate love!" Lindsay Anderson, in his 1958 review of *A Taste of Honey*, compares Jo to Holden Caulfield of J.D. Salinger's *A Catcher in the Rye*. "Like Holden, Josephine is a sophisticated innocent," notes Anderson. "Precious little surprises her; but her reactions are pure and direct, her intuitions are acute, and her eye is very sharp. . . . But Josephine is luckier than Holden in some ways: she is tougher, with common-sense,

Lancashire working-class resilience that will always pull her through. And this makes her different too from the middle-class angry young man, the egocentric rebel. Josephine is not a rebel; she is a revolutionary." Rather than being a social philosopher who deliberately tries to move an audience with didactic messages, D. is a careful and compassionate observer of life; her audiences are moved to ponder the implications of what they see.

D.'s second (and, to date, only other) play, *The Lion in Love*, was originally presented in September 1960 at the Belgrade Theatre, Coventry, for a run outside London before moving to the Royal Court in late December. The script draws its title from an Aesop fable which moralizes, "Nothing can be more fatal to peace than the ill-assorted marriages into which rash love may lead." Naturalistic in style, the play examines a strained marriage, problems and difficulties of each generation in search of what it wants, and the "waywardness of life itself." Unlike *A Taste of Honey*, the play incorporates a large cast, a complex interweaving of story-lines, and direct statements of social-consciousness by a number of the characters. It was not a popular success and received mixed critical reactions. Although most reviewers considered it verbose, poorly constructed, and thematically unfocused, Kenneth Tynan found the realistic qualities of the piece to have "authenticity, honesty, restraint and . . . a prevailing sense of humor." John Russell Taylor found some merit in the characterization, particularly the mature perspicuity of one of the play's young females, but hoped *The Lion in Love* would eventually prove only a transitional work.

In 1963, D. published a collection of autobiographical short stories entitled *Sweetly Sings the Donkey*. Reviewers thought the writing uneven, but, at its best, composed "in that same arresting voice," in Marion Magid's words, "without literary pretension, honest to the point of brutality, that made Miss Delaney's first work so striking." Since 1963, she has written screenplays for two films—*The White Bus* (1966) and *Charlie Bubbles* (1968)—and several scripts for television including "The House That Jack Built" (1977), which was performed without accolade in 1979 as a stage production Off-Broadway.

WORKS: *A Taste of Honey* (1958; screenplay 1961). *The Lion in Love* (1960). *Sweetly Sings the Donkey* (1963). *The White Bus* (1966). *Charlie Bubbles* (1968). "Did Your Nanny Come from Bergen?" (1970). "St. Martin's Summer" (1974). "The House That Jack Built" (1977). "Find Me First" (1981). "So Does the Nightingale" (1981).

BIBLIOGRAPHY: Anderson, L. *Encore* (July-August 1958). Clurman, H. *The Naked Image*. (1966). Ippolito, G.J. *Drama Survey* (1961). Kerr, W. *The*

Theatre in Spite of Itself (1963). Kitchin, L. *Mid-Century Drama* (1962). Lumley, F. *New Trends in 20th Century Drama* (1972). MacInnes, C. *WSCC* (1966). Marowitz, C., T. Milne, and T. Hale, eds. *New Theatre Voices of the Fifties and Sixties* (1965). Noel, J. *RLV* (1960). Simon, J. *Hudson Review* (1961). Taylor, J.R. *Anger and After* (1962; rev. 1963; rev. as *The Angry Theatre: New British Drama*, 1969). Tynan, K. *Tynan Right and Left* (1968). Wandor, M. *Look Back in Gender: Sexuality and the Family in Post-War British Drama* (1987). Wellwarth, G. *The Theatre of Protest and Paradox* (1964).

For articles in reference works, see: *CA. CD. Crowell's Handbook of Contemporary Drama* (1971). *McGraw-Hill Encyclopedia of World Drama* (1972). *Modern World Theatre* (1970). *WA.*

Paul D. Nelsen

Mary Granville Pendarves Delany

BORN: 14 May 1700, Coulston, Wiltshire.
DIED: 15 April 1788, Windsor.
DAUGHTER OF: Bernard Granville.
MARRIED: Alexander Pendarves, 1718; Patrick Delany, 1743.
WROTE UNDER: Mary Granville, M. Pendarves, Mrs. Delany.

When the adolescent D. was being courted by a man of whom her parents disapproved, they sent her to live with an aunt and uncle, Lord Lansdowne, who arranged the marriage of D. to Alexander Pendarves, 68, a wealthy Cornish landholder. After the marriage in 1718 the couple lived mostly in Cornwall. At her husband's death in 1725, D. moved to London where she earned the affection and enjoyed the society of the court. While visiting Swift in Ireland, she met Patrick Delany, a widower, an Irish Anglican clergyman, and Dean of Down whom she married. When Delany died in 1768, D. again established residence in London, this time as a member of the Bluestocking circle with Elizabeth Montagu, Frances Boscawen, and others. She met Fanny Burney at this time and became her patron. The paper mosaics she cut during this period, evidence of her patience, skill, and artistry, remain in the British Library. A constant associate of the members of the royal family, D. received a pension and lived in a "grace and favour" house at Windsor.

Acquainted with Burke, Handel, and Rousseau, D. wrote often to Swift and to her sister Ann Dewes and other relatives and friends. Her letters show the concerns and occupations of privileged women of the eighteenth century. She criticizes women who waste their time playing cards and urges women to appreciate attentive and honest husbands. Swift noted that D.'s "want of ignorance" did not make her affected and generalized his admiration: "To say the truth, the ladies in general are extremely mended both in writing and reading since I was young." Like Walpole and Mary Wortley Montagu, D. was aware of the literary quality of a fine letter. Of Ann Granville's letter "dated Easter Eve," D. says, "You never wrote a better; I cannot say more in its praise." Her own letters to her sister are sometimes instructive, as when she offers advice on learning French: "Wherever you go take some French book with you, and the dictionary, and read for every day half an hour." D.'s candidness lightens descriptive passages; "I have [a garden] as big as your parlour at Gloucester," she boasts to her sister, "and in it groweth *damask-roses*, *stocks* variegated and plain, some purple, some red, *pinks*, *Philaria*, some dead some alive; and *honey-suckles* that never blow. But when you come to town to weed and water it, it shall be improved after the new taste, but till then it shall remain dishevelled and undrest."

WORKS: *A Catalogue of Plants Copied from Paper Mosaick, Finished in the Year 1778, and Disposed in Alphabetical Order, According to the Generic and Specific Names of Linnaus* (1778). *Letters from Mrs. Delany . . . to Mrs. Frances Hamilton* (1820–1821). *Autobiography and Correspondence* (ed. Lady Llanover, 1861–1862, rev. and ed. by Sarah Chancey Woolsey, 1879). *Mrs. Delany at Court and Among the Wits, Being the Record of a Great Lady of Genius in the Art of Living*, ed. R.B. Johnson (1925). *Aspasia: The Life and Letters of Mary Granville, Mrs. Delany* (1700-1788) ed. C.E. Vulliamy, 1935.

BIBLIOGRAPHY: Dewes, S. *Mrs. Delany* (1904). Dobson, A. *Side-walk Studies* (1902). Hayden, R. *Mrs. Delany, Her Life and Her Flowers* (1980). Symonds, E.M. *Mrs. Delany (Mary Granville), a Memoir, 1700-1788* (1900).

For articles in reference works, see: *Allibone. BA19C. DNB. DLEL. Longman. NCLEL. OCEL.*

Mary Comfort

Monica Dickens

BORN: 10 May 1915, London.
DAUGHTER OF: Fanny Runge Dickens and Henry Charles.
MARRIED: Roy Stratton, 1951.

As becomes the great-granddaughter of Charles Dickens, D. has been a prolific writer of fiction. Her literary career began with an autobiographical work in 1939 (*One Pair of Hands*), and her latest works are either nonfiction or autobiography (*Cape Cod, Talking of Horses,* and *An Open Book*), but the majority of her extensive production has been fiction. Her full-length works for adults number 23, and there are 10 works written for children.

A Roman Catholic, she was educated at St. Paul's School for Girls and travelled abroad before joining a dramatic school. After she was presented at court in 1935, she rejected the life of the famous by seeking employment as a maid and cook in private homes in London for two years. She also worked as a nurse and a mechanic in an aircraft engine repair factory. She later married a retired U.S. naval officer and moved to Cape Cod, Massachusetts, where she has remained.

D.'s rebellion against her social upbringing is reflected particularly in her later works which are often concerned with urban poverty, child abuse, and other social ills. Although she has spent many years in the United States, D.'s first book with an American setting was *The Room Upstairs* in 1966. The reviews were mixed; typical is the one from the *New York Times*, which extolled the "excellent characterization of a New England matriarch," but found the "psychic phenomena . . . more of a distraction than an interest." In fact, the reviews of her novels are often mixed. For example, *Winds of Heaven*, written eleven years earlier, prompted the reviewer of the *Sunday Tribune* to applaud her "acute observation of human conduct" and "witty comments" while criticizing her inability to "plumb the depths of human experience."

The problems of suicide have been the center of interest for D. during the most recent years. Once in England for research purposes, she was impressed by a group called the Samaritans, a group that takes phone calls and "listens" to those contemplating suicide. D. founded this group in the United States in Boston, Cape Cod, and Providence and is still profoundly involved in the mental health group. This concern has made its way into her fiction, but even with such devoted interest, her books on the subject have failed to get the accolades she hoped for. *The End of the Line* in 1971, for example, was described in the *New York Times Book Review* as a novel in which the main characters, "these Samaritans, their involvements and the difficulties of their clients are so intermingled it's sometimes hard to decide who needs more help."

While D. has obviously been devoted to her profession, her success has been limited in terms of positive critical response.

WORKS: One Pair of Hands (1939). The Moon Was Low (1940). One Pair of Feet (1942). Edward's Fancy (1943). Thursday Afternoons (1945). The Happy Prisoner (1946). Joy and Josephine (1948). Flowers on the Grass (1949). My Turn to Make the Tea (1950). The Nightingales Are Singing (1953). The Winds of Heaven (1955). The Angel in the Corner (1956). Man Overboard (1958). Cobbler's Dream (1963). Kate and Emma (1964). The Room Upstairs (1966). My Fair Lady (1967). The Landlord's Daughter (1968). The Great Fire (1970). The End of the Line (1970). The Listeners (1970). The Great Escape (1971). Summer at World's End (1971). Follyfoot (1971). World's End in Winter (1972). Cape Cod (1972). Talking of Horses (1973). Follyfoot Farm (1973). Spring Comes to World's End (1973). An Open Book (1978).

BIBLIOGRAPHY: For articles in reference works, see: *CA. Catholic Authors. CN. Longman. NCHEL. WA.*

Miriam Quen Cheikin

Margaret Drabble

BORN: 5 June 1939, Sheffield, Yorkshire.
DAUGHTER OF: John Frederick and Marie Bloor Drabble.
MARRIED: Clive Swift, 1960; Michael Holroyd, 1982.

Widely read and well received by both critics and the general audience, D. plays a lively role in British culture. In addition to nine novels, she has written several stories, screenplays, and a biography of Arnold Bennett. She has written or edited several books on literary subjects and scores of reviews and other pieces for journals, newspapers, and magazines. She writes on popular and literary topics for both school children and adults, for both scholars and laymen. Frequently interviewed and photographed, the subject of several feature articles as well as much critical commentary, she also appears on televised literary programs, participates on governmental councils and Arts Council tours, and teaches adult education one day a week at Morley College.

D. went from The Mount, a Quaker boarding school in York, to Newham College, Cambridge University, on scholarship, receiving a brilliant starred First in English literature. While her fiction is located within, enriched by, and played off against the literary language, traditions, and characters she knows so well, D. deliberately chooses not to be a high-culture artist disengaged from day-to-day realities. Eminently accessible and readable, she is attuned to herself and to ordinary experience, vividly rendering the ordinary with intelligence and learning, insight, and humor. Her informal, intimate, personal voice seems to speak directly for a whole generation of readers, particularly women, in Great Britain, the United States, and other countries.

The protagonists of D.'s novels have followed the course and concerns of her own life: young women leaving university, getting married and separated, birthing children, having affairs, raising progressively older children, reaching midlife, and wondering what next. The surface lucidity of D.'s early novels and the seeming candor of her first-person narrators have misled some readers into assuming that little critical distance separates the author and her narrators. In fact, the tension between surface and meaning gives to D.'s work an unresolved, exploratory quality quite different from the popular women's fiction it deceptively resembles. D.'s fiction at its best is a virtual "double-voiced discourse" exemplifying the tension that many women experience who are struggling to define themselves within a patriarchal frame of reference. She examines with subtlety and moral acuity the very tissue and structure of women's lives. From her first comparatively slight novel, *A Summer Bird-Cage* (1963), D.'s first-person characterizations grow in depth and subtlety, reaching their culmination in the portrait of Jane Gray in her most technically experimental narrative, *The Waterfall* (1969). Whereas each of these narrators lives in a solipsistic world and uses her body as a decorative front and self-protective retreat from external realities, *The Waterfall* records Jane Gray's orgasmic breaking out of the constrictions of female identity. The significance of this experience is equivocally examined by Jane, as are the lives and experiences of the narrators who proceed her.

The third-person novels of D.'s middle period move further out of the solipsistic spaces of the early novels. They record a more graphic exodus from the constricting world of childhood: its geography, class-bound values, moral outlook.

Northern landscapes are rejected in each novel for the cosmopolitan environment of London, duplicating the journey D. herself made from Sheffield to London. While born into a liberal, professional, middle-class family, D. draws from her family's rural, working-class roots in her fiction, dramatizing particularly the "need to escape" from oppressive provincial limitations. "By will and by strain" her characters create new selves and new worlds out of preconceived "golden" fantasies: a golden Jerusalem, a Bunyanesque holy city, realms of gold. Literary influence continues to be important: *Jerusalem the Golden* (1967) was, D. admits, "profoundly affected" by Bennett and by his character Hilda Lessways. *The Needle's Eye* (1972) is characterized by its skillful adaptation of Jamesian central intelligence and its probing psychological and moral complexities. The interconnected network of characters, images, literary allusions, and levels of reference of *The Realms of Gold* (1975) initiates D.'s more expansive later style.

While these novels link up to the sociomoral tradition of the English novel—which D. outspokenly values over modernist experiments—they, like her earlier work, continue to be in many ways double-voiced and equivocal, mediating between traditional realistic humanism and modern perspectives. "Omniscience has its limits," the narrator of *The Realms of Gold* candidly admits, calling attention to the fictionality of this carefully constructed world. Similarly, character is not at all stable, and perhaps not knowable. Because the characters' lives are such a composite of psychological determinism and willful self-creation, the boundaries between the real and the imagined are equivocal for characters and readers alike. Furthermore, D.'s use of houses and landscapes as objective correlatives of mental states lends considerable subtlety and depth to these works, dramatizing her intense preoccupation with the "effect of landscape upon the soul." Where D. is resolutely traditional is her liberal belief that the individual must link up to something larger than the self—a place, a community, shared values, the past. All of her work is about the conflict between free will and determinism, between the search for free feeling and the desire for some measure of control and judgment. The search for a suitable moral and human habitation is the compelling genesis of her art. The tension within these middle novels resides in the apparent freedom of the individual to create a new self coupled with his or her necessary circumspection within geographical, communal, and historical contexts.

In her last two novels, *The Ice Age* (1977) and *The Middle Ground* (1980), D. focuses on the commonly shared contexts and experiences of urban middle-class life, detailing the texture, the trends, and the trappings of mass culture. The most vividly memorable passages of both books depict the dehumanized, noisy, dirty, ugly, and graffiti-ridden world that is modern urban Britain. The environment in which characters live is largely shaped from without. The individual may be, like Anthony Keating in *The Ice Age*, no more than a "weed upon the tide of history" doomed to enact a drama which differs only in particulars from other members of his or her generation.

Like their author, the characters, successful in their professional lives, are now experiencing a midlife reappraisal of self. The characters are less obsessed with the past than they are with the quality and significance of the lives they are now leading, lives which strikingly resemble those of their associates. D.'s characters crave connection, and in midlife the connection they seek is increasingly social and metaphysical. What is happening to individuals reflects, in turn, what is happening to the British nation as a whole, which is getting older, tired, staid, facing crises, going through some strange and disorienting metamorphosis. *The Ice Age* is highly controlled, a visibly plotted work, and so too are the lives of the characters it chronicles, whereas *The Middle Ground* is plotless and shapeless; the novel's structure is open to contingency just as the lives of its characters are.

Because D. refuses to stay in the same spot, her fiction is constantly nourished by her own personal development. As a result, D., perhaps more than any other contemporary British woman novelist, has the opportunity to produce a distinctively female work which surpasses gender limitations. Her mediating position between "male" and "female" concerns and traditions, literary and popular issues and perspectives, the literary and the real, the traditional and the modern gives equivocal resonance and strength to her

fiction. Her attempt to "only connect" these diverse strains is the generating energy of her work.

WORKS: A Summer Bird-Cage (1963). The Garrick Year (1964). The Millstone (1965). Wordsworth (1966). Jerusalem the Golden (1967). The Waterfall (1969). The Needle's Eye (1972). Virginia Woolf: A Personal Debt (1973). Arnold Bennett: A Biography (1974). The Realms of Gold (1975). The Ice Age (1977). For Queen and Country: Britain in the Victorian Age (1978). A Writer's Britain: Landscape in Literature (1979). The Tradition of Women's Fiction: Lectures in Japan (1982). The Radiant Way (1987).

BIBLIOGRAPHY: For the most complete listing of extensive primary and secondary sources, see "A Margaret Drabble Bibliography" by J.S. Korenman in *Critical Essays on Margaret Drabble* (1984). Books on Drabble include: Creighton, J.V. *Margaret Drabble* (1985). Hannay, J. *The Intertextuality of Fate: A Study of Margaret Drabble* (1986). Moran, M.H. *Margaret Drabble: Existing Within Structures* (1983). Myer, V.G. *Margaret Drabble: Puritanism and Permissiveness* (1974). Rose, E.C. ed. *Critical Essays on Margaret Drabble* (1984). Rose, E.C. *The Novels of Margaret Drabble: Equivocal Figures* (1980). Roxman, S. *Guilt and Glory: Studies in Margaret Drabble's Novels 1963-1980* (1984). Sadler, L.V. *Margaret Drabble* (1986). Schmidt, D., ed. *Margaret Drabble: Golden Realms* (1982).

For articles in reference works, see: *CA. CLC. CN. DLB. EWLTC. MBL. WA.*

Other references: Bromberg, P.S. *Journal of Narrative Technique* (1986). Olshanskaya, N.L. *ZAA* (1986).

Joanne V. Creighton

Lucie Duff-Gordon

BORN: 24 June 1821, London.
DIED: 14 July 1869, Cairo, Egypt.
DAUGHTER OF: John Austin and Mary Taylor.
MARRIED: Sir Alexander Cornwall Duff-Gordon, 1840; mother's name not known.

A woman of strong temperament, independent mind, and uncommon munificence, D. achieved renown as a travel writer. Her *Letters from Egypt* record with moving sympathy Arab customs and manners, and especially the indigence of the *fellahin* (peasants) who came to esteem her as "Sitt el Kebeer," the great lady. This superb transcript is not only marked by the vigor of her commentary but by a rare regard for her

subject, a point noted by George Meredith who wrote in his preface to the 1902 edition of her travel letters, "Hers was the charity which was perceptive and embracing." Nettled by the colonial arrogance of some of the English, D., who openly confessed that "my heart is with the Arabs," asked pointedly, "Why do the English talk of the beautiful sentiment of the Bible and pretend to feel it so much and when they come and see the same life before them, they ridicule it?"

Praised widely for her statuesque and majestic beauty, D. was the model for Tennyson's poem "The Princess." A personal friend of Heine, Thackeray, Dickens, and Kinglake, she became during the mid-nineteenth century a cultural figure of scintillating brilliance. Her home in London and then at "Gordon Arms" in Esher was one of England's acclaimed salons to which Guizot fled across the Channel after the Revolution of 1848. Kinglake, the famed traveler to the Levantine who entranced her with his rich vein of reminiscence, spoke for many of her admirers when he wrote, "But she was so intellectual, so keen, so autocratic, sometimes even so impassioned even in speech, that nobody, feeling her powers, could well go on feebly comparing her to a mere Queen or Empress."

The breadth of her interests and the charm of her personality are partly products of a roving childhood. At the age of five, D. traveled to Bonn with her parents, mastering German with great alacrity. In later years she was known for her enviable ability to out-talk Carlyle on German literature, a not inconsiderable achievement. While still a youngster, she met Heinrich Heine at Boulogne who remembered her at the end of his life when she came to visit him in his "mattress grave" in Paris. D. has left a moving account of the great German lyrical poet in Lord Houghton's *Monographs Personal and Social* (1873).

Her literary career began in 1839, appropriately with a translation of Barthold Georg Niebuhr's *Studies of Ancient Grecian Mythology*. While yet a child she heard the respected German classical scholar recount these tales to his son while she was in Bonn with her parents. In 1844 she translated Meinhold's *Mary Schweidler, the Amber Witch*, a narrative with derivations from a seventeenth-century chronicle, followed by *Narrative of Remarkable Criminal Trials* by Anselm Ritter von Feuerbach, father of the famous theologian and philosopher, Friedrich von Feuerbach, whose theory of religious anthropomorphism was a major precursor of Marxism. In collaboration with her husband, Sir Alexander Cornwall Duff-Gordon, whom she married in 1840, she translated *Memoirs of the House of Brandenburg* by Leopold von Ranke, a much-respected historian who numbered among the illustrious figures to visit her in London.

The Duff-Gordons diffused such charm that their democratic hospitality included the humble and undistinguished as much as those of reputation and rank. Even abroad, D. was a glowing star, drawing luminaries into her orbit. When she lived in the Rue Chaillot in Paris in 1857, she was befriended by a roster of French geniuses including Victor Cousin, Alfred de Vigny, Barthelmy St. Hilaire, Auguste Comte, and Leon de Wailly, whose *Stella and Vanessa* she had translated and published in 1850. The life of ideas inspired by these associations enhanced a social conscience already brought to an extraordinary level of acuity.

Her health, always frail—she had nearly died of consumption in 1849 after the birth of a son, Maurice—declined vertiguously around 1860,

forcing her to abandon England for the more clement weather of the Cape of Good Hope. There she made many loyal friends among the Malays who had originally been brought across the Indian Ocean as slaves by the Dutch East India Company and who had been set free under the British Slave Emancipation Act of 1834. Here, as later in Egypt, she was to champion the downtrodden and win their hearts by a concern and tenderness of sympathy atypical for a Westerner of the period. Her sharply etched observations of her South African sojourn are recorded in *Letters from the Cape*, which were printed in Francis Galton's *Vacation Tourist*, during 1862–1863.

The aggravation of her consumption forced her removal to the dry climate of Egypt. A good many of her seven years of residence in the nominally Turkish province were spent at Luxor in an old house built over an ancient Egyptian temple. She took an avid interest in the multicolored life and manners of the natives and filled her famed *Letters from Egypt* with ethnological remarks on the differences between the Arabs and the Turks, the kindness of the Copts, the calligraphic beauty of Arab art, and the pictorial complexity and splendor of its architecture. Despite the widely regarded despotism of the East, she argued that in the Levant "social equality" existed to a greater degree than elsewhere. Ever amazed at the expanse and depth of Egypt, she wrote, "This country is a palimpsest in which the Bible is written over Herodotus, and the Koran over that. In the town the Koran is most visible, in the country Herodotus."

D. died of consumption in 1869 and lies buried in the English Cemetery in Cairo. Her *Letters from Egypt* are the most memorable of her productions, indicative of a preternatural acuity of observation and judgment, and for a while boasted a considerable circulation among the English literati and orientalists. Her trenchant commentary and her open distaste for colonialism give much of her writing a contemporary ring.

WORKS: (trans.) *Studies of Ancient Grecian Mythology*, by B.G. Niebuhr (1839). (trans.) *Mary Schweidler, the Amber Witch*, by W. Meinhold (1844). (trans.) *Narrative of Remarkable Criminal Trials*, by A.R. von Feuerbach (1844). (trans.) *Stella and Vanessa*, by L. de Wailly (1850). (trans.) *History of Prussia; Ferdinand I and Maximilian II of Austria; State of Germany after the Reformation*, by L. von Ranke (1853). *Letters from the Cape* (1863). *Letters from Egypt* (1865). *Last Letters from Egypt* (1875).

BIBLIOGRAPHY: Etherington-Smith, M. and J. Pilcher, *The "It" Girls: Elinor Glyn, Romantic Novelist, and Lucy, Lady Duff-Gordon. Lucile, the Couterière* (1986). Gendron, C. *Ariel* (1986). Norton, C. *Macmillan's Magazine* (1869).

Michael Skakun

Maureen Duffy

BORN: 21 October 1933.
DAUGHTER OF: Grace Wright and Cahia P. Duffy

Raised in an impoverished London family, D. began writing seriously at thirteen, and when asked to "Say us a piece" by family visitors, often successfully passed off her own poetry as "real" writing. Her autobiographical first novel, *That's How It Was*, described the grinding poverty of her childhood as well as the positive influence of her mother's love and encouragement. D. was educated at state schools and at King's College, London (B.A., honors, 1956), and taught school for five years. She has published ten novels, five plays (all produced), a television play, six books of poetry, and three nonfiction works, as well as editing, translating, and writing reviews of nonfiction and music for *The New Statesman*. Active on various British arts councils that have increased funding for authors, she is also deeply involved in the anti-vivisection cause.

The main characters of her novels are often outsiders: a writer who has left his family to spend a bitter winter alone on a houseboat (*The Paradox Players*); a wealthy, precocious and Oedipal adolescent (*The Love Child*); a group of Lesbians who frequent a bar in London (*The Microcosm*); a convict released from prison by a group of anti-vivisectionists so that he can free animals from their cages (*All Heaven in a Rage*); and a half-human, half-gorilla child (*Gor Saga*). D. describes herself as a writer for whom the most poignant image is "the nose pressed against the glass. The very curious sort of flattening that happens and the way you see things inside as though under water and both more attractive and more frightening. This whole image is just not there for people who haven't spent their childhoods waiting outside pubs." Frequent themes in her novels are education, "social engineering," and love as a redeeming force; however imperfect our world—and she registers those imperfections with a deadly accurate eye—D.'s novels warmly suggest

that since this is the only world we have, we must try to look at it not only clearly but constructively.

D. has always been acknowledged for the excellence of her writing, especially for her ability to imagine compellingly specific moments of her characters' lives. Criticism has been directed at her allowing consciously learned sections to interrupt her story (*Love Child*) and for an awkward mix of literary styles (*The Microcosm*). The most common criticism has been of a lack of focus in some of her works. Her novels seem to have moved toward a smooth blend of her proletarian background—"What you escaped from feeds you," she believes—her knowledge of philosophy, and her facility with literary forms. In *Housespy*, an espionage thriller, and *Gor Saga*, she has achieved that blend and a place as one of the few British novelists who is rooted in the England of ordinary people, with the versatility needed to portray that reality in compelling and intelligent ways.

WORKS: *Josie* (1961). *The Lay Off* (1962). *That's How It Was* (1962). [trans.] *A Blush of Shame*, by D. Rea (1963). *The Single Eye* (1964). *The Microcosm* (1966). *The Silk Room* (1966). *The Paradox Players* (1967). *Lyrics for the Dog Hour* (1968). *Wounds* (1969). *Rites* (in *New Short Plays 2*, 1969). *Solo, Olde Tyme* (1970). *The Venus Touch* (1971). *Love Child* (1971). *The Erotic World of Faery* (1972). *Actaeon* (1973). *I Want to Go to Moscow: A Lay* (American title: *All Heaven in a Rage*, 1973). *A Nightingale in Bloomsbury Square* (1973, published in *Factions*, 1974). *Evesong* (1975). *Capital* (1975). *The Passionate Shepherdess: Aphra Behn, 1640-1689* (1977). *Housespy* (1978). *Memorials of the Quick and the Dead* (1979). *Inherit the Earth: A Social History* (1980). *Gor Saga* (1981). *Collected Poems* (1985).

BIBLIOGRAPHY: Interview with D. Barber, *Transatlantic Review* (Spring 1973). Rule, J. *Lesbian Images* (1982).

For articles in reference works, see: *CA. CD. CN. CP. DLB. WA. Who's Who in Twentieth Century Literature.*

Katherine A. Allison

Dame Daphne Du Maurier

BORN: 13 May 1907, London.
DAUGHTER OF: Gerald Du Maurier and Muriel Beaumont.
MARRIED: Lt.-Gen. Sir Frederick Browning, 1932.

D. is the granddaughter of George [Louis Palmella Busson] Du Maurier (1834–1896), author of *Peter Ibbetson*, *Trilby*, and *The Martian*, and daughter of the actor-manager Sir Gerald [Hubert Edward] Du Maurier (1871–1934) and his co-star in *The Admirable Crichton* in 1902, Muriel Beaumont (1881–1957). She has done much to preserve the reputation of her colorful forebears (whom one critic in *The New Statesman and Nation* in 1937 said she regards "on the whole, with much kindliness and some condescension") and to build a fame of her own as a novelist, playwright, and short-story writer.

She began writing about 1928, and her first published novel, *The Loving Spirit*, already indicated the direction she was to take and exhibited (according to Helen Grosse) a talent "full of promise." She followed with *I'll Never Be Young Again* (1931) and *The Progress of Julius* (1932) and hit her stride with the romantic adventures of *Jamaica Inn* (1936). Then came perhaps her best-known work: *Rebecca* (1938), called by some "the twentieth-century *Jane Eyre*" and by *TLS* as "a lowbrow story with a middlebrow ending."

In *Rebecca*, D.'s talent for well-researched and melodramatic atmosphere and romantic settings, her deft way with an inventive and mysterious plot embroiling innocent heroine and moody hero, her characters conflicted by dual natures or sudden forced changes of circumstance—in fact all the armamentarium of the modern Gothic novel—is at the peak. Though *Rebecca* has been accused of plagiarism because of its fairly close resemblance to Carolina Nabuco's *A Sucesora* (a novel in Portuguese about a second wife) and Edwina Macdonald's "I Planned to Murder My Husband" and *Blind Windows*, it really simply partakes of the basic material of the romantic genre. The moping hero melancholy mad is as old as the Byronic Hero (or older), the distressed heroine right out of the melodramas of the Victorian theatre, the mysterious mood as ancient as Walpole, Holcroft, Collins, Radcliffe, Mary Shelley, and others. Within this format, even *TLS* had to admit, D. is "extraordinarily bold and confident, eloquent and accomplished" and "merits genuine respect."

In Menabilly (her own manor house at Par in Cornwall) D. created commercial family sagas (such as *The Loving Spirit* and *Hungry Hill*, for which she also wrote the screenplay), thoroughly reliable and exciting historical novels (such as *The King's General* set in the English Civil War, or *The Glass Blowers* set in the French Revolution), plays (*Rebecca*, *The Years Between*, *September Tide*), a screenplay (*Hungry Hill* with Terence Young and Francis Crowdry), a television play ("The Breakthrough"), novels warmly received by book clubs (*Frenchman's Creek*, *Rule Britannia*, etc.) and Hollywood (*Rebecca*, *My Cousin Rachel*), macabre stories, and more.

D. has perhaps not received the praise she deserves for her short fiction, eclipsed by her blockbuster best-sellers, but she is the author of *Happy Christmas* (1940), *Come Wind, Come Weather* (1940), *Nothing Hurts for Long, and Escorts* (1943), *Consider the Lilies* (1943), *Spring Picture* (1944), *Leading Lady* (1945), *London and Paris* (1945), *Early Stories* (1954), *The Breaking Point: Eight Stories* (1959, as *The Blue Lenses and Other Stories*, 1970), *The Treasury of Du Maurier Stories* (1960), *Not After Midnight* (1971; U.S. *Don't Look Now*, 1971), *Echoes from the Macabre: Selected Stories* (1976), *The Rendezvous and Other Stories* (1980), and the short novel *The Apple Tree* (with other stories, 1952) and *Kiss Me Again, Stranger: A Collection of Eight Stories Long and Short* (1953). She has also edited an anthology of the short story. Had she never written *The Parasites*, *Mary Anne*, *The Scapegoat*, completed Sir Arthur Quiller-Couch's novel *Castle Dor* (1962), or written any of her better-known novels, her short fiction alone would earn her a respected place in any guide to women writers. Especially in those stories in which she can concentrate her ability to evoke the eerie, so often a part of her longer works, she is masterful. While novels such as *The Parasites* may be (as Antonia White remarked) "not, unfortunately, a work of art" in the best sense, her stories are seldom ineffective and often memorable. They do not often depend upon the incredible as do some of her novels (in *The Scapegoat* an Englishman passes himself off as a Frenchman and the Frenchman's intimates do not even notice the deception) but do exploit the mysterious.

The best of D.'s novels have, at least while one is engrossed in them, a powerful charm and exciting and well-managed plots. *My Cousin Rachel* is typically melodramatic and essentially hollow. Sober literary critics may well find Rachel Ashley, unknown even to herself, too trite a bundle of contradictions and Gothic claptrap, but the market for transpontine melodrama, which did not end with the Victorian era, continues to be in vogue today; one cannot really say that after half a century D. is out of date.

D. is also notable as family biographer (*Gerald: A Portrait* [1934], editor of the letters of *The Young Du Maurier* [1951], and chronicler of *The Du Mauriers* [1937]) and autobiographer (*Growing Pains* [1977], published in the U.S. as *Myself When Young*, and *The Rebecca Notebook and Other Memories* [1980]). She has also written about *The Infernal World of Branwell Brontë* (1960) and the dashing Sir Francis Bacon (*Golden Lads* [1975] is about Sir Francis and his brother Anthony, *The Winding Stair* [1977] about Sir Francis himself). All of these are solid, readable, commendable.

"Every book is like a purge," D. told the eager fans in *Ladies' Home Journal* (November 1956), "at the end of it one is empty . . . like a dry shell on the beach, waiting for the tide to come in again." But for many years and with great reliability the tide kept coming in for her, so she gave her adoring readers book after book that could excite and entertain. Whether she gave them something approaching science fiction (*The House on the Strand*) or fantasy (*Rule Britannia* involves Britain threatened with an American invasion), whether she made her readers feel that they were drenched with Italian sunlight or the mists of the Cornish coast, she knew how to spin a yarn that kept adolescents from their play and matrons from their bridge tables. Frequently she gave them more than they sought in escapist fiction. She inherited her grandfather's pictorial sense and her father's theatrical sense and made good use of both in her own version of the arena in which both of her ancestors had made a name for themselves: popular entertainment. Her work, or some of it, is likely to live longer than theirs.

WORKS: *The Loving Spirit* (1931). *I'll Never Be Young Again* (1932). *The Progress of Julius* (1933). *Gerald: A Portrait* (1934). *Jamaica Inn* (1936). *The Du Mauriers* (1937). *Rebecca* (1938; as play, produced London 1940, New York 1945, published 1943). *Happy Christmas* (1940). *Come Wind, Come Weather* (1941). *Frenchman's Creek* (1941). *Hungry Hill* (1943; as screenplay 1947). *Nothing Hurts for Long, and Escorts* (1943). *Consider the Lilies* (1943). *Spring Picture* (1944). *The Years Between* (produced Manchester 1944, London 1945, published 1945). *Leading Lady* (1945). *London and Paris* (1945). *The King's General* (1946). *September Tide*

(produced Oxford and London 1948, published 1949). *The Parasites* (1949). *My Cousin Rachel* (1951). *The Apple Tree: A Short Novel and Some Stories* (1953). *Early Stories* (1954). *Mary Anne* (1954). *The Scapegoat* (1957). *The Breaking Point* (1959). *The Treasury of Du Maurier Stories* (1960). *The Infernal World of Branwell Brontë* (1960). *Castle Dor* (1962). *The Glass Blowers* (1963). *The Flight of the Falcon* (1965). *Vanishing Cornwall* (1967). *The House on the Strand* (1969). *Not After Midnight* (1971). *Golden Lads: Sir Francis Bacon, Anthony Bacon, and Their Friends* (1975). *The Winding Stair: Francis Bacon, His Rise and Fall* (1976). *Rule Britannia* (1976). *The Breakthrough* (1976). *Echoes from the Macabre* (1977). *Growing Pains: The Shaping of a Writer* (1977). *The Rebecca Notebook and Other Memories* (1980). *The Rendezvous* (1980). *Classics of the Macabre* (1987).

BIBLIOGRAPHY: Bakerman, J.S. *And Then There Were Nine . . . More Women of Mystery*, ed. J.S. Bakerman (1985). Kelly, R. *Daphne DuMaurier* (1987).

For articles in reference works, see: *CA. CLC. CN. Longman. MBL. TCA* and *SUP. TCC&MW. TCRGW. TCW.*

Other references: Auerbach, N. *Critical Inquiry* (1981). Banta, M. *Studies in the Literary Imagination* (1983). Bromley, R. *Literature and History* (1981).

Leonard R.N. Ashley

Nell Dunn (pseudonym for Nell Mary Sandford)

BORN: 1936, London.
MARRIED: Jeremy Sandford, 1956.

"In 1959 Nell Dunn, a Chelsea heiress, crossed the Thames and went to live in Battersea, a working-class district of London." So noted the *Library Journal* in first introducing its readers to an eyebrow-raising literary study of slum life produced by a young writer of aristocratic pedigree. D.'s experiences with and observations of the *indigenes*, particularly the women, of the blue-collar ghetto formed the foundation of her writing career. "There is a lot of observation in what I write," she has stated. "I don't make very much up. What I do, really, is listen for about two years, and then, with what I've heard and what I've thought, I make something."

D.'s first book was a collection of short sketches, *Up the Junction* (1963), about life around the Clapham Junction commercial center of Battersea. The vignettes are candid pictures of routines among the denizens of Clapham: girls

putting on their makeup for a night out; sexual flirtations at the local pub; life around a home for unwed mothers; and bawdy conversations and unthinking chit-chat among women who work in a small candy factory. The author's "coolly observant narrative" endeavors to document the character of their existence, finding stories in the little struggles which color their lives, without shrinking from the vulgarity of the milieu of which she writes.

Up the Junction's most effective writing, according to D.A.N. Jones in *The New Statesman*, conveys a "miserable comment on English class relations," and Edgar Z. Friedenberg praised D.'s successful "use of ethnology" in her accounts of "lower-depths poverty." Many critics, however, accused her of "slumming" and snubbed the book as more spectacularly coarse than socially illuminating. "In this underworld of varicose veins and sleazy plastic," wrote James R. Frakes, "where nobody is frightened of death since 'you can't get hurt when yer dead' and the ultimate compliment you can pay a bird is 'you smell as if you never sweated in yer life,' the dawn that slides over the gasworks illuminates only a junkyard landscape of total hopelessness, pop culture at its most rancid." *Up the Junction* won the John Llewellyn Rhys Memorial Prize for a short-story collection in 1964; was adapted for a feature film; and in 1966 received its first publication in the United States.

Talking to Women, a 1965 collection of interviews, and *Poor Cow*, a novel published in 1967, are also outgrowths of her Battersea "research." In these works, D. focuses on the struggles and passions of working-class women, quoting the brutal dialect with which they try to communicate, revealing obscenity and preoccupation with indelicate matters of sex as simple verities of a complex stratum of British society. Like *Up the Junction*, *Poor Cow* is a loosely assembled series of sketches but with the difference of a pervasive central character—a bawdy adventuress named Joy.

Although *Punch* dismissed Dunn's effort as "just taking the lid off a slum and leaving it at that," V.S. Pritchett considered *Poor Cow* an accurate picture of "the exposed, unsupported, morally anonymous condition of people who have nothing that can really mean much to them except the vagaries of the sexual itch, what the telly says, and what is lit up in the supermarkets and pubs." "Based on the kind of true confessions that Nell Dunn collected in her *Talking to Women*," wrote the *Times Literary Supplement*, "this is a serious and moving little book, but it is scarcely a novel nor, quite, an original substitute for one." *The New Yorker* praised *Poor Cow* saying, "Whether [this] is a novel . . . does not matter. What does matter is that this young writer is possessed of a high degree of talent, and, beyond that, that there is something unforgettable about her work—some quality so individual and gentle that her writing is irresistible." At a time before feminism had become a popular movement, D., based on personal observations of exploited women of the working class, had written three works—representing sometimes startling, feminist points of view—that provoked critical interest in her blend of candor and compassion.

During the next dozen years, D. wrote or collaborated on a half-dozen books as well as a screenplay, with director Kenneth Loach, for a film adaptation of *Poor Cow*. With Susan Campbell she produced a book for children in 1969, and in 1971 she published another novel, *The Incurable*. The following year a collaboration with Adrian Henri was published as *I Want*. From 1974 through 1978, Dunn completed three more books, *Tear His Head off His Shoulders*, a novel, *Living Like I Do*, a documentary work, and another novel, *The Only Child*. None of these works received the critical attention of her early books nor the international praise which came in 1981 with the production of her first play, *Steaming*.

Dunn's only prior link to the stage was through her maternal grandfather, the Earl of Rosslyn, who had owned a London theatre. Weary of "scribbling away by herself in a tiny upstairs workroom," she decided to write a play to force her out of her "cocoon" and "spent about a year going to plays and reading them" in order to learn the craft of the playwright. *Steaming* opened July 1 at the famous fringe playhouse, Theatre Royal Stratford East, drew immediate and nearly universal acclaim from the press, and by the end of August was playing to enthusiastic audiences at The Comedy Theatre in the West End.

In *Steaming*, D. follows the pattern of her early work and "listens in" on a group of women talking. The setting is the "Turkish Lounge" of dilapidated Public Baths in the East End of London, a place of escape where the play's five principal characters meet to relax and share their troubles. "As they take off their clothes," notes Sylviane Gold, "they also shed their inhibitions, and they compare notes on men, on sex, on what matters most in their lives. Although their accents range from genteel to Cockney, their concerns, it turns out, are not all that different. And Miss Dunn unites the characters politically as well, when the baths are threatened with demolition."

Some critics complained that the play's feminist polemics were superficially represented; other observations focused on the "creaky theatrical devices" and transparent plot contrivances employed by an inexperienced playwright to structure the work. Nevertheless, the popular success of *Steaming*, in America and Australia as well as in England, reflected the charm of its "lively, ribald humor" and "homely sincerity." D. was awarded the 1981 Susan Smith Blackburn Prize, a highly regarded award given to a female writer for "a work of outstanding quality for the English-speaking theatre." In an interview for the *New York Times* at the time *Steaming* opened in New York in December 1982, Dunn stated that she found drama to be a stimulating medium and suggested that her next writing venture would also be for the stage.

WORKS: *Up the Junction* (1963). *Talking to Women* (1965). *Poor Cow* (1967; with Kenneth Loach, screenplay, 1968). *Freddy Gets Married* (with Susan Campbell, 1969). *The Incurable* (1971). *I Want* (with Adrian Henri, 1972). *Tear His Head off His Shoulders* (1974). *Living Like I Do* (1976). *The Only Child* (1978). *Steaming* (1981).

BIBLIOGRAPHY: *Library Journal* (1 November 1966). *New Statesman* (22 November 1966). *New Yorker* (11 November 1967). *NYRB* (18 May 1967). *NYT* (12 and 13 December 1982). *NYTBR* (6 November 1966). *Punch* (26 April 1967). *TLS* (4 May 1967). *Yale Review* (Spring, 1968).

For articles in reference works, see: *CA. CN.*

Paul D. Nelsen

Emily Eden

BORN: 3 March 1797, London.
DIED: 5 August 1869, Richmond, Surrey.
DAUGHTER OF: William and Eleanor Elliot Eden.

E. lived her life in the aristocratic surroundings she depicts in her two novels. She was the twelfth child and seventh daughter of the 1st Baron Auckland, a commissioner in America after the Revolutionary War, Chief Secretary in Ireland, Minister-Plenipotentiary to Versailles, and Ambassador to both Spain and Holland. E.'s uncle, Robert Eden, was the last colonial governor of Maryland. Her family's descendants were equally illustrious: novelist Eleanor (Lena) Eden was her niece; Violet Dickinson, friend of Virginia Woolf and Vita Sackville-West, was her great-niece; and Prime Minister Anthony Eden was her great-great nephew.

E. was well educated by governesses and then by the same tutor who taught her brother Robert. She was conversationally at ease amid topics of Whig politics and foreign affairs. E. never married, a personal choice rather than an effect of the growing surplus of women over men as the nineteenth century advanced. She and her sister Frances (Fanny) lived with her brother George (later Lord Auckland), first in London, where he was First Lord of the Admiralty, and then, from 1835 to 1842, in India, where George was Governor-General and E. and Fanny served as his "first ladies." Two of her books describe this experience. "Up the Country": Letters Written to her Sister from the Upper Provinces of India (1866), is an account of E.'s two and one half year tour of India. Although she was largely unconscious of her brother's role in initiating the nadir of British rule in India through his mismanagement of the First Afghan War, E. does give an accurate contemporary glimpse into the life of the British in India, including a sympathetic comprehension of the Indian dislike of British arrogance and self-righteousness. "Up the Country" was E.'s most popular work and has continued to be of interest to contemporary travelers to India, with modern reprintings in 1930, 1978, and 1983.

Portraits of the Princes and People of India (1843) is a beautifully printed volume of E.'s sketches and watercolors, which elicited praise for her as "one of the most accomplished amateur artists in India in the early nineteenth century." Her drawings were highly enough regarded that they received a showing by the Viceroy of India in 1916, and some 200 of them are still on display in the Victoria Memorial in Calcutta. Her portrait of Ranjit Singh has influenced subsequent portraitists.

It is for her novels, however, that E. is most enduringly remembered. The Semi-Detached House (1859) and The Semi-Attached Couple (1860) have both been readily available since their initial publication, most recently in Virago Press editions. In them E. shows an Austenesque love-and-marriage market among the very rich. In House young Lady Blanche Chester awaits the birth of her son, establishes herself as a force in country society, and comes to know the Hopkinsons and to help promote the marriages of Janet and Rose, thwarting meanwhile the snobbery of Baroness Sampson. The semi-detachment of the house reflects E.'s democratic belief in human worth and relatedness despite class differences. Couple details the difficulties that a young married couple face in learning to know one another; romance takes a back seat to very real differences of upbringing, sensitivity, and activity, as Lord Teviot's hearty loving frightens young Helen. In addition, the houseguests, hunting, and ambassadorial duties incumbent upon their lifestyle make it impossible for the couple to become intimate. In the midst of a borough election, Helen learns both how to yield and how to stand up for herself, and Teviot sees the roughness of his prideful ways. In both books the dry drollery of E.'s presentation remains as fresh and captivating as it was over a century ago. She is aptly characterized as a minor Jane Austen.

WORKS: Portraits of the Princes and People of India (1843). The Semi-Detached House (1859). The Semi-Attached Couple (1861). The Journals and Correspondence of William, Lord Auckland, ed. G. Hogge (1861–1862). "Up the Country": Letters Written to Her Sister from the Upper Provinces of India (1866; reprinted as Letters From India 1872). Catalogue of Exhibition of Paintings by the Hon. Miss Eden (at Victoria Memorial Exhibition, Belvedere, Calcutta, 1916). Miss Eden's Letters, ed. V. Dickinson (1919).

BIBLIOGRAPHY: Archer, W.G. Paintings of the Sikhs (1966). DNB. Dunbar, J. Golden Interlude: The Edens in India 1836–1842 (1955).

Loralee MacPike

Maria Edgeworth

BORN: 1 January 1768, Black Bourton, Oxford-shire.
DIED: 22 May 1849, Edgeworthstown, Ireland.
DAUGHTER OF: Richard Lovell and Anna Maria Elers Edgeworth.

In the "General Preface" to his *Waverley Novels* Sir Walter Scott wrote: "Without being so presumptuous as to hope to emulate the rich humor, pathetic tenderness, and admirable tact which pervade the work of my accomplished friend, I felt that something might be attempted for my own country, of the same kind with that which Miss Edgeworth so fortunately achieved for Ireland." E.—an Anglo-Irish novelist, short story writer, dramatist, and educational essayist—is known chiefly for her work in the tradition of the novel of manners although she is also remembered for her contributions to educational theory. Her reputation as a novelist has suffered from inevitable comparisons to Jane Austen; however, literary historians have long acknowledged her many innovations to English fiction.

Much of E.'s work was inspired and motivated by her father, a politician, inventor, and educator. Married four times, he fathered twenty-two children. Besides her responsibilities as agent and secretary of the family estate (Edgeworthstown, Ireland, where she lived from age fifteen until her death), E. had control of her father's ever-increasing family. To entertain them she composed stories, first on a slate and then, if they approved, in ink. In this manner E. perfected her skills as a storyteller.

Formal collaboration between E. and her father occurred on only two books, most notably *Practical Education*, which espouses many ideas on education taken from Rousseau, but her father's hand is noticeable in almost all her work. Not only did he urge her to write moralistic and didactic stories, but he edited her manuscripts, deleting and inserting, rearranging and rewriting to his own taste. Most critics agree that his presence within E.'s work is more of a hindrance than a help. Yet some maintain that the dichotomy of highly imaginative fiction with extreme pragmatism creates an interesting puzzle.

Castle Rackrent: An Hibernian Tale (1800) is considered by most to be E.'s best work. Written while her father was travelling, the novel is free from the overt didacticism of much of Edgeworth's other works. Although surpassed in many of her efforts by later writers, E. implemented several new narrative techniques in *Castle Rackrent*. Of major importance is her narrator, Thady Quirk. Not only is he active rather than passive but the narrative is presented from his perspective (a narrative device later adopted by Austen). The first regional novel, *Castle Rackrent* depicts speech, mannerisms, and activities of a specific group—a technique which greatly influenced Scott as well as others such as William Thackeray and James Fenimore Cooper. Ivan Turgenev said that his *Sportsman's Sketches* were also influenced by *Castle Rackrent* in their full development of lower-class characters.

E.'s other Irish tales are also considered to be worthy of note. *Belinda* is a picture of society at the close of the eighteenth century and is commented on by Austen in *Northanger Abbey*. Also included in this group is *The Absentee* and *Ormond*. Concerned with social and economic problems and showing great understanding for Irish culture, these are generally grouped among E.'s best work.

Thus, because of her innovations to narrative technique in the English novel, her sensitivity to local atmosphere, and her sympathetic portrayal of national character, E. influenced some of England's best-known authors (most notably Austen and Scott) and is an important figure in the history of the English novel.

WORKS: *Adalaide and Theodore* (1783). *Letters for Literary Ladies* (1795). *The Parent's Assistant* (1796). *Practical Education*, with R.L. Edgeworth (1798). *Castle Rackrent* (1800). *Early Lessons* (1801). *Moral Tales* (1801). *Belinda* (1801). *The Mental Thermometer* (1801). *Essay on Irish Bulls* (1802). *Popular Tales* (1804). *The Modern Griselda* (1805). *Leonora* (1806). *Essays on Professional Education*, with R.L. Edgeworth (1809). *Tales of Fashionable Life* (1812). *Patronage* (1814). *Continuation of Early Lessons* (1814). *Comic Dramas* (1817). *Harrington*, a tale; and *Ormond*, a tale (1817). *Rosamond: a Sequel to Early Lessons* (1821). *Frank: a Sequel to Frank in Early Lessons* (1822). *Harry and Lucy Concluded: being the last part of Early Lessons* (1825). *Thoughts on Bores, Janus* (1826). *Little Plays for Children* (1827). *Garry-Owen* (1829). *Helen, a tale* (1834). *Orlandino* (1848). *The Most Unfortunate Day of My Life* (1931).

BIBLIOGRAPHY: Butler, M. *Maria Edgeworth: A Literary Biography* (1972). Owens, C., ed. *Family Chronicles: Marie Edgeworth's "Castle Rackrent"* (1987).

For articles in reference works, see: *Allibone. BAKC. Cassell. CBEL. Chambers. ChPo. DIL. DLEL. DNB. Longman. NCLC. NCHEL. OCEL.*

Lynn M. Alexander

Amelia Ann Blanford Edwards

BORN: 7 June 1831, London.
DIED: 15 April 1892, Weston-super-Mare.

Although noted as a novelist, journalist, and Egyptologist, E. was not formally educated. Her talents, however, were early recognized by her mother, who sent E.'s poem, "The Knights of Old," written by the seven-year-old, to a penny weekly where it was published. At the age of nine, she won a prize for a temperance story. Her second published work, "The Story of a Clock," was written when she was twelve and republished in the January 1893 *New England Magazine.* Not only a talented writer, E. was also adept in music and drawing. A manuscript she sent to George Cruikshank for *The Omnibus* had such impressive pencillings on the back that he called on its author, surprised to find these caricatures the work of a fourteen-year-old girl.

She began her career as a journalist after sending a story to *Chambers' Journal* for which she was paid. Thereafter she wrote regularly for *Household Words* and *All the Year Round,* often supplying the ghost story for the Christmas issues. E. also served on the staff of the *Saturday Review* and *Morning Post,* sometimes contributing the leading articles and often the music, drama, and art reviews. She wrote, too, for the *Graphic* and the *Illustrated News.*

E. also wrote a number of novels, the first of which (*My Brother's Wife: A Life History*) was published in 1855. Another novel (*The Ladder of Life: A Heart-History*) followed in 1857, but her earliest popular success was *Barbara's History,* published in 1864, which went through three editions, was published in the American magazine, *Harper's,* and translated into German, French, and Italian. Her most popular novel was *Lord Brackenbury,* published in 1880. The novel, which originally came out in the *Graphic* with illustrations by Luke Fildes, subsequently ran through fifteen editions and was translated into Italian, French, German, and Russian.

E. also wrote works of nonfiction. Her interest in history is reflected in two works she published in 1856 summarizing English and French history, with a continuation of her summary of French history published in 1880. She published her own *Ballads* in 1865. In addition, she edited two anthologies of poetry, both published in 1879. She wrote several travel books as well, one about her tour through northern Belgium (1862), another about a trip through the Black Forest. A third travel book, based on a trip to the Dolomites, was published with illustrations from her own sketches (1873).

It was, however, her next major excursion, a trip to Egypt in the winter of 1873–1874, that altered the future course of her life. From then on, the study of Egypt became her consuming interest. Her *A Thousand Miles up the Nile,* published in 1877, included facsimiles of inscriptions, plans, maps and over eighty of her own illustrations. This book became a popular guide book, and a second edition was published in 1889. In 1882, E. founded the Egypt Explorer's Fund whose purpose was to prevent the destruction of antiquities, with herself and Reginald Stuart Poole as joint honorary secretaries; the Fund sponsored annual expeditions to Egypt for excavations. From this time on, E. wrote about Egypt for many journals and newspapers. She contributed over one hundred scholarly articles on Egypt to the *Academy* alone, and wrote frequently on the subject for *The Times* as well as various journals, both scholarly and popular. Her article, "Lying in State in Cairo," published in *Harper's Magazine* for July 1882, describes in detail the discovery of the royal mummies at Thebes.

E. attended the Orientalist Congress in Leyden in 1884, where she read a paper, later published as a pamphlet, titled "On a Fragment of Mummy-Case," illustrated by her. At the Orientalist Congress in Vienna the following year, she read a paper on "The Dispersion of Antiquities," a subject which greatly concerned her and which was again the topic of her paper in 1886. In 1888, she presented an important paper detailing the contents of private and provincial collections of antiquities in England. She toured America in 1889, with the lectures she delivered published two years later under the title *Pharoahs, Fellahs and Explorers.*

E.'s egyptological writing was valued and admired for its accessibility to the general reader as well as for its reliability as careful scholarship, and she is credited with popularizing egyptology. She bequeathed her egyptological library and antiquities to University College, London, with an endowment to found a chair of Egyptologies, the only such chair in England. Most of her books, however, she bequeathed to Somerville Hall, Oxford. A marble bust by Percival Ball, sculpted in Rome in 1873, was bequeathed to the National Portrait Gallery, London; her photograph provides the frontispiece of "The Queen of Egyptology," a biographical sketch by W.C. Winslow first published in *The American Antiquarian Magazine.*

WORKS: *My Brother's Wife: A Life History* (1855). *A Summary of English History: from the Roman Conquest to the Present Time* (1856). *The*

History of France from the Conquest of Gaul by the Romans to the Peace of 1856 (1856). *The Ladder of Life: A Heart-History* (1857). *The Young Marquis* (1857). *Hand and Glove* (1858). (trans.) *A Lady's Captivity Among The Chinese Pirates*, by F. Loviot (1858). *Sights and Stories: Being Some Account of a Holiday Tour through the North of Belgium* (1862). *A Night on the Borders of the Black Forest* (n.d.). *The Story of Cervantes, who was a Scholar, a Poet, a Soldier, a Slave Among the Moors, and the author of "Don Quixote"* (1863). *The Eleventh of March* (1863). *Barbara's History: A Novel* (1864). *Ballads* (1865). *Half a Million of Money* (1865). *Miss Carew: A Novel* (1865). *The Four-Fifteen Express* (1867). *Debenham's Vow* (1870). *Untrodden Peaks and Unfrequented Valleys: A Midsummer Ramble in the Dolomites* (1873). *In the Days of My Youth* (1873).

Monsieur Maurice: a New Novelette and Other Tales (1873). *A Thousand Miles up the Nile* (1877). *A Poetry-Book of Elder Poets* (1879). *A Poetry Book of Modern Poets* (1879). *Lord Brackenbury: A Novel* (1880). *The History of France from the Conquest of Gaul by the Romans Continued to the Death of the Prince Imperial* (1880). (trans.) *Egyptian Archeology*, by G.C.C. Maspero (1887). *Pharoahs, Fellahs, and Explorers* (1891). (trans.) *Julia Kavanagh*, by K.S. Macquoid (1897). (trans.) *Manual of Egyptian Archeology*, by G.C.C. Maspero (1902).

BIBLIOGRAPHY: Winslow, W.C. *The American Antiquarian Magazine* (November, 1892).

For articles in reference works, see: *DNB. Webster's New Biographical Dictionary.*

Gale Sigal

George Eliot (*pseudonym of Mary Ann Evans*)

BORN: 22 November 1819, South Farm, Arbury, Warwickshire.
DIED: 22 December 1880, London.
DAUGHTER OF: Robert and Christiana Pearson Evans.
MARRIED: John Walter Cross, 1880.

In his recollection of E., F.W.H. Myers wrote: "She . . . taking as her text the three words . . . *God, Immortality, Duty*,—pronounced, with terrible earnestness, how inconceivable was the *first*, how unbelievable the *second*, and yet how peremptory and absolute the *third*." E. herself recognized something of the kind in her work as the following comments reflect:

The idea of God, so far as it has been a high spiritual influence, is the ideal of a goodness entirely human (i.e., an exaltation of the human).

I am just and honest, not because I expect to live in another world, but, because having felt the pain of injustice and dishonesty towards myself, I have a fellow-feeling with other men, who would suffer the same pain if I were unjust or dishonest towards them.

If art does not enlarge men's sympathies, it does nothing morally; I have had heart-cutting experience that opinions are a poor cement between human souls: and the only effect I ardently long to produce by my writings is, that those who read them should be better able to imagine and to feel the pains and the joys of those who differ from themselves in everything but the broad fact of being struggling, erring, human creatures.

Born Mary Ann Evans, E. was the daughter of a Warwickshire land agent, a man of strong Evangelical Protestant feeling. She and her father became very close after her mother's death in 1836, but in 1842 an emotional conflict developed that severed communication between them: E. refused to attend church with her father. In the early 1840s E. became familiar with Higher Criticism, the new biblical and theological scholarship from Germany that applied science and history to the Bible. In 1844 E. began to translate Strauss's *Das Leben Jesu*, published in 1846 as *The Life of Jesus, Critically Examined*. Three years later she began translating Spinoza's *Tractatus Theologico-Politicus*. In May 1849 her father died, and E. decided to accompany the Charles Bray family to the Continent.

When E. returned to England in 1850, she met John Chapman and lived for much of 1851–1853 (under difficult emotional circumstances) as a resident of his London house. E. became assistant editor of the *Westminster Review* when Chapman bought it in 1851, a post she held until 1854. It was at this time that she became a close friend of Herbert Spencer, with whom she believed herself in love, and through him met George Henry Lewes. In 1853 E. began translating Feuerbach's *Das Wesen des Christenthums* (published as *The Essence of Christianity* in 1854).

The year 1853 also marked the beginning of one of the most famous liaisons in nineteenth-century Victorian England, that of E. and Lewes. Although Lewes was separated from his wife, the laws of the time made divorce impossible. However, E.'s union with him lasted until his death in

1878. They called themselves man and wife and were accepted as such by their friends.

E. was in her mid-thirties when she finally gave in to the urging of Lewes and tried her hand at writing fiction. It was in 1857 that the pseudonym of George Eliot was adopted, chiefly to avoid notoriety following the publication of her first three short stories in *Blackwood's Edinburgh Magazine*—"Amos Barton," "Mr. Gilfil's Love-Story," and "Janet's Repentance," published together in 1858 as *Scenes of Clerical Life*. This same year E. also began working on her first novel, *Adam Bede* (1859).

The plot of *Adam Bede* is based on a story about a confession of child murder made to E.'s aunt, Elizabeth Evans, by a girl in prison. Elizabeth Evans was a Methodist preacher and the original of the Dinah Morris character. With its pairings of contrasting characters—the two brothers, Adam and Seth, and Dinah and Hetty—the novel provides an early example of E.'s skill at characterization. Likewise, the garrulous Mrs. Poyser is a memorable supporting character.

The Mill on the Floss, published in 1860, is viewed by many scholars as E.'s most autobiographical work. The heroine, Maggie Tulliver, is highly strung and intelligent, of intense sensibility, and possessing artistic and poetic tastes. From conflicting temperaments within her family and the incongruity of Maggie's character with her surroundings spring unhappiness and ultimate tragedy. Her love for her brother, Tom, is thwarted by his lack of understanding, and the intellectual and emotional sides of her nature are starved. Eventually Maggie is turned out of her brother's house and ostracized by the community after being innocently but irremediably compromised by her cousin's fiancé. The situation appears irreconcilable; but a flood descends upon the town, and Maggie courageously rescues Tom from the Mill. There is a moment of revelation for Tom before the boat is overwhelmed and both brother and sister are drowned.

With the publication of *Silas Marner* in 1861 E. again focuses on the innocent individual wrongly driven out of a seemingly virtuous community. Gradually Marner finds happiness through his love for an orphan, Eppie. A solemn and somewhat bleak story, E. intended *Silas Marner* "to set in a strong light the remedial influences of pure, natural, human relations."

Romola (1863), Eliot's only historical novel, is set during the Italian Renaissance. According to Lewes, contemporary reviewers met it "with a universal howl of discontent." E., however, thought it her best work. "There is no book of mine," she wrote, "about which I more thoroughly feel I could swear by every sentence as having been written with my best blood."

With her next book, *Felix Holt, the Radical* (1866), E. again departed from her usual rendering of rural communities and townsfolk, this time capturing the urban environment in her only overtly political novel. In the novel E. provides a political model for reforms: Felix is noble-minded and self-sacrificing, deliberately choosing the life of a humble artisan in order to show his fellow workers that the hope of improving their condition lies in education and learning to think for themselves, not in legislative programs.

E. returned to the rural with her next, and finest, novel, *Middlemarch* (1871-1872). Originally conceived as two separate works, "Miss Brooke" and "Middlemarch," the novel presents a broad canvas of community life with parallel plots concerning unhappy marriages with one partner outgrowing the other, and false hopes of scientific discoveries prevented or marred because of the arbitrariness of time, medical and social reforms blocked because of ignorance, and the cancerous effect of money on human relationships. Despite the broad scope and complications of intertwining stories, *Middlemarch* presents some of E.'s strongest characterizations and plotting. Subtitled "A Study of Provincial Life," it is a complex panoramic work focusing on the social, religious, economic, political, and personal interrelationships among a number of characters. E. states her basic premise in the work's "Prelude": a natural conflict occurs between personal growth and ambition when an individual is faced with social or other adversaries. Hence her provincial characters are concerned more with materialism and conformity than with personal substance, and her two protagonists, Dorothea Brooke and Tertius Lydgate, must overcome apathy and intolerance to exercise their idealism. E.'s handling of plot, as a carefully worked-out organic whole with every character and incident forming a "contributory and integral part," as David Cecil called it, is excellent, as are her many carefully delineated, psychologically complex characters, her sensitivity to setting, her complete awareness of the cultural and intellectual currents of her day. E.'s concern above all for a rational approach to life enables her to see the shallow hypocrisies and narrow prejudices of the majority of the people in the world she describes. Compared to the overwhelming novels of her day, as F.R. Leavis noted, *Middlemarch* can be best compared with the work of Tolstoy.

Between *Felix Holt* and *Middlemarch*, E. tried her hand at writing a closet drama, *The Spanish Gypsy* (1868). Although contemporary reviews were positive, Henry James's evaluation of the work reflects the attitude of most modern critics: "*The Spanish Gypsy* is not a genuine poem," he declared. "It lacks the hurrying quickness, the palpitating warmth, the bursting melody through a glass smoked by the flame of meditative vigils."

E.'s last novel, *Daniel Deronda* (1876), is considered by many critics to be one of the finest, most sensitive portrayals of Jewish life ever created by a non-Jewish writer. Two years after its publication, Lewes died, and on 6 May 1880 E. married John Cross, a clergyman. She became ill in October the same year and died on 22 December.

E.'s fiction centered around moral problems and the moral growth and development of her characters. This preoccupation with moral dilemmas gives her work an overt didacticism that many twentieth-century readers find heavy-handed. Yet few fail to admire her ability to construct on a vast scale while maintaining a close attention to detail. Her works are carefully crafted and capture much of the rugged beauty and hardships of rural nineteenth-century England.

WORKS: (trans.) *The Life of Jesus Critically Examined*, by D.F. Strauss (1846). (trans., as by Marian Evans) *The Essence of Christianity, by L. Feuerbach* (1854). *Scenes of Clerical Life* (1858). *Adam Bede* (1859). *The Mill on the Floss* (1860). *Silas Marner* (1861). *Romola* (1863). *Felix Holt, the Radical* (1866). *The Spanish Gypsy* (1868). *Middlemarch* (1871-1872). *Daniel Deronda* (1876). *Letters*, ed. G. Haight (1955). *A Writer's Notebook, 1819-1880, and Uncollected Writings*, ed. J. Wiesenfarth (1981). (trans.) *Ethics*, by B. Spinoza, ed. T. Deegen (1981). (trans.) *Tractatus Theologico-Politicus*, by B. Spinoza (unpub.)

BIBLIOGRAPHY: Bennett, J. *George Eliot: Her Mind and Her Art* (1948). Carpenter, R.M. *George Eliot and the Landscape of Time: Narrative Form and*

Protestant Apocalyptic History (1986). Cross, J.W., ed. *George Eliot's Life as Related in Her Letters and Journals* (1885). David, D. *Intellectual Women and Victorian Patriarchy: Harriet Martineau, Elizabeth Barrett Browning, and George Eliot* (1987). Dentith, S. *George Eliot* (1986). Haight, G. *George Eliot: A Biography* (1968). Haight, G., ed. *The George Eliot Letters* (1955). Hardy, B. *The Novels of George Eliot: A Study in Form* (1959, 1963). Harvey, W.J. *The Art of George Eliot* (1961). Kitchel, A.T. *George Lewes and George Eliot: A Review of Records* (1933). Kroeber, K. *Styles in Fictional Structure: The Art of Jane Austen, Charlotte Brontë, and George Eliot* (1971). Leavis, F.R. *The Great Tradition: George Eliot, Henry James, Joseph Conrad* (1960). Paris, B.J. *Experiments in Life: George Eliot's Quest for Values* (1965). Prentis, B. *The Brontë Sisters and George Eliot* (1987). Redinger, R.V. *George Eliot: The Emergent Self* (1975). Thale, J. *The Novels of George Eliot* (1959). Thomas, J. *Reading "Middlemarch": Reclaiming the Middle Distance* (1987). Uglow, J. *George Eliot* (1987).

For articles in reference works, see: *Allibone SUP. BA19C. DLB.*

Other references: Adams, H.F. *Nineteenth Century Fiction* (1984). Bevan, E. *Victorian Institute Journal* (1984). Court, F.E. *Victorian Newsletter* (1963). Damm, R.F. *Victorian Newsletter* (1969). Hagan, J. *Nineteenth-Century Fiction* (1961). McConnell, J. *Genre* (1982). Willey, B. *Nineteenth-Century Studies: Coleridge to Matthew Arnold* (1949). Woolf, V. *The Common Reader* (1925).

Lynn Alexander

Queen Elizabeth I

BORN: 7 September 1533, Greenwich.
DIED: 24 March 1603, Richmond.
DAUGHTER OF: Henry VIII and Anne Boleyn.

After a youth that saw her mother's execution in 1536, her brother's accession to the throne in 1547, and her own imprisonment under her Catholic sister's reign, E. began her rule of England in 1558, bringing a long period of relative peace, military success, and enhanced political importance to the nation. Her popularity at home was matched with a sometimes grudging respect from allies and enemies abroad, not only for her political astuteness but for her learning.

Roger Ascham and his pupil William Grindal, both leading Protestant humanist scholars, educated her and praised her aptitude. While queen, E. continued to study history and classical literature, but it was her capabilities as a linguist

that produced the largest portion of her writings. She was expert enough in Greek, Latin, French, and Italian to write *A Book of Devotions* in English and these tongues. Probably compiled in the 1570s, even these private prayers show her as conscious of her political image.

E.'s linguistic ability also produced translations from all four of these foreign languages at various times in her life. She rendered the 13th Psalm into English tetrameter verse and Marguerite de Navarre's *Le Miroir de L'Ame Pecheresse* into prose (*The Mirror of the Sinful Soul*) when only about eleven years old. When sixty-five, she tackled Horace's "Ars Poetica." Her most polished piece, an early one done in verse, is of 90 lines from Petrarch's "Trionfo Dell'Eternita," and her longest is of Boethius's *De Consolatione Philosophiae* (1593). In many of these works, the alliteration may alienate the modern ear, but certain passages have considerable vigor. The great speed at which she translated may account for some mistranslations and a rhythmically awkward Latinate word order, but the devotion of effort to such a task amid state duties is remarkable.

E. also wrote original poems, though not all those subsequently ascribed to her. Of the six definitely genuine pieces, three are only two-to-four-line epigrams, and the others under twenty lines. This small body of work, nonetheless, has distinct characteristics: the poems touch her particular situations, political and personal. They do not so much complain against fortune as assert her determination to overcome it. One, perhaps the latest, relies on the paradoxes of Petrarchan love poetry, while the two other main pieces have the occasional alliteration and rougher meters characteristic of mid-century lyrics.

E.'s numerous letters penned in her roles as princess and queen exhibit a variety of styles suited to the particular situations and correspondents. She could be remarkably direct, even with other monarchs, but could, when her own feelings were ambivalent or when her purposes required that she not commit herself, write in a cloudy language of high diction, extended metaphors, and philosophical aphorisms.

Over a dozen of E.'s speeches survive, and though their occasions vary, they typically express trust in her people's good-will and a desire for their security. While some rhetorical features, like a dependence on deductive reasoning and a penchant for comparisons and metaphors, remain fairly constant, her style changes. Early speeches rely on an obfuscating adorned prose. When E.'s political confidence increases, later performances grow more bold, if only in stating her evasiveness.

In one case, she herself calls her response to a request an "answer answerless." The two most famous speeches, that at Tillbury to her troops as the Spanish Armada approached and her final "Golden" oration to Parliament, are unusually direct and dramatic.

E.'s political position and talents have made her literary fame more as a subject of masterpieces like Spenser's *Faerie Queene* than as an author in her own right. Her contemporaries recognized, however, that she was immensely learned and a skillful writer in a wide variety of forms.

WORKS IN MODERN EDITIONS: *A Book of Devotions Composed by Her Majesty Elizabeth R*, trans. A. Fox and intro. J. Hodges (1970). *Mirror of the Sinful Soul*, ed. P. Ames (1897). *Queen Elizabeth's Englishings of Boethius . . . Plutarch . . . Horace*, ed. C. Pemberton (1899, rpt. 1973). *The Poems of Queen Elizabeth I*, ed. L. Bradner (1964). *The Letters of Queen Elizabeth I*, ed. G. Harrison (1935, rpt. 1968). G. Rice, *The Public Speaking of Queen Elizabeth I: Selections* (1951, rpt. 1966).

BIBLIOGRAPHY: Erickson, C. *The First Elizabethan* (1983). Hodges, J. *The Nature of the Lion* (1962). Johnson, P. *Elizabeth I: A Study in Power and Intellect* (1974). Levine, J. *Great Lives Observed: Elizabeth I* (1969). Neale, J. *Queen Elizabeth* (1934, rpt. 1957). Plowden, A. *The Young Elizabeth* (1971). Ridley, J. *Elizabeth I* (1987).

For annotated bibliography, see: Hageman, E., *ELR* (1984).

Other references: Brooke, T. *HLQ* (1939). Haugaard, W., *SCJ* (1981). Heisch, A. *Signs* (1975).

Sayre N. Greenfield

Elizabeth of York

BORN: 11 February 1465, Westminster Palace.
DIED: 11 February 1503, Tower of London.
DAUGHTER OF: Edward IV and Elizabeth Woodville.
MARRIED: Henry VII, 1486.

In an age of bitter struggle over dynastic succession, E., daughter of King Henry VII, was a figure of central importance. She was first promised to George Nevill in 1469, but when his father turned against the King the match was cancelled. Next, her marriage to the French Dauphin was a condition of peace between Edward and Louis XI, but this too was called off. While engaged to the Dauphin she was also offered to Henry, then Earl of Richmond, as a ploy to lure him into Edward's control. Henry, then a refugee in Brittany, did not take the bait. When the King died in 1483, the

family entered Westminster for sanctuary from Richard, duke of Gloucester, where they remained for ten months. When they left, E. was treated so well at court that rumors spread concerning herself and Richard III. After Richard was killed at Bosworth fields, Henry became King Henry VII and married E. on 18 January 1486. She was crowned queen on 25 November 1487.

As a youth she read widely from among the books William Caxton was printing at Westminster Abbey—books of history, philosophy, theology, and literature. She could read and write French and Spanish. Although none of E.'s writing survives, her letters appear to have played an important role in politics. In a letter reported by Sir George Buck in the seventeenth century (the document has not been seen by anyone else), she encourages Richard III in the hope that he may marry her after his queen dies. Though the letter cannot be verified, it is true that rumors of Richard's intentions were so widespread that in April of 1485 he made a dramatic public denial of them before the Lord Mayor and aldermen of London.

A group of letters was sent to Henry, Earl of Richmond, while E. was staying at Sheriff Hutton Castle in Yorkshire, still under Richard's guard. According to the popular "Song of the Lady Bessy" by Humphrey Brereton (a servant of Lord Stanley), E. hated Richard and sent messages to Henry encouraging him and promoting his uprising. She sent a letter with a ring to Henry in Brittany, and Henry pledged himself to her at Vannes Cathedral on Christmas Day 1483.

In 1492 King Henry VII invaded France and laid siege to Boulogne. Bernard Andreas, the royal historiographer, indicates that E. sent numerous letters to Henry in France and had no small influence on his decision to return to England.

All indications are that their married life was a happy one. She is said to have been beautiful, with a fair complexion and golden hair. She appears to have enjoyed music, dancing, cards, dice, and hunting. Of her seven children three died as infants. The oldest son, Prince Arthur, died in 1502, causing both parents such grief that it is said to have led to E.'s death after the birth of her last child, Catherine, in 1503. Her daughter Mary became queen of Louis XII of France, and her second son became Henry VIII of England. Sir Thomas More wrote an elegy on her death.

WORKS: none surviving.

BIBLIOGRAPHY: Harvey, N.L. *Elizabeth of York: Tudor Queen* (1973). Leland, J. *De Rebus Britannicus Collectanae* (1770). Nicolas, N.H. *Privy Purse Expenses of Elizabeth of York* (1830). Strickland, A. *Lives of the Queens of England* (1863).

For articles in reference works, see: *DNB.* Routh, C.R.N., *Who's Who in History* (1964).

Richard Poss

Sarah Stickney Ellis

BORN: 1799 (?), Holderness, Yorkshire.
DIED: 16 June 1872, Hoddesdon, Hertfordshire.
DAUGHTER OF: William and Esther Richardson Stickney.
MARRIED: William Ellis, 1837.
WROTE UNDER: Sarah Stickney, Sarah Ellis, Sarah Stickney Ellis, Mrs. Ellis.

E. wrote scores of novels, poems, and moral tales, but she achieved her greatest success with *The Women of England* (1839) and other conduct manuals. In many ways, her life approaches the Victorian ideal of womanhood which her books disseminated. Raised a Quaker on her father's farm in East Riding, she learned the duties of the sickroom by nursing her sisters and numerous other relatives through their fatal illnesses. Instead of getting to "act the bride," she plunged into the "trials, perplexities, and hard work" of marriage at the age of thirty-eight when she became the second wife of author and missionary William Ellis (1794–1872). An admirer of Elizabeth Fry, E. performed the good deeds appropriate for middle-class women: she gave bazaars, visited the poor, and directed a Sunday-school. Yet her letters reveal the discrepancy between prescription and practice. Although her advice books warned against vanity, E. delighted in having her portrait done. She advised women to conceal their gifts (talent, she wrote, is "a jewel which cannot with propriety be worn"), but she became acquainted with her husband by submitting poetry to an annual he edited; he encouraged her work and relied on her editorial assistance, especially after his health began to fail. E. recommended deference to male authority but resisted much of her husband's advice about religion and writing. In her books, women are sheltered from economic competition; letters show she kept a keen eye on sales and resented relatives who tried to borrow money. She exhorted women to make the home pleasant for others; in her house, she wanted a room of her own for painting and other art projects.

As a writer, E. intended to inculcate truth and earn money. E. admired Shakespeare, Milton, Byron, Tennyson, Margaret Oliphant, and Harriet Beecher Stowe; she felt that Charlotte Brontë, another Yorkshire writer, had a special hold upon her. Since sales for *The Negro Slave* (1830) and other privately printed early works were disappointing, she followed the advice of her friend Mary Howitt and contacted Thomas Pringle in 1832. When he made her a good offer to write for the circulating libraries, she quickly agreed, provided she could include "a certain degree of moral or religious sentiment." An experienced portrait painter, she often supervised the illustrations for her books. Apart from friendship with Mary Howitt and Mary Sewell, E. had little contact with other writers. Despite her husband's interest in her work, E. suspected that literary achievement and marital happiness were antithetical: the How-itts offered a hopeful model for literary marriage, but the unhappy situation of Anna Jameson suggested that there was "no luck with authoress-wives." When E. became a formidable figure in the mid-century marketplace, she still complained about "the bondage of writing." Preferring to spend her time on educational endeavors, she founded a school at Rawdon House (1845), where she lectured for twenty years; spoke frequently to women's groups; and at the age of seventy-one wrote with enthusiasm about setting up new classes for young women.

E. helped turn the novel away from romance and toward domestic realism. Her "Apology for Fiction" is contained in her first collection of tales, *Pictures from Private Life* (1833–1837). Anticipating religious objections, she cited allegory and scripture as evidence that fiction could be used "as a means of reproof and conviction." "Fiction," she said, "may be compared to a key, which opens many minds that would be closed against a sermon." E. endorsed "lawful" fictions, "drawn from the scenes of every-day life, animated with our feelings, weak with our frailties, led into our difficulties, surrounded by our temptations, and altogether involved in a succession of the same causes and effects which influence our lives." Virtue must be flawed according to the demands of realism, but it must also be rewarded. Thwarting the reader's expectations for romantic endings, E. tries to create ideal goodness in the midst of everyday life. The heroine of "The Hall and the Cottage" overcomes vanity, ambition, and desire, but she meets "no belted knight, no steel-clad warrior, no prince in disguise"; instead she ends her days as a "respectable old maid" exuding "unbounded benevolence" in humble surroundings. Later novels, such as *The Brewer's Family* (1863), describe the dreadful consequences of drinking and parental neglect. *Home, or The Iron Rule* (1836) is a lesson to fathers who make their children's obedience a matter of compulsion rather than a choice of the heart. *The Mother's Mistake* (1856) is a warning to mothers lest they misread their children's characters and channel their energies in the wrong directions.

Addressing her conduct manuals to "women" rather than "ladies," E. attacks the "false notions of refinement" which were making modern women "less influential, less useful, and less happy" than in the past. E. urges the reader to be content with her proper sphere, to practice the "art of accommodation," to make prudent use of material resources. Laying aside "her very *self*," and putting away "all personal feeling," the Christian woman should dedicate herself to making time "pass pleasantly and profitably for others." The charm—and indeed, the moral duty—of "the

true English woman" is found in "diffusing happiness, without appearing conspicuously as the agent of its diffusion." E. did not advocate unlimited sacrifices for irresponsible husbands, but she did maintain that women's interests were best served by ministering to men.

E.'s work is fraught with contradiction. Women are said to constitute the "fabric of society," but they are rendered silent and invisible as their identities are submerged in others. E. believed that women should establish intimate bonds with one another through the shared suffering of their lives, but she instructed them to shape their education, conversation, and conduct to men's needs. The enormous popularity of *The Women of England* and its sequels indicates how well E. understood the needs of middle-class women to redefine their roles in a newly industrialized and very competitive society. Driven by religious zeal, some writers on women's influence would soon argue for rebellion and reform. But as the debate on the woman question evolved, E. remained loyal to existing social and economic structures, limiting her advice to "the minor morals of domestic life."

WORKS: *The Negro Slave* (1830?). *The Poetry of Life* (1835). *Pictures of Private Life* (1833–37). *Home; or, The Iron Rule* (1836). *Pretension* (1837). *The Women of England* (1839). *The Sons of the Soil* (1840). *Summer and Winter in the Pyrenees* (1841). *The Daughters of England* (1842). *Family Secrets* (1842). *The Mothers of England* (1843). *The Wives of England* (1843). *The Irish Girl and Other Poems* (1844). *Look at the End* (1845). *Temper and Temperament* (1846). *The Island Queen* (1846). *Prevention Better than Cure* (1847). *Social Distinction* (1848). *Fireside Tales for the Young* (1848). *Pique: A Tale of the English Aristocracy* (1850). *Family Pride* (185–?). *Self-Deception* (1851). *The Education of Character* (1856). *The Mother's Mistake* (1856). *Friends at Their Own Fireside; or, Pictures of the Private Life of the People Called Quakers* (1858). *The Mothers of Great Men* (1859). *The Widow Green and the Three Nieces* (1859). *Janet: One of Many* (1862). *The Brewer's Family* (1863). *William and Mary* (1865). *Share and Share Alike* (1865). *The Beautiful in Nature and Art* (1866). *Northern Roses* (1868). *Education of the Heart* (1869). *The Brewer's Son* (1881).

BIBLIOGRAPHY: Colby, V. *Yesterday's Woman: Domestic Realism in the English Novel* (1974). *The Home Life and Letters of Mrs. Ellis Compiled by Her Nieces* (1893).

For articles in reference works, see *Allibone.* Boase. *CBEL. DNB. Europa. NCBEL. VB.*

Robin Sheets

Una Mary Ellis-Fermor

BORN: 20 December 1894, London.
DIED: 24 March 1958, London.
DAUGHTER OF: Joseph Turnley Ellis-Fermor and Edith Mary Katherine Ellis-Fermor.
WROTE UNDER: U.M. Ellis-Fermor, Una Ellis-Fermor, Una Mary Ellis-Fermor, and (pseudonym) Christopher Turnley.

E., one of the most versatile literary critics of the English Renaissance, wrote the majority of her work during the 1930s and 1940s. Major contributions were her analysis of Christopher Marlowe's satanic overreachers, her analysis of the literary history of Jacobean drama, and her research on William Shakespeare's use of imagery and characterization. Her long writing career, beginning in 1927 with *Christopher Marlowe*, was honored in 1946 when she was invited to become General Editor for *The Arden Shakespeare* editions of the plays, a role she filled until her death in 1958. Although E.'s criticism placed too much emphasis on characterization, especially in her discussions of Elizabethan and Jacobean drama, her contributions to the study of drama have not been sufficiently acknowledged. Few people are able to write about such a wide range of literary topics as Marlowe, Shakespeare, Ibsen, and the early twentieth-century Irish dramatic movement.

Ellis-Fermor was so careful a scholar as to edit, meticulously, the 1930 edition of Marlowe's *Tamburlaine* (Parts One and Two); but she could also write theoretically in *The Frontiers of Drama*, where she questions the generic limits of the drama's subject matter and type of conflict. She was also able to translate several of Ibsen's plays and to speculate, in *Masters of Reality*, on the value of imagination in controlling one's life. She was a poet who wrote two collections, *Twenty-Two Poems* (1938) and *Sharpness of Death* (1939) under the pseudonym Christopher Turnley, a combination of Christopher Marlowe and Joseph Turnley Ellis-Fermor. Surprisingly, given all of her talent and achievements, few of the standard British or American reference works carry articles about her work. The reason her work was neglected is unclear, unless her emphasis on character as revealing the author's personality was already suspect when she was writing.

E. began her study of drama at Somerville College, Oxford, where she received the B. Litt. and M.A. degrees, and at the University of London where she received the D. Lit. Aside from a position at Manchester University, most of her career was spent at Bedford College, University of London, first as Reader in English Literature and, from 1947 until her death, as Hildred Carlile Pro-fessor of English. She spent several years in the United States, first as Rose Sidgwick Fellow at Yale and Columbia Universities (1922–1923), then as a Fulbright scholar in 1951. She also received the Rose Mary Crawshay Prize for Literature in 1930.

In E.'s first work, *Christopher Marlowe* (1927), she attempts to trace the development of Marlowe's art as revealed in his surviving work and to draw some conclusions about his personality. She considers Marlowe's early translations, *Tamburlaine, Faustus, The Jew of Malta, The Massacre at Paris, Edward II*, and *Hero and Leander*, arguing that in most of his plays Marlowe was interested in large questions concerning the nature of man and his part in the universe. *Tamburlaine*, for example, embodies a vision of the power of the human will; *Faustus* records the loss of harmony between a man's mind and the forces surrounding him. All of Marlowe's work, she concludes, investigates man's relationship not to other men but to God and the universe. She places perhaps too much emphasis on Marlowe's personality in determining his characters' ambitions.

One of E.'s lasting contributions is her in-depth study of the plays and lives of the major Jacobean dramatists. *The Jacobean Drama: An Interpretation* attempts to consider the outstanding plays during the years 1598 to 1625 that share literary and dramatic techniques. Her book treats Chapman, Marston, Jonson, Dekker, Middleton, Tourneur, Webster, Greville, Beaumont and Fletcher, and Ford. Writing in very general terms, E. argues that the mood of the drama during 1598 to 1625 passed through three phases: 1) worship of the vitality, the expansion and elation of the mind, 2) a sense of defeat, 3) much apprehension in social and political life after Elizabeth's death—a sense of futility in man's achievements and a preoccupation with death.

With some trepidation, E. next investigates the drama, in *The Irish Dramatic Movement* (1939), of the early twentieth-century movement in Ireland begun by Yeats, Lady Gregory, Synge, and the group who supported and followed them at the Abbey Theatre. The book is, however, more concerned with Yeats than any other member of the movement. E.'s major interest in this drama was its ability, she argued, to bring back high poetry to English-language literature. She believed that poetic drama, which had been in decline since Jacobean times, was restored by the Irish Dramatic Movement to the living theater. The leaders' Irish revival was made in large terms; it was not limited to one country. For E., Yeats was the movement's fountainhead of poetic ideals.

Imagination became the pre-eminent human faculty for E. in her speculative *Masters of Reality* (1942). The book describes the functions of the imagination in the daily lives of the English people. She asserts that the use of the imagination, far from being an irresponsible escape, may be a determining factor for the survival of civilization itself. In England, she argues, there is an unfortunate valuation of the unimaginative and suppressed. Such habits of mind, when combined with over-reliance on machines, lead to passivity and fatalism, indifference and dullness. Beset by machines, we lose our capacity for wonder; our need for stimulation becomes more and more exaggerated.

In her only theoretical study, *The Frontiers of Drama* (1945), E. examines plays whose themes and subject matter defy common beliefs in what is appropriate for the theater. Although she believes that the drama imposes some inevitable limits, she is interested in the very few plays that manage to transcend these limitations. Attempts at religious drama have usually had disastrous results because religious emotion, what she calls "beatitude," is a condition free from conflict, upon which drama depends.

Shakespeare the Dramatist (1961) is a volume of Ellis-Fermor's critical essays. Kenneth Muir, who edited this collection and compiled a careful bibliography, believed that her work on Shakespeare was E.'s greatest contribution to literary criticism. She believed that the specifically dramatic qualities in Shakespeare's art were passion, thought, and a poetic imagination which "irradiates" the mind of the poet. Fullest expression of the drama comes from within the characters, and Shakespeare is able to speak from within all of his characters; his art is the most consistently dramatic of English dramatists.

Although some of E.'s observations about Shakespeare's characterization were familiar to her audience, she wrote intelligently and perceptively about the ways in which Shakespeare, and the other dramatists, presented characters to the audience. Her greatest contribution as a literary critic was her work on drama, especially her two excellent introductory guides, one to the Jacobean plays and another to the Irish Dramatic Movement.

WORKS: *Christopher Marlowe* (1927). *The Jacobean Drama: An Interpretation* (1936; Second Edition, 1947; Third Edition, 1953; Fourth Edition, 1958). *Some Recent Research on Shakespeare's Imagery* (1937). *Twenty-Two Poems.* By Christopher Turnley (pseudonym) (1938). *The Irish Dramatic Movement* (1939; Second Edition, 1954). *Sharpness of Death.* By Christopher Turnley (pseudonym) (1939). *Masters of Reality* (1942). *The Frontiers of Drama* (1945; Second Edition, 1946; Third Edition, 1948). *The Study of Shakespeare* (1948). (trans.) *Three Plays*, by Ibsen (1950). (trans.) *The Master Builder and Other Plays*, by Ibsen (1958). *Shakespeare the Dramatist and Other Papers.* Edited by K. Muir (1961).

BIBLIOGRAPHY: Muir, K. *A Select List of the Published Writings of Una Ellis-Fermor.* In *Shakespeare the Dramatist and Other Papers* (1961).

For articles in reference works, see: *Biographical Master Index. NCBEL. NCHEL. Who Was Who, 1951-1960.* Vol. 5 (345–46). *Who Was Who Among English and European Authors.*

Other references: *Books and Bookmen* (August 1965). *British Book News* (October 1981). *Choice* (March 1965, April 1968). *Observer* (30 July 1967). *Renaissance Quarterly* (1975). *Reprint Bulletin Book Reviews* 23 (1978). *Sewanee Review* (1982). *Spectator* (9 October 1965). *TLS* (30 December 1965).

Laura Niesen de Abruña

Elizabeth Elstob

BORN: September 1683, Newcastle-on-Tyne.
DIED: 30 May 1756, Bulstrode.
DAUGHTER OF: Ralph and Jane Elstob.

E. is the first (known) female scholar of Anglo-Saxon. Her father, a merchant in Newcastle, died when she was three; her mother, whom E. herself described as "a great admirer of learning, especially in her own sex," began to teach her daughter Latin, but she died when E. was eight.

We do not know precisely how the "Anglo-Saxon nymph," as she was dubbed in her own day, subsequently acquired her remarkable learning. After her mother's death she was raised by an uncle, a Prebendary of Canterbury, who like most men of his time objected to the education of women. Her brother William was a student and later Fellow of University College, Oxford; biographers speculate that E. may have joined him at Oxford, and in fact one tradition has it that she was the "first home student" there. In any case, she was certainly her brother's companion in London from 1702 (when E. was 19) until the time of his death in 1715. William presumably trained E. in Anglo-Saxon at some point, and her scholarly writings all date from the latter half of her days in London (1708–15).

E.'s first work was an anonymous translation of Mlle. de Scudery's *Essay upon Glory*. A year later (1709) she published her first work in Anglo-Saxon, an edition of an Old English sermon, titled in full *An English-Saxon Homily on the Birthday of St. Gregory: Anciently used in the English-Saxon Church. Giving an Account of the Conversion of the English from Paganism to Christianity.* In a lengthy preface to this pioneering edition, E. defends both her right as a woman to learning and the importance of her subject matter (which was at the time often ridiculed as too arcane), as well as its theological interest. Despite criticism of her work—or more likely of its apparatus—as a "Farrago of Vanity," E.'s edition was apparently well-enough received to encourage her to plan the publication of a "Saxon homilarium," a much larger project including most of Aelfric's sermons. In the early eighteenth century, scholarly editions of this sort were funded by subscribers, and E. published preliminary plans and appeals for subscription in pamphlet form in 1713. The Homilarium, however, was never completed, though proofs of the first few pages survive in the British Museum. In 1715, E.'s final scholarly publication appeared, the first grammar of Old English written in modern English, entitled *The Rudiments of Grammar for the English-Saxon Tongue.* Modern readers will again be interested, as in the case of the *English-Saxon Homily*, in E.'s discursive notes and in the Preface, which is noteworthy for two reasons. First, E. explicitly addresses her work to a female audience. She says that she was motivated to write the text after meeting with an unnamed "young lady" in Canterbury who wanted to become her pupil and that she writes her grammar "considering the Pleasure I myself had reaped from the Knowledge I have gained from this Original of our Mother Tongue, and that others of my own Sex might be capable of the same Satisfaction." Second, E. defends the validity of Anglo-Saxon studies, this time attacking among other detractors Jonathan Swift, whose *Proposal for Correcting, Improving, and Ascertaining the English Tongue* criticizes English for its tendency to become monosyllabic and disparages the study of the language's history and development. E.'s defense of her philological work against "Pedagogues who huff and swagger in the height of their arrogance" has been called by one modern scholar "a bravura display of vast learning and wide reading."

In the same year in which E.'s grammar was published personal disaster struck, and the precariousness of the female scholar's career becomes evident. E.'s brother William died, and so did her most important scholarly supporter, George Hickes. For almost two decades afterwards, E. virtually disappears from the record. There is some evidence that she remained in London for two or three years after her brother's death, attempting to carry on her work and publish her Homilarium, and then to avoid debtor's prison she was forced to leave the city, perhaps heading north, changing her name, and becoming a domestic servant. She re-emerges in the 1730s as a careworn schoolmistress in Evesham. With the help of a few friends (including Mary Pendarves Delany, who was Swift's friend and later Fanny Burney's patroness), the unsuitability of E.'s position was finally brought to the attention of Queen Caroline, who intended to patronize E. but died in 1737. After various trials and failures, E. became a governess in 1739 in the house of the Duchess of Portland, where she remained until her death in 1756.

In 1738, at the request of her friend George Ballard, tailor and author of *Memoirs of Learned Ladies* (1752), E. wrote a brief, still unpublished memoir. Through the efforts of Ballard and a few others, she was not completely forgotten by antiquarians and scholars in her own day, but her work as governess for 17 years afforded her no more scope and time for renewed scholarly activities than did the years in which she vanished from society. She appears to have been fond and proud of her noble young pupils but told friends that "my acquaintance and interest is reduced to a very narrow compass." She wrote to Ballard, advising him against the notion of compiling a book about female scholars, "For you can come into no company of Ladies and Gentlemen, where you shall not hear an open and vehement exclamation against Learned Women, and by those women who read much themselves, to what purposes they know best." One material reminder of E.'s career survives: Oxford University Press still owns punches and matrices of an Anglo-Saxon type known as the "Elstob" font, presumably used in the printing of her English-Saxon Grammar.

WORKS: (trans.) *Essay on Glory* by Mlle. De Scudery (1708). *An English-Saxon Homily on the Birth-Day of St. Gregory* (1709). *Some Testimonies of Learned Men, in Favour of the Intended Edition of the Saxon Homilies* (1713). *The Rudiments of Grammar for the English-Saxon Tongue* (1715; facsimile edition by Scholar Press, 1968).

BIBLIOGRAPHY: Contemporary accounts: Delany, Mary. *Autobiography and Correspondence* (1861–62). E.'s memoirs in Ballard MSS., Bodleian Library. Hearne, Thomas. *Remarks and Collections*

(1885–1921). "Memoirs of the Learned Saxonists Mr. Wm. Elstob and His Sister." Nichols' *Bibliotheca Topographica Britannica* (1790). Thoresby, Ralph. *Diary and Correspondence* (1832). Modern biographical studies: Ashdown, M. *MLR* (1925). Green, M.E. *Female Scholars: A Tradition of*

Learned Women Before 1800, ed. J.R. Brink (1980). Reynolds, M. *The Learned Lady in England, 1650-1750* (1920). Wallas, A. *Before the Bluestockings* (1929).

Elaine Tuttle Hansen

Juliana Horatia Ewing

BORN: 3 August 1841, Ecclesfield, Yorkshire.
DIED: 13 May 1885, Bath.
DAUGHTER OF: the Rev. Alfred and Margaret Gatty.
MARRIED: Major Alexander Ewing, 1867.
WROTE UNDER: J.H.G., Juliana Horatia Ewing, J.H. Ewing.

A storyteller, poet, and illustrator, E. is best known for the stories she wrote for children. Many of these stories appeared first in *Aunt Judy's Magazine for Children*, a respected periodical founded by E.'s mother and later run by E. and her sister. Randolph Caldecott and George Cruikshank illustrated some of the stories E. wrote.

Many of E.'s letters have been published, including those she wrote when she and her husband were stationed in Canada. She wrote that she liked the works of Sir Walter Scott and especially William Shakespeare. However, she did not fully admire important Victorian writers. She found Charles Dickens and Henry James imperfect writers although interesting, and she criticized George Eliot for her limited imagination and unnatural characters.

E. herself preferred to write stories with an explicit moral. She also believed modern fairy tales should reflect the oral tradition of older fairy tales. To this end, "The Brownies" and "Amelia and the Dwarfs" are moralistic tales with a character who acts as storyteller.

E.'s best known stories include "The Story of a Short Life" and "Jackanapes," but the former is too rambling and saccharine for modern tastes. Because the tone and structure of "Jackanapes" are more controlled, it is a better work of art. As E. stated in the conclusion of "Jackanapes," the hero shows the importance of patriotism. To the modern reader the moral is less interesting than the characterization of Jackanapes, an impish orphan, who grows up to face death fearlessly.

E. was a very popular writer during her day. Some of her stories such as "Jackanapes" are still interesting for their characterization, but most are too sentimental and didactic for the modern reader.

WORKS: *A Bit of Green* (18??). *Old-Fashioned Fairy Tales* (18??). *Melchior's Dream and Other Tales* (1862). *Mrs. Overtheway's Remembrances* (1869). *The Brownies and Other Tales* (1870). *Lob Lie-by-the Fire* (1874). *A Very Ill-Tempered Family* (1874–1875). *Six to Sixteen* (1876). *Jan of the Windmill* (1876). *Master Fritz* (188?). *A Flat Iron for a Farthing* (1880). *We and the World* (1880). *The Story of a Short Life* (1882). *Brothers of Pity* (1882). *Blue and Red* (1883). *A Week Spent in a Glass Pond* (1883). *Jackanapes* (1883). *A Soldier's Children* (1883). *The Blue Bells on the Lea* (1884). *Daddy Darwin's Dovecot* (1884). *Dandelion Clocks and Other Tales* (1887). *The Peace Egg and a Christmas Mumming* (1887). *Mother's Birthday Review and Seven Other Tales in Verse* (1888). *Snap-Dragons* (1888). *Works* (1890). *Jackanapes and Other Tales* (1890). *Last Words* (1891). *Lob Lie-by-the-Fire, The Brownies and Other Tales* (1892). *Jackanapes, Daddy Darwin's Dovecot and Other Stories* (1893). *Verses for Children and Songs for Music* (1895). *A Great Emergency* (1897). *The Trinity Flower and Other Stories* (1897). *The Land of the Lost Toys* (1900). *Mary's Meadow* (1900). *Madam Liberality* (1901). *Juliana Horatia Ewing's Works* (1909). *Jackanapes and the Story of a Short Life* (1909). *Jackanapes and Other Stories* (ed. S.C. Bryant, 1917). *Stories by Juliana Horatia Ewing* (1920). *Jackanapes and the Peace Egg* (1928). *The Ewing Book* (ed. E.M. Allsopp, 1930). *Three Christmas Trees* (1930). *Timothy's Shoes and Two Other Stories* (1932). *The Brownies and Other Stories* (1954). *Canada Home* (ed. M.H. Blom and T.E. Blom, 1983).

BIBLIOGRAPHY: Avery, G. *Mrs. Ewing* (1961). Eden, H.K. (Gatty). *Juliana Horatia and Her Books* (1885). Laski, M. *Mrs. Ewing, Mrs. Molesworth, and Mrs. Hodgson Burnett* (1950). Maxwell, C. *Mrs. Gatty and Mrs. Ewing* (1949).

For articles in reference works, see: *BA19C. Cassell. Everyman's Dictionary of Literary Biography*, ed. D.C. Browning (1965).

Margaret Ann Baker

Ruth Fainlight

BORN: 2 May 1931, New York City.
DAUGHTER OF: Leslie Alexander and Fanny
    Nimhauser Fainlight.
MARRIED: Alan Sillitoe, 1959.

F. was educated in America and England before attending Birmingham and Brighton Colleges
of Arts and Crafts. Except for travels to France,
Spain, Morocco, Israel, and Majorca, she has lived
most of her adult life in London where she married the novelist and poet Alan Sillitoe. Best
known as a poet, she is also a short-story writer,
translator, and adapter of dramas. Her claim to
literary accomplishment, however, rests with a
series of poetry collections published steadily since
1958.

F.'s poetry is most often characterized by a
sense of quietness. Her rhythms are smooth, her
language measured, and her voice controlled, all of
which is surprising, given the nature of her subjects. Like Sylvia Plath, who dedicated "Elm" to F.,
her poems are often about death, suicide, madness,
imprisonment, and the frustrations of housewives. She also shares Plath's interest in children,
the English countryside, gardening, and the holocaust, and in her earlier books her poetry has a
particularly Plathian sound: "I am the seer who
reads her own entrails:/ I search for signs of what
the future means/ in the past's hot reek"; or
"Perhaps I'll bleed to death./ Appropriate, if I still
seek a role./ Then I will be/ As clean as any
animal/ My family eats." Her affinity for the sort
of subjects that attracted Plath is indicated in such
titles as: "The Vampire Housewife," "The
Screaming Baby," and "The Infanticide," all from
Cages.

F.'s earlier books often have a brooding quality, an obsession with death, guilt, and anxiety
over growing old without having had one's say.
Her recent books, however, although meditations
on similar themes, replace an earlier measured
despair with a more subtle sense of strength. As
the title poem of her fourth collection attests, she
wishes "To See the Matter Clearly," even when
the matter is intense self-preoccupation. Instead
of being "overwhelmed by giant agony," she remains a survivor, not by avoiding the anguish of
life but by her ability to "turn down the sound."

As a result, her later poems, while continuing
to echo some of Plath's subjects, create a sense of
control, even as her poetic forms become more
prose-like. In "Hospital Flowers," for instance, she
writes: "Unless the nurses take them/ away,
day after day they wilt in regulation/ vases or
commandeered drinking glasses, reminders/ of
the friends who brought them, and that fear/
which, though omni-present, looms clearer here/

than in the world outside, the place where/ flowers are forced especially for this purpose." The
first half of *Sibyls and Others* is taken up with a
series of variations on the theme of the sibyl, a
series that echoes the mixture of Jewish and
Christian prophecy common to both the *Sibylline
Books* and to F.'s family origins in Austro-Hun-
gary, England, and America.

Eventually a series of personal subjects
emerge from the body of her work: she is particularly drawn to the moon, hair, mirrors, babies,
allusions to classical mythology, and as she continues to write, to an uneasy acceptance of age and
rural life, lyrically rendered in poems that find
relief in the cyclical pattern of nature and in the
victory of natural death over suicidal impulses.

Although some reviewers see F.'s voice as
being too restrained, others have applauded her
tone, her determination to examine a personal
situation which in many ways parallels Plath's.
Like her more famous friend, F. is an expatriate
American living in England, struggling to write
poetry while fulfilling the difficult role of wife of a
well known British author and mother of young
children. F., who wrote in a poem titled "Un-
seemly," "I left my race and family/ To learn
about myself," has managed to survive her situation and to find a home for herself within it. The
result is a body of poetry centered around the
major problems of twentieth-century women, expressed in a voice that commands our attention,
despite its quietness, a voice "Between fineness
and toughness," qualities she called "my own special markings."

WORKS: *A Forecast, A Fable* (1958). *Cages* (1966).
18 Poems from 1966 (1967). (trans. and adapted
with A. Sillitoe) *All Citizens Are Soldiers,* by Lope
de Vega (1967). *To See the Matter Clearly and Other
Poems* (1968). *Poems* (with Alan Sillitoe and Ted
Hughes, 1971). *Daylife and Nightlife* 1971). *The
Region's Violence* (1973). *Twenty One Poems*
(1973). *Another Full Moon* (1976). *Two Fire Poems*
(1977). *The Function of Tears* (1979). *Sibyls and
Other Poems* (1980). *Coral* (translated from the
poetry of Sophia de Mello Breyner, 1982). *Climates*
(1983). *Fifteen to Infinity* (1983).

BIBLIOGRAPHY: For articles in reference works,
see: *CA. CP.*

Other references: *Letters Home by Sylvia Plath,*
ed. Aurelia Schober Plath (1980). *New Statesman*
(12 March 1976, 9 May 1980). *Poetry* (1978). *TLS*
(8 April 1977, 23 May 1980).

Timothy Dow Adams

Anna Maria Falconbridge

FIRST TRACED: Bristol, 1790.
LAST TRACED: Bristol, 1794.
MARRIED: Alexander Falconbridge, 1790; Isaac Dubois, 1793.

Most information about F. comes from her 1794 *Narrative of Two Voyages to the River Sierra Leone*. In 1790 she married former ship's surgeon Alexander Falconbridge, whose abolitionist activities led them to West Africa in 1791 in an attempt to reestablish a small anti-slavery colony. Her husband succeeded in arranging a new site for the colony, and F.'s narrative is lively and cheerful as she describes her visits to African villages, the royalty she meets, the strange animals and insects, the scenery, her liking for African food, and even the privations and illnesses of the colonists. Keeping herself out of the account at most times, she is factual and detailed, quick with sarcasm, and careful to blend observations with interesting anecdotes.

Five months later the F.'s returned to England after a three-month voyage marked by storms, disease, and near starvation. The Sierra Leone Company promoted her husband to Commercial Agent and persuaded F. to return with him. In Africa, F. noted desperate shortages and daily death tolls, but her husband had to answer to a self-important Council whose members did little to encourage agriculture or provide land for a group of new colonists, black Americans who had previously moved to Nova Scotia because of the revolution. From Company letters we know that her husband was impossible: his "hot, rash, and impetuous" temper, lack of commercial qualifications, and habitual drunkenness finally forced the Company to replace him. F. defended his actions but had few regrets at his subsequent death: "his conduct to me for more than two years past was so unkind (not to give a harsher term) as long since

to wean every spark of affection or regard I ever had for him."

As conditions in the colony degenerated further, F.'s account becomes increasingly critical. She scorns the religious idealism of the Company at a time when the necessities of life were often lacking in the colony. Shortly after her husband's death she married Isaac Dubois, the town planner, and several months later they left for Jamaica, which she compared unfavorably to Sierra Leone. In Jamaica, however, the treatment of the slaves seems better to her than that of "three fourths" of Africans under tribal rule, and she finds her former circle "bigoted for the abolition."

From Jamaica, F. and Dubois returned to England, where she fought for money due her at Mr. F.'s death. The last section of her account protests the Company's broken promises to the black colonists and to herself, and she appends a letter urging her rights. With the exception of a month of journal entries, the rest of the *Narrative* is epistolary. F. says it was written for publication, and she could have heard through colony Governor Clarkson of the remunerative vogue for travel accounts. The detail and clarity with which she records events and registers her opinions make the *Narrative* a delight to read as well as a historical treasure.

WORKS: *Two Voyages to the River Sierra Leone During the Years 1791-2-3* (1794).

BIBLIOGRAPHY: Clarkson, R.N. *Sierra Leone Studies* (1927), also excerpted in Ingham, E.G., *Sierra Leone After a Hundred Years* (1894). Mackenzie-Grieve, A. *The Great Accomplishment* (1953).
For articles in reference works, see: *DNB*. Todd.

Marie E. McAllister

Lady Anne Fanshawe

BORN: 25 March 1625, London.
DIED: 30 January 1680.
DAUGHTER OF: Sir John and Margaret Harrison.
MARRIED: Sir Richard Fanshawe, 1644 or 1645.

F.'s *Memoirs* are her only literary legacy. Originally intended as both a family history and as an ethical guide for her last surviving son, the work has since been estimated as a "charming" collection of "remarkable actions and accidents" revealing a wife and mother "of conjugal devotion, of maternal

excellence, and of enduring fortitude under calamities."

According to her chronicles, F. initially enjoyed a privileged and pleasant childhood as the daughter of a devoted Royalist until unfavorable consequences of the Civil War forced the family to move from St. Olan's Hart Street, London (her birthplace) to a poor baker's house in Oxford. The series of reverses continued with the death of F.'s mother in 1650 and the loss of William, the second of three brothers, as a result of injuries sustained during a skirmish with the Earl of Essex's retinue. F.'s father, having refused a Baronetcy "on the grounds of poverty," was subsequently arrested and confined as a political prisoner. Marriage to Sir Richard Fanshawe, a career diplomat and integral member of the Prince of Wales' assemblage, only served to increase opportunities for privation and danger, which she describes in detail throughout her *Memoirs.*

F.'s writings trace her husband's loyalty to the royal family with vivid accounts of her family's jaunts to each of Sir Richard's diplomatic posts. F.'s admiration for her husband at this time is only exceeded by her endurance and strength: F.'s fourteen pregnancies were often jeopardized by constant changes of residence, and only five children survived.

Each account of F.'s adventures is depicted in gentle, gracious tones. Scenes of deprivation or tragedy have a matter-of-fact quality as if almost anyone else could claim similar experiences. One particular event seems almost operatic. Between 13 September to 28 November 1651, Sir Richard was imprisoned at Whitehall. Every day, at 4 A.M., F. spoke with him under the cell window. Daily, she demanded, from his keepers, a certificate of ill health, which she finally received and used to petition council for his release.

Sir Richard died during his last post as Ambassador to Madrid. Refusing the queen mother's generous offers of wealth, honor, and a permanent residence if she embraced the Catholic faith, F. sold many possessions to bring her children and the body of her husband back to England.

In addition to fulfilling her original intentions, the *Memoirs* serve several other functions. They elicit the essentials required of a public servant, unrequited obedience and unfailing dedica-tion to duty; they present "lively and entertaining" asides on personal and national history; and they serve as a treatise on the conditions in court after the Restoration (which F.'s publisher considers "the most disgraceful in the annals of [England]" in his addition to a later printing). The *Memoirs* also added to the "evidence which exists of the total want of principle which characterised the court of Charles the Second."

There are variations in dates within the notations, as the inaccuracies were difficult for the publisher to correct "because the Authoress sometimes used the old and sometimes the new style, and now and then speaks of things out of the order in which they happened." An amended addition, including excerpts from Lord Fanshawe's correspondence, was published in 1829 and edited by Sir N. Harris Nicolas. A further reprint was developed in 1907 from an original manuscript possessed by a descendant of the family.

The dedication in the initial printing indicates the family's appreciation of their mother's nobility. F.'s son, Charles, addresses the Duchess of Clarence and notes the Fanshawe heritage of loyalty and courage: "These qualities still animate the hearts and steel the hands . . . 'Like men to conquer, or like Christians fall.'"

WORKS: *Memoirs of Lady Fanshawe; Wife of the Right Hon. Sir Richard Fanshawe, Bart.; Ambassador from Charles the Second to the Court of Madrid in 1665,* ed. Sir N. Harris Nicolas (1829).

BIBLIOGRAPHY: For articles in reference works see: *BAB1800. CHEL. Chambers. DNB.*

Zelda Provenzano

Eleanor Farjeon

BORN: 13 February 1881, Hempstead.
DIED: 5 June 1965, Hempstead.
DAUGHTER OF: Margaret Jefferson Farjeon and Benjamin Leopold Fargeon.
WROTE UNDER: Eleanor Farjeon, Tom Fool, Chimaera.

F. was a prolific writer whose best-known works were children's short stories and poems written for the most part between the two world wars. These numerous works share an interest in children's fantasy and a deep-seated belief in the essential goodness of humanity. These traits have led many commentators to compare her work with that of her contemporary and friend, Walter de la Mare. Her work, which has been translated into twelve European languages as well as He-brew and Japanese, is now known mainly through anthologies.

F. grew up in a thoroughly literary family, her father being a prolific novelist and her mother the daughter of Joseph Jefferson, a celebrated American actor. Two of her brothers became writers, and the third taught music at the Royal Academy. F. educated herself by reading widely in the family library and listening to the conversations among writers, musicians, and actors who were frequent guests in her home. As she explains in *A Nursery in the Nineties* (1935), her early life, filled with fantasy games, was essential to her development as a person and as a writer. These fantasy games were so realistic that it became second nature for her to create and inhabit worlds of her own.

Although she wrote stories and poems as a child, her serious career as a writer began when her father died in 1903. At first, she wrote humorous or topical verse for *Punch, The Daily Herald,* and *Time and Tide.* At this time, she was also beginning to publish stories and verse, first *Dream-Songs for the Beloved* (1911) and then *The Soul of Kol-Nikon* (1914). This early work was completed with the encouragement and guidance of the poet Edward Thomas and his wife.

After Thomas's death in 1917, she rented a cottage in Sussex for two years, during which time she wrote *Martin Pippin in the Apple Orchard* (1921), one of her best-known works. This collection of tales was intended for an adult audience, but reviewers read it as a children's book, and it was reissued as such in 1952. By 1925, she was writing her first stories intended for children, and by 1930 she was fully established as a writer. From 1930 to 1944 she wrote plays, musicals, and humorous verse in collaboration with her brother Herbert, as well as publishing many collections of retold tales like *Tales from Chaucer* (1930).

The 1950s marked another productive period for her, a time when much of her earlier work was reissued. During the fifties, she published her major collections of poetry as well as her award-winning story collection, *The Little Bookroom* (1955). This collection earned the Carnegie Medal and the Hans Christian Andersen Medal in 1956.

F.'s work is diverse and uneven. Certainly her best work is her short stories, notably the two collections centering on the minstrel character of Martin Pippin, *Martin Pippin in the Apple Orchard* (1921) and *Martin Pippin in the Daisy-Field* (1937), the latter of which includes her famous story "Elsie Piddock Skips in Her Sleep." This simple story is typical of F.'s work in that its fairy-tale plot demonstrates the triumph of good over evil, freedom over restriction. In the story, a man threatens to build a factory on the children's playground, but he allows one last skipping rope contest to be held there. He will not break ground, he says, until the last jump-rope skipper has stopped. In order to save the playground, an old woman, Elsie Piddock, skips endlessly with the aid of her fairy jump rope. Many of F.'s other story collections, like *Jim at the Corner* (1934), are strung together by a single theme or a single character. Her most famous story collection is *The Little Bookroom* (1955), which contains 27 stories including "The Glass Peacock" and "I Dance Mine Own Child," two of her more successful realistic tales. In addition to these original stories, F. published several new versions of old tales including *Tales from Chaucer* (1930), *Ten Saints* (1936) and *The Wonders of Herodotus* (1937).

F.'s poems are collected in several volumes, including *Silver-Sand and Snow* (1951), *The Children's Bells* (1957), and *Then There Were*

Three (1942). In addition, *Nursery Rhymes for London Town* (1916) reproduces all her poems from *Punch* (which she later set to music), and *Kings and Queens* (1932) and *Heroes and Heroines* (1933) are farcical poems on historical subjects that she wrote in collaboration with her brother Herbert. With Herbert, she also wrote several plays including *The Glass Slipper* (1944), a rendition of the Cinderella story.

Not all of her books were for children, however. She wrote several novels and collections of stories for adults including *Ladybrook* (1931), *Humming Bird* (1936), *Miss Granby's Secret* (1940), and *Ariadne and the Bull* (1945). But more interesting are her two autobiographical memoirs that paint vivid pictures of life in Victorian and Edwardian England. The first, *A Nursery in the Nineties* (1935), includes biographies of her parents and recounts her life until her father's death in 1903. The second volume, *Edward Thomas: The Last Four Years* (1958), was intended as the first in a series of autobiographical works and covers her early writing career and her relationship with Thomas.

F. will probably be best remembered as a writer of children's books that present fascinating characters in fully realized fantasy worlds. In recognition of this work, she was awarded the American Regina medal in 1959. But she is also a fascinating study of the female writer. Indeed, most books about F. address her personal rather than her literary merits. In her memory, the Children's Book Circle in England awards the Eleanor Farjeon award each year for "distinguished service to children's books."

WORKS: *Floretta* (1894). *The Registry Office* (1900). (with H. Farjeon) *A Gentleman of the Road* (1903). *Pan-Worship and Other Poems* (1908). *Dream-Songs for the Beloved* (1911). *Trees* (1914). *Nursery Rhymes of London Town* (1916). *More Nursery Rhymes of London Town* (1917). *All the Way to Alfriston* (1918). *Sonnets and Poems* (1918). (with H. Farjeon) *A First Chapbook of Rounds* (1919). (with H. Farjeon) *A Second Chapbook of Rounds* (1919). *Singing Games for Children* (1919). *Gypsy and Ginger* (1920). *Martin Pippin in the Apple Orchard* (1921). *Songs for Music and Lyrical Poems* (1922). (trans.) *Four Comedies,* by C. Goldoni (1922). *Tunes of a Penny Piper* (1922). *All the Year Round* (1923). *The Soul of Kol-Nikon* (1923). *The Country Child's Alphabet* (1924). *Mighty Men* (1924). *The Town Child's Alphabet* (1924). *Faithful Jenny Dove and Other Tales* (1925). *Songs from 'Punch' for Children* (1925). *Tom Cobble* (1925). *Young Folk and Old* (1925). *Italian Peepshow and Other Tales* (1926). *Joan's Door* (1926). *Nuts and May* (1926). *Singing Games from Arcady* (1926). *Come Christmas* (1927). *King's Barn* (1927). *Mill of Dreams* (1927). *The Wonderful Knight*

(1927). *Young Gerard* (1927). *ABC of the B.B.C.* (1928). *An Alphabet of Magic* (1928). *Kaleidoscope* (1928). *Open Winkins* (1928). *A Bad Day for Martha* (1928). *A Collection of Poems* (1929). *The King's Daughter Cries for the Moon* (1929). *The Perfect Zoo* (1929). *The Tale of Tom Tiddler* (1929). *Tales from Chaucer* (1930). *Westwoods* (1930). *Ladybrook* (1931). *The Old Nurse's Stocking-Basket* (1931). (with H. Farjeon) *Kings and Queens* (1932). *The Fair of St. James* (1932). *Katy Kruse at the Seaside* (1932). *Perkin the Pedlar* (1932). *Ameliaranne and the Magic Ring* (1933). (with H. Farjeon) *Heroes and Heroines* (1933). *Ameliaranne's Prize Packet* (1933). *Over the Garden Wall* (1933). *Pannychis* (1933). *Ameliaranne's Washing Day* (1934). *The Clumber Pup* (1934). *Jim at the Corner* (also issued as *The Old Sailor's Yarn Box*) (1934). *And I Dance Mine Own Child* (1935). *A Nursery in the Nineties* (issued as *Portrait of a Family* in America) (1935). (with H. Farjeon) *The Two Bouquets* (1936). *Humming Bird* (1936). *Jim and the Pirates* (1936). *Ten Saints* (1936). *Martin Pippin in the Daisy-Field* (1937). *Paladins in Spain* (1937). *The Wonders of Herodotus* (1937). *One Foot in Fairyland* (1938). (with H. Farjeon) *Songs of Kings and Queens* (1938). *Sing for Your Supper* (1938). *Grannie Gray* (1939). *A Sussex Alphabet* (1939). *Miss Granby's Secret* (1940). *Brave Old Woman* (1941). *Magic Casements* (1941). *The New Book of Days* (1941). *Cherrystones* (1942). *Then There Were Three* (1942). *The Fair Venetian* (1943). *Golden Coney* (1943). *Ariadne and the Bull* (1945). *Dark World of Animals* (1945). *The Mulberry Bush* (1945). *A Prayer for Little Things* (1945). (with H. Farjeon) *The Glass Slipper* (1946). *First and Second Love* (1947). *Love Affair* (1947). *The Two Bouquets* (1948). *The Starry Floor* (1949). *Mrs. Malone* (1950). *Poems for Children* (1951). *Silver-Sand and Snow* (1951). (with R.F. Birch) *Roundelay* (1952). (with H. Farjeon) *Aucassin and Nicolette* (1952). *The Silver Curlew* (1953). *The Little Bookroom* (1955). *The Glass Slipper* (1955). *The Children's Bells* (1957). *Elizabeth Myers* (1957). *Edward Thomas: The Last Four Years* (1958). *Mr. Garden* (1966). *Around the Seasons* (1969).

BIBLIOGRAPHY: Blakelock, D. *Eleanor: Portrait of a Farjeon* (1966). *A Book for Eleanor Farjeon: A Tribute to Her Life and Work*, ed. N. Lewis (1966). Cameron, E. *The Green and Burning Tree* (1962). Colwell, E. *Eleanor Farjeon* (1961). Farjeon, A. *Morning Has Broken: A Biography of Eleanor Farjeon* (1986).

For articles in reference works, see: *CA. DNB. Longman. TCA* and *SUP. TCCW. TCW.*

Tori Haring-Smith

Eliza Fay

BORN: 1756, perhaps at Blackheath.
DIED: September 1816, Calcutta, India.
FAMILY NAME: unknown.
MARRIED: Anthony Fay, late 1770s.

Though very little is known of her life, F.'s *Original Letters from India—1779-1815* contributes to our record of the British in Calcutta in the late eighteenth century. As the new bride of Anthony Fay, an advocate at the Supreme Court, F. went to India in 1779 via France, Italy, and Egypt. After her husband failed at law and fathered an illegitimate child, they divorced; F. returned to England in 1782. She had, however, business schemes of her own based on mantua-making and the cloth trade and eventually returned to Calcutta in 1784, in 1796, and in 1816. Each time, her financial plans went awry. After she died in debt in 1816, the administrator of her estate published letters which she had been gathering in hopes of paying off her creditors. The letters were published in Calcutta in 1817, reprinted in 1821, and re-edited there in 1908. The 1908 edition came to the attention of E.M. Forster who found it troublesome because both prose and punctuation had been altered by the Rev. W.R. Firminger. Forster restored the original text and wrote the introduction and notes to the 1925 edition.

F.'s one great Indian adventure, which required all her resourcefulness and pluck, came when she first arrived in India and was imprisoned for fifteen weeks by Hyder Ali at Calicut. All in all, however, her letters have relatively little to do with India; indeed, her attitude towards Indians and Indian customs is generally supercilious. Her theme is her life with the Anglo-Indians—setting up house; going to dinners, balls, the races, and the theater; sorting out marital and financial difficulties; the long journeys to and from India. Thus her book is a valuable social document. Beyond that, we are attracted to it, as was E.M. Forster, because of F.'s idiosyncratic, piquant—and even catty—prose style.

In response to renewed interest in travel literature and the Raj, Forster's edition of *Original Letters from India* was re-issued in 1986 with a new introduction by M.M. Kaye.

WORKS: *Original Letters from India—1779-1815* (1817, 1821, 1908, 1925, 1986).

BIBLIOGRAPHY: Beyer, K.C. *The Aligarh Journal of English Studies* (1983). Forster, E.M. *Cornhill* *Magazine* (May 1924). Forster, E. M. *Egyptian Gazette* (5 and 16 April, 11 May 1917); revised and reprinted in *Pharos and Pharillon* (1923).

Kathleen Collins Beyer

Elaine Feinstein

BORN: 24 October 1930, Bootle, Lancashire.
DAUGHTER OF: Isidore Cooklin and Fay Compton Cooklin.
MARRIED: Arnold Feinstein, 1957.

A poet, translator, writer of fiction, television playwright, biographer, and editor, F. has published a dozen books of her own verse in addition to well-received translations of poetry by Russian writers, notably Marina Tsvetayeva, and she has won a number of prizes for both fiction and poetry. She began writing poetry in the 1960s when she taught at Essex University. She was, she says, consciously influenced by such American poets as William Carlos Williams, Wallace Stevens, Emily Dickinson, and Robert Creeley, "at a time when the use of line, and spacing, to indicate the movement of poetry was much less fashionable than it is now among young British poets." She also states that her translations of Tsvetayeva gave her her "true voice" as a poet and that the Russian made her "attend to a strength and forward push, *against* and *within* a formal structure."

Though raised in the same period as "the angry young men" and others of the 1950s who felt socially displaced and guilt-ridden, she knew little of the anxieties of the time because of her cultural background. F. received her B.A. and M.A. from Newnham College, Cambridge. She took law examinations, worked as an editor for Cambridge University Press, taught at several schools, worked as a journalist, and in 1957 married a biochemist specializing in immunology.

Her Cambridge experience enabled her to meet Donald Davie, a well-known poet, and when he moved to Essex University, she taught there as well. She first read Russian literature at Essex and was part of a poetry group that included Ed Dorn, a group that planned, unsuccessfully, to be similar to the Black Mountain group in the United States. Their support and criticism helped her and enabled her to become more conscious of her non-British roots.

She published her first book of verse, *In a Green Eye*, in 1966, and her first two novels, *The Circle* and *The Amberstone Exit*, in the early 1970s. These works relate to each other because of F.'s similar techniques: wide spaces between groups of words, unusual syntax, and similar attempts to imitate actual speech rhythms and pauses. Her first two novels use language economically as a means of expressing the constricted lives of her characters. In *The Circle*, through Lena and other women and their children, F. suggests the fragmented existences of the characters and their variously successful abilities to find their own niches or "private worlds" in life. *The Amberstone Exit*, similarly, describes a woman seeking her own "space," as she tries, only partially successfully, to find security in London and as she reflects on her earlier life in the small town of the title.

The Magic Apple Tree (1971), like most of F.'s verse, uses imagery, color, speech rhythms, and, again, broken syntax to capture the vivid patterns of everyday life; her emphasis on the visual can be seen in the title poem (based on a painting), in "Out" (citing Buster Keaton), "West" (hinting at Mae West), and "I Have Seen Worse Days Turn" (the weather), as well as in echoes of earlier poets, such as in "Our Vegetable Love Shall Grow" (an echo of Andrew Marvell's "The Garden"). *At the Edge* (1972) continues F.'s exploration of personal discovery, as does the long title poem in *The Celebrants and Other Poems* (1973), which not only considers love, religion, and poetry as forces governing human survival but moves into new territory as well, a more somber tone and touches of mordant humor.

In 1973 F. published *The Glass Alembic*, titled *The Crystal Garden* in the United States. Written after a year's stay in Switzerland, the novel is set in Basel and focuses on the drug culture of the 1960s as this contrasts with the more traditional Swiss society. The central characters, Matthew and Brigid and their teenage son and daughter, experience a variety of sexual and familial disappointments before the near death from drugs of one of Matthew's laboratory colleagues, and hovering always are the "ghosts" of such earlier residents of Basel as Erasmus and Paracelsus.

Although descended from Russian immigrants from Odessa, F. was not particularly aware of Jewishness. Her gradual interest in her heritage, both Jewish and Russian, grew after her parents' deaths in 1973, resulting first in *The Children of the Rose* (1975), about Polish Jews who survived the war and were financially successful but who subsequently lived in different countries: the insatiable Alex lives an emancipated life in France, while the troubled Lalka lives in London and learns to live with the past by revisiting Poland.

F.'s next two novels are satiric attempts to use the conventions of such popular genres as science fiction and fantasy while still centering on her Jewish heritage and the search for roots. *The Ecstacy of Dr. Miriam Garner* (1976) is a wildly absurdist foray into a woman's psychic "journey" to medieval Spain, when Jews, Arabs, and Christians lived easily with each other, unlike the situation she, as a specialist in Islam, finds in the modern world. *The Shadow Master* (1978) is similarly farcical while exploring a serious situation—a new messiah comes to modern Istanbul—but the novel's metaphysical framework gets bogged in excessive digressions, in both geography and character. It is less successful than its predecessor.

F.'s other collections of verse include *Some Unease and Angels* (1977), which attempts a synthesis between incompatible human and natural forces through the use of poetic language, and *The Feast of Euridice* (1980), which uses myth—as in the poems about Dido and Aeneas—to contrast mortal and immortal love; in both collections F. experiments with longer verse forms than she did in her earlier collections. In 1980 F. published her only collection of stories, *The Silent Areas*, with the shorter form, like her verse, enabling her to avoid the relative lack of focus and control the more expansive novel led to in *The Shadow Master*.

It is F.'s translations, however, that have brought her the greatest degree of recent critical attention. Her *Three Russian Poets: Margarita Aliger, Yunna Moritz, Bella Akhmadulina* (1979) was noted for its idiomatic accuracy, but *The Selected Poems of Marina Tsvetayeva* (1971, 1987), as well as her *A Captive Lion: The Life of Marina Tsvetayeva* (1987), have given her a much wider audience than any of her own poetry or fiction. Tsvetayeva's poetry has been called "incredibly difficult to translate" because of its syntactical and linguistic complexity; F.'s translation is considered the standard. The biography, however, has been welcomed for its obvious love for its subject but criticized severely for its lack of scholarship and awareness of recent work on Tsvetayeva.

F. has grown as a writer, particularly as a poet and translator of poetry by others, but her work in a number of genres suggests her versatility, talent, and willingness to consider new alternatives for her creative impulses.

WORKS: *In a Green Eye* (1966). *The Circle* (1970). *The Magic Apple Tree* (1971). (trans.) *The Selected Poems of Marina Tsvetayeva* (1971, 1986). *At the Edge* (1972). *Matters of Chance* (1972). *The Amberstone Exit* (1972). *The Celebrants and Other Poems* (1973). *The Glass Alembic* (1973; in the U.S. as *The Crystal Garden*, 1974). *Children of the Rose* (1975). *The Ecstasy of Dr Miriam Garner* (1976). *Some Unease and Angels: Selected Poems* (1977). *The Shadow Master* (1978). (trans.) *Three Russian Poets: Margarita Aliger, Yunna Moritz, Bella Akhmadulina* (1978). *The Feast of Euridice* (1980). *Matters of Chance* (1980). *The Silent Areas: Short Stories* (1980). *The Survivors* (1982). *The Border* (1984). *Bessie Smith* (1985). *Badlands* (1986). *Mother's Girl* (1987). (trans.) *First Poems*, by Nika Turbina (1987). *A Captive Lion: The Life of Marina Tsvetayeva* (1987).

BIBLIOGRAPHY: Mitchell, D. *British Poetry Since 1970: A Critical Survey*, ed. P. Jones and M. Schmidt (1980).

For articles in reference works, see: *CA. CN. CP. DLB.*

Other references: *Books and Bookmen* (January 1977, September 1984, January 1986). *Encounter* (September 1984). *Harper's* (June 1974). *Listener* (10 August 1972, 21 June 1973, 24 April 1975, 28 September 1978, 28 February 1980, 11 March 1982, 21 June 1984, 5 December 1985). *New Statesman* (4 August 1972, 11 April 1975, 4 June 1976, 22 September 1978, 15 February 1980, 26 February 1982, 8 June 1984, 15 November 1985). *NYT* (25 February 1974, 21 August 1987). *NYTBR* (19 May 1974, 4 November 1979, 20 September 1987). *Observer* (20 August 1972, 13 May 1973, 27 May 1973, 10 March 1974, 20 April 1975, 30 May 1976, 10 September 1978, 3 February 1980, 28 February 1982, 10 June 1984, 3 November 1985). *Spectator* (5 June 1976, 24 September 1977, 23 September 1978, 16 June 1979, 9 February 1980). *TLS* (11 August 1972, 29 June 1973, 7 December 1973, 25 April 1975, 4 June 1976, 6 October 1978, 22 February 1980, 18 January 1980, 26 February 1982, 8 June 1984). *WLT* (Spring 1980).

Paul Schlueter

Susan Edmonstone Ferrier

BORN: 7 September 1782, Edinburgh.
DIED: 5 November 1854, Edinburgh.
DAUGHTER OF: James Ferrier and Helen Coutts Ferrier.

F. was the tenth and last child of James Ferrier, writer to the signet, and Helen Coutts Ferrier, who died when F. was fourteen. As a child and a young woman, F. knew and visited many people (in Edinburgh society and elsewhere in Scotland), a number of whom turn up later as thinly disguised characters in her novels. Among the homes she visited was that of the Duke of Argyle, where she established a friendship with Charlotte Clavering that was to develop into a very productive literary relationship. Clavering and F. initially considered joint authorship, but differing tastes and writing styles precluded this. Clavering did contribute a chapter to F.'s first novel, *Marriage* (1818), but her main value to F. the writer was as a keen and thoughtful critic.

F. has been grouped with the Scottish didactic novelists (Brunton, Hamilton, etc.), and with the Scottish regionalists (Galt, Porter, Scott), and has even been termed the Scottish Austen. However, in the end it is the considerable merits of her own novels that have maintained F.'s vitality as a writer. Her novels are pointedly witty studies of Scottish society, animated by the sprightly dialogue of wonderfully comic characters although occasionally the energy is checked and the sparkle dimmed by long tendentious moral commentary. F. wrote three novels: *Marriage, The Inheritance* (1824), and *Destiny* (1831). Critics generally agree that the novels successively diminish in spontaneity, freshness, and originality while they increase in technical control, artistic shaping, and overall stylistic mastery. It should not be surprising, then, that the middle novel, *The Inheritance*, is generally regarded as F.'s best.

Marriage opens with an encounter between the very elegant and very squeamish Englishwoman, Lady Juliana, and her husband's Highland relatives, including his three eccentric aunts and his five "great purple" sisters. This group of deliciously odd creatures is reinforced by their still odder neighbor, Lady MacLaughlan. The result is a mighty clash of culture, sentiments, and values. Juliana is horrified and disgusted by this Highland family and its homeland, but the family itself remains cheerfully oblivious to her attitude. Juliana flees from stingy Scotland to extravagant London, where she raises one of her twins to be even more spoiled and self-centered than she herself and leaves the other twin, Mary, to be raised in the Highlands by her gentle and sensible sister-in-law, with predictably different results. The second part of the book brings Mary to her mother's house, where she is highly unwelcome and out of place. Mary is eventually rewarded for her patient endurance and her charity. She marries the MacLaughlans' heir and returns to her beloved Highlands.

The next novel, *The Inheritance*, is less a study of manners in conflict than a history of a young woman, Gertrude St. Clair, who nearly forfeits her inheritance by choosing a lover of whom the lord disapproves. Gertrude, while of good instincts and generous heart, is too easily led by her selfish lover. Consequently, she lives extravagantly for several years until she learns that she is really the child of Mrs. St. Clair's nurse and an heiress only by fraud. Instantly repudiating her wealth and title, she loses her false lover, who can now inherit in his own right. After a period of despair, she is helped to mature by her cantankerous but kindly Uncle Adam and by her true lover who at once restores her to position and wealth. The book offers acute insights about a heroine who struggles vainly against the skilled and ruthless manipulation of her "mother" and the more overt tyranny of her guardian. The only hope for a woman to be happy and worthy alone, F. suggests, is to devote herself to a higher master and to a life of faith and good works, as do Mrs. St. Clair's unmarried sisters.

F. owes obvious debts to Austen, and the opening line of *Inheritance*, "It is a truth universally acknowledged, that there is no passion so deeply rooted in human nature as that of pride," has often been cited. But the differences between the two writers are more marked than their similarities. This very quotation is symptomatic, since F.'s line is pedantic and moralistic. She seems completely to have missed the light irony in the original line. Nor does F.'s wit resemble Austen's; it is consistently broader, more acerbic, and more dependent on caricature and farce in the Smollettian tradition.

F.'s final novel, *Destiny*, was written after her life had become increasingly narrowed by the loss of many of her siblings and by her own long confinement with her ill father. Critics generally maintain that her gallery of originals was exhausted and her material wearing thin. The novel is precisely articulated and symmetrical almost to a fault. Providence, in keeping with the title, is the justification for the remarkable coincidences of the book, but it remains difficult fully to admire the strong authorial hand. For all this, the book remains quite readable, and the great comic clergyman, Mr. McDow, makes amends for pages of overly sentimental prose. What critics find the most original aspect of the book, setting F. apart from other Scottish regionalists, is her portrait of the petty, selfish, irascible Glenroy who is fiercely proud of his family name and unforgivably blind to his daughter's virtues, her love for him, and even her basic needs for survival. Here, for once, is an unromantic portrayal of a Highland chieftain. Here, too, is the charming Mrs. Macauley, who is generally agreed to be one of the few completely realized and fully successful sentimental figures in literature. And here, finally, is the aging society belle, Lady Elizabeth Waldegrave, Glenroy's English wife, who provides her own contribution to the humor, although she also elicits more pity than did her predecessor, Lady Juliana.

Readers should not ignore F.'s letters. As Barbara Hardy claims, they are "sprightly, clever, intelligently and fluently communicative, arch and facetious, generating a flow of images, anecdotes, and projects."

Walter Scott, an old friend, assisted F. in negotiating terms for the publication of *Destiny*. She visited Abbotsford late in life, but besides this visit and trips to London about her failing vision, F.'s later life was almost entirely homebound. She declined requests that she write another work,

although she did make revisions for the 1849 reappearance of her books in Bentley's Standard Novels.

WORKS: *Marriage* (1818). *The Inheritance* (1824). *Destiny, or the Chief's Daughter* (1831).

BIBLIOGRAPHY: Cullinan, M. *Susan Ferrier* (1984). Grant, A. *Susan Ferrier of Edinburgh: A Biography* (1957). Parker, W. *Susan Ferrier and John Galt* (1965).

Other references: Bushnell, N.S. *Studies in Scottish Literature* (1968). Colby, V. *Yesterday's Women* (1974). Craik, W. *Scott: Bicentenary Essays*, ed. A. Bell (1973). Douglas, G. *The Blackwood Group* (1897). Foltinek, H. Introduction to *Marriage* (1971). Gwynn, S. *Macmillan's Magazine*, (April 1899). Hamilton, C.J. *Women Writers* (1892). Hardy, B. *TLS*, (7 June 1985). Hart, F.R. *The Scottish Novel* (1978). Irvine, J. Preface, *Marriage* and *The Inheritance* (1985). Johnson, R.B. *The Women Novelists* (1918; rpt. 1972). Kestner, J. *Wordsworth Circle* (1979). Paxton, N. *Women and Literature*, (1976). Sackville, Lady M. Introduction to *Works* [Includes *Memoir and Correspondence*, by J.A. Doyle (1898)] (1928; rpt. 1970).

Kathleen Fowler

"Michael Field"

Katharine Harris Bradley

BORN: 27 October 1846, Birmingham.
DIED: 26 September 1914.
WROTE UNDER: Michael Field, Arran Leigh.

Edith Emma Cooper

BORN: 12 January 1862, Kenilworth, Warwickshire.
DIED: 13 December 1913.
WROTE UNDER: Michael Field, Isla Leigh.

B. and C. were constant companions from 1865, when B. joined the household of her invalid older sister, C.'s mother, and assumed the care and tutelage of her niece. B. corresponded with John Ruskin between 1875 and 1880; she and C. came to disagree with the "speckled silliness in Ruskin's dealings with women." In 1878 the family moved to Bristol, where B. and C. attended University College together, participating in debate societies, women's suffrage organizations, and antivivisectionist activities. By the time C. was twenty years old, the two women had sworn "Against the world, to be/ Poets and lovers evermore." For the remainder of their lives, they collaborated on more than twenty-five tragic dramas and eight volumes of lyrics; after their deaths, their journal

Works and Days revealed the great joy they had found in the life they led.

The first volume issued under the pseudonym "Michael Field" was a pair of tragic dramas, *Callirrhoë and Fair Rosamund* (1884). Like most of B. and C.'s plays, these were never performed, but the book was hailed by the popular press as the work of a promising new writer, comparable in some respects to William Shakespeare. When it was revealed that the author was not a man ("some avatar of Waring"), but a spinster aunt and her spinster niece, public acclaim quickly subsided. Nevertheless, praise from Robert Browning, George Meredith, and other late nineteenth-century poets encouraged B. and C. to continue. Their many plays, mostly on classical or historical subjects, are slow and stiff, though well researched and often at least mildly feminist in theme. The only one that was performed in their day failed immediately.

B. and C.'s poetry, on the other hand, compares with that of Oscar Wilde and George Moore (both of whom they knew) in its turn-of-the-century aestheticism. *Long Ago* (1889), for example, is a collection of intense and sensuous verses based on Sappho; this volume also contains "Tiresias," a passionate appreciation of feminine "receptivity of soul" and "the mystic raptures of the bride." *Underneath the Bough* (1893) includes "A Girl," B.'s rhapsodic description of C.; this poem concludes with an explanation of the deeply collaborative method of F.'s poems: "our souls so knit,/ I leave a page half-writ—/ The work begun/ Will be to heaven's conception done,/ If she come to it." In "Stream and Pool," B. elaborated on this theme: "Mine is the eddying foam and the broken current,/ Thine the serene-flowing tide, the unshattered rhythm." Although B. wrote many of the poems in *Underneath the Bough* and in *Mystic Trees* (1913) and C. wrote *Poems of Adoration* (1912), the majority of their work, including the journal *Works and Days*, was a joint effort.

Near the end of their lives, fearing the separation of death, the two women converted to Roman Catholicism, with its promise of everlasting life together. When C. subsequently developed cancer, B. nursed her until her death; then she herself died of the same illness within six months. Their relationship has been cited as an example of the "romantic friendships" common among women in the nineteenth century. *Works and Days*, originally written for a personal rather than a public audience, was entrusted to T. Sturge Moore, who was asked to open it at the end of 1929 and publish whatever seemed fitting; he did so. The journal offers many insights into the self-definition and self-concept of two talented and mutually devoted women artists who stood together at the crossroads of the nineteenth and twentieth centuries.

WORKS: The New Minnesinger and Other Poems by Arran Leigh (1875). Bellerophon and Other Poems by Arran and Isla Leigh (1881). Callirrhoë; Fair Rosamund (1884). The Father's Tragedy; William Rufus, Loyalty or Love (1885). Brutus Ultor: A Play in Verse (1886). Canute the Great; The Cup of Water (1887). Long Ago (1889). The Tragic Mary (1890). Stephania: A Trialogue (1892). Sight and Song (1892). Underneath the Bough: A Book of Verses (1893). A Question of Memory: A Play in Four Acts (1893). Attila, My Attila: A Play in Verse (1896). The World at Auction: A Drama in Verse (1898). Noontime Branches (1899). Anna Ruina: A Drama in Verse (1899). The Race of Leaves (1901). Julia Domna: A Drama in Verse (1903). Borgia: A Period Play (1905). Queen Marianne: A Play (1908). Wild Honey from Various Thyme: Poems (1908). The Tragedy of Diane (1911). The Accuser; Tristran de Léonois; A Messiah (1911). Poems of Adoration (1912). Mystic Trees (1913). Dedicated: An Early Work of Michael Field (1914). Whym Chow, Flame of Love (1914). Deirdre; A Question of Memory; Ras Byzance (1918). In the Name of Time: A Tragedy (1919). The Wattlefold: Unpublished Poems (1930). Works and Days: Extracts from the Journals of Michael Field (1934).

BIBLIOGRAPHY: Ricketts, C. *Michael Field*, ed. P. Delaney (1976). Sturgeon, M. *Michael Field* (1922).

For articles in reference works, see: *BA19C. The Distaff Muse: An Anthology of Poetry Written by Women*, ed. C. Bax and M. Stewart (1949). *The Poets and the Poetry of the Century*, ed. A.H. Miles, vol. 8 (1892). *The Women Poets in English: An Anthology*, ed. A. Stanford (1972).

Other references: Faderman, L. *Surpassing the Love of Men: Romantic Friendship and Love between Women from the Renaissance to the Present* (1981). Foster, J. *Sex Variant Women in Literature* (1956). Hickok, K. *Representations of Women: Nineteenth-Century British Women's Poetry* (1984). Marble, A.R. *Pen Names and Personalities* (1930). Maynard, T. *Carven from the Laurel Tree* (1919). Moore, T.S. "Introduction" to *A Selection from the Poems of Michael Field* (1923). Moriarty, D.J. in *Nineteenth-Century Women Writers of the English-Speaking World*, ed. R.B. Nathan (1986). Sturgeon, M. *Studies of Contemporary Poets* (1920).

Kathleen Hickok

Sarah Fielding

BORN: 1710, East Stour, Dorset.
DIED: 9 April 1768, Bath.
DAUGHTER OF: Edmund and Sarah Gould Fielding.
WROTE UNDER: "A Lady," "The Author of David Simple."

F. spent her girlhood as a middle child in a family of six children; their mother died when F. was seven and a half, and her father's remarriage caused a breach in the family resulting in F.'s grandmother, Lady Gould, concerned about inheritance rights and the children's upbringing, filing a Bill of Complaint in the Court of Chancery. The five younger children subsequently lived with their grandmother in Salisbury, with Henry (the oldest) joining them on holidays from Eton. F. and her three sisters attended a boarding-school in Salisbury, "in order to be educated and to learn to work and read and write and to talk French and Dance and be brought up as Gentlewomen." F.'s reading was extensive as is indicated by frequent allusions in her novels to authors such as Shakespeare, Milton, Horace, Virgil, Pope, and Montaigne. During this girlhood, F. met Jane Collier, the daughter of a family acquaintance, who became her lifelong friend.

When Lady Gould died in 1733, F., who was then twenty-three, remained in the house with her sisters for several years, with an aunt as chaperone. In 1737, the family estate at East Stour was sold and divided among the six children. Off and on during the 1740s, F. lived with Henry, helping him care for his children. By 1754, she appears to have settled in the vicinity of Bath, in a house provided by Ralph Allen (Squire Allworthy of Henry's *Tom Jones*).

In 1742, F. likely wrote the Letter from Leonora to Horatio in Henry's *Joseph Andrews*, and one year later, she seems to have written Anna Boleyn's story for Henry's *Journey from this World to the Next*. In May 1744, when she was thirty-four years old, F. published her first novel, *The Adventures of David Simple . . . by a Lady*, which she preceded with this note: "Perhaps the best Excuse that can be made for a Woman's venturing to write at all, is that which really produced this Book—Distress in her Circumstances, which she could not so well remove by any other Means in her Power. If it should meet with Success, it will be the only Good Fortune she ever has known." Immediately popular, the novel came out in a second edition that autumn, in a form "revised and corrected" by Henry.

F.'s innovative genius, political consciousness, and interest in psychology are reflected in her seven novels, each of which experiments with the form of fiction in order to examine the damage to the human psyche incurred by the mid-eighteenth-century system of patriarchal capitalism. Her fictional experiments include writing the first children's novel and first British fictional autobiography, as well as creating a new genre she called "dramatic fable." In the 1744 *David Simple*, she experiments with urban picaresque as a vehicle for apologue, and in the completion of this novel, *Volume the Last* (1753), she draws her apologue to its dark conclusion through the use of domestic tragedy. She uses satire throughout, its light stroke in the 1744 work sharpening to a painful edge in the last volume. She condemns the system we know as patriarchal capitalism for the greed and mistrust it fosters in families and communities and through such professionals as lawyers and financiers. In particular, she depicts the insidious effects of internal oppression, damning the supposed feminine virtues of innocence, passivity, and privacy for the illness and failure they allow to fester unto death.

In 1746, H. likely wrote a story for the March 18-25 issue of her brother's journal, *The True Patriot*. One year later, she published her epistolary collection, *Familiar Letters Between the Principal Characters in "David Simple,"* and her children's novel, *The Governess, or, The Little Female Academy*, was published in 1749 after readings in manuscript by both Samuel Richardson and Jane Collier, with a second edition the same year. Using formal realism in combination with such modes as fable, fairy tale, and parable, *The Governess* illustrates the connection of womanly community to female identity. In the female academy, young girls learn to bring their own powers of analysis to everyday situations and to tell their own stories as a way of articulating identity. Also in 1749, F. seems to have published the pamphlet *Remarks on Clarissa, Addressed to the Author*, and in 1752, she likely contributed two pieces to Henry's *Covent-Garden Journal*, Numbers 63 and 64. During this time, she must also have been writing *The Adventures of David Simple: Volume the Last*. Grief for the deaths of her three sisters, who had died within eighteen months of each other, in 1750-51, may have inspired the dark vision of *Volume the Last*, in which despair for a healthy society is emphasized through repeated illnesses and deaths of innocent people.

At this same time, F. and her friend Jane Collier were at work on *The Cry: A New Dramatic Fable*, which they published in 1754. *The Cry* is a work of metafiction, examining parameters of responsibility and dialogue between author and audience and focusing on woman's effort to define herself in a world that demands her self-effacement. Assuming "a certain freedom in writing, not strictly perhaps within the limits prescribed by rules," F. and Collier here shape a unique genre, one which employs the essay form as well as drama and fable, a shifting angle of vision, narrative within narrative, and frequent satiric/comic sallies.

In 1757, F. published by subscription *The Lives of Cleopatra and Octavia*, a fictional autobiography in which F. employs the device of paired women in order to illustrate internal oppression and its various corruptions of the female psyche. In writing *Cleopatra and Octavia*, F. drew upon her knowledge of classical history and literature and told the story of these parallel lives through the use of epistolary fiction, first-person narration, and fantasy set in the underworld.

The History of the Countess of Dellwyn was published in 1759. Employing satire and domestic tragedy, F. here tells the devastating story of a woman whose corruption by the marriage market is such that she becomes goods-for-sale, even to herself. Her outward humiliation, culminating in the shame of a public divorce, is petty compared to the spectacle of her total loss of self and consequent inability to love. *The History of Ophelia*, published in 1760, experiments with a Richardsonian plot, the Gothic, and satire of a type which looks forward to Burney and Austen. Opening with bitter condemnation of the sexual oppression of women, the novel explores the effects of the feminine "virtues" in perpetuating female sexual vulnerability.

Although F. worked to earn her own way, all her life she was a needy gentlewoman, and the plight of others like herself is a theme in her novels. In *The Countess of Dellwyn*, she offers a solution, a community of women. In January of 1768, when she was fifty-eight, F. was invited by her friends Elizabeth Montagu and Sarah Scott to join just such a household, which they were planning to establish, but by then she was too ill to leave her cottage and in April she died.

WORKS: *The Adventures of David Simple: Containing an Account of his Travels thro' the Cities of London and Westminster, in the Search of a Real Friend. By a Lady* (1744). *The Adventures of David Simple . . . The Second Edition, revised and corrected, with Alterations and Additions; and a Preface by Henry Fielding Esq.* (1744, 1775 [abridged]). *Familiar letters between the principal Characters in David Simple, and some others . . . To which is added, A Vision. By the Author of David Simple* (1747). *The Governess; or, Little Female Academy* (1749). *Remarks on Clarissa, Addressed to the Author* (1749). *The Adventures of David Simple, Volume the Last* (1753). *The Cry: A New Dramatic Fable* (1754). *The Lives of Cleopatra and Octavia* (1757). *The History of the Countess of Dellwyn* (1759). *The History of Ophelia* (1760). tr., *Xenophon's Memoirs of Socrates* (1762). Attributions: *The History of Charlotta Summers* (1749). *The History of Betty Barnes* (1753). *The Histories of Some of the Penitents in the Magdalen House* (1760).

BIBLIOGRAPHY: Baker, E.A., ed. and intro. *The Adventures of David Simple* (1904). Cross, W. *The History of Henry Fielding* (1918). Dudden, F.H. *Henry Fielding: His Life, Work, and Times* (1952). Grey, J.E., ed. and intro. *The Governess* (1968). Grey, J.E., ed. and intro. *Sarah Fielding: 1710-1768* (1968). Johnson, R.B., ed. and intro. *The Lives of Cleopatra and Octavia* (1928). Kelsall, M., ed. and intro. *The Adventures of David Simple* (1969). McKillop, A.D. *Samuel Richardson, Printer and Novelist* (1936). MacCarthy, B. *The Female Pen. Vol. 1: Women Writers: Their Contribution to the English Novel, 1621-1744* (1944). Schofield, M.A., ed. and intro. *The Cry* (forthcoming).

For articles in reference works, see: *DNB. OCEL. Todd.*

Other references: Barker, G.A. *MLS* (1982). Battestin, M.C. *Novel* (1979). Black, C. *Gentleman's Magazine* (1888). Downs-Miers, D. *Children's Literature Association Quarterly* (1985). Downs-Miers, D. *Fetter'd or Free? British Women Novelists, 1670-1815*, ed. M.A. Schofield and C. Macheski (1985). Horner, J.M. *Smith College Studies in Modern Languages* (October 1929). McKillop, A.D. *MP* (1934). Hunting, R.S. *Boston University Studies in English* (1957). Johnson, R.B. *TLS* (11 April 1929). Reynolds, M. *The Learned Lady in England* (1929). Utter, R.P., and G.B. Needham, *Pamela's Daughters* (1937). *TLS* (4 April 1929). Watt, I. *The Rise of the Novel* (1965). Woodward, C. in *Transactions of the Samuel Johnson Society of the Northwest* (1984).

Carolyn Woodward

Eva Figes

BORN: 15 April 1932, Berlin.
DAUGHTER OF: Emil Eduard and Irma Cohen Unger.
MARRIED: John George Figes, 1954.

Born to affluent, German-Jewish parents in Berlin shortly before Hitler assumed power, Eva Unger lived her first seven years in Germany before escaping, with her parents and brother, to England (1939). There she excelled in studies and won a scholarship to read literature at Queen Mary College, London, from which she received a B.A. (with honors) in 1953. From 1952 until 1967 she worked as an editor for several publishing houses; during that time she married John George Figes (1954) and had two children. The breakup of her marriage led to her writing her first novel, *Equinox* (1966). Divorced in 1967, F. left publishing and devoted her energies to writing and translating. Her second novel, *Winter Journey* (1967), won the Guardian Fiction Prize. Six novels and three scholarly studies (*Patriarchal Attitudes* [1970]; *Tragedy and Social Evolution* [1976]; *Sex and Subterfuge* [1976]), and an autobiography (*Little Eden* [1978]), followed.

F.'s fiction is experimental, intricate, sometimes obscure and challenging; for some readers it is simply inaccessible—for others it is singularly unsatisfying. Two points need be noted. First, F. is a feminist; *Patriarchal Attitudes: Women in Society* is a classic historical study, convincing in its presentation of how men have sought to subjugate women. Her opposition to traditional sexual stereotypes runs parallel to her pronounced dissatisfaction with traditional forms of fiction. Second, because of this dissatisfaction, F.'s fiction is marked by three sometimes troubling qualities: lack of traditional, identifiable plot structure; an often unreliable narrator/protagonist; and a prose style that is frequently dense, allusive, and obscure—and sometimes deliberately manipulative. All are attributable to her experimentation.

Winter Journey is a short, 119-page novel narrated by a confused, failing elderly man, Janus Stobbs. The story of one day in his life, the novel succeeds in depicting an old man's pain-wracked efforts just to keep moving. *Konek Landing* (1969) reveals F.'s debt to Kafka: a stateless orphan suffers through a complex series of interior monologues and nightmares in an often incomprehensible struggle; a Central European Jew who narrowly escaped the Holocaust, F. here expresses a profound sense of survivor's guilt in an attempt to make some sense of this ghastly period of human history. *B.* (1972), a metafictional experiment documenting the creative angst of an alienated writer, received a cool critical reception. Likewise, *Days* (1974), a 113-page stream-of-consciousness tale told by a nameless female narrator lying in a hospital, lacks convincing narrative unity and is marred by heavy-handed allegorizing.

In *Nelly's Version* (1977), F.'s fondness for ambiguity pervades a tale of lost identity. The narrator, a middle-aged female amnesiac, functions as a video/audio cassette recording the people and places of typical English landscapes. The novel shows the influence of Pinter and Beckett as well as Kafka; read as a thriller, it invites comparison with Hitchcock's films.

With her most recent two novels, *Waking* (1981) and *Light* (1983), F. has realized a stunning poetic lyricism. *Waking* chronicles that hazy period between sleep and full awakening at seven times in the life of an unnamed female narrator whose interior monologues reveal her as intensely preoccupied with self, a woman who feels herself defiled by contact with others. *Light*, a 91-page novella limning one day in the life of the French Impressionist painter Claude Monet, offers an integrated, more traditional narrative. F.'s poetic prose, impressionistic and sensuous, perfectly matches the subject with an evocative power sufficient to make light the chief character of this work, as it was in Monet's.

In somewhat oversimplified fashion, we might divide F.'s novels into two groups: the first comprises *Equinox, Winter Journey, Konek Landing, B., Days,* and *Nelly's Version*; the second, *Waking* and *Light*. The novels of the first group are essentially fables of identity whether personal, racial, or artistic with unreliable, fallible narrators wandering in space and time. They live in constricted worlds of social isolation, weighted down by the past. Oppression, the product of political and sexual forces, abounds.

Waking, while taking its subject matter from these previously explored areas of identity and oppression, offers a more accessible narrative structure, organized chronologically. F.'s powerful lyric language delineates a woman-in-process; here, Woolf's rhythmic rendering of character finds new expression.

In *Light*, F.'s preoccupations with time, identity, and creativity merge. Though creativity and identity have intersected before (*B.*), they've never met forcefully, nor could they, except in the person of Monet, a consummate artist who sought to capture fugitive light before time stole it from him. Likewise, F. attempts to capture light and time in her creation. Her pointillistic, poetic language embraces the experience of time: we live with and through Monet, as well as the members of his household, for twenty-four hours.

Light seems to point in a new direction for F. Monet is an isolated, rather than alienated, figure. He moves freely away from and back toward his family and household at Giverny. His excursions on the water are nearly solitary; though accompanied by a sleepy boyhood friend, he is, for all intents and purposes, surrounded by silence and light as he paints. His individual perceptions are transmuted into art; temporarily finished, a canvas is laid aside, until another day, and the painter returns to his small, vital human community. *Light* is a poetic distillation of F.'s probing not only inner consciousness but the unconscious, where the springs of creativity swirl. It is her finest novel to date.

WORKS: *Equinox* (1966). *The Musicians of Bremen* (1967). *Winter Journey* (1967). (trans.) *He and I and the Elephants*, by B. Grzimek (1967). (trans.) *Little Fadette*, by G. Sand (1967). *Konek Landing* (1969). (trans.) *Family Failure*, by R. Rasp (1970). *Patriarchal Attitudes: Women in Society* (1970). *Scribble Sam: A Story* (1971). *B.* (1972). *Days* (1974). *Sex and Subterfuge* (1976). *Nelly's Version* (1977). *Tragedy and Social Evolution* (1976). *Little Eden* (1978). *Waking* (1981). *Light* (1983). *The Seven Ages* (1986). *Little Eden: A Child at War* (1987).

BIBLIOGRAPHY: For articles in reference works, see: *CA. CLC. CN. DLB. DLEL.*

Other references: *Commonweal* (2 April 1971). *Library Journal* (15 November 1983). *Nation* (31 December 1983, 7 January 1984). *New Yorker* (8 June 1968). *NYRB* (22 July 1971, 12 May 1982). *NYT* (23 February 1982). *NYTBR* (28 April 1968, 28 February 1982, 16 October 1983). *Observer* (9 April 1967). *TLS* (24 April 1967, 31 July 1970, 23 January 1981, 26 August 1983). *Spectator* (30 June 1977). *Yale Review* (January 1984).

Robert E. Hosmer, Jr.

Anne Kingsmill Finch, Countess of Winchelsea

BORN: April 1661.
DIED: 5 August 1720, London.
DAUGHTER OF: William and Anne Kingsmill.
MARRIED: Heneage Finch, 1684.
WROTE UNDER: Anne, Countess of Winchelsea; A Lady.

The best thing that ever happened to F., or more precisely to her poetry, was the deposition of James II in 1688. She and her husband, Heneage Finch, had held positions in James's court, he as gentleman of the bedchamber, she as maid of honor to Mary of Modena. With the exile of James, those at court were required to take an oath of allegiance. This the Finches could not do, meaning that their public lives were over.

Heneage Finch was the uncle of the Earl of Winchelsea. When in 1690 the Earl invited F. and husband to the family seat in Kent, F. found an environment conducive to poetry: a circle of literate and literary friends (she knew Nicolas and Elizabeth Rowe as well as John Gay, Alexander Pope, and Jonathan Swift, all of whom recognized her talents); the devotion and encouragement of a loving husband (Heneage became Earl of Winchelsea when his nephew died in 1712); beautiful natural surroundings; alternation between London and Kent with the social season; and plenty of free time.

This is not to suggest that her way was completely smooth. F. had the inner tensions that produce good poetry; some of these had to do with the fears and frustrations of a woman who wishes to enter the male-dominated world of literature. It is true that as a woman of rank she was exempt to some extent from real critical calumny, but even a cursory reading of her work reveals her deep wish to be taken seriously. Many ruling-class women of her time dabbled in verse, but F. set herself apart with a genuine desire, not to say need, to write. Writing was literally her life, all the more so after the Finches left court. If we can believe her poem "Ardelia to Melancholy," her writing was therapy for and a retreat from recurrent bouts of depression. She herself, however, considered her poetry far more than therapy. F. kept informed of the major intellectual and artistic currents of the Augustan age, and her poetry shows genuine poetic sensibility together with a keen interest in ideas.

There are really three divisions of F.'s work. The first is the occasional poems, devotionals, and songs that she wrote between 1680 and 1700. These she either kept private out of fear of ridicule or published anonymously in anthologies. During this period she wrote "The Spleen"

(1701), a fine Augustan Pindaric ode and one of the best meditations on melancholy in English.

Many of these early poems appeared in *Miscellany Poems on Several Occasions, Written by a Lady* (1713). This book marks a second division in F.'s work because her decision to publish was in itself remarkable. On one hand, she was shy and retiring; her fear of ridicule was not the convention it may appear to be in some of her poems. She genuinely abhorred the labels of female versifier or dilettante scribbler. In "The Introduction" F. writes that the prospect of facing the critical establishment, intimidating enough to any writer, must appear worse still to a woman: "So strong the opposing faction still appears,/ The hopes to strive can ne'er outweigh the fears." Her next line might well be taken as her personal and literary credo: "Be cautioned then, my Muse, and still retired."

Miscellany Poems indeed does show the work of a cautioned muse. Here, F.'s poems steer clear of confrontation and controversy; rather, they are public poems, showing her talent and versatility in many of the popular Augustan modes, including dramatic verse, fables, meditations, and odes. In this volume she is already an accomplished poet, with a flexible line, a sensitive ear, and the knack for *dispositio* that other writers strove for in this age of "rational" poetic utterance.

There is also a distinctive sensibility striving to be expressed that is most apparent in the manuscript of poems she left for posthumous publication, the third division in F.'s work. Here, she felt freer to condemn the exclusion of women from public life, the male contempt for women poets, and (in the poem "The Unequal Fetters") the unjust double standard that makes marriage the end of a woman's life and only an intermittent obligation for a man. Although individual poems from this collection did appear in print, the entire manuscript was not published until 1913.

In this manuscript F. largely writes from the feminine perspective, which in itself would be enough to set her apart. She writes of her relation to other women and other women writers, of her quite happy marriage, and of the rigors of writing. "Ardelia's Answer to Ephelia" is the only Augustan poem to attempt a serious moral judgment of women; F. satirizes the empty-headed followers of fashion as women without much inner content, and, perhaps most exciting, she portrays the ideal of woman as rational and moral. Such a thing had certainly never been done by any of her contemporaries, and only seldom, if at all, before then: F.'s models were mostly by, for, and about the ideal *man*, and thus she may be said to have been writing without precedent.

Miscellany Poems had been prefaced by "Mercury and the Elephant," a conventional poem of self-effacement. We need only compare it to the later "Introduction" to measure the difference in the two volumes. The first twenty lines of "The Introduction" are a list of the stock criticisms leveled at the woman writer, culminating with the bitter words "the dull manage of a servile house/ Is held by some our utmost art and use." This poem is F. at her most tough-minded. Yet there is a note of despair at the end, a fear that her poems may never have been meant for the "laurel groves" of established literature.

F. cannot be said to have had much of a reputation for the rest of the century, for her real poetic career begins when Wordsworth rediscovers her. When we read "A Nocturnal Reverie," we can see why Wordsworth felt she was a kindred spirit. She had anticipated by almost a century the paradigm of the Romantic meditation on nature. The poet finds a solitary spot one evening, and, by devoting rapt attention to the reality of nature, discovers ease, release, and, ultimately, the desire "to seek/Something, too high for syllables to speak." F.'s meditation is different, however, from Shelleyan ecstasy or Byronic fury. She emphasizes that the speaker's spirit feels a "sedate content" and that the soul discovers a "solemn quiet." This is not the spontaneous overflow of Wordsworth, though the emotions revealed are indeed powerful. Still, it is remarkable that F. anticipated so much of the Romantic program in this and in other poems (such as "The Petition for an Absolute Retreat," where the poet seeks isolation in nature for meditation). And in "A Nocturnal Reverie" we may feel that F. observes nature far more precisely than some Romantics did: at twilight, "a paler hue the foxglove takes/ Yet checkers still with red the dusty brakes"; odors "through temperate air uninterrupted stray"; in a startlingly modern line, "swelling haycocks thicken up the vale." In the end, F. may have been right. Her poems, so Augustan, were not for the Augustan age but for later readers, better equipped with the open mind needed to appreciate them.

WORKS: *The Poems of Anne Countess of Winchelsea*, ed. M. Reynolds (1903). "Poems by Anne Finch," ed. E. Hampsten, *Women's Studies* 7 (1980). *Selected Poems of Anne Finch, Countess of Winchelsea*, ed. K.M. Rogers (1979).

BIBLIOGRAPHY: Brower, R.A. *Studies in Philology* (1945). Messenger, A. *English Studies in Canada* (1980). Messenger, A. *Restoration: Studies in English Literary Culture, 1660–1700* (1981). Rogers, K.M. *Shakespeare's Sisters*, ed. S. Gilbert and S. Gubar (1979). Sena, J.F. *Yearbook of English Studies* (1971). Thompson, D. *PN Review* (26 June 1982).

John Timpane

Penelope Fitzgerald

BORN: 17 December 1916, Lincoln.
DAUGHTER OF: Edmund and Christina Hicks Knox Valpy.
MARRIED: Desmond Fitzgerald, 1941.

F.'s family was distinguished by achievement in letters and religion. Her father was the editor of *Punch* and her mother the niece of Monsignor Ronald Knox, the acclaimed biblical scholar. At Somerville College, Oxford, she read English and received a degree with first-class honors in 1939. She has worked as a journalist, as a programmer for the BBC, and as a tutor. Before her first work of fiction in 1977, she published two biographies, one of Edward Burne-Jones, the other of her uncles, the four Knox brothers. She has also written *Charlotte Mew and her Friends* and edited *The Novel on Blue Paper*, an incomplete work by William Morris.

The author of six novels to date, F. has enjoyed popular and critical success, most especially in England since only *The Golden Child* (1977) has been published in the United States. Though she published no fiction until age sixty-one, from the beginning she demonstrated a remarkably economical, fluent prose style. Without oversimplifying or undervaluing her fiction, we might say that her work is characterized by several telling qualities: careful illumination of a small world; unsentimental, though not unsympathetic, delineation of characters, particularly the young and the aged; a concern for articulating sound moral values; and finally, a decided comic richness that unifies character, language, and narrative.

The Golden Child, a thriller set "in the great hive of the [unnamed] Museum with the Golden Treasure at its heart," presents the stifling world of that museum with its competing personalities of varying backgrounds and interests as a metaphor for society. F.'s characters, with the exception of only a few, most notably Sir William Livingstone Simpkin, are detached from ordinary human concerns, viewing the museum as a kind of secret treasure chest, open only when absolutely necessary to viewing by outsiders. Simpkin, with his sympathy for the crowds of cold children queued up around the building, waiting for admission to the exhibition with the golden child, is the humane and moral center of gravity for the novel. Knowing that the golden treasures are fakes, he shuns any role in the commercial spectacle and dies when crushed between two steel shelves in the Museum's library. In an explosive climax, the glass case containing the golden child breaks and "reveals the ancient royal child as an undernourished, recently deceased African child."

Likewise, in F.'s next novel, *The Bookshop* (1978), the focus falls on an individual of courage and conviction living within a world of competing forces. Here the social context is nearly as static as the Department of Funerary Art at the museum: the town of Hardborough is a depressed area, victim to the hard times that hit Britain in the late 1950s. Florence Green decides to open a bookshop in the Old House, a damp, haunted structure at the atrophied heart of the town. From the outset, physical setting, economic conditions, and social context collaborate against her, yet their victory is no quick conquest. Old Mr. Brundish and young Christine Gipping lend considerable, though ultimately ineffectual, support to Florence. In her unsentimental depiction of these three characters, F. creates a carefully localized drama of individual courage and determination assaulted by inhospitable natural forces and knowing political powers. Mr. Brundish dies after pleading Florence's case; Christine's work at the shop may have caused her poor showing on her exams; Florence loses her bookshop and leaves town. Flecked with wonderfully comic episodes and a poetic recreation of land- and seascape, *The Bookshop* is a novel about the oppression imposed by divisions of class, education, and individual consciousness.

In her third novel, *Offshore* (1979), for which she won the Booker Prize, F.'s powers of specificity and richly atmospheric description enable her to present a whole world in the space of only 133 pages. Set in 1961 within a kind of utopian community of houseboat dwellers, a classless cast of characters living on the tidal Thames at Battersea Reach, the novel presents these men and women living in a divided world, half the time mired in the mud, half the time drifting. As in her depiction of Florence Green, F. is interested in the ways in which human beings live within particular contexts; some succeed, some do not, and once again F. is particularly successful at creating children who are knowing survivors in an adult world. But F. gathers rather too many characters on board to keep things afloat with her typical buoyancy. *Offshore* ends neither at sea nor on dry land but in ceaseless flux, subject to the threat of cruel tides on the one hand and gelatinous mud on the other.

Human Voices (1980) is perhaps F.'s least engaging novel. This time the fictional microcosm is the BBC's Recorded Programmes Department; the time is summer and autumn, 1940. Very much like the museum of *The Golden Child*, the department is a hive of power games and territorial intrigue, and here, too, there is "the pride and bitter jealousy which is the poetry of museumkeeping," though rhetorical concerns are naturally of greater moment in this context. Dialogue, which comprises the bulk of the novel, etches character and delineates conflict; silence emphasizes and amplifies. More than in any other F. novel, style functions as content; in her use of both speech and silence, in her attempts to capture the nuances and peculiarities of human communication, F. has extended the range of her own voice, but it is open to question whether her attempt to broaden the meaning and relevance of her miniature set-piece, the BBC's RPD, succeeds.

With the delightful *At Freddie's* (1982), F. returned to the world of aged eccentrics and knowing children, in this case the Temple Stage School, founded and run by Miss Freddie Wentworth, a snappy, Kate Hepburn-type character. For nearly forty years she has trained child actors for the London theatre; the roguish band of children studying at Freddie's in 1964 comprises talented characters who are professional but not prematurely adult. A crisis occurs when the government decides to establish a National Stage School; realizing that she'll be out of business, Freddie orchestrates a letter-writing campaign to *The Times*. In the end, though the government's plans are shelved, the savvy Freddie decides that she'll henceforth train her charges for television commercials. Like Florence Green, Freddie is a survivor; unlike her, she is a successful survivor. This novel is marvelously entertaining, seamless in construction, knowing in character development, and brightly human, though not Pollyannish in its optimistic outlook.

The readers of F.'s fiction must resist the temptation to dismiss it as mere light entertainment. While not expressive of the serious, metaphysical concerns presented by Muriel Spark, to whom she is often compared, F.'s work is distinguished by undeniable excellences of style, by sharply-focused insights into character, and by a consistent, humane concern for the moral dimension of human existence. Too wise to manipulate elements of fiction to create a fable-like world in which good always wins, F., like Florence Green, knows full well that the world is divided into exterminators and exterminatees, but unlike her she knows that comedy is therapeutic and ultimately triumphant.

WORKS: *Edward Burne-Jones: A Biography* (1975). *The Knox Brothers* (1977). *The Golden Child* (1977). *The Bookshop* (1978). *Offshore* (1979). *Charlotte Mew and Her Friends* (1979). *Human*

Voices (1980). *William Morris: The Novel on Blue Paper* (1981). *At Freddie's* (1982). *Innocence* (1986). *Offshore* (1987).

BIBLIOGRAPHY: For articles in reference works, see: *CA. CLC. DLB. Who's Who.*
Other references: *Books and Bookmen* (December 1979). *Encounter* (January 1981). *Listener* (23 November 1978, 2 October 1980). *London Magazine* (February 1980). *London Sunday Times* (28 March 1982) *New Statesman* (7 October 1977, 7 September 1979). *Observer* (2 September 1979, 28 March 1982). *Spectator* (27 March 1982). *TLS* (17 November 1978, 23 November 1979, 26 September 1980).

Robert E. Hosmer, Jr.

Margaret Forster

BORN: 25 May 1938, Carlisle.
DAUGHTER OF: Arthur Gordon and Lilian Hind Forster.
MARRIED: Hunter Davies, 1960.

After her upbringing in the northern English city of Carlisle, F. won an open scholarship to Somerville College, Oxford, graduating with a degree in history. She married writer Hunter Davies in 1960 and became the mother of two daughters and a son. Primarily a novelist, F.'s published works to date include twelve novels and three historical-biographical volumes. In addition, F. served from 1977–1980 as the chief non-fiction reviewer for the London *Evening Standard* and has contributed to *Punch*. In 1966, one of F.'s early novels, *Georgy Girl*, was turned into a successful film for which she co-authored the script with Peter Nichols.

Perhaps because her manner is realistic, her storytelling apparently straightforward, F.'s writing has attracted no critical attention more extensive than reviews. Yet her writing has been consistently published in the United States as well as in England and has been, for the most part, favorably reviewed. Auberon Waugh, for example, in a *TLS* (22 January 1971) assessment of F.'s *Mr. Bone's Retreat*, remarked that "she has become as good as anyone writing in the English language."

The four earliest novels (*Dame's Delight, Georgy Girl, The Bogeyman,* and *The Travels of Maudie Tipstaff*), and some of the later ones (*Miss Owen-Owen Is at Home, The Seduction of Mrs. Pendlebury*), delineate exceptionally strong-willed and not particularly attractive characters. The writing in *Dame's Delight* and *Georgy Girl* is clinical and sharply satirical; while this style continues as an element, the later novels, from *Bogeyman* onward, display a more complex vision of the human condition. F.'s monsters have human needs and motivations; her conventional characters act, on occasion, as compulsively as the strong-willed.

A few generalizations can be made about F.'s fiction. She is primarily a novelist of character. Her stories deal with their characters' response to modern life. The books' scale is small, usually limited to the relationships of a single group of people brought closely together by marriage, by physical proximity (neighbors in *The Seduction of Mrs. Pendlebury*), or by an organizational bond (the country high school in *Miss Owen-Owen*). Their time, with the exception of *Fenella Phizackerly*, is concentrated.

These generalizations fail to account for readers' perceptions of both strength and variety in F.'s fiction. F. experiments with form, from the tight patterning of the nonetheless realistic *Maudie Tipstaff*, to the mock fairytale of *Fenella Phizackerly*, to the overt romance of *The Bride of Lowther Fell*, to the complex realistic structure of *Mother, Can You Hear Me?*. F. also explores an unusually varied range of protagonists, from young or middle-aged middle-class women to the elderly of every class and both sexes.

F.'s non-fiction has received mixed reviews. *The Rash Adventurer* has been praised as the best biography of Bonnie Prince Charlie, though the later years of the prince's life were exceptionally dull and the biography cannot enliven them. In *Memoirs of a Victorian Gentleman*, F. imitates Thackeray's voice in a pseudo-autobiography, an experiment some readers appreciated and others heartily disliked. F.'s most recent book, *Significant Sisters*, offers rather tame though well-told lives of several illustrious women, including Florence Nightingale, Elizabeth Cady Stanton, and Emma Goldman. The book's intention was to make these formidable women accessible; in doing so, it somewhat dims their fires.

F.'s works are pleasing, astute, skilled and powerful enough to deserve the careful critical assessment they have not yet received.

WORKS: *Dame's Delight* (1964). *Georgy Girl* (1965, film script, 1966). *The Bogeyman* (1965). *The Travels of Maudie Tipstaff* (1967). *The Park* (1968). *Miss Owen-Owen Is at Home* (1969, In U.S. published as *Miss Owen-Owen*). *Fenella Phizackerly* (1970). *Mr. Bone's Retreat* (1971). *The Rash Adventurer: The Rise and Fall of Charles Edward Stuart* (1973). *The Seduction of Mrs. Pendlebury* (1974). *William Makepeace Thackeray: Memoirs of a Victorian Gentleman* (1978). *Mother, Can You Hear Me?* (1979). *The Bride of Lowther Fell* (1980). *Marital Rites* (1981). *Significant Sisters: The Grassroots of Feminism 1839-1939* (1984).

BIBLIOGRAPHY: For articles in reference works, see: *Who's Who* (1985).

Ellen Laun

Jessie Fothergill

BORN: June 1851, Cheethem Hill, Manchester.
DIED: 28 July 1891, Berne, Switzerland.
DAUGHTER OF: Thomas Fothergill and Anne Coultate Fothergill.
WROTE UNDER: Anonymous, Jessie Fothergill, J.F.

Eldest child of a cotton industry businessman, F. resided in the Manchester area all her life. She was educated first in a small private school in Bowdon, later studying several years at a boarding school in Harrogate. When F. was a child, the death of her father brought financial hardship, and the family moved to a house near a cotton mill in Littleborough. F. suffered from a chronic lung complaint throughout her life. Most of her later years were spent abroad, e.g., Germany, Italy, Switzerland, America, often for health reasons.

F.'s father was a Yorkshireman, a yeoman, and a Quaker, and the last influenced F. even though her father left the church when he married. F.'s first book, *Healey* (1875), and a later work, *Kith and Kin* (1881), present sympathetic portraits of the Quakers and their lifestyle. Her Quaker background surfaces also in the austerity of many of her protagonists, reminiscent of her own lifestyle, and in her inherent distrust of characters who love luxury and need material comforts.

After finishing her studies at Harrogate, F. returned to her family. An early nonconformist, she turned aside from the pursuits of conventional young ladies. She read omnivorously, wandered about the Tadmorden Valley, studied the lives of the people at the cotton mill, and wrote stories in her attic. Several of her works relate to this period of her life: *The Lasses of Leverhouse* (1888), narrated by a literary-minded adolescent, is the tale of an impoverished, boisterous family; *Healey* (1875) and *Probation* (1879) focus on the cotton industry and the lives of its people. The latter is especially noteworthy for its vivid and sympathetic portrayal of the lives of the workers; it also covers the cotton famine of 1862.

F.'s most popular novel, *The First Violin* (1877), was published anonymously (although later editions bore her name)—presumably because her Quaker family may have been unhappy with the author's excessive romanticism and the non-judgmental handling of a married woman's involvement with another man. The novel, narrated by a naive English girl observing life in Düsseldorf, is melodramatic. The protagonist, Eugen Courvoisier, hiding under an assumed name, has accepted disgrace and exile to shield another's guilt. F. began this work during a fifteen-month sojourn in Düsseldorf with her sister and two friends, and the book is filled with her impressions. All subsequent novels generally included episodes reflecting her interest in Germany and its music.

Although *The First Violin* went through many editions and brought F. fame, it is an uneven romantic work. It is, however, still readable and, of course, because of its extreme popularity, is particularly interesting to scholars of the period.

Unlike the imaginative and clearly fictional *The First Violin*, F.'s other novels are realistic, focusing mainly on the scenes, situations, and people in the Manchester area. Her settings are those of her ancestors and her family: the Yorkshire moors and the manufacturing towns. Littleborough is the Hamerton in *Healey* and *The Lasses of Leverhouse*; Rochedale is Thanshope in *Probation*; Manchester is Darkinford in *Peril* and Irkford in *Kith and Kin*.

The author's characters, too, are substantive, endemic to their milieu, universal in nature. Wilfred Healey (*Healey*) is a mill owner; Godfrey Noble (*A March in the Ranks*) is a medical man like her grandfather. Through him F. exposes the charlatanism of a hydropathic establishment, the popular contemporary "rest cure." (One may assume that F.'s chronic ill health would have led her to such institutions.)

F.'s heroines are not as believable as their male counterparts, possibly because they often personify the "dream" rather than the "actual," the exception rather than the standard, for most Victorian women. Frequently "masculine" by the conventions of the time, these heroines are interested in political and social issues; they work at "men's" work: Katherine Healey (*Healey*) helps run her brother's business; Alison Blundell (*A*

March in the Ranks) manages the estate and affairs of her invalid brother. Reality for the Victorian woman was often frustrating, however, whatever the achievement, and more in keeping with the truth are Helena Spenceley in *Probation* and Peril in the novel of that name, evidencing the stress and revolt experienced by women of ability and strength restricted by established, inferior roles.

Overall, F.'s protagonists are strong and independent. They lean toward agnosticism, and her laxness concerning religion offended some of her reviewers. Politically, they were liberal, even radical.

It is in this vivid and concrete depiction of the people she knew and observed in her immediate area that F.'s literary strength lies. Contemporary reviewers criticized her weak plots, but modern readers may construe that weakness constructively: F. centered her attention on a particular human situation, e.g., an individual struggling against the restraints of class, poverty, or tradition, or lovers defying barriers of status, money, or previous commitments. F., like Chekhov, focused on internal rather than external tension. At her best F. can be favorably compared—as she was—with other regional writers such as the Brontës and Gaskell.

WORKS: *Healey* (1875). *Aldyth* (1877). *The First Violin* (1877). *Probation* (1879). *The Wellfields* (1880). *Kith and Kin,* (1881). *Made or Marred* (1881). *Peril* (1884). *Borderland: A Country-town Chronicle* (1886). *The Lasses of Leverhouse* (1888). *From Moor Isles. A Love Story* (1888). *A March in the Ranks* (1890). *Oriole's Daughter* (1893).

BIBLIOGRAPHY: Black, H.C. *Notable Women Authors of the Day* (1906). Crisp, J. *Jessie Fothergill* (Victorian Fiction Research Guides II) (1980). De la Mare, W. *The Eighteen-Seventies,* Ed. H. Granville-Barker (1929). Fothergill, C. "Preface," *Aldyth* (1891). Gardiner, L. *Novel Review,* n.s. (1892). O'Conor, W.A. *Manchester Quarterly* 2 (1883).

For articles in reference works, see: *Allibone,* (1891). *Century Cyclopedia of Names,* Ed. B. Smith (1894). *Dictionary of Biographies of Authors,* ed. R. Johnson (1927). *DNB. New Century Cyclopedia of Names,* ed. Clarence L. Barnhart (1954). *NCHEL.*

Other references: *Athenaeum* (1 August 1891). *Critic* (New York), (29 August 1891). Gettmann, R.A. *A Victorian Publisher: A Study of the Bently Papers* (1960). *Illustrated London News,* (8 August 1891). Speight, H. *Romantic Richmondshire* (1897). *Times* (London) (31 July 1891). Wright, M.B. *Literary World* (Boston) (1891).

Phyllis J. Scherle

Pamela Frankau

BORN: 3 January 1908, London.
DIED: 8 June 1967 Hampstead, London.
DAUGHTER OF: Gilbert Frankau and Dorothea Drummand (Black) Frankau.
MARRIED: Marshall Dill, Jr., 1945.
WROTE UNDER: Eliot Naylor.

Journalist, novelist, short story writer, World War II major, lecturer, broadcaster, F. was the youngest offspring of her father's first marriage. Her early years were spent in Windsor with her mother and sister, Ursula. After graduating from Stapleton with first scholastic honors and forced to forego entrance to Cambridge due to financial shortages stemming from her mother's severe illness, F. began her literary career at eighteen, as a member of the London staff of the *Woman's Journal.* She later advanced to feature writer for the *Daily Sketch* and the *Mirror.* Though eventually regretting this practical decision, one which almost alienated F. from her father's influence and affection, she used the time spent traveling to and from work in a third-class rail carriage to create her first novel, *Marriage of Harlequin* (1927), reputedly using a scarlet pen on paper taken from the office supply. *The New York Herald Tribune*

considered this semi-biographical novel, about a sophisticated debutante and a wily fortune hunter in post World War I London, almost "too well written" for one so young.

With the publication of her first work, F. became the third member of her family to achieve literary recognition. Grandmother Julia, as "Frank Denby," wrote *Pigs in Clover* and other well-received fiction. F.'s father, though considered "an admirable novelist for ordinary people," was acclaimed during his lifetime as one of the world's best-selling authors.

F.'s next few novels reflected her strong admiration for Michael Arlen's fiction, with its development of breezy, energetic characters in "smart," unconventional settings. *Three* (1929), for example, concerns the adventures of Janet James. While engaged to an English officer, she enjoys a prolonged vacation on the Italian Riviera where she meets, and falls in love with, Count Fermi. After a year's liaison, she finally rejects romance for security and returns to her fiancé.

Another novel, *Born at Sea* (1932), involves a wealthy but neurotic egotist determined to succumb to the sea while on a South African voyage, but his despair is alleviated by three female passengers. Though criticized as somewhat superficial, it signals the onset of more mature and complicated plots somewhat removed from the Arlen influence.

F.'s most commended work, *The Willow Cabin* (1949), represents the culmination of her early period. Its plot deals with a twenty-two-year-old British woman's rejection of a promising career when she becomes the mistress of a journalist twice her age. At his death, she insists on meeting her former lover's estranged wife to untangle inevitable emotional complexities. The writing is sharper, more precise, and highly polished and earned accolades from *The New York Times.*

Perhaps the most important influence was F.'s father. After her parents' divorce, F.'s novels contained several villains whose careers and philosophies mocked the older novelist, but in *Pen to Paper*, her second autobiography, she includes a posthumous apology "for all the times we had worn masks in each other's company." When they weren't at odds, F. often consulted her father on a particular turn of a plot or argued with him about a character's motivation and occasionally took his well-intended advice.

In 1942, F. converted to the Roman Catholic Church. Three years later, she married Marshall Dill and moved to the United States. Their only child died soon after birth. Despite her religious convictions, F. divorced her husband in 1961. Other forms of writing included essays, newspaper articles, serial fiction and short stories. She also read manuscripts and wrote reviews for the Book Society. F. carefully avoided any form of pleasure that might deter her from writing at least 3000 words a day.

An interest in psychic phenomena pervaded F.'s later fiction. A trilogy, *The Clothes of a King's Son*, provided a distinctive creative experience. Its protagonist, Thomas Weston, is given the ability to discover the differences between good and evil through the use of extrasensory perception. *Slaves of the Lamp*, the second volume, is an exercise in manipulation, as she manages to keep myriad plots moving while highly articulate characters—almost artificial, some critics claimed—infuse the narrative with their upper-class morality.

F.'s thirty-first and last novel, *Colonel Blessington*, edited by her cousin, Diana Raymond, and published posthumously, involves the disappearance of the leading character. F. died as she was completing this work, her most complicated mystery, but Raymond's attention to F.'s notes produced a worthy member of the author's prolific library.

WORKS: *Marriage of Harlequin* (1927). *Three* (1929). *She and I* (1930). *Letters from a Modern Daughter to Her Mother* (1931). *Born at Sea* (1932). *Women Are So Serious* (1932). *I Was the Man* (1932). *Walk into My Parlour* (1933). *The Foolish Apprentices* (1933). *Tassel-Gentle* (1934). *Fly Now, Falcon* (1934). *I Find Four People* (1935). *Villa Anodyne* (1936; in U.S. as *Laughter in the Sun*). *Fifty-Fifty and Other Stories* (1936). *Some New Planet* (1937). *Jezebel* (1937). *No News* (1938). *The Devil We Know* (1939). *A Democrat Dies* (1939). *Appointment with Death* (1940). *Shaken in the Wind* (1948). *The Willow Cabin* (1949). (as Eliot Naylor) *The Off-Shore Light* (1952). *The Winged Horse* (1953). *To the Moment of Triumph* (1953). *A Wreath for the Enemy* (1954; also as *The Duchess and the Smugs*). *The Bridge* (1957). *Ask Me No More* (1958). *Road Through the Woods* (1960). *Pen to Paper: A Novelist's Notebook* (1961). *Sing for Your Supper* (*Clothes of a King's Son*, Part I, 1963). *Slaves of the Lamp* (*Clothes of a King's Son*, Part II, 1965). *Over the Mountains* (*Clothes of a King's Son*, Part III, 1967). (Completed and ed. D. Raymond) *Colonel Blessington* (1968).

BIBLIOGRAPHY: For articles in reference works see: *CA. Catholic Authors. DLB. Longman. TCA.*
Other references: *NYT* (9 June 1967). *SR* (1 January 1966).

Zelda Provenzano

Antonia Fraser (Lady Antonia Pinter)

BORN: 27 August 1932, London.
DAUGHTER OF: 7th Earl of Longford and Countess of Longford (Frank and Elizabeth Harmon Pakenham).
MARRIED: Rt. Hon. Sir Hugh Charles Fraser, 1956; Harold Pinter, 1980.
WRITES UNDER: Antonia Fraser, Antonia Pakenham.

F. received her university degree from Lady Margaret Hall, Oxford, in 1953; she grew up in Oxford where her father was an Oxford don before his elevation to the peerage. It is no surprise, therefore, that the family is popularly known as the "literary Longfords." Lord Longford wrote the first biography of John F. Kennedy to be published in Great Britain, but he is better known by the nickname of "Lord Porn" for his exhaustive inquiries into pornography. F.'s mother, Elizabeth Longford, has written successful biographies of Queen Victoria and Lord Wellington, and two sisters and a brother are also published authors. F., however, maintains that her family was not the only factor in determining her career. In *Maclean's* she says, "I don't say it very often, but I began to write to help support our family [the children she had with Fraser]. There's no better inspiration than that." Although her first work, *King Arthur and the Knights of the Round Table*, was published in 1954, F.'s distinction as a biographer was established with *Mary, Queen of Scots* (1969), which won the James Tait Black Memorial prize for biography. In addition to her outstanding biographies, F. has written a succession of well-received mysteries. Her literary prestige has earned her invitations to serve as a member of The Arts Council of Great Britain, 1970–1972; English PEN, 1979––; and the Crimewriters' Association, 1980––.

To date F. has written four biographies of prominent historical figures: *Mary, Queen of Scots* (1969), *Cromwell Our Chief of Men* (1973), *King James: VI of Scotland, I of England* (1974), and *King Charles II* (1979), also published as *Royal Charles*. On the basis of these four works, F.'s literary reputation has been labeled "ambiguous" by one critic, and Mel Gussow in the *New York Times Magazine* says that "her work receives respectful reviews for her impressive research and readability. Her primary strength is her sense of narrative. At the same time some professional historians consider her approach a storybook view of history." F. does spend an impressive amount of time in research. She devoted three years to *Mary, Queen of Scots* and four years to *Cromwell*. Almost every reviewer calls attention to the amount of exact detail which F. includes. Her most valuable contribution seems to be in the mass of detail concerning Mary Stuart's health, which F. uses to explain many of the charges relating to the queen's scandalous behavior. Although F. invested the same quantity of energy in the biography of Cromwell, it met with more mixed critical reaction. F.'s intention is to make her subjects seem more human, and this she does very well. For example, Paul Johnson comments that this book goes "a long way to redress the distortion from which Cromwell has suffered." It is this "humane" approach, however, which bothers critics the most. Jane Majeski remarks that F.'s "emphasis on Cromwell as a typical country gentleman leaves one with the implausible impression that he stumbled on the throne of England by accident." Even Johnson charges that F.'s treatment of the political situation is "skimpy" and "cursory."

Although the two biographies of kings, *James VI* and *Charles II*, were best sellers, F. did not spend as much time in research, and neither book is as extensive as the two earlier works. Once again critical reaction is mixed. Alden Whitman writes that *King James VI* is "thoroughly readable as a character study" and that "on superficial levels . . . [F.] has cleared away some of the unjust accusations leveled against James that have persisted over the years." Jane Majeski claims that the book "lacks the thorough research and depth" of the earlier biographies. With *Cromwell*, critics—Majeski in particular—had charged F. with failing to deal adequately with the political situation; in contrast with *King James VI*, these same critics comment that F. "would have done better to have written a thorough analysis of James's character . . . and to have left aside the political complications."

F.'s latest biography, *King Charles II*, has elicited the same diverse response. Writing in the *Economist*, one critic says that "Antonia Fraser's greatest achievement is her dissection and reconstruction of the king's political and personal character." On the other hand, Peter Prescott in *Newsweek* calls the book "a revisionist work, a highly intelligent but partisan reinterpretation." F.'s contribution in biography has been to investigate highly controversial historical figures, dispel many of the myths surrounding these figures, and produce immensely readable, provocative best sellers.

With the 1977 publication of her first mystery novel, *Quiet as a Nun*, F. introduced Jemima Shore, investigator. Frequently referred to as an adult Nancy Drew or a new Miss Marple, Jemima, a reporter for Megalith Television, finds herself investigating mysteries surrounding the subjects she has been assigned to cover. Using settings familiar to her, F. places *Quiet as a Nun* in a Roman Catholic convent similar to the one where F. attended school. *Wild Island* (1978) is set in the Scottish Highland retreat of the Fraser family, and *Oxford Blood* (1985) is in F.'s childhood home of Oxford. Continuing to draw upon her own experiences, *Cool Repentance* (1982) is set amid a group of actors in a provincial drama festival. The conflicts and tensions among the festival group certainly mirror those she has encountered as the wife of Harold Pinter. T.J. Binyon notes that the novels have an "unobtrusive *roman à clef* element." In addition, the description of the victim in *A Splash of Red* (1981) could also be of F. herself. Chloe Fontaine had looks which "hid a considerable talent as a novelist" and "there had been a series of admirers, lovers, and husbands. . . . Her friends sometimes remarked on the odd contrast of her disorderly private life and the careful formality of her work." Although critics found her early mysteries too predictable, all five novels have been best sellers. *Quiet as a Nun* was a "Mystery!" presentation on PBS, and another series based on the Jemima Shore stories has been produced.

As a result of her research on the biographies, as well as a feeling of affinity for the people of the seventeenth century, F. wrote *The Weaker Vessel* (1984), an exploration into the position of women in that century. Christopher Lehmann-Haupt in *The New York Times* says that "it appears to gather up almost everything one could possibly think of to ask about women in the century that began with the death of Queen Elizabeth in 1603 and ended with the accession of Queen Anne in 1702." In this book, which could be classified biography, history, or even women's studies, F. recounts actual experiences of women from the alehouse to the palace, from the church, the academy, and the prison. Referring to the work as a "breakthrough" for F., Mel Gussow says that this is the first time F. "has dealt foursquare with feminist issues and the first time that she has felt a kind of missionary zeal." Summing up her investigations in the epilogue, F. notes that despite a rise in women's stature in the middle decades, at the end of the century it was back on the same level it had been at the death of Queen Elizabeth. F. comments, "This cyclical pattern . . . is perhaps worth bearing in mind; as with all forms of liberation, of which the liberation of women is only one example, it is easy to suppose in a time of freedom that the darker days of repression can never come again."

In spite of the notable scholarly quality of her biographies, F.'s lively presentation of what could be dull historical fact has attracted a large reading public. Her creation of the contemporary, racy, liberated Jemima Shore is not a contrast to her earlier work but an obvious extension. F.'s work has the possibilities of joining the ranks of writers such as Dorothy L. Sayers, someone whom F. greatly admires.

WORKS: *King Arthur and the Knights of the Round Table* (as Antonia Pakenham) (1954). *Martyrs in China* by Jean Monsterleet (trans.) (1956). *Robin Hood* (1957). *Dior by Dior: The Autobiography of Christian Dior* (trans.) (1957). *Dolls* (1963). *A History of Toys* (1966). *Mary, Queen of Scots* (1969). *Cromwell Our Chief of Men* (1973, also published as *Cromwell, The Lord Protector*). *Mary, Queen of the Scots, and the Historians* (1974). *King James: VI of Scotland, I of England* (1974). *Quiet as a Nun* (1977). *The Wild Island* (1978). *King Charles II* (1979, also published as *Royal Charles*). *A Splash of Red* (1981). *Cool Repentance* (1982). *The Weaker Vessel* (1984). *Oxford Blood* (1985). *Jemima Shore's First Case and Other Stories* (1987).

BIBLIOGRAPHY:

For articles in reference works, see: *CA. DLEL. TCC&MW. WA.*

Alice Lorraine Painter

Helen Louise Gardner

BORN: 13 February 1908, London.
DAUGHTER OF: Charles Henry and Helen Mary Roadnight Cockman Gardner.

G. is a distinguished literary critic and scholar who has, during the past fifty years, deeply influenced many readers' perceptions of British poetry, especially of the late sixteenth and early seventeenth centuries. She is particularly credited for her careful interpretive and textual work in preparing several editions of John Donne's poetry and prose: *The Divine Poems* (1952, 2nd. Ed. 1978), *Selected Prose* (1967), and *The Elegies and the Songs and Sonnets* (1965). An important T.S. Eliot scholar as well, G. has written three critical studies on this twentieth-century poet, who also had the major influence on her own criticism: *The Art of T.S. Eliot* (1949), *T.S. Eliot and the English Poetic Tradition* (1966), and, most recently, *The Composition of "Four Quartets"* (1978), which analyzes both the drafts of *Four Quartets*, especially as marked by John Hayward, and Eliot's process of textual emendation. G. has also written on John Milton and on Shakespeare's tragedies.

G.'s critical methodology brings an impeccably well-informed and sensitive mind to a literary work and is eclectic, ignoring neither a work's historical context, the author's personal habits of mind, the relationship of a work to its time, nor the meaning we can logically deduce from the relationship of the parts of a work to its whole structure. In two works, *The Business of Criticism* (1959) and *In Defense of the Imagination* (1982), G. states that her twenty-five and then fifty years of experience with literature have formed her belief in the critic's responsibility to elucidate a work's meaning, its relationship to an historical context, and, inevitably, to make a judgment of its value.

G.'s literary education began at North London Collegiate School. She received the B.A. in 1929 from St. Hilda's College, Oxford, where she was granted the M.A. in 1935. Although she had begun a thesis on the medieval mystic writer Walter Hilton, she took a job as an assistant lecturer at the University of Birmingham, 1930–31, remaining at Birmingham until 1941 when Oxford offered her the position of tutor in English literature at her alma mater, St. Hilda's College. She was a Fellow of St. Hilda's from 1942 to 1966 and

University Reader in Renaissance English Literature, Oxford University, from 1954 to 1966. She became Merton Professor of English Literature and a Fellow of Lady Margaret Hall, Oxford, both from 1966–75. She is now an Honorary Fellow of Lady Margaret Hall and St. Hilda's College. Beginning in 1954 with an invited lectureship at the University of California, Los Angeles, G. has lectured throughout the United States, most recently at Harvard University where she delivered the 1979–80 Charles Eliot Norton Lectures (later published as *In Defense of the Imagination*). She is a member of the Royal Academy, the American Academy of Arts and Sciences, and the Royal Society of Literature.

In the two works in which she examines her beliefs about literature and the role of the critic, *The Business of Criticism* and *In Defense of the Imagination*, G. explains her purpose in writing. G. eschews any attempt to measure the amount of poetic value or to rank one poem as more valuable than another. The critic's task, or judgment, is to uncover the meaning the author intended the work to embody and to read the poem in that light. But the critic does not create readings for her audience; she simply assists other readers to read for themselves. Her strategy, similar to T.S. Eliot's "impersonal" theory of poetry, is to divest one's reading from the biases of personal prejudices and emotion.

G. also argues for the necessity of an historical approach to works of literature, which places the poem in the context of its time period. Yet we cannot simply equate a specific work's meaning with an idea that was historically popular, both because of the illogicality of such a simplistic equation and the possibility of the writer's opinions being unusual or exceptional for that time. The modern critic must recognize the historical nature of his or her own approach: it, too, is conditioned by the time period, about which we have no balanced perspective.

In her most recent work, *In Defense of the Imagination*, G. reviews her positions, professional regrets, and achievements, and gives her opinion of recent literary theories and the state of the profession. In the essay "Present Discontents" G. expresses dissatisfaction with the "new New Criticisms" that have arisen during the last twenty years, usually in France. She finds that the work of structuralists, deconstructionists, and psychoanalytic theorists is damaging to the reader's pleasure in experiencing a work of the imagination. She finds that modern criticism is insecure about the worth of its own activity; she links this both to the disease of the time and to the emphasis universities now place on publication. Both tempt young scholars to do something to the text rather than elucidate it for students or other interested readers who may not know the jargon of literary theorists. She recommends that universities lessen the "over-production" of scholarly publications by shifting their focus to good teaching, which to Gardner is the ability to elucidate a text and to add to students' enjoyment of literature. Despite her long and varied bibliography, G. still considers herself, after fifty years of publishing and teaching, primarily a teacher: "I would wish to be considered as a teacher or as nothing."

Since G. did not write about her own teaching, or on pedagogy, she will be remembered by most for her sensitive and careful scholarship on John Donne, Shakespeare, John Milton, and T.S. Eliot. Some critics have been uneasy with her insistence on "judgements" in analyzing literary works; and others have criticized her admitted belief that the concerns of Shakespearian tragedy are often "Christian." In the 1980s we might have hoped for a more discriminating analysis of recent critical theories than she admits in "Present Discontents." But, using Gardner's own tenet of consistency, one finds her recent position a logical outgrowth of her earlier insistence on the integrity and impersonality of a poem. The value of her scholarship will survive the current critical tempest.

WORKS: The Art of T.S. Eliot (1949). *The Limits of Literary Criticism: Reflections on the Interpretation of Poetry and Scripture* (1956; rpr. in *The Business of Criticism*, 1959). *The Business of Criticism* (1959). *Edwin Muir* (1961). *A Reading of Paradise Lost* (1965). *T.S. Eliot and the English Poetic Tradition* (1966). *King Lear* (1967). *Literary Studies* (1967). *Religion and Literature* (1971). *Poems in the Making* (1972). *The Waste Land 1972* (1972). *The Composition of "Four Quartets"* (1977, 1978). *In Defense of the Imagination* (1982).

BIBLIOGRAPHY: Carey, J., ed. *English Renaissance Studies Presented to Dame Helen Gardner in Honour of Her Seventieth Birthday* (1980). For an autobiographical essay, see "Apologia Pro Vita Mea" (138–64) from *In Defense of the Imagination* (1982).

For articles in reference works, see: *CA. CLC. WA. Who's Who.* (1985).

Other references: *Choice* (November 1978). *Commonweal* (12 May 1972). *New Statesman* (27 August 1971; 5 May 1978). *New Yorker* (21 October 1950). *NYT* (27 October 1972). *NYTBR* (15 October 1972). *Observer Review* (11 April 1969). *Poetry* (October 1950). *TLS* (6 April 1967; 13 July 1967; 17 August 1967; 1 September 1972).

Laura Niesen de Abruña

Constance Garnett

BORN: 1862, Brighton.
DIED: 18 December 1946, the Cearne, Richmond.
DAUGHTER OF: David Black and Clara Patten Black.
MARRIED: Edward Garnett, 1889.
WROTE UNDER: C[onstance]. C[lara]. Black, Constance Garnett.

Wife of critic and scholar Edward Garnett, mother of novelist and autobiographer David Garnett, G. is now the most famous of her eminently literary family. Her translations into English of important Russian novels, plays, and tales filled seventy volumes and greatly promoted the appreciation of Russian literature in England and America. G. inherited part of her interest in things Russian: her grandfather, Peter Black, had served as Naval Architect to Czar Nicholas I, and her father had grown up in Russia before studying law in London, living briefly in Canada, and settling in Brighton, where he became coroner. G.'s mother—devoted to her eight children and domestic duties—was the daughter of Prince Albert's portrait-painter-in-ordinary and had been accustomed before her marriage to travel in intellectual and artistic circles.

To her mother and her older siblings G. owed much of her early education. Like the typical middle-class Victorian girl, however brilliant, G. was kept at home as a child; because she had contracted tuberculosis of the hip (which was cured by the time she was seven), her family regarded her as particularly delicate. She managed nevertheless to master mathematics, basic science, geography, French, German, and Latin before reaching her teens. G.'s formal education began inauspiciously with a brief stay at a boarding school, where she was suicidally depressed by her isolation: her characteristic shyness was compounded by the school's policy of separating G. from the other girls in class because she was so intellectually advanced, as well as separating her from them in their dormitories because—a lifelong atheist—she refused to say her prayers. At seventeen she won a scholarship to Newnham College, Cambridge, then in its first year of existence, where she was ecstatically happy. Although Cambridge granted no degrees to women until 1947, G. took first-class honors on her final examination, the Classical Tripos, in 1883.

When her studies were complete G. lived in London, first with two of her sisters, then alone in the East End. She became librarian at the People's Palace, joined the Fabian Society, married Edward Garnett in 1889, and supported his literary endeavors with the income from her library job for the following three years, when she resigned to have a child. While G. was pregnant with David, her only child, she began to learn Russian, under the encouragement of Felix Volkhovsky, a house guest who had recently escaped imprisonment in Siberia. To alleviate the post-partum depression resulting from a particularly difficult birth, G. worked in 1892 on her first translation, Goncharov's *A Common Story*. She proceeded to an essay of Tolstoy's and then to the works of Turgenev, whom—as one of her very favorite authors—she later regretted having tackled at so early and inexperienced a stage in her career. For over 35 years, G. worked constantly on translations of Russian texts, never once publishing an original composition.

G. associated with several Russian revolutionaries in exile, among them N. Tchaykovsky, Prince Peter Kropotkin, Prince Tcherkessov, and Sergey Stepniak. At Stepniak's urging, she travelled alone to Russia in 1894, officially to deliver famine relief funds that had been raised in England but actually to deliver letters from the exiles to fellow revolutionaries. Though she had personal ties to proponents of the revolution, as well as philosophical leanings to socialism, G. never became a communist. She believed that *Das Kapital* held only very limited truth and ultimately she had no respect at all for the Bolsheviks. When G. returned to Russia with her son in 1904, her enthusiasm was waning; in 1907, when she met Stalin, Lenin, and Trotsky at the Russian Social Democratic convention in England, she declined even to serve as interpreter for Lenin's public address.

Her devotion to Russian literature, however, remained fervent. She translated continuously, even though her always weak eyesight was permanently impaired by her unstinting work on *War and Peace*. In later years she would dictate her English translations to an assistant who read the Russian originals aloud to her. G.'s major translations included thirteen volumes of Chekhov's tales and two volumes of his plays, seventeen of Turgenev, thirteen of Dostoyevsky, six of Gogol, four of Tolstoy, and six of Herzen as well as scattered volumes of Goncharov and Ostrovsky. G.'s translations are not now universally accepted as definitive; G.'s theory of translating required that she render the language in a style appropriate to the period of the author, which somewhat "dates" her works. But as the most authoritative and comprehensive (not, in every case, the first) English translations of major Russian works in her day, they played an enormous role in influencing modern British and American writers.

WORKS: C.C. Black [Garnett] and O. Dymond. *Catalogue of the Books in the Library of the People's Palace for East London* (1889).

TRANSLATIONS: Goncharov. *A Common Story* (1893). Tolstoy. *The Kingdom of God Is Within You* (1894). Turgenev. *The Complete Works* (1894–1899). Ostrovsky. *The Storm* (1899, 1917). Tolstoy. *Anna Karenina, War and Peace*, and tales (1901–1904). Feldman, K. *The Revolt of the "Potemkin"* (1908). Dostoevsky. *The Brothers Karamazov* (1912). *The Idiot* (1913). *Letters from the Underground* (1913). *The Possessed* (1914). *Crime and Punishment* (1914). *The House of the Dead* (1915). *The Insulted and Injured* (1915). *A Raw Youth* (1916); stories (1917–1920). Chekhov. *Complete Plays and Tales* (1904–1912). *Letters* (1920–1926). Tolstoy. *Christianity and Patriotism* (1922). Gogol. *Complete Works* (1922). Herzen, A.J. *My Past and Thoughts* (1924).

BIBLIOGRAPHY: Garnett, D. *The Golden Echo* (1954). Heilbrun, C.G. *The Garnett Family* (1961). Muchnic, H. *Dostoevsky's English Reputation (1881-1936), Smith College Studies in Modern Languages*, (1939). Rubinstein, R. *Colorado Quarterly* (1974).

Articles in reference works: *The Europa Biographical Dictionary of British Women* (1983). *Oxford Companion to English Literature* (1967).

Other references: *NR* (6 January 1947). *Time* (30 December 1946). *TLS* (2 January 1954, 30 April, 1954, 16 July 1954).

Robyn R. Warhol

Elizabeth Gaskell

BORN: 29 September 1810, London.
DIED: 12 November 1865, Holybourne, Hampshire.
DAUGHTER OF: William and Elizabeth Holland Stevenson.
MARRIED: William Gaskell, 1832.
WROTE UNDER: Mrs. Gaskell, Cotton Mather Mills, Esq.

In November 1865, when reporting her death, *The Athenaeum* rated G. as "if not the most popular, with small question, the most powerful and finished female novelist of an epoch singularly rich in female novelists." Today G. is generally considered a lesser figure in English letters remembered chiefly for her minor classics *Cranford* and *Wives and Daughters: An Every-day Story.* G.'s early fame as a social novelist began with the 1848 publication of *Mary Barton: A Tale of Manchester Life*, in which she pricked the conscience of industrial England through her depiction and analysis of the working classes. Many critics were hostile to the novel because of its open sympathy for the workers in their relations with the masters, but the high quality of writing and characterization were undeniable, and critics have compared *Mary Barton* to the work of Friedrich Engels and other contemporaries in terms of its accuracy in social observation. The later publication of *North and South*, also dealing with the relationship of workers and masters, strengthened G.'s status as a leader in social fiction. G.'s fiction was deeply influenced by her upbringing and her marriage. The daughter of a Unitarian clergyman who was a civil servant and journalist, G. was brought up after her mother's death by her aunt in Knutsford, a small village that served as the prototype not only for Cranford but also for Hollingford in *Wives and Daughters* and the settings of numerous short stories and novellas. In 1832 she married William Gaskell, a Unitarian clergyman in Manchester in whose ministry she actively participated and with whom she collaborated to write the poem "Sketches Among the Poor" in 1837.

"Our Society at Cranford," now the first two chapters of *Cranford*, appeared in Dickens' *Household Words* on 13 December 1851 and was itself a fictionalized version of an earlier essay, "The Last Generation in England." Dickens so liked the original episode that he pressed G. for more; at irregular intervals between January 1852 and May 1853 eight more episodes appeared.

Two controversies marred G.'s literary career. In 1853 she shocked and offended many of her readers with *Ruth*, an exploration of seduction and illegitimacy prompted by anger at moral conventions that condemned a "fallen woman" to ostracism and almost inevitable prostitution—a topic already touched on in the character of Esther in *Mary Barton*. The strength of the novel lies in its presentation of social conduct within a small Dissenting community when tolerance and rigid morality clash. Although some element of the "novel with a purpose" is evident, G.'s sensitivity in her portrayal of character and, even more, her feel for relationships within small communities and families show a developing sense of direction as a novelist. Although critics praised the soundness of the novel's moral lessons, several members of G.'s congregation burned the book and it was banned in many libraries. Even G. admitted that she prohibited the book to her own daughters, but she nevertheless stood by the work.

The second controversy arose following the 1857 publication of *The Life of Charlotte Brontë*. The biography's initial wave of praise was quickly followed by angry protests from some of the people dealt with. In a few instances legal action was threatened; however, with the help of her husband and George Smith the problems were resolved without recourse to law. The most significant complaint resulted from G.'s acceptance of Branwell Brontë's version of his dismissal from his tutoring position (he blamed it on his refusal to be seduced by his employer's wife) and necessitated a public retraction in *The Times*, withdrawal of the second edition, and a revised third edition, the standard text. Despite the initial complications and restrictions necessitated by conventions of the period (G. did not, for example, deal with Brontë's feelings for Constantin Heger), *The Life of Charlotte Brontë* has established itself as one of the great biographies; later biographies have modified but not replaced it.

During 1858 and 1859 G. wrote several items, mainly for Dickens, of which two are of particular interest. *My Lady Ludlow*, a short novel cut in two by a long digressive tale, is reminiscent of *Cranford*, yet the setting and social breadth anticipates *Wives and Daughters*. The second work, *Lois the Witch*, is a somber novella concerning the Salem witch trials which prefigures G.'s next work, *Sylvia's Lovers*, by its interest in morbid psychology. *Sylvia's Lovers* is a powerful if somewhat melodramatic novel. The first two volumes are full of energy; they sparkle and have humor. The ending, however, shows forced invention rather than true tragedy. Regarded by G. as "the saddest story I ever wrote," *Sylvia's Lovers* is set during the French Revolution in a remote whaling port with particularly effective insights into character relationships.

Most critics agree that *Cousin Phillis* is G.'s crowning achievement in the short novel. The story is uncomplicated; its virtues are in the manner of its development and telling. *Cousin Phillis* is also recognized as a fitting prelude for G.'s final and most widely acclaimed novel, *Wives and Daughters: An Every-Day Story*, which ran in *Cornhill* from August 1864 to January 1866. The final installment was never written, yet the ending was known and the novel as it exists is virtually complete. The plot of the novel is complex, relying far more on a series of relationships between family groups in Hollingford than on dramatic structure. Throughout *Wives and Daughters* the humorous, ironical, and sometimes satirical view of the characters is developed with a heightened sense of artistic self-confidence and maturity.

G. was hostile to any form of biographical notice of her being written in her lifetime. Only months before her death, she wrote to an applicant for data: "I disapprove so entirely of the plan of writing 'notices' or 'memoirs' of living people, that I must send you on the answer I have already sent to many others; namely an entire refusal to sanction what is to me so objectionable and indelicate a practice, by furnishing a single fact with regard to myself. I do not see why the public have any more to do with me than buy or reject the ware I supply to them" (4 June 1865). After her death the family sustained her objection, refusing to make family letters or biographical data available.

Critical awareness of G. as a social historian is now more than balanced by awareness of her innovativeness and artistic development as a novelist. While scholars continue to debate the precise nature of her talent, they also reaffirm the singular attractiveness of her best works.

WORKS: *Mary Barton: A Tale of Manchester Life* (1848). *Lizzie Leigh: A Domestic Tale* (1850). *The Moorland Cottage* (1850). *Cranford* (1853). *Ruth* (1853). *Lizzie Leigh and Other Tales* (1855). *North and South* (1855). *The Life of Charlotte Brontë* (1857). *My Lady Ludlow* (1858). *Right at Last and Other Tales* (1860). *Lois the Witch and Other Tales* (1860). *Sylvia's Lovers* (1863). *A Dark Night's Work* (1863). *Cousin Phillis: A Tale* (1864; republished as *Cousin Phillis and Other Tales*). *The Grey Woman and Other Tales* (1865). *Wives and Daughters: An Every-Day Story* (1866). *The Letters of Mrs. Gaskell*, ed. J.B.V. Chapple and A. Pollard (1966).

BIBLIOGRAPHY: Craik, W.A. *Elizabeth Gaskell and the English Provincial Novel* (1975). Easson, A. *Elizabeth Gaskell* (1979). Ffrench, Y. *Mrs. Gaskell* (1949). Ganz, M. *Elizabeth Gaskell: The Artist in Conflict* (1969). Gerin, W. *Elizabeth Gaskell: A Biography* (1976). Hopkins, A.B. *Elizabeth Gaskell: Her Life and Work* (1952). Lansbury, C. *Elizabeth Gaskell: The Novel of Social Crisis* (1975). Pollard, A. *Mrs. Gaskell: Novelist and Biographer* (1966). Rubenius, A. *The Woman Question in Mrs. Gaskell's Life and Works* (1950). Sanders, G.D. *Elizabeth Gaskell* (1929). Selig, R.L. *Elizabeth Gaskell: A Reference Guide* (1977). Sharps, J.G. *Mrs. Gaskell's Observation and Invention: A Study of Her Non-Biographic Work* (1970). Stoneman, P. *Elizabeth Gaskell* (1987). Welch, J. *Elizabeth Gaskell: An Annotated Bibliography, 1929-75* (1977). Wright, E. *Mrs. Gaskell: The Basis for Reassessment* (1965).

For articles in reference works, see: *Allibone SUP. DLB. DNB.*

Other references: Lucas, J. *Tradition and Tolerance in Nineteenth-Century Fiction: Critical Essays on Some English and American Novels* (1966). Mews, H. *Frail Vessels: Woman's Role in Women's Novels from Fanny Burney to George Eliot* (1969). Minto, W. *Fortnightly Review* (1 September 1878). Shorter, C.K. *The Bookman* (June 1896). Warhol, R.R. *PMLA* (1986).

Lynn M. Alexander

Pam Gems

BORN: 1 August 1925, Bransgore, Hampshire.
DAUGHTER OF: Jim and Elsie Mabel Annetts Price.
MARRIED: Keith Gems, 1949.

G. is a prolific and frequently produced playwright whose best-known plays, *Dusa, Fish, Stas and Vi* (1976), *Queen Christina* (1977), *Piaf* (1978), and *Camille* (1984), show that neither generosity, majesty, talent, nor beauty can free women from the special choices imposed by gender roles. Finding women "very funny, coarse, subversive," G. provides major roles for actresses that reveal women's changing lives with intelligence and compassion for both sexes.

G. was the first child of working-class parents. Her mother brought up her daughter and two younger sons alone after their father's death in the workhouse in 1929. G. won a scholarship to Brockenhurst County Grammar School but left school to join the Women's Royal Naval Service (WRENS) in World War II. She describes her war years on the south coast of England as "all sex and high adrenalin" because of the risk, particularly for the men, of being killed. Her war service provided the means for attending Manchester University, where she took a degree in psychology in 1949. That same year she married Keith Gems, a model manufacturer. Living at first in Paris and then on the Isle of Wight, the family moved to London after the birth of their fourth child.

G. had worked briefly for the BBC after the birth of her first two children, writing three plays for television, of which only *A Builder by Trade* (1961) was produced. Living in London, G. began to work with lunchtime theatres and with the feminist movement. In 1973 she wrote *My Warren* (about aging and sexuality) and *After Birthday* (about instant infanticide) for Al Berman's Almost Free Theatre and *The Amiable Courtship of Miz Venus and Wild Bill* for Almost Free's Women's Season.

Dusa, Fish, Stas and Vi (1976), her first play to reach the West End, was originally called *Dead Fish*. Rich and radical Fish shares her flat with Dusa, searching for the children her divorced husband has kidnapped; Stas, working as a physiotherapist by day and a party girl by night; and Vi, reveling in anorexia. Warm and tough, the women support each other, but they cannot overcome Fish's depression when her lover, and fellow radical organizer, leaves her to marry a more submissive woman. Fish ends her masochistic obsession by poisoning herself, an act discovered, ironically, just as the women's joint efforts have recovered Dusa's children. The women have no positive relationship with men: Dusa's husband takes her children; Fish's lover envies her skills as a speaker; Stas's johns give her gonorrhea along with the money she wants for graduate study; and Vi would rather starve. Fish's suicide note recognizes that it will be harder to change male-female relations than to change women's lives: "We don't do as they want any more, and they hate it. What are we to do?" Fish models herself on Rosa Luxemburg, another middle-class socialist, and is partly modeled, according to Colin Chambers, on Buzz Goodbody, the brilliant young director of The Royal Shakespeare Company's Other Place, who killed herself in 1975.

The Other Place in Stratford produced G.'s *Queen Christina* in 1977 after the Royal Court had turned it down because it was too sprawly, expensive, and slanted toward women. Christina of Sweden (1626–1689), brought up to rule as a man, learns that only power is respected and abdicates rather than accept her woman's duty to provide an heir. She travels south to Rome where she embraces Catholicism and tries to embrace a cardinal. Finally, offered military power as a surrogate male, she feels cheated of her woman's life and refuses further violence. Christina's transformation shows her that women's lives produce bread and children rather than power and corpses, shows her that she was wrong to despise women. Yet Irving Wardle praised the play, ironically, as "a most masculine performance" in its "energy, fair-mindedness and bold construction." What Christina wanted, but could not achieve with all her brilliance and power, was scope for her "masculine" talents and energy, and for her emotions. The point is not that she made the wrong choice but that she should not have had to choose between achievement and nurturing.

In 1977 G. produced a one-act play called *Franz into April* about the director of a mental health institute and a repressed Englishwoman. The following year, the Royal Shakespeare Company produced *Piaf*, the first full-length play she wrote (1973), her second play to reach the West End, and her first to cross the Atlantic to Broadway, in 1981. As Piaf, the Parisian streetwalker who became a cabaret star without denying her background, Jane Lapotaire was funny and desperate, vulgar and elegant, addicted to morphine and to a series of lovers. Piaf's only lasting relationship is with her woman-friend Toine, from the same background. In structure, the play is deliberately episodic, joined by songs, to the satisfaction of London critics but not of New Yorkers. Lapotaire, however, received a Tony award for her role.

While *Piaf* was running, G.'s adaptations of

Uncle Vanya and then *A Doll's House* were produced. In 1982 *The Treat*, set in a French brothel, portrayed the cruel enactments of male fantasies with grotesque humor. The gentler fantasies of literary male transvestites enliven *Aunt Mary* (1982). A television producer who would exploit them on her show as a cage of odd birds is defeated by the campy, anarchic, generous community of writers.

Returning to the Parisian floating world, a century earlier than *Piaf*, G.'s version of *Camille* was first produced at The Other Place in Stratford in 1984, then at the Comedy in London, and in 1986 at the Long Wharf in New Haven. Her Camille first gives up her livelihood for love, threatening her circle of dependents, and then gives up her lover when his father promises to educate her son for a place in the secure class. In England the play provided a vehicle for Frances Barber to temper passion with pragmatism, and in New Haven for Kathleen Turner.

G.'s *The Danton Affair* (1986) is adapted from the stage chronicle by Stanislawa Przybyszewska, and produced at the Barbican by the Royal Shakespeare Company. A very large cast acts out bread riots and faction fights that lead Danton to challenge Robespierre. In contrast to the better-known play by Georg Büchner, *Danton's Death*, G. makes the sea-green incorruptible Robespierre more admirable than Danton, whose credibility on her stage is undercut by his forced attentions to his peasant-born child-bride. Several critics praised Ian McDiarmid as Robespierre, but few liked the three-hour play. Still, G. has brought her concern for the complex connections between private and public lives from lunchtime theatre to the main stage of the Barbican.

WORKS: *A Builder by Trade* (1961). *Betty's Wonderful Christmas* (1972). *My Warren* (1973). *After Birthday* (1973). *The Amiable Courtship of Miz Venus and Wild Bill* (1974). *Go West, Young Woman* (1974). *Up in Sweden* (1975). *The Project* (1976). *Dead Fish*, later called *Dusa, Fish*, *Stas and Vi* (1976). *Guinevere* (1976). (trans.) *My Name Is Rosa Luxemburg*, by M. Auricoste (1976). (trans.) *The Rivers and Forest*, by M. Duras (1976). *Queen Christina* (1977). *Franz into April* (1977). *Piaf* (1978). *Sandra* (1979). *Ladybird, Ladybird* (1979). (adaptation) *Uncle Vanya*, by A. Chekhov (1979). (adaptation) *A Doll's House*, by H. Ibsen (1980). *Pasionaria* (1982). *The Treat* (1982). *Aunt Mary* (1982). (adaptation) *The Danton Affair*, by S. Przybyszewska, original trans. B. Toborski (1986).

BIBLIOGRAPHY: Bassnett-McGuire, S.E. *Semiotics of Drama and Theatre: New Perspectives in the Theory of Drama and Theatre*, ed. H. Schmidt and A. Van Kesteren (1984). Carlson, S.L. *Drama, Sex and Politics* (1985). Keyssar, H. *Feminist Theatre* (1985). Wandor, M. *Understudies* (1981). Wandor, M. *Carry On, Understudies* (1986). Wandor, M. *Look Back in Gender: Sexuality and the Family in Post-War British Drama* (1987).

For articles in reference works, see: *CA. CD. DLB. WD. Who's Who in the Theatre*.

Other references: *British Booknews* (February 1986). Chambers, C. *Other Spaces* (1980). Itzin, C. *Stages in the Revolution* (1980).

Mary R. Davidson

Lady Grace Norton Gethin

BORN: 1676, Abbots Leigh, Somerset.
DIED: 11 October 1697.
BURIED: Hollingbourne, Kent.
DAUGHTER OF: Sir George Norton and Lady Frances Freke Norton.
MARRIED: Sir Richard Gethin.

After G. died in October 1697 in her twenty-first year, a monument to her memory was erected in the south aisle of Westminster Abbey. Within two years, writings taken from her commonplace book were published as *Reliquiae Gethinianae, or Misery Is Virtue['']s Whetstone*, probably at the instigation of her mother, Lady Frances Norton. The book begins with "A Poem in Praise of the Author" by W.C., very likely William Congreve, and is followed by brief essays, generally no longer than a page, on various subjects, such as "Of Friendship," "Of Love," and "Of Gratitude." Only later was it discovered that most of these essays originated in the works of earlier writers and were mistakenly thought to be written by G., who must simply have copied them for her own edification, occasionally adding brief comments. In spite of its derivative nature, *Reliquiae Gethinianae* went through three editions in four years, and in the 1703 edition there is a second elegant poem, this time signed by Congreve, "Sacred to the Memory of Grace Lady Gethin."

A collation of *Reliquiae Gethinianae* with Bacon's *Works* shows that many passages are indeed taken from the *Essays*; another source is probably Bishop Hall as suggested in the eighteenth-century marginalia of the first edition (British Library copy, 12269.bbb.17).

G. was survived by her husband as well as her

parents, but it was her mother Lady Frances Norton, described by one eighteenth-century writer (Ballard, *Learned Ladies*) as "a lady of great piety and uncommon abilities," who seems to have grieved most over her daughter's death. Although one cannot be certain, it is perhaps true that Lady Frances was unaware that her daughter's writings were not original and, ironically enough, had *Reliquiae Gethinianae* published as a tribute to G.'s integrity. On the other hand, it is just as plausible that Lady Frances—who seems to have been responsible for her daughter's moral education—wished to use the commonplace book as an example of how a virtuous education can be based on ethical readings.

But there were other memorials. In 1700 came a funeral sermon for G. (printed after being preached in Westminster Abbey) and a third edition of *Reliquiae Gethinianae* in 1703. More remarkable, at age 65 Lady Frances had two additional books published in 1705. Both of these volumes, *Applause of Virtue* and *Momento Mori*, or *Meditations on Death*, are mostly quotations on ethical subjects from the Bible, several church fathers, and ancient classical writers. Thus she became a compiler, if not a writer, of two books under her own name, perhaps to mitigate her sorrow for her recently deceased daughter, G. Before Lady Frances's death at the age of ninety-one, she had outlived three husbands and three children, and she left three books compiled on the subject of "virtuous living and holy dying."

WORKS: *Reliquiae Gethinianae* (1699, 1700, 1703).

BIBLIOGRAPHY: Ballard, G. *Memoires of Several Ladies . . . , who have been Celebrated for their Writings* (1752). Birch, P. *Sermon Preached at Westminster Abbey on 28 Mar 1700*. Collinson, J. *History of Somersetshire* (1791). *DNB*. Stanley, A.P. *Historical Memorials of Westminster Abbey*, 5th ed. (1882).

Susan Garland Mann
and David D. Mann

Stella Gibbons

BORN: 5 January 1902, London.
DAUGHTER OF: Telford Charles and Maud Williams Gibbons.
MARRIED: Allan Bourne Webb, 1933.

If G.'s name is recognized at all today, it is usually for her comic novel *Cold Comfort Farm* (1932), whose good-natured parody of the pastoral novel of the early twentieth century has created for her a small but staunch cult following. In fact, G. is the author of twenty-five novels, three volumes of short stories, and four volumes of poetry—most of them refreshing, original, and good enough to reward re-reading.

Cold Comfort Farm, G.'s first novel, won the Femina Vie Heureuse Prize for 1933 and, according to *Choice*, "belongs in any collection of modern British fiction." In it, Flora Poste opens the mental as well as physical doors of a gloomy Surrey farm, dispels the family ghosts, and sends everyone off to his or her own happiness. The somewhat disappointing sequel, *Conference at Cold Comfort Farm*, brings a married Flora back to the farm sixteen years later, where she presides over a comic conference of Independent Thinkers. She also once again saves the farm, which had been bought out by the National Trust and renovated into a nightmare of cuteness, and brings the seven Starkadder brothers back from South Africa to restore Cold Comfort Farm to its primal brutality.

In her other novels, G. proves herself a careful chronicler of the modern era. She writes of young love with that mixture of sensibility and romance unique to those who lived through both World Wars; *Nightingale Wood* rewards the naive honesty of a shopgirl by a fairy-tale marriage to a rich and handsome landowner. Nancy Leland in *The Wolves Were in the Sedge* and Nell Sely in *Here Be Dragons* show the utter surrender possible only to romantics with hope, while Margaret Steggles in *Westwood* and Una Beaumont in *The Weather at Tregulla* deal with the failure of romance. G. also shows the condition—it is not dire enough to be called a *plight*—of middle-aged women with uncertain financial futures in *Bassett*, *Miss Linsey and Pa*, and *The Charmers*. (G.'s married, middle-class, middle-aged women, such as Lucy in *The Swiss Summer* and Alda in *The Matchmaker*, often turn out to be petty and unlikable.)

G.'s work is particularly valuable because it provides an intimate and detailed chronicle of life during World War II. *White Sand and Grey Sand* unravels the mystery of a Belgian foundling raised during the war. *The Bachelor* and *The Matchmaker*, set in the war-torn British countryside, capture England's grim winter existence during the last years of the war. G. is at her best describing the painful ordinariness of life under siege, and her war novels offer a fine supplement to historical accounts.

Several of G.'s works venture into the occult. Most unusual is *Starlight*, which begins as a sympathetic portrayal of elderly London slum dwellers and ends with a startling exorcism; in *The Shadow of a Sorcerer*, the eerily charming hero just might be the devil himself.

In spite of her attentiveness to the details of contemporary life, G. is not a "problem" novelist. As she says of her novelist character Amy Lee in *My American*, her novels contain "no deep psychological problems or social analysis." What they do contain is an extremely fine cast of charming, *nice* people who linger in the reader's mind long after her often weak plots are forgotten. She has a rare ability to enter into the feelings of the uncommunicative and to bring to life the emotions of the unremarkable. Her comic genius, too, has been recognized both in the timeless popularity of *Cold Comfort Farm* and in the reissue of *Ticky* in 1984 as part of Sutton's "Classics of Humor" series.

G.'s shorter works do not match the quality of her novels. The short stories present a *tranche de vie* much in the style of Katherine Mansfield but too often without Mansfield's incisive characterization. G.'s poems are slight lyrics, describable in her own words (from *Conference at Cold Comfort Farm*) as "show[ing] a nice nature but technically weak." They tend toward classic, even archaic, diction, and only occasionally do they show flashes of the novels' wit. *The Untidy Gnome* is her lone sally into children's stories.

Before beginning her forty-year career as a novelist and poet, G. was a cable decoder for British United Press and a journalist in London, most notably for the *Evening Standard* (1920–1930). She was elected a Fellow of the Royal Society of Literature in 1950.

WORKS: *The Mountain Beast* (1930). *Cold Comfort Farm* (1932). *Bassett* (1934). *The Priestess* (1934). *The Untidy Gnome* (1935). *Enbury Heath* (1935). *Miss Linsey and Pa* (1936). *Roaring Tower* (1937). *Nightingale Wood* (1938). *The Lowland Venus* (1938). *My American* (1939). *Christmas at Cold Comfort Farm* (1959). *The Rich House* (1941). *Ticky* (1943). *The Bachelor* (1944). *Westwood* (1946). *Conference at Cold Comfort Farm* (1949). *The Matchmaker* (1949). *Collected Poems* (1950). *The Swiss Summer* (1951). *Fort of the Bear* (1953). *Beside the Pearly Water* (1954). *The Shadow of a Sorcerer* (1955). *Here Be Dragons* (1956). *White Sand and Gray Sand* (1958). *A Pink Front Door* (1959). *The Weather at Tregulla* (1962). *The Wolves Were in the Sledge* (1964). *The Charmers* (1965). *Starlight* (1967). *The Snow Woman* (1969). *The Woods in Winter* (1970).

BIBLIOGRAPHY:

For articles in reference works, see: *CA. TCA.* Other references: *SR* (1946). *Leader* (28 April 1945). *PW* (May 1934). *Books of Today* (May 1949).

Loralee Mac Pike

Penelope Gilliatt

BORN: 25 March 1932, London.
DAUGHTER OF: Cyril and Mary Douglas Conner.
MARRIED: R.W. Gilliatt, 1954; John Osborne, 1963.

Novelist, short story writer, critic, and playwright, G. has established a considerable reputation as a woman of letters. G. grew up in Northumberland, the daughter of a prominent barrister and his Scots wife. G.'s education, divided as it was between Queen's College, University of London (1942–47) and Bennington College (1948–49), foreshadowed her transatlantic career, for she continues to divide her time between England and the United States. She worked for several magazines in London, most prominently *Vogue*, becoming features editor there, and for the *Observer*, for which she served as film critic (1961–64) and drama critic (1964–67). After a stint as guest film critic for *The New Yorker* in 1967, G. became regular film critic for that magazine, taking six-month turns with Pauline Kael until 1979 when she resigned. Since then, G. has continued to write, concentrating her energies on stories and profiles for *The New Yorker* and novels, though an opera libretto and other pieces have appeared as well.

G.'s first major publication, a novel, *One by One*, appeared in 1965; it would be the first of four: *A State of Change* (1967); *The Cutting Edge* (1978); and *Mortal Matters* (1983). The first three show striking similarities, while the fourth is a departure of sorts. Each of these novels is concerned with establishing those coping mechanisms necessary to integrate the past and order the present; G.'s sense of this finds clearest expression in a letter from one brother to another in *The Cutting Edge*: "Oh to have the Lord's capacity of language and themes, and to reduce the bickering world to order with each stroke of the keys." Memory is an essential adjunct as well; somehow, in G.'s scheme of things, memory is a repository of values for survival and language a means of activating those values.

One by One focuses attention on a trio of characters: Joe, married to Polly, and Coker, Joe's lifelong friend. Set in contemporary London during a fictional plague which provides G. with ample opportunity to offer political commentary, the novel documents the disintegration of Joe's and Polly's marriage and his descent into a madness that results in suicide. While G.'s talent for limning characters with telling psychological accuracy manifests itself here with haunting precision, her mixing of elements from allegory and parable as she layers conflicts of all sorts—emotional, physical, social, and political—produces a narrative altogether too tentative and diffuse.

A State of Change likewise dwells on a relationship among three characters: Kakia, a Polish cartoonist who comes to London in the 1950s; Don Clancy, a BBC star; and Harry Clopton, a physician. Kakia seeks political and artistic freedom but is caught in the paradox of trying to maintain that while bound in a cramping relationship with Harry. Like an avant-garde drama, *A State of Change* offers minimal plot; indeed, 75% of the novel seems to be conversation, bright but brittle word games, with characters and scenes functioning as mere props.

In *The Cutting Edge* we meet Peregrine and Benedick Corbett, brothers so deeply attached that by novel's end each has altered his physical appearance to resemble the other. Born and brought up in the Northumbrian border country, they live their whole lives on the edge, both geographically and existentially. The inevitable third person is Joanna, sometime wife to Benedick, who becomes Peregrine's mistress; rather than severing the brothers' relationship, this *ménage à trois* only joins Peregrine and Benedick more significantly. Here, too, G. shows an acute ear for dialogue and an infectious enthusiasm for words as exchanges sparkle with wit and letters, diaries, and journals become large slices of narrative.

Mortal Matters concerns the life of Lady Averil Corfe, widow of a shipping magnate and central character. In a novel of eleven chapters, the first and last are set in the present while those in between constitute an elaborate flashback sequence to Averil's years in Northumberland as a child, wife, and mother, chronicling her mother's, as well as her own, involvement in the social/political struggle for women's rights. G. has incorporated substantial historical research to make this an evocative portrait of an extraordinary woman and her age. While *Mortal Matters* illuminates the role of the past in shaping the present, in personal as well as social and political terms, and while it displays G.'s characteristic verbal virtuosity, this novel marks a departure with its focus on one pivotal character and its optimistic conclusion.

Though this last novel may be a more satisfying effort, G. is not a novelist of the first rank. While Anthony Burgess has rightly praised her as "intelligent, economical, poignant, highly contemporary, and innovative," he has, in noting that G. likes "to shunt plot elements to a perfunctory margin and allow the characters to play word games," discerned something which, if not a weakness, is certainly an indication of fiction for a very special taste.

The short story, a literary form calling for economy, intensity, and narrowed focus, suits G.'s talents far better. All five of her collections demonstrate those virtues which have earned a reputation for being the quintessential *New Yorker* writer; indeed, of the 48 collected stories, 38 originally appeared in that magazine.

The nine stories in *Come Back If It Doesn't Get Better* (1969), published in England as *What's It Like Out?* (1968), are character studies which show G.'s interest in the workings of the disintegrating human psyche. The eight stories and one play in *Nobody's Business* (1972) follow suit, both in concentration on character and in mood. The stories of Frank, the "Family Robot Adapted to the Needs of Kinship," Izolska, the little girl whose connection with the world is limited to a telephone hooked to a computer, and Max, Peg, and Abberly, three aging patients immobilized and attached to electrocardiograph machines, are typical of the collection. Characters in all these stories struggle with the dehumanizing forces of technocracy. Each story's focus on a particular situation imparts a static quality only slightly relieved by verbal sophistication, humor, and an uncanny choice of the most revealing remark or exchange.

Splendid Lives (1978) contains nine stories, virtually all about the last years of aged characters, none more memorable than the Bishop of Hurlingham, aged 92, of the title story. This "cousin three times removed of Queen Victoria," who spent some of his early years going to jail with suffragettes, is now obsessed by the problem of his racehorse being off his feed. The Bishop's involvement in anti-Vietnam and anti-Rhodesia protests illustrates a political dimension prominent in nearly all the stories in *Splendid Lives* and strikes, riots, and unemployed workers figure in some of the stories.

Quotations from Other Lives (1981), with its eleven stories and one play, continues G.'s examination of lives in contemporary England and America. Many are tales of lovers, whether young, vital, and displaced or geriatric and fixed, all share a desire to escape from pervasive loneliness, but none is particularly memorable. G.'s stock of plots has been depleted; she repeats not only names and jokes but even remarks.

They Sleep Without Dreaming (1985), a collection of ten stories and one play, breaks no new ground. There are tales of mental imbalance, for example, "The Purse," which features an upper-middle class bag lady with a son who is a Fellow of

All Souls, Oxford, of irreconcilable character types in exile ("The Hinge"), and of adults overcoming painful childhoods to make considerable names for themselves ("The Windchild Factor" and the title story).

Reading all the novels and collected short stories of G. brings an awareness of deficiencies as well as excellences. The flaws become obvious and irritating. An essential emptiness of plot, while less noticeable in a short story, is fatal in a novel. Then, too, G. is given to repetition, not just of theme but of devices and descriptions. She borrows not only from herself but from other writers, and to little point. Moreover, a reader seeking emotional engagement must look elsewhere, for G.'s writing is rather cerebral entertainment. Her excellences are mainly stylistic: flashing remarks, witty conversation, and language economical, evocative, and precise enough to sketch important characters with rhetorical flourish.

The best story in each of G.'s last four collections turns out to be a play, and, given her talent for description, dialogue, and close-up analysis, that is not surprising. The world of film and theatre engages her sensibilities and employs her skills best, whether in original work or criticism. Certainly her finest creative work produced the screenplay *Sunday Bloody Sunday* (1971), which treats the lives of a trio of characters: Daniel Hirsh, a homosexual Jewish physician; Alex, a divorced businesswoman; and Bob, a young artist who is lover to both. While little happens in *Sunday Bloody Sunday*, for it is simply the story of Bob leaving Daniel and Alex behind to go to America, the juxtaposition of carefully rendered personalities and the shifting dynamics of their interaction make for riveting drama.

G.'s critical writing about film and theatre spans her entire professional career. She has published two collections of reviews, *Unholy Fools: Wits, Comics, Disturbers of the Peace: Film and Theater* (1973) and *Three-Quarter Face: Reports and Reflections* (1980). The first is a gathering of short, lively pieces ranging from reviews of Royal Shakespeare Company productions to profiles of great comics like Keaton, Chaplin, and Lloyd to

pieces on the film version of the *Tales of Beatrix Potter* and new films from Poland and Czechoslovakia. Two of the profiles in this volume became full-length studies: *Jean Renoir: Essays, Conversations, Reviews* (1975) and *Jacques Tati* (1976). Both demonstrate that though G. does not ignore technical matters, she is clearly more interested in the film as fictional narrative. The keen biographical interest shown in *Renoir* and *Tati* emerges again in *Three-Quarter Face*, essentially a study of two dozen or so directors and entertainers. G. seeks to uncover that one-quarter face of the artist hidden from public view because she believes it essential to understanding the work.

WORKS: *One By One* (1965). *A State of Change* (1967). *What's It Like Out?* (1968; published in the U.S. as *Come Back If It Doesn't Get Better*, 1969). *Sunday Bloody Sunday* (1971). *Nobody's Business* (1972). *Unholy Fools* (1973). *Jean Renoir: Essays, Conversations, Reviews* (1975). *The Western* (1975). *The Method* (1975). *Living on the Box* (1975). *The Flight Fund* (1975). *Jacques Tati* (1976). *Splendid Lives* (1977). *The Cutting Edge* (1978). *In the Unlikely Event of an Emergency* (1979). *Three-Quarter Face: Reports and Reflections* (1980). *Nobody's Business* (1980). *Property* (1980). *In Trust* (1980). *Quotations from Other Lives* (1981). *Beach of Aurora* (1981). *Mortal Matters* (1983). *They Sleep Without Dreaming* (1985).

BIBLIOGRAPHY:
For articles in reference works, see: *CA. CLC. CN. DLB. WA.*

Other references: *Book Week* (18 July 1965). *London Magazine* (February 1979). *New Statesman* (30 April 1965, 27 October 1978). *New Yorker* (7 November 1983). *NYT* (15 June 1969, 3 October 1971). *NYTBR* (25 April 1965, 10 September 1972, 29 January 1978, 21 January 1979). *Observer* (25 April 1965, 24 September 1972, 6 November 1983, 3 February 1985). *Spectator* (30 April 1965, 7 January 1984). *TLS* (29 April 1965, 20 August 1982, 29 November 1985). *Washington Post* (21 January 1979).

Robert E. Hosmer, Jr.

Hannah Glasse

BORN: 1708, Holborn, London.
DIED: 1770, Newcastle.
DAUGHTER OF: Isaac and Hannah Allgood.
MARRIED: John (Peter?) Glasse, 1725.
WROTE UNDER: A Lady.

G.'s father was the son of the Rev. Major Allgood, rector of Simonsburn; her mother was

the daughter of Isaac Clark, London vintner. She and her husband, son of a Scotswoman and an Irishman, had six or eight children, half of whom died in infancy. G.'s half-brother Lancelot Allgood (1711–1782) was knighted in 1760. G. may be the "Hannah Glass of St. Paul's Co. Garden" on the 1754 bankruptcy list in the *Gentleman's Magazine*.

The author of *The Compleat Confectioner* and *The Servant's Directory*, G. is best known for *The Art of Cookery, Made Plain and Easy*. First published in 1747 as "by a lady" and claimed in the 4th edition in 1751 by G. identifying herself as "Habit Maker to Her Royal Highness the Princess of Wales, in Tavistock Street, Convent Garden," the cookbook first bore G.'s name in 1788, by which time it had appeared in over ten editions and had become popularly associated with her. While some questioned her originality and others accused her of extravagance, the book was generally acclaimed for its clarity and its organization. Listing 200 subscribers in 1747, *ACPS* had by 1812 appeared in 26 editions, two in America.

Although she promises not to be so "pertinent" as to "direct a Lady how to set out her Table," her advice frequently goes beyond measurements and ingredients as she urges cooks to consider economy, to be flexible, and to attend to the appearance of their dishes. French cooks and cookery often appear as the negative examples of kitchen economy. She warns, "If Gentlemen will have *French* Cooks, they must pay for *French* Tricks." While one French cook "used six Pounds of Butter to fry twelve Eggs," G. reminds her readers, "Every Body knows, that understands Cooking, that Half a Pound is full enough." Although she offers specific instructions, she recognizes the need to make changes based on variations in ingredients. "The strength of your Beer must be according to the Malt you allow more or less, there is no certain Rule." Similarly, times for roasting a pig cannot be specified exactly. "If just kill'd, an Hour; if kill'd the Day before, an Hour and a Quarter." For all pigs, however, "the best Way to judge is when the Eyes drop out." Cooks must prepare food to be admired as well as eaten. Pickled red cabbage is a "Pickle of little Use, but

for garnishing of Dishes, Sallats and Pickles, tho' some People are fond of it." To make a tart, "fill it with what Fruit you please, lay on the Lid, and it is done; therefore if the Tart is not eat, your Sweetmeat is not the worse, and it looks genteel."

Although G. recommends that a few eels stewed in broth may remedy "weakly and consumptive constitutions," she does not, as do many authors of eighteenth-century cookbooks, emphasize medicinal uses of food. Nor does she flippantly ignore the exigencies of her recipes with the advice, long attributed to her, that the cook "First Catch your Hare."

WORKS: *The Art of Cookery, Made Plain and Easy; Which Far Exceeds Anything of the Kind Ever Yet Published, etc.* [by a lady] (1747). *The Compleat Confectioner: or, the whole art of confectionary made plain and easy* (c. 1760). *The servant's directory, or house-keeper's companion: wherein the duties of the chamber-maid, nursery-maid, house-maid, laundery-maid, scullion, or under-cook . . . to which is annexed . . . directions for keeping accounts. etc.* (1760).

BIBLIOGRAPHY: Hope, M. *Archeologia Aeliana*, (1938). Aylett, M., and O. Ordish. *First Catch Your Hare: A History of the Recipe-makers* (1965). Willan, A. *Great Cooks and Their Recipes: From Taillevent to Escoffier* (1977).

For articles in reference works, see: *DNB. IDWB. NCHEL. OCEL.*

Other references: Heal, A. *N & Q* (1938). Drake, T.G.H. *Journal of the American Dietetic Association*, (1952). Cf. notes on "Glasse, Hannah." *A Short-Title Catalogue of Household and Cookery Books published in the English Tongue 1701–1800* (1981).

Mary Comfort

Caroline Glyn

BORN: 27 August, 1947.
DAUGHTER OF: Sir Anthony and Lady Susan Rhys Williams Glyn.

Great-granddaughter of Elinor Glyn (prolific author of *Three Weeks*, *It*, and other novels and screenplays), G. became, at age fifteen, the *wunderkind* of the 1960s with the publication of her first novel, *Don't Knock The Corners Off* (1963). Encouraged by parents who are similarly gifted (Sir Anthony, a writer; Lady Susan, an artist), G. began writing short stories and poetry at the age of six. At nine she was recognized for another talent when one of her designs received an award

from *Good Housekeeping*. Other, unique honors followed: Poem-Tilling First Prize, 1959, and second prize, "Jeune Espoir," for a painting, France, 1964.

G. has worked as a teenage correspondent for the color supplement of *The Observer*, and her poems have been published in numerous journals, including *Cornhill*. In 1983, she and her mother penned an article for *Stained Glass* concerning their familial and artistic relationships.

Don't Knock the Corners Off was, for the most part, a critical success. Astonished at G.'s talent for unselfconscious narration, many reviewers went overboard in their praise; one even cited it as "the best novel by a fifteen-year-old ever written," and it received the La Libre Belgique award for best foreign novel. Using the first-person, G.'s narrator, Antonia Rutherford, a somewhat aloof, shy, and clever young girl, describes her grammar and primary school experiences, especially the indignities she suffers as the brunt of her peers' taunting behavior. Antonia tries to resolve the differences between her somewhat relaxed home environment and the structured, middle-class conformities deemed necessary for survival in a scholastic atmosphere. At novel's end, the narrator's acceptance into an art school presents hope for a much-needed escape: "Art students still have their corners on. . . . Everything's going to be all right after all," Antonia concludes.

When sixteen, G. followed her parents to Paris and was admitted into the Ecole Superieure des Arts Moderns. Here, she literally dogged the footsteps of her more financially-privileged classmates, at first admiring their independence, then despairing over their pretentiousness. Winston Hosanna, the West Indian Negro who is the hero of G.'s second novel, *Love and Joy in the Mabillon* (1966), also attempts to enter a society of wealthy young artists whose world-weary existence is lightened by visits to sidewalk cafes like the Mabillon. Winston is disheartened as his natural longings (love and joy) are declined by an upper-class "ice princess." He finally realizes that he will only be marginally permitted into the farthest perimeters of their blasé lives. Once more, G. is able to reproduce conflicting views of a particularly youthful, yet deplorable, society. The novel was runner-up for the Society of Authors award to young writers in 1966.

While completing her third novel, *The Unicorn Girl* (1966), G. explained to an interviewer that the teen-aged heroine would also become the leading character in two other, related works, *Heights and Depths* (1968) and *The Tree* (1969). She also promised to take a more opti-

mistic tone, and the results indicate that a less despairing attitude now pervades her philosophy.

One of G.'s more enjoyable occupations has been working as a long-distance operator in London. The position enables G. to have some financial freedom while she completes her novels. G. also enjoys travelling and has visited the United States with members of her family.

G. has created sufficient material for several one-man art shows in England and France. When asked about her interest in these varied forms of expression, she stated that her "painting and writing complement each other, and I could not live without either. I paint trees, stars, and religious abstracts, and my books come into being while I am about it."

In 1979, G. revealed that Wordsworth and Blake were important influences, "believing in the redemption of the earth—as it undergoes visible destruction—by the visionary principle in man, true imagination. By this power, which is love, the world is being remade, a spiritual world, in which all is restored. All my books are on this theme; and I like to think that, by writing them, I have shared in the great work. . . .'"

WORKS: *Dream Saga* (1962). *Don't Knock the Corners Off* (1963). *Love and Joy in the Mabillon* (1965). *The Unicorn Girl* (1966). *Heights and Depths* (1968). *The Tree* (1969). *The Tower and the Rising Tide* (1971). *The Peacemakers* (1974). *In Him Was Life* (1975). *A Mountain at the End of Night: Stories of Dream and Vision* (1977).

BIBLIOGRAPHY: Glyn, S. *Studia Mystica* (Winter 1981).

For articles in reference works, see: *CA. DLEL*.

Other references: *Life* (13 May 1966). *New Statesman* (19 Sept. 1969, 8 July 1977). *NYTBR* (5 January 1964). *Observer* (21 September 1969, 11 July, 1971, 7 August 1977). *SR* (4 January 1964). *Seventeen* (July 1964). *Stained Glass* (Fall 1983). *Time* (3 January 1964).

Zelda Provenzano

Elinor Glyn

BORN: 17 October 1864, Jersey, Channel Islands.
DIED: 23 September 1943, London.
DAUGHTER OF: Douglas and Elinor Saunders Sutherland.
MARRIED: Clayton Glyn, 1892.

G. was a prolific novelist who wrote more than twenty books, several of which were made into silent films starring such legendary performers as Gloria Swanson, Clara Bow, John Gil-

bert, and Rudolph Valentino. She was raised by her mother after her father died of typhoid fever when G. was only a few months old, received only the minimal education available in local schools, and in 1892 married Clayton Glyn, a wealthy entrepreneur.

In 1899 G. published her first book, *The Visits of Elizabeth*, an epistolary novel. This book, published anonymously and serialized in *The World*, was quite successful. According to her biographer, her grandson Anthony Glyn, G. got great pleasure from listening to her friends trying to guess the name of the author, especially the friend who declared that G. could not be the author because "a really clever person must have written these letters." With her earnings, G. traveled to Italy, France, and Egypt. The style of G.'s second novel, *Reflections of Ambrosine* (1902), is similar to that of *Visits of Elizabeth*. This book is the "autobiography," written in diary form, of Ambrosine Eustasie, Marquise de Galincourt, who was guillotined in 1793. In *Reflections*, G. exhibits considerable historical knowledge as well as great empathy for her protagonist. Now proud of her success as a novelist, G. includes a note at the front of *Ambrosine* stating that she will no longer write anonymously: "Everything I write will be signed."

Among G.'s most unusual books is *The Damsel and the Sage: A Woman's Whimsies* (1903), a series of witty exchanges between a "fun-loving" Damsel and a misanthropic Sage who hates women and lives in a cave, contemplating the mysteries of the universe. The two eventually fall in love, and the Damsel convinces the Sage to leave his cave and "Remember the tangible now." *The Damsel and the Sage* is clever in that the characters debate whether to "seize the day" in much the same way as Marlowe's Shepherd and Ralegh's Nymph, but the male and female roles are reversed and the Damsel wins the debate.

G.'s most popular book nearly ended her writing career. *Three Weeks* (1907) was called too "sensational" and was viciously attacked by nearly every London critic. The love scenes, tame by modern standards, were too explicit for what was still a Victorian press. Thought by Anthony Glyn to be partly autobiographical, *Three Weeks* is the story of Lady Henrietta, who marries for money, falls in love with a man she meets in Egypt, has a child by her lover (which she passes off as her husband's), and spends her life helping her son succeed. By 1916 over two million copies had been sold, and *Three Weeks* had been translated into virtually every European language. The financial success of *Three Weeks* was fortunate for G. because her husband had lost all his money by 1908, making G. the sole support of her family.

During 1907 and 1908 G. toured the United States, dividing her time between New York City and the mining areas of Colorado, Nevada, and California. As a result of her travels, G. wrote another epistolary novel, *Elizabeth Visits America* (1909), which she illustrated herself. G. hoped to regain her reputation with the critics by returning to the style of her first novel, but she was only moderately successful.

His Hour (1910) was the result of six months G. spent in St. Petersburg and Moscow as the guest of the Grand Duchess Vladimir. This novel, which finally restored G. to the critics' favor, is the story of an English widow, Tamara Loraine, who,

while traveling in Egypt, falls in love with Prince Gritzko Milaslavski. She follows him to St. Petersburg, where, after overcoming numerous obstacles, they eventually marry. Probably because of G.'s first-hand knowledge of St. Petersburg and the customs of the Russian Imperial Court, *His Hour* suffers from none of what Crosland calls the "effusive vagueness" of most romance novels.

After G.'s husband died in 1915, she increased the volume of her work and in 1917 signed a lucrative contract with William Randolph Hearst for the American rights to her novels. G. and Hearst became close friends despite an "artistic disagreement" over *The Career of Katherine Bush* (1917). According to Anthony Glyn, Hearst asked G. to make her heroine "more lovable." G. steadfastly refused, and Hearst eventually gave in.

G.'s career as a filmwriter began in 1920, when Famous Players-Lasky asked her to write the screenplay for *The Great Moment*, starring Gloria Swanson. G.'s own novel *Beyond the Rocks* (1906) was filmed in 1922 and featured Gloria Swanson and Rudolph Valentino. G.'s other film credits include *Three Weeks* (1923), *His Hour* (1924), *Man and Maid* (1925), *Love's Blindness* (1925), *The Only Thing* (1926) and *Ritzy* (1927). *Ritzy*, based on G.'s short story "It" in which she gave her own definition of "personal magnetism," led to Clara Bow, the star of the film, being known forever after as the "It Girl." G. left Hollywood in 1929 after the failure of her only non-silent film, *Such Men Are Dangerous.*

During the 1930s, G. lost most of her money in a failed attempt to start her own film production company. Both of the movies she produced (and financed), *Knowing Men* and *The Price of Things*, were financial disasters. She returned to writing full-time and continued publishing novels until her death in 1943.

WORKS: *The Visits of Elizabeth* (1900). *Reflections of Ambrosine* (1902; in the U.S. as *The Seventh Commandment*, n.d.). *The Damsel and the Stage* (1903). *Beyond the Rocks* (1906; as screenplay, 1924). *Three Weeks* (1907; as screenplay, 1923). *The Sayings of Grandmama and Others* (1908). *Elizabeth Visits America* (1909). *His Hour* (1910; in the U.S. as *When His Hour Came*, 1915; screenplay with K. Vidor and M. Fulton, 1924). *The Reason Why* (1911). *Halcyone* (1912; in the U.S. as *Love Itself*, 1924). *The Sequence* (1913; in the U.S. as *Guinevere's Lover*, 1913). *The Contract and Other Stories* (1913). *Letters to Caroline* (1914; in the U.S. as *Your Affectionate Godmother*, 1914). *The Man and the Moment* (1914; as screenplay, with A.C. Johnson and P. Perez, 1929). *Three Things* (1915). *The Career of Katherine Bush* (1916). *Destruction* (1918). *The Price of Things* (1919; in the U.S. as *Family*, 1919). *Points of View* (1920). *The Philoso-*

phy of Love (1920). *The Great Moment* (screenplay
with M.M. Katterjohn, 1921; book, 1923). *Man and
Maid—Renaissance* (1922; in the U.S. as *Man and
Maid*, 1922; as screenplay, 1925). *The Elinor Glyn
System of Writing* (1922). (with C. Campbell and
G. Bertholon) *The World's a Stage* (screenplay,
1922). *The Philosophy of Love* (1923; in the U.K. as
Love—What I Think of It, 1928). *Six Days* (1924).
(with C. Wilson) *Three Weeks* (The Romance of a
Queen) (1924). (with D.Z. Doty and G. Carpenter)
How to Educate a Wife (1924). *Letters from Spain*
(1924). *This Passion Called Love* (1925). *The Only
Thing* (1925). *Love's Blindness* (1926; as screenplay,
1926). (with others) *Ritzy* (1927). (with others) *It*
(screenplay, 1927). *It and Other Stories* (1927). *The
Wrinkle Book: or, How to Keep Looking Young*
(1927; in the U.S. as *Eternal Youth*, 1928). (with
others) *Three Week-Ends* (screenplay, 1928). (with
E. Vajda) *Such Men Are Dangerous* (screenplay,
1930). (with E. Knoblock) *Knowing Men* (screenplay, 1930). *The Flirt and the Flapper* (1930). *Love's*

Hour (1932). *Glorious Flames* (1932). *Sooner or
Later* (1933). *Did She?* (1934). *Saint or Satyr? and
Other Stories* (1933; in the U.S. as *Such Men Are
Dangerous*, 1933). *Romantic Adventure* (1936). *The
Third Eye* (1940).

BIBLIOGRAPHY: Davson, G. ("A. Glyn"), *Elinor
Glyn: A Biography* (1955). Haskell, M. *From Rever-
ence to Rape: The Treatment of Women in the
Movies* (1974). Crosland, M. *Beyond the Lighthouse*
(1981). Etherington-Smith, M., and J. Pilcher. *The
"It" Girls: Elinor Glyn, Romantic Novelist, and Lucy,
Lady Duff Gordon, Lucile, the Couteriere* (1986).

For articles in reference works, see: *CB.
Chambers. DNB. Film 2: Women Who Make Movies. Longman. TCA* and *SUP. TCRGW.*

Other references: Bennett, A. *Books and
Persons* (1917). Davson, G. *Good Housekeeping*
(April 1955). Mosley, L.O. *Curzon: The End of an
Epic* (1960).

Kate Beaird Meyers

(Margaret) Rumer Godden

BORN: 10 December 1907, Sussex.
DAUGHTER OF: Arthur Leigh Godden and
   Katherine Hingley Godden.
MARRIED: Laurence S. Foster, 1934; James
   Haynes Dixon, 1949.
WRITES UNDER: P. Davies, Rumer Godden

G. is a child of England and of India, and her
fifty-year career as a novelist and writer of children's books reflects this dual influence. G. was
born in Sussex, but as a small child she lived on
the banks of India's greatest river which, according to *Twentieth-Century Authors,* she preferred
to the "dull and colorless life in a cold South Coast
town." In the 1930s G. founded and operated a
children's dancing school in Calcutta, India, and
began her long career with a book about a Chinese
man and a Pekingese dog called *Chinese Puzzle,*
published under the pseudonym of P. Davies in
1936.

Three themes seem predominant in G.'s
world. First, she writes about the vulnerability and
fragility of children and about their innate toughness and spunk. *An Episode of Sparrows* (1955),
for instance, is the story of Lovejoy Mason, deserted by her man-hungry actress mother in a
London slum. Lovejoy is a feisty, determined tomboy who battles both the natural elements and the
slum's inhabitants in her efforts to create a beauti-

ful garden in a bombed-out churchyard. *The
Greengage Summer* (1958) describes the more
amusing (but sometimes bittersweet) adventures
of five English siblings on their own in the unfamiliar world of a French *pension.* There are similarities in the thematic structure of these and
other Godden novels about children. The youngsters are always initially bereft and cut off from
adult authority and strength, but they are, finally,
resourceful, courageous, and competent. The English children in *Breakfast with the Nikolides*
(1942), saddled with a neurotic, unhappy mother
and an angry but idealistic father, prove to be
more insightful than either parent. The English
children in *The Battle of the Villa Fiorita* (1963)
are determined to extricate their forty-two-year-
old mother from her romance with an Italian film
director. In league with the director's young
daughter, Pia, they force the lovers apart, which
leaves the reader with a sense of surprise and
disappointment.

G., a Roman Catholic, has produced several
books that deal with the lives of cloistered nuns.
Black Narcissus (1939) is about an Anglican sisterhood in India. *In This House of Brede* (1969)
and *Five for Sorrow, Ten for Joy* (1979) both deal
with women who become nuns in their middle
years. In the first of these, Philippa Talbot, an
English superwoman type, is a widowed executive

who speaks Japanese, who has mastered the intricacies of both the commercial and real estate markets, and who enters Brede, an enclosed convent of upper-middle class Benedictine nuns. This novel is an encyclopedia of details about first clothings, simple and solemn professions, discipline, prayer, and politics in an English convent. Lise Ambard (in *Five for Sorrow, Ten for Joy*), a thirty-seven-year-old ex-prostitute, also chooses "enclosure" at Saint Etienne and Béthanie in France, as do the nuns in *The Dark Horse* (1981), set in India. G. seems to be fascinated with walls and with both the enervating and invigorating effects of limits. Her houses and hotels protect, but they often imprison as well.

G.'s third theme is the contrast of divergent cultures. She is particularly gifted in pointing out both the confusion of multilingual and multiethnic India, a land of many religions and an entrenched caste system. But her India is also wise and accepting, beautiful and vibrant. As Paul Zimmerman of *Newsweek* has pointed out, "Rumer Godden remains among the last British novelists to be influenced by the colonial experience in India," and her books reflect "the enlightenment and catholic vision acquired from those early years along the banks of the great accepting rivers of the sub-continent."

G. has written more than fifteen books for children, many of which have dolls as their protagonists. The most famous are *The Doll's House* (1947) and *Impunity Jane* (1954), in which a doll falls into the hands of a gang of boys. *The Mousewife* (1951), based on an entry in Dorothy Wordsworth's *Journal*, is the story of a friendship between a caged dove and a mouse.

At least six of Godden's novels have been made into successful films for TV or the movies because she is, in the final analysis, a perceptive and sympathetic teller of tales. Her novels will remain popular because they are about basic human nature in England, India, and elsewhere.

WORKS: (as P. Davies) *Chinese Puzzle* (1936). (as P. Davies) *The Lady and the Unicorn* (1938). *Black Narcissus* (1939). *Gypsy, Gypsy* (1940). *Breakfast with the Nikolides* (1942). (as P. Davies) *Rungli-Rungliot* (1944). *Bengal Journey 1939–1945* (1945). *Take Three Tenses: A Fugue in Time* (1945). *The River* (1946). *The Doll's House* (1947). *A Candle for St. Jude* (1948). *In Noah's Ark* (1949). *A Breath of Air* (1950). *The Mousewife* (1951). *Kingfishers Catch Fire* (1953). *Impunity Jane: The Story of a Pocket Doll* (1954). *Hans Christian Andersen: a Great Life in Brief* (1954). *An Episode of Sparrows* (1955). *The Fairy Doll* (1956). *Mooltiki* (1957). *Mouse House* (1957). *The Story of Holly and Ivy* (1958). *The Greengage Summer* (1958). *Candy Floss* (1960). *St. Jerome and the Lion* (1961). *Miss Happiness and Miss Flower* (1961). *China Court: The Hours of a Country House* (1961). *Prayers from the Ark* (1962). *The Creatures' Choir* (1962). *Little Plum* (1963). *The Battle of the Villa Fiorita* (1963). (with J. Godden) *The Feather-Duster: A Fairy-Tale Musical* (1964). *Home Is the Sailor* (1964). *Two Under the Indian Sun* (1966). (with M. Bell) *Round the Day: Poetry Programmes for the Classroom or Library* (1966). (with M. Bell) *Round the Year: Poetry Programmes for the Classroom or Library* (1966). (with M. Bell) *The World Around: Poetry Programmes for the Classroom or Library* (1966). *The Kitchen Madonna* (1967). (with M. Bell) *A Letter to the World: Poems for Young People* (1968). *Mrs. Manders' Cook Book* (1968). *Gone: A Book of Stories* (1968). *Operation Sippacik* (1968). *In this House of Brede* (1969). *The Raphael Bible* (1970). *The Tale of Tales: The Beatrix Potter Ballet* (1971). *Shiva's Pigeons* (1972). *The Old Woman Who Lived in a Vinegar Bottle* (1972). *The Diddakoi* (1972). *Mr. McFadden's Hallowe'en* (1975). *The Peacock Spring* (1975). *The Rocking Horse Secret* (1977). *The Butterfly Lions: The Story of the Pekingese in History, Legend and Art* (1978). *Five for Sorrow, Ten for Joy* (1979). *The Dark Horse* (1981). *A Time to Dance, No Time to Weep* (1987).

BIBLIOGRAPHY: Frey, J.R. *JEGP* (1947). Prescott, O. *In My Opinion* (1952). Simpson, R.G. *Rumer Godden* (1973). Smaridge, N. *Famous British Women Novelists* (1967). Tindall, W.Y. *EJ* (1952).

For articles in reference works, see: *CA. CN. DEL. Longman. MBL. NCHEL. TCA SUP. TCCW. TCW.*

Other references: *Atlantic* (October 1969). *Books and Bookmen* (December 1967, August 1968, December 1971). *Book Week* (29 September 1963). Boyd, J.D. *New Catholic World* (July–August 1985). *Commonweal* (10 November 1978). *Economist* (20 December 1975, 26 November 1983). *Harper's* (May 1968). Hartley, L. *Mahfil: A Quarterly of South Asian Literature* (1966). *Listener* (12 July 1979, 24 September 1981). *NR* (24 November 1979, 23 June 1982). *New Statesman* (2 June 1972, 10 November 1972, 19 May 1978, 2 December 1983). *Newsweek* (30 September 1963, 4 April 1976, 6 December 1982, 9 December 1985). *NYHTBR* (18 December 1949, 8 October 1950). *NYTBR* (9 July 1939, 7 February 1965, 12 June 1966, 7 January 1968, 30 June 1968, 1 June 1969, 21 September 1969, 13 February 1972, 7 May 1972, 4 June 1972, 5 November 1972, 25 April 1976, 29 April 1979, 16 December 1979, 15 November 1981, 24 June 1982, 18 November 1984). *Observer* (2 October 1966, 14 July 1968, 2 November 1969, 25 April 1971, 28 May 1972, 28 September 1975, 23 November 1975, 7 December 1975, 6 February 1977, 21 December 1980, 17 January 1982, 1 December 1985, 16 December 1984). *Progressive* (May 1980). *PW* (10 November 1969). Sharma, V. *Indian P.E.N.* (1975). *Spectator* (3 November 1967, 13 November 1971, 11 November 1972, 4 October

1975, 6 December 1975, 17 October 1981). *SR* (3 December 1955, 4 October 1969, 17 June 1972). *Time* (17 July 1939, 12 August 1940, 11 October 1963, 14 November 1969, 19 April 1976). *TLS* (30 November 1967, 3 April 1969, 12 May 1972, 14 July 1972, 3 November 1972, 5 December 1975, 30 January 1976, 16 December 1977). *Washington Post* (29 November 1969, 3 December 1979).

Mickey Pearlman

Catherine Grace Frances Moody Gore

BORN: 1800, London.
DIED: 29 January 1861, Linwood, Lynhurst, Hampshire.
DAUGHTER OF: C. Moody.
MARRIED: Charles Arthur Gore, 1823.
WROTE UNDER: Mrs. Gore, Albany Poyntz, Anonymous.

When G. died in 1861, the *London Times* praised her as "the best novel writer of her class and the wittiest woman of her age." She was known throughout novel-reading Britain, particularly among women, as the author of more than sixty "fashionable novels," works that portray the manners, romances, and scandals of high society. Yet G. also published plays, poems, short stories, literary sketches, songs, and even a gardener's manual on roses. Among those who knew her personally, including Mary Russell Mitford, Thackeray, and Dickens, she was renowned for her learned and clever conversation.

Raised in East Retford, Nottinghamshire, and in London, G. began writing at an early age and published her first novel, *Theresa Marchmont, or The Maid of Honour*, in 1824, a year after her marriage, and 1829 saw the appearance of her *Hungarian Tales*, narratives blending fact and fiction. But it was in 1830, with the publication of *Women As They Are, or Manners of the Day* that G. joined the ranks of the "Silver-Fork School" of novelists; she ultimately became its most prolific, and possibly most popular, writer. In *Women As They Are* and dozens of subsequent novels of fashion, G. depicts the gay leisure class of Regency England, complete with strutting dandies, arrogant parvenus, scheming mamas, and hopeful girls decked out in the family jewels. G.'s novels appealed both to the fashionables about whom she wrote and to middle-class readers as well. The romances portrayed in her works often play out the middle-class female daydream of marrying into aristocracy, and her pages are crowded with the minute details about shops, dress, and etiquette craved by those struggling themselves to rise in society. However, G. also brought to her novels a sharp wit and keen insight into the pretensions and absurdities of the fashionable world; in fact, one reviewer cautioned her not to be too reckless in her exposure of hypocrisy.

Following the appearance of *Women As They Are*, G. turned out work at an astonishing rate, producing six books and several plays in 1831 and 1832 alone. Toward the end of this period, she published *The Fair of May Fair* (1832), a collection of short stories. It was not well-received, and G.'s correspondence indicates she was stung by the bad reviews, particularly by suggestions that she was wasting her talents. G. had privately referred to herself as a writer of "rubbish," but in the face of public criticism, she fiercely defended the fashionable novel, contending that "every picture of passing manners, if accurate, is valuable from the drawing room to the alehouse." However, when she published *A Sketchbook of Fashion* anonymously, in 1833, G. requested that the book be given no notice at all and confessed to her publisher that she had grown rather ashamed of her novels of fashion. Hoping to redeem her name and remind readers of her earlier success at a more serious form of literature, G. also produced a collection of historical stories in 1833 and announced them as "*Polish Tales*, by the authoress of *Hungarian Tales*."

In 1832, the Gores had moved to Paris, where G. presided over a Sunday salon frequented by literary and political personalities. She published little more until 1836, when a flurry of novels appeared, occasioned, most likely, by a financial crisis. Years later, G. expressed her belief that "even from an iron intellect the sparks are only elicited by collision with the flints of this world." But in G.'s case, necessity tended to result in the frivolous novels for which she was famous rather than the serious work to which she sporadically returned.

By 1841, the Gores had returned to England, and G. published her best-known novel: *Cecil: or Adventures of a Coxcomb*. At her insistence, the novel was published anonymously to encourage readers in the belief that an exciting new talent had appeared: it created just the sensation G. had hoped for. Purporting to be the autobiography of a dandy, a friend and companion of Lord Byron, *Cecil* displays an intimate acquaintance with London clubs as well as a greater knowledge of Greek and Latin than would ordinarily be attributed to a woman. Hence, no one imagined it had been written by G., who probably got her information about the clubs from her friend William Beckford. Throughout the novel, G. mercilessly satirizes dandyism, although she also uses Cecil's travels to show off her own acquaintance with Parisian manners, cuisine, and politics.

In the same year that *Cecil* appeared, G. began a series of articles in *Bentley's Miscellany* under the pseudonym "Albany Poyntz." In one of the earliest of these articles, "The Children of the Mobility versus the Children of the Nobility," G. bitterly contrasts the "freedom" of poor children with the "deprivations" and discomforts supposedly suffered by the gaudily dressed children featured in the currently popular "Portraits of the Nobility." The Albany Poyntz articles also include a series of satirical sketches of members of the upper-class entourage—"The Standard Footman," "The Lady's Maid," etc.—but even in some of these, G. reveals an understanding of and compassion for the hardships of the poor.

G.'s efforts at playwriting met with considerably less success than her novels and sketches. Although *The School for Coquettes* was a hit in 1831, G.'s most highly publicized play, *Quid Pro Quo, or The Day of the Dupes*, was a theatrical disaster. The play won a lucrative prize in 1844 as the best comedy of British life and manners, but when it was produced the play was hooted off the stage and assailed by the press.

In 1846, G.'s husband died, and four years later she received an inheritance from another family member that allowed her to relax her demanding pace. G. had regularly turned out novels over the previous decade, but none had met with the same success as *Cecil*—not even its sequel, *Cecil, A Peer* (1841), or *Adventures of Borneo* (1849), another fictional autobiography, this time in the style of *Robinson Crusoe*. Interest in the fashionable novel was waning, but when G. fell victim to a bank scandal in 1855, she cunningly reissued her 1843 novel about a corrupt banker, *The Banker's Wife, or Court and City*—omitting, of course, the appreciative dedication she had made, ironically enough, to her own trusted banker, who later involved her funds in the scandal; 1855 also saw the appearance, fittingly, of G.'s *Mammon, or The Hardships of an Heiress*. G. published her last novel in 1858. Her eyesight began to fail and she died in 1861.

The comparison of G.'s life and her work produces some odd contradictions: she courted high society even as she satirized it, and despite her own financial hardships and hard-headed business sense, her novels celebrate the virtue of womanly submission and chronicle the disastrous consequences of women's attempts at independ-

ence. G. herself alternately disparaged and defended her fashionable writing. Had she not been driven by financial necessity, she might have produced works of more lasting stature; still, her *oeuvre* provides a revealing portrait of the follies of her era.

WORKS: *Theresa Marchmont, or The Maid of Honour: A Tale* (1824). *The Bond: A Dramatic Poem* (1824). *Richelieu, or the Broken Heart* (1826). *The Lettre de Cachet: A Tale*, with *The Reign of Terror: A Tale* (1827). *Hungarian Tales* (1829). *Romances of Real Life* (1829). *Women As They Are, or The Manners of the Day* (1830). *The Historical Traveller* (1831). *The School for Coquettes* (1831). *Pin Money: A Novel* (1831). *The Tuileries: A Tale* (1831). *Mothers and Daughters: A Tale of the Year 1830* (1831). *The Opera: A Novel* (1832). *The Fair of May Fair* (1832). *The Sketchbook of Fashion* (1833). *Polish Tales* (1833). *The Hamiltons, or The New Era* (1834). *The Maid of Croissey, King O'Neil, and The Queen's Champion* (in *Webster's Acting National Drama*, 1835). *The Diary of a Désennuyée* (1836). *Mrs. Armytage, or Female Domination* (1836). *Picciola, or Captive Creative* (by X. B. Saintine, ed. and trans. by G., 1837). *Memoirs of a Peeress, or the Days of Fox* (ed. C. Bury, 1837). *Stokeshill Place, or The Man of Business* (1837). *The Rose Fancier's Manual* (1838). *Mary Raymond and Other Tales* (1838). *The Woman of the World: A Novel* (1838). *The Cabinet Minister* (1839). *The Courtier of the Days of Charles II, with Other Tales* (1839). *A Good Night's Rest, or Two O'Clock in the Morning* (in *Duncombe's British Theatre*, 1839). *Dacre of the South, or The Olden Time: A Drama* (1840). *The Dowager, or The New School for Scandal* (1840). *Preferment, or My Uncle the Earl* (1840). *The Abbey and Other Tales* (1840). *Greville, or a Season in Paris* (1841). *Cecil, or The Adventures of a Coxcomb: A Novel* (1841). *Cecil, a Peer* (1841). *Paris in 1841* (1842). *The Man of Fortune and Other Tales* (1842). *The Ambassador's Wife* (1842). *The Money-Lender* (1843). *Modern Chivalry, or A New Orlando Furioso* (1843). *The Banker's Wife, or Court and City: A Novel* (1843). *Agathonia: A Romance* (1844). *Marrying for Money* (in *Omnibus of Modern Romance*, 1844). *The Birthright and Other Tales* (1844). *Quid Pro Quo, or The Day of the Dupes: A Comedy* (1844). *The Popular Member: The Wheel of Fortune* (1844). *Self* (1845). *The Story of a Royal Favorite* (1845). *The Snowstorm: A Christmas Story* (1845). *Peers and Parvenus: A Novel* (1846). *New Year's Day: A Winter's Tale* (1846). *Men of Capital* (1846). *The Debutante, or The London Season* (1846). *Sketches of English Character* (1846). *Castles in the Air: A Novel* (1847). *Temptation and Atonement and Other Tales* (1847). *The Inundation, or Pardon and Peace: A Christmas Story* (1847). *The Diamond and the Pearl: A Novel* (1849). *Adventures in Borneo* (1849). *The Dean's Daughter, or*

The Days We Live In (1853). *The Lost Son: A Winter's Tale* (1854). *Transmutation, or The Lord and the Lout* (1854). *Progress and Prejudice* (1854). *Mammon, or The Hardships of an Heiress* (1855). *A Life's Lessons: A Novel* (1856). *The Two Aristocracies: A Novel* (1857). *Heckington: A Novel* (1858).

BIBLIOGRAPHY: Anderson, B. *JPC* (1976). Farrell, J.F. *Library Chronicle of the University of Texas* (1986). Gettman, R.A. *A Victorian Publisher: A Study of the Bentley Papers* (1960). Horne, R.H., ed. *A New Spirit of the Age* (1872). Rosa, M.W. *The Silver-Fork School: Novels of Fashion Preceding Vanity Fair* (1936).

For articles in reference works, see: *DNB. NCBEL.*

Other references: *The Archives of Richard Bentley and Sons 1829-1898*, Part Two (Somerset House microfilm, reel 32, 1977). *Illustrated London News* (16 February 1861). *London Athenaeum* (9 February 1861, 16 February 1861). *New Monthly Magazine* (June 1833, March 1837, June 1852). *Times* (London) (4 February 1861).

Cynthia Merrill

Eva Gore-Booth

BORN: 22 May 1870, Lissadell, County Sligo, Ireland.
DIED: 30 June 1926, London.
DAUGHTER OF: Sir Henry Gore-Booth and Georgina Hill.

The Irish Literary Revival, the British movement for Woman's Suffrage, and the Women's Peace Crusade during World War I all fed G.'s imagination as a political writer, a poetess, and a dramatist.

Born in the shadow of "Knocknarea," the legendary burial cairn of Queen Maeve, G. spent her childhood learning about the people and legends of Connaught. In addition to this familiarity with the Irish, she was tutored in German, English, and French literatures and led a typical Anglo-Irish girlhood, preparing to enter aristocratic society with a strong background in the arts. But her father, Sir Henry Gore-Booth, who accompanied A.H. Markham on an expedition to the North Pole in 1879 as a scientist and who showed an equally active social conscience in that same year by generating aid for County Sligo's severe famine, was unprecedented in his concern as a landlord for the needs of the local Irish peasantry. G.'s early travels outside Ireland included a voyage to the Caribbean and North America with Sir Henry in 1894. In the following year, the father and daughter made the traditional tour of the European Continent that carried them from the Wagner Festival at Bayreuth to the theater in Oberammergau to northern Italy's cathedrals and museums.

G. and her sister, Constance, attracted a circle of literary acquaintances during the 1890s. W.B. Yeats often visited the ancestral Gore-Booth estate, "Lissadell," Irish for "the Court of the Blind Man"; in the thirteenth century it had been the home of a famous blind piper whose prominence in legend along with the reputed beauty of the

Gore-Booth sisters may have attracted Yeats from his nearby home. G. also socialized with the novelist Julian Sturgis, who introduced her to Andrew Lang. It was through Lang that her early poems reached the editor of *Longman's Magazine* where her work first appeared. G.'s first, slim book of verse entitled *Poems* appeared in 1898. Yeats wrote to her of its final four lines as being "really magical" and concluded, "I think it is full of poetic feeling and has great promise." In addition, *The Irish Homestead, The New Irish Review, The Nineteenth Century, The Yellow Book,* and *The Savoy* published poems by G. before the close of the 1890s.

In 1903, George Russell (A.E.) anthologized poems by G. in *New Poems: A Lyric Selection by A.E.,* with poetry from seven others among whom were Padraic Colum and Katherine Tynan. Russell's preface to the collection speaks of the "new ways the wind of poetry listeth to blow in Ireland today." By this time, G. had entered into the spirit of the Celtic Twilight, a spirit generated by images of ethereal "winds" whose composers saw themselves as prophets taking up the role left them by ancient, mystical Irish bards. G.'s best-known work, "The Little Waves of Breffny," invokes this spirit: ". . . the haunted air of twilight is very strange and still,/ And the little winds of twilight are dearer to my mind," treating this vague and airy "twilight" as a romantic symbol of Ireland's occult past. In 1904, James H. Cousins remarked, in a letter to Yeats, of the awkwardness involved in staging one of G.'s plays because "difficulties of stage management, such as getting a crow to fly across the stage, and a fog to enter and condense into a human figure, were too much even for our enthusiasm."

G.'s adult life was divided between participation in the Irish Literary Revival and her political activities in Britain. In 1896 she met Esther Roper with whom she lived in Northern England and whom she joined as a joint secretary to the Women's Textile and Other Workers' Representation Committee. From 1896, G. was engaged in protesting British trade union policies, which excluded women from joining unions and exploited women by hiring them to replace the more expensive, organized male workers. She organized, wrote, and spoke in all parts of England, submitting deputations to Cabinet Ministers and to Members of Parliament. She edited a paper called *The Women's Labour News* and acted as a representative of the women workers to the Manchester Education Committee. She ran reading classes for workers as well as dramatic societies. G. sustained her literary career simultaneously with her political activities. In 1906 she published *The Egyptian Pillar*, assimilating the imagery of her politics to Christian and Islamic themes; "The Good Samaritan," for example, seems to indicate her respect for the proletariat: "Stone-breakers resting from their toil/ Have poured out wine and oil./ The miner hurrying from his mine/ Has seen a flash of light divine,/ And every tired laborer/ Has given a helping hand . . . ." Another book of poems, *The Agate Lamp*, appeared in 1912 with more variations upon Irish themes, and another play, *The Death of Fionovar*, was substantially revised in 1916.

G.'s plays treated themes from Ulster's *Red Branch Cycle*. Her dramatic skit, "The Death of Cuchulain," from her book, *Unseen Kings*, was performed at the Abbey Theater, and her sister, Constance, produced a version of the entire *Unseen Kings* for The Independent Theatre Company in January of 1912. Constance was also an enthusiast of G.'s drama, *The Buried Life of Deirdre* (1908), which G. re-wrote and illustrated while Constance was being tried and imprisoned in 1916 for her part in the Easter Uprising. She was sentenced as Constance Markievicz (the wife of a Polish count) to life imprisonment; her male counterparts were executed. Prior to this, G. had been a devoted pacifist. She traveled widely in Britain to protest Britain's involvement in World War I, and she attended tribunals and courts martial of conscientious objectors to offer her support.

When her militant sister was tried and incarcerated for I.R.A. involvement, G. supported her by writing letters, visiting, and working in the name of her sister's cause, although she disagreed with any kind of war. Constance would outlive G., confined to Dublin's Kilmainham Jail where she died in 1927.

Christian ideals consumed G.'s interests during the 1920s. *A Psychological and Poetic Approach to the Study of Christ in the Fourth Gospel* was published in 1923 while she was studying Latin and Greek to become closer to the Scriptures. *The Shepherd of Eternity* was a book of poetry that followed in 1925. *The Inner Kingdom* (1926) and the unfinished, final book, *The World's Pilgrim* (1927), were both published posthumously. G. died on 30 June 1926, writing poetry and promoting peace to her final day.

G. is probably best known through W.B. Yeats' elegy, "In Memory of Eva Gore-Booth and Con Markievicz." Yeats summons images of a pastoral Lissadell, and G.'s youthful beauty is described as that of a "gazelle" only to be contrasted with the later image of her, "withered old and skeleton gaunt,/ An image of such politics."

WORKS: *Poems* (1898). *Unseen Kings* (1904). *The One and the Many* (1904). *The Three Resurrections and the Triumph of Maeve* (1905). *The Egyptian Pillar* (1906). *The Sorrowful Princess* (1907). *The Agate Lamp* (1912). *Broken Glory* (1918). *The Sword of Justice* (1918). *The Psychological and the Poetic Approach to the Study of Christ in the Fourth Gospel* (1923). *The Shepherd of Eternity* (1925). *The House of Three Windows* (1926). *The Inner Kingdom* (1926). *The World's Pilgrim* (1927). *Poems of Eva Gore-Booth* (1926). *The Buried Life of Deirdre* (1930).

BIBLIOGRAPHY: Fox, R.M. *Rebel Irishwomen* (1935). VanVorris, J. *Constance deMarkievicz: In the Cause of Ireland* (1967).

For articles in reference books, see: *DIL. Longman. The Modern Irish Drama: A Documentary History*, eds. R. Hogan and J. Kilroy (1976).

John E. Lavin, Jr.

Elizabeth de Beauchamp Goudge

BORN: 24 April 1900, Wells, Somerset.
DIED: 1 April 1984, near Henley-on-Thames.
DAUGHTER OF: Ida de Beauchamp Collenette and Henry Leighton Goudge.

G., novelist, playwright, artist, and teacher of handicrafts, was a prolific and popular, though somewhat old-fashioned, writer of books for both adults and children. She was especially recognized for her precise ability to depict the English countryside and for her characterization. The best known of her nearly fifty books—*Green Dolphin Country* (1944; published in the U.S. as *Green Dolphin Street*), *The Little White Horse* (1947), *Gentian Hill* (1949), and *The Child from the Sea* (1970)—have been compared favorably to Victorian novels; like most of her work, they are explicitly religious, reflective of G.'s active Anglicanism. After studying art, she taught design and applied art from 1922 to 1932 in Ely (where her father became a canon in 1911) and Oxford (where her father become Regius Professor of Divinity in 1923) and lived with her parents until her father died in 1939 and her mother in 1944.

Her first works were plays, including one about the Brontës that was produced in London when she was thirty-two; when she was advised to try writing fiction, she succeeded with her third effort, *Island Magic*, published in 1934. She thereafter wrote stories for such periodicals as *The Strand* and continued writing plays (which she preferred) and novels. In the mid-1930s she had a nervous breakdown; after her mother's death, she moved to Henley-on-Thames, where she lived till her death in 1984.

G. wrote in a variety of forms, including historical fiction, children's works, nonfiction works on religion, and, most often, novels celebrating particular locales. *Island Magic*, for example, told of her maternal grandparents' lives on Guernsey in the Channel Islands and was the first of a number of works dealing with specific British locations. Several works are set in cathedral towns, including *A City of Bells* (1936), a contemporary novel set in Wells (but called "Torminster"), *Towers in the Mist* (1938), set in sixteenth-century Oxford, and *The Dean's Watch* (1960), set in nineteenth-century Ely.

Her best-known adult novel, the long historical romance *Green Dolphin Country*, is again about a member of her family, in this case a great-uncle, also from Guernsey, who emigrated to New Zealand; he writes home for a wife but because of confusion over her name gets her sister instead. The novel won several awards, was bought for $125,000 by M.G.M., and was made into a popular motion picture under its American title. Other historical novels include *Gentian Hill*, set in the Napoleonic era, and *The Child from the Sea*, about Lucy Waters, the secret wife of Charles II.

G. wrote a series of novels set in Devon about the several generations of the Eliot clan of Damerosehay; these emphasized family and spiritual values. G.'s favorite, *The Bird in the Tree* (1940), depicts the matriarch of the clan, Lucilla, trying to persuade her actor grandson, David, to end his affair with his uncle's ex-wife, Nadine, so she can return to her family. *The Herb of Grace* (1948), about an inn of that name, shows how Nadine finally renounces David and he returns to the family home. David is also the focus of *The Heart of the Family* (1953), in which he learns to forgive the actions of others through the intervention of a concentration-camp survivor; David had participated in the 1945 bombing of Hamburg, in which the survivor's family was killed, and after their

encounter David can be fully restored to his family as Lucilla's heir.

G.'s children's books—which she started writing, unsuccessfully, even before entering art school (*The Fairies' Baby and Other Stories*, 1919)—gave her more pleasure, she said, than anything else she wrote, even though they now seem excessively sentimental. Most of these books, both novels and collections of stories, appeared relatively early in her career, as with the best-known, *Henrietta's House* (1942; in the U.S. as *The Blue Hills*) and *The Little White Horse* (1947), but she maintained her interest up to 1971 (*The Lost Angel*). In addition, G. wrote numerous explicitly religious works, including *God So Loved the World* (1951), a biography of Jesus, and *My God and My All* (1959), a biography of Francis of Assisi, as well as others on prayer, peace, Christmas, and faith.

G. has often been criticized for her reliance on happy endings, didacticism, and sentimentality. She once stated that though such endings are "inartistic," they are the only kinds she can write; given the amount of tragedy in life, she said, "we don't want it in the story books to which we turn when we are ill or unhappy." She acknowledges that her books are escapist, and she knows that she writes primarily for the old, the young, and the sick. Her explicitly Christian emphasis assumes a hierarchical, planned universe in which everyone—even evil people—works toward the good. Yet at her best her works show a remarkable insight into character (again, especially the young and the old) and place, and her children's works, along with one or two adult historical novels, are likely to remain popular.

WORKS: *The Fairies' Baby and Other Stories* (1919). *Island Magic* (1934). *The Middle Window* (1935). *A City of Bells* (1936). *A Pedlar's Pack and Other Stories* (1937). *Towers in the Mist* (1938). *The Sister of the Angels: A Christmas Story* (1939). *There Plays: Suomi, The Brontës of Haworth, and Fanny Burney* (1939). *Smoky House* (1940). *The Bird in the Tree* (1940). *The Golden Skylark and Other Stories* (1941). *The Well of the Star* (1941). *The Castle on the Hill* (1941). *Henrietta House* (1942; in the U.S. as *The Blue Hills*). *The Ikon on the Wall and Other Stories* (1943). *Green Dolphin Country* (1944; in the U.S. as *Green Dolphin Street*). *The Elizabeth Goudge Reader*, ed. R. Dobbs (1946; in the U.K. as *At the Sign of the Dolphin: An Elizabeth Goudge Anthology*, 1947). *The Little White Horse* (1947). *Songs and Verses* (1947). *At the Sign of the Dolphin* (1947). *The Herb of Grace* (1948; in the US. as *Pilgrim's Inn*). *Gentian Hill* (1949). *Make-Believe* (1949). *The Reward of Faith and Other Stories* (1950). *The Valley of Song* (1951). *God So Loved the World: A Life of Christ* (1951). *White Wings: Collected Short Stories* (1952). *The Heart of the Family* (1953). *David, the Shep-*

herd Boy (1954). *The Rosemary Tree* (1956). *The Eliots of Damerosehay* (1957). *The White Witch* (1958). *Saint Francis of Assisi* (1959; in the U.S. as *My God and My All: The Life of St. Francis Assisi*). *The Dean's Watch* (1960). *The Scent of Water* (1963). *Linnets and Valerians* (1964). *Three Cities of Bells* (1965). *The Chapel of the Blessed Virgin Mary, Buckler's Hard, Beaulieu* (1966). *A Christmas Book* (1967). *I Saw Three Ships* (1969). *The Ten Gifts* (1969). *The Child from the Sea* (1970). *The Lost Angel* (1971). *The Joy of the Snow: An Autobiography* (1974). *Pattern of People* (1976).

BIBLIOGRAPHY: Goudge, E. *The Joy of the Snow: An Autobiography* (1974). Leasor, J. *Author by Profession* (1952).

For articles in reference works, see: *CA. CB. Longman. Something About the Author. TCA* and *SUP. TCCW. TCR&GW. TCW. Writer's Directory.*

Other references: *Books and Bookmen* (May 1972). *Christian Century* (3 November 1976). *Christian Science Monitor Magazine* (8 June 1940). Dobbs, R. "Introduction." *The Elizabeth Goudge Reader*, ed. R. Dobbs (1946). Marsden, M. *Images of Women in Fiction: Feminist Perspectives*, ed. S.K. Cornillon (1972). *New Statesman* (27 September 1974). *NYHTBR* (7 October 1951). *NYT* (27 April 1984). *Observer* (8 September 1974, 21 July 1985). *Scholastic* (4 March 1939). *Time* (4 September 1944). *Times* (London) (3 April 1984). *TES* (14 December 1979). *TLS* (6 April 1973).

Paul Schlueter

Sarah Grand (pseudonym of Frances Elizabeth [Clarke] McFall)

BORN: 10 June 1854, Donaghadee, County Down, Northern Ireland.
DIED: 12 May 1943, Calne.
DAUGHTER OF: Edward John Bellenden Clarke and Margaret Bell Sherwood Clarke.
MARRIED: David Chambers McFall, 1870.

One of five children, G. was born in Ireland of English parents, but when her father, a naval officer, died in 1861, her mother moved the family back to England. G. was educated at home until she was fourteen when she was sent to boarding school for more discipline. She escaped from school at sixteen by marrying a naval surgeon twenty-three years her senior, apparently an unhappy match. After *Ideala* (1888) was published, she moved from her husband and son to live in London, where her career flourished, and when her husband died in 1898, G. joined the Women Writers' Suffrage League and became active in the women's suffrage movement in Tunbridge Wells. In 1922, two years after moving to Bath, she became that city's mayoress for six years. She died in 1943 in Calne, where she had moved for safety during the war.

One of the "New Women" writers of the 1890s who criticized the oppression of women, G. used her ample experience and acute observation, as well as her travels to the Far East, in writing her novels, which can be read as arguments for the need to reform society's treatment of women, the way women themselves behave, and the economic system. Besides her novels, G. wrote many short stories and articles for women's magazines, such

as "Is It Ever Justifiable to Break Off an Engagement?" and "Should Irascible Old Men Be Taught to Knit?"

G.'s first successful novel, *Ideala*, forms a trilogy with *The Heavenly Twins* (1893) and *The Beth Book* (1897). *Ideala*, a first-person narrative about Ideala by a male friend, examines a number of social problems as well as the question of the proper goal for women: to be or to act. In G.'s first best-seller, *The Heavenly Twins*, she experiments with her narrative voice, producing some disconcerting breaks. Otherwise, the novel is well worth reading since it introduces many of G.'s themes. The inadequacy of women's education and its disastrous effects are graphically revealed in this novel, which does, however, show some characters rising above and conquering the hardships society has given them. The title refers to the twins Angelica and Diavolo, female and male, and their upbringing, but the novel actually focuses on Evadne, a highly intelligent and self-educated woman who, through being kept in ignorance by her parents, inadvertently marries a brutish man with a sordid past. This is also a novel within a novel, and plots and sub-plots abound, intertwining with each other to produce a complete world in which many young people are joining to improve society.

The Beth Book (1897) is G.'s best novel, primarily because of the strong, fascinating character of Beth herself and the detailed description of the Victorian upbringing of a young girl. Based loosely on G.'s own life, the first half of the novel deals with Beth's life from birth through adolescence (one reason the novel was scorned by critics when it was first published), but instead of being a pathetic, sentimental account of the oppression of female children, the novel presents Beth unexpectedly refusing to submit, a refreshing change from conventional novels of the day. Indeed, G.'s heroines often succeed in spite of society rather than succumbing to their oppressors. But *The Beth Book* does have problems. Besides occasional overexplanation, the problems are mainly accounted for by the narrative point of view. Sometimes G. creates awkward scenes when she tries to develop other characters while retaining Beth's point of view. In one scene, for example, Beth trails her corrupt Uncle James around his estate, unseen, yet close enough to hear his conversations, for an unbelievably long time. On the other hand, the absence of a sense of time in the passages from Beth's early childhood seems similar to the experiments with point of view of modern writers such as Faulkner.

Although G. had a social purpose for writing, her characters are not stereotypes. In fact, she goes so far in her attempts to portray even minor characters as complex individuals that inconsistencies sometimes develop, such as the abrupt change in Mr. Caldwell, Beth's father, from a harsh, domineering and critical husband ("not to disturb him was the object of everybody's life") to a patient, appreciative and understanding father to Beth shortly before his death. The advice he gives Beth is necessary for the continuation of the novel, but the change in his personality is explained only perfunctorily in a few hasty scenes in the garden. Nevertheless, G.'s short character descriptions and pithy statements are honed with irony and truth.

Unlike her trilogy, *Singularly Deluded* (1893) caused little controversy and was even praised for its vivid description of a fire at sea; unfortunately it is much less interesting than the other novels and offers little satisfaction besides finding out how it ends. G.'s next two major novels, *Adnam's Orchard* (1912) and *Winged Victory* (1916), deal with the problem of land reform. In these novels

G. branches out to focus for the first time on characters who are not all members of nobility. In doing so, G. considers at length what makes a person "noble." How much is heredity and how much environment? In *Adnam's Orchard* we see a land laid waste by its unambitious noble landowners, the workers and their families either out of work or scraping by in substandard housing. The absurdity of the landowners' raising the rent as soon as tenants make any improvements in the property is apparent. *Winged Victory* follows the life of Ella Banks, a character in *Adnam's Orchard*, and her attempts to improve the lives of women workers in the sweat shops.

G. is intelligent enough not to prescribe one path for everyone. She accepts individuality and wants only a society that also recognizes individuality in its members instead of forcing them all, both men and women, into pre-ordained roles. Her novels provoked controversy. Although critics severely criticized both subject matter and style, G.'s novels were very popular among readers and were praised by, among others, Mark Twain and George Bernard Shaw. Indeed, she has lapses; yet when read today, her novels resound with common sense.

WORKS: *Two Dear Little Feet* (1880). *Ideala: A Study From Life* (1888). *A Domestic Experiment* (1891). *Singularly Deluded* (1892; 1893). *The Heavenly Twins* (1893). *Our Manifold Nature* (1894). *The Beth Book* (1897). *The Modern Man and Maid* (1898). *Babs the Impossible* (1900). *Emotional Moments* (1908). *Adnam's Orchard* (1912). *Winged Victory* (1916). *Variety* (1922).

BIBLIOGRAPHY: Cunningham, G. *The "New Woman" and the Fiction of the 1890's* (1978). Huddleston, J. *Sarah Grand: A Bibliography* (1979). Showalter, E. *A Literature of Their Own* (1977).

For articles in reference works, see: *TCA.*

Other references: *Journal of Women's Studies in Literature* (1979). *Mark Twain Journal* (Summer 1972). *Modern Drama* (December 1971).

Carol Pulham

Kate Greenaway

BORN: 17 March 1846, Hoxton, London.
DIED: 6 November 1901, Hampstead, London.
DAUGHTER OF: John and Elizabeth Jones Greenaway.
WROTE UNDER: K.G., Kate Greenaway.

Primarily known for her illustrations of children's books, G. wrote verse and other texts as well. Her children's rhymes and drawings of chil-

dren and English gardens were very popular in Europe and in America. G.'s parents recognized her budding talent at twelve and provided art lessons for her, but her formal education alternated between visiting tutors and girls' schools. Her first published works, in 1868, were designs for Christmas and Valentine cards. She soon began illustrating little books and continued this work throughout her life.

But G.'s writings alone would not have gained entry into the publishing world. Her writings fall into five categories: illustrated verses, datebooks, nonfiction, correspondence, and miscellaneous poetry. Her popular illustrated verses still have a special innocent charm, the almanacs and datebooks brought her some notoriety, and G. also illustrated texts for art lessons and game rules.

The only two children's rhyme books that G. both wrote and illustrated were *Under the Window* (1878) and *Marigold Garden* (1885). Her *An Apple Pie* (1885) has been considered original, but the text is very close to standard nursery alphabet rhymes. *Under the Window* is a series of outside scenes spotlighting Victorian emerging ladies and gentlemen, reflecting in words and images the whimsy and innocent fantasy of childhood. The rhyme is sing-songy, and the theme is a combination of fantasy and etiquette. *Marigold Garden*, also manners-conscious, was more successful in capturing the fancy of a child's perspective. The illustrations and text form a complementary whole so that the picture of the stuffy woman with her constrained, dutiful grandchildren matches the tone of the verse.

These works' popularity was a reflection of the Victorian Age of which G. was certainly a part. In many ways, the innocence and beauty of G.'s children, who in no way resemble the chimneysweeps and other poor waifs then on the streets, are directly influenced by the Pre-Raphaelite movement. G. not only admired the paintings of John Everett Millais, Rossetti, and Hunt, but was a disciple of John Ruskin. The Ruskin–G. correspondence spanned 1880, when he wrote about the *Under the Windows* exhibition, and 1900, when he died; he wrote about 500 letters, and she wrote 1000 or more. Ruskin, the authoritarian art critic, offered advice and friendship and devoted a lecture to G. called "Fairyland" on 30 May 1883. Feeling that G. was wasting much effort on her illustrations and datebook art, he encouraged G. to paint larger works, which she did. G. subsequently illustrated over twenty books written by others. In addition to a collection of cat poems edited by Ruskin, *Dame Wiggins of Lee and Her Seven Wonderful Cats* (1885), G.'s best known collaborators were Bret Harte (*The Queen of the Pirate Isle*, 1886) and Robert Browning (*The Pied Piper of Hamelin*, 1888).

G.'s unpublished poems fill up four volumes of manuscripts, though several were subsequently published in a biography about her. Most of her poems are unpolished and amateurish, and G. never was satisfied with them. They are not, however, the nursery rhymes. They are lyrics, some in sonnet form, on a number of different themes, many serious and sad, and many others verses about love.

The artist described by her biographers was "sincere, modest, patient, intelligent, bighearted, sensitive, forgiving, and humorous," and Ruskin said that G. was able to "re-establish throughout gentle Europe the manners and customs of fairyland."

WORKS: Self-illustrated: *Under the Window: Pictures and Rhymes for Children* (1878). *Art Hours: After K. Greenaway* (1882). *Steps to Art: After Kate Greenaway* (1882). *Kate Greenaway's Almanac for 1883–95, 1897* (14 vols., 1882–1896). *Language of Flowers* (1884). *Kate Greenaway's Alphabet* (1885). *Marigold Garden: Pictures and Rhymes* (1885). *An Apple Pie* (1886). *Kate Greenaway's Book of Games* (1889). *Kate Greenaway's Pictures from Originals Presented by Her to John Ruskin and Other Personal Friends* (1921). *The Kate Greenaway Treasury: An Anthology of the Illustrations and Writings of Kate Greenaway*. ed. E. Ernest and P. Lowe (1967). *The Kate Greenaway Book*, ed. B. Holme (1976).

BIBLIOGRAPHY: Engen, R. *Kate Greenaway* (1976). Ernest, E., ed. *The Kate Greenaway Treasury* (1967). Holme, B. *The Kate Greenaway Book* (1976). Moore, A. *A Century of Kate Greenaway* (1946). Ruskin, J. *Works*, ed. E. Cook. (1903–1912). Spielmann, M., and G. Layard, *Kate Greenaway* (1905). Tarbox, A. *Magic Land of Kate Greenaway* (1968).

For works in reference books, see *DNB. Illustrators of Children's Books, 1744–1945*, ed. B. Mahony, (1947). *NCHEL. OCEL. Who's Who of Children's Literature*, ed. B. Doyle (1968). *Yesterday's Authors of Books for Children 2*, ed. A. Commire (1978).

Other references: *Horn Book* (March 1946).

Marilynn J. Smith

Lady Augusta Gregory

BORN: 15 March 1852, Roxborough, Ireland.
DIED: 22 May 1932, Coole.
DAUGHTER OF: Dudley Persse and Francis Barry.
MARRIED: Sir William Gregory, 1880.

A playwright, director, folklorist, historian, translator, biographer, and co-founder of the Irish National Theatre, Lady Gregory was an important figure in the Irish Literary Renaissance of the early twentieth century. Although born into and married within the Protestant land-owning ascendancy, she developed early in life an imaginative empathy with Irish Catholic peasantry, an empathy which, along with her goal of literary nationalism, exerted the formative influence on her large and varied oeuvre.

G.'s literary use of Irish peasants and peasant dialect formally began with her study of Gaelic in 1894. Excited by the growing interest in folklore, she began visiting the peasants around her estate, listening to and recording their oral poems and stories. W.B. Yeats, whom she met in 1896 and who became a close friend, encouraged her work, and, in 1902, she published her translations of some of the native Irish epics in *Cuchulain of Muirthemne*. She went on to translate other works from the Gaelic, some of which influenced important Irish writers of the time. In 1920 she published her serious folklore study, *Visions and Beliefs in the West of Ireland*, which earned her the epithet "mother of folklore" from Thomas Wall of the Irish Folklore Commission.

G. later used her folklore stories and her studies of dialect to full advantage in her plays. A co-founder of the Abbey Theater (its name and location were her suggestions), she was one of the theater's most important playwrights, contributing more plays than any other author in the group and serving, with Synge and Yeats, as one of the three major directors in the theatre. Writing primarily one- and two-act plays, G. worked with tragedies, comedies, and farces. She wrote peasant plays, folk history plays, a passion play, and adaptations (as well as translations) from Molière and Goldoni. Like Synge, she generally wrote in the distinctive English of the peasants of Western Ireland, a dialect rich in concrete images and metaphors and odd grammatical constructions.

G.'s plays are characterized by her rich gift for dialogue, her ear for the saying that reveals character, and her skill in creating taut dramatic plots from simple anecdotes. She often created comic effects by writing dialogue as two monologues and was talented at raising an anecdote from the particular to the universal. In plays like *Kincora*, *Dervorgilla*, and *Grania*, she also gives intriguing studies of frustrated women, in the last presenting the Irish counterpart to the Deirdre figure used by both Synge and Yeats in their plays.

An advocate of home rule and a defendant of free speech (she defended Synge's *Playboy of the Western World* on opening night although she did not care for the play), G. also evidenced political and national concerns in plays such as *Caravans, The Wren Boys,* and *The Deliverer*. After her son's death in World War I, she turned her talents to children's plays, fairy plays, and a biography of her nephew, Hugh Lane. Her passion play, *The Story Brought by Bridget,* was written following the Irish Civil War and treats of the futility of hatred as a motivating force. Her memoirs of the Abbey's history, *Our Irish Theatre,* still serve as an important historical source. G.'s last act at the Abbey was her direction of Sean O'Casey's *The Plough and the Stars.* In her last years, G. lived on at her estate at Coole Park. She died in 1932.

Long recognized for the help she offered other writers, G. is now being appreciated for her own creative works. In her plays, folklore collections, biographies, memoirs, essays, and translations and in her efforts to establish the Abbey as a successful theatre, she was, she said, "a beggar at many doors." But her work left some of the finest one-act plays in English, provided materials other writers drew upon for their works, and introduced many English readers to the Irish sagas and native literature. Her "series of enthusiasms," only begun when she was forty-four, has left the Irish nation and all of us with a rich and varied literary heritage.

WORKS: *Arabi and His Household* (1882). *Cuchulain of Murithemne* (1902). *Poets and Dreamers* (1903). *Gods and Fighting Men* (1904). *Kincora* (1905). *A Book of Saints and Wonders* (1906). *The Kiltartan History Book* (1909). *The Kiltartan Wonder Book* (1910). *The Kiltartan Molière* (1910). *Our Irish Theatre* (1913). *The Kiltartan Poetry Book* (1918). *Visions and Beliefs in the West of Ireland* (1920). *Hugh Lane's Life and Achievement* (1921). *Coole* (1931). *Collected Plays 1: The Comedies* (1970). *Collected Plays 2: The Tragedies and Tragic-Comedies* (1970). *Collected Plays 3: The Wonder and Supernatural Plays* (1970). *Collected Plays 4: The Translations and Adaptations* (1970). *Seventy Years: Being the Autobiography of Lady Gregory* (1976). *Journals,* ed. D.J. Murphy (Vol. I, 1978; Vol. II, 1987).

BIBLIOGRAPHY: Adams, H. *Lady Gregory* (1973). Adams, H. *PMLA* (1957). Ayling, R. *Shaw Review* (September 1961). Bowen, A. *Southern Folklore Quarterly* (1939). Clement, W.M. *Colby Literary Quarterly* (March 1978). Howarth, H. *The Irish Writers, 1880-1940* (1959). Kopper, E.A. *Lady Isabella Persse Gregory* (1970). McHugh, R. *James Joyce Quarterly* (1970). Ramaswamy, S. *Indian Journal of English Studies* (1969). Mikhail, E.H. *Lady Gregory: An Annotated Bibliography of Criticism* (1982). Saddlemyer, A. *In Defence of Lady Gregory, Playwright* (1966). Saddlemyer, A. and C. Smythe, Ed. *Lady Gregory: Fifty Years After* (1987). Stevenson, M.L. *Journal of the Rutgers University Library* (1978). Weygandt, C. *Irish Plays and Playwrights* (1913).

For articles in reference works, see: *DIL. Dictionary of Irish Writers,* ed. C. Brian (1967). *Longman. MBL. MWD.*

Other references: *Birmingham Post* (16 May 1970). *Hibernia* (26 June 1970). *Modern Drama* (1965). *SR* (10 December 1967).

Glenda Wall

Elizabeth Griffith

BORN: 11 October 1727, Dublin.
DIED: 5 January 1793, Millicent County, Kildare, Ireland.
DAUGHTER OF: Thomas and Jane Foxcroft Griffith.
MARRIED: Richard Griffith, 1752.
WROTE UNDER: "Frances," Mrs. Elizabeth Griffith, Mrs. Elizabeth Griffiths.

A playwright and novelist, G. wrote primarily for the support of her family. She married Richard Griffith secretly in 1752 after guiding him toward marrige for six years. Over the next three years, G. appeared on the stage in Dublin and London. She began to write plays in 1765 and in 1769 succeeded in attracting the attention of David Garrick, who successfully produced two of her plays and to whom she dedicated her longest work, *The Morality of Shakespeare's Drama Illustrated* (1775). From 1764 G. lived in London while her husband spent much time in Ireland. After many years of marriage, her husband seduced a wealthy young woman with whom he lived until his death. G. died in 1793 at her son Richard's house, in County Kildare.

G.'s original plays and translations enjoyed success in her day, but none have been produced subsequently. Although they lack originality, all show her characteristic delicacy of feeling. She believed that gentleness and magnanimity are the best equipment for life and that marriage should be founded upon love and esteem. *The School for Rakes* (1769; translated, at Garrick's suggestion, from Beaumarchais's *Eugénie*) shows G.'s characteristic delicacy. Although the heroine has already been tricked into a sham marriage by the hero, the couple refuse a forced marriage because they love each other. In *The Platonic Wife* (1765; adapted from Marmontel's *L'Heureux Divorce*), the falsely suspected wife is virtuous; in *A Wife in the Right* (1772), the husband proves he loves only his wife; in *The Times* (1780; adapted from Goldoni's *Bourru Bienfaisant*), the wife's extravagance is cured when she realizes the damage it has done her husband.

G.'s first publication was *A Series of Genuine Letters Between Henry and Frances* (1757), a selection from her correspondence with her husband before their marriage. Though overly sentimental, it is perceptive on books, men, and manners. Encouraged by the moderate success of this production, the couple published later correspondence in four more volumes. G. also wrote three epistolary novels, each of which links several slightly related stories to a main plot. In *The*

Delicate Distress (1769), a companion novel to her husband's *The Gordian Knot* (1770), the husband's former mistress almost recaptures him, but his wife's selfless nursing of him through a fever, even after she knows of his divided affections, makes him realize his love for her. *The History of Lady Barton* (1771) and *The Story of Lady Juliana Harley* (1776), less well constructed and more melodramatic, revolve around forced and loveless marriages. G. also edited *A Collection of Novels* (1777), by Aphra Behn, Eliza Haywood, and Penelope Aubin, and *Novellettes* (1780), which included thirteen of her stories. Her last work, *Essays Addressed to Young Married Women* (1782), contains thoughts on the education of the young, affection for a husband, and the wife's necessary fortitude, charity, economy, and accomplishments.

Although marred by excessive sensibility as well as loose structure and derivative plotting, G.'s work offers a broad and generous moral perspective, common sense, and distinctive and humorously drawn characters.

WORKS: *A Series of Genuine Letters Between Henry and Frances* (1757). (trans.) *Memoirs of Ninon de l'Enclos* (1761). *Amana: A Dramatic Poem* (1764). *The Platonic Wife* (1765; adapted from Marmontel). *The Double Mistake* (1766). (trans.) *The School for Rakes*, by Beaumarchais (1769). *The Delicate Distress* (1769). (trans.) *Memoirs, Anecdotes, and Characters of the Court of Louis XIV* (1770). (trans.) *The Shipwreck and Adventures of Monsieur Pierre Viaud* (1771). *The History of Lady Barton* (1771). *A Wife in the Right* (1772). (trans.) *The Fatal Effects of Inconstancy: or, Letters of the Marchioness de Syrce, the Count of Mirbeele* [sic; Mirbelle] *and Others*, by C.J. Dorat (1774). *The Morality of Shakespeare's Drama Illustrated* (1775). *The Story of Lady Juliana Harley* (1776). (trans.) *The Barber of Seville* by Beaumarchais (1776). (trans.) *A Letter from Monsieur Desenfans to Mrs. Montague* (1777). (trans.) *The Princess of Cleves* by Segrais [Mme. de La Fayette] (1777). (trans.) *Zayde, A Spanish History* by Segrais [Mme. de la Fayette] (1780). *The Times* (1780; adapted from Goldoni). *Essays Addressed to Young Married Women* (1782).

BIBLIOGRAPHY: MacCarthy, B.G. *Later Women Novelists, 1744-1818* (1947). Whitmore, C.H. *Women's Work in English Fiction* (1910).
For articles in reference works, see: Chalmers. *DNB.* Todd.

Kate Browder Heberlein

Elizabeth Grymeston or Grimston

BORN: Before 1563, North Erpingham, Norfolk.
DIED: 1603, London (?).
DAUGHTER OF: Martin and Margaret Flint Bernye.
MARRIED: Christopher Grymeston, 1584.

A recusant Catholic, G. published only one work, *Miscelanea. Meditations. Memoratives.* A series of short essays interspersed with poetry, *Miscelanea. Meditations. Memoratives.* follows the Boethian tradition of theodicy, borrowing directly from the work of another Norfolk recusant, Robert Southwell (1561–95), as well as from *Englands Parnassus* (1600).

Published posthumously, the work had four editions between 1604 and 1618 [?]; the later editions have six additional chapters of meditation and prayer on such subjects as the cross, murder, and the role of judges. The earlier editions, which may come closer to the author's intention in their structure, begin with a fascinating letter from G. to her son, Bernays Grymeston, that explains the circumstances of composition and gives personal advice. This opening letter is followed by chapters that consider death, affliction, and God's role in human affairs; other chapters are interior monologues by such characters as Dives and Heraclitus. Chapters XI–XIII offer religious poetry by others with G.'s meditations on their verse. The final chapter is a collection of moral maxims.

The literary quality of G.'s work does not lie in its originality for, like others who wrote meditative literature, she borrows extensively, practicing the tradition of *imitatio*. Instead its strength is the vivid development she gave to the ideas of others and the emotional intensity of her style. The work moves us because of G.'s situation. Her life was difficult; not only was she persecuted as a recusant, she also watched eight of her nine children die and fought bitterly with her mother. Writing to Bernays from her sickbed, G. knew she was dying and believed that her mother's "undeserved wrath so virulent" had fatally aggravated the consumption that was killing her. Further, she thought that her mother had tried repeatedly to murder her husband, Christopher.

Despite her troubles, G. writes with good sense, affection, and humor, urging Bernays to marry wisely and live temperately. In the essays that follow the letter, she turns to her own fate and that of all humans, regarding pain and affliction without discouragement and death without fear. Given her suffering and the nearness of her end, her sincerity and self-possession work with her rhetorical skills to make *Miscelanea. Meditations. Memoratives.* a fine example of meditation literature.

WORKS: Miscelanea. Meditations. Memoratives. (1604, STC 12407).

BIBLIOGRAPHY: Fletcher, B.Y., and C.W. Sizemore. *The Library Chronicle*, (1981). Hughey, R., and P. Hereford. *The Library* (1934–1935). Mahl, R., and H. Koon. *The Female Spectator* (1977).

For articles in reference works, see: *DNB*.

Frances Teague

Charlotte E.B. Guest

BORN: 19 May 1812, Uffington House, Lincolnshire.
DIED: 15 January 1895, Canford Manor, Dorset.
DAUGHTER OF: Albemarle Bertie, ninth Earl of Lindsey, and Charlotte Layard.
MARRIED: Sir Josiah John Guest, 1833; Charles Schreiber, 1855.
WROTE UNDER: Lady Charlotte Guest, Lady Charlotte E. Guest, Lady Charlotte Elizabeth (Bertie) Guest, Lady Charlotte Schreiber, Lady Charlotte Elizabeth Schreiber.

G. is usually remembered for her scholarly, annotated translation of *Mabinogion* into English. An avid collector of china, fans, and playing cards, she made extensive contributions from her collections to the holdings of the Victoria and Albert museum and to the British Museum. She produced several catalogues containing detailed descriptions of her collections. G. also kept a journal from 1822 until 1891 in which she recorded events in her daily life along with her impressions of contemporary political, social, and economic issues.

G. recorded that her childhood was an unhappy one due to the death of her father in 1818 and her mother's remarriage in 1821 to her tyrannical cousin, the Reverend Peter William Pegus. It was only after G.'s marriage in 1833 to the wealthy ironmaster Josiah Guest, by whom she had ten children, that she had the freedom to indulge her varied interests. She studied ancient and modern European and Middle Eastern languages, taking an especial interest in Welsh and translating the *Ma-*

binogion from 1838 until 1846. Her three-volume edition, with notes and the original Welsh text, was published in 1849, and a second abridged edition, which omitted the Welsh text, appeared in 1877. In 1881 she published *The Boy's Mabinogion; Being the Earliest Welsh Tales of King Arthur in the Famous Red Book of Hergest.*

Besides languages, G. studied music and art. She was an accomplished pianist, harpist, and etcher on copper plate. Her interest in Welsh culture led her to work on various projects for the improvement of the living conditions of Welsh workers, including the founding of several schools for the poor. She also took an active part in the administrative affairs of her husband's ironworks at Dowlais in Wales, acting as his private secretary and completely taking over the management of the works upon his death in 1852.

In 1855 she married Charles Schreiber, a member of Parliament for Cheltenham and Poole. It was during her second marriage that she became less actively involved with business and reform activities although she gave much support to the Turkish Compassionate Fund between 1877 and 1880, the period in which her son-in-law, Sir Austen Henry Layard, was ambassador to Turkey. Her chief interest throughout the second half of her life was her art collections, and it was in 1865 that she began to collect china, frequently traveling throughout Europe in search of rare pieces. She later developed an interest in collecting playing cards and fans.

It was upon the death of her husband in 1884 that she presented her collection of English china and Battersea enamels in his memory to the South Kensington Museum, which is now the Victoria and Albert Museum. She catalogued the two thousand pieces in the Schreiber collection in the same year, and her catalogue was printed in 1885. She also published two folio volumes entitled *Fans and Fan Leaves collected and described by Lady Charlotte Schreiber.* The first volume was published in 1888, contains 161 illustrations, and describes her English fans. The second volume appeared in 1890, contains 153 illustrations, and describes her foreign fans. She presented her collection to the British Museum in 1891, the same year she was presented with the freedom of the Fanmakers' Company. A catalogue of her fan collection was printed in 1893. In 1892 she published the first volume of her *Playing Cards of Various Ages and Countries,* the same year in which she received the honorary freedom of the Company of Makers of Playing Cards. Her first volume presents English, Scottish, Dutch, and Flemish cards; her second volume (1893), French and German cards; her third volume (1895), Swiss and Swedish cards. She grew blind during her work on the volumes of fans and playing cards and died on 15 January 1895, leaving to the British Museum those cards

in her collection for which the museum did not already have specimens.

Lady Charlotte Schreiber's Journals: Confidences of a Collector of Ceramics & Antiques Throughout Britain, France, Holland, Belgium, Spain, Portugal, Turkey, Austria & Germany from the Year 1869 to 1885, was edited by her son, Montague J. Guest, and published in 1911 in two volumes that contain over one hundred illustrative plates of objects from her collections. *Lady Charlotte Guest: Extracts from Her Journal, 1833-1852* and *Lady Charlotte Schreiber: Extracts from Her Journal 1853-1891* were published in 1950 and 1952, respectively, by the Earl of Bessborough. Together, her published entries form a valuable picture of life in Victorian England, covering everything from workers' strikes to political economy to Whig controversies to society dinner parties to social mores. G.'s style is often florid and sentimental, as was typical of her age. The entry she made on the day of her wedding to Josiah Guest begins, "A Journal! Again dare I commence a journal, and with what hope of continuing it?" Yet the incidents she recorded reveal an energetic personality consisting of equal parts romantic emotionalism and hard-headed business practicality. Upon concluding business affairs left unresolved by the death of her first husband, she wrote that she clasped his marble bust for some minutes and kissed its cold lips. A few months later she quelled a pending workers' strike at Dowlais.

It is not for her political or business activities that G. is remembered, however, or for her immense journal, but for her work as a translator and collector. Although inaccuracies have been pointed out in her translation, such as her incorrect use of *mabinogion* as the plural of *mabinogi,* and her incorrect application of the term to the entire contents of the Red Book of Hergest, contemporary scholars still refer to her work. Her collections are still being held in the Victoria and Albert Museum and in the British Museum.

WORKS: *The Mabinogion: From the Llyfr Coch o Hergest, and Other Ancient Welsh Manuscripts, with an English Translation and Notes, by Lady Charlotte E. Guest* (1849). *The Boy's Mabinogion: Being the Earliest Welsh Tales of King Arthur in the Famous Red Book of Hergest* (1881). *Catalogue of English Porcelain, Earthenware, Enamels, &c., Collected and Described by Charles Schreiber, Esq., M.P., and the Lady Charlotte Elizabeth Schreiber, and Presented to the South Kensington Museum in 1884* (1885). *Fans and Fan Leaves Collected and Described by Lady Charlotte Schreiber,* 2 vols. (1888–90). *Playing Cards of Various Ages and Countries, Selected from the Collection of Lady Charlotte Schreiber,* 3 vols. (1892–95). *Lady Charlotte Schreib-*

er's Journals: Confidences of a Collector of Ceramics and Antiques Throughout Britain, France, Holland, Belgium, Spain, Portugal, Turkey, Austria & Germany from the Year 1869 to 1885, 2 vols., ed. M.J. Guest (1911). Lady Charlotte Guest: Extracts from Her Journal, 1833-1852, ed., the Earl of Bessborough (1950). Lady Charlotte Schreiber: Extracts from Her Journal, 1853-1891, ed., the Earl of Bessborough (1952).

BIBLIOGRAPHY: G. Jones and T. Jones, trans., The Mabinogion (1974).
For articles in reference works, see: DNB.

Karen Michalson

Susannah Minifie Gunning

BORN: 1740, Fairwater, Somersetshire.
DIED: 28 August 1800, London.
DAUGHTER OF: James Minifie; Mother's name not known.
MARRIED: Captain, later Lieutenant General, John Gunning, 1768.
WROTE UNDER: Miss Minifie, Mrs. Gunning; also wrote anonymously.

The "Miss Minifies" (Susannah and her sister, Margaret) were well-known as the authors of four novels, all published before G.'s marriage in 1768. With the initiative that marks G.'s entire career, she and her sister arranged for their first effort, The Histories of Lady Frances S—— and Lady Caroline S——, to be published by subscription in 1763. Subsequent collaborations, The Picture, Family Pictures, and The Cottage, were printed by commercial publishers. These early novels were poorly constructed, markedly sentimental and conventional in plot. G. published her first independent work, Barford Abbey (1768), the year of her marriage to Captain John Gunning, and its improvement over the earlier works may derive from autobiographic content.

It is tempting to compare Miss Warley's marriage to Lord Darcey in Barford Abbey with G.'s marriage to the son of a viscount's daughter. The epistolary story begins when Miss Warley's "mother" dies, leaving her the ward of Lady Mary, whose directions she receives from a German "spaw." During a visit to Lord and Lady Powis, the heroine attracts the attentions of their ward, whom Lord Powis is determined to marry prudently. The opposition between love and patrilineal prudence is resolved when Lord Powis's estranged son returns; the father/guardian blesses both the Lord Darcey–Miss Warley match and his son's clandestine marriage. But before the denouement can be settled, a set of contradictions must be resolved. Miss Warley, still in doubt about Lord Darcey's intentions, leaves to meet Lady Mary in France and is thought to have been lost in a shipwreck. Meanwhile, a birth mystery unravels by which she is discovered to be Mr. and Mrs. Powis's daughter, heiress to Lord and Lady Powis.

Miss Warley found safe and restored to her family, the novel concludes in marriage.

After the publication of The Cottage (1769), The Hermit (1770), and a second edition of Barford Abbey in 1771, it was 1783 before G. published her next novel, Coombe Wood. Read biographically, the novel bears evidence of G.'s own marital difficulties, for marriage, rather than an ideal denouement, has become a target for satire.

The scandal for which the Gunnings became famous began when their daughter Elizabeth was accused of forging a letter that forwarded her own schemes of marriage with her cousin, the Marquis of Lorne. G.'s response was a public letter to the Marquis' father denying her daughter's guilt. With societal approval, General Gunning ejected his wife and daughter, only to become embroiled in his own scandal when he was fined £5000 for "criminal conversation" with his tailor's wife. His response was also literary, his Apology (1792)—written in exile from Naples—boasting of many conquests. Five years later, however, a letter from Elizabeth prompted him to change his will, leaving his £8000 estate to her and her mother.

For the next several years, G. turned these family details to good use in her fiction. The novels Anecdotes of the Delborough Family (1792) and Memoirs of Mary (1793) and the poem Virginius and Virginia (1792) are particularly susceptible of biographic interpretation. Memoirs of Mary, probably the best of G.'s novels, had achieved a third edition by 1794.

Much like Fanny Burney's Evelina, Memoirs of Mary begins with a history of the heroine's early life as her grandmother's ward on a country estate. An interpolated tale explains her parents' courtship and death; after a secret marriage, Mary's father served briefly with a regiment in America. Mary's social life begins when she is sent to live with the Duke and the Duchess of Cleveland. A cousin who envies her inheritance connives against Mary's impending marriage with Henry Lexington, nephew and heir of the Duke of Cleveland. Eventually, the plot resolves in Mary's favor, but not before G. has exposed the dissipations of fashionable life.

The novel combines biographical allusions and elements of gothic. G.'s canvas foregrounds the courtship story, it is true, yet the attendant family squabbles and plottings form a much broader backdrop than the typical woman's novel of the period. For analogues, one must look back to Richardson or forward to Edgeworth and Austen. Another stroke of originality is Mary's suitor, who not only is developed more fully than the usual ancillary hero but is allowed to be witty. *Memoirs of Mary*, a cleverly written epistolary novel, which relieves the stasis of letters with idiomatic expressions and clever plotting, is one of the better minor novels of its period.

In 1796, G. turned away from the family scandal to write *Delves*, a picaresque tale set in Wales, and *The Forester*, an "adaptation" from the French. With *Love at First Sight* (1797) and *Fashionable Involvements* (1800), G. returned to the novel, but these late efforts were less successful, hackneyed tales of manners. At her death in 1800, G. left unfinished *The Heir Apparent* (1802), which her daughter Elizabeth (later Plunkett) revised, augmented, and published.

WORKS: *The Histories of Lady Frances S——— and Lady Caroline S———* (1763). *Family Pictures* (1764). *The Picture* (1766). *Barford Abbey* (1768). *The Cottage* (1769). *The Hermit* (1770). *Coombe Wood* (1783). *A Letter from Mrs. Gunning, addressed to . . . the Duke of Argyll* (1791). *Anecdotes of the Delborough Family* (1792). *Virginius and Virginia* (1792). *Memoirs of Mary* (1793). *Delves* (1796). *The Foresters* (1796). *Love at First Sight* (1797). *Fashionable Involvements* (1800). *The Heir Apparent* (1892).

BIBLIOGRAPHY: Todd, J. *SVEC* (1983). For articles in reference works, see: Todd.

Catherine S. Green

Anne Murray Halkett

BORN: 4 January 1622, London.
DIED: 22 April 1699, probably in Scotland.
DAUGHTER OF: Thomas Murray and Jane Drummond.
MARRIED: Sir John Halkett, 2 March 1656.
WROTE UNDER: Anne Lady Halkett, Lady Halkett.

A Royalist and a writer on religious subjects, H. left more than twenty volumes of manuscripts at her death. In 1701, a volume of her religious meditations was published along with her autobiography that she had written a quarter of a century earlier.

H. came by her Royalist enthusiasms naturally. Her father, the Earl of Tullibardin, had been appointed by James I to be preceptor to his son, Charles I. Until his death in 1625 when H. was three years old, her father was provost of Eton College. Her mother, who was related to the noble family of Perth, was governess to the Duke of Gloucester and to Princess Elizabeth, the children of Charles I. Both H. and her sister Jane were educated by their mother, who, as H. writes, "paid masters for teaching my sister and me to write, speak French, play on the lute and virginals, and dance, and kept a gentlewoman to teach us all kinds of needlework." In her autobiography, H. notes that her mother oversaw their religious training: they read the Bible and attended "divine service at five o'clock in the morning in summer and six o'clock in the winter" (p. 3). In keeping with the noblewoman's lot, H. studied physic and surgery to help the poor. Her success at treating the sick was legendary. She drew patients not only from England but from the continent as well.

In 1644, when she was twenty-two, H. quarrelled with her mother who discouraged a match with Thomas Howard, the eldest son of Edward, beause H. was without a fortune. Reluctantly submitting to her mother's wishes that she never see Howard again, H. insisted she would marry no one else. In a way she kept her promise: when she said goodby to Howard who was sent off to relatives in France, she wore a blindfold. So distressed was she that she asked her cousin who was a consul in Holland whether she could enter a Protestant nunnery there. The cousin gave his answer to H.'s mother, who was again angry with her daughter. H. explains: "since I found nothing would please her that I could do, I resolved to go where I could most please myself, which was in a solitary retired life." That same year, Howard not only privately married Lady Elizabeth Mordaunt, a much richer woman, substantiating the expectations of the age, but he also publicly humiliated H. She writes: "Is this the man for whom I have suffered so much?" While her mother laughed at her despair, H. was sad and indignant. Looking back on those events, H. writes in her memoir that Howard's wife "miscarried several children before she brought one to the full term, and that one died presently after it was born; which may be a lesson to teach people to govern their wishes."

In 1647, during the Civil War, H. met Joseph Bampfield who enchanted and influenced her for the next nine years. In a dramatic moment, H. had women's clothing made to fit the fourteen-year-old Duke of York for the boy's escape to the continent. H. met the future king at the water's edge and helped him dress. She also provided him with some food and cake. Later, Bampfield enlisted her help as a courier to carry his letters to the king. Their dangerous activities united them so that Bampfield's proposal of marriage was not a surprise. His duplicity was: when he proposed he explained that his wife was dead. Not until 1649 did she learn the truth—that his wife was alive. It was about that time, too, that she learned that Bampfield had been arrested. Sickened almost to death by the news of Bampfield's wife and his arrest, H. did not recover until she heard of his escape.

In 1650, she travelled to Scotland to recover a part of her inheritance. Reaching Edinburgh on 6 June, she found that Bampfield was already there. About that time she met Charles II, encountered wounded soldiers after the battle of Dunbar, and spent a few days at Kinross attending them. At Perth, the king thanked her and gave her £50. For the next two years she remained in Aberdeenshire where she treated the sick and the wounded who came to her.

In 1652 H. returned to Edinburgh where she tried to recover the portion left to her by her mother. She also assisted Bampfield in Royalist plots until he left for the north. News reached H. that Bampfield's wife was in London. By 1653, H. met Sir James Halkett who convinced her to take charge of his two daughters and to promise to marry him. In 1654 when H. visited London, Bampfield called on her and asked if she were married to Halkett. With extraordinary efforts to be honest, "She said, 'I am' (out loud), and secretly said 'not.'"

Married on 2 March 1656, at her sister's house in Charleton, H. and her husband returned to Scotland. It was there that H. wrote her first tract. She was understandably fearful of childbirth; she was, after all, thirty-four years old. H. wrote "The Mother's Will to her Unborn Child," while she was pregnant with her first child. H. wrote a tract during each of her subsequent pregnancies providing a Mother's Instructions to be used in the chance that she died.

After the Restoration, H. received £500 in recognition of the £412 annual interest that she had lost after the death of Charles I. In addition she received £50 from the Duke of York. In 1676 her husband died, leaving her without enough income to provide for their children. She began to teach upper-class children in her home, and in 1685 James II provided her with £100 annually because of her help to him during the Civil War.

Her devotional writing is tied closely to events in her life. She lost three or four children in their infancy, and her prayers and meditations reflect her grief and her loss. Her twenty volumes contain material that is of interest to the historian as well as the biographer of women of the seventeenth century. Her work is personal and vivid. According to James Sutherland, H. could have provided Samuel Richardson "with all the material he could possibly need for another novel; for Lady Halkett, intelligent, lively, resourceful, far from indifferent to moral and religious scruples, and yet placed in an equivocal position by her love for an adventurer, was the sort of heroine Richardson could not have failed to appreciate. To her own friends, Colonel Bampfield may never have appeared to be anything better than a Lovelace, but she herself continued to believe in his integrity. . . ." Sutherland finds that her work is not only of historical interest but of considerable human value.

WORKS: Bound in one volume entitled by the binder as *Lady Halket* are the following works, all of which are dated 1701: "Instructions for Youth . . . For the use of those young noblemen and gentlemen whose education was committed to her care" (18 pp.), "Meditations and Prayers, upon the first; with observations on each day's creation: and considerations of the seven capital vices, to be oppos'd: and their opposit vertues to be studied and practised" (50 pp.). "Meditations on the twentieth and fifth Psalm. By one who had found how beneficial it was to have the soul continually placed upon divine objects, and therefore made choice of this Psalm to raise her contemplations" (48 pp.). "The Life of the Lady Halkett." *Meditations upon the seven gifts of the Holy Spirit mentioned Isaiah XI. 2, 3, as also meditations upon Jabez, his request, I Chron. IV, 10, together with sacramental meditations on the Lord's Supper and prayers, pious reflections and Observations* (1702). *Meditations on the 25th Psalm . . . wrote in the year 1651-2. By a Lady* (rpt. 1788, 1806; 1771). *The Autobiography of Anne Lady Halkett.* ed. by J.G. Nichols (1875 by Camden Society, N.S. XIII). *The Memoirs of Anne, Lady Halkett, and Ann, Lady Fanshawe,* ed. with an intro. by John Loftis (1979 rpt. of Nichols' 1875 ed.).

BIBLIOGRAPHY: Bottrall, M.S. *Personal Records: A Gallery of Self-Portraits* (1961). Cumming, L.M. *Blackwood's Magazine* (November 1924). Fraser, A. *The Weaker Vessel* (1984). Reynolds, M. *The Learned Lady in England, 1650-1760* (1920). Stenton, D.M. *English Women in History* (1957). Sutherland, J. *English Literature of the Late Seventeenth Century* (1969).

For articles in reference works, see: *CBEL. DNB.* Todd.

Sophia B. Blaydes

Anna Maria Fielding Hall

BORN: 6 January 1800, Dublin.
DIED: 30 January 1881, Devon Lodge, East Moulsey.
DAUGHTER OF: Sarah Elizabeth Fielding.
MARRIED: Samuel Carter Hall, 1824.
WROTE UNDER: Anonymous, Mrs. S.C. Hall.

H. is known primarily for Irish sketches and novels; she also wrote short stories, plays, and children's books. She was born in Ireland, residing for most of her first fifteen years in the house of her step-grandfather, George Carr of Craigie, Wexford, her mother being left a widow. In 1815, Anna Marie and her mother came to England, becoming permanent residents. At twenty-four she married Samuel Carter Hall. She published her first work, "Master Ben," five years later and continued to write until her death.

"Master Ben" was the first of a series of Irish sketches based on the author's recollection of areas and persons familiar during her early years in Ireland, later offered in one volume, Sketches of Irish Character. Although H. presented the Irish milieu, she was never popular in Ireland, for she did not identify solely with either of the political factions, the Orangemen or the Roman Catholics, impartially commending and criticizing both.

She devoted much time in beneficent efforts, being instrumental in establishing the Hospital for Consumption at Brompton, the Governesses' Institute, the Home for Decayed Gentlewomen, and the Nightingale Fund. She worked for women's rights, the friendless, the fallen, and for temperance causes. She was known for her friendliness toward street musicians. Ironically, although she remained a dedicated and devout Christian throughout her entire life, she embraced spiritualism with equal fervor. Marian, oftren considered the best of her nine novels, displays a knowledge of Irish character comparable in quality to the writings of Maria Edgeworth, her contemporary; Midsummer Eve, A Fairy Tale of Love has been touted as her most beautiful book.

Several of H.'s tales were dramatized rather successfully: "The Groves of Blarney," first published as one of a series under the title Lights and Shadows of Irish Life in New Monthly Magazine (edited by H.'s husband), ran for a whole season at the Adelphi in 1938 (adapted especially for Tyrone Power). Other productions were The French Refugee, running for ninety nights at the St. James's Theatre in 1836, and Mabel's Curse, featuring John Pritt Harley (same theatre). The sole copy of one of her dramas, Who's Who, was lost at sea in 1841.

H.'s works contain fine rural descriptions; they are delicately humorous and have a high moral tone. She often contributed to the publications her husband edited and was herself an editor of the St. James Magazine from 1862–63.

WORKS: Sketches of Irish Character (1829, second series, 1831). The Juvenile Forget-me-Not (edited by Mrs. S.C. Hall, 1829 and 1862). Chronicles of a School-Room (1830). The Buccaneer (1832). The Outlaw (1835). Tales of a Woman's Trials (1835). Uncle Horace (1837). St. Pierre, the Refugee (1837). Lights and Shadows of Irish Life (1838). The Book of Royalty: Characteristics of British Palaces (1839). Tales of the Irish Peasantry (1840). Marian, or a Young Maid's Fortunes (1840). The Hartopp Jubilee (1840). (with S.C. Hall) A Week at Killarney (1843). (with S.C. Hall) Ireland, Its Scenery, Characters &c (1841–43). The White Boy, a Novel (1845). (with J. Foster) Stories and Studies from the Chronicles and History of England (1847). Midsummer Eve, A Fairy Tale of Love (1848). The Swan's Egg, a Tale (1850). Pilgrimages to English Shrines (1850). Stories of The Governess (1852). (with S.C. Hall) Handbooks for Ireland (1853). The Worn Thimble, a Story (1853). The Drunkard's Bible (1854). The Two Friends (1856). A Woman's Story (1857). The Lucky Penny and Other Tales (1857). Finden's Gallery of Modern Art, with Tales by Mrs. S.C. Hall (1859). (with S.C. Hall) The Book of the Thames (1854). The Boy's Birthday Book (1859). Daddy Dacre's School (1859). (with S.C. Hall) Tenby (1860). (with S.C. Hall) The Book of South Wales (1861). Can Wrong be Right? A Tale (1862). The Village Garland: Tales and Sketches (1863). Nelly Nowlan and Other Stories (1865). The Playfellow and Other Stories (1866). The Way of the World and Other Stories (1866). The Prince of the Fairy Family (1867). Alice Stanley and Other Stories (1868). Animal Sagacity (1868). The Fight of Faith, A Story (1869). Digging a Grave with a Wineglass (1871). Chronicles of a Cosy Nook (1875). Boons and Blessings: Stories of Temperance (1875). Annie Leslie and Other Stories (1877). (with S.C. Hall) A Companion to Killarney (1878). Grandmother's Pockets (1880).

BIBLIOGRAPHY: Colburn's New Monthly Magazine (August 1838). Dublin University Magazine (August 1840). Fraser's Magazine (June 1836). Hale's Woman's Record (1855). Hall, S.C. A Book of Memories (1876). Hall, S.C. Retrospect of a Long Life (1883). Howitt, M.B., An Autobiography (1889). Illustrated London News (12 February 1881). Illustrated News of the World (1861). Thomas, J. Universal Pronouncing Dictionary of Biography and Mythology (1901). Times (1 February 1881).

For articles in reference works, see BA19C.

Phyllis J. Scherle

Radclyffe Hall

BORN: 1886, Bournemouth, Hampshire.
DIED: 11 October 1943, London.
DAUGHTER OF: Radclyffe and Mary Jane Radclyffe-Hall.

H., christened Marguerite Hall, was the daughter of Radclyffe Radclyffe-Hall, whom she barely knew but who left her a large inheritance when she turned seventeen. H. was raised by her flighty mother and a moody Italian stepfather, parents who often subjected her to emotional and even physical abuse.

H. started her writing career at the age of three when she wrote her first poem. Between 1906 and 1915, she published five volumes of poems. Her work improved in the later volumes, though becoming increasingly personal, and the poems' lyrical qualities enabled several composers, including Coleridge Taylor, Liza Lehmann, Woodesforde Finden, Mrs. George Batten, and Coningsby Clarke, to set them to music.

Her first novel, *The Forge*, was a brief social comedy published in 1924, followed by *The Unlit Lamp* later the same year. This early work hints at incest and the subject of lesbianism, which she returned to in *The Well of Loneliness*, but the treatment is so muted that the book attracted little public notice. Nevertheless, the writing is powerful in its bleakness. H. published *A Saturday Life*, a novel, in 1925, and another novel, *Adam's Breed*, the next year. Although *Adam's Breed* is overly sentimental, the protagonist, Gian-Luca, a headwaiter, again demonstrates a character struggling against conforming to society's demands. The story is presented with H.'s usual honesty and won several awards, including the American Eichelberger Humane Award.

In 1928 H. published her famous novel of "sexual inversion," *The Well of Loneliness*. The novel became a *cause célèbre* as people either defended or condemned the book, which was banned in England because, said the Magistrate, it portrayed "unnatural and depraved relationships." Whether the story of Stephen Gordon and her lover, Mary, is a good novel is another matter. Havelock Ellis claims it shows "poignant situations . . . set forth so vividly." Yet Leonard Woolf and Rebecca West, both of whom fought for its publication, consider the work flawed. Woolf states that the characters "appear to be the creation of the intellect, and for the reader they have no emotional context." West is even harsher in her remarks, saying it is "not a very good book . . . A novel which ends a chapter with the sentence 'And that night they were not divided' cannot redeem itself by having 'they' mean not what it usually does." West's complaint underlies the fact that despite its subject matter, the novel is still encased in Victorian trappings. However, regardless of its flaws, the work is important because, as Jane Rule says, it "remains *the* lesbian novel." H. later returned to the subject in her short story, "Miss Ogilvy Finds Herself."

H. was a devout Christian, although maintaining a strong interest in psychic research, and this became the topic of her next novel, *The Master of the House* (1932). Christophe Bénédit is the son of a carpenter, Jousé, has a mother named Marie, and has a cousin, Jan. The parallel to the Holy Family is obvious, and though some critics questioned the propriety of modernizing Christ's life, H. considered this to be her finest work.

In 1934 she published *Miss Ogilvy Finds Herself*, a collection of five stories. Her last novel, *The Sixth Beatitude*, was published in 1936. The protagonist, Hannah Bullen, a servant, is an unwed mother of two children by different fathers, who, nevertheless, is presented, as the title implies, as being pure of heart. The novel, like much of H.'s better fiction, is grim and unrelenting.

Before dying of cancer in 1943, H. spent her last thirty years living with her lover, Lady Una Troubridge, who called H. by the name John.

WORKS: *'Twixt Earth and Stars* (1906). *A Sheaf of Verses* (1908). *Poems of the Past and Present* (1910). *Songs of Three Counties, and Other Poems* (1913). *The Forgotten Island* (1915). *The Forge* (1924). *The Unlit Lamp* (1924). *A Saturday Life* (1925). *Adam's Breed* (1926). *The Well of Loneliness* (1928). *The Master of the House* (1932). *Miss Ogilvy Finds Herself* (1934). *The Sixth Beatitude* (1936).

BIBLIOGRAPHY: Baker, M. *Our Three Selves: The Life of Radclyffe Hall* (1985). Brittain, V. *Radclyffe Hall: A Case of Obscenity?* (1969). Dickson, L. *Radclyffe Hall at the Well of Loneliness: A Sophic Chronicle* (1975). Ellis, H. "Commentary." *The Well of Loneliness* (1928). Omrod, R. *Una Trowbridge: The Friend of Radclyffe Hall* (1985). Pritchett, V.S. *New Statesman* (15 December 1961). Radford, J. In *The Progress of Romance: The Politics of Popular Fiction*, ed. J. Radford (1986). Rule, J. *Lesbian Images* (1975). Troubridge, U. *The Life of Radclyffe Hall* (1961). West, R. *Ending in Earnest: A Literary Log* (1931). Woolf, L. *Nation* (August 4, 1928).

For articles in reference works, see: *CA. Longman. MBL. TCA. TCLC.*

Louis J. Parascandola

Elizabeth Hamilton

BORN: 25 July 1758, Belfast, Ireland.
DIED: 23 July 1816, Harrogate.
DAUGHTER OF: Charles and Katherine Mackay Hamilton.

H. was separated from her older sister, Katherine, and brother, Charles, when H.'s father died in 1759; their mother died in 1767. An active child and a voracious reader, H. was raised on a Stirlingshire farm by her paternal aunt, Mrs. Marshall. She was educated at a school for both boys and girls at Stirling and also received training in the usual "female accomplishments." In 1772, H. met her brother, and they began a correspondence which she termed "a second education." When Charles sailed for India, the Marshalls took up residence in Ingram's Crook, Scotland, where H. for some time led a very quiet life. She visited the Highlands, producing a journal which was published in a local magazine, and then began a historical novel on Arabella Stuart. In December 1785 she published an essay in The Lounger.

On Charles' return in 1786, H. assisted him with his translations, acquiring thereby an interest in and knowledge of Indian literature and customs, and they moved to London with their sister the same year, living there until Charles' death in 1792.

In 1796 H. published (under her own name) Hindoo Rajah, partly to honor her brother, who appears there as Captain Percy; she herself appears as Charlotte. This book, in the tradition of Goldsmith's Citizen of the World, traces the education of the Rajah Zaarmilla in English mores, which are contrasted, often unfavorably, with the noble customs of the Hindoos. There is some real wit here, especially in H.'s satire on modern philosophers ("men who, without much knowledge, either moral or natural, entertain a high idea of their own superiority from having the temerity to reject whatever has the sanction of experience and common sense").

In 1800, this time anonymously, H. returned to her attack on the Godwinian circle in the Memoirs of Modern Philosophers. The "editor" claims that the book's unknown (male) author had died unpublished and that "missing" early chapters had served to wrap fish. The "heroine," the ugly and foolish Bridgetina Botherim—a malicious portrait of Mary Hays, author of Emma Courtnay—is duped by the vicious Vallaton (an unattractive caricature of Rousseau), by Glib (another Godwinian portrait) and by others. Again H. scores brilliantly off her targets, using their own words in absurd contexts to render them ridiculous. (Curiously, H. does praise Wollstonecraft, only regretting the excess of her zeal.)

The novel begins lightly but hardens quickly into an unsatisfactory mix of acidic Juvenalian satire and highly sentimental tragedy, freighted with heavy moralizing; its "message" is that society's rules for women are essential protections rather than undesirable restraints. Perhaps H.'s severe attack of gout, which interrupted the composition of Memoirs, explains the work's disunity and shift in tone.

Residing at Bath for her health, H. found herself lionized for Memoirs. In the following years, despite periodic illness, she wrote a number of works on educational philosophy, proper conduct for women, and education of the poor. H. maintains that observation and experience are as vital to education as reading. In The Memoirs of Agrippina, H. tries to illustrate her educational principles through biography. Her final work, Hints, proposes a partial adoption of Pestalozzi's educational system. Robert Colby sees H.'s educational philosophy as consonant with Edmund's in Austen's Mansfield Park. Vineta Colby praises H.'s psychological insights, especially in Popular Essays, which emphasizes the goal of self-improvement through self-examination. "Without writing many novels herself," says Colby, "Mrs. Hamilton laid down the ideological principles of the evangelical–domestic novel."

H.'s active philanthropy included helping to establish a House of Industry in Edinburgh, where she lived for a time. There she wrote The Cottagers of Glenburnie, a comic novel designed to combat ignorance and laziness among her Scottish neighbors. This lively book, drawing on H.'s Stirling memories, won praise from Scott, among others, for its fine character sketches and dialectal humor. After various experiences, the narrator—the pious, generous, and garrulous Mrs. Mason—goes to live with the MacClartys of Glenburnie and tries to overcome their indolence and parental indulgence. Spurning her advice, the family is finally ruined, and Mrs. Mason establishes a school which successfully inculcates cleanliness, piety, and industry. The book is highly sentimental, moralizing, and didactic, and the reader must sympathize somewhat with the MacClartys' annoyance at Mrs. Mason's meddling. Still, it remains the most readable of H.'s works.

H. also wrote several poems (quoted in Benger's Memoirs) and a popular song, "My Ain Fireside." Her private journal and extensive correspondence are extracted in Benger. In 1812 H.'s failing health led her to return to England where she died in 1816.

WORKS: Translation of the Letters of a Hindoo Rajah (1796). Memoirs of Modern Philosophers

(1800). *Letters on the Elementary Principles of Education* (1801–1803). *Memoires of the Life of Agrippina, the Wife of Germanicus* (1804). *The Cottagers of Glenburnie* (1808). *Rules of the Annuity Fund for the Benefit of Governesses* (1808). *Letters Addressed to the Daughter of a Nobleman* (1806). *Exercises in Religious Knowledge* (1809). *Popular Essays Illustrative of Principles Connected with the Improvement of the Understanding, the Imagination and the Heart* (1813). *Hints Addressed to Patrons and Directors of Schools* (1815).

BIBLIOGRAPHY: Benger, E. *Memoirs of The Late Mrs. Elizabeth Hamilton* (1818).

For articles in reference works, see: *Allibone. BA19C. CBEL. CHEL. DNB.*

Other references: Baker, E. *The History of the English Novel* (1929, rpt.: 1967). Black, F. *The Epistolary Novel in the Late Eighteenth Century* (1940). Butler, M. *Jane Austen and the War of Ideas* (1975). Colby, R. *Fiction with a Purpose* (1967). Colby, V. *Yesterday's Woman* (1974). Elwood, Mrs. *Memoirs of the Literary Ladies of England* (1843); *Stirling Natural History and Archaeological Society* (1932). Keddie, H. (pseud. Sarah Tytler), and J.L. Watson. *Songstresses of Scotland* (1871). MacCarthy, B. *The Later Women Novelists* (1947). Mews, H. *Frail Vessels* (1969). Moler, K. *Jane Austen's Art of Allusion* (1968). Renwick, W. *English Literature, 1789-1815* (1963). Tompkins, J. *The Popular Novel in England.* Wilson, M. *Jane Austen and Some Contemporaries* (1938).

Kathleen L. Fowler

Mary Ann Hanway

BORN: Mary Ann Vergy (?) between 1756–1770 (?).
DIED: Between 1823–1825 (?), London (?).
MARRIED: Hanway Hanway, 26 May 1788, St. Marylebone, St. Mary's Parish, Middlesex (?).

Of H.'s life virtually nothing is known, and the critics have entirely neglected her. A contemporary review indicates that her husband (unnamed) is nephew to Jonas Hanway, the eighteenth-century English philanthropist (Hanway Hanway, né Balack, is actually his great-nephew and heir). An inscription in one of her novels mentions a niece named Mrs. Hitchcock. From the prefaces to her novels, we know that H. lived in Manchester in 1800 and in Blackheath (now part of London) in 1808 and 1814. H. wrote four novels: *Ellinor* (1798), *Andrew Stuart* (1800), *Falconbridge Abbey* (1809), and *Christabelle* (1814). One other work, the anonymous *Journey to the Highlands of Scotland* (1776?), has been attributed to her but probably erroneously.

H.'s novels, while heavily didactic, are closer to the sentimental/romantic novel than to the usual style of contemporary moral novelists. *Ellinor*, especially in the early volumes, is a novel of manners distinctly in the Fanny Burney style although it becomes increasingly romantic, improbable, and sentimental as it progresses. Like *Evelina*, *Ellinor* relates the story of a young woman in quest of her identity (and, incidentally, her ideal mate). It is frequently witty and generally well written, if overly long, and offers a wonderful character study in Lady John Dareall, an outspoken feminist who protects Ellinor.

The next novel, *Andrew Stuart*, is a grabbag of stories (not all successfully integrated) written in a highly florid and sentimental style. *The Antijacobin Review* could not resist parodying its pretentious vocabulary: "The wrongs of the gentle-hearted Isabella, *incarcerated* in a *castellated* mansion, *intenerated* not our rigid feelings; nor did the vulgarity of the emaciated Orpington's *cher ami* excite our souls to laughter." However, even in this book, H. occasionally exhibits a pointed and skillful satiric style. Speaking of the progress of an idle young nobleman, for example, H. reports that from "being an idle dissipated lounger [he] was . . . become an abandoned libertine, a professed *roué*, a gamester at the Cocoa-Tree, a knowing one on the turf, and frequently an umpire at boxing matches." The book recounts the adventures of Stuart, the Northern Wanderer, who, having run off to sea as a child, later rescues Isabella Newton from her tormenting sister. On the morning of their wedding day, Isabella is abducted by Lord Lorimore, and Stuart is shipped off in chains to India. Stuart wins his freedom there and falls in love with his cousin; Isabella is rescued and falls in love with her new saviour. The novel ends with weddings all around. This saccharine close is relieved in part by the brilliantly apposite fate of the vicious Lord Lorimore, who is forced to marry his now-despised and discarded mistress.

Falconbridge Abbey represents a new level of achievement for H. Although the longest of all her works, the novel is relatively tight, often clever, and largely effective. It is a study of the havoc wrought among the noble Falconbridges, Berenvilles, and Glenallens by two unscrupulous Elizas (mother and daughter). These women, especially the younger, are splendidly selfish, ruthless, and ambitious. They anticipate Becky Sharp in their Machiavellian talent for manipulating words, people, and situations. A number of other convincing characters and a greatly improved sophistication in style and figuration make this a readable, and at points even powerful, work.

H. repeatedly praised verisimilitude in writing and maintained that she herself was faithful to human nature, society, probability, and even to facts. The subtitle of *Christabelle*, for instance, is "A Novel Founded on Facts." However, the book, which traces the history of another daughter of unknown parents amid the tumult of the French Reign of Terror, suffers from no taint of realism. It is thoroughly romantic in its notions and its style and relies heavily on elaborate plot contrivances. Virtuous characters are veritable paradigms, and villainous figures are innocent of any redeeming qualities. *Christabelle* swarms with gothic devices: a foreign and Catholic setting, anarchists, revolution, imprisonment and peremptory trials, miraculous interventions, a determined ravisher who repeatedly (and unsuccessfully) abducts the heroine, a sea capture, and the like.

H.'s favorite themes are the folly of family pride, the failure of parents (in myriad forms), and the inevitable triumph of virtue. Intermingled with these principal concerns are her abhorrence of slavery, war, and dueling; her admiration for liberty, religious tolerance, individual merit, and education; and her profound ambivalence toward women. While H. urges proper conduct, especially for young women—her heroines are all faultless—she clearly delights in racy, energetic older

women like Miss Helen Nesbit in *Andrew Stuart* and Lady John in *Ellinor*, who not only advocate the rights of women but enact them as far as possible.

Ellinor and *Falconbridge Abbey* are well worth reading, and *Christabelle* is a fascinating document in the study of England's response to the French Revolution. None of H.'s novels had been reissued since the early nineteenth century until 1974. Nonetheless, H. deserves some attention not only as a possible influence on other writers but also as an author who was in some ways unusual, in other ways quite typical of her period.

WORKS: *Ellinor, or the World as It Is: A Novel in Four Volumes* (1798). *Andrew Stuart, or the Northern Wanderer: A Novel in Four Volumes* (1800). *Falconbridge Abbey: A Devonshire Story in Five Volumes* (1809). *Christabelle, the Maid of Rouen: A Novel Founded on Facts in Four Volumes* (1814). *Possible: A Journey to the Highlands of Scotland. With Occasional Remarks on Dr. Johnson's Tour. By a Lady* (1776?).

BIBLIOGRAPHY: *A Biographical Dictionary of the Living Authors of Great Britain and Ireland* (1816). Copeland, E. *Modern Language Studies,* 9 (1979). Gregory, A. *The French Revolution and the English Novel* (1915). Luria, G. Introduction to *Ellinor* (1974). Ward, W.S. *Literary Reviews in British Periodicals: 1789-1797: A Bibliography* (1979).

Kathleen L. Fowler

Barbara Hardy

BORN: June 1924, Swansea, Wales.
DAUGHTER OF: Maurice Nathan and Gladys Nathan.
MARRIED: Ernest Dawson Hardy, n.d.

H., one of Britain's foremost literary critics, is a teacher, critic, poet, and professor of English. After receiving her bachelor's and master's degrees at the University of London, she held visiting teaching positions at Northwestern, Princeton, Dijon, and Stockholm universities and since 1965 has been a professor of English at Royal Holloway and Birkbeck colleges at the University of London. She is an honorary member of the Modern Language Association and the Welsh Academy and has lectured at universities in Japan, the Soviet Union, Canada, the United States, and Scandinavia.

H.'s scholarly work has been primarily concerned with arguing theoretical and generalized views of narrative form and genre through textual

analysis. Her early books modified and revised then current concepts of fictional form, and she has continued to elaborate and extend analysis to lyric poetry and Shakespearian drama. She is also interested in examining the sociological and moral imagination of writers, especially Thackeray and Austen as well as Shakespeare and Henry James. Narrative is emphasized in all her writing, though in greatest detail in *Tellers and Listeners: The Narrative Imagination* (1975), in which H. discusses such forms of narrative as jokes, daydreams, gossip, memoirs, and boasting, among others, as these serve to make up longer narrative patterns.

Her most significant body of work is her analysis of nineteenth-century writers, notably Thomas Hardy, George Eliot, Thackeray, Austen, and Dickens. Her *The Moral Art of Dickens* (1970) has been praised for its incisive treatment of Dickens's "moral transformation" in his novels. *The Exposure of Luxury: Radical Themes in*

Thackeray (1972) was similarly cited for H.'s perceptive handling of Thackeray's psychological insights.

Her first book, *The Novels of George Eliot: A Study in Form* (1959), remains one of her most distinguished. In addition to H.'s thorough knowledge of Eliot's work, H. demonstrates a wide-ranging familiarity with numerous influences on Eliot, in particular such problems of the day as education, Positivism, and political reform. H. also draws parallels to and applies a wide variety of writers to Eliot, including Dickens, Freud, Shakespeare, Wordsworth, and Henry James.

H. is especially concerned with interpreting Eliot's concern with "form" in a broad sense to include everything that helps the reader to see how Eliot's work reflects both a coherent, disciplined structure and a profound understanding of human nature. Indeed, "form" is a recurrent emphasis in H.'s writings, from her second book, more specifically on novelistic structure, *The Appropriate Form: An Essay on the Novel* (1964), through *Forms of Feeling in Victorian Fiction* (1985).

In addition to the many books she has written or edited, H. has also contributed to numerous journals, including *The New Statesman, The Guardian*, the *Times Literary Supplement*, and *Victorian Studies*, and her verse has appeared in *Poetry Wales, New Poets, Critical Quarterly*, and *London Review of Books*, among others. She has written on a broad range of authors for various collections, symposia, and journals, including James Joyce, W.H. Auden, Elizabeth Gaskell, John Donne, W.B. Yeats, Emily Brontë, William Shakespeare, William Empson, and Virginia Woolf, as well as the craft of fiction in general.

WORKS: *The Novels of George Eliot: A Study in Form* (1959). *The Appropriate Form: An Essay on the Novel* (1964). *Charles Dickens: The Later Novels* (1968). *The Moral Art of Dickens* (1970). *The Exposure of Luxury: Radical Themes in Thackeray* (1972). *Tellers and Listeners: The Narrative Imagination* (1975). *A Reading of Jane Austen* (1975). *The Advantage of Lyric: Essays on Feeling in Poetry* (1976). *Particularities: Readings in George Eliot* (1982). *Forms of Feeling in Victorian Fiction* (1985). *Narrators and Novelists: The Collected Papers of Barbara Hardy.* Vol. 1. (1987).

BIBLIOGRAPHY:

For articles in reference works, see: *CA. CLC.* Other references: *Encounter* (July 1977). *New Statesman* (24 October 1975). *NYRB* (8 October 1970). *NYTBR* (11 September 1977). *TLS* (18 January 1968, 5 February 1970, 25 December 1970, 6 October 1972, 23 April 1976, 16 January 1976). *Virginia Quarterly Review* (Summer 1971, Winter 1973). *Washington Post* (30 December 1970).

JoAnna Stephens Mink

Brilliana Harley

BORN: 1600, Brill, Holland.
DIED: October 1643, Brampton Bryan, Herefordshire.
DAUGHTER OF: Sir Edward Conway and Dorothy Tracy.
MARRIED: Sir Robert Harley, 1623.

H. remains a paradoxical figure. Known in her own time for the successful military defense of Brampton Bryan castle during the Civil War, for which she became something of a hero to the Roundheads, she is principally remembered today for her extraordinary letters to her son, which present her as an attentive mother consumed with domestic activities.

She was named after the town in Holland, Brill, where she was born; her father, Sir Edward Conway, was then Lieutenant-Governor of the Netherlands, and the family returned to England in 1606. H. received an unusual education; she was well read and knew both Latin and French. She married Sir Robert Harley in 1623, his third wife, and bore seven children between 1624 and 1634. Her husband served in parliament under James I and Charles I. Both she and her husband were Calvinist and sided with the parliamentary forces during the Civil War. After her marriage and until her death she resided principally at Brampton Bryan castle in Herefordshire, which she successfully held against royalist forces in 1643. In December 1642, shortly after hostilities had begun, the royalist governor, knowing her Puritan sympathies, demanded that she surrender the castle to the king's forces, to which request she refused.

During her lifetime H. wrote numerous letters, none of which were published. In the 1850s, however, a descendant, Lady Frances Vernon Harcourt, discovered a cache, which included 205 letters, mainly to her son Ned, subsequently published as *Letters of Lady Brilliana Harley* in 1854. The first letter is dated 30 September 1625, and the last, 9 October 1643, shortly before her death. Eight letters—the first in the collection—are to her husband, the remainder to her son. They provide vivid information about the daily life of an upper-class family of the period. While not as intense as the letters of Madame de Sévigné to her daughter, written a few decades later, they nevertheless evince considerable maternal affection. Often she sends him folk medicinal recipes, such as: "beare boyled with licorisch; it is a most excelent thinge for the kidnee" (14 December 1638). Or: "It is an excelent thinge to carry a littell peece of meer in your mouth, to keep you from any infection" (19 April 1641). She comments regularly on various members of the household receiving bloodlettings. Occasionally, she sends him pies, cakes and cheeses; he, in turn, sends her books. One, a copy of "The Man in the Moune," she finds "some kine to Donqueshot" [Don Quixote] (30 November 1638), an indication of the breadth of her own reading. In short, the letters are an important document of

social history, giving us a rare and charming glimpse of a seventeenth-century woman at ease, relaxed and in conversation.

The final letters record her anxieties about the siege. On 25 August she wrote: "The gentill men of this cuntry have . . . [brought] an army against me." And in her last letter she remarked, "I have taken a very greete coold, which has made me very ill thees 2 or 3 days, but I hope the Lord will be mercifull to me . . . ." (9 October 1643).

WORKS: Letters of Lady Brilliana Harley (1854).

BIBLIOGRAPHY: Fraser, A. The Weaker Vessel (1984). Lewis, T.T. Introduction and Notes to the Letters of Lady Brilliana Harley (1854).

For articles in reference works, see: DNB.

Josephine Donovan

Mary St. Leger (Kingsley) Harrison

BORN: 4 June 1852, Eversley, Hampshire.
DIED: 27 October 1931, Tenby, Wales.
DAUGHTER OF: Charles Kingsley and Frances Grenfell Kingsley.
MARRIED: William Harrison, 1876.
WROTE UNDER: Lucas Malet.

The youngest daughter of Charles Kingsley, eminent Christian Socialist clergyman, novelist, and poet, H. became a popular and controversial novelist. At Eversley the rectory was filled with celebrities—intellectuals, royalty, creative spirits—and during H.'s years of growing up with her two brothers, Maurice and Genville, and her elder sister, Rose, the Kingsley children found themselves in an atmosphere where individualism and learning were equally emphasized. When the Prince of Wales came to tea, H. stayed away, for she had determined that it was not appropriate to curtsy to another human. H. attended the Slade School to study art; although she was considered to show exceptional promise, she abandoned this career in 1876 when she married her father's curate, William Harrison, and went with him to North Devon, where he had been appointed rector of Clovelly. Unhappy in her marriage, H. later legally separated from her husband and began a writing career. Not wishing to trade too heavily on the fame of her father and uncle, H. chose as her pen name two family names, so that it was as "Lucas Malet" that she made her mark in English letters, although her identity was no secret.

Her first novel, Mrs. Lorimer: A Sketch in Black and White (1882), attracted little attention, but her second, Colonel Enderby's Wife (1885), established her reputation, which was strength-

ened by The Wages of Sin (1891). These novels, based on her experiences in Devon and in London's artistic circles, were considered somewhat daring and unpleasant by some critics. Another novel, The Carissima: a Modern Grotesque (1896), was even more shocking as it details, in a somewhat Jamesian style, the trauma of a young man who fails to prevent a dog from eating a baby and his continuing obsession with the event.

A handsome woman and brilliant conversationalist, she was friend to Henry James and the critic W.L. Courtney and, during her years on the Continent, of Romain Rolland. When her husband died in 1897, H. bought a house in Eversley, adopted her cousin Gabrielle Vallins, and spent most of her time in France and Switzerland with yearly visits to England. It was on such a visit that she died in 1931. H. became a Roman Catholic in 1902 and revised her early novels, but her postconversion writings continue to puzzle, shock, or enrage critics. Her middle and late novels focused on one or more moral dilemmas inherent in relations between men and women and often contained elements of the Gothic. Some, such as The Gateless Barrier (1900), in which the heroine is a ghost endeavoring to bring her former lover to self-knowledge, and The Tall Villa (1920), which concerned ancestral ghosts and their effect on the living, were more Gothic than psychological.

H. inherited Charles Kingsley's literary remains, although she did not obtain possession of them for sixteen years. Finding a fragment of a novel, Alcibiades, she completed it, prefaced it with an essay in which she discusses her theory of fiction, comparing it to that of her father, and published it under the title of The Tutor's Story in 1916.

It is in her novels decribing the effects of a moral dilemma in naturalistic terms but coming to a religio-romantic conclusion that she made a major impact. *Sir Richard Calmady* (1901) is an ambitious attempt to explore the different relationships that three women have with the same man, somewhat shocking in the early twentieth century for the outspoken, but not explicit, sexual nature of these relationships. *Adrian Savage* (1911) developed a triangle of widow, daughter, and young poet, which ends with the suicide of the daughter. A critic in the *Times Literary Supplement* called it "ugly and brutal." *Damaris* (1916) and *Deadham Hard* (1919) tell the story of Damaris from age five to eighteen. In the first, Damaris's father wants his mistress to bring up the child, and in the second, Damaris learns to cope with the knowledge that she has an illegitimate half-brother. In these dark-toned novels, women trained to be toys from childhood both suffer and cause suffering to others. Despite the seeming naturalism of the subject matter, critics describe H. as romantic in approach and like George Meredith in style. It seems, however, H. herself saw her fiction as more than entertainment, rather as a forum for discussing humanity's hard choices.

WORKS: *Mrs. Lorimer: A Sketch in Black and White* (1882). *Colonel Enderby's Wife* (1885). *A Counsel of Perfection* (1888). *Little Peter: A Christ-* *mas Morality* (1888). *The Wages of Sin* (1891). *The Carissima: A Modern Grotesque* (1896). *The Gateless Barrier* (1900). *The History of Sir Richard Calmady: A Romance* (1901). *The Far Horizon* (1906). *The Score* (1909). *The Golden Galleon* (1910). *Adrian Savage* (1911). *The Tutor's Story: An Unpublished Novel by Charles Kingsley, Revised and Completed by Lucas Malet* (1916). *Damaris* (1916). *Deadham Hard, A Romance* (1919). *The Tall Villa* (1920). *Da Silva's Widow and Other Stories* (1922). *The Survivors* (1923). *The Dogs of Want: A Modern Comedy of Errors* (1924). *The Private Life of Mr. Justice Syme* (1932; completed by G. Vallins).

BIBLIOGRAPHY: Archer, W. *Real Conversations* (1904). Chitty, S. *The Beast and the Monk* (1974). Collums, B. *Charles Kingsley: The Lion of Eversley* (1975). Courtney, W.L. *Feminine Notes in Fiction* (1904). Kingsley, F., ed. *Charles Kingsley, His Letters and Memories of His Life, Edited by His Wife* (1877). Pope-Hennessy, U. *Canon Charles Kingsley* (1948). Thorp, M.F. *Charles Kingsley, 1819-1875* (1937).

For articles in reference works, see: *DNB. Dictionary of Catholic Biography. Women Novelists, 1891-1920.*

Other references: *NYT* (6 July 1885). *Times* (London) (29 October 1931).

Eleanor Langstaff

Frances Ridley Havergal

BORN: 14 December 1836, Astley.
DIED: 3 June 1879, Swansea, Wales.
DAUGHTER OF: The Rev. William Henry and Jane Head Havergal.
WROTE UNDER: F.R.H., Frances Ridley Havergal.

A prolific poet and writer of religious tracts, H. is remembered chiefly for her hymns and her saintly life. This reputation, strongest among Evangelicals, has unjustly obscured her stature as a minor Victorian poet. She wrote some 75 hymns, also composing tunes for many of them, and had a hand in editing three books of hymns and tunes. A dozen or so of her hymns, such as "Consecration Hymn" ("Take my life") and "A Worker's Prayer" ("Lord, speak to me"), are still in use. But her collected verse, running to some 850 pages, includes sonnets, odes, mottoes, epigrams, narrative poems, a cantata, translations from the German, meditations, some political verse, and various other forms.

The quality of her work is uneven. Too much of it tries too hard to teach a lesson or achieve still more utilitarian ends, such as fund-raising for one of her many causes. She wrote verse fluently, starting at age seven, and verse became her natural vehicle to commemorate birthdays and other family events, stirring mountain scenery, memorable experiences, and the like; and she would usually try to honor anyone's request for a poem on a given theme. Writings of this sort she herself tended to dismiss as containing "not a spark of poetry." Take them all away, however, and sparks enough remain—her intense appreciation of nature, her flashes of gentle wit, as in "Evening Song," which occasionally relieve the sometimes overwhelming earnestness, her eye for the apt metaphor and, often, the allegorical application that rings true, her strong intellect organizing the movement of thought in a poem, her attention to technical detail.

Thanks to the technical discipline, very little of what H. wrote—even if uninspired, even the floral greeting card verse for which she was much sought after—can be called mere doggerel or cliché. Though her themes invited sentimental treatment, at her best the artistry firmly controlled the emotion. Besides the hymn-like stanza forms which predominate, she used the "Locksley Hall" meter, acrostics, blank verse, and other patterns. "Yesterday, To-day, and for Ever" is "a Greek acrostic, thrice tripled"—nine triplets, each an acrostic on the word AEI "always." She sometimes changed meter within a poem and speculatively linked the esthetic effect of doing so with key modulation in music.

Music in fact played an important part in her artistic life. One poem, "The Moonlight Sonata," includes a quite creditable verbal description and imitation of Beethoven's composition; the ode "Threefold Praise" is inspired equally by a Prayer Book text and by oratorios of Haydn, Mendelssohn, and Handel. A satire, "To the Choir of Llangryffyth," criticizes practices in church music. Of a distinguished musical family—her father and brother were composers and the former, an Anglican clergyman, pioneered the revival of older English church music—she was a talented pianist and singer, who gave up a promising concert career to devote her talents entirely to God's service. The lines "Take my voice, and let me sing/ Ever, only, for my King" ("Consecration Hymn") she meant quite literally. Vocation was a frequent theme in early poems—e.g., "The Ministry of Song," where music is implicitly a metaphor for poetry, and "The Poet's Zenith"—and a continuing struggle later in recurrent periods of failed inspiration. "Poetry is not a trifle,/ Lightly thought and lightly made," she wrote ("Making Poetry"); "the songs that echo longest" must be written "with your life-blood." Requisite is "suffering before you sing."

Other prominent themes in H.'s poetry are the praise of God, his goodness, trust in his providence despite affliction, seeking God's will and obeying it—her favorite terms for him are "king" and "master"—and the certainty of eternal things as opposed to the evanescence of the temporal. To be sure, H. dashed off dozens of occasional verses, whether based on a holy-day (Christmas, New Year's, Easter) or on a text used as a starting point for meditation. Yet as the early poem "Our Hidden Leaves" suggests, as well as the title of her second collection, *Under the Surface* (1874), she strove to penetrate beyond the obvious and probe true feelings and motivations. She brooded on the extreme difficulty of revealing or even knowing one's inner self ("Autobiography," "How Should They Know Me?").

Yet her writings reflect a remarkable depth of spiritual insight, gained both from introspection and from the Scriptures which she studied incessantly. Reared in an Evangelical vicarage, she experienced a spiritual awakening at fourteen, and much later, after years of intense activity in teaching and personal evangelism, she made a more profound act of surrender to God (see her booklet *Such a Blessing*). Her mysticism has been likened to that of St. Teresa of Avila. Despite repeated long illnesses she had a remarkable cheerfulness and buoyancy, and her pastimes included mountaineering in Switzerland—which furnished some of her best imagery.

H.'s many text-based poems—often taking a phrase from Scripture and applying it personally in allegorical fashion—owe much to her seriousness as a scholar. She committed several books of the Bible to memory, including most of the New Testament. Though her classroom schooling, including the Luisenschule in Düsseldorf, totaled less than two years, she knew several modern languages and habitually used the Hebrew and Greek texts in Scripture study. The typological method had an especial attraction for her. She had a high regard for the English seventeenth-century poets and divines, and glimpses of Herbert and Milton may be seen in her work.

Much of H.'s time in her last decade, beyond the demands of an immense correspondence, was given to writing prose books and leaflets. Viewing her supreme calling as ministry to others, she devoted her writing talent to that end. Her causes included circulating Irish-language Bibles in Ireland (*Bruey*), keeping Bible studies in the English curriculum (*An Educated Topsy*, verse satire), furthering the Young Women's Christian Association (*Holiday Work, All Things*), and promoting devotional exercises through daily and weekly guides (*My King*, the "Royal" series, *Starlight Through the Shadows* for invalids, *Pillows and Bells* for children). *Kept for the Master's Use* (1879), a line-by-line prose commentary on her "Consecration Hymn," has maintained its place in evangelical devotion down to the present.

Such works enjoyed immense popularity, as did articles and poems published separately in magazines and leaflets, some with a combined circulation close to half a million. After her death the demand continued: more than 60 posthumous anthologies of extracts from her writings have been published (of which the list of "Works" below contains only a selection), and many single poems in lavishly illustrated format.

An autobiographical sketch written at twenty-two is incorporated in her sister's *Memorials*, and letters—many of them replete with theological insight and spiritual counsel—there and in other biographies; later journals and autobiography are extant in manuscript.

WORKS: *The Ministry of Song* (1869). *Sacred Songs for Little Singers* (1870). *Bruey: A Little Worker for Christ* (1872). *Such a Blessing* (1873). *Holiday Work* (1873). *An Educated Topsy* (1873). *Under the Surface* (1874, publ. in United States as

Our Work and Our Blessings). The Four Happy Days (1874). Hints for Lady Workers at Mission Services (1874?). Little Pillows; or, Good-Night Thoughts for the Little Ones (1875). Morning Bells; or, Waking Thoughts for the Little Ones (1875). My King; or, Daily Thoughts for the King's Children (1877). Royal Commandments; or, Morning Thoughts for the King's Servants (1877). Royal Bounty; or, Evening Thoughts for the King's Guests (1877). The Royal Invitation; or, Daily Thoughts on Coming to Christ (1878). Loyal Responses; or, Daily Melodies for The King's Minstrels (1878). Kept for the Master's Use (1879). Echoes from the Word for the Christian Year (1879). Under His Shadow: the Last Poems, ed. M.V.G. Havergal (1879). Morning Stars; or, Names of Christ for His Little Ones (1879). (Musical setting) Loving All Along, by S.G. Prout (1879?). Life Mosaic, illus. by H. von Cramm (1879). All Things (1880). Life Chords, illus. by H. von Cramm (1880). Most Blessed for Ever, ed. M.V.G. Havergal (1880). Poems (1881). Swiss Letters and Alpine Poems, ed. J.M. Crane (1881). Starlight through the Shadows and Other Gleams from the King's Word, ed. M.V.G. Havergal (1881). My Bible Study: for the Sundays of the Year, ed. H. Bullock (1882). Specimen Glasses for the King's Minstrels: Papers on Modern Hymn Writers, ed. C. Bullock (1882). Ben Brightboots and other True Stories, Hymns and Music, ed. M.V.G. Havergal (1883). Life Echoes, ed. M.V.G. Havergal (1884). Ivy Leaves, ed. F.A. Shaw (1884). Letters, ed. M.V.G. Havergal (1885). Treasure Trove: Extracts from Unpublished Letters and Bible Notes, ed. E.P. Shaw (1886). Seven Songs for Eastertide (1886). Streamlets of Song for the Young, ed. J.M. Crane (1887). Blossoms from a Believer's Garden (1888). Fellowship: Letters Addressed to My Sister Mourners (18—?). Birthday Blessings: A Havergal Birthday Book (1904). The Havergal-Murray Daily Text-book (1927). Opened Treasures, comp. W.J. Pell (1962).

BIBLIOGRAPHY: Bullock, C. Near the Throne: Frances Ridley Havergal, Sweet Singer and Royal Writer (189—?). Darlow, T.H. Frances Ridley Havergal: A Saint of God. A New Memoir, with a Selection of Extracts from Her Prose and Verse (1927). Duffield, S.W. English Hymns (1886). Fairchild, H.N. Religious Trends in English Poetry, vol. 4 (1957). Grierson, J. Frances Ridley Havergal: Worcestershire Hymnwriter (1979). Havergal, M.V.G. Memorials of Frances Ridley Havergal (1880). (Wrenford, J.T.) A Brief Memorial of One of the King's Daughters (1879).

For articles in reference works, see: Allibone. BA19C. British Library Catalogue. DNB. Encyclopaedia Britannica, 11th ed. Julian, J. A Dictionary of Hymnology (1891). Routley, E. An English-Speaking Hymnal Guide (1979). Routley, E. A Panorama of English Hymnody (1979).

Other references: Christianity Today (1979). Miles, A.H. The Poets and Poetry of the Century, vol. 10: Sacred, Moral, and Religious Verse (1897). Nicholson, D.H.S., and A.H.E. Lee, eds. The Oxford Book of English Mystical Verse (1916).

Charles A. Huttar

Eliza Fowler Haywood

BORN: 1693, London.
DIED: 25 February 1756, London.
DAUGHTER OF: London shopkeeper and his wife.
MARRIED: The Rev. Valentine Haywood, 1711.
WROTE UNDER: T.B., Exploralibus, E.H., E. Haywood, Eliza Haywood (or Heywood), Mrs. Eliza Haywood, Justicia (?), Mira.

Author of over sixty narratives, translations, plays, and periodicals, H. was a major figure in the rise and growth of the popular novel in eighteenth-century England. H.'s career spans nearly half a century; her works reflect both the changing demand for fiction in the eighteenth century and her consistent concern for the economic and educational constraints faced by women in this period.

H. occasionally appealed to readers' generosity on the basis of her minimal "female" education but more often claimed to be better educated than the average women of her day. She launched her highly successful writing career in 1719 with the racy romance, Love in Excess; or, the Fatal Inquiry. In 1721 H.'s husband, a Norfolk clergyman, advertised in the Post Boy that she had left him without his consent and that he would not be responsible for her debts. H. seems to have spent the rest of her life in or around London, working as a writer and actress and for a time in the 1740s setting up her own publishing business. In addition to her own novels, plays, and periodicals, she translated several novels from the French, often drawing attention to places where she has elaborated and "improved" the original.

In her numerous short novels of the 1720s,

H. created a form that combined the expansive, emotionally rich texture of seventeenth-century French romances with the day-to-day problems of and dangers to English women in the early eighteenth century. Haywood's characters often derive from songs and ballads of the period—the rake, the endangered innocent, loyal lovers betrayed and manipulated by their own jealousy. By using repeatable and to some extent popular forms, H. was able to appeal to a wide audience. At the same time she manipulated romance conventions to explore and develop the emotional side of women's economic and sexual vulnerability, an emphasis that became central to the epistolary fiction of the 1740s.

Often, H.'s novels contrast the experience of "good" and "bad" heroines to create a context in which women are able to speak honestly about their sexual desire and their experience of danger in love. In *The British Recluse* (1722), Cleomira and Belinda meet and share their stories of betrayal; they end the novel living together in the country seeking "revenge" on the world of love that has betrayed them. Similarly, by way of accident or abandonment, H.'s upper-class heroines often travel to remote parts of the world, where, in order to survive, they must dress as men or as peasant women. In *Philidore and Placentia* (1727) such a period of wandering and disguise allows the heroine's emotional education and eventual ability to negotiate her own marriage settlement. Although most of H.'s plots end either in a happy marriage or in a series of tragic deaths, they often maintain the possibility of other sexual arrangements—bigamy, homosexuality, celibacy—right up to the end. This fantasy structure has strong affinities with and is perhaps the precursor of the twentieth-century "Harlequin romance," which some critics consider to be a genre of women's erotic literature. Versions of this structure are pervasive in the eighteenth century, informing works by later women novelists such as Charlotte Lennox, Fanny Burney, and Jane Austen.

We have much less information about H.'s writing in the 1730s because the bulk of it was published anonymously. In 1725 she began a series of direct stabs at the ruling elite with the politically scandalous *Memoirs of a Certain Island* .... Based on Delariviere Manley's *The New Atalantis* (1709), *Memoirs of a Certain Island* presents thinly veiled contemporary figures in a series of sexual and political exploits. H.'s funny but deadly serious political satires were probably part of what incited Pope's wrath and his damning her as a half-naked woman surrounded by illegitimate children in *The Dunciad* (1728). Her best political satire, the anti-Walpole *Adventures of Eovaii, Princess of Ijaveo* (1736), is dedicated to the Duchess of Marlborough and calls

itself a "Pre-Adamitical History." Here, H. indicts everything from spying to the sexual inequities built into language and firmly advocates republicanism and sexual freedom instead. During the 1730s H. also acted in, wrote, and collaborated on several plays including *The Opera of Operas* (1733).

After the Licensing Act closed Henry Fielding's "little theatre" in Haymarket, effectively silencing political and satirical theatrical performances, H. returned to writing fiction with *Anti-Pamela; or, Feigned Innocence Detected* (1741), one of numerous spin-offs from Samuel Richardson's best-selling novel *Pamela* (1740). Appealing to the advocates as well as the opponents of the new conduct literature, H. wrote a number of her own books and periodicals in this area. These range from *A Present for a Servant-Maid* (1743), which suggests how to fend off a master's sexual advances, to the highly successful and decorous *Female Spectator* (1744–46), which was presented in the form of a ladies' discussion circle but was probably written entirely by Haywood.

—These two kinds of writing—that which advocates proper female conduct and that which satirizes and subverts it—come together in H.'s later novels, especially in the delightful *History of Miss Betsy Thoughtless* (1751). Betsy Thoughtless is one of the great naughty heroines of all time, "thoughtless" because she repeatedly ignores her own danger, as well as others' concerns, in pursuing her own freedom and experience. Betsy is nearly raped several times, and only learns how vulnerable she is—both sexually and economically—by her disastrous marriage to the cruel and selfish Munden. In *Betsy Thoughtless* and again in *The Wife* (1756), H. suggests that because divorce was all but legally impossible women should leave, if necessary, in order to free themselves of bondage within marriage. A writer of incredible range, passion, and political insight, H. deserves to be republished and read seriously in our own time.

SELECTED WORKS: *Love in Excess; or, the Fatal Enquiry* (1719–1720). *Letters from a Lady of Quality to a Chevalier* (trans., 1721). *The Fair Captive: a Tragedy* (1721). *The British Recluse; or, the Secret History of Leomira, Suppos'd Dead* (1722). *The Injur'd Husband; or, the Mistaken Resentment* (1723). *Idalia; or, the Unfortunate Mistress* (1723). *Lasselia; or, the Self Abandoned* (1723). *A Wife to be Lett: A Comedy* (1724). *The Rash Resolve; or, the Untimely Discovery* (1724, rpt. 1973). *The Arragonian Queen: A Secret History* (1724). *The Fatal Secret; or, Constancy in Distress* (1724). *A Spy upon the Conjurer* (1724). *The Surprise; or, Constancy Rewarded* (1724). *La Belle Assemblee; or, the Adventures of Six Days* (trans., 1724–1726). *The Tea-*

Table; or, a Conversation between Some Polite Persons of Both Sexes, at a Lady's Visiting Day (1724). The Masqueraders; or, Fatal Curiosity (1724). The Works of Mrs. Eliza Haywood (1724). The Memoirs of Baron de Brosse (1725). Memoirs of a Certain Island Adjacent to the Kingdom of Utopia . . . (1725; rpt. 1972). The Unequal Conflict; or, Nature Triumphant (1725). Mary Stuart, Queen of Scots: Being the Secret History of her Life, and the Real Cause of her Misfortunes (1725). Bath Intrigues (1725). Secret Histories, Novels and Poems (1725). The Mercenary Lover; or, the Unfortunate Heiresses (1726). The City Jilt; or, the Alderman Turn'd Beau (1726). Secret History of the Present Intrigues of the Court of Caramania (1727, rpt. 1972). Letters from the Palace of Fame (1727). The Fruitless Enquiry (1727). Cleomelia; or, the Generous Mistress (1727). The Life of Mme. Villesache (1727). Love in its Variety (trans., 1727). Philidore and Placentia, or L'Amour trop delicat (1727, rpt. 1963). The Agreeable Caledonian; or, Memoirs of Signiora di Morella, a Roman Lady (1728). Irish Artifice; or, The History of Clarina (1728). Persecuted Virtue, or the Cruel Lover (1728). The Perplex'd Dutchess; or, Treachery Rewarded (1728). Frederick, Duke of Brunswick-Lunenburgh: A Tragedy (1729). The Fair Hebrew (1729). Love-Letters on All Occasions Lately Passed between Persons of Distinction (1730). Secret Memoirs of the Late Mr. Duncan Campbell (1732). The Opera of Operas; or, Tom Thumb the Great (1733). L'Entrien des Beaux Esprits: Being the Sequel to La Belle Assemblee (trans., 1734). The Adventures of Eovaai, Princess of Ijaveo (1736, rpt. 1972). Anti-Pamela; or, Feign'd Innocence Detected (1741, rpt., 1975). The Virtuous Villager; or, Virgin's Victory (trans., 1742; rpt. 1975). A Present for a Servant-Maid; or, The Sure Means of Gaining Love and Esteem (1743). The Fortunate Foundlings: Being the Genuine History of Colonel M--rs and His Sister, Madam du P--y (1744, rpt. 1974). The Female Spectator (1744-1746; rpt. 1929). The Parrot (1746). Life's Progress Through the Passions; or, the Adventures of Natura (1748, rpt. 1974). Epistles for the Ladies (1749-1750). The History of Miss Betsy Thoughtless (1751; rpt. 1986). The History of Jemmy and Jenny Jessamy (1752; rpt. 1974). The Invisible Spy (1754). The Wife (1756). The Husband, In Answer to the Wife (1756). The History of Miss Leonora Meadowson (1788). Plays of Eliza Haywood (1979). Four Novels of Eliza Haywood (1983).

BIBLIOGRAPHY: Beasley, J.C. Novels of the 1740s (1982). Doody, M.A. A Natural Passion (1974). Eaves, T.C.D., and Kimpel, B.D. Samuel Richardson (1971). Horner, J.M. The English Women Novelists and Their Connection with the Feminist Movement (1688-1797) (1930). MacCarthy, B.G. Women Writers: Their Contribution to the English Novel (1621-1744) (1944). Reeve, C. The Progress of Romance (1785). Richetti, J.J. Popular Fiction Before Richardson: Narrative Patterns 1700-1739 (1969). Rogers, K. Feminism in Eighteenth-Century England (1982). Schofield, M.A. Quiet Rebellion: The Fictional Heroines of Eliza Fowler Haywood (1982). Spencer, J. The Rise of the Woman Novelist (1986). Whicher, G.F. The Life and Romances of Mrs. Eliza Haywood (1913).

For articles in reference works, see: DLB. DNB. Todd.

Other references: Bulletin de la Societe d'Etudes Anglo-americaines des XVIIe et XVIIIe Siecles (1978). Huntington Library Quarterly (1978). N&Q (1973). Romance Notes (1969). SP (1973). Studies in Eighteenth-Century Culture (1983). TSLL (1964).

Carol L. Barash

Annie French Hector

BORN: 23 June 1825, Dublin.
DIED: 10 July 1902, London.
DAUGHTER OF: Robert French and Anne Malone.
MARRIED: Alexander Hector, 15 April 1858.
WROTE UNDER: "Mrs. Alexander," Annie French Hector.

The only daughter of a Dublin barrister, H. was educated under governesses and was widely read. After some financial difficulties, her family left for Liverpool and after much moving about finally settled in London; H. returned only once to Ireland. She established many literary friendships in London, notably with Eliza Lynn and W.H. Wills, editor of Household Words. It was in this magazine that she first attracted attention with an article "Billeted in Boulogne" (1856). She had previously written two novels which went unnoticed.

After her marriage to an ambitious explorer and merchant, H. wrote little since her husband thought it unwomanly. After his health began to fail, however, she published Which Shall It Be? (1866), and shortly before he died in 1875, she published her best known novel, The Wooing O't, which had appeared in installments in Temple Bar in 1873 and as a three-volume work under her pseudonym, Mrs. Alexander. The story is a wholesome Cinderella-like tale of a thoroughly good but poor young girl who marries well at the end of the novel.

Left alone with three daughters and a son, H. began to write in earnest to support her family. They lived for six years in Germany and France, an experience reflected in her novels; after three years in St. Andrews, they moved in 1885 to London where H. occupied herself with writing. *Saturday Review* had judged *The Wooing O't* to be "a book of healthy tone and pleasant feeling, womanly but not sentimental," but her many later novels were judged to be "dry" and "without life." For example, *Her Dearest Foe* (1876) reads now as a rather hackneyed story of a young widow's struggle to regain her husband's property from a gentleman with whom she falls in love and eventually marries.

A number of H.'s novels were popular in America as well as in Britain, and eleven were printed in second editions. *The Freres* (1882) was translated into Spanish, *By Woman's Wit* (1886) into Danish, and *Mona's Choice* into Polish. Her final novel, *Kitty Costello* (1904), describing an Irish girl's experience in England, contains autobiographical details. Perhaps the most outstanding characteristic of H.'s novels is their blandness, which makes them pleasant and light entertainment.

WORKS: *Agnes Waring* (1854). *Kate Vernon* (1855). *Which Shall It Be?* (1866). *The Wooing O't* (1873). *Ralph Wilton's Weird* (1875). *Her Dearest Foe* (1876). *The Heritage of Langdale* (1877). *Maid, Wife or Widow* (1879). *A Peep at Presburg and Perth* (1879). *The Australian Aunt* (1882). *At Bay* (1882). *The Freres* (1882). *Look Before You Leap* (1882). *Valerie's Fate* (1882). *The Admiral's Ward* (1883). *The Executor* (1883). *Second Life* (1883). *Beaton's Bargain* (1884). *Mrs. Vereker's Courier Maid* (1884). *By Woman's Wit* (1886). *Forging the Fetters* (1887). *Mona's Choice* (1887). *A Life Interest* (1888). *A Crooked Path* (1889). *A False Scent* (1889). *Blind Fate* (1890). *A Woman's Heart* (1890). *Mammon* (1891). *Well Won* (1891). *What Gold Cannot Buy* (1891). *The Snare of the Fowler* (1892). *For His Sake* (1892). *Found Wanting* (1893). *Broken Links* (1894). *A Choice of Evils* (1894). *A Ward in Chancery* (1894). *A Fight with Fate* (1896). *A Winning Hazard* (1896). *Barbara, Lady's Maid and Peeress* (1897). *A Golden Autumn* (1897). *Mrs. Chrichton's Creditor* (1897). *V.C. Brown* (1899). *The Cost of Her Pride* (1899). *A Missing Hero* (1900). *The Step Mother* (1900). *Through Fire to Fortune* (1900). *The Yellow Fiend* (1901). *Stronger than Love* (1902). *Kitty Costello* (1904).

BIBLIOGRAPHY: Black, H. *Notable Women Authors of the Day* (1893).

For articles in reference works, see: *DNB*.

Carole M. Shaffer-Koros

Felicia Dorothea Browne Hemans

BORN: 25 September 1793, Liverpool.
DIED: 16 May 1835, Dublin.
DAUGHTER OF: George and Felicity Wagner Browne.
MARRIED: Captain Alfred Hemans, 1812.
WROTE UNDER: Felicia Browne, Felicia Hemans, Mrs. Hemans.

The most popular woman poet of the nineteenth century, H. spent most of her life in Wales, where her family moved after her father's business failures. A beautiful, precocious child, she was educated at home under her mother's direction. She studied French, Spanish, Italian, Portuguese, German, and Latin. She read Shakespeare at six, began writing poetry at eight, and published her first volume at fourteen—dedicated to the Prince of Wales and listing over nine hundred subscribers, including her future husband. Her marriage lasted less than six years. Shortly before the birth of their fifth son, Captain Hemans went to Rome "for the sake of his health," and was never seen again. Pursuing "uninterrupted domestic privacy," she devoted herself to her sons and mother.

American writer Lydia Sigourney attributed H.'s success to the influence of "maternal culture": "by her prolonged residence under the maternal wing, she was sheltered from the burden of those cares which sometimes press out the life of song." The mother's death in 1827 seems to have marked the beginning of her own decline. H. died of tuberculosis at forty-two, mourned by Wordsworth as "that holy Spirit,/ . . . who, ere her summer faded/ Has sunk into a breathless sleep."

H. produced numerous volumes of poetry, songs, translations, and some periodical essays. Her five-act tragedy, *The Vespers of Palermo*, failed at Covent Garden but was produced more successfully in Edinburgh with the assistance of Sir Walter Scott. H. read, and often quoted, Shakespeare, Petrarch, Lope de Vega, Tasso, Gibbon, Schiller, Novalis, Goethe, Byron, Shelley, and Mme. de Staël. *Corinne*, she said, "has a power over me which is quite indescribable. Some passages seem to give me back my own thoughts and feelings, my whole inner being." She corresponded with Joanna Baillie and Mary Howitt, and in 1829, she visited Sir Walter Scott at Abbotsford. At the instigation of Maria Jewsbury, she also became acquainted with William Wordsworth, whom she visited in 1830 at Rydal.

Although she set most of her long poems in exotic places—Moorish palaces, Carthaginian ruins, Spanish castles—and invoked stories of political rebellion and war, her real concerns are domestic. Her chosen themes are, in Sigourney's words, "the loveliness of nature, the endearments of home, the deathless strength of the affections, the noble aims of disinterested virtue, the power of that piety which plucks the sting from death." Maternal love is a prevailing concern, especially in *The Records of Woman*, poetical tales written shortly after her mother's death.

H. provides insight into the critical values and popular taste of the nineteenth century. She was acclaimed by such prominent reviewers as Francis Jeffrey and recommended for study in the schools by Matthew Arnold (her poems, he said, "have real merits of expression and sentiment"). In America, where H. was the most frequently anthologized English writer in the gift books and annuals, critics Andrews Norton and Andrew Peabody ranked her work above Milton's and Homer's. Essay after essay defines her as the perfect lady poet.

Assuming that the "nature of this poetess is more interesting than her genius, or than its finest productions," reviewers evaluate the poetry in terms of her personality. She is applauded for living in retirement and maintaining proper "feminine reserve." Readers note her "tremulous sensibility," "delicate organization," and "intense susceptiveness," but conclude that she keeps her feelings under control. "The calm mistress of her stormiest emotions," H. exudes the right amount of melancholy and reveals "no unsatisfied cravings." Moreover, she has little sense of artistic self-consciousness. As Lydia Sigourney said, "Sympathy, not fame, was the desire of her being." H. proclaimed that she was determined not to become "that despicable thing, a woman living upon admiration!" In "Properzia Rossi," a celebrated woman sculptor decries her fame as "worthless" because her statue has no effect on the knight she adores.

Being "a genuine woman, and, therefore, a true Christian," H. is commended for dispensing religious and moral sentiments. According to William Michael Rossetti, she had "that love of good and horror of evil which characterize a scrupulous female mind." Her favorite poem, *The Forest Sanctuary*, concerns a sixteenth-century Spaniard who flees to North America in search of religious freedom. *The Sceptic*, a poem arguing for the necessity of deism, infuriated Byron ("too stiltified

& atmospheric—& quite wrong"), but most readers saw it as appropriate for women to act as "natural guardians of morality and faith."

Women also praised H. in extravagant terms. Author Maria Jewsbury idolized her as "a Muse, a grace, a variable child, a dependent woman, the Italy of human beings." George Eliot, who quoted "our sweet Mrs. Hemans" frequently during the early 1840s, called *The Forest Sanctuary* "exquisite!" Elizabeth Barrett Browning and Letitia Landon wrote elegies for H., while Sigourney and other American "poetesses" claimed her as their precursor. Indeed, it has been suggested that H. "ought to be read at length before trying any of the great woman poets of the nineteenth century." Despite an awkward situation that left her living without her husband, H. proved that it was possible to be a poet, a lady, a mother, *and* a great popular success. But the gushing praise for her poetry reveals a double critical standard that would limit the aspirations and diminish the achievements of women poets throughout the century.

WORKS (Selected): Poems (1808). England and Spain, or Valour and Patriotism (1808). The Domestic Affections and Other Poems (1812). The Restoration of the Works of Art to Italy (1816). Translations from Camoens and Other Poems (1818). Stanzas to the Memory of the Late King (1820). Dartmoor (1821). Welsh Melodies (1821). The Vespers of Palermo (1823). The Forest Sanctuary and Other Poems (1825). Records of Woman (1828). Songs of the Affections (1830). Hymns for Childhood (1834). National Lyrics and Songs for Music (1834). Scenes and Hymns of Life (1834).

BIBLIOGRAPHY: Chorley, H.F. Memorials of Mrs. Hemans (1836). Cruse, A. The Victorians and Their Reading (1935). Helsinger, E., Sheets, R., and Veeder, W. The Woman Question: Literary Issues (1983). Hickok, K. Representations of Women: Nineteenth-Century British Women's Poetry (1984). Hughes, H.M.B. Memoir of the Life and Writings of Mrs. Hemans (1839). Kaplan, C. Salt and Bitter and Good (1975). Ritchie, A.T. Blackstick Papers (1908). Rossetti, W.M. "Prefatory Notice." The Poetical Works of Mrs. Felicia Hemans (1837). Sigourney, L.H. "An Essay on Her Genius." The Works of Mrs. Hemans (1840). Trinder, P.W. Mrs. Hemans (1984). Walker, C. The Nightingale's Burden: Women Poets and American Culture before 1900 (1982).

For articles in reference works, see: Allibone. CBEL. DNB. Europa. NCBEL. OCCL.

Robin Sheets

Georgette Heyer

BORN: 16 August 1902, London.
DIED: 4 July 1974, London.
DAUGHTER OF: George and Sylvia (Watkins) Heyer.
MARRIED: George Ronald Rougier, 1925.
WROTE UNDER: Georgette Heyer, Stella Martin.

H., the eldest of three children and the only daughter of George and Sylvia Heyer, was privately educated and did not attend university. When H. was seventeen she wrote a story, as she said, "to relieve my own boredom, and my brother's." Although she had written merely to entertain her brother Boris while he was recovering from an illness, her father, who himself had written several articles for *Punch*, liked the story and encouraged her to work on it for publication. She did, and in 1921 H.'s first novel, *The Black Moth*, was published.

Despite her early success, she cared little for publicity. Throughout her writing career of over 50 years, she made no appearances and never granted an interview, even in the interest of increasing book sales. She used the pseudonym Stella Martin for her third book but thereafter retained the name of H. That she was an early success would, however, prove to be especially important in 1925. When her father died she became the principal means of financial support for her mother and two younger brothers.

In 1925 she married a mining engineer; in 1927 she joined him in Africa, but he was unhappy with his job and H. was unhappy with their travels, so in 1929 they returned to England. There, with his wife's encouragement, he began studying to be a barrister, something he had long wished for; H.'s writing was now providing the basic financial support not only for her mother's family but for her own.

H. was a prolific writer. Best known for her Regency novels, her publishers noted that she "worked quickly, . . . and made few corrections, soaking herself in the Regency Period—becoming an expert on the history and manners of that time." Indeed, she kept copious notes and sketches of Regency life and fashion. This attention to detail did not encumber her style, which is marked by a verve and wit that at times has been compared to that of Jane Austen. Instead, the details of dress and use of Regency slang lend a viable sense of scene to these novels in which the functions of social class, manners, and romance figure predominantly. A 1948 *New York Times* review captured the tone of these novels when the reviewer said of H. that she "writes cheerful and highly unorthodox historical novels, set in Regency England,

in which people never lose their lives, their virtue, or even their tempers."

Such a novel is *The Nonesuch* (1962) in which Sir Waldo Hawkridge comes to Broom Hall, setting the countryside in a turmoil as families rush to entertain him with the most stylish and engaging parties, mothers and daughters concoct matchmaking schemes, and the young men of the town try desperately to emulate this paragon of style known as the "Nonesuch." The story contains common elements of the romance genre. The hero suddenly appears in a small town, unknown but by his reputation, and falls in love with Ancilla Trent, governess of the feisty and coquettish Miss Tiffany Wield. Tiffany, "a most accomplished flirt," determines to charm the Nonesuch and at least capture the heart of the young Lord Julian. Yet in the end it is the "very gentle" but courageous Miss Patience Chartley who takes Lord Julian's heart.

H., here as in many of her Regency romances, relieves the potential melodrama of these situations with humor, wit, and a refreshing use of common sense. Characters are well-defined and even the most annoying Tiffany is likeable. H. develops the potential of the genre by mirroring characters and relationships—the Nonesuch and Ancilla Trent with the young Lord Julian and Patience Chartley, the coquette with the gentle beauty, fashion with foppery. The humorous romantic complications are enlivened by the overriding satire of the society that busies itself in frenzied albeit always clumsy attempts to marry off the Nonesuch or to imitate his fashion and skill. Good manners, "tradition, and upbringing" are the measure of the nobility of character in these novels that exemplify the best elements of the romance genre right up to the climax when the runaway Tiffany must be rescued and finally taught a lesson by the Nonesuch.

While H. is best known for these Regency novels, she also published a dozen mysteries, the first being *Footsteps in the Dark* (1932). Her husband, while studying for the bar, frequently collaborated with her on these novels by helping with the plot. The wit, clear characterization, and closely defined social scene that marked her Regency novels were also important elements of her detective novels. Two of H.'s characters—Scotland Yard detectives Superintendent Hannasyde and Inspector Hemingway—make return appearances in eight of these novels as they frequently confront eccentric characters whose humor enlivens both the investigation and the novel.

While H. at times criticized her own work as not being "real" literature, she summarized many readers' responses as she noted that "it's unquestionably good escapist literature . . . its period detail is good, . . . and . . . I will say that it is very good fun."

WORKS: *The Black Moth* (1921). *The Great Roxhythe* (1922). *The Transformation of Philip Jettan* (as Stella Martin, 1923). *Instead of the Thorn* (1923). *Simon the Coldheart* (1925). *These Old Shades* (1926). *Helen* (1926). *The Masqueraders* (1928). *Beauvallet* (1929). *Pastel* (1929). *The Barren Corn* (1930). *The Conqueror* (1931). *Footsteps in the Dark* (1932). *Devil's Cub* (1932). *Why Shoot a Butler?* (1933). *The Unfinished Clue* (1934). *The Convenient Marriage* (1934). *Death in the Stocks* (1935). *Regency Buck* (1935). *Behold, Here's Poison!* (1936). *The Talisman Ring* (1936). *They Found Him Dead* (1937). *An Infamous Army* (1937). *A Blunt Instrument* (1938). *Royal Escape* (1938). *No Wind of Blame* (1939). *The Spanish Bride* (1940). *The Corinthian* (1940). *Envious Casa* (1941). *Faro's Daughter* (1941). *Penhallow* (1942). *Friday's Child* (1944). *The Reluctant Widow* (1946). *The Foundling* (1948). *Arabella* (1949). *The Grand Sophy* (1950). *Duplicate Death* (1951). *The Quiet Gentleman* (1951). *Detection Unlimited* (1953). *Cotillion* (1953). *The Toll-Gate* (1954). *Bath Tangle* (1955). *Sprig Muslin* (1956). *April Lady* (1957). *Sylvester: or The Wicked Uncle* (1957). *Venetia* (1958). *The Unknown Ajax* (1959). *Pistols for Two and Other Stories* (1960). *A Civil Contract* (1961). *The Nonesuch* (1962). *False Colours* (1963). *Frederica* (1965). *Black Sheep* (1966). *Cousin Kate* (1968). *Charity Girl* (1970). *Lady of Quality* (1972). *My Lord John* (1975).

BIBLIOGRAPHY: Hodge, J.A. *The Private World of Georgette Heyer* (1984).

For articles in reference works, see: *CA TCC&MW*.

Other references: *NYT* (6 June 1974). *NYTBR* (21 March 1948).

Paula Connolly

Octavia Hill

BORN: 3 December 1838, Wisbeck.
DIED: 12 August 1912, London.
DAUGHTER OF: James Hill and Caroline Southwood Smith.

H. was a social reformer whose work and writing centered primarily on the reform of urban housing and the improvement of the quality of urban life. She was the eighth of eleven children. In 1851, her mother, an educator, was obliged by financial necessity to move to London with her five daughters, taking a position as manager of the Ladies' Cooperative Guild, an organization founded by the Christian Socialists. In 1852, at the age of fourteen, H. began attending meetings of the Christian Socialists where she met the Reverend F.D. Maurice, who offered her her first post in another Christian Socialist venture, taking charge of the "ragged children" employed in a toy-furniture making operation; her first article, published in *Household Words* in 1856, was an account of the lives of the poverty-stricken toy-makers. H.'s success with the toymakers led F.D. Maurice to employ her to teach arithmetic at the newly established classes of working women at the Working Men's College and, when the Ladies' Cooperative Guild failed, Maurice offered her a salaried post as Secretary to the Women's Classes. In 1862, the Hills started a school for girls at their new home in Nottingham Place that thrived for 24 years. H. received her certificate from Queen's College in 1864.

Through her association with the Christian Socialists, H. met Ruskin, who gave her artistic training and commissioned work from her for the next ten and one half years. For Ruskin, H. copied pictures for *Modern Painters*, the Society of Antiquaries, and the National Portrait Gallery. H.'s association with Ruskin proved fruitful not only because he commissioned her copying work; he also assisted her in her next and most important venture, which was to launch her future career and in which she found her true vocation. In 1865, Ruskin purchased three tenanted slum-houses in Paradise Place, a court not far from H.'s home that she was to manage and improve. She improved the properties, gradually rehabilitating both living quarters and their occupants. In 1866, Ruskin further aided H.'s schemes, purchasing a row of cottages; later that year, H. had four more dilapidated houses placed in her management. Her first article specifically about housing appeared in the *Fortnightly Review* in November 1866 and was followed by a series of others on the same subject.

In 1865, H. was involved in the founding of the London Association for the Prevention of Pauperization and Crime (which later became the Charity Organization Society) to which Ruskin contributed generously. H. read her paper, "The Importance of Aiding the Poor Without Almsgiving," at an 1869 meeting, and thereafter the Reverend W. Freemantle invited H. to take charge of the very poor Walmer Street District in his parish. Her successful management of all these properties led to more and more similar undertakings, and her fame began to spread beyond Marylebone where her first properties were situated and soon beyond London altogether. She was asked to manage properties in Leeds (1874), Liverpool (1879), and Manchester.

In 1875, H. became a member of the Central Council of the Charity Organization Society, and with the demands for her property management growing, she found it necessary to train workers to whom she could delegate her increasing responsibilities. Soon her renown spread beyond England, and women from Berlin, Munich, Sweden, Holland, Russia, and America were in her training. Her system of property management was introduced by these delegates into many towns and cities outside of England. Also in 1875, five of her articles were published as a book in America under the title *Homes of the London Poor.* This work, later translated into German by Princess Alice of Hesse, led to the founding of the "Octavia Hill Verein" in Berlin. In that year, H. became a member of the Executive Council of the Commons Preservation Society. In 1877, she and her sister, Miranda, were among the founding members of the Kyrle Society, H. functioning as treasurer and her sister as president. These societies worked toward the creation and improvement of public spaces; it was, for example, largely due to H.'s efforts that Parliament Hill was secured for public use.

She is also remembered today for her part in the founding in 1895 of the National Trust, along with Robert Hunter and Canon Rawsley, which secured many important properties, including the Cliff at Barmouth, Tintagel, portions of the Lake district, and Mariners Hill, for public use and enjoyment. In 1898, J.S. Sargent painted the portrait of H. which hangs in the National Portrait Gallery. In 1905, H. became a member of the Royal Commission on the Poor Laws.

WORKS: *Further Account of the Walmer Street Industrial Experiment* (1872). *Letter to my Fellow-Workers Accompanying the Account of Donations Received for Work Amongst the Poor During 1872(-1911)* (1873 [-1912]). *Homes of the London Poor* (1875). *District Visiting* (1877). *Our Common Land and Other Short Essays* (1877). *Colour, Space and Music for the People* (1884). *An Open Space for Deptford: An Appeal* (1892). "Preservations of Commons: Speech at a Meeting for Securing West Wickham Common." Kent and Surrey Committee of the Commons Preservation Society (1892). *Memorandum on the Report of the Royal Commission on the Poor Laws and Relief of Distress* (1909). *Report of an Attempt to Raise a Few of the London Poor Without Gifts* (n.d.).

BIBLIOGRAPHY: Bell, E.H.C.M. *Octavia Hill* (1942). Hill, W.T. *Octavia Hill, Pioneer of the National Trust and Housing Reformer* (1956). Hill, W.T. *Octavia Hill* (1956). Loch, C.S. *In Memoriam: Miss Octavia Hill* (1913). Ouvry, E.S., ed. *Extracts from Octavia Hill's "Letters to Fellow-Workers," 1864-1911* (1933). Maurice, C.E. *Life of Octavia Hill as Told In Her Letters* (1913). Maurice, E.S., ed. *Octavia Hill: Early Ideals From Letters* (1928). Tabor, M.E. *Pioneer Women: Octavia Hill* (1927).

For articles in reference works, see: *DNB. Webster's New Biographical Dictionary.*

Other references: Cockburn, J. *The Quarterly Review* (1939). Jardine, afterwards White, E. *Women of Devotion and Courage* (no. 5, Octavia Hill) (1925). Kent, M. *Cornhill Magazine* (1928). Ruskin, J. "Supplement to the *Report* [*by Octavia Hill*] *of an Attempt to Raise a Few of the London Poor Without Gifts* ... Being a Letter from J. Ruskin" (c. 1930).

Gale Sigal

Susan Hill

BORN: 5 February 1942, Scarborough.
DAUGHTER OF: R.H. and Doris Hill.
MARRIED: Stanley Wells, 1975.

In 1985 H. was first seen on American television rather than in bookshops in her own dramatization—for *Masterpiece Theatre*—of "A Bit of Singing and Dancing," the title story of a collection she published in 1973. It is typical of H.'s emphasis: the plight of an abused, proud, gullible person suddenly released from responsibilities (parental, economic) late in life and therefore willing, even anxious, to avoid loneliness even if it means accepting "second best." Typically choosing seaside resorts, H. follows in the footsteps of her admired Elizabeth Bowen and Elizabeth Taylor, whose spas are lined with respectable older folk and not so respectable day trippers. Esme in "A Bit of Singing and Dancing" accepts a mysterious lodger after her mother finally dies, a Mr. Amos Curry, who appears very "right" in dress and manner, the perfect gentleman lodger for *her* "part of town." In fact Esme one day weeks later stumbles on him poignantly reliving his earlier music-hall profession at a busy intersection of the seafront: There he is tap dancing and singing, a cap for coins at his feet, coins that eventually, she realizes, pay her rent.

Television and radio plays, reviews, talk shows, chatty columns in literary papers, in 1983 a chilling ghost story the length of *The Turn of the Screw*—called *The Woman in Black*—but no major novel since 1974 despite the promise of the reviews, the showering of literary prizes. H.'s novels are kept in print, however, especially by Penguin, while many of her contemporaries disappear after a season in the sun.

She chooses as characters people outside the usual list of friends and relations. They are often very young boys, sometimes deaf and dumb, often maimed in some way. They can be at the other end of life, too: elderly but alone, retired, their isolation making them nearly pathological. But H. in her spare, economic way never treats her folk like psychotics: she instills in them an isolated dignity that borders on the heroic whatever their age (the boy victim in *I'm King of the Castle*). They are the misfits, the disadvantaged to be sure, but they are also the ones who care and think about others; they possess a sense of value absent around them. Put in political terms, they are the minority group just barely tolerated by the majority, the normal, the confident. In *The Bird of Night* older, gifted men (a scientist, a poet) seek refuge from the world in each other, one over-fastidious, the other paranoid, almost "mad." The possibility of their abnormal relationship is vaguely assumed but not developed. It is what society has done to them, how society has isolated them, that concerns H. She is also concerned with the inexpressible pain of loss a woman feels, newly married, at the sudden death of her husband. The only person in the community who understands her is a youngster, her brother-in-law. As in so many of her novels and stories, the isolated central character turns to nature, even to animals and birds, for solace.

A limit is met in the most extraordinary story of all, "The Albatross." A terrible burden is placed on a rather simple son by a dominant mother who issues commands from her wheelchair. Set again on the seashore of a northern fishing village, the sea and the elements become almost a character in the story. Duncan, the son, finally discovers the possibility of relief: escape to become apprenticed to Ted Flint, a fisherman, a strong, important person in the pub and in the town. Ted quite casually lets Duncan know he is a person. Indeed, the setting reminds one of a Benjamin Britten opera: the boats, the sea, the life of the villages reduced to survival through fishing. The sea pounds the shore, pounds the village; the mother's words pound at the consciousness of the child. The intensity reaches a screaming point, and we nearly rejoice when Duncan puts his mother in her wheelchair in the middle of the night and pushes her over the end of the jetty. The language H. chooses to use is understated, quiet. The matter-of-factness of the murder provides a catharsis in its almost atonal cadence.

It might be argued that the controlled tension H. generates in her long stories is more appropriate than when applied to the novel. *I'm King of the Castle*, a sado-masochistic story of two youngsters, becomes almost unbearable in its later pages: its passionate factual development of hate becomes suffocating. The gothic quality becomes an end in itself rather than a reference to a more substantial generalization. That generalization seems to surface in "The Albatross" and in some of the earlier radio plays.

Finally, the attachment H. obviously has for birds and for the countryside reminds one of Hardy, whose stories she has edited. At her best she integrates the setting with the plight of the characters. She is both off-beat and concerned, gothic but humane. Anti-heroes in many instances, these off-center folk are not scarecrows because they are so deeply felt. We see them vividly; we sympathize with them.

WORKS: *The Enclosure* (1961). *Do Me a Favour* (1963). *Gentleman and Ladies* (1968). *A Change for the Better* (1969). *I'm King of the Castle* (1970). *Miss Lavender Is Dead* (1970). *Taking Leave* (1971). *The End of Summer* (1971). *Lizard in the Grass* (1971). *Strange Meeting* (1971). *The Albatross and Other Stories* (1971). *The Custodian* (1972). *The Bird of Night* (1972). *The Cold Country* (1972). *A Bit of Singing and Dancing* (1973). *White Elegy* (1973). *Consider the Lilies* (1973). *In the Springtime of the Year* (1974). *A Window on the World* (1974). *Strip Jack Naked* (1974). *The Cold Country and Other Plays for Radio* (includes *The End of Summer, Lizard in the Grass, Consider the Lilies, Strip Jack Naked*) (1975). *Lanterns Across the Snow* (1987).

BIBLIOGRAPHY: Jackson, R. *Twentieth-Century Woman Novelists*, ed. T.F. Staley (1982).

For articles in reference works, see: *CA. CD. CLC. CN. DLB. DNB.*

Other references: *English Journal* (1983). *Listener* (11 February 1971, 14 September 1972, 29 March 1973, 24 January 1974, 15 May 1975, 22 September 1983, 29 November 1984). *London Review of Books* (17 November 1983). *New Statesman* (28 October 1983, 7 December 1984). *NYTBR* (30 March 1969, 27 May 1973, 10 June 1973, 2 December 1973, 5 May 1974, 17 May 1985). *Observer* (21 September 1969, 21 December 1969, 6 September 1970, 14 February 1971, 17 October 1971, 17 September 1972, 1 April 1973, 20 January 1974, 8 February 1976). *Punch* (7 December 1983). *PW* (6 July 1970, 23 February 1976, 8 March 1976, 19 April 1983, 19 October 1984). *Spectator* (16 September 1972, 19 May 1973, 15 May 1982, 29 October 1983, 5 November 1983). *TLS* (25 September 1969, 30 October 1970, 5 March 1971, 29 October 1971, 15 September 1972, 30 March 1973, 25 January 1974, 30 November 1984).

Ernest H. Hofer

Molly Holden

BORN: 7 September 1927, London.
DIED: 5 August 1981, Bromsgrove.
DAUGHTER OF: Conor Henry and Winifred (Farrant) Gilbert.
MARRIED: Alan W. Holden, 1949.

Although H. wrote several novels and children's books, she is best known for her nature poetry. H. was an atheist, but a sense of power and order prevails in her truthful, unsentimental portrayal of nature. She especially admires its toughness. In "Pieces of unprofitable land," it is asserted that "their vigour justifies all wastes and weeds." Nature's fierceness and heroism are demonstrated in poems such as "Hare":

> But he is no more than flesh and blood,
> living all his speedy life with fear,
> only oblivious of constant danger
> at his balletic time of year
> when spring skies, winds, the greening furrows
> overcome hunger, nervousness, poor sight,
> fill him with urgent, huge heroics,
> make him stand up and fight.

It is this tenacity which most attracts H. It is why the speaker in "Giant decorative dahlia" says of the "unnamed tuber, offered cheap" that "I could not deny it love if I tried."

H.'s poems show similarities to the verse of Edward Thomas, John Clare, and Thomas Hardy (though without his sense of irony). H. was aware of these influences and proudly acknowledged them, as in her poem for Hardy, "T.H." She praises the wariness of the author who "saw everything he needed/ about his fellow-men and the world, marking it all/ upon the full-mapped country of his mind and memory." In fact, her poems often contain literary and artistic references. The influence of earlier writers may account for the great number of poems using rhyme, as for example, in the volume To Make Me Grieve. This rhyme often has a startling simplicity. The conclusion of "Every May" is one example: "But now and then I notice/ in May's sweet cold,/ the comfortable heat of humans./ I grow old."

H. was disabled by multiple sclerosis in 1964, ironically at the same time her poetic powers ripened. Her affliction is sometimes the subject of her work, for instance, "Illness" and "Adjustment." But she is never self-pitying. She rejects the temptation to "raise my voice and howl/ at what has been done to me." In "Hospital" we see that religion is no comfort for her sickness. She is "seeking inside not out for a human grace/ that would give me a strength and a courage for enduring/ against great odds in a narrow place." The comfort must come from an inner strength, much like the force that runs through her nature poetry. For this reason, it is not surprising that in such poems as "The seven bushes" there is a oneness between the speaker and nature: "we share this soil with mutual wariness."

H. possesses a strong narrative sense, but there can be a certain uniformity of tone in her work. Regardless of this possible flaw, she has been one of England's greatest nature poets of this century. Her poems have a quiet, subtle distinctiveness. As John Cotton asserts, Holden's poems "steadily grow on you." Before her death in 1981, she was awarded the Arts Council Award in 1970 and the Cholmondeley Award in 1972.

WORKS: The Bright Cloud (1964). To Make Me Grieve (1968). The Unfinished Feud (1971). Air and Chill Earth (1971). A Tenancy of Flint (1971). White Rose and Wanderer (1972). Reivers' Weather (1973). The Speckled Bush (1974). The Country Over (1975). Selected Poems, with a memoir by A. Holden (1987).

BIBLIOGRAPHY: Byers, M. British Poetry Since 1960, ed. M. Schmidt and G. Lindop (1972).
For articles in reference works, see: CA. CP. DLB.
Other references: Alma, R. Poetry Nation 2 (1974).Observer Review (19 January 1969). New Statesman (28 February 1969). London Magazine (July 1969).

Louis J. Parascandola

Winifred Holtby

BORN: 23 June 1898, Rudstone, Yorkshire.
DIED: 25 September 1935, London.
DAUGHTER OF: David and Alice Holtby.

H., novelist and essayist, was a prolific writer on numerous subjects. Born to a father who worked as a farmer and a mother who served as

alderman of East Riding, Yorkshire, H. was a precocious child, publishing a volume of poems, My Garden and Other Poems, at the age of thirteen. Her schoolmistress encouraged her parents to send her to Somerville College, Oxford, where she was an exceptional student. Her studies were interrupted for a year during World War I while she served in a post of the signals branch of the Women's Auxiliary Army Corps.

After she graduated, H. joined Lady Margaret Rhondda as an editor of *Time and Tide*, eventually (after 1926) as director. She traveled extensively throughout Europe, lecturing for the League of Nations Union. In London she lived with Vera Brittain, whom she had met at Oxford; their friendship was to endure until H.'s death at the age of thirty-seven. When Brittain married, H. shared her home, caring for Brittain's children as her own. Though H. never married, she had an extended relationship that culminated with her engagement on her deathbed. Both overwork and heart disease have been cited as responsible for her early death. Indeed, H., dedicated to her writing even when she knew death was imminent, barely completed her best-known novel, *South Riding*, working rapidly during her last four weeks of life.

At her death, H. had published six novels, two volumes of stories, a book of verse, two volumes of satire, a study of Virginia Woolf, a book about women, and a play that she saw produced. Moreover, she was an active journalist, turning out many articles for such publications as the *Manchester Guardian*, the *News Chronicle*, and *Time and Tide*, and she campaigned actively for black rights in South Africa. Though her talents as a critic and essayist are often noted, it is as a novelist that she is remembered today.

H.'s best novels are usually considered to be *Poor Caroline* (1931), *Mandoa! Mandoa!* (1933), and *South Riding* (published posthumously in 1936). *Poor Caroline* tells of the Christian Cinema Company and especially of its founder, Caroline Denton-Smyth, a vigorous but self-deluded woman who tackles projects that have no hope of being completed. A heavily ironic story, it describes especially well how Denton-Smyth and her company affect others who depend on them for their livelihoods. *Mandoa! Mandoa!* is even more heavily satiric; in it, an aggressive British travel agency attempts to advertise and market a small, isolated community in Africa, with H. in the process offering thoughtful, barbed comments about the contrasts between an industrial civilization and a less developed one.

South Riding: An English Landscape is considerably more complex, suggesting H.'s likelihood of achieving even more significant fiction had she lived. It is set in H.'s native Yorkshire, with the title a reference to a fictional part of the county (Yorkshire has only north, east, and west "ridings," or administrative divisions) and with H.'s mother's experiences as a member of the County Council especially relevant. The county, gradually becoming urbanized, is reflective of England in its contrasts between country and city, older ways of thinking versus the newer, and tra-

ditional ways contrasted with more innovative. The County Council, in its "apparently impersonal" (Brittain's term) deliberations and decisions, affects the lives of all local citizens; as H. wrote in her preface (addressed to her mother), "The complex tangle of motives prompting public decisions, the unforeseen consequences of their enactment of private lives, appeared to me as part of the unseen pattern of the English landscape."

In *South Riding*, H. shows how the conservative councillor, Robert Carne, and the relatively unconventional new teacher, Sarah Burton, necessarily clash in their differing approaches to education and to life. Carne comes to love Burton, but no liaison occurs because of his heart condition. H. offers numerous lesser though equally dramatic vignettes, such as those involving a bright, impoverished girl who must quit school to care for her family, a dying woman who tries to protect her husband from the truth about her condition, a councillor who fears tuberculosis, a woman who dreads death in childbirth, and a shopkeeper whose wife withholds sexual activity and who is blackmailed by his lover.

The book has been compared favorably to the work of Arnold Bennett and other writers, with the *Literary Digest* calling it a "magnificent epitaph" for H. and with Brittain comparing it to Ibsen's *An Enemy of the People*. Without any doubt, H. was growing in skill and confidence, thus making her death—at an earlier age, as Brittain noted, than George Eliot, John Galsworthy, or Bernard Shaw had been before they had accomplished anything of note—especially premature. Her diverse interests, balanced as they were between her public life, including her friends and their families, and her need for time alone in order to write, made for a remarkably full and varied life. Though she focused on Yorkshire, her work has had remarkable success in both England and the United States, with a motion picture version of *South Riding* (released in 1938) contributing to her reputation.

WORKS: *My Garden and Other Poems* (1911). *Anderby Wold* (1923). *The Land of Green Ginger* (1928). *Eutychus; or, The Future of the Pulpit* (1928). *Poor Caroline* (1931). *Virginia Woolf, A Critical Study* (1932). *The Astonishing Island* (1933). *Mandoa! Mandoa!* (1933). *Truth Is Not Sober and Other Stories* (1934). *Women and a Changing Civilisation* (1934). *The Frozen Earth and Other Poems* (1935). *South Riding: An English Landscape* (1936). *Pavements at Anderby: Tales of South Riding and Other Regions* (1937). *Letters to a Friend* (1937). *The Crowded Street* (1938). *Take Back Your Freedom* (1939) *Women* (1941). *The Letters of Winifred Holtby and Vera Brittain, 1920-1935*, ed. by V. Brittain and G. Handley-Taylor (1960). *Testament of a Generation: The Journalism* of *Vera Brittain and Winifred Holtby*, ed. P. Berry and A. Bishop (1985).

BIBLIOGRAPHY: Brittain, V. *Testament of Friendship* (1940). Handley-Taylor, G. *Winifred Holtby: A Concise and Selected Bibliography Together with Some Letters* (1955). White, E. *Winifred Holtby as I Knew Her* (1938).

For articles in reference works, see: *MBL. TCA* and *SUP. TCW.*

Other references: *Christian Century* (30 October 1935). Gray, J. *On Second Thought* (1946). Green, M. *A Mirror for Anglo-Saxons* (1950). Heil-brun, C. "Introduction." V. Brittain. *Testament of Friendship* (1981). *Literary Digest* (11 April 1936). *Ms.* (June 1986). O'Faolain, S. *London Mercury* (April 1936). *Publishers' Weekly* (12 October 1935). *Punch* (25 November 1981). *Scholastic* (22 January 1938). Scott-James, V. *London Mercury* (May 1937). *Spectator* (6 February 1982). *TLS* (25 December 1981, 18 July 1986). *(Village) Voice Literary Supplement* (May 1986). *Wilson Library Bulletin* (April 1934, November 1935).

Paul Schlueter

Susanna Harvey Hopton

BORN: 1627.
DIED: 12 July 1708, Hereford, Herefordshire.
DAUGHTER OF: (?) Harvey, of an old Staffordshire family, and (?) Wiseman, of an Essex family.
MARRIED: Richard Hopton.

H., devotional writer and benefactress, was born Susanna Harvey in 1627. The Harveys were of ancient Staffordshire stock. In her youth, she converted to Roman Catholicism; but, after a careful analysis of the opposing arguments advanced by Roman Catholic writers and by Anglican authorities, she returned to the Anglican faith. She married Richard Hopton of Kington, Herefordshire, a barrister and judge, with whom she lived happily until his death in 1696. They were childless. She died in Hereford at the age of eighty-one and was buried next to her husband at Bishop's Frome.

She was known for her charity to those in need near her home in Kington and in distant places, as evidenced by the letters of gratitude found among her papers. Her executor, William Brome, writes concerning her good work that "she was charitable to the poor in the highest degree, and hospitable to her friends in a generous manner." Her dedication to her church is revealed in her bequest of £800 to suffering clergymen.

Her devotion to God's work extended to the conduct of her own spiritual life, which was both demanding and disciplined. Each day she awakened at four in the morning for the first of her five worship sessions, a course of devotions she maintained throughout most of her life. Her extraordinary commitment included the world of learning; for, although she had little formal education, she read deeply in the devotional books in her own library and conversed at length with "the best Divines," so that "she attained," according to her friend and editor Nathaniel Spinckes, "to a very considerable knowledge in Divinity; and has been a Benefactress to the Age, by the religious and instructive Works she has left behind her."

Her literary survivals are all of a religious nature. Her *Daily Devotions*, published in 1673, consists of thanksgivings, confessions, and prayers, which she describes in "The Preface to the Reader" as "Rational, Comprehensive, and Emphatical." Even a brief passage like the following reveals her vigorous, straightforward style: "Shake the earth of my Heart with terror at the approach of every sin; that I may die rather than commit one known wilful sin against thee more." Less dramatic, yet quietly powerful, is her Prayer for the Ninth Hour, which closes with these words: "O by this death of thine, have mercy upon me, let it kill, crucifie, and destroy all sin in me, let me die unto the World, and live henceforth only unto thee."

Devotions in the Ancient Way of Offices, published in 1700, was "reformed" by H. for the use of Anglicans from the earlier work of the same title by John Austin, a Roman Catholic, originally published in Paris in 1668. The work provides psalms, hymns, and prayers "for every Day of the Week" and "for our Saviour's Feasts," "the Holy Ghost," "the Saints," and "the Dead." George Hickes, editor of the work, fails to identify H. as the reformer; however, the description in "To the Reader," with its reference to self-education and to a successful book of devotions, fits H. In addition, in his Preface to *Controversial Letters* (1710), Hickes attributes the work to her.

A letter to Father Henry Turbeville, published by Hickes in 1710 in his *Second Collection of Controversial Letters*, is a carefully-reasoned argument justifying her return from the Church of Rome to the Church of England. Spinckes, in describing the letter, writes that she "gave such reasons for her return, as not only will justify it before all intelligent and impartial persons, but may be of very good use to others. . . ."

In 1717, Spinckes published *A Collection of Meditations and Devotions, in Three Parts*, which consisted of H.'s *Hexaemeron, or Meditations on the Six Days of Creation, Meditations and Devotions on the Life of Christ*, and another edition of *Daily Devotions*. In *Hexaemeron*, she reveals in her discussion of the six days of creation how God made man in His likeness, endowed him with the gifts of reason and understanding, and brought him into a world that was provided with all necessities for subsistence, comfort, delight, and ultimate salvation. She raises the question, how, in view of such kindness, could man fail to give thanks? *Meditations . . . on the Life of Christ* is a logical sequel to *Hexaemeron* in its examination of God's gifts, including the Son and the nature of the sacrifice.

Although H.'s works are not readily available except in research libraries, they do warrant attention because they reflect a sensitive, dedicated woman's overcoming the lack of formal education and recording her thoughts in clear, powerful prose. In addition, she herself is important as a seventeenth-century woman who managed to get her books published and who impressed religious thinkers like George Hickes and Nathaniel Spinckes with her superior qualities of mind and spirit.

WORKS: Daily Devotions Consisting of Thanksgivings, Confessions, and Prayers (1673). Devotions in the Ancient Way of Offices (1700). Letter to Father Turbeville, in George Hickes. Second Collection of Controversial Letters (1710). Hexaemeron, or Meditations on the Six Days of the Creation and Meditations on the Life of Christ, in Nathaniel Spinckes. Meditations and Devotions (1717).

BIBLIOGRAPHY: Ballard, G. Memoirs of Several Ladies of Great Britain (1752; ed. R. Perry, 1985). Hickes, G. Preface. Linguarum Vetterum Septentrionalium Thesaurus (1705). Hickes' Prefaces to Daily Devotions, (1673). Devotions in the Ancient Way of Offices (1700). Second Collection of Controversial Letters (1710). Jordan, R. D. Yearbook of English Studies (1982). Spinckes, N. In [John Wilford]. Memorials and Characters of Two Hundred Eminent and Worthy Persons . . . of Great Britain (1744; rpt. Spinckes, N. Preface. A Collection of Meditations and Devotions [1717]).

For articles in reference works, see: *DNB*. Ireland, N.O. *Index to Women of the World* (1970). Stenton, D.M. *The English Woman in History* (1957). Todd.

Philip Bordinat

Elizabeth Jane Howard

BORN: 26 March 1923, London.
DAUGHTER OF: David Liddon and Katharine Margaret Somervell Howard.
MARRIED: Peter Scott, 1942; James Douglas Henry, 1960; Kingsley Amis, 1965.

Educated privately at home, H. later studied acting at the London Mask Theatre and in the Scott Thorndyke Student Repertory, and she performed at Stratford-upon-Avon and in repertory theatre in Devon. During World War II, she served as an air raid warden and at the same time worked in radio and television broadcasting and as a model. Writing was a secret "vice" from age fourteen; however, she did not enter the literary profession until the 1950s when her novels began to appear and she worked as an editor for London publishing houses.

Known for both her long and short fiction, H. considers herself to be "in the straight tradition of English novelists." Her fiction deals with character and manners in elegant, irreverent, witty, lightly satirical prose. H.'s milieu is the carefully described, devastatingly detailed world of the middle class in which she deftly delineates the often tacit but nonetheless excruciating conflicts among family members: husbands and wives, siblings, children and parents, grandparents and grandchildren. Her central characters are frequently alienated young women or men whose internal sense of emptiness and inadequacy spill over into other lives, disrupting and complicating them, particularly as the young people seek through these others the elusive chimeras of love and security. Occasionally striving too hard for resolution, H. provides cheerful endings inappropriately, but her most serious studies, especially the gem of black comedy, *Odd Girl Out* (1972), conclude more ambivalently. Because even H.'s most substantial novels are comic and unpretentious, she has not received the critical attention she deserves. Auberon Waugh comments about *Odd Girl Out*, "she may not have written a highbrow novel, to be approved of by the tiny and extraordinarily unintelligent untalented circle of people in London who like to think of themselves as highbrow, but she has written a thunderingly good novel."

H. says, "I write about 300 words a day with luck and when I am free to do so. I do it chiefly because it is the most difficult thing I have tried to do."

WORKS: *The Beautiful Visit* (1950). (with R. Aickman) *We Are for the Dark: Six Ghost Stories* (1951). *The Long View* (1956). (with A. Helps) *Bettina: A Portrait* (1957). *The Sea Change* (1959). *After Julius* (1965). *Something in Disguise* (1970). *Odd Girl Out* (1972). *Mr. Wrong* (1975). *Getting It Right* (1982). (with T. Maschler) *Howard & Maschler on Food* (1987).

BIBLIOGRAPHY: For articles in reference works, see: *CA. CLC. CN. MBL* and *SUP. SF&FL. WA*.

Other references: *New Statesman* (21 September 1957, 11 July 1975). *Newsweek* (29 December 1975). *NYT* (9 January 1966). *NYTBR* (22 February 1976). *Spectator* (8 April 1972, 26 July 1975). *TLS* (20 November 1959, 24 March 1972).

Carey Kaplan

Henrietta Hobart Howard

BORN: c. 1688 Bickling, Norfolkshire.
DIED: 26 July 1767, in Twickenham, Middlesex.
DAUGHTER OF: Sir Henry Hobart and Elizabeth Maynard Hobart.
MARRIED: Charles Howard, 2 March 1706; George Berkeley, 26 June 1735.

H., later the Countess of Suffolk, was a letter-writer, courtier, and mistress to George II of England. She was born c. 1688 in Bickling, Norfolkshire, the first daughter of Sir Henry Hobart, Baronet, and Elizabeth Maynard, whose grandfather had been commissioner of the great seal under William III. In 1706, while still in her teens, H. married the Hon. Charles Howard, who twenty-five years later would become the ninth Earl of Suffolk. Seeing few opportunities for immediate advancement in England, the young couple traveled to Hanover where they came to the attention of Prince George Augustus and Princess Caroline of Ansbach, who, on the death of Queen Anne of England in 1714, would become the Prince and Princess of Wales. In October of 1714, Princess Caroline appointed H. as one of the women of the bedchamber, commencing a relationship that would continue until H. retired in 1734. During many of these years that she served Caroline, H. served the husband as well. Horace Walpole, the close friend of her twilight years, writes of H.'s relationship to the King that she diverted "the channel of his inclinations to herself." Indeed, she became the prince's mistress and continued the liaison after he became king. He visited her in her lodgings at the same time each day and spent hours walking and talking with her in the gardens of St. James and Richmond, where she resided at Richmond Lodge.

After a number of years, the King financed the construction for her at Twickenham of an elaborate villa, Marble Hill, which was completed in 1724. Her neighbor, Alexander Pope, helped design the gardens. Here was the perfect setting for entertaining the monarch when they were away from St. James and for conversing with her many friends, among them some of the most exciting personalities from the worlds of English letters, politics, and society. Yet the pleasures of such encounters were sometimes marred by tensions arising from ambitions and jealousies. For example, ambitious to gain royal patronage, Jonathan Swift, John Gay, and Aaron Hill sought to use the friendship of H. to their advantage. Although Gay received small favors and Swift had an audience with Queen Caroline, when he spoke vigorously for his own and for Ireland's welfare, the material results of such appeals were insignificant. Unfortunately, H.'s lack of success on Swift's behalf spoiled their friendship. The "Character of Mrs. Howard," written in 1727, reflects in characteristic Swiftian tones his bitterness. Although Swift achieved a measure of vengeance for what he believed to be H.'s disloyalty, her friends, including Gay and Pope, defended her, recognizing, no doubt, that though she had the ear of royalty, she had little real influence.

When the eighth Earl of Suffolk died without an heir in 1731, Charles Howard succeeded to the title, a development that allowed H. to be called Lady Suffolk; at this time she was appointed Groom of the Stole to the Queen, a position with a stipend of £800 a year. Two years later, on 28 September 1733, her husband died, and the following year she petitioned the King and Queen to be allowed to retire. The Queen, referring to her as the best of servants, insisted that H. take a week to reconsider. However, H., now in her mid-forties and quite deaf, stood by her decision and left the royal service.

Although she had severed her royal connections, H., during the more than three decades of life that remained to her, continued to entertain important people at Marble Hill and in her London residence at 27 Saville Street, now Saville Row. In 1735 she married the Hon. George Berkeley, who was described by Lord Hervey as "neither young, handsome, healthy, nor rich." Yet their marriage was apparently happy, being marked by frequent visits from their many friends, among them Pope, until his death in 1744; young William Pitt, at the start of his illustrious career; and Horace Walpole, after H.'s husband died in 1746.

H.'s modest place in literature depends on her correspondence, which was published in two volumes in 1824 under the title *Letters to and from Henrietta, Countess of Suffolk, and her Second Husband, the Hon. George Berkeley; from 1712 to 1767.* The work was edited anonymously by George Wilson Croker, who is remembered chiefly for his devastating attack on Keats's *Endymion.* Croker acquired the manuscripts of the letters from Lord and Lady Londonderry, who could trace their family back to H. Croker provides a representative selection from the five folio volumes of Suffolk papers that currently reside in the British Library (Add. MS. 22,625–29).

The edition opens with the editor's biographical notice, followed by Swift's character of H. and Pope's poem "To a Certain Lady at Court." The preliminaries conclude with a poem by the Earl of Peterborough, who exclaims, "O wonderful creature!" The letters, chronologically arranged and copiously annotated, span more than half a century, from 1712 to 1767. Only thirty of the nearly two hundred and fifty were written by H. The others were usually directed to her by her friends who were involved in literature, politics, and society. Swift, Gay, Pope, Arbuthnot, Chesterfield, Pitt, Glenville, Peterborough, Bolingbroke, and Horace Walpole were among the men, and the Duchesses of Buckingham, Marlborough, and Queensbury were among the women who corresponded with the Countess. The cumulative effect upon the reader is involvement in the social milieu. One must look elsewhere for comment on the major issues of the times.

For the reader who would arrive at an independent assessment of the merits of H.'s correspondence, the task is complicated because there has been no edition since Croker's in 1824, although in 1924 Lewis Melville reprinted in *Lady Suffolk and Her Circle* a considerable number of the letters plus some not previously printed. Fortunately, the reader can sample the correspondence in modern editions of the letters of Walpole, Pope, Swift, and Chesterfield.

A reading of H.'s correspondence provides access to the social worlds of the eighteenth-century English court and of the English aristocracy. In process, the reader encounters key figures in literature, politics, and society as they touched the life of one of the fascinating women of the times. The portrait of H. that emerges is intrinsically interesting. Her characteristic qualities are captured by comments made over forty years apart by two of her dearest friends. In c. 1725, Pope wrote of her, "I know a Reasonable Woman/ Handsome and witty, yet a Friend"; and in 1767, shortly after her death, Walpole wrote, "I never knew a woman more respectable for her honour and principles, and have lost few persons in my life whom I shall miss so much."

WORKS: *Letters to and from Henrietta, Countess of Suffolk, and Her Second Husband, the Hon. George Berkeley; from 1712 to 1767. With Historical, Biographical, and Explanatory Notes,* ed. John Wilson Croker (1824).

BIBLIOGRAPHY: Aitken, G. *The Life and Works of John Arbuthnot* (1892). Arkell, R.L. *Caroline of Ansbach: George the Second's Queen* (1939). Brightfield, M. *John Wilson Croker* (1940). *Burke's Peerage* (1970). Chesterfield, Earl of. *The Letters of Philip Dormer Stanhope, Earl of Chesterfield* (1845). *Edinburgh Review* (March 1824). *Gentleman's Magazine* (July 1767). Kippis, A. *Biographica Britannica* (1778). Melville, L. [*pseud.* L.S. Benjamin]. *Lady Suffolk and Her Circle* (1924). Pope, A. *Correspondence* (1956). Pope, A. *Minor Poems* (1954). *Quarterly Review* (January 1824). Quennell, P. *Caroline of England: An Augustan Portrait* (1939). Swift, J. *Correspondence* (1963). Swift, J. *Prose Works.* (1962). Walpole, H. *Correspondence* (1961). Walpole, H. *Memoirs* (1852). Walpole, H. *Memoirs of the Reign of King George the Second* (1846). Walpole, H. *Selected Letters* (1973).

For articles in reference works, see: *DNB.*

Other references: Dobrée, B. *English Literature of the Early Eighteenth Century* (1959). Ireland, N.O. *Index to Women of the World* (1957). Melville, L. [*pseud.* L.S. Benjamin]. *Maids of Honour* (1917). Sherman, R. *World's Great Love Letters* (1917). Stenton, D.M. *The English Woman in History* (1957).

Philip Bordinat

Mary Botham Howitt

BORN: 12 March 1799, Coleford, Gloucestershire.
DIED: 30 January 1888, Rome.
DAUGHTER OF: Samuel and Ann Wood Botham.
MARRIED: William Howitt, 16 April 1821.

A prolific author, producing, sometimes in collaboration with her husband, over 110 books and scores of articles, H. was a novelist, nature writer, children's book author, editor, and translator. She was the daughter of strict Quaker parents, and, along with her sister Anna, eighteen months older, was first educated at home, until both girls were sent to a school run by neighbor Mary Parker. Samuel Botham required, however, that his daughters sit apart from the other girls lest they acquire un-Quaker-like ideas and habits. In 1809 the two girls attended a Society of Friends school in Croyden until their mother's illness caused them to return to Uttoxeter. Study at a Friends school in Sheffield in 1811 was followed by a brief period of instruction from tutors at home in 1812, after which H. was left to self-education. Because Samuel Botham was a firm believer in the Quaker prohibition against art and literature, the Botham daughters had to study both secretly. In 1818 H. met fellow Quaker William Howitt, who shared her interest in literature and in writing. They were married in a Quaker ceremony at Uttoxeter on 16 April 1821. William worked briefly in his own chemist's shop, but soon the couple depended on writing, translating, and editing for their income. Their first works, *The Forest Minstrel, and Other Poems* (1823) and *The Desolation of Eyam, and Other Poems* (1827), began a collaboration that continued throughout their lives. Like much of their subsequent work, these poems show the influence of the Romantics, of whom they were early popularizers. H. and her husband became friends with Wordsworth, and they also admired Keats and Byron, defending the latter against detractors after his death.

One of their early joint editing ventures was *Howitt's Journal*, which began 2 January 1847 but lasted only a year and a half because of financial difficulties. H. was a friend of Elizabeth Gaskell, whose earliest stories were published in *Howitt's Journal* under the pseudonym Cotton Mather Mills. H. and her husband also encouraged Gaskell in her first novel, *Mary Barton*, working to arrange its publication. H. was also a friend of Fredrika Bremer and was the first to translate her Swedish novels into English, starting with *Neighbours* in 1842. She also translated Hans Christian Andersen's stories and the work of several German authors, and with her husband produced a history of Scandinavian literature, *The Literature and Romance of Northern Europe* (1852). Her children's stories include *The Children's Year* (1847) and *Our Cousins in Ohio* (1849), based on letters from her sister Emma, who had moved to the United States. She wrote for most of the major and minor periodicals of Victorian England, including *Athenaeum, Household Words*, and *All the Year Round*.

Her reputation during her lifetime was considerably stronger than it has been since; in the United States she was especially well regarded for her poems, a collection of which appeared in an American edition along with the work of Keats and Henry Hart Milman. Most of her work has been out of print in the twentieth century except for her *Autobiography* and her Bremer translations.

Her life reflects the struggles and concerns common to Victorians and to women. She supported the 1856 proposal for a Married Women's Property Act, working with friends such as Barbara Leigh Smith Bodichon and Octavia Hill, with whom H. pasted together the signed petitions. She also had a lifelong concern for social, educational, and political reform and for the peace movement. In addition to writing, translating, and editing, H. managed a family that included five children who survived infancy; four of them reached adulthood. Family responsibilities and the need to earn a living undoubtedly affected the quality of her work; she anticipated Virginia Woolf's *A Room of One's Own* by more than seventy-five years, regretting in 1848 that a new house gave her "no little working-room to myself," but that she could "bear interruptions" better than other members of her family (*Autobiography*, II, 46). Her life also reflected the crisis of faith experienced by many Victorians: having been raised in the Society of Friends, she later became involved in Unitarianism and spiritualism and in her old age joined the Church of Rome (26 May 1882).

Her *Autobiography* remains one of her most readable works, the record of an energetic and thoughtful woman, a keen observer of nature, a writer who worked for the rights of working people and women, for copyright reform, for broader educational opportunities, and for peace.

WORKS: (with W. Howitt) *The Forest Minstrel, and Other Poems* (1823). (with W. Howitt) *The Desolation of Eyam; The Emigrant, a Tale of the American Woods: and Other Poems* (1827). *The Seven Temptations* (1834). *Sketches of Natural History* (1834). *Tales in Prose* (1836). *Tales in Verse* (1836). *Wood Leighton; or, A Year in the Country*

(1836). *Hymns and Fire-Side Verses* (1839). *Hope On, Hope Ever!* (1840). *Strive and Thrive* (1840). *Sowing and Reaping; or, What Will Come of it?* (1841). *Little Coin, Much Care; or, How Poor Men Live* (1842). *Which Is the Wiser; or, People Abroad* (1842). *Work and Wages; or, Life in Service* (1842). (trans.) *The Neighbours: A Story of Every-Day Life,* by F. Bremer (1842). *Alice Franklin* (1843). *Love and Money* (1843). *No Sense Like Common Sense; or, Some Passages in the Life of Charles Middleton* (1843). (trans.) *The Home . . . ,* by F. Bremer (1843). *My Uncle the Clockmaker* (1844). *The Two Apprentices* (1844). (trans.) *The Rose of Tistelon,* by E. Carlen (1844). (trans.) *The H. Family,* by F. Bremer (1844). (trans.) *New Sketches of Every-Day Life,* by F. Bremer (1844). (trans.) *The Picture of the Virgin,* by J.C. von Schmid (1844). (trans.) *The Child's Picture and Verse-Book* by O. Spektor (1844). (trans.) *The Curate's Favourite Pupil,* by K. Stober (1844). *Fireside Verses* (1845). (trans.) *The Improvisatore,* by H.C. Andersen (1845). (trans.) *Only a Fiddler!* by H.C. Andersen (1845). (trans.) *O. T. or Life in Denmark,* by H.C. Andersen (1845). *Who Shall Be Greatest?* (1845). *My Own Story; or, The Autobiography of a Child* (1845). (trans.) *Wonderful Stories for Children,* by H.C. Andersen (1846). (trans.) *The Citizen of Prague,* by T. Thyrnau (1846). (trans.) *A Diary; the H-- Family, etc.,* by F. Bermer (1846). (trans.) *The Home; or, Life in Sweden,* by F. Bremer (1846). (trans.) *The Neighbours . . . and Other Tales,* by F. Bremer (1846). (trans.) *The President's Daughter, including Nina,* by F. Bremer (1846). *The Heir of Wast-Way-lan* (1847). *Ballads and Other Poems* (1847). (trans.) *The True Story of My Life,* by H.C. Andersen (1847). (trans.) *Genevieve: A Tale,* by A. de Lamartine (1847). (trans.) *Pictures of Life,* by A. Stifter (1847). (trans.) *Brothers and Sisters,* by F. Bremer (1848). *The Children's Year* (1847, rev. 1864; rev. as *The Story of a Happy Home; or, The Children's Year, and How They Spent It,* 1875). *The Childhood of Mary Beeson* (1848, 1870). *The Steadfast Gabriel* (1848). (trans.) *The Peasant and His Landlord,* by S.M. von Knorring (1848). *Our Cousins in Ohio* (1849). (with W. Howitt) *Stories of English and Foreign Life* (1849). (trans.) *The Midnight Sun . . . ,* by F. Bremer (1849). *How the Mice Got Out of Trouble and Other Tales* (1850). (trans.) *An Easter Offering,* by F. Bremer (1850). (with W. Howitt) *The Literature and Romance of Northern Europe* (1852). *The Dial of Love* (1852). (trans.) *Jacob Bendixen, the Jew,* by M.A. Goldschmidt (1852). (trans.)

The Homes of the New World, by F. Bremer (1853). *Birds and Flowers and Other Country Things* (1855). *The Picture Book for the Young* (1855). (trans.) *Trust and Trial,* by B.M. Bjornson (1858). (trans.) *Hertha . . . ,* by F. Bremer (1859). *Marion's Pilgrimage: A Fire-Side Story, and Other Poems* (1859). (trans.) *Father and Daughter,* by F. Bremer (1859). *A Popular History of the United States of America, from the Discovery of the American Continent to the Present Time* (1859). *The Blackbird, the Parrot, the Cat, and Other Stories* (1861). *Adventures of Jack and Harry* (1861). (trans.) *Two Years in Switzerland and Italy,* by F. Bremer (1861). (with Mrs. S.C. Hall) *The Favourite Scholar and Other Tales* (1861). *Lillieslea; or, Lost and Found* (1861). *Little Arthur's Letters to His Sister Mary* (1861). *A Treasury of New Favourite Tales for Young People* (1861). (with W. Howitt) *Ruined Abbeys and Castles of Great Britain* (1862). (trans.) *Travels in the Holy Land,* by F. Bremer (1862). *The Poet's Children* (1863). (trans.) *Greece and the Greeks,* by F. Bremer (1863). *The Story of Little Cristal* (1863). (with W. Howitt) *The Wye: Its Ruined Abbeys* (1863). *The Cost of Caergwyn* (1864). *Stories of Stapleford* (1864). *Mr. Rudd's Grandchildren* (1864). (with W. Howitt) *The Ruined Abbeys of the Border* (1865). (with W. Howitt) *The Ruined Abbeys of Yorkshire* (1865). *Our Four-Footed Friends* (1867). (trans.) *Behind the Counter* [*Handel und Wandel*], by J.W. Hackländer (1867). *John Oriel's Start in Life* (1868). *Pictures from Nature* (1869). *Vignettes of American History* (1869). *A Pleasant Life* (1871). *Birds and Flowers* (1871). *Birds and Their Nests* (1872). *Natural History Stories* (1875). *Tales for All Seasons* (1881). *Tales of English Life* (1881). *An Autobiography* (1889).

BIBLIOGRAPHY: de Groot, H.B. *Blake Studies* (1971). Lee, A. *Laurels and Rosemary: The Life of William and Mary Howitt* (1955). Paston, G. [E.M. Symonds]. *Little Memoirs of the Nineteenth Century* (1902). Walker, M.H. *Come Wind, Come Weather: A Biography of Alfred Howitt* (1971). Woodring, C.R. *Victorian Samplers, William and Mary Howitt* (1952). Woodring, C.A. *Harvard Library Bulletin* (Spring 1951).

For entries in reference works, see: *BA19C. DNB.*

Other references: *Blake Studies* (1971). Butler, J.A., *ELN* (1975). *Country Life* (30 April 1981). *Harvard Library Bulletin* (Spring 1951).

Carol A. Martin

Margaret Hamilton Wolfe Hungerford

BORN: c. 1855, Cork, Ireland.
DIED: 24 January 1897, Bandon, Ireland.
DAUGHTER OF: Canon Fitzjohn Stannus Hamilton, Vicar-Choral of St. Faughman's Cathedral and Rector of Ross Co., Ireland.
MARRIED: Edward Argles, 1872; Thomas Henry Hungerford, 1882.
WROTE UNDER: Anonymous, "Author of Phyllis," "Mrs. Hungerford," or the pseudonym "The Duchess."

Eldest daughter of an old and distinguished family, H. began writing as a young child and won many prizes in composition at school. She enjoyed telling her friends fairy tales and ghost stories, which she made up, and decided to write seriously at eighteen, publishing her first novel, Phyllis, in 1877. Typical of the many novels that followed, the work is light, full of wit, humor, and pathos. It focuses on the affairs of the human heart and ends happily.

H. wrote more than forty-six works. Her best-known novel is Molly Bawn (1878), the tale of a frivolous, petulant Irish girl, a flirt, who arouses her lover's jealousy and naively ignores social conventions.

H.'s works deal with conventional stories and situations. Slighting plot, she writes of the country society almost exclusively on the level of landlords, ignoring the peasant class. She does not analyze character; her common subject is romantic love and the frivolous interplay between couples in love before marriage. H. conveys these trivial incidents of passion and turmoil largely through dialogue. She provides interest with flirtations and delicate love scenes (never offensive even to the most prudish). She does not pursue political issues or social concerns, and, unlike some of her contemporaries, she is not didactic. She does have a sensitive ear for language, sometimes using dialect as well as slang. With artistic skill she includes vivid descriptions of nature as in "A Week in Killarney" and "Moonshine and Marguarites." Her occasional movement from prose to verse often distracts rather than intensifies the tone.

Although largely superficial, sentimental, and clearly lacking in serious intent, H.'s works are still readable, even somewhat entertaining. Adept at recreating the social milieu of her day, H. has imaginatively recorded the small-talk of her fashionable contemporaries residing at country estates like St. Brenda's, where she had lived with her second husband till her death from typhoid fever in 1897.

WORKS: Phyllis: A Novel (1877). Molly Bawn. By the Author of Phyllis (1878). Airy Fairy Lilian (1879). Beauty's Daughters (1880). Mrs. Geoffrey (1881). Faith and Unfaith (1881). Portia (1882). Loÿs, Lord Beresford, and other Tales (1883). Rossmoyne (1883). Doris (1884). O Tender Dolores (1885). A Maiden All Forlorn, and other Stories (1885). In Durance Vile (1885). Lady Branksmere (1886). A Mental Struggle (1886). Lady Valworth's Diamonds (1886). Her Week's Amusement (1886). Green Pastures and Gray Grief (1886). A Modern Circe (1887). The Duchess (1887). Undercurrents (1888). Marvel (1888). Hon. Mrs. Vereker (1888).

BIBLIOGRAPHY: Black, H.C. Notable Women Authors of the Day (1893). Dorland, Wm. A.N. The Sum of Feminine Achievement (1917). Showalter, E. A Literature of Their Own: British Women Novelists from Brontë to Lessing (1977). The Englishwoman (April 1897).
For articles in reference works, see: Allibone. The Bibliophile Dictionary. Biographical Dictionary and Synopsis of Books Ancient and Modern. British Authors of 19th Century. Brown, S.J. Ireland in Fiction: A Guide to Irish Novels, Tales, Romances, and Folk-lore (1969). Dictionary of Irish Writers, Vol. 1; Index to Women of the World from Ancient to Modern Times. Roberton, W. The Novel Reader's Handbook (1899).
Other references: Athenaeum (31 August 1878). Illustrated London News (30 January 1897). NYT (25 January 1897) Spectator (1855, 1878). Strand Magazine (October 1893). Times (London) (25 January 1897).

Phyllis J. Scherle

Violet Hunt

BORN: 28 September 1862, Durham.
DIED: 16 January 1942, South Lodge, Campden Hill.
DAUGHTER OF: Alfred William Hunt and Margaret Raine Hunt.
WROTE UNDER: I[sobel]. V[iolet]. Hunt; Violet Hunt.

Her mother a novelist and her father a famous Pre-Raphaelite painter, H. has been remembered more for the company she kept in youth and adulthood than for her novels, biographies, and autobiography. Growing up in a family where Browning, Millais, Burne-Jones, Ruskin, and the Rossettis were familiar visitors, H.

studied painting from her earliest years to please her father, who hoped she would become an artist. H. was ultimately more influenced by the literary side of her background; she sought Christina Rossetti's reaction to her earliest poems.

At twenty-eight H. published her first book, "a novel in dialogue," *The Maiden's Progress* (1894). A modest experiment in narrative technique, the novel includes passages of interior monologue as well as stage-comedy banter. Its light-hearted reliance on slang and formula jokes (e.g., "illusions, like wisdom teeth, are last to come and first to go") typifies H.'s early work and, though genuinely amusing, is probably responsible for the general appraisal of her writings as dated and superficial. Parodying novels of initiation, it traces the social successes of eighteen-year-old Moderna, who, an admirer says, can "take the impress of every passing wave of modern thought and yet preserve [her] individuality." Moderna likes playing practical jokes and rebuffing suitors; still unmarried at twenty-seven, she begins to worry that she may have "no heart." The flamboyantly happy ending rewards her with a man she had rejected at eighteen: this time, he announces, "I simply take you."

The traditional woman's reward that H. gave her first heroine was never to become her own. Though H. did not marry, her famous liaison with novelist Ford Madox Ford (then Ford Madox Hueffer) lasted from 1909–1919, indelibly marking her life and work. H. had renewed her acquaintance with Ford (who shared her Pre-Raphaelite roots) when he published an early story of hers in his *English Review*. When their affair began, Ford's wife refused to divorce him. H. went so far as to travel with Ford to Germany in 1911 and return calling herself "Mrs. Hueffer"; when various London newspapers referred to H. by that name, Ford's wife sued, bringing the affair to the scandalized attention of the public. Eventually Ford was estranged from H. when he fell in love with one of her younger friends. H.'s bitterness over their hostile parting is openly expressed in her unpublished diary of the period (now at the Pennsylvania State University Library), and colors her autobiography, *The Flurried Years* (1926; published in America as *I Have This to Say*).

Before and during her time with Ford, H. achieved her own fame for her weekly columns for the *Pall Mall Gazette*; her parties in London and at her country home, South Lodge; and her fiction, especially the occult and bizarre *Tales of the Uneasy* (1911). She raised funds for women's suffrage. She worked for Ford's *Review*, and shares with him the credit for "discovering" D.H. Lawrence, whose career they promoted by publishing his early poems. In 1916 she and Ford collaborated on *Zeppelin Nights*, a frankly patriotic collection of framed tales (explicitly comparing itself to the *Decameron*) which concludes that even poets must "do something" for the war effort by enlisting.

White Rose of Weary Leaf (1907), often considered H.'s best novel, is the long and melodramatically sad story of Amy Stevens, "a common person's child—a unit of no particular value." Showing the influence of Ford's literary circle, the novel emphasizes the importance of early impressions: the unfortunate Amy's childhood memories include images of a prison, a paralyzed woman, and a crucifix. Her story plays out these obvious symbols of frustration, helplessness, and martyrdom as she strives to support herself in occupations as diverse as secretary, actress, and director of a boys' home. Unconventional and unattached, she is known as an "adventuress" but manages at last to find a permanent situation as companion in a family where she inevitably falls in love with the father. Unconsummated for years, their affair consists of intellectual but intimate conversations that is—surprisingly—not at all ironic in tone: "'Learn that men are brutes,' said her master gently." Their menage collapses under the pressure of his wife's jealousy; when at last Amy becomes pregnant, she disappears to begin a new, solitary life. Optimistic, she enjoys her independence and the comfort of not having broken up her lover's family. When her lover learns in the extravagantly tragic last scene that Amy has died in childbirth, he commits suicide. The novel holds up very little hope for the fate of the resourceful but unattractive single woman who has neither money nor position of her own.

H. may have come to see herself as a similarly tragic figure. Her last book, a biography called *The Wife of Rossetti* (1932), reveals her bitterness. According to Thomas C. Moser, H. "identifies wholly with the barbarously treated Lizzie Siddal." As a younger, successful novelist she may have been, as Ford called her, "cheerfully heartless," but her later work still reflects Moderna's private fear that a woman without a man—a woman, perhaps, without a heart—cannot find fulfillment. The recent scholarship of Marie and Robert Secor promotes appreciation of H.'s literary accomplishments, as well as treating her experiences from H.'s own point of view rather than from that of the man who so much affected her perspective.

WORKS: The Maiden's Progress (1894). *The Celebrity at Home* (1894). *A Hard Woman* (1895). *The Way of Marriage* (1896). *Unkissed, Unkind!* (1897). *The Human Interest: a Study in Incompatibilities* (1899). *Affairs of the Heart* (1900). *The Memoirs of Jacques Casanova de Seingalt* (tr. and ed. by I.V. Hunt and A. Farley, 1902). B. Tosti, *The Heart of Ruby* (tr. by V. Hunt, 1903). *Sooner or Later: the Story of an Ingenious Ingenue* (1904). *The Cat* (1905). *The Workaday Woman* (1906). *White Rose* of *Weary Leaf* (1907). *The Wife of Altamont* (1910). *Tales of the Uneasy* (1911). *The Doll: a Happy Story* (1911). *The Governess* (begun by H.'s mother, Margaret Hunt; finished by V. Hunt, 1912). *The Desirable Alien* (with a preface and two chapters by F.M. Hueffer, 1913). *The Celebrity's Daughter* (1913). *The House of Many Mirrors* (1915). *Their Lives* (1916). *Zeppelin Nights* (with F.M. Hueffer, 1916). *The Last Ditch* (1918). *Their Hearts* (1921). *The Tiger Skin* (1924). *More Tales of the Uneasy* (1925). *The Flurried Years* (in America, *I Have This to Say*, 1926). *The Wife of Rossetti* (1932).

BIBLIOGRAPHY: Adcock, A. St. J. *The Glory That Was Grub Street* (1928). Goldring, D. *South Lodge: Reminiscences of V. Hunt, etc.* (1943). Patmore, B. *My Friends When Young* (1968). Richards, G. *Memories of a Misspent Youth* (1932). Secor, M. *English Literature in Transition* (1976). Secor, M. and R. *F.M. Ford and V. Hunt's 1917 Diary* (1983). Secor, M. and R. *The Pre-Raphaelite Review* (1979). Secor, M. and R. *The Return of the Good Soldier*. Secor, M., and R. *Women & Literature* (1978). Secor, R. *Browning Institute Studies in Victorian Literary and Cultural History* (1979). Secor, R. *Texas Studies in Literature and Language* (1979). Sinclair, M. *English Review* (1922).

Works on F.M. Ford that refer to H.: Goldring, D. *Trained for Genius* (1949). MacShane, F. *The Life and Work of F.M. Ford* (1965). Mizener, A. *The Saddest Story* (1971). Moser, T.C. *The Life in the Fiction of F.M. Ford* (1980).

For articles in reference works, see: *Longman. TCA* and *SUP*.

Other references: *Bookman* (October 1931, June 1932). *Times* (London) (19 January 1942). *The Windmill* (1947).

Robyn R. Warhol

Lucy Apsley Hutchinson

BORN: 29 January 1620, London.
DIED: after 1675.
DAUGHTER OF: Sir Allen Apsley and Lucy St. John.
MARRIED: John Hutchinson, 1638.

Along with her contemporary, Margaret Cavendish, the Duchess of Newcastle, H. is one of the first significant women prose writers in English. She was born 29 January 1620 in the Tower of London, where her husband was later imprisoned in 1663. H.'s father, Sir Allen Apsley, was Lieutenant of the Tower at the time of her birth, and her mother, Lucy St. John, was Apsley's third wife. They had ten children; H. was the fourth, following three boys.

Though she is best known for her biography of her husband, the *Memoirs of the Life of Colonel Hutchinson*, her most interesting extant piece is an autobiographical fragment: "The Life of Mrs. Hutchinson Written by Herself." This work gives a rare inside glimpse into the lives of upper-class young women in the early seventeenth century. It opens with a grim prefiguration of what was to be the central historical event in the lives of her and her husband—the English Civil War: "The land was then at peace [at the time of her birth] . . . if that quietness may be called a peace, which was rather like the calm and smooth surface of the sea, whose dark tomb is already impregnated with a horrid tempest." This statement is a fairly typical example of H.'s style, which, despite her Puritan inclinations, retained a Latinate sophistication, derived no doubt from the strong classical training she received as a child.

That education, very unusual for a woman at that time, H. received partly because she was very precocious and partly because her mother doted on her. Having had three sons, her mother "received me with a great deal of joy" and learning that the child might not live "became fonder of me." H. was taught French and English simultaneously by a French "day-nurse" and could read English by the age of four. She had an excellent memory and recited sermons verbatim, much to the delight of the adults. By the age of seven she had eight tutors in such fields as languages, music, dancing, writing, and needlework, but her bent was already toward serious reading. Her mother feared that her zeal for studies would "prejudice" her health, but even during periods of prescribed play, "I would steal into some hole or other to read." In Latin she "outstripped" her brothers who were at school, even though her tutor was a "pitiful dull fellow." "Play among other children I despised," and she neglected the traditional feminine accomplishments: "and for my needle I absolutely hated it."

H.'s mother met her father when he was forty-eight and she was sixteen. After their marriage they lived in the Tower, where Mrs. Apsley became active in caring for prisoners. She funded "experiments" in "chemistry" done by Sir Walter Raleigh (then in prison) and others, "Partly to comfort and divert the poor prisoners, and partly to gain the knowledge of their experiments, and the medicines to help such poor people as were not able to seek physicians. By these means she acquired a great deal of skill." She evidently taught some of her medicinal knowledge to her daughter, who ministered to the enemy wounded during the Civil War despite criticism by one of her husband's fellow officers. H.'s sympathy for the poor and disabled was clearly a factor in her support of the Puritan cause. In the *Memoirs* she notes with enthusiasm how under the Republic her husband, as a member of the Council of State (from 1649–51), was able to take "such courses that there was very suddenly not a beggar left in the country, and all the poor [were] in every town so maintained and provided for, as they were never so liberally . . . before nor since."

The interest in the *Memoirs of Colonel Hutchinson* lies in the anecdotes that illuminate the social life of the time as well as the character of the actors in the drama she unfolds. For example, we learn that on the day of her engagement she came down with smallpox. Despite the fact that "all that saw her were affrighted," her fiancé stood by her, the marriage took place, and "God recompensed his justice and constancy by restoring her . . . as well as before."

Much of the *Memoirs*, however, is a rather dry exposition of the events of the Civil War in which her husband was personally involved, such as the defense of Nottingham against the royalists, a strategic battle which preserved the north-south passage for the forces of parliament. H. clearly sees herself as writing military history and rejects temptations to elaborate romantic episodes. The work was written in the third person, ostensibly to recount her husband's life to her children and not intended for publication. She proposed that "a naked, undressed narrative speaking the simple truth of him, will deck him with more substantial glory, than all the panegyrics [of] the best pens." However, the weakness in the work lies in its relentless enthusiasm for her husband's improbably impeccable character. As a follower of Cromwell, Hutchinson was out of favor during the Restoration and in 1663 was arrested; he died in prison eleven months later. H. wrote the *Memoirs* shortly thereafter, probably between 1664 and 1671. It was not published until 1806, but thereafter reprinted several times, remaining one of the most popular of the Civil War memoirs.

Its author herself lived into the late 1670s, having presented a translation of Lucretius' *De Rerum Natura* in 1675, which had been written much earlier. The dedication to that work is largely a recantation of having committed "the sin of amusing myself with such vain philosophy" as Epicureanism. She asserts, however, that she did the translation only as a diversion: "I did not employ any serious study . . . for I turned it into English in a room where my children practised . . . with their tutors, and I numbered the syllables of my translation by the threads of the canvas I wrought in"—a further glimpse into the early milieu of the woman writer. She also completed a partial translation of the *Aeneid* and wrote two treatises on religion: "On the Principles of Christian Religion," written for her daughter, and "On Theology," which were published in 1817. An earlier manuscript narrative of the events of her husband's life remains in the British Museum and some additional writings on moral and religious subjects were still privately owned in the early 1900s.

WORKS: Memoirs of the Life of Colonel Hutchinson (1806). The Life of Mrs. Hutchinson Written by Herself (1806). On the Principles of the Christian Religion; Addressed to Her Daughter; and on Theology (1817).

BIBLIOGRAPHY: Firth, C.M. Introduction to the *Memoirs of Colonel Hutchinson* (1906). Handley, G.M. *Notes on the Memoirs of Colonel Hutchinson* (1905).

For articles in reference works, see: *DNB*.

Other references: *Contemporary Review* (1949). *Evangelical Quarterly* (1959). MacCarthy, B. *Women Writers: Their Contribution to the English Novel* (1944). *N&Q* (1955).

Josephine Donovan

Elizabeth Simpson Inchbald

BORN: 15 October 1753, Stanningfield, Suffolk.
DIED: 1 August 1821, Kensington.
DAUGHTER OF: John and Mary Rushbrook Simpson.
MARRIED: Joseph Inchbald, 1772.
WROTE UNDER: Elizabeth Inchbald, Mrs. Inchbald.

I. was eighth child in a family of nine. She ran away from home at nineteen to seek her fortune on the London stage. As a beautiful woman with a pronounced stammer, I. faced formidable obstacles in her aspirations. The stammer she could control when delivering carefully rehearsed lines, but her beauty caused difficulties of another kind, for it marked her as prey to such unscrupulous actors as James Dodd, who attempted to molest her when she applied to him for help.

The experience of independence was so thoroughly frightening that, three months after her arrival, I. accepted the proposals of Joseph Inchbald, whom she had earlier rejected. Seventeen years her senior, Joseph provided I. the security of marriage with a fellow Roman Catholic as well as automatic access to the stage. Ironically, or perhaps intentionally, I.'s Bristol debut as Cordelia to Joseph's Lear capitalized on their age difference, and this was a role she was to repeat many times. For the first four years of their marriage, I. served an apprenticeship in the regional theaters of England and Scotland, but finally, in July 1776, Joseph having quarreled with the Edinburgh audience, they moved to Paris, where he tried to earn a living by his avocation, painting, and she tried writing comedies, only to return to Brighton in September.

It was at this low period that the Inchbalds befriended Sarah Siddons and her brother, John Philip Kemble, and I. fell in love with the latter, but I. never remarried after her husband's death in June 1779.

One of I.'s earliest known literary efforts was an outline of *A Simple Story*, which she circulated among friends in 1777. By 1779, I. had completed the first version of the novel, which she offered for publication several times over the next ten years. Meanwhile, she began to succeed in her dramatic writing, earning 100 guineas from the sale of her first play, *The Mogul*, which played ten days at the Haymarket in 1784. After this first play, inspired by the French craze for ballooning, I. received consistently high fees for her subsequent plays, most of which were produced and printed. I.'s humanitarian interests are revealed in her most successful plays. Under the guise of a light summer comedy, *I'll Tell You What* (1786) raised questions about marriage and divorce. *Such Things Are* (1787), which brought £900, probed social issues by portraying, in the character Haswell, the prison reformer John Howard. Today I.'s best-known play may be *Lover's Vows*, a rendering of a Kotzebue play that scandalizes Fanny Price in *Mansfield Park*.

Although her first gainful writing was for the theater, I. is better known for her novels, *A Simple Story* (1791) and *Nature and Art* (1796). When she failed to locate a publisher for her early version of *A Simple Story*, I. began a second novel in 1779, yet it was not until she combined the stories ten years later that she succeeded in selling the book to a publisher for £200. *A Simple Story*, well-received by the public, praised for its realism and its dramatic qualities, may be read autobiographically, the Dorriforth-Miss Milner relationship reminiscent of I.'s infatuation with Kemble (another Catholic who studied for the priesthood).

As a Catholic, I. intentionally subverted the usual vilification of her religion by depicting a sympathetic priest whose tender and virtuous relationship with his ward ripens into love. Dorri-

forth is torn between his "prospect of futurity" in heaven and his recognition of his ward's failings on the one hand and his earthly love for Miss Milner and his desire to reform her on the other. The struggle is resolved when he inherits an earldom and, forgiven his priestly vows, is encouraged to marry as a family duty. But in the second part of the novel (set some 16 years later) Dorriforth's first instincts are proven correct, when his wife, still bent on testing the extent of his tolerance, slips into an affair in his absence. Although she dies shortly thereafter with a deathbed repentance, Dorriforth's unyielding morality continues to prosecute the sins of the mother in their daughter until the shock of her near abduction effects a reconciliation.

Nature and Art, frankly revolutionary in tone, is less psychologically acute and thought less successful now, though I.'s contemporaries praised it highly. The story begins with two brothers who make their way after their father's death. Henry, a fiddler, supports William until the latter has risen to a deanship; the resentment he receives in return prompts him to leave England for Africa. Later, Henry's "naturally" educated son returns to live under his uncle's protection in England and there meets his cousin, William, whose "artificial" education has molded him in the image of his own calculating father. The opposition between the two persists as William seduces a virtuous woman and later (as judge) sentences her for the prostitution he forced on her, and Henry first delivers his father from his African exile and then marries his faithful Rebecca.

I. continued writing for the London stage until 1805, her last production being the comedy, *To Marry, or Not to Marry* (1805). In the fall of that year, she turned to editorial work, writing a series of 125 biographical and critical prefaces for *The British Theatre* (1806–1808), a twenty-five volume collection published by Longman. She then selected plays for a seven-volume *Collection of Farces* (1809) and a ten-volume *The Modern Theatre* (1811). I. also wrote articles and reviews for the *Edinburgh Review* and the *Artist*, declining other offers to write for the *Quarterly Review* and to edit *La Belle Assemblee*. I. lived the last two years of her life in Kensington House, a Roman Catholic residence for ladies, dying there on 1 August 1821.

Self-tutored and remarkably successful, I. achieved an unusual degree of recognition for a professional woman writer of her period. She was an active playwright for more than twenty years, earning the respect of Richard Brinsley Sheridan, who commissioned *The Wedding Day* (1794). Her first novel, *A Simple Story*, praised by her contemporaries, has continued to be reissued since its publication.

WORKS: *Appearance Is Against Them* (1785). *I'll Tell You What* (1786). *The Widow's Vow* (1786). *Such Things Are* (1788). *The Mogul Tale* (1788). *Animal Magnetism* (1788). *A Simple Story* (1791). *The Massacre* (1792). *Everyone Has His Fault* (1793). *The Wedding Day* (1794). *Nature and Art* (1796). *Wives as They Were, and Maids as They Are* (1797). *To Marry, or Not to Marry* (1805).

BIBLIOGRAPHY: Boaden, J. *Memoirs of Mrs. Inchbald* (1833). Joughin, G.L. *University of Texas Studies in English* (July 1934). Littlewood, S.R., *Elizabeth Inchbald and Her Circle* (1921). McKee, W., *Elizabeth Inchbald, Novelist* (1935). Tompkins, J.M.S., ed. *A Simple Story* (1967).

For articles in reference works, see: *BAB1800. DLB.* Todd.

Other references: Kelly, G. *The English Jacobin Novel, 1780–1805* (1976). Rogers, K.M., *Eighteenth Century Studies* (1977). Sigl, P. *N&Q* (1982).

Catherine S. Green

Jean Ingelow

BORN: 17 March 1820, near Boston, Lincolnshire.
DIED: 20 July 1897, London.
DAUGHTER OF: William and Jean Kilgour Ingelow.
WROTE UNDER: Jean Ingelow, Orris.

I. has been called a "lost Pre-Raphaelite." Her poetry and prose, published during the second half of the nineteenth century, exhibit the form, style, and subject matter characteristic of Pre-Raphaelite art. I. and her numerous brothers and sisters were educated at home by their mother, who encouraged their creativity; together they produced a family periodical, where I. first saw her poems "in print." However, it was financial exigency that prompted her to begin publishing in earnest, in the 1850s: mostly children's tales, under the pen name "Orris" (these were illustrated by John Millais), and an anonymous book of poems.

Her second volume of poetry, published in 1863, went through thirty editions. In this book many of her best poems appeared, including "Songs of Seven" and "Divided," a wistful tale about a couple walking on opposite sides of a streamlet that becomes ever wider and faster, until it divides them absolutely and forever. The natural descriptions and the emotional authenticity in this poem made it one of her best loved and most quoted pieces. It is comparable in content, style, and quality to Christina Rossetti's "An Echo from Willow-Wood."

"Divided" led I.'s biographer, Maureen Peters, to conclude that in her youth I. must have lost a sweetheart herself. It is true that I. never married; a spinster aunt Rebecca who was anti-marriage may have influenced I.'s opinions on the subject. And though she was essentially conservative, in many of her poems I. expressed reservations about marriage: e.g., "Katherine of Aragon to Henry VIII" (1850), "Brothers, and a Sermon" (1863), and "Wedlock" (1867). On the whole, however, her numerous narratives of love, court-ship, and marriage are more similar to Coventry Patmore's *The Angel in the House* than, say, George Meredith's *Modern Love*.

"The High Tide on the Coast of Lincolnshire, 1571" (1883), a ballad about a sixteenth-century disaster, was her most popular poem. Contemporary readers were also moved by her poems about childhood deaths; the best of these is probably "Katie, Aged Five Years," written for her friend (and first editor) the Rev. Edward Harston, who had lost three children in rapid succession. In her later years I. wrote mostly fiction, including several novels—*Off the Skelligs* (1872) and *Sarah de Berenger* (1879)—and numerous children's tales. Her most successful children's story is *Mopsa the Fairy* (1869), written in a graceful, Pre-Raphaelite style reminiscent of George MacDonald or William Morris and in a fantasy mode comparable to *Alice in Wonderland* or "Goblin Market."

I. was on friendly terms with Ruskin, Longfellow, and Tennyson, as well as Christina Rossetti and Jane and Ann Taylor of Ongar. When Tennyson died in 1892, I. was mentioned as a candidate for the poet laureateship though she was actually better known in the United States than in England. Some people belived it was I.'s popularity in America, combined with her female gender, that prompted Queen Victoria to offer the laureateship to Alfred Austin instead.

WORKS: *A Rhyming Chronicle of Incidents and Feelings*, ed. E. Harston (1850). *Allerton and Drieux; or the War of Opinion* (1857). *Tales of Orris* (1860). *Poems* (1863). *Studies for Stories* (1864). *Stories Told to a Child* (1865). *Home Thoughts and Home Scenes* (1865). *Songs of Seven* (1866, 1881). *The Wild Duck Shooter and I Have a Right* (1867). *A Story of Doom and Other Poems* (1867). *A Sister's Bye-Hours* (1868). *Mopsa the Fairy* (1869). *The Little Wonder-Horn* (1872). *Off the Skelligs* (1879). *Fated to be Free* (1875). *One Hundred Holy Songs, Carols and Sacred Ballads* (1878). *Sarah de Berenger* (1879). *Poems* (1880). *Don John: A Story* (1881). *The High Tide on the Coast of Lincolnshire, 1571* (1883). *Poems: Third*

Series (1885, 1888). *Poems of the Old Days and the New* (1885). *John Jerome, His Thoughts and Ways: A Book Without Beginning* (1886). *Very Young and Quite Another Story* (1890). *A Motto Changed* (1894). *The Old Man's Prayer* (1895).

BIBLIOGRAPHY: Anon. *Some Recollections of Jean Ingelow and Her Early Friends* (1901). Lewis, N. *TLS* (8 December 1972). Peters, M. *Jean Ingelow, Victorian Poetess* (1972). Stedman, E.A. *An Appreciation* (1935). Symons, A. *SR* (1897).

For articles in reference works, see: *BA19C. English Poetesses*, ed. E.S. Robertson (1883).

Notable Women Authors of the Day, Ed. Helen C. Black (1893). *Our Living Poets,* Ed. H.B. Forman (1871). *The Poets and the Poetry of the Century*, Ed. Alfred H. Miles, (1892).

Other references: *Athenaeum* (24 July 1897). Hearns, L., in *Appreciations of Poetry*, Ed. J. Erskine (1916). Hickok, K., *Representations of Women: Nineteenth-Century British Women's Poetry* (1984). King, H.D., *N&Q* (30 August 1952). Singers-Biggers, G., *English* (1940). *Times* (London) (21 July 1897).

Kathleen Hickok

Phyllis Dorothy James (White)

BORN: 3 August 1920, Oxford.
DAUGHTER OF: Sidney Victor James and Dorothy Amelia (Hone) James.
MARRIED: Ernest Conner Bantry White, 1941.
WRITES UNDER: P.D. James.

J.'s formal education ended at the age of sixteen in 1937 after attending Cambridge High School for Girls. Although J. wanted to attend college, her father, a tax officer, did not believe in educating girls. J. first worked in a tax office and then as assistant stage manager of the Cambridge Festival Theatre until her marriage in 1941. After her husband returned home following World War II, he began to suffer from a mental illness, and he was confined to psychiatric hospitals until his death in 1964. J. was consequently forced to return to work in 1949 in order to support herself and her two daughters. She took a job with the National Health Service and worked her way up to principal administrative assistant of the North West Metropolitan Regional Hospital Board in London, moving in 1968 to the Home Office-Criminal Policy Department.

At the age of forty she decided to fulfill her long-time dream of becoming a writer, and to this day J. has never received a rejection slip. In addition, half of her novels have won awards, such as The Silver Dagger of the British Crime Writers Association; *Innocent Blood, The Skull Beneath the Skin*, and *A Taste for Death*, all written in the 1980s, have been best sellers; and at least two of her novels—*Death of an Expert Witness* and *A Shroud for a Nightingale*—have been made into television serials. J. was granted an OBE (Officer, Order of the British Empire) award in 1983.

In the classic detective novel tradition, J. has created two major central detective characters: Adam Dalgliesh, who dominates seven novels, and Cordelia Gray, who figures in two stories.

Dalgliesh, a professional policeman who rises through the ranks during the course of the novels, is an intelligent, sensitive individual and a published poet. Cordelia Gray, the central character in *An Unsuitable Job for a Woman* and *The Skull Beneath the Skin*, is more of an amateur because her career as a private detective is just getting started. In fact, Gray finds herself suddenly thrust into running the agency on the unexpected death of her mentor and boss. Throughout *An Unsuitable Job for a Woman*, Adam Dalgliesh remains in the background quietly guiding Gray through her first case.

In reviewing *Cover Her Face* (1966), J.'s first novel, Anthony Boucher writes that the novel is "modeled firmly upon the detective story of thirty years ago at its dullest. No forward plot, nothing but 80,000 words of relentless (and non-procedural) investigation leading to the final assembly of all characters and the unbelievable confession. . . . When I keep urging a return to the formal detecive story, this is *not* what I mean." J. is sometimes criticized for following the detective novel canon, but other critics find no fault with this. For example, Jean White reviewing *An Unsuitable Job for a Woman* comments that this novel "honorably carries on in the tradition of the classic English mystery—literate, intelligent, with shrewdly observed characters and sound plotting." J. herself, in an October 1987 interview on National Public Radio (NPR), cheerfully admitted that she writes to a formula. She stated that working within the formula allows her creative imagination to develop realistic characters and to focus on socially relevant themes.

All of J.'s novels are set in a closed society. In three, the setting is a village and, in addition, in the conventional "country house." *Cover Her Face* is in the village of Chadfleet near London, *Unnatural Causes* in a village in Suffolk, and *An Unsuitable Job for a Woman* in the Callender

Laboratory and Summertrees—a country house near Cambridge. As an outcome of her hospital and police experiences, J. sets *A Mind to Murder* in the Steen Psychological Clinic in London, *A Shroud for a Nightingale* in Nightingale Hospital and House, *Black Tower* in a nursing home for victims of multiple sclerosis, and *Death of an Expert Witness* in the Hoggatt Forensic Laboratory.

One of the reasons J. always rejects the comparison made between her novels and those of Agatha Christie is the difference in the treatment of death. In her NPR interview, J. maintained that Christie's corpses were just blood-splattered bodies lying on a floor. She stated that she herself was interested in how the person died, but that Christie was only interested in the puzzle created by the death. It is J.'s characterization that has so often drawn favorable critical comment. In reviewing *Death of an Expert Witness*, Barbara Bannon writes that J.'s "insight into sexual fears and needs . . . is profound, and she makes of even her murderers and his victims, human beings whom one can, in the end, deeply pity."

Another break with tradition occurs with J.'s focus on illness and dying. In *Cover Her Face*, the father of the family is terminally ill and in a coma; in *Unnatural Causes*, one of the characters is a paraplegic; many of the characters in *Black Tower* suffer from multiple sclerosis; and in *A Mind to Murder*, the mother of the victim had been mentally ill for years and had been treated by the medical director of the clinic. Even when the critics find her novels disappointing, as many did with *Black Tower*, they praise her compassionate and perceptive handling of such difficult themes.

J.'s one movement outside the traditional confines of the detective novel, *Innocent Blood*, has received the most widely divergent critical comment. *Innocent Blood* was J.'s first best seller, became a Book-of-the-Month Club main selection, and made the writer financially secure. On the other hand, critics such as Julian Symons charge that the book "shows among other things the risks of too much ambition. . . . And judged by its characters . . . is strikingly implausible." Writing in the (London) *Times Literary Supplement*, Paul Bailey says, "There are two novels fighting for dominance within the covers of *Innocent Blood*." One, he says, "conveys something of the messiness involved in being human," and the other "look[s] at crime through a dusty lorgnette. For most of the book, the two go their separate ways, but every so often they merge—with embarrassing consequences."

Innocent Blood is the story of Philippa Palfrey's search for her real parents. During the course of the novel, there is strangulation, death by automobile and cancer, suicide, rape of a child, a child battering, incest, and revenge. In addition,

the novel ends happily. Writing in the *New York Times*, Christopher Lehmann-Haupt says that J.

> has burst the bounds of her territory. . . . she has gone far beyond the conventional limits of the whodunnit . . . and written a novel that is subtle, rich, allusive and positively Shakespearean in its manipulation of such symbols as blindness, bastardy and flowers, and in its preoccupation with Guilt and Innocence, Good and Evil, Justice and Revenge, and the competing claims of Blood and Environment.

Although the elements of the detective story are present, for Philippa does follow certain clues, *Innocent Blood* can be more easily compared with the psychological novels of Ruth Rendell, whom J. often reviews. With an ending more hopeful than many of Rendell's, J.'s main character learns to love and forgive while exploring the extremes of happiness and disappointment in a human relationship. It is interesting to note that J. followed *Innocent Blood* with *The Skull Beneath the Skin*, the second Cordelia Gray novel. Gray and Philippa Palfrey have a number of characteristics in common, notably their wish to be strong, determined women.

J. compares her novels to those of Dorothy L. Sayers and Margery Allingham, and there is no doubt in her reader's mind that her novels carry on in that same tradition. It is for J., however, to continue to take the mystery novel on to greater triumphs. In an article in *The Writer*, J. says that she has used "the setting to fulfill all the functions of place in detective fiction." She concludes the article by saying,

> And it is surely the power to create this sense of place and to make it as real to the reader as is his own living room—and then to people it with characters who are suffering men and women, not stereotypes to be knocked down like dummies in the final chapter—that gives any mystery writer the claim to be regarded as a serious novelist.

This J. has accomplished.

WORKS: *Cover Her Face* (1966). *A Mind to Murder* (1967). *Unnatural Causes* (1967). *Shroud for a Nightingale* (1971). (with T.A. Critchley) *The Maul and the Pear Tree: The Ratcliffe Highway Murders, 1811* (1971). *An Unsuitable Job for a Woman* (1973). *The Black Tower* (1975). *Death of an Expert Witness* (1977). *Innocent Blood* (1980). *The Skull Beneath the Skin* (1982). *A Taste for Death* (1987).

BIBLIOGRAPHY: Bakerman, J.S. *Clues: A Journal of Detection* (1984). Benstock, B. *Twentieth Century Women Novelists*, ed. T.F. Staley (1982). Harkness, B. *Art in Crime Writing: Essays on Detective Fiction*, cd. B. Benstock (1983). Hubley, E. *Clues: A*

Journal of Detection (1982). Hubley, E. *Modern Fiction Studies* (1983). Joyner, N.C. *Ten Women of Mystery*, ed. E.F. Bargainnier (1981). Salwak, D. *Clues: A Journal of Detection* (1985). Siebenheller, N. *P.D. James* (1982). Smyer, R.I. *Clues: A Journal of Detection* (1982).

For articles in reference works, see: *CA. CB. CLC. TCC&MW.*

Other references: Campbell, S.E. *Modern Fiction Studies* (1983). *TLS* (5 June 1981). Winks, R.W. *NR* (31 July 1976).

Alice Lorraine Painter

Anna Brownell Jameson

BORN: 19 May 1794, Dublin.
DIED: 17 March 1860, London.
DAUGHTER OF: Denis Brownell Murphy.
MARRIED: Robert Sympson Jameson, 1825.

Art historian, social and cultural critic, author of a novel and many essays, J. helped shape the popular taste of Victorian England and America. As a child, she lived in a world of dreams, which she later denounced as "unhealthy." "I was always a princess heroine in the guise of a knight, a sort of Clorinda or Britomart, going about to redress the wrongs of the poor, fight giants, and kill dragons; or founding a society in some far-off solitude or desolate island . . . where there were to be no tears, no tasks, and no laws—except those which I made myself." She loathed the religious stories of Hannah More, and the illustrations to *Pilgrim's Progress* gave her nightmares. J. liked nature poetry, fairy tales (especially "The Arabian Nights") and Shakespeare. She read books, not for their "contents, but for some especial image or picture I had picked out of them and assimilated to my own mind and mixed up with my own life." J. wrote her earliest tales to amuse her sisters and asked her father, an Irish miniature painter, to comment on her poems. She became a governess at sixteen and remained in the employment of wealthy families until her ill-fated marriage in 1825.

J. was encouraged to seek publication by her husband, barrister Robert Jameson. Her novel, *The Diary of an Ennuyee* (1826), was based on journals of a European tour she had begun in 1821 after her engagement to Jameson was temporarily broken off. Situating her text in relationship to Evelyn's *Diary*, de Staël's *Corrine*, and Lady Morgan's *Italy*, the narrator records her responses to the beauties of Italian art and broods about a mysterious passion which eventually kills her.

J.'s early essays are biographical sketches of women who have been immortalized in poetry, like Petrarch's Laura, and queens, like Cleopatra and Catherine II. Writing for ladies who are "fair, pure-hearted, delicate-minded, and unclassical," J. is timid, self-deprecating, and reluctant to criticize. She gained confidence in addressing a general audience with the favorable reception of *Characteristics of Women* (1832), an analysis of Shakespeare's heroines based on the assumption that the characters are "complete individuals" who "combine history and real life."

Winter Studies and Summer Rambles in Canada (1838) resulted from J.'s 1836 trip to Canada. She went hoping to resolve differences with her husband, who was soon to be appointed Vice-Chancellor of Upper Canada; she returned with an allowance of £300 a year, a guarantee that she could live separately from her husband, and material for one of the century's most interesting travel memoirs. *Winter Studies* contains essays on German culture; *Summer Rambles* recounts her strenuous journey to Sault Ste. Marie. "The woman of the bright foam," as the Indians called her, was exhilarated by new friends, such as Indian authority Henry Schoolcraft and his Chippewa wife, and by the wild beauty of the land. "O how passing lovely it was," she said of Mackinaw, "how wondrously beautiful and strange." Realizing that she had been thrown "into relations with the Indian tribes, such as few European women of refined and civilised habits have ever risked, and none have recorded," J. described clothing, agricultural implements, religious rituals, stories, and songs. Having set out "to see, with my own eyes, the condition of women in savage life," she soon took issue with the accounts of Indian women prepared by "gentlemen travellers." The squaw performed heavy physical labor, but by "providing for her own subsistence and the well-being of society," she attained dignity. J. argued that "the woman among these Indians holds her true natural position relatively to the state of the man and the state of society; and this cannot be said of all societies." Chastity was not highly valued among the Indians, but prostitution was unknown. Given the lack of real property and the absence of class divisions, Indian life offered a kind of rough equality. Indeed, J. observed that the squaw's life was "gracious" in comparison with that of a factory girl or servant in London.

As a social critic, J. was particularly concerned with women's need for employment. J. believed that women's work, including writing, was necessitated by men's failure to provide them with financial and emotional support. When she knew her own marriage was failing, she observed, "Only in the assiduous employment of such faculties as we are permitted to exercise, can we find health and peace, and compensation for the wasted or repressed impulses and energies more proper to our sex." The government's 1842 report on factories and mines prompted J. to take a broader perspective on the consequences of industrialization. Women forced into such exhausting and degrading work could not fulfill their domestic responsibilities. "'Woman's mission,' of which people talk so well and write so prettily, is irreconcilable with woman's position, of which no one dares to think, much less to speak," she charged. She called for better education, here and in a 1846 pamphlet in support of the Governesses' Benevolent Association. She encouraged the founding of the *Englishwoman's Journal*, and she made her home a gathering place for young feminists—her "adopted nieces." In the 1850s, she lectured on "sisterhoods," Protestant communities that would provide women with training in nursing and social service. J.'s feminism assumes sympathetic understanding between the sexes. "At the core of all social reformation, as a necessary condition of health and permanence in all human institutions, lies the working of the man and the woman together, in mutual trust, love, and reverence." Invoking the family model, she argues for the extension of "motherly and sisterly" influence into the state.

Between 1840 and 1860, she wrote primarily about art. J. wanted to introduce the English public "to that *many-sided* and elevated spirit in criticism with which the Germans have long been familiar." Showing increased professionalization and a greater awareness of herself as a specialist, she produced several important guidebooks and a very influential account of early Italian art. In *Poetry of Sacred and Legendary Art* (1848), the first part of her tetralogy, she set out to interpret the symbolism of Christian art in historical rather than religious terms. Her *Legends of the Madonna* (1852) constitutes the "first extensive study

of the imagery of the Virgin in the literature of art."

An energetic and emotionally impulsive traveller, J. had a wide range of friends. She sought Fanny Kemble's advice on Shakespeare, supported Ottilie von Goethe through the birth of her illegitimate child, participated in Lady Byron's intrigues, joined the Brownings on their honeymoon trip, gave Elizabeth Gaskell advice about her novels, and at the age of sixty-eight toured Hawthorne around Rome. Despite the popularity of her books, she was often under financial pressure. When her husband's retirement and death left her in precarious straits, friends secured pensions for her. Her works, said Harriet Martineau, "will remind a future generation that in ours there was a restless, expatiating, fervent, unreasoning, generous, accomplished Mrs. J."

WORKS (selected): *The Diary of an Ennuyee* (1826). *The Loves of the Poets* (1829). *Memoirs of Celebrated Female Sovereigns* (1831). *Characteristics of Women* (1832). *Visits and Sketches at Home and Abroad* (1834). *Winter Studies and Summer Rambles in Canada* (1838). *Memoirs of the Early Italian Painters* (1845). *Memoirs and Essays* (1846). *The Poetry of Sacred and Legendary Art* (1848). *Legends of the Monastic Orders* (1850). *Legends of the Madonna* (1852). *A Commonplace Book of Thoughts, Memories, and Fancies* (1854). *Sisters of Charity* (1855). *The Communion of Labour* (1856). *History of Our Lord* (1864).

BIBLIOGRAPHY: Erskine, B., ed. *Anna Jameson: Letters and Friendships*, 1812-1860 (1915). Holcomb, A. *Women as Interpreters of the Visual Arts*, ed. C. Sherman (1981). Halcomb, A. *Art History* (1983). Killham, J. *Tennyson and "The Princess": Reflections of an Age* (1958). Macpherson, G. *Memoirs of Anna Jameson* (1878). Needler, G., ed. *Letters of Anna Jameson to Ottilie von Goethe* (1939). Thomas, C. *Love and Work Enough: The Life of Anna Jameson* (1967). York, L.M. *Mosaic* (1986).

For articles in reference works, see: *BA19C. BDBF. DNB. Europa. VB.*

Robin Sheets

Storm Jameson

BORN: 8 January 1891, Whitby, Yorkshire.
DIED: 30 September 1986, Cambridge.
DAUGHTER OF: William Storm and Hannah Margaret Jameson.
MARRIED: (?) Clark, 1914; Guy Patterson Chapman, 1926.
WROTE UNDER: James Hill, William Lamb, Storm Jameson.

Although she wrote over fifty novels, J. asserted in her autobiography, *Journey from the North* "novels, for all the intense pains taken with them—are not serious, not worth a tear." She often deprecated her work, most often being too hard on herself (her work does vary somewhat widely in quality). J. also spoke often of her hatred of settled domestic life, passed down, she felt, from her mother, who often accompanied her sea-captain husband on his travels. She continued this practice after J.'s birth and settled down only after the number of children made travel cumbersome. When she settled, she chose the seaport of Whitby, Yorkshire, where the Jameson ancestors had lived and where J. had been born. Whitby had been a fishing and shipbuilding port but was reduced by the time of J.'s birth to a minor harbor on the North Sea. J. endured a poor yet ambitious childhood. Her own intense desire for an education and her mother's support led her to earn a rare county scholarship, which enabled her to attend Leeds University. There she took first class honors in English language and literature in 1912. Granted a research scholarship to University College, she transferred to King's College—which she felt was more interesting than the pedantic University College—where she earned an M.A. in 1914, writing her thesis (later published) on Modern Drama in Europe.

True to her dislike of settled life, J. traveled and moved around a great deal. Her first marriage gave her a son whom she loved deeply and a husband unsuited to her. Her husband found a way of life he loved while in the army during World War I as J. painfully separated herself from her child in order to take jobs. She began to publish her novels, work as a copywriter for an advertising agency, and edit the *New Commonwealth*, a weekly. She met her second husband, Guy Chapman, while working for the Alfred A. Knopf publishing company as their English representative. Her relationship with Chapman lasted until his death in 1972.

J. was an active member of P.E.N. International and president of its English Centre from 1938-1945. This work took her over much of Europe aiding refugee writers. As a result, her own work was banned by the Nazis. Her later novels reflect this interest and atmosphere. A book unlike most of her work, *In the Second Year* (1936), is a futuristic story of the takeover of England by fascists. In the late 1930s J. lost many of her friends as her pacifist stand gave way to support for England's war effort against Nazism.

J. wrote furiously most of her life. Many of her novels are set in Yorkshire dealing with families involved in shipbuilding or sailing. Her *Triumph of Time* and *Mirror of Darkness* series cover four generations of Yorkshire families. The three books in the *Triumph of Time* and the five in *The Mirror of Darkness* are realistic in every detail of setting and character. Mary Hervey, the main character of *The Triumph of Time* trilogy—*The Lovely Ship*, *The Voyage Home*, and *A Richer Dust*—is head of a shipbuilding firm; the story covers her life from 1841 to 1923 and follows shipbuilding from sail to steam to turbines to war boom. *The Mirror of Darkness* saga centers

on Mary Hervey Russell, a character close to J. herself in many ways. J. used transcripts of arguments between herself and her first husband for dialogue in some of these works.

Her two-volume autobiography, *Journey from the North* (1969-1970) is possibly her best work and an excellent preparation for a study of her fiction. In it she describes her eyes as "a darker clouded grey-blue: I fit badly into my skull, and while my eyes are taking you in my brain is trying to guess what you are thinking and what will keep you at a safe distance." She tells of her hatred of domesticity, her decision to write novels: "I have a strong, patient brain, but it is myopic and slightly mad. It reminds me of a young horse I once rode, which was blind in one eye and under the delusion that it could jump walls." The autobiographical narrative of Jameson's life reads as lively as any of her novels or short stories as it explores, with a relentless truthfulness few are capable of, the forces that formed her.

Aware that she was writing too quickly, midway through her *Mirror of Darkness* series J. took on two successive male pennames in an attempt to change her pace and direction in a way that was not really successful. Much of her work is criticized for being too socially motivated and pedantic, while her stories of the Yorkshire families remain the most popular. Much of J.'s later work, such as *Cousin Honoré* and *Europe to Let* is set in Europe. In 1974 she was awarded the English Centre of International P.E.N. award for *There Will Be a Short Interval*.

J. worked in several genres other than that of the novel. She translated Guy de Maupassant, wrote such non-fiction as *The Georgian Novel and Mr. Robinson* (1929), *The Decline of Merry England* (1930), *The Soul of Man in the Age of Leisure* (1935), *The Novel in Contemporary Life* (1938), *The Writer's Situation and Other Essays* (1950), and *Speaking of Stendhal* (1979), a work of literary criticism. She worked as editor with her husband on his autobiography, *A Kind of Survivor* (1975), as well as producing short stories and television plays.

J. is only now beginning to gain the kind of popularity she had in her heyday, due partly to reprints of her major works.

WORKS: *The Pot Boils* (1919). *The Happy Highways* (1920). *Modern Drama in Europe* (1920). *The Clash* (1922). *The Pitiful Wife* (1923). *Lady Susan and Life: An Indiscretion* (1924). (trans.) *Mont-Oriol* by G. de Maupassant (1924). (trans.) *Horla and Other Stories* by G. de Maupassant (1925). *Three Kingdoms* (1926). *The Lovely Ship* (1927; *The Triumph of Time* I). *Farewell to Youth* (1928). *The Georgian Novel and Mr. Robinson* (1929). *Full Circle* (1929). *The Decline of Merry England* (1930). (trans., with E. Boyd) *88 Short Stories* by G. de

Maupassant (1930). *The Voyage Home* (1930; *The Triumph of Time* II). *A Richer Dust* (1931; *The Triumph of Time* III). *The Single Heart* (1932). *That Was Yesterday* (1932). *A Day Off* (1933). *Women Against Men* (1933; includes *A Day Off*, *The Delicate Monster*, and *The Single Heart*). *No Time Like the Present* (1933). *Company Parade* (1934). *The Soul of Man in the Age of Leisure* (1935). *Love in Winter* (1935). *In the Second Year* (1936). *Now Turn Back* (1936). *The Delicate Monster* (1937). *Moon Is Making* (1937). (as William Lamb) *The World Ends* (1937). (as James Hill) *Loving Memory* (1937). (as James Hill) *No Victory for the Soldier* (1938). *The Novel in Contemporary Life* (1938). *Here Comes a Candle* (1938). *A Civil Journey* (1939). *Farewell Night, Welcome Day* (1939; in the U.S. as *The Captain's Wife*). *Europe to Let: The Memoirs of an Obscure Man* (1940). *Cousin Honoré* (1940). *The End of This Year* (1941). *The Fort* (1941). *Then We Shall Hear Singing: A Fantasy in C Major* (1942). *Cloudless May* (1943). *The Journal of Mary Hervey Russell* (1945). *The Other Side* (1946). *Before the Crossing* (1947). *The Black Laurel* (1947). *The Moment of Truth* (1949). *The Writer's Situation and Other Essays* (1950). *The Green Man* (1952). *The Hidden River* (1955). *The Intruder* (1956). *A Cup of Tea for Mr. Thorgill* (1957). *A Ulysses Too Many* (1958). *Days Off: Two Short Novels and Some Stories* (1959). *Last Score; or, The Private Life of Sir Richard Ormston* (1961). *Morley Roberts: The Last Eminent Victorian* (1961). *The Road from the Monument* (1962). *A Month Too Soon* (1963). *The Aristide Case* (1964; in the U.S. as *The Blind Heart*). *The Early Life of Stephen Hind* (1966). *The White Crow* (1968). *Journey from the North* (1969, 1970). *Parthian Words* (1970). *There Will Be a Short Interval* (1973). *Speaking of Stendhal* (1979).

BIBLIOGRAPHY: Burdett, O. *English Review* (May 1935). Gindin, J. *Centennial Review* (1978). "S.O." *English Review* (January 1921). Taubman, R. *New Statesman* (26 January 1962).

For articles in reference works, see: *CA. CN. DLB. MBL. SF&FL. TCA* and *SUP. TCW.*

Other references: *Books and Bookmen* (May 1970). *Christian Science Monitor* (29 September 1937, 19 July 1969). *NR* (13 March 1971). *NYHTBR* (8 April 1962). *NYTBR* (9 May 1971). *Spectator* (25 October 1969).

Robin Sheets

(Patricia) Ann Jellicoe

BORN: 15 July 1927, Middlesborough, Yorkshire.
DAUGHTER OF: John Andrea Jellicoe and Frances Jackson Henderson.
MARRIED: C. E. Knight-Clarke, 1950; David Roger Mayne, 1962.

During the decade or so that followed the momentous 1956 arrival of John Osborne's *Look Back in Anger* at London's Royal Court Theatre, J. achieved critical recognition as one of a group of young playwrights whose innovative works were revitalizing British drama. Although J.'s reputation is associated almost exclusively with the success in 1961 of her eccentric comedy, *The Knack* (particularly Richard Lester's 1965 film adaptation of the script), her distinctive contribution to the "New Drama" generation may be more broadly related to nonliterary elements she includes within the body of her scripts—a factor clearly rooted in J.'s interest and experience with directing. These script notes may suggest opportunities for actors to improvise; they may describe specific visual action or rhythmic noises and nonverbal vocalization and often evoke a feeling of ritual or mystical ambiguity. "These are not loose effects" J. comments; "They are introduced to communicate with the audience directly through their senses to reinforce the total effect of the play, and they are always geared to character and situation." Nevertheless, readers of J.'s early plays must be prepared to employ the imagination of a stage director, thus conjuring a *mise-en-scene* in their heads, in order to comprehend fully the character of the drama she creates.

Because J. boldly colors her scripts with elements integral to her training and ambitions as a director, critic John Russell Taylor describes her writing as ". . . certainly exotic, and perhaps unique among the younger dramatists" writing scripts at the time her first full-length play, *The Sport of My Mad Mother*, made its debut on the stage of The Royal Court. In contrast with Osborne, John Arden, Arnold Wesker, Shelagh Delaney, Harold Pinter, even the significant tradition of British playwriting, "Jellicoe was trying," Taylor observes, ". . . to make her play primarily something which happened in front of an audience and made its effect as a totality, rather than a piece of neatly carpentered literary craftsmanship which would 'read well' and work largely by way of its dialogue's appeal to the mind." Her influence as an individual playwright cannot be measured precisely, but the nonliterary emphasis of her style of script composition anticipated a trend in works for the stage that took hold in the early

60s throughout Europe and America and remains today a recognizable genre of dramaturgy.

J. was born in the north of England; her parents were separated when she was eighteen months old. "My childhood," she has stated, ". . . was rather unpleasant [and] spent mostly at boarding school which, as I now realise, is a system designed to make children conform, to mould them into a standard pattern. At the time I could never understand why I was so unpopular, unhappy and out of step. I thought they were right and I was wrong, and I tried very hard to be like everyone else. To some extent I succeeded and after I left school it took me more than ten years to discover what sort of person I really was, and what my ideas were."

From 1943 to 1947, J. studied acting in war-ravaged London at the Central School of Speech and Drama, winning most of the prizes she was eligible for. When she completed her studies, she traveled extensively through Europe and discovered in herself a facility for learning languages—an ability that would serve her later when she completed translations and adaptations of plays by Ibsen and Chekhov and so, she explains, "earned the time and independence to write my own work."

In 1950, she became the founding director of the Cockpit Theatre Club in London as an extension of a commission she had received to develop a study of the relationship between theatre practice and theatre architecture. "For the first time in my life," she has commented, "I began to think deeply about the nature of theatre; this led to an interest in the open stage (audience on three sides) and I founded a theatre club to experiment with the form." After over two years of intensive work at the Cockpit, which included production of a one-act play and two translations of her own, J. returned in 1953 to the Central School of Speech and Drama to teach and direct and remained there until 1955. "When I left it was chiefly because you were never free to concentrate on trying to achieve an absolute work of art. . . . About this time *The Observer* newspaper organised a play-writing competition; the conditions of entry showed they wanted something new and different. . . . I saw that if I didn't write a play now I never would, so I sat down and wrote *The Sport of My Mad Mother*, which won third prize and was produced at the Royal Court in 1958. So I became a playwright."

Kenneth Tynan described *The Sport of My Mad Mother* as "a tour de force that belongs in no known category of drama. It stands in the same relationship to conventional play-making as jazz does to conventional music: in an ideal production it would have the effect of spontaneous improvisation, or of a vocal *danse macabre* that makes up its own rules and language as it goes along." The

play portrays a London street gang of Teddy-boys led by Greta, an earth-mother figure associated with the Indian goddess Kali, force of destruction and creation (the play's title is based on a Hindu hymn: "All creation is the sport of my mad mother Kali"). The essentially unstructured plot progresses in waves of unmotivated violence where word and cries are repeated, evolving into ritualized manifestations of abstract menace. Its original production was co-directed by J. and George Devine (founding director of the English Stage Company) and was curtly dismissed by all but a few critics with a nose for the avant-garde.

J. wrote her next play on commission from the Girl Guides' Association, providing them with a spectacular pageant-like fantasy entitled *The Rising Generation*. The piece envisioned a fabulous creature called Mother who decries the crimes of men, proclaims that the best of life is rooted in the spirit of womankind—"Shakespeare was a woman; Milton was a woman; . . . Newton was a woman . . ."—and devises to reform the ills of life by invoking the spirit of open-mindedness and cooperation to carry a select group of girls and boys into outer space to colonize a braver, newer world. The Girl Guides declined producing the provocative work, but this feminist pageant did finally reach the stage of the Royal Court in 1967, nearly a decade after its original commission, and was "warmly received."

"With her next play, *The Knack*," notes John Russell Taylor, "Ann Jellicoe scored one of the most resounding popular successes of the New Drama." The play was first presented by the English Stage Company at the Arts Theatre, Cambridge in October of 1961, made its Royal Court premiere the following March, with J. co-directing, and saw its New York debut in May 1964 in an off-Broadway production with Brian Bedford and George Segal in a cast directed by Mike Nichols. The title alludes to the focus of the play's driving spirit—the obsession of young men with the knack of seducing women. Within a loosely structured whirligig of often zany antics, the action develops around three male housemates—Tom, Tolen, and Colin—representing a wide range of sexual résumés, and their competition to win the favor of Nancy, an apparently innocent young woman who stops at the window of their domicile, seeking directions to the Y.W.C.A. In the most frequently cited scene of the play, Tom and Colin charm Nancy into a game fantasy in which they pretend the bed is a Bechstein (piano) and "play it" in a wild incantation of "pings" and "plongs" to the tune of "The Blue Danube" waltz. Beneath the surface ebullience of the action, however, one senses the anxieties and frustrations of young innocents in a maze of sexual bewilderment. The climactic images of the play involve a ritualized chase scene, accompanied by the cacophonous clang of pot covers and repeated howls of "Rape," where games and rivalries resonate with undertones of primal violence. Although events are stopped short of brutality, these final movements, when well performed, hold the potential of being immensely stirring.

The plays that have followed *The Knack* have met with little critical enthusiasm. In *Shelley; Or, The Idealist* (1965), J. offers "an almost documentary account," in conventional dramaturgical form, of the poet's life. *The Giveaway* (1968) playfully examines the goings-on in a family that has just won a ten-year supply of corn flakes. *London Times* critic Irving Wardle saw it as "an honest and logical effort to extend her work into popular territory" but, nonetheless, did not find the piece rewarding comedy. *You'll Never Guess,* another attempt at reviving the distinctive zaniness of her early work, opened in London in 1973 under J.'s direction to poor notices. A handful of short plays she has written since have been similarly disappointing and, in the words of John Russell Taylor who was among the first critics to celebrate her work, "rather give the impression of marking time. Now perhaps we may hope that she will return to a subject within the center of her most personal style and range—that area where she is just not at all like anyone else."

WORKS: *Rosmersholm* (adaptation of play by Ibsen, 1952; revised 1959). *The Sport of My Mad Mother* (1958; revised 1964). *The Rising Generation* (1960). *The Lady from the Sea* (adaptation of play by Ibsen, 1961). *The Knack* (1961). *The Seagull* (adaptation of play by Chekhov, with Ariadne Nicolaeff, 1964). *Der Freischütz* (translation of libretto by Friedrich Kind, music by Weber, 1964). *Shelley; Or, The Idealist* (1965). *Some Unconscious Influences in the Theatre* (1967). *The Giveaway* (1968). *You'll Never Guess* (1973). *Two Jelliplays: Clever Elsie, Smiling John, Silent Peter* and *A Good Thing or a Bad Thing* (1974). *Devon: A Shell Guide* (1975). *The Reckoning* (1978). *The Tide* (1980). *Community Plays: How to Put Them On* (1987).

BIBLIOGRAPHY: *New Theatre Magazine* (1960). *New Theatre Voices of the Fifties and Sixties,* ed. C. Marowitz and others (1965). *NYT* (30 June 1965). Taylor, J.R., *Anger and After* (1962). *Village Voice* (8 June 1967).

For articles in reference works, see: *CA. CD. Crowell's Handbook of Contemporary Drama* (1971). *McGraw-Hill Encyclopedia of World Drama* (1972). *Modern World Theatre* (1970). *WA.*

Other references: *At the Royal Court,* ed. R. Findlater (1981).

Paul D. Nelsen

Elizabeth (Joan) Jennings

BORN: 18 July 1926, Boston, Lincolnshire.
DAUGHTER OF: Henry Cecil Jennings, mother's name not known.

J. was born into a Roman Catholic physician's family and grew up in Oxford (where she still lives), graduating from St. Anne's College at Oxford with honors in English. She wrote her first meaningful poem when she was thirteen, after reading a work by G.K. Chesterton, and found rhythm and alliteration "exciting" enough to try writing poetry herself. Her uncle suggested that she avoid "writing [about] experiences one has never had," and the encouragement he offered led to a simple honesty in her verse throughout her career as poet, critic, and translator. She acknowledges the influence of W.H. Auden and T.S. Eliot and is fond of Edwin Muir, Wallace Stevens, and especially W.B. Yeats.

During the eight years she worked as a librarian, her first published efforts appeared: *Poems* (1953) and *A Way of Looking* (1955), both of which won prizes. These volumes were criticized as somewhat monotonous, limited in scope, and imitative of Eliot's free verse, though her admitted power in creating verse of a meditative nature was readily acknowledged by critics. She subsequently published several other volumes in the 1950s and the early 1960s, most of which reflected her involvement with a short-lived group of poets identified with Robert Conquest's *New Lines* collection; while others in the group, such as Philip Larkin, Thom Gunn, and Kingsley Amis subsequently diverged from the group's emphasis on understated emotion, J. has continued to write with an ostensible lack of feeling while actually demonstrating controlled though subdued power.

J.'s breakdown and attempted suicide in the early 1960s led to hospitalization and psychotherapy and the writing of *Recoveries* (1964) and *The Mind Has Mountains* (1966), which also won a literary prize. The poems in the latter collection (with a title from a poem of Gerard Manley Hopkins) deal primarily with such phenomena as suicide, hysterical behavior, and madness and are as understated as her previous volumes. The self-conscious poems in this volume reflect the struggle of a troubled soul for enlightenment, but they are not self-pitying, only restrained, searching, and ultimately triumphant in celebrating J.'s overcoming depression.

When her *Collected Poems* appeared in 1967, it not only enabled readers and critics to see her career to that date at a glance but even more to evaluate her strengths. Terry Eagleton noted that in this collection J.'s mind "works in exact congruence with the poetic structure she uses, so that this pared, precise, aesthetic yet morally sensitive structure seems to reproduce the structure of her thinking and feeling," with this "congruence" serving as both her strength and her weakness since the lack of tension results in a "passive, abstract and energyless verse." Her limited emotional range was frequently noted, as was the genuineness of her convictions. She frequently writes about Catholic saints (St. John of the Cross, St. Teresa of Avila, St. Catherine, St. Augustine) and biblical figures and events (Jesus, Mary, "Annunciation," "The Visitation"), as well as various artists (Rembrandt, Rouault, Cezanne, and especially van Gogh).

In addition to other volumes of verse for both adults and children, J. has written various works of criticism, including *Let's Have Some Poetry* (1960), for children; *Poetry Today* (1961), an overview of contemporary British poetry; books taking a religious approach to literature, *Every Changing Shape* (1961) and *Christianity and Poetry* (1965; published in the United States as *Christian Poetry*); a biography of Robert Frost; a well-received translation of *The Sonnets of Michelangelo* (1961, 1969); and *Seven Men of Vision: An Appreciation*, about Yeats, D.H. Lawrence, Lawrence Durrell, St.-John Perse, David Jones, Antoine de St. Exupery, and Boris Pasternak (1976), among many other books.

J. has found that as an insecure, solitary person, poetry can help her relate to the larger world and is in fact a form of prayer for her; even her poems of exaltation and celebration reflect her concern with isolation and the effects of the passing of time on "the mind," a term she uses frequently. Her quiet, mystical poems suggest in their metrical formality and precise, understated diction an admittedly subdued voice, but equally acknowledged emotional conviction, and spiritual power.

WORKS: *Poems* (1953). *A Way of Looking: Poems* (1955). *A Child and the Seashell* (1957). *A Sense of the World* (1958). *Let's Have Some Poetry* (1960). *Every Changing Shape* (1961). *Poetry Today 1957-60* (1961). *Song for a Birth or a Death and Other Poems*

(1961). (trans.) *The Sonnets of Michelangelo* (1961, 1969). (with L. Durrell and R.S. Thomas) *Penguin Modern Poets I* (1962). *Recoveries: Poems* (1964). *Frost* (1964). *Christianity and Poetry* (1965; in the U.S. as *Christian Poetry*). *The Mind Has Mountains* (1966). *The Secret Brother and Other Poems for Children* (1966). *Collected Poems* (1967). *The Animals' Arrival* (1969). *Lucidities* (1970). *Hurt* (1970). (with others) *Folio* (1970). *Relationships* (1972). *Growing-Points: New Poems* (1975). *Seven Men of Vision: An Appreciation* (1976). *Consequently I Rejoice* (1977). *After the Ark* (1978). *Moments of Grace: New Poems* (1979). *Selected Poems* (1979). *Winter Wind* (1979). *Moments of Grace* (1980). *A Dream of Spring* (1980). *Celebrations and Elegies* (1982). *Extending the Territory* (1985). *In Shakespeare's Company* (1985). *Collected Poems, 1953-1985* (1986).

BIBLIOGRAPHY: Allott, K., ed. *Penguin Book of Contemporary Verse* (1962). Byers, M. *British Poetry Since 1960*, ed. M. Schmidt and G. Lindop (1972). Orr, P., ed. *The Poet Speaks* (1966). Schmidt, M. *An Introduction to 50 Modern British Poets* (1979). Schofield, M.A. *Notes on Contemporary Literature* (1983). Stürzl, E.A. *On Poetry and Poets, Fifth Series*, ed. J. Hogg (1983). Wheeler, M. *Hopkins Among the Poets: Studies in Modern Responses to Gerard Manley Hopkins* (1985).

For articles in reference works, see: *CA. CLC. CP. EWL. MBL* and *SUP. TCW. WA.*

Other references: *Books and Bookmen* (December 1972, February 1980). *Encounter* (January 1980). Fraser, G.S. *The Modern Writer and His World*, rev. ed. (1964). *Listener* (23 July 1964, 22 March 1973, 30 October 1975, 13 October 1977, 31 January 1980, 5 May 1986). *London Magazine* (February 1962, November 1964). *Mademoiselle* (January 1955). *New Statesman* (13 October 1967, 29 September 1972, 30 May 1975, 2 November 1979, 15 November 1985). *Observer* (27 April 1975, 1 September 1985). *Poetry* (December 1956, November 1959, March 1977). *Poetry Review* (Spring 1967). *Spectator* (1 December 1979, 19 October 1985). *Stand* (1968). *TES* (24 November 1978, 30 July 1982). *TLS* (4 July 1975, 30 December 1977, 1 February 1980, 16 July 1982, 28 November 1986). *WLT* (Spring 1979). *Yale Review* (Summer 1959).

Paul Schlueter

Geraldine Ensor Jewsbury

BORN: 22 August 1812, Measham, Derbyshire.
DIED: 23 September 1880, London.
DAUGHTER OF: Thomas Jewsbury.

A popular and controversial novelist, journalist, and reviewer and promoter of women's

causes, J. was six when her mother died in 1818 and was raised, along with her three brothers, by her sister Maria Jane, twelve years her elder. Maria Jane managed in spite of her housekeeping responsibilities to write to great critical acclaim, her first book being published in 1824 when J. was twelve. This stimulating literary environment, which included visits to and from literary notables both English and American, continued until 1833 when Maria Jane married and sailed for India and J. assumed the responsibilities of the household until her father's death in 1840.

J.'s two great philosophical mentors were George Sand and Thomas Carlyle. J. discovered Carlyle's writings, notably *Past and Present*, at a time of spiritual crisis, and they affected her so profoundly that she wrote to him, perhaps following the example of her sister, who had early been encouraged by Wordsworth and other influential literary critics and writers but who had died in 1833 in India. Perhaps J. felt she must take up her career where her sister's had ended, but instead of following the Wordsworthian example, J. proposed a woman's right to full equality, especially independence and equal education, sexual freedom, and secular thinking as themes for her writing.

In 1841 she visited Thomas and Jane Carlyle in Cheyne Row and began a lifelong friendship with both of them that was at times tempestuous. Although demanding the support of the Carlyles, J. refused to be wholly guided by them, disgusting Carlyle by her enthusiasm for George Sand. She returned to Lancashire to keep house for her favorite brother, Frank, and where she wrote her first novel, *Zoe* (1845). J. spent the next decade in Lancashire, housekeeping, entertaining visiting writers such as Ralph Waldo Emerson and George Henry Lewes, and writing. "Faith and Scepticism" was sent to the *Westminster Review* by Lewes on her behalf in 1849 and made a strongly favorable impression in certain literary circles. In 1854 she moved to Chelsea to be near the Carlyles and continued to write for the periodicals and to produce novels until 1859. In 1866, after the death of Jane Carlyle, she removed to Kent where she lived in retirement but continued to read for the publishing house of Bentley and Sons and to review for the *Athenaeum* until illness forced her back to London where she died in 1880.

J. enjoyed a full career as a journalist, but her true influence over the course of English reading was as a reader for Bentley and Sons from 1858 to 1880 and as a reviewer of more than 1800 books for the *Athenaeum*.

While history sees J. as a writer of popular fiction, she saw herself as a serious writer of social novels although she spent only 12 years of a long career producing them. The hero's conflict between religion and love in *Zoe* is used as a means to question the validity of organized religion and made the book an instant success. While the development of the hero was influenced by J.'s interest in the Oxford Movement, the heroine was an exploration of passion along George Sand lines.

The Half-Sisters (1848) showed a woman rising above her illegitimate birth and lack of social standing to a respected place in society. *Marian Withers* (1851) discussed women's education and society's requirement that a woman establish herself by an appropriate marriage. George Henry Lewes described it, to J.'s annoyance, as a reply to *Mary Barton*. *The Sorrows of Gentility* (1851) explores society's approbation of a husband's exploitation of his wife. *Constance Herbert* (1855) details the fate of a woman who chooses power over other possible human relationships. In *Right or Wrong* (1856), J.'s last novel, she returns to religion in a denunciation of priestly celibacy in the Roman Catholic Church. In all her novels the pace was brisk, the characters well drawn, the descriptions vivid, and the tone didactic. George Eliot criticized her for making all women heroines and all men villains as she espoused the cause of unmarried women. J. also wrote two children's books, *The History of an Adopted Child* (1852) and *Angelo, or the Pine Forest in the Alps* (1855), as well as numerous children's stories in *Juvenile Budget* and *Household Words*. Selections of her letters to Jane Welsh Carlyle have been published, and Virginia Woolf has written of their friendship.

WORKS: *Zoe: The History of Two Lives* (1845). *The Half-Sisters: A Tale* (1848). *Marian Withers* (1851). *The History of an Adopted Child* (1853). *Constance Herbert* (1855). *Angelo; or, The Pine Forest in the Alps* (1855). *Right or Wrong* (1856). *The Sorrows of Gentility* (1856). *Selections from the Letters of Geraldine Ensor Jewsbury to Jane Welsh Carlyle, Edited by Mrs. Alexander Ireland . . . Prefaced by a Monograph on Miss Jewsbury by the Editor* (1892).

BIBLIOGRAPHY: Cary, M. *Research Studies* (1974). Fahnestock, J.R. *Nineteenth Century Fiction* (1973). Fryckstedt, M.C. *Geraldine Jewsbury's "Athenaeum" Reviews: A Mirror of Mid-Victorian Attitudes Toward Fiction* (1986). Fryckstedt, M.C. *Research Studies* (1983). Griest, G.L. *Mudie's Circulating Library and the Victorian Novel* (1970). Howe, S. *Geraldine Jewsbury, Her Life and Errors* (1935). Mercer, E. *Manchester Quarterly* (1898). Thomson, P. *George Sand and the Victorians: Her Influence and Reputation in Nineteenth-Century England* (1977).Woolf, V. *Collected Essays*, v. 2 (1967).

Eleanor Langstaff

Maria Jane Jewsbury

BORN: 25 October 1800, Measham, Derby-shire.
DIED: 4 October 1833, Poona, India.
DAUGHTER OF: Thomas Jewsbury.
MARRIED: William Kew Fletcher, 1832.

Vivacious friend of William Wordsworth and his daughter, Dora, J. received some early formal education at Mrs. Adams' School, Shenstone, but returned home for health reasons at the age of fourteen. At eighteen, upon the death of her mother and the family's removal to Manchester, she took charge of her younger sister Geraldine and her three brothers, one an infant. In spite of her intellectual isolation, she burned to achieve a literary career, writing to Felicia Hemans, "the ambition of writing a book, being praised publicly and associating with authors, seized me."

Alaric A. Watts, editor of the *Manchester Courier*, encouraged her in her ambition and sponsored her first book, *Phantasmagoria, or Sketches of Life and Character*, published at Leeds in 1824 with a dedication to Wordsworth, whom she did not as yet know. The resulting correspondence began a lifelong friendship with the Wordsworth family, especially with Dora Wordsworth. Wordsworth appreciated J. as an accurate observer of simple people. After reading "The Young Gleaner and His Cousin," he urged her to abandon poetry and write about life and manners, advice that she took to heart.

The youthful, lively, satirical tone of *Phantasmagoria* was generally faulted by the reviewers even while assuring their attention. A poem written at the same time, "Song of the Hindoo Women While Accompanying a Widow to the Funeral," reflects the love of exoticism of the period as well as a universal approach to the "woman question."

After J. fell very ill in the summer of 1826, the tone of her work became less satirical and more serious and religious. *Letters to the Young* (1828), a meditative work, discusses belief in God, intellectual snobbery, and "the true end of education." Its popularity required a second edition in 1829 and a third in 1832. *Lays of Leisure Hours* appeared in 1829 and *The Three Histories* in 1830; subtitled *The History of an Enthusiast, the History of a Nonchalant, the History of a Realist*, the latter work is considered by modern scholars to owe much to Madame de Staël's *Corrine ou l'Italie*.

She was praised for her eloquent style by Miss Landon and Christopher North, and her work appeared frequently in the *Atheneum* from 1830–1832. But in keeping with her new seriousness and religious fervor, she married William Kew Fletcher, a chaplain for the East India company, in August of 1832. As a closing to her life in English letters (though she kept a diary of her trip to India, parts of which were later published), she wrote to Hemans that she regretted her early reputation and desire for premature publication. She died of cholera in October 1833 in Poona, India, without seeing Wordsworth's "Liberty" which he had dedicated to her and of which she was the subject.

WORKS: *Phantasmagoria, or Sketches of Life and Character* (1825). *Letters to the Young* (1928). *Lays of Leisure Hours* (1829). *The Three Histories: The History of an Enthusiast, the History of a Nonchalant, the History of a Realist* (1830). Extracts from her journal of her voyage and early days in India were published in *Lancashire Worthies*, ed. F. Espinasse (1874).

BIBLIOGRAPHY: Howe, S. *Geraldine Jewsbury, Her Life and Errors* (1939). Fryckstedt, M.C. *Bulletin of the John Rylands University, Library of Manchester* (1984).

For articles in reference works, see: *DNB*.

Eleanor Langstaff

Ruth Prawer Jhabvala

BORN: 7 May 1927, Cologne, Germany.
DAUGHTER OF: Marcus and Eleanor Prawer.
MARRIED: C.S.H. Jhabvala, 1951.

J. has lived major portions of her life in four countries. Born in Cologne, Germany in 1927 to a Polish Jewish lawyer and his German Jewish wife, J. fled from Germany to England in 1939 with her parents and brother. In 1951, after graduating from the University of London with an M.A. in English literature, she married Cyrus Jhabvala, an Indian architect, and moved with him to Delhi, India. There the Jhabvalas raised three daughters. For both professional and personal reasons and with her husband's encouragement, J. left India in 1975 and moved to the United States.

The personal reasons that caused J. to leave are presented in a powerful essay, reprinted as the introduction to *An Experience of India*. Essentially India, so exhilarating at first, had become oppressive to J. She uses the image "living on the back of an animal" to represent her irritation at India's extreme and inescapable poverty and her inability either to affect or to overlook it.

J. chose New York because its pressures and variety somehow drew together for her the experiences of the Europe of her youth and the India of her adulthood. She also chose it because it was the home of her cinematic collaborators, James Ivory and Ismail Merchant. Ivory, an American director, and Merchant, an Indian producer, had come to India in 1961 to ask J. to write the filmscript for her novel, *The Householder*. Since that time the team has produced fourteen films, including two based on J.'s novels. J., Merchant, and Ivory are personal friends as well as colleagues, all living in the same apartment house. J.'s recent story, "Grandmother," and novel, *In Search of Love and Beauty*, probably explore this friendship.

To date, J.'s writings on India still constitute the main body of her work. Of her novels, only the most recent, *In Search of Love and Beauty*, does not have an Indian setting. In India, J. is often considered with others writing about India in English, such as Kamala Markandaya. Indian reviews are not always favorable, finding J.'s writing able but unsympathetic.

In fact, J.'s earliest novels, *Amrita* and *The Nature of Passion*, while comic and satiric, present Indian life with considerable delight. However, the mood of *Esmond in India*, J.'s third novel, is darker. In it a pretty, naive Indian heroine, much like her counterparts in the earlier novels, feels modern enough to make her own matrimonial choices. But her story, unlike theirs, does not close happily: at novel's end she is left pursuing a damaging affair with Esmond, a selfish Englishman already married to an Indian woman who had made a similar choice.

The bitterness of *Esmond* lies less in the Indian life depicted than in the effects of the intersection of Indian and Western ways. The next novel, *The Householder*, returns to more purely Indian life. There Western figures appear but only as exotic yet finally irrelevant interlopers. J.'s last novel concerned mainly with Indian family life and told from an Indian point of view is *Get Ready for Battle*. In mood it is closer to the first novels than to *Esmond*.

The next three novels, *A Backward Place*, *Travelers*, and *Heat and Dust*, reflect J.'s declaration in *An Experience of India* that she is no longer interested in India but in herself (as symbolic of the westerner) in India. The central characters in these novels are westerners who have come to India for varied reasons. Judy, of *A Back-ward Place*, is an English girl married to an Indian actor. Because she has come without an agenda—neither to find herself as Lee of *Travelers* wishes to do, nor to have India give up its secrets, as the central character of *Heat and Dust* wants—Judy remains healthy and becomes more assimilated into India than any of the other westerners. Yet Judy, J. suggests, is not a complicated girl, and other westerners because of their natures are more likely to become trapped by India's sensuality or its mystical religions (as do Lee and the narrator of *Heat and Dust*. Or they may be unable to leave their western background behind enough to enter into Indian life. The true meeting of East and West, J.'s fiction suggests, is a rarity, and the path to that meeting is fraught with danger to travelers in either direction.

Most recently, J. has been writing more filmscripts than fiction, a kind of writing that she reports to be less taxing. Writing for films has influenced her novels. The later books tend to be written in distinct scenes with sharp cuts between people and places; a similar change has taken place in her short fiction. J.'s later work, then, seems more modern than her earlier, but it is also colder and more distancing, reflecting perhaps J.'s increasing sense of her own rootlessness. However, J.'s last published story, "Farid and Farida," makes it difficult to predict her future direction, for it deals once again with Indian subjects and ends with the possibility of hope.

WORKS: To Whom She Will (1955; published in United States as *Amrita*). *The Nature of Passion* (1956). *Esmond in India* (1958). *The Householder* (1960; as filmscript, 1963). *Get Ready for Battle* (1962). *Like Birds, Like Fishes* (1964). *A Backward Place* (1965). *Shakespeare Wallah* (1965). *A Stronger Climate* (1968). *The Guru* (1969). *Bombay Talkie* (1970). *An Experience of India* (1971). *A New Dominion* (1973; published in U.S. as *Travelers*). *Heat and Dust* (1975; as filmscript, 1983). *Autobiography of a Princess* (1975). *How I Became a Holy Mother and Other Stories* (1976). *Roseland* (1977). *Hullabaloo over Georgie and Bonnie's Pictures* (1978). *The Europeans* (1979). *Jane Austen in Manhattan* (1980). *Quartet* (1981). *In Search of Love and Beauty* (1983). *A Room with a View* (1985). *Three Continents* (1987).

BIBLIOGRAPHY: Gooneratne, Y. *Ariel: A Review of International Literature* (April 1984). Gooneratne, Y. *Language and Literature in Multicultural Contexts* (1983). Gooneratne, Y. *Westerly* (December 1983). Gooneratne, Y. *WLWE* (1979). Hayball, C. *Journal of Indian Writing in English* (July 1981). Kandala, N.R. *Journal of European Studies* (1978). King, B.A. *The New English Literatures* (1981). Rao, R.K. *Journal of European Studies* (1982). Rubin, D. *MFS* (1984). Rutherford, A., and K.N. Peterson. *WLWE* (1976). Shahane, V.A.

Aspects of Indian Writing in English. ed. M.K. Naik (1980). Shahane, V.A. *Journal of Commonwealth Literature* (August 1977). Shahane, V.A. *Ruth Prawer Jhabvala* (1976). Singh, R.H. *The Indian Novel in English: A Critical Study* (1977). Souza, E. *Awakened Conscience*, ed. C.V. Narasimhaiad (1979). Williams, H.M. *TCL* (1969).

For articles in reference works, see: *CA. CLC. CN. NCHEL. TCW. WA.*

Other references: Bell, P.K. *NYTBR* (4 April 1976). Grimes, P. *NYT* (30 October 1977). Kaplan, J. *Commentary* (November 1973). King, B.A. *Sewanee Review* (Winter 1977). Nott, K. *Encounter* (February 1983). Pritchett, V.S. *New Yorker* (16 June 1973). Weingarten, R. *Midstream* (March 1974). Weintraub, B. *NYTMag* (11 September 1983).

Ellen Laun

Elizabeth Jocelin

BORN: 1596 in Norton, Chester.
DIED: 21 October 1622, Cambridgeshire.
DAUGHTER OF: Sir Richard and Joan Chaderton Brooke.
MARRIED: Tourell Jocelin, 1616

J.'s only work was a popular advice book, *The Mothers Legacie to her unborne Childe*. Between 1624 and 1625, it had three editions and other English editions followed; a Dutch translation appeared by 1699 and a German one by 1748. The chief interest of this book is the contrast between the education that J. suggests is appropriate for her child and the education that J. herself had.

In an essay prefixed to *The Mothers Legacie*, Thomas Goad makes it clear that J. had an unusually thorough education for a Renaissance woman. As a consequence of her parents' separation, J. was reared in the household of her grandfather, William Chaderton, bishop of Lincoln, where she studied religion, history, and languages. In particular, Goad praises her memory for both English and Latin; she seems to have had almost total recall of the sermons she heard in church.

When she became pregnant with her first child, J. feared she would die in childbirth. She therefore wrote *The Mothers Legacie*, giving advice about the education of her unborn child. The actual schedule that she suggests draws no distinction between what is appropriate for a son or daughter: the morning and evening are given to

meditation, study, and prayer, while the afternoon is spent in discourse and social pursuits. But in advice to her husband, J. urges him to allow a son formal study, which, she hoped, would lead him to the ministry. A daughter, however, was to have a limited education. A girl should be literate, so she might read the Bible, and to learn "good housewifery . . . and good workes: other learning a woman needs not." This advice, of course, is inconsistent with J.'s own experience.

One can account for this inconsistency by noting that J. praises educated women who are also humble. She may have urged a limited education for her daughter to protect the child from pride, which J. regarded as the most dangerous of sins. Furthermore, J. wrote in a period of intense misogyny, when such women as Lady Mary Wroth and Rachel Speght were under attack for their writing, so *The Mothers Legacie* may reflect an awareness of this anti-feminist bias.

On 12 October 1622, J. gave birth to a healthy daughter, Theodora; nine days later, J. died.

WORKS: *The Mothers Legacie to her unborne Childe* (1624, STC 14624).

BIBLIOGRAPHY: Clarke. S. *The Lives of Sundry Eminent People* (1683). Sizemore, C.W. *University of Dayton Review* (1981).

For articles in reference works, see: *DNB.*

Frances Teague

Esther Johnson ("Stella")

BORN: 13 March 1681, near Richmond, Surrey.
DIED: 28 January 1728, Dublin.
DAUGHTER OF: Edward and Bridget Johnson.
MARRIED: Jonathan Swift, 1716(?).

The mysterious character of the liaison between J. and Jonathan Swift, much speculated about when they were alive, has inspired meticu-

lous but inconclusive scholarly activity ever since. It is certain that Swift met J. at Moor Park, the country home of Sir William Temple when J., the housekeeper's daughter, was only eight and Swift, Temple's newly engaged secretary, twenty-two. It is also established that Temple was fond of both, offering each preferential treatment over others associated with his household staff. The theory that J. and Swift were both illegitimate children of their benefactor, however, seems to have lost prestige in the most recent biographical research.

In 1701, two years after Temple's death, Swift helped arrange for the nineteen-year-old J. to establish herself permanently in Ireland with her life-long companion Rebecca Dingley. The motive was, as Swift to the end insisted, to ease the women's financial difficulties by enabling them to live where goods and services could be had for much better prices than were then current in England. But several scholars interpret the move as evidence of a pact or a promise or perhaps even a type of engagement in some way preliminary to marriage or to something like it. The complicated arguments cast complex patterns of light and shadow upon our understanding of Swift the lover and Swift the writer.

Despite the paucity of extant proofs of her talents, Swift scholars all acknowledge J. as a writer meriting notice in her own right. They see J.'s role in relation to Swift as a telling one. They point out that Swift himself recognized her talent on numerous occasions. Indirect evidence, they also argue, suggests that her skill in writing, as in conversation, must have been quite considerable to have sustained Swift's respect through a relationship (sometimes painfully stressful) lasting nearly forty years. All speculation aside, the facts stand as a stark challenge to literary historians: only one poem by J. and only one letter from J. to Swift remain. Some idea of her characteristic style may be garnered from phrases Swift appears to attribute to her from 1710 to 1713 in his *Journal to Stella*. The rest of what she wrote is lost, destroyed perhaps by Swift himself. Whatever the case, the extant letter (a perfunctory thank you note) can hardly be called witty. Dated 25 May 1723, it is conventionally polite, almost exaggeratedly humble and grateful, only hinting at strengths of character in the measured emphatics of "to be sure you did exstreamly right to give a receipt in full of all demands." The log Swift kept of letters received from J. is nothing more than a tantalizingly long list of postmark dates.

On the other hand, the poem—"Stella to Dr. Swift on his Birth-day, November 30, 1721"—handsomely repays close reading in the light of scholarly research because the gratitude J. ex-

presses is laced through with a saucy piquancy that might well escape the casual reader but that comports with Swift's otherwise mystifying practice of addressing J. as "Sirrah" and of teasing her with such sobriquets as "Admirable Bitch." Hardy identifies the quality in J. that Swift could not do without once he had cultivated it in her: "a certain hardness . . . to combat his egotism." Other women (J. writes in her poem, with evident self-satisfaction) must eventually lose their place in Swift's regard and come "tumbling down Time's steep hill,/ While Stella holds her station still." Rich in gallantry, J.'s captious lines to Swift ("My early and my only guide") are slender evidence of her power over him but strong evidence of her rapier wit:

> O! turn your precepts into laws,
> Redeem the women's ruin'd cause,
> Retrieve lost empire to our sex,
> That men may bow their rebel necks.

If Swift had anything to do with the eradication of J.'s *oeuvre*, might these two pieces by J. have survived because they express gratitude for his attentions, but not too much gratitude? They do not, in any case, contradict the spirit of Swift's elegaic prose piece *On the Death of Mrs. Johnson*, which he wrote the night of J.'s death.

WORKS: "To Dr. Swift, on his Birth-day, November 30, 1721," in *The Poems of Jonathan Swift*, ed. H. Williams, 2nd. ed., (1958).

BIBLIOGRAPHY: Davis, H.J. *Stella: A Gentlewoman of the Eighteenth Century* (1942). Ehrenpreis, I. *Swift, the Man, His Works, and the Age*, 3 Volumes (1962, 1967, 1983). Donoghue, D., ed., *Jonathan Swift: A Critical Anthology* (1971). Gold, M. B., *Swift's Marriage to Stella: Together with Unprinted and Misprinted Letters* (1937). Hardy, E. *The Conjured Spirit, Swift: A Study in the Relationship of Swift, Stella, and Vanessa* (1949). Le Brocquy, S. *Swift's Most Valuable Friend* (1968). Nokes, D. *Jonathan Swift: A Hypocrite Reversed, A Critical Biography* (1985). Swift, J. *Journal to Stella*, ed. H. Williams, (1948). Swift, J., *Stella's Birth-Days: Poems* (1967).

For articles in reference works, see: *DNB*, (under "Swift, Jonathan"). *Europa*.

R. Victoria Arana

Pamela Hansford Johnson

BORN: 29 May 1912, London.
DIED: 18 June 1981, London.
MARRIED: M. Gordon Neil Stewart, 1936; C.P. Snow, 1950.

The novels of J.'s second husband, centrally concerned as they are with questions of might and right, paradoxes in the corridors of power, decisions and machinations in hierarchies and bureaucracies, are better known than hers. Where he writes of the political environment, she writes of the psychological. She is concerned with decision and dilemma, too, but her focus is upon the individual rather than the institution and how he or she reacts to the moral questions. This is true of all her career, from her very first novel, *This Bed Thy Centre* (1935), written when she was just twenty-two.

The Last Resort (1956), for instance, contrasts ordinary people with saints and martyrs, and writing of the book Anthony Burgess has summed it up as "they commit themselves to the big terrible decisions; we hold back." In *The Humbler Creation* (1959) we see the struggle of an Anglican clergyman with an unhappy married life, which drives him, rather unwillingly, into adultery that he is hardly equipped to revel in. In *An Error of Judgement* (1962), a highly successful doctor examines his innermost heart and admits to himself that it was sadism that determined his choice of profession. He gives it up and turns to altruism: he will help delinquent youth. Then he encounters a "worthless" little monster, a boy who has committed a ghastly crime, got away with it, feels no remorse whatever, and is not unlikely to do worse in the future. The doctor kills the boy, and we are left to decide whether it was "an error" or not, to judge him but also to keep firmly in mind that this is not a world of black and white, that circumstances alter facts, that good deeds can be done for bad reasons as well as bad ones for good reasons. If Snow's series *Strangers and Brothers* shows us a very complicated world of power, J.'s works show us one of no less complexity, no more cut and dried motivations.

The picture she gives us of modern people caught up in a struggle of good and evil, between us, within us, perplexed by the challenges of morality and ethics in situations as doubtful and diverse as those in her novels *The Unspeakable Skipton* (1958) and *A Summer to Decide* (1948), *The Family Pattern* (1942), *An Impossible Marriage* (1954), and *Catherine Carter* (1952) definitely places her in that select group of modern writers of fiction such as Graham Greene, William Golding, Anthony Burgess, P.H. Newby, and Patrick White who address the large issues of theology as they affect moral dilemmas. In her best-known novel, the "unspeakable" writer Skipton lives by his wits and amuses us by his audacity, but even he raises (as do more sober characters in other novels from her pen) touchy questions of amorality and immorality. Some people struggle with private demons. Some are trapped in incomplete or "impossible" marriages. Some are baffled by the problems of hopeless affairs (as in *The Sea and the Wedding*, also titled *The Last Resort*). Avoiding both unnecessary complexity or popular

easy answers, J. tackles questions quite as serious as her husband, actually more serious than the jockeying for a university position of power in *The Masters*. Though J.'s insights are often startling, her characters are usually ordinary. It is the predicament they may be in, seen both in their own terms and also against a standard of judgment that may be said to be more objective (or more middle-class orthodox), that engages our attention, even sympathy.

Before her marriage to Snow she wrote the play *Corinth House*, and after her marriage she collaborated with him on plays such as *The Supper Dance, Family Party, Spare the Rod, To Murder Mrs. Mortimer, The Pigeon with the Silver Foot, Her Best Food Forward* and *The Public Prosecutor* (produced 1967, printed 1969, after Georgi Dzhagarov). With Kitty Black (after Jean Anouilh, produced 1961) she did *The Rehearsal*, and she authored half a dozen "reconstructions" for radio of characters from Proust. All her plays show her interest in middle-class mores and her skill with dialogue. None is exceptionally good but all are adequate.

She edited *Winter's Tales 7* (1961, modern Russian short stories, with her husband) and wrote *Personalia* (1974), a charming and intelligent book about things "important" to her personally. Her novels, however, are the real basis for her literary reputation. Americans will wince at *Night and Silence, Who Is Here?*, a novel set in New Hampshire on a college campus and worthy to rank with those ascerbic pictures of academia drawn with a certain malice by such authors as Mary McCarthy, Randall Jarrell, and Anthony Burgess. Belgians will appreciate the Belgian settings of *Too Dear for My Possessing* (1940), *The Holiday Friend* (1972), and *The Unspeakable Skipton* (in which a "Baron Corvo" sort of ne'er-do-well is resident not in Venice but in Bruges). Londoners will applaud the accuracy of the settings of *This Bed Thy Centre, The Survival of the Fittest* (1963), and the truly nasty but hilarious send-up of London literary life in her "novel in bad taste," *Cork Street, Next to the Hatter's* (1965).

After she wrote *Too Dear for My Possessing* (1940), she briefly collaborated with her then husband (Stewart) on *Tidy Death* (1940) and *Murder's a Swine* (1943, also published as *The Grinning Pig*). Then, after her own *The Family Pattern* (1942), *Winter Quarters* (1943), and *The Trojan Brothers* (1944), she added to *Too Dear for My Possessing* two more novels to make a trilogy: *An Avenue of Stone* (1947) and *A Summer to Decide* (1948). Margaret Willy in a brief appreciation of J. in *Great Writers of the English Language: Novelists* (1979) makes the point that the narrator of the trilogy is a man—

The Unspeakable Skipton, The Survival of the Fittest, and *The Good Listener,* etc., also have male central characters—and writes:

> Pamela Hansford Johnson has a talent, comparatively rare among women novelists, for subtle and convincing depiction of the viewpoints, thought-processes, and emotional responses of the opposite sex. Indeed her whole breadth of subject and treatment is peculiarly masculine in its detachment, expressing a shrewd yet compassionate acceptance of many aspects of human frailty.

But men and women speak differently, and the male characters in J., however keenly observed and central, speak an oddly non-"masculine" prose, male dialogue as written by someone who cannot speak or reproduce the male language, just as most males cannot write like women. But all readers can agree that J. masters plot with careful construction and involves readers with moral dilemmas.

WORKS: *Symphony for Full Orchestra* (1934). *This Bed Thy Centre* (1935). *Blessed Above Woman* (1936). *Here Today* (1937). *World's End* (1937). *The Monument* (1938). *Girdle of Venus* (1939). *Too Dear for My Possessing* (1940). *Tidy Death* (with G.N. Stewart) (1940). *The Family Pattern* (1942). *Winter Quarters* (1943). *Murder's a Swine* (with G.N. Stewart) (1943). *An Avenue of Stone* (1947). *A Summer to Decide* (1948). *The Duchess at Sunset* (1948). *Hungry Gulliver; An English Critical Appraisal of Thomas Wolfe* (1948). *The Philistines* (1949). *Ivy Compton-Burnett* (1951). *The Supper Dance* (with C.P. Snow) (1951). *Family Party* (with C.P. Snow) (1951). *Spare the Rod* (with C.P. Snow) (1951). *To Murder Mrs. Mortimer* (with C.P. Snow) (1951). *The Pigeon with the Silver Foot* (with C.P. Snow) (1951). *Her Best Foot Forward* (with C.P. Snow) (1951). *Catherine Carter* (1952). *Swann in Love* (1952). *An Impossible Marriage* (1954). *Madame de Charlus* (1954). *Albertine Regained* (1954). *Saint-Loup* (1955). *The Last Resort* (1956). *A Window at Montjarrain* (1956). *The Sea and the Wedding* (1957, retitled *The Last Resort*). *Proust Recaptured* (1958, collecting the radio plays based on Proust). *The Humbler Creation* (1959). *The Unspeakable Skipton* (1959). *The Rehearsal* (1961, with Kitty Black after Jean Anouilh). *An Error of Judgement* (1962). *Night and Silence, Who Is Here?* (1963). *Cork Street, Next to the Hatter's* (1965). *On

Iniquity: Some Personal Reflections Arising out of the Moors Murder Trial (1967). *The Survival of the Fittest* (1968). *The Public Prosecutor* (1969, with C.P. Snow after Georgi Dzhagarov). *The Honours Board* (1970). *The Holiday Friend* (1972). *Important to Me: Personalia* (1974). *The Good Listener* (1975).

BIBLIOGRAPHY: Halperin, J. *C.P. Snow: An Oral Biography Together with a Conversation with Lady Snow (Pamela Hansford Johnson)* (1983). Lindblad, I. *Pamela Hansford Johnson* (1982). Quigly, I. *Pamela Hansford Johnson* (1968).

For articles in reference works, see: *CLC. CN. LLC. Longman. MBL* and *SUP. TCA SUP. TCW.*

Other references: Allen, W. *Tradition and Dream* (1964; in U.S. as *The Modern Novel in Britain and the United States*). *AS* (Fall 1971). *Atlantic* (November 1965, July 1968). *Books and Bookmen* (October 1965, July 1968, March 1969, October 1970, February 1973, May 1975, January 1978). Borowitz, A. *Innocence and Arsenic: Studies in Crime and Literature* (1977). Brophy, B. *Mosaic* (1968). *Commonweal* (11 February 1966). *Contemporary Review* (May 1967). Dick, K. *Friends and Friendship: Conversations and Reflections* (1974). Franks, M.M. *Bulletin of Bibliography* (1983). *Harper's* (November 1965, April 1967). *Listener* (16 May 1968, 16 March 1967, 13 August 1970, 26 October 1972, 19 June 1975, 3 October 1974, 26 October 1978, 7 May 1981). *Nation* (19 August 1968). Newquist, R. *Counterpoint* (1964). *NR* (25 March 1967). *New Statesman* (1 October 1965, 17 May 1968, 24 March 1967, 14 August 1970, 27 October 1972, 20 September 1974, 4 July 1975). *Newsweek* (27 May 1968). *NYTBR* (14 November 1965, 7 July 1968, 20 September 1970, 28 September 1975, 14 September 1975). *Observer* (3 October 1965, 19 May 1968, 16 August 1970, 29 October 1972, 22 September 1974, 22 June 1975, 22 October 1978, 19 April 1981). Rabinowitz, R. *The Reaction Against Experiment in the English Novel, 1950-60* (1967). Raymond, J. *The Doge of Dover* (1960). *Spectator* (1 October 1965, 10 March 1967, 17 January 1969, 15 August 1970, 4 November 1972, 21 June 1975, 30 May 1981). *SR* (9 October 1965, 3 August 1968, 15 April 1967, 24 October 1970). *Time* (19 November 1965, 7 April 1967, 28 September 1970). *TLS* (30 September 1965, 16 May 1968, 14 August 1970, 27 October 1972, 20 June 1975, 3 January 1975, 2 May 1975, 3 November 1978, 1 May 1981). *Vogue* (1 March 1961).

Leonard R.N. Ashley

Jennifer Johnston

BORN: 12 January 1930, Dublin.
DAUGHTER OF: Denis Johnston and Shelegh Richards.
MARRIED: Ian Smyth, 1951; David Gilliland, 1976.

Daughter of one of Ireland's foremost playwrights and a noted actress-director-producer, J. has received wide praise and a number of awards for her seven novels, several of which have also been produced as television dramas. Her novels are all set in the Republic of Ireland or Northern Ireland (where she lives) and are chiefly concerned with differences in class, religion, or politics. She has also consistently been sensitive to the gradual ability of an adolescent to understand old age and the corresponding indifference and cruelty of adults. Her protagonists often find themselves in situations in which their social, political, or religious restrictions become a source of confrontation and growth.

J. uses multiple points of view in her fiction, with diary entries as well as shifting perspectives in voice and time supporting her interest in the effects of the historical past upon the present. Her use of these techniques to apply to Ireland's periods of "troubles" enables her novels, according to the *TLS*, to "convey more about her country than whole volumes of analysis and documentation."

Her first completed novel, *The Gates*, was rejected because publishers considered it too short; after the success of her first published work, *The Captains and the Kings* (1972), however, *The Gates* was accepted and published in 1973. *The Captains and the Kings* won several prizes as best first book. It focuses on the decay of the Anglo-Irish "Big House" tradition in the years prior to the Irish Rebellion. The elderly Charles Prendergast, whose youth and marriage were emotionally empty, finds the past impinging on the present; haunted by memories he cannot control, he limits himself to one bare room of his home. Prendergast befriends a local youth, who is coerced into accusing Prendergast of sexual abuse, but just as the police come to arrest the innocent old man, he dies. The novel opens with the guards leaving the police station to make the arrest and closes with their arrival.

The Gates also uses a complex structure to show how sixteen-year-old Minnie McMahon, daughter of a Communist journalist, reluctantly learns the importance of living in Ireland. J. shows that Minnie's misplaced affections and near escape from a derelict existence like that she sees around her results from youthful idealism and romanticism, not overwhelming conviction. Through the use of diary entries to open each

chapter, followed by an omniscient narrative perspective and dialogues between Minnie and a ghost or other people, J. offers a sometimes confusing but incisive account of the dilemma the young in Ireland face; a subplot concerned with the stealing of manorial gates suggests again the decline of the Anglo-Irish estates.

Though part of the action of *How Many Miles to Babylon?* (1974) occurs on such an estate, the emphasis is not on the decline of the "Big House." The novel is set during World War I and vividly depicts front-line horrors, but the emotional desperation surpasses the physical in its treatment of Alexander Moore. Moore shot his only friend, a lower-class Irish youth, to save him from execution for desertion; he now awaits his own death, offering a first-person narrative of his simultaneous coming-of-age and death. The book was widely praised for its handling of war scenes and was compared favorably to work by writers ranging from Stephen Crane to Siegfried Sassoon and Wilfred Owen.

Shadows on Our Skin (1977) is set in contemporary Londonderry (where J. currently lives); it centers on Protestant-Catholic relations, in this case through a young woman teacher, a Protestant, and a twelve-year-old Catholic boy who wishes to write poetry. The boy's older brother, active in the Irish Republican Army, at first believes himself in love with the teacher, but after learning that she plans to marry a British soldier, he and his I.R.A. friends attack her as a means of persuading her to leave the country. But the boy himself and his attempt to use poetic language as a means of overcoming the political and religious divisiveness in the outside world are J.'s primary concerns.

J. returns to Ireland in the 1920s in *The Old Jest* (1979), with her viewpoint again shifting between diary entries and a third-person narrator and with another adolescent nearing adulthood as protagonist. Nancy Gulliver, age eighteen, reflects through her diary on her grandfather's onetime greatness in the Boer War and his subsequent senility as well as on her friend, an Irish terrorist who is killed by the British. Nancy, another would-be writer, confuses love with emotional security, knowing she cannot endure the pain of the adult world. After the terrorist's death, she is better able to make adult decisions.

The Christmas Tree (1981), set in contemporary Dublin, focuses on Constance Keating, age forty-five and dying of leukemia less than a year after bearing an illegitimate child. She reflects on her unsatisfactory life and her desire to write, but other narrative viewpoints are also brought in, including a servant's comments after her death and flashbacks; her life thus becomes the novel she wishes she could have written.

In *Fool's Sanctuary* (1987), J. returns to the "Big House" theme and again has an adolescent protagonist, Miranda, who cannot envision life away from the estate—or, for that matter, life ever changing. Her father knows that independence is imminent and wishes to make amends for his family's centuries of abuse. Miranda's love, a Dublin student, talks of fighting rather than love, and her brother, a British soldier, even more fervently advocates violence. At novel's end, Miranda stays in the house, emotionally unable to leave or to accept her own limited maturity as she herself approaches death. Based on a play, *Indian Summer* (produced in Belfast in 1983), the novel in most respects returns in emphasis and technique to J.'s earlier works.

At her best, J. constructs her novels carefully and methodically, and her skill at handling several narrative points of view simultaneously is excellent. She is also able to develop character superbly, especially in her fully drawn characters' ability to grapple with both their own and their country's struggles for identity. She continually shows how the past, personally as well as nationally, impinges upon the present, thus making her fiction considerably more effective than would be the case were it merely historical fiction. Though character types and incidents of which she has limited personal knowledge have sometimes been criticized as little more than unrealistic caricature, at her best her compact, tightly structured novels are powerful and deeply realized.

WORKS: *The Captains and the Kings* (1972). *The Gates* (1973). *How Many Miles to Babylon?* (1974). *Shadows on Our Skin* (1977). *The Old Jest* (1979). *The Christmas Tree* (1981). *Fool's Sanctuary* (1987).

BIBLIOGRAPHY: Benstock, S. *Twentieth Century Women Novelists*, ed. T.F. Staley (1982). Burleigh, D. *Irish Writers and Society at Large*, ed. M. Sekine (1985). Connelly, J. *Eire* (1986). Imhof, R. *Etudes Irlandaises* (1985). O'Toole, B. *Across a Roaring Hill: The Protestant Imagination in Modern Ireland: Essays in Honour of John Hewitt*, ed. G. Dawe and E. Longley (1985). Connolly, J. *Eire-Ireland* (1986).

For articles in reference works, see: *CA. CLC. DIB. DIL. DLB.*

Other references: *Cosmopolitan* (November 1980). *Irish Times* (3 March 1973). *New Statesman* (19 January 1973, 15 March 1974, 15 April 1977). *NYTBR* (27 October 1974, 12 January 1975, 26 March 1978, 16 March 1980). (London) *Observer Magazine* (26 October 1975). *Spectator* (29 January 1972). *TLS* (26 January 1973, 1 March 1974, 15 April 1977, 18 September 1981, 1 May 1987). *Yale Review* (1975).

Paul Schlueter

Julian of Norwich

BORN: 1343.
DIED: after 1416.

One of the outstanding theological and mystical writers of the church, J. composed two versions of her book in 16 chapters (or showings), *Revelations of Divine Love*. The first version was probably written shortly after she experienced her 16 visions, and the longer text some 20 years later.

J. evidences familiarity with mystical texts both from England and the Continent as well as a thorough knowledge of the Vulgate and of the writings of St. Gregory and St. Augustine. She was also recognized for her talents at spiritual counseling, as is evident from Margery Kempe's account of their meeting. Well-educated, erudite, and blessed with remarkable intellectual skills, J. not only recorded but also interpreted her visions. Unlike the bourgeois (and uneducated) Margery Kempe, whose revelations are nonanalytic, J. explained her mystical experiences in clear theological terms.

Like most medieval mystics, J. strove for the perfect union through love with the Godhead. Concerned with the spiritual welfare of her readers and intent upon sharing her message of hope, she emphasized the limitless nature of divine love and compassion by contemplating the motherhood of God. "God as Mother," or rather, Christ, the creative force of the Trinity, the *natura creatrix*, is eulogized by J. as the ultimate (because tender and self-sacrificing in love) embodiment of true love:

The Mother may tenderly lay her child to her breast, but our Mother, Jesus, may familiarly lead us into His blessed breast by His Sweet open side. . . . This fair and lovely word, Mother, is so sweet and so kind in itself that it may not truly be said of anyone but Him and Him Who is the very life of all things. To the property of motherhood belong nature, love, wisdom, and understanding and it is God.

J. has earned an eminent and well-deserved place in the history of Roman Catholic mysticism; in her we have a visionary of remarkable literary and imaginative powers and a compassionate, fascinatingly complex human being. Her spirituality is essentially optimistic; her message is one of hope in divine benevolence; her revelations are theologically and analytically sound, and her style is memorable.

WORKS: Colledge, E., and J. Walsh, eds. *A Book of Showings to the Anchoress Julian of Norwich* (1978). Glasscoe, M., ed. *Revelations of Divine Love.* (1976). Reynolds, S.A., ed. *A Shewing of God's Love: The Shorter Version of Sixteen Revelations by Julian of Norwich* (1958). Walsh, J., ed. *The Revelations of Divine Love.* (1961). Walters, C., ed. *Revelations of Divine Love* (1966).

BIBLIOGRAPHY: Bradley, R. *Downside Review* (1986). Clay, R.M. *The Hermits and Anchorites of England* (1914). Colledge, E., and J. Walsh. *Medieval Studies* (1976). Colledge, E. *The Mediaeval Mystics of England* (1961). Foss, D.A. *Downside Review* (1986). Knowles, D. *The English Mystical Tradition* (1961). Meech, S.B., and H.E. Allen, eds. *The Book of Margery Kempe* (1940). Molinari, P. *Julian of Norwich: The Teaching of a Fourteenth-Century Mystic.* (1958). Panichelle, D.S. *Downside Review* (1986). Reynolds, F. *Pre-Reformation of English Spirituality*, ed. J. Walsh, (1966). Reynolds, F. *Leeds Studies in English and Kindred Languages* (1952). Riehle, W. *The Middle English Mystics.* Trans. Bernard Standring (1981). Siegmund-Schultze, D. *ZAA* (1986). Stone, R.K. *Middle English Prose Style: Margery Kempe and Julian of Norwich* (1970).

Katharina M. Wilson

Katherine of Sutton

BORN: Abbess of Barking, near London, from 1363–1376.

K., abbess of the Barking nunnery in the fourteenth century, is the first known woman playwright in England. She composed her liturgical plays for ardently religious and pragmatically didactic reasons. She wished to dramatize the Eastern offices, she says, in order to "dispel the sluggish indifference of the faithful" and to increase devotion, interest, and piety among people attending the services. Her adaptations in Latin of the traditional liturgical ceremonies at Easter are recognized to constitute a far more impressive effort in the way of dramatic realism than do other contemporary ventures. K.'s *Depositio Crucis*, celebrated at the close of the Matins, contains such animated and realistic details as the removal of Christ's figure from the cross and the cleansing of His wounds with wine and water by Joseph and Nicodemus. Her adaptation of the *Elevatio Hostiae* contains a representation of the *Harrowing of Hell* whereby members of the convent (representing the patriarchs in Hell awaiting the coming of Christ) wait behind closed doors at the chapel of Mary Magdalene and come forth, carrying palm-leaves, after the priest (representing Christ) had knocked on the door three times.

K.'s *Visitatio Sepulchri* also contains several inventions. The three Marys, for example, are played by nuns and not, as was usual, by clerics; Mary Magdalen converses with a second angel after the other two Marys had entered the tomb; and the three Marys engage in a dialogue with the clergy representing the disciples. In her copious rubrics preceding the play, K. gives directions for the three nuns representing the three Marys to be dressed, confessed, and absolved by the Abbess before the play.

K.'s imaginative adaptations are especially noteworthy for their attempt at representation (though not quite impersonation) and her elaboration of and addition to the speeches by the characters of her plays.

WORKS (modern editions): Tolhurst, J.B.L., ed. *The Ordinale and Customary of the Benedictine Nuns of Barking Abbey.* (1977-78). Young, K. *The Drama of the Medieval Church.* (1933). Young, K. *Transactions of the Wisconsin Academy of Sciences, Arts and Letters* (1910).

BIBLIOGRAPHY: Cotton, N. *Women Playwrights in England c. 1363-1750* (1980). Young, K. *The Drama of the Medieval Church* (1933).

Katharina M. Wilson

Anna Kavan (Helen Woods Edmonds)

BORN: 10 April 1901, Cannes, France.
DIED: 5 December 1967, London.
DAUGHTER OF: Claude Charles Edwards Woods and Helen Eliza Bright.
MARRIED: Donald Ferguson, c. 1920; Stuart Edmonds, c. 1930.
WROTE UNDER: Helen Ferguson, Anna Kavan.

K.'s experimental novels and short stories place her in the realm of literary modernism. During her sixty-seven years she wrote 18 books, worked as an assistant editor for *Horizon* magazine and as a military psychiatric worker, raised bulldogs, and designed houses; she was also an accomplished painter. Her writings, many of them cryptic and symbolic, have been called "before their time" in both technique and content. As an author, K. exhibits skill in description and a penchant for unusual narrative designs. She employs a variety of forms such as dreams, parables, allegories, and tales. Her style is characterized by economy, clarity, and concreteness. Her most successful novel, *Ice* (1967), presents a futuristic vision of the end of the world by ice and a man's harrowing search for a thin helpless blonde girl as the ever-encroaching ice gets closer and closer. This work, sometimes classified as science fiction, is told in a narrative of fluctuating reality where the distinctions between reality and unreality have become blurred.

As a child K. was financially but not emotionally well provided for. Her father committed suicide when K. was quite young, and her mother felt K.'s birth to be an intrusion on her privacy and an embarrassment to her youth. She both dominated and neglected the child, leaving her with relatives and strangers and then reappearing to whisk her off on a cross-continental or cross-Atlantic excursion that could last for months before returning her to England again. K. was educated in a Church of England school, by private tutors, and in California, New York, and France. She enjoyed being physically active and showed a talent for both writing and painting.

When she was in her late teens, to escape the mother's dominance and to gain independence, K. married a wealthy Scotsman, Donald Ferguson, who was in the foreign service. K. went to Burma with him in the early 1920s, but it was not a happy marriage. By 1926, she had returned to England with her two-year old son, Brian. According to her unpublished diaries, she felt nothing but hatred for the father of her child. In this same year she began an emotional affair with Englishman Stuart Edmonds whom she subsequently married around 1930. Edmonds encouraged K. to enroll in the

Central Academy of Art in London. K. believed that creativity and productivity were essential to existence and so she was eager to select her life-work. However, she considered herself to be a failure as she had already tried "medicine, writing, and marriage" and was a success at none.

By 1929 she was able to publish her first novel, *A Charmed Circle*, which examines the problem of two sisters attempting to achieve independence and self-fulfillment in a hostile environment of familial disapproval and cultural disarray. She published this book and the five subsequent ones under her first married name, Helen Ferguson. These early works, including *Let Me Alone* (1930), *The Dark Sisters* (1930), *A Stranger Still* (1935), *Goose Cross* (1936) and *Rich Get Rich* (1937), represent a particular segment of K.'s career; these books, exploring the subject of "suburban neurosis," are written in a conventional manner with named characters and logical plots. They reflect the author's interest in descriptive and lyrical writing, psychological representation, and social issues.

K.'s marriage to Edmonds was happy at first, but as he went through a transformation from bohemian artist to successful real estate agent and Sunday painter, she began to be bored with him. As they drew farther apart K. lapsed into mental illness. She had begun using drugs during the late twenties, mostly for the treatment of insomnia, and her drug use, combined with a suicidal tendency, manifested itself into a series of mental breakdowns and two incarcerations. After her second period in a mental institution, following the dictum of the surrealist, André Breton, "Changez la vie!", K. died her hair blonde, grew very thin, and changed her name to Anna Kavan. She also registered herself with the British authorities as a drug addict, which enabled her to receive heroin by prescription. Divorcing Edmonds sometime in the late 1930s, K. assumed her previous lifestyle and spent much of her time traveling. She went to New York and New Zealand and then returned to London where she worked for a year in a military psychiatric unit taking case histories. In 1943 she was hired as an editorial assistant on the avantgarde literary magazine, *Horizon*, edited by Cyril Connolly.

Kavan, who had taken her name from one of her own characters in *Let Me Alone* and *A Stranger Still*, published five books during the 1940s, a period marking the beginning of her mature style. As she changed from suburban characters to inmates in a mental institution, she sharpened the narrative focus on internal psychological processes. *Asylum Piece* (1940) and *I Am Lazarus* (1945) are collections of short stories that probe the psyches of the mentally ill and the emotionally disturbed.

Kavan's main concern during this period was the importance of the individual's rights to maintain dissenting views in a rapidly changing British society. Having gained the reputation as an expert on psychological methods, K. was also critical of certain psychological treatments such as insulin shock therapy, the effects of which she portrays in her story "I Am Lazarus," published in *Horizon* in 1943. Some of Kavan's other fictional interests include natural history and the presentation of dreams. These two elements come together in her masterly two-page short story "The Gannets" in *I Am Lazarus*, a gruesome nightmarish vision of the tragic post-war world.

In 1948 K. published *Sleep Has His House*, an experimental novel that attempts to delineate the existence of "a nighttime world" and a character whose predominant existence is in the world of dreams. This book's lack of critical success was a disappointment for K. so, other than a brief collaboration with her friend and doctor, K.T. Bluth, on a short novel, *The Horse's Tale*, K. spent her time traveling to Switzerland and South Africa and considered a return to painting as her profession.

In 1956, her publishing connections in a bad state, she partially subsidized a small press to publish *A Scarcity of Love*, an exploration of the effects on personality development of the absence of genuine affection. The book received a favorable review by Edwin Muir in the London *Sunday Times*, but before it could be distributed the publisher went bankrupt and the book was pulped. In 1957 K. published the first of the three novels that are her best work, *Eagle's Nest*. With strong undertones of Kafka, K. creates a nightmare vision of confusion and misfortune. This dream-technique was used again in her 1963 novel, *Who*

Are You?, which is actually a re-write of the early work *Let Me Alone*. Her final dream work, *Ice*, brought her literary recognition since it was published in both England and the United States and translated into French and Italian.

The increased interest in modernist writing by women has created a new interest in K.'s works. Her elliptical narratives seem to baffle more than please critics, but K.'s carefully constructed tales and visions yield an excellent but gloomy commentary on the state of the twentieth-century world.

WORKS: As Helen Ferguson: *A Charmed Circle* (1929). *Let Me Alone* (1930). *The Dark Sisters* (1930). *A Stranger Still* (1935). *Goose Cross* (1936). *Rich Get Rich* (1937). As Anna Kavan: *Asylum Piece and Other Stories* (1940). *Change the Name* (1941). *I Am Lazarus* (1945). *Sleep Has His House* (1948). *The Horse's Tale* (1949—with K.T. Bluth). *A Scarcity of Love* (1956). *Eagle's Nest* (1957). *A Bright Green Field* (1958). *Who Are You?* (1963). *Ice* (1967). *Julia and the Bazooka* (1970). *My Soul in China* (1975).

BIBLIOGRAPHY: Crosland, M. *Beyond the Lighthouse* (1981). Davis, R. Preface to *Let Me Alone* (1975). Davis, R. Introduction to *Julia and the Bazooka* (1970). Owen, P. Prefatory Note to *Asylum Piece* (1972).

For articles in reference works, see: CA. *Critical Survey of Long Fiction* (1983). WA.

Other references: Aldiss, B. *Billion Year Spree: The True History of Science Fiction* (1973). Byrne, J. *Extrapolation* (Spring 1982). Centing, R. *Under the Sign of Pisces* (Summer 1970). Gornick, V. *Village Voice* (2-8 December 1981). Muir, E. *Sunday Times* (5 April 1956). Nin, A. *The Novel of the Future* (1968).

Priscilla Dorr

Julia Kavanagh

BORN: 1824, Thurles, Ireland.
DIED: 28 October 1877, Nice, France.
DAUGHTER OF: Peter Morgan Kavanagh.

Novelist and biographer, K. lived much of her early life in France, the scene of many of her novels. Settling in London in 1844, she began her writing career partially as a support for her invalid mother, partially because of her interest in social amelioration. Her family life was not very satisfactory. Although a lifelong invalid requiring a daughter's constant supervision, her mother survived her by a decade; her father, himself a writer and self-styled philologist, damaged her growing

literary reputation in 1857 by passing off a poor novel of his own, *The Hobbies*, as one of hers.

K.'s second book, *Madeleine* (1848), based on the life of a peasant girl of Auvergne, brought her to the notice of critics and public alike. K. continued to utilize her detailed knowledge of France in a collective biography, *Woman in France During the Eighteenth Century* (1850) and in many of her novels. Charlotte Brontë praised *Nathalie* (1850), whose heroine—small, defenseless, deprived of compatible intellectual companionship—possibly suggested Brontë's Lucy Snowe in *Villette*. Rose, the heroine's sister, Brontë thought to be autobiographical. *Nathalie*, set in a girls' school in northern France, addresses itself to the question of whether experience is self-fulfillment or the expiation for sin it is seen to be in a convent where young women are taught to submit to the rules of society.

Although her fresh French material gave K. her first hearing, the condition of England, rather than the exotic landscape of France, seized her imagination as she became acclimatized to England as an adult. In *Rachel Grey; A Tale Founded on Fact* (1856) she depicted, through the eyes of an orphaned working girl, how relentless striving for success affected both the working and managerial classes of northern England. Rachel, struggling to survive in her shabby-genteel world, was constantly under attack by both the workers and managers who were driven by the standard of success imposed upon them. Rachel departs from the typical stereotype of the Victorian heroine by learning to work well with her male relations and outsiders. Although George Eliot's review faulted this novel as literature, *Rachel Grey* is considered to have influenced her own work. Having elected to set the novel in a part of England Eliot knew well, K. is justifiably criticized by an expert for not being at home with the speech and folkways of her characters.

Whether set in England or on the continent, K.'s novels reached a large audience as serialized in periodicals or published as multivolume novels. She figured prominently in the Tauchnitz series of British novel reprints, and although considered a woman's novelist, and thus meant only to entertain, K. nonetheless addressed herself consistently to the problems of women in an unreformed but reformable society.

WORKS: *The Montyon Prizes* (1846). *The Three Paths: A Story for Young People* (1848; U.S. ed. *Saint-Gildes; or, The Three Paths,* 1856). *Madeleine: A Tale of Auvergne* (1848). *Nathalie: A Tale* (1850). *Woman in France During the Eighteenth Century* (1850). *Women of Christianity Exemplary for Acts of Piety and Charity* (1852). *Daisy Burns: A Tale* (1853). *Grace Lee: A Tale* (1855). *Rachel Gray: A Tale Founded on Fact* (1856). *Adèle: A Tale* (1858). *A Summer and Winter in the Two Sicilies* (1858). *Seven Years and Other Tales* (1860). *French Women of Letters: Biographical Sketches* (1863). *English Women of Letters: Biographical Sketches* (1863). *Queen Mab: A Novel* (1863). *Beatrice: A Novel* (1865). *Sybil's Second Love: A Novel* (1867). *Dora: A Novel* (1868). *Silvia* (1870). *Bessie: A Novel* (1872). *John Dorrien: A Novel* (1875). *The Pearl Fountain and Other Fairy Tales* (1876). *Two Lilies: A Novel* (1877). *Forget-me-not* (1878).

BIBLIOGRAPHY: Colby, R. *Fiction with a Purpose* (1967). DNB. Foster, S. *Etudes Anglaises: Grande-Bretagne, Etats-Unis* (1982).

Eleanor Langstaff

Sheila Kaye-Smith

BORN: 4 February 1887, St.-Leonard's-on-the-Sea.
DIED: 14 January 1956, near Rye, Sussex.
DAUGHTER OF: Edward Kaye-Smith; mother's name not known.
MARRIED: Theodore Penrose Fry, 1924.

K. was a popular, prolific regional novelist between the World Wars who continued writing, though less successfully, to the end of her life. Most of her forty-six books are novels. She also collaborated on two studies of Jane Austen and wrote various other volumes, including autobiographical and bibliographical works, poetry, and stories. She was raised in Sussex (the area about which she wrote most frequently), the daughter of a country physician and a French Huguenot whose parents had emigrated from France. A bright child, she wrote from childhood on, publishing her first novel, *The Tramping Methodist* (1908), when she was twenty-one. From the beginning she was compared favorably to Thomas Hardy and Maurice Hewlett, who also wrote about rural England. Though raised in a Protestant family, she became first an Anglo-Catholic and then, with her husband, a Church of England clergyman, a convert to Roman Catholicism.

K. published six additional novels (mostly melodramatic and sentimental) before succeeding with *Sussex Gorse* (1916), still considered one of her finest books. After this work K. avoided the sentimental, strove for greater realism, and began to emphasize regionalism and stronger characterization of the rural men and women who peopled her novels. She depicts Reuben Backfield, a nineteenth-century landowner, as being so obsessed with developing his land that he becomes hateful and isolated; once his plan succeeds, however, with all his family and friends having deserted him, he dies at age eighty-five, a happy man. *Sussex Grove* received consistent high praise, despite some critics' feeling that Sussex was too limited a source for fiction.

With *Joanna Godden* (1921), K. wrote her first book with a strong female protagonist, about a tenacious woman who must take control of her dead father's prosperous farm. Her success exceeds her expectations, making the property more valuable than ever (despite other, male, farmers' efforts) and simultaneously maintaining a complicated personal life. Joanna Godden is presented vividly and memorably, and despite defeats and heartbreaks, she prevails.

The End of the House of Alard (1923) was K.'s first best seller and focused on her Anglo-Catholicism. Set immediately after World War I, the novel concerns class conflicts on hereditary estates as well as conflicts between Low Church and High Church Anglicanism. Her rather stereotyped characters in this novel tended toward flatness, as L.P. Hartley noted, and the "painful" book seemed to him to be based on a false assumption about a family's living so "steadfastly and stupidly in the past" that K.'s superb handling of the clashes, not the issues themselves, dominate. As the Alard family dies out, the void is filled by previously *déclassé* people who look to the future, not the past.

Shortly after she converted to Roman Catholicism, K. wrote *The History of Susan Spray, the Female Preacher* (1931), about a woman raised in a free-church religious tradition derived from Calvinism who serves as an itinerant preacher, presumably by inspiration of God but actually, at first, as rationalization for her unwillingness to work at physical labor. So persuaded is she of her inspiration, though, that she eventually achieves high status as a prophet as well as enduring personal complications. Her behavior may be hypocritical, or it may be based on true conviction; either way, she is successful and uses her talents effectively.

Rarely did K. permit her personal religious convictions to intrude into her fiction, other than in *The End of the House of Alard* and, to a lesser extent, in *Gallybird* (1934) and *Superstition Corner* (1934), both of which use her Roman Catholicism to suggest the progressive decline in the sixteenth and seventeenth centuries of the same Alard family whose end she wrote about previously. K. eloquently defended her use of her Catholicism as foundations for her fiction (in her autobiographical *Three Ways Home*, 1937). None of her more than a dozen novels after *Gallybird* and *Superstition Corner* were as eloquent a defense, nor did any make much of an impact as fiction.

K. wrote a number of non-fiction works as well, notably *Talking of Jane Austen*, (1943; published in the United States as *Speaking of Jane Austen*, 1944) and *More About Jane Austen* (1949; published in the United Kingdom as *More Talk of Jane Austen*, 1950), both written in alternating chapters with G.B. Stern and both charming, conversational sets of impressions, quizzes, and analyses of characters. She also wrote *John Galsworthy* (1916), *Anglo-Catholicism* (1925),

Mirror of the Months (1931), *All the Books of My Life: A Bibliography* (1956), and *The Weald of Kent and Sussex* (1953).

It is for her novels, however, for which K. is best remembered, and despite her occasional two-dimensional characters with their explicitly doctrinaire religious views and excessive ambitions, her excessively detailed settings, and her dependence on overly complicated plots, she is at her best a natural storyteller who writes about her native Sussex with obvious affection and knowledge. Like Hardy, she is a fine regionalist and social historian, even if she lacks much of the tragic element that makes Hardy's novels so enduring. Still, three or four of her many novels are likely to endure as accurate, moving portraits of life in provincial England before the encroachment of the modern world.

WORKS: *The Tramping Methodist* (1908). *Starbrace* (1909). *Spell Land: The Story of a Sussex Farm* (1910). *Isle of Thorns* (1913). *Willow's Forge and Other Poems* (1914). *Three Against the World* (1914; in the U.S. as *The Three Furlongers*). *John Galsworthy* (1916). *Sussex Gorse: The Story of a Fight* (1916). *The Challenge to Sirius* (1917). *Little England* (1918; in the U.S. as *The Four Roads*, 1919). *Tamarisk Town* (1919). *Green Apple Harvest* (1920). *Joanna Godden* (1920). *Saints in Sussex* (1923). *The End of the House of Alard* (1923). *The George and the Crown* (1924). *Anglo-Catholicism* (1925). *The Mirror of the Months* (1925). *Joanna Godden Married and Other Stories* (1926). *Iron and Smoke* (1928). *The Village Doctor* (1929). *Sin* (1929). (with J. Hampden) *Mrs. Adis, and The Mock-Beggar* (1929). *Shepherds in Sackcloth* (1930). *Mirror of the Months* (1931). *Songs Late and Early* (1931). *The History of Susan Spray, the Female Preacher* (1931; in the U.S. as *Susan Spray*). *The Children's Summer* (1932; in the U.S. as *Summer Holiday*). *The Ploughman's Progress* (1933; in the U.S. as *Gipsy Wagon: The Story of a Ploughman's Progress*). *Superstition Corner* (1934). *Gallybird* (1934). *Selina Is Older* (1935; in the U.S. as *Selina*). *Rose Deeprose* (1936). *Three Ways Home* (1937). *Faithful Stranger and Other Stories* (1938). *The Valiant Woman* (1938). *Ember Lane: A Winter's Tale* (1940). *The Hidden Son* (1941; in the U.S. as *The Secret Son*, 1942). (with G.B. Stern) *Talking of Jane Austen* (1943; in the U.S. as *Speaking of Jane Austen*, 1944). *Tambourine, Trumpet and Drum* (1943). *Kitchen Fugue* (1945). *The Lardners and the Laurelwoods* (1947). *The Happy Tree* (1949; in the U.K. as *The Treasure of the Snow*, 1950). (with G.B. Stern) *More About Jane Austen* (1949; in the U.K. as *More Talk of Jane Austen*, 1950). *Mrs. Gailey* (1951). *Quartet in Heaven* (1952). *The Weald of Kent and Sussex* (1953). *The View from the Parsonage* (1954). *All the Books of My Life: A Bibliography* (1956).

BIBLIOGRAPHY: Allen, W.G. Irish *Ecclesiastical Record* (1947). Doyle, P.A. *English Literature in Transition* (1972, 1973, 1974, 1975). Hopkins, R.T. *Sheila Kaye-Smith and the Weald Country* (1925). Walker, D. *Sheila Kaye-Smith* (1980).

For articles in reference works, see: *The Book of Catholic Authors. CA. Catholic Authors. CN. Cyclopedia of World Authors. DLB. Modern British Literature. TCA* and *SUP. TCLC. TCW.*

Other references: Adcock, A.St.-J. *Gods of Modern Grub Street: Impressions of Contemporary Authors* (1923). Alexander, C. *The Catholic Literary Revival: Three Phases in Its Development from 1845 to the Present* (1935). Anderson, R. "Introduction" to *Joanna Godden* (reprint, 1983). Bowen, R.O. *Renascence* (Spring 1955). Braybrooke, P. *Some Catholic Novelists: Their Art and Outlook* (1931). Braybrooke, P. *Some Goddesses of the Pen* (1927). Cavaliero, G. *The Rural Tradition in the English Novel, 1900-1939* (1977). Cowley, M. *The Dial* (February 1920). Dalglish, D.N. *Contemporary Review* (January 1925). Drew, E.A. *The Modern Novel: Some Aspects of Contemporary Fiction* (1926). George, W.L. *Literary Chapters* (1918). Hartley, L.P. *The Spectator* (15 September 1923). Johnson, R.B. *Some Contemporary Novelists (Women)* (1920). Kernahan. C. *Five More Famous Living Poets: Introductory Studies* (1928). Lawrence, M. *The School of Femininity* (1936). Mackenzie, M. *Thought* (June 1931). Malone, A.E. *Living Age* (1924). Malone, A.E. *Fortnightly Review* (2 August 1926). Mansfield, K. *The Athenaeum* (12 September 1919). Montefiore, J. "Introduction" to *The History of Susan Spray: The Female Preacher* (reprint, 1983). *North American Review* (December 1916). *NYT* (16 January 1956). *NYTBR* (5 February 1922). O'Brien, J.A. *The Road to Damascus* (1949). Pendry, E.D. *The New Feminism of English Fiction: A Study in Contemporary Women-Novelists* (1956). Quigley, J. *The Fortnightly Review* (1 October 1923). Roberts, R.E. *The Bookman* (London) (March 1923). Smaridge, N. *Famous British Women Novelists* (1967). *SR* (London) (3 May 1930). Stack, M. *Commonweal* (18 January 1935). Stern, G.B. *And Did He Stop and Speak to You?* (1958). Stern, G.B. *Yale Review* (October 1925). Swinnerton, F. *The Georgian Literary Scene, 1910-1935* (1935; rev. 1969). *Times* (London) (16 January 1956).

Paul Schlueter

Molly Keane (Mary Nesta Skrine Keane)

BORN: 4 July 1904, County Kildare, Ireland.
DAUGHTER OF: Walter Clarmont and Agnes Shakespeare Higginson Skrine.
MARRIED: Robert Lumley Keane, 1938.
WROTE UNDER: M.J. Farrell, Molly Keane.

K., one of five children born to Anglo-Irish gentry, has had a successful, though intermittent, literary career as both novelist and playwright; that career can be divided into two periods: 1928-1961 (ten novels, four plays); and 1981-present (two novels). During the first period, K. wrote under the pen name "M.J. Farrell," in order, she says, "to hide my literary side from my sporting friends." Her novels were favorably received by press and public alike. Her first two plays, *Spring Meeting* (1938) and *Ducks and Drakes* (1942), directed by John Gielgud, prompted comparison with Noël Coward's bright, sophisticated comedies.

The tragic death of her husband at the age of thirty-six and the failure of her fourth play, *Dazzling Prospect* (1961) led to her withdrawal from the world of letters for a time. Nearly three decades after the publication of her tenth novel, *Treasure Hunt* (1952), K. appeared with a new novel, *Good Behaviour* (1981), quickly followed by *Time After Time* (1983).

The world of K.'s early years is the world of her novels: the Ireland of stately, if decaying, houses, interminable hunts, and high-spirited horses. Reared in an atmosphere of benign neglect by a father impervious to cold and pain and a mother more interested in poetry than children, K. and her four siblings developed close, lasting relationships. Their lives revolved around the pleasures of the hunt and of a social life circumscribed by class and culture with a particular code dictating good behavior.

Young Entry (1928), a gothic tale of two young women entering the adult world, displays K.'s sharp eye for description, particularly of landscape and animal life, keen insight into character, and acute ear for dialogue. *Taking Chances* (1929) offers a witty comedy of manners: four key characters and a fifth, who ruins the lives of all, trade love and venom in an Irish countryside of dogs, horses, fox hunting, and martinis. In *Mad Puppetstown* (1931), place is dominant: Puppetstown, a wild and romantic Irish country house belonging to the Chevingtons, is the central character, exerting magnetic force in the plot. Likewise, *Point-to-Point* (1932) is light on plot and character; it is really a study of the savage, brutal appeal of blood sport among the Anglo-Irish gentry.

Both *Devoted Ladies* (1934) and *Full House* (1935) demonstrate K.'s acid wit; with satiric edge she attacks the pseudo-literary and -artistic world of London, creating a memorable rogues' gallery of characters in the process. The emphasis in *Full House* is also on satire: locale recedes as character occupies center stage in this novel, which studies inherited insanity. In *The Rising Tide* (1937), K. traces the fortunes of the French-McGrath family during the first two decades of this century, telling a poignant tale of power and pain.

K.'s current reputation rests on her two recent novels. She began this second literary career after widowhood and the marriage of her daughters because, she says, "I had time on my hands and a lack of money . . . and a wish to write again and prove myself." *Good Behaviour*, which was shortlisted for the Booker Prize in 1981, is a black comedy that opens with a chilling death scene. Miss Aroon St. Charles, the obese, unmarried, only surviving child of an Anglo-Irish family, kills her mother by feeding her rabbit quenelles. The rest of the novel, a flashback told by Aroon, a naive and unreliable narrator, details life at Temple Alice, the family house, with a philandering amputee of a father, an elegant, malicious mother, a homosexual brother, and a cast of roguish retainers. The death of the brother and the father's stroke rearrange the household; Aroon, though victimized and dominated by her mother, takes charge, vindicated in the end when her father leaves Temple Alice to her, not to her mother. Consistently misinterpreting most events, Aroon nonetheless practices the "good behaviour" expected by her narrow social world, deluded into believing that "all my life so far I have done everything for the best reasons and the most unselfish motives."

Time After Time returns to the same basic plot structure of *Taking Chances*: four characters whose lives are ruined by the actions of a fifth. April, May, June, and Jasper Swift, aged Irish siblings living at Durraghglass, are visited by their blind Jewish cousin Leda. Each of the Swifts is disfigured in some way: April, deaf, vain, and addicted to exotic diets; May, a kleptomaniac with a deformed hand; June, mentally slow and dyslexic; Jasper, blind in one eye from a childhood mishap. Confined in their once-grand country house, the four survive in malicious balance by torturing each other with petty cruelties. Even their various dogs and cats reflect their owners' love-hate dependency. But it is spiritual, not physical, deformity that makes each of these characters so repulsive. K. catalogues their sins, foibles, and shortcomings; in some ways the chaos, filth, and decay of their house

are metaphors for the states of their souls. K. spins a narrative with perfect timing, carefully revealing the shameful secret each Swift harbors and bringing everything to a head in a wonderfully vicious "true confessions" scene orchestrated by Leda at breakfast one morning.

These two dark comedies, frequently called modern classics by contemporary critics, are illuminated by K.'s poetic descriptions of the world of nature. Her specialty is the use of the unreliable narrator, a technique that invites the reader to discover truths about the characters and events in her novels that the characters themselves are unable (or unwilling) to see. In these last two novels K. tells her story with renewed wit, devastating irony, and comic detachment, her novelist's powers undiminished. She deserves greater recognition for her ability to portray scenes from a vanished way of life; though her canvas is small, she renders all her subjects, whether human or animal, with attention to detail and considerable zest.

WORKS: *Young Entry* (1928). *Taking Chances* (1929). *Mad Puppetstown* (1931). *Conversation Piece* (1932; in the U.S. as *Point-to-Point*). *Red-Letter Days* (1933). *Devoted Ladies* (1934). *Full House* (1935). *The Rising Tide* (1937). *Spring Meeting* (1938). *Two Days in Aragon* (1941). *Ducks and Drakes* (1941). *Treasure Hunt* (1950; as play, 1952). *Loving Without Tears* (1951; in U.S. as *The Enchanting Witch*). *Dazzling Prospect* (1961). *Good Behaviour* (1981). *Time After Time* (1983).

BIBLIOGRAPHY: Blackwood, C. *Harper's & Queen* (November 1985). Kreilkamp, V. *Massachusetts Review* (1987). O'Toole, B. *Across a Roaring Hill: The Protestant Imagination in Modern Ireland, Essays in Honour of John Hewitt*, ed. G. Dawe and E. Longley (1985).

For entries in reference works, see: *CA. CLC.* Higginson, A.H. *British and American Sporting Authors* (1949).

Other references: *Harper's* (January 1984). *Newsweek* (15 January 1981). *NR* (6 June 1981, 30 January 1984). *New York* (16 January 1984). *NYHTBR* (10 March 1929). *NYRB* (12 April 1984). *NYT* (10 January 1981). *NYTBR* (16 February 1930, 19 June 1932, 9 April 1933, 10 June 1934, 27 October 1935, 9 August 1981, 22 January 1984). *SR* (London) (12 February 1938). *TLS* (22 March 1928, 25 July 1929, 10 September 1931, 9 October 1981).

Robert E. Hosmer, Jr.,
and Marjorie Podolsky

Adelaide Kemble

BORN: c. 1814, London.
DIED: 4 August 1879, Warsash House, Hampshire.
DAUGHTER OF: Charles Kemble and Maria Theresa deCamp.
MARRIED: Edward John Sartoris, 1843.
WROTE UNDER: Adelaide Sartoris.

During her lifetime, K. achieved public recognition primarily as a dramatic vocalist; her career as an author was secondary to and perhaps brought about by experiences related to her life as an opera singer. She was the younger daughter of famous parents, both actors with long careers and important reputations. Her sister, Frances Anne (Fanny), was an extremely popular actress who later published three volumes of reminiscences. She had two brothers, John Mitchell, poet and archaeologist, and Henry, neither of whom was involved in theatre, and her mother was born in Vienna to a family of musicians and dancers.

Fanny Kemble later wrote of her sister that she had an "unquenchable musical genius" which alone sustained her "timid disposition" through her early years of vocal training, since their mother was critical of her efforts. Consequently, she was taught by her Aunt Adelaide ("Dal"), who was a patient teacher. K. sang professionally for the first time at a concert of ancient music on 13 May 1835 and at the York Festival the following September. She toured Germany and then Italy, where she met and studied with Guidetta Pasta, the great Italian singer for whom Bellini composed *Norma*; K. introduced that opera to England after her return in 1841, where it was met with great enthusiasm. K. received critical acclaim for her operatic talent, based not so much on the quality of her voice as on the nature of her personality and her sensitivity as an interpreter of dramatic roles. She was said to be the "greatest though not the best English singer of the century."

Her musical career over after 1842, she married and raised her children. She sang frequently on social occasions, but never returned to the stage, and began directing her creative energy to writing. She is known to have written some songs, but none were published.

Her first literary work, *A Week in a French Country House*, first appeared in the *Cornhill* and then was published as a book in 1867. Described by its author as "more than a sketch and less than a story," it is said to have attained popularity in its time because of the portraits of the celebrities it contained. Her reputed lighthearted personality

and sensitivity are evidenced by the book's lively representation of nineteenth century family life, social customs, furnishings, and food. English readers are taught about the rituals of the hunt in France, including the costumes, technique, and terminology. The characters are full of anecdotes, interestingly and realistically related. K. was correct, though, in her assessment of the work as falling short of a real novel; while Bess, the first-person narrator, and her fiancé of eleven years finally manage to obtain the financial means to marry, there is no true plot. The details of that romance are essential to the entire work but are not the primary focus of the book.

Woven into that story as a kind of cautionary tale, however, is the case of a couple who did not marry: Ursula and René. Although Bess is the narrator, it is the spirited Ursula who most resembles K. The two women together represent K.'s divided feelings about leaving her career to marry and raise children. Unlike Bess, though, Ursula is self-determined and boldly honest while confronting the male members of the party who hold that "Heaven has gifted men in a manner which has been denied" to women, who are childlike; "What woman," the two are asked, "has ever brought to perfection any serious work?" Bess admits to herself that the only example she can think of is *Aurora Leigh*; she does not reply to the question, however, because the men would "only throw Milton and Shakespeare" at her. Ursula's answer to the challenge, on the other hand, is fervent and intelligent: "What sort of intellectual nourishment do women get? What is called their education consists for the most part of nothing but a series of abridgments filtered through miserable smatters." René, a flamboyant individualist, confides to Bess that women adore the "masculine element" in Ursula but predicts that men will never adore her. He professes a desire for a weak, dependent, "feminine" woman, which Bess so obviously is, and then proposes to Ursula, who refuses. By speaking in Bess's voice, K. indicates that she had indeed given up those "early adventurous times," expressing her ambivalence over the prospect of doing so through the yet-untamed Ursula.

K.'s second book, *Medusa and Other Tales*, was published in 1868. It is a collection of short pieces, none of which is as developed and lively as *Week* nor approaches the earlier work in popular appeal. It was republished with additions, which included some poetry, in 1880 under the title *Past Hours*, with a preface by K.'s daughter.

WORKS: *A Week in a French Country House* (1867). *Medusa and Other Tales* (1868).

BIBLIOGRAPHY: Butler, F.K. *Records of a Girlhood* (1830). Butler, F.K. *Records of a Later Life* (1846). Chorley, H.F. *Thirty Years of Musical Recollections* (1862). Ritchie, A.T. "Preface" in 1903 edition of *Week*. "Preface" of 1880 edition of *Past Hours* (republication of *Medusa*) by M.E. Gordon.

Dolores DeLuise

Fanny (Frances Anne) Kemble

BORN: 27 November 1809, London.
DIED: 15 January 1893, London.
DAUGHTER OF: Charles Kemble and Marie Therese De Camp.
MARRIED: Pierce Butler, 1834.
WROTE UNDER: Fanny Kemble, Mrs. Kemble.

Born into England's first family of the theatre, K. exemplifies what was possible for talented, assertive nineteenth-century women. Remembered chiefly for her incomparable readings of Shakespeare in England and America, she also received attention for her inspired acting and for her literary output. Her writings, spanning the Victorian era, include journals, poetry, letters, essays, historical dramas, and one novel, as well as translations of works by Schiller and Dumas.

K. was the third generation of Kembles to work in the theatre, although she always preferred writing to acting. Niece of John Philip Kemble and Sarah Siddons and daughter of the actor-proprietor of Covent Garden and an actress, K. made her acting debut as Juliet in 1829 at Covent Garden, at the urgings of her family, to help stave off debt. Though she was an instant success, her efforts did not save her father from bankruptcy, and in 1832, father and daughter left for a two-year American theatrical tour to recoup funds. K. was wildly successful in America, but she most ardently desired a literary career like that of Scott, Byron, or Keats. In April 1834, she gladly rejected a stage career in favor of marriage to Pierce Butler, an American who had avidly pursued her since seeing her act in Philadelphia two years before. As K. later wrote to Anna Brownell Murphy Jameson nearly five months after her wedding, "In leaving the stage, I left nothing that I regretted."

Two years after their marriage, Butler inherited a Georgia plantation that made him one of the state's largest slaveholders, and he and K. went to live briefly at Sea Islands. This sojourn began the inexorable destruction of their marriage and, ironically, also provided the impetus for the work her admirer Henry James was to call her best prose work, *Journal of a Residence on a Georgia Plantation in 1838-1839*. The book, based on K.'s one hundred days in Georgia, was not published until 1863, when it joined the debate over slavery at a crucial juncture in the North's will to triumph. Though K. wished only to bury her past, she was impelled to publish the journal to counteract the British interest in entering the Civil War. Though her book undoubtedly contributed to that decision, it came too late to play the decisive role her biographers have attributed to it. Though subsequently neglected, the work deserves to be read as an important document in American cultural history. It argues passionately against slavery and includes many brutally realistic passages describing conditions on a southern plantation before the Civil War. It is also noteworthy for its fascinating insights into the life and mind of a talented Victorian personality.

Noting in 1839 that she had been entirely ignorant of her husband's "dreadful possessions," K. found herself increasingly unable to overlook his values or unconventional life-style, though it is clear during these years that she most valued and passionately desired an intact family, especially after the birth of her two daughters. She moved away from her concern with abolition to fight to keep her family whole, but her effort failed in 1849, when Butler sued for divorce and won custody of their children until the girls came of age. Emotionally wounded by the sensational court case, K. returned to England, where she filled the next decade of her life by writing *A Year of Consolation* and returning to the stage. After appearing in several plays, K. settled into an extremely lucrative career staging readings of Shakespeare in England and America that won her universal praise and a secure financial future.

After her anti-slavery journal was published in 1863, K. lived for thirty more years, deriving satisfaction from closeness to her daughters and their families. Her first grandchild, Owen Wister, Jr., was later to continue the literary tradition of his grandmother by writing *The Virginian*. K. read Shakespeare on stage, enjoyed the company of literary greats such as Robert Browning, Henry Wadsworth Longfellow, Henry James, and Edward FitzGerald, and published a play, poems, and her autobiographical *Records of a Girlhood* and *Records of Later Life*. James, her friend in old age, called these journals "one of the most animated autobiographies in the language." At eighty, she became a novelist for the first time, publishing *Far Away and Long Ago*, a curious work that correlates with her earliest expressions of desire for a life of love and adventure. Though not carried off as she had wished in girlhood—"The death I should prefer would be to break my neck off the back of a good horse at a full gallop on a fine day"—she did manage to live life to the fullest, in good Romantic fashion, ranging over England and America in stage performance and trying her hand at fiction, poetry, drama, essays, and journals. Her active life as mother, writer, actress, and political activist correctly entitles her to an early biographer's subtitle, "a passionate Victorian." Both her life and literary works await definitive scholarly study.

WORKS: *Francis the First: An Historical Drama* (1832). *Journal of F.A. Butler* (1835). *The Star of Seville, A Drama in Five Acts* (1837). *Poems* (1844). *A Year of Consolation* (1847). *Journal of a Residence on a Georgian Plantation in 1838-1839* (1863). *Plays: An English Tragedy, Mary Stuart* (Translated from the German of Schiller), *Mademoiselle de Belle Isle* (Translated from the French of Dumas) (1863). *Poems* (1866). *Records of a Girlhood: An Autobiography* (1878-1879). *Notes upon Some of Shakespeare's Plays* (1882). *Records of Later Life* (1882). *Adventures of John Timothy Homespun in Switzer-land: A Play Stolen from the French of Tartarin de Tareascon* (1889). *Far Away and Long Ago* (1889). *Further Records, 1848-1883* (1890). *Fanny, The American Kemble: Her Journals and Unpublished Letters*, ed. F.K. Wister (1972).

BIBLIOGRAPHY: Armstrong, M. *Fanny Kemble: A Passionate Victorian* (1938). Bobbe, D. *Fanny Kemble* (1931). Buckmaster, H. *Fire in the Heart* (1948). Driver, L. *Fanny Kemble* (1933). Furnas, J.C. *Fanny Kemble: Leading Lady of the Nineteenth-Century Stage* (1982). Gibbs, H. *Affectionately Yours, Fanny: Fanny Kemble and the Theatre* (1945). Marshall, D. *Fanny Kemble* (1977). Stevenson, J. *The Ardent Years* (1960). Wister, F.K., ed. *Fanny, The American Kemble: Her Journals and Unpublished Letters* (1972). Wright, C.C. *Fanny Kemble and the Lovely Land* (1972).

For articles in reference works, see: *American Authors, 1600-1900. American Women Writers. BA19C. DAB. DLB. Library of Southern Literature. Notable American Women.*

Other references: James, H. *Essays in London and Elsewhere* (1893). Lee, H. *Atlantic Monthly* (May 1893). McMahon, E. *Living Age* (1983). Pope-Hennessey, U. *Three English Women in America* (1929). Scott, J.A. "Introduction" to *Journal of a Residence on a Georgian Plantation in America in 1838-1839* (1984).

Rhoda L. Flaxman

Margery Kempe

BORN: c. 1373, Bishop's Lynn (today King's Lynn), Norfolk.
DIED: c. 1439.
DAUGHTER OF: John Brunham or Burnham.
MARRIED: John Kempe, c. 1393.

Often labeled "fanatic" and "hysterical," K. is perhaps one of the most immediate, personal, and fascinating religious mystics in England. Illiterate, she dictated her autobiography, *The Book of Margery Kempe*, in old age to an amenuensis, probably a priest. *The Book of Margery Kempe* is the first vernacular autobiography in England, and it relates K.'s life, sufferings, conversion, and subsequent conversations (dalliances) with God the Father, Christ, the Holy Spirit, the Virgin Mary, St. Catherine, St. Bridget, and other saints in great and lively detail. Throughout the book K. refers to herself almost invariably in the third person as "this creature" in apposition to God her Creator whose glorification is ultimately the purpose of her book. K.'s visions are characterized by their vivid conciseness and are accompanied by sensual experiences (smells, sounds, and other sensations).

In her autobiography, K. reveals herself as a headstrong, determined woman. Her first vision of Christ came at the end of a long period of tribulations: an apparently very difficult birth was followed by hallucinations in which devils threatened and tortured her and Christ came to her aid, consoling, calming and healing her. This experience triggered her religious enthusiasm and initiated her path of piety, which, though frequently interrupted at the onset by worldly ambitions and self-doubts, culminated in her lively dalliances with Christ and His saints.

Having failed in several commercial ventures (brewing, milling), which she interpreted as God's punishment for her ostentation and worldly cares, she focused all her energies and determination on her religious experience. Her frequent fits of uncontrollable cryings, sighs, and lamentations not only in Church but on pilgrimages and other public places as well earned her much scorn and criticism, occasionally even the accusation of hypocrisy. Nevertheless, firm in her faith (though not always sure of the genuineness of her revelation) and encouraged, too, by her confessors and spiritual counselors, Philip Repyngdon, bishop of Lincoln, and the Anchoress Julian of Norwich, among them, she pursued her religious career with a dogged determination and unfaltering decisiveness.

In 1413, as a result of her long insistence, she and her husband took vows of mutual continence and shortly thereafter she set out for the first of her long series of pilgrimages both abroad and in England. Her travel to the Holy Land, beset with various trials and difficulties but rich, too, in excruciatingly intense visionary experiences, is particularly informative. Accused more than once of Lollardy, because her brand of popular pietism smacked of heresy to the clerical class, she was vindicated every time as orthodox.

What makes *The Book of Margery Kempe* an invaluable literary and historic document is her uncompromising honesty even toward herself and her exuberantly vivid, clear style, devoid of theological and philosophical reflections but abounding in physical and psychological details that make K. and her world come alive even to today's readers.

WORKS: Butler-Bowden, W., ed. *The Book of Margery Kempe: A Modern Version* (1944). Meech, S.B., and H.E. Allen, eds. *The Book of Margery Kempe* (1940).

BIBLIOGRAPHY: Atkinson, C. W. *Mystic and Pilgrim: The Book and World of Margery Kempe* (1983). Beckwith, S. *Medieval Literature: Criticism, Ideology, and History*, ed. D. Aers (1986). Boyd, B. *Mystics Quarterly* (1986). Collis, L. *The Apprentice Saint* (1964). Cross, C. *Medieval Women*, ed. D. Baker (1978). Goodman, A. *Medieval Women*, ed. D. Baker (1978). Knowles, D. *The English Mystical Tradition* (1961). Provost, W. *Medieval Women Writers*, ed. K. M. Wilson (1984). Stone, R. K. *Middle English Prose Style: Margery Kempe and Julian of Norwich* (1970).

Katharina M. Wilson

Margaret Moore Kennedy

BORN: 23 April 1896, London.
DIED: 31 July 1967, Adderbury, Oxfordshire.
DAUGHTER OF: Charles Moore Kennedy and Elinor Marwood Kennedy.
MARRIED: David Davies, 1925.
WROTE UNDER: Margaret Kennedy.

K. was a lifelong writer, beginning before she could read or write with a "play" performed with other children and including five novels and three plays (all destroyed) written before she entered Somerville College, Oxford. In her half-century of active writing as an adult, she wrote a textbook on modern European history as well as some thirty novels, plays, memoirs, and other non-fiction, in addition to film scripts (such as *The Little Friend*, written with Christopher Isherwood in 1936). From the start she was known as a writer who was able to combine the major social issues and developments of her era with excellent storytelling talents.

K.'s first published novel, *The Ladies of Lyndon* (1923), was set in post-World War I England; it is a conventional, though perceptive, account of a "decorative" woman raised to be merely a suitable wife for a man; set on an English estate, the novel analyzes upper-class British society through the lives of a materialistic family. *The Constant Nymph* (1924, adapted for the stage, with Basil Dean, two years later) is also about an unhappy love affair, in this case about the naive daughter, Tessa Sanger, of a composer (ostensibly based on the artist Augustus John) thrown into emotional chaos when her father dies and she has to fend for herself in her love for a musician: K.'s most popular novel, it was made into a 1943 film starring Charles Boyer and Joan Fontaine.

Red Sky at Morning (1927) also reflects an essentially romantic view of elegant life: a Victorian housekeeper keeps her dead husband's reputation alive, though he was little more than a hack writer, as she cares for her own children and their cousins, who, unlike her husband and her offspring, reflect greater talent, imagination, and freedom. K.'s somewhat contrived romantic relationships and maudlin conclusion make the novel less convincing as art but still valuable as social commentary.

The Fool of the Family (1930) is also about Tessa Sanger's family, in this case about two of her brothers, one a great artist, the other honest but dull. The two compete for the same woman, who is herself incapable of understanding love. An artist and his craving for success is also the subject of *Return I Dare Not* (1931), but this is generally considered too serious a handling of essentially comic material, as the playwright-protagonist desperately appeals for support from party-goers. The same privileged world is the setting for *The Midas Touch* (1938), *Troy Chimneys* (1952), and *The Heroes of Clone* (1957; in the U.S. as *The Wild Swan*), among K.'s other books, suggesting that her range in both setting and subject changed little over her career. K. often wrote of artists, particularly those who are misunderstood by society or who try to nurture wealthy benefactors.

K.'s last books suggest a certain sense of loss, not only of the England she had known as a young woman, but also of the values she herself knew. Her allegorical novel about the "seven deadly sins" (*The Feast*, 1950) was her first since 1938. Most of those that followed had flat characters and anachronistic viewpoints, only occasionally heightened by a sense of understanding of the modern world; in *The Forgotten World* (1961), for example, she sensitively describes the plight of a woman no longer needed by her family and who tries, not wholly successfully, to find a life of her own.

K.'s novels are characterized by excessively romantic situations and characters and by widely divergent settings (Greek islands, the Austrian Alps, Welsh country houses, a woman's college). Though her ostensible subject is the ability to survive in the modern world, she often hearkens back to a simpler era. She was never in any particular literary group, though she had attended college with Vera Brittain and Dorothy Sayers, was friends with L.P. Hartley and Elizabeth Bowen, and was related to Joyce Cary. Her work was popular and respected during her lifetime but has not retained much popularity since.

WORKS: *A Century of Revolution, 1789-1920* (1922). *The Ladies of Lyndon* (1923). *The Constant Nymph* (1924; as play, with B. Dean, 1926). *A Long Week-End* (1927). *Red Sky at Morning* (1927). *Dewdrops* (1928). *The Game and the Candle* (1928). (with B. Dean) *Come With Me* (1928). *The Fool of the Family* (1930). *Return I Dare Not* (1931). *A Long Time Ago* (1932). *Escape Me Never! A Play in Three Acts* (1934). *Together and Apart* (1936). *The Midas Touch* (1938). (adapted by K. and G. Ratoff from I. Surguchev) *Autumn* (1940). *Where Stands a Winged Sentry* (1941). *The Mechanized Muse* (1942). *Who Will Remember?* (1942). *The Feast* (1950). *Jane Austen* (1950). *Lucy Carmichael* (1951). *Troy Chimneys* (1952). *The Oracles* (1955; in the U.S. as *Act of God*). *The Heroes of Clone* (1957; in the U.S. as *The Wild Swan*). *The Outlaws on Parnassus* (1958). *A Night in Cold Harbour* (1960). *The Forgotten World* (1961). *Not in the Calendar: The Story of a Friendship* (1964). *Women at Work* (1966).

BIBLIOGRAPHY: Beauman, N. "Introduction" to *The Ladies of Lyndon* (1981). Birley, J. "Introduction" to *Together and Apart* (1981). Powell, V. *The Constant Novelist* (1983).

For articles in reference works, see: *CA. CLC. DLB. DNB. MBL. Modern World Drama. TCA* and *SUP. TCR&GW. TCW. WA* and *SUP.*

Other references: *Antiquarian Bookman* (28 August 1967). *Arts and Decoration* (May 1925). *Bookman* (October 1925). *Books Abroad* (Spring 1968). *Life* (10 February 1941). Mackenzie, C. *Literature in My Time* (1933). *NYHTBR* (5 August 1951). *NYTBR* (19 March 1950). *NYT* (1 August 1967). *Time* (11 August 1967). *TLS* (24 June 1955).

Paul Schlueter

Anne Killigrew

BORN: 1660, London.
DIED: 16 June 1685, London.
DAUGHTER OF: Dr. Henry Killigrew; mother's name not known.

Anne Killigrew, a poet and a painter, was a member of a family "prominent in the court of Charles II." Her father was a theologian and Master of the Savoy; her uncle Thomas, a playwright, was "court wit" and author of *The Parson's Wedding*. K. (as did Anne Finch) served as a Maid of Honour to Mary of Modena, Duchess of York.

K. received, according to George Ballard, a "polite education," indicating that she was taught the "accomplishments" necessary to a woman of her social situation. Evidently, however, she did learn something of the classics as her paintings demonstrate a knowledge of Greek and Roman mythology and literature. Germaine Greer asserts that "Her scenes with sacred groves and nymphs and satyrs are allegorical as well as fantastic: her understanding of their function raises her above the throng of the King's artisans."

John Dryden admired K.'s paintings and praised them in the prefatory poem he composed for a posthumous collection of her poems:

Her Pencil drew, what e'er her Soul design'd,
And oft the happy Draught surpass'd the Image
in her Mind.

In the same poem, Dryden also describes K.'s landscape paintings, which are now lost. Myra Reynolds believes that if the paintings were as "truly English" in subject and tone as Dryden said, K. could be placed "at the very inception of English landscape art."

K.'s poetry has often been dismissed as imitative, a criticism perpetuated by a probably well-intentioned remark in Dryden's prefatory poem: 'Such Noble Vigour did her Verse adorn, / That it seem'd borrow'd, where 'twas only born." In actuality, K. was simply following the seventeenth-century conventions she observed in the work of other poets, not an unusual technique for any beginning writer. Unfortunately, K. did not live long enough to develop a distinctive style of her own.

More interesting than her "style," however, is the subject matter of K.'s poetry. Reynolds accurately describes K. as pessimistic, scornful, rather hard and drastic in her judgments, an "anomaly." Although K. was an active participant in the festive life surrounding the court of Charles II, she learned early on that "all this world has to offer will turn to dust and ashes in the mouth." Her poetry usually included "invectives" against greed, ambition, unbridled love, atheism, and war. She often seemed to long for death, as in her poem "On Death":

> Tell me thou fastest End of all our Woe,
> Why wreched Mortals do avoid thee so:
> Thou gentle drier o' th' afflicteds Tears,
> Thou noble ender of the Cowards Fears;
> Thou sweet Repose to Lovers sad dispaire,
> Thou Calm t' Ambitions rough Tempestuous Care.

K. herself encapsulated the meaning of her life and work in "An Epitaph on her Self":

> When I am Dead, few Friends attend my Hearse,
> And for a Monument, I leave my VERSE.

K. died of smallpox on 16 June 1685, at the age of twenty-five. K.'s father published a memorial edition of her collected works as *Poems* (1686). The small volume, to which an engraving of K.'s self-portrait is prefixed, contains the prefa-tory ode by Dryden, "To the Pious Memory of the Accomplisht Young LADY Mrs. Anne Killigrew, Excellent in the two Sister-Arts of Poesie, and Painting," as well as a memorial tribute in verse ("On the Death of The Truly Virtuous Mrs. Anne Killigrew") signed by E.E., assumed to be Edmund Elys, a scholarly poet and writer of theological pamphlets.

WORKS: *Poems* (1686).

BIBLIOGRAPHY: Bernikow, L. *The World Split Open* (1974). Greer, G. *The Obstacle Race: The Fortunes Of Women Painters and Their Work* (1979). Morton, R. Intro. to *A Facsimile Reproduction of K.'s Poems* (1967). Reynolds, M. *The Learned Lady in England 1650–1760* (1920; rpt. 1964). Rowton, F. *The Female Poets of Great Britain* (1853; rpt. 1981).

For articles in reference works, see: *CBEL. DNB.* Todd.

Other references: Ballard, G. *Memoirs of Several Ladies of Great Britain* (1752; rpt. 1985). Bryan, M. *Bryan's Dictionary of Painters and Engravers* (1903–1905). Clayton, E. *English Female Artists* (1867). Costello, L. *Memoirs of Eminent Englishwomen*, Vol. 3 (1844). Fine, E. *Women and Art* (1978). Hale, S.J. *Woman's Record* (1855; rpt. 1970). Hays, M. *Female Biography; or Memoirs of Illustrious and Celebrated Women* (1807). Stanford, A. *The Women Poets in English: An Anthology* (1972). Waters, C. *Women in the Fine Arts, From the Seventh Century B.C. to the Twentieth Century A.D.* (1904).

Kate Beaird Meyers

Mary Henrietta Kingsley

BORN: 13 October 1862, Islington
DIED: 3 June 1900, Simonstown, South Africa
DAUGHTER OF: Mary Bailey and Dr. George Kingsley.

K. was a celebrated traveller, ethnologist, and naturalist, whose two trips to West Africa yielded three books as well as numerous articles and lectures. Of the Victorian lady travellers, she was among the most political, firmly opposing many missionary activities, the common patronizing attitude toward the Africans, and the Crown Colony system of governing West Africa. Her writings are notable for their unusual combination of vivid poetic description, self-deprecating humor, and cool scientific prose.

K.'s first thirty years were spent in relative isolation, running the house for her mother and brother while her father travelled as personal physician to a number of English noblemen. Although her brother was given an education at Cambridge, she was self-educated. In her father's library, she found delight in scientific writings (many of the amusingly archaic), travel tales, eighteenth-century picaresque novels, and the writings of Dickens and Twain. Except for one brief visit to Paris, she did not travel until after her parents died within a few months of each other in 1892.

A combination of professional and personal concerns moved her to travel, and she went to one of the few continents not visited by her father. Her first trip to West Africa began in August 1893 in the company of British traders. During this voyage, she learned the habits of traders and Africans alike and became an accomplished naturalist. She left no record of this trip although it is alluded to in letters and in her later writings. Her second trip to Africa, begun in December of 1894, took her through rarely travelled areas, brought her in close contact with several tribes, some of which were cannibalistic, and concluded with an ascent of Mungo Mah Lobeh, a 13,760-foot mountain.

Throughout these travels, she firmly adhered to the dress codes and etiquette of an English lady even as she forded leech-filled swamps up to her neck in muck or tumbled into fifteen-foot deep animal traps. Her travel books are filled with accounts of taking tea in the most unlikely of places. But she carried little else from England with her as she waded through malarial swamps, faced aggressive crocodiles and gorillas, and slept in filthy huts. She learned how to trade in rubber and oil and partially supported herself by this commerce. Her preference for travelling in native fashion suited her meager means, and so she announced at one point that one of her most prized accomplishments was learning to paddle a native canoe.

When she returned from her second trip, she found that she was quite a celebrity, and she lectured and wrote extensively before the publication of her two major books, *Travels in West Africa* (1897) and *West African Studies* (1899). She intended to return to West Africa but became embroiled in political discussions about appropriate forms of government for that area. Although she did not oppose colonization, she firmly objected to a system of rule that violated African culture and interfered with trade in the area. Instead of rule from Whitehall, she proposed a system of colonial government administered by traders and based on existing tribal politics. Her books, articles, and lectures consistently depict the Africans as a wise and rational people, different from whites more in kind than in degree.

Her political involvement and her devotion to her brother kept her in England until early in 1900, during which time she completed a short narrative history of West Africa, *The Story of West Africa* (1900), and completed her brother's aborted attempts at editing her father's *Notes on Sport and Travel* (1900). In March of 1900 she travelled to South Africa, nominally to collect more specimens of African wildlife but in fact to nurse soldiers from the Boer War. After only two months of work in a hospital, she herself died from enteric fever and, in accordance with her wishes, was buried at sea.

Her first book, *Travels in West Africa*, combines a travel narrative with the presentation of scientific information about Africa. Although her lack of education made her unsure about her writing ability, she resisted editing the final manuscript heavily because she wanted her voice to sound natural. And indeed it did. Her colloquial tone and rambling, episodic narrative recall the style of Twain and the structure of the picaresque novels that she loved. She described her method as showing the reader "a series of pictures of things" in the hope that the reader would divine from them "the impression which is the truth." Addressing both the scientific community and the public at large, the persona in the book shifts rapidly from a professional naturalist to a self-abnegating female traveller to a confident and even aggressive seaman. She assigned herself both male and female gender, calling herself a "trading man" and then, a few sentences on, insisting on her femininity. In addition to concerns about her style, K. worried about whether she would be credible as a scientist, and so she avoided sensationalism and omitted accounts of her outstanding bravery from this narrative.

Clearly one underlying purpose in this book and her second, more scholarly *West African Studies* was to depict the humanity that the Africans and Europeans shared. She consistently identified herself with Africa, calling herself a "firm African." By explaining African customs by analogy to British manners, she strongly combatted the notion that Africans are naive or child-like. She described her friendship with the Africans, saying, "We recognized that we belonged to that same section of the human race with whom it is better to drink than to fight. We knew we would each have killed the other, if sufficient inducement were offered, and so we took a certain amount of care that the inducement should not arise." This passage is typical of the fine, understated humor that pervades K.'s work.

The many articles that K. published in journals like *The National Review* and *Cornhill Magazine* made her an influential figure in late nineteenth-century colonial politics and earned her the designation of "new woman," a title that she disliked as strongly as she opposed female suffrage.

K.'s dry wit, warm humanity, and poetic description make her travel books stand out among those of her contemporaries. Although her political stance is complex and outdated, her stories of human interaction are timeless.

WORKS: *Travels in West Africa* (1897). *West African Studies* (1899). *The Story of West Africa* (1899).

BIBLIOGRAPHY: Campbell, O. *Mary Kingsley* (1957). Frank, F. *A Voyager Out: The Life of Mary Kingsley* (1986). Gwynn, S. *The Life of Mary Kingsley* (1933). Howard, C. *Mary Kingsley* (1957). Hughes, J. *Invincible Miss* (1968). Middleton, D. *Victorian Lady Travellers* (1965). Stevenson, C.B. *Victorian Women Travel Writers in Africa* (1982). Wallace, K. *This Is Your Home* (1956).

For articles in reference works, see: *DNB*.

Tori Haring-Smith

Lady Caroline Lamb

BORN: 13 November 1785, London.
DIED: 24 January 1828, London.
DAUGHTER OF: Sir Frederick, 3rd earl of Bessborough, and Henrietta Spencer Ponsonby.
MARRIED: William Lamb, later Lord Melbourne, 1805.
WROTE UNDER: Anonymous, Caroline Lamb.

L., an aristocratic novelist and poet of the early nineteenth century, is chiefly remembered as the flighty married woman who fell in love with Byron and who ungraciously accepted his decision to terminate their liaison. Brought up in a social class in which titled family connections and elegance ruled, L. was given no formal education because a doctor had advised that she "should not be taught anything or placed under any restraint." When she married William Lamb at 20, L. was described as a model of fashion and of pale, delicate complexion.

The liaison with Byron flourished under the class system of literary soirées in which the evening's amusement is to complete the verses for a partner. L. met Byron shortly after the success of his *Childe Harold* in 1812. She met him at a ball, exchanged gifts and letters, and they appeared in public together for about nine months. As the relationship slowly and tortuously died before L.'s eyes, Byron married Anne Isabella Milbanke 2 January 1815. His marriage ended in scandal when Lady Byron signed separation papers; he subsequently left England for good. There are numerous references to L. in his correspondence.

Meanwhile L.'s in-laws were plotting to separate her legally from William by having her declared insane. During this period she secretly wrote *Glenarvon*, a *roman à clef* about her affair with Byron. She published it anonymously in 1816, but the particulars were immediately well discovered. As a novel, its chief interest is to Byron scholars. The complicated plots and "innumerable subsidiary characters" make the book confusing, one of L.'s biographers said. There are some scenes which bring a scene or emotion to life, but basically it was L.'s "sole comfort" during a time when she and her husband were ostracized. The parallels between her life and her novel are easily drawn. Calantha, young, ingenious, and irresponsible, falls in love with Lord Avondale and marries him. Over time, Calantha's wild behavior and Avondale's negligence create a weak marriage. She associates with several London society ladies, all easily recognizable to L.'s contemporaries. While Avondale is away to quiet a political disturbance, Calantha meets Glenarvon, a stranger who has appeared to lay claim to some property. They are attracted to each other and exchange gifts and letters. After numerous calamities Glenarvon marries and leaves.

Her second novel, *Graham Hamilton*, finished in 1820, is not as complicated or emotionally charged as her first. Consequently, little attention has been given to it. Her third novel, *Ada Reis*, finished in 1823, was inspired by exotic Eastern tales such as *Vathek* and was well received in its day. Jenkins says that Ugo Foscolo, the exiled Italian writer, encouraged her to write something that "would not offend." Ada Reis becomes a pirate, settles in Arabia, and meets Kabarra, a spirit of darkness, who becomes his mentor. And L.'s poems, mostly autobiographical, are generally technically stilted and cliché ridden, as for example, "William Lamb's Return from Paris, Asking Me My Wish."

Always of delicate health, her final years were relatively quiet. In 1824, however, she happened to pass the cortege carrying Byron's body, and popular legend reports that L.'s emotional stability broke as a result. Actually, she reports having been troubled at the sight, but what caused her the most pain was the biography of Byron written by Thomas Medwin shortly after the poet's death. In it, according to Jenkins, she had to "endure . . . the new anguish of seeing herself for the first time as she had been held up to the scorn of Byron's friends, and now to that of the public." Even her obituary notice in the *London Gazette* could not allow her liaison with Byron to sink into oblivion: "The world is very lenient to the mistresses of poets, and perhaps not without justice, for their attachments have something of excuse; not only in their object but in their origin, they arise from imagination, not depravity." Other writers she knew intimately were Benjamin Constant and Mme de Staël, and beginning in 1825, the young Bulwer-Lytton.

WORKS: *Glenarvon* (anon., 1816; reissued as *The Fatal Passion*, 1865). *Verses from Glenarvon; To Which is Prefixed the Original Introduction* (1816). *A New Canto* (anon., 1819). *Graham Hamilton* (anon., 1822). *Ada Reis: A Tale* (anon., 1823). *Fugitive Pieces and Reminiscences of Lord Byron with Some Original Poetry*, ed. I. Nathan (1829).

BIBLIOGRAPHY: Blyth, H.C. *Caro: The Fatal Passion* (1972). Jenkins, E. *Lady Caroline Lamb* (1932). Paul, C. *William Godwin: His Friends and Contemporaries* (1876). Sadleir, M. *Life of Bulwer-Lytton* (1931). Smiles, S. *A Publisher and His Friends* (1891). Strickland, M. *The Byron Women* (1974).

For articles in reference works, see: *BA19C. DNB. Biographie Universelle* (1870). *Lives of the Georgian Age*, ed. W. Gould (1978).

Other references: *Ariel* (October 81). *Irish University Review* (1980). *N&Q* (1974). *Wordsworth Circle* (1979).

Marilynn J. Smith

Mary Ann Lamb

BORN: 3 December 1764, London.
DIED: 20 May 1847, London.
DAUGHTER OF: John and Elizabeth Field Lamb.
WROTE UNDER: Anonymous, M.B., Sempronia, "Author of *Mrs. Leicester's School.*"

L. is known chiefly as the sister of Charles Lamb, a writer of the early Romantic period. Having intermittent bouts with mental illness throughout her adult years, she worked on several publishing projects to help support herself and Charles. Of the work attributed to Charles, L. was responsible for 14 of the 20 tales in their children's Shakespeare book, all but three of the stories in *Mrs. Leicester's School*, and a third of the poems in a small volume of children's poems. In addition, she wrote an article addressing the issue of the woman's role in nineteenth-century England.

L. had two brothers: Charles, born when she was 11 years old, and John, one year her senior. The family spent many years living in quarters in the Temple, property once owned by the Knights Templar, where the father was a factotum of a prominent lawyer, Samuel Salt, who had chambers in the Temple. Through Salt, John and Charles received scholarships to attend Christ's Hospital, where Charles met Coleridge. L.'s only formal schooling was briefly at William Bird's Day school.

It was necessary that the young L. had to assist her parents through L.'s taking care of Charles and through needlework, and as her parents aged, she nursed them at home. On 27 September 1796, at the age of 32, however, exhausted from the physical and emotional strain of caring for her aging parents, L. became hysterical. In a knife-wielding charge against a young apprentice, L. stabbed her mother, who was trying to stop the fracas. The wound killed Mrs. Lamb, but it wasn't for several days that L. remembered the incident at all. Declared a lunatic, she stayed in an asylum until the following April, when she was placed under Charles' guardianship and moved to a private home, not returned home until the death of her father in 1799. From the day of the collapse she was never able to discuss the incident of her mother, and she experienced occasional upsets, some of which necessitated hospital care.

Upon joining her brother in new lodgings, L. and Charles received their friends on regular Wednesday evening parties and developed their writing interests. They visited regularly with Coleridge, the Wordsworths, and the Hazlitts; later they knew Leigh Hunt and Robert Southey. For L., one association that prepared her literary career was with the Godwins. She did not know William Godwin (1756-1836) before the death of his first wife, Mary Wollstonecraft, but she did know his second wife, Mary Jane Godwin, who began publishing and selling juvenile books. She commissioned L. to write *Tales from Shakespear*, which appeared in 1807. L. wrote fourteen comedies and histories, and Charles did the six tragedies, but only Charles' name appeared on the title page. The prose tales taken from some of Shakespeare's plays have been well received and are probably the best-known work of the Lambs.

Mrs. Godwin also published two other collaborations in 1809: *Mrs. Leicester's School* and *Poetry for Children*. Although unverified, approximately a third of the poems may have been L.'s and all but three of the stories were L.'s. This time, the title page listed no author; the stories are "autobiographical" accounts told by different school girls at the school. The book was well received, running into eight editions by 1823.

L.'s article "On Needlework," appearing in *The British Lady's Magazine* in April 1815, addressed the issue of women's duties and how best to meet them. L. proposes ways that a woman, within the framework of her feminine world, can add to the comfort and income of her household. Noting that "women have of late been rapidly advancing in intellectual improvement" and that "workwomen of every description were never in so much distress for want of employment," L. recommends selling the needlework so many women do to fill leisure hours. Her idea of feminine duty is to "be accounted the helpmates of *men*; who, in return for all he does for us, expects, and justly expects, us to do all in our power to soften and sweeten life." Unless parents can foresee a daughter's need for future self-sufficiency, L. wrote, there is no need to "strain every nerve in order to bring them up to a learned profession." By doing needlework for money, "so much more nearly will woman be upon an equality with men as far as respects the mere enjoyment of life."

WORKS: *Tales from Shakespear* (1807; L. wrote "The Tempest," "A Midsummer Night's Dream," "The Winter's Tale," "Much Ado About Nothing," "As You Like It," "The Two Gentlemen of Verona," "The Merchant of Venice," "Cymbeline," "All's Well that Ends Well," "The Taming of the Shrew," "The Comedy of Errors," "Measure for Measure," "Twelfth Night," and "Pericles, Prince of Tyre"). *Mrs. Leicester's School; or the History of Several Young ladies, related by Themselves* (anon., 1807; L. wrote Elizabeth Villiers, Louisa Manners, Ann Withers, Elinor Forester, Margaret Green, Emily Barton, Charlotte Wilmot). *Poetry for Children* (by the author of "Mrs. Leicester's School", 1809). "On Needleworking," The British Lady's Magazine (by Sempronia, April, 1815; reprinted Gilchrist, 244-254). Mary and Charles Lamb: Poems, Letters, and Remains (ed. W. Hazlitt, 1874). The Works of Charles and Mary Lamb, E.V. Lucas (1903-05). The Works of Charles and Mary Lamb, ed. T. Hutchinson (1924). The Letters of Charles and Mary Lamb, ed. E.W. Marrs, Jr. (1975-1978).

BIBLIOGRAPHY: Anthony, K. The Lambs: A Story of Pre-Victorian England (1945). Courtney, W.

Young Charles Lamb: 1775-1802 (1982). Frend, G. The Lambs, Fanny Kelly and Some Others (1926). Gilchrist, A. Mary Lamb (1883). Hazlitt, W. Mary and Charles Lamb (1874).

For articles in reference works, see: BA19C. CHEL. SATA.

Other references: SAQ (January 1948). Transactions of the Royal Society of Canada (1928). TLS (21 August 1924, 20 September 1947).

Marilynn J. Smith

Letitia Elizabeth Landon

BORN: 14 August 1802, Chelsea.
DIED: 15 October 1838, Cape Coast, Africa.
DAUGHTER OF: John Landon.
MARRIED: George Maclean, 1838.
WROTE UNDER: L., L.E.L.

L. is a memorable figure in British literary history for various reasons. First, her poetry perfectly illustrates the standards of popular taste for women's verse in the nineteenth century in subject matter, style, and tone. Second, the years of her greatest popularity correspond exactly to the hiatus in English poetry between the Romantic and Victorian eras. Finally, her career illustrates the vicissitudes of fame and fortune for an aspiring literary woman in nineteenth-century England.

L.'s prolific output of verse was marked by a constant tone of melancholy and sentimentalism although in person, by all accounts, she was quite a cheerful and pragmatic young woman. In a preface to her Poetical Works L. explained, "Aware that to elevate I must first soften, and that if I wish to purify I must first touch, I have ever endeavored to bring forward grief, disappointment, the fallen leaf, the faded flower, the broken heart, and the early grave. . . . [As to] my frequent choice of Love as my source of song, I can only say that, for a woman, whose influence and whose sphere must be in the affections, what subject can be more fitting than one which it is her peculiar province to refine, spiritualize, and exalt?"

Educated at the same school in Chelsea as Mary Mitford and Lady Caroline Lamb, L. was considered a child prodigy. When William Jerden ran across some of her early poems, he was so impressed that in 1820 he launched her career in his Literary Gazaette. L. was just 18 years old. Her verses were so well received that she went on to publish five full volumes of poetry between 1821 and 1828: The Fate of Adelaide (1821), The Improvisatrice (1824), The Troubadour (1825), The

Golden Violet (1827), and The Venetian Bracelet, The Lost Pleiad, A History of the Lyre, and Other Poems (1828). Her work was acclaimed by contemporary critics and awaited eagerly by readers who romanticized the life of the mysterious L. in accord with the recurrent subjects of her poems. She was hailed as a female Byron, raising expectations that she could never fulfill.

The immense popularity of L.'s poetry has been explained by critic Lionel Stevenson as a function of her success in capturing the "surface characteristics" of Romanticism at a time when all the great Romantic writers had died or lost their poetic vitality and of her anticipation of the emerging moralism of Victoran verse. Equally significant, however, was the extent to which her continual characterizations of self-sacrificing femininity captured the new social ideal of womanhood. Regarding L., Blackwood's "Tickler" asked in 1825, "Does she not throw over her most impassioned strains of love and rapture a delicate and gentle spirit from the recess of her own pure and holy woman's heart?" Answered North, "She does."

Yet L. thought of herself as a professional writer, motivated by the financial need of her family. Thus in addition to half a dozen volumes of poetry, five novels, and a book of moral tales, she also published numerous fugitive pieces in various annuals and periodicals, including the Drawing-Room Scrapbook, Keepsake, and Friendship's Offering. A few of these she edited or coedited with the Countess of Blessington and others.

Her unguarded professional relationships with editors William Jerdan and William Maginn damaged her personal reputation and may have caused biographer John Forster to break off his engagement to marry her. To the astonishment of her friends, she responded by secretly marrying George Maclean, the governor of Cape Coast Castle, and setting sail with him for a three-year term in Africa, despite rumors that Maclean already had an African wife. A few months later, she was found dead in her room with a bottle of prussic acid in her hand. Whether she died by accident, suicide, or murder was never determined.

The extensive recognition accorded to L. in her teens encouraged her to conceive of writing as a spontaneous, improvisatory act rather than as a conscious discipline. Consequently, she wrote effusively and seldom revised; often the sublime effect she aimed for collapsed into triteness and sentimentality. In "Erinna" (1826), however, abandoning her usual rhymed couplets for blank verse, she wrote a truly autobiographical poem. In this dramatic monologue on the subject of the ancient "poetess," L. revealed her own frustrations as a woman writer. Finally, in a poetical fragment found among her papers after her death, L. lamented, "Alas! that ever / Praise should have been what praise has been to me— / The opiate of the mind." Sadly, L.'s untimely death forestalled whatever maturation of her talents might have followed from this revelation.

WORKS: *The Fate of Adelaide: A Swiss Romantic Tale, and Other Poems* (1821). *The Improvisatrice and Other Poems* (1824). *The Troubadour* (1825). *The Golden Violet* (1827). *The Venetian Bracelet, The Lost Pleiad, A History of the Lyre, and Other Poems* (1828). *Romance and Reality* (1831). *Frances Carrara* (1834). *The Vow of the Peacock, and Other Poems* (1835). *Traits and Trials of Early Life* (1836). *Ethel Churchill, or The Two Brides* (1837). *A Birthday Tribute, Addressed to the Princess Alexandrina Victoria* (1837). *Duty and Inclination: A Novel, Edited by Miss Landon* (1838). *Flowers of Loveliness*, with Lady Blessington and T.H. Bayley (1838). *The Easter Gift: A Religious Offering* (1838). *The Zenana, and Minor Poems of L.E.L.*, with a memoir by E. Roberts (1839). *Life and Literary Remains of L.E.L.*, ed. S. L. Blanchard (1841). *Lady Anne Granard: or Keeping Up Appearances* (1842). *Poetical Works*, with a memoir of the author (1850). *Complete Works* (1856). *Poetical Works*, ed. W.B. Scott (1873). *The Gift of Friendship*, with contributions by L.E.L. (1877).

BIBLIOGRAPHY: Ashton, H. *Letty Landon* (1951). Courtenay, J. *The Adventurous Thirties* (1933). Enfield, D.L. *A Mystery of the Thirties* (1928). Sheppard, S. *Characteristics of the Genius and Writings of L.E.L.* (1841). Stevenson, L. *Modern Language Quarterly* (1947).

For articles in reference works, see: *Allibone. English Poetesses*, ed. E.S. Robertson (1883). *The Poets and the Poetry of the Century*, ed. A.H. Miles (1892).

Other references: Bethune, G. *The British Female Poets* (1848). *Blackwood's* (August 1824, September 1825). Elwin, M. *Victorian Wallflowers* (1934). Elwood, A.K., *Memoirs of the Literary Ladies of England* (1843). Hall, S.C. and A.M. *Atlantic* (March 1865). Hickok, K. *Representations of Women: Nineteenth-Century British Women's Poetry* (1984). Jerdan, W. *Autobiography of William Jerdan* (1852-53). *New Monthly Magazine* (December 1831).

Kathleen Hickok

Marghanita Laski

BORN: 24 October 1915, London.
DIED: 6 February 1988.
DAUGHTER OF: Neville J. and Phina Gaster Laski.
MARRIED: John Eldred Howard, 1937.
WROTE UNDER: Marghanita Laski, Sarah Russell.

L. left Somerville College with an Oxford M.A. in 1936. After growing up under the influence of a maternal grandfather who was the chief rabbi for the Portuguese and Spanish Jews in England and an uncle, Harold Laski, a well-known English liberal, L. tried careers in fashion design and philological research before turning to writing in 1944. With a varied background and working life—dairy farming, nursing, publishing, intelligence, and radio and television broadcasting—it does not seem strange that L.'s journalistic career should also reflect diverse interests. Having established a reputation as novelist, critic, and journalist, L. held positions on several prestigious committees: the Annan Committee of Inquiry into the Future of Broadcasting, 1974-77; the Arts Council of Great Britain, 1979—; Chairman of the Literature Advisory Panel, 1980-84; and Chairman of the Arts and Films Committees, 1984-86. She was also named an Honorary Fellow of Manchester Polytechnic, 1971.

L.'s novelistic career began in 1944 with two works of fantasy. *Love on the Supertax* (1944), L.'s first novel, is a science-fiction account of an England altered by war. In her third novel, *Tory Heaven* (1948), also published as *Toasted English*, L. satirizes government by creating a mock utopia based upon the caste system. Emmett Dedmon in the *Chicago Sun* comments that Laski's satire is "in the tradition of Jonathan Swift, that is to say literate, enjoyable and with a purpose." Similarly, C. J. Rolo in *Atlantic Monthly* praises the book as "a scorching indictment of a hierarchical society." The critical response to Laski's satire is not unanimous, however. Writing in the *Christian Science Monitor*, Ruth Chapin charges that "Miss Laski is betrayed by her own system. . . . Her satirical intent has been blurred by her sheer delight in reconstructing the mores of the Victorian upper classes."

Little Boy Lost (1949), L.'s first serious novel, is set against a background of France after World War II and involves a father's search through a wilderness of orphanages for his missing son. By the end of the novel the father has also found himself. As with *Toasted English*, critical reaction ranges from Sylvia Norman's favorable comment in the *Spectator* that "*Little Boy Lost* has a simplicity like that of a Blake poem—less naive than ultimate. . . . Character, action, and atmosphere are as one here" to Elizabeth Jenkins' conflicting opinion in the *Manchester Guardian* that "the ring is false" although "the writing is always accomplished."

L. returns to her earlier theme of class consciousness in *The Village* (1952). In this humorous novel, the author depicts two lovers from different social classes in a small English village battling the snobbery of their parents. Written during a period when English society was undergoing pressure for reform, Robert Riley in *Catholic World* comments, the novel is "a most perceptive comedy of manners in the English tradition" and that "it delineates . . . the quiet but implacable social revolution which is now taking place within that tradition."

In *The Victorian Chaise-Longue* (1953), L.'s last adult novel, she turns from humor to terror. After falling asleep on an antique chaise, a young woman suffering from tuberculosis has a nightmare during which she finds herself changed into the chaise's original owner, a Victorian lady dying of the same disease. Antonia White in the *New Statesman and Nation* says that this "device enables Miss Laski to create an authentic sense of terror and frustration" and gives "one a genuine feeling of nightmare." Called "a little jewel of horror" by J.H. Jackson in the *San Francisco Chronicle*, this suspense novel can certainly be favorably compared to those of more recent psychological-thriller writers such as Ruth Rendell.

After establishing herself as primarily a writer of fiction, L. turned to other fields. With the publication of *Mrs. Ewing, Mrs. Molesworth, and Mrs. Hodgson Burnett* (1950), *Jane Austen and Her World* (1969), and *George Eliot and Her World* (1973), critics now consider L. a capable biographer and critic. The first volume is a study of three Victorian writers of children's books, another area of her literary interest. However, it is the work on Jane Austen that established her

reputation as biographer. Writing in the *Times Literary Supplement*, a critic remarks that "readers of this book will put it down knowing almost everything there is to know about Jane Austen. Miss Laski has written a scholarly and immensely readable account of Jane Austen's life, her family, friends, and surroundings. No short biography could be better done." In addition, a reviewer in the *New Yorker* comments that L.'s book "brings the first fully enduring English novelist into a reasonably satisfactory focus."

With two books on the same scientific study, *Ecstasy: A Study of Some Secular and Religious Experiences* (1962) and *Everyday Ecstasy* (1974), Laski turns to an exploration into the way in which intense human experiences are triggered, how they affect society, and whether or not they should be approved. The conclusions in the earlier volume came as a result of a questionnaire sent to sixty-three people, with their responses then compared to various literary and religious examples. The critical reaction, as with most of her work, is diverse. Frances O'Brien writing in *Saturday Review* particularly calls attention to L.'s use of her own criteria and original terminology as well as her controversial use of the word "trigger" to include nature, art, and sexual love. Maurice Richardson in the *New Statesman* refers to the book as "a useful descriptive catalogue" which deserves a place in the library with William James. On the other hand, Alan Brien in the *Spectator* maintains that "by the end of the book, the reader is still not convinced that the patterns may not be accidental, or illusory, because he cannot be certain that the minimum laboratory conditions for any kind of scientific study have been observed."

The later work, *Everyday Ecstasy*, is a published series of lectures given at Kings College, London. In these lectures, L. explores the effects of ecstasy on society. In the *Times Literary Supplement* Mary Warnock refers to the "paradoxes" which "mar the book." One paradox, Warnock charges, is Laski herself who Warnock calls "the most rational, anti-enthusiastic, unsentimental, conventional person . . . to explore the subject of ecstasy." The worst paradox, however, according to Warnock, concerns the style. L. fails to treat her subject "with gentleness and subtlety," and by the end of the work, "there is a terrible sense that the concept of pleasure has somehow been irrevocably lost."

In addition to her major works, L. also wrote a three-act play, *The Offshore Island* (1959); edited several anthologies for young people: *The Patchwork Book* (1946), *Stories of Adventure* (1946), and *A Chaplet for Charlotte Yonge* (1965); contributed to *Survivors: Fiction Based on Scientific Fact*, published by the Campaign for Nuclear Disarmament (1960); wrote a children's novel, *Ferry the Jerusalem Cat* (1983); and edited a book of reviews, *Palm to Pine* (1987).

Although not widely known outside her own country, Laski's reputation as writer, critic, and lecturer has continued to grow in Great Britain since the 1940s. Until her death she continued to be a contributor of articles and reviews to periodicals and newspapers, including the *London Times*, and to the *Oxford English Dictionary*.

WORKS: *Love on the Supertax* (1944). *The Patchwork Book* (1946). *To Bed with Grand Music* (as Sarah Russell) (1946). *Tory Heaven*, also published as *Toasted English* (1948). *Little Boy Lost* (1949). *Mrs. Ewing, Mrs. Molesworth, and Mrs. Hodgson Burnett* (1950). *The Village* (1952). *The Victorian Chaise-Longue* (1953). *The Offshore Island* (1959). *Ecstasy: A Study of Some Secular and Religious Experiences* (1961). *A Chaplet for Charlotte Yonge* (1965). "The Secular Responsibility" (Conway Memorial Lecture) (1967). *Jane Austen and Her World* (1969). *George Eliot and Her World* (1973). *Everyday Ecstasy: Some Observations on the Possible Social Effects of Major and Minor Ecstatic Experiences in our Daily Secular Lives* (1980). *Ferry the Jerusalem Cat* (1983). *From Palm to Pine* (1987).

BIBLIOGRAPHY:
For articles in reference works, see: *CA. CB. Longman. MBL. TCA.*

Other references: *AS* (Summer 1976). *Books and Bookmen* (August 1973). *Economist* (19 May 1973). *Kenyon* (15 May 1977). *Listener* (29 May 1980). *MLR* (April 1974). *New Statesman* (25 July 1969). *New Yorker* (1 August 1977). *NYT* (26 April 1978). *NYTBR* (27 July 1986). *Observer* (12 August 1973, 11 May 1980). *Spectator* (16 August 1980). *TES* (25 July 1980). *TLS* (28 August 1969, 29 June 1973, 6 June 1980).

Alice Lorraine Painter

Mary Lavin

BORN: 11 June 1912, Walpole, Massachusetts.
DAUGHTER OF: Thomas and Nora Mahon Lavin.
MARRIED: William Walsh, 1942; Michael MacDonald Scott, 1969.

Author of many volumes of short stories and recipient of numerous literary awards, L. is one of Ireland's foremost writers of short fiction. The only child of Irish emigrants, she spent the first ten years of her life in Walpole, Mass. In 1921 L. and her mother returned to her mother's family's home in Athenry, and the following year when her father returned the family settled in Dublin. As a young woman, L. attended the Loretto Convent, then University College Dublin, where her M.A. thesis on Jane Austen was awarded high honors. She started a dissertation on Virginia Woolf but abandoned the project to devote herself to writing fiction, publishing five volumes of short stories and two novels before her husband's death in 1954, leaving L. with three young children to raise and a farm to manage. After several difficult years, a Guggenheim Fellowship for 1959-1961 provided L. with time and support for writing, and the next two decades were productive years. She served as writer-in-residence at the University of Connecticut in 1967 and 1971, and in 1969 she married a close friend from her college days.

Although she has written two novels as well as two books for children, the short story is Lavin's genre. Her stories examine the often-troubled relationships of families, friends, and lovers and the conflicts arising from strictures and conventions of class, religion, a society. In her narration of the seemingly ordinary and insignificant events surrounding the lives of her predominantly Irish middle-class characters, L. dramatizes and explores the loneliness and isolation, the regrets and sorrows, of common experience. Characteristically, the stories are told in the third person from the point of view of a central consciousness, over half of which are told from a female perspective. In the most effective stories, her technique is one of inconclusiveness, implication, and suggestion, and the complexity of experience and emotion is evoked with sympathy and understanding.

Her career began in 1939 when *Dublin Magazine* published her first story, "Miss Holland," the first of three to appear in that periodical. These stories drew attention and support, and in 1942 her first volume of short stories, *Tales From Bective Bridge*, was published with a preface by Lord Dunsany; the following year it was awarded the James Tait Black Memorial Prize. Two of the stories from this period—"A Cup of Tea" (*The Long Ago*, 1944) and "A Happy Death" (*The Becker Wives*, 1946)—are among her best. In "A Cup of Tea," a mother anticipates and prepares for her daughter's return from college. The awaited evening ends, however, in anger and bitter silence between them, a result of the mother's resentment toward her husband and the daughter's inattentiveness to the mother. The father never appears in the story, and the couple's incompatibility is revealed through the thoughts and exchanges of mother and daughter. "A Happy Death," a long, beautifully crafted story, moves between present and past to unfold the story of a failed marriage and of broken dreams, of youthful love that yielded to smoldering resentment and misunderstanding. The need for husband and wife to know and to empathize with each other separates the two even at the moment of the husband's death. His peaceful vision of the two of them in the carefree days of their youthful love brings to the husband a happy death; to his wife it brings remorse over his failure to turn his thoughts to eternal salvation.

Of the stories that L. wrote in the fifties, many are generally considered to be flawed by intrusive authorial commentary and by excessively artificial contrivances, a frequent criticism of her novels as well. Revised versions of some of these stories, however, reveal the author's awareness of these flaws.

During the sixties and seventies, L. published nine volumes of short stories, became a regular contributor to the *New Yorker*, and won the Katherine Mansfield Prize for the title story of *The Great Wave and Other Stories* (1961). Several stories in these volumes have widows for their central characters and explore the isolation and loss as well as the determination and endurance of the woman suffering through the death of her husband. "In the Middle of the Fields" (*In the Middle of the Fields,* 1967) portrays a widow so terrified of the darkness that she retreats upstairs every evening at nightfall. She is, at the same time, sufficiently assertive and self-assured to demand a fair deal from a local workman and to fend off his bumbling, though threatening, advances. "The Cuckoo's Spit," from the same volume, offers scenes from the encounters of a widow and a much younger man to dramatize difficulties of their developing intimacy.

The stories of widows have obvious autobiographical overtones. However, in one story, "Tom" (*The Shrine*, 1977), L. presents a completely autobiographical narration, a first-person reminiscence of her father and "the gold spikes of love with which he pierced me to the heart." In this story, a series of evocative recollections, she speaks of the "not happy marriage" of her parents and recounts a trip that she and her father made to his native Roscommon. As is the case with much of L.'s fiction, the effectiveness of "Tom" lies in her power to suggest and reveal a great deal more than appears in a few scenes, dialogues, and details.

Only since the mid-1970s has L.'s fiction received full-length critical treatment. Unlike many Irish writers, she rarely treats the issue of nationalism (the story "The Patriot Son" is an exception). She depicts with precision the social and physical settings inhabited by her Irish characters, but her works belong to a larger literary context. In his preface to *Tales from Bective Bridge,* Lord Dunsany compared her stories to the works of the great Russian writers. Of tradition and influence, L. herself has said: "Anything I wanted to achieve was in the traditions of world literature. . . . As for influences perhaps I owed most to Edith Wharton, the pastoral works of George Sand, and especially to Sarah Orne Jewett." Indeed, in both Jewett's and L.'s fictions, one finds embodied in the local and ordinary the universal endurance of the human spirit and the courage of the individual. Perhaps the best statement of these qualities comes from one of L.'s characters in "A Tragedy" (*The Patriot Son,* 1956). Of the victims of an air crash, the character reflects: "not one of them . . . but would fling back, if he could, his mantle of snow and come back to it all: the misunderstandings, the worry, the tensions and cross-purposes." It is this affirmation of life and experience that underlines L.'s fiction.

WORKS: *Tales from Bective Bridge* (1942). *The Long Ago and Other Stories* (1944). *The House in Clewe Street* (1945). *The Becker Wives* (1946). *At Sallygap* (1947). *Mary O'Grady* (1950). *A Single Lady and Other Stories* (1951). *The Patriot Son and Other Stories* (1956). *A Likely Story* (1967). *Selected Stories* (1959). *The Great Wave and Other Stories* (1961). *The Stories of Mary Lavin,* volume I (1964). *In the Middle of the Fields and Other Stories* (1967). *Happiness and Other Stories* (1970). *Collected Stories* (1971). *The Second Best Children in the World* (1972). *A Memory and Other Stories* (1972). *The Stories of Mary Lavin,* volume II (1973). *The Shrine and Other Stories* (1977). *A Family Likeness* (1985).

BIBLIOGRAPHY: Bowen, Z. *Mary Lavin* (1975). Dunleavy, J.E. *The Uses of Historical Criticism,* ed. R.H. Canary, C. Huffmann, and H. Kuzicki (1974). Kelly, A.A. *Mary Lavin: Quiet Rebel* (1980). O'Connor, F. *The Lonely Voice: A Study of the Short Story* (1963). Peterson, F. *Mary Lavin* (1978). Pritchett, V.S. "Introduction." *Collected Stories* (1971).

For articles in reference works, see: *CA, Catholic Authors CLC. CN. DIL. DLB. DLEL. Longman. MBL SUP. NCHEL. TCA SUP.*

Other references: *Eire-Ireland* (1968, 1972). L. issue (includes bibliography), *Irish University Review* (Autumn 1979). *Kilkenny Review* (Spring 1965). *MFS* (1978). *St. Stephen's* (1967). *Studies* (Winter 1963).

Patricia A. O'Hara

Frieda (von Richthofen) Lawrence

BORN: 11 August 1879, Metz (Lorraine), Germany.
DIED: 11 August 1956, Taos, New Mexico.
DAUGHTER OF: Baron Friedrich von Richthofen and Anna Marquier.
MARRIED: Ernest Weekley, 1899; David Herbert Lawrence, 1914; Angelo Ravagli, 1950.

An editor, correspondent, and memoirist, L. is best known as the "noble, healthy, fertilizing influence" on the work of her second husband, D.H. Lawrence. Her three marriages divided her career into distinct phases. She did not begin personal writing until the 1930s. Raised in the German garrison town of Metz and surrounded by admiring young soldiers, L. early displayed her inexhaustible capacity for enjoying life. Following her youthful marriage to and three children by Ernest Weekley, a professor of romance languages at University College, Nottingham, she grew restless; under Weekley's encouragement, she edited Schiller's *Secret Ballads* (1902) and *Bechstein's "Märchen"* (1906) for Blackie's Little German Classics.

In 1912, L. ran off with the novelist D.H. Lawrence, and as the fertilizing influence on his work led a passionate, peripatetic life for the next eighteen years. L. accompanied Lawrence on his search for the "life experience," which took them throughout Europe, India, Australia, Mexico, and America, where they lived on a farm near Taos, New Mexico. During this period L. did not write, but her letters to friends and Lawrence's editors are filled with astute criticism of the novelist's work. Lawrence himself claimed that what was creative in his work sprang from L. as much as from himself.

L.'s writing began shortly after Lawrence's death in 1930. In an effort to clarify for others her life with Lawrence, she wrote "*Not I, But the Wind . . .*" (1934), the title taken from one of his poems. Of their marriage she wrote of "the certainty of the unalterable bond between us, and the everpresent wonder of the world around us." Most poignant is L.'s account in "Nearing the End" of Lawrence's death and burial in Vence.

In 1931, L. returned to Kiowa Ranch near Taos with Angelo Ravagli, an Italian soldier and former landlord whom she married in 1950. Here, L. began her memoir. In "And the Fullness Thereof . . ." using pseudonyms for herself, family, and friends, L. recalled Christmas celebrations in Metz, her adolescence, her English marriage, and an account of her first year with Lawrence, which records her anguish at being separated from her beloved children. But she also wrote of the present as she recorded life and travels with "Angelino." Although never finished, the memoir is, according to Tedlock, "a complete record of her adventure, and constitutes an important human and literary document. Like her speech, the writing is simple, candid, and forceful, rising to climaxes of intense feeling and characteristic wit. Through it run the elemental force and the fierce honesty with which she responded to everyday experience and the crises of her life."

L.'s wide circle of friends and correspondents included literati from two continents, among them Edward and David Garnett, Bertrand Russell, Lady Cynthia Asquith, S.S. Koteliansky, Witter Bynner, Rhys Davies, Mabel Dodge Luhan, Dorothy Brett, William York Tindall, John Middleton Murry, Katherine Mansfield, Harry T. Moore, Richard Aldington, and Aldous Huxley. She died on her 77th birthday and is buried on Kiowa Ranch in front of the shrine she and Ravagli built for Lawrence's ashes.

WORKS: *Not I, But the Wind* (1934). *The Memoirs and Correspondence*, ed. E.W. Tedlock (1964).

BIBLIOGRAPHY: Green, M. *The von Richthofen Sisters: The Triumphant and the Tragic Modes of Love. Else and Frieda von Richthofen, Otto Gross, Max Weber and D.H. Lawrence, in the years 1870–1970* (1974). Lawrence, D. H. *Look! We Have Come Through* (1917). Lucas, R. *Frieda Lawrence* (1973). Moore, H.T. *The Intelligent Heart: The Story of D.H. Lawrence* (1960). Moore, H.T. and D.B. Montague. *Frieda Lawrence and Her Circle: Letters from, to and About Frieda Lawrence* (1981).

Other references: *NYT* (12 August 1956); *Times (London)* (13 & 16 August 1956).

Judith C. Kohl

Jane Ward Lead[e]

BORN: March 1623, Norfolk.
DIED: 19 August 1704, London.
DAUGHTER OF: Schildknap Ward of Norfolk.
MARRIED: William Leade, c. 1644.

A religious mystic, L. had her first religious experience at the age of fifteen when she heard a voice whispering to her during the Christmas revels at her father's house. L., who had at least a rudimentary education, lapsed into a melancholic state, which abated when she was eighteen due to a vision of "a pardon with a seal on it" which absolved her from a trifling lie she had told earlier in her life. At twenty-one, she married a distant relative, William Leade, with whom she lived happily for 27 years. They had at least one daughter, Barbara, who lived to adulthood. William Leade died in February of 1670, and L. devoted the remainder of her life to religion, becoming "a widow of God."

In 1663, L. met Dr. John Pordage, a follower of Jacob Boehm, and the acquaintance may have solidified her belief in the value of mystic revelation. Her mystical experiences increased until in 1670 she had almost nightly visions, which are recorded in her journal, *A Fountain of Gardens*. In 1681, L.'s first book, *The Heavenly Cloud Now Breaking*, was published and excited a great deal of interest in both Holland and Germany. Her second book, *The Revelation of Revelations*, was published in 1683, and the Dutch and German editions, translated by Loth Fischer of Utrecht, were published in 1694 and 1695. Dr. Francis Lee, an Oxford scholar, heard of L. in Holland and visited her upon his return to England. The visit developed into a lifelong friendship between the two. L. later adopted Lee as a son, and he married her daughter, allegedly as the result of a divine order.

In 1694, Lee and L. inaugurated the Philadelphian Society, which was partially financed by Baron Knyphausen of Germany. Richard Roach, also an Oxonian, joined them, and he and Lee published the society's monthly periodical, *Theosophical Transactions by the Philadelphian Society*. The Philadelphians were adamant that they were not a group of Dissenters, and they stressed the fact that they were in complete agreement with the authorities and were not religious revolutionaries. Nevertheless, they aligned themselves with those movements that stressed an increase in spiritual life.

L., with the help of Lee and Roach, was the center of the Philadelphian Society, receiving her directions from God. Though she originally kept accounts of her visions for her own edification, she began publishing them when commanded by God to do so. Due to L.'s blindness in her later years, many of her works were dictated to Lee and are chiefly remarkable for complex sentence structure, strained metaphors, and lengthy titles. Her talent for transforming her thoughts into concrete images not only secured her position as head of the Philadelphian Society but likely contributed to the elaborate images that distinguish her prose.

L. died in 1704, "in the 81st year of her age, and 65th of her vocation to the inward life," and was buried in Bunhill Fields. After her death, Lee wrote *The Last Hours of Jane Lead, by An Eye and Ear Witness* which, along with her own writings, gives a full account of L.'s life and beliefs. L.'s importance lies less in the artistry of her work than in her position as head of the English contingent of Behmenists, a subgroup illustrative of the religious controversy of the seventeenth century.

WORKS: *The Heavenly Cloud Now Breaking. The Lord Christ's Ascension-Ladder sent down* (1681). *The Revelation of Revelations, &c.* (1683). *The Enochian Walks with God, found out by a Spirituall Traveller, whose Face towards Mount Sion above was set. With an Experimental Account of what was known, seen, and met withal there* (1694). *The Laws of Paradise given forth by Wisdom to a Translated Spirit* (1695). *The Wonders of God's Creation manifested in the variety of Eight Worlds, as they were made known experimentally unto the Author* (1695). *A Message to the Philadelphian Society whithersoever dispersed over the whole Earth* (1696). *The Tree of Faith, or the Tree of Life springing up in the Paradise of God, from which all the Wonders of the New Creation must proceed* (1696). *The Ark of Faith, a supplement to the Tree of Faith* (1696). *A Fountain of Gardens watered by the Rivers of Divine Pleasure, and springing up in all the Variety of Spiritual Plants, blown up by the Pure Breath into a Paradise, sending forth their Sweet Savours and Strong Odours for Soul Refreshing* (1696-1701). *A Revelation of the Everlasting Gospel Message* (1697). *The Ascent to the Mount of Vision,* (n.d.) *The Signs of the Times: forerunning the Kingdom of Christ, and evidencing when it is to come* (1699). *The Wars of David and the Peaceable Reign of Solomon* (1700). *A Second and Third Message to the Philadelphian Society* (n.d.). *A Living Funeral Testimony, or Death overcome and drowned in the Life of Christ* (1702). *The First Resurrection in Christ* (1704).

BIBLIOGRAPHY: *British Quarterly Review* (July 1873). *Dawn: A Journal of Social and Religious Progress* (December 1862). *DNB.* Reynolds, M. *The Learned Lady in England* (1964). *N&Q* (17 December 1870). Thune, N. *The Behmenists and The Philadelphians* (1948).

S.A. Winn

Mary Leapor

BORN: 16 February 1722, Marston St. Lawrence, Northamptonshire.
DIED: 12 November 1746, Brackley, Northamptonshire.

The daughter of Judge John Blencowe's gardener, L. is thought to have been either a cook or a cookmaid in a gentleman's family. She was educated by her mother and showed an early aptitude for poetry, which was encouraged by her parents for a while and then discouraged because they felt the pursuit would cause unhappiness in her station in life. However, L. persisted in writing poetry, exhibiting a keen admiration for the works of Alexander Pope. She acquired a library of 17 books, which included the works of both Pope and Dryden, and her own poems are primarily imitations of Pope.

L. was described as being "courteous, obliging to all, chearful, good-natured, and contented in the Station of Life in which providence had placed her." Her poetry is remarkable for its tolerant humor, though her satire was sometimes as pointed as Pope's. She apparently was sensible but vivacious and quick-witted and showed remarkable talent for one so young.

L.'s book *Poems Upon Several Occasions* was published by subscription in 1748, two years after her death. The list of subscribers is liberally sprinkled with members of the nobility, including several earls, dukes, and countesses, and David Garrick is said to have written the prospectus. The poems reveal Pope's influence but are definitely written from a female point of view. "Dorinda at her Glass," written in heroic couplets, is a delightful comment on aging belles. "The Fox and The Hen" is apparently influenced by Chaucer, and "The Ten-Penny Nail" is a dream vision reminiscent of the "The Dream of the Rood." The nail, however, is not a religious object but an emblem of workaday life and as such it admonishes the poet to stop dreaming and get on with her work. L.'s criticism of elegant dress in "The Sow and The Peacock" is much more pointedly satirical than her other poems, and her Essays on Friendship, Happiness, and Hope are rather inferior imitations of Pope. The volume also contains several pastorals, one of which, "Damon and Strephon. A Complaint," is a pastoral elegy on the death of a great poet, presumably Pope who died in 1744. A second volume, containing letters to patrons, a tragedy in blank verse entitled "The Unhappy Father," and a few acts of another drama, was published in 1751. L.'s poems also predominate in *Barber's Poems By Eminent Ladies*, published in 1755.

L. died of measles at the early age of twenty-four, two days after the death of her mother. Most of her poems are satires in the Horatian vein, and they are so good-natured and cheerful that they succeed where more spiteful satire might have failed. L.'s witty comments on the social foibles of her day should secure her a place among the minor satirists of the eighteenth century.

WORKS: Poems Upon Several Occasions, I & II (1748, 1751)

BIBLIOGRAPHY: DNB. Hays, M. *Female Biography*, (1803). Reynolds, M. *The Learned Lady in England* (1964).

S.A. Winn

Queenie Dorothy Leavis

BORN: 7 December 1906, London.
DIED: 17 March 1981, Cambridge.
MARRIED: Frank R. Leavis, 1929.
WROTE UNDER: Q.D. Leavis.

A respected literary critic, L. was widely regarded as an educator of sensibilities, an amaneunsis of the great tradition of English literature, and a stout defender of standards much reduced by the coarsening of mass culture. Co-editor of the quarterly review *Scrutiny*, founded by her husband and collaborator Frank Raymond Leavis, she sought to stem the floodtide of dinginess sweeping across the world of letters. Her unerring vigilance led to an elitist view of culture with *Scrutiny* serving in the words of one American commentator as "the graveyard of a thousand literary reputations, ancient as well as modern, incorruptible guardian of standards in a decadent culture, upholder of seriousness in a frivolous age."

Cambridge-educated, L. accepted in toto Ford Madox Ford's position that modern industrial civilization would of necessity restrict high culture to a select few who were to be conscious of the privilege of their station and the responsibility with which they were invested. Her small output was marked by a strong ethical impulse or as some of her detractors came to term it a moral fastidiousness. Although an admirer of Edith Wharton's sharp wit and lancing style, she faulted the American "literary aristocrat" for lacking "the natural piety, that richness of feeling and sense of moral order, of experience as a process of growth, in which George Eliot's local criticisms are embedded and which give the latter her large stature." Sensitive to every leap of the mind, L. was most attuned to the moral poise that she found at the center of all great writers.

Dismissive of cheap psychologizing and haute vulgarization equally endemic on both sides of the Atlantic, she hoped to find in the critical idiom a restoration of values. *Fiction and the Reading Public* (1932) bemoans the division between writers and the public, the apparently impassible gulf between sensibility and self-indulgence. The gross multiplication of inferior genres (in L.'s words the cinema, the circulating library, the magazine, the newspaper, the dance hall) keep the majority jovially impervious to taste, quality, and depth. Her views are congruent with those of T.S. Eliot who came to regard romanticism as a demoralizing and ultimately degenerating literary phenomenon.

Far from retreating to a sterile classicism, L. sought meaning in the confluence of character and narrative that served as the spawning ground for the kind of creative force that lent itself to genius. Taking the broad view, she esteemed Dickens as a force to contend with. Disagreeing vividly with Edmund Wilson who viewed the Victorian novelist as a misfit and disaffected with the moral obliquity of his age, the Leavises in their joint effort, *Dickens the Novelist*, insisted on a corrective optic that "will enforce . . . the conviction that Dickens was one of the greatest of creative writers, that with the intelligence inherent in creative genius, he developed a fully conscious devotion to his art, becoming a popular and fecund but yet profound, serious and wonderfully resourceful practising novelist. . . ."

For her the past was never dead, and in the capacious pocket of her beautifully educated memory there was a special place for writers who could dramatically resolve moral equivocations. Although never slighting the importance of sociological themes in the novels she elevated into critical consideration, L. preferred the complexity of character delineation in which narrative reaches its most passionate pitch of perfection. In "A Fresh Approach to *Wuthering Heights*," an essay addressed to an American audience during her visit to the United States in 1966, she sought to turn attention to "the human core of the novel, to

recognize its truly human centrality" while never forsaking its firm moral effect. In this novel of hopeless, tragic renunciation, L. professed to see the resolution of the highest moral principles not by didactic instruction but rather by the subtle art of indirection, through such technical instrumentalities as contrast and parallelism. *Wuthering Heights* obtains a Leavisian imprimatur precisely because of its sustained complexity and textural richness, which adds dimension to historical portraiture. She makes her point by contrasting Emily Brontë's novel with Henri-Pierre Roche's popular but lesser work, *Jules and Jim*, which falls prey to that "moral vacuum in which the characters merely exhibit themselves."

Accused of fostering a kind of cultural mandarinism in which the great works of literature succeed each other as if engraved in a splendid frieze, L. regarded her often severe principles of consideration as tending to a new "social and ethical hygiene." To obtain a completeness of response, the signature of a *Scrutiny* critic, called for a vigorous abstention from mystic rapture or self-absorption. Her anxious pursuit of moral rigor created unhappiness in circles where aesthetic appreciation received greater sympathy; her obdurate disregard for the sensuous in language, a perhaps too unyielding espousal of high thinking and plain living to the exclusion of literature's mellower pleasures, has led to a loss in her reputation.

L.'s standing has been hurt by charges that her writing lacks bite and originality. F.W. Bateson has lamented "the curious absence in the typical *Scrutiny* critic of creative talent." Although literary criticism provided her, much as it did her husband, with the test for life and sheer concreteness—ultimately attaining the status as the "central organon for humanistic studies"—it never escapes the partriarchalism of the very conscious moral intention.

WORKS: *Fiction and the Reading Public* (1932). *Lectures in America* (with F.R. Leavis, 1969). *Dickens the Novelist* (with F.R. Leavis, 1970).

BIBLIOGRAPHY: Greenwood, E. *F.R. Leavis* (1978). Walsh, W. *F.R. Leavis* (1980).

For articles in reference works, see: *CA. CLC.*

Michael Skakun

Sophia Lee

BORN: 1750, London.
DIED: 13 March 1824, Clifton, Bristol.
DAUGHTER OF: John Lee and Mrs. Lee.

One of five daughters of the actor and theater manager John Lee, L. lost her mother at an early age and had to be a mother to the younger family members. One of her earliest literary efforts was *The Chapter of Accidents* (1780), a five-act play based on Diderot's *Le Père de Famille*. It was first produced at the Haymarket Theatre on 5 August 1780 and later at Drury Lane and Covent Garden.

It was published in 1780, and there were subsequent editions and reprintings as well as a French and a German translation. From the play's profits, L. established a school for young ladies at Belvidere House, Bath, where her sisters, including Harriet (also a novelist and playwright), came to reside. In 1803, L. gave up the school, and after a residence in Monmouthshire near Tintern Abbey she settled at Clifton, Bristol.

L. also wrote one of the first English historical romances, *The Recess, or a Tale of Other Times*, a literary landmark whose first volume appeared in 1783, with the second and third volumes following in 1785. A year later, L. published *Warbeck, a Pathetic Tale*, a translation of Baculard D'Arnaud's *Varbeck* which, like *The Recess*, blended historical fact with sentimental fiction. A ballad in 156 stanzas entitled *A Hermit's Tale, Recorded by His Own Hand and Found in His Cell* followed in 1787. A second play, a tragedy in blank verse called *Almeyda; Queen of Granada*, was produced at Drury Lane in 1796. Although her sister Harriet conceived and executed the design of *The Canterbury Tales* (1797–1805), L. contributed the introduction and two stories, "The Young Lady's Tale, the Two Emilys" and "The Clergyman's Tale, Pembroke," which together comprised one and one-half volumes of the total five volumes. Although it was not published until 1804, *The Life of a Lover*, a six-volume epistolary narrative with autobiographical overtones, constituted L.'s earliest literary effort. The comedy *The Assignation*, L.'s final work, was produced at Drury Lane in 1807, but it was unfavorably received due to its satirical treatment of certain public figures.

L.'s literary reputation rests upon *The Recess*, one of the earliest and most influential examples of historical Gothic writing. Although this literary genre was pioneered by Thomas Leland's *Longsword, Earl of Salisbury* (1762), it was *The Recess* that inaugurated a lengthy train of successors. This work is set during the reign of Queen Elizabeth I, who figures as one of the major characters, along with Sir Philip Sidney, Sir Francis Drake, Lord Burleigh, and Lady Pembroke. The plot is as convoluted and labyrinthine as the subterranean recess that gives the novel its name. Briefly, *The Recess* tells of the extended sufferings of two fictitious daughters of Mary, Queen of Scots, by a clandestine marriage to Thomas, fourth Duke of Norfolk. The two daughters, Ellinor and Matilda, are raised in secrecy in a subterranean recess within the precincts of an abandoned abbey. Their retirement ends abruptly with the entrance of the Earl of Leicester, his secret marriage to Matilda, and the removal of both sisters from seclusion to court. There Ellinor falls in love with the Earl of Essex, but their union is thwarted. The rest of the narrative recounts the persecution both

sisters undergo at the hands of a villainous Elizabeth, who discovers in their noble birth a threat to the security of her own throne.

L.'s novel clearly is indebted to the English Gothic writers, Sir Horace Walpole and Clara Reeve, as well as the French writers of historical romance, Abbé Prévost and Baculard D'Arnaud. Like Reeve and Walpole, L. presents herself as the editor, rather than the author, of an authentic and antique manuscript that chronicles a by-gone era. Like Prévost and D'Arnaud, L. interweaves fictitious and factual events with a free hand; like them, she casts over this concoction a distinctly Gothic gloom, employing such standard Gothic themes as death, incest, and madness and conventions like subterranean vaults, trapdoors, and monastic ruins. In *The Recess* history affords a basis for suggestion rather than knowledge, and dates are confused or ignored, perhaps by design, perhaps by accident. Neither L. nor her readers seem disturbed by a rewriting of history that places the Armada invasion before the execution of Mary, Queen of Scots. The explanation behind historical events is shown to be personal and private rather than political and public. (For example, love controls Essex's behavior in Ireland and causes Sidney's death at Zutphen.) L. deflates the grand panoramic sweep of history and brings it within the comprehension of her contemporary reading public. L. reveals this intention in the novel's advertisement: "History, like painting, only perpetuates the striking features of the mind, whereas the best and worst actions of princes often proceed from partialities and prejudices, which live in their hearts and are buried with them." The narrative seeks to demonstrate not only the intensely personal motives comprising history but also the subjectivity inherent in our interpretations of history. The narrative is made up of two long letters, one by each sister, each bringing to bear strikingly different viewpoints on essentially similar occurrences.

In its own time, *The Recess* was well received, with four editions by 1792, a fifth in 1804, an Irish edition in 1791, and various printings and abridgements in 1800, 1802, 1824, 1827, and 1840 as well as French and Portuguese versions. The German play *Maria Stuart und Norfolk* by actor and romanticist Christian Heinrich Speiss owed its inspiration to L.'s novel. The writing of historical romances flowered after the publication of *The Recess*, and a number of works clearly took L.'s book as their model: Mrs. Harley's *St. Bernard's Priory* (1786), Anne Fuller's *Alan Fitz-Osborne, an Historical Tale* (1787), and Rosetta Ballin's *The Statue Room* (1790). The art of Sir Walter Scott and Ann Radcliffe also bear the impress of L.'s achievement. Her use of the rationally explained supernatural reached its perfection in Radcliffe, and the strain of historical romance that L. inaugurated culminated in Scott's novels.

WORKS: *The Chapter of Accidents* (1780). *The Recess, or a Tale of Other Times* (1783-1785). *Varbeck* by Baculard D'Arnaud (translated by Lee as *Warbeck, a Pathetic Tale*, 1786). *A Hermit's Tale, Recorded by His Own Hand and Found in His Cell* (1787). *Almeyda; Queen of Granada* (1796). Introduction, "The Young Lady's Tale, The Two Emilys" and "The Clergyman's Tale, Pembroke," in *The Canterbury Tales* by Harriet and Sophia Lee (1797-1805). *The Life of a Lover* (1804). *The Assignation* (stage performance only, 1807).

BIBLIOGRAPHY: Punter, D. *The Literature of Terror: A History of Gothic Fictions from 1765 to the Present Day* (1980). Summers, M. *The Gothic Quest: A History of the Gothic Novel* (1938). Tompkins, J.M.S. *The Popular Novel in England 1770-1800* (1932). Varma, D. Introduction to *The Recess, or a Tale of Other Times* (1972).

For articles in reference works, see: *BAB1800*.

Eileen Finan

Rosamond Lehmann

BORN: 3 February 1901, Bourne End, Buckinghamshire.
DAUGHTER OF: Rudolph Chambers and Alice Marie Davis Lehmann.
MARRIED: Leslie Ruciman, 1923; Wogan Philipps, 1928.

Born into an unusually intellectually and artistically gifted family, L. fit in well with her younger sister, Beatrix, who became a well-known actress, and her youngest brother, John, who became a critic, poet, founder of *New Writing*, and, for a time, manager of Leonard and Virginia Woolf's Hogarth Press. L.'s father, an editor of *Punch* and a regular contributor of verse and prose to that magazine, also entertained many literary figures at his home. Educated privately, L. went to Girton College, Cambridge, in 1919 to study modern languages, returning home in 1922.

Partly because most of her important work was published by 1947, L.'s reputation does not live up to early expectations that ranked her with Elizabeth Bowen and Virginia Woolf although she has consistently enjoyed critical esteem. Those who have objected to aspects of her writing have chided her for confining herself to the world of "feminine sensibility" in which, in technically impeccable but mannered and highly charged emotional prose, women and girls are faced with disillusionment, loss of innocence, and betrayal by love and life.

Despite these problems, L.'s novels profoundly and lyrically investigate aspects of women's lives that are frequently ignored: for example, lesbian relations, infidelity, suicide, hatred, and power manipulations. In her first highly acclaimed novel, *Dusty Answer*, published a year before Radclyffe Hall's *Well of Loneliness*, L. treated the theme of adolescent lesbianism with sensitivity and candor, using her own college ex-

periences. *A Note in Music* and *The Weather in the Streets* both deal with the drabness and disillusionment accompanying unfulfilled middle age, an accomplishment especially in an era when there were even fewer novels than there are today depicting lives of women over thirty. *The Ballad and the Source* is L.'s best-known and most critically acclaimed novel. Stylistically breathtaking and structurally complex, full of Jamesian experimentation with point of view, the book presents a charismatic but egomaniacal central character, the aging Mrs. Sybil Anstey Herbert Jardine, who comes to dominate the consciousness of a progressively unillusioned adolescent, Rebecca Landon, who learns variations of the story of Mrs. Jardine's life—a tale encompasing adultery, madness, suicide and hatred—from four people who knew her. A theme introduced in this novel that remains important in L.'s later writing is that of the mystical and transcendent influence of the self on others. Many critics have praised L.'s ornate, romantic, lyrical prose. L. said of herself that she wrote in a "half-trance," experiencing herself as "a kind of preserving jar in which float fragments of people and landscapes, snatches of sound, [but] there is not one of these fragile shapes and serial sounds but bears within it the explosive seed of life."

After her daughter's death of poliomyelitis in 1958, L. turned increasingly to spiritualism, which she discusses in *The Swan in the Evening*, a disquieting, even embarrassing but moving personal memoir.

WORKS: *Dusty Answer* (1927). *A Note in Music* (1930). *Letter to a Sister* (1932). *Invitation to the Waltz* (1932). *The Weather in the Streets* (1936). *No More Music* (1945). *The Ballad and the Source* (1945). *The Gipsy's Baby and Other Stories* (1947). *The Echoing Grove* (1953). *A Man Seen Afar* (with W. Tudor Pole) (1965). *The Swan in the Evening:*

Fragments of an Inner Life (1967). (with Cynthia Hill Sandys) *Letters from Our Daughters* (1972). *A Sea-Grape Tree* (1977).

BIBLIOGRAPHY: LeStourgeon, D. *Rosamond Lehmann* (1965).

For articles in reference works, see: *CA. CN. DLB. EWLTC. TCA SUP.*

Other references: *Contemporary Literature* (1974). *TCL* (1981). *Virginia Woolf Quarterly* (Spring 1973).

Carey Kaplan

Dorothy Kempe Leigh

BORN: n.d. [c. 1616]; Finchingfield, Essex.
DAUGHTER OF: Robert Kempe (or Kemp), Esquire of Spainshall, and Elizabeth, daughter of Sir Clement Higham of Barrowhall, Suffolk.
MARRIED: Ralph Leigh (or Lee), a Cheshire gentleman and soldier under the Earl of Essex at Cadiz, n.d.

An English gentlewoman of the middle class, L. authored one work, *The Mothers Blessing*, for her three sons. The book is a fine example of the advice book, a genre then in vogue. It is evident that L.'s advice book reflects the results of both the humanist and religious advocates of education for women. In fact, her book forwards their attitudes as she urges her sons to educate their wives and servants, stressing knowledge of the Bible and practical skills. Little is known of L.'s life or that of her family except that she was pious, a Puritan, and a dedicated mother. She is unlisted in the *DNB*. She married Ralph Leigh (or Lee) and had three sons, George, John, and William. Her son William may have become Rector of Groton near Hadleigh, appointed by John Winthrop.

L.'s book is divided into four sections. The first is a dedication to Princess Elizabeth who is asked to serve as "protectoresse" of the work. Part II of the tract is a letter to her sons explaining her reasons for writing. The third section of the work is an Introductory Epistle, which is composed in an eight-line stanza. The epistle is controlled and indicates some poetic merit. Possibly as a reflection of her country life, L. employs images of

nature, such as bees and flowers, which are then incorporated into a parable of the busy bee wherein L. urges her sons to model themselves after the busy rather than the idle bee. Part IV is the longest section of the work, presenting in 45 brief chapters L.'s concerns with personal behavior, choice of wife, and education. Her advice to her sons, though practical, is primarily religious. Each of the chapters opens with a biblical quotation.

The book was extremely popular as evidenced by the publication of seventeen editions between 1616 and 1640 and its continued printing into the last quarter of the century. Although popular, the book did not seem to have much literary influence, though it may have had social influence. It did, however, presage Milton, also a Puritan, in its attitude toward education, especially of women, and in the belief that a wife functions chiefly as a companion.

WORKS: *The Mothers Blessing* (1616, STC 15402).

BIBLIOGRAPHY: Sizemore, C. *SAB* (1976). Sizemore, C. *The University of Dayton Review* (1981). Travitsky, B., ed. *The Paradise of Women: Writings by Englishwomen of the Renaissance* (1981). Travitsky, B. *The Lost Tradition: Mothers and Daughters in Literature*, ed. E.M. Broner and C.N. Davidson (1979).

Marcia Davis

Doris Lessing

BORN: 22 October 1919, Kermanshah, Persia.
DAUGHTER OF: Alfred Cook Tayler and Emily McVeagh Tayler.
MARRIED: Frank Wisdom, 1939; Gottfried Lessing, 1944.
WRITES UNDER: Doris Lessing, Jane Somers.

When L. entered the literary scene in 1950 with the conventionally realistic *The Grass Is*

Singing, she began a career devoted to exploring the psychic wholeness missing in the "fragmented" modern world. In her novels, as well as in numerous stories and work in other genres, L. has been for many readers a kind of Cassandra or conscience of the modern age. L. has produced fiction of many forms, including a multi-volume *Bildungsroman*, works focusing on characters seeking inner knowledge or independence, an ongoing "space fiction" series, books about a young terrorist and a career woman working in the world of fashion—in short, a wide literary canvas peopled with earnest characters who have had considerable impact on intelligent readers around the world.

L.'s first novel, *The Grass Is Singing*, published after L. emigrated from Rhodesia to London, is set in, and clearly deeply concerned with, the colonial world L. knew as a child. Mary Turner is seen in flashback as incapable of adjustment to white "superiority" on the impoverished farm she and her husband run, and her cruelty and insecurity result in her being killed by her black houseboy. Africa is also the setting for four of the five parts of L.'s "Children of Violence" series (published from 1952 through 1969); Martha Quest is depicted from adolescence to old age and death, from colonial expectations during World War II through failed marriages and child raising, political and social involvement, emigration to England, and psychic complexities in a world hurtling rapidly toward destruction (in *The Four-Gated City*, 1969) at the end of the twentieth century.

The Golden Notebook (1962) is by common consent L.'s masterpiece. More overtly concerned with the fragmented soul than any of L.'s other books, this novel shows how Anna Wulf divides her life into notebook narratives (black for her life in colonial Africa, red for her life as a Communist, yellow about an alter ego, and blue, a factual diary), all of which culminate in a golden one serving as therapy and reconciliation of her various "selves." In addition, several "Free Women" sections comprise a short conventional novel, also about Anna Wulf but "written" by her as counterpoint to her "real" life. Erroneously considered by some critics to be L.'s own "confessions," the novel is instead a rich, multi-layered, endlessly rewarding account of a woman's search for wholeness through Jungian therapy as well as through sex, marriage, dreams, politics, writing, and incessant analysis of news reports and of herself.

L.'s forays into "inner space" continued with *Briefing for a Descent into Hell* (1971), a claustrophobic work somewhat indebted to Scottish psychiatrist R.D. Laing in its concern with mental imbalance and psychic phenomena. Charles Watkins, one of the few male protagonists in L.'s novels, is a classics professor who "travels" psychically to a gathering of Greek deities (hence the book's title, with "hell" equated with earth), to World War II Yugoslavia (where he fights with partisans), and, most startling, to a raft on the ocean that lands him in a prehistoric city where strange species of animals fight and from which he escapes to "reality." After the amnesiac Watkins is found wandering in London, he is hospitalized, able to recall his various "existences" but not his "real" life; after therapy, he is restored to

"sanity," but not to wholeness, freedom, and human harmony.

Restoration of psychic health is also L.'s concern in *The Summer Before the Dark* (1973) and *Memoirs of a Survivor* (1974). The first is a realistic, somewhat clichéd account of Kate Brown's gradual awakening at age forty-five into a self-conscious "liberation"; she goes away from home and family for a series of experiences one summer that culminate in her returning, chastened and reconciled, to her routine life. The latter work, though, is an important study of a woman's solitary survival following the ultimate war; inexplicably, she must care for a pre-adolescent girl who rapidly matures into a sexually liberated woman and who, with her lover and a strange hybrid pet, pioneer in helping other survivors endure the end of civilization. Most impressive in the book, however, are those passages in which the narrator "walks" through a wall to "see" a series of tableaux about her own earlier life by which she rids herself of behavior and thinking invalid in her world.

L.'s series of "space fiction" narratives (five novels published to date), "Canopus in Argos: Archives," depict earth's history as a battleground for opposing forces of ageless beings. *Shikasta* (1979) is a prolix sequence of documents, reports, and records presenting earth's history from a cosmic perspective; as allegory, the work shows how humanity flounders helplessly from catastrophe to catastrophe, but as a novel it is unconvincing. *The Marriages Between Zones Three, Four and Five* (1980), however, is a fascinating fable that, although allegorical, also offers a convincing love story and psychological analysis of the rise and fall of civilizations. *The Sirian Experiments* (1981) contains many documents about earth's early history, but it also offers a female demi-god who slowly changes as she understands the "group mind" that runs the universe and the effects this has on and for earth. *The Making of the Representative for Planet 8* (1982) concerns the freezing death of a world whose inhabitants must prepare for their promised removal to another planet; even the "Overlords," though, are subject to inexorable cosmic forces that radically diminish earthly concerns with nationalism and historical pride. Finally, *Documents Relating to The Sentimental Agents in the Volyen Empire* (1983) again includes various documents but is also an ineffectual attempt at satire regarding the debasement of language as mere "rhetoric" in the rise and fall of societies.

In 1983 L. attempted a hoax by publishing *The Diary of a Good Neighbour* under the name "Jane Somers," and *If the Old Could . . .* under the same name the year after; her intent in the experiment was to see whether novels could be published on their merits instead of on an author's name and reputation. But neither realistic book, one focusing on a fashion magazine editor's relationship with a dying older woman, the other on a non-consummated love affair and relationship with her niece, is very good: characters are banal, plots are sentimental, and insights into any larger world view are limited. It seems as if L. had both a narrower purpose and a more unquestioning attitude toward human behavior in these pseudonymous works than in her earlier books.

The Good Terrorist (1985) is a return to a realistic approach; it concerns a young insecure middle-class woman who works with (and supports) a gang of would-be terrorists; they prefer to fight the "system" through parasitic behavior and endless discussions and demonstrations while she works as a drudge cleaning up after them, abusing her own parents, and, through misguided idealism, taking the revolution into her own hands. Topical though the book is, it lacks emotional liveliness and compelling characters.

L.'s work has obviously changed radically over the years, especially as she has taken chances in trying new approaches and subjects. Her high prophetic seriousness (as reflective of her recent interest in Sufism) and relative lack of a sense of humor have often been noted, but at her best, when she focuses on a solitary, compulsive person (usually a woman) who has been forced to a moment of crisis, she effectively dramatizes a revaluation of personal identity. Though her fiction is often repetitive, prolix, didactic, and trivial, her depth of character presentation and sense of character commitment have secured her place among the most powerful and compelling writers of the century.

WORKS: *The Grass Is Singing* (1950). *This Was the Old Chief's Country* (1951). *Martha Quest* ("Children of Violence" I) (1952). *Five: Short Novels* (1953). *A Proper Marriage* ("Children of Violence" II) (1954). *Retreat to Innocence* (1956). *The Habit of Loving* (1957). *Going Home* (1957). *A Ripple from the Storm* ("Children of Violence" III) (1958). *Each His Own Wilderness*, in *New English Dramatists: Three Plays*, ed. E.M. Browne (1959). *Fourteen Poems* (1959). *In Pursuit of the English: A Documentary* (1960). *Play with a Tiger* (1962). *The Golden Notebook* (1962). *A Man and Two Women* (1963). *African Stories* (1964). *Landlocked* ("Children of Violence" IV) (1965). *Particularly Cats* (1967). *The Four-Gated City* ("Children of Violence" V) (1969). *Briefing for a Descent into Hell* (1971). *The Story of a Non-Marrying Man and Other Stories* (1972; in U.S. as *The Confessions of Jack Orkney and Other Stories*). *The Singing Door*, in *Second Playbill Two*, ed. A. Durband (1973). *The Summer Before the Dark* (1973). *Memoirs of a Survivor* (1974). *A Small Personal Voice: Essays, Reviews, and Interviews*, ed. P. Schlueter (1974).

Collected Stories (1978; in U.S. as *Stories*). *Shikasta* ("Canopus in Argos: Archives" I) (1979). *The Marriages Between Zones Three, Four and Five* (Canopus in Argos: Archives" II) (1980). *The Sirian Experiments* ("Canopus in Argos: Archives" III) (1981). *The Making of the Representative for Planet 8* ("Canopus in Argos: Archives" IV) (1982). *Documents Relating to the Sentimental Agents in the Volyen Empire* ("Canopus in Argos: Archives" V) (1983). (as Jane Somers) *The Diary of a Good Neighbour* (1983). (as Jane Somers) *If the Old Could . . .* (1984). *The Good Terrorist* (1985). *Prisons We Choose to Live Inside* (1986). *The Wind Blows Away Our Words* (1987).

BIBLIOGRAPHY: Brewster, D. *Doris Lessing* (1965). Burkom, S. and M. Williams, *Doris Lessing: A Checklist of Primary and Secondary Sources* (1973). Draine, B. *Substance Under Pressure: Artistic Coherence and Evolving Form in the Novels of Doris Lessing* (1983). Fishburn, K. *The Unexpected Universe of Doris Lessing: A Study in Narrative Technique* (1985). Holmquist, I. *From Society to Nature: A Study of Doris Lessing's "Children of Violence"* (1980). Knapp, M. *Doris Lessing* (1984). Morris, R.K. *Continuance and Change: The Contemporary British Novel Sequence* (1972). Pratt, A., and L.K. Dembo, ed. *Doris Lessing: Critical Studies* (1974). Rose, E.C. *The Tree Outside the Window: Doris Lessing's Children of Violence* (1976). Rubenstein, R. *The Novelistic Vision of Doris Lessing* (1979). Sage, L. *Doris Lessing* (1983). Schlueter, P. *The Novels of Doris Lessing* (1973). Seligman, D. *Doris Lessing: An Annotated Bibliography of Criticism* (1981). Spiegel, R. *Doris Lessing: The Problem of Alienation and the Form of the Novel* (1980). Sprague, C., and V. Tiger, ed. *Critical Essays on Doris Lessing* (1986). Sprague, C. *Rereading Doris Lessing: Narrative Patterns of Doubling and Repetition* (1987). Steele, M. C. *Children of Violence and Rhodesia: A Study of Doris Lessing as Historical Observer* (1974). Taylor, J., ed. *Notebooks/Memoirs/Archives: Reading and Rereading Doris Lessing* (1982). Thorpe, M. *Doris Lessing* (1973). Thorpe, M. *Doris Lessing's Africa* (1978).

For articles in reference works, see: *CA. CD. CN. DLB. MBL.* and *SUP. TCW. WA.*

Other references: Ahearn, M. *Proceedings of the Fifth National Convention of the Popular Culture Association* (1976). Barnouw, D. *Contemporary Literature* (1973). Bazin, N.T. *Modern Fiction Studies* (1980). Bolling, D. *Contemporary Literature* (1973). Burkom, S. *Critique* (1969). Cederstrom, L. *Mosaic* (1980). Christ, C. *Diving Deep and Surfacing: Women Writers on Spiritual Quest* (1980). Drabble, M. *Ramparts* (February 1972). Draine, B. *Modern Fiction Studies* (1980). Eder, D.L. *Contemporary Literature* (1973). Fishburn, K. *The Lost Tradition: Mothers and Daughters in Literature*, ed. C.N. Davidson and E.M. Brown (1980).

Gindin, J. *Postwar British Fiction* (1962). Hardin, N.S. *Contemporary Literature* (1973). Hinz, E. and J. Teunissen. *Contemporary Literature* (1973). Hynes, J. *Iowa Review* (1973). Kaplan, S.J. *Feminine Consciousness in the Modern Novel* (1975). Kaplan, S.J. *Twentieth Century Women Novelists*, ed. T.F. Staley (1982). Karl, F.J. *Contemporary Literature* (1972). Karl, F.J. *Old Lines, New Forces: Essays on the Contemporary British Novel, 1960-1970*, ed. R.K. Morris (1976). McDowell, F.P.W. *Arizona Quarterly* (1965). Magie, M. *College English* (1977). Mulkeen, A.M. *Studies in the Novel* (1972). Pickering, J. *Modern Fiction Studies* (1980). Porter, N. *World Literature Written in English* (1973). Rigney,

B.H. *Madness and Sexual Politics in the Feminist Novel* (1978). Schlueter, P. *Contemporary British Novelists*, ed. C. Shapiro (1965). Schweichkart, P.C. *Modern Fiction Studies* (1985). Showalter, E. *A Literature of Their Own: British Women Novelists from Brontë to Lessing* (1977). Sprague, C. *Modern Fiction Studies* (1980). Stimpson, C. *The Voyage In: Fictions of Female Development*, ed. E. Abel and M. Hirsch (1983). Vlastos, M. *PMLA* (1976). Watson, B.B. *Old Lines, New Forces: Essays on the Contemporary British Novel, 1960-1970*, ed. R.K. Morris (1976).

Paul Schlueter

Amy Levy

BORN: 10 November 1861, London.
DIED: 10 September 1889, London.
DAUGHTER OF: Lewis Levy and Isabelle Levin.

Born in London of well-to-do Anglo-Jewish parents, L. showed early talent and brilliance with the publication of "Ida Grey," a chivalric ballad, which was published in the *Pelican* magazine in January 1875. Four years later, she became the first Jewish woman admitted to Newnham College, Cambridge, where she continued to publish poetry and short stories while still an undergraduate.

The first of these, "Euphemia, a Sketch," appeared in the *Victoria Magazine*, of August 1880. The following year, a collection of poetry, *Xantippe and other Verse*, was published. Originally appearing in the *Dublin University Magazine*, *Xantippe* reveals another side to the usual depiction of Xantippe as the "nagging wife" of Socrates; L. presents the woman's own point of view. The poem is tragically beautiful and can be seen as a feminist view of traditional marriage.

Upon completing her studies at Newnham College, L. travelled to the continent where she wrote articles about Jewish populations in other countries. These articles, especially one on the Ghetto of Venice, express her observations on the uncomplicated life of the confined inhabitants as opposed to the difficulties experienced by more assimilated populations.

These difficulties appear as the theme of her most important work, the novel *Reuben Sachs* (1888). The tension between the perceived materialism of middle-class Jewish society and the scholarly idealism of Jewish history are personified in the relationships between the Sachs and Leuniger families. Leo Leuniger appears again in L.'s last published short story, *Cohen of Trinity* (1889). He has attained acceptance in the aristo-

cratic environment of a British university. Cohen, the member of a family of whom Leuniger says "were not people that one 'knew,'" publishes a book and receives wide acclaim. This recognition does not compensate him for the snubs he had previously received, and after a dinner at which he is flattered by the "smart-set," he commits suicide.

The story dramatically prefigures L.'s own untimely end. While *Reuben Sachs* received excellent notices from contemporary critics, L. was severely excoriated by members of the Jewish community for her criticism of some of its constituents. Most writers have felt that this was the explanation for L.'s suicide.

But the critic Richard Garnett, who (with his wife Constance) was a close friend of hers, views the suicide in an entirely different light. In his entry about L. in the *DNB*, Garnett said: "Incapacity for pleasure was a more serious trouble than her sensitiveness to pain: it deprived her of the encouragement she might have received from the success which . . . attended her remarkable novel *Reuben Sachs* (1888). . . . She was indeed frequently gay and animated, but her cheerfulness was but a passing mood that merely gilded her habitual melancholy, without diminishing it by a particle, while sadness grew upon her steadily, in spite of flattering success and the sympathy of affectionate friends."

L. numbered among these friends Oscar Wilde, to whose magazine *Woman's World* she was a frequent contributor. In addition to such literary notables as Garnett and Wilde, L. maintained a close friendship with Olive Schreiner. Active in radical and feminist organizations such as the Men & Women's Club, L. was politically controversial. This and the negative feelings engendered in some quarters by *Reuben Sachs* and *Cohen of Trinity* may explain why her writing, which has such artistic merit, has been suppressed. Her inclusion in the *DNB* is testimony to the degree of excellence of her work but her exclusion from anthologies and re-publication lists is even more significant.

WORKS: Xantippe and Other Verse (1881). *A Minor Poet and Other Verse* (1884). *The Romance of a Shop* (1888). *Reuben Sachs* (1889). *A London Plane Tree* (1900).

BIBLIOGRAPHY: Abrahams, B.A. *A.J.A. Quarterly.* Modder, M.F. *The Jew in the Literature of England* (1939). Showalter, E. *A Literature of Their Own* (1977). Zatlin, L.G. *The 19th Century Anglo-Jewish Novel* (1981).

For articles in reference works, see: *DNB.*

Gail Kraidman

Elizabeth Lynn Linton

BORN: 10 February 1822, Cumberland.
DIED: 14 July 1898, London.
DAUGHTER OF: the Reverend James and Charlotte Lynn.
MARRIED: William James Linton, 1858.

L. a prolific writer and social critic, wrote no fewer than twenty-four novels and thirteen other books in addition to scores of journal articles, essays, and reviews. Her novels were often thinly-cloaked polemics centering primarily on moral conflicts, the theme of class consciousness, or the Woman Question. An outspoken, energetic writer, she was an observant and accurate chronicler of the age in which she lived.

She left Cumberland for London in 1845, spending that year reading in the British Museum and writing her first novel, *Azeth the Egyptian* (1846). Her second novel, *Amymone: A Romance of the Days of Pericles* (1848), received favorable reviews by Walter Savage Landor and others. On the basis of an article she submitted to the *Morning Chronicle* titled "Aborigenes," she was hired as a salaried staff writer, the first woman to hold such a position, and between August 1849 and February 1851 wrote at least 80 articles and 36 reviews. During this time she met Landor, with whom she became very close, and through him she met Charles Dickens and John Forster.

Leaving the *Morning Chronicle* in 1851, she began work on her third novel, *Realities*, which she dedicated to Landor and published that same year. During 1851 she also met Marian Evans (George Eliot). After the poor reception of her third novel, she toured the Continent and in 1852 took the post of Paris correspondent for *The Leader*, also writing articles for Dickens' *Household Words*. On her return to England in 1854, she published an essay in praise of Mary Wollstonecraft in *The English Republic*, the monthly run by her future husband. Soon thereafter, however, she wrote "Rights and Wrongs of Women" in *Household Words*, which expressed strong views against "the emancipated woman."

In 1858 she married William James Linton, engraver, writer, and reformer, then a widower with seven children. In 1864 L. collaborated with her husband on *The Lake Country*, she writing the text and he illustrating it. They lived apart from 1865 on, and her husband spent much of the rest of his life in America.

From 1865 until her death, L. published a novel a year. In *Grasp Your Nettle* (1865) and *Lizzie Lorton* (1866), she criticized village life, with *Lizzie Lorton*, set in L.'s native Cumberland, receiving high praise. Among the thirty-three articles she contributed to *The Saturday Review* in 1868 is the one for which she became best known, her anonymous "Girl of the Period"; L. vehemently attacked the idea of female emancipation, arguing primarily against what she characterized as the frivolity and vulgarity of the advanced woman and arguing in favor of the ideals of feminine charm and domesticity. She also decried the overriding selfishness and immorality of the "Girl of the Period," whose concern with fashion, cosmetics, and luxury she denounced.

In addition to writing regularly for *The Saturday Review* and contributing to other journals, she also published *Ourselves: Essays on Women* (1869), which carried on her attacks against feminine emancipation. Despite her criticism of "the Girl of the Period," L. did argue in favor of economic and legal rights for married and divorced women. When Forster's *The Life of Landor* came out in 1869, which slighted her importance in Landor's life, L. wrote a scathing review and published an article on Landor.

In 1872, L. published *Joshua Davidson*, her most successful and popular novel. An adaptation of the gospel story to the condition of modern life, it attacked Christian morality and the position of the Church of England. Her next novel, *The Atonement of Leam Dundas*, was among her favorite works but was one of her least commercially successful and was harshly reviewed. For the next several years, L. travelled on the Continent, turning out a stream of articles as well as writing several novels, *The World Well Lost* (1877), *Under Which Lord?* (1879), *The Rebel of the Family* (1880), a three-volume collection of long short stories titled *Within a Silken Thread* (1880), and *My Love* (1881). In 1883 her famous "Girl of the Period" essays were published under her own name in two volumes with the title, *The Girl of the Period and Other Social Essays*. Although these volumes gave her lasting fame, they did not sell well at the time. In 1883 she also published her novel, *Ione*, dedicated to Swinburne.

In 1885 she published another notable novel, the one she considered her best, *The Autobiography of Christopher Kirkland*, an autobiography in the shape of a three-volume novel in which the protagonist was male. Again focusing on the Woman Question, the novel was neither a popular nor critical success. Before the end of the year she also published a short novel, *Stabbed in the Dark*, contributed an essay on George Eliot to *Temple Bar*, and produced other articles. In 1886 she published *Paston Carew, Millionaire and Miser*, which she had begun in 1884, and in 1889 *Through the Long Night*. In the next years, L. continued writing social criticism as well as novels. Her public prominence is apparent in the fact that in 1890 she was one of the three contributors to a symposium on *Candour in English Fiction* in the *New Review*; the other two contributors were Walter Besant and Thomas Hardy.

In 1891 she published *An Octave of Friends*, and one of her best essays, "Our Illusions," was published in the April issue of the *Fortnightly Review*. *One Too Many*, another virulent attack upon female emancipation and higher education for women, was serialized in the *Lady's Pictorial* in 1893 and published as a book the next year. In 1893, Helen Black published a collection of interviews with "Notable Women Authors," and L., at the age of 71, was the first woman interviewed for the series.

In 1896, L. was elected to the Society of Authors and was honored by being the first woman to serve on its committee. She was still steadily contributing essays on the relations between the sexes, asserting in the January 1896 issue of *Woman at Home* the impossibility of platonic friendships between man and woman as well as women's inferiority and weakness. Early in 1897, she wrote an appreciation of George Eliot for a series entitled *Women Novelists of Queen Victoria's Reign* and began work on her last novel, an autobiographical work, *The Second Youth of Theodora Desanges*, which was published posthumously in 1900, as was her final work, a collection of reminiscences, *My Literary Life*.

WORKS: *Azeth the Egyptian* (1846). *Amymone: A Romance of the Days of Pericles* (1848). *Realities: A Tale* (1851). *Witch Stories* (1861). *The Lake Country* with map and illustrations by W.J. Linton (1864). *Grasp Your Nettle* (1865). *Lizzie Lorton of Greyrigg* (1866). *Sowing the Wind* (1867). *The Girl of the Period* (1868). *Ourselves: A Series of Essays on Women* (1869). *The True History of Joshua Davidson* (1872). *Patricia Kemball* (1875). *The Mad Willoughbys, and Other Tales* (1876). *The Atonement of Leam Dundas* (1876). *The World Well Lost* (1877). *A Night in the Hospital* (1879). *Under Which Lord?* (1879). *The Rebel of the Family* (1880). *Within a Silken Thread and Other Stories* (1880). *My Love* (1881). *Ione: A Novel* (1883). *The Girl of the Period and Other Social Essays* (1883). *Stabbed in the Dark: A Tale* (1885). *The Rift in the Lute: A Tale* (1885). *The Autobiography of Christopher Kirkland* (1885). *Paston Carew, Millionaire and Miser* (1886). *The Philosophy of Marriage* (1888). *Through the Long Night* (1889). *Was He Wrong?* (serialized only, 1889). *Youth of Theodora Desanges* (1900). *Sowing the Wind* (1890). *About Ireland* (1890). *An Octave of Friends with Other Silhouettes and Stories* (1891). *About Ulster* (1892). *Freeshooting: Extracts from the Work of Mrs. Lynn Linton*, selected and arranged by G.F.S. (Mrs. Gulie Moss) (1892). *In Haste and at Leisure: A Novel* (1895). *Twixt Cup and Lip: Tales* (1896). *Dulcie Everton* (1896). *My Literary Life* (1899). *The Second Youth of Theodora Desanges* (1900). A list of her articles is found in H. Van Thal's biography, *Eliza Lynn Linton: The Girl of the Period* (1979), pp. 229-230.

BIBLIOGRAPHY: Anderson, N.F. *Women Against Women in Victorian England: A Life of Eliza Lynn Linton* (1987). Linton, E.L. *My Literary Life* (1899). Smith, F.B. *Radical Artisan: William James Linton* (1973). Van Thal, H. *Eliza Lynn Linton: The Girl of the Period* (1979).

For articles in reference works, see: *DNB*.

Other References: Anderson, N. *Eliza Lynn Linton and the Woman Question in Victorian England* (1973). Aria, B. *My Sentimental Self*. Bellflower, J. *The Life and Career of Elizabeth Lynn Linton 1822-1898* (1967). Bevington, M. *The Saturday Review 1855-1868* (1941). Black, H.C. *Notable Woman Authors of the Day* (1893). Bullet, G. *George Eliot* (1947). Carr, J. *Some Eminent Victorians* (1908). Clodd, E. *Memories*. Cockran, H. *Celebrities and I* (1902). Crow, D. *The Victorian Woman* (1971). Edel, L. *Henry James: The Conquest of London 1870-1833* (1962). Elwin, M. *Landor: A Replevin* (1958). Gettman, R.A. *A Victorian Publisher: A Study of the Bentley Papers* (1960). Granville-Barker, H., ed. *The Eighteen-Seventies* (1929). Haight, G.S. *George Eliot* (1968). Layard, G.S. *Mrs. Lynn Linton, Her Life, Letters and Opinions* (1901). Linton, W.J. *Memories* (1895). Paget, Lady W. *In My Tower*. Royle, E. *Victorian Infidels* (1974). Spencer, H. *Autobiography* (1904). Swinburne, A. *Letters*. Thomson, P. *The Victorian Heroine* (1956). Yates, E. *Recollections and Experiences* (1884).

Gale Sigal

Anne Vaughan Locke

BORN: early 1530s.
DIED: after 1590.
DAUGHTER OF: Stephen Vaughan.
MARRIED: Henry Locke (Lok), 1552(?); Edward Dering, 1573; Richard Prowse, before 1583.
WROTE UNDER: A.L., Anne Prowse.

Best known for her close friendship with the Scottish reformer John Knox, L. had a lifelong devotion to the Protestant cause and contributed to it in small but significant ways. Her father, governor of the English merchants in Antwerp from 1538 to 1546, had been a friend of Tyndale. Left a minor at his death in London c. 1550, she married Henry Locke, a cloth merchant, a year or two later. The first of her six children (two of whom lived to adulthood) was born in 1553. Shortly before this time she first met Knox, who was in London as one of the chaplains of King Edward VI. Knox, who became her spiritual counselor, described her as "honest" and "poor." After the Catholic queen Mary ascended the throne in August 1553, Knox lived with the Lockes, then fled to the Continent early in 1554. In 1556, established as English pastor in Geneva, he wrote to persuade her to join the colony of exiles there. She arrived the next spring, with children and a servant; her husband's business interests presumably occupied him elsewhere on the Continent. She remained in Geneva for nearly two years, rejoining Henry in Frankfurt in 1559 and returning to London.

While in Geneva L. heard, or saw in manuscript, four sermons on chapter 38 of Isaiah, preached by John Calvin in the fall of 1557. She translated these into English, publishing the translation soon after returning to London—two years ahead of the printing in Geneva of the original French version. Her translation, though very close—"I have rendred it so nere as I possibly might, to the very wordes of his text, and that in so plaine Englishe as I could expresse"—is quite readable. Appended to this text she published a stanzaic meditation, almost certainly by Knox, on Psalm 51, with the verses of the psalm supplied in the margins. These, which match no known English prose translation, are presumed to be her own work.

L.'s correspondence with Knox continued until at least 1562. In his letters Knox entrusted her with messages for the Puritan community, requests for books and money, news of the progress of reformation in Scotland, and a manuscript copy of another of his unpublished works.

Widowed in 1571, L. was married in 1573 to the rising Puritan preacher Edward Dering, who died of consumption three years later at the age of 36. Her third husband was Richard Prowse, a well-to-do draper, sheriff in Devon, mayor of Exeter, and member of Parliament.

In 1590 she published another translation from French, a recent tract first addressed to persecuted Protestants in the Netherlands, now "augmented by the Author" and chosen by L., no doubt, for its applicability to the circumstances of English Puritans.

L. was the mother of the minor Elizabethan poet Henry Lok.

WORKS: Sermons of John Calvin, vpon the songe that Ezechias made after he had bene sicke, and afflicted by the hand of God, translation from French (1560). Of the marks of the children of God, and of their comforts in afflictions, by Jean Taffin, translation from French (1590).

BIBLIOGRAPHY: Collinson, P. Studies in Church History (1965). Lupton, L. A History of the Geneva Bible, vol. 4 (1972) and 8 (1977).

For articles in reference works, see: DNB (under "Henry Lok").

Charles Hutter

Marie Adelaide Belloc Lowndes (Mrs. Belloc Lowndes)

BORN: 1868, La Celle Saint Cloud, France.
DIED: 14 November 1947, Eversley Cross, Hampshire.
DAUGHTER OF: Louis Belloc and Bessie Parkes Belloc.
MARRIED: Frederic Sawrey A. Lowndes, 1896.
WROTE UNDER: Mrs. Belloc Lowndes, Philip Curtin, Elizabeth Rayner.

Born late in life to an English mother and a French father, L. was the sister of the well-known Catholic writer Hilaire Belloc and the great-great-granddaughter of Joseph Priestley. L. and her brother were born in France, where she spent large portions of her young life. Her later and married life was spent primarily in England. Fluent in French, she confessed to a lifelong attachment to France and her French family. L.'s father died at 42 and left her mother to raise the two children alone. Bessie Parkes Belloc moved her family back to England, where she made a bad investment, and the family had to live on a modest income.

Although L.'s education was somewhat untraditional (she had only two years of formal education at a convent school), she was drawn to writing. At the age of sixteen, L. decided to make writing her career. She obtained her first writing job in 1888 when she was made a part author of a guide to the Paris Exhibition of 1889 by W.T. Stead, editor of the *Pall Mall Gazette*. Between 1889 and 1895 she continued to write for the *Gazette* and a number of other publications, and her life during this period, according to her accounts, was a relatively free and liberated one for a woman of that time. During those early writing years, she made numerous trips to France and met many French literary figures, including Edmond de Goncourt, Paul Verlaine, Alphonse Daudet, Anatole France, Emile Zola, and Jules Verne. She was also quite interested in the French theater of the time.

Throughout her life, L. was a prolific writer. Her publications begin in the 1890s and continue through the 1940s, though a few works were published posthumously, including *The Young Hilaire Belloc* (1956). Among her numerous publications were articles, sketches, memoirs, biographies and autobiographies, and plays. Her greatest production, however, was in fiction, both short stories and novels.

L. wrote more than forty novels, mostly mysteries or novels of crime—*The Lodger* (involving the story of Jack the Ripper) and *The Chink in the Armour* are probably her best known—and several short story collections. She also wrote two works under pseudonyms—*Noted Murder Mysteries* by Philip Curtin and *Not All Saints* by Elizabeth Rayner. Her daughters in the "Foreword" to the *Diaries and Letters of Marie Belloc Lowndes, 1911-1947* note that L. "did not consider it to be the business of a novelist to inculcate moral lessons . . . [but] believed that 'who breaks, pays.'" Her novels "depict the reactions of ordinary persons to sudden violence in their own circle. . . . The reader soon knows who is guilty, and so watches the reactions of the people in the story, with an ever deepening sense of horror and suspense." Her settings are varied and her topic is people, people involved in love, mystery, crime, the supernatural, and life. Her strengths are plot, character, and the ability to hold the interest of the casual mystery reader. Her weakness for the modern reader may be her slant toward the melodramatic and her somewhat sanitized view of crime.

WORKS: *The Life and Letters of Charlotte Elizabeth, Princess Palatine* (1889). *Edmond and Jules De Goncourt, with letters and Leaves from Their Journals*, compiled and translated by M.A. Belloc and M. Shedlock (1894). *King Edward the Seventh* (1898).

The Philosophy of the Marquise (1899). *T.R.H. The Prince and Princess of Wales* (1902). *The Heart of Penelope* (1904). *Barbara Rebell* (1905). *The Pulse of Life* (1908). *The Uttermost Farthing* (1908). *Studies in Wives* (1909). *When No Man Pursueth* (1910). *Jane Oglander* (1911). *The Chink in the Armour* (1912). *Mary Pechell* (1912). *The End of her Honeymoon* (1913). *The Lodger* (1913). *Studies in Love and in Terror* (1913). *Noted Murder Mysteries, by Philip Curtin* (1914). *Not All Saints, by Elizabeth Rayner. Good Old Anna* (1915). *Price of Admiralty* (1915). *Lilla, a Part of Her Life* (1916). *The Red Cross Barge* (1916). *Told in Gallant Deeds: A Child's History of the War* (1916). *Love and Hatred* (1917). *Out of the War (Gentleman Anonymous)* (1918). *From the Vasty Deep* (1920). *The Lonely House* (1920). *What Timmy Did* (1921). *Why They Married* (1923). *The Terriford Mystery* (1924). *Bread of Deceit* (1925). *Some Men and Women* (1925). *What Really Happened* (1926). *Thou Shalt Not Kill* (1927). *The Story of Ivy* (1927). *Cressida, No Mystery (Love's Revenge)* (1928). *Love's Revenge* (1929). *One of Those Ways* (1929). *The Second Key, Possibly The Key: A Love Drama in Three Acts* (1930). *With All John's Love* (1930). *Why Be Lonely* (1931). *Love is a Flame* (1932). *The Reason Why* (1932). *Duchess Laura, Certain Days of Her Life* (1933). *Duchess Laura, Further Days of Her Life* (1933). *The House by the Sea (Vanderlyn's Adventure—U.S.A.)* (1931). *Letty Lynton* (1931). *Why Be Lonely* (1931). *Jenny Newstead (An Unrecorded Instance—U.S.A.)* (1932). *Another Man's Wife* (1934). *The Chianti Flask* (1934). *Who Rides on a Tiger* (1935). *And Call It Accident* (1936). *Her Last Adventure* (1936). *The Second Key* (1936). *The Marriage Broker (The Fortune of Bridget Malone—U.S.A.)* (1937). *The Empress Eugenie* (1938). *Motive (Why It Happened—U.S.A.)* (1938). *The Injured Lover* (1939). *Lizzie Borden* (1939). *Reckless Angle* (1939). *The Diamond* (1940). *Before the Storm* (1941). *I, Too, Have Lived in Arcadia* (1941). *What of the Night* (1943). *Where Love and Friendship Dwelt* (1943). *The Merry Wives of Westminster* (1946). *A Passing World* (1948). *She Dwelt with Beauty* (1949). *The Young Hilaire Belloc* (1956).

BIBLIOGRAPHY: Lowndes, S., ed. *Diaries and Letters of Marie Belloc Lowndes, 1911-1947* (1971). Mansfield, K. *Novels and Novelists* (1930).

For articles in reference works, see: NCBEL. NCHEL. TCA.

Other references: *Baker Street Journal* (1978). *TLS* (1 October 1971). *Toward a Feminist Tradition: An Annotated Bibliography of Novels in English by Women*, Eds. D. Daims and J. Grimes (1982).

Evelyn A. Hovanec

Mina Loy

BORN: 27 December 1882, London.
DIED: 25 September 1966, Aspen, Colorado.
DAUGHTER OF: Sigmund and Julia Bryan Lowy.
MARRIED: Stephen Haweis, 1903; Arthur Cravan (Fabian Avenarius Lloyd), 1918.

L., a painter and designer as well as poet, wrote a relatively small amount of poetry that had a significant influence on modern poetic technique. Although she deprecated herself and deliberately chose obscurity toward the end of her life, she was a major force in introducing the ideas of pre-World War I European writers and artists to America. She was formally uneducated except for art classes, where she excelled, but extraordinarily intelligent, sensitive, and bold, her intellect stimulated by and challenging to Futurist artists Marinetti, Papini, and others in Mabel Dodge Luhan's circle in Florence, where L. lived and painted from 1906 to 1916.

After the end of her marriage to Stephen Haweis, she lived intermittently in New York and Paris from 1916 to 1923 and designed lampshades, painted, modeled, acted in dadaist plays, frequented literary salons, and, famous for her talent and beauty, was a center of attraction in avant-garde artistic circles, wittily recorded in "O Marcel . . . Otherwise I Also Have Been to Louise's." Critics praised her poems, which appeared in magazines such as *Rogue, Others* and *Contact.* In 1918 she married dadaist artist Arthur Cravan, nephew of Oscar Wilde, in Mexico, where Cravan disappeared late that year; she never got over his loss; their daughter Fabi was born in 1919. In 1923 L. returned to Paris and for the next seven years was in contact with modernist writers there—Joyce, Breton, Stein, et al.—although an increasing sense of isolation besieged her. In the 1930s she published only two poems but worked on her painting and prose and in 1936 returned to the United States where she lived in New York and Aspen, near her daughters, until her death.

L.'s first poems, published from 1914 on and collected in *Lunar Baedecker* [sic] in 1923, shocked her early readers. She refused rhyme and fixed meter, used extremely short uncapitalized lines, and made explicit sexual references, pioneering in techniques which are now familiar in twentieth-century poetics. In 1918 Ezra Pound commented that L.'s verse, like Marianne Moore's, is "a dance of the intelligence among words and ideas . . . a mind cry rather than a heart cry." In this review Pound also said, evidently ignorant of L.'s English parentage, that her work was "distinctly American in quality," but her poems are more accurately seen as international modernist in style, not tied to any one national culture, in their tight construction, sharp satiric thrust, punning word-play, and references to other arts and artists.

An early poem, "Apology of Genius," contains an artistic manifesto similar to James Joyce's; L. says: "In the raw caverns of the Increate / we forge the dusk of Chaos / to that imperious jewelry of the Universe / —The Beautiful—." In another poem, "Der Blinde Junge," she sees a war-blinded beggar-boy on the streets of Vienna, "drowned in dumfounded instinct," as an emblem and warning: "Listen! / illuminati of the coloured earth / How this expressionless 'thing' / blows out damnation and concussive dark / Upon a mouth-organ."

Excessive alliteration—excess for L. is a virtue—always characterizes her work, creating the effect of intense involvement startlingly combined with unsentimentalized distance. "Lunar Baedeker," the poem which first brought her literary notice, mocks romanticism's treatment of the moon, indicating a new irrationality and colder view of both love and art: "in the oxidized Orient / Onyx-eyed Odalisques / and ornithologists / observe / the flight / of Eros obsolete" and concludes: "Pocked with personification / the fossil virgin of the skies / waxes and wanes." In "The Black Virginity" her cubist visualization of young priests strolling in a park—"Fluted black silk cloaks / Hung square from shoulders / Truncated juvenility"—expresses her antiauthoritarianism and hatred of religious hypocrisy.

L. was also a feminist. Even as a child in England she rejected the traditional feminine dress and behavior urged on her because of her physical beauty and chose to leave home as soon as possible for the artist's life abroad. Although she said that contact with Marinetti's vitality "added twenty years to my life," she broke with the Futurists in 1915 and wrote: "What I feel now are feminist politics." "The Effectual Marriage," "At the Door of the House," and "Parturition" reflect these concerns. Her "Feminist Manifesto," now collected with other prose in *The Last Lunar Baedeker* (1982), shows her ahead of her time: "*there is nothing impure in sex* except the attitude toward it." She advises women: "Leave off looking to men to find out what you are *not.* Seek within yourselves to find out what you *are.*"

A continual seeker and thinker, she scrutinized the sources of her own independent intellect and creativity in the remarkable long autobiographical poem, *Anglo-Mongrels and the Rose.* Published in segments between 1923 and 1925, it describes her Jewish father, a tailor, called in the poem Exodus, her mother, the English rose, called Ada, and herself, Ova. She sees herself at birth as a

". . . mystero-chemico Nemesis / . . .The isolate consciousness / projected from back of time and space / pacing its padded cell" and records the genesis of this consciousness through the baby's visual impressions. She saw her parents as "armored towers"; the green of a cat's-eye brooch associated with ivy taught her the link between the color and the word "green"—an essential moment in the artist's development.

The growing child suffers from the indifference of her angry anti-sexual mother and from the cruelty of her father. She is moved by a housemaid's story of Gentle Jesus and is later impressed by a church crucifix with its feet "wounded with red varnish." Her religious feelings mature into the Swiftian antitheology of the poem's last segment, in which a post-God deity, the Tailor, remakes the human race: "conscience / disappears / in utter / bifurcate dissimulation / leaving / only those inevitable yet more or less circumspect / creasings / in the latest in trouserings." Thus we see that L.'s forms unite with content deep in her consciousness. The literary roots of her poems may lie in the French "art for art's sake," but she goes beyond that position while never denying the integrity of the artist. Her compression and formal innovation spring from the passionate conviction that no other mode will serve to penetrate intellectually and philosophically as far as she wants to go.

Later poems, written after she moved to the United States, such as "Property of Pigeons," "On Third Avenue," "Idiot Child on a Fire-Escape" and "Mass Production on 14th Street," record her fascination with the American scene. Her theological concerns continue, with more emphasis on death under the shadow of World War Two, as in "Aid of the Madonna": "Skies once ovational / with celestial oboes . . . / are skies in clamor / of deathly celerities— / the horror of diving obituaries / under flowers of fire." For years she lived on the Bowery in New York; in "Hot Cross Bum" she looks ruthlessly at the derelicts there yet strangely identifies with them. Coinages, witty puns, and powerfully condensed images continue to enliven her work: "a dull-dong bell / thuds out admonish-

ment / . . .waylaying for branding / indirigible bums / with the hot-cross / of ovenly buns." As she saw the blind beggarboy in Vienna long before, so she sees the bum as emblematic of a degraded world and loss of the genuine, yet with some unironic remnant of hope in his imitation of love: "he's lovin' up the pavement /—interminable paramour / of horizontal stature / Venus-sans-vulva— / A vagabond in delirium / aping the rise and fall / of ocean / of inhalation / of coition." From what she early called "civilized wastes" and from the most unpromising materials, L. reclaims moments of hope and vitality without sacrificing truth through her combination of humane vision and brilliant language.

WORKS: *Auto-Facial Constructions* (1919). *Psycho-Democracy* (1920). *Lunar Baedecker* [sic] (1923). *Lunar Baedeker and Time-Tables: Selected Poems of Mina Loy* (1958). *The Last Lunar Baedeker* (1982).

BIBLIOGRAPHY: Benstock, S. *Women of the Left Bank: Paris, 1900-1940* (1986). Burke, C. In *Coming to Light: American Women Poets of the Twentieth Century* (1985). Burke, C. *Feminist Studies* (1985). Burke, C. *Poetics Journal* (1984). Burke, C. In *Silence and Power* (1985). Burke, C. *Women's Studies* (1980). Conover, R. Introduction to *The Last Lunar Baedeker* (1980). Guggenheim, P. *Out of This Century* (1946). Hunting, C. *Sagetrieb* (Spring 1983). Kouidis, V. *Boundary 2* (Spring 1980). Kouidis, V. *Mina Loy: American Modernist Poet* (1980). Kreymborg, A. *A History of American Poetry: Our Singing Strength* (1934). Pound, E. *The Little Review* (March 1918). Winters, Y. *Yvor Winters: Uncollected Essays and Reviews*, ed. Francis Murphy (1973).

For articles in reference works, see: *CA* (although this work erroneously lists Loy's birthname as Lowry instead of Lowy). *CLC. DLB.*

Other references: *Contemporary Literature* (1961). *HOW(ever)* (1985). *Los Angeles Times Book Review* (22 August 1982). *Nation* (27 May 1961). New York *Evening Sun* (13 February 1917). *NYTBR* (16 November 1980, 16 May 1982). *Southern Review* (July 1967).

Jane Augustine

Joanna (Jane) Fitzalan Lumley

BORN: 1537(?), presumably in Sussex.
DIED: 1576 (or 1577), presumably in the Fitzalan family home on the Strand.
DAUGHTER OF: Henry Fitzalan, twelfth earl of Arundel, and Katherine Grey Fitzalan.
MARRIED: John, first baron Lumley, of the second creation, c. 1549.

L., the older of the two unusually learned

daughters of Henry Fitzalan, earl of Arundel, may have been highly educated with the expectation that she would marry into the royal family, but was married around age twelve to John Lumley, her brother's classmate at Cambridge. She was fortunate in being matched to a man of a very learned turn, who, like her father, became high steward of Oxford, a member of the Elizabethan Society of Antiquities, and an amasser of a noteworthy library.

It is possible that Lord and Lady L. worked at similar study, side by side. The combined Fitzalan and L. libraries became part of the Royal Library after Lumley's death, and it is in this collection, now in the British Library, that L.'s manuscript compositions (MS. Reg. 15. A. ix.) are preserved.

It is not surprising that her translations from Greek and Latin literature were not printed, since even highly eduated Tudor "prodigies" hesitated to put their writings into print; those brave women who did so overwhelmingly produced religious translations. The chief of L.'s productions is her abridged prose translation of about 1550 of Euripides' *Iphigenia at Aulis*, first printed, by the Malone Society, in 1909. Although it is not a polished translation, it is a remarkable achievement, since, in England, Renaissance scholarship was concentrated heavily on Latin materials; the remaining translations by L. in the quarto volume containing the *Iphigenia* are from Latin. Her translation of Euripides is the earliest known translation from Greek to English of a Greek drama.

WORKS: (trans.) "The Tragedie of Euripides called Iphigenia translated out of Greke into Englisshe" (Br. L. MS. Reg. 15. A. ix.; rpt. Malone Society, ed. Harold H. Child, 1909).

BIBLIOGRAPHY: Ballard, G. *Memoirs of Several Ladies of Great Britain. . . .* (1752). Cotton, N. *Women Playwrights in England c. 1363-1750* (1980). Crane, F.D. *Classical Journal* (1944), *DNB* (entry for "Gordon Goodwin, Fitzalan, Henry, twelfth earl of Arundel [1511-1580]"). Greene, D.H. *Classical Journal* (1941). Hays, M. *Female Biography. . . .* (1807). Hogrefe, P. *Tudor Women. . . .* (1975). Reynolds, M. *The Learned Lady in England, 1650-1760* (1920). Stenton, D. *English Women in History* (1957). Warnicke, R.M. *Women of the English Renaissance and Reformation* (1983). Williams, J. *Literary Women of England . . . .* (1861).

Betty Travitsky

(Emilie) Rose Macaulay

BORN: 1 August 1881, Rugby.
DIED: 30 October 1958, London.
DAUGHTER OF: George and Grace Macaulay.
WROTE UNDER: Rose Macaulay.

The second of seven children, M. was a tomboy who believed she would grow up to be a man; in her early twenties she still hoped to join the Navy. This sense of gender ambiguity, both playful and serious, pervades her fiction. In 1887 the Macaulays left Rugby, where M.'s father was an assistant master, and moved to Italy. In the seacoast town of Varazze, the children led an exciting and undisciplined life before the family returned to England in 1894. M. attended Oxford High School and later Somerville College, Oxford, where she read modern history. After graduating in 1903, she lived with her parents, first in Aberystwyth and afterwards in Cambridge. By late 1905 she had had several poems published and was at work on her first novel, *Abbots Verney*, (1906).

M.'s early novels combine a witty, aphoristic style with themes of loss and isolation from society. *The Lee Shore* (1912) concludes by urging philosophical detachment from failure and the "lust to possess": "The last, the gayest, the most hilarious laughter begins when, destitute utterly, the wrecked pick up coloured shells upon the lee shore." After the success of this novel (which won first prize and £1000 in a competition organized by its publisher), M. moved to London where she mingled with writers and intellectuals. During "this pre-war golden age," as she once called it, M.

published *The Making of a Bigot*, a comic novel about the necessity of compromising the "many-faced Truth" in order to get on in the world, and her first book of poems, *The Two Blind Countries*, which reflects the influence of Walter de la Mare and other Georgians but succeeds in registering her own peculiar sense of the instability of institutions and social structures, which she figures as "the transient city."

M. worked as a nurse for part of the First World War, and in 1916 became a civil servant in the War Office, dealing with exemptions from service and conscientious objectors. In *Non-Combatants and Others* (1916), the heroine Alix comes to realize that her pacifist mother, Daphne—one in a series of exuberant, confident, worldly women in M.'s fiction—is right in campaigning for a "positive" peace, "a young peace, passionate, ardent, intelligent, romantic, like poetry, like art, like religion." The novel also contains an early and sensitive study of the psychological effects of trench-fighting. Early in 1918, M. was transferred to the Ministry of Information. Here she met and fell in love with Gerald O'Donovan, a married novelist with whom she had a relationship that lasted until his death in 1942. His stimulus and criticism were of much importance to her career.

During the 1920s M. established her reputation for trenchant, clear-eyed social satire. Her first best-seller, *Potterism* (1920)—an attack on the popular press and the muddleheaded emotionalism it exploits—is dedicated to "the unsentimental precisians in thought, who have, on this confused, inaccurate, and emotional planet, no fit habitation." In *Crewe Train* (1926), London society and its malicious gossip are exposed through the silent, anarchic figure of Denham, who, much against her husband's will, prefers to live alone in a Cornish cottage and explore the caves beneath it. But "Life" is too strong for her; her self-sufficiency gives way to social and marital pressures. She relinquishes her cottage and the cave of her own and returns to her husband.

In the 1930s M. became increasingly absorbed in the study of the seventeenth century and wrote a refreshing, informed biography of Milton. More important is her historical novel *They Were Defeated* (1932), set in the early 1640s and featuring the poet Robert Herrick. M. restricted the characters' vocabulary to words known to have existed at the period, and the dialogue is remarkably credible and fluent. The novel elegizes the Cavalier tradition and movingly portrays Herrick, whose verses celebrating simple rural joys go unheeded in a world where Donnian "conceit" is all the rage. Most poignant are the "defeats" involving women. A harmless old eccentric is hunted down as a witch; and Julian Conybeare, a brilliant and poetically gifted girl, becomes the mistress of the poet John Cleveland only to discover that he wants her to give up ideas and poetry and assume her proper role in life. Her protest, "It makes no differ, being a maid," does not avail. The story ends with her tragic, absurd death. In *Crewe Train* M. had described Denham as "the Silent Woman"; Julian might be called "the silenced woman."

M. visited Portugal and Spain and produced two works of great learning and wit based on her travels, *They Went to Portugal* (1946) and *Fabled Shore* (1949). In 1948, M. began writing *The World My Wilderness* (1950), her first novel in almost a decade. The central symbol—the London Blitz ruins—is a variation of the cave motif used in *Crewe Train*. Barbary, a girl resembling Denham in many ways, leaves her home in a tiny French port to live in "civilized" London. But her earlier life and her participation in the French underground have made her unfit for all this, and she is at home only in the bombed-out buildings of the city. Here, the "cave" is more a symbol of widespread moral decline than an image of personal freedom.

All her life M. was fascinated by religious questions, and much of her work reflects this. She had stopped receiving Communion in 1922 because of her involvement with the married O'Donovan. Yet she always considered herself an "Anglo-Agnostic," and in 1950 she began exchanging letters with an Anglican priest named Johnson. M.'s letters to him fill two books—*Letters to a Friend* and *Last Letters to a Friend*—and trace her return to the Anglican Communion under his spiritual guidance.

In 1956, M. published *The Towers of Trebizond*, which John Betjeman considered "the best book she has written, and that is saying a lot." Partly inspired by a trip to Turkey in 1954, the novel is a masterful and picaresque compendium of M.'s beliefs and interests, written in what she called a "rather goofy, rambling prose style." This allows her to sketch a scene swiftly or digress at length (on the history of mistresses, e.g.). The eccentric Father Chantry-Pigg, along with an insane camel and a trained ape, provide hilarity, but the work also reflects, in part, M.'s crisis of faith. The narrator Laurie—who does not reveal herself to be a woman until the end—yearns for the Byzantine city of Trebizond, which symbolizes the Church, but her adulterous relationship prevents her from making "the pattern and the hard core" of the city her own. At the end she is still outside the city.

"Ignorance, vulgarity, cruelty" were M.'s "three black jungle horrors." In contrast, her work consistently offers a voice that is civilized, ironic, playful, canny, and sane. Her satire is sometimes accused of flippancy, but this is because her narrative "mimicry" and use of authorial voice are not yet properly understood. Nor are her feminism and her play on gender expectations fully appreciated. What Katherine Mansfield called "her offhand, lightly-smiling manner" thinly disguises intense commitment to difference and eccentricity and equally intense religiosity. Her pluralistic mind, like the Anglican Church as she describes it in *The Towers of Trebizond*, was "very wonderful and comprehensive." M. was made a Dame Commander of the British Empire in 1958.

WORKS: *Abbots Verney* (1906). *The Furnace* (1907). *The Secret River* (1909). *The Valley Captives* (1911). *Views and Vagabonds* (1912). *The Lee Shore* (1912). *The Two Blind Countries* (1914). *The Making of a Bigot* (1914). *Non-combatants and Others* (1916). *What Not: A Prophetic Comedy* (1919). *Three Days* (1919). *Potterism: A Tragifarcical Tract* (1920). *Dangerous Ages* (1921). *Mystery at Geneva* (1922). *Told by an Idiot* (1923). *Orphan Island* (1924). *A Casual Commentary* (1925). *Crewe Train* (1926). *Catchwords and Claptrap* (1926). *Keeping Up Appearances* (1928; in U.S., *Daisy and Daphne*). *Staying with Relations* (1930). *Some Religious Elements in English Literature* (1931). *They Were Defeated* (1932; in U.S., *The Shadow Flies*). *Going Abroad* (1934). *Milton* (1934). *The Minor Pleasures of Life* (1934). *Personal Pleasures* (1935). *An Open Letter to a Non-Pacifist* (1937). *I Would Be Private* (1937). *The Writings of E.M. Forster* (1938). (with Daniel George) *All in a Maze* (1938, anthology). *And No Man's Wit* (1940). *Life Among the English* (1942). *They Went to Portugal* (1946). *Fabled Shore: From the Pyrenees to Portugal* (1949). *The World*

My Wilderness (1950). *Pleasure of Ruins* (1953). *The Towers of Trebizond* (1956). *Letters to a Friend: 1950-1952* (1961). *Last Letters to a Friend: 1952-1958* (1962). *Letters to a Sister* (1964).

BIBLIOGRAPHY: Babington Smith, C. *Rose Macaulay* (1972). Bensen, A. *Rose Macaulay* (1969). Crosland, M. *Beyond the Lighthouse: English Women Novelists of the Twentieth Century* (1981). Mansfield, K. *Novels and Novelists* (1930). Monro, H. *Some Contemporary Poets* (1920). Sherman, S. *Critical Woodcuts* (1926). Sturgeon, M. *Studies of Contemporary Poets* (1919). Swinnerton, F. *The Georgian Literary Scene* (1935).

For articles in reference works, see: *CA. The Chelsea House Library of Literary Criticism: Twentieth Century Literature 3, 1783-1791. DLB.*

Other references: *Bookman* (May 1927). Fromm, G. G. *New Criterion* (October 1986). Nicholson, H. et al. *Encounter* (March 1959), Nicholson H. *Observer* (6 May 1949). Swinnerton, F. *Kenyon* (November 1967). *TLS* (12 May 1950).

Robert Spoo

Elizabeth Mackintosh

BORN: 25 June 1896, Inverness, Scotland.
DIED: 13 February 1952, London.
DAUGHTER OF: Colin and Josephine Horne Mackintosh.
WROTE UNDER: Gordon Daviot, Josephine Tey.

M. is best known as the author, as Josephine Tey, of several extraordinary novels of detection. More extensive, however, and in her own estimation more central to her career as a serious writer, was her output of fiction, plays, and biography under the pseudonym Gordon Daviot.

Born in Inverness, Scotland, she attended the Royal Academy there but declined to go on to university or art school ("I balked, too, at art—my talent is on the shady side of mediocre"). Instead she studied three years at Anstey Physical Training College, Birmingham, worked briefly as a physiotherapist, and taught physical education at schools in Scotland and England. Called home in 1923 to attend her dying mother, she remained in Inverness living with her father. She took long annual holidays in England and developed some friendships in London theatrical circles but shunned publicity and was generally reclusive. She continued her work through the year of illness that preceded her early death. Found among her papers were two novels and thirteen plays, since published.

The career of "Gordon Daviot" began about 1925 with contributions to magazines and continued in 1929 with two novels including a detective story, *The Man in the Queue*. M. then turned to drama but, on the rejection of her first effort, reworked it as a romantic novel, *The Expensive Halo* (1931). Finally in 1932 came *Richard of Bordeaux*; running in London for over a year, starring John Gielgud, as well as in New York, this remained M.'s most successful play. In Gielgud's opinion "she improved on Shakespeare . . . by giving [King] Richard [II] a sense of humour." *Richard* was followed by twelve other full-length plays, five of which were produced in her lifetime (Laurence Olivier played Bothwell in *Queen of Scots*), and thirteen shorter plays, including several radio broadcasts. Nearly half her plays retell stories from history or the Bible (Sarah and Hagar, Joseph, Moses, Rahab). The latter group should not be considered religious plays: it was the story that interested M., and her reading of it was typically nonsupernaturalist. Romantic themes appear occasionally in her plays; more prominent is a vein of tart satire, especially of politicians. M. also wrote two historically based prose works, a biography of the seventeenth-century Scottish royalist Viscount Dundee (*Claverhouse*, 1937) and a novel about the pirate Henry Morgan (*The Privateer*, 1952).

The pseudonym "Josephine Tey" first appeared in 1936 with *A Shilling for Candles*, and M. reserved it for detective fiction, which she deprecated as her "yearly knitting." From 1947 to 1952, indeed, one Tey novel did appear each year. These works, exhibiting M.'s skill in dialogue (honed by writing for the stage) and attention to characterization, not only rank high in classic "golden age" detective fiction but belong to the mainstream of the novel. Exploration of character is M.'s chief interest. Insight into motive and the perception of such typically "criminal" character traits as vanity are always, for her, key elements in detection, and when her detectives err, as often happens, it is by suppressing such insight and trusting more traditional, apparently objective, kinds of evidence. (One oddity in M.'s presentation of character is the obsessive notion that it can be read infallibly in trivial details of facial features and expression. Her Scotland Yard inspector Alan Grant relies heavily on this method, applying it no less accurately with photographs or portraits than in the flesh. But curiously, M. hardly ever describes Grant himself.) Thematically, M. develops romance interests in some of the Tey novels and, with delightful asperity of tone, makes fun of the vanity and shallow

303

life-style of the theatre and arts crowd. Another serious theme uniting these works is that of identity, ranging from initial difficulty in identifying the corpse (*Queue, Sands*) through the morally neutral effort of a prodigal to escape disgrace by resuming his old name (*Shilling*), to imposture (teenage harlot posing as innocent victim in *Franchise*, foundling cousin posing as heir in *Brat*, transvestite disguise in *Love*).

Moreover, M. feels free to depart from golden age formulas, often in ways suggesting a more skeptical postmodern sensibility. Only half the eight novels have corpses; in two no one dies, and in two long-closed cases are reopened. Especially remarkable is *The Daughter of Time*, in which a bedridden detective conducts an academic investigation into the fate of the young princes in the Tower and concludes that Henry VII, not Richard III, had them murdered. Here and twice more (*Miss Pym Disposes, The Franchise Affair*) M. ends not with order satisfyingly restored by justice but with innocence suffering and society powerless to punish the wrongdoers adequately if at all.

Among the sufferers are M.'s detectives, who may be physically (*Daughter*) or emotionally (*Sands*) ill, prone to play God—hence the title *Miss Pym Disposes*—but inept, or themselves involved in crime though fundamentally honest (*Brat*). For all M.'s favorable, even sympathetic treatment of him, Grant is unusually fallible. He wastes time chasing the wrong suspect, and sometimes (*Shilling, Franchise*) it takes an amateur detective to correct his errors. Three cases (*Queue, Pym*, and *Sands*) are solved by the murderer's confession, not the detective's sleuthing, though in the last, to do Grant justice, the confession merely anticipates his independent solution; and in *The Daughter of Time*, the verdict against King Henry inherently must lack the external corroboration standard for the genre.

If the police have trouble drawing the right conclusions, all the more easily is the general public hoodwinked. M.'s skepticism on this score unites the Tey and the Daviot *oeuvres*. Frequently she attacks gullibility in the face of fraudulent piety, whether that of the rogue "monk" in *A Shilling for Candles* or that of the Covenanters in *Claverhouse*. Misled public opinion drives an innocent into exile in *The Franchise Affair* (a fictionalized version of an eighteenth-century case) and, in the one-act play *Leith Sands*, hangs a man for a murder that never occurred. Much of Grant's case in *The Daughter of Time* consists of questioning the reliability of accepted "evidence" and citing parallel instances of historians' naive credulity. This book is M.'s best known in academic circles, being used as a textbook for raising questions on historical method. M. handled the same story in dramatic form in *Dickon*. She especially enjoyed rehabilitating characters vilified by history (Dundee, Morgan, Richard III) and,

in fiction, portraying the character type of the honest rogue (*Kif, Brat*).

Other links between Tey and Daviot are consistent patterns in the treatment of women and a cinematic quality in M.'s writing. She loved movies, habitually attending twice weekly, and several of her novels have been dramatized in film (e.g., Hitchcock's *Young and Innocent*) or television.

WORKS: (as Gordon Daviot) *The Man in the Queue* (1929, rpt. 1953 under Josephine Tey). (as Gordon Daviot) *Kif: An Unvarnished History* (1929). (as Gordon Daviot) *The Expensive Halo* (1931). (as Gordon Daviot) *Richard of Bordeaux* (produced 1932, published 1933, rpt. 1958 in Penguin Plays). (as Gordon Daviot) *The Laughing Woman* (1934). (as Gordon Daviot) *Queen of Scots* (1934). (as Josephine Tey) *A Shilling for Candles* (1936). (as Gordon Daviot) *Claverhouse* (1937). (as Gordon Daviot) *The Stars Bow Down* (1939). (as Gordon Daviot) *Leith Sands* [broadcast 1941] *and Other Short Plays* (1946). (as Josephine Tey) *Miss Pym Disposes* (1947). (as Josephine Tey) *The Franchise Affair* (1948). (as Josephine Tey) *Brat Farrar* (1949). (as Josephine Tey) *To Love and Be Wise* (1950). (as Josephine Tey) *The Daughter of Time* (1951). (as Josephine Tey) *The Singing Sands* (1952). (as Gordon Daviot) *The Privateer* (1952). (as Gordon Daviot) *Plays*, 3 vols., foreword by J. Gielgud (1953-54; *The Pen of My Aunt*, rpt. in *Eight Short Plays* [1968]; *Dickon* ed. with intro., historical commentary and notes by E. Haddon [1966]). *Three by Tey* (*Miss Pym Disposes, The Franchise Affair, Brat Farrar*), intro. by J. Sandoe (1954). *Four, Five and Six by Tey* (*The Singing Sands, A Shilling for Candles, The Daughter of Time*) (1958).

BIBLIOGRAPHY: Champion, L. *A Fair Day in the Affections: Literary Essays in Honor of Robert B. White, Jr.*, ed. J. Durant and M. Hester (1980). Mann, J. *Deadlier Than the Male* (1981). Rollyson, C. *The Daughter of Time." Iowa State Journal of Research* (August 1978). Roy, S. *Josephine Tey* (1980). Talburt, N.E. *10 Women of Mystery*, ed. E. Bargainnier (1981).

For articles in reference works, see: Barzun, J., and W.H. Taylor, *A Catalogue of Crime* (1971). *CA. DLB. Encyclopedia of Mystery and Detection* (1976). *NCBEL*, vol. 4, under Daviot. *Penguin Companion to English Literature* (1971). *TCA SUP. TCC&MW.* (1980). *TCLC. Who's Who* under Daviot (1936 through 1952).

Other references: *The Armchair Detective* (Summer 1977, Fall 1977, Spring 1981). Charney, H. *The Detective Novel of Manners* (1981). Clues (*Fall-Winter 1980*). *NR* (14 March 1934, 20 September 1954). *NYTBR* (14 December 1980). *Washington Post Book World* (21 December 1980).

Charles A. Huttar

May McKisack

BORN: 30 March 1900, Belfast, Northern Ireland.
DIED: 14 March 1981, Oxford.
DAUGHTER OF: Audley John M. and Elizabeth McCullough.

An eminent scholar and teacher of medieval English history, M., having studied under several distinguished women historians, published three major books and influenced the lives and careers of undergraduates, research students, and scholars in both Europe and America.

Widowed early, M.'s mother moved her two children, M. and her brother Audley, knighted in 1958, from Belfast to Bedford, England, where M. studied with Agnes Sandys at the highly regarded Bedford School for Girls during 1910-1919. M. continued her studies at Somerville College, Oxford, as Mary Ewart Scholar as a pupil of Maude Clarke, earning her B.A. with Second Class Honors and Final Honors, in the School of Modern History in 1922. For the next two years M. remained at Somerville as Mary Somerville Research Fellow completing her B.Litt., *Parliamentary Representation of the English Boroughs in the Middle Ages*, later published as a volume in the Oxford Historical Series. After teaching history for a year in high school, she served as lecturer in medieval history at Liverpool University from 1927-1935. In 1936 she returned to Somerville, where she remained for the next two decades. During this period, the Oxford tutorial system enabled her to develop close ties with her students while she continued her research in medieval English political history. In 1955, M. was installed as Professor of History, Westfield College, University of London. Her inaugural lecture, *History As Education*, reveals her love not only of the subject but also of those who study it. As Professor of History at Westfield, M. exercised the same concern and leadership in department and college matters that had served so many students at Somerville. Her sure hand guided Westfield through a period of rapid growth while she instituted in the London Honours Program a new special subject on the reign of Richard II. Retirement from Westfield allowed M. to accept a Visiting Professorship of History at Vassar College in 1967-68, where she again brought medieval topics and people alive for undergraduates and forged new friendships with American colleagues. M. retired to Oxford where she made her home with Dame Lucy Sutherland and was often visited by friends and former pupils.

M.'s distinguished teaching career was highlighted by several influential publications. In 1932, her *Parliamentary Representations of the English Boroughs in the Middle Ages* challenged current interpretations of the topic and established her reputation as a careful researcher. In this volume she argued that representation of boroughs did not decrease for the fourteenth century and showed an increase in the fifteenth century. Her research corrected the view that burgesses did not attend Parliament and argued that burgesses were not as subordinate to knights as was generally thought by modern historians.

M.'s most widely read work, *The Fourteenth Century*, appeared in 1959 as volume five of the Oxford History of England. The great strength of this balanced and detailed survey was its clear presentation of institutional developments and political events. Revising current interpretations, she suggested that the aristocracy did not expand dangerously during this period. The volume has remained the most authoritative treatment of fourteenth-century England.

In 1971, M. published her third book, *Medieval History in the Tudor Age*. Using manuscripts in the royal, diocesan, and university collections, she documented England's awakening interest in her medieval past during the sixteenth century. In the same year, she was honored by a volume of essays from her former pupils and colleagues on the reign of Richard II.

WORKS: *Parliamentary Representation of the English Boroughs* (1932). *History As Education*, An Inaugural Lecture (1956). *The Fourteenth Century* (1959). *Medieval History in the Tudor Age* (1971).

BIBLIOGRAPHY: Du Boulay, F.R.H., and C.M. Barron, eds. The *Reign of Richard II: Essays in Honour of May McKisack* (1971).

Other references: Podel, J., ed. *The Annual Obituary 1981* (1982). *Who's Who* (1980).

Judith C. Kohl

Sara Maitland

BORN: 27 February 1950, London.
DAUGHTER OF: Adam and Hope Maitland.
MARRIED: Donald Hugh Thomson Lee, 1972.

M. is the second of six children, raised in London and Scotland. Educated privately, she went on to attend St. Anne's College, Oxford. M.

has worked as a free-lance academic researcher, journalist, writer, and lecturer. As a feminist socialist, M. has been involved with the Women's Liberation Movement since 1970 and has been active in various campaigns such as the Women's Lobby, Women's Aid, and the Christian Feminist Network. She has also lectured on feminist theology, women's history, and contemporary literature in England and the United States. In 1972 M. married an Anglican priest; they now live in an East London vicarage with their two children.

M.'s first novel, *Daughter of Jerusalem*, won the Somerset Maugham Award in 1979. The novel's nine chapters, an ironic parallel with the nine months of pregnancy, describe the protagonist's obsessive desire to bear a child. When Elizabeth and her husband Ian are unable to conceive after five years of marriage, she turns to a medical specialist. The dichotomies of heart and mind, soul and body, come under close scrutiny because Dr. Marshall insists that Liz, reluctant to become a "Real Woman" by embracing a stereotypical definition of femininity, psychologically represses ovulation. The novel depicts how Liz's obsession with child-bearing pervades every aspect of her life, compelling her to view her promiscuous past as punishment for her present barrenness, to rethink her feminist principles, and to reassess personal relationships (marriage with a gay man, parental relations, and friendships with various members of a feminist discussion group). Narrative devices, such as the abrupt fluctuation from present to past through flashbacks or from an objective third-person to inner thoughts, give the novel a claustrophobic intensity. *Daughter of Jerusalem* establishes the sorts of themes that M. will explore again: fatherly approval and self-doubt, patriarchal authority, and feminist disobedience. M. incorporates her continuing interest in Christianity and feminism by concluding each chapter with the re-telling of Biblical stories, feminist re-readings, for instance of Sarah and Abraham, Samson and Delilah, or Mary and Joseph.

Virgin Territory, M.'s second novel, opens with the rape of a American Catholic nun, which functions as the catalyst for protagonist Sister Anna's nervous breakdown. Anna eventually arrives in London (to perform research on another sort of rape, the plunder and enslavement of native tribes by the Conquistadors) where, as a motherless daughter, she confronts the omnipresent voice of the Fathers. M. both invokes and subverts the standard pattern of enclosure and escape, and the intense third-person narrative renders Anna's extended struggle with these inner voices all the more violent and disturbing. Anna's relationships with Karen (a lesbian to whom she is attracted) and with Cara (a brain-damaged child who serves as another mouthpiece for patriarchal authority) sustain her through a painful search for

an authentic female identity. In juxtaposing two seemingly different sorts of women's communities, lesbians and nuns, M. expands the meaning of virgin territories to portray female sexuality in depth.

M.'s first published writings appear in *Tales I Tell My Mother*, an anthology of short stories and essays by the members of a feminist collective (including Zoe Fairbairns, Valerie Miner, Michele Roberts, and Michelene Wandor). M. is fascinated with the act of writing and the process of writing as a feminist collective. In examining the impact of the women's movement and the way that it affects the outlook of both women and men, M. argues that "art is a way of organizing experience in order to clarify it." M. tests definitions of female and feminists by using a variety of literary forms and techniques, inner dialogue, letters, and myths. In *Telling Tales*, a collection of her own short stories, M. rewrites myths and tales of the past to challenge the patriarchal view of women's place in history while focusing, at the same time, on present issues that concern contemporary women. *Weddings and Funerals*, co-written with Aileen La Tourette, shows her continuing interest in writing as a collective experience and in the short story form as a means to present ideas in a concentrated way.

In addition to fiction, M. has written two important, distantly related works of nonfiction. The first, *A Map of the New Country: Women and Christianity*, is an impressive analysis of the predicament the Church poses for Christian feminists (this very phrase an oxymoron to some members of each respective group). The study includes an overview of the history of women and the church, communities of religious women, women's ordination, women in the church hierarchy, and a critique of sexism in religious language and spirituality. M. argues that feminism offers a unique "way forward, a way of healing our dangerous divisions and a way back to the Christian truth of service, equality, justice, and the renunciation of power through love." In combining systematic research and a coherent argument with a subjective voice and personal interviews collected in Britain and the United States, M. not only fills a gap in religious and women's studies but further demonstrates the potential for a specifically feminist scholarly approach that avoids the preferred objective voice of traditional scholarship.

The second work of nonfiction, M.'s biography of *Vesta Tilley*, is a contribution to the Virago Pioneers series, an ambitious feminist history project designed to introduce and reassess women of the past and examine their lives and contributions from a feminist perspective. Vesta Tilley (1864-1952), actress, singer, and male impersonator, was a fascinating figure of the Victorian music hall who used maleness to attain a higher social position. Such an "extraordinary woman," M. writes, "deserves a brassy book," and M.'s narrative style is a perfect match. The biography blends careful research with a relaxed and jovial narrative style, and, perhaps most importantly, M. uses the opportunity of telling Tilley's life to probe larger questions on gender and culture.

In "A Feminist Writer's Progress" (in *On Gender and Writing*, ed. M. Wandor, 1983), M. characterizes her development as a writer in terms of a mock-quest where the heroine must discover suitable companions (the Feminist Writers' Group), negotiate perilous straits between great writing and politics, and find the voice of the wise animal (her daughter). Though incomplete, this pseudo-quest identifies the special difficulties faced by the feminist writer and encapsulates M.'s principal themes and concerns. By re-telling the old stories, whether mythic or biblical, M. works effectively to resolve the tension that arises when the patriarchy collides with a feminist sensibility. Within M.'s determination to explore the possible and important connections between the seemingly irreconcilable, especially between feminism and Christianity, both the strengths and limitations of her writing are evident.

WORKS: *Introduction 5* (1973). *Daughter of Jerusalem* (1978; repub. as *Languages of Love* in 1981). *Tales I Tell My Mother* (with four other writers, 1978). *A Map of the New Country* (1983). *Telling Tales* (1983). *Weddings and Funerals* (with A. La Tourette, 1984). *Virgin Territory* (1984). *Vesta Tilley* (1986). *More Tales I Tell My Mother* (with four other writers, 1987). *A Book of Spells* (1987). *Arky Types* (with M. Wandor, 1987).

BIBLIOGRAPHY: *Contemporary Review* (October 1983). *Harper's* (April 1981). *New Statesman* (4 March 1983, 1 July 1983, 21 December 1984, 23 May 1986). *NYTBR* (29 June 1986). *TLS* (1 December 1978, 15 April 1983, 9 November 1984).

Other reference: *CA*.

Laura L. Doan

Bathsua Pell Makin

BORN: 1608 (?) at Southwick, Sussex.
DIED: 1675 (?)
DAUGHTER OF: John and Mary Holland Pell.

M. was the daughter of a minister who died in 1616; her mother died the following year. One of M.'s brothers, Thomas Pell, was a "gentleman of the bedchamber" to Charles I before emigrating to America in 1635, where he settled on a farm near Fairfield, Connecticut. M.'s other brother, John Pell, was a well-known mathematician. Although no record exists of M.'s ever having attended a school, she apparently knew Greek, Latin, Hebrew, Spanish, French, Italian, and mathematics. J.R. Brink speculates that M. probably tutored her brother John in those subjects before he entered Trinity College, Cambridge, at the age of only thirteen.

During some part of the 1640s M. served as the tutor of Princess Elizabeth (1635-1650), the daughter of Charles I. In fact, the Princess Elizabeth's expertise with languages was much admired throughout Europe, and, as her teacher, M. became known as the "most learned Englishwoman of her day." At around this same time, M. began corresponding with Anna Marie van Schurman (Dutch, 1607-1678), whom Brink refers to as the "most famous woman scholar of her time in Europe"; she not only knew Latin, Greek, and Hebrew but also Syriac, Arabic, Chaldee, and Ethiopic as well as having studied geography, philosophy, mathematics, the sciences, and religion. Two letters written in Greek and signed by M. were found among Schurman's papers. Proficiency in Greek was rare among women at that time.

Money was evidently a problem for M. during most of her adult life. On 24 September 1646, she published a pamphlet entitled "The Malady and Remedy of Vexations and Unjust Arrests and Actions," in which she outlined the six points of law that should be changed to ensure equitable treatment for all persons accused of indebtedness. Her concern was that many innocent people were imprisoned because they could not afford "a full hearing of their causes."

Only sketchy information has been uncovered about the events of M.'s later life. She was, according to the *DNB*, keeping "schools or colleges of the young gentlewomen" at Putney in 1649. In that same year M. wrote the first of two poems now held in the Hastings Collection of the Huntington Library, a Latin elegy on the death of Henry, Lord Hastings, the son of M.'s friend Lucy Hastings, the Countess of Huntingdon. On 2 May 1664, M. wrote the second poem, an elegy on the death of the Countess's daughter, entitled "Upon the much lamented death of the Right Honourable, the Lady Elizabeth Langham." In the letter accompanying that poem, M. described herself as a widow; however, no record of her marriage has been found. In another letter, dated 24 October 1668, M. indicated that she had a son.

In 1673, while she was mistress of a school at Tottenham High Cross, M. published her most important work, "An Essay to Revive the Ancient Education of Gentlewomen," a piece of writing that Myra Reynolds calls "admirable propaganda," a document that "tossed off the unmeaning arguments of opponents with . . . contemptuous ease." The essay, dedicated to "all Ingenious and Virtuous Ladies, more especially to her Highness the Lady Mary, the eldest daughter to his Royal Highness the Duke of York," is prefaced by two (probably fictitious) letters, the first written by a man who is supportive of women's education, the second by a man who says educating women is "preposterous." M. begins "An Essay" by listing the names of many learned women who have made contributions to the arts and sciences. The list is followed by such comments as:

> Had God intended women only as a finer sort of cattle, He would not have made them reasonable. Brutes, a few degrees higher than . . . monkeys . . . might have better fitted some men's lust, pride, and pleasure; especially those that desire to keep them ignorant to be tyrannized over.

M. specifies all the subjects in which women should be educated, such as grammar and rhetoric, logic, physic, languages (especially Greek and Hebrew), mathematics, geography, and the arts (music, painting, and poetry). She says that "women thus instructed" will be of profit to themselves, to their relations, and to the nation. M. concludes the essay by calling on all who read it to

> Let a generous resolution possess your minds, seeing men in this age have invaded women's vices; in a noble revenge, reassume those virtues which men sometimes unjustly usurped to themselves, but ought to have left them in common to both sexes.

WORKS: "The Malady and Remedy of Vexations and Unjust Arrests and Actions" (1646). "Upon the much lamented death of the right Honourable, the Lady Elizabeth Langham" (1664). "An Essay to Revive the Antient [sic] Education of Gentlewomen" (1673; rept. 1980).

In Manuscript: More poetry and other personal papers, Hastings Collection at the Huntington Library.

BIBLIOGRAPHY: Brink, J.R. *Female Scholars, A Tradition of Learned Women Before 1800* (1980). *The Female Spectator: English Women Writers Before 1800*, Eds. M. Mahl and H. Koon (1977). Reynolds, M. *The Learned Lady in England 1650-1760* (1920; rpt. 1964).

For articles in reference works, see: *DNB*. Todd.

Other references: Gardner, D. *English Girlhood at School* (1929). Watson, F. *Atalanta* (1895).

Kate Beaird Meyers

(Mary?) Delariviere Manley

BORN: 6 or 7 April 1663[?] or 1667–72, Jersey.
DIED: 11 July 1724, London.
DAUGHTER OF: Sir Roger Manley.
MARRIED: John Manley, c. 1688.

Much is problematic about the early years of M., including whether Mary was her first name and when and where she was born. Her own testimony, given in thinly fictionalized autobiographical narratives, is unreliable; and the little remaining documentary evidence is ambiguous. We do know that she was born in the latter part of the seventeenth century in England, possibly on the island of Jersey, or possibly at sea between Jersey and Guernsey, the daughter of Sir Roger Manley, who was Lieutenant-Governor of Jersey, a Stuart sympathizer, and an author of histories. She had three sisters and a brother. Her mother died in M.'s youth and her father c. 1688, apparently leaving her the ward of a cousin, John Manley, who later married her under false pretenses (he was already wed) and abandoned her with a son. This "bigamous marriage," which M. recounts in *The New Atlantis* (1709) and *The Adventures of Rivella* (1714), seriously damaged her social reputation.

Shortly thereafter she became the companion of Barbara Palmer, the Duchess of Cleveland, who figures in various M. works. They soon quarreled, and M. retired to Exeter, having discovered, as she put it in *The Adventures of Rivella*, that "her Love of Solitude was improved by her Disgust of the World." In Exeter she wrote the first of her works: two plays—*The Lost Lover*, a comedy, and *The Royal Mischief*, a tragedy—and an epistolary protonovel entitled *Letters Written by Mrs. Manley* (1696; retitled *A Stage Coach Journey to Exeter* in 1725). At about this time she had an affair with Sir Thomas Skipworth, who produced her plays in London in 1696. *The Lost Lover*, presented at Drury Lane c. March 1696, had little success, but the tragedy, which appeared a month or so later at Lincoln's Inn Fields, helped to establish M.'s reputation and yielded her a financial profit. Both plays were preceded by important feminist prefaces. Only "prejudice against our Sex," she maintained, prevented the plays from receiving a more enthusiastic reception. Partly as a response to these statements, Drury Lane shortly thereafter exposed M. and other women playwrights of the period to public ridicule by presenting a burlesque of the production of *The Royal Mischief* entitled *The Female Wits.* Whether this play had a chastening effect on M. is unclear, but she gave up writing (or at least publishing) for nearly a decade. During this period she became romantically involved with John Tilly, who was married and the warden of the Fleet Street prison. Tilly was the great love of her life, but she gave him up after several years to allow him to make a financially advantageous liaison with a rich widow.

It was shortly after this (1702) that M. began producing her most celebrated works, a series of fictionalized satires written partly to vindicate herself, partly to promote her Tory political interests, and partly to make money. The first of these, which most scholars attribute to her, is *The Secret History of Queen Zarah, and the Zarazians* (1705). It includes an important theoretical preface, which provides a critique of the then popular heroic romance. *Queen Zarah* has the distinction of being the first *roman à clef* written in English. The work is a political satire in the form of a picaresque romance, directed against Sarah Churchill, the Duchess of Marlborough, who with her husband was an influential Whig member of the court of Queen Anne. In *Queen Zarah* Sarah is portrayed as ambitious, cruel, greedy, rude, and guilty of various sexual improprieties. Perhaps because of the explicitness of the latter descriptions the book was extraordinarily popular, selling several thousand copies. In 1706 M. produced another play, *Almyna*, considered her best tragedy.

M.'s most celebrated work, *Secret Memoirs and Manners . . . from the New Atlantis*, appeared in 1709. Like *Queen Zarah*, this satire was a kind of *roman à clef* that recounted political intrigue and sexual scandal, mainly among members of the Whig aristocracy. The work includes scenes of homosexual, as well as heterosexual, orgy, drunkenness, rape, and incest, which have given it a sensationalist reputation. The second volume, for example, opens with a piece on the New Cabal, a group of wealthy lesbians. M. was arrested for libel on 29 October 1709 but was released under the newly enacted *habeus corpus* writ on 5 November, and the case was eventually dropped in 1710. As in all M.'s works, *The New Atlantis* reveals the author's talent at realistic description, of dress, manners, and psychological motivation, as well as her wry, sarcastic wit. The last of M.'s political works, *Memoirs of Europe*, appeared in 1710, and *Court-Intrigues*, in 1711. During this period M. published *The Female Tatler*, a journal of political satire, and in 1711 succeeded Jonathan Swift, a fellow Tory, as editor of *The Examiner*.

Probably of most interest to the modern reader is M.'s *Adventures of Rivella* (1714), which remains an important early precursor to the novel. Essentially autobiographical, Rivella's (M.'s) story is narrated by Sir Charles Lovemore to a Chevalier d'Aumont, who is an admiring Rivella/(M.) reader. Like many later novels, the central character is presented as an innocent victim of circumstances—mainly financial—and of prejudice against women. M. is particularly exercised by the double standard: "*If she had been a Man, she had been without Fault*: But the Charter of that Sex being much more confin'd than ours, what is not a Crime in Men is scandalous and unpardonable in Woman." In addition to a feminist perspective, the work expresses a kind of cynicism reminiscent of Là Rochefoucauld (whom, indeed, Rivella reads) that contributes to the growing tradition of realism in literature. The world is portrayed as a decidedly unromantic jungle where people operate primarily according to self-interest.

Her final works included a play, *Lucius, The First Christian King of Britain*, produced at Drury Lane in 1717, *The Power of Love: in Seven Novels* (1720), and *Bath Intrigues* (1725), published posthumously; the latter may not be hers.

Her contribution lies in having forged an authentically feminist realism, in creating vigorous true-to-life characters whose psychological behavior is finely tuned, and in having braved the negative currents that opposed women's entrance into the field of dramatic and fictional literature. She is one of the pioneers of women's literature in English, but her work has yet to receive the serious critical attention it deserves.

WORKS: *Letters Written by Mrs. Manley* (1696) (reprinted as *A Stage Coach Journey to Exeter* in 1725). *The Lost Lover; or, The Jealous Husband* (1696). *The Royal Mischief* (1696). *The Secret History of Queen Zarah, and the Zarazians* (1705). *Almyna; or, the Arabian Vow* (1707). *Secret Memoirs and Manners of Several Persons of Quality of Both Sexes, from the New Atlantis, an Island in the Mediterranean* (1709). *Memoirs of Europe, toward the Close of the Eighth Century* (1710). *Court Intrigues, in a Collection of Original Letters from the Island of the New Atlantis* (1711). *The Adventures of Rivella; or, the History of the Author of the Atlantis by Sir Charles Lovemore* (1714). *Lucius, the First Christian King of Britain* (1717). *The Power of Love: in Seven Novels* (1720). *Bath Intrigues* (attributed to M.) (1725). *The Novels of Mary Delariviere Manley*, ed. with an introduction by P. Köster (1971).

BIBLIOGRAPHY: Clark, C. *Three Augustan Women Playwrights* (1986). Lock, F. P. *Woman in the Eighteenth Century and Other Essays* ed. P. Fritz and R. Morton (976). MacCarthy, B. *Women Writers: *Their Contribution to the English Novel* (1944). Richetti, J.J. *Popular Fiction Before Richardson: Narrative Patterns 1700-1739* (1969).

    For articles in reference works see: *DLB. DNB.* Other references: *Bookman's Journal* (1925). *Eighteenth Century Life* (June 1977). *Huntington Library Quarterly* (1948-1949, 1951). *MLN. MP*

(1930, 1931, 1936, 1937). *Philological Quarterly* (1934, 1936, 1973). *PMLA* (1937). *Review of English Studies,* (1978). *Transactions of the Samuel Johnson Society of the Northwest,* (1971). *Women and Literature* (Spring 1978). *Women's Studies* (1979).

Josephine Donovan

Ethel Mannin

BORN: 11 October 1900, London.
DIED: 5 December 1984, Devon.
DAUGHTER OF: Robert and Edith Gray Mannin.
MARRIED: J.A. Porteous, 1920; Reginald Reynolds, 1938.

M. wrote over one hundred books in her fifty-year literary career: novels, travel books, autobiographies, and memoirs as well as works on education, religion, politics, and morality. She was a woman with definite views. "A writer's business," she wrote, "is essentially with truth, to interpret life in its infinite complexity, to illuminate, to communicate."

From the outset M. believed in the importance of the individual and the inadequacy of the existing social system. During the twenties she was concerned with freedom of the individual, during the thirties she became involved in political movements that promised to change society, and by the forties she was the champion of an unpopular view, upholding the individualist creed of "pacifist-anarchist," a view she has maintained. Her immense canon is a detailed document of her personal growth and a record of the changes in the world around her. "I am one of those who believe that the writer should concern himself with current affairs, be of his time, concerned with its problems, social and political," she said.

M. was born to working-class parents of Irish descent (her father was a post office sorter), and from her early life drew a belief in the value of the working-class point of view. Educated at state school, she began writing at age seven, left school at age fifteen, and got a job in an advertising agency as a stenographer. By age seventeen she was editing in-house publications and the *Pelican,* a theatrical and sporting paper. In 1920 she married J.A. Porteous by whom she had a daughter, Jean. At first she established herself as a free-lance journalist by writing for the women's market. Her first serious literary recognition came with the publication of her third novel, *Sounding Brass* (1926), a satire of the advertising world. It created a stir on Fleet Street because the hero of the novel was thought to be her former employer.

Her literary career underway, M. in 1928 was "emancipated from marriage into independence" by divorcing Porteous. In the late twenties and early thirties M. mingled with the Jazz Age crowd, traveling to America where she encountered A.S. Neill, going frequently to the continent, especially Paris and Vienna, "because running around Europe was the vogue with the young intelligentsia of the period," and writing more than a dozen books in damp hotels and dismal flats as well as in her "Very Jazz Age" decorated suburban cottage. Her first important book of this period was *Confessions and Impressions* (1929), an autobiography and memoir, called by the author (in retrospect) a "rash and brash account" of the twenties scene. It contains sketches and portraits of "people who have interested me," including Osbert Sitwell, Tamara Karsavina, D.H. Lawrence, Bertrand Russell, and A.S. Neill.

Neill's progressive ideas on child education had a profound effect on M. When she went to America in 1926, she sent her six-year old daughter to his school. M. wrote about Neill's school in her 1928 novel, *Green Willow,* and, in 1930, wrote her first book on child education, *Common Sense and the Child,* for which Neill wrote the preface; M. also wrote two other books in this series: *Common Sense and the Adolescent* and *Common Sense and Morality,* which also included a preface by Neill.

For M. the end of her twenties was important in terms of personal development. During the years 1929-30 she began her regular rhythm of literary output: a novel and a non-fiction book each year. In the early thirties M., like other members of her generation, became involved in political movements. This change in focus is evident in the kinds of novels M. wrote during this decade, such as *Linda Shawn* and *Venetian Blinds,* both of which are concerned with social rather than romantic themes. In 1933 she joined the International Labour Party, which was Marxist by ideology. One of the major tenets of the ILP was "critical support of the Soviet Union." *Cactus* and *The Pure Flame* are the culmination of Mannin's Marxist sympathies, portraying the struggle of the classes against the forces of imperialism. In 1934, when she toured a Russian commune, she was very impressed with the progress of the Communist project. However, when she returned to Russia in 1935, an unguided trip to the collective at Samarkand proved to be a disillusioning experience. She found that the Russian experiment was riddled with the power interplay that she was rejecting in her own country as an opponent of imperialism and capitalism. Her disappointment was portrayed in the travel book *South to Samarkand* and the novel, *Comrade, O Comrade; or, Low-Down on the Left*.

The involvement with the ILP coincided with M.'s association with the pacifist movement. It was at an ILP meeting that she met her future husband, a Quaker pacifist and former student of Gandhi. With him she participated in nonviolent activities, speaking at public meetings, writing articles, raising funds, and distributing literature for freedom groups. At the end of the decade, as an opponent of fascism, M. was involved with fundraising activities for the Spanish anarchists and Emma Goldman. M.'s *Women and the Revolution* discusses the involvement of women in the anarchist experiment in Catalonia, Spain, and *Red Rose* is a slightly romanticized and highly readable novel about the life of Emma Goldman.

When war broke out in England, M. and her husband declared themselves pacifists and refused to take part in the war effort. This unpopular view prevented M. from acquiring a travel permit, so she spent the war years in England and continued her amazing productivity. One of her most interesting political books was *Bread and Roses: An Utopian Survey and Blue-Print*, which outlines a program for a Utopian world based on the political philosophy of anarcho-syndicalism, "the practical expression of anarchism." The basic concept, which organized each trade and industry into syndicates controlled by the workers, had been put into practice in Catalonia and was eventually crushed by the forces of power operative in the Spanish Civil War. M. was convinced that "man must find a new way of living or perish," which must have seemed self-evident in London during the war. This new way of living was to come to the pacifist-anarchist conclusion that a revolution must occur in the mind of man that would enable him to seek out a world controlled by the ideals of brotherhood. The object of political striving then was to construct a new culture with man living harmoniously with man in a free ungoverned society. The book, however, was at first difficult to publish and then when in print received little notice. It is a singular document, laying down in clear but idealized language the dreams of this philosophical view. It serves as an indicator of M.'s creed, which was not to change for the next thirty years of her writing.

In the post-war world Mannin continued to be involved in international political issues. Traveling to Germany and Austria to observe hunger problems there, for example, resulted in *German Journey*, a travel book, and *Bavarian Story*, a novel. She also wrote *The Dark Forest*, about the invasion of a neutral country. In order to publish it M. had to modify the epilogue, which suggested that one occupying army in a neutral country was very like another. M. and her husband also traveled to India, Morocco, Burma, and Japan. Each of these journeys resulted in a travel book in which M. told not only of her experiences but also informed the public of the living conditions, from a liberal perspective, in the various countries. M. and Reynolds were not extremely popular for their views, which included supporting the Arab cause as opposed to the Jewish Palestinian one and sponsoring the independence of India. Each of these journeys also produced a novel such as *The Living Lotus, The Road to Beersheba, The Night and Its Homing, The Midnight Street*, and *Mission to Beirut* as well as several travel books.

In 1958 her husband died of a cerebral hemorrhage while on a journey to Australia. M.'s *Brief Voices* ends with a discussion of his death and how she never expected the book to end that way. The immediacy of her life to her writing is evident from the ending of the book. After Reynolds' death, M. continued her literary career. She continued to travel, to write of her travels, and to write more novels. In 1971 she wrote *Young in the Twenties*, which serves as a commentary of her first piece of autobiography, *Confessions and Impressions*. She also wrote *Stories from My Life* and, in 1977, published *Sunset over Dartmoor: A Final Chapter of Autobiography*. During the same twenty-year period she wrote fourteen novels, four juvenile books, travel books on Japan, Egypt, Jordan, America, and two on England. She also wrote books on the revolt of the individual, loneliness, and the human phenomenon of love. M. lived in Devon until her death.

M.'s books are highly readable and informative and she is always concerned with presenting the prevailing view, tempered by her own liberal attitude. She has received little critical attention, perhaps due to her radical politics, highly individualized manner, and working-class status. An author of diverse talents and interests, M.'s most important achievement is as a chronicler of the experiences of the twentieth century.

WORKS: Martha (1923, rev. 1929). *Sounding Brass* (1925). *Green Willow* (1928). *Confessions and Impressions* (1930, rev. 1936). *Common-Sense and the Child: A Plea for Freedom* (1931). *Green Figs* (1931). *The Tinsel Eden and Other Stories* (1931). *Bruised Wings and Other Stories* (1931). *Ragged Banners: A Novel with an Index* (1931). *All Experience* (1932). *Venetian Blinds* (1933). *Dryad*

(1933). *Men Are Unwise* (1934). *Forever Wandering* (1934). *The Falconer's Voice* (1935). *Cactus* (1935, rev. 1944). *The Pure Flame* (1936). *South to Samarkand* (1936). *Common-Sense and the Adolescent* (1937, rev. 1945). *Women Also Dream* (1937). *Rose and Sylvie* (1938). *Darkness My Bride* (1938). *Women and the Revolution* (1939). *Privileged Spectator: A Sequel to "Confessions and Impressions"* (1939, rev. 1947). *Julie: The Story of a Dance-Hostess* (1940). *Red Rose: A Novel Based on the Life of Emma Goldman* (1941). *Christianity—or Chaos? A Re-Statement of Religion* (1941). *Commonsense and Morality* (1942). *Captain Moonlight* (1942). *The Blossoming Bough* (1943). *No More Mimosa* (1943). *Bread and Roses: An Utopian Survey and Blue-Print* (1944). *Proud Heaven* (1944). *Lucifer and the Child* (1945). *The Dark Forest* (1946). *Selected Stories* (1946). *Comrade, O Comrade; or, Low-Down on the Left* (1947). *Connemara Journal* (1947). *German Journey* (1948). *Late Have I Loved Thee* (1948). *Every Man a Stranger* (1949). *Bavarian Story* (1949). *Jungle Journey* (1950). *At Sundown the Tiger . . .* (1951). *The Fields at Evening* (1952). *The Wild Swans and Other Tales Based on the Ancient Irish* (1952). *Moroccan Mosaic* (1953). *So Tiberius* (1954). *Land of the Crested Lion: A Journey Through Modern Burma* (1955). *The Living Lotus* (1956). *Fragrances of Hyacinths* (1958). *Brief Voices: A Writer's Story* (1959). *The Flowery Sword: Travels in Japan* (1960). *Sabishisa* (1961). *Curfew at Dawn* (1962). *A Lance for the Arabs: A Middle East Jour-*

ney (1963). *Rebels' Ride: A Middle East Journey* (1964). *The Road to Beersheba* (1964). *The Burning Bush* (1965). *The Lovely Land: The Hashemite Kingdom of Jordan* (1965). *Loneliness: A Study of the Human Condition* (1966). *The Night and Its Homing* (1966). *The Lady and the Mystic* (1967). *An American Journey* (1967). *England for a Change* (1968). *Bitter Babylon* (1968). *The Midnight Street* (1969). *Practitioners of Love: Some Aspects of the Human Phenomenon* (1969). *England at Large* (1970). *Free Pass to Nowhere* (1970). *Young in the Twenties: A Chapter of Autobiography* (1971). *The Curious Adventure of Major Fosdick* (1972). *Stories from My Life* (1973). *Mission to Beirut* (1973). *Kildoon* (1974). *An Italian Journey* (1974). *Sunset over Dartmoor: A Final Chapter of Autobiography* (1977).

BIBLIOGRAPHY:

For articles in reference works, see: *CA. CN. DIL. Longman. TCA* and *SUP.*

Other references: *Bookman* (August 1926). *Book Week* (30 August 1964). *Commonweal* (12 November 1948). *New Statesman* (10 January 1932). *NYT* (20 June 1926, 7 October 1928, 26 June 1932, 16 June 1935, 25 July 1937, 10 October 1948, 1 September 1957). *SR* (24 July 1926, 13 October 1928, 15 July 1950). *TLS* (13 November 1924, 27 April 1933, 12 September 1936, 2 April 1938, 3 August 1967, 14 May 1970, 25 August 1972). *Times* (London) (8 January 1985). *Washington Post* (10 December 1984).

Priscilla Dorr

Olivia Manning

BORN: 1911 (?) or 1915 (?), Portsmouth.
DIED: 23 July 1980, Isle of Wight.
DAUGHTER OF: Oliver and Olivia Manning.
MARRIED: Reginald Donald Smith, 1939.

Though best known for her novels, particularly *The Balkan Trilogy* (1965), M. also wrote stories, humor, history, travel, and other works, as well as numerous essays and reviews for the (London) *Times* and such journals as *Horizon, Spectator, Punch, New Statesman*. Little biographical information is available for her, and until her death even an approximate year of her birth was unknown. Her father was a commander in the Royal Navy and her husband a BBC drama producer. She served in the press office in the U.S. embassy, Cairo (1942), in the Public Information Office, Jerusalem (1943-1944) and in the British Council Office, Jerusalem (1944-1945). She was also a painter; indeed, Walter Allen once noted that she had a "painter's eye for the visible world"

that "enabled her to render particularly well the sensual surface of landscape and places."

M.'s first novel, *The Wind Changes* (1938), dealt with the Irish uprising but differs from most other fictionalized accounts of the "troubles" in its focus on the conflicts within the central characters, a woman and two men, rather than on larger political and social issues. Her insightful handling of mental states was praised for its clarity and careful pacing, and her style, especially dialogue, was compared favorably to the work of Hemingway. The characters, however, were said to be indistinguishable in mood or act simply because of her emphasis on thought processes.

M.'s precise observation and description seemed to limit her efforts to present people and their actions adequately. Though her other early novels (*Artist Among the Missing*, 1949, *School for Love*, 1951, and *A Different Face*, 1953) were respectfully received, none made any appreciable impact. Yet all seem in retrospect to be leading, through her acknowledged gifts of humor, precision of language, sweeping sense of history, and keen appreciation of place, toward her *Balkan Trilogy*. *School for Love* is set in Jerusalem during World War II as experienced by a stranded sixteen-year-old boy. *A Different Face*, by contrast, is set on the English coast and concerns a man who discovers that his investment in a school has disappeared. In both cases, these early novels reflect M.'s skill at dramatizing essentially pessimistic, even hopeless, situations with a sharp eye for the telling detail, the vivid phrase, the ironic perspective, even though her dispassionate distance from her subjects sometimes displeased both readers and critics.

Each of these works was deservedly praised for its broad canvas, juxtaposition of individual fates against the backdrop of great European conflicts, and careful placement of characters in particular historical contexts; yet here, too, M.'s handling of her central characters came in for repeated criticism. Her acknowedged skill in penetrating the male psyche was often noted, but the individual, male or female, seemed wholly overwhelmed by the sheer magnitude of world events, so much so, in fact, that readers sometime found the books more persuasive as historical documents than as fiction.

The Balkan Trilogy includes *The Great Fortune* (1960), *The Spoilt City* (1962), and *Friends and Heroes* (1965). *The Great Fortune* (the title presumably refers to life itself) presents a husband and wife (Guy and Harriet Pringle) in Bucharest who see how the older world is doomed but who, of course, are incapable of altering the inevitable. The cosmopolitan Guy (as seen through Harriet's eyes) is considered one of the most complex, appealing, full-bodied characters in all of modern literature; Anthony Burgess considers him a "kind of civilization in himself." Bucharest is the "spoilt city" of the second novel; in this work, Guy tries to save the city during its occupation by the Germans, though he is scarcely able to save himself and can never wholly fathom the radical changes he is witnessing. The same emphasis on the uncertainty of events is found in *Friends and Heroes*, in which the Pringles, now in Athens, find themselves still surrounded by flux and discord; M. seems to suggest that never again will Europe—or the world—be able to experience the previous world of stability and order.

M. subsequently completed an additional three volumes about World War II. Also considered fine examples of the *roman fleuve* (series or sequence novel), the *Levant Trilogy* (made up of *The Danger Tree*, 1977, *The Battle Lost and Won*, 1978, and *The Sum of Things*, 1980) continues the story of the Pringles, now stranded in Egypt and soon to wander through Palestine and Syria. M.'s

excellent sense of atmosphere continues to dominant her characters' perceptions, though critics noted her more conventional reliance on routine descriptions and incidents as they experience the sharp contrast between England and Egypt, the rich and the poor. The soberly realistic Middle East descriptions avoid the poetic or exotic temptations of, say, Lawrence Durrell's *Alexandria Quartet* as M. dryly, wittily captures the world of military hospitals, markets, religious shrines, and cafes.

M.'s other novels include *The Rain Forest* (1974), set on an island in the Indian Ocean, again focusing on the gradual dissolution of a colonial way of life. She necessarily utilizes details of a steamy, oppressive climate as she contrasts incompetent British authority and the forbidden forest of the title. Her protagonists are a married couple who after struggling against both humans and nature are able to go on together, while others find the forest itself a primeval refuge.

M.'s talent was widely recognized, and her ambitious series novels are likely to endure as her most important works. Her concern was not with shifting political loyalties or historical topicality, despite the specific settings of her best novels, so much as with a quiet but vivid sense of the effects of setting on sensitive characters' awareness of the dissolution of empires.

WORKS: *The Wind Changes* (1938). *The Remarkable Expedition: The Story of Stanley's Rescue of Emin Pasha from Equatorial Africa* (1947; in the U.S. as *The Reluctant Rescue*). *Growing Up: A Collection of Short Stories* (1948). *Artist Among the Missing* (1949). *The Dreaming Shore* (1950). *School for Love* (1951). *A Different Face* (1953). *The Doves of Venus* (1955). *My Husband Cartwright* (1956). *The Great Fortune* (1960). *The Spoilt City* (1962). *Friends and Heroes* (1965). *A Romantic Hero and Other Stories* (1967). *Extraordinary Cats* (1967). *The Play Room* (1969; as screenplay, 1970; in the U.S. as *The Camperlea Girls*). (with others) *Penguin Modern Stories 12* (1972). *The Rain Forest* (1974). *The Danger Tree* (1977). *The Battle Lost and Won* (1978). *The Sum of Things* (1980). *The Play Room* (1984). *The Weather in the Streets* (1986).

BIBLIOGRAPHY: Allen, W. *Tradition and Dream: The English and American Novel from the Twenties to Our Time* (1964; in the U.S. as *The Modern Novel in Britain and the United States*, 1965). Burgess, A. *The Novel Today* (1963; in the U.S. as *The Novel Now: A Guide to Contemporary Fiction*, 1967). Mooney, H.J., Jr. *Twentieth Century Women Novelists*, ed. T.F. Staley (1982). Morris, R.K. *Continuance and Change: The Contemporary British Novel Sequence* (1972).

For articles in reference works, see: *CA. CLC. CN. MBL* and *SUP. TCW. WA.*

Other references: *Books and Bookmen* (August 1971). *British Book News* (January 1981). *Christian Science Monitor* (9 April 1979). *Encounter* (May 1960). *John O'London's* (18 February 1960). *Listener* (25 September 1980). *London Magazine* (October–November 1974). *Manchester Guardian* (17 May 1962). *New Statesman* (11 April 1969, 5 April 1974, 17 November 1978, 26 September 1980). *NYTBR* (3 April 1938, 9 October 1977). *SR* (London) (9 April 1938). *SR* (New York) (17 November 1956). *Time and Tide* (22 December 1956). *TLS* (29 January 1960, 24 November 1978, 19 September 1980).

Paul Schlueter

Katherine Mansfield

BORN: 14 October 1888, Wellington, New Zealand.
DIED: 9 January 1923, Paris.
DAUGHTER OF: Harold and Annie Dyer Beauchamp.
MARRIED: G.C. Bowden, 1909; John Middleton Murry, 1918.

A master of the short story, M. was born in New Zealand, the fourth child of wealthy parents. She received her education in London at Queen's College, where she first encountered the writings of the symbolists (an important influence on her own work) and began her writing career on the school magazine. After graduation, she returned to New Zealand with her parents, determined to become a writer and return to Europe. In 1908 she persuaded her father to let her return with a modest allowance. She never saw New Zealand again.

Some of M.'s first stories appeared from 1910–12 in the Fabian-Socialist magazine *The New Age*. There she published sharp, satirical sketches, literary parodies, feminist polemics, and the "Bavarian Sketches," later collected under separate cover as *In A German Pension*. She met J.M. Murry, whom she later married, in 1911 and with him established a new periodical called *Rhythm*. It was while writing for *Rhythm* that she met such figures as D.H. Lawrence and Leonard and Virginia Woolf. The news of her brother's death in 1915, which drove her into deep despair, sparked her interest in her native New Zealand. In a burst of creativity she produced "Prelude," published in 1917 as one of the first publications of Virginia and Leonard Woolf's Hogarth Press. Other stories such as "The Man Without a Temperament" and "Je ne parle pas français," written at this time, helped to enhance her growing reputation as a short story writer.

M.'s move from what Woolf called the literary "underground" to the canon of accepted modern writers was accompanied by the discovery of her tuberculosis. Realizing that the diagnosis was her death sentence, she spent much of her remaining time writing. In 1920 she published *Bliss and Other Stories*, and in 1922 the *Garden Party and Other Stories*. From 1921–22, as death neared, she worked with great power and intensity, completing enough short stories for two posthumous collections later published by her husband. She died in 1923 at the Gurdjieff Institute in Paris.

A many-faceted craftswoman, M. wrote satirical pieces, feminist literature, and touching stories of her childhood New Zealand, in which over half of her stories are set. Greatly influenced by the symbolist writers and often described as a writer of "lyrical" quality, she was interested not in social contexts and realities but in evoking an atmosphere or mood created through a network of concrete images and the power of the idealizing imagination. Like most Symbolists, she was also a tireless experimenter in literary form. Her stories are the quintessential modern format, with conscious epiphanies serving as focal points for the portrayal of internal crisis. Among her favorite devices are internal monologues, parallelisms, contrasts, flashbacks, and daydreams. In her later career she also experimented with the short-story cycle, in which separate stories are linked by character, setting, and repeating images and motifs.

Among M.'s favorite themes were the flowering of the self, sexual corruption, the terrors of childhood, the female artist, solitude, and death. From her symbolist roots she also inherited a keen interest in expanding the poetic potentials of the prose genre, and many of the short stories are written in a lyrical prose, exploiting rhythm, image, and sound as aids to convey meaning.

M. used her exquisite and delicate sensibility to create stories of solid and well-crafted structure, dealing with themes of weighty implications. Since her death, critical commentary has been unfortunately and intimately intertwined with comments on her personality. On one hand, Lawrence's picture in *Women in Love* and on the other her husband's portrait in the patiently edited and rearranged editions of her notebooks have muddied the critical waters. Today, however, critics are displaying new interest in her art and her contribution to the short story form.

M. once said, "The false writer begins as an experimenter; the true artist ends as one." Her death at thirty-four cut short both her life and that experimentation, leading Elizabeth Bowen to call M. "our missing contemporary."

WORKS: *In a German Pension* (1911). *Prelude* (1918). *Je ne parle pas français* (1918). *Bliss, and Other Stories* (1920). *The Garden-Party, and Other Stories* (1922). *The Dove's Nest, and Other Stories* (1922). *Poems* (1923). *Something Childish, and Other Stories* (1924). *The Aloe* (1930; rev. 1984). *Novels and Novelists* (1930). *Juliet* (1970). *The Letters and Journals of Katherine Mansfield, A Selection* (1977). *The Complete Stories of Katherine Mansfield* (1978). *The Urewera Notebook* (1978). *Collected Letters*, v. 1 (1984). *Critical Writings*, ed. C. Hanson (1987). *Collected Letters*, v. 2 (1987).

BIBLIOGRAPHY: Alpers, J. *The Life of Katherine Mansfield* (1980). Berkman, S. *Katherine Mansfield: A Critical Study* (1951). Clarke, I.C. *Katherine Mansfield: A Biography* (1944). Daly, S.R. *Katherine Mansfield* (1965). Gordon, I.A. *Katherine Mansfield* 1971). Hankin, C.A. *Katherine Mansfield and Her Confessional Stories* (1983). Hanson, C., and A. Gurr. *Katherine Mansfield* (1981). Magalaner, M. *The Fiction of Katherine Mansfield* (1971). Meyers, J. *Katherine Mansfield: A Biography* (1978). Moore, J. *Gurdjieff and Mansfield* (1980). Rohrberger, M. *The Art of Katherine Mansfield* (1977). Tomalin, C. *Katherine Mansfield: A Secret Life* (1987).

For articles in reference works, see: *CA. MBL* and *SUP. MCL. TCA* and *SUP.*

Other references: *Adam International Review* (1965, 1973-73). Gubar, S. *The Representation of Women in Fiction*, ed. C.G. Heilbrun and M. Higonnet (1983). Kaplan, S.J. *Women's Language and Style*, ed. D. Butturff and E. Epstein (1978). Meyers, J. *Journal of Modern Literature* (1979). Neaman, J.S. *TCL* (1986). Wright, C.T. *MP* (1954).

Glenda Wall

Marie de France

BORN: 1160? Probably French by birth.
DIED: 1215?

In the epilogue to her fables she says: "Marie ai num, si suis de France," generally interpreted to mean that she was of the Ile de France. She spent most of her life in England. Several attempts have been put forth to identify her: she may have been the illegitimate daughter of Geoffrey of Anjou (later abbess of Shaftesbury) or the abbess of Reading or Marie de Meulan, daughter of Count Waleron de Beaumont. M. wrote at or for the English court of Henry II and Eleanor of Aquitaine.Her works enjoyed popularity in the Middle Ages: Denis Piramus (1170-1180) mentions her in his *Vie Seint Edmund le Rey* saying that she was one of the most popular authors with lords and ladies, and her lais were translated into various languages during the Middle Ages.

M. is the first known woman writer to compose vernacular narrative poetry; she is often praised as the author of the best short vernacular fiction before Boccaccio. Her trademark, as has been repeatedly observed, is her sophisticated use of symbolic creatures or artifacts around which the lais' action revolves. Functioning almost as *Leitmotivs*, these symbolic entities enable M. to craft multidimensional, often ambiguous narratives that explore the nature of love, fidelity, loyalty, and sacrifice. Her themes center on the need for self-fulfillment both for men and women and the unlimited power of the imagination and of love to make one's wish and desire come true.

Her twelve lais, all in octosyllabic couplets, range in length from 118 lines ("Chevrefoil") to 1184 lines ("Eliduc") and were probably intended for oral recitation. Based on Celtic tales and transmitted orally by Breton bards, they were composed between 1160-1199. "Guigemar" depicts the psychological and sexual growing up of the protagonist in a fairy-tale setting. The young hero, oblivious to the attractions of women, is wounded by a deer and can only be healed by a woman's love. "Le Fresne" concerns the selfless love of an abandoned girl, which is ultimately rewarded by recognition by her parents and marriage to her beloved. "Bisclavret," M.'s tale of a werewolf, centers on betrayal and loyalty, and "Lanval" presents the ennobling effects of love in the tale of a noble knight and his fairy sweetheart set against the ignoble court of Arthur and his lascivious and cruel queen. "Les Deus Amanz," a tragic tale, celebrates the all-embracing joy of true love, while "Yonec" paints a virtuous lady's escape from her marital prison through her imagination, manifested in her bird-knight-lover. "Milun" tells of long-lasting love and of a father's encounter with his unknown son, while "Chaitivel" recounts the sad story of an indecisive lady who loses all her lovers. "Equitan," the most didactic of the lais, explores the nature of reciprocal responsibilities and loyalties. "Laüstic" is the tragic story of a lady deprived of all joy in her marriage, and "Eliduc" is the classic triangle story of a man caught between two women and two lords.

M.'s fables, translated into French from English, are all characterized by a marked sense of social obligations and social justice and compassion for the oppressed. Yet even here M. does not fall prey to over-simplifications: wickedness is sometimes committed by the oppressed as well as the oppressor, and corruption is not the exclusive domain of the rich and the powerful. *L'Espurgatoire Saint Patrice,* finally, is a translation from Latin into French depicting the otherworldly journey of the Irish knight Owein. Having witnessed the tremendous pain and suffering of the souls in purgatory as well as the bliss of earthly paradise, he returns to earth to lead an exemplary life.

M.'s strength as a writer lies with her lively style, psychological astuteness, and economy of expression. Throughout her works she avoids easy and over-simplified generalizations. She is an exciting, intense, suggestive, and talented storyteller, able to present archetypal themes in engaging contemporary guise.

WORKS: The Lais of Marie de France, ed. J.M. Ferrante and R.W. Hanning (1978). *Fables,* ed. and trans. H. Spiegel (1987).

BIBLIOGRAPHY: Burgess, G. *Marie de France: An Analytical Bibliography* (1977). Le Mée, K.W. *A Metrical Study of Five Lais of Marie de France* (1978). *Malvern, M.M. Tulsa Studies in Women's Literature* (1983).

Katharina M. Wilson

Florence Marryat

BORN: 9 July 1837, Brighton.
DIED: 27 October 1899, St. John's Wood, London.
DAUGHTER OF: Frederick Marryat and Catherine Shairp.
MARRIED: T. Ross Church, 1854; Francis Lean, 1890.

M., the sixth daughter of Captain Frederick Marryat, the celebrated writer of sea adventures, was a prolific popular novelist of Victorian England. Early in life she evinced an interest in writing and published her first novel, *Temper,* at age twenty-two. She scored a success five years later with *Love's Conflict,* written to distract herself while nursing her children who had come down with scarlet fever.

She married young, wedding Colonel T. Ross Church of the Madras Staff Corps when she was sixteen. Her extensive travels with him in India resulted in *"Gup": Sketches of Anglo-Indian Life and Character* (1868) ("Gup" is Hindustani for "gossip"). While emerging as a popular fiction writer of the 1870s, she also found time to publish her father's correspondence (the two-volume *Life and Letters of Captain Marryat,* 1872), to which she contributed a biographical portrait, and to edit the monthly periodical *London Society* (1872–1876).

In the 1880s and 1890s M. added drama and spiritualism to her growing interests, writing and starring in a comedy, *Her World* (1881), and producing among other such works *There Is No Death* (1891), a detailed account of seances and interviews with mediums. By 1890, when she married Colonel Francis Lean of the Royal Marine Light Infantry, there seemed no end to her accomplishments: she was an operatic singer, entertainer, public speaker, and manager of a school of journalism.

M. is remembered as a practitioner of the "sensation novel," a semi-Gothic literary form of the 1860s and 1870s featuring sinister family secrets and daring anti-heroines. Her novel *Love's Conflict* (1865) employs these elements in the story of Helen Du Broissart, a social climber and the daughter of an adulteress, who marries into the wealthy Treherne family only to be murdered by her former lover. Like her fellow sensationalists, Mary Elizabeth Braddon and Mrs. Henry Wood, M. both paid fascinated attention to the fallen woman and prudently punished her by the end of the story. M. treated another favorite character, the cynical aristocrat who skirts immorality, in *The Confessions of Gerald Estcourt* (1867), one of a string of popular works.

Many of M.'s almost sixty novels were widely read in the United States and translated into a number of languages, including Swedish and Russian. Her fluid style (such sentences as "The affections will be their own judges" came effortlessly to her narrators), sharp eye for social pretension, and travel writer's observation of place earned her a certain success with a readership avid for details of aristocratic houses and the *mésalliances* that occurred in them.

WORKS: Temper (1859). *Love's Conflict* (1865). *Woman Against Woman* (1865). *Too Good for Him* (1865). *For Ever and Ever: A Drama of Life* (1866). *The Confessions of Gerald Estcourt* (1867). *"Gup": Sketches of Indian Life and Character* (1868). *Nelly Brooke* (1868). *Veronique* (1869). *The Girls of Feversham* (1869). *Petronel* (1870). *The Prey of the Gods* (1871). *Her Lord and Master* (1871). *Life and Letters of Captain Marryat* (1872). *Mad Dumaresq* (1873). *Sybil's Friend, and How She Found Him* (1874). *No Intentions* (1874). *Open! Sesame!* (1875). *Fighting the Air* (1875). *My Own Child* (1876). *Hidden Chains* (1876). *Her Father's Name* (1876). *A Harvest of Wild Oats* (1877). *Christmas*

Leaves (1877). *Our Villas* (1877). *Written in Fire* (1878). *A Little Step-son* (1878). *Her World Against a Life* (1879). *A Star and a Heart* (1879). *Out of His Reckoning* (1879). *The Poison of Asps* (1876). *A Scarlet Sin* (1880). *The Root of All Evil* (1880). *The Fair-Haired Alda* (1880). *Her World* (1881). *With Cupid's Eyes* (1881). *My Sister the Actress* (1881). *Phyllida, a Life Drama* (1882). *How They Loved Him* (1882). *Facing the Footlights* (with Sir C.L. Young) (1882). *A Moment of Madness, and Other Stories* (1883). *Peeress and Player* (1883). *The Heir Presumptive* (1886). *The Master Passion* (1886). *Tom Tiddler's Ground* (1886). *Mount Eden* (1889). *The Nobler Sex* (1890). *A Fatal Silence* (1891). *Gentleman and Courtier* (1891). *The Risen Dead* (1891). *There is No Death* (1891). *How Like a Woman* (1892). *Parson Jones* (1893). *The Spirit World* (1894). *A Bankrupt Heart* (1894). *The Hampstead Mystery* (1894). *The Beautiful Soul* (1895). *The Heart of Jane Warner* (1895). *The Strange Transfiguration of Hannah Stubbs* (1896). *A Rational Marriage* (1899). *The Folly of Allison* (1899). *A Crown of Shame* (189?). *There Is No Death* (1920).

BIBLIOGRAPHY: *Athenaeum* (4 November 1899). Showalter, E. *A Literature of Their Own* (1977).

For articles in reference works, see: *Allibone*. *DNB*. Hays, F. *Women of the Day* (1885). Plarr, V. *Men and Women of the Time* (1895). *Times* (London) (28 October 1899).

Laura Hapke

Ngaio Marsh

BORN: 23 April 1899, Christchurch, New Zealand.
DIED: 18 February 1982, Christchurch, New Zealand.
DAUGHTER OF: Henry Edmund and Rose Elizabeth Seager Marsh

In the mid-thirties, when M. came on the literary scene with a detective novel, the appearance of a woman writer in the genre was not unusual. In the twenties, for instance, readers of the kind of fiction that stretched back to Poe and Wilkie Collins, Conan Doyle, and the rest had been introduced to Agatha Christie (*The Mysterious Affair at Styles*, 1920), the Lord Peter Wimsey of Dorothy L. Sayers (*Whose Body?*, 1923), the Albert Campion of Margery Allingham (*The Crime at Black Dudley*, 1929), and more. But soon, especially with *Death in a White Tie* (1938) and *Overture to Death* (1939), it was clear that M. was going to carve herself a special place in this field of popular literature.

While some critics (such as Edmund Wilson) attacked detective fiction, the public on the whole loved it, and they loved the work of M. Wilson might say authoritatively that M., even Sayers, padded books and mangled prose, but readers did not care, and they strongly resented Wilson describing her prose as "unappetizing sawdust" or her characters in *Overture to Death* as "faked-up English country people who are even more tedious than those of [Sayers'] *The Nine Tailors*." The fact is that M.'s prose is sub-literary, but with Christie in competition that will hardly be noticed. Moreover, though she does "fake-up" her characters at least her detectives (such as Inspector Alleyn) are ordinary, not blind, fat, foreign, or otherwise odd. Most of all, as with Christie, no one reads M. for the syntax or the psychology; people read her for the plot.

Though it is true that the plot may hinge on a gun being rigged up inside a piano to kill someone who pushes down a pedal, and though it is also true that *Death in a White Tie* has a story that can politely be described as intricate, such is M.'s talent that it works and reading the novels is a distinct pleasure. M. can do more than make a mere puzzle; she can make an entertaining detective story.

M. was not a scholar like Sayers (who translated Dante, *The Song of Roland*, and other literature) but she received a D. Litt. from the University of Canterbury (New Zealand) and was awarded first a C.B.E. (1948) and then a D.B.E. (1966), became a Fellow of The Royal Society of Arts, won various prizes (such as the coveted Grand Master Award from the Mystery Society of America, 1978), and retired to her native land having won the hearts of Britain, America, and the whole English-speaking world.

Born in New Zealand, she was educated there and went into the theatre as actress, producer, and writer. She was in London as an interior designer 1928–1932 and dabbled in writing. So well was her work received early on that she decided to write professionally. But "full-time" to a woman of her energy left plenty of time for wartime service with the Red Cross, post-war theatrical producing, lecturing, and many other activities. In her autobiography, *Black Beech and Honeydew* (1965), M. has a busy story to tell and in fact stresses not her detective story writing but her theatre work. She is the author not only of detective novels but of books on play production (1946 and 1960), on New Zealand (1942, 1960, 1964), some plays (often from her own novels), a couple of juvenile entertainments (*The Christmas Tree*, 1962, *A Unicorn for Christmas*, 1965), a television play (*Evil Liver*, 1975), etc.

It is, however, for thirty novels from *A Man Lay Dead* (1934) to *A Grave Mistake* (1978) that she is famous. Some, such as *Colour Scheme* (1943), do not really qualify as detective fiction, but most are centered on crimes solved by Inspector Roderick Alleyn, a sleuth who combines the aristocracy of such as Lord Peter Wimsey with the practicality featured in more recent "police procedurals." As Conan Doyle's Sherlock Holmes had his Dr. Watson, so Inspector Alleyn often has Inspector Fox or friend Nigel Bathgate; they act as foils. Neither they nor M.'s central character are as deliberately peculiar as Christie's Hercule Poirot or Miss Marple, or the strange detectives that other writers place in pathology labs, wheelchairs, and so on.

M. puts her solid Inspector Alleyn and other characters into settings that are often vivid, some coming from M.'s personal experience as actress, theatrical producer, or playwright (as in *Opening Night*, also published as *Night at the Vulcan*). If only a few of her detective stories give evidence of life as she knew it in New Zealand, it may be because her readership has always been primarily British and American.

M. once said that "intellectual New Zealand friends tactfully avoid all mention of my published work" and that it was pleasant for her to appear on British radio and be asked about detective story writing as "a tolerable form of reading by people whose opinion one valued." Maybe she fell, as she told *The Writer* (1977), into detective story writing pretty much as James Fenimore Cooper fell into writing (he read a book and announced he could do better than that), but that day in 1933 when M. put down her reading (she tactfully refuses to say whether it was Christie, Sayers, or another mistress of mystery) was a bright one for her and her coun-

trymen and for the readers everywhere of detective stories. Her first novel she constructed on the plan of the popular parlor game of the time called "Murder." For forty years afterwards she wrote essentially the same kind of book, and each one of them was welcomed and enjoyed by the public, so that (as the *Spectator* said on 4 May 1974) she has really "now reached that classic state where she is almost above criticism."

WORKS: *A Man Lay Dead* (1934). *Enter a Murderer* (1935). *Artists in Crime* (1936). (with H. Jellett) *Nursing Home Murder* (1936). *Vintage Murder* (1937). *Death in Ecstasy* (1937). *Death in a White Tie* (1938). *Overture to Death* (1939). *A Wreath for Rivera* (1940). *Death at the Bar* (1940). *Death of a Peer* (1940). *Death and the Dancing Footman* (1941). (with R.M. Burden) *New Zealand* (1942). *Colour Scheme* (1943). *Died in the Wool* (1945). *A Play Toward: A Note on Play Production* (1946). *Final Curtain* (1947). (with O.B. Howell) *Surfeit of Lampreys* (1950). *Night at the Vulcan* (1951). *Spinsters in Jeopardy* (1953). *Scales of Justice* (1955). *Death of a Fool* (1956). *Singing in the Shrouds* (1958). *False Scent* (1959 as play, 1961). *Play Production* (1960). *Perspectives: New Zealand and the Visual Arts* (1960). *The Christmas Tree* (1962). *Hand in Glove* (1962). *Dead Water* (1963). *New Zealand* (1964). *A Unicorn for Christmas* (1965). *Killer Dolphin* (1966). *Black Beech and Honeydew: An Autobiography* (1966). *The Clutch of Constables* (1969). *When in Rome* (1970). *Murder Sails at Midnight* (1972). *Tied Up in Tinsel* (1972). *Black as He's Painted* (1973). *Evil Liver* (1975). *LastDitch* (1977). *Grave Mistake* (1978). *Photo Finish* (1981). *Light Thickens* (1983).

BIBLIOGRAPHY: Bargainner, E.F. *Armchair Detective* (1978). Bargainner, E.F. *Ten Women of Mystery* (1981).

For articles in reference works, see: *CA. CLC. CN. TCA* and *SUP. TCC&MW. TCW.*

Leonard R. N. Ashley

Anne Marsh-Caldwell

BORN: 1791, Linley Wood, Staffordshire.
DIED: 5 October 1874, Linley Wood, Staffordshire.
DAUGHTER OF: James and Elizabeth Stamford Caldwell.
MARRIED: Arthur Cuthbert Marsh, 1817.
WROTE UNDER: Anne Marsh, Anne Marsh-Caldwell, Mrs. Marsh.

M., a mid-nineteenth-century domestic novelist, launched her literary career under the direc-

tion of Harriet Martineau. Daughter of a Staffordshire landholder and lawyer, wife of a failed banker, and mother of seven children, she had often written stories for her own amusement. When Martineau came to visit, M. read her "The Admiral's Daughter," a story of a young woman's adultery. After a fit of crying, Martineau expressed her amazement and admiration; after rereading the manuscript at home, she agreed to help M. find a publisher. The author's name was withheld from the public at the direction of her husband.

"A father of many daughters," explained Martineau, "did not wish their mother to be known as the author of what the world might consider second-rate novels." Although "The Admiral's Daughter" was a sensational success, M. continued to publish anonymously. Some reviewers knew her name; others simply referred to her as "the authoress." Very little is known about the circumstances of her life. Although some attributions are still in doubt, she seems to have produced over twenty novels, two books of stories, a history of the Protestant Reformation in France, and some translations from French. When her brother died in 1858, she succeeded to her family's property at Linley Wood and resumed the surname of Caldwell. She died on the estate where she was born, "lady of the manor, landholder, like her father," said the *Athenaeum* obituary.

M.'s best-known works were "The Admiral's Daughter" and *Emilia Wyndham.* As Margaret Oliphant observed, "Her first and most ambitious work is not addressed to her audience of young ladies." Its protagonist, a beautiful woman of Spanish descent, drifts into an illicit affair with her husband's friend. She is, therefore, a "worm," "an empty casket," a "worthless withered rose." Ridden with guilt, she can no longer feel comfortable in attending church or caring for their children. She must face a duel, her husband's fatal injury, and her lover's suicide. In contrition and love, she disguises herself as a nurse to attend her dying husband; dressed as a governess, she supervises her daughters' education. No book produced "more solemn silent showers than that heart-rending story," said one paper. While Harriet Martineau believed that "the singular magnificence of that tale was not likely to be surpassed," most readers preferred the pure and patient heroines of her later novels.

In *Emilia Wyndham,* for example, "the charm of the story is the character of its heroine—her trials—her patience—her fidelity." Emilia dreams "of Una and her lion—or Clarinda and her lance," but she must follow her mother's instructions and achieve heroism in "the heavy, wearying every-day evils of every-day actual life . . . combining patience, perseverance, endurance, gentleness, and disinterestedness." "A highminded, devoted girl," she does not err; she rescues others. M. dedicated the novel to William Wordsworth in recognition of "the fine influence of his poetry" and prefaced it with an essay on domestic realism. The indisputable quality of the novel, she argued, is "that it should convey the sense of reality—that the people we read of should be to us as actual beings and persons—that we should believe in them." Without overstepping the bounds of easy probability, the novelist should bring "causes and their consequences into obvious connexion."

Like other domestic novelists, M. sometimes criticized the way men abused their power within the family. In *Emilia Wyndham,* she took issue with Douglas Jerrold's characterization of the nagging wife in *Mrs. Caudle's Curtain Lectures,* a series of satirical sketches in *Punch.* "Any vulgar penny-a-liner can draw Mrs. Caudle, and publish her in a popular journal; and with such success that she shall become a by-word in families, and serve as an additional reason for that rudeness and incivility, that negligent contempt, with which too many Englishmen still think it their prerogative, as men and true-born Britons, to treat their wives." Her heroine must confront a tyrannical father who torments his daughter and wife. At the end of the novel, she asks, "Is it not just possible, think you, that *some* of the discomforts of married life—a *very* small proportion, of course—might be ameliorated, if husbands now and then received a lesson in their turn, and learned to correct themselves as well as their wives?" *Punch* retaliated with a parody.

At a time when fiction was still regarded with considerable suspicion, M. seemed safe. She "writes as an English gentlewoman should write; and what is better still, she writes what English gentlewomen should read," said James Lorimer, having commended her for avoiding metaphysical precipices, moral volcanos, and "the odours of the workhouse." She was, according to Oliphant, "orthodox and proper beyond criticism." Indeed, one conservative journal saw her popularity as evidence of the nation's moral integrity. But if she helped make fiction respectable, she also made it dull: she and her heroines were "a *wee, wee* bit prosy." Moreover, she was not able to sustain her early achievements. Writing in 1855, Oliphant concluded, "She has taken to making books rather than to telling stories, and has perceptibly had the printing-press and certain editorial censors before her." A modern literary historian theorizes that M.'s situation was typical of many other popular women writers of the time: working in isolation and drawing upon her own fantasies, she produced one book of considerable promise; entering the literary world and receiving suggestions from editors and readers, she lapsed into a formulaic fiction.

WORKS: *The Old Men's Tales: "The Deformed" and "The Admiral's Daughter"* (1834). *Tales of the Woods and Fields* (1836). *The Triumphs of Time* (1844). *Mount Sorel: Or, The Heiress of the de Veres* (1845). *Father Darcy* (1846). *Emilia Wyndham* (1846). *Norman's Bridge: Or, The Modern Midas* (1847). *The Protestant Reformation in France: Or, The History of the Hugonots* (1847). *Angela* (1848). *Mordaunt Hall: Or, A September Night* (1849). *Tales of the First French Revolution* (1849). *Lettice Arnold* (1850). *The Wilmingtons* (1850). *Ravenscliffe* (1851). *Time the Avenger* (1851). *Castle Avon* (1852). *The Longwoods of the*

Grange (1853). *Aubrey* (1854). *The Heiress of Houghton: Or, The Mother's Secret* (1855). *Woman's Devotion* (1855). *Margaret and Her Bridesmaids* (1856). *The Rose of Ashurst* (1857). *Mr. and Mrs. Ashton* (1860). *The Ladies of Lovel-Leigh* (1862). *Chronicles of Dartmoor* (1866). *Lords and Ladies* (1866).

BIBLIOGRAPHY: Colby, V. *Yesterday's Woman: Domestic Realism in the English Novel* (1974).

Cruse, A. *The Victorians and Their Reading* (1936). Martineau, H. *Autobiography* (1877). Mitchell, S. *The Fallen Angel: Chastity, Class and Women's Reading, 1835–1880* (1981).

For articles in reference works, see: *Allibone.* Boase. *CBEL. DNB. NCBEL. VB.*

Robin Sheets

Harriet Martineau

BORN: 12 June 1802, Norwich.
DIED: 27 June 1876, Birmingham.
DAUGHTER OF: Thomas and Elizabeth Rankin Martineau.

The study of M.'s life affords the student of nineteenth-century English and American society a view not only of an exceptional woman but of the transformations taking place during this era in politics, views of child-rearing and education, and the strain inherent in a woman's life if that woman happens to defy convention by following a calling beyond her designated sphere. Although M.'s discerning eye and prolific ease with the written word earned her the respectful title of "The first sociologist," her accomplishments were at times threatened by debilitating disease, conflicting feelings regarding family responsibilities, and the volatile reaction of her readers on the many controversial issues she deigned to explore and popularize in her fifty-year literary career.

M. was described as a delicate and difficult child, the latter adjective a result perhaps of her mother's seeming indifference to her sixth child. M.'s experience, however, was like that of many in the early 1800s when scrupulous attention was paid material and educational needs while emotional and nurturing components were virtually ignored. Early bouts with digestive and nervous disorders and the partial loss of hearing justify the term "delicate."

Rather than letting her past embitter or impede her personal development as an adult, M. used her own childhood experiences (described in detail in *Household Education* [1849] and *Autobiography with Memorials by Maria Weston Chapman* [1877]), as a catalyst for a lengthy and impassioned articulation of the deficiences of early nineteenth-century beliefs on children and childhood education; in so doing, M. became an early popularizer of the theories of John Locke and David Hartley. Other examples of M.'s use of personal experience as a basis for broad social texts are *Life in the Sickroom* (1844), a description of invalidism, common of women in the nine-

teenth century, a book which also reads like a home-care nursing manual, and *Our Farm of Two Acres* (1865), which describes M.'s brief venture into rural living.

Much of M.'s writing appeared in journals and newspapers such as the *Edinburgh Review, Westminster Review, National Anti-Slavery Standard*, and, most especially, the *Monthly Repository*. In 1864 her essays published in the *Daily News* were compiled into a book, *Biographical Sketches*, many of which are formal obituaries of historical personages of her time. These miniature biographies eulogize such women as Amelia Opie, Charlotte Brontë, Mrs. Wordworth, and Mrs. Marcet, and, as such, offer contemporary readers historical and biographical information regarding other women, known and unknown, of this era.

M.'s first pieces, "Female Writers on Practical Divinity" and "On Female Education," published in 1827 and 1823, reflect a constant theme of her work, that is, that any discrepancy in women and men's capabilities was due to a disparity in education, and although M. believes that educating women would certainly enhance women's status in their domestic sphere, she in no way believed that women should be relegated to that area.

Women were indeed an important subject in M.'s most noted work, *Society in America* (1837). Her keen observations regarding the status of women in a nation professing freedom of opportunity for all was certainly one of the main factors in the mixed reaction of her readership in both countries. *Society in America* as well as *Retrospect of Western Travel* (1838), a more readable tract of her observations during her two-year visit to America, and *How to Observe: Morals and Manners* (1838) are considered some of the earliest instances of the science of comparative sociology, and as such won her the distinction of innovator in a field previously uncharted. Besides remaining one of the best sources of descriptive information regarding the early years of the American republic, *Society in America* is also an honest chronicle of one woman's discovery of the discrepancies between political theory and the actualities of people's lives within any social system.

M.'s reputation as a writer, which preceded her coming to America in 1834, was based principally on her *Illustrations of Political Economy*. In this series, written between 1832 and 1834, she defined and illustrated, in rather stilted story form, the unfolding principles of *laissez-faire* capitalism and the concepts of progress and opportunity based upon ability rather than ancestry. These popular works were originally written as separate booklets and were directed specifically at the working class in England, though they were read widely by all. Her idealistic enthusiasm regarding the mutually beneficial relationship possible between labor and capital interests was based in part on her belief that if all members of such a system understood the principles of political economy, corruption within the system was less apt to occur.

M. was first and foremost a natural journalist, never editing or changing her thoughts once they were committed to the page. This resulted in a prolific legacy (over fifty books and pamphlets) on a surprising range of subjects and in many styles; she is considered at her best with social descriptions and at her worst with fictional accounts. *The Hour and the Man* (1841), an example of her fiction, recreates the life of a black Haitian revolutionary and that nation's struggle for freedom from white domination. Fiction also offered a "respite" from her usual journalistic style, said M., in describing *Deerbrook* (1839), a three-volume love story.

People responded to the mature M. in extremes, from intense dislike, as was the case with George Eliot, to the devoted admiration of Maria Weston Chapman, her first biographer. Her passionate dual personality and frankness caused the loss of many friendships throughout the years, as did her association with such controversial issues as abolition, women's rights, and nontraditional forms of healing. M. remained, however, a teacher in the broadest sense of the word, an activist early called to share her observations and experiences with others through the written word. She never married but rather developed into a happily independent woman, consumed not by relationships but by her work.

WORKS: *Devotional Exercises* (1823). *Illustrations of Political Economy* (1832–1834). *Society in America* (1837). *How to Observe; Morals and Manners* (1838). *Retrospect of Western Travel* (1838). *Deerbrook* (1839). *The Hour and the Man* (1841). *Life in the Sickroom* (1844). *Household Education* (1849). *Biographical Sketches* (1864). *Our Farm of Two Acres* (1865). *Autobiography with Memorials by Maria Weston Chapman* (1877). *Harriet Martineau's Letters to Fanny Wedgewood*, ed. E. Arbuckle (1983). *Harriet Martineau on Women*, ed. G.G. Yates (1984).

BIBLIOGRAPHY: Bosenquet, T. *Harriet Martineau: An Essay in Comprehension* (1927). David, D. *Intellectual Women and Victorian Patriarchy: Harriet Martineau, Elizabeth Barrett Browning, and George Eliot* (1987). Miller, F.B. *Harriet Martineau* (1884). Neville, J. *Harriet Martineau* (1943). Pichanick, V., ed. *Harriet Martineau: The Woman and Her Work* (1980). Sanders, V. *Reason Over Passion: Harriet Martineau and the Novel* (1986). Thomas, G. *Harriet Martineau* (1985). Webb, R.K. *Harriet Martineau: A Radical Victorian* (1960). Weiner, G. *Feminist Theorists*, ed. D. Spender (1983). Wheatley, V. *The Life and Work of Harriet Martineau* (1957).

For articles in reference works, see: *Allibone* and *SUP. BA19C. Cassell. Chambers, DLB. Junior Book of Authors. Moulton's. NCHEL. OCEL. Yesterday's Authors.*

Other references: Colson, P. *Victorian Portraits* (1932). Dentler, R. *Midcontinent American Studies Journal* (1962). Horne, R.H. *A New Spirit of Age* (1844). Lever, T. *Brontë Society Transactions* (1974). Lohrli, A. *SSF* (1983). Mineka, F.E. *The Dissidence of Dissent: "The Monthly Repository,"* 1806–1838 (1944). Morley, J. *Critical Miscellanies* (1909). Myers, M. *Women's Autobiography: Essays in Criticism*, ed. E.C. Jelinek (1980). Pichanick, V. *Women's Studies* (1977). Richardson, B. *PLL* (1984).

V. Kim Duckett

Charlotte Mew

BORN: 15 November 1869, London.
DIED: 24 March 1928, London.
DAUGHTER OF: Frederick Mew and Anna Kendall Mew.

The life of M. lacked outward event, but her inner life possessed enormously complex vitality and intensity of feeling. Incompatible emotions warred within her, as the *personae* in her writings reveal. Whenever sexual desire arises, religious or moral renunciation blocks its expression. Obsession with death dominated everything she wrote. For none of her deepest longings could she find satisfying outlets in her life; she could only find them in her writing. Erotic love, religion, and death are the three great irreconcilable themes which create almost unbearable tensions in her poetry and prose. Although her output is quantitatively small—sixty-eight poems, eighteen stories and thirteen essays—it is of the highest quality, utterly genuine and moving, deserving the praise it won from writers and critics in her lifetime and after. If she had written nothing but the seventeen poems of *The Farmer's Bride,* Louis Untermeyer commented, they "would have been sufficient to rank her among the most distinct and intense" of modern poets.

The bare facts of M.'s biography do little to explain her accomplishments. Her father, Frederick Mew, an architect, married his partner's daughter: of their seven children, two died in infancy, one died at the age of five and two finished their lives in mental institutions. M. grew close to her remaining sister, Anne, four years her junior. Believing their siblings' insanity to be hereditary, they both pledged not to marry lest their offspring inherit the family madness. This pledge must have been costly to M., for her writing shows an appreciation and enjoyment of children and also a profound intuition of the human need for sexual intimacy. Her inner religious standards, high and severe, must, however, ultimately account for her constricted life.

M. began writing short stories in the 1890s. She published the first of these, "Passed," in *The Yellow Book* in 1894 and between 1900 and 1912 also published some poetry. In 1913 she met the novelist May Sinclair, who admired and encouraged her work, and Alida Monro, wife of Harold Monro, owner of the Poetry Bookshop and publisher of her collection, *The Farmer's Bride* (1916). The volume received discriminating critical notice and made a strong impression on such writers as Virginia Woolf, Hugh Walpole, the poet laureate Robert Bridges, and especially on Thomas Hardy, who invited M. to visit him at Max Gate. Hardy was the one writer who, of all her contemporaries, she most admired, and to whose work her own is most often compared.

M.'s mother and sister both became ill early in the 1920s and, as caring for them absorbed all her energies, she wrote very little from then on. Their financial situation was desperate until 1922 when Hardy, John Masefield, and Walter de la Mare procured for M. a Civil List pension of £75 a year. Her mother died in 1923 and her sister in 1927. In 1928, M. entered a nursing home for treatment of neurasthenia and there, apparently fearing that she, too, was losing her mind, committed suicide by drinking half a bottle of Lysol.

Death following renounced or thwarted love is a predominant motif in all her work. Sometimes religious principle causes the renunciation, as in the stories "An Open Door" and "In the Curé's Garden." Sometimes, as in the stories "The China Bowl," "A Wedding Day," and "White World," parental love jealously opposes marital love; only death brings resolution. Missed opportunity is an abiding theme, as in "Passed" and "The Bridegroom's Friend." Even in the fairy tale "The Smile," the struggling heroine dies as she reaches the goddess of happiness, for the goddess happened not to be watching the struggle and so could not reward it, a paradigm of M.'s life.

Irreconcilable conflict between sexual desire and spiritual aspiration is also a principal theme of her poems, which are excellently crafted, economical in language, and usually in the form of rhymed odes. Often the poem is an interior monologue expressing the intense subjectivity of a *persona* clearly not the poet herself. These *personae* are often drawn from the fishing villages of England or France, since M. was deeply attracted to French literature and to Catholic France, as is seen in the essay "Notes in a Brittany Convent" and the poem "The Little Portress (St. Gilda de Rhuys)." Although Christian in her thinking, she never became Roman Catholic.

Rural settings also enabled her to express her profound love of the natural world, which she described in her essay, "A Country Book," and the long poem "Madeleine in Church," the interior monologue of a prostitute, a modern Mary Magdalen, expresses M.'s doubts concerning God's forgiveness and eternal life. The motif of "really seeing," of the intense look, recurs frequently in M.'s work. The eyes of two beings meet in passionate contact to express boundless emotions beyond speech, as in "Ken," a poignant poem about an idiot-madman taken to an institution. The intense look also often signals falling in love, as in "The Fête," the monologue of an enamoured adolescent boy who feels "half-hidden, white unrest" watching a circus performer.

Sexual love is characteristically linked to and countermanded by its inevitable contrary, religious feeling. Sexual love is by no means always the debased activity of a Madeleine or a Pécheresse. Often it is a sublime ideal of union precluded by death, as in the moving poem, "In Nunhead Cemetery." This interior monologue is spoken by a male *persona*, a husband to a dead wife, but, as Nunhead Cemetery is the actual burial place of M.'s brother Henry, the emotions in it may be seen as transmutations of her own. Here, as often in M., grief is mixed with and heightened by sexual longing put in terms of burning. Burning suggests flames, the color red, and the red rose, all of which she uses with the traditional symbolism of sexual passion, as in "The Quiet House," a poem which she described as "perhaps the most subjective to me" of the poems in *The Farmer's Bride.* The female *persona*, a daughter kept home to care for an ailing father, muses: "When you are burned quite through you die./ Red is the strangest pain to bear;/ . . . A rose can stab you across the street/ Deeper than any knife:/ And the crimson haunts you everywhere—"

M. once said of herself: "I have a scarlet soul." Here the *persona* continues: "I think that my soul is red/ Like the soul of a sword or a scarlet flower:/ But when these are dead/ They have had their hour./ I shall have had mine, too,/ For from head to feet,/ I am burned and stabbed half through,/ And the pain is deadly sweet." The oxymoron of "deadly sweet pain" sums up M.'s being. The poem's final words convey her strange premonitory self-understanding and read almost as an epitaph:" . . . No one for me—I think it is myself I go to meet;/ I do not care; some day I *shall* not think; I shall not *be*!"

WORKS: *The Farmer's Bride* (1916). *Saturday Market* (1921). *The Rambling Sailor* (1929). *Collected Poems* (1953). *Collected Poems and Prose*, ed. V. Warner (1981).

BIBLIOGRAPHY: Meynell, V., ed. *Friends of a Lifetime: Letters to Sydney Carlyle Cockerell* (1940).

Monro, A. "Charlotte Mew—A Memoir." *Collected Poems of Charlotte Mew* (1953). Monroe, H. *Some Contemporary Poets* (1920). Moore, V. *Distinguished Women Writers* (1934). Schmidt, M. *A Reader's Guide to Fifty Modern British Poets* (1979). Swinnerton, F. *The Georgian Literary Scene, 1910 - 1935: A Panorama* (1950). Untermeyer, L. *Modern British Poetry* (1962). Warner, V. Introduction to *Charlotte Mew: Collected Poems and Prose* (1981). Williams-Ellis, A., *An Anatomy of Poetry* (1922).

For articles in reference works, see: *CP. TCA. TCLC.*

Other references: *Bookman* (May 1928). *Bulletin of the New York Public Library* (September 1970 and September 1971). *Bulletin of Research in the Humanities* (Winter 1978). *Encounter* (June 1954). *Nation* (8 July 1916). *NYTBR* (19 June 1921).

Jane Augustine

Alice Meynell

BORN: 11 October 1847, Barnes.
DIED: 17 November 1922, London.
DAUGHTER OF: Christiana Weller and Thomas James Thompson.
MARRIED: Wilfred Meynell, 1877.
WROTE UNDER: A.C. Thompson, Alice Meynell.

Though M.'s literary output also included essays, art history, travel writing, literary criticism, translations, anthologies, and editorial work, it was primarily her poetry that brought M. fame in her day. A prominent late Victorian and mid-Georgian writer, her reputation, along with that of Christina Rossetti, whose aesthetic and religious interests she generally shares, suffered eclipse in the twentieth century. Critical admiration for her restrained, stylistically simple, and rhythmically disciplined verse is now returning, and her oeuvre is ripe for reevaluation.

In recent years feminist literary critics have become increasingly drawn to the story of M.'s life as an example of an "early superwoman" who successfully fused a marriage of equal partners with a family (seven living children) and career while working on women's issues such as suffrage and peace. A woman of passionate attachments to male mentors—most prominently, a Father Dignam (her early spiritual guide), Francis Thompson, Coventry Patmore, and George Meredith—she managed to maintain her marriage, busy social life, and maternal obligations while turning out a large and varied body of writing.

The daughter of independently wealthy, culturally enlightened parents, M. was educated by daily tutorials and a life lived, in alternate seasons, in northern Italy and England. Brought up among adults and books, she wrote poems as early as seven years old and resolved to be a poet. Her famous protest, written in her diary at age eighteen, signals her seriousness of purpose: "Of all the crying evils in the depraved earth . . . the greatest, judged by all the laws of God and humanity, is the miserable selfishness of men that keeps women from work." But her diaries also reveal her struggle to balance her dedication to work with an equal interest in an active life among people.

Converting to Catholicism at the age of twenty, she caught the eye of Aubrey de Vere, and, through his interest, of Patmore, Tennyson, and Henry King, who admired her work. *Preludes* (1875), her first book of poems, earned praise from John Ruskin, Christina Rossetti, George Eliot, and others, placing her as a late-Romantic of notable stylistic economy. Her poetic themes in this first volume foreshadow her consistent poetic interests throughout her life: love, time, process, religious faith, poetic inspiration, and nature.

Her marriage to Wilfred Meynell in 1877 presages the shift in her attention from poetry to journalism, piece work against deadlines that she evidently found most compatible with raising seven children. The Meynells established and co-edited the short-lived *Pen: A Journal of Literature* (1880); in 1881 her husband became owner and editor of *The Weekly Register*, a stable source of income for the next eighteen years. In addition, he founded *Merry England*, a literary magazine. M.

wrote for these journals as well as for *The Spectator, The Saturday Review, The Scots* (later, *The
National*), *The Observer, The Tablet,* and
The Pall Mall Gazette. Turning to prose writing
in the 1880s and 1890s, she suspended poetry
publishing until 1896.

When her husband sold *The Weekly Register*
in 1899, M. began to travel again, lecturing across
the United States in 1901-1902, the date of her
Later Poems. She remained an active writer for
the rest of her life. Between 1903 and 1911 her
literary output included brief essays on Wordsworth, Tennyson, Robert and Elizabeth Barrett
Browning, Shelley, Keats, Herrick, Coleridge,
Cowper, Arnold, Christina Rossetti, Jean Ingelow,
and Blake for Blackie's Red Letter Library. *Poems*
(1913) contained reissued poems as well as several
new ones. In spite of her busy family life, she
published four books of poetry during World War
I. Though in failing health, she wrote twenty-five
new poems in the last three years of her life, dying
in 1922 at the end of a long and productive literary, social, and family life.

Modern critics fault M.'s essays for humor-
lessness, overprecious satirical slant, and impressionistic and underdeveloped ideas. Most of her
essays, composed to fit the format of the editorial
column, lack elaborately reasoned arguments. Yet
it was just these qualities that earned her the
praise of contemporaries as one of the first successful female literary critics and popular essay-
ists, one who never overwrote and who left room
for the reader's interpretation.

The key to both her life and art lies in the
word "discipline." Among her elegant, austere lyrics, her religious poems have earned special attention for their highly controlled expression of
moral, rather than mystical, religious consciousness and their lack of sentimentality. Her poetic
ideas about religion emphasize a life of renunciation and understated stoicism, and she was regarded as one of England's most important
Roman Catholic poets of her day.

M.'s important ties to many of the famous
writers of her period occasion her biographer's
description of her as a woman paradoxically surrounded by friends and admirers, and yet solitary
at the core. Contemporary accounts suggest that
no one in her circle really felt he or she knew M.
She was somewhat of an enigma to those closest
to her, both welcoming relationships and protecting her privacy. In the midst of an unusually rich
and interesting private life among gifted writers,
she produced her highly disciplined poems and
economical essays that shield as much as they
reveal.

WORKS: (as A.C. Thompson) *Preludes* (1875).
The Poor Sisters of Nazareth (1889). (with F.W.
Farrar) *William Holman Hunt, His Life and Work*
(1893). *Poems* (1893, 1896). *The Rhythm of Life
and Other Essays* (1893, 1896). (trans.) *Lourdes:
Yesterday, To-Day and To-Morrow,* by D. Barbe
(1894). *The Colour of Life and Other Essays on
Things Seen and Heard* (1896). *Other Poems*
(1896). *The Children* (1897). *London Impressions*
(1898). *The Spirit of Place and Other Essays* (1899).
John Ruskin (1900). (trans.) *The Madonna,* by
A. Venturi (1901). *Later Poems* (1902). *Children of
the Old Masters: Italian School* (1903). (trans.) *The
Nun,* by R. Bazin (1908). *Ceres' Runaway and Other
Essays* (1909). *Mary, the Mother of Jesus* (1912,
1923). *Childhood* (1913). *Poems* (1913). *Essays*
(1914). *The Shepherdess and Other Verses* (1914).
(trans.) *Pastoral Letter of His Eminence Cardinal
Mercier, Archbishop of Malines, Primate of Bel-
gium, Christmas* (1914). *Ten Poems* (1915). *Poems
on the War* (1916). *Hearts of Controversy* (1917). *A
Father of Women and Other Poems* (1917). *The
Second Person Singular and Other Essays* (1921).
The Last Poems of Alice Meynell (1923). *The Poems
of Alice Meynell,* Complete Edition (1923). *Essays of
To-day and Yesterday* (1926). *Wayfaring* (1929).
Selected Poems of Alice Meynell, ed. F. Meynell
(1930). *The Poems of Alice Meynell,* ed. F. Page
(1940). *The Poems of Alice Meynell, 1847-1923,*
Centenary Edition, ed. F. Meynell (1947, 1955).
Alice Meynell: Prose and Poetry, Centenary Edition,
ed. F. Page, V. Meynell, O. Sowerby, and F. Meynell
(1947). *The Wares of Autolycus: Selected Literary
Essays,* ed. P.M. Fraser (1965).

BIBLIOGRAPHY: Badeni, J. *The Slender Tree: A
Life of Alice Meynell* (1981). Connolly, T.L., ed.
Alice Meynell Centenary Tribute, 1847-1947 (1947).
*The Letters of George Meredith to Alice Meynell,
1896-1907,* ed. E. Meynell (1923). Meynell, V. *Alice
Meynell: A Memoir* (1929). Meynell, F. *Alice Meynell, 1847-1922: Catalogue of the Centenary Exhibition of Books, Manuscripts, Letters and Portraits*
(1947). Meynell, V. *Francis Thompson and Wilfred
Meynell, A Memoir* (1952). Tuell, A.K. *Mrs. Meynell
and Her Literary Generation* (1925).

For articles in reference works, see: *DLB.*

Other references: Bluen, H. *Aryan Path* (May
1966). Fairchild, H.N. *Religious Trends in English
Poetry* (1962). Meynell, F. *My Lives* (1971).
Moore, V. *Distinguished Women Writers* (1934).
Schlack, B.A. *Women's Studies* (1980).

Rhoda Flaxman

Grace Sherrington Mildmay

BORN: 1553, Laycock Abbey, Wiltshire.
DIED: July 1620, Apethorpe, Northampton-
shire.
DAUGHTER OF: Sir Henry and Lady Sher-
rington.
MARRIED: Sir Anthony Mildmay, 1567.

According to Retha Warnicke, only three
journals kept by Elizabethan women survive, and
the longest of these journals is M.'s. M. began
keeping the journal when she was about seventeen, three years after her marriage to Anthony
Mildmay, and continued to keep it until a few
years before she died at age sixty-seven. In it she
recorded meditations, advice, and autobiography.

The autobiographical sections suggest M.'s
compliant nature. One of three daughters, M. was
reared by her mother and by a much-loved governess, Mrs. Hamblyn. As in many Renaissance
households, her mother believed in education by
beating and "never so much as for lying." M. herself
felt that corporal punishment was a sign of love
and concern that led her to value the truth for its
own sake. Under this tutelage M. learned the usual
Elizabethan accomplishments: needlework, the
lute, household management, and good behavior. In
her journal M. has much to say on this last topic,
explaining how she was taught that a woman
should always be quiet, modest, and industrious.

Her father was a Protestant (he had been
associated with Thomas, Baron Seymour of Sudeley, who served as Edward VI's Lord High Admiral and wooed Elizabeth), and as a consequence of
his faith his daughters were taught to be devout—
and literate—Anglicans. This circumstance has
two consequences for M.'s work. First of all, because M. was taught to read and write, so that she
could study her Bible, she was predisposed to
value education, including education for women.
Second, she concentrated on her religious faith in
her journal.

M.'s marriage, a very good match, was arranged, and her husband's interests included hunting and war; nor was he intellectually negligible, if
we can judge from a successful speech he made at
Peterhouse, Cambridge, during Queen Elizabeth's

visit in 1564. Like M., her husband came from a
Protestant family that valued education; his father
had served as Chancellor of the Exchequer under
Elizabeth and founded the Puritan Emmanuel College, Cambridge. Nevertheless, Sir Anthony was
unwilling to marry until his father assured him of
financial support. The early years of M.'s marriage
were not happy ones; the couple had little money,
and Sir Anthony was often away on diplomatic
business. When he was home, he often seems to
have been harsh. During these years, M., prompted
both by her respect for her father-in-law and by her
education in obedience, "could not find it in [her]
heart to challenge him for the worst worde or deede
which ever he offered [her] in all his lyfe." Instead
she withdrew into herself, studying religious books,
writing down household remedies and recipes, or
educating her one child, Mary. As the years passed,
M.'s life grew happier. Her husband's affection for
her increased, their financial position improved,
and her daughter made a brilliant marriage to Sir
Francis Fane, later the Earl of Westmorland. M.
concerned herself more and more with her beloved
grandchildren as well as with the household and
her charitable works.

The journal gives details of M.'s life, but her
writing also suggests that she combined spiritual
and practical interests. The bulk of her journal is a
series of Protestant meditations, interrrupted
from time to time by her notes on her life. In
addition to the journal, M. collected cures and
recipes; some occur in her household books and
others were copied after her death by her daughter. The picture M.'s writing presents is one of a
quiet, devout, and useful life.

WORKS: *Lady Grace Mildmay's Journal and Papers*
(1570-1617, unpublished), Northampton Public Library.

BIBLIOGRAPHY: Bush, D. *English Literature in
the Earlier Seventeenth Century, 1600-1660* (1962).
Warnicke, R. *Women of the English Renaissance
and Reformation* (1983). Weigall, R. *Quarterly Review*, (1911).

Frances Teague

Harriet Hardy Taylor Mill

BORN: 8 October 1807, London.
DIED: 3 November 1858, Avignon, France.
DAUGHTER OF: Thomas and Harriet Hurst
Hardy.
MARRIED: John Taylor, 1826; John Stuart
Mill, 1851.

M. was an intellectual woman who spent her
life energies encouraging a man but who herself
has all but disappeared from history. Born into a
wealthy, contentious London doctor's family, she
had little formal education and married a London
druggist when she was eighteen. Knowledge of

the young M. is sketchy since her life before John Stuart Mill has not been of importance to scholars. Her first husband was well-to-do and of a liberal (radical) persuasion and attended the Unitarian South Place Chapel, where her friend William Johnson Fox, the preacher, became the trustee of the Flower sisters, Eliza and Sarah, in 1829, with Eliza ultimately becoming his housekeeper and common-law wife. The resultant scandal forced Fox to spend less time in the church and to put more effort into his political and journalistic endeavors. He was the owner and editor of the *Monthly Repository*, the Unitarian radical journal; the intellectual coterie surrounding that journal was the center of M.'s life before and for several years after she met John Mill.

M. was twenty-three when Fox brought Mill to dinner at the Taylors' house in 1830; she had been married four years and had two sons. Many stories are told of that first meeing (including reminiscences by Harriet Martineau, also a dinner guest that night), but it is certain that the two were drawn to each other.

M. was already writing poetry after her last child, Helen, was born in 1831, and soon her contributions—both poetry and reviews—began appearing in the *Monthly Repository*. Her most prolific year was 1832; after that time she published little under her name. Since her relation with Mill was becoming intense, she and Taylor agreed to a trial separation in 1833; they agreed at the end of six months that she would both continue to live with Taylor and keep on seeing Mill. Mill and M. continued this intellectual romantic arrangement for nearly 20 years, until Taylor's death (1849); two years later they were married. M. always insisted that Mill was her *Seelefreund* (soul-mate), implying that they were never physical lovers. For Victorian Britishers this arrangement was certainly possible, although the couple's outward behavior even before marriage—they worked together, traveled abroad together, wrote daily love letters when apart, dined together, and appeared socially together—did little to keep scandal from appearing.

From the beginning M. spent her best energies on Mill's intellectual projects, and many of his works are co-produced with her. He acknowledges her influence and her help, detailing the kind of editorial and compositional assistance she made—sometimes her ideas, sometimes her wording, sometimes whole sentences—but she has never been given co-authorship credit for *On Liberty,* the *Autobiography*, or any other of Mill's works. Only "The Enfranchisement of Women," first published in 1851, was acknowledged to be in fact written by M. There are differences between M.'s ideas and Mill's. M. was always much less tentative than Mill, more certain, in some ways more rational. A correspondence exists, for example,

between Mill and Auguste Comte in which Mill takes Comte to task for his stand against women's rights. But in the ensuing discussion, Mill is almost apologetic in his position. M., in going over this series with him in 1844, castigates him for this tendency, and Mill determines, as a result, not to publish the letters at all.

Two early pieces, one by Mill and one by M. (first published in 1951), suggest more specific differences. M. argues that there should be no marriage laws at all, that a woman should simply take responsibility for her own children, thus removing the child custody problem from divorce issues. Mill calls for a postponement of childbearing so that couples could determine if their choice of a mate was a good one. In the case of the divorce of parents with children, Mill advocated a kind of joint custody within a supportive community. A second and more striking difference is found in their attitude toward increased education for women. For M., women should be well educated so that all occupations will be open to them, but her husband cautiously argued that woman's education had the goal of creating a better wife and mother, that only in exceptional cases (single women, widows) should women enter the labor force at all. M. wanted education for its own sake for women; he wanted women's education for men.

M. continued to do her own intellectual work through Mill even after they were married. She suggested that he write on religion (*Three Essays on Religion*), and she wrote a long outline of what should be in that work. She suggested and then added the chapter "On the Probable Future of the Labouring Classes" in *Political Economy*, a chapter emphasizing the domestic slavery of women and stressing working women's need to be freed from that double burden. *On Liberty* was evidently a joint venture from its very conception, with M. writing, revising, and suggesting throughout its creation. The *Autobiography*, not published until many years later (1873), was actually written and revised while M. was still alive (during 1853-54); many conversations and letters attest to the detailed care that she gave to that work.

On Liberty, Mill's most famous and enduring work, is also the one on which M. did the most work; according to Mill, it should be considered a "joint production," since this essay packed all the "intellectual pemican" that the couple thought liberal thinkers might need for posterity. The concept of political freedom was translated into individual, everyday situations, and the basic tenet of "liberal conservatism" was enunciated: the liberty of an individual can only be interfered with if it constitutes a danger to society or to other individuals; otherwise the individual is sovereign. The book is a balanced, rational argument against tyranny. Great stress was placed on women and children as the two groups most tyrannized and least protected by law. The essay strongly advocates a system of universal education for all children (both boys and girls) to be required and provided by the parents, the State only paying the costs for those who cannot afford it. Examinations should be confined to factual matters, and great care must be exercised to assure that the State's bias on politics and religion not be determining factors.

Although the couple had continued to work on the essay for several years, refining concepts, changing words or sentences, it had not yet been completed to their satisfaction at the time of M.'s death. After that time, Mill could not bring himself to make any further changes and published it as it was as a kind of memorial. In the next few years Mill wrote *The Subjection of Women*, attributing most of the inspiration and ideas of the essay to M. (although he did not publish it until 1869, when, he said, the climate of opinion was more favorable). Like many women, M.'s creative and intellectual efforts were spent in assisting a man. Although Mill did not hesitate to give her credit, for over a century a doubting and suspicious world has refused to take his tributes seriously.

WORKS: "On Marriage and Divorce" (1832). "The Enfranchisement of Women" (1851). Joint authorship, with J. S. Mill, of *Principles of Political Economy* (1848); *On Liberty* (1859); *The Autobiography* (1873); *Letters*, first published in Hayek (1951).

BIBLIOGRAPHY: Hayek, F.A. *John Stuart Mill and Harriet Taylor: Their Friendship and Subsequent Marriage* (1951). Himmelfarb, G. *On Liberty and Liberalism* (1974). Kamm, J. *John Stuart Mill in Love* (1977). Mill, J.S. and H. *Essays on Sex Equality*, ed. A. Rossi (1970). Pugh, E.L. *Canadian J. of History* (1978). Spender, D. *Women of Ideas* (1983).

Margaret McFadden

Naomi Mitchison

BORN: 1 November 1897, Edinburgh.
DAUGHTER OF: John Scott and Kathleen (Trotter) Haldane.
MARRIED: Gilbert Richard Mitchison, 1916.
WRITES UNDER: Naomi Mitchison, Naomi Margaret Mitchison, Naomi Haldane Mitchison.

Since the 1920s M. has been writing on an astonishing variety of subjects—from classical antiquity to contemporary African politics, from birth control to Byzantine historiography, from the oil and herring industries in Scotland to her own girlhood in the Edwardian Age. A prolific professional author known for her crystalline expository prose, M. is also recognized in Great Britain as a playwright, a poet, and, perhaps especially, as a novelist with a flair for historical fiction.

M. has related the most important incidents of her life in a series of autobiographies. These convey a sense of life lived to the fullest: in them, she recalls Edwardian grandmothers and country places, describes the health hazards of serving as a volunteer nurse during World War I, analyzes her life as the young wife of a Labour Party member of Parliament, narrates the circumstances of her research in Botswana, remembers her friendships with such people as Aldous Huxley, W.H. Auden, and D.H. Lawrence, characterizes both the Socialists and the Nazis she met in Vienna in the 1930s, evokes images of herself watching the natives in Beirut, Karachi, the Kalahari, Arkansas, and the Soviet Union, and gives an account of her participation in local Scottish political life after World War II as a member of the Argyll County Council. Many of these experiences found their way into book-length essays, novels, and books for children.

M.'s evident thirst for an understanding of human life in the twentieth century led her to engage in a sustained study of African history and cultures; her research and personal observations culminated in one of the best general introductions to the continent ever written (*The Africans*, 1970) as well as in a number of local histories and folklore anthologies.

Over the long course of her career as a writer, M. also masterminded a number of literary projects aimed at synthesizing up-to-date reports on the current state of human knowledge; these— (for example, *An Outline for Boys and Girls* and *What the Human Race Is Up To*)—included many contributions by such brilliant thinkers as J.B.S. Haldane (her brother) and W.H. Auden. "Our ideas . . . are . . . on the move," wrote M. by way of introduction to her encyclopedic *What the Human Race is Coming To*. A progressive at heart, M. devoted her long writing career to the building of bridges—bridges between Western and Third-World cultures, between the elder and the younger generations, between scientists and humanists, between businesses and community interests.

In recognition of her nearly two decades of service and friendship, the Bakgatla tribe of Botswana honored M. in 1963 by bestowing on her the honorific title "Tribal Mother." Characteristically, in 1980, M. returned the compliment by publishing a collection of stories entitled *Images of Africa.* "To my mind, much of the communication between Europe and Africa is either superficial or has been deflected by a clash of values," she wrote, adding that only "imagination bridges differences." A poetic work, *Images of Africa* offers parables of race relations and cultural history from the African point of view, based on stories borrowed from the Kgatleng, the Bushmen of the Kalahari, and the people of Botswana and Zambia.

The principal quality of M.'s over eighty book-length publications—the lively candor with which she addresses human experience—has been spilling over refreshingly from work to work for over six decades. Whatever her topic or genre, her writing radiates a joyful recognition of human potential and a clear-eyed awareness of human frailty. Her attitude is far from sentimental. M. has repeatedly voiced the need for active responsibility, creative intelligence, and ultimate hopefulness.

WORKS: *The Conquered* (1923). *When the Bough Breaks and Other Stories* (1924). *Cloud Cuckoo Land* (1925). *The Laburnum Branch* (1926). *Black Sparta: Greek Stories* (1928). *Nix-Nought-Nothing: Anna Commena* (1928). *Four Plays for Children* (1928). *Barbarian Stories* (1929). *Comments on Birth Control* (1930). *The Hostages and Other Stories for Boys and Girls* (1930). *Boys and Girls and Gods* (1931). *The Corn King and the Spring Queen* (1931). (with L.E. Gielgud) *The Price of Freedom* (1932). *The Powers of Light* (1932). *The Delicate Fire: Short Stories and Poems* (1933). *The Home and a Changing Civilization* (1934). *Naomi Mitchison's Vienna Diary* (1934). *Beyond This Limit* (1935). *We Have Been Warned* (1935). *The Fourth Pig* (1936). (with R.H.S. Crossman) *Socrates* (1937). *An End and a Beginning and Other Plays* (1937). *The Moral Basis of Politics* (1938). *The Kingdom of Heaven* (1939). (with L.E. Gielgud) *As It Was in the Beginning* (1939). *The Blood of the Martyrs* (1939). *Not By Bread Alone* (1943). *The Bull Calves* (1947). (with D. Macintosh) *Men and Herring* (1949). *The Big House* (1950). *The Corn King* (1950). (with D. Mac-

intosh) *Spindrift* (1951). *Lobsters on the Agenda* (1952). *Travel Light* (1952). *Graeme and the Dragon* (1954). *The Swan's Road* (1954). *To the Chapel Perilous* (1955). *The Land the Ravens Found* (1955). *Little Boxes* (1956). *The Far Harbour* (1957). *Behold Your King* (1957). *Other People's Worlds* (1958). *Five Men and a Swan* (1958). *Judy and Lakshmi* (1959). *The Rib of the Green Umbrella* (1960). *Karensgaard: The Story of a Danish Farm* (1961). *Presenting Other People's Children* (1961). (with G.W.L. Paterson) *A Fishing Village on the Clyde* (1961). *The Young Alexander the Great* (1961). *The Young Alfred the Great* (1962). *Memoirs of a Space Woman* (1962). *The Fairy Who Couldn't Tell a Lie* (1963). *Alexander the Great* (1964). *Henny and Crispies* (1964). *Ketse and the Chief* (1965). *When We Become Men* (1965). *Friends and Enemies* (1966). *Return to the Fairy Hill* (1966). *Highland Holiday* (1967). *The Big Surprise* (1967). *African Heroes* (1968). *Don't Look Back* (1969). *The Family at Ditlabeng* (1969). *The Africans* (1970). *Sun and Moon* (1970). *Cleopatra's People* (1972). *The Danish Teapot* (1973). *Sunrise Tomorrow: A Story of Botswana* (1973). *Small Talk: Memories of an Edwardian Childhood* (1973). *A Life for Africa: The Story of Bram Fischer* (1973). *Oil for the Highlands?* (1974). *All Changes Here: Girlhood and Marriage* (1975). *Sittlichkeit* (1975). *Solution Three* (1975). *Snake!* (1976). *The Brave Nurse and Other Stories* (1977). *The Two Magicians* (1978). *The Cleansing of the Knife* (1979). *Images of Africa* (1980). *You May Well Ask* (1980). *The Vegetable War* (1980). *Mucking Around: Five Continents over Fifty Years* (1981). *What Do You Think Yourself?* (1982).

BIBLIOGRAPHY: Nellis, M.K. *Studies in Medievalism* (Fall 1983).

For articles in reference works, see: *CA. CN. ConSFA. MBL. TWCA* and *SUP.*

Other references: *Horn Book* (June 1961). *NYT* (28 October 1923). *NYTBR* (28 May 1961). *TLS* (5 June 1980, 24 July 1981).

R. Victoria Arana

Mary Russell Mitford

BORN: 16 December 1787, Alresford.
DIED: 10 January 1855, Swallowfield.
DAUGHTER OF: Dr. George Mitford and Mary Russell.

The author of *Our Village* was born into relatively favored circumstances; her mother was an heiress and her father a physician. But because of her father's profligacy, M. spent much of her

life on the edge of poverty. Indeed, it was a desperate need for money that prompted her profuse literary production, which began in the 1820s: historical dramas and the "sketches" of rural life that made her famous.

A precocious only child, M. could read by the age of three. Her mother's fortune had already been dissipated by her father by the time M. was six or seven, so because of their straitened financial situation, the Mitfords moved first to London and later to Reading. While in London (in 1797) M. herself won a lottery prize of £20,000, which put the family back on a sound financial track for some years. The following year she matriculated at a "ladies' school" in London run by a French emigré, St. Quintin, where she won various prizes. Throughout her life she remained a voracious reader; she was conversant in French and knew some Italian and Latin. She studied at the school for over four years, after which she returned to live with her parents.

Her first publications were a collection of poems in 1810, followed by several longer poetic works. "Christina," which concerned a romance that developed in the wake of the mutiny on the "Bounty," appeared in 1811 and was very popular, especially in the United States, and went through several editions. "Blanch of Castile" followed in 1812 and "Narrative Poems on the Female Character" in 1813. These years are documented in a series of letters M. wrote, some to her parents, most to Sir William Elford, a dilettante painter who became a kind of mentor. They now comprise the first volume of her collected letters, published in 1869, a mine of information on nineteenth-century manners and attitudes. The first volume reveals M. to be a lively, frank intelligence, given to irreverent humor, whose talent for moving descriptions of rural life is apparent early in her life. The conversational mode which M. used in her letters became the hallmark of her fictional style, about which she once wrote: ". . . we are free and easy in these days, and talk to the public as a friend . . . we have turned over the Johnsonian periods . . . to keep company with the wigs and hoops"— an indication that M. saw herself as part of the democratization of art that was a central aspect of romantic literary theory.

M., however, remained ambivalent about the works of her romantic contemporaries, Wordsworth, Coleridge, and Byron, though she reveled in Wordsworth's and Coleridge's praise of her work. Her preference, not surprisingly (given the similarity between their work and hers), was for the prose fiction of Maria Edgeworth and Jane Austen; the other major influence on her was Washington Irving. In 1824, as the first series of Our Village was about to be published, she explained that the book "will consist of essays and characters and stories, chiefly of country life, in the manner of the 'Sketch Book,' but without sentimentality or pathos—two things which I abhor." Throughout her correspondence M. iterates her distaste for romantic sentimentalism and her preference for realism. That she herself occasionally indulged in sentimentalism reflects the romantic cast of the era but may also be due to her need to appeal to popular taste.

By 1820 the family, reduced to near destitu- tion, had to move to humbler quarters in Three Mile Cross, a small village near Reading where M. was to live for more than thirty years and which she was to endow with international celebrity as the site of "our village." The first of these sketches appeared in the Lady's Magazine in 1819. At the same time M. turned her hand to a completely different literary form, tragedy. Her first attempt at drama, Fiesco, was not accepted, but shortly thereafter Julian was presented at Covent Garden on 15 March 1823 with William Charles Macready, an eminent actor, in the title role. It ran for eight performances and evidently received much sexist criticism.

Foscari, her second work, was completed in 1821 but not produced until 4 November 1826, when it ran for fifteen performances at Covent Garden with Charles Kemble in the lead. Coincidentally, Byron had put forth a tragedy on the same subject in 1821, which caused M. considerable consternation. Her most successful play was Rienzi, another romantic historical tragedy set in Renaissance Italy and concerning rival noble families who contend for power and containing a "Romeo and Juliet" subplot. Critics consider this her best play, and audiences evidently agreed, for it had thirty-four performances in London in the fall of 1828 and was very successful on the road in the United States where Charlotte Cushman played the lead female role. M.'s other dramatic works include: Inez de Castro (1831), Mary, Queen of Scots (1831), Charles the First (1834), and an opera, Sadak and Kalasrade (1836).

Meanwhile, M. had begun publishing Our Village, the work that was to establish her as an international celebrity, in five volumes published in 1824, 1826, 1828, 1830, and 1832. She described it as "not one connected story, but a series of sketches of country manners, scenery, and character, with some story intermixed, and connected by unity of locality and of purpose." This is in fact an accurate description of the work, which did not fit into traditional notions of genre but instead created a new form, "village fiction," and provided the basis for a dominant nineteenth-century women's literary tradition, that of the local color writers. Particularly strong in the United States, it included such writers as Caroline Kirkland, Harriet Beecher Stowe, Rose Terry Cooke, and Sarah Orne Jewett—all of whom were directly influenced by Mitford. She also had an effect on American writer Catherine Sedgwick, with whom she corresponded, Irish writer S.C. Hall (Sketches of Irish Character), and Elizabeth Gaskell, whose Cranford is a direct descendant of Our Village.

Our Village is narrated by a persona who guides the reader through the streets of her town, describing in detail the surrounding vegetation, housing, and landscape as well as the various "characters" who inhabit the village. Their stories are sketched in, as well, which provides what little plot *Our Village* may be said to have. Writing in the heyday of romanticism, it is not surprising that M. saw the rural world as a kind of pastoral Utopia that nurtured authentic people who spoke truths born of their intimate experience of nature. She favors such characters and their eccentricities and resists any sign of encroaching urban homogenization. *Our Village* became a popular rage. M. was for years besieged by visitors and correspondents wanting to see or learn more about the original model for such characters. Children were named after them; flowers were named after M. herself.

M. continued her studies of rural life with *Belford Regis* (1834), *Country Stories* (1837), and *Atherton* (1854). In 1836 she met Elizabeth Barrett (later Browning) with whom she was to form a strong friendship; numerous letters between them are extant. Despite her industrious literary production, M. remained impoverished in the latter years of her life, finally forced to move to a small cottage in Swallowfield, also near Reading, where she died. A charming stylist and a pioneer of an important direction in women's literature, M.'s current obscurity is undeserved.

WORKS: Poems (1810). Christina, the Maid of the South Seas; a Poem (1811). Blanch of Castile (1812). Narrative Poems on the Female Character, in Various Relations of Life (1813). Julian (1823). Our Village: Sketches of Rural Character and Scenery, 5 vols. (1824, 1826, 1828, 1830, 1832). Foscari (1826).

Dramatic Scenes, Sonnets, and Other Poems (1827). *Rienzi, A Tragedy* (1828). *Mary, Queen of Scots* (1831). *Inez de Castro* (1831). *Charles the First, an Historical Tragedy* (1834). *Belford Regis, or Sketches of A Country Town,* (1835). *Sadak and Kalasrade; or the Waters of Oblivion* (1836). *Country Stories* (1837). *The Works of Mary Russell Mitford: Prose and Verse* (1841). *Recollections of A Literary Life* (1852). *Atherton and Other Tales* (1854). *The Dramatic Works of Mary Russell Mitford* (1854). *The Life of Mary Russell Mitford . . . Related in a Selection from Her Letters to Her Friends,* ed. A.G.K. L'Estrange (1869). *Letters of Mary Russell Mitford,* ed. Henry Chorley (1872). *Correspondence with Charles Boner and John Ruskin,* ed. Elizabeth Lee (1914).

BIBLIOGRAPHY: Agate, J.E. Mary Russell Mitford (1940). Austin, M. Mary Russell Mitford: Her Circle and Her Books (1930). Hill, M.C. Mary Russell Mitford and Her Surroundings (1920). Johnson, R.B. The Women Novelists (1919). Jones, C.M.D. Miss Mitford and Mr. Harness (1955). L'Estrange, A.G.K., ed. The Friendships of Mary Russell Mitford as Recorded in Letters from Her Literary Correspondents (1882). Roberts, W.J. Mary Russell Mitford (1913). Watson, V. Mary Russell Mitford (1949).

For articles in reference works, see: DNB.

Other references: British Museum Quarterly (1965). Bulletin of the John Rylands Library (1957). SB (1959). SSF (1968).

Josephine Donovan

Nancy Mitford

BORN: 28 November 1904, London.
DIED: 30 June 1973, London.
DAUGHTER OF: David Bertram Ogilvy and Sydney Bowles Freeman-Mitford.
MARRIED: Peter Rodd, 1923.

M. was the oldest of the Earl of Redesdale's seven children. Though she came from a family of writers, as well as politicians and historians, her parents were convinced she needed no education, and so she (like her writer sister Jessica) got none. This contributed to her independent nature and perhaps to a certain eccentricity. She did not, however, become a fascist like two of her five sisters (one of whom married Sir Oswald Moseley, who led the British Union of Fascists). Her amusement at her family's odd behavior is reflected in her entertaining novel *The Pursuit of Love* (1945), where she treats her relatives as almost Dickensian caricatures; they were also the "hons. and rebels" Jessica wrote about.

M.'s most familiar novels are probably *Love*

in a Cold Climate (1949), *The Blessing* (1951), and *Don't Tell Alfred* (1960), but she was also the author of fiction of the Thirties: *Highland Fling* (1931), *Christmas Pudding* (1932), and *Wigs on the Green* (1935). They were appreciated in their day for a witty style and a facile, sometimes farcical, humor, and today they are read because of the fame of her later work.

In *Highland Fling* a huntress, Jane Dacre, goes after Albert Gates, despite the fact that when he invited her to see his etchings he was really thinking about art. In *Christmas Pudding* we have "one of those houses which abound in every district of rural England, and whose chief characteristic is that they cannot but give rise, on first sight, to a feeling of depression." In the house, however, is the lively young lady Philadelphia Bobbin, in search of romance. In *Wigs on the Green* Poppy St. Julien knows that Jasper Aspect has neither propects nor scruples—which makes him irresistible to her. Reissued in the 1970's (with *Pigeon Pie* of 1940, in which a bored sophisticate, Sophia

Garfield, is out to cheer up the dreariness of war-time with a skirmish in the war between the sexes), these early novels are a little dated but still have some charm.

Especially dated is *Pigeon Pie*, written at the time of the "phony war" and joking about things such as espionage, sabotage, and propaganda that were soon to become serious matters. But the intrigue of the book is, in fact, like the country house and the London "smart set" backgrounds of the other books, truly incidental. Essentially the books are all satires of the Sweet Young Things, now called The Beautiful People. "Cracks in the upper crust," ran a blurb on the Penguin edition of one of M.'s novels, were "almost Nancy Mitford's private literary domain."

M. knew the upper crust. As the wife of the son of a former British ambassador to Italy, M. lived in Paris and reported the social life there for the *Sunday Times*. She set *Love in a Cold Climate* and some other work in Parisian diplomatic circles: Alfred in *Don't Tell Alfred* is the British ambassador to France. Most undiplomatically, Fanny, the narrator and Alfred's wife, is really M. herself and writes (as Norman Collins said in the *Observer*) "of the heart with a most engaging heartlessness." Fanny/Nancy satirizes the surfaces of life at least in the upper echelons (said a critic in the *Spectator*) "with more truth, more sincerity, and more laughter than a year's output of novels in the bogus significant style."

M. had no desire to attempt the "bogus significant" and knew she was not penetrating, that she was clever but not profound. She never gets very deeply into characters; she is at her best with eccentrics such as the couple in *The Blessing*. She is Grace Allingham, who has lived with her dashing husband only 10 days in 7 years and nonetheless adores him. He is a French marquis who loves her—and any other beautiful women he can get his hands on. Another writer might make a tragedy of this material, but M. plays it for laughs. She lacks the bite that makes serious satire better (if bitter); she is content to jest about aristocratic friends and foes and their horrible children and their trendies and toadies.

Horsemanship and French, she said, was all the knowledge her parents' weird ideas about education gave her to work with. The French she used to make *The Little Hut* (1951) out of André Roussin's pleasant little play and to research solid studies of *Madame de Pompadour* (1954, revised 1968), *Voltaire in Love* (1957), and *The Sun King: Louis XIV at Versailles* (1966). She also translated Mme. de Lafayette's classic *The Princess of Clèves* (1950). She educated herself widely and was able to write the essays in *The Water Beetle* (1962), a popular biography of *Frederick the Great* (1970), and *Noblesse Oblige: An Enquiry into the Identifiable Characteristics of the English Aristocracy*

(1956), which made her widely known in connection with the differences between "U" and "non-U" speech. She edited the letters of Maria Josepha, Lady Stanley of Aderley, and her daughter-in-law (Henrietta Maria Stanley) as *The Ladies of Aderley* and *The Stanleys of Aderley* (both 1938), throwing interesting sidelights on Victorian women. But, like many self-educated persons, in all her work she seems attracted to curious detail rather than the large picture, to gossipy anecdotes, to flash and filigree, peculiarities rather than profundities. At the same time she is nobody's fool, and she can always limn a character deftly when she wants to or conjure up the costumes and scenery of a bygone age convincingly.

M. lacked not so much education as malice. She would have been a better writer had she some of the nastiness of, say, Evelyn Waugh. As it is, her satire is never scathing and one wonders if there is enough salt in it to preserve it for posterity. The "hons. and rebels" are fast fading. There was a time, M.'s mother once said, that whenever she saw "Peer's Daughter" in a sensational banner headline she knew it was "going to be something about one of you children." Today Unity (with her fascination with the Nazis) and some of the other Redesdale brood (one of whom married royalty) are far less likely to ring a bell in memory than M. Whether the interest in her pre-war world and her post-war eccentrics will last, or whether M. herself will continue to be of interest because of the autobiographical elements in *The Pursuit of Love*, remains to be seen.

One hopes M.'s fun will not be forgotten. There was more to the Thirties than strikes and depression and, though one might not know it from reading most modern fiction, not all the world is lower class or middle class.

WORKS: *Highland Fling* (1931). *Christmas Pudding* (1932). *Wigs on the Green* (1935). *The Stanleys of Aderley* (1938). *The Ladies of Aderley* (1938). *Pigeon Pie* (1940). *The Pursuit of Love* (1945). *Love in a Cold Climate* (1949). [trans.] *The Princess of Clèves*, by Mme. de Lafayette (1950). *The Blessing* (1951). *The Little Hut* (1951). *Madame de Pompadour* (1954, 1968). *Voltaire in Love* (1957). *Don't Tell Alfred* (1960). *The Water Beetle* (1962). *The Sun King: Louis XIV at Versailles* (1966). *Frederick the Great* (1970). *A Talent to Annoy: Essays, Journalism, and Reviews*, ed. C. Mosley (1968). *Selima Hastings* (1985).

BIBLIOGRAPHY: Acton, H. *Mitford: A Memoir* (1975). Hastings, S. *Nancy Mitford: A Biography* (1986).

For articles in reference works, see: *CA. Great Writers of the English Language: Novelists* (1979). *Longman. MBL. TCA SUP. TCW.*

Leonard R.N. Ashley

Elizabeth Montagu

BORN: 2 October 1720, York.
DIED: 25 August 1800, London.
DAUGHTER OF: Matthew and Elizabeth Drake Robinson.
MARRIED: Edward Montagu, 1742.

Essayist and Shakespearean critic M. was also a prolific letter-writer. Her witty and vividly descriptive correspondence, spanning two-thirds of the eighteenth century, recreates the diverse activities in which she excelled, from the London establishment of scholarly forums to the management of Berkshire farmlands and Northumberland collieries. Additionally, the letters reveal her political interests, such as her concern for the welfare and advancement of women and her discomfort with the ethical implications of the century's newly developing capitalism. Finally, her letters tell the story of her more private life—her relationship with her husband and her several intimate and steadfast friendships.

M. was the fourth child and first daughter in a large family which was wealthy, socially prominent, and well-educated. In her adolescence, she was energetic and gregarious, and when she was 22, she married Edward Montagu, nearly 30 years her senior. Shortly after his death in 1775, M. adopted her young nephew Matthew Robinson (later Montagu) as her heir, who after her death became custodian of her correspondence, bringing out collections of her letters in 1809 and 1813.

M.'s first published work consisted of three dialogues she contributed anonymously to her friend Lord Lyttelton's *Dialogues of the Dead* (1760), with the delightful "Dialogue between Mercury and a modern Fine Lady" influenced by Elizabeth Carter's "Modish Pleasures" (*Rambler*, 2 March 1751). Also during 1760, M., with Carter's encouragement, began a second project, an extended essay in response to Voltaire's attack on Shakespeare in his *Dictionnaire philosophe*. In 1768, M. wrote to Carter, "Between attending Mr. Montague in his very infirm state, domestic Orders for the regulation of a family consisting of about thirty persons, letters of business, and my authorlike duties, I have sometimes a great hurry, and I have also some sick patients for whom I am obliged to make up Medicines, that being in some cases not to be trusted to another; poor Shakespear is last served." But she persevered, and in 1769 her *Essay on the Writings and Genius of Shakespeare* was published anonymously. Her identity almost immediately known, M. became highly esteemed as a Shakespearean critic. The *Essay* went to several editions and was translated into French and Italian.

Besides time spent in Berkshire and North-umberland, Montagu travelled in Scotland, the Rhineland, and the Low Countries, and often visited France. An enthusiastic patron of the arts, she supported many writers, architects, and painters. Among the women writers she assisted were Sarah Fielding, Hester Chapone, and Hannah More. At one point, she proposed the establishment of a women's college, and in 1767 she and her sister Sarah Scott (q.v.) were working on a plan to provide a home for unmarried gentlewomen. Among M.'s several close female friends, Elizabeth Carter may have been the most important. The two exchanged many letters, sometimes travelled together, often visited one another, and planned to share a home in later life. But although M. settled a pension on Carter immediately after her husband's death, the two friends never lived together. Affectionate friendship marked the Bluestocking women, that group of London ladies with perhaps Montagu at the center, which created a forum for social, literary, artistic, and intellectual interests (see Elizabeth Vesey entry). The Bluestockings looked to one another for intellectual support, and in their self-sufficiency demonstrated the strengths of womanly community. Through her Bluestocking parties, M. brought together women and men of diverse backgrounds, interests, and beliefs to share ideas: "I have always pitied a certain set of people who some years ago called themselves the 'little world,' it is so much better to be of the general world . . . . to be able to converse with ease, and hearken with intelligence to persons of every rank, degree and occupation."

WORKS: Lyttelton, G.L. *Dialogues of the Dead.* 3rd ed. (1760). *An Essay on the Writings and Genius of Shakespeare, Compared with the Greek and French Dramatic Poets.* 6th ed., corrected, to which are added *Three Dialogues of the Dead* (1810). *Letters of Mrs. Elizabeth Montagu, with Some of the Letters of Her Correspondents,* ed. M. Montagu (1809-13). *Letters from Mrs. Elizabeth Carter to Mrs. Montagu Between the Years 1755 and 1800,* ed. M. Pennington (1817). Gaussen, A.C.C. *A Later Pepys: The Correspondence of Sir W.W. Pepys 1758-1825, with . . . Mrs. Montague . . . and Others* (1904). *Elizabeth Montague, the Queen of the Bluestockings: Her Correspondence from 1720 to 1761,* ed. E.J. Climenson (1906). Blunt, R., ed. *Mrs. Montagu, "Queen of the Blues"* (1923). Anson, E. and F. *Mary Hamilton at Court and at Home* (1925; contains letters from M.). Johnson, R.B., ed. *Bluestocking Letters* (1926).

BIBLIOGRAPHY: Busse, J. *Mrs. Montagu, Queen of the Blues* (1928). Doran, J. *A Lady of the Last Century* (1893). Fellowes, E.H. and E. Pine, eds. *The Tenbury Letters* (1943). Halsband, R. *The Lady of Letters in the Eighteenth Century,* ed. I. Ehrenpreis and R. Halsband (1969). Hornbeak, K.G. *The Age of Johnson: Essays Presented to C.B. Tinker* (1949). Huchon, R.L. *Mrs. Montagu and Her Friends, 1720-1800* (1907). Hufstader, A.A. *Sisters of the Quill* (1978). Jones, W.P. *Huntington Library Quarterly* (1952). Ross, I. *Huntington Library Quarterly* (1965). Scott, W.S. *The Bluestocking Ladies* (1947). Tinker, C.B. *The Salon and English Letters* (1915). West, R. *From Anne to Victoria*, ed. B. Dobree (1937). Wheeler, E.R., *Famous Bluestockings* (1910).

For articles in reference works, see: *DNB*. Todd.

Other references: Beatty, J.M., Jr. *MLN* (1926). Boulton, J.T. *Burke Newsletter* (1961-62). de Castro, J.P. *N&Q* (1941). Harmsen, T.G. *N&Q* (1958). Hegeman, D.V. *Kentucky Foreign Language Quarterly* (1957). Hufstader, A.A. *Musical Quarterly* (1961). Jones, C.E. *N&Q* (1946). Jones, W.P. *N&Q* (1958). Larson, E.S. *Studies in Eighteenth-Century Culture* (1986). Phillips, G.L., *RES* (1949). *TLS* (20 September 1941).

Carolyn Woodward

Mary Wortley Montagu

BORN: 1689, London.
DIED: 21 August 1762, London.
DAUGHTER OF: Evelyn Pierrepont and Lady Mary Fielding.
MARRIED: Edward Wortley Montagu, Esq., 1712.
WROTE UNDER: MWM, M. Wortley Montagu, Mary Wortley Montagu.

After their mother died in 1693, M. and three siblings were left to the care of paternal grandparents and a governess, who, says M., "took so much pains from my infancy to fill my head with superstitious tales and false notions, it was none of her fault I am not at this day afraid of witches and hobgoblins, or turned Methodist." Educated in part by tutors, M. was largely self-taught and began writing poetry when she was twelve. In 1712 she eloped with Edward Wortley Montagu, appointed Ambassador Extraordinary to the Court of Turkey in 1716. Journeying with her husband to Constantinople, M. began to write the letters that would establish her reputation as an author. The couple returned to England in 1718 and, encouraged by Pope, M. settled at Twickenham with their two children, Mary, who married John Stuart and became Lady Bute, and Edward, whose marriages and profligate spending constantly embarrassed his family. Resuming her travels in 1739, in part at the invitation of the Italian Count Algarotti, M. resided first at Avignon and then at Lovere; she returned in January 1762, after the death of her husband and at the request of her daughter, and died in August.

A vigilant observer of human nature in society and politics, M.'s poetry, essays, and letters show her concerns as a feminist and as a moralist. As a *bel esprit*, M. eschewed publication, but she circulated much of her writing in manuscript, and both the pirated printings and the unpublished works met with acclaim from contemporaries including her friend Lord Hervey, Pope, Walpole, Johnson, and Burns. Contemporary publication of M.'s works, therefore, was sporadic and not au-

thoritative, but her literary reputation was firmly established during her lifetime.

In her essays, some of which she published anonymously, she often started by exposing a fashionable error, an intellectual misstep. A longing for honesty and integrity in all human relationships frequently underlies her focus on specific public personalities. The voice and intention of her persona are defined in an essay from 24 January 1738: "I keep up to the character I have assum'd, of a Moralist, and shall use my endeavors to relieve the distress'd, and defeat vulgar prejudices whatever the event may be." On 28 July 1714, M.'s essay justifying the light-heartedness of some widows appeared in the *Spectator*. In *The Nonsense of Common-Sense*, a series of nine essays published as a weekly newspaper from December 1737 to March 1738, M. defends Walpole against attacks in the Opposition paper, *Common Sense*. On 3 January, justifying Walpole's attempts to tax wine and tobacco, she writes, "The highest Perfection of Politicks, they say, is to make the Vices of the People contribute to the Welfare of the State." In her poetry, M.'s Augustan forms and her consistently satiric tone attest to her respect for the models of her contemporaries. But her opinions and insights shape her poems, frequently occasioned by personal and public events.

Written in 1715 during a literary liaison with Pope and John Gay, three of her *Court Eclogues* were printed anonymously without her permission by Edmund Curll in 1716 as *Court Poems*. In 1718 Pope presented M. with his autograph copy of her manuscript of the eclogues, and Walpole printed an annotated edition of all six eclogues in 1747. The subject of the third eclogue, "The Drawing Room," shows the wisdom of M.'s decision to circulate poetry only among friends, for in it she criticizes the morality of Princess Caroline's court: "A greater miracle is daily view'd,/A virtuous Princess with a court so lewd."

M. is best known for her letters. Most famous are her Embassy letters, the value of which was recognized by Mary Astell whose preface shows her characteristic encouragement and admiration of M. and identifies the unique quality of M.'s voice. "To how much better purpose the Lady's Travel than their Lords. . . . A Lady has the skill to strike out a New Path and to embellish a worn-out Subject with variety of fresh and elegant Entertainment. . . . besides that Purity of Style for which it may justly be accounted the Standard of the English tongue, the Reader will find a more true and accurate Account of the Customs and Manners of the several Nations with whom the Lady Convers'd than he can in any other Author. . . . Her Ladyship's penetration discovers the inmost follys of the heart, . . . treating with the politeness of a Court and gentleness of a Lady, what the severity of her Judgment cannot but Condemn."

In addition to the descriptive letters themselves, M. brought back from Turkey an enthusiastic and convincing tale of inoculation against smallpox. In a letter to Sarah Chiswell, in which she recalls her discovery, she shows her disdain for professional irresponsibility and betrays her own desire to be more assertive. "I should not fail to write to some of our doctors very particularly about it if I knew any one of 'em that I thought had virtue enough to destroy such a considerable branch of their revenue for the good of mankind, but that distemper is too beneficial to them not to expose to all their resentment the hardy wight should undertake to put an end to it. Perhaps if I live to return I may, however, have courage to war with 'em. Upon this occasion, admire the heroism in the heart of your friend."

In her letters to her sister Frances, the Countess of Mar, M. creates whimsical sketches of her social life. Similar subjects become polished commentary in letters to the Countess of Oxford and the Countess of Pomfret. Although they differ in their views on morality and propriety, M. and Lady Bute correspond openly on issues of feminism and child raising. M. gracefully defends having emphasized domestic training for her own daughter and then urging scholarly training for her granddaughter. "The ultimate end of your education was to make you a good wife. . . ; hers ought to make her happy in a virgin state." M.'s individualized feminism takes its direction from the status quo: "I have heard it lamented that boys lose so many years in mere learning of words: this is no objection to a girl, whose time is not so precious: she cannot advance herself in any profession, and has therefore more hours to spare." M.'s evaluation only lightly conceals an ironic complaint about women's limited options, but her *carpe diem* response, based on practicality and preference, precludes bitterness.

Letters to Lady Bute lament "the general want of invention which reigns amongst our writ-ers." She wonders if England "has not sun enough to warm the imagination." Only Congreve and Fielding, M. concludes, show originality, but, because they must publish in order to make a living, they fall short of their potential genius. "The greatest virtue, justice, and the most distinguishing prerogative of mankind, writing, when daily executed do honor to human nature, but when degenerated into trades are the most contemptible ways of getting bread." And although she participates herself in a literary battle with Pope, she insists that authors should, instead of "stigmatizing a Man's name, . . . confine their censure to single Actions . . . [instead of] Satyrs and Panegyricks."

M.'s *A Comedy/Simplicity* is a translation and adaptation of *Le Jeu de l'amour et du hasard*, a French play written by Pierre de Marivaux.

In her practical feminism M. urges readers to consider that reform benefits the oppressor as well as the oppressed. She writes, "Amongst the most universal Errors I reckon that of treating the weaker sex with a contempt, which has a very bad Influence on their conduct, who, many of them, think it excuse enough to say, they are Women, to indulge any folly that comes into their Heads, and also renders them useless members of the common wealth, and only burdensome to their own Familys." It is little wonder that with a pen so merciless in exposing folly, M.'s friends' and family's responses varied from profound affection to violent antagonism. Modern audiences discover in M.'s writing a sensitive and sensible response to significant issues of the eighteenth-century.

WORKS: *Six Town Eclogues. With some other Poems* (ed. H. Walpole, (1747). *A Collection of Poems* (printed for R. Dodsley, 1748). *Works* (ed. J. Dallaway, 1803). *Letters and Works* (ed. Lord Wharncliffe, 1837). *Letters and Works*, ed. W. Moy Thomas (1861). *The Nonsense of Common-Sense* (ed. R. Halsband, 1947). *Complete Letters of Lady Mary Wortley Montagu*, 3 vol. (ed. R. Halsband, 1965-67). *Essays and Poems and Simplicity, A Comedy* (ed. R. Halsband and I. Grundy, 1977). *The Best Letters of Lady Mary Wortley Montagu* (ed. T. Octave, 1978). *Court Eclogs, Written in the Year Seventeen Sixteen: Alexander Pope's Autograph Manuscript* (ed. R. Halsband, 1977).

BIBLIOGRAPHY: Barry, I. *Portrait of Lady Mary Montagu* (1928). Gibbs, L. *The Admirable Lady Mary* (1949). Halsband, R. *The Life of Lady Mary Wortley Montagu* (1957). Huchon, R. *Mrs. Montagu & Her Friends, 1720-1800* (1907; repr. 1983). Leslie, D. *A Toast to Lady Mary* (1968). Melville, L. *Lady Mary Wortley Montagu: Her Life and Letters* (1925). Paston, G. *Lady Mary Wortley Montagu & Her Times* (1907).

For articles in reference works, see: *Cassell. DBPP. IDWP.*

Other references: *AR* (Fall 1981). *BLR* (February 1981). Bradford, G. *Portrait of Women* (1916). Ehrenpreis, I. *The Lady of Letters in the Eighteenth Century* (1969). *GR* (Winter, 1983). Holmes, W. *Seven Adventurous Women* (1953). Melville, L. *Maids of Honour* (1917). *N&Q* (1958). *New States-man* (1958). *PMLA* (1965). *PQ* (1965, 1966). *RES* (1972). Rogers, K., ed. *Before Their Time: Six Women Writers of the Eighteenth Century* (1979). Rubenstein, J. *Prose Studies* (1986). *SB* (1958). Thomson, K. *The Queens of Society* (1861).

Mary Comfort

Hannah More

BORN: 2 February 1745, Stapleton, Gloucestershire.
DIED: 7 September 1833, Windsor Terrace, Clifton.
DAUGHTER OF: Jacob and Mary Grace More.
WROTE UNDER: Anon., Hannah More.

M. lived through two eras, a fact that both defined and limited her impact as a writer. Born in the century of Johnson, she died at the end of the Romantic age. Toward the close of her life she was a celebrated anachronism, refusing to accept the fundamental social and philosophical changes that accompanied Romanticism. To the last she defended what, in effect, was already gone. Yet in her own way she had helped to create change just as surely as she had tried to stop it. Too conscientious to ignore things as they were, M. was too conventional to opt for radical transformation. Still, her attempts to preserve the status quo while modifying it for the better struck a chord in the hearts of an entire generation.

One of five sisters who ran a successful boarding school in Bristol, M. had since childhood shown a gift beyond the others for communication in all its forms. Too, she had the peculiar distinction of having the great personal crisis of her life done with early on. Jilted three times by the rich landowner to whom she had been engaged for six years, M. learned firsthand the value of compassion. Around 1773 she firmly rejected her erstwhile fiancé's pleas for another chance, but she never turned bitter. Instead, she sublimated her feelings into her religion, her family, and her ever-widening circle of friends.

While recovering from the stress of the broken engagement, M. visited London in 1773 or 1774. There her intellectual and conversational gifts won over David Garrick and his wife, who introduced her to a large number of London celebrities. There M., who had begun her career as a poet and playwright in Bristol, found fame with the production of her drama *Percy* (1777), a tragedy that was the triumph of its season. Garrick edited and promoted the play for his protegée, and its success was surely due in large part to his efforts. On its own, *Percy* is neither poetic nor dramatic, merely a bland imitation of Cor-

neille. After Garrick's sudden death in 1779, M. lost interest in the stage. She produced another play, *The Fatal Falsehood* (1779), and she published *Sacred Dramas* (1782), a set of Biblical stories done as closet drama; but her attention had turned elsewhere.

Wherever her attention turned, she met further success. Over her lifetime she made some £30,000 as an author, most of it predicated on her ability to communicate equally well with the great and the unknown. In London M. was quickly accepted as a Bluestocking, a friend of Edmund Burke, Joshua Reynolds, and Samuel Johnson. She pleased them all with "Bas Bleu" (1782), a poem saluting London's female intellectuals, past and present. She could have continued writing such elegant trifles for the rest of her life.

Instead, in a series of didactic works, she urged the upper classes to embrace true Christianity, by which she meant an Evangelical form of the Anglican faith. As M. grew older, she became convinced that human corruption and divine redemption were the key elements in Christianity and that the true Christian must not only establish a personal relationship with God but also demonstrate it in his every act. This kind of enthusiasm seemed almost Methodistic to more conservative Anglicans, and it left M. open to criticism within her own Tory group; but it also gave her the strength to press that group for moderate reform. Thus, in *Thoughts on the Importance of the Manners of the Great to General Society* (1788), she urged the wealthy to respect the Sabbath as it was intended. In *An Estimate of the Religion of the Fashionable World* (1790), she held that Christianity must be embraced in its entirety rather than in part. In *Strictures on the Modern System of Female Education* (1799), she suggested that women should be trained as circumstances require and as a Christian society demands.

William Cobbett once called M. an "old bishop in petticoats," and she was something of the sort. She was as well, however, a parson to the poor. Following William Wilberforce, she worked for the abolition of slavery, a cause she championed in her poem "The Slave Trade" (1788). Following Robert Raikes, she and her sisters established a string of Sunday schools for the neglected rural poor. Nonetheless, even with her doctrinal leanings toward reform, she remained a staunch Tory who feared and despised the French Revolution. In 1792 she wrote "Village Politics," her first pro-government, anti-revolution tract. In simple language that deliberately aped the chapbook style, she justified the English system and reviled the French. Widely praised, this bit of anti-Jacobin propaganda led to a series of *Cheap Repository Tracts* (1795-98), distributed by the rich to the poor in an effort to quell their unrest. A prime mover in this cause, M. wrote at least fifty of these tracts. How successful they were as an antidote to the "French poison" is debatable; what is certain is that they were widely circulated among a people whose concerns eventually led to reform rather than to revolution.

In 1808 M. published her only novel, *Coelebs in Search of a Wife*, meant as an alternative to the romances then in fashion. The alternative was another huge success, with dozens of editions printed in England and America. Like the rest of M.'s work, *Coelebs* is too didactic to be good reading now. Ostensibly the story of a bachelor seeking a spouse, it is in fact a general statement of M.'s beliefs. Characters do not so much converse as lecture on her favorite subjects: women, education, children, charity, and above all, Christianity as the center of existence.

After *Coelebs* the old "female bishop" wrote several other works on pious subjects; but though everything sold well, something was different. The Romantic age had superseded the Johnsonian era; and if Romanticism was more than revolution, its politics and metaphysics were quite distasteful to an Evangelical Tory. Romantics like Coleridge and De Quincey found M. equally distasteful. Though she was still revered by many when she died quietly in 1833, England and the world had left her in another century. Yet by her work for reform she, too, had a place, not just in the past but in the continuum of those who work for the welfare of humanity.

WORKS: *The Search After Happiness* (1773). *The Inflexible Captive* (1774). *Essays for Young Ladies* (1777). *Percy* (1777). *The Fatal Falsehood* (1779). *Sacred Dramas* (1782). *Thoughts on the Importance of the Manners of the Great to General Society* (1788). *An Estimate of the Religion of the Fashionable World* (1790). *Cheap Repository Tracts* (1795-98). *Strictures on the Modern System of Female Education* (1799). *Hints Towards Forming the Character of a Young Princess* (1805). *Coelebs in Search of a Wife* (1808). *Practical Piety* (1811). *Christian Morals* (1813). *An Essay on the Character and Practical Writings of St. Paul* (1815). *Stories for Persons of the Middle Ranks, and Tales for the Common People* (1819). *Moral Sketches of Prevailing Opinions of Manners, Foreign and Domestic, with Reflections on Prayer* (1819). *Bible Rhymes* (1821). *The Spirit of Prayer* (1825). *Works* (8 vols., 1801; 19 vols., 1818-19; 11 vols., 1830; 6 vols., 1833-34; 2 vols., 1848). *Poems* (1816, 1829).

BIBLIOGRAPHY: Brown, F.K. *Fathers of the Victorians* (1961). Hopkins, M.A. *Hannah More and Her Circle* (1947). Jones, M.G. *Hannah More* (1952). Pickering, S. *SSF*, 12 (1975). Roberts, A., ed. *Mendip Annals* (1859). Roberts, W. *Memoirs of the Life and Correspondence of Mrs. Hannah More* (1834).

For articles in reference works, see: *DNB. Europa.*

Other references: Myers, M. *Fetter'd or Free? British Women Novelists, 1670-1815*, ed. M.A. Schofield and C. Macheski (1986). Pedersen, S. *Journal of British Studies* (1986).

Mary Ferguson Pharr

Penelope Ruth Mortimer

BORN: 19 September 1918, Rhyl, Flint, Wales.
DAUGHTER OF: A.F.G. and Amy Caroline Fletcher.
MARRIED: Charles Dimont, 1937; John Clifford Mortimer, 1949.
WRITES UNDER: Penelope Dimant, Penelope Mortimer.

In her poetic autobiography, *About Time*, M. reveals important insights into growing up in rural England between the First and Second World Wars as well as chronicling her parents' lives, both of whom were born in the last quarter of the nineteenth century. M., the younger of two children, was reared as an only child, since her brother, four years older, was sent away to school at four.

Her novels, following *Johanna* (1947), which was unsuccessful, have built her reputation solidly as one of Britain's finest living writers. In 1979 she received the Whitbread Award for non-fiction. M. has also written short stories and screenplays and was a critic-journalist and former Lonely Hearts columnist for London's *Daily Mail*, where she used the pseudonym Ann Temple. From 1967-70 she was movie critic for *The Observer*.

Throughout her novels, she uses the lives of women as a metonym of human vulnerability. In women's roles, as daughters, mothers, mistresses, wives, sisters, the shabby shelters of the self seem most tentative. M. chooses again and again the image of the house to convey the structure of self emblematic of women's roles, as suggested by her titles: *The Villa in Summer*; *The Bright Prison* ("shades of the prison house falls upon the growing boy"); *Cave of Ice*; *The Pumpkin Eater*; *My Friend Says It's Bullet-Proof*; *The Home*; *Long Distance* (from home); and *The Handyman* (the role of a man around the house). The image of architecture and the sound of voice identified in nursery rhymes and fairy tales carry her themes.

In 1972 she wrote: "The canvas of my fiction is narrow—domestic, mainly concerned with sexual and parental relationships—but I hope makes up in depth what it lacks in breadth. So far, I am almost entirely concerned with individuals' motives and the development of their personalities from an early age (*Pumpkin Eater* and *The Home*, particularly). Rather obviously (though not necessarily) I write through the eyes and ears of a woman. My men, I think, are getting better, and maybe I will someday venture to try to put myself inside a man's head and write from there. I believe that comedy is absolutely essential to tragedy, and I hope my books are almost as funny as they are (I'm told) sad or depressing. I would like to enlarge my scope, but not if it's at the expense of depth." In many of M.'s plots, the self is threatened in its relationships, feels captured, shelled, shelved, eaten. The depth of the heroine's mind is plumbed to reveal that the "I" is lost in its "we" relationships and that power flows from men. The lyric self of childhood memories and egoism is lost in the passage of time, and love cannot rescue it. M.'s stories and novels explore the conflict and theme of identity in transition.

About Time: An Aspect of Autobiography (1979) discloses the origins of M.'s lyric self, the *persona* of the novels. M.'s voice recounting her girlhood is fond, bemused, and deadly honest in its portrayal of her parents and their siblings, even when the truth is difficult and painful. For example, she reports her father's pitiful attempts to seduce her at eight and her own provocative behavior toward him when she turned sixteen. This incestuous and competitive relationship is reported in a truly disinterested voice. Her gentleness and independence serve her well in investigating her parents' generation. Many scenes drawn from memory recur in the fiction and are memorable; her uncle's rope factory and the dance with Mr. Fox, who was "at least forty-five, heavily married, and had a nasty little black mustache." Yet more indelible than the drawing of character, later caricatured in comedy, is M.'s disclosure of the details of provincial life that improbably represent the full range of human emotion in her fiction.

Her three early novels, *A Villa in Summer* (1955), *The Bright Prison* (1957), and *Daddy's Gone A-Hunting*, center on the case of the emo-

tionally overcommitted woman caught in a failing marriage: he withdraws, she frantically pursues. Adultery is a symptom of betrayal within the self. M. is interested not in the war between the sexes but in the war within the self. Two individuals may never become one in marriage, but each may romantically count on becoming one whole person. This failed dream sets up the blaming which turns the plot in all three. Marriage is the "bright" prison, the confining institution that hosts children's birthday parties and sexual infidelities. In *Daddy's Gone A-Hunting*, guilt for her part in the couple's failure to find unity in sexual fidelity paralyzes its heroine. She suffers, but cannot change her own plight or, more damaging, protect her daughter from her "hunter"-husband, Rex.

The Pumpkin Eater (1962), M.'s best-known novel, was adapted as a film by Harold Pinter and starred Anne Bancroft and Peter Finch. After three marriages end in divorce, the heroine meets and falls in love with Jake who welcomes marriage and family life, embracing the many children of his new wife. To say that purpose for the unnamed heroine amounts to having babies shows how M. simplifies a narrative of desire to its fairy-tale structure. To keep Jake happy and fed, to keep her own sanity which is linked to his happiness, she must terminate her last pregnancy. For her, it is the murder of desire and sanity. An abortion and sterilization are prescribed to remedy her depression. The displacement of motive and the manipulation of wills foment madness whose horror is simulated in the novel's fragmentation and dissolution.

My Friend Says It's Bullet-Proof (1968) demonstrates how "comedy is absolutely essential to tragedy" and how the novelist deepens her themes of isolation and identity by genre exploration. Comedy integrates character through change. In *Bulletproof* and *The Home* (1972), the heroines face their dissolving marriages and de-selved roles with comic verve. They are obsessed with recording their loss. Rather than finding a recognizable self in the record, a new self emerges in the recording.

If *Bulletproof* is comedy and *The Home* realism, then M.'s eighth novel, *Long Distance*, is allegory and fabulation, the journey into the past by way of madness. Again, the "I" of *Long Distance*, like Jake's wife in *The Pumpkin Eater*, has no given name; she speaks directly to a "you" who seems to be the eternal judging and deserting male. Read as a sequel to *The Pumpkin Eater*, the "action" follows the nightmare of shock treatments, drugs, and psychoanalytic therapy after her breakdown. M. has been criticized for her mishandling of fantasy and the fantastic landscape, but the image of the woman as a lost child, a long distance from home, making her escape to the gardener's shed to confess her incestuous love to this gardener-father is a terrifying Alice with her trick looking-glass. The novel attempts to render the terrors of madness by poetically concentrating the familiar and customary roles in erotic associations. All characters are figments of her mind and, therefore, highly stylized: for example, the old witch-sibyl-mother, the gardener-seducer-father, and her young dream lover, Simon, her son in reality.

John Updike called M.'s most recent novel, *The Handyman* (1985) a "lovely book—fierce in its disillusion, poetic and carefree in its language, comic and horrifying and deeply familiar all at once." The novel tells the story of Phyllis Muspratt who in her middle sixties is thrust into change and choice after her husband Gerald suddenly drops dead of a heart attack. Muspratt has an optimistic nature and life-long energetic habits that allow her to cope with her grown children and enjoy her grandchildren, especially her adored grandson. She is a woman who relies on traditional wisdom and roles. When she moves to the country, it is as though the civilized past is left behind because citizenship has been perverted into an underworld or an underground economy. It feels like a ruthless cowboy economy run by hired bullies with one strong-man leader, Wainwright, calling the shots.

It is almost fair to say that M.'s last novel is her first novel. Technically, she works like a poet, reinforcing brevity of plot and episode with character density and depth. Her language is deft, hinting at associations with imagery, allusive discourse, tracing details. In the early books, the vulnerable self is identified with women's roles whenever and wherever they serve others: lovers, wives, mothers. The creative self in her early novels is covert: the voice of the mad housewife. In *The Handyman*, the traditional woman and the independent woman—little Phyllis Muspratt of private life and Rebecca Broune of public life—are allowed to speak. Neither is lesser. What we hear are two original voices of spirit, dignity, and courage, noble heroines, both, in a splendid, notable novel.

WORKS: *Johanna* (as Penelope Dimont, 1947). *A Villa in Summer* (1954). *The Bright Prison* (1956). *With Love and Lizards* (with John Mortimer, 1957). *Daddy's Gone A-Hunting* (1958; U.S. edition published as *Cave of Ice*, 1959). *The Renegade* (1961). *Saturday Night with the Brownings* (1960). *The Pumpkin Eater* (1962). *Bunny Lake Is Missing* (with John Mortimer, 1965). *Ain't Afraid to Dance* (1966). *My Friend Says It's Bullet-Proof* (1967). *The Home* (1971). *Three's One* (1973). *Long Distance* (1974). *The Handyman* (1985).

BIBLIOGRAPHY: Rubenstein, R. *Boundaries of the Self: Gender, Culture, Fiction* (1987).

For articles in reference works, see: *CA. CN. TCW. WA.*

Other references: *Book Week* (1 September 1985). *Listener* (14 July 1983). *London Journal* (August 1985). *London Review of Books* (21 July 1983). *New Statesman* (20 May 1983). *NYTBR* (19 August 1979). *Observer* (22 May 1983).

Brett Averitt

(Jean) Iris Murdoch

BORN: 15 July 1919, Dublin.
DAUGHTER OF: Wills John Hughes and Irene Alice Richardson Murdoch.
MARRIED: John O. Bayley, 1956.

Born of Protestant Anglo-Irish parents in Dublin, M. grew up in London but has retained an active interest in Ireland, especially as setting for some of her novels. She studied Classics, Ancient History, and Philosophy at Oxford before World War II, worked during the war for the British government, and later helped refugees for the United Nations. She continued her study of Philosophy at Cambridge after the war and subsequently became a fellow at Oxford. She married John Bayley, poet, critic, novelist, and also a fellow at Oxford, in 1956.

In addition to specialized papers on linguistic analysis and existentialism, she has written a number of less technical works on ethics, aesthetics, and similar moral issues, including *Sartre, Romantic Rationalist* (1953), *The Sovereignty of Good* (1970), *The Fire and the Sun: Why Plato Banished the Artists* (1977), and *Acastos* (1986), Platonic dialogues. Though she has tried to keep her philosophic work distinct from her literary output (over twenty novels as well as stories and plays), her philosophic bent is immediately evident in her fiction.

M.'s fiction is characterized by a remarkable sense of humor, particularly wit and word play, farce (including wild chases), burlesque, dependence on split-second timing, and unforeseen plot twists. Her sense of parody and satire is less obvious, but her balance among various comic modes, including gentle satiric thrusts, combined as these are with serious, even polemical concerns, makes her work considerably more complex than it first appears.

She has repeatedly stated that she identifies with the tradition of George Eliot. Though she has acknowledged Henry James's influence, she has also stated that she prefers the non-Jamesian "open" novel (a spontaneous gathering of eccentric characters engaged in casual, seemingly uncontrolled activities), a claim not wholly borne out by her tightly structured books. She has used the term "transcendental realism" (in her essay "Against Dryness: A Polemical Sketch") to apply to her fiction, a term suggesting an initial acceptance of conventional concepts of plot, character, and setting with a subsequent explosion of absurd, wildly outrageous, and richly unconventional occurrences and "messy" characters. Despite the seemingly anarchic tone and nature of her novels, M. is evidently pessimistic about transient humanity's chances of survival in a formless, directionless universe.

M.'s fiction, consequently, focuses on individuals who are required by some circumstance (possibly violent or absurd) to ponder the nature of personal freedom and commitment. They must then realize that they can know neither love nor freedom unless they accept the radical "contingency" and ultimate pointlessness of existence as prerequisite to relations with others. M.'s first novel, *Under the Net* (1954), for example, offers a protagonist, Jake Donaghue, who discovers the sheer joy and unknowable wonder of life through some wildly comic adventures involving continual misunderstanding of other people. *The Flight from the Enchanter* (1956), a more complex, original novel, contrasts the fascinating but amoral Mischa Fox, who uses other people, with Rosa Keepe, who barely escapes his influence.

The Bell (1958), commonly considered (with *A Severed Head*, 1961) the best of M.'s earlier works, follows a variety of ordinary characters who retreat to a monastery to escape human limitations and failure, especially at love. Unable to live either in the world or out of it, they individually work out their destinies. *A Severed Head* is a remarkably effective comic account of the same efforts to understand the nature of human freedom; one of M.'s familiar clumsy male protagonists, Martin Lynch-Gibbon, reluctantly learns about love and sex in a series of wildly incongruous sexual couplings.

Following *A Severed Head*, M. published seven novels in quick succession. *An Unofficial Rose* (1962) is a family chronicle about an elderly man's reflections on his past and his desires for his son's future; *The Unicorn* (1963) is a slight though heavily philosophical work concerned with the ambiguity of relationships, especially sexual ones; *The Italian Girl* (1964) is a short, more Gothic work set in a Scottish household; *The Red and the Green* (1965) is a historical work set in Dublin during the 1916 Easter uprising; *The Time of the Angels* (1966), M.'s "God is dead" novel closely related to *The Unicorn* in its concern with metaphysical concepts, is a fascinat-

ing, sensational, Gothic exploration into the nature of evil; *The Nice and the Good* (1968) is a return to M.'s earlier concern with the conflicts inherent in spiritual and sexual love; and *Bruno's Dream* (1969) is a somewhat surrealistic account of an old man's dying thoughts as he feebly attempts to understand the world and death.

In the 1970s M. continued her rapid production, with *A Fairly Honourable Defeat* (1970) an appropriate name for the position many of her characters accept in their metaphysical quest. Though this novel breaks no new ground for M., she is more detailed in her evident knowledge of cuisines and cultural allusions, and this and several of her subsequent works are more expansive in scope and bulk. *An Accidental Man* (1971) focuses on the contrast between the search for love and the search for power through a kind of parallel novel-within-a-novel. *The Black Prince* (1973) is more experimental in its obsessive handling of a middle-aged man's lust for a twenty-year-old woman and with other sexual pairings reminiscent of *An Accidental Man*. *The Sacred and Profane Love Machine* (1974) is also about a man obsessed, in this case with his two loves, his wife (the sacred) and his mistress (the profane); this book, by far M.'s most violent, raises numerous moral questions but resolves few of them satisfactorily. The protagonist in *A Word Child* (1975) discovers that his adultery has been indirectly responsible for the deaths of two others and that his past is returning to haunt him; desperate to touch and love others, he eventually tries to purge his guilt by contacting the man he cuckolded.

The more thoughtful *Henry and Cato* (1976) focuses on two men who attempt individually to reconcile private impulses, especially the need for love: one, a self-exile in the United States until his brother's death, returns to England and echoes of his earlier life; the other, his boyhood friend turned Anglican priest, wrestles with forbidden love. Both men are complicated, both have muddled emotional lives, and both learn about pure evil in the forms of "fallen angels" who tempt them. *The Sea, The Sea* (1978) has been compared by Margaret Drabble to *The Tempest* and also to Homer; it deals with a theatre director who retires to the seashore but who slowly entraps his old circle of friends in his sexual obsessiveness.

The 1980s have shown a continuation of M.'s prolific productivity, with no diminution of her philosophical interests but with greater abstraction in characterization. The first word of *Nuns and Soldiers* (1980) is "Wittgenstein," who has frequently been invoked in analyses of M.'s work; the speaker, dying on Christmas eve, hosts an entourage of friends who later intrude possessively between would-be lovers, the widow, and one of the friends. *The Philosopher's Pupil* (1983) presents an overly didactic allegorical struggle between good and evil, even to the point of identifying the narrator by an initial; similarly, *The Good Apprentice* (1985) is both allegorical and muddled, though it is much more emphatic about the protagonist's suffering through personal irresponsibility toward a friend.

M.'s books have steadily grown longer and more turgid, though with greater concern with her character's experiential growth and breadth. She has often written about her characters' sexuality, even promiscuity, and she has dealt with such sexual taboos as incest. As her books have grown more abstract and philosophical, they have also grown less interesting as fiction, with recent characters less memorable than those of the 1960s.

Yet she remains a fertile writer, with undiminished vigor and productivity, with meticulous detail, and above all with dense, austere, unromantic, and pessimistic perspectives on her characters' lives. These characters are not tragic, just pathetic or terrible, and comedy helps the reader to see how enslaved they are, trapped by the ideas M. forces them to bear. At her best she is both entertaining and intellectually challenging; at her worst she is abstract to the point of obscurity. She deals primarily with concepts such as love, freedom, and power, and the "morality" she offers through her characters is limited in part by their own limitations, in part by the opposition of a host of authority figures, but almost always by some form of love and moral commitment.

WORKS: Sartre: Romantic Rationalist (1953, 1980). Under the Net (1954). The Flight from the Enchanter (1955). The Sandcastle (1957). The Bell (1958). A Severed Head (1961; as play, with J.B. Priestley, 1964). An Unofficial Rose (1962). The Unicorn (1963). The Italian Girl (1964; as play, with J. Saunders, 1968). The Red and the Green (1965). The Time of the Angels (1966). The Nice and the Good (1968). Bruno's Dream (1969). A Fairly Honourable Defeat (1970). The Sovereignty of Good (1970). The Servants and the Snow (1970). An Accidental Man (1971). The Three Arrows (1972). The Black Prince (1973). The Sacred and Profane Love Machine (1974). A Word Child (1975). Henry and Cato (1976). The Sea, the Sea (1978). The Fire and the Sun: Why Plato Banished the Artists (1977). A Year of Birds (1978). Nuns and Soldiers (1980). Art and Eros (1980). The Philosopher's Pupil (1983). The Good Apprentice (1985). Acastos (1986).

BIBLIOGRAPHY: Baldanza, F. *Iris Murdoch* (1974). Byatt, A.S. *Degrees of Freedom: The Novels of Iris Murdoch* (1965). Conradi, P.J. *Iris Murdoch: The Saint and the Artist* (1986). Dipple, E. *Iris Murdoch: Work for the Spirit* (1982). Gerstenberger, D. *Iris Murdoch* (1975). Hague, A. *Iris Murdoch's Comic Vision* (1979). Johnson, D. *Iris Murdoch* (1987). Todd, R. *Iris Murdoch* (1986). Todd, R. *Iris Murdoch: The Shakespearian Interest* (1979). Wolfe, P. *The Disciplined Heart: Iris Murdoch and Her Novels* (1966).

For articles in reference works, see: *CA. CD. CLC. CN. DLB. EWLTC. MBL & SUP. TCR. WA.*

Other references: Bellamy, M. *Contemporary Literature* (1977). Biles, J.I. *Studies in the Literary Imagination* (1978). Blum, L.A. *Philosophical Studies* (1986). Bradbury, M. *Possibilities: Essays on the State of the Novel* (1973). Brans, J. *Southwest Review* (1985). *Chicago Review* (Autumn 1959). Conradi, P.J. *Critical Quarterly* (1981). Culley, A. *Modern Fiction Studies* (1969). *Encounter* (January 1961). Jaidev. *Punjab University Research Bulletin (Arts)* (October 1985). Jefferson, D. *The Uses of Fiction: Essays on the Modern Novel in Honour of Arnold Kettle,* ed. D. Jefferson and G. Martin (1982). Moss, H. *Grand Street* (1986). *Partisan Review* (1959). Pears, U.F., ed. *The Nature of Metaphysics* (1957). Sage, L. *Critical Quarterly* (1977). Scholes, R. *The Fabulators* (1967; rev. as *Fabulation and Metafiction,* 1979). Tucker, L. *CL* (1986). Widman, R.L. *Critique* (1967). Widmer, K. *Twentieth Century Women Novelists,* ed. T.F. Staley (1982). *Yale Review* (1959).

Paul Schlueter

Carolina, Baroness Nairne

BORN: 16 August 1766, Gask, Perthshire.
DIED: 27 October 1845, Gask.
DAUGHTER OF: Laurence Oliphant and Margaret Robertson.
MARRIED: William Nairne, 1806.
WROTE UNDER: Mrs. Bogan of Bogan, B.B.

Raised by ardent Jacobites and named for Prince Charles Stuart, N. spent her early life listening to tales of her Jacobite kin, the Robertsons, Murrays, Drummonds, and Graemes, and learning the music that was a particular pleasure to her upper-class family. Her grandfather was a veteran of the rebellion of 1715; both her grandfather and her father were veterans of the 1745 rebellion, and her maternal grandfather was Duncan Robertson, chief of the clan Donnochy. Such distinguished lineage no doubt influenced the young woman, as did the music that played an important part in her homelife from early childhood when the children would sing a song before going to bed. N. and her two sisters were all able to play musical instruments and often entertained at social gatherings. This background provided the inspiration when "pretty Miss Car" began writing Jacobite songs as a young woman.

She enthusiastically welcomed the poetry of Robert Burns and persuaded her brother, Laurence, to subscribe to an edition of his poems which was published in 1786. N. was interested in Burns' method of providing new lyrics for old Scottish tunes because she felt that some of the old lyrics were too earthy. In 1792, she persuaded her brother to present her own anonymous version of "The Ploughman" or "The Pleuchman" to a group of his tenants. It became very popular, and in succeeding years N. wrote a number of humorous and patriotic songs, among which were "John Tod," "Jamie the Laird," and "The Laird o' Cockpen." In 1798, N. sent a copy of "The Land o' the Leal" to her friend Mrs. Campbell Colquhoun when the latter's child died. The song, a lament for a dead child that promises a better life in heaven, was for many years thought to be Burns' deathbed song because N. insisted on anonymity with regard to her lyrics.

In 1806, N. married her kinsman William Murray Nairne, who was heir to a peerage but whose lands and title were forfeit under the Act of Attainder. The couple had one son, and N. continued writing lyrics as part of a committee of women dedicated to purifying the national minstrelsy. The committee published *The Scotish Minstrel* with N. contributing to the collection under the name of Mrs. Bogan of Bogan. Her songs were signed B.B., and even the publisher did not know her true identity because she disguised herself as an old gentlewoman when she held interviews with him. Though she admired Burns, she thought some of his songs "tended to inflame the passions" and asked to have his "Willie brewed a peck o'maut," a drinking song, removed from *The Scotish Minstrel.* At this time, she was composing Jacobite songs for her aged uncle, the Chief of Strowan, and songs of the working classes for Nathaniel Gow, son of the famous Perthshire fiddler Neil Gow, among which was "Caller Herrin" about a Newhaven fishwoman. The tune of the song represents the chimes of Iron Church in Edinburgh.

N.'s husband was restored to the peerage by George IV in 1824, and N. became Baroness Nairne. Lord Nairne died in 1830, after which N. took her ailing son to Ireland where she wrote several songs, the best known of which is "Wake, Irishmen, Wake," a political protest against the oppressiveness of the Catholic Church in Ireland. N.'s son died in 1837 in Brussels, and from that time on, she often commented on her joy in the rapid passing of time so she could rejoin her husband and son in the afterlife.

At the age of thirty-one, when she had a mystical experience, N. became very devout and, disapproving of the lyrics of the old Scottish songs, resolved to rewrite them in a more modest vein. Her efforts, though welcomed in her own time, have been criticized by modern commentators as mere contributions "to the sentimental pietism and the genteel falsification of the working-class that overtook Scottish culture in the early nineteenth century." Such a charge may be leveled at "The Land o' the Leal" and perhaps "Caller Herrin," but it is not valid with regard to N.'s patriotic airs. "Will ye no' come back again?" beautifully expresses the desolation of the Jacobites at the exile of their Prince, and "The Hundred Pipers," though apocryphal, is a thoroughly rousing portrayal of the crossing of the Esk by Scottish troops.

Before her death, N. agreed to have her songs published anonymously, and the book was in preparation at her death. With the approval of her sister, the songs were subsequently published in 1846 as *Lays from Strathearn* by Carolina, Baroness Nairne, and N.'s lifelong secret was at last revealed. N.'s songs, some of which rival Burns' best, are important reminders of the humor, the piety, and the patriotism of the Scottish nation.

WORKS: *The Scotish Minstrel* (1821). *Lays from Strathearn* (1846).

BIBLIOGRAPHY: Crichton, A. *"The Land o' the Leal": Who Wrote It, Lady Nairne or Burns?* (1919). Keddie, H. [pseud. Sarah Tytler] and J.L. Watson. *Songstresses of Scotland* (1871). Rogers, C. *The Life and Songs of the Baroness Nairne* (1869). Simpson, M.S. *The Scottish Songstress Caroline Baroness Nairne* (1894).

Articles in reference works: *DNB. Penguin Companion to World Literature.*

Other references: Montgomerie, W. *Scottish Studies* (1957, 1959).

S.A. Winn

Edith Nesbit

BORN: 15 August 1858, London.
DIED: 22 April 1924, Dymchurch.
DAUGHTER OF: John Callis Nesbit and (?) Alderton.
MARRIED: Hubert Bland, 1880; Thomas Terry Tucker, 1917.

WROTE UNDER: Fabian Bland, E. Bland, Edith Nesbit.

N. was the youngest of four surviving children born to an agricultural chemist and the principal of an agricultural college in Kennington, a rural suburb of London, who died when N. was only three. Her widowed mother managed the college for a time but then decided to take her family abroad. This was an unsettled time for N., who hated the continental schools so much that she ran away from one of them. Her one happy time was in Brittany, where she stayed with a French family who had a daughter her own age. When she was thirteen, her family returned to England, settling in a large country house in Kent which she loved, but soon her mother ran out of money, necessitating a move to London.

When N. was twenty, she met Hubert Bland, a bank clerk, whom she married a year later. When her husband became ill with smallpox and his partner absconded with his funds, the family was left penniless. N., who had been publishing verse occasionally, was forced to support her children by selling poems and stories. The Blands both became socialists and were founders of the Fabian Society. They were the center of a literary salon, entertaining friends in Bohemian but intellectual gatherings. In spite of her domestic responsibilities with four children to support, N. was a prolific writer, publishing many short stories and other hack work. Her well-known books for children, which distinguished her career as a fiction writer, were not written until her forties. In 1897 she became famous for *The Story of the Treasure Seekers*, a collection of short pieces about the Bastable family, which had appeared in *Pall Mall* and *Windsor* magazines. This success also brought her prosperity and a new period of happy life at Well Hall in Kent, a moated sixteenth-century house. The second Bastable book, *The Wouldbegoods*, appeared in 1901.

The best known of her children's novels, still popular today, are *Five Children and It* (1902), *The Phoenix and the Carpet* (1904), and *The Story of the Amulet* (1906). In *Five Children and It*, the children discover the Psammead, or sandfairy, which grants them wishes every morning and revoking the effects each evening at sunset. In *The Phoenix and the Carpet* children find a phoenix egg rolled up in a carpet. Both magical creatures, the testy, cynical Psammead and the haughty, pompous phoenix, are memorable creations. *The Story of the Amulet* is a well-researched novel in which the quest for a missing half of an amulet takes the children on a series of time travels to ancient civilizations. Unlike most of her predecessors, N. was not didactic in her novels for children. Not concerned with moral issues, she rather took delight in the sheer variety of experience, particularly the comic and the fantastic. Influenced by Charles Dickens, whom she greatly admired, and by Victorian fantasist F. Anstey (Thomas Anstey Guthrie), N. in turn has influenced modern children's writers, including Edward Eager who praised and imitated her technique of introducing magic into ordinary daily life.

In spite of her tremendous output—fifteen novels for children, nine novels for adults, and over forty other books—N. continued to be in financial straits and her husband's death in 1914 left her desolate, though she was awarded a modest civil pension in 1915 for her literary achievement. In 1917 she remarried and settled with her new husband, a widowed, retired marine engineer and an old friend, in a bungalow on the Kent coast, where she died in 1921 at the age of sixty-five.

N. regarded herself as one of those who remain children in a grown-up world. This quality of perceiving life from a child's point of view clearly influenced her effective portrayal of children and her convincing excursions into the realm of fantasy.

WORKS: *The Prophet's Mantle* (as Fabian Bland, with Hubert Bland, 1895). *Lays and Legends* (1886-92). *The Lily and the Cross* (1887). *The Star of Bethlehem* (1887). *The Better Part and Other Poems* (1888). *By Land and Sea* (1888). *Easter-Tide: Poems* (with Caris Brooke, 1888). *Landscape and Song* (1888). *Leaves of Life* (1888). *The Message of the Dove: An Easter Poem* (1888). *The Time of Roses* (with Caris Brooke and others, 1888). *Corals and Sea Songs* (1899). *The Lilies Round the Cross: An Easter Memorial* (with Helen J. Wood, 1889). *Life's Sunny Side* (with others, 1890). *Songs of Two Seasons* (1890). *Sweet Lavender* (1892). *The Voyage of Columbus, 1492: The Discovery of America* (1892). *Flowers I Bring and Songs I Sing* (as E. Bland, with H.M. Burnside and A. Scanes, 1893). *Grim Tales* (1893). *Listen Long and Listen Well* (with others, 1893). *Our Friends and All About Them* (1893). *Something Wrong* (1893). *Sunny Tales for Snowy Days* (with others, 1893). *Told By Sunbeams and Me* (with others, 1893). *The Butler in Bohemia* (with Oswald Barron, 1894). *Fur and Feathers: Tales for All Weathers* (with others, 1894). *Hours in Many Lands: Stories and Poems* (with others, 1894). *Lads and Lassies* (with others, 1894). *Tales That Are True, for Brown Eyes and Blue* (with others, 1894). *Tales to Delight from Morning to Night* (with others, 1894). *Doggy Tales* (1895). *Dulcie's Lantern and Other Stories* (with Theo Gift and Mrs. Worthington Bliss, 1895). *Holly and Mistletoe: A Book of Christmas Verse* (with Norman Gale and Richard Le Gallienne, 1895). *A Pomander of Verse* (1895). *Pussy Tales* (1895). *Rose Leaves* (1895). *Tales of the Clock* (1895). *Treasures from Storyland* (with others, 1895). *As Happy As a King* (1896). *In Homespun* (1896). *The Children's Shakespeare* (1897). *Dinna Forget* (1897). *Royal Children of English History* (1897). *Tales Told in Twilight: A Volume of Very Short Stories* (1897). *Dog Tales, and Other Tales* (with A. Guest and Emily R. Watson, 1898). *Songs of Love and Empire*

(1898). *Pussy and Doggy Tales* (1899). *Secret of the Kyriels* (1899). *The Story of the Treasure Seekers, Being the Adventures of the Bastable Children in Search of a Fortune* (1899). *The Book of Dragons* (1900). *Nine Unlikely Tales for Children* (1901). *Thirteen Ways Home* (1901). *To Wish You Every Joy* (1901). *Five Children and It* (1902). *The Red House* (1902). *The Revolt of the Toys and What Comes of Quarreling* (1902). *The Wouldbegoods, Being the Further Adventures of the Treasure Seekers* (1902). *The Literary Sense* (1903). *Playtime Stories* (1903). *The Rainbow Queen and Other Stories* (1903). *Cat Tales* (with Rosamund Bland, 1904). *The New Treasure Seekers* (1904). *The Phoenix and the Carpet* (1904). *The Story of the Five Rebellious Dolls* (1904). *Oswald Bastable and Others* (1905). *Pug Peter: King of Mouseland, Marquis of Barkshire, D.O.G., P.C. 1906, Knight of the Order of the Gold Dog Collar, Author of Doggerel Lays and Days* (1905). *The Rainbow and the Rose* (1905). *The Incomplete Amorist* (1906). *Man and Maid* (1906). *The Railway Children* (1906). *The Story of the Amulet* (1906). *The Enchanted Castle* (1907). *Twenty Beautiful Stories from Shakespeare: A Home Study Course* (1907). *Ballads and Lyrics of Socialism 1883-1908* (1908). *The House of Arden* (1908). *Jesus in London* (1908). *The Old Nursery Stories* (1908). *Cinderella* (1909). *Daphne in Fitzroy Street* (1909). *Harding's Luck* (1909). *Salome and the Head: A Modern Melodrama* (1909). *These Little Ones* (1909). *Fear* (1910). *The Magic City* (1910). *Ballads and Verses of the Spiritual Life* (1911). *Dormant* (1911). *My Sea-Side Book* (with George Manville Fenn, 1911). *The Wonderful Garden, or The Three C's* (1911). *Children's Stories from Shakespeare* (1912). *Garden Poems* (1912). *The Magic World* (1912). *Our New Story Book* (1913). *Wet Magic* (1913). *Children's Stories from English History* (with Doris Ashley, 1914). *The Incredible Honeymoon* (1916). *The New World Literary Series, Book Two* (1921). *The Lark* (1922). *Many Voices* (1922). *To the Adventurous* (1923). *Five of Us—And Madeline* (ed. Mrs. Clifford Sharp, 1925). *Long Ago When I Was Young* (1966). *Fairy Stories* (ed. Naomi Lewis, 1977).

BIBLIOGRAPHY: Bell, A. *E. Nesbit* (1960). Briggs, J. *A Woman of Passion: The Life of E. Nesbit, 1858-1924* (1987). Moore, D.L. *E. Nesbit: A Biography* (1933, rev. ed. 1966). Streatfeild, N. *Magic and the Magician: E. Nesbit and Her Children's Books* (1958).

For articles in reference works, see: *More Junior Authors* (1963). *OCCL. TCCW.*

Other references: Manlove, C. *The Impulse of Fantasy Literature* (1984).

Charlotte Spivack

Florence Nightingale

BORN: 12 May 1820, Florence, Italy.
DIED: 13 August 1910, London.
DAUGHTER OF: William Edward and Frances Smith Nightingale.

"I had so much rather live than write; writing is only a supplement for living," N. told a friend. "I think one's feelings waste themselves in words; they ought all to be distilled into actions, and into actions which bring results." N. won her place in history through her heroic actions during the Crimean War, but her reasons for rebelling against society's expectations for women, her religious justifiction of her conduct, and her proposals for reforming health care and sanitation are all formulated in words: diaries, letters, government reports, journal articles, addresses to nursing students, more than two hundred books and pamphlets. For N., writing was a means to self-knowledge and an instrument for social change.

Educated at home by their wealthy, well-bred father, N. and her older sister Parthenope studied history, philosophy, mathematics, and classics; they also wrote weekly compositions. At the urging of classical scholar Benjamin Jowett, she prepared an anthology of writings by medieval mystics prefaced with the statement, "This reading is good only as a preparation for work." N. objected to writers who failed to understand the importance of work: poets who ignored poverty and disease in order to celebrate "the glories of this world"; "female ink-bottles" who spewed out pages of useless polemics; novelists who lured young women into fantasies of romantic love. Without action, the imagination could be dangerously self-indulgent. Dreaming, which N. regarded as an all-consuming activity for many women, was a sign of despair and frustration, an alternative rather than a prelude to accomplishment.

Writing served a therapeutic function in N.'s private life. Early journals describe her anger and frustration with the idle life of an upperclass Englishwoman. N. believed she had a call from God to undertake a life of heroic service, while her family asked her to write letters, play the piano, and entertain company, so writing enabled her to break with her family and begin her work in nursing. She told her father, "I hope now I have come into possession of myself." "Cassandra," an autobiographical fragment from this period, criticizes Victorian family structure, analyzes the ways women's time and talents are wasted, and prophesies the coming of a female Christ who will arise in the midst of suffering and complaint. Although the work remained unpublished during N.'s lifetime, John Stuart Mill incorporated some of her criticism of domestic routine into *The Subjection of Women*. N. continued to write "spiritual meditations" throughout her life: confessions of guilt, apologies for her self-obsession, communings with God.

Suggestions for Thought, the work from which "Cassandra" is derived, is, according to Elaine Showalter, "a major document of Victorian religious thought, which should be studied alongside Newman's *Apologia Pro Vita Sua*." In 1852, N. declared, "I have remodelled my whole religious belief from beginning to end. I have learnt to know God. I have recast my social belief; have them both written for use, when my hour is come." Rejecting Anglicanism, Catholicism, Protestantism, and Positivism, N. argued that the laws of God could be discovered by experience, research, and analysis. God is the Universal Being who is Law, "a Being who, willing only good, leaves evil in the world solely in order to stimulate human faculties by an unremitting struggle against every form of it." N. tried to impose order—digests with elaborate divisions and subdivisions, running titles, marginal glosses—but the massive manuscript is marred by rambling digressions and repetitions. N. sent her jumbled "Stuff," as she called it, to Mill, who advised publication, and Jowett, who called for extensive revision. Although N. had a few copies privately printed in 1860, she lost interest in revising the book for a general audience. *Suggestions* had served its purpose: she had formulated a theological justification for her commitment to self-development and public service.

In the public sphere, N. wrote her way into positions of power. Although N. was a public idol when she returned from the Crimean in 1856, she had no official standing with the military or governmental agencies investigating British losses in the war. She had also become an invalid. Arrogant, manipulative, and almost demonically energetic, she used her pen to attack the administrative chaos and poor sanitary conditions in the British Army. When a report was omitted from the government's publication, she paid to have five hundred copies printed in the form of a parliamentary blue book and circulated among her influential acquaintances. *Notes on Matters Affecting the Health, Efficiency, and Hospital Administration of the British Army* (1858) resulted in the establishment of a Royal Commission and passage of many of N.'s recommendations. Recognizing her brilliant analytic skills and knowledge of statistics, government leaders frequently sought N.'s advice, especially on matters of public health in India. When necessary, N. could organize tre-

mendous public support through adroit use of the press.

Notes on Nursing: What It Is, and What It Is Not (1860) was N.'s most popular book, selling 15,000 copies in a few months and receiving scores of enthusiastic reviews; according to Harriet Martineau, it was "a work of genius." N.'s advice on domestic hygiene was intended for a wide audience, for she defined a nurse as anyone who has responsibility for another's health. N.'s belief that all disease is "more or less a reparative process" meant that the nurse must "put the patient in the best condition for nature to act upon him." The doctor's duties were diminished by N.'s adamant opposition to the germ theory and her conviction that "nature alone cures." N.'s prose is clear, concrete, often epigrammatic in style, and occasionally satiric in tone; through related image patterns, she fuses moral fervor and scientific authority.

N. carefully cultivated her image as the noble, self-sacrificing "lady with the lamp," but she also identified with Jesus, Joan of Arc, Correggio's Magdelen, and Queen Victoria. A skilled mythmaker, she made the nurse into a figure of epic proportions. "Una and the Lion" (1868) invokes Spenser's *Faerie Queene* to eulogize Agnes Jones, a woman who died while nursing in a workhouse, as "Una in real flesh and blood—Una and her paupers, far more untameable than lions." In actuality, N. thought Jones was inept; in print, she saw an opportunity to satisfy her own ego needs and win converts to Christian service.

N. was reluctant to align herself with women, perhaps because of unresolved conflicts with her mother and sister. She supported married women's property rights, but she resisted Mill's appeals for help in the suffrage campaign, remarking that she herself exerted more influence on government than if she "had been a borough returning two M.P.'s" Having money, position, and great personal strength, N. claimed to be "brutally indifferent to the wrongs or rights of my sex." But even as she urged readers to keep clear of "both jargons"—the jargon about women's rights, "which urges women to do all that men do," and the jargon about woman's mission, "which urges women to do nothing that men do"—she set an example and gave advice that enabled many women to set out upon independent lives: "Oh, leave these jargons, and go your way straight to God's work, in simplicity and singleness of heart."

WORKS: *Notes on Matters Affecting the Health, Efficiency, and Hospital Administration of the British Army* (1858). *Notes on Hospitals* (1859). *Notes on Nursing: What It Is and What It Is Not* (1860). *Suggestions for Thought* (1860). *Observations on the Evidence Contained in the Stational Reports Submitted to Her by the Royal Commission on the*

Sanitary State of the Army in India (1863). "How People May Live and Not Die in India" (1863). "Una and the Lion" (1868). *Florence Nightingale to Her Nurses* (1914). *Selected Writings of Florence Nightingale,* ed. L.R. Seymer (1954). "Cassandra," ed. Myra Stark (1979).

BIBLIOGRAPHY: Bishop, W.J., and S. Goldie. *A Bio-Bibliography of Florence Nightingale* (1962). Boyd, N. *Three Victorian Women Who Changed Their World* (1982). Cook, E.T. *The Life of Florence Nightingale* (1914). Forster, M. *Significant Sisters: The Grassroots of Active Feminism, 1839-1939* (1984). Holton, S. *Social Analysis* (1984). Pugh, E.L. *Journal of British Studies* (1982). Rosenberg, C.E. *Healing and History,* ed. C.E. Rosenberg (1979). Showalter, E. *Signs* (1981). Smith, F.B. *Florence Nightingale: Reputation and Power* (1982). Vicinus, M. *Independent Women: Work and Community for Single Women, 1850-1920* (1985). Woodham-Smith, C. *Florence Nightingale* (1950).

For articles in reference works, see: *BDBF. DNB. Europa.*

Robin Sheets

Duchess of Northumberland (Elizabeth Percy)

BORN: 1716.
DIED: 5 December 1776, Alnwick Castle.
DAUGHTER OF: Algernon, Baron Percy and Francis Thynne.
MARRIED: Hugh Smithson, 1740.

A leading figure in English society, N. remains interesting to political and social historians, students of architectural and landscape history, and connoisseurs of travel writing. With her husband, N. supported the arts, worked to institute reforms on their estates, and campaigned against Wilkes during the 1767 Westminster elections. A friend of Walpole's and a correspondent of Boswell's, N. served as Lady of the Bedchamber to her friend Queen Charlotte until the Queen took umbrage, Walpole says, at N.'s parading "before the Queen with more footmen than her Majesty."

From 1752 to 1776 N. kept detailed diaries of political and social events and of her visits to country houses, a principal entertainment even when ill health forced her to spend increasing amounts of time on the continent. N. made her own country house, Syon, into England's finest, and kept a list of over 150 questions with which she noted the details of estates she visited. The descriptions she kept have helped scholars identify architects, flesh out their knowledge of vanished houses, and trace the tastes of the century, including N.'s own liking for gothic.

A Short Tour, taken from the travel diaries, may have been unauthorized; neither author's nor publisher's name appears in the volume. The excerpt is unremarkable, revealing N.'s eye for detail but little of her sharp wit. Other portions of the diaries describe her two years in Ireland, where the then-Earl of Northumberland served as Lord Lieutenant, her many journeys on the continent, and a brief visit to Voltaire, whom she found "like all the busts," but plumper.

A minor versifier, N. contributed what Walpole labelled "bouts rimes on a buttered muffin" to a miscellany by Bath socialite and travel writer Anna Miller. Johnson, while defending the right of "a lady of her [N.'s] high rank" to do anything she pleased, also scorned the book.

N's style in the diaries sometimes founders under the weight of innumerable details, but she can be direct, gossipy, or stingingly clever. A new acquaintance is "the biggest puppy I ever met," and on a country visit she must kiss "an ugly Cousin and a sweaty Brother of Lord Balhavens." In France, she has "the advantage of a reeking Dunghill under the Window" of her inn; "I really thought I should have hanged myself...." She revels in pomp, enthuses over scenery, and delights in news of Lady Harriet eloping with her footman or Madame de Boufller's husband being "so complaisent as to dye" shortly before rumors that her lover, the Prince de Conti, planned to marry her.

No complete edition of N.'s works has yet appeared. Grieg's edition contains excellent notes but concentrates on the social and political, omitting most of N.'s architectural descriptions and the common events of her days. N.'s papers remain at the ancestral home, Alnwick Castle.

WORKS: Diaries and notebooks (unpublished). Extracts from diaries in Grieg, J., ed., *Diaries of a Duchess* (1926). *A Short Tour Made in the Year 1771* (1775). "The pen, which now I take and brandish." *Poetical Amusements at a Villa Near Bath* (ed. A.R. Miller, 1775).

BIBLIOGRAPHY: Hesselgrave, R. *Lady Miller and the Batheaston Circle* (1927). Northumberland, Duke of. "Introduction" *Diaries of a Duchess,* ed. J. Grieg (1926). Percy, V., and G. Jackson-Stops, *Country Life* (31 January, 7 February, 14 February 1974).

For articles in reference works, see: Todd.

Other references: Boswell, J., *Life of Johnson* (1791). Walpole, H. *Letters* (1937-1983).

Marie E. McAllister

Frances (Freke) Norton

BORN: 1640, Hannington, Wilts.
DIED: 20 February 1731.
DAUGHTER OF: Ralph Freke and Cecilia Colepepper (Culpepper).
MARRIED: Sir George Norton, c. 1672; Colonel Ambrose Norton, 1718; William Jones, 1724.

The third daughter of Ralph and Cecilia Freke of Hennington, Wiltshire, N. was a devotional writer and poet who was familiar with Latin and Greek and wrote verses of extraordinary piety. N. was so acclaimed that on her death she was buried in Westminster Abbey. Her life, however, was fraught with the pain and melancholy that seemed the lot of so many women of her time. Apparently married first about 1672 to Sir George Norton, knight of Abbots Leigh, Somerset, N. gave birth to three children: George and Elizabeth, who died young, and Grace, afterwards Lady Gethin. It was said of N.'s first husband that he had concealed Charles II in his home during the battle of Worcester. The marriage between N. and her Royalist husband survived the first few years, but just barely. N. left her husband after Grace was born. Grace died in 1697, and two years later N. published her daughter's manuscripts in a volume called *Misery's Virtues Whetstone*. Praised by critics such as William Congreve and later Edmund Gosse, the volume was re-

printed in 1700 as *Reliquiae Gethinianae*. In 1705, N. published two of her own works in small quarto volumes: *The Applause of Virtue, in four parts*, and *Memento Mori, or Meditations on Death*. So affected by the death of her daughter, N. explains in the preface that her essays served as "melancholy divertisement." Each of the works is a collection of quotations on moral lessons from ancient and modern writers.

After her first husband's death on 26 April 1715, N. married again on 23 April 1718, possibly to Colonel Ambrose Norton, who died in 1723, and in 1724 she probably married William Jones. In 1714, she produced her *Miscellany of Poems*, religious poems that she also preserved in needlepoint that she signed.

WORKS: *The Applause of Virtue. In four parts. Consisting of several divine and moral essays towards the obtaining of true virtue* (1705). *Memento Mori: or, Meditations on Death* (1705). *Miscellany of Poems* (1714).

BIBLIOGRAPHY: Ballard, G. *Memoirs of Several Ladies. . . , who have been Celebrated for their Writings* (1752). Collinson, J. *History of Somersetshire* (1791).
    For articles in reference works, see: *DNB. Fifty Famous Women* (n.d.). Todd.

Sophia B. Blaydes

Kathleen (Cecilia) Nott

BORN: 1910, London.
DAUGHTER OF: Philip and Ellen Nott.
MARRIED: Christopher Bailey, 1929.

N., poet, critic, philosopher, and novelist, has written in many genres but considers herself primarily a poet. She studied philosophy extensively, especially ethics and aesthetics, at the universities of London and Oxford. She was a social worker among poor Jews in London's East End during the 1930s and out of her experiences wrote her first novel, *Mile End* (1938). She has since written numerous volumes of verse, fiction, philosophy, and criticism, the best known of which is *The Emperor's Clothes* (1953), an attack upon the "dogmatic orthodoxy" of such writers as C.S. Lewis, T.S. Eliot, and Dorothy Sayers. In addition, N. has written for many journals, including the *Times* (London) *Literary Supplement*, *Observer*, *Spectator*, and *Time and Tide*. She has long been active with P.E.N., as editor of one of its publications and in various executive positions.

Mile End, N.'s longest novel, attempts to span three generations of East London Jews torn between their own heritage and the demands of the larger, non-Jewish world. This work was criticized for its common first-novel excesses, both in style and in length, as well as for N.'s repeated reliance on philosophizing rather than on action, but it successfully captures the dilemmas faced by her characters. Her conclusion—that neither set of rigid orthodoxies is preferable—leads to her characters simply opting for "Life."

The Dry Deluge (1947) and *Private Fires* (1960) are generally considered lesser fictional efforts because of problems with narrative perspectives as well as continued reliance on authorial commentary. *The Dry Deluge* describes the creation of an underground socialistic Utopia, run by an eccentric but charismatic professor and devoted to planning for and practicing immortality, and *Private Fires* focuses on various unusual characters in London immediately after World War II. In neither case are N.'s characters fully dimensional or believable, nor are her contrived conclusions convincing.

N.'s fourth novel, *An Elderly Retired Man* (1963), is by common consent her best, primarily because N. seems in greater control of her materials. Her title character, Roden Cluer, a civil servant, attempts belatedly to resolve his lifetime of doubts and uncertainties; for the first time he realizes the necessity—and painful difficulty—of accurately assessing his marriage, friends, and loyalties, especially as he contemplates the ways in which his one deeply emotional attachment affects his and his wife's situation. Unlike her earlier novels, in which N. tried to force the reader's conclusions, this one is perceptive, convincing, and moving.

The Emperor's Clothes was N.'s attempt to expose the "New Philistinism" represented by the religious and cultural orthodoxy of Eliot, Lewis, Graham Greene, Walter Allen, and, by implication, others who also show what N. perceives as hostility to and inability to grasp the meaning of science. Vigorously defending the "humanism" that has dominated Western thought for the past 300 years, N. defends such writers as Jacob Bronowski and Bertrand Russell while criticizing those she calls "Augustinian novelists." N. is fully as dogmatic in rejecting Christian orthodoxy as are those she attacks, and her sometimes sarcastic tone serves less to defend the "Two Cultures" concept of C.P. Snow and more to suggest a certain close-mindedness. *Philosophy and Human Nature* (1970), by contrast, is a more balanced assessment of the various philosophies (including existentialism and Eastern thought) that appeal to modern men and women, with N.'s own allegiance to logical positivism (and the linguistic analysis of A.J. Ayer) clearly uppermost in her mind.

N.'s other works in philosophy include *Objections to Humanism* (1963; written with others); *A Soul in the Quad* (1969), which she describes as what she conceives "the relations of poetry and philosophy to be" in an "autobiographical and intellectual-social setting"; and *The*

Good Want Power: An Essay in the Psychological Possibilities of Liberalism (1977).

N.'s poetry reflects her philosophical tendencies; she regards poetry as a "special language and an existential one," the "language of beings of rather peculiar physiological and psychological organization," and the "most favourable . . . highly authentic personal vision." Her four volumes of verse have been noted for their rhythm more than for their use of conventional forms and criticized for their imprecise and forced diction and confused resolution of the ideas prompting the poems.

Most likely N. will be remembered as a writer on philosophical topics more than as a poet or novelist, with her most contentious work, *The Emperor's Clothes*, especially prominent, though more because of her targets' lasting reputations than her own persuasive observations.

WORKS: *Mile End* (1938). *The Dry Deluge* (1947). *Landscapes and Departures* (1947). (trans.) *Northwesterly Gale*, by L. Chauvet (1947). *The Emperor's Clothes: An Attack on the Dogmatic Orthodoxy of T.S. Eliot, Graham Greene, Dorothy Sayers, C.S. Lewis and Others* (1953). *Poems from the North* (1956). (trans.) *Son of Stalin*, by R. Baccelli (1956). (trans.) *The Fire of Milan*, by R. Baccelli (1958). *Creatures and Emblems* (1960). *Private Fires* (1960). *A Clean Well-Lighted Place: A Private View of Sweden* (1961). *An Elderly Retired Man* (1963). (with others) *Objections to Humanism* (1963). (with others) *What I Believe* (1966). *A Soul in the Quad* (1969). *Philosophy and Human Nature* (1970). *The Good Want Power: An Essay in the Psychological Possibilities of Liberalism* (1977). *Elegies and Other Poems* (1981).

BIBLIOGRAPHY: Holloway, J. *The Colours of Clarity: Essays on Contemporary Literature and Education* (1964).

For articles in reference works, see: *CA. CN. CP. Science Fiction Encyclopedia. WA.*

Other references: *TLS* (3 December 1938, 24 May 1947, 7 June 1947).

Paul Schlueter

Edna O'Brien

BORN: 15 December 1930, Tuamgraney, County Clare, Ireland.
DAUGHTER OF: Michael and Lena Cleary O'Brien.
MARRIED: Ernest Gebler, 1951.

O., an Irish expatriate, has been sexually candid in her works. These attributes, plus being a woman, have added to her appeal to her reading

public, especially in the United States, where she has had to endure the peculiar fate of a woman writer criticized as much as she is celebrated. Her professional readers are, it seems, on the lookout for the least echo of Joyce, the least emotional excess, the least indication of derivative lyricism or self-indulgence. Scrutiny has been even more intense because she writes so well so often.

O. writes best about what she knows, and

much of her best writing draws from her personal experience. Therefore she writes better stories about Ireland than she does about London, better stories about village life than city life, and best about women facing and abandoning a Catholic, Irish heritage for a secular, passionate life in search of what O. is never ashamed to call "true love." The word "girl" surfaces and resurfaces in her writing, calling up the pain involved in callow girls' traumatic education for living. For many of her women, this abandoned heritage remains in the psyche and the flesh forever; one never stops being an Irish Catholic, a daughter, a village girl.

Thus O. has forged a body of work parallel to her real life. The *Country Girls* trilogy (*The Country Girls*, 1960; *The Lonely Girl*, 1962; *Girls in Their Married Bliss*, 1964), begun shortly after O. had moved to London, deals with growing up, breaking ties, and learning about (and failing in) love. Her novels of the late sixties, especially *August Is a Wicked Month* (1965) and *Casualties of Peace* (1966), address the consequences of marriage's collapse. (O. herself was divorced in 1964.) In 1977 she published *Johnny I Hardly Knew You*, which she has said was an exploration of the older woman's attraction for younger men, a search to re-establish the unambiguous mother-son relationship through the ambiguous medium of sex. That book may also take revenge on males in general when the heroine murders her handsome younger lover.

By the 1980s O. was ensconced in a large house in Maida Vale, a largely Irish residential district in London. Her expatriation appears in two ways in her fiction: in the less successful stories about urban life collected in *A Fanatic Heart* (1984) and an exploration of things Irish in her nonfiction, including *Mother Ireland* (1976), *James and Nora* (1981), and *Returning* (1982).

O. is famous for writing well (and frequently) about sex. She has taught women writers how to write lyrically and honestly about physical and emotional intimacy, but she has been most convincing when she portrays sex as part of a woman's total existence, something involving her education, her childhood, her hopes, even her career. Thus her depictions of sexual relations in stories such as "The Love Object" and "Paradise" are less convincing than those in "A Rose in the Heart of New York," "A Scandalous Woman," or in novels such as *Country Girls* or *Night* (1972).

O. explores human emotions through a richly lyrical confessional prose. Perhaps the height of her lyric mode was reached in the interior monologues of Mary Hooligan in *Night*. Lyricism and confessionalism arise from the Irish narrative tradition as does her very Irish sensibility: she is looking for the very rhythms of the human soul and the rules of life. There is an intoxication with the dangers at hand for any Irish writer: senti-mentality, maudlin self-absorption, facile lyricism, blather, blarney. And if she sometimes succumbs to these temptations—"That night their lovemaking had all the sweetness and all the release that earth must feel with the long-awaited rain"—there are riches that more than balance the lapses.

The conviction and authenticity of superior fiction come through so often that O. must be considered as one of the most important writers of her time. The *Country Girls* trilogy is, as a whole, quite successful, even if there is a loss of energy and descent into pessimism in the last novel, the too obviously titled *Girls in Their Wedded Bliss*. Kate and Baba of the *Country Girls* books are perhaps O.'s best-known characters. Kate, one of her most sympathetic and frustrating creations, is, quite simply, a victim of romance; as we watch her mature, we follow her through a series of amorous disappointments and disasters, realizing that her unrealistic expectations of love disqualify her for happiness. Her friend and opposite, Baba, a reckless ironist, prospers in the ironic world of intimacy. True love fails for Baba, too, but she is resilient and hard enough to settle for a series of non-genuine attachments, culminating in a marriage to a rich man she does not love. One of the rewards of the *Country Girls* books is that O. as author identifies ideals in which she passionately wishes to believe—and allows them to fail. By the end of the trilogy, none of these ideals are left standing. Kate fails because of her devotion to the love ideal, and Baba succeeds because of a complete absence of ideals.

Of her stories, the two best are possibly "Sister Imelda" and "A Rose in the Heart of New York." "Sister Imelda" describes a nun and her schoolgirl pupil, both obsessed with the quest for purity, who fall in love with each other and with the intensity of their quest. One of O.'s best moments occurs when the girl realizes she must turn away from her mentor and toward a worldly future. "Rose," also about turning away, is a careful tracing of the relation of mother and daughter. If there is a single best moment in O.'s fiction, it may well be the moment when the daughter discovers some money her dead mother has left for her.

O. has also written successfully in other genres. She has written screenplays for film versions of her novels, including *The Girl with Green Eyes* (1964), and *X, Y, and Zee* (1971). Her play *Virginia* (1981) is a very successful study of Virginia Woolf, and she is also an excellent essayist.

O.'s independent mind has put her at odds with other women writers who have expected her to be a spokesperson for the feminist viewpoint. "I don't feel strongly about all the things they feel strongly about," she has said. "I feel strongly about childhood, truth or lies, and the real expression of feeling." She has insisted on a real difference between the sexes. Especially unfeminist is her conviction that there is "both a conscious and an unconscious degree of submission in a woman." However, O. feels that women can and must fight this submissiveness. For her future fiction, O. has said that her goal is to create a truly great female character. She wishes not only to match the best of literature's women (ironically, created mostly by male authors) but also to create a truly believable heroine, a "woman who succeeds," if only to show that success is possible.

WORKS: *The Country Girls* (1960). *The Lonely Girl* (1962; rpt. as *Girl with Green Eyes*, 1964; screenplay by O., 1964). *A Cheap Bunch of Nice Flowers*, in *Plays of the Year*, ed. J.C. Trewin (1963). *Girls in Their Married Bliss* (1964). *August Is a Wicked Month* (1965). *Casualties of Peace* (1966). *Time Lost and Time Remembered* (screenplay with D. Davis from O.'s story "A Woman at the Seaside," 1966). *Three into Two Won't Go* (screenplay by O. from the novel by A. Newman, 1968). *The Love Object* (1969). *A Pagan Place* (1970). *Zee & Co.* (screenplay by O. for the film *X, Y, and Zee*, 1971). *Night* (1972). *A Pagan Place* (1973). *The Gathering* (1974). *A Scandalous Woman and Other Stories* (1974). *Mother Ireland* (1976). *Johnny I Hardly Knew You* (1977; in U.S. as *I Hardly Knew You*, 1978). *Arabian Days* (1978). *The Collected Edna O'Brien* (1978). *Mrs. Reinhardt and Other Stories* (1978). *A Rose in the Heart* (1979). *James and Nora* (1981). *Virginia: A Play* (1981). *Returning* (1982). *A Fanatic Heart* (1984). *The Country Girls Trilogy and Epilogue* (1986).

BIBLIOGRAPHY: "Dialogue with Edna O'Brien." *Under Bow Bells: Diaglogues with Joseph McCulloch* (1974). Eckley, G. *Edna O'Brien* (1974). "Edna." *Talking to Women*, ed. N. Dunn (1965). Kiely, B. *Conor Cruise O'Brien Introduces Ireland*, ed. O. Edwards (1969). O'Brien, D. *Twentieth Century Women Novelists*, ed. T. Staley (1982).

For articles in reference works, see: *CA. CLC. DIL. DLB.*

Other references: *Bookviews* (January 1978). *Eire-Ireland* (1967, 1977). *Irish University Review* (1977). *James Joyce Quarterly* (1966). *The Nation* (14 May 1973). *Observer* (18 January 1981); *The New Yorker* (12 February 1972). *NR* (7 January 1985, 30 June 1986). *NYT* (7 April 1976, 11 October 1977, 27 June 1978, 12 November 1984). *NYTBR* (1 January 1978, 18 November 1984). *SR* (1 February 1979). *TLS* (23 April 1982). *Village Voice* (1 July 1986).

John Timpane

Kate O'Brien

BORN: 3 December 1897, Limerick, Ireland.
DIED: 13 August 1974, Faversham, Kent.
DAUGHTER OF: Thomas and Catherine (Thornhill) O'Brien.
MARRIED: Gustaaf Renier, 1923.

O. was an Irish novelist and playwright, who, unlike most Irish writers of her time (who wrote about the poor and the working class), concentrated her work on the cultured Irish middle class and the emotional tensions created for them by the "puritanism" of the Catholic Church in Ireland. O.'s work is, according to Eavan Boland, "our only link in literature" with:

... an Ireland of increasing wealth and uneasy conscience, where the women wore stays and rouged their cheeks, had their clothes made by Dublin dressmakers and tried to forget the hauntings of their grandparents. This was Catholic Ireland; it was never nationalist Ireland. Its citizens were wealthy merchants, and it perished overnight when the ghosts of their ancestors walked again in their hunger and their anger.

In 1903, when O. was five, her mother died. O. was sent to school at the Laurel Hill Convent, Limerick, where she lived for twelve years. In 1915 she won a scholarship to study Arts at University College, Dublin. During World War I, O. moved to England and worked as a journalist in Manchester and London; she then spent a year in Spain, employed as a governess. She married Gustaaf Renier, a Dutch journalist, in 1923, but the marriage lasted only a few months. Afterward, she devoted her time to writing short stories and plays. O.'s reputation as a playwright was established with the success of her first play, *Distinguished Villa*, in 1926. Her second play, *The Bridge*, was produced in 1927.

The first of O.'s nine novels, *Without My Cloak* (1931), was highly praised, and for it she won both the Hawthornden and the James Tait Black Prizes for literature. *Without My Cloak* is set in a fictional town called "Mellick" (probably Limerick), also the setting of O.'s second novel, *The Ante-Room* (1934), considered one of O.'s best works, which tells a story of love and marriage among the Irish-Catholic bourgeoisie of the early twentieth century. O., as Boland points out, views "the world of her birth with the eyes of an exile." By doing so, Boland says, O. manages "to make us love these selfish merchant souls. They are dross. We know they are dross. But by the end of the book we have spent such golden hours in their company that they look different."

O. spent the early 1930s working as a journalist in Bilbao, Spain, but returned to England at the start of the Spanish Civil War. Three of O.'s books, *Mary Lavelle* (1936) and *That Lady* (1946), both novels, and *Farewell Spain* (1937), a "romanticized" travel book, are based on her experiences in Spain. *Mary Lavelle* is the story of a young Irishwoman spending a year as a governess in Spain before marrying her childhood sweetheart in Mellick. Mary falls in love, predictably, with the married son of her employer, but there is no sentimental happy ending. What makes *Mary Lavelle* an important book is O.'s sympathetic portrayal of a lesbian character, Agatha Conlon, who falls in love with Mary. Both *Mary Lavelle* and O.'s later book, *The Land of Spices* (1941), in which the protagonist discovers that her father is homosexual, were banned in Ireland for "immorality."

That Lady (1946, published as *For One Sweet Grape* in the United States), is an historical novel based on the relationship between Ana de Mendoza, the Princess of Eboli, and Philip II of Spain, a story O. discovered in the letters of St. Teresa of Avila, about whom she would later publish a monograph (1951). In its concern with an illicit love affair, *That Lady* exemplifies what Tamsin Hargreaves calls the "unorthodox" nature of O.'s work:

> Kate O'Brien's novels are unorthodox; her heroines are driven by personal need and they struggle to reach modes of behaviour and thought which are true to themselves, even if, at times, this means going against the teaching of the Catholic Church. All Kate O'Brien's major novels describe love . . . which in orthodox terms is illicit and forbidden and which is therefore deeply problematic.

For Ana de Mendoza, human love comes to mean less "than her own spirituality"—a spirituality that includes personal freedom. Ultimately, she enters a convent and finds peace by isolating herself from "the passions of human loving." Al-

though the book was very successful, both a play (1949) and a movie (1955) based on the story failed.

In addition to her plays and novels, O. also wrote several non-fiction pieces, of which *English Diaries and Journals* (1943), a combination of history and criticism, is one of the most interesting. O. examines the diaries of many famous people as well as those of relatively obscure historical figures, including Samuel Pepys, John Evelyn, John Wesley, Fanny Burney, Queen Victoria, Sir Walter Scott, and Katherine Mansfield. O.'s comments on Burney are quite perceptive: "We cannot but wonder why she never took herself in hand and became a great novelist, as great as Jane Austen." The reason may have been Burney's "benevolent" but "rather foolish" father.

In 1947, O. was elected to the Irish Academy of Letters and was made a Fellow of the Royal Society of Literature. She lived most of her life at Roundstone, County Galway, but moved in 1961 to Faversham. She published *My Ireland*, a travel book, in 1962, and *Presentation Parlour*, her autobiography, in 1963.

WORKS: *Distinguished Villa* (1926). *The Bridge* (1927). *Without My Cloak* (1932). *The Ante-Room* (1934). *Mary Lavelle* (1936). *Farewell Spain* (1937). *Pray for the Wanderer* (1938). *The Land of Spices* (1941). *The Last of Summer* (1943). *English Diaries and Journals* (1943). *That Lady* (1946). *Teresa of Avila* (1951). *The Flower of May* (1953). *As Music and Splendour* (1958). *My Ireland* (1962). *Presentation Parlour* (1963).

BIBLIOGRAPHY: Boland, E. preface to *The Ante-Room* (rpt. 1982). Dalsimer, A.M. *Eire* (1986). Hargreaves, T. preface to *Mary Lavelle* (rpt. 1984). Reynolds, L. *Kate O'Brien: A Literary Portrait* (1987).

For articles in reference works, see: *Authors and Writers. CA. CBEL. DIL. TCA* and *SUP.*

Other references: Lawrence, M.M. *The School of Feminism, or We Write as Women* (1930). Nathan, G.J. *Theatre Book of the Year, 1949-1950* (1950).

Kate Beaird Meyers

Julia O'Faolain

BORN: 6 June 1932, London.
DAUGHTER OF: Sean and Eileen O'Faolain.
MARRIED: Lauro Martines.

Writer of fiction, translator, editor, and reviewer, O. is most accomplished in the short story, the form that won her father international recog-

nition. She was educated in Dublin by Sacred Heart nuns, graduated from University College, Dublin, and continued her schooling in Rome and Paris. She is married to the American historian, Lauro Martines, and maintains residences in London and Los Angeles.

Although many of her works reflect her Irish

heritage, O.'s fiction has an international scope, as many of her stories and novels are set on the Continent and in America. A writer with definite feminist sympathies, O. poses questions about the role of women in society and delineates the repression of women in a male-dominated world. Her fiction deals honestly, sometimes almost brutally, with sexual and religious hypocrisy; the toughness and frankness of her prose has been the object of both critical acclaim and disapproval. A more compassionate humanity and refined sense of humor, however, have surfaced in some of her more recent works.

The stories in O.'s first collection, *We Might See Sights* (1968), introduce concerns that are to reappear throughout her subsequent fiction. The Irish stories, in which O. reveals little sympathy for her homeland, explore such subjects as adolescent sexuality and suppression of the passions. The softer Italian stories center on the intricate links between the past and present and on the sadness of loneliness and old age.

O.'s first novel, *Godded and Codded* (1970), received a mixed critical response. The work, entitled *Three Lovers* in America, recounts the sexual initiation of a young Irishwoman in Paris during the Algerian troubles. While the characterizations tend to be shallow, O. shows talent as a caricaturist of Left Bank life and convincingly conveys the protagonist's victimization by men. In 1973 she published *Not in God's Image* (subtitled "Women in History from the Greeks to the Victorians"), which she edited with her husband. In their efforts to study the subjection of women in western civilization, the editors compiled selections from a variety of primary sources, ranging from diary entries to excerpts from literary works, accompanied by commentary. Termed by one critic as "in a class quite of its own," this volume was especially praised for its scholarship.

The vast array of problems besetting individuals as they attempt to deal with sexuality dominate the stories of *Man in the Cellar* (1974). Serious social concerns inform some pieces, such as the title story, in which a battered wife locks her husband in their cellar, thus gaining revenge and regaining a sense of identity. In other selections O. reveals a gift for black comedy.

Woman in the Wall (1975) constitutes O.'s most ambitious, and, perhaps, most successful achievement to date. Basing her novel on the historical account of Queen Radegund, patron saint of prisoners and captives, who with St. Agnes founded the monastery of the Holy Cross, O. has transformed original manuscript material into a vivid recreation of life in sixth-century Gaul. Ingunda, the fictional daughter of St. Agnes and a poet-priest, walls herself up to expiate her

parents' sin, but the title has implications that reach far beyond this act. The figurative "walling-up" of the characters' intellects, spirits, and individuality are caused by the blend of violence, politics, and mysticism pervading the novel's world. O.'s concern with the powerful force of sexuality and the buried life of women brings to the novel a strong sense of contemporaneity.

The positive and negative features of Irish politics, from the Troubles through the 1970s, are the subject of O.'s third novel, *No Country for Young Men* (1980). As she shifts between past and present throughout the novel, she studies the changes that Ireland has undergone since gaining its independence. While the work has been commended for its apprehension of the political reality of Ireland, it has been criticized for an uncertainty of purpose, a looseness of form, and a tendency towards melodrama.

In *The Obedient Wife* (1982), O. places her Italian heroine, Carla, in a contemporary Los Angeles suburb. Carla emerges as an admirable, sensitive, and stable force in a world that is permeated with moral, sexual, and religious disintegration and hypocrisy. O. explores the obsessive and frequently destructive powers of the passions in her most recent, critically acclaimed collection of stories, *Daughters of Passion* (1982). She often reveals sympathy for her characters, though she examines with critical distance the degree to which their passions have enslaved them.

A major voice in British letters today, O. has produced works of intellectual and imaginative complexity, notable for their understanding of human nature and their attention to significant contemporary social issues.

WORKS: *We Might See Sights and Other Stories* (1968). *Godded and Codded* (1970; American ed. *Three Lovers*, 1971). *Not in God's Image* (edited by O. with L. Martines, 1973). *Man in the Cellar* (1974). *Women in the Wall* (1975). *Melancholy Baby and Other Stories* (1978). *No Country for Young Men* (1980). *The Obedient Wife* (1982). *Daughters of Passion* (1982). *The Irish Signorina* (1984). *No Country for Young Men* (1987).

BIBLIOGRAPHY: Burleigh, D. *Irish Writers and Society at Large*, ed. M. Sekine (1785). Weekes, A. *Eire* (1986).

For articles in reference works, see: *CA. CLC. DIL. DNB.*

Other references: *Economist* (17 February 1973). *New Republic* (10 May 1975). *NYTBR* (9 May 1971). *Spectator* (1 January 1983). *TLS* (23 January 1969, 16 August 1974, 23 July 1982).

Peter Drewniany

Margaret Oliphant

BORN: 4 April 1828, Wallyford, near Mussel-
burgh, Midlothian.
DIED: 25 June 1897, Eton.
DAUGHTER OF: Francis Wilson and Mar-
garet Oliphant.
MARRIED: Francis Oliphant, 1852.

The last of several children born to cousins,
O. spent her early years in Lasswade, near Edinburgh. Her two much older brothers, the only
other surviving children of the family, went to
school in Edinburgh and for much of the time O.
was the focus of her mother's attentions. Her
mother, descended from the Oliphants of Kellie
Castle in Fife, was an excellent story-teller and a
dedicated reader and was one of the major influences on O.'s literary tendencies.

When O. was six years old, the family moved
to a large and gloomy house in Glasgow. The
lugubrious surroundings and the lack of social contacts increased her voluminous reading; Q.D. Leavis notes that at "seven or eight [O.] was already a
confirmed novel-reader," and what Henry James
called her "immensity of reading" led naturally to
an "easy flow" of writing. This "easy flow" led to
an output both prodigious and varied. She published over one hundred books of fiction, criticism,
translations, travel guides, and biography. In addition, the articles and essays she produced for many
periodicals, chiefly *Blackwood's*, amount to at least
another hundred volumes.

The first of her published works, *Passages in
the Life of Mrs. Margaret Maitland* (1849), was
written while the family was living in Liverpool,
where her father had a position in the Customs
House. During this period, O. became engaged to
a young man who was going to America for three
years, after which they were to have been married,
but the engagement was broken following a year
of quarrelsome letters. In her *Autobiography*, O.
refers to this time as one of "depression and sadness." It was also a time when her mother became
ill and O. sat silently at her mother's bedside and
began to write in order to amuse herself. Her
brother, living in London, took the manuscript of
her first book to the publishing firm of Colburn,
where it was accepted for publication.

The £150 O. earned for the novel financed
her first trip to London, where she had gone to
await its publication and to look after her eldest
brother, who was perpetually in debt. Thus began
the pattern of her life, ceaseless literary labors in
the support of her male relatives. Ironically, it was
at this time that she became acquainted with her
cousin Francis Oliphant, whom she would marry
in 1852. He was an artist who had designed the
stained glass windows in the Houses of Parlia-

ment, but like her father, brothers, and sons, he
was never as financially successful as she was to
become.

On the morning of her wedding, she received
the page proofs of her novel *Katie Stewart*, published by Blackwood, an association which was to
last forty-five years until her death in 1897. Her
marriage to Francis Oliphant, however, lasted
only seven years and ended with his death in
Rome in 1859. The Oliphants had gone to Italy in
search of a more healthful climate for Francis,
who was suffering from consumption. The family,
which by this time included a daughter and a son,
settled in Florence where the weather was cold
and damp, but Francis' health did not improve.
The preceding years had been difficult for O.; she
had given birth to four children, only two of
whom survived, and her mother, her greatest
source of strength and support, had died shortly
after the second child. Throughout this tragic
time, she published dozens of articles for
Blackwood's and at least two or three novels each
year. Her third child was born six weeks after the
death of her husband.

She returned to Scotland and continued with
her writing, beginning what was perhaps her
most famous series of novels, *The Chronicles of
Carlingford*. The first two, *The Rector and the
Doctor's Family* and *Salem Chapel*, were published in 1863; *The Perpetual Curate* (1864) and
Miss Marjoribanks (1866), continued the series.
The latter is considered by most critics to be her
best work and the one which was most influential
upon the work of other writers. Ironic, satirical,
and comedic, the novel was written following the
death of her twelve-year-old daughter Margaret.
The success of the Carlingford series had enabled
her to travel again to Italy, where the child succumbed to an attack of fever.

O. returned to England and lived near Eton
where she had enrolled her sons. The expenses of
their education and the support of her brother
Frank and his family necessitated an unending
literary output, notably the concluding volume in
the Carlingford series, *Phoebe Junior* (1876). The
last years of her life were as unfortunate personally as the earlier ones had been. She outlived both
of her sons, who had never fulfilled her hopes for
them. Her nephew, whom she had educated,
showed promise as an engineer but died of typhoid in India.

The tragedies of her personal life have
tended to obscure her unique accomplishments as
a writer. The heroines in her novels do not conform to the usual Victorian stereotypes; they are
practical, clever, and articulate, and they worked
(as O. herself had always done). The first writer to

note the "feminine cynicism" in Austen's novels, she was an original and perceptive critic.

Her last major work, the first two of the three-volume *Annals of a Publishing House* (1897), a history of Blackwood, remains as one of the most detailed, accurate, and engaging works of its kind. Her last journal article for *Blackwood's*, "'Tis Sixty Years Since," published in May 1897, honored the long reign of Queen Victoria in anticipation of the Queen's Jubilee, which was to be held in June. When she had completed the article, her doctor told her she was dying. With typical Scottish fortitude, she clung to life until two days after the celebration. She died as she had lived, pleasing others through the efforts of her pen but never totally satisfying her own desires.

WORKS: *Passages in the Life of Mrs. Margaret Maitland* (1849). *Katie Stewart* (1853). *Zaidee, A Romance* (1856). *Literary History of England in the End of the Eighteenth and Beginning of the Nine-*teenth *Century* (1882). *The Ladies Lindores* (1883). *Lady Car: The Sequel of a Life* (1889). *The Victorian Age of English Literature* (1892). *The Sorceress* (1893). *A Child's History of Scotland* (1895). *The Sisters Brontë* (1897). *Autobiography and Letters of Mrs. Margaret Oliphant*, ed. A.L.W. Coghill (1899). *Selected Short Stories of the Supernatural*, ed. M.K. Gray (1986).

BIBLIOGRAPHY: *Autobiography and Letters of Mrs. Margaret Oliphant*, ed. A.L.W. Coghill (1899). Clarke, J.S. *Margaret Oliphant: A Bibliography* (1986). Williams, M. *Margaret Oliphant: A Critical Biography* (1986).

For articles in reference works, see: *BA19C*.

Other references: Moore, K. *Victorian Wives* (1974). Showalter, E. *A Literature of Their Own* (1977). Stebbins, L.P. *A Victorian Album: Some Lady Novelists of the Period* (1946).

Gail Kraidman

Amelia Opie

BORN: 12 November 1769, Norwich.
DIED: 2 December 1853, Norwich.
DAUGHTER OF: James Alderson and Amelia Briggs.
MARRIED: John Opie, 1798.

A novelist who brought heightened pathos and mournful tenderness to the domestic novel and a small gift to poetry, O. reached the apogee of her fame in the three-volume *Adeline Mowbray*, a tale suggested in part by the colorful history of William Godwin and Mary Wollstonecraft. High spirited, convivial, with a self-acknowledged love of society and luxury, she came in later years to recoil from the sumptuary side of life, devoting her best energies to befriending the mentally ill, developing republican sympathies, and ultimately turning to the asceticism of the Quakerism of her native Norwich. She found favor with prominent English radicals and won the admiration of Kosciusko, Benjamin West, and Maria Edgeworth. In Paris, the *illustrati* of the day applauded her as much for the strength of her compassionate instincts as for her literary achievements. Although not nearly as subtle and steady a reader of character as Jane Austen, her near contemporary, O. achieved a limited mastery over style and setting. Twentieth-century critical estimations have been harsh, ranking her far beneath the realm of the distinguished.

As a child, she imbibed the radical politics and utilitarianism of her father, a physician and the grandson of a dissenting minister. Her educa-tion was brief but richly supplemented by reading and the graces of French and dancing. Her juvenilia include poems and a tragedy, "Adelaide," mounted for the amusement of her local friends. At the age of fifteen, becoming mistress of her father's house upon the death of her mother, she entered local society, regaling it with wit and song. Acting as hostess to such famous visitors as William Godwin and James Macintosh matured her political awareness and gave her a larger sense of life.

Part of her fame can be attributed to the numerous portraits painted of her by her husband, John Opie, often referred to as the English Rembrandt. Sir Joshua Reynolds thought his numerous court commissions and such genre canvases as "Cornish Beggar" representative of a talent of "Caravaggio and Velasquez in one." After his marriage to O. in 1798, his work, it is commonly agreed, was enhanced by a certain grace it lacked before. Indeed, it was John Opie who encouraged O. to take up the pen, for he hoped thus to wean her of her love of society. Her first acknowledged work appeared three years after her marriage. *Father and Daughter* achieved a certain fame as a moral tale, leading Sir Walter Scott to confess shedding tears upon reading it. Once she assumed the role of author, she became steadfast at her craft, putting in eight to ten hour days at her writing desk. She remained devoted to John Opie and after his death in 1807 prepared a memoir later prefixed to her edited version of his *Lectures on Painting*, which are acknowledged to be among the most brilliant and original presented at the Royal Academy.

O.'s renown in her day, since greatly diminished, resulted from her inclusion in the orbit of William Godwin's circle. Inspired by the radical beliefs of the French *philosophes*, Godwin was an inveterate system builder and espouser of radical politics. O. first met Godwin in 1793 at Norwich, and the most extreme of British revolutionary philosophers took a pronounced liking to her. Her most important novel, *Adeline Mowbray* (1804), is based on the career of the proto-feminist, Mary Wollstonecraft, author of *A Vindication of the Rights of Women*, who lived with William Godwin. Harriet Westbrook gave this multi-volume work to Shelley in a successful bid to convince him to undertake the vows of marriage.

O.'s literary career came to a halt in 1825 when she was formally inducted into the Society of Friends. The renewal of her early acquaintance with Joseph John Gurney, "the Quaker pope," gave definite shape to her hitherto amorphous religious beliefs and convinced her to renounce novel writing.

Her last novel, *Madeline*, was published in two volumes in 1822. When O. donned the grey habit of the Friends she declined to finish *The Painter and his Wife*, which was under contract. Her last work, *Lays for the Dead*, poems in memory of departed relatives and friends, was entirely different in character, devotional and elevating. It was in keeping with her daily round of visiting hospitals, ministering to the poor, and helping ameliorate workhouse conditions. Every consideration gave way to the imperative claim of her newfound religious convictions. Complete self-abnegation, however, was beyond her reach for she entertained the love of society and its pleasures too much to effect a complete and irreparable break. Not surprisingly, Harriet Martineau noted in 1839 that O. could not resist "a spice of dandyism" in the demure peculiarity of her dress. During the socially restricted years of her Quakerism, she still continued to meet such notables as La-

fayette, Benjamin Constant, Cuvier, Segur, and Mme. de Genlis.

Although she accepted the renunciation of her craft with philosophic calm, her old habits were not so easily dismissed. Even when invested in the full canonicals of her newfound calling, O. could not bow to all the strictures of Quakerism, certainly not those which would darken her vivacity and irrepressible wit. Her social conscience remained with her to the last, for injustice was a conception her mind refused to admit. She was active in antislavery circles, and in her advanced years, when she had long abandoned the life of the writer, she attended the London Antislavery Convention of 1840 as a Norwich delegate.

Dismissed by her peers as too "lachrymose" a novelist and too sentimentally gushing a poet, O. remained a sympathetic and congenial personality of her age, extending the dominion of the domestic novel by perfecting the tone and timbre of social dialogue. Her poetry, although not of the first order except possibly for "Elegy to the Memory of the Late Duke of Bedford," possesses a warbling persuasiveness and sweetness that lend it charm and color.

WORKS: "Adelaide" (1787). *Father and Daughter* (1801). "An Elegy to the Memory of the Duke of Bedford" (1801). *Adeline Mowbray* (1804). *Simple Tales* (1806). *The Warrior's Return and other Poems* (1808). *Temper, or Domestic Scenes* (1812). *Tales of Real Life* (1813). *Valentine's Eve* (1816). *Tales of the Heart* (1820). *Madeline* (1822). *Lays for the Dead* (1833).

BIBLIOGRAPHY: Brightwell, C.L., ed. *Memorials of the Life of Amelia Opie* (1854). Howells, W.D. *Heroines of Fiction* (1901). Macgregor, M.E. *Smith College Studies in Modern Language* (1933). Ritchie, A.I.T. *A Book of Sibyls: Mrs. Barbauld, Miss Edgeworth, Mrs. Opie and Miss Austen* (1883). Wilson, J.M. *Amelia: The Life of a Plain Friend* (1937).

For articles in reference works, see: *Allibone*. *BA19C*. *DNB*. Todd.

Michael Skakun

Dorothy Osborne

BORN: 1627, Chicksands Priory, Bedfordshire.
DIED: January 1695, Moor Park, Surrey.
DAUGHTER OF: Sir Peter Osborne and Dorothy Danvers.
MARRIED: Sir William Temple, 1655.

Included in the *DNB* in the entry for her husband, O. began to receive attention in her own name after extracts from forty-two of her letters

were printed in T.P. Courtenay's *Memoirs of . . . Sir William Temple* in 1836. Containing "personal rather than literary charm," according to the *DNB*, the letters appealed to Thomas Babington Macaulay, whose enthusiasm sparked the Honourable Judge Parry to edit them in a separate volume in 1888. Since then Parry's edition has been reprinted frequently, and other editions have followed.

The appeal of the letters extends beyond the limits suggested by the *DNB*, providing for readers today insights into the life of an intelligent seventeenth-century woman who could recreate a period for readers centuries later through a scene or a character. Not designed for publication, the letters were written for O.'s future husband, and they contain intimate details and descriptions of the Interregnum not found elsewhere. Exhibiting the literary qualities and immediacy of the diaries of Pepys and Evelyn, the letters focus upon the dilemmas of a young Royalist woman whose affections have been captured by a Puritan.

O.'s father was the Royalist Governor of Guernsey who had defended the Castle Cornet. Sir William Temple's father, however, was a Puritan who sat in the Long Parliament. The couple met by chance in 1648 at the Isle of Wight when Temple was on his way to a diplomatic assignment in France. After O.'s brother wrote some anti-Puritan graffiti on a window, Temple watched as O., upon being arrested by Puritans, confessed that she did it. Courageously, O. trusted that the Puritan officer was gallant enough that he would not punish a young woman for such a prank. She was right. All who had been arrested, including O., were released. The incident occurred when O. was twenty-one and Temple, twenty. Their courtship, a long and unlikely one, had begun.

For the next seven years the two corresponded, Temple from the Continent, O. in England. Both families objected to their union, and both urged more advantageous matches; yet O. remained constant. She was considered to be a good match and was courted by others, even though her father was an impoverished Royalist. One of the suitors she rejected was Oliver Cromwell's fourth son, Henry. Her account to Temple of Henry's attempt to woo her by giving her a greyhound is both informative and amusing. Young Cromwell did not mourn; within a few months after he had been rejected by O., he was married to another. O.'s family, especially her youngest brother, Henry, urged her to break her vow with Temple and to marry another man. In her letters, O. writes of her isolation and her unhappiness; despite her misery, she remains stoical and patient, writing secretly to her future husband. When the marriage finally did take place, O. was severely scarred by smallpox. Married in 1655 by a Justice of the Peace at St. Giles, Middlesex, the couple left that year for Ireland, not returning to England until 1663. In 1666 Temple became a baron.

The letters cover only the first years of their courtship. The rest of O.'s life remains in the shadow cast by her husband's more evident achievements. He continued his distinguished diplomatic career, negotiating for the monarchs.

Through his essays, romances, and histories, he secured his reputation as a writer. Adding to his subsequent importance in the literary history of England was his secretary, his cousin, Jonathan Swift.

Throughout her life, O. remained deeply attached to Temple, apparently coping with a more dominant figure in the household, her sister-in-law, Lady Giffard. Through her letters and events later in her life, O. is revealed as a gentle, unpretentious woman who actively helped her husband, and who, once again, on a voyage from Ireland to England in 1671 (*CSPD* 1670-1671), exhibited the unusual courage that Temple had admired years earlier.

Only O.'s letters to Temple written from 1652 to 1654 have survived. Even though they give only half of the correspondence, the letters are valuable. Preserved by Temple and the couple's descendants, the letters are reflective, witty, and informative. They demonstrate O.'s belief that "All Letters mee thinks should bee free and Easy as ones discourse, not studdyed, as an Oration, nor made up of hard words like a Charme." Katherine Rogers recently noted that O.'s letters reveal the seventeenth-century woman's lack of education. By the eighteenth century those elements that are problematic in O.'s letters improved, especially the spelling, punctuation, sentence structure, and paragraphing.

Despite errors and problems with composition, the letters remain part of that personal literature that arose in the seventeenth century. O. richly describes everyone, not just herself. Her commentaries on her family, her friends, and her views of her future husband are illuminating, sympathetic, and delightful. As Douglas Bush suggested, one would need to go "far to find another such individual mixture of Juliet, Rosalind, and Jane Austen." Through the letters we see an intimate view of a young woman in an unsettled age. O. writes of people she knew, of the books she read, and, perhaps most important to her, of love, marriage, and filial duty. It is through O. that we learn of the reception of the Duchess of Newcastle's first book, published in 1653, and of the horror with which society viewed a woman who published; it is through O. that we discover the aversion that well-bred young women had of passion, "that whereso'ever it comes destroys all that entertain it"; and, it is through O. that we learn how Royalists sought refuge from the chaos of England in the 1650s.

WORKS: *Memoirs of . . . Sir William Temple*, ed. T.P. Courtenay (1836). *Letters from Dorothy Osborne to Sir William Temple, 1652-54*, ed. E.A. Perry (1888, revised and enlarged 1903). *The Love Letters of Dorothy Osborne to Sir William Temple, 1652-54*, ed. E.A. Parry (1901). *The Love Letters of Dorothy to Sir William Temple, Newly Edited from the Original Manuscripts,* ed. I. Gollancz (1903). *The Letters of Dorothy Osborne to William Temple,* ed. G.C. Moore Smith (1928). *Martha, Lady Giffard, Her Life and Correspondence (1664-1722), A Sequel to the letters of Dorothy Osborne,* ed. J.G. Longe, with preface by Judge Parry (1911). *The Letters of Dorothy Osborne to Sir William Temple, 1652-54,* ed. K. Hart (1968).

BIBLIOGRAPHY: Cecil, D. *Two Quiet Lives* (1948). Hewlett, M. *Last Essays* (1924). Irvine, L.L. *Ten Letter Writers* (1932). Lerch-Davis, G.S. *Texas Studies in Language and Literature* (1978). Lucas, F.L. *Studies French and English* (1934). Marburg, C. *Sir William Temple: A Seventeenth Century "Libertin"* (1932). Reynolds, M. *The Learned Lady in England 1650-1760* (1920). Smith, G.C.M. "Introduction" to *The Letters of Dorothy Osborne to William Temple* (1928). Woolf, V. *The Second Common Reader* (1932).

For articles in reference works, see: Balch, M. *Short Biographies* (1945). Bottrall, M. *Personal Records* (1962). Browning, D.C. *Cassell. DNB. Everyman's Dictionary of Literary Biographies: English and American,* rev. ed. (1962). Stenton, D.M. *English Women in History* (1957).

Other references: Donovan, J. *Women and Language in Literature and Society* (1980). Wade, R. *Contemporary Review* (1986).

Sophia B. Blaydes

Sydney Owenson, Lady Morgan

BORN: 25 December 1776/1778?, on the Irish Sea.
DIED: 16 April 1859, Pimlico.
DAUGHTER OF: Robert and Jane Hill Mac-Owen.
MARRIED: Charles T. Morgan, 1812.
WROTE UNDER: Sydney Owenson and (after her marriage) Lady Morgan.

O. was the first financially successful professional woman writer. A fast, prolific producer of what Scott praised (and imitated in *Waverley*) as "national and picaresque fiction," as well as travel books, history, and essays, O. was a celebrated social, literary, and political figure for half a century. In 1837 she became the first woman to receive a pension (£300 a year from Lord Melbourne) "in acknowledgment of the services rendered by her to the world of letters."

The eldest child of actors, O. claimed to have been born on board a ship on the Irish Sea. She was educated at various schools in Dublin and was employed as a governess from 1798-1800. After her third novel, *The Wild Irish Girl* (1806), made her famous, she rose quickly in Dublin society and became a member of the household of the Marquis of Abercorn. Here she met Charles Morgan, their physician, whom she married in 1812 despite her fears of losing her independence. Morgan supported her literary endeavors throughout a long, childless, and happy marriage. After he died in 1843, she remained a force in London literary and political circles until her death in 1859.

O.'s first two novels, *St. Clair, or the Heiress of Desmond* (1802) (an imitation of *Werther*) and *The Novice of St. Dominick* (1803), were popular enough to procure her a £300 advance on her third, *The Wild Irish Girl,* which went into seven

editions in two years. O.'s fresh, original tone and lively powers of description were praised, her carelessness and her sometimes bombastic style criticized. The book created a political controversy because of its nationalistic sentiments, its sympathy for the dispossessed heirs of the ancient rulers of Ireland, and its extensive, well-documented passages on Irish history, legend, and art. Glorvina, the heroine, is an Irish princess whose natural grace and refinement have not been corrupted by erroneous education but whose knowledge of Irish history is extensive. Like her creator, she is adept at singing, dancing, and playing the harp.

O.'s other patriotic Irish novels include *O'Donnel* (1814), an attempt to describe "the flat realities of life" in Ireland; *Florence Macarthy* (1818), best remembered for its satire of John Wilson Croker (one of the most vicious of the critics who had attacked *O'Donnel* in the pages of the *Quarterly Review*); and *The O'Briens and the O'Flahertys* (1827). All were undertaken to promote the emancipation of the Catholics of Ireland. O. initiated the genre of the political romance, a mixture of sensibility, nationalism, the sublime, and the picturesque. She defended the use of fiction for political ends in the preface to *O'Donnel*: "A novel is specially adapted to enable the advocate of any cause to steal upon the public."

O.'s other novels include *Woman, or Ida of Athens* (1809), *The Missionary* (1811, revised and re-issued as *Luxima the Prophetess,* 1859), and *The Princess* (1835).

Her *France* (1817) was very popular; in 1818 she traveled through Italy to research *Italy* (1821), which Byron called "fearless and excellent." Also of interest is *Woman and her Master* (1840), a critique of the treatment of women from barbaric times to the Middle Ages and a plea for women's rights.

Although O.'s writing suffers from an inflated style, sarcasm, and careless execution, she deserves to be remembered for her vigor and originality, for her role as Irish advocate and historian, and for her creation of the political romance.

WORKS: *Poems by a Young Lady Between the Age of 12 and 14* (1801). *Deep in Love* (1802). *St. Clair, or The Heiress of Desmond* (1803). *The Novice of St. Dominick* ((1804). *A Few Reflections* (1805). *The Wild Irish Girl* (1806). *Patriotic Sketches of Ireland Written in Connaught* (1807). *The First Attempt* (1807). *The Lay of an Irish Harp, or Metrical Fragments* (1807). *Woman, or Ida of Athens* (1809). *The Missionary: An Indian Tale* (1811). *O'Donnel: A National Tale* (1814). *France* (1817). *Florence Macarthy: An Irish Tale* (1818). *Italy* (1821). *Letter to Reviewers of "Italy"; Including an Answer to a Pamphlet Entitled "Observations upon the Calumnies and Misrepresentations in Lady Morgan's 'Italy'"* (1821). *The Life and Times of Salvatore Rosa* (1824). *Absenteeism* (1825). *The O'Briens and the O'Flahertys: A National Tale* (1827). *The Book of the Boudoir* (1829). *France in 1829-30* (1830). *Dramatic Scenes from Real Life* (1833). *The Princess, or The Beguine* (1835). *Woman and Her Master: A History of the Female Sex from the Earliest Period* (1840). *Book Without a Name* (1841). *Letter to Cardinal Wiseman in Answer to His Remarks on Lady Morgan's Statements Regarding St. Peter's Chair* (1851). *Luxima the Prophetess: A Tale of India* (1859). *An Odd Volume: Extracted from an Autobiography* (1859). *Lady Morgan's Memoirs: Autobiography, Diaries and Correspondence* (1862).

BIBLIOGRAPHY: Fitzpatrick, W.J. *Lady Morgan* (1860). Kavanagh, J. *English Women of Letters* (1863). Murch, J. *Mrs. Barbauld and Her Contemporaries* (1877). Stevenson, *The Wild Irish Girl* (1936). Spender, D. *Mothers of the Novel* (1986). Whitmore, C.H. *Women's Work in English Fiction* (1910). Wilson, M. *These Were Muses* (1924).

For articles in reference works, see: *DNB*.

Kate Browder Heberlein

Violet Paget

BORN: 14 October 1856, Boulogne-sur-Mer, France.
DIED: 13 February 1935, San Gervasio, Italy.
DAUGHTER OF: Henry Hippolyte Ferguson Paget and Matilda Lee-Ferguson, née Adams.
WROTE UNDER: Mlle. V.P., Vernon Lee.

From the Victorian to the modern period, P. wrote consistently about aesthetics and the arts. A figure of importance to the artists who surrounded her, she is mentioned in Browning's poem "Asolando" (1889) and Anatole France's *Le Lys Rouge* (1894), as well as being commented on by Walter Pater, Henry James, Edith Wharton, Wyndham Lewis, I.A. Richards, Bernard Shaw, Aldous Huxley, and H. G. Wells, among others.

Brought up on the continent, where her family travelled from one watering place to another, P. first lived in Germany, later Italy, where the family stayed in 1868 and eventually settled. Rome at that time was, as depicted in *The Marble Faun*, a center for artists, and P. began there a lifelong interest in the arts, fostered by her acquaintance with the family of John Singer Sargent, a childhood friend, whose painting of P. is in the Tate Gallery. P.'s acquaintance with the artistic community in Italy led, when she finally started visiting England in 1881, to her being immediately introduced to a circle of writers including Henry James, Oscar Wilde, Walter Pater, and others. In England, which she visited yearly while residing in Florence, P. was to become a kind of *enfant terrible.* Wearing a black tailor-made dress and Gladstone collar, her hallmark, she expressed her opinions freely and aggressively on all subjects. Henry James described her as having a "monstrous cerebration" and as being a "tiger-cat." She repeatedly gave offense through her outspokenness, right up to the end of her life when her unpopular public statements on pacifism during World War I made her new enemies. P. never married but had long-lasting friendships with women artists, first with Mary Robinson and later with Kit Anstruther-Thomson; both relations caused her intense pain when they were broken off.

P.'s first piece of writing, "Les Aventures d'une Piece de Monnaie" (1870), appeared when she was thirteen and is characteristic of her later interests. It describes in first person from a coin's point of view its history from Hadrian's time to the Victorian era, a device that allows P. to explore imaginatively various cultures and time periods. P.'s first serious work, *Studies of the Eighteenth Century in Italy* (1880), a book of essays on music and literature, began a series of such works, including *Euphorion* (1884), which contains an essay on Shakespeare and Renaissance Italy, and *Renaissance Fancies and Studies* (1895). Work on the separate branches of the arts led P. to aesthetics in general, about which she was to write a series of books beginning with *Belcaro* (1881), which examines the relation of artistic form to pleasure. In *Juvenilia* (1887), P. moved to the Tolstoyan question of art's use for the lower classes; in *Beauty and Ugliness* (1912) and *The Beautiful* (1913) to the overall question of the psychological response of the viewer; and finally in *Music and Its Lovers* (1932) to interviewing a series of listeners about why they loved music. These books, though stylistically difficult, introduced ideas that were taken very seriously by critics of the time, as, for example, by I. A. Richards who disagrees with P. in *Principles of Literary Criticism*.

P. was less successful with her fiction. *Miss Brown* (1884), a satire against the aestheticism of the Pre-Raphaelites, and *Vanitas* (1892) offended London literary society, particularly Henry James, who was represented in the second, because the fictional characters were easily identifiable as real figures. P. seems to have been unaware of the offensiveness of these works as she wrote them. Described as "better with place than with people," she was more successful with her play, *Ariadne in Mantua* (1903), a lyric drama about concepts of love which evokes the atmosphere of Italy, and her essays on travel, *Genius Loci* (1899), perhaps her two best-known works. Her satiric allegory about the need for peace, *Satan the Waster* (1920), is also effective polemical writing.

The range of P.'s intelligence was her most impressive characteristic. Henry James said of her that "the vigour and sweep of her intellect are most rare and her talk superior altogether," Walter Pater that if she could overcome the difficulties of her style, she would stand "among the very few best critical writers of all time."

WORKS: *Studies of the Eighteenth Century in Italy* (1880). *Tuscan Fairy Tales* (1880). *Belcaro: Being Essays on Sundry Aesthetical Questions* (1881). *The Prince of the Hundred Soups* (1883). *Ottilie: An Eighteenth Century Idyll* (1883). *Euphorion: Being Studies of the Antique and the Medieval in the Renaissance* (1884). *The Countess of Albany* (1884). *Miss Brown* (1884). *Baldwin: Being Dialogues on Views and Aspirations* (1886). *A Phantom Lover: A Fantastic Story* (1886). *Juvenilia: Being a Second Series of Essays on Sundry Aesthetical Questions* (1887). *Hauntings: Fantastic Stories* (1892).

Vanitas: Polite Stories (1892). *Althea: A Second Book of Dialogues on Aspirations and Duties* (1894). *Renaissance Fancies and Studies: Being a Sequel to Euphorion* (1895). *Limbo, and Other Essays* (1897). *Genius Loci: Notes on Places* (1899). *Ariadne in Mantua* (1903). *Penelope Brandling: A Tale of the Welsh Coast* (1903). *Pope Jacynth, and Other Fantastic Tales* (1904). *Hortis Vitae: Essays on the Gardening of Life* (1904). *The Enchanted Woods, and Other Essays* (1905). *Sister Benvenuta and the Christ Child* (1906). *The Spirit of Rome: Leaves from a Diary* (1906). *The Sentimental Traveler: Notes on Places* (1908). *Gospels of Anarchy, and Other Contemporary Studies* (1908). *Laurus Nobilis: Chapters on Art and Life* (1909). *Vital Lies: Studies of Some Varieties of Recent Obscurantism* (1912). (with Clementine Anstruther-Thomson) *Beauty and Ugliness, and Other Studies in Psychological Aesthetics* (1912). *The Beautiful: An Introduction to Psychological Aesthetics* (1913). *Louis Norbert: A Two-fold Romance* (1914). *The Tower of Mirrors: And Other Essays on the Spirit of Places* (1914). *The Ballet of Nations: A Present-day Morality* (1915). *Satan the Waster: A Philosophical War Trilogy* (1920). *The Handling of Words: And Other Studies in Literary Psychology* (1923). *The Golden Keys, and Other Essays on the Genius Loci* (1925). *Proteus: Or the Future of Intelligence* (1925). *The Poet's Eye* (1926). *For Maurice: Five Unlikely Stories* (1927). *A Vernon Lee Anthology* (selected by I.C. Willis, 1929). *Music and Its Lovers* (1932). *Letters.* (intro. I.C. Willis, 1937). *The Snake Lady, and Other Stories.* (intro. H. Gregory, 1954). *Supernatural Tales* (1955). *Pope Jacynth and More Supernatural Tales* (1956).

BIBLIOGRAPHY: Baring, M. *The Puppet Show of Memory* (1922). Gardner, B. *The Lesbian Imagination (Victorian Style): A Psychological and Critical Study of "Vernon Lee"* (1987). Gunn, P. *Vernon Lee: Violet Paget 1856–1935* (1964). Lewis, P. W. *The Lion and the Fox* (1927). Mannocchi, P.F. *WS* (1986). Richards, I. A. *Principles of Literary Criticism* (1922).

For articles in reference works see: *CA. DNB.* Other references: *ELT* (1983). *JDECU* (1981–82). *PMLA* (1953, 1954). *RES* (1982).

Elsie B. Michie

Emmeline Goulden Pankhurst

BORN: 14 July 1858, Manchester.
DIED: 14 June 1928, London.
DAUGHTER OF: Robert Goulden and Jane Quinn.
MARRIED: Richard Marsden Pankhurst, 1879.

P. was one of eleven children born to ardent abolitionists who provided both a loving home and a model for the life of political activism she led. After her marriage in 1879 to an extremely liberal activist barrister, she and her husband raised a family and fought for suffrage and other social reform.

P. received her education in Paris under the direction of Mlle. Marchef-Girard, returning to Manchester at eighteen to begin a lifelong commitment to public office, political and social militancy, and motherhood. P. and her daughter Christabel frequently spoke publicly, marched in rallies, and were arrested and imprisoned together. P. reported that after meeting Susan B. Anthony in 1902, Christabel declared, "It is unendurable to think of another generation of women wasting their lives begging for the vote. We must not lose any more time. We must act."

Act they did. The Pankhurst name is inextricably linked to the fight for suffrage in England as well as to reform for laborers, poor and unemployed persons, children, prisoners, indeed, all powerless and disenfranchised groups. P. was a Fabian Socialist, a member of the Manchester school board, founder of the Women's Social and Political Union, originator of the Women's Parliament of 1907, member of the Chorlton Board of Guardians, and founder of a Committee for the Relief of the Unemployed. She was a part of every reform movement of her time; as she says in the opening of her autobiography, "those men and women are fortunate who are born at a time when a great struggle for human freedom is in progress. . . . I am glad and thankful that this was my case."

Her autobiography, *My Own Story* (1914), documents her participation in public speeches, rallies, marches, and addresses to Parliament as well as two trips to the United States to meet American feminists. She reports incidents of public police brutality, deplorable imprisonment, and political ridicule. She responded always with incredible strength through the physical suffering, with hunger and thirst strikes while in prison, and with a determined attitude placing "votes for women" above all else. For a short time following her husband's death in 1898 P. retired from public militancy. Upon receiving the position of registrar of births and deaths, however, she was brought back into public life, and in 1909 when her friend and comrade Keir Hardie was elected to Parliament, her political activity was revived and continued till her death in 1928, the year British women received the vote.

WORKS: *The Importance of the Vote* (1908). *The Causes of the Revolt of the Women in England* (1909). *Verbatim Report of Mrs. Pankhurst's Speech Delivered November 13, 1913 at Parsons' Theatre, Hartford, Conn.* (1913). *Why We Are Militant: A Speech Delivered by Mrs. Pankhurst in New York, October 21, 1913* (1914). *My Own Story* (1914).

BIBLIOGRAPHY: Pankhurst, E.S. *The Life of Emmeline Pankhurst* (1935). Pankhurst, E.S. *The Suffragist Movement* (1931). Spacks, P.M. *Women's Autobiography: Essays in Criticism*, ed. E.C. Jelinek (1980).

For articles in reference works, see: *Longman. McGraw-Hill Encyclopedia of World Biography.*

Anne-Marie Ray

Catherine Parr

BORN: 1513, Westmoreland.
DIED: 1548, Sudeley, Wiltshire.
DAUGHTER OF: Sir Thomas Parr and Maud Green Parr.
MARRIED: Edward Brugh, Lord Brugh, 1525; Sir John Nevill, Lord Latimer, 1533; Henry Tudor, King of England, 1543; Sir Thomas Seymour, (later) Lord High Admiral, 1547.

The sixth and surviving wife of Henry VIII, P. proved a nurturing stepmother to his children, Mary Tudor (daughter of Catherine of Aragon), Elizabeth Tudor (daughter of Anne Boleyn), and Edward Tudor (daughter of Jane Seymour). A learned woman, inclined to study and to serious religiosity, she restored sobriety to Henry's court, surrounding herself with a coterie of like-minded noblewomen, and supported such religious reformers as Coverdale, Latimer, and Pankhurst. She sponsored a translation of the Bible into the vernacular and published two works emanating from her own religious experience. *The lamentacion or complaynt or a sinner . . .* (1547) is a moving account of her own religious odyssey, and *Prayers, or Meditations . . .* (1545) is a collection of her own religious exercises. Both works were extremely popular and both were reprinted within the century.

P. united learning, intelligence, and a personal sympathy which brought light into the tossled lives of her stepchildren, quiet and peace into the life of her difficult, invalid husband, King Henry, and encouragement to the religious scholars of her time. That she was able to persuade her Roman Catholic stepdaughter, Mary Tudor, to contribute a translation to the edition of the New Testament that she sponsored is a measure of her personal gifts. That Henry valued her is shown by his appointment of her as regent while he campaigned in France in 1544. She also overcame a plot laid against her by intriguing courtiers.

After Henry's death, P., then thirty-four,

married the swashbuckling Thomas Seymour, a former suitor. Accounts of the success of this marriage vary, but it was, in any case, shortlived. P. died in September, 1548, six days after the delivery of her only child, a daughter.

P.'s moving *Lamentacion* is interesting in combining simple and humble statements of Catherine's perception of herself as a feeble individual, struggling to escape from the coils of sin and justified only by faith, with politically and personally astute (and possibly sincere) statements of support for Henry's leadership of the English church.

The admiration of her contemporaries for P. is attested to by the preface by William Cecil to the 1548 edition of her *Lamentacion*. It reads, in part, "Here mayest thou se one, if the kynde may moove the a woman, if degre may provoke thee a woman of highe estate, by byrthe made noble, by mariage mooste noble, . . . refusyng the worlde wherin she was loste, to obteyne heaven, wherin she may be saved; . . . remoovyng supersticion, wherwith she was smothered, to enbrace [sic] true regilion [sic], wherwith she may revive."

WORKS: Prayers, or Meditations, wherein the mynd is stirred, paciently to suffre all afflictions here, to set at nought the vaine prosperitie of this worlde, and always to longe for the everlasting felicitie: collected out of holy woorkes by the most vertuous and gracious Princess Katherine queene of Englande, Fraunce, and Irelande (1545). The lamentacion or complaynt of a sinner, made by the most vertuous Ladie, Quene Caterin, bewayling the ignoraunce of her blind life: set forth and put in print at the instaunt desire of the righte gracious ladie Caterin Duchesse of Suffolke, & the earnest requeste of the right honorable Lord, William Parre, Marquesse of North Hampton (1547).

BIBLIOGRAPHY: Ballard, G. *Memoirs of Severall Ladies of Great Britain. . . .* (1752). *DNB* (James Gairdner, "Catherine Parr [1512-1548], sixth and last queen of Henry VIII"), III, 1217-1221. Foxe, J. *Actes and monuments of these latter and perillous dayes. . . .* (1563). Gordon, M. *A Life of Queen Katherine Parr* (1951). Haugaard, W.P. *RQ* (1969). Hays, M. *Female Biography. . . .* (1807). Hoffman, C. Fenno, Jr. *HLQ* (1960). Hogrefe, P. *Tudor Women. . . .* (1975). *Hogrefe, P. Women of Action in Tudor England. . . .* (1977). Hughey, R. *Library*, 4th Series (1934). King, J.N. In *Silent but for the Word. . . .* Ed. M.P. Hannay. (1985). Mahl, M.R., and H. Koon, eds. *The Female Spectator. . . .* (1977). Levin, C. *International Journal of Women's Studies* (1980). Strickland, A. *Lives of the Queens of England from the Norman Conquest* (1842). Travitsky, B., ed. *Paradise of Women. . . .* (1981). Warnicke, R.M. *Women of the English Renaissance and Reformation* (1983). Williams, J. *Literary Women of England. . . .* (1861). *Writings of Edward VI, William Hugh, Queen Catherine Parr, Anne Askew, Lady Jane Grey, Hamilton and Balnaves* (1842).

For articles in reference works, see: *Allibone. DNB.*

Betty Travitsky

Margaret Paston

BORN: 1423.
DIED: 1482.
DAUGHTER OF: John Mauteby.
MARRIED: John Paston, c. 1440.

Prior to her marriage to John Paston, nothing is known of P.'s life except that she was the daughter of a wealthy landowner of Norfolk. From the day of her first meeting with her future husband, however, she became one of a handful of medieval women—or medieval men—whose individual experiences were recorded and preserved for future generations, in her case in a vast collection of Paston family correspondence and papers spanning almost a century. Had she married anyone else, P. might or might not have ever written a letter, but in either event her experience would have been completely lost to us, and so in a very real sense the P. we now reconstruct epitomizes the extent to which a woman's life was determined by the particular role of wife to which she was assigned. As P.'s own words reveal, this role (for a woman of her class and times) was circumscribed and subordinate, but in no way was it marginal or powerless. Her central and formidable responsibility included and is manifest in her letter writing, but it may be misleading to think of P. as a "woman writer" without an initial word of qualification. There is no evidence that P. was in the least bit learned or interested in reading and writing in ways that we would understand; it is not even possible to be sure that she was able to write, since the 104 extant letters sent in her name were written in a number of different hands. It is most probable that she could and did write herself, but like most affluent men and women in the fifteenth-century more often hired a scribe to take dictation. It is a voice rather than a hand, then, that speaks in her letters.

A single, not extraordinary circumstance (for the fifteenth century) occasioned both P.'s most remarkable activities and many of her letters: for a good deal of their married life, her husband was away from home. John Paston was a student at Cambridge when he married and left his wife with his in-laws while he finished his studies there and then went on to the Inner Temple in London. Later he spent many months of each year in London, when the courts were in session, and on a few occasions he was detained in Fleet prison as a result of the vagaries of his complex property claims and political maneuvers. The nature of the disputes in which the Pastons were involved often left P. to defend, in a literal sense, their properties. One of the early struggles centered on a mansion in Gresham that they bought from Geoffrey Chaucer's son Thomas, to which a rival baron also laid claim. In 1449-50, John Paston seized the property and left his wife in charge while he went to London to take further legal action. The rival claimants soon retook the house with armed forces, physically removing P. from the premises and then looting and partially destroying the house. Similarly, when a decade later the Pastons inherited Caister Castle from John Fastolf (Shakespeare's Falstaff, and apparently a distant relative of P.'s), they were subsequently sued and attacked by various claimants. P. was again left to fend off enemies for long periods of time, and no settlement of this private war took place until after her husband's death in 1466.

P. also bore at least eight children, six of whom survived, and even when her husband was at home planned for and orchestrated all the daily needs of a large household of family and servants. Modern biographers often comment on what is perceived by our standards as her harshness and lack of affection for her children, and her relationship with one of her daughters is often cited. When it became known that her daughter had secretly exchanged a vow of marriage with the Pastons' bailiff, P. attempted to block official sanction of the unapproved match. When her efforts failed, she formally refused to let her daughter back into her home, and the daughter was sheltered in a nunnery until the wedding took place.

But her function as mother and even as "housewife," in the broadest sense of the term, is not a dominant theme in P.'s writing, though occasionally she requested that her husband buy

certain food or clothes for her and her family. Her letters center, however, on her part in the public spheres of property management, politics, and local warfare; Virginia Woolf described them as "the letters of an honest bailiff to his master." Her writing was never an incidental part of her life, a leisure pastime, or a vehicle of self-expression; instead, it was an integral and essential part of the job she undertook. She acted repeatedly in her husband's place to manage his large estate and the complex affairs it entailed, buying and selling goods, negotiating with her tenants and enemies, holding courts, and pleading his cases. She reported on what she had done and agreed (or in some cases refused) to perform future services for him. She passed on appeals and information from others and kept him well-advised on what was happening on the local front, since affairs of all sorts affected their family peace and prosperity. She sometimes asked for money and sometimes agreed to send him funds. In all this, she played a crucial advisory role, evaluating and proposing strategy and recommending action.

After her husband's death, most of P.'s extant letters were written to two of her sons, the eldest, Sir John Paston, and the younger John Paston. While still carrying out Sir John's occasional orders and always acting and plotting on his behalf, she advised her sons more directly and authoritatively than she did their father on increasingly troublesome financial and political matters and even resorted to threats in her efforts to force the titular head of the family to act as she thought he should. Her letters to her eldest son are filled with reproaches for spending too much, failing to work hard, forgetting to write or come home, selling off family property to pay for personal indulgence, and neglecting to buy a tombstone for his father's grave. In the later letters, she spoke more and more openly with disappointment and bitterness as well as with characteristic anxiety, as her son failed to take the charge and care to which she, for his and his name's sake, devoted her entire life.

WORKS: The Paston Letters and Papers of the Fifteenth Century, ed. N. Davis (1971).

BIBLIOGRAPHY: Bennett, H.S. *The Pastons and Their England* (1932). Bennett, H.S. *Six Medieval Men and Women* (1955). Woolf, V. *Collected Essays*, Vol. III (1925). Gies, F. and J. *Women in the Middle Ages* (1978).

Elaine Tuttle Hansen

Emily Jane Davis Pfeiffer

BORN: 26 November 1827, Montgomeryshire, Wales.
DIED: 23 January 1890, Putney.
DAUGHTER OF: R. Davis.
MARRIED: Jurgen Edward Pfeiffer, 1853.

P. was the daughter of R. Davis, an army officer. Although her father recognized and encouraged P.'s early talent as a painter and poet, his financial mismanagement burdened his family with poverty and prevented her from receiving a thorough and systematic education. When P. married J.E. Pfeiffer, a prosperous German merchant who had settled in England, she acquired the financial means and leisure to educate herself. The result, despite constant bouts of ill health and insomnia, was ten volumes of poetry and two of prose.

In general, P. wrote about the pressures on women, their victimization and ways they might escape it. She expressed solidarity with women unlike herself—single women, working-class women, "fallen" women, foreign women, etc. In addition, she was very conscious of being a woman artist and often wrote about the constraints on female aspiration and achievement in the nineteenth century as well as the great social need she perceived for women's particular contributions to art, politics, and education.

Her first serious publication, in 1873, was *Gerard's Monument*, a romantic poetic narrative of love and death set in medieval times. Here as elsewhere, P. characteristically portrayed the sexual passion of lovers as both a natural and a spiritual experience. In *Poems* (1876), her religious inspiration is evident as she expresses her hopes for an egalitarian future—for herself personally, for women in general, for the working poor, and indeed for the entire human race. "The Winged Soul"—an image P. returns to throughout her career—portrays the pain and frustration of the creative human spirit born into the captivity of class or gender.

P.'s best poetry appeared in the 1880s: *Sonnets and Songs* (1880, revised and enlarged in 1886), *Under the Aspens, Lyrical and Dramatic* (1882), *The Rhyme of the Lady of the Rock* (1884), and *Flowers of the Night* (1889). This poetry evidences a mature, feminist perspective on women's lives and problems. P. sometimes speaks in her own voice (as in many of her sonnets) and sometimes in a metaphorical, dramatic, or historical/mythological mode. *The Wynnes of Wynhavod* (1881), though never staged, is a very readable full-length blank-verse drama of nineteenth-century life. Among the most interesting of P.'s works is *The Rhyme of the Lady of the Rock* (1884), a complex narrative addressing various social issues, such as the marriage market, marital rape, domestic tyranny, and the nature of female heroism. In this piece, which is structurally similar to Tennyson's *The Princess* (1847), the heroine recites to an audience of mixed class, gender, education, and political perspective her own poetic retelling of a local legend, pausing frequently to entertain their commentary on the morality of the action and the quality of the poetry. In the framing narrative, the poet heroine confides to her readers (though not to her listening audience) about the anxieties she experiences regarding her poetic authority and competence.

In many ways P. seems a "modern" poet; she addresses issues still alive today and with a markedly female focus and tonality. Yet she is also very much a woman of her own times, bound in many ways by nineteenth-century artistic and social norms. Among the writers she most admired were Jane Austen, Charlotte Brontë, George Eliot, and Elizabeth Barrett Browning; she cited their literary achievements as evidence of women's equality with men in the area of creative thought and expression. "The Lost Light" (1880) is a moving eulogy for George Eliot. In general, the ideals that emerge from P.'s poetry are personal courage and integrity, faith, idealism, freedom, and achievement.

In addition to poetry, P. also published political essays. In 1885, after completing an extensive tour of Asia and America, she published *Flying Leaves from East and West*, a collection of political and artistic commentaries in travelog form. In this book P. wrote, "The lion has so long been the painter, that he is apt too wholly to ignore the aspect which his favourite subject may take from the point of view of the lioness. If the latter will sometimes tell the truth, and tell, not what she thinks she ought to see, but of what she really sees, many an intellectual picture which has hitherto satisfied the sense of mankind, may be found to be somewhat out of focus" (p. 68). Among the political topics she addressed in this volume were class and race relations in the United States and the degraded status of women in harems in Turkey.

It was also during the 1880s that P. wrote most of her numerous articles on the subjects of women and education, work, suffrage, and trade unionism, published in periodicals such as the *Cornhill Magazine* and the *Contemporary Review*. Many of these essays were collected in *Women and Work* (1887), where she attacked the physiological, pseudoscientific theories that claimed women were not strong enough to work and called for more occupational opportunities and more competitive wages for women.

When her husband died in 1889, P. was devastated; she did not survive him much more than a year. In the last year of her life, she made plans to found an orphanage, which was opened after her death, and provided funds for a School of Dramatic Art for women. In addition to a fine collection of her paintings, which she bequeathed to her niece, she left £2000 for higher education for women, which was used in 1895 to erect Aberdare Hall, the first dormitory for women students at University College, Cardiff, in South Wales.

WORKS: *Valisneria; or a Midsummer Night's Dream* (1857). *Margaret, or the Motherless* (1861). *Gerard's Monument and Other Poems* (1873, enlarged 1878). *Poems* (1876). *Glân-Alarch: His Silence and Song* (1877). *Quarterman's Grace and Other Poems* (1879). *Sonnets and Songs* (1880, revised and enlarged 1886). *The Wynnes of Wyn-havod: A Drama of Modern Life* (1881). *Under the Aspens: Lyrical and Dramatic* (1882). *The Rhyme of the Lady of the Rock and How It Grew* (1884). *Flying Leaves from East and West* (1885). *Women and Work: An Essay* (1887). *Flowers of the Night* (1889).

BIBLIOGRAPHY: For articles in reference works, see: *BA19C. DNB. English Poetesses*, ed. E.S. Robertson (1883). *The Poets and the Poetry of the Century*, ed. A.H. Miles, vol. 7 (1892). *Victorian Poets*, ed. E.C. Stedman (1875, 1887, 1903).

Other references: *Academy* (1 February 1890). *Athenaeum* (1 February 1890). Hickok, K. *Representations of Women: Nineteenth-Century British Women's Poetry* (1984). Sackville-West, V. *The Eighteen Seventies*, ed. H. Granville-Barker (1929). *Western Mail* (8 October 1895).

Kathleen Hickok

Katherine Philips

BORN: 1 January 1632, London.
DIED: 22 June 1664, London.
DAUGHTER OF: John and Katherine Oxenbridge Fowler.
MARRIED: James Philips, 1648.
WROTE UNDER: Katherine Philips, Orinda, Mrs. K.P.

Although P. was born to a middle-class family in London and instructed nearby at Mrs. Salmon's school for girls, her life and poetic activities centered in southwest Wales. About four years after her father died in 1642, her mother married Sir Richard Phillipps of Pembroke. P. herself, at age sixteen, married his kinsman and former son-in-law, 54-year-old James Philips. They settled at Cardigan, but she traveled several times to London and once to Dublin. P. was writing verse as early as 1650, and by the time of her death at thirty-two from smallpox, she had gained a considerable literary reputation, distributing poems among her acquaintances. Her two most intimate friends, often addressed in the poems by pseudo-classical names, were Mary Aubrey (Rosania) and Anne Owen (Lucasia). Other members of her circle included the Master of Ceremonies for Charles II, Sir Charles Cotterell (Poliarchus), her husband (Antenor), and, at least peripherally, such admirers as the Earl of Orrery, the theologian Jeremy Taylor, and the poets Henry Vaughan and Abraham Cowley.

P.'s extant literary works consist of approximately 120 original poems, five poems translated from French, and two translations of Corneille's dramas, *Pompey* and *Horace* (the latter incomplete). All these, except for one poem that appeared in both Tutin (1905) and Elmen (1951) and three that surfaced in 1977 (one in Mahl and Koon, two in Mambretti), were printed in her 1667 collected works. (For other uncertain attributions, see Mambretti.) An edition of 74 poems had appeared without P.'s consent in 1664, and a very few poems saw print earlier, the first prefixed to William Cartwright's works in 1651 and two in Henry Lawes's 1655 *Second Book of Ayres*.

Of her plays, *Pompey* had been published twice in 1663, after opening successfully at Dublin's Smock Alley during the 1662–63 season, and probably in London as well. *Horace*, completed by John Denham, was performed at court, February, 1668, and nearly a year later enjoyed a London theater run. P.'s letters also attracted interest, enough for two eighteenth-century editions of those written to Cotterell and for four others to have been anthologized in 1697.

P.'s reputation rests mostly on her poetry, but she is less original in style than subject. Her verse sticks mostly to regular meters in such regular forms as heroic couplets, tetrameter stanzas, and a few ballad stanzas. As a late Cavalier poet, she has an inclination for metaphysical conceits but usually avoids sharp incongruities and rough rhythms. Like Cartwright, who influenced her greatly, she gives most of her verse, but not necessarily her best, a smooth courtliness.

P.'s great theme is friendship, adapted from the Cavalier poets' treatment of Platonic love but, under the influence of the French *Précieuse* society, turned to Platonic friendship between women. Her poems elevate her friends, particularly Rosania and Lucasia, to the heights of beauty and goodness and exclaim her own devotion to them. Men, she sometimes felt, could not possibly deserve such a sublime being in marriage: "She is a public Deity, / And were't not very odd / She should depose herself to be / A petty household god?"

When not praising or remonstrating with her adored friends, P. frequently lauds other acquaintances or, after the Restoration, members of the court. If these verses are insipid, two Interregnum pieces that suggest Royalist leanings, one complaining of "The dying Lion kick'd by every ass," have more power. In fact, in one poem, she angrily and wittily defends her husband, an official under Cromwell, from the taint of such verses. Though her upbringing and marriage should have put her in the Puritan camp, she had opposite political loyalties, perhaps through a youthful association with Royalist literati.

Personal relationships and situations dominate P.'s poetry, and her own isolation from London's literary and social scene may account for a minor strain of *contemptus mundi* verse. These poems, especially her translation of Saint-Amant's "Solitude," are often superior to her panegyrics. Occasionally, such subjects lead her away from personal verse to abstract philosophical poems, among the first instances of this genre in English. Though she is no master of the poetic essay, rare couplets, like, "Mean, sordid things, which by mistake we prize, / And absent covet, but enjoy'd despise," achieve a power of antithesis even the great eighteenth-century poets might not have scorned.

WORKS: *Pompey* (1663). *Poems By the Incomparable, Mrs. K.P.* (1664). *Poems By the most deservedly Admired Mrs. Katherine Philips The matchless Orinda* (1667). *Letters from Orinda to Poliarchus* (1705, enlarged 1729).

MODERN EDITIONS: Complete verse (excluding recent discoveries, plays): G. Saintsbury, ed., *Minor Poets of the Caroline Period* (1905). Collections of 25 and 15 poems: J. Tutin, ed., *Selected Poems* (1904, 1905). Recent anthologies with small selections of verse and letters: M. Ferguson, ed., *First Feminists* (1985); M. Mahl and H. Koon, eds., *The Female Spectator* (1977); A. Stanford, ed., *The Women Poets in English* (1972).

BIBLIOGRAPHY: *Aubrey's Brief Lives* (1898). Gosse, E. *Seventeenth Century Studies* (1897). Morgan, F. *The Female Wits: Women Playwrights of the Restoration* (1981). Souers, P. *The Matchless Orinda* (1931).

For articles in reference works, see: *An Annotated Bibliography of Twentieth-Century Critical Studies of Women and Literature, 1660-1800*, eds. P. Backscheider, F. Nussbaum, P.S. Anderson (1977). *English Literature in the Earlier Seventeenth Century 1600-1660*, ed. D. Bush. (1962). Todd.

Other references: Brashear, L. *Restoration* (1986). Elmen, P. *PQ* (1951). Limbert, C. *ELR* (1986). Mambretti, C. *PBSA* (1977). Roberts. W. *ELN* (1964). Roberts W. *PQ* (1970).

Sayre N. Greenfield

Laetitia Pilkington

BORN: 1712, Dublin.
DIED: 29 July 1750, Dublin.
DAUGHTER OF: Dr. and Mrs. Van Lewen.
MARRIED: Matthew Pilkington, 1730.
WROTE UNDER: Mrs. Meade, Laetitia Pilkington.

Although P. was confident that her poetry would bring her immortality, she is today remembered for her three-volume *Memoirs* (1748-54). Beginning with the claim that with Pope she "lisped in numbers" as a child, the *Memoirs* chronicles a life seen completely in terms of literature and literary production. The daughter of a Dutch obstetrician and a woman distantly related, through the Meades, to the Irish nobility, P. married Matthew Pilkington, an impoverished parson twelve years her senior. Pilkington himself had literary pretensions (his *Poems on Several Occasions* was published in 1730), and with his help and that of a few skillfully-aimed verses, P. managed to gain admittance to the inner circle of

Jonathan Swift, who had recently retired to Dublin. Her account of their unusual friendship remains a primary source for biographers from Thackeray to the present seeking information on Swift's declining years.

It is at this point that P., "the harmless household dove," disappears and P., the "notorious prostitute" of the broadsides, appears. P.'s love of learning, it seems, caused her to be caught in her bedchamber at "an unseasonable hour" in the company of a man, whom, she explains, possessed the "attractive charms of a new Book, which the gentleman would not lend me, but consented to stay until I read it through." She was immediately expelled from her husband's house, and, Dublin soon growing too hot, she left for London in 1738 to attempt to be the first female professional writer after Aphra Behn.

Volume I of the *Memoirs* was written, like so many of the "scandalous" memoirs that proliferated at the beginning of the eighteenth century, both for vindication and out of financial need. It relates the story of P.'s life up until her arrival in London, including her version of her break with her husband, whose jealousy of her literary ability she cites as the real reason for the collapse of their marriage, along with a number of quotations and original poems sprinkled liberally throughout the text. The verse often furnishes an interesting counterpoint on the prose. P.'s poem, "The Statues," for example, was not published until 1739 but was inserted in the *Memoirs* at a point in the early 1730s where it comments upon both Swift's peculiar reaction to women and her own disintegrating marital relationship. The scandal that resulted when the book was published in 1748 was further abetted by the paper wars that were waged between P. and various other writers, most of whom were suspected to be Pilkington himself.

Volume II, which appeared as Volume I had gone into its second printing, tells of P.'s attempts to support herself by furnishing epithets and verses to fashionable London. For a time she was successful, as much, she admits, for the novelty of being a charming young woman as for her poetic ability, many examples of which are included in the text. Her virtue, however, did not stand her in good stead, and she gradually sank on the social scale until she was imprisoned for debt and had to be bailed out by her friend Colley Cibber. With the money left over from this adventure, P. opened a print and pamphlet shop, where she was reunited with her son, John Carteret Pilkington.

Volume III was written while P. was on her deathbed in order to furnish a legacy for her son. At this point the narrative breaks down completely into a random collection of ripostes, reminiscences, and poems—anything, Virginia Woolf comments, "to fill a page and earn her a guinea." The volume appeared in 1754, four years after P.'s death, with a long postscript describing her final illness appended by her son.

Despite the fact that P. is remembered mainly as the author of a "scandalous" memoir, her uniqueness as a writer is defined rather by her refusal to capitulate to the social forms that are necessary for such qualities of scandal and appropriateness to exist. Declaring herself to be "an heteroclite, or irregular verb, which can neither be declined or conjugated," P. aspired to live her life on a plane beyond the social, in the meritocracy of literary production. Even after he repudiated her, Swift remained a symbol of this standard of value by which her poetry would be given what she had been denied during her lifetime.

WORKS: *The Memoirs of Mrs. Letitia Pilkington, Wife to the Rev. Mr. Matthew Pilkington. Written by Herself. Wherein are Occasionally Interspersed All Her Poems; with Anecdotes of several eminent persons, Living and Dead. Among others Dean Swift, Alexander Pope, Esq; &c. &c. &c.,* Vol. I (1748), vol. II (1749), vol. III (1754).

BIBLIOGRAPHY: Barry, I. "Introduction." *The Memoirs. . . .,* ed. I. Barry (with bibliography by J. Isaacs) (1928). *Gentlemen's Magazine* (1748–49) (summarizes and excerpts the Memoirs and provides moral commentary). Nussbaum, F. *The New Eighteenth Century: Theory/Politics/English Literature,* ed. F. Nussbaum and L. Brown (1987). *The Parallel* (1748) (a comparison of the Memoirs of P. and those by Teresia Constantia Phillips). Shumaker, W. *English Autobiography: Its Emergence, Materials, and Form* (1954). Stauffer, D.A. *The Art of Biography in Eighteenth-Century England* (1941). Woolf, V. *The Common Reader* (1925).

Susan Pavloska

Hester Lynch Salusbury Thrale Piozzi

BORN: 16 January 1741, Bodvel, Carnarvonshire, Wales.
DIED: 2 May 1821, Clifton.
DAUGHTER OF: John Salusbury and Hester Cotton Salusbury.
MARRIED: Henry Thrale, 1763; Gabriel Piozzi, 1784.
WROTE UNDER: Mrs. Piozzi, Hester Lynch Thrale Piozzi, "An Old Acquaintance of the Public."

Informally educated in Bodvel by doting parents, P. showed early signs of intelligence and wit. She spent the earliest years of her twenty-one-year marriage to Henry Thrale at Streatham Park near London. Of twelve pregnancies, five daughters survived infancy, four to adulthood. Although her own children and her associates in the Bluestocking circle objected to her second marriage to an Italian singer and music teacher, she managed to reconcile family and society to some extent as she pursued a career as an author, at her best in characterizing through dialogue.

Long an enthusiastic diarist, P. kept her first diary as a record of the progress of her daughter Queeney. Gradually, the diary expanded to include commentary about her growing family. Encouraged by Samuel Johnson's suggestion and Thrale's gift of an empty volume as repository, she began the diary she called *Thraliana* on 15 September 1776. A rich collection of anecdotes and conversations occasionally unified by her narrative,

Thraliana provides insight into English society. P. selects her materials carefully, recording the words of famous persons or the compelling comments of relatively unknown associates. A connoisseur of conversation, she supplements overheard, spontaneous dialogue with discussions she has herself prompted and guided, especially in her salon among the members of the Bluestocking circle and with Johnson, a constant companion during the years of her marriage to Thrale. It also shows P. was concerned less with recording daily in strict chronological order than with aligning the rhythm of historical event with personal circumstance. Posterity would inherit not historicity but vivid moments captured in their entirety. While her emphasis on the personal and individual makes her writing more colloquial than orderly or authoritative, it recalls the rich texture and variety of a domestic life made vibrantly intellectual by the vigilant diarist's search for materials.

Much of *Thraliana* recalls Johnson's extended visits, but the *Anecdotes* and *Letters* to and from Johnson more consistently interest Johnson scholars. P.'s collections include Johnson's minor poetry as well as details of his daily life and sayings. When Johnson, disapproving her marriage to Piozzi, terminated a long and mutually inspirational relationship with P., he freed her to consider more objectively his personality and thought. Thus she tells of a different Johnson than the man portrayed by Boswell, with whom she had several battles during the publication of numerous early reminiscences of Johnson.

An innovative author, P. discovered subjects for research and writing throughout her lifetime. With Johnson, she began translating Boethius, and she began a discussion of art and philosophy, abandoning the project after writing over 100 pages. Other writings chronicle travel to Wales and France. P.'s verse is effective as satire, if not as poetry, a judgment she makes of her own work when she compiles it in *Thraliana*. Her ability to create compelling dialogue has been noted in her imitation of Swift's poems on his own death ("Three Dialogues on the Death of Hester Lynch Thrale") and in a two-act comedy. Readers note in

British Synonymy political commentary, in *Observations and Reflections* a popularizing of travel literature, and in *Retrospection* the leavening of history with anecdote and commentary.

WORKS: *Anecdotes of the Late Samuel Johnson, LL.D. During the Last Twenty Years of His Life* (1786). *Letters to and from the Late Samuel Johnson, LL.D. to Which Are Added Some Poems Never Before Printed* (1788). *Observations and Reflections Made in the Course of a Journey Through France, Italy, and Germany* (1789). *The Three Warnings* (1792). *British Synonymy; or an Attempt at Regulating the Choice of Words in Familiar Conversation. Inscribed, With Sentiments of Gratitude and Respect, to such of her Foreign Friends as Have Made English Literature their Peculiar Study* (1794). *Three Warnings to John Bull before He Dies. By an Old Acquaintance of the Public* (1798). *Retrospection: or a Review of the Most Striking and Important Events, Characters, Situations, and Their Consequences, Which the Last Eighteen Hundred Years Have Presented to the View of Mankind* (1801). *Autobiography, Letters and Literary Remains*, ed. A. Hayward (1861). *Thraliana, the Diary of Mrs. Hester Lynch Thrale, Later Mrs. Piozzi* (ed. K.C. Balderson) (1942).

BIBLIOGRAPHY: Broadley, A.M. *Doctor Johnson and Mrs. Thrale* (1910). Clifford, J.L. *Hester Lynch Piozzi, Mrs. Thrale* (1952). Hyde, M.M. *The Impossible Friendship: Boswell and Mrs. Thrale* (1972). McCarthy, W. *Hester Thrale Piozzi: Portrait of a Literary Woman* (1985). Mangin, E. *Piozziana . . . Recollections by a Friend* (1833). Merritt, P. *The True Story of the So-Called Love Letters of Mrs. Piozzi* (1927). Thomson, K.B. *Queens of Society* (1860). Vuliamy, C.E. *Mrs. Thrale of Streatham* (1939).

For articles in reference works, see: *Allibone. BA.B1800. Cassell. DNB. ELB. NCHEL. OCEL.*

Other references: Adelman, J. *Famous Women. BJRL* (1974). DeMorny, P. *Best Years of Their Lives* (1955). Dorland, W. *The Sum of Feminine Achievement* (1917). Hammerton, J.A. *Concise Universal Biography. MLR* (1972). *MR* (1942). *N&Q* (1943). *RES* (1946, 1948). Stanton, D. *English Women in History.* Thomson, K. *The Queens of Society* (1860).

Mary S. Comfort

Ruth Pitter

BORN: 7 November 1897, Ilford, Essex.
DAUGHTER OF: George and Louisa R. Murrell Pitter.

P.'s poetry is often compared to the work of such seventeenth-century poets as Vaughan, Tra-

herne, and Carew, as well as the work of such others as Spenser, Blake, Clare, and Hopkins. Her lyrical verse deals with such traditional subjects as the natural world and religion, and her clear awareness of sensory stimuli and concern for metaphysics seem to derive at least in part from the influence of her friend C.S. Lewis, though her long identification with and precise knowledge of the English countryside, the joys of gardening, and her long life of physical exertion contribute uniquely to her verse.

Oldest of three children born to two London elementary school teachers, P. started writing poetry at age five and published her first poem at thirteen, in A. R. Orage's *New Age* (later renamed *New English Weekly*). She worked as a War Office clerk in World War I; after the war she mastered such crafts as woodworking and painting before operating, with a partner, a gift shop in London until 1945. She then retired to Aylesbury, Bucks., where she still lives.

Her poetic appeal is to both heart and mind, and her lyrics often seem deceptively simple though admittedly deeply felt and balanced. Many of her poems reflect what Hilaire Belloc called her "perfect ear and exact epithet," with some, such as "The Fishers" and "The Cygnet," typical of her contemplations on and celebrations of what she calls the "secret dynamism of life." "The Cygnet," for example, uses two swans as suggestive of the soul's victory over evil. Other contemplative poems include "Urania," "The Eternal Image," and "The Downward-Pointing Muse." But she is also capable of witty, satiric verse, as in *The Rude Potato* (1941) and *On Cats* (1947), the latter collection less "old-maidish" (her term) and rollicking than the similar volume by her acquaintance T.S. Eliot.

P. is not experimental, preferring instead to depend on traditional meters and forms. Nor does the frantic world around her throughout most of her life intrigue her to any appreciable degree, though her "The Military Harpist" offers a subdued, sardonic commentary on war. Rather, she celebrates silence and contemplation through an emphasis on natural splendor and on life itself as reflective of the contrast between mere daily existence and the Christian hope.

Widely praised by other poets and by many critics—Belloc was one of her first supporters, and she has been praised by Louise Bogan, Louis Untermeyer, Gorham Munson, Walter de la Mare, Gilbert Murray, Osbert Sitwell, John Masefield, and others—P. has had an enduring though unpretentious poetic career. She has won such awards as the Hawthornden Prize (1937), the Heinemann Award (1954), and the Queen's Gold Medal for Poetry (1955); in 1979 she received the Commander of the British Empire honor. Never a fashionable or popular writer and a member of no poetic "school," P. has lived in comparative though wholly unjustified obscurity.

WORKS: *First Poems* (1920). *First and Second Poems, 1912-1925* (1930). *Persephone in Hades* (1931). *A Mad Lady's Garland* (1934). *A Trophy of Arms: Poems 1926-1935* (1936). *The Spirit Watches* (1939). *The Rude Potato* (1941). *Poem* (1943). *The Bridge: Poems 1939-1944* (1945). *On Cats* (1947). *Urania* (1951). *The Ermine: Poems 1942-1952* (1953). *Still By Choice* (1966). *Poems 1926-1966* (1968; American ed. titled *Collected Poems*). *End of Drought* (1975). *A Heaven to Find* (1987).

BIBLIOGRAPHY: Gilbert, R. *Four Living Poets* (1944). *Poetry Northwest* (special P. issue, winter, 1960). Russell, A., ed. *Ruth Pitter: Homage to a Poet* (1969). Watkin, E.I. *Poets and Mystics* (1953).

For articles in reference works, see: *CA. CP. DLB. EWLTC. TCW. TWA* and *SUP*.

Other references: Bogan, L. *Poetry* (1937). Kunitz, S. *A Kind of Order, a Kind of Folly: Essays and Conversations* (1975). Munson, G.B. *Commonweal* (1929). Scott-James, R.A. *Fifty Years of English Literature: 1900-1950* (1951). Shahani, R.G. *Poetry* (1942). Swartz, R.T. *Poetry* (1940). Wain, J. *Listener* (1969).

Paul Schlueter

Mary Pix

BORN: 1666, Nettlebed, Oxfordshire.
DIED: 1709, London(?).
DAUGHTER OF: Roger and Lucy Berriman Griffith.
MARRIED: George Pix, 1684.

Daughter of an Oxfordshire vicar, P. married at eighteen a London merchant tailor; her only child died in 1690. In 1696, at the age of thirty, she became a professional writer, producing in one year a tragedy, *Ibrahim*, which, according to a contemporary, made audiences weep; a successful comedy, *The Spanish Wives*; and a romantic novel, *The Inhumane Cardinal*, in which a cardinal disguises himself in order to seduce a young girl.

Her initial success, coupled with her association with two other new women playwrights, Delariviere Manley and Catherine Trotter, caused her to be satirized in an anonymous play, *The Female Wits* (1696), in which P. appears as Mrs. Wellfed, "a fat Female Author," a tippler, unlearned but amiable and unpretentious. In 1697-98 P. was involved in a plagiarism dispute with George Powell, an actor and sometimes playwright for the United Company at Drury Lane, who copied her play *The Deceiver Deceived* in his *The Imposture Defeated*. William Congreve and Thomas Betterton of the Lincoln's Inn Fields playhouse were partisans of P. Except for these two occasions, her public and personal life was inconspicuous.

A professional playwright of modest abilities and moderate success, P. wrote twelve plays—six comedies and six tragedies. Her tragedies, which continued the Fletcherian tradition, are undistinguished, written in inflated prose printed as blank verse. Her one overt attempt at stage reform, *The False Friend* (1699), was a muddle of melodrama and moralizing. Her tragedies point forward in the increasing prominence of the heroines and of fatal accidents to love; their popularity probably rested on her knack for alternating scenes of rant with melting love scenes in which a mighty hero languished at his lady's feet.

P.'s best works are her comedies, especially *The Spanish Wives* (1696) and *The Adventures in Madrid* (1706). *The Spanish Wives* is a lively, amusing farce skillfully double-plotted to contrast the situations of two young wives. The lady of the old governor of Barcelona is given unusual liberty by her husband; touched by this goodness, she resists the advances of a young English colonel. Elenora, kept locked up by a jealous and avaricious husband, escapes to marry her former fiancé. Music, song, dance, and disguise proved stage spectacle. In *The Adventures in Madrid* two English gentlemen intrigue with and eventually marry two Spanish ladies in spite of the complications provided by the villainies of the supposed husband of one of the ladies.

P.'s comedies contain lively intrigues, much stage business, many surprises, and some pleasant songs. Her encomium of the English merchant in *The Beau Defeated* (1700) suggests Lillo and the bourgeois drama of the next generation. Forced or unhappy marriages appear frequently and prominently in the comedies. P. is not, however, writing polemics against the forced marriage but using it as a plot device and sentimentalizing the unhappily married person, who is sometimes rescued and married more satisfactorily. Occasionally the unhappy wife or husband seems erring but is really virtuous. P.'s use of sentimentalized characters in intrigue comedies, while causing oddities of plotting, reflects the changing theatrical taste that called for less emphasis on cuckolding and more on virtuous love. P.'s attempt to write a mixture of hard and soft comedy is characteristic of playwrights under pressure for stage reform at the turn of the century.

WORKS: *Ibrahim* (1696). *The Spanish Wives* (1696). *The Inhumane Cardinal* (1696). *The Innocent Mistress* (1697). *The Deceiver Deceived* (1697; reissued 1699 as *The French Beau*). *Queen Catherine* (1698). *The False Friend* (1699). *The Beau Defeated* (1700). *The Double Distress* (1701). *The Czar of Muscovy* (1701). *The Different Widows* (1703). *Violenta* (1704). *The Conquest of Spain* (1705). *The Adventures in Madrid* (1706). *Plays*, ed. E.Steeves (1982).

BIBLIOGRAPHY: Cotton, N. *Women Playwrights in England c. 1363–1750* (1980). *The Female Wits*, ed. L. Hook (1967). Clark, C. *Three Augustan Women Playwrights* (1986).

Other references: *MLN* (1933). *RECTR* (May 1976). *RES* (July 1930). *WS* (1980).

Nancy Cotton

Anna Maria Porter

BORN: 1780, Durham.
DIED: 21 September 1832, Bristol.
DAUGHTER OF: William and Jane Blenkinsop Porter.
WROTE UNDER: Anonymously, a young lady eighteen years of age, Anna Maria Porter, Miss Anna Maria Porter, Miss A.M. Porter, Miss Anna Porter.

P. was the younger sister of two artists. Jane Porter, also a novelist, collaborated with P. on two works, *Tales Round a Winter Hearth* (1826) and *Coming Out and the Field of Forty Footsteps* (1828). Sir Robert Ker Porter, her brother, was a painter who designed the frontispiece of P.'s first published work, *Artless Tales* (1793). P. had a friendship with a third artist, Sir Walter Scott.

Both writers of historical romances, they likely influenced each other's art.

A traditional writer without feminist interests, P. preferred male protagonists who suffer because of a deceitful woman before finding happiness with a selfless, beautiful woman. This plot is evident in three of her most popular novels, *The Hungarian Brothers* (1807), *Don Sebastian* (1809), and *Walsh Colville* (1833).

The Hungarian Brothers, a historical romance, concerns two brothers who overcome poverty, war, unworthy women, and deceitful men until they at last marry the women they love. While the novel lacks vivid sensory detail and the plot is clumsily handled at times, the contrast between the two brothers is effective. Charles, the older brother, is the prudent, brave soldier, while

Demetrius is delicate and thoughtless. It is the younger brother who reflects the moral stated in the novel's introduction: "to shew youth the destructive tendency of uncontrolled passions. . . ."

Don Sebastian or the House of Braganza, a romantic tale of palace intrigue, has two plots: Don Sebastian's efforts to regain the throne of Portugal and his adventures in love. Excessive pathos, anti-Catholic sentiment, and repetitive episodes make this work unappealing to modern readers.

Like *The Hungarian Brothers* and *Don Sebastian*, *Walsh Colville* is an early example of a *Bildungsroman*. After leaving home, the title character of this romance must learn to tell the difference between the duplicity and genuine affection of the men and women he encounters. The portrayal of the protagonist as a naive, earnest young man is effective, but the reformation of his deceitful friend Stanhope is unconvincing. Moreover, P.'s narrative style is uneven, alternating between well-delineated and hastily described scenes.

Plot and characterization are well executed in *Ballad Romances and Other Poems* (1811) although the language is unimaginative and trite. Two of the better poems, like P.'s novels, depict the duplicity of women. In "Eugene," a woman, after losing the man she loves to her sister, secretly murders her nephew. In "The Knight of Malta," a woman's lie leads the hero to kill his own brother.

A novelist, poet, and writer of short fiction, P. is best remembered today for making an early contribution to sentimental romances.

WORKS: *Artless Tales* (1793). *Original Poems on Various Subjects* (1789). *Airs, Duets, Choruses, Etc.* (1803). *The Lake of Killarney* (1804). *A Sailor's Friendship and a Soldier's Love* (1805). *The Hungarian Brothers* (1807). *Don Sebastian* (1809). *Ballad Romances and Other Poems* (1811). *The Recluse of Norway* (1814). *Tales of Pity on Fishing, Shooting and Hunting* (1814). *The Knight of St. John* (1817). *The Fast of St. Magdalen* (1818). *The Village of Mariendorpt* (1821). *Roche-Blanche* (1822). *Honor O'Hara* (1826). *Tales Round a Winter Hearth*, with Jane Porter (1826). *Coming Out and the Field of Forty Footsteps*, with Jane Porter (1828). *The Barony* (1830). *Walsh Colville* (1833). *Octavia* (1833).

BIBLIOGRAPHY: Elwood, A.K. *Memoirs of Literary Ladies of England* (1843).

For articles in reference works, see: *Allibone. BA19C.* (1875). *A Dictionary of Literature in the English Language*, ed. R. Myers (1970). *Everyman's Dictionary of Literary Biography*, ed. D.C. Browning (1965). *NCHEL.*

Margaret Ann Baker Graham

Jane Porter

BORN: 1776.
DIED: 24 May 1850, Bristol.
DAUGHTER OF: William and Jane Blenkinsop Porter.

Novelist and playwright, daughter of an army officer and sister of Dr. William, Anna, and Sir Robert, P.'s Edinburgh education was enhanced by an avid interest in Scottish myths and legends, many narrated to her by a poor neighbor, Luckie Forbes.

In 1797, P. and Anna assisted Thomas Frognall Dibdin in the publication of *The Quiz*, a short-lived periodical. Following its failure, the family moved to a London residence formerly owned by Sir Joshua Reynolds, where, it is believed, P. wrote her early biographical fiction. The first romance, *Thaddeus of Warsaw* (1803), was considered a product of her youthful exuberance and natural sympathy for the influx of Polish citizens seeking refuge. An equally vital source of inspiration was Robert's description of a personal meeting with the Polish hero, Thaddeus Kosciuszko, during the general's visit to England. P. wrote that her first herioc tale was "founded on the actual scenes of Kosciuszko's suffering and moulded out of his virtues," though she masks her protagonist as a young descendant of John Sobieski. Many other characters are thinly disguised versions of various friends and family members. Acclaimed as a "work of genius" and later recognized as "the best and most enduring" of P.'s fiction, the novel achieved wide acceptance and was published in several translations.

The ninth edition of *Thaddeus of Warsaw* and the initial printing of *The Scottish Chiefs* occurred in 1810. The latter publication, a five-volume work, is based on the life of the Scotch patriot, William Wallace. This heroic romance incorporates the childhood legends P. loved as well as an old poem by Henry the Minstrel (Blind Harry) and bits of information on Wallace's life received from Campbell the Poet, who also supplied a list of recommended references. Wallace's career as an outlaw began when he killed an Englishman who had insulted him. As his band of brigands increased in number, they engaged the British army several times, notably at Stirling Bridge, and almost succeeded in liberating Scotland until a reinforced troop of British soldiers overpowered Wallace's men at Falkirk. Although he escaped capture at this time, he was eventually arrested, tried, and executed as a traitor, but his death provided inspiration for the country's next hero, Robert Bruce, who successfully achieved Wallace's dream of independence. P.'s interpretation of this much-loved legend found instant favor with her readers and its fame rivaled the predecessor, with numerous translations printed throughout Europe and parts of India.

The Scottish Chiefs was dubiously "honored" by Napoleon who attempted to have its translation banned in France. It is considered one of the few historical novels printed prior to Scott's *Waverly* to have survived and has had several reprints since its initial publication.

After writing a three-volume novel dealing with the Stuart clan, *The Pastor's Fireside* (1815), P. wrote several plays. One, *Egmont: or the Eve of St. Alyne*, sent to Edmund Kean, famed Shakesperean tragedian, was denied production by his fellow-actors, and it was never published. *Switzerland* (1819) and *Owen: Prince of Powys* (1822) were eventually presented at Drury Lane but considered "lamentable failures."

George IV suggested the subject of her next novel, *Duke Christian of Lüneburg*, which she dedicated to the monarch. Her final publication, *Sir Edward Seaward's Narrative of His Shipwreck and Consequent Discovery of Certain Islands in the Caribbean Sea* (1831), harbors the mystery of its origin. Purported to have developed from an actual diary account and edited by P., it was described by the *Quarterly* as a well-written work of fiction. P. insisted that the account was genuine and had been given to her by the writer's family, yet an inscription in Bristol Cathedral, supposedly placed there by P., cites her brother William as the actual author.

P., a strikingly good looking woman, received many honors and invitations, especially for her first two works. She was made a Lady of the Chapter of St. Joachim and given the gold cross of the order from Württemberg. In 1844, an organization composed of American authors, publishers, and booksellers sent a rosewood armchair "as an expression of admiration and respect," but these gifts did not alleviate the family's financial difficulties, a fact which she repeatedly noted in her unpublished diaries.

P. seriously regarded her literary skill as a "religious duty" and painfully extracted each word. She often envied her sister, Anna, who had a facility for free expression and a more relaxed approach. P. insisted that the major changes in the English novel originated with her works, rather than with the creations of Sir Walter Scott—ironically, a childhood playmate—as her reputation was in its zenith long before his first novel reached publication. P. defended her ability to unite "the personages and facts of real history or biography with a combining and illustrative machinery of the imagination" although later critics deplored her manipulation of various events in order to secure the novel's development.

The public, however, is the final critic, and its delight in P.'s enthusiastic exaggerations cannot be denied. Scottish children, normally denied the reading of romantic stories, were encouraged to enjoy her tales, and P.'s unique blends of legend, myth, and reality remain landmark contributions to the art of fiction.

WORKS: *A Defence of the Profession of an Actor* (1800). *Thaddeus of Warsaw* (1803). *Sketch of the Campaign of Count A. Suwarrow Ryminski* (1804). *The Scottish Chiefs* (1810). *The Pastor's Fireside* (1815). *Switzerland* (1819). *Owen: Prince of Powys* (1822). *Duke Christian of Lüneberg* (1824). *Tales Round a Winter Hearth* (with A.M. Porter) (1826). *The Field of the Forty Footsteps* (1828). *Sir Edward Seaward's Narrative of His Shipwreck* (1831).

BIBLIOGRAPHY: Elwood, A.K. *Memoirs of the Literary Ladies of England* (1843). Hall, A.M. *Pilgrimages to English Shrines* (1854). Hall, S.C. *A Book of Memories of Great Men and Women of the Age* (1871). MacLise, D. *The Maclise Portrait Gallery* (1873). Vaughn, H.M. *From Anne to Victoria* (1967). Wagenknecht, E. *Cavalcade of the English Novel* (1954).

For articles in reference works, see: *BA19C. Chambers. DNB.*

Other references: *Scottish Review* (April 1897).

Zelda Provenzano

Beatrix Potter

BORN: 28 July 1866, Bolton Gardens, Kensington.
DIED: 22 December 1943, Sawrey.
DAUGHTER OF: Rupert and Helen Leech Potter.
MARRIED: William Heelis, 1913.

Born into a family whose fortune was already well established, P. led a carefully guarded childhood. Unlike her younger brother Bertram, P. was not sent to school and had virtually no friends. At an early age P. showed a talent for illustration and was encouraged by her governess to practice her artwork. P. found subject material first at local museums and later in nature when her family took extensive summer vacations in Scotland and the Lake District.

P.'s attachment to nature was by no means sentimental; she often dissected dead animals when she found them and had a keen eye for ecological and biological detail. Her illustrations in *Wayside and Woodland Fungi* (1967) are the work of a skilled and knowledgeable naturalist. P. maintained a tie with nature even in the austere home of her parents by keeping a small menagerie. Most notable among her pets, which included mice, bats, frogs, and snails, were two of her rabbits, Peter Rabbit and Benjamin Bunny, and her hedgehog, Mrs. Tiggy-Winkle.

In 1893 the son of one of P.'s former governesses took ill. To amuse the boy during his recovery, P. sent him illustrated letters which traced the adventures of her pets. The letters circulated among friends and P. was encouraged to prepare the story of Peter Rabbit as a book. Failing to find a publisher, P. had *The Tale of Peter Rabbit* printed privately in 1900. A second private printing followed in 1902 along with a private edition of *The Tailor of Gloucester*. By this time the firm of Frederick Warne & Co. offered to publish *Peter Rabbit* if P. would do color illustrations. The success of *Peter Rabbit* established P. as an important children's writer, and with each successive work, usually in the same miniature format as the first, her reputation and popularity grew.

The association between P. and Warne & Co. was a long and happy one which lasted over the publication of 24 of her books. P. was particularly close to Norman Warne who worked in his father's firm. In 1905 Norman proposed and P., in spite of her parents' strenuous objections, accepted. Unfortunately, Warne died shortly after their engagement was announced. During this period P. bought Hill Top, a farm near the village of Sawrey, using both the earnings from her books and a small legacy. Still under the rule of her parents, P. leased the farm, under generous terms, to a tenant farmer and visited it only occasionally. The legal concerns of her property brought P. into contact with William Heelis, a local solicitor, whom she married in 1913.

Although some books did appear after her marriage, P.'s career as a writer was essentially over. She immersed herself in the concerns of her farm and was respected enough to be elected president of the Herdwick Sheep-Breeders' Association shortly before her death. As Mrs. Heelis, P. shunned fame, and though she referred to accolades of her work as "great rubbish," there is no question of her stature or the extent of her influence in children's literature.

P.'s stories have a simplicity that is complemented by a sense of realism and of humor. Her characters, who live in a world that can be both comforting and threatening, learn to appreciate the former by experiencing the latter. The impact of her stories is consistently emphasized by the deft accuracy and subtle playfulness of her artwork.

WORKS: *The Tale of Peter Rabbit* (1902). *The Tale of Squirrel Nutkin* (1903). *The Tailor of Gloucester* (1903). *The Tale of Benjamin Bunny* (1904). *The Tale of Two Bad Mice* (1904). *The Tale of Mrs. Tiggy-Winkle* (1905). *The Pie and the Patty-pan* (1905). *The Tale of Mr. Jeremy Fisher* (1906). *The Story of a Fierce Bad Rabbit* (1906). *The Story of Miss Moppet* (1906). *The Tale of Tom Kitten* (1907). *The Tale of Jemima Puddle-Duck* (1908). *The Roly-Poly Pudding* (1908; later *The Tale of Samuel Whiskers*, 1926). *The Tale of the Flopsy Bunnies* (1909). *Ginger and Pickles* (1909). *The Tale of Mrs. Tittlemouse* (1910). *Peter Rabbit's Painting Book* (1911). *The Tale of Timmy Tiptoes* (1911). *The Tale of Mr. Tod* (1912). *The Tale of Pigling Bland* (1913). *Tom Kitten's Painting Book* (1917). *Appley Dapply's Nursery Rhymes* (1917). *The Tale of Johnny Town-Mouse* (1918). *Cecily Parsley's Nursery Rhymes* (1922). *Jemima Puddle-Duck's Painting Book* (1925). *Peter Rabbit's Almanac for 1929* (1928). *The Fairy Caravan* (1929). *The Tale of Little Pig Robinson* (1930). *Sister Anne* (1932). *Wag-by-Wall* (1944). *The Tale of the Faithful Dove* (1956). *The Journal of Beatrix Potter* (1966). *Wayside and Woodland Fungi* (illustrations only, 1967). *Letters to Children* (1967). *A History of the Writings of Beatrix Potter* (1971).

BIBLIOGRAPHY: Anderson, C. *Proceedings of the 7th Annual Conference of Children's Literature* (1980). Crouch, M. *Beatrix Potter* (1960). Greene, G. *Collected Essays* (1951). Lane, M. *The Magic Years of Beatrix Potter* (1978). Lane, M. *The Tale of Beatrix Potter* (1946). Nere, C. *Country Life* (1972). Nesbitt, E. *A Critical History of Children's Literature* (1953). Sicroff, S. *Children's Literature* (1973). Taylor, J. *Beatrix Potter: Artist, Story-Teller, and Countrywoman* (1986).

For articles in reference works, see: *Children's Literature Review* (1946). *DNB. Yesterday's Authors of Books for Children* (1977).

Other references: *International Fiction Review* (1977). Hamer, D. *N&Q* (1969). *Horn-Book* (1941, 1944, 1977, 1978). Nere, C. *Country Life* (1972). Sicroff, S. *Children's Literature* (1973).

Alan Rauch

Barbara Pym

BORN: 2 June 1913, Oswestry, Shropshire.
DIED: 11 January 1980.
DAUGHTER OF: Frederic Crampton and Irena Thomas Pym.

After receiving her B.A. with honors in English Literature from St. Hilda's College, Oxford, P. served with the Women's Royal Naval Service in England and Italy from 1943 to 1946. She then began her long career working for the International African Institute where she became assistant editor of its journal, *Africa*, while writing novels in her spare time.

Her first six novels, published between 1950 and 1961, achieved critical recognition and a small but loyal following. These books established Pym as the chronicler of a world small in scope but wide in relevance, the world of spinsters dedicated to the church and to more or less worthless curates; the world of small office workers, librarians, anthropologists, the Church of England clergy; and persons on the outskirts of academic life. This world of little people, especially women, leading quiet lives of compromise, resignation, and acceptance is recorded with compassion, irony, dry wit, an evocative attention to details, and an absolute absence of sentimentality.

Incredibly, P. could not find a publisher after 1961, although she continued to write fiction, seeing it increasingly as a personal and private exercise. Despite great fortitude, though, she began to question the value of her early work. In 1974 she retired from her editorial position and went to live with her sister in an Oxfordshire village.

In February 1977, responding to an invitation from the *Times Literary Supplement* to a number of literary figures to name the most underrated and overrated writers of the century, Lord David Cecil and Philip Larkin both named P., suddenly catapulting her to fame and international publication after sixteen years of oblivion. Her frequently rejected novel, *Quartet in Autumn*, a small ironic masterpiece on the theme of aging, was bought by Macmillan, while Jonathan Cape reissued all her out-of-print books. *The Sweet Dove Died* followed, and *A Few Green Leaves* was published posthumously after P.'s death from cancer.

A reserved person who described her avocations as "reading, domestic life and cats," P. was also a traditionalist in feeling that what mattered most to her in life were the Church of England and the English poetic tradition. Nonetheless, and despite a calm, conventional, though highly crafted, style, P.'s art is radical in that she insists on telling the truth about women's lives, albeit with gentle scepticism and satire. Typical is this comment in *Less Than Angels*: "It would be a reciprocal relationship—the woman giving the food and shelter and doing some typing for him and the man giving the priceless gift of himself."

Her themes are consistent throughout her books and help explain the recent upsurge in interest, especially among feminist scholars: the (often unmet) need for an appropriate and responsive recipient of one's love; the necessity for humorous acceptance of a confining existence; and the pathos of lives being lived without affection or any other aesthetic framework to dignify, amplify, and explain their significance.

WORKS: *Some Tame Gazelle* (1950). *Excellent Women* (1952). *Jane and Prudence* (1953). *Less Than Angels* (1955). *A Glass of Blessings* (1959). *No Fond Return of Love* (1961). *The Sweet Dove Died* (1978). *A Few Green Leaves* (1980). *A Very Private Eye: An Autobiography in Diaries and Letters* (1985). *An Academic Question* (1986). *Civil to Strangers and Other Writings*, ed. H. Holt (1987).

BIBLIOGRAPHY: Benet, D. *Something to Love: Barbara Pym's Novels* (1986). Burkhart, C. *The Pleasure of Miss Pym* (1987). Brother, S.B. *Twentieth-Century Women Novelists*, ed. T.F. Staley (1982). Long, R.E. *Barbara Pym* (1986). Salwak, D. ed., *The Life and Work of Barbara Pym* (1987). Rossen, J. *The World of Barbara Pym* (1987). Staley, T.F., ed., *Twentieth Century Women Novelists* (1982).

For articles in reference works, see: *CA. CAP. DLB.*

Other references: *Commonweal* (14 March 1980). Cooley, M. *TCL* (1986). *Encounter* (May 1987). Kane, P. *SDR* (1986). Kaufman, A. *TCL* (1986). *NYTBR* (15 August 1982). *PW* (14 March 1980). *Research Studies* (1981). Rubenstein, J. *MFS* (1986). Sadler, L.V. *WVPP* (1986). *Time* (26 September 1983).

Carey Kaplan

Ann Ward Radcliffe

BORN: 9 July 1764, London.
DIED: 7 February 1823, London.
DAUGHTER OF: William and Ann Oates Ward.
MARRIED: William Radcliffe, 1787.

The mysteries and ironies of R.'s life are somehow appropriate for the woman who perfected the Gothic suspense tale. Arguably the most popular writer of her time, she lived a reclusive life and stopped writing for publication altogether when her mother's will made her financially comfortable. Her best novels are set in a romanticized Italian landscape, but she never traveled to Italy. Though contemporaries and writers of the next generation would tell jokes at her expense, they would also imitate her. She bequeathed more to the Romantic imagination in terms of sensibility and vocabulary than the Romantics would ever admit. By all accounts, she lived as a dutiful wife, daughter, and niece; her novels, however, are powerful explorations of female fantasy. In many of her tales apparently supernatural events arouse suspense and terror, which are alleviated when the explanation is found to be purely natural. However, her own mind tended toward melancholy and outright depression, perhaps even to madness near the end of her life.

R.'s family included famous physicians and scholars. However, her father was a haberdasher, salesman, and businessman. She often visited her uncle, Thomas Bentley, who knew many eminent poets, scientists, and travelers. In her obituary her husband would write that these visits to her uncle were a major influence on her imagination. Otherwise, her education was standard. When living in Bath, R. may have been a student of Sophia Lee, who ran a woman's school there. If R. did not meet Lee, she certainly read and was deeply influenced by Lee's novel The Recess. That book had marked a departure from the standard domestic sentimental novel. There is an interest in madness, in passion and mystery, in the psychology of the romantic sensibility. What was new about Lee's novel was its freedom from the constraints of "realism," which in most cases meant the depiction of house, home, and duty expected in women's fiction. Female characters could now be placed in wild and unpredictable circumstances, and the depiction of their perils and emotions could be freer. Thus, fantasy of a powerful kind was given a new latitude. These developments, along with an interest in the dark and the macabre (R. frequently reread Macbeth), left its mark on R.'s subsequent literary work.

In 1787 R. married William Radcliffe, a law student turned journalist, who encouraged her to write and critiqued her work. Her novels were almost immediately popular, and by The Romance of the Forest (1791), she was a well-known literary figure. R. achieved true fame with The Mysteries of Udolpho (1794), a book that earned her the nickname "The Great Enchantress."

R.'s novels have been considered in several ways. Earlier critics, wishing to get around R. as quickly as possible, either dismissed her work as trash or praised it faintly as the precedent for much better novels, such as Jane Eyre and Wuthering Heights. Lately, critics have begun to attribute a great deal of importance to R. Her novels can be seen as the first perfection of an enduringly popular genre (witness the recent vogue for "romance novels"). R. also wrote the first novels whose main aim was to elicit emotions of terror, horror, and suspense. Lately she has been recognized as a writer whose main theme was female fantasy—specifically, the fantasy in which the virtuous and beleaguered heroine triumphs over insurmountable difficulties to achieve her own happiness and vindicate the essential goodness of the divine order.

Clearly, R. was a writer with a formula. Keats was responding to R.'s depiction of nature when he lampooned her as a writer who will "cavern you and grotto you, and waterfall you and wood you, and immense-rock you." R. concocted a mixture of medieval and contemporary romance that brought ruined castles, houses with secret passageways, cryptic messages that explain everything, and dark, half-understood portents in nature into fiction; she also resurrected the apparatus of Renaissance romance, including the low-born heroine who discovers that she is nobly born, woods lushly responsive to the excesses of the heroine's emotions (as is the case with Adeline of The Romance of the Forest, 1791), and the reunion of deserving lovers after eventful separation. There is also a cast of characters that has become too familiar: a lonely maiden, an older authoritarian male figure who sooner or later becomes an out-and-out villain, a loyal servant, and a virtuous hero.

Yet R. deserves to be remembered for more than these clichés. Her writing reveals a genuine interest in the extremes of human psychology. She is acutely sensitive to the aspects of life that make us anxious and afraid. And there is a moral purpose to the excitation of terror in the reader, for terror is a test of reason, an index of the extent to which the reader trusts herself and her world. As mentioned above, the point of most of her novels is that all the terror has a natural explanation. Her heroines are heroines because they triumph over great difficulties to discover this; her villains are villains because, like La Motte of *The Romance of the Forest*, they often know the secret and try to prevent the heroine from discovering it. These villains often enjoy tormenting the unknowing heroine over their half-understood world. The extent of their evil is revealed at the end, when the heroine understands that world more clearly and has a more complete control over her life. Thus La Motte keeps the true origin of Adelie's birth from her, and Montoni of *The Mysteries of Udolpho* tries to wheedle his dead wife's money out of her daughter Emily. Emily triumphs over Montoni and over La Motte because of self-reliance and inner strength.

One need not belabor the patterns that emerge so clearly from these novels—of male figures denying female figures essential information and essential power, of revelations that change the place of woman in the world. When in *Udolpho* the veil is lifted over the mysterious picture, the key to it all, Emily faints; it is as if she, allowed to see the real truth, must escape somehow from its impact. Most importantly, R.'s heroines do it themselves: in the end they act to change their worlds and break free of the dark, often unconscious fetters of fear.

Part of all the fantasy is the undeniably attractive nature of some of the villains. Some readers have been quick to find Electra complexes throughout R.'s fiction. More to the point, her villains are brooding, isolated, full of a mysterious inner conflict. R. refined and refined this character until she perfected it in Father Schedoni of *The Italian* (1797). He has been recognized as the prototype of the aloof, preoccupied Romantic hero, a proto-Manfred: "there was something in [Schedoni's] air, something almost superhuman." Though Ellena triumphs over Schedoni in the end and marries the virtuous Vivaldi, it is his character that remains the most striking thing in a very striking novel.

The Italian was the last of R.'s novels to be published during her lifetime. A year later, her father died and her husband fell ill. In March 1800, her mother died, leaving R. alone, despondent, "the last leaf on the tree." Although she wrote one more novel, *Gaston de Blondeville* (1826), she had lost the desire to publish, possibly even to be read. According to her husband's obituary, she died in a delirium.

R. is a writer who has had a remarkable and enduring impact on fiction both serious and popular. Of her works, *The Romance of the Forest* and *The Italian* hold up the best. They are still enjoyable for their suspense and attractive for their substance. Though she wrote very little about her personal life, one imagines that she would have appreciated readers who could see the moral intent of all the wildness, the twists of plot, the romance, and the fantasy. She virtually discovered a form of myth that, however it may embarrass or distress us, is still very powerful.

WORKS: *The Castles of Athlin and Dubayne* (1789). *A Sicilian Romance* (1790). *The Romance of the Forest* (1791). *The Mysteries of Udolpho* (1794). *A Journey made in the Summer of 1794 through Holland and the Western Frontiers of Germany, with a return down the Rhine, to which are added Observations during a tour to the Lakes of Lancashire, Westmoreland and Cumberland* (1795) (travel journal). *The Italian, or the Confessional of the Black Penitents* (1797). *Gaston de Blondeville, or the Court of Henry III Keeping Festival in Ardenne* (1826). *St. Alban's Abbey* (1826).

BIBLIOGRAPHY: Grant, A. *Ann Radcliffe* (1920). McIntyre, C.F. *Ann Radcliffe in Relation to Her Time* (1920). Murray, E.B. *Ann Radcliffe* (1972). Ware, M. *Sublimity in the Novels of Ann Radcliffe* (1963). Weiten, A.S.S. *Mrs Radcliffe, Her Relation Towards Romanticism* (1926).

For articles in reference works, see: *Annual Biography and Obituary for 1824* (1824).

Other references: Durant, D. *SEL* (1982). Flaxman, R.L. *Fetter'd or Free? British Women Novelists, 1670-1815*, ed. M.A. Schofield and C. Macheski (1986). Krely, R. *The Romantic Novel in English* (1972). London, A. *Eighteenth-Century Life* (1986). Nichols, N. *The Female Gothic*, ed. J.E. Fleenor (1983). Ruff, W. *The Age of Johnson: Essays Presented to C.B. Tinker* (1949). Scott, W. "Introduction" to *The Novels of Ann Radcliffe* (1824). Smith, N.C. *SEL* (1973). Spencer, J. *The Rise of the Woman Novelist* (1986). Tamkin, L.E. *Heroines in Italy* (1985). Tomkins, J.M.S. *The Popular Novel in England: 1770-1800* (1932). Varma, D.P. *The Gothic Flame* (1957).

John Timpane

Kathleen Raine

BORN: 14 June 1908, Ilford.
DAUGHTER OF: George and Jessie Raine.
MARRIED: Hugh Sykes Davies; Charles Madge.

R. has won many awards for her poetry and criticism, in particular for her many books on William Blake. Daughter of two London school teachers, R. received an M.A. in natural sciences from Girton College, Cambridge University, in 1929 and was briefly married to two Cambridge professors. R., along with her second husband and William Empson, were part of a group of Cambridge poets in the 1930s, though the group was less well known than a comparable group at Oxford University which included W.H. Auden, Stephen Spender, C. Day Lewis, and Louis MacNeice. R. has been a research fellow at Girton College, a lecturer at Morley College, London, and Andrew Mellon Lecturer at the National Gallery of Art, Washington, D.C.

R.'s earliest verse was warmly praised for her precise observations of nature, which at least in part resulted from her scientific studies; all of her poetry is distinguished by her lucid, introspective awareness of the physical universe as this affects human life, by a use of diction that is sometimes archaic and intentionally unembellished, and by a persistent meditative attitude. She has self-consciously chosen to use the term "symbolic language" traditionally used by the British Romantic poets for her own work, and her neo-Platonic concern with such universal themes as birth and death, nature and eternity, distinguish her work from that of most other modern poets. In the introduction to her *Collected Poems* (1956), she said that "the ever-recurring forms of nature mirror eternal reality; the never-recurring productions of human history reflect only fallen man, and are therefore not suitable to become a symbolic vocabulary for the kind of poetry I have attempted to write."

Her emphasis on the natural world's transcendence over mere human concerns has led to many volumes of what she calls "soul-poetry," traditional verse that reflects Platonic reality and objectivity. Unlike many modern poets, she has never emphasized wit or self-conscious confessionalism; rather, her smooth, graceful lyricism and precise diction subordinates what she calls "mere human emotion" to the "Perennial Philosophy" (i.e., to an expression of ancient truths in a modern world). Among the writers with whom she shares the greatest affinities are Blake, Edmund Spenser, Thomas Taylor, and William Butler Yeats.

Her major critical work, *Blake and Tradition* (1962), is an exhaustive analysis of Blake's visionary language and cosmology in which she shows how Blake's symbolic language derives from and is directly in the line of anti-materialistic philosophy dating from Plotinus and Plato. In *Defending Ancient Springs* (1967), R. argues that genuine poets "learn" a symbolic language as a means of grasping "the beautiful order of 'eternity.'" Her three-volume autobiography—*Farewell Happy Fields* (1973), *The Land Unknown* (1975), and *The Lion's Mouth* (1978)—is important both for a detailed analysis of her literary theories and for vivid accounts of her rural youth, Cambridge in the 1930s, her marriages and other relationships, and her incessant seeking after transcendant truth, a search that led to a brief conversion to Roman Catholicism.

Both her verse and her criticism thus reflect a visionary attempt to return to the roots of modern experience and thought. Some of her best poems, such as "The Speech of Birds," are especially successful in depicting man's separation from nature. The universal, Jungian symbols and images she uses (as in her dream or meditational poems) are constant reminders of this separation. At her least effective, she relies too heavily on wistful, escapist, and self-consciously mystical experience; at her best she effectively reminds the reader of those poets she considers her masters.

WORKS: *Stone and Flower* (1943). *Living in Time* (1946). *The Pythoness and Other Poems* (1949). *William Blake* (1951; rev. 1965, 1969). *Selected Poems* (1952). *The Year One* (1952). *Coleridge* (1953). *Collected Poems* (1956). *Poetry in Relation to Traditional Wisdom* (1958). *Christmas 1960: An Acrostic* (1960). *Blake and England* (1960). *Blake and Tradition* (1962). *The Hollow Hill and Other Poems* (1965). *The Written Word* (1967). *Defending Ancient Springs* (1967). *Six Dreams and Other Poems* (1969). *Life's a Dream* (1969). *On the Mythological* (1969). *Poetic Symbols as a Vehicle of Tradition* (1970). *William Blake* (1971). *The Lost Country* (1971). *Faces of Day and Night* (1972). *Yeats, The Tarot, and the Golden Dawn* (1972, rev. 1976). *Hopkins, Nature, and Human Nature* (1972). *Faces of Day and Night* (1972). *Farewell Happy Fields* (1973). *On a Deserted Shore* (1973). *Three Poems Written in Ireland* (1973). *Death-in-Life and Life-in-Death* (1974). *David Jones: Solitary Perfectionist* (1974). *A Place, A State* (1974). *The Land Unknown* (1975). *The Inner Journey of the Poet* (1976). *Waste Land, Holy Land* (1976). *Berkeley, Blake, and the New Age* (1977). *Blake and Antiquity* (1977). *The Oval Portrait and Other Poems* (1977). *Fifteen Short Poems* (1978). *From Blake to "A Vision"* (1978). *The Lion's Mouth* (1978). *David Jones and the Actually Loved and Known* (1978). *Blake and the New Age* (1979). *Cecil Collins: Painter of Paradise* (1979). *What is Man?* (1980). *The Oracle in the Heart* (1980). *The Celtic Twilight* (1981). *Collected Poems: 1935-80* (1981). *The Human Face of God: William Blake and The Book of Job* (1982). *The Inner Journey of the Poet and Other Papers* (1982). *The Chaldean Oracles of Zoroaster* (1983). *Blake and the City* (1984). *The Matter of Britain* (1984). *The Lipstick Boys* (1984). *Yeats the Initiate: Essays on Certain Themes in the Writings of W.B. Yeats* (1985). *The Presence: Poems 1984-87* (1987).

BIBLIOGRAPHY: Grubb, F. *A Vision of Reality* (1965). Mills, R.J., Jr. *Kathleen Raine* (1967). Grigson, G. *The Contrary View* (1974). Netterville, H.E. *Kathleen Raine: The Heart in Flower* (1981). Rosemergy, J.M.C. *Kathleen Raine, Poet of Eden: Her Poetry and Criticism* (1982). *Poetry and Prophecy* (*Lindisfarne Letter* #9, 1979, special issue). Duncan, E. *Unless Soul Clap Its Hands: Portraits and Passages* (1984).

For articles in reference works, see: *CA. CLC. CP. EWLTC. MBL* and *SUP. TCW.*

Other references: *Book Forum* (1981). *English Studies* (1961). Olney, J. *NR* (18 December 1976). *Poetry* (1952). *Spring 1982: An Annual of Archetypal Psychology and Jungian Thought* (1982). *TLS* (14 August 1981). *TXSE.* (1958).

Paul Schlueter

Marie Louise de la Ramée (Ouida)

BORN: 1 January 1839, Bury St. Edmunds.
DIED: 25 January 1908, Viareggio, Italy.
DAUGHTER OF: Louis and Susan Sutton Ramé.
WROTE UNDER: Ouida.

An only child, R. was left by the long and frequent absences of her French father to be raised almost entirely by her English mother and grandmother. The family liked to believe that the mysterious M. Ramé was involved in opposition politics in his native land and that he died during the days of the Commune. R.'s fierce pride in her French heritage soon combined with her fantasizing temperament to inflate her surname to de la Ramée.

Her fantasies having long outgrown the narrow provinciality of Bury St. Edmunds, R. welcomed the move to London with her mother and grandmother in 1857. After being introduced to Harrison Ainsworth, then editor of *Bentley's Miscellany*, she began her writing career as "Ouida" (her childhood mispronunciation of "Louise"). She followed up the success of her "Dashwood's Drag; or the Derby and What Came of It," which appeared in *Bentley's* for April and May 1859, with a series of similar tales of high society and sporting life, many collected in *Cecil Castlemaine's Gage, and Other Novelettes* (1867). *Granville de Vigne*, serialized in Ainsworth's *New Monthly Magazine* and reprinted as *Held in Bondage* (1863), typified R.'s early fiction. Its formula of dashing military life, extravagant luxury, tortuous romantic intrigue, and a hero of almost impossible beauty, courage, and style reached its epitome in *Under Two Flags* (1867). The public attention (and financial rewards) such fiction attracted allowed R. to live out the fantasies otherwise denied by her lack of beauty and social status. Adorned in Worth gowns and surrounded by hothouse flowers, she held court to largely male audiences in the Langham Hotel during the seventies; in later years she frequently dressed to resemble the heroines of her latest novel. Although essentially conventional in her own behavior, she flouted Victorian codes of respectability by encouraging people to smoke throughout dinner and by remaining with the men over

brandy and cigars, collecting material for her novels from their conversation. *Tricotrin* (1869) and *Folle-Farine* (1871) added a new element to her fictional formulas: the peasant heroine who becomes tragically enmeshed in the snares of high society, a device she would exploit again in *Two Little Wooden Shoes* (1874).

In 1871 R. traveled to Europe, producing *A Dog of Flanders and Other Stories* (1872) from her observations of the Belgium peasantry and a series of novels set in Italy, among them *Pascarèl* (1873), *Signa* (1875), *In a Winter City* (1876), and *Ariadnê* (1877). She lived in the Villa Farinola outside Florence from 1871 to 1888. Of the several novels featuring fashionable members of Florentine society, the most notorious was *Friendship* (1878). Its main characters were recognized to represent R., the Marchese della Stuffa (a gentleman-in-waiting to the Italian court whom she had pursued with unrequited passion), and Mrs. Janet Duff Gordon Ross, Stuffa's avowed mistress. R.'s insistence that the novel was based on absolute truth made its idealization of her own role and its vilification of her rival all the more outrageous. Her personal disappointments helped turn her attention from the glamor to the failings of polite society. *Moths* (1880), perhaps her most successful work, shows the social fabric being eaten away by the vice and hypocrisy of society's fashionable "moths." She would increasingly lament the upper classes' failure to live up to the ideals of taste and breeding she set for them as well as their surrender to the values of the vulgar and social climbing middle classes she had all her life detested. She sentimentalized the Italian peasantry as victims abandoned by the aristocracy to the tyranny of the bourgeois bureaucracy in *A Village Commune and Other Stories* (1881). *The Massarenes* (1897) most directly condemns the *nouveaux riches* and the "smart" set that collaborated with them.

As the eighties waned, so, too, did R.'s popularity with an audience turning from three-decker romances to more realistic one-volume works. Her extravagant life-style continually outran her income, leaving unpaid bills and pending law suits behind her as she moved from place to place, her only companions after her mother's death being a faithful servant or two and the pack of spoiled dogs on which she lavished her affection. In her final years only a Civil List Pension, awarded in appreciation for her contributions to literature, stood between her and real poverty. During the nineties she turned increasingly to criticism and commentary: many of her analyses of British and European writers and her vendettas against publishers, plagiarists, cruelty to animals, female suffrage, Italian misgovernment, the Boer War, and the rising tide of vulgarity and ugliness brought on by the ascendancy of middle-class money and values were collected in *Views and Opinions* (1895) and *Critical Studies* (1900).

R. owed her considerable success in the 70s and 80s in part to her abundant imagination for sensational plotting, vivid detail, and local color, in part to the expanding market for fiction created by lending libraries and railway bookstalls. Her eccentricity, her egotism, and her flamboyance were always straining against the prosaic and sometimes sordid reality of her life; her wish-fulfilling fictions fed her own and her audience's longing for the glamour, romance, and luxury forever beyond their reach.

WORKS: *Held in Bondage* (1863). *Strathmore* (1865). *Chandos* (1866). *Cecil Castlemaine's Gage, and Other Novelettes* (1867). *Under Two Flags* (1867). *Idalia* (1867). *Tricotrin* (1869). *Puck* (1870). *Folle-Farine* (1871). *A Dog of Flanders and Other Stories* (1872). *Pascarèl* (1873). *Two Little Wooden Shoes* (1874). *Signa* (1875). *In a Winter City* (1876). *Ariadnê* (1877). *Friendship* (1878). *Moths* (1880). *Pipistrello, and Other Stories* (1880). *A Village*

Commune and Other Stories (1881). *Bimbi: Stories for Children* (1882). *In Maremma* (1882). *Wanda* (1883). *Frescoes: Dramatic Sketches* (1883). *Princess Napraxine* (1884). *Othmar* (1885). *A Rainy June* (1885). *Don Guesaldo* (1886). *A House Party* (1887). *Guilderoy* (1889). *Ruffino and Other Stories* (1890). *Syrlin* (1890). *Santa Barbara, and Other Tales* (1891). *The Tower of Taddeo* (1892). *The New Priesthood: A Protest against Vivisection* (1893). *Two Offenders and Other Tales* (1894). *The Silver Christ and A Lemon Tree* (1894). *Toxin* (1895). *Views and Opinions* (1895). *Le Selve, and Other Tales* (1896). *The Massarenes* (1897). *Dogs* (1897). *An Altruist* (1897). *La Strega, and Other Stories* (1899). *The Waters of Edera* (1900). *Critical Studies* (1900). *Street Dust, and Other Stories* (1901). *Helianthus* (1908).

BIBLIOGRAPHY: Beerbohm, M. *More* (1899). Bigland, E. *Ouida the Passionate Victorian* (1950). Elwin, M. *Victorian Wallflowers* (1934). Ffrench, Y. *Ouida: A Study in Ostentation* (1938). Lee, E. *Ouida: A Memoir* (1914). Stirling, M. *The Fine and the Wicked: The Life and Times of Ouida* (1958). Van Vechten, G. *Excavations* (1926). Yates, E. *Celebrities at Home*, 1st series (1877).

For articles in reference works, see: *BA19C*. *DLB*. *DNB*. Hays, F. *Women of the Day* (1885). Platt, V. *Men and Women of the Time* (1899).

Other references: *Bulletin of Research in the Humanities* (1978). *Publishing History* (1978). Street, G.S. *Yellow Book* (1895). *Times* (London) (27 January 1908).

Rosemary Jann

Clara Reeve

BORN: 23 January 1729, Ipswich.
DIED: 3 December 1807, Ipswich.
DAUGHTER OF: William and Hannah Reeve.

R. led a quiet and retired life; her birth and death took place in the same town where her forebears had long resided. Her mother was the daughter of the goldsmith and jeweller to George I; her father was a clergyman, as was his father before him. R. was educated by her father (rather than by her mother or a governess), and her reading included parliamentary debates, Rapin's *History of England*, Cato's *Letters*, Plutarch, and Greek and Roman history. This was a more masculine and classical education than most of her female contemporaries would have received.

Not surprisingly, one of R.'s first literary endeavors was a translation from the Latin of Barclay's romance *Argenis*, published as *The Phoenix* (1772). In 1777 she published semi-

anonymously her most famous original work, *The Champion of Virtue*, and its title page identified her only as the editor of *The Phoenix*. A second edition appeared in 1778, revised by Mrs. Bridgen, Samuel Richardson's daughter, and renamed *The Old English Baron*, with R. now clearly identified as the author. (Subsequent editions have all borne this title.)

R. also wrote five other romances. *The Two Mentors* (1783) and *The School for Widows* (1791) both have contemporary settings; *The Exiles, or Memoirs of the Count de Cronstadt* (1788), *Memoirs of Sir Roger de Clarendon* (1793), and *Destination: or, Memoirs of a Private family* (1799) are set in earlier historical periods. In addition, R. is known for her literary criticism, *The Progress of Romance* (1785) which, presented in the form of a conversation between fictional characters, comments on both ancient and modern romances. In *Plans of Education, with Remarks on the Systems of Other Writers* (1792), R. offers her educational views under the guise of an exchange of letters between friends.

But R. is most remembered for her first novel, *The Old English Baron.* A composite of three genres, this work blends the marvels of the medieval romance with the credibility of the novel of manners and the emotional appeal of sentimental fiction. R. takes Sir Horace Walpole's *Castle of Otranto* as both her model and her point of departure. In her preface to the second edition, R. calls her work the "literary offspring of the Castle of Otranto," both written to unite "the most attractive and interesting circumstances of ancient Romance and modern Novel." At the same time, R. criticizes *Otranto*'s violent supernatural machinery, claiming that the story should have been "kept within the utmost *verge* of probability." Her work seeks to use the marvelous to arrest the reader's attention and so direct it to some morally useful end.

While contemporary reviews awarded moderate praise to this endeavor, other writers found fault with her compromise between the rational and the supernatural. Walpole found the result an "insipid dull-nothing," and Mrs. Barbauld concurred that the manipulation of the supernatural should have been "more artful, or more singular." The reading public, however, was much taken with this tale of a young man's discovery of his noble origins and the restoration of his title and estates, despite the scheming efforts of envious kinsmen. From 1778-1886 thirteen editions were published; in 1787 the book was translated into French; in 1799 it was dramatized (although never presented) for the stage; and during this period, it inspired several chapbooks as well.

Underlying R.'s works, both her didactic fiction and her fiction-like expository prose, is a profound conservatism. *The Old English Baron* presents a rigidly stratified society in which the hero's obscure but noble birth triumphs inevitably. *Plans of Education,* although published in the same year as Mary Wollstonecraft's *Vindication of the Rights of Women,* advocates an education for women less progressive than R.'s own: "There is no education for daughters equal to that which they receive under the eye of a good mother, who

herself gives, or superintends it, according to her degree and station." The education that women receive should emphasize "virtue, modesty, and discretion," instill religious principles, and agree with their "gradations of rank and fortune." Like *The Old English Baron,* the *Plans of Education* reveals a society in which each class must maintain its place in order to ensure the harmonious regulation of the whole.

R.'s ideological conservatism is of interest because it tells us of the historical context in which she wrote, but she is more properly appreciated for her role in the development of the Gothic novel. R. is credited with introducing the conventions of the haunted suite, the portentous dream, and the identifying token of jewelry. In her attempt to curb the supernatural powers that Walpole unleashed in full force, R. is an important precursor of Ann Radcliffe, whose novels of terror effect the consummate compromise between the marvelous and the probable by placing apparently supernatural occurrences within the framework of individual psychology and rational explanation.

WORKS: *Original Poems on Several Occasions* (1769). *Argenis* by Barclay (translated by Reeve as *The Phoenix,* 1772). *The Champion of Virtue* (1777; reissued as *The Old English Baron,* 1778). *The Two Mentors* (1783). *The Progress of Romance* (1785). *The Exiles, or Memoirs of the Count de Cronstadt* (1788). *The School for Widows* (1791). *Plans of Education, with Remarks on the Systems of Other Writers* (1792). *Memoirs of Sir Roger de Clarendon* (1793). *Destination: or, Memoirs of a Private Family* (1799).

BIBLIOGRAPHY: Punter, D. *The Literature of Terror: A History of Gothic Fictions from 1765 to the Present Day* (1980). Scott, Sir W. Preface to vol. 5 of *Ballantyne's Novelists' Library* (1823). Summers, M. *The Gothic Quest: A History of the Gothic Novel* (1938). Tompkins, J.M.S. *The Popular Novel in England 1770-1800* (1932). Trainer, J. Introduction to *The Old English Baron* (1967). Varma, D. *The Gothic Flame* (1957).

For articles in reference works, see: *BAB1800.*

Eileen Finan

Lynne Reid Banks

BORN: 31 July 1929, London.
DAUGHTER OF: James and Muriel Marsh Reid Banks.
MARRIED: Chaim Stephenson, 1965.

R., daughter of a physician and an actress, was evacuated to Canada during World War II.

After returning to England, she acted in repertory theatres for several years, worked as a secretary, journalist, and television reporter, and was employed as a news and script writer for England's Independent Television News (1955-1962). She taught English on an Israeli kibbutz (1962-1971) and married a sculptor in 1965. Since 1971 she has been a full-time writer and by 1987 had written over twenty novels, both adult and children's.

R. is best known for *The L-Shaped Room* (1961, 1977), made into a film in 1963, and its two sequels, *The Backward Shadow* (1971) and *Two Is Lonely* (1974). The three novels describe the experiences of a single mother as she is faced in each novel with a new challenge that requires her to re-evaluate her standards and renew her life. *The L-Shaped Room* displays R.'s gift for fully developed, convincing characterization, apt descriptive details, and accurate dialogue. The plot concerns Jane Graham, twenty-seven, single, and pregnant, who lives in a crowded rooming house. When she decides to have her child, the other residents of the rooming house get emotionally involved, on one side of her situation or another, with the birth offering a kind of coherence otherwise missing from their lives.

As in all of R.'s books, the narrative is straightforwardly linear; R.'s writing is highly colloquial, without conscious stylistic flourishes. Many of R.'s books share the theme of renewal, depicting women (particularly young, single women) who must reconstruct their lives following a disaster of some sort. R.'s heroines are typically ordinary, middle-class women, not exceptionally beautiful or talented, who find in themselves the ability to face changed circumstances with courage and humor.

Several of R.'s novels draw on her Israeli experiences, notably *An End to Running* (1962) and *Children at the Gate* (1969). These novels combine R.'s theme of renewal with a resonant handling of the Israeli setting. In *An End to Running*, the move from London to an Israeli kibbutz serves as a backdrop for the main character's emotional metamorphosis. *Children at the Gate* depicts a bitter, disillusioned woman's spiritual reawakening when she becomes responsible for three children in the Arab section of a city in Israel.

In *Dark Quartet: The Story of the Brontës* (1976) and *Path to the Silent Country: Charlotte Brontë's Years of Fame* (1978), R. fictionalized the lives of Anne, Emily, and Charlotte Brontë. Although the books do not offer any new insights about the Brontës, R. uses her gift for creating strong, vividly characterized women to good effect and evokes the atmosphere of Victorian England with some skill.

R.'s juvenile and young adult novels, including *The Indian in the Cupboard* (1980) and *The Writing on the Wall* (1981), are also noteworthy; R.'s spare, unsentimental writing makes for refreshing, lively children's reading.

R.'s writing has many merits. Her characterizations of deceptively ordinary women are invariably intriguing and entirely convincing. R.'s prose, unstylishly conversational and unmannered, is a joy to read, and sharply delineated evocations of specific incidents, times, and places fill the novels. But reductive treatments of gender roles and obtrusive racism and homophobia mar many of R.'s works, and she has been rightly criticized for her naive, clichéd solutions to the moral issues she raises.

Each of R.'s novels has met with mixed responses from critics. Aside from reviews, R. has received virtually no critical or scholarly attention; she is seldom mentioned in discussions of significant contemporary British writers. Nonetheless, despite their serious flaws, her works deserve attention as literature. R. demonstrates the expressive potential of colloquial, everyday English even as she illuminates the courage with which "ordinary" women face the turning points in their lives.

WORKS: (with V. Madden) *Miss Pringle Plays Portia* (1954). *It Never Rains* (1954). *All in a Row* (1956). *The Killer Dies Twice* (1956). *The L-Shaped Room* (1961, 1977). *Already It's Tomorrow* (1962). *An End to Running* (1962; in the U.S. as *House of Hope*). *The Gift* (1965). *Children at the Gate* (1969). *The Backward Shadow* (1971). *One More River* (1973). *Two Is Lonely* (1974). *Sarah and After* (1975). *The Adventures of King Midas* (1976). *The Farthest-Away Mountain* (1976). *Dark Quartet: The Story of the Brontës* (1976). *My Darling Villain* (1977). *Path to the Silent Country: Charlotte Brontë's Years of Fame* (1978). *I, Houdini: The Autobiography of a Self-Educated Hamster* (1978). *Letters to My Israeli Sons: A Personal View of Jewish Survival for Young Readers* (1979). *The Indian in the Cupboard* (1980). *The Writing on the Wall* (1981). *Defy the Wilderness* (1981). *Torn Country: An Oral History of the Israeli War of Independence* (1982). *Maura's Angel* (1982). *The Warning Bell* (1984). *The Fairy Rebel* (1985). *Casualties* (1986). *The Return of the Indian* (1986).

BIBLIOGRAPHY:

For articles in reference works, see: *CA. CLC. CN. TCCW.*

Other references: *Books and Bookmen* (September 1968). *Commonweal* (11 November 1977). *Contemporary Review* (April 1977). *Listener* (11 April 1974). *Observer* (9 August 1970, 7 April 1974). *New Statesman* (12 November 1960, 26 July 1968, 7 August 1970, 18 April 1975, 16 October 1981). *New Yorker* (8 June 1968). *NYTBR* (9 April 1961, 12 May 1968, 8 November 1970, 16 October 1977). *Punch* (7 August 1968). *TES* (24 November 1978). *Times* (London) (13 August 1984). *TLS* (22 March 1974, 10 December 1976, 2 October 1981).

Jane Weiss

Mary Renault (pseudonym of Eileen Mary Challans)

BORN: 4 September 1905, London.
DIED: 15 December 1983, Cape Town, South
Africa.
DAUGHTER OF: Frank Challans and Clemen-
tine Baxter.

R. was the daughter of an English Puritan
descendant and a medical doctor. She received her
early education in Bristol, graduated from St.
Hugh's College, Oxford, and later completed nursing training at Radcliffe Infirmary, Oxford. She
turned to nursing to observe human life first hand
since she noted that her earlier writings were
purely derived from other people's books. Her
first novel, *The Purposes of Love,* published in the
United States as *Promise of Love,* was drawn from
R.'s hospital nursing experience. Her next three
novels, love stories with well-drawn character
portrayals, were written off duty. The last of
these, *Return to Night,* described by one critic as
"everything Hollywood could possibly want,"
earned her an MGM $150,000 prize in 1947. The
story is told from the male doctor's point of view,
leading T. Sugrue to comment that "the objectivity of which she is so proud is a negation of
feminine tenderness. . . ." This work established
R.'s reputation in America.

After her nursing service during the war, R.
moved to Natal, South Africa and began extensive
travels through Italy, France, Greece, and the Ae-
gean. She was most impressed with Greece, the
setting for her first historical novel, *The Last of
the Wine,* a taut and absorbing narrative. In 1959
The Charioteer appeared in the United States, a
book which, according to H. Saal, enters "the
shadowy world of the homosexual" whose character's "untiring delicacy becomes—like a steady diet
of English lady writers, tiresome—and the intrusion of some good old-fashioned heterosexual vulgarity welcome." Other critics, however, praised
her sensitive delineation of love among men. She
also touched upon contemporary issues by introducing conscientious objectors and the subject of
pacifism into the novel.

Her 1962 novel, *The Bull from the Sea,* is a
sequel, dealing with the death of Theseus. The
structure is episodic, held together by the presence
of the hero. At this point critics began to debate
whether R. might best be considered a writer of
historical novels or historical romances. In spite of
her appended "historical notes" and scholarly bibliographies, much of R.'s writing, especially in the
dialogues, is pure fiction. A unifying motif of a
number of the novels is the sacrificial death of a
king. R. makes the mythological personal and hu-

manized through her use of the first-person narrative.

The Persian Boy (1972) received mixed reviews. A panoramic view of the Asian and African
conquests of Alexander the Great, the tale is told
from the point of view of a castrated Persian slave
whose understanding of the historical moment is
unbelievable. R. pursued her interest in the conqueror with a biography, *The Nature of Alexander* (1975). In *The Praise Singer,* R. returned to
her earlier formula of presenting a story from the
point of view of an obscure but historically representative figure, Simonides the Poet, who laments
the passing of traditional Greek values in the sixth
century B.C. R. ended her Alexander trilogy with
Funeral Games, a complex story with a preface of
forty-five "Principal Persons." An especially vivid
character is the Amazonian Eurydice who fails as a
"masculine" warrior. The presence of such a figure in R.'s final novel is an interesting one. While
the theme of homosexuality is a frequently recurring one in R.'s works, the characters were usually
masculine. Indeed, many critics reacted rabidly to
these characters, one, H. Kenner, referring to R.
as "a male impersonator," in spite of the fact that
homosexuality is always dealt with in a delicate,
natural fashion throughout her work. Such attacks
were perhaps directed at R. personally because of
her life-long relationship with a friend she had
met during nurses' training. In spite of this kind
of criticism, R.'s novels, especially *The Last of the
Wine* and *The Mask of Apollo,* continue to enjoy
popularity as novels of historical and entertaining
value.

WORKS: *Purposes of Love* (1939; republished as
Promise of Love). *Kind Are Her Answers* (1940).
The Friendly Young Ladies (1944; republished as
The Middle Mist, 1945). *Return to Night* (1947).
North Face (1948). *The Charioteer* (1953). *The Last
of the Wine* (1956). *The King Must Die* (1958). *The
Bull from the Sea* (1962). *The Lion in the Gateway*
(1964). *The Mask of Apollo* (1966). *Fire from
Heaven* (1969). *The Persian Boy* (1972). *The Nature
of Alexander* (1975). *The Praise Singer* (1978).
Funeral Games (1981).

BIBLIOGRAPHY: Burns, L.C. *Critique* (1963–64).
Dick, B. *The Hellenism of Mary Renault* (1972).
Wolfe, P. *Mary Renault* (1969).

For articles in reference works, see: *CA. CN.
MBL SUP. Modern Commonwealth Literature. WA.*
Other references: *Atlantic* (December 1972).
Book Week (6 November 1966). *Christian Science
Monitor* (17 July 1958, 6 November 1975).
Commonweal (1 August 1958). *Economist*

(4 October 1975). *NR* (19 November 1966). *NYHTBR* (14 October 1956, 13 July 1958, 18 February 1962). *New Yorker* (19 April 1947). *NYT* (12 March 1939, 20 April 1947, 13 July 1958, 14 December 1983). *NYTBR* (18 February 1962, 30 October 1966, 14 December 1969, 31 December 1979). *Sewanee Review* (Autumn 1973). *SR* (12 July 1958, 17 February 1962, 1 October 1966, 9 December 1972). *TLS* (25 February 1939, 29 June 1956, 19 September 1958, 16 March 1962, 15 December 1966, 11 December 1970, 3 November 1972). *Virginia Quarterly Review* (summer 1973, summer 1976). *Washington Post Book World* (23 November 1969).

Carole Shaffer-Koros

Ruth Rendell

BORN: 17 February 1930, London.
DAUGHTER OF: Arthur Grasemann and Ebba Elise (Kruse) Grasemann.
MARRIED: Donald John Rendell, 1950; remarried Rendell, 1977.
WRITES UNDER: Ruth Rendell, Barbara Vine.

Soon after completing her formal education at Loughton High School, Loughton, Essex, R. became a newspaper reporter and subeditor for the *Essex Express and Independent* from 1948 to 1952. In an interview with Diana Cooper-Clark, R. recounts how she had written a number of novels before her first one was accepted. After finally submitting one—a drawing room comedy—which was rejected, she sent in a detective story that she had written just for fun. This became her first published novel, *From Doon with Death* (1964). R. reports:

> It was quite successful for a first novel, and I was caught up really because of this success with the genre. Having now established for myself a means of livelihood, I was constrained to work within the detective genre and doing so I found that I preferred to deal with the psychological, emotional aspects of human nature rather than the puzzles, forensics, whatever most seem to come within the ambience of the detective novel.

Since that first novel, R. has written twenty-nine novels and four collections of short stories under her own name as well as two novels under the pseudonym of Barbara Vine. Her novels fall into two groups: the Wexford series and the psychological thrillers sometimes referred to as the non-Wexford novels. She has won several awards for her work including the Mystery Writers of America Edgar Allan Poe Award in 1974, 1984, and 1986; the Gold Dagger from the Crime Writer's Association for *A Demon in My View* in 1977; the Arts Council of Great Britain book award for a genre novel in 1981; and an Arts Council bursary, also in 1981.

R.'s publisher refers to her as "The New First Lady of Mystery," and some critics have called her the new Agatha Christie. Although R. maintains that she writes in the classic detective tradition, she dislikes being compared to Christie or to P.D. James, another frequent comparison. In fact, R.'s development of her series character, Detective Chief Inspector Reginald Wexford, is more in the style of Ngaio Marsh's Roderick Alleyn. Inspector Wexford and his assistant Michael Burden are down-to-earth policemen with private lives and families. Both men have family problems that become subplots in many of the detective novels. In the early works there is a certain amount of antagonism between Wexford and the Chief Constable of Kingsmarkham. As a result of this conflict, Wexford sometimes goes off in the wrong direction following unproductive leads. Wexford is not an infallible Hercule Poirot. During the course of the novels, the reader becomes involved with Wexford's coming to terms with the marriage vs. career concerns of his two grown daughters and follows Burden's coping with the sudden death of his wife, problems of raising two adolescents on his own, and his own needs as a man. Both characters are drawn into sexual liaisons. Wexford's in *Shake Hands Forever* (1975) is more a suggestion than a reality. David Lehman in a review refers to Wexford as "sane, shrewd, a good family man, a reassuring father figure." In the same review, R. says, "I get letters from women who would like to marry him [Wexford] if his wife ever dies."

R.'s Wexford novels are classic detective stories only in the sense of the Sherlock Holmes and Dr. Watson type of relationship between Wexford and Burden, as well as the need to follow a series of clues in order to solve a murder. Otherwise, R., despite her dislike of the comparison, is similar to P.D. James in her development of theme or social comment. In *A Sleeping Life* (1978), Wexford's married daughter leaves her husband and brings her small sons home to live. The marital break occurs when Sylvia decides that she needs to be more than cook, housekeeper, and nursemaid, a subplot providing a brief examination of the women's liberation movement. Another timely theme appears in *Some Lie and Some Die* (1973), where the murder takes place during a rock music festival. Wexford's understanding and tolerant handling of a generation quite different from his own provides a subtle balance to Burden's stiff, heavy-handed, and more typical approach.

Family relationships, or relationships in general, could be said to be a theme in all of R.'s work. Arthur, the main character in *A Demon in My View* (1976), is an estranged child. In *Murder Being Once Done* (1972) and *The Best Man to Die* (1969), R. uses Wexford's relationship with his younger daughter Sheila as a contrast to the selfish attitudes of another family. The employee/employer relationship is the focal point of *A Judgement in Stone* (1977). R. says that family relationships are important to her. She comments in an interview with Diana Cooper-Clark: "Relationships in general interest me and I am always watching them and how people react to each other. The family relationship is very important as an impetus to murder. . . ."

Although R.'s Wexford novels are skillfully written, with ingenious plots and subtly handled themes, it is with her psychological thrillers that she creates her best work. Newgate Callendar calls R. "a master at bringing horror to ordinary situations." Similarly, David Lehman says that R. "communicates an almost palpable sense of impending disaster. Her novels are mesmerizing studies in psychopathology. The culprits, victims, and bystanders of crime are frequently ordinary people who slip (or are pushed) into madness."

All of the non-Wexford novels are disturbing. Arthur in *A Demon in My View*, for example, strangles a department store mannequin over and over in order to control his desire to kill for real. Dolly in *The Killing Doll* (1984) creates an effigy of her stepmother; after she persuades her brother Pup to disembowel it with satisfactory results, the stepmother is found dead after an accident with a syringe. *The Tree of Hands* (1984) focuses on a young single mother, Benet Archdale, whose baby dies suddenly while she is still suffering from postnatal depression. Benet's mother, also suffering from a mental illness, kidnaps a child briefly left alone on the street by his own single mother. Benet keeps the child and convinces herself it is her own. *Heartstones* (1987) is narrated by a disturbed sixteen-year-old girl who says, "In those days I had never given a thought to poisoning and I can be sure of this, that I had nothing to do with our mother's death." This is the only thing she and the reader can be sure of as Elvira describes her obsession with her father, the

sudden death of her father's fiancée, a time in a mental hospital, and the deteriorating mental state of her younger sister Despina. When asked about the main characters in her thrillers, R. replied, "I do think there are a lot of people in a sad psychotic state. . . . It seems that a number of people believe that most people that one encounters in this world were leading happy, rational, lucid and logical lives, but I don't find that." Certainly one does not find rational characters in R.'s novels.

Although not all of her novels have been universally applauded by the critics, R.'s expert characterization is widely admired. One critic sums up her accomplishment by saying, "Concern with character and its development is perhaps the greatest of her many strengths as a writer. Each personality is clearly drawn; each is believable because each is honestly motivated." In addition, R. is also acclaimed for her technique in building suspense. Newgate Callendar comments, "Nothing much seems to happen, but a bit here, a bit there, a telling thrust, and suddenly we are in a sustained mood of horror. Rendell is awfully good at this kind of psycho-suspense." If R. is not "The New First Lady of Mystery" or "The Queen of Crime"—another title she dislikes—she has certainly carved out her own place among crime writers. In the words of Callendar, "Her writing style is muted, purposely so, and that makes the extraordinary situations all the more biting. She has worked out a special field for herself, and she continues to pursue it with ingenuity."

WORKS: *From Doon with Death* (1964). *To Fear a Painted Devil* (1965). *Vanity Dies Hard* (1965; in U.S. as *In Sickness and in Health*, 1966). *A New Lease of Death* (1967; in the U.S. as *Sins of the Fathers*, 1970). *Wolf to the Slaughter* (1967). *The Secret House of Death* (1968). *The Best Man to Die* (1969). *A Guilty Thing Surprised* (1970). *No More Dying Then* (1971). *One Across, Two Down* (1971). *Murder Being Once Done* (1972). *Some Lie and Some Die* (1973). *The Face of Trespass* (1974). *Shake Hands Forever* (1975). *A Demon in My View* (1976). *The Fallen Curtain and Other Stories* (1976). *A Judgement in Stone* (1977). *A Sleeping Life* (1978). *Make Death Love Me* (1979). *Means of Evil and Other Stories* (1979). *The Lake of Darkness* (1980). *Put on by Cunning* (1981; in the U.S. as *Death Notes*). *Master of the Moor* (1982). *The Fever Tree and Other Stories* (1982). *The Speaker of Mandarin* (1983). *The Killing Doll* (1984). *The Tree of Hands* (1984). *An Unkindness of Ravens* (1984). *The New Girl-Friends* (1985). *Live Flesh* (1986). (as Barbara Vine) *A Dark-Adapted Eye* (1986). (as Barbara Vine) *A Fatal Inversion* (1987). *Heartstones* (1987). (as Barbara Vine) *Collected Short Stories* (1987). *Talking to Strange Men* (1987).

BIBLIOGRAPHY: Bakerman, J. *Armchair Detective* (1978). Bakerman, J. *The Mystery Nook* (1977). Bakerman, J. *Ten Women of Mystery*, ed. E. Bargainnier (1981). Barnard, R. *Armchair Detective* (1983). Carr, J.C. *The Craft of Crime: Conversations with Crime Writers* (1983). Cooper-Clark, D. *Armchair Detective* (1978). Miller, D. *The Mystery Nook* (1977).

For articles in reference works, see: *CA. CLC. TCC&MW.*

Alice Lorraine Painter

Jean Rhys (pseudonym of Ella Gwendolyn Rees Williams)

BORN: 24 August 1890, Roseau, Dominica, British West Indies.
DIED: 14 May 1979, Exeter.
DAUGHTER OF: William Rees Williams and Minna Lockhart Williams.
MARRIED: Jean Lenglet, 1919; Leslie Tilden-Smith, 1932; Max Hamer, 1947.

The daughter of a Welsh doctor and his Scottish-Dominican wife, R. was educated at a convent in Roseau, Dominica, until she left the island to attend the Perse School in Cambridge, England. She studied later at the Royal Academy of Dramatic Art but left school after her father's death. Over her family's objections, she remained in England and worked as chorus girl in a musical comedy company touring the provinces. Some of her later jobs included modeling, tutoring, translating, and ghostwriting a book on furniture. She began to write after her first marriage in 1919. A member of the Royal Society of Literature, she received the Arts Council of Great Britain Award for Writers in 1967 and the W.H. Smith Award for the publication of *Wide Sargasso Sea.* Queen Elizabeth II honored R. with a Commander of the British Empire designation in 1978.

R. wrote for many years before Ford Madox Ford encouraged her to publish her first book, *The Left Bank and Other Stories.* These stories, and most of her later works as well, depict her experiences as a child growing up in Dominica and as a young woman living in London and Paris. Although there is a fine line in her work between life and art, her prose transcends autobiography by capturing the impressions of an unrepresented class in literature, those cast out by society. In his preface to *The Left Bank,* Ford characterized R.'s innovation as "an almost lurid! [sic] passion for stating the case of the underdog." Ford also praised her sensitive ear for dialogue and her careful eye for form in fiction, stylistic qualities that reveal R.'s conviction that one must write from life in order to portray truth in fiction. As she stated in a 1968 interview, "I am the only truth I know."

In the four novels written in the 1920s and 1930s, R. describes the same lonely female figure at different stages of life. In her first novel *Postures* (R. preferred the American title *Quartet*), she presents the *ménage à trois* of an English couple and Marya Zelli, a young married woman whose husband has been jailed. Seen by critics to be a *roman à clef* of the difficult relationship of R., Ford, and Ford's common-law wife Stella Bowen, the novel details the cruel treatment of the unprotected single woman by "respectable" people, a theme that recurs often in R.'s works. In her second novel, *After Leaving Mr. Mackenzie,* Julia Martin, the former mistress of the title character, has been pensioned off by her lover and ekes out a lonely existence in a Paris hotel room. The typical R. heroine, like Julia, ends up alone, friendless, and broke, without the protection of a man. R.'s own favorite of the early novels, *Voyage in the Dark,* is the story of Anna Morgan, a chorus girl taken as mistress by an older man and then discarded when she asserts her independence. In R.'s fictional world, women who abhor the hypocrisy of respectability are always at odds with those, usually men, who have law and money on their side. Women of a certain type struggle desperately for money that provides them with security, but they lose or spend money freely when they have it. Although the aging Sasha Jansen in *Good Morning, Midnight* manages, through the generosity of a friend, to live well during a trip to Paris, she cannot let down her guard to trust a gigolo who eventually reveals himself to be as vulnerable as she is. Sasha's experiences with love have scarred her and left her emotionally bankrupt.

R.'s early novels, re-issued after the success of *Wide Sargasso Sea,* gained a wider audience in the 1960s and 1970s when critics pointed out that she had been a pioneer in addressing the difficulties faced by a single woman in a male-dominated society. Although in interviews R. revealed her opposition to a strictly feminist reading of her fiction, she raises the issue of the powerlessness of women in the nineteenth century in her last novel.

R. receded from the public in the 1940s and 1950s and lived in obscurity in Cornwall; she was rediscovered in 1957 when the B.B.C. produced a radio version of *Good Morning, Midnight* and placed an advertisement in the *New Statesman* seeking its author. She had worked for years on a number of short stories and a novel based on the character of Antoinette Cosway, the mad wife of Rochester in Charlotte Brontë's *Jane Eyre*. Characteristically searching for the most appropriate words for her ideas, R. rewrote the novel many times with some chapters having as many as eleven versions. R.'s careful craftsmanship forbade her from publishing what she considered to be inferior work, and she continued to revise the manuscript of *Wide Sargasso Sea* until its publication in 1966, when it was hailed by critics as one of the greatest English novels. R. said she wrote the story of the Caribbean-born Antoinette in order to revise Brontë's nineteenth-century interpretation of the West Indian woman and to vindicate the madwoman in the attic. *Wide Sargasso Sea* is a painfully compelling story of violence and madness that questions the definition of the word "primitive" in classifying English and Caribbean culture. While her earlier novels present the alienation of the foreigner in a European setting, the portrayal of Antoinette centers on the distorted view of Caribbean culture held by the English and the ambiguous status of the white West Indian who is not at home in either culture.

In the last years of her life, R. published two collections of short stories and worked on her autobiography. These collections of short stories are technically superior to her first book, which R. felt did not merit re-publication although she allowed selected stories to re-appear in *Tigers Are Better-Looking*. The later stories in this collection are more developed and polished than the earlier sketches, but R. continued to focus on the themes of an unmarried woman struggling to get along and the alienation of the West Indian living in England who is subject to British prejudices. In her last book, *Sleep It Off, Lady*, R. ordered the stories chronologically according to the stages of her life. Stories of the Caribbean are followed by those that treat of her encounter with England, and the collection ends with the story of an old woman reviled by the inhabitants of a small English village. In her unfinished autobiography, *Smile Please*, R. described the real-life versions of some of these stories and revealed how closely her work is tied to her life. *The Collected Short Stories*, a volume which includes some previously uncollected stories, was published posthumously. R. refused to have her biography written, but the stories, novels, and her own autobiographical impressions represent articulately her courageous spirit in living.

Called by A. Alvarez in 1974 "the best living English novelist," R.'s work has been compared to that of Françoise Sagan in their common ability to portray sadness. Although in her youth a voracious reader of Byron and Dickens, R. did not in later years keep up with other writers' work and thus remained outside literary movements. Her contribution to literature bridges two traditions, the British and the Caribbean, but she does not rest securely in either, as her work is at its best when it considers those who do not belong and who spit in the face of respectability.

WORKS: *The Left Bank and Other Stories* (1927). *Perversity*, by Francis Carco (1928; translated from the French by R., although attributed to F.M. Ford). *Postures* (1928; published in United States as *Quartet*, 1929). *After Leaving Mr. Mackenzie* (1931). *Barred*, by Edward de Nève (1932; translated from the French by R.; de Nève was a pseudonym of Jean Lenglet). *Voyage in the Dark* (1934). *Good Morning, Midnight* (1939). *Wide Sargasso Sea* (1966). *Tigers are Better-Looking, with a Selection from the Left Bank* (1968). *Penguin Modern Stories I* (1969). *My Day* (1975). *Sleep It Off, Lady* (1976). *Smile Please: An Unfinished Autobiography* (1979). *The Letters of Jean Rhys*, ed. by F. Wyndham and D. Athill Melly (1984). *The Collected Short Stories* (1987).

BIBLIOGRAPHY: Angier, C. *Jean Rhys* (1985). James, L., *Jean Rhys* (1978). Nebeker, H. *Jean Rhys, Woman in Passage: A Critical Study of the Novels* (1981). O'Connor, T.F. *Jean Rhys: The West Indian Novels* (1986). Plante, D., *Difficult Women: A Memoir of Three* (1983). Staley T., *Jean Rhys* (1979). Wolfe, P., *Jean Rhys* (1980).

For articles in reference works, see: *CA. CB. CLC. WA.*

Other references: *Ariel* (July 1977). *Atlantic Monthly* (January 1975, June 1980). *Book World* (5 April 1970). Borinski, A. *Poetics Today* (1985). *Chicago Review* (Spring 1981). *CL* (Spring 1979, Fall 1983). *Critical Inquiry* (Autumn 1985). *Georgia Review* (Spring 1981). *Guardian* (8 August 1968). *Ms.* (January 1976). *NR* (31 May 1980; 25 May 1987). *New Statesman* (15 February 1980). *NYRB* (18 May 1972; 11 November 1976). *NYTBR* (17 March 1974; 25 May 1980). *New Yorker* (10 December 1984). *Sewanee* (Winter 1977). Smilowitz, E. *Ariel* (1986). *Studies in the Novel* (Summer 1984). *TCL* (Winter 1982). *TLS* (21 December 1979). Wilson, L. *MFS* (1986).

Carol Colatrella

Mary Boyle Rich, Countess of Warwick

BORN: 8 November 1625, Youghal, Cork, Ireland.
DIED: 12 April 1678, Leighs.
DAUGHTER OF: Richard Boyle, first Earl of Cork, and Catherine Fenton.
MARRIED: Charles Rich, 1641.

Renowned for her piety and philanthropy, R. began her life in the home of the powerful and wealthy Boyle family. She was the seventh daughter and the thirteenth child of the prominent Royalist family. Her brother was the eminent Robert Boyle. Less than three years old when her mother died in 1628, B. and her younger sister, Margaret, were brought up by the wife of Sir Randall Clayton. In 1638 Lord Cork tried to marry his young daughter to James Hamilton, the only son of James, first viscount Clandeboye, later earl of Clanbrassil. In the most well-known gesture of her life, young B. rejected her suitor. Her father saw the twelve-year-old as an "unruly child."

R.'s early resistance to her father's authority took on a more serious tone when she permitted herself to be wooed and won by Charles Rich, the second son of Robert, third earl of Warwick. Lord Cork disapproved of the match because the young man lacked a fortune, in contrast to his other six daughters for whom he had arranged brilliant matches. He banished R. to the family's house in a little country seat near Hampton Court, where Rich secretly visited her. They were quietly married in 1641, her father bestowing on her a generous dowry of £7000 per year.

R. spent the rest of her life with her husband's family and on the Warwick estate at Leighs Priory. Within a short time, she bore two children, a girl who died in infancy and a son who lived until 1663. In 1671 R. was already recognized for her piety. Her life seemed to be devoted to meditation, works of charity, and the occasional entertainment of her husband's associates. In 1671, her husband inherited the Warwick title and lands. For twenty years he had suffered with painful and debilitating attacks from gout. He died 24 August 1673, leaving his entire estate to R. The last five years of her life R. spent as she had spent most of her years of marriage—piously and privately.

Upon her death, she was hailed by Anthony Walker, her minister, as a generous and pious woman. Her "soul father" during her life, Walker fittingly preached the sermon, "The Virtuous Woman Found," at her funeral. It was published in 1686 in London along with three works by R.: "Rules for a Holy Life, in a Letter to George, Earl of Berkeley," "Occasional Meditations upon Sundry Subjects," and "Pious Reflections upon Several

Scriptures." R.'s piety and the quality of her life are also revealed in the diary that she kept from July 1666 to November 1677. The thoughtfulness, religious fervor, and profound sense of guilt and suffering that defined R.'s adult life permeate each day's entry and each prayer. Of special interest is her need to control her emotions when she felt particularly burdened or punished. On 28 August 1671, for example, she writes:

> After dinner got an opportunity of speaking to my lord about his soul's concernments, and I did much beseech him to be more careful for his soul's good, and told him of his offending God by his passions, and the sad effects of it. Afterwards my lord in a dispute fell into a great passion with me, upon which I found in myself a sudden violent eruption of passion, which made me instantly go away, for fear it should break out, and by so doing I was kept from having my lord hear me say anything; but to myself I uttered some passionate words, which though no other heard yet, O Lord, thou didst; oh, humble me for it.

The diaries, like her meditations, were not published until after R. died. Given the title *Occasional Meditations*, the diaries passed into the hands of Thomas Woodroffe, R.'s personal chaplain. It is believed that he annotated the diaries after R.'s death. In 1847 the Religious Tract Society published selections from or an abridgement of R.'s diary by Woodroffe or a Mr. Barham entitled *Memoir, of Lady Warwick: Her Diary, From A.D. 1666 to 1672. Now First Published. To Which Are Added, Extracts from her Other Writings.* Then in 1848 Thomas Crofton Croker collected "Some Specialties" that he published for the Percy Society under the title *Autobiography of Mary Countess of Warwick.* In 1866 the British Museum acquired the diaries (Additional MSS. 27351-8).

Although R. did not write for publication, she left an important document for her twentieth-century readers, particularly those who wonder about the life of a woman of spirit and intellect in the seventeenth century. Her accounts are vivid and effective. R. writes with simplicity and purpose, leaving her readers with a better understanding of those turbulent years and of an aristocratic woman's irreconcilable problems and her efforts to find peace.

WORKS: *The Virtuous Woman Found;* (1) *Rules for a Holy Life, in a Letter to George, Earl of Berkeley,* (2) *Occasional Meditations upon Sundry Subjects,* (3) *Pious Reflections upon Several Scriptures* (1686). *Memoir of Lady Warwick: Also Her Diary, from A.D. 1666 to 1672, Now First Published; To*

Which Are Added, Extracts from Her Other Writings, (1847). *Autobiography of Mary Countess of Warwick*, ed. T.C. Croker (1848).

BIBLIOGRAPHY: Budgell, E. *Memoirs of the Lives and Characters of the Illustrious Family of the Boyles* (1737). Fell-Smith, C. *Mary Rich, Countess of Warwick (1625-1678): Her Family and Friends* (1901). Kleinbord, E. *The Myth of the Heroine: The*

Female Bildungsroman in the Twentieth Century . . . (1987). Palgrave, M. E., *Mary Rich, Countess of Warwick (1625-1678)* (1901).

For articles in reference works, see: Aubrey, J. *Brief Lives* (1898). *BAB1800*. Rogers, K.M. *Feminism in Eighteenth-Century England* (1982). Todd.

Sophia B. Blaydes

Dorothy Richardson

BORN: 17 May 1873, Abingdon, Berkshire.
DIED: 17 June 1957, Beckenham, Kent.
DAUGHTER OF: Charles and Mary Taylor Richardson.
MARRIED: Alan Odle, 1917.

R.'s home life, outwardly conventional and prosperous, at least until R. was twenty and her father went bankrupt, was inwardly disrupted by pretention and madness: her father urgently longed to transcend his merchant-grocer origins and be a gentleman; her mother, depressed for many years, ultimately killed herself in 1895 while on vacation with R. At age five, R. learned to read and spell, her only interests, at a small private school. Later she was educated, first at home by a governess whom she detested, then at Southborough House, London, an intellectually lively institution where R. particularly revelled in the study of logic. Poverty forced her to become a pupil-teacher in Germany in 1891 and a governess from 1891 to 1895, experiences treated in the first volumes of *Pilgrimage*. After her mother's death, longing for independence and freedom from what she perceived as the horrors of woman's lot in a middle-class domestic setting and having learned that teaching was far too confining for her, R. accepted a post as a dental assistant at £1 per week and began her long romance with London. At this time she met H.G. Wells, her friend for many years and lover for a few, husband of a school friend. Wells encouraged her to write as did others. She began with journalism and went on to nonfiction and finally to her masterwork, *Pilgrimage*. At the age of forty-four she married Alan Odle, a talented but highly eccentric and unworldly artist sixteen years younger than she, with whom she lived amicably but maternally until his death.

From the publication of *Pointed Roofs*, the first chapter or volume of *Pilgrimage*, R. received enthusiastic and awed critical recognition. Even Virginia Woolf, who felt competitive with her, acknowledged that R. had "invented or . . . developed and applied to her own use, a sentence which we might call the psychological sentence of the femi-

nine gender." In histories of the novel, R. is consistently coupled with Proust, Joyce, and Woolf as a major early innovator in technique and subject and an early practitioner of the stream-of-consciousness method. Many books and studies have been written about R., particularly in recent years. Remarkably, though, she remains a very nearly unread writer. Ford Madox Ford fulminated that she was "the most abominably unknown contemporary writer," and Elizabeth Bowen insists that "until Dorothy Richardson has been given her proper place, there will be a great gap in our sense of the growth of the English novel."

Pilgrimage, the work to which she devoted most of her life, is a twelve-volume (or chapter, as she preferred) work charting and capturing the flow of consciousness through Miriam Henderson as she grows and changes from adolescence to young womanhood. At the same time, without being remotely didactic, the work gives an incomparable portrayal of the consciousness of an era. Unlike Joyce, R. is faithful to the waking, coherent, rational mind, despite her record of the profusion of experience. And, unlike Proust, she records without attempting to analyze. Her constant low-key awareness of the specialness of the female mind and of complex issues confronting that mind at a period of rapid and radical emancipation is highly congenial to modern feminist readers. R.'s anti-Semitism, on the other hand, even if perceived as a reflection of the times, is unsympathetic since it is so badly presented with no irony, detachment, or distance, particularly in the last chapter-volumes.

R. herself knew that her work was highly original and groundbreaking but contemptuously dismissed the critical attempt to define her technique: "What do I think of the term 'Stream of Consciousness'. . . .? Just this: that amongst the company of useful labels devised to meet the exigencies of literary criticism it stands alone, isolated by its perfect imbecility."

WORKS: *The Quakers Past and Present* (1914). *Gleanings from the Works of George Fox* (1914). *Pointed Roofs* (1915). *Backwater* (1916).

Honeycomb (1917). *The Tunnel* (1919) *Interim* (1919). *Deadlock* (1921). *Revolving Lights* (1923). *The Trap* (1925). *Oberland* (1927). *John Austen and the Inseparables* (1930). *Dawn's Left Hand* (1931). *Clear Horizon* (1935). *Pilgrimage* (including *Dimple Hill*), 4 vols. (1938). *Pilgrimage* (including *March Moonlight*), 4 vols. (1967).

BIBLIOGRAPHY: Blake, C.R. *Dorothy Richardson* (1960). Fromm, G. *Dorothy Richardson: A Biography* (1977). Gregory H. *Dorothy Richardson: An Adventure in Self-Discovery* (1967). Hanscombe, G. *The Art of Life: Dorothy Richardson and the Development of Feminist Consciousness* (1982). Kleinbord, E. *The Myth of the Heroine: The Female Bildungsroman in the Twentieth Century: Dorothy Richardson, Simone de Beauvoir, Doris Lessing, Christa Wolf* (1987). Staley, T.F. *Dorothy Richardson* (1976).

For articles in reference works, see: *CA. Cyclopedia of World Authors* (1958). *EWLTC. TCLC.*

Other references: *Journal of Women's Studies in Literature* (Winter 1979). *International Journal of Women's Studies* (Winter 1978).

Carey Kaplan

Charlotte Eliza Lawson Cowan Riddell

BORN: 30 September 1832, Carrickfergus, County Antrim, Ireland.
DIED: 24 September 1906, Hounslow, London.
DAUGHTER OF: James Cowan and Ellen Kilshaw.
MARRIED: James H. Riddell, 1857.
WROTE UNDER: F.G. Trafford, Charlotte Riddell.

R., the youngest daughter of the High Sheriff of Carrickfergus, Ireland (1830-37), was self-educated and began her writing career at age fifteen with her first novel, *The Moors and the Fens* (1858), published unter the pseudonym F.G. Trafford, which she used until 1864.

Throughout her life R. suffered much misfortune, beginning in her youth with her father's lingering illness and eventual death, at which time she and her mother were forced to leave their old home. They lived for some while in County Down, where R. later set her novel *Berna Boyle* (1884) as well as three other Irish novels, *The Earl's Promise* (1873), *The Nun's Curse* (1888), and *Maxwell Drewitt* (1865). Shortly after their arrival in London, R.'s mother became an invalid; R. tried desperately to sell her stories, and when at last she successed in selling *The Moors and the Fens*, her mother died. Her wanderings through London at this time gave her an intimate knowledge of the city which is reflected in a number of her later novels.

After her marriage in 1857, R. frequently consulted her gifted civil-engineer husband on chemistry, engineering, and other topics she incorporated into her novels. His struggle to make a fortune in business led to severe financial difficulties, the business details of which R. incorporated into novels such as *The Race for Wealth* (1866) and *Mortomley's Estate* (1874). In spite of the struggles, R. managed to have a large family and succeeded in making a profit with her novels. Her first major success was *George Geith of Fen Court* (1865); between 1864 and 1902, and under her own name, she wrote thirty novels, most of which went into second and third editions. Most had a background of city and commercial life, which was unusual for England in the 1860s when businessmen were looked down upon. R. tried to prove that "a man did not lose caste for engaging in business"; however, by 1902 the new generation conceded the point, making R.'s novels antiquated.

R.'s works are sensation novels, mostly in three volumes, which are carefully written and reflect much insight into character. Both male and female characters value passion and assertive action. *George Geith*, republished in 1886, was dramatized into a popular play in 1883 by W. Reeve. With time, however, the dramatic force of the reappearance of the "dead" wife was lost. R. also displayed a bright sense of humor in *A Mad Tour, or A Journey Undertaken in an Insane Moment through Central Europe on Foot* (1891). Some of her work, however, is spoiled by anti-semitic diatribes.

R. cleverly retained her book copyrights. By 1867 she achieved a powerful and influential position as co-proprietor and editor of *St. James Magazine*. She also edited a magazine called *Home* and wrote fairly successful stories for the Christian Knowledge Society and Routledge's Christmas Annuals, but her short stories never were as popular as her novels.

WORKS: *Zuriel's Grandchild* (1855). *The Ruling Passion* (1857). *The Moors and the Fens* (1858). *Rich Husband* (1858). *Too Much Alone* (1860). *City and Suburb* (1861). *The World in the Church* (1863). *George Geith of Fen Court* (1864). *Maxwell Drewitt* (1865). *Phemie Keller* (1866). *The Race for Wealth* (1866). *Far Above Rubies* (1867). *The Miseries of*

Christmas (1867). *Austin Friars* (1870). *A Life's Assize* (1871). *The Earl's Promise* (1873). *Home, Sweet Home* (1873). *Mortomley's Estate* (1874). *Frank Sinclair's Wife and Other Stories* (1874). *The Uninhabited House* (1875). *Above Suspicion* (1876). *Her Mother's Darling* (1877). *The Haunted River: A Christmas Story* (1877). *Fairy Water* (1878). *The Disappearance of Mr. Jeremiah Redworth* (1878). *The Mystery of Palace Gardens* (1880). *The Curate of Lowood* (1882). *Daisies and Buttercups* (1882). *The Prince of Wales's Garden Party and Other Stories* (1882). *Idle Tales* (1882). *A Struggle for Fame* (1883). *Susan Drummond* (1884). *Weird Stories* (1884). *Berna Boyle: A Love Story of County Down* (1884). *Mitre Court* (1885). *For Dick's Sake* (1886). *Miss Gascoigne* (1887). *The Nun's Curse* (1888).

Princess Sunshine and Other Stories (1889). *The Head of the Firm* (1892). *The Rusty Sword* (1894). *A Silent Tragedy* (1893). *The Banshee's Warning and Other Tales* (1894). *Did He Deserve It?* (1897). *A Rich Man's Daughter* (1897). *Handsome Phil and Other Stories* (1899). *The Footfall of Fate* (1900). *Poor Fellow* (1902).

BIBLIOGRAPHY: Black, H.C. *Notable Women Authors of the Day* (1893). Ellis, S.M. *Wilkie Collins, Le Fana, and Others* (1931).

For articles in reference works, see: *DNB*.

Other references: *Times* (London) (26 September 1906).

Carole M. Shaffer-Koros

Anne Ridler

BORN: 30 July 1912, Rugby, Warwickshire.
DAUGHTER OF: Henry Christopher and Violet Milford Bradby.
MARRIED: Vivian Ridler, 1938.
WRITES UNDER: Anne Bradby, Anne Ridler.

In fifty years R. has amassed a substantial *oeuvre* in poetry, drama, and criticism. At Faber & Faber in the late thirties she was T.S. Eliot's secretary (see her "Personal Reminiscence" in *Poetry Review*, 73 [1983]), assisting in the editing of *Criterion*, and a reviewer of manuscripts submitted for publication. Her own first collection, *Poems* (1939), was published by Oxford, but after she left Faber's Eliot urged her to submit a manuscript, and Faber's has since published four volumes of her poetry, four of plays, and three anthologies. She has received two prizes (1954, 1955) for work published in *Poetry* (Chicago).

Most of R.'s poems are distillations from ordinary experience. She writes with tenderness of married love, both beginning and grown over the years, of the pain of separation (her husband was an RAF intelligence officer in World War II), the awe of parenthood, the tensions and joys of family life, and, especially recently, aging and death. With great subtlety she observes human relationships in poems like the early "On Being Asked Pardon" and the late "A Pirated Edition." Places, associated with homes or holidays, often inspire her meditative insights; so also, in her 1951 collection, do works of music and art. A few poems address contemporary moral decay.

Tensions between doubt and faith inform "Deus Absconditus," a rare example of R.'s dealing directly with religious experience. Oftener, her antennae for epiphanies in the quotidian will draw profound theological insight from an astonishing range of everyday events: "For a Child Expected," "Blood Transfusion Centre," and "Corneal Graft" are salient examples. Such, she believes, is the function of poetry, whose "lifeblood" is symbolism; symbols are the "hiding places of power." In "Taliessin Reborn" she explores the power of poetry to awaken realizations of the "other world"; in a sonnet for Eliot's 60th birthday ("'I Who Am Here Dissembled'"), its power to sound the depths of human emotion. Yet aware as she is of the tragic dimension of existence, for R. "still the raw material of pain / Is changed into joy" ("Exile"). "All art is not tragedy, and music / Cries of a haven, over the storm swell. / Where did they find their faith, the serene masters, / Their crazy word, that all shall yet be well?" ("Reading the News"). That echo of Eliot reveals one of R.'s formative influences, but the interrogative form is typical of her quietly honest balance of affirmation and doubt.

Contributing to the realization of epiphanies is R.'s gift for fresh description. An azalea indoors in winter is an "explosion of sunsets, archangels on a needle-point, / Red parliament of butterflies." To a loafing boy in summer, the river is "cool as lemon squash"; clouds are "the lazy yachts of the sky" ("Evenlode"). Fresh too in its effect is her deft word play, sometimes bilingual. In "Deus Absconditus" God "absconds from every promised land." The sea ("Mare Nostrum"), a "changeable beast with rumpled fur of foam," "plunges along the land, / Held by a moonstring, yet by solid rock / Hardly contained."

The heir of (among others) Wyatt, the Metaphysical poets, Hopkins, Charles Williams, and Auden, she commands great metrical variety and writes with polish, believing that "the poet will do his work better if he has his conscious mind occupied with technical problems."

At home from the start with dramatic forms

("Dialogue Between Three Characters and a Chorus" in *Poems* [1939]), R. has written several works for stage and radio performance. In 1945 she was one of three poets chosen for the New Plays by Poets series (Mercury Theatre). *The Trial of Thomas Cranmer* (1956) was commissioned for broadcast on the 400th anniversary of Cranmer's martyrdom; full performance followed in St. Mary's church, Oxford, where Cranmer had been tried. Since 1970 all her dramatic writing has been for musical accompaniment, including libretti for productions of Italian opera in translation.

Most of R.'s original plays are religious in orientation. *Cranmer* is a tough-minded modern hagiography, *Cain* a re-seeing of sacred myth, "For a Christmas Broadcast" (*The Golden Bird* [1951]) and *The Jesse Tree* festal observances. *The Missing Bridegroom*, like *Cranmer*, was originally designed for performance in a church. *The Shadow Factory*, externally social satire—critics compare it to work by Galsworthy or Orwell—centers on a factory Christmas pageant and looks for social solutions first in personal, only then in structural, change. (Even that hope is extremely cautious: "We must make the best of a bad job"—a line that anticipates Eliot's *Cocktail Party*.) *The Mask, Henry Bly*, and "The Golden Bird" develop folktales to bring out religious overtones. "Evenlode," however (in *A Matter of Life and Death* [1959]), charmingly replays but does not christianize Greek myth.

Recurrent themes in R.'s plays include the ultimate self-destructiveness of self-enthronement and self-indulgence and, related to that, the rarity of genuine relationships between selves—difficult and costly at best, and sometimes simply refused. Both these themes are central to *Cain*; the second is especially prominent in *The Shadow Factory, How Bitter the Bread*, and—emphasizing frustrated love—*A Mask*, "Evenlode," and *Who Is My Neighbour?* The last of these also explores themes of responsibility, forgiveness, and the movement of souls after death, a theme found also in "The Departure" (*Some Time After* [1971]). Alongside these themes is that of redemptive grace able to triumph even over perverse self-destructiveness. The delightful *Henry Bly* best exemplifies this vein. It is grace also that makes of Cranmer's death at the stake what his wife can credibly call "his happy ending." There and elsewhere, thanks to Williams's influence, the theme of substitution and exchange is also prominent.

R. has been much concerned with the relations of music and poetry and with the technical problems of verse drama. Her first play experimented with varied forms: blank verse for Adam and Abel, alliterative for Cain, commonsensical prose for Eve. In keeping with the rejection of naturalism which poetic drama implies, she employs such other devices as prologues and epilogues directly addressing the audience, choric characters who become part of the plot (Witness in *Cranmer*, Prompter in *The Mask*, Verger in *The Missing Bridegroom*), masque-like stylization (*The Jesse Tree*), and liturgy-like incantation.

In her editorial work at Faber's, R. was known as a sensitive critic. Most of her published criticism is scattered in reviews, prefaces and introductions, and letters to *TLS*. In edited works selection, of course, is implicit criticism; her most substantial explicit scholarship is in the editions of Thomson, Darley, Austin, and the first two of Williams.

WORKS: *Poems* (1939). *A Dream Observed and Other Poems* (1941). *The Nine Bright Shiners* (1943). *Cain* (1943). *The Shadow Factory: A Nativity Play* (1945, publ. 1946). *Henry Bly* [prod. 1947] *and Other Plays* (1950). *The Golden Bird and Other Poems* (1951). *The Trial of Thomas Cranmer* (1956). *A Matter of Life and Death* (1959; title poem alone rpt. in limited ed., 1982). *Selected Poems* (1961). *Who Is My Neighbour?* [prod. 1961] *and How Bitter the Bread* (1963). *Olive Willis and Downe House: An Adventure in Education* (1967). *The Jesse Tree: A Masque in Verse* (1970, publ. 1972). *Some Time After and Other Poems* (1972). Cavalli, F. *Rosinda* (libretto translated by Ridler, produced 1973, unpublished). *The King of the Golden River* (1975). Monteverdi, C. *Orfeo* (libretto translated by Ridler, 1975; rev. ed. 1981). Cavalli, F. *Eritrea* (libretto translated by Ridler, 1975). *Italian Prospect: Six Poems* (1976). *The Lambton Worm* (1978, publ. 1979). Monteverdi, C. *Return of Ulysses* (libretto translated by Ridler, produced 1978, unpublished). Cesti, A. *Orontea* (libretto translated by Ridler, produced 1979, unpublished). Handel, G. *Agrippina* (libretto translated by Ridler, produced 1981, unpublished). Cavalli, F. *Calisto* (libretto translated by Ridler, produced 1984, unpublished).

BIBLIOGRAPHY: Allott, K., ed. *The Penguin Book of Contemporary Verse 1918 –60* (1962). Jennings, E. *Poetry Today* (1961). Kliewer, W. *Approach* (1964). Morgan, K.E. *Christian Themes in Contemporary Poets* (1965). Nicholson, N. *Man and Literature* (1943). Spanos, W.V. *The Christian Tradition in Modern British Verse Drama* (1967). Thwaite, A. *Contemporary English Poetry* (1959). Warr, T. *Poetry Review* (1983). Weales, G. *Religion in Modern English Drama* (1961).

For articles in reference works, see: *CA. CD. CP. DLB. International Who's Who in Poetry*, ed. E. Kay (6th ed., 1982).

Other references: *Drama* (Autumn 1956). *Faber Book of Modern Verse*, 3rd ed. rev. by D. Hall (1965). *New Statesman* (24 November 1951). *Poetry* (Chicago) (March 1963). Speaight, R. *Christian Theatre* (1960). *TLS* (10 June 1939, 6 November 1959, 21 April 1972).

Charles A. Huttar

Lady Anne Thackeray Ritchie

BORN: 9 June 1837, Hyde Park, London.
DIED: 26 February 1919, "The Porch," Freshwater.
DAUGHTER OF: William Makepeace and Isabella Shawe Thackeray.
MARRIED: Richmond Thackeray Ritchie, 1877.

The elder of the two Thackeray daughters, R. grew up in a thoroughly literary environment. Shortly after the birth of R.'s sister Minny (Harriet Marrion Thackeray, b. 1840), Mrs. Thackeray began to show signs of the mental instability that would result in lifelong institutionalization. The daughters were therefore sent to live with their grandmother and step-grandfather, the Charmichael-Smyths, in Paris. Thackeray remained close with his daughters even when they were away and in 1846 he brought them back to live with him in London. Although she had no rigorous education, R. showed an early awareness of contemporary culture and politics; by the age of fourteen she was assisting Thackeray as his amanuensis.

During Thackeray's tours of America his daughters returned to their grandmother in Paris. Although there was an effort by Mrs. Charmichael-Smyth to provide the girls with the moral and religious education she thought they were lacking, the sisters remained open and broadminded. Reminiscences of R.'s travels in Europe at this time, her friendship with the Dickens children (who were also in Paris), and of her acquaintances in Paris are recounted in *Chapters from Some Memoirs* (1894). R. joined her father in London when he returned from America and continued to act as his secretary. Her London acquaintances included Tennyson, the Carlyles, the Brownings and even, in her 1850 visit, Charlotte Brontë (". . . a tiny, delicate, serious, little lady, pale with fair straight hair and steady eyes").

When she was twenty-three, R.'s first story, "Little Scholars," was published (with the consent of publisher George Smith) in her father's new and prestigious *Cornhill Magazine*. According to Thackeray, the firm of Smith and Elder was "in raptures about Anny's style," and in 1862, R.'s first novel, *The Story of Elizabeth*, was serialized in the *Cornhill*. The novel, a convoluted romance centered around an impetuous heroine, was an immediate success.

In 1863, on Christmas Eve, William Thackeray died leaving his daughters well off but very much alone (their grandmother died within a year). Among the ever-increasing circle of friends who watched over the Thackeray sisters was the Stephen family, and in 1867 Minny was married to Leslie Stephen. R. lived with her sister and

brother-in-law until 1875 when Minny died. This period was R.'s most productive in terms of fiction. In 1867 *The Village on the Cliff*, a novel in which a woman must come to grips with unrequited love, was published. It remained one of R.'s favorite works. Other works of fiction followed, including *Old Kensington* (1873), *Bluebeard's Keys and Other Stories* (1874), *Miss Angel* (1875), as well as a collection of essays (*Toilers and Spinsters and Other Essays*, 1874).

Following Minny's death, R. and Stephen, who called her "the most sympathetic and sociable of beings," shared a residence at Hyde Park. Here she met and was courted by her cousin Richmond Thackeray Ritchie, who though seventeen years her junior proposed and was accepted. Although Ritchie had an "uneventful" career in the India Office, his work was solid enough to merit a knighthood in 1907 and appointment as permanent Undersecretary for India in 1909, three years before he died. The Ritchies had two children.

R. was active until her death. She wrote introductions to the works of Mary Russell Mitford, Elizabeth Gaskell, and Maria Edgeworth. Some of her later reminiscences are recorded in *Blackstick Papers* (1908) and *From the Porch* (1913). But the most consuming project of her later years by far were the introductions she prepared for her father's collected works.

Virginia Woolf, R.'s "niece," describes her aunt in the character of Mrs. Hilbery in the novel *Night and Day* (1919). In the obituary she prepared for the *Times Literary Supplement*, Woolf praised R.'s work for its "surprisingly sharp edges." "It is Lady Ritchie," says Woolf elsewhere in the obituary, who "will be the un-acknowledged source of much that remains in men's minds about the Victorian age."

WORKS: *The Story of Elizabeth* (1863). *The Village on the Cliff* (1867). *Five Old Friends* (1868). *Old Kensington* (1873). *Bluebeard's Keys and Other Stories* (1874). *Toilers and Spinsters and Other Essays* (1874). *Miss Angel* (1875). *To Esther and Other Sketches* (1876). *Madame de Sévigné* (1881). *Miss Williamson's Divagations* (1881). *A Book of Sibyls* (1883). *Mrs. Dymond* (1885). *Little Esme's Adventure* (1887). *Records of Tennyson, Ruskin, and Robert and Elizabeth Browning* (1892). *Alfred Lord Tennyson and His Friends* (1893). *Chapters from Some Memoirs* (1894). *Lord Amherst and the British Advance Eastward to Burma* (1894). *Chapters from Some Unwritten Memoirs* (1895). *Blackstick Papers* (1908). *A Discourse on Modern Sibyls* (1913). *From the Porch* (1913). *From Friend to Friend* (1919).

BIBLIOGRAPHY: Fuller, H.R., and V. Hammersley. *Thackeray's Daughter* (1951). Gerin, W. *Anne Thackeray Ritchie* (1981). Lewis, N. *A Visit to Mrs. Wilcox* (1957). Ritchie, H. *Thackeray and His Daughter* (1924).

For articles in reference works, see: *Allibone. DNB.*

Other references: Callow, S. *Virginia Woolf Quarterly* (1979). Woolf, V. *TLS* (6 March 1919). Zucherman, J. *Virginia Woolf Quarterly* (1973).

Alan Rauch

Mary Darby Robinson ("Perdita")

BORN: 27 November 1758, College Green, Bristol.
DIED: 26 December 1800, Englefield Cottage, Surrey.
DAUGHTER OF: Captain [?] and Elizabeth Seys Darby.
MARRIED: Thomas Robinson, 1774.
WROTE UNDER: Perdita, Mrs. Robinson.

The daughter of a whaling ship captain of Irish descent, R. became an actress, a playwright, a poet, and a novelist. She was also, for a brief time, the mistress of the Prince of Wales, later George IV.

R. was introduced by the dancing-master at Mrs. Hervey's to David Garrick, who asked R. to play Cordelia to his Lear. Although R. served a period of internship at Drury Lane Theatre, her acting debut was postponed by her marriage to Thomas Robinson, a law student. After a period of high living in London, Robinson, who proved to be a scoundrel, was sent to debtors' prison, where R. and her infant daughter, Maria, spent ten months with him.

Shortly after her marriage, R. began writing poetry. With the help of her patroness, Georgianna Cavendish, the Duchess of Devonshire, R. published her first collection of poems, *Verses*, in 1775. Cavendish was R.'s only female visitor in prison, a fact that led R. to develop a bitter dislike for members of her own sex. In her *Memoirs*, R. said: "During my long seclusion from society . . . not one of my female friends even inquired what was become of me. . . . Indeed, I have almost found my own sex my most inveterate enemies; I have experienced little kindness from them; though my bosom has often ached with the pangs inflicted by their envy, slander, and malevolence."

Upon her husband's release from prison, R. resumed her acting career and enjoyed four highly successful seasons at Drury Lane, but her fourth season, 1779–1780, was her last. On 3 December 1779, R. played the part of Perdita in *The Winter's Tale*. Her performance so captivated the Prince of Wales that he fell in love with her, and R. was permanently nicknamed "Perdita." R. shortly became the Prince's mistress but was soon replaced. Humiliated by the Prince's rejection, R.

abandoned the stage and fled to France, where she was befriended by Marie Antoinette, in whose honor R. later composed "Monody to the Memory of the Late Queen of France." When R. returned to England, she formed a lasting liaison with Colonel Tarleton (Sir Banastre), an officer of the British army in America.

The early 1780s marked the high point of R.'s public fame. She regularly toured the fashionable sections of London in an "absurd chariot with a basket shaped like a coronet attached to the side," driven by her current "friend"; her husband and other hopeful admirers sat in the side-car. But R.'s life changed drastically in 1784 when she contracted an "unknown" disease, probably rheumatoid arthritis or infantile paralysis, that left her lower body weakened and partially paralyzed. R. remained an invalid for the rest of her life and devoted herself completely to her writing.

Though much of R.'s poetry now seems too affected and too sentimental, with an over-abundance of eighteenth-century apostrophizing, a number of R.'s contemporaries, most notably Samuel Taylor Coleridge, had high praise for R.'s work and found her "a woman of undoubted genius." Coleridge not only admired R.'s poems but imitated one of them himself: his "The Snow-Drop" was originally entitled "Lines written immediately after the perusal of Mrs. Robinson's Snow Drop." Coleridge was also very much impressed with R.'s "Haunted Beach," a poem vaguely reminiscent of his own "Rime of the Ancient Mariner." As a final tribute, Coleridge's "The Stranger Minstrel" was subtitled: "Written [to Mrs Robinson] a few weeks before her death." From 1788 to 1791, R. was part of the Della Cruscan movement led by Robert Merry. R., and other female followers of Merry (Hester Thrale Piozzi and Hannah Cowley) were viciously attacked, both personally and professionally, by literary critic William Gifford in his *Baviad*.

R. spent her last years in London, where she belonged to a circle of "radical" women that included Mary Wollstonecraft, Mary Hays, Charlotte Smith, and Helen Maria Williams, all of whom were accused by the Reverend Richard Polwhele, an anti-feminist, anti-"Jacobin" critic, of trying to "taint" their young female readers with the "demon democracy." It was due, in part, to the influence of the Wollstonecraft circle that R. published two feminist tracts, "Thoughts on the Condition of Women" and "A Letter to the Women of England on the Injustice of Mental Subordination, with Anecdotes by Anne Frances Randall," in 1799. R. was also a close friend of William Godwin, whose influence can be seen in R.'s most widely-read novel, *Walsingham; or, The Pupil of Nature* (1797). *Walsingham*, basically a sentimental novel, though it does touch on political and ethical questions similar to those posed in Godwin's works, was especially popular in France. At the time of her death in 1800, R. was writing her autobiography. The work was completed by R.'s daughter and published posthumously in 1801 as *Memoirs of the Late Mrs Robinson, Written by Herself*.

WORKS: *Verses* (1775). *Poems* (1777). *The Lucky Escape* (1779). *Poems* (1791). *Vaucenza; or the Dangers of Credulity* (1792). *Nobody* (1794). *The Widow* (1794). *Angelina* (1796). *The Sicilian Lover* (1796). *Sappho and Phaon* (1796). *Hubert de Sevrac* (1796). *Walsingham; or, the Pupil of Nature* (1797).

The False Friend (1799). "A Letter to the Women of England on the Injustice of Mental Subordination, with Anecdotes by Anne Frances Randall" and "Thoughts on the Condition of Women" (1799). *Effusions of Love* (R.'s correspondence with the Prince, n.d.). *Lyrical Tales* (1800). *The Mistletoe* (1800). *Memoirs of the Late Mrs. Robinson, Written by Herself* (edited by M. Robinson, 1801). *Poetical Works of the Late Mrs Mary Robinson* (edited by M. Robinson, 1806).

BIBLIOGRAPHY: Bass, R. *The Green Dragoon: The Lives of Banastre Tarleton and Mary Robinson* (1957). Hargreaves-Mawdsley, W.N. *The English Della Cruscans and Their Time, 1783-1828* (1967). Luria, G. Intro. to *Walsingham; or The Pupil of Nature* (1797, rpt. 1974). Makower, S. *Perdita [Mary Robinson]; A Romance in Biography* (1908). Robinson, M. Preface to *Poetical Works of the Late Mrs. Mary Robinson* (1806, rpt. 1828). Robinson, M. *Memoirs of the Late Mrs. Robinson, Written by Herself* (1801).

For articles in reference works, see: *DNB*. Other references: *Drama* (Summer 1950).

Kate Beaird Meyers

Margaret More Roper

BORN: 1505, Bucklersbury (London).
DIED: 1544.
DAUGHTER OF: Sir Thomas and Jane More.
MARRIED: William Roper, 1521.

Although recognized in her own day as an accomplished scholarly woman, R. has received little attention since then. Three of her father's early biographers—William Roper, R.'s husband (c. 1556), Nicholas Harpsfield (c. 1557) and Thomas Stapleton (1588)—all singled out R. from among the four siblings as the most scholarly and virtuous of his children. By eighteen years of age, R. had excelled at Greek and Latin studies of classics and patristics, and Stapleton listed her accomplishments as Latin and Greek verse, "elegant and graceful" Latin speeches, a "clever" exercise in imitation of Quintilian's oratory, meditations on *The Four Last Thynges*, and "eloquent" Latin and English letters. Well aware of both her accomplishments and the predicament of a female scholar, her father writes, "the incredulity of men would rob you of the praise you so richly deserved . . . as they would never believe when they read what you have written that you had not often availed yourself of another's help."

Only a small elite circle knew R. as a scholar; however, her gentle personality and excellent scholarship did have a profound effect on several Re-

naissance humanists in their consideration of a classical education for women. Erasmus, after living with the More family for an extended period, wrote G. Budé, specifically mentioned R.'s written work as the basis for his new belief in higher education of women. Richard Hyrde in a dedicatory letter prefacing the *Devout Treatise* speaks to a young woman, advocating a good education, referring to R. as "proof evident enough, what good learning can do, where it is surely rooted."

Few of her works are extant: several letters and the *Devout Treatise Upon the Pater Noster*. One of the letters written to her step-sister, Lady Alice Alington, and likely written in cooperation with her father when he was imprisoned in the Tower of London awaiting execution is an artfully crafted dialogue patterned after Plato's *Crito*. Like the Platonic defense for Socrates' position shortly before his execution, R.'s dialogue provides the defense for her father's conscientious stand against the desires of Henry VIII.

R.'s *A Devout Treatise*, though considered a translation of Erasmus' Latin meditations on the Lord's Prayer, is, in fact, an expression of her own voice and emphases. She goes well beyond a mere literal translation. Her sentence structure is independent of the original, with added phrases and clauses, and she creates parallel structures indicative of an expertise in composition not frequently found in the English prose of the early sixteenth century. But particularly in the sense of the work, R. has contributed her own expression, emphasizing the contrast between man's unworthiness and vileness against God's goodness and gentleness far more than the original work suggests.

WORKS: Letter found in E.F. Rogers, *The Correspondence of Sir Thomas More* (1947), No. 206. *A Devout Treatise Upon the Pater Noster* (1526?), STC 10477; reprinted in R.L. De Molen, ed., *Erasmus of Rotterdam* (1971), pp. 93-124.

BIBLIOGRAPHY: Reynolds, E.E. *Margaret Roper* (1960). Robineau, M.C. Donnelly, G.J. Marc'hadour, G. and E.E. Reynolds. *Moreana* (1966). Stapleton. T. *The Life and Illustrious Martyrdom of Sir Thomas More* (1588), trans. P.E. Hallett (1928; reprinted, ed. E.E. Reynolds, 1966). Verbrugge, R.M. *Silent but for the Word: Tudor Women as Patrons, Translators, and Writers of Religious Works*, ed. Margaret Hannay (1985).

Rita M. Verbrugge

Christina Rossetti

BORN: 5 December 1830, London.
DIED: 29 December 1894, London.
DAUGHTER OF: Gabriele and Frances Polidori Rossetti.
WROTE UNDER: Ellen Alleyn.

R., the foremost female poet of religious verse and orthodox Christianity in nineteenth-century England, has been ranked with John Donne, George Herbert, and Gerard Manley Hopkins as one of the great religious poets.

R. was the youngest of four children born into a gifted, literary Italian-English family; the Pre-Raphaelite poet and painter Dante Gabriel Rossetti was her oldest brother, and R.'s first book, *Verses* (1847), was printed by her grandfather on his own press when she was sixteen. R. suffered from chronic ill health throughout her life, a condition which allowed her to escape the odious work as a governess that her sister Maria undertook to help support the family. On two occasions R. assisted her mother in conducting a day school, in 1851–52 and again in 1853, and from 1860–70 she worked at a House of Charity for "fallen" women run by Anglican nuns.

Family and religion formed the dominant centers of R.'s life. She was strongly attached to her mother, with whom she lived most of her life. Like her mother and sister, R. was influenced by the Oxford Movement and became a fervent Anglo-Catholic. In 1850 R. broke her engagement to the Pre-Raphaelite painter James Collinson because of religious differences, and again in 1866 she refused to marry a close friend, the linguist Charles Bagot Cayley, ostensibly because he did not share her religious views. Significantly, perhaps, R. served as the model for Mary in several of her brother's paintings.

In 1850, seven of R.'s poems appeared in the Pre-Raphaelite journal *The Germ*, all under the pseudonym of Ellen Alleyn. D.G. Rossetti eagerly promoted his sister's poems, sending them in 1861 to the Victorian critic John Ruskin, who judged that no publisher would take them because they were too full of "quaintnesses and offences." But in the same year Macmillan accepted R.'s manuscript of *Goblin Market and Other Poems* (1862), the success of which established R. as a leading English poet. A moral allegory of sensual temptation, fall, and redemption through sisterly love and self-sacrifice, this work is considered by some critics to be R.'s major claim to literary immortality. The subject of sisters, who frequently embody contrasting states of mind, occurs in a number of R.'s poems from the 1850s and 1860s.

The title poem of R.'s next collection, *The Prince's Progress and Other Poems* (1866), is a richly textured Pre-Raphaelite allegorical pilgrimage of a soul and the moral crisis that results from worldly self-indulgence.

A mood of world-weariness echoes through many of R.'s poems. The themes of unhappy or unrequited love, renunciation, regret at a wasted life, and musings on death and eternal life are common. Rarely does a note of joyous exultation break through, as it does in her early and famous love poem "A Birthday" (1857). Of her more than 1,000 poems, nearly half are devotional and nearly half her poems deal with death, either as an end to suffering or as a prelude to the happier afterlife of the Christian resurrection. R. renounced the fulfillment of earthly love in devotion to an ideal of spiritual love. That R.'s love of heaven presented her with no easy consolation but with a difficult journey is apparent in her well-known poem "Uphill" (1858).

A different side of R. emerges in her poems for children, published as a collection in *Sing-Song: A Nursery Rhyme Book* (1872). These verses consist of light instructional rhymes, poems about animals, flowers, and the natural world, lullabies, Christmas carols, and a few nonsense rhymes. R.'s most famous poem for children, "Who has seen the wind?", is still widely anthologized, as is the carol "In the bleak mid-winter."

R.'s two collections of short stories, *Commonplace* (1870) and *Speaking Likenesses* (1874), were not popular and are of interest chiefly for their characterizations of people in the Rossetti circle. More successful as an autobiographical portrait is R.'s youthful novella *Maude* (1897), written when she was nineteen but published posthumously. Maude, suffering from R.'s own character flaws of overscrupulousness and a very human and impenitent pride in her poetic accomplishments, dies when she falls out of a carriage. R. presents in the story several alternative female roles and fates, though Maude's own fate is clearly the most romantic.

"Monna Innominata," a sonnet sequence on the theme of unhappy love, was originally published in *A Pageant and Other Poems* (1881). Like Elizabeth Barrett Browning before her, R. intentionally reverses the male poetic tradition in these fourteen sonnets and lets the "unnamed lady" of so many love sonnets express her own love in her own voice. Another sonnet sequence published in *A Pageant and Other Poems* is "Later Life," twenty-eight poems that are essentially religious and hortatory in tone. Here, as in other poems, R. uses the cycle of nature to represent the cycle of despair and of hope for rebirth in the human spirit.

R.'s religious prose does not reveal the intensity of spiritual struggle shown in many of her poems and is often merely dutiful in tone. But works like *Annus Domini* (1874), *Called To Be Saints* (1881), and *The Face of the Deep* (1892) reflect her intimate knowledge of the Bible and the Apocrypha, and *Time Flies: A Reading Diary* (1885) is of interest for its reflections on incidents and details from R.'s life.

Although many readers have regarded R. as one of the world's finest religious poets and some have called her the greatest English woman poet of the nineteenth century, her vision and power were limited by the restrictions of the Victorian world. The deep conflict between R.'s instinctive temperament and the demands of Victorian womanhood and authoritarian religion resulted in her withdrawal from direct experience of life into an intense and often anguished inner life. Thus much of her poetry deals, as Ralph Bellas has said, with "the self-consciousness of suffering rather than the dramatic presentation of suffering itself." Yet from within her limited angle on the world, R. produced a number of memorable poems whose acute musicality, technical mastery, and expressive tenderness assure her of literary immortality.

WORKS: *Verses* (1847). *Goblin Market and Other Poems* (1862). *The Prince's Progress and Other Poems* (1866). *Poems* (1866). *Commonplace and Other Stories* (1870). *Sing-Song: A Nursery Rhyme Book* (1872 and 1893). *Annus Domini: A Prayer for Each Day of the Year, Founded on a Text of Holy Scripture* (1874). *Speaking Likenesses, with Pictures Thereof by Arthur Hughes* (1874). *Goblin Market, The Prince's Progress, and Other Poems* (1875). *Seek and Find: A Double Series of Short Studies on the Benedicite* (1879). *A Pageant and Other Poems* (1881). *Called to be Saints: The Minor Festivals Devotionally Studied* (1881). *Letter and Spirit: Notes on the Commandments* (1883). *Time Flies: A Reading Diary* (1885). *Poems* (1890). *The Face of the Deep: A Devotional Commentary on the Apocalypse* (1892). *Verses: Reprinted from "Called to be Saints," "Time Flies," "The Face of the Deep"* (1893). *New Poems, Hitherto Unpublished or Uncollected* (1896). *Maude: A Story for Girls* (1897). *The Poetical Works of Christina Georgina Rossetti, with Memoir and Notes*, ed. W.M. Rossetti (1904). *The Complete Poems of Christina Rossetti*, (ed. R.W. Crump. (1979-). Rossetti, W.M., ed. *Rossetti Papers 1862-1870* (1903). Rossetti, W.M., ed. *The Family Letters of Christina Georgina Rossetti* (1908). Troxell, J.C., ed. *Three Rossettis. Unpublished Letters to and from Dante Gabriel, Christina, William* (1937).

BIBLIOGRAPHY: Battiscombe, G. *Christina Rossetti: A Divided Life* (1981). Bell, M. *Christina Rossetti* (1898). Bellas, R.A. *Christina Rossetti* (1977). Crump, R.W., *Christina Rossetti: A Reference Guide* (1976). Fairbanks, C. *More Women in Literature: Criticism of the Seventies* (1979). Fredeman, W.E. *The Victorian Poets: A Guide to Research* (1968). Garlitz, B. *PMLA* (1955). Hunt, H.W. *Pre-Raphaelitism and the Pre-Raphaelite Brotherhood* (1905). Kent, D.A., ed. *The Achievement of Christina Rossetti* (1987). Leder, S. and A. Abbott. *The Language of Exclusion: The Poetry of Emily Dickinson and Christina Rossetti* (1987). Mermin, D. *Victorian Poetry* (1983). Packer, L.M., *Christina Rossetti* (1963). Rosenblum, D. *Victorian Poetry* (1982). Woolf, V. *The Second Common Reader* (1932).

For articles in reference works, see: *BA19C. DLB. DNB. NCLC.*

Other references: Keane, R.N. *Nineteenth-Century Women Writers of the English-Speaking World* (1986). Knoepflmacher, U.C. *Nineteenth Century Fiction* (1986).

Jean Pearson

Susanna Rowson

BORN: 1762, Portsmouth, Hampshire.
DIED: 2 March 1824, Boston, Massachusetts.
DAUGHTER OF: William Haswell and Susanna Musgrave Haswell.
MARRIED: William Rowson, 1786.
WROTE UNDER: Susanna Haswell; Mrs. Rowson of the New Theatre, Philadelphia; Susanna Rowson.

Though born in England, R. achieved her fame in America: one of the first professional woman writers in the United States, she wrote the first American best-selling novel, *Charlotte Temple: A Tale of Truth* (1791). Enormously productive and virtually self-supporting, she worked at various times as governess, novelist, dramatist, actress, poet, lyricist, editor, essayist, textbook writer, and mistress of one of the most successful American girls' boarding schools of her time.

Many reference works that mention Rowson classify her as an American author, but her early experiences were distinctly British. Her mother died in childbirth and R.—an only child—stayed in England when her father, a lieutenant in the Royal Navy, went to America to serve as a collector of Royal Customs. Having remarried and settled in Nantasket, Massachusetts, he returned to England in 1767 to bring his daughter to his new home. Because he was an officer of the Crown, his property was confiscated during the Revolutionary War; impoverished, the family returned to England in 1778.

Already resourceful in her late teens, R. became a governess (eventually working for the Duchess of Devonshire) and began to write. She published *Victoria*, an epistolary novel interspersed with verse, in 1786. In that year she married a hardware merchant, William Rowson, and continued writing at an impressive rate. The five novels she produced in England during the first six years of her marriage include the famous *Charlotte* as well as *Rebecca: or The Fille de Chambre* (1792), a very popular novel that draws on R.'s experiences in England and America during and after the war.

Reasonably popular in England, *Charlotte Temple* was phenomenally successful in the United States and went through some 200 editions. A moralizing account of a fallen woman "for the perusal of the young and thoughtless of the fair sex," the novel was presented as being "not merely the effusion of Fancy, but . . . a reality" based on the true experience of acquaintances of the author's. Whether its appeal arose—as many critics have assumed—from its apparent veracity, from its scandalous story, from its metaphoric treatment of the themes of filial rebellion and paternal forgiveness (so close to the consciences of Americans), or from

a literary merit that twentieth-century critics have been slow to ascribe to R.'s writing, *Charlotte* in many ways resembles Richardson's *Clarissa*.

The story of the sixteen-year-old daughter of devoted British parents, it details her seduction by an army lieutenant whom her parents dislike. Corrupted by the influence of an immoral French teacher, Mlle. La Rue, Charlotte elopes to America with her lover, only to be disappointed in her expectation of marriage. Falsely convinced that Charlotte is unfaithful, her lover rejects her in favor of a respectable American girl; Charlotte dies in childbirth, in the arms of her forgiving father and to the regret of her penitent seducer. Following as it does the outlines of *Clarissa*, the novel is astonishingly short: only about 130 pages in modern editions. R.'s style is relatively terse, relying on dialogue and dramatic presentation of scenes and using comparatively little narrative intervention to underline her moral points. Nevertheless, *Charlotte* inspired many tears and led faithful readers for decades to place flowers on the grave of the heroine's supposed original in Trinity Churchyard in New York.

R.'s husband's business failed in 1792, and the couple took the unusual course of making their living on the stage, first in Britain, then in America; R. was the more successful actor of the two. In 1793 they joined the New Theater in Philadelphia, for whom R. wrote plays in addition to acting character parts (she was, for example, Audrey in *As You Like It*, the Nurse in *Romeo and Juliet*, Mrs. Quickly in *Merry Wives of Windsor*, Lady Sneerwell in *School for Scandal*). Her first play, *Slaves in Algiers* (1794)—a comedy promoting liberation of black slaves and equal rights for women—created a controversy in the American press; her subsequent plays were also topical. The Rowsons moved to the Federal Street Theater in Boston, where R.'s creditable acting career ended with her retirement in 1797.

R. opened a girls' school in 1797 that was to absorb much of her energy for 25 years. During this period she nevertheless wrote the lyrics for around 40 popular songs (with titles as diverse as "America, Commerce, and Freedom," "Will You Rise, my Beloved," "Orphan Nosegay Girl," and "He Is not Worth the Trouble"). She also published textbooks, poems, religious writings, and several more novels, including a very popular sequel to *Charlotte*, known variously as *Charlotte's Daughter: The Three Orphans; Lucy Temple*; and *Love and Romance: Charlotte and Lucy Temple* (1828). From 1802–1805 R. also edited and contributed to the *Boston Weekly Magazine*. As a writer and as an educator R. can fairly be called one of the more productive and influential women of her age, in England or America.

WORKS: Victoria (1786). The Inquisitor; or, Invisible Rambler (1788). Poems on Various Subjects (1788). A Trip to Parnassus; or, The Judgement of Apollo on Dramatic Authors and Performers (1788). The Test of Honour (1789). Charlotte; A Tale of Truth (1791; as Charlotte Temple, 1794). Mentoria; or, The Young Lady's Friend (1791). Rebecca; or, the Fille de Chambre (1792; as The Fille de Chambre, 1793). Slaves in Algiers; or, A Struggle for Freedom (1794). The Female Patriot; or, Nature's Rights (from the play The Bondman by P. Massinger, 1795). The Standard of Liberty: A Poetical Address (1795). Trials of the Human Heart (1795). The Volunteers: A Musical Entertainment (1795). The American Tar (1796). Americans in England; or Lessons for Daughters (1797; as The Columbian Daughters; or, Americans in England, 1800). Reuben and Rachel; or Tales of Old Times (1798). Miscellaneous Poems (1804). An Abridgement of Universal Geography, Together with Sketches of History (1805). A Spelling Dictionary (1807). Hearts of Oak (1810). A Present for Young Ladies, Containing Poems, Dialogues, Addresses (1811). Sarah; or, The Exemplary Wife (1813, originally serialized in Boston Weekly Magazine as "Sincerity"). Youth's First Step in Geography (1818). Biblical Dialogues Between a Father and His Family (1822). Exercises in History, Chronology, and Biography, in Question and Answer (1822). Charlotte's Daughter; or, The Three Orphans (1828; as Lucy Temple: One of the Three Orphans, 1842; as Love and Romance: Charlotte and Lucy Temple, 1854).

BIBLIOGRAPHY: Adams, O.F. Christian Register, 17 March 1913. Bowne, E.S. A Girl's Life Eighty Years Ago (1887). Brandt, E.B. Susanna Haswell Rowson: America's First Best Selling Novelist (1975). Cobbett, W.A. Kick for a Bite (1795). Dall, C.W.H. The Romance of the Association; or, One Last Glimpse of Charlotte Temple and Eliza Wharton (1875). Knapp, S.L. Charlotte's Daughter (1828). Nason, E. A Memoir of Mrs. Susanna Rowson (1870). Parker, P.L. Studies in Short Fiction 13 (1976). Sargent, M.E. Medford Historical Register April 7, 1904. Swanwick, John. A Rub from Snub (answer to Cobbett, 1795). Vail, R.W.G. Proceedings of the American Antiquarian Society 42 (1932). Weil, D. In Defense of Women: Susanna Rowson (1762-1824) (1976).

For articles in reference works, see: Allibone. American Authors 1600-1900, A Biographical Dictionary of American Literature (1938). Cambridge History of American Literature (1917). Great Writers of the English Language: Novelists and Prose Writers (1979). Quinn, A.H. A History of the American Drama from the Beginning to the Civil War (1923). Seilhamer, G.O. History of the American Theatre: New Foundations (1888-1891).

Other references: Brown, H.R. The Sentimental Novel in America, 1789-1860 (1940). Cowie, A. The Rise of the American Novel (1948). Dauber, K. Criticism (1980). Dunlap, W. History of the American Theatre and Anecdotes of the Principal Actors (1963). Durang, C. Philadelphia Dispatch (15 October 1854). Fiedler, L. Love and Death in the American Novel (1969). Loshe, L.D. The Early American Novel (1907). Martin, W. Women's Studies (1974). Rourke, C. The Roots of American Culture (1942). Pattee, F.L. The First Century of American Literature, 1770-1870 (1935). Petter, H. The Early American Novel (1971).

Robyn R. Warhol

Vita (Victoria Mary) Sackville-West

BORN: 8 March 1892, Knole, Sevenoaks, Kent.
DIED: 2 June 1962, Sissinghurst, Cranbrook, Kent.
DAUGHTER OF: Lionel Edward and Victoria Sackville-West.
MARRIED: Harold Nicolson, 1913.

"I will get myself into English Literature." As S.-W. herself might appreciate, her prominence therein relies upon a notoriously unconventional life as well as upon prodigious—if essentially non-"modernist"—literary works. Early in life she imagined her name in histories of literature: "Sackville-West, V., poet and novelist." Excluding juvenilia (eight novels and five plays between 1906 and 1910), S.-W. produced twelve novels, five biographies, two long poems, much other poetry, and assorted travel, garden/country, and critical writing.

Anomalous among her works is the short experimental novel Seducers in Ecuador (1924), which Virginia Woolf praised for its "fantasticallity." It remains a delightful and disconcerting text, probably intended as a compliment to Woolf's style. In S.-W.'s English Georgics, The Land (which poem won the 1927 Hawthornden Prize), and superb novel, The Edwardians (1930)—both enormously popular—her literary conservatism triumphs: she sings the cycle of her country's year in rurally erudite verse, and recreates in brilliant, often satiric prose the overblown vie-en-rose of aristocrats during her childhood. S.-W.'s best writing treats the extremes of gentry life, fields, and salons alike. Her other work is less achieved artistically, betraying a lack of "central transparency" (in Woolf's phase) and giving "the effect of having been done from the outside" (in S.-W.'s)—perhaps the aesthetic price for ingrained snobbery and indirect narcissism.

That her *oeuvre* should continue to intrigue readers is hardly surprising, however, if only for what it reveals about S.-W. and her relations with both *beau monde* and Bloomsbury. "I am an incredible egoist, that's the long and the short of it"; fascinated by her own personality (or personalities) and sexuality (or sexualities), S.-W. reflected creatively upon her forty-nine-year marriage to diplomat-politician Harold Nicolson and her lifelong series of love affairs with women, including Woolf. The "Author's Note" to *The Edwardians* advises, "No character in this book is wholly fictitious"; early S.-W. novels such as *Challenge* (written in 1919) suggest psychobiographical readings of the author's fictionalized self-representation as either male or tellingly split between two characters of different gender.

S.-W.'s mixed Spanish-English heritage also divided her. Born and raised on a colossal estate held by centuries of Sackvilles (one of whom coauthored *Gorboduc* and wrote the Induction to *A Mirror for Magistrates*), S.-W. considered it her life's tragedy as an only daughter to watch her beloved Knole pass to an uncle and a cousin. The literary compensation for this loss was extraordinary: Woolf's *Orlando* (1928), which has been called the longest love-letter in history. Given an early copy (and later the manuscript, beautifully bound), S.-W. read it on publication day, overwhelmed and flattered to be consoled for her father's death and identified with Knole for posterity.

S.-W. was more ambivalent about her maternal past. She adored and feared her mother, by turns an impulsively generous "Bonne Maman" and cruelly imperious Lady Sackville (who called Woolf "that wicked Virgin Wolf"). At midlife S.-W. wrote *Pepita* (1937), a biography of her grandmother, the Spanish dancer whose supposed Gypsy blood S.-W. associated with the wanderlust and passionate nature she was finally beginning to control in herself. Henceforth, "heart of darkness" themes—even latent sado-masochism, notably in *The Dark Island* (1934)—gave way to themes of leavetaking (adumbrated in 1931 by the splendid novel *All Passion Spent*), solitude (the title of a 1938 poem), and saints' lives (those of Joan and the two Teresas). S.-W. would explore "the power of being alone," specifically, in her poetics of place, "the power of being alone with earth and skies."

A prolific correspondent, S.-W. wrote daily to Nicolson for most of their lives. Her letters to Woolf alone fill a volume. She kept a rich diary, and a long autobiographical memoir about her traumatic affair with Violet (Keppel) Trefusis was published posthumously in *Portrait of a Marriage*, together with explanatory chapters by son Nigel amounting to a panegyric of his parents' marriage.

That relationship has been mythologized by all concerned, its ability to withstand both partners' series of homosexual lovers elevated to a principle of "caring without interference." S.-W. and Nicolson spoke about marriage on the B.B.C. and on tour in the United States of America; in transcripts (and elsewhere) one notes the slippage in S.-W. between feminist and aristocratic/egoistic self-assertion, between rights for all women, as women, and independence for exceptional selves who transcend gender through personal privilege. S.-W. became conservative with age and her experience of World War II (like Woolf, she lived under the bombing path across southern England). She was surprised that one of her young female relatives wanted a career, for example. Yet in her last novel, *No Signposts in the Sea* (1961), S.-W. speaks through a narrator lower class in background to challenge the wealth-based assumptions of a woman who prescribes against "squalour" in marriage by recommending separate bedrooms. *Signposts* also returns to the cruise-of-life metaphor of *Seducers*.

Not generally considered a professional writer, S.-W. in fact wrote most deliberately for money: she supported herself, and often Nicolson; sent her sons to Balliol (Oxford); paid for Long Barn and Sissinghurst Castle; and financed the creation of the celebrated Sissinghurst Garden. (She was nonetheless loyal to the Hogarth Press, ignoring mid-career other publishers' lucrative offers.) Weekly *Observer* gardening columns brought S.-W. more contemporary recognition than her poetry and novels put together, and she was awarded the Royal Horticultural Society's Gold Medal (which, in her words, "generally goes to old men over eighty, who have devoted the whole of their lives to horticulture").

Some find paradoxical S.-W.'s devotion to "country notes," truth-in-platitude, and formal gardens after a nonconformist youth (the "splendid arson of my reckless days" [*The Garden*]). Hugh Walpole characterizes her as a romantic hedonist. Given British social history, however, S.-W.'s defiant independence can be seen in a tradition of licensed aristocratic eccentricity. She took pains to avoid overt "scandal," keeping her lesbian affairs semi-secret and withdrawing *Challenge*—with its portraits of Trefusis as Eve, S.-W. as Julian—from publication. Her "open" marriage had an Edwardian aspect: members of the upper-class, including S.-W.'s parents, had always tolerated discreet adultery. Her literary works reflect a personal progress towards restraint, service, and reclusivity; the result is balanced prose of great beauty brought up to match her consistently decorous poetry. S.-W.'s career conjoins distinguished writing with an idiosyncratic life of struggle against sexual norms.

WORKS: *Chatterton* (1909). *Constantinople: Eight Poems* (1915). *Poems of East and West* (1917). *Heritage* (1919). *The Dragon in Shallow Waters* (1921). *Orchard and Vineyard* (1921). *The Heir* (1922). *Knole and the Sackvilles* (1922). *Challenge* (1923 U.S.A., 1974 U.K.). *Grey Wethers* (1923). *The Diary of Lady Anne Clifford* (ed., 1923). *Seducers in Ecuador* (1924). *The Land* (1926). *Passenger to Teheran* (1926). *Aphra Behn* (1927). *Twelve Days* (1928). *King's Daughter* (1929). *The Edwardians* (1930). *Sissinghurst* (1931). *Invitation to Cast Out Care* (1931). *Rilke* (translations, 1931). *All Passion Spent* (1931). *The Death of Noble Godavary and Gottfried Kunstler* (1932). *Thirty Clocks Strike the Hour* (1932). *Family History* (1932). *Collected Poems* vol. I. [no vol. II] (1933). *The Dark Island* (1934). *Saint Joan of Arc* (1936). *Pepita* (1937). *Some Flowers* (1937). *Solitude* (1938). *Country Notes* (1939). *Country Notes in Wartime* (1940). *English Country Houses* (1941). *Grand Canyon* (1942). *The Eagle and the Dove* (1943). *The Woman's Land Army* (1944). *Another World Than This* (with H. Nicolson, 1945). *The Garden* (1946). *Nursery Rhymes* (1947). *Devil at Westease* (1947). *In Your Garden* (1951). *In Your Garden Again* (1953). *The Easter Party* (1953). *More for Your Garden* (1955). *Even More for Your Garden* (1958). *A Joy of Gardening* (1958). *Daughter of France* (1959). *No Signposts in the Sea* (1961). *Faces: Profiles of Dogs* (1961). *V. Sackville-West's Garden*

Book, ed. P. Nicolson (1968). *Dearest Andrew: Letters from V. S.-W. to Andrew Rieber, 1951-62*, ed. N. MacKnight (1979). *The Letters of Victoria Sackville-West to Virginia Woolf*, ed. L. DeSalvo and M.A. Leaska (1984).

BIBLIOGRAPHY: Brown, J. *Vita's Other World: A Gardening Biography of V. S.-W.* (1985). Glendinning, V. *Vita: The Life of V. S.-W.* (1983). Nicolson, N. *Portrait of a Marriage* (1973) [incl. 1920 S.-W. MS]; ed., *The Diaries and Letters of Sir Harold Nicolson* (1966-1968). Stevens, Michael. *V. S.-W.: A Critical Biography* (1973) [incl. definitive List of Published Works, Index of Reviews, some unpub. S.-W. poems]. Watson, S.R. *V. S.-W.* (1972).

Other references: Ames, C. *Studies in Literary Imagination.* Cohen, E.H. *ELN* (December 1981). DeSalvo, L.A. *Virginia Woolf Miscellany* (1979). DeSalvo, L.A. *Signs* (Winter 1982). DeSalvo, L.A. *Women Writers and the City*, S.M. Squier, ed. (1984). Edgar, S. *Quadrant* (March 1984). Fone, B.R.S. *The Gay Academic*, ed. L. Crew (1978). Gindin, J. *SN* (1980). Haight, G.S. *Yale Review.* Heilbrun, C. *Ms.* (1974). Klaitch, D. *Woman + Woman: Attitudes towards Lesbianism* (1974). Miles, R. *The Fiction of Sex* (1974). Pomeroy, E.W. *TCL* (Fall 1982). Ruas, C. *Book Forum* (1979). Rule, J. *Lesbian Images* (1975). Schaefer, J. O. *Virginia Woolf Quarterly* (1976). Stimpson, C.R. *Nation*, 30 November 1974. Tomalin, C. *New Statesman*, 23 September 1977. Trautman, J. *The Jessamy Brides: The Friendship of Virginia Woolf and V. S.-W.* (1973).

Catherine Milsum

Dorothy L. Sayers

BORN: 13 June 1893, Oxford.
DIED: 17 December 1957, Witham, Essex.
DAUGHTER OF: Henry Sayers and Helen Leigh.
MARRIED: Oswald Arthur Fleming, 1926.

Sayers is best known for her Lord Peter Wimsey detective novels, witty mysteries that portray English society between the wars. The only child of The Rev. Henry Sayers and Helen Leigh Sayers, she was born 13 June 1893 in Oxford. After an isolated childhood, largely in the Fens, she went up to Somerville College in 1912; many of her contemporaries at Oxford died in the trenches of World War I. In 1915 she won first class honors in modern languages but no degree because of her sex; in 1920 she was awarded both the B.A. and the M.A. with the first group of women to be granted degrees from the University of Oxford. Blackwell's published her first work, two volumes of poetry, *Op. I* (1916) and *Catholic*

Songs (1918); she worked at Blackwell's as an editor, taught at a boys' school in southern France, and then in 1922 joined Benson's Advertising Agency in London as a copywriter. In 1924 she managed to hide her pregnancy from her family and close friends; after her marriage to Captain Oswald Arthur (Mac) Fleming in 1926, she legally adopted her own son without revealing his parentage.

Whose Body?, a rather conventional detective puzzle, introduced Lord Peter Wimsey in 1923. Wimsey's flippant delight in the corpse was gradually replaced by an attitude of moral responsibility in the later books. In *Clouds of Witness* (1926) he saved his brother, the Duke of Denver, from a murder conviction by brilliant sleuthing that included a daring cross-Atlantic flight just prior to Lindbergh's. *Unnatural Death* (*The Dawson Pedigree* in the US, 1927) introduced Wimsey's resourceful ally, Miss Climpson. *Unpleasantness at the Bellona Club* (1928) concerns the effects of World War I on veterans, a theme which reoccurred in the series as Lord Peter's own war service and subsequent breakdown were gradually revealed. (Sayers's own husband suffered psychologically from his war experience; she supported him for most of their marriage, which lasted until his death in 1950.) By 1928, Lord Peter had made her famous. In that year she published *Lord Peter Views the Body*, a collection of twelve short stories, and edited *Great Short Stories of Detection, Mystery and Horror* (*The Omnibus of Crime* in the United States), supplying a significant essay analyzing the detective tradition.

When her father died in 1928, leaving her a small legacy, Sayers bought a home in Witham, Essex, a pleasant train journey from her London publishers. With Anthony Berkeley, G.K. Chesterton, and other mystery writers, she founded the Detection Club, complete with rituals such as swearing a sacred oath on a skull named "Eric." She also completed *Tristan in Brittany*, a translation of the twelfth-century *Romance of Tristan* (1929). The following year she collaborated on *The Documents in the Case* with "Robert Eustace" (pseud., probably for Eustace Fraser Rawlins; see Trevor Hall's book on S.) and published *Strong Poison*, the novel which introduced Harriet Vane as a mystery writer suspected of poisoning her lover. In 1931 Sayers published *The Five Red Herrings*, edited another volume of detective stories, and collaborated on *The Floating Admiral*, a detective parody written by members of the Detection Club, including G.K. Chesterton and Agatha Christie. *Have His Carcase* (1932) was a less successful Wimsey/Vane story; leaving out the "love interest" Sayers wrote two masterful mysteries, *Murder Must Advertise* (1933), set in an advertising agency rather like Benson's, and *The Nine Tailors* (1934), set in the Fen country where she had spent her childhood.

After giving a speech at the Somerville College Gaudy (reunion) in 1934, she published *Gaudy Night* (1935), a Wimsey/Vane novel set in a women's college at Oxford. Her best novel, it focuses on the theme of intellectual integrity and explores the conflict between head and heart. By telling the story from Harriet Vane's perspective, Sayers is able to present Wimsey as a fully-rounded character, beset with fears about the European situation and about his own aging; the book ends with Wimsey's famous proposal in Latin on Magdalen bridge. In the following year, Sayers collaborated with her friend Muriel St. Clare Byrne to produce *Busman's Honeymoon* on stage (1936), portraying the start of Harriet's life as Lady Peter Wimsey; the subsequent novel version was appropriately sub-titled "A Love Story with Detective Interruptions." That was the end of the published Wimsey saga, except for some short stories and a few wartime essays and advertisements. Later her friend Wilfred Scott-Giles published *The Wimsey Family*, telling the history of the Wimseys since 1066, a saga that Sayers and her friends had made up as a game. An unfinished Wimsey/Vane novel, *Thrones, Dominations*, begins just after the honeymoon; the manuscript is in the Marion E. Wade Collection at Wheaton College (Illinois).

In 1937 Sayers "turned from her life of crime," as one schoolboy put it, and devoted her writing to theological drama. *The Zeal of Thy House* followed her friend T.S. Eliot's *Murder in the Cathedral* at the Canterbury Festival (1937). Other dramas include *The Devil to Pay*, a reworking of the Faust legend for the Canterbury Festival (1939); *The Just Vengeance* (Litchfield Festival, 1946); *The Man Born to Be King*, a series of 12 radio dramas on the life of Christ, broadcast in monthly segments in 1941–1942 and published 1943; and *The Emperor Constantine* (Colchester Festival Play, 1951). She also wrote several radio plays for children; *Love All*, a farce staged in London (1940); several volumes of short stories featuring Lord Peter or her other detective, Montague Egg; a book on aesthetics, *The Mind of the Maker* (1941); a series of witty essays on theology and social issues, including feminism; a translation of *The Song of Roland* (1957); and an unfinished biography of Wilkie Collins (1977).

Her final years were primarily devoted to Dante. One night on her way to the air raid shelter, she grabbed a copy of *The Divine Comedy* in the original Italian and was entranced. She subsequently translated *Hell* (1949) and *Purgatory* (1955) for Penguin classics in a lively *terza rima*, documented with erudite and witty notes. At the invitation of her friend Barbara Reynolds, Sayers gave a series of lectures at Cambridge, later published as *Introductory Papers on Dante* (1954) and *Further Papers on Dante* (1957). While at work on the *Paradiso*, she died suddenly in her home on 17 December 1957; the translation was completed by her friend Barbara Reynolds.

Although she wrote in many genres, Sayers's work is unified by a concern with craftsmanship, with the value of worthwhile work done well. Appropriately, her memorial tablet in Somerville College is inscribed, "Praise Him that He hath made man in His own image, a maker and craftsman like Himself."

WORKS: *Op. 1* (1915). *Catholic Tales and Christian Songs* (1918). *Whose Body?* (1923). *Clouds of Witnesses* (1926). *Unnatural Death* (1927). *The Unpleasantness at the Bellona Club* (1928). *Lord Peter Views the Body* (1928). (tr.) *Tristan in Brittany* (1929). (with Robert Eustace) *The Documents in the Case* (1930). *Strong Poison* (1930). *The Five Red Herrings* (1931). (with others) *The Floating Admi-*

ral (1931). *Have His Carcase* (1932). *Murder Must Advertise* (1933). *Hangman's Holiday* (1933). *The Nine Tailors* (1934). *Gaudy Night* (1935). (as edited by M. Wimsey) *Papers Relating to the Family of Wimsey* (1936). *Busman's Honeymoon* (1937). *The Zeal of Thy House* (1937). *The Greatest Drama Ever Staged* (1938). *Double Death* (1939). *Strong Meat* (1939). *The Devil to Pay* (1939). *In the Teeth of the Evidence* (1939). *He That Should Come* (1939). *Begin Here* (1940). *Creed or Chaos?* (1940). *The Mysterious English* (1941). *The Mind of the Maker* (1941). *Why Work?* (1942). *The Other Six Deadly Sins* (1943). *The Man Born To Be King* (1943). *Even the Parrot* (1944). *The Just Vengeance* (1946). *Unpopular Opinions* (1946). *Making Sense of the Universe* (1946). *Creed or Chaos and Other Essays* (1947). *Four Sacred Plays* (1948). *The Lost Tools of Learning* (1948). (tr.) *The Comedy of Dante Alighieri the Florentine: Cantica I: Hell* (1949). *The Emperor Constantine* (1951). *The Days of Christ's Coming* (1953). *Introductory Papers on Dante* (1954). *The Comedy of Dante Alighieri the Florentine: Cantica II: Purgatory* (1955). *Further Papers on Dante* (1957). (tr.) *The Song of Roland* (1957). *The Comedy of Dante Alighieri the Florentine: Cantica III: Paradise* (1962). *The Poetry of Search and the Poetry of Statement* (1963). *Christian Letters to a Post-Christian World* (1969). *Lord Peter: A Collection of All the Lord Peter Wimsey Stories* (1972). *Talboys* (1972). *A Matter of Eternity* (1973). *Striding Folly* (1973). *Wilkie Collins: A Critical and Biographical Study* (1977). *The Wimsey Family* (1977).

BIBLIOGRAPHY: Brabazon, J. *Dorothy L. Sayers: A Biography* (1981). Dale, A. *Maker and Craftsman: The Story of Dorothy L. Sayers* (1978). Durkin, M.B. *Dorothy L. Sayers* (1980). Hall, T. *Dorothy L. Sayers: Nine Literary Studies* (1980). Hannay, M. ed. *As Her Whimsey Took Her: Critical Essays on the Work of Dorothy L. Sayers* (1979). Harmon, R. and M.A. Burger. *An Annotated Guide to the Works of Dorothy L. Sayers* (1977). Hitchman, J. *Such a Strange Lady* (1975). Hone, R.E. *Dorothy L. Sayers: A Literary Biography* (1979). Tischler, N. *Dorothy L. Sayers: A Pilgrim Soul* (1980).

For articles in reference works, see: *CA. DLB. DNB. Modern British Dramatists. MBL* and *SUP. TCA* and *SUP. TCCr&MW. TCLC. TCW.*

Other references: Bander, E. *Armchair Detective* (1977). Brody, M. *Style* (1985). Campbell, S.E. *MFS* (1983). Elliott, J.R., Jr., and D.L. Sayers. *Seven* (1981). Gregory E.R. *Christianity and Literature* (1975). Hannay, M. *Mythlore* (1979). Heilbrun, C. *AS* (Autumn 1982). Hone, R. *Seven* (1985). Klein, K.G. *10 Women of Mystery*, ed. E. Bargainnier (1981). Mascall, E.L. *Seven* (1982). Marshall, D.G. *Seven* (1983). Merry, B. *Art in Crime Writing: Essays on Detective Fiction*, ed. B. Benstock (1983). Morris, V.B. *MFS* (1983). Ohanian, S. *JPC* (1980). Ralph, G. *Seven* (1986). Reynolds, B. *Seven* (1980). Sayers, D.L., and K. Nott. *Seven* (1982). Scott, W.M. *Armchair Detective* (1979). Scowcroft, P.L. *Seven* (1984). Stock, A. *American Benedictine Review* (1985). Taylor, D.J. *Seven* (1982). Webster, R. *Seven* (1981).

Margaret Hannay

Janet Schaw

BORN: c. 1730, Lauriston, Scotland.
DIED: c. 1801.
DAUGHTER OF: Gideon Schaw and Anne Rutherfurd.

In October, 1774, S. set sail from Scotland with her brother Alexander, two servants, and the children of an American relation. Before the letters documenting that journey begin, we know little of S.'s life: she was born near Edinburgh and can be traced there again in 1778, two years after her return to Scotland; she had five siblings and was a distant relative of Sir Walter Scott; she was a well-educated gentlewoman who could quote poets and natural philosophers easily and claim to know "all the descriptions that have been published of America."

The letters collected into S.'s *Journal of a Lady of Quality* compensate for our limited knowledge. Beautifully written, they offer lively descriptions of the four stages of S.'s journey: an arduous

trip to the West Indies, the stay there, her subsequent residence in the Cape Fear colony, and her escape to Lisbon on the eve of the American Revolution. The first of these sections is tightly structured and novelistic, with its vivid images of storms and shipboard conditions, the pathetic tale of an emigrant family on board, and occasional passages in the present tense reminiscent of Richardson's "writing to the moment."

S. not only romanticized but enjoyed her voyage, and her letters become less dramatic once she reaches land. While Alexander Schaw prepared to assume the post of customs agent, S. relished the social life, the food, and the sights of Antigua and St. Kitts. Her racism and Presbyterian prejudices surface here, as her loyalist feelings do in America, but she nonetheless comes across as a witty and appreciative observer.

To return the young people and to see their brother Robert, the Schaws soon sailed for North Carolina, where S.'s predictions were borne out:

"people talk treason by the hour." Though able to mock her out-of-place British finery, S. could not forgive the rebellion brewing around her. She scoffs at American manners and agriculture, wishes for a few good British troops, and refuses to believe that landowners might support the revolutionaries. As tensions increased, Alexander returned abruptly to England, Robert and other loyalists were ordered to take arms for the Americans, news came south of the battle of "Bunkershill," and S. managed to make her escape with the young Rutherfurds. A pet bear came with them: "We were afraid he would join his brethren of the [rebel] congress, and as he has more apparent sagacity than any of them, he would be no small addition to their councils."

A pleasant trip to Lisbon returned S. to Scottish friends, and her final, least interesting, letters mingle description of Portugal with tales of balls and sightseeing tours. The letters from North Carolina are heavily relied on by revolutionary historians, and, prejudices apart, have proven highly accurate. The comic touches and colorful images of S.'s account make exciting reading. The manuscript is written to a Scots friend and was copied for private circulation, though not published during the author's lifetime.

WORKS: *Journal of a Lady of Quality . . . 1774 to 1776*, ed .E.W. Andrews in collaboration with C.M. Andrews. (1921, rev. ed., 1939). Letters (unpublished).

BIBLIOGRAPHY: Andrews, above. Hubbell, J. *The South in American Literature, 1607-1900* (1926).

For articles in reference works, see: Joint Committee of the North Carolina Teachers' Assn. and the N.C. Library Assn. *North Carolina Authors* (1952). Todd.

Marie E. McAllister

Olive Emilie Albertina Schreiner

BORN: 24 March 1855, Wittebergen, Basutoland (now Lesotho).
DIED: 11 December 1920, Wynberg, South Africa.
DAUGHTER OF: Gottlob and Rebecca Lyndall Schreiner.
MARRIED: Samuel "Cron" Cronwright, 1894.
WROTE UNDER: Mrs. S.C., Ralph Iron, O. Schreiner, Olive Schreiner, Olive Cronwright-Schreiner.

Known primarily for her feminist novel, *The Story of an African Farm* (1883), and for *Woman and Labour* (1911), the "Bible" of the early twentieth-century British women's suffrage movement, S. was probably the first white woman to write novels about the African colonial situation.

The ninth of her missionary parents' twelve children and named for three dead brothers, S. was often estranged from her religious family. She claimed that she became a mystical "free thinker" after the death of her younger sister and that this early impulse was further shaped by reading the works of Darwin, Herbert Spencer, John Stuart Mill, Shelley, Goethe, and Emerson, from whom she probably derived her pseudonym, Ralph Iron. S. had a little bit of education at home but never attended public school. When her family's home broke up because of poverty, S. was shuttled between older siblings until she left to become a governess. It was at this time that S. began to write seriously. In seven years of loneliness and isolation, she wrote the bulk of three novels—*Undine* (1929), *The Story of an African Farm*, and *From Man to Man* (1926)—the manuscripts of which she took with her when she left South Africa for England in 1881.

The Story of an African Farm has two major sections, childhood and adulthood, which are separated by a long, meditative passage about the birth and growth of a mystical belief shared by the novel's central characters, Lyndall and Waldo. Lyndall's understanding of Victorian culture's construction of masculinity and femininity is both passionate and profound. However, like the heroine Rebekah in *From Man to Man*, Lyndall seems unable to act on her feminist impulses, choosing instead a brief, masochistic liaison which ends in her shame and death. While S.'s best male characters often incorporate Victorian women's tasks into their own sense of work—they nurture the women they love and think of their creations as offspring—her ugliest, most vicious characters are usually women and many of her women characters, such as Em in *African Farm* and Bertie in *From Man to Man*, seem emotionally as well as economically tied to a system that treats them as commodities for men's aggrandizement and exchange.

Soon after it was published, *The Story of an African Farm* pushed S. to the center of London's literary and intellectual circles. She was an early member of the Men and Women's Club, an elite group which met weekly to discuss sexual reform and "sex morality," and she became close friends with group members Edward Carpenter, Havelock Ellis, and Karl Pearson. S.'s intense and dependent relationship with Ellis in particular is traced in *The Letters of Olive Schreiner* (1924). S. chose to live among prostitutes while in London, but she seems to have had few close women friends, with the notable exceptions of Eleanor Marx and the suffragist Constance Lytton.

S. suffered from severe attacks of asthma, which may have been psychological in origin and which often prevented her from writing, talking, or traveling. Although she struggled to finish *From Man to Man* and an introduction to Mary Wollstonecraft's *A Vindication of the Rights of Woman* (1792), the only works S. completed in England were short, allegorical pieces, collected in *Dreams* (1890), *Dream Life and Real Life* (1893), and the posthumous *Stories, Dreams and Allegories* (1923). Although her husband radically edited the original letters and destroyed what he did not publish, the *Letters* and *The Life of Olive Schreiner* (1924) remain important sources in understanding her work.

When she returned to South Africa in 1889, her writing became primarily political. *Trooper Peter Halket of Mashonaland* (1897) is a bitter parody of Cecil Rhodes in which a Dutch soldier sacrifices his own life to free a black man who has been convicted and sentenced to death because of British racism. Here, as in *An English South African's View of the Situation* (1899) and *Thoughts on South Africa* (1923), S.'s criticism of anti-native colonial policies was radical for her time. She claimed that blacks act as a laboring class on which the South African economy depends, that race is a metaphysical as well as a physical reality, and that women understand what unites the races better than men because of their common experience of mothering. On the other hand, S. tended to idealize her own culture, particularly the traditional beliefs and roles of Boer women, in her attempt to imagine an interracial South Africa. In her later years S. remained in contact with the militant suffragists and with Gandhi's nonviolent *satyagraha* movement. She broke with the Cape Colony Women's Enfranchisement League when it failed to endorse native men's and women's, along with white women's, suffrage.

Although it is no longer well-known, S.'s *Woman and Labour* was read by thousands of women in pre-War England. *Woman and Labour* brought together S.'s allegorical and political impulses; she considered it her most significant work. Stories are told of suffragettes' reading *Woman and Labour* to one another in jail and of women's "conversion" to feminism from reading

S.'s work. The work addresses women's emotional complicity in their economic oppression, making scathing attacks on what S. calls "parasitic" upper-class women and prostitutes. As the title suggests, *Woman and Labour* tends to elide women's labor in the work force with their reproductive labor, implying that the knowledge gained from mothering should both enable and transform other kinds of professional work. S. argues that men and women will benefit equally from women's improved economic status and that equality will lead to improved sexual relations between women and men. Many of S.'s arguments continue to inform contemporary feminist theory.

When S. married Samuel Cronwright in 1894, he changed his name to Cronwright-Schreiner, but for most purposes she did not. Because of her asthma and her political involvement, she spent long periods of time away from her husband. A month after her fortieth birthday, S. gave birth to a child that lived less than a day. This dead daughter remained a haunting presence in S.'s life and later writing, and she chose to be buried next to the child overlooking the *kopje* that inspired *The Story of an African Farm*. S. has been an influence on numerous white African writers, including Doris Lessing and Nadine Gordimer.

WORKS: *The Story of an African Farm* (1883). *Dreams* (1890). *Dream Life and Real Life* (1893, rpt. 1977). *The Political Situation* (with S.C. Cronwright-Schreiner, 1896). *Trooper Peter Halket of Mashonaland* (1897, rpt. 1974). *An English South African's View of the Situation. Words in Season* (1899). *A Letter on the Jew* (1906). *Closer Union* (1909). *Olive Schreiner's Thoughts About Women* (1909). *Woman and Labour* (1911, rpt. 1979). *Thoughts on South Africa* (1923). *Stories, Dreams and Allegories* (1923). *The Letters of Olive Schreiner* (edited by S.C. Cronwright-Schreiner, 1924). *From Man to Man; or, Perhaps Only . . .* (1926, rpt. 1982). *Undine* (1929). *A Track to the Water's Edge: The Olive Schreiner Reader*, ed. H. Thurman (1973), *Olive Schreiner Reader*, ed. C. Barash (1987). *Letters, Vol. I: 1871-1899*, ed. R. Rive (1987).

BIBLIOGRAPHY: Beeton, R. *Olive Schreiner, a Short Guide to her Writings* (1974). Berkman, J. *Olive Schreiner: Feminism on the Frontier* (1979). Cronwright-Schreiner, S.C. *The Life of Olive Schreiner* (1924). Davis, R. *Olive Schreiner 1920-1971: A Bibliography* (1972). First, R., and A. Scott, *Olive Schreiner, A Biography* (1980). Friedmann, M. *Olive Schreiner: A Study in Latent Meanings* (1955). Jacobsen, D. Intro. to *Story of an African Farm* (1971). Lessing, D. Intro. to *Story of an African Farm* (1976). Meintjes, J. *Olive Schreiner: Portrait of a South African Woman* (1965). Showalter, E. *A Literature of Their Own* (1977). Smith, M. and Maclennan, D. *Olive Schreiner and After* (1983). Verster, E. *Olive Emilie Albertina Schreiner* (1946). Winkler, B. *Victorian Daughters* (1980).

For articles in reference works, see: *Biography and Genealogy Master Index. CA. Longman. Modern Commonwealth Literature. TCA* and *SUP. TCLC.*

Other references: *Contemporary Review* (April 1984). *Contrast* (1979). *Dalhousie Review* (1979). *Doris Lessing Newsletter* (1976). *English in Africa* (1979, 1985). *History Workshop Journal* (1986). *Journal of Commonwealth Literature* (August 1977). *Journal of South African Studies* (1968). *MS.* (1977). *Quarterly Bulletin of the South African Library* (1977). *Research in African Literatures* (1972). *Standpunte* (1980). *SN* (1972). *Texas Quarterly* (1974, 1978). *TLS* (15 August 1980). *Women's Studies International Forum* (1986). *ZAA* (1984).

Carol Barash

Sarah Scott

BORN: 21 September 1723, Yorkshire.
DIED: 3 November 1795, Catton (near Norwich).
DAUGHTER OF: Matthew and Elizabeth Drake Robinson.
MARRIED: George Lewis Scott, 1751.
WROTE UNDER: Henry Augustus Raymond, "a Gentleman on His Travels," Sarah Scott.

Known best today for her feminist utopian novel *A Description of Millenium Hall*, S. also wrote four other novels, one translation, two historical works, and one biography. The most significant period in her life seems to have been the ten years during which she and her close friend Lady Barbara Montagu lived together. During these years, the two women established and ran a school for twenty-four working-class girls and boys, and S. wrote and published five of her works.

S. was the sixth child and second daughter of a family of twelve children, nine of whom survived to adulthood. The family was wealthy, socially prominent, and well educated. When S. was four, her mother inherited the family estate of Mount Morris in Kent, and the family moved there. Although the girls were not sent to school, Sarah and her elder sister Elizabeth read avidly, enjoying Shakespeare, Marivaux, Bacon, Sidney, and Virgil. When she was eighteen, she suffered an attack of smallpox, which left her face disfigured. Later, of a character in *Millenium Hall*, she wrote that the "features and complexion have been so injured by smallpox, that one can but just guess that they were uncommonly fine."

Sometime in her late teens or early twenties, S. began to take an active interest in politics, education, and economics, interests she continued all her life. Also during this period, she wrote and published *The History of Cornelia*, a melodramatic novel in imitation of Marivaux's *Marianne*. As was every one of her books, *Cornelia* was published anonymously.

At the age of twenty-two, S.'s sister Elizabeth married Edward Montagu, nearly thirty years her senior, and was later much admired for her Blue-stocking parties and stylish, energetic letters; interestingly, letters from S. to Elizabeth often employ figurative language and humor, devices generally absent from her published works. In 1751, the twenty-eight-year-old S. married George Lewis Scott, with whom she had been friends for six years. But in April of 1752, S. was "taken from her house and husband by her father and brothers." S. retained half her dowry and received one hundred pounds a year from her husband, from whom she remained separated. S. had met Lady Barbara (Bab) Montagu in 1748 and the two had become such dear friends that Lady Barbara had accompanied S. and George on their wedding trip and had lived with them for a time. After separating from George, S. went to Bath, partly for her ill health and partly to be near Lady Barbara's home.

In 1754, S. and Lady Barbara began living together, in a "most charmingly situated farm house" in the village of Batheaston. That same year, S. published *A Journey Through Every Stage of Life*, thought possibly to be a translation, and *Agreeable Ugliness, or the Triumph of the Graces*, a translation of the French novel *La Laideur Aimable* by Pierre-Antoine de La Place. Of the latter, S. wrote to Elizabeth that even her publisher Dodsley could "have no guess at the translator." S. next wrote *The History of Gustavus Erickson, King of Sweden* (1761) and *The History of Mecklenburgh* (1762).

Millenium Hall, written in about one month's time, was also published in 1762. A didactic novel, it tells the story of five women who pool their resources and live together in the West of England, where they establish a charity school to educate both girls and boys: girls study reading, writing, arithmetic, and needlework and are taught household management. Millenium Hall also shelters the elderly and the deformed, offers work training for needy gentlewomen, and provides paid employment for disabled persons. S. next wrote *The History of Sir George Ellison* (1766), in which the narrator of *Millenium Hall* founds a school for boys. Her last two works, published in 1772, were an epistolary novel, *A*

Test of Filial Duty, and a biography, *The Life of Theodore Agrippa D'Aubigné*.

Financial insecurity was part of the life that S. and Lady Barbara shared, as were recurring illnesses in each of the women. In 1765, Lady Barbara died. After her friend's death, S. seems to have wandered, living short periods in Hitcham, London, Tunbridge Wells, Canterbury, and Sandleford. She finally settled in 1787 in the village of Catton, near Norwich, where she continued to lead an active social and intellectual life. She died in 1795.

WORKS: *History of Cornelia* (1750). *Agreeable Ugliness, or the Triumph of the Graces* (1754). *A Journey Through Every Stage of Life* (1754). *The History of Gustavus Erickson, King of Sweden* (as by Henry Augustus Raymond, Esq.) (1761). *The History of Mecklenburgh* (1762). *A Description of Millenium Hall. By a Gentleman on His Travels* (1752). *The History of Sir George Ellison* (1766; in abridged form as *The Man of Real Sensibility, or the History*

of Sir George Ellison*, 1797). *A Test of Filial Duty* (1772). *The Life of Theodore Agrippa D'Aubigne* (1772). [letters] Blunt, R., *Mrs. Montagu, Queen of the Blues* (1923). [letters] Climenson, E., *Elizabeth Montagu, Queen of the Blues* (1906). [letters] Doran, J., *Lady of the Last Century* (1873). [unpublished letters: Elizabeth Montagu Collection, Huntington Library]

BIBLIOGRAPHY: Beach, J.W. *JEGP* (1933). Crittenden, W.M. "Introduction" to *Millenium Hall* (1955). Crittenden, W.M. *The Life and Writings of Mrs. Sarah Scott, Novelist (1723–1795)* (1932). Faderman, L. *Surpassing the Love of Men* (1980). Grow, L.M. *Coronto* (1972). Reynolds, M. *The Learned Lady in England, 1650–1760* (1920). Schnorrenberg, B.B. *Women's Studies* (1982).

For articles in reference works, see: Todd. Other references: *TLS* (12 August 1955). *MLN* (1955). *Personalist* (1957).

Carolyn Woodward

Florida Scott-Maxwell

BORN: 24 September 1883, Orange Park, Fla.
DIED: 6 March 1979, Exeter.
DAUGHTER OF: Anna Elizabeth Pier and Robert MacChesney.
MARRIED: Scott John Scott-Maxwell, 1910.
WROTE UNDER: Florida Pier, Florida Scott-Maxwell.

S. was raised by her nominal father's family, the Piers, in Pittsburgh, Pa. Primarily self-educated, she attended Pittsburgh Public Schools from the ages of ten to thirteen, then art school for a time. At fifteen, she trained at a drama school in New York City, and at sixteen began a career as a player of minor roles in the Edwin Mayo Theatre Company. In 1903, she began writing short stories, published in *Harper's* and *Century* magazines, and became the first woman staff member of the *New York Evening Sun* with a weekly column.

S. married in 1910 and lived at Ballieston house, near Glasgow, for the next sixteen years, bearing four children and working for women's suffrage. During this time she published only a feminist play, *The Flash Point*. Divorced in 1929, she settled in London and again supported herself by writing: women's columns, short stories, fiction reviews, and a play, *Many Women*, produced at The Arts Theatre in 1932. She also collaborated on an autobiographical account of a White Russian nurse's experiences during World War I, *The Kinsmen Knew How to Die*.

By 1935, she was involved in Jungian analysis

and afterward trained as an analyst herself. In 1939, she published *Toward Relationship*, which examines the difficulties women must face in filling expected feminine roles and also existing as individuals. *Toward Relationship* anticipated such major feminist themes as woman as "other" and the crucial value of the "feminine" in a world too much concerned with achievement and progress, at great cost to human relationships. She did not, however, picture men taking on part of the "feminine" task of relating and thus feared that the necessity for women to develop as individuals would deprive society of valued skills.

S. spent World War II immersed in her analytic practice in Edinburgh; it was only at the war's end that she began to write again—an experimental play, *I Said to Myself*, produced at the Mercury Theatre in 1946. Critics agreed that the idea—different actors playing the parts of one personality—was exciting, but questioned the play's ultimate stageability. After World War II, S. settled in Exeter, practicing as an analyst, writing, and giving broadcasts for the BBC on such subjects as aging, loneliness, and sex roles. Her second Jungian book, *Women and Sometimes Men*, further explored the ideas of *Toward Relationship*. Though the book was praised for its wisdom and perceptiveness, critics felt that it included too many generalizations and questioned the value of the masculine-feminine categorizations as related to character traits.

After a writing career plagued by all the silences common to women writers, due to marriage, immersion in nurturing roles, discouragement at criticism, and feelings of lack of authority due to lack of education, S at eighty-five published her oft-quoted journal, *The Measure of My Days*, which has been praised as an honest, impassioned, and sentient view of the aging process.

WORKS: *The Flash Point* (1914). *The Kinsmen Knew How to Die* (with Sophie Batcharsky) (1931). *Many Women* (1932). *Toward Relationship* (1939).

I Said to Myself (1946). *Women and Sometimes Men* (1957). *The Measure of My Days* (1968).

For articles in reference works, see: *Who's Who Among American Women*, 1958.

Other references: *New Statesman* (8 October 1932). *NYHTBR* (6 October 1957). *NYT* (22 September 1957). *SR* (26 October 1957). *Spectator* (11 July 1947). *Washington Post* (4 March 1972).

Katherine A. Allison

Anna Seward

BORN: 12 December 1742, Eyam, Derbyshire.
DIED: 25 March 1809, Lichfield, Staffordshire.
DAUGHTER OF: Thomas and Elizabeth Hunter Seward.
WROTE UNDER: Benvolio, Anna Seward.

A minor celebrity who believed herself a major poet but never understood her own limitations, S. was the mistress of a kind of ornate verse that revealed the excesses of eighteenth-century sentimentalism. Hailed as the "Swan of Lichfield," this spirited, opinionated Bluestocking was the very model of a provincial English *précieuse*. That is, she had little judgment and limited talent but an unending capacity to feel and an intense desire to express those feelings. Her work was vivid enough to attract a coterie of admirers and a degree of fame. All that she lacked was genius.

A precocious child, she showed an early aptitude for poetry. When she was in her teens, her fledgling verse was encouraged and influenced by Erasmus Darwin, then practicing in Lichfield. Not yet famous as a naturalist, Darwin was a poet of the ornamental school, but S. would eventually surpass him in floridity.

As a young woman, she seemed as interested in her familial and social obligations as in her budding verse but although she had suitors she never married. Instead, she busied herself with the romances of her sister Sarah (who died just before she was to wed) and her adopted sister Honora (who married a man S. detested) and poured out her grief in her poetry. When she fell in love with the married vicar choral of the Lichfield Cathedral, the hopelessness of the situation could only have sharpened her grief.

Grief, mistaken perhaps for sensitivity, made the elegy an appropriate form for S. to try. In 1780 she published an *Elegy on Captain Cook*, a well-received tribute to the slain explorer that may have been written in part by Darwin. The next year S. offered a *Monody on the Death of Major André*, an elegy to the young Englishman hanged in the Benedict Arnold affair. Since S. had known

and truly liked André, she managed to make her poem's sentiments sincere. The *Monody* made her famous as it reached Britons everywhere and provided an outlet for their frustration over the American Revolution. It was no wonder Darwin called S. the inventor of the epic elegy.

For the rest of her life, S. poured out numerous epitaphs and short verses for her friends. In 1784 she published something longer: *Louisa*, a poetical novel in epistolary form. The story of lovers whose virtues first separate then reunite them, *Louisa* exemplifies the sensibility that was seminal to its author. She called herself an enthusiast, and since *Louisa* finally went through five editions, others must have shared her enthusiasm.

Always confident of her ability, S. published a series of Horatian imitations (*Odes*) in the *Gentleman's Magazine* of 1786 that were immediately controversial since their author, who knew no classical languages, had merely paraphrased prose translations of Horace. That same year and the next S. wrote and published a set of letters signed "Benvolio," in which she criticized the character of the late Samuel Johnson. A native of Lichfield, Johnson had been taught by S.'s grandfather and was remotely related to her mother. Nonetheless, S. did not care for him, and after James Boswell queried her for Johnsonian anecdotes, he rejected the material (mostly negative) that she offered. In the 1790s the two became embroiled in a further and quite public series of disputes over Johnson which showed neither S. nor Boswell to much advantage.

What S. lacked in discretion she made up for in emotionalism. Deeply affected by the Welsh retreat of two eccentric Irish spinsters, she wrote *Llangollen Vale* (1796), a stylized description of what she perceived as an exotic refuge for two sublime hermits. Her one hundred *Sonnets* (1799), Miltonic in style, are structurally sound but somewhat cloying in tone. Though her circle admired them, even they had trouble admiring her prose *Memoirs of the Life of Dr. Darwin* (1804). Inaccurate at points and inarticulate throughout, the *Memoirs* did nothing for its author's reputation.

As the nineteenth century began, S. was losing touch with the times. Though she championed the early work of Robert Southey, Walter Scott, and Samuel Taylor Coleridge, what she liked in these first-generation Romantics were their most conventional aspects. She had no grasp of Romanticism as a movement that had broken with her school of ornate sentimentality. After her death Scott performed the gentlemanly task of editing her poetical works, and Constable published her later letters (both acting on requests from S. before she died); but there was no great call for either poems or letters.

WORKS: *Elegy on Captain Cook* (1780). *Monody on the Death of Major André* (1781). *Poem to the Memory of Lady Miller* (1782). *Louisa: A Poetical Novel in Four Epistles* (1784). *Variety: A Collection of Essays* (1788). *Llangollen Vale, with Other Poems* (1796). *Original Sonnets on Various Subjects and Odes Paraphrased from Horace* (1799). *Memoirs of the Life of Dr. Darwin* (1804). *Poetical Works*, ed. W. Scott (1810, rpt. 1974). *Letters of Anna Seward Written Between the Years 1784 and 1807* (1811, rpt. 1975).

BIBLIOGRAPHY: Ashmun, M. *The Singing Swan* (1931). Lucas, E.V. *A Swan and Her Friends* (1907). Monk, S.H. *Wordsworth and Coleridge: Studies in Honor of George McLean Harper* (1939). Woolley, J.D. *MP*, 70 (1972-73).

For articles in reference works, see: *DNB. Europa.*

Mary Ferguson Pharr

Anna Sewell

BORN: 30 March 1820, Yarmouth.
DIED: 25 April 1878, Old Catton, near Norwich.
DAUGHTER OF: Isaac and Mary Wright Sewell.

The obscure author of only one book, the classic horse story *Black Beauty*, S. experienced a typical Victorian upbringing in a strict Quaker family. Except for two sojourns at spas in Germany and several extended visits with relatives, she remained at home, never married, and was nursed during her slow decline and last illness by her devoted and domineering mother, the writer Mary Sewell. From earliest childhood, S. displayed a lively interest in horses and fierce outrage at any mistreatment of animals. At age fourteen she fell while running and seriously injured her ankles, which brought to an end her brief attendance at a local day-school; inappropriate medical treatment caused her to become a semi-invalid for the rest of her life, and S. came to depend on horses for companionship as well as freedom of movement.

During S.'s year-long medical treatment in Boppard, Germany, in 1856, her mother began to write ballads for children and working people. S. helped her prepare several collections of verse and prose for publication, and two of Mary Sewell's ballads (including "Mother's Last Words") became unprecedented bestsellers. In the town of Wick, near Bath, where the family lived from 1858-64, S. and her mother founded a library, a Temperance Society, a Hall for Mothers' Meetings, and an Evening Institute for Working Men, where mother and daughter taught reading, writing, and natural history three times a week. S.

liked to improvise little humorous stories in verse which were occasionally written down and kept by friends, but one serious poem by her survives from this period.

At age fifty-one, S.'s health deteriorated to the point that she gave up her own horse. To repay her debt of gratitude to the many horses she had ridden throughout her adult life, she began to write a book that would show "what gentle and devoted friends horses can be." At first she dictated the book to her mother, but gradually she felt strong enough to write the story of *Black Beauty* down in pencil, which her mother then transcribed. Between Nov. 1871 and Aug. 1877, only three entries in S.'s journal note her progress on her famous story. The book was published in 1877 and began to be widely and enthusiastically reviewed in January 1978. When S. died three months later, 91,000 copies had been sold and she was happily aware that her work was a success.

S. designated *Black Beauty* as "the autobiography of a horse" with herself as the translator "from the original equine," and wrote the book not for children but for working men who dealt daily with horses. Her aim was not to create a lasting work of literature but "to induce kindness, sympathy, and an understanding treatment of horses." The title character is a thoroughbred stallion who falls to lowest social station of hired carthorse through no fault of his own but through human mistreatment. The book contains much technical information on the care and training of horses; so accurate were the descriptions of horse care that one expert horseman declared the book to be written by a veterinarian.

Black Beauty is an "improving" book of the

kind that was popular in the Victorian era. That *Black Beauty*'s fame has survived while the vast majority of such books are now forgotten testifies to the originality and sincerity of S.'s story-telling. She wished particularly to portray the difficult situation of London cabmen, but although she sought practical alleviation for the working class, S. subscribed to an inherently feudal, hierarchical ordering of the world, with the benevolent master at the head of both family and society. She considered it the duty of the lower classes to serve the upper, just as horses were created to serve men. It was the responsibility of the masters, in turn, to look after those beneath them and to prevent cruelty, wrong-doing, and suffering wherever they occurred. S. disliked the changes brought about by the Industrial Revolution and technology, and the city represents corruption and evil for Black Beauty. Of social evils, alcoholism is the worst,

often the cause of cruelty to horses. The ethic of humaneness, however, is clearly heralded throughout the novel in the words and behavior of compassionate men, women, and children.

WORKS: *Black Beauty: His Grooms and Companions. The Autobiography of a Horse* (1877).

BIBLIOGRAPHY: Baker, M.J. *Anna Sewell and Black Beauty* (1956). Bayly, Mrs. M. *The Life and Letters of Mrs. Sewell* (1889). Chitty, S. *The Woman Who Wrote Black Beauty* (1971). Montgomery, E.R. *Story Behind Great Books* (1946). Starrett, V. "'Black Beauty' and Its Author," in *Buried Caesars* (1923, reprinted 1968).

For articles in reference works, see: *Something About the Author.* Ed. A. Commire (1981).

Jean Pearson

Margery Sharp

BORN: 1905, Malta.
DAUGHTER OF: J.H. Sharp.
MARRIED: Major Geoffrey L. Castle, 1938.

S., who was born to British parents and raised on the island of Malta, began to write novels after her graduation, with honors, from London University with a degree in French. For over forty years she has had a successful and prolific double career—as a writer of adult fiction and also as the creator of Miss Bianca and the prisoners Aid Association of Mice. Miss Bianca, an engaging white mouse, beloved of Bernard the Brave, has ventured in subsequent volumes to the Salt Mines, the Orient, the Antarctic, and elsewhere.

From 1930 to 1970 S. published over twenty novels, many of which contain zany, unconventional, and offbeat characters (usually female), who must function in tradition-laden, socially stratified, and conservative English settings. Julia Packett, the star of her seventh novel, *The Nutmeg Tree*, is a typical product of S.'s angle of vision. Her theory, S. has said, is "that people often aren't bad but circumstances sometimes make them so . . . Julia, particularly, [is] a warm-hearted and completely amoral person who was perfectly good in her way, but if placed in a completely conventional society she looked bad. In fact, she *was* bad for them because she broke up all their patterns."

Cluny Brown, made into a motion picture in 1946, is, similarly, about a young, restless heroine, a plumber's niece. She is charming and predictably unpredictable; she likes pipes and tools more than featherdusters and aprons. Cluny is sent as a par-

lor maid to a family in Devon where everyone keeps reminding the reader that "the trouble with young Cluny is she don't know her place." This is, indeed, the case, since she ends up with a distinguished Polish professor for a husband.

Alice Bensen has pointed out in *Contemporary Novelists* that S.'s "satire of social assumptions lacks bitterness" and that the "off-beat characters . . . are basically sound, and the conventional persons are basically kind." But there is still a wry edge to S.'s work. In *The Faithful Servants* (1975), for instance, she creates the Copstock Foundation, established in 1860 to help support "the honest and faithful superannuated maidservants in the City of Westminster." Predictably, it is the monied, educated, and sometimes titled trustees of the Foundation who become dependent on the very servants who apply for financial aid. The trust is named after Emma Copstock, the archetypal, faithful housekeeper of Jacob Arbuthnot, "a womanizer approaching eighty." As S. notes, Arbuthnot had "womanized for far longer than appears credible, let alone decent," and when "medical opinion [pronounced] him off the hooks [he] took the warning in good part, and sent for the lawyer." Emma Copstock becomes the first "superannuated maidservant" to apply to the Foundation and is followed in the next one hundred years by a potpourri of saintly, corrupt, devious, immoral, and virtuous female servants, all, in the final analysis, shrewder and stronger than the masters and mistresses they have served.

This idea of reversal dominates *The Foolish Gentlewoman* as well. Here Isabel Brocken, a daffy dowager type familiar in British novels, gives the family wealth over to her annoying and obnoxious second cousin, Tilly Cuff, much to the consternation of both her indignant brother-in-law and her heir. Every expectation of the reader is upset by the novel's end; nothing happens as S.'s audience would expect it to, and yet the overturned events are believable. The cloying, even repulsive Tilly, for many years a paid companion to various gentlewomen, dominates the book. She is a precursor of the often devious, vulgar, and manipulative servants who emerge in the more recent fiction of Muriel Spark and Iris Murdoch.

S. will be remembered for her intelligent perceptions into the psyches and motivations of all classes of English people because, in her light and entertaining novels, there is insight as well as froth.

WORKS: *Rhododendron Pie* (1930). *Fanfare for Tin Trumpets* (1932). *The Nymph and the Noble-man* (1932). *Meeting at Night* (1934). *Flowering Thorn* (1934). *Sophie Cassmajor* (1934). *Four Gardens* (1935). *The Nutmeg Tree* (1937). *Harlequin House* (1939). *Stone of Chastity* (1940). *Three Companion Pieces* (1941). *Lady in Waiting* (1941). *Cluny Brown* (1944). *Britannia Mews* (1946). *The Foolish Gentlewoman* (1948). *Lise Lilly-white* (1951). *The Gipsy in the Parlour* (1954). *The Birdcage Room* (1954). *The Tigress on the Hearth* (1955). *Eye of Love* (1957). *The Rescuers* (1959). *Melisande* (1960). *Something Light* (1960). *Martha in Paris* (1962). *Miss Bianca* (1962). *The Turret* (1963). *Martha, Eric and George* (1964). *Lost at the Fair* (1965). *The Sun in Scorpio* (1965). *Miss Bianca in the Salt Mines* (1966). *In Pious Memory* (1967). *Rosa* (1970). *Miss Bianca in the Orient* (1970). *Miss Bianca in the Antarctic* (1971). *Miss Bianca and the Bridesmaid* (1972). *The Innocent* (1972). *The Lost Chapel Picnic* (1973). *Children Next Door* (1974). *The Magical Cockatoo* (1974). *The Faithful Servants* (1975). *Bernard the Brave* (1977).

BIBLIOGRAPHY: R. Newquist, *Counterpoint* (1964).

For articles in reference works, see: *CA*. *CN*. *TwCA* and *SUP*. *TwCCW*. *Who's Who*.

Other references: *CSM* (4 May 1967). *Harper's* (August 1937). *NatRev* (27 June 1967). *N.Y.* (22 June 1967). *NYTBR* (April 1967).

Mickey Pearlman

Mary Wollstonecraft Shelley

BORN: 30 August 1797, London.
DIED: 1 February 1851, London.
DAUGHTER OF: William Godwin and Mary Wollstonecraft.
MARRIED: Percy Bysshe Shelley, 1816.
WROTE UNDER: "The Author of Franken-stein," Mary Wollstonecraft Shelley.

Of his wife S., Percy Bysshe Shelley wrote in the dedication to *The Revolt of Islam*, "They say that thou wert lovely from thy birth, / Of glorious parents, thou aspiring child." William Godwin, radical philosopher, and Mary Wollstonecraft, author of *A Vindication of the Rights of Women*, were those "glorious parents." Wollstonecraft had died as a result of giving birth to S., and Godwin's remarriage to widow Mary Jane Clairmont four years later created bitter feelings and resentment for S. These feelings and her strong attachment to her father led to her removal to Scotland in 1812 to ease tensions in the family, which included S., Fanny Imlay (Wollstonecraft's "love child"), Charles, Jane (later Claire), and William.

In 1812 S. met the poet Shelley and his wife, Harriet Westbrook. S. was nearly seventeen when she and Shelley met again in May 1814; he and his wife were estranged by this time, and almost immediately S. and Shelley became lovers. By July she was pregnant, and the couple eloped to the Continent. S.'s first book, *History of a Six Weeks' Tour*, published anonymously in 1817, describes the trip through France, Switzerland, and Germany that S., Shelley, and S.'s stepsister Claire Clairmont took following the elopement. S.'s earlier writing has all been lost, but with Shelley's aid and encouragement, her best-known work would be published the following year.

Frankenstein; or, The Modern Prometheus was published anonymously in 1818. Shelley, S., and Claire had taken residence in Geneva near Byron (Claire's somewhat reluctant lover) and John Poli-dari. *Frankenstein*, a novel of the scientific creation of life severed from moral concerns and social affiliation, became a literary sensation in London. It apparently grew in S.'s imagination in response to a casual competition to create a ghost story as well as to a conversation about contemporary experiments with galvanic electricity on dead tissue. *Frankenstein*, according to Ellen Moers, "is most interesting, most powerful, and most feminine: in the motif of revulsion against newborn life, and the drama of guilt, dread, and fright surrounding birth and its consequences."

For S., the consequence of giving birth was tragedy. Before she reached the age of twenty-two, she had given birth to three children, all of whom had died. These deaths separated her emotionally from Shelley. Her only surviving child was born in

1819. In addition, her half-sister Fanny Imlay had committed suicide in 1816, as did Harriet Shelley (abandoned by Shelley earlier the same year and pregnant by an unknown lover). Harriet's death freed Shelley to wed S. two weeks later. Her greatest loss, however, was the death by drowning of Shelley himself in July 1822. Still somewhat emotionally estranged from him at this time, S., an impoverished widow at twenty-four, attempted through her grief and guilt to establish Shelley's literary reputation (against his father's express wishes) and to support her son through her writing.

S. wrote other novels, several biographies, and many stories, most of which were published in *The Keepsake*; some have elements of science fiction while others are Gothic. Among them is the novella *Mathilda* (1819), in which Shelley is fictionalized as Woodville. This largely biographical work explores the estrangement between S. and Shelley after their daughter Clara's death at age one.

Valperga (1823) and *The Last Man* (1826) are widely considered S.'s best work after *Frankenstein*. *The Last Man* represents a creative landmark in S.'s work. Though marred by overwriting and excessive length, the book commemorates her husband as she was unable to do in a biography. Her characterization of Adrian, second Earl of Windsor, is the only acknowledged portrait of Shelley: "I have endeavoured, but how inadequately, to give some idea of him in my last published book—the sketch has pleased some of those who best loved him." This idealized view of Shelley, a variation on the "Noble Savage" motif, is set in the future and describes the gradual destruction of the human race by plague; its narrator, Lionel Verney, begins life as a shepherd boy and after many years finds himself amid the ruined grandeur of Rome in the year 2100.

The same theme is found in *Lodore* (1835): the heroine Ethel is taken as a child by her father, Lord Lodore, to the wilds of Illinois and raised amid the grandest objects of Nature, after which she returns to a life of romance and penury in a London reminiscent of S.'s early years. S. also wrote *The Fortunes of Perkin Warbeck* (1830) and *Falkner* (1837) and another novella, *The Heir of Mondolfo* (published posthumously in 1877). In addition to her many stories, S. also wrote biographical and critical studies of continental authors and published several editions of her husband's work. She also worked on, but never completed, biographies of Shelley and her father. In short, S. spent her widowhood as a productive and successful woman of letters.

In 1844 S.'s father-in-law died, leaving his title and estate to S.'s son. Only then was she secure financially. The devotion of her son and his marriage to her friend Jane St. John made her last years comfortable. She died 1 February 1851, eight days after falling into a coma.

WORKS: (with P.B. Shelley) *History of a Six Weeks' Tour Through a Part of France, Switzerland, Germany, and Holland, with Letters Descriptive of a Sail round the Lake of Geneva and of the Glaciers of Chamouni* (1817). *Frankenstein* (1818). *Mathilda* (1819). *Valperga; or, The Life and Adventures of Castruccio, Prince of Lucca* (1823). *The Last Man* (1826). *The Fortunes of Perkin Warbeck. A Romance* (1830). *Lodore* (1835). (with others) *Lives of the Most Eminent Literary and Scientific Men of Italy, Spain, and Portugal* (1835-1837). *Falkner: A Novel* (1837). (with others) *Lives of the Most Eminent Literary and Scientific Men of France* (1838). *Rambles in Germany and Italy in 1840, 1842, and 1843* (1844). *The Swiss Peasant* (in *The Tale Book*, with others, 1859). *The Choice. A Poem on Shelley's Death* (1876). *The Heir of Mondolfo* (1877). *Tales and Stories*, ed. R. Garnett (1891). *The Romance of Mary W. Shelley, John Howard Payne, and Washington Irving* (1907; the Payne-Shelley letters, ed. F.B. Sanborn). *Letters, Mostly Unpublished* (1918, ed. H.H. Harper). *Proserpine and Midas. Two Unpublished Mythological Dramas* (1922; ed. A. Koszul). *Letters*, ed. F.L. Jones (1944). *Mathilde*, ed. E. Nitchie (1959). *Journals*, ed. L. Robinson (1947). *My Best Mary: The Selected Letters*, ed. M. Spark and D. Stanford (1953). *Collected Tales and Stories*, ed. C.E. Robinson (1976). *Letters*, ed. B.T. Bennett. vol. 1 (1980), vol. 2 (1983). *Journals 1814-44*, ed. P.R. Feldman and D. Scott-Kilvert (1987).

BIBLIOGRAPHY: Bigland, E. *Mary Shelley* (1959). Church, R. *Mary Shelley* (1928). Gerson, N.B. *Daughter of Earth and Water: A Biography of Mary Shelley* (1973). Grylls, R.G. *Mary Shelley, A Biography* (1938). Levine, G., and U.C. Knoepflmacher, ed. *The Endurance of "Frankenstein": Essays on Mary Shelley's Novel* (1979). Lyles, W.H. *Mary Shelley: An Annotated Bibliography* (1975). Marshall, F.A., ed. *The Life and Letters of Mary Wollstonecraft Shelley* (1889). Moore, H. *Mary Wollstonecraft Shelley* (1886). Nitchie, E. *Mary Shelley: Author of "Frankenstein"* (1953). Norman, S. *On Shelley* (1938). Small, C. *Ariel Like a Harpy: Shelley, Mary, and "Frankenstein"* (1972; in the U.S. as *Mary Shelley's "Frankenstein": Tracing the Myth*). Spark, M. *Child of Light* (1952). Spark, M. *Mary Shelley: A Biography* (1987). Thornburg, M.K.P. *The Monster in the Mirror: Gender and the Sentimental/Gothic Myth in "Frankenstein"* (1987). Tropp, M. *Mary Shelley's Monster: The Story of "Frankenstein"* (1977). Walling, W. *Mary Shelley* (1972).

For articles in reference works, see: *Allibone. BA19C. DNB. Moulton.*

Other references: Bloom, H. *Partisan Review* (1965). Callahan, P.D. *Extrapolation* (December 1972). Cude, W. *Dalhousie Review* (1972). Fleck, P.D. *Studies in Romanticism* (1967). Goldberg, M.A. *Keats-Shelley Journal* (Winter 1959). Gubar, S.

Women and Men: The Consequences of Power, ed. D.V. Miller and R.A. Sheets (1977). Hill, J.M. *American Imago* (1975). Jones, F.L. *PMLA* (1946). Kiely, R. *The Romantic Novel in England* (1972). Kmetz, G. *Ms.* (15 February 1975). Levine, G. *Novel* (1973). Lovell, E.J., Jr. *UTSE* (1951). Mays, M.A. *Southern Humanities Review* (1969). Moers, E. *NYRB* (21 March 1974, 4 April 1974). Newman, B. *English Literary History* (1986). Norman, S. *Shelley and His Circle*, ed. K.N. Cameron (1970). Peck, W.E. *PMLA* (1923). Philmus, R.M. *Into the Unknown: The Evolution of Science Fiction from Francis Godwin to H.G. Wells* (1970). Pollin, B.R. *Comparative Literature* (1965). Poovey, M. *PMLA* (1980). Reeve, H. *Edinburgh Review* (1882). Sherwin, P. *PMLA* (1981). Spark, M. *Listener* (22 February 1951). Veeder, W. *Critical Inquiry* (1986).

Anne-Marie Ray

Frances Sheridan

BORN: 1724, Dublin.
DIED: 26 September 1766, Blois, France.
DAUGHTER OF: Philip and Anastasia Whyte Chamberlaine.
MARRIED: Thomas Sheridan, 1747.

S., forbidden by her father to learn to write, was educated in Latin and botany as well as in written English by her older brothers. When she was fifteen years old, she wrote her first novel, *Eugenia and Adelaide*, on paper given to her for the household accounts. In 1743, when she was nineteen, she entered the fray of a pamphlet war, defending a man whom she had not yet met but was later to marry. Both the pamphlet, "A letter from a Young Lady to Mr. Cibber," and a poem, "The Owls," published in the *Dublin News Journal*, were in protest to the attacks of Theophilus Cibber on Thomas Sheridan, a popular actor and manager of the Theatre Royal, Smock Alley, Dublin.

In 1747, S. married Thomas Sheridan, but she did not again write for publication until 1759. During these years she was made intimately aware of birth and death. She bore six children, two of whom died, her beloved uncle died, both her parents died, and her close friend, Miss Pennington, died. S. herself was plagued with illness; lame since childhood, she was stricken in her early thirties with maladies which stayed with her until her death, variously described as rheumatism in the head, violent headaches, disorders of the stomach, and fainting seizures. Yet she was noted for her vivacity and charm, and from 1759 until her death she worked steadily at the profession of writing.

To get away from Dublin theatre disturbances and from financial debts, S. and her husband settled in London in 1754. S. became friends with Samuel Johnson, David Garrick, and Samuel Richardson, and with several literary women, such as Hester Mulso Chapone, Sarah Fielding, and Catherine Macauley. Samuel Richardson read *Eugenia and Adelaide*, contemplated but decided against publishing it, and encouraged S. to begin writing again.

During the winter of 1759/60, busy with household management and with supervision of her children's education, grieving for Miss Pennington's death, and suffering from her own illnesses, S. wrote her novel *The Memoirs of Miss Sidney Bidulph*. It was published in March in both London and Dublin, and by July a second London edition came out. Her next effort was a comedy, *The Discovery*, which in late 1762 opened at Drury Lane, where it played to packed houses for seventeen nights. The following year, she wrote another comedy, *The Dupe*, which opened in December at Drury Lane. Although it closed after only three performances, sales of the printed play were so brisk that she was paid £100 above the usual copyright fee.

In September of 1764, in response to S.'s worsening health and to continuing financial distress, the family moved to France. Over the next two years, she wrote four works. For some time her health seemed to improve, but in early September 1766 she was seized with fainting fits and a fever and died two weeks later. An autopsy revealed, as her husband wrote, that "all the noble parts were attacked, and any one of four internal maladies must have proved fatal." Two works were published posthumously in 1767: *Nourjahad*, an exotic moral tale, and a two-volume continuation of *Sidney Bidulph*; a dramatic tragedy based on this continuation was lost in manuscript. A third comedy, *A Journey to Bath*, was refused by Garrick and not published until 1902, at which time a three-act fragment, credited to her, was included in W. Fraser Rae's edition of her son Richard Brinsley Sheridan's plays.

S.'s youthful effort, *Eugenia and Adelaide* (published 1791), depicts the gothic adventures of two girlhood friends. *Sidney Bidulph*, noted by Johnson for its power of feeling, was immensely popular during the eighteenth century, running to five London editions and at least one Dublin edition. In translation, it was avidly read on the continent: for instance, twenty years after its first publication, a French bookseller remarked that she had sold more copies of *Sidney Bidulph* than of any other novel. Here, S.'s interest is in exploring the passions, perhaps encouraged as much by grief for the deaths of loved ones as by the inspiration of Richardson's *Clarissa*. The plot is sentimentally tragic, but S.'s language is energetic and direct and comic interludes break the general air of sorrow. One such interlude, the story of a rich relation from the West Indies who disguises himself as a beggar in order to test the kindness of Sidney and her brother, was picked up by S.'s son Richard Brinsley in *The School for Scandal*. Themes in the novel are the powerlessness of women in patriarchy and the bonds of consolation formed among women. A destructive kindness exists between Sidney and her mother; oppression as women binds Sidney and the maidservant Patty Main, while class difference separates them; and romantic friendship offers solace but no hope for change. In the 1767 continuation, Sidney's powerlessness is destructive to her own daughters.

As early as mid-1763, *The Discovery* had been published in London, Dublin, and Edinburgh, with a second London edition printed before the year was out; the play saw repeated revivals during the eighteenth century, was anthologized and adapted well into the nineteenth century, and in 1924 Aldous Huxley offered a modern version. In *The Discovery*, women assure harmony through placating and indirectly guiding villainous or foolish men. Here, as in her other comedies, S. achieves effect through an awareness of language from which her son learned much. For instance, the contrasting personalities of Lord Medway and Sir Anthony are caught by the language they use: Lord Medway, "the shorter we make the wooing—women are slippery things—you understand me!" Sir Anthony, "Your Lordship's insinuation, though derogatory to the honour of the fair-sex, (which I very greatly reverence) has, I am apprehensive, a little too much veracity in it." Aptly, Sir Anthony's nephew refers to him as "uncle Parenthesis."

The Dupe might have been a stage success half a century earlier, but in 1763, its satire offended the moral sensibilities of its bourgeois audience. The play closed to "an almost universal hiss" from the critics, who found it "low and vulgar" and who censured its author for "conduct so unbecoming, so unfemale." In the printed version, S.'s language was sanitized. For instance, "Spawn of a Chimney Sweeper" and "Cinder Wench" are expunged, and the description of the name of *wife* as worse "than ten thousand blistering Plaisters" dwindles to "worse than ten thousand daggers."

In *A Journey to Bath*, Mrs. Surface, a landlady whose parlor is "a Mart of Scandal," uses language hypocritically. S. had her most fun, however, with Mrs. Tryfort, who later metamorphosed into Mrs. Malaprop. Among her frequent linguistic man-

glings are these: "to teach my Lucy, and make her illiterate," "Oh in everything ma'am he is a progeny! a perfect progeny!" and "But my Lord Stewkly is so embelished, Mrs. Surface! No body can be embelished that has not been abroad you must know. Oh if you were to hear him describe contagious countries as I have done, it would astonish you. He is a perfect map of geography."

Nourjahad, which S. had planned as the first in a series of Oriental moral tales, is a whimsical fable with a complicated plot having a true surprise ending. In the story, a young man who values pleasure above all else is granted his desire for eternal youth and wealth; but the world remains mortal and he learns what loss is. Gradually he discovers new values. The tale was often reprinted in the eighteenth and nineteenth centuries and as recently as 1927.

Criticism of S.'s work focuses on what her son learned from her, which was significant. But S.'s work has more to offer than evidence of her son's comedic training. *Sidney Bidulph* is fascinating for the ways in which it questions how completely woman's life is bound by patriarchy. The comedies are lively explorations of the use and misuse of language. Finally, *Nourjahad* is a delight in its inventive plot, its finely sketched characterization, and its tone of poignant simplicity.

WORKS: *A Letter from a Young Lady to Mr. Cibber* (1743; in *Cibber and Sheridan*). *The Owls: A Fable* (1743; in *Dublin News Letter*). *Memoirs of Miss Sidney Bidulph* (1761). *The Discovery* (1763). *The Dupe* (1764). *The History of Nourjahad* (1767). *Eugenia and Adelaide* (1791). *Letters and Ode to Patience* (1799; In *A Miscellany*). *A Journey to Bath*, in *Sheridan's Plays . . . and His Mother's Unpublished Comedy*, ed. W.F. Rae (1902). *Verses on Thomas Sheridan*, in *Sheridan*, ed. W. Sichel (1909). *The Plays of Frances Sheridan*, ed. R. Hogan and J.C. Beasley (1984).

BIBLIOGRAPHY: Baker, E.A. *The History of the English Novel* (1924-36). Fitzgerald, P. *The Lives of the Sheridans* (1886). LeFanu, A. *Memoirs of the Life and Writings of Mrs. Frances Sheridan* (1824). Nicoll, A. *A History of Late Eighteenth-Century Drama, 1750-1800* (1925). Wilson, M. *These Were Muses* (1924).

For articles in reference works, see: *Biographica Dramatica. DIL. DNB. Todd.*

Other references: Baker, D.E. *The Companion to the Play-House* (1764). Butt, J. *The Mid-Eighteenth Century*, ed. G. Carnall (1979). Chew, S.P. *PQ* (1939). Doody, M.A. *Fetter'd or Free? British Women Novelists, 1670-1815*, ed. M.A. Schofield and C. Macheski (1986). Horner, J.M. *Smith College Studies in Modern Languages* (1929-30). Russell, N.E. *Book Collector* (1964).

Carolyn Woodward

Mary Sidney, Countess of Pembroke

BORN: 27 October 1561, Penshurst, Kent.
DIED: 25 September 1621, Crosby Hall.
DAUGHTER OF: Sir Henry Sidney and Mary Dudley.
MARRIED: Henry Herbert, Earl of Pembroke, 1577.

S. was born to a family of power in Elizabeth's court. Her mother was the daughter of John Dudley, Duke of Northumberland, who had died for his attempt to put Lady Jane Grey on the English throne. Northumberland's surviving sons—Robert Dudley, Earl of Leicester, and Ambrose Dudley, Earl of Warwick—were primary patrons for Protestant writings in England, supported Elizabeth against her Catholic rivals, and advocated military intervention on the Continent in behalf of Protestants there. Northumberland's daughters married men who strongly supported the Protestant cause: Katherine Dudley married the Earl of Huntington, Lord President of the Council in the North; Mary Dudley herself married Sir Henry Sidney, Lord President of the Marches of Wales and Lord Deputy of Ireland, who had been educated with the young King Edward. Among them, S.'s father and uncles ruled approximately two thirds of the land under Elizabeth's rule.

After the death of her older sister, Ambrosia, S. went to Elizabeth's court at the Queen's express invitation. Her uncle Robert Dudley, Elizabeth's favorite and reputedly the most powerful man in England, arranged for her marriage at age fifteen as the third wife of one of the great Protestant lords, the middle-aged Henry Herbert, Earl of Pembroke, and contributed substantially to her dowry. As the Countess of Pembroke and the mistress of huge estates near Salisbury, in Wales, and in London, she used her money and influence to encourage such writers as Edmund Spenser, Abraham Fraunce, and Samuel Daniel.

Her brother, Sir Philip Sidney, was the hope of Protestants on the Continent. Endeavoring to influence Elizabeth to support the Huguenots against the Catholic Valois in the French religious wars, the Earls of the Dudley/Sidney alliance met at her London home to plan a letter dissuading Elizabeth from marrying the Duc d'Anjou. Philip served as spokesman for the alliance, infuriating the Queen, who forced him to leave the court. Philip spent his time of enforced idleness with S. at Wilton, her country estate. There he wrote the *Arcadia*, the most popular prose fiction in English for two centuries. After Philip died, S. edited the *Arcadia* for publication (1593) as well as his sonnet sequence *Astrophil and Stella* (1598).

S. also helped to create a hagiography, establishing Philip as a Protestant martyr. She wrote two poems mourning his death, "The Doleful Lay of Clorinda," published with other elegies for Philip in Spenser's *Colin Clouts Come Home Again*, and "To the Angell Spirit of the most excellent Sir Philip Sidney," which exists in one manuscript copy, a presentation copy of her Psalms. Her other two original poems praise Elizabeth. "A Dialogue between two shepheards . . . in praise of Astrea" was written for the Queen's visit to Wilton; it is unfortunately undated. "Even now that care" dedicates S.'s translation of the Psalms to Queen Elizabeth (1599).

In addition to these original poems, she translated four works in the 1590s: Robert Garnier's *Marc Antonie*, Philippe de Mornay's *A Discourse on Life and on Death*, Petrarch's *Trionfo della Morte*, and the Psalms of David. The first three works deal with the theme of death, which was particularly appropriate to her at that time; her three-year-old daughter Katherine had died the same day her son Philip was born in 1584; her father, mother, and her brother Philip all had died in 1586; by 1595, her youngest brother Thomas and all of her powerful uncles had died as well.

S.'s major literary achievement was her translation of the Psalms. Philip had translated the first 43 psalms into sophisticated English verse patterns modeled on the French psalter of Clemont Marot and Theodore de Beze. After his death, S. revised some of those psalms and translated the rest. Rarely repeating a verse pattern, her work is a triumph of English prosody and consists more of meditations on the Psalms than of literal translations. John Donne praised her Psalms, saying "They tell us *why*, and teach us *how* to sing," a statement more accurate than hyperbolic, as recent studies of George Herbert and others have recognized.

The Psalms were never presented to the Queen, and S.'s prestige waned with her husband's. Pembroke had long been plagued with ill health and in his physical weakness had lost most of his power in Wales. In January 1601 he died, leaving his widow the castle and town of Cardiff, Wales, along with some other properties. When he came of age, her son William, third Earl of Pembroke, assumed S.'s role as patron of writers; the first folio edition of Shakespeare, for example, is dedicated to her sons William and Philip. Although both William and Philip attained great wealth and power in the court of James I, S. largely retired from court life after the accession festivities. She attempted to put down insurrections in Cardiff, continued her literary friendships, and spent much time taking the waters for her health in the fashionable Continental town of Spa.

Her continued, although diminished, importance as a patron is seen in Aemilia Lanyer's dedication of *Salve Deus Rex Judaeorum* to her (and other women of her circle) in 1611. She died in 1621 at the advanced age of fifty-nine and was buried "in a manner befitting her degree."

Samuel Daniel had prophesied that by her Psalms S.'s name would live even when her great house at Wilton "lies low levell'd with the ground." In 1647, Wilton burned, destroying most of the records of her life and quite possibly some additional writings alluded to in contemporary correspondence. Nevertheless, her Psalms do stand as one of the most significant poetic achievements in Elizabeth's reign.

WORKS: *A Discourse of Life and Death; Antonius: A Tragoedie* (1592; *The Countess of Pembroke's Antonie*, ed. A. Luce, 1897; *Narrative and Dramatic Sources of Shakespeare* 5, ed. G. Bullough (1966). "A Dialogue Between Two Shepheards . . . in Praise of Astrea." *A Poetical Rhapsody*, ed. F. Davison (1602). *The Psalms of Sir Philip Sidney and the Countess of Pembroke*, ed. J.C.A. Rathmell (1963). *The Triumph of Death and Other Unpublished and Uncollected Poems by Mary Sidney, Countess of Pembroke (1561-1621)*, ed. G.F. Waller (1977). *The Countess of Pembroke's Translation of Philippe de Mornay's "Discours de la Vie et de la Mort,"* ed. D. Bornstein (1983).

BIBLIOGRAPHY: Hannay, M. *Philip's Phoenix: Mary Sidney, Countess of Pembroke* (1989). Waller, G., ed. and intro. *The Triumph of Death and*

Other Unpublished and Uncollected Poems by Mary Sidney, Countess of Pembroke (1561-1621). Young, F.B. *Mary Sidney, Countess of Pembroke* (1912).

Other references: Bornstein, D. *Silent But for the Word: Tudor Women as Translators, Patrons and Writers of Religious Works*, ed. M. Hannay (1985). Brennan, M.G. *RES* (1982). Fisken, B.W. *Silent But for the Word: Tudor Women as Translators, Patrons and Writers of Religious Works*, ed. M. Hannay (1985). Freer, C. *Music for a King: George Herbert's Style and the Metrical Psalms* (1971). Freer, C. *Style* (1971). Hannay, M. *Silent But for the Word: Tudor Women as Translators, Patrons and Writers of Religious Works*, ed. M. Hannay (1985). Hannay, M. *Spenser Studies* (1985). Hogrefe, P. *Women of Action in Tudor England* (1977). Kinnamon, N.J. *George Herbert Journal* (1978). Lamb, M. *ELR* (1982). Lamb, M. *Yearbook of English Studies* (1981). Lewalski, B.K. *Protestant Poetics and the Seventeenth-Century Religious Lyric* (1979). Martz, L. *Poetry of Meditation* (1962). Rathmell, J.C.A. "Introduction." *The Psalms of Sir Philip Sidney and the Countess of Pembroke* (1963). Roberts, J.A. *ELR* (1984). Smith, H. *HLQ* (1946). Waller, G. *The Triumph of Death and Other Unpublished and Uncollected Poems by Mary Sidney, Countess of Pembroke (1561-1621)* (1977). Waller, G. *Wascana Review* (1974). Woods, S. *Natural Emphasis: English Versification from Chaucer to Dryden* (1984).

Margaret P. Hannay

Catherine Sinclair

BORN: 17 April 1780, Edinburgh.
DIED: 4 August 1864, London.
DAUGHTER OF: John Sinclair and Catherine McDonald.

Born the fourth daughter of a baronet, S. is best known today as the author of *Holiday House* (1839), a pioneering children's book credited with ushering in the reign of the nonsense tale and marking the triumph of imaginative literature for children over pious moral tracts.

S.'s father was the first president of the Board of Agriculture and she, too, took part in philanthropic life, establishing drinking fountains, having seats set up in crowded thoroughfares, and serving as her father's secretary until his death in 1835. Although she never married, S. would often tell stories to her nieces and nephews, and this is considered the origin of many of her stories.

Holiday House is a loosely connected series of episodic adventures that has its genesis in Sir

Walter Scott's remark to S. that "in the rising generation there would be no poets, wits, or orators because all the play of imagination is now carefully discouraged and books written for young persons are generally a mere dry record of facts, unenlivened by any appeal to the heart, or any excitement to fancy." In addition to an appeal to the imagination, S. also has a fairly unorthodox view of children. Critics have pointed out that she makes a distinction between naughtiness and wickedness, believing that children can be forgiven for the former, which is natural, and corrected, not punished, for the latter. Her sibling protagonists, Harry and Laura, get into various escapades: Harry almost burns down the house and Laura cuts off all her hair. The villain of the piece, though, is the governess, Mrs. Crabtree, who believes that one could make children good by whipping them; the author's mouthpiece is their grandmother who declares that "Parents are appointed by God to govern their children as he governs us, not carelessly indulging their faults, but wisely correcting them." The work is equally well known because it contains Uncle David's "Nonsensical Story About Giants and Fairies"; often anthologized separately, the tale is one of the very first nonsense stories in the language.

Other children's books include *Charles Seymour* (1832), which critics have found more sedate, and *Sir Edward Graham* (1849), a sequel to *Holiday House*, presenting many of the same characters (and which was reissued in 1854 under the title *The Mysterious Marriage*). The *Letters*, begun in 1861, were a series of six stories in letter form with pictures printed in color by W.H. McFarlane; advertised as "warranted to keep the noisiest child quiet for half an hour," they proved her most popular success.

Though remembered mostly as a children's writer, S. also wrote novels for adults, beginning with *Modern Accomplishments* (1836) and its sequel, *Modern Society* (1837). Both were commercially successful and were still in print in the 1870s, though today critics see them as excessively wordy and moralistic. S. wrote several volumes of travel literature, beginning with a descriptive tour of Wales, *Hill and Valley* (1840). In addition, she wrote stories that were issued separately between January and April of 1853 under the title "Common Sense Tracts" and published as a collection, *London Homes*.

While successful in her day at all the forms she tried, in this century only *Holiday House* remains in print. Though intended as a reaction against didacticism in children's literature, recent critics have pointed out that the work preaches a conventional morality by paying homage to the family and that S.'s remarkably permissive attitude applies only to children of respected classes.

WORKS: *Charles Seymour; or the Good Aunt and the Bad Aunt* (1832). *Modern Accomplishments, or the March of Intellect* (1836). *Modern Society, or the March of Intellect* (1837). *Holiday House* (1839). *Hill and Valley* (1840). *Scotland and the South* (1840). *Shetland and the Shetlanders* (1840). *Modern Flirtations, or a Month at Harrowgate* (1841). *Jane Bouverie, or Prosperity and Adversity* (1846). *The Journey of Life* (1847). *Sir Edward Graham, or the Railway Speculators* (1849). *Lord and Lady Harcourt, or Country Hospitalities* (1850). *Beatrice, or the Unknown Relatives* (1852). *London Homes* (1853). *Cross Purposes* (1855). *The Picture Letter* (1861). *Another Letter* (1862). *The Bible Picture Letter* (1862). *The Crossman's Letter* (1862). *The Sunday Letter* (1862). *The First of April Letter* (1864).

BIBLIOGRAPHY: Darnton, F.J.H. *Children's Books in England* (1962). Green, R.L. *Teller of Tales* (1965). Gryllis, D. *Guardians and Angels* (1978). Thwaite, M. *From Primer to Pleasure* (1963). Townsend, J.R. *Written for Children* (1975).

For articles in reference works, see: Bingham, J. and G. Sholt, *15 Centuries of Children's Literature* (1980). DNB. Sadleir, M. *19th Century Fiction: A Bibliographical Record.*

Tony Giffone

Mary Amelia St. Clair Sinclair

BORN: 24 August 1863, Rock Ferry, Higher Bebington, Cheshire.
DIED: 14 November 1946, Aylesbury, Buckinghamshire.
DAUGHTER OF: William and Amelia Hind Sinclair.
WROTE UNDER: Anonymous, Julian Sinclair, M.A. St. C. Sinclair, Mary Sinclair, May Sinclair.

S. wrote twenty-four novels and two major works of philosophy, as well as numerous poems, short stories, translations, and reviews. She was one of the most popular novelists of the early twentieth century and, speaking of Dorothy Richardson's *Pilgrimage* (1915), the first to apply William James's term "stream of consciousness" to the psychological force of modern literature.

All but ignored in England until *The Divine Fire* (1904) was successful in the United States, S. was the only daughter in a strictly religious Victo-

rian family with five sons. When her shipowner father's business collapsed and he became an alcoholic, S.'s parents separated and S. cared for her ailing and dogmatic mother until her death in 1901. She attended Cheltenham Ladies' College between 1881 and 1882 and began studying philosophy with the headmistress, Dorothea Beale. The autobiographical novel *Mary Olivier: A Life* (1919), which S. considered her best work and which was originally serialized beside James Joyce's *Ulysses* in the *Little Review*, reveals the competition and the orthodoxy that haunted S.'s childhood. The philosophies of Plato, Spinoza, and Kant became ways to resist Christian dogma and to search for a more universal truth. *Mary Olivier* is one of fiction's most sustained studies of the mother-daughter relationship.

S. began translating from the Greek tragedies while writing dense narrative and argumentative poems and abstract philosophical pieces for journals in the 1880s. Her first stories and novels bring together the strengths of these two genres: the compact, imagistic language of poetry and the hard, moral questioning of idealist philosophy. Several of S.'s early works—*Mr. and Mrs. Nevill Tyson* (1898), *The Helpmate* (1907), *The Judgement of Eve* (1908), and *Kitty Tailleur* (1908)—explore bad Victorian marriages and the ways disappointment in love leads to illness, brutality, and death. *The Helpmate* shocked many Edwardian readers with its scene of a husband and wife talking in bed. In *The Divine Fire* (1904) and *The Creators* (1910), S. depicts a variety of creative personalities; she shows sensory and sensual experiences inspiring creative work, and she portrays a variety of women choosing for and against marriage and family ties as they attend to their impulse to write.

In the 1910s and 1920s S. was one of the few advocates of the younger modern writers. She and Arnold Bennett, who was probably the model for *Taskor Jevons* (1916), were the only two established writers to protest publicly the banning of D.H. Lawrence's *The Rainbow* (1915). In addition, S. introduced Ezra Pound to the editor Ford Madox Hueffer (Ford) in 1909 and wrote one of the first positive reviews of T.S. Eliot's *Prufrock and Other Observations* (1917). She published a poem, "After the Retreat," in the April 1915 Imagist number of the *Egoist*, and she encouraged the avant-garde writing of numerous women—Hilda Doolittle, Dorothy Richardson, Violet Hunt, and Charlotte Mew—both privately and in print. Like these younger writers, S. strove to uncover the mysteries of the individual psyche and the differences between the individual woman and the individual man.

A member of the Women Writers Suffrage League, S. wrote a pamphlet, *Feminism* (1912), and several letters to the editor on behalf of women's freedom to work. In 1914, she traveled with a Red Cross ambulance corps to Belgium, from which she derived *A Journal of Impressions in Belgium* (1915). *The Tree of Heaven* (1917) was one of the first novels to explore the psychological impact of the Great War.

She tried, in her biography of the Brontë sisters, *The Three Brontës* (1912), to disentangle them from a web of hostile and often conflicting critical views. S., the first to see the relationship between Emily's Gondal poems and the novel *Wuthering Heights* (1847), also considered Anne's *The Tenant of Wildfell Hall* (1848) the first feminist novel. She praised Charlotte's *Jane Eyre* (1847) as a novel without precedent and Lucy Snowe, the heroine of *Villette* (1853), as the forerunner of the psychological realism of George Meredith and Henry James. Also derived from S.'s fascination with the Brontës' family life in the Yorkshire moors, *The Three Sisters* (1914) breaks radically from her earlier works to show the ongo-

ing psychological impact of women's social and political inequality.

S. was a member of both the Society for Psychical Research and Dr. Jessie Margaret Murray's Medico-Psychological Clinic, the first group to practice Freudian analysis in England. Various contemporary theories of "psychology"—from the individual's almost passive psychic development, to mysticism, to the spiritual responsibility to discover and to apply absolute truth—work against one another in S.'s works of fiction and philosophy. S. underwent at least partial analysis; she discusses the changes in her style and form resulting from the study of psychoanalysis in the introduction to *The Judgement of Eve and Other Stories* (1914).

In *A Defense of Idealism* (1917), S. uses Indian mysticism, through the poetry of Rabindranath Tagore, to challenge Bertrand Russell's reigning realism. *The New Idealism* (1922) distinguishes between primary and secondary consciousness (the self's knowing the objective world and the self's knowing that it knows) and the "ultimate consciousness" of order, unity, and presence. On the basis of her work in philosophy S. was named a member of the Aristotelian Society for the Systematic Study of Philosophy in 1923.

Many of S.'s short stories, especially those in *Uncanny Stories* (1923), hinge on one character's ability to communicate with the spirit world, to perceive and to extend unity, or to link the living and the dead. *The Dark Night* (1924), a novel in blank verse, includes a powerful evocation in the "Grandmother" section. On the other hand, with the exception of *Life and Death of Harriett Frean* (1922) and *Arnold Waterlow: A Life* (1924), S.'s later novels became more hardened and satirical than the experimental, psychological works of her middle period. *Mr. Waddington of Wyck* (1921) tells of a provincial aristocrat and *A Cure of Souls* (1923) of a lazy, materialistic rector who prefers not to mix the untidy death of the poor with the propriety and order of afternoon tea. Several of S.'s works were rewritten by others for the stage; *The Combined Maze* (1913) had a short run in London in 1927.

In the 1930s S. retired from London with her nurse and companion, Florence Bartrop. She died of Parkinson's disease in 1946 after a long and painful illness.

WORKS: Nakiketas and Other Poems (1886). Essays in Verse (1892). Outlines of Church History (trans., 1895). Audrey Craven (1897). Mr. and Mrs. Nevill Tyson (1898, U.S.: The Tysons, (1906). England's Danger, The Future of British Army Reform (trans., 1901). Two Sides of a Question (1901). The Divine Fire (1904). Thoughts from Goethe (trans. and ed., 1905). The Helpmate (1907). The Judgement of Eve (1908). Kitty Tailleur (1908, U.S.:

The Immortal Moment). The Creators: A Comedy (1910). *Feminism* (1912). *The Flaw in the Crystal* (1912). *The Three Brontës* (1912). *The Combined Maze* (1913). *The Judgement of Eve and Other Stories* (1914). *The Three Sisters* (1914). *The Return of the Prodigal and Other Stories* (1914). *America's Part in the War* (1915). *A Journal of Impressions in Belgium* (1915). *Tasker Jevons: The Real Story* (1916, U.S.: *The Belfry*). *The Tree of Heaven* (1917). *A Defence of Idealism: Some Questions and Conclusions* (1917). *Mary Olivier: A Life* (1919). *The Romantic* (1920). *Mr. Waddington of Wyck* (1921). *Anne Severn and the Fieldings* (1922). *Life and Death of Harriett Frean* (1922). *The New Idealism* (1922). *Uncanny Stories* (1923). *A Cure of Souls* (1924). *Arnold Waterlow: A Life* (1924). *The Dark Night: A Novel in Verse* (1924). *The Rector of Wyck* (1925). *Far End* (1926). *The Allinghams* (1927). *History of Anthony Waring* (1927). *Fame* (1929). *Tales Told by Simpson* (1930). *The Intercessor and Other Stories* (1931).

BIBLIOGRAPHY: Aldington, R. *Life for Life's Sake* (1941). Allen, W. *The Modern Novel: in Britain and the United States* (1964). Boll, T.E.M. *Miss May Sinclair: Novelist* (1973). Brewster, D., and Birrell, A. *Dead Reckonings in Fiction* (1924). Chevalley, A. *The Modern English Novel* (1921). Cooper, F.T. *Some English Story Tellers* (1912). Doolittle, H., *Bid Me to Live* (1960). Gorsky, S. in Cornillon, S., ed. *Images of Women in Fiction: Feminine Perspectives* (1972). Frierson, W. *The English Novel in Transition 1885-1940* (1942). Gould, G. *The English Novel of Today* (1924). Kaplan, S. *Feminine Consciousness in the Modern British Novel* (1975). Kumar, S. *Bergson and the Stream of Consciousness Novel* (1963). Myers, W. *The Later Realism* (1927). Phelps, W. *The Advance of the English Novel* (1916). Radford, J. Intro. to *Mary Olivier: A Life* (1980). Raikes, E. *Dorothea Beale of Cheltenham* (1908). Stevenson, L. *History of the English Novel* (1967). Swinnerton, F. *The Georgian Scene* (1934). Taylor, C. *A Study of May Sinclair* (1969). Tynan, K. *The Middle Years* (1916). Zegger, H. *May Sinclair* (1976).

For articles in reference works, see: *CA. TCA.*
Other references: *Arts and Decoration* 21 (July 1924). *Bulletin of the New York Public Library* (September 1970). *Comparative Literature* (Spring 1959). *CL* (1972). *ELT* (1973, 1978). *Literary Digest International Book Review* (1924). *Proceedings of the American Philosophical Society* (August 1962). *Psychoanalytic Review* (April 1923). *TCL* (1980). *University of Pennsylvania Library Chronicle* (1961).

Carol L. Barash

Dame Edith Sitwell

BORN: 7 September 1887, Scarborough, Yorkshire.
DIED: 11 December 1964, London.
DAUGHTER OF: Sir George and Lady Ida Denison Sitwell.

S., a poet and public figure who provoked controversy, was associated with avant-garde styles and thought for fifty years. S. became a public figure because she not only read her poems on lecture tours but wrote and performed poetry designed to be accompanied to music.

A child of an aristocratic family, she and her younger brothers Osbert and Sacheverell were brought up in legendary elegance. S. was educated at home and was introduced to French symbolist poetry, especially Rimbaud's, through her governess Helen Rootham, with whom she lived in the 1920s. When S. moved to London, she published at her own expense her first volume, *The Mother and Other Poems* (1915), and edited the annual volumes of *Wheels* (1916-1921).

S. also became notorious by performing her poems in *Façade* (1922), set to music by William Walton, in a concert hall. Many of the titles of these poems were dance names such as "Waltz," "Polka," or "Fox Trot." S. not only explored the rhythms of word order but the sounds as well. In "Waltz," for example, the sound and rhythm create the 1-2-3 beat of the dance: "Daisy and Lily,/ Lazy and silly,/ Walk by the shore of the wan grassy sea—/ Talking once more 'neath a swan-bosomed tree." Criticism, much of it hostile, responded to the seemingly meaningless poems and the theatricality of her performance. Other poems published in the 1920s also reflect her experimentation in synesthesia and the social disillusionment of the times, and her friends of the period included T.S. Eliot, Aldous Huxley, and Virginia Woolf.

In the 1930s much of S.'s work was written to support herself, so there are several anthologies and general prose works: a study of Pope (1930), a book about Bath (1932), *English Eccentrics* (1933), *Aspects of Modern Poetry* (1934), a biography of Queen Victoria (1936), and a novel about Jonathan Swift's loves, *I Live Under a Black Sun* (1937). She resumed writing poetry in 1938.

Poems after World War II reflect a change in style and philosophies, as in *Green Song & Other Poems* (1944), *Song of the Cold* (1945), *Shadow of Cain* (1947). In these poems, lines are longer and her despair over the destruction of life through the bomb "rains" can be seen in her openly pacifist poems. "The Shadow of Cain," S. insists in her introduction to her *Collected Poems* (1954), shows her outrage at the bombing of Hiroshima: "This poem is about the fission of the world into warring particles, destroying and self-destructive."

Later poems are more metaphysical and spiritual. In 1955 S. was accepted into the Roman Catholic Church, and many poems of the late 1940s and 50s seek to "give holiness to each common day." In her 1962 *The Outcasts* S. called poetry the "deification of reality."

In her last years honors and praise made her well-known. In 1948 and 1950 S. toured the United States reading her poems, which contributed to her reputation. In 1951 the University of Oxford gave her an honorary D. Litt., and in 1954 the Queen made S. a Dame Commander of the Order of the British Empire. Most of her manuscripts, sold in auction at Sotheby's, were sent to the library of the University of Texas.

WORKS: *The Mother and Other Poems* (1915). *Twentieth-Century Harlequinade and Other Poems* (with Osbert Sitwell, 1916). *Clowns' Houses* (1918). *The Wooden Pegasus* (1920). *Façade* (1922). *Bucolic Comedies* (1923). *The Sleeping Beauty* (1924). *Troy Park* (1925). *Poor Young People* (with Osbert and Sacheverell Sitwell, 1925). *Poetry and Criticism* (1925). *Elegy on Dead Fashion* (1926). *Rustic Elegies* (1927). *Gold Coast Customs* (1929). *Alexander Pope* (1930). *Collected Poems* (1930). *Bath* (1932). *The English Eccentrics* (1933; rev. and enl., 1957). *Five Variations on a Theme* (1933). *Aspects of Modern Poetry* (1934). *Victoria of England* (1936). *Selected Poems* (1936). *I Live Under a Black Sun* (1937). *Poems New and Old* (1940). *Street Songs* (1942). *English Women* (1942). *A Poet's Notebook* (1943,

1950). *Green Song & Other Poems* (1944). *The Song of the Cold* (1945). *Fanfare for Elizabeth* (1946). *The Shadow of Cain* (1947). *The Canticle of the Rose* (1949). *Poor Men's Music* (1950). *Façade and Other Poems, 1920-1935* (1950). *Selected Poems* (1952). *Gardeners and Astronomers* (1953). *Collected Poems* (1954). *The Outcasts* (1962). *The Queens of the Hive* (1962). *Taken Care of* (1965). *Selected Poems of Edith Sitwell*, ed. J. Lehmann (1965).

BIBLIOGRAPHY: Bowra, C. *Edith Sitwell* (1947, 1973). Brophy, J. *Edith Sitwell: The Symbolist Order* (1968). Daiches, D. *Poetry and the Modern World* (1940). Deutsch, B. *Poetry in Our Times* (1956). Elborn, G. *Edith Sitwell* (1981). Glendinning, V. *Edith Sitwell: A Unicorn Among Lions* (1981). Mills, R. *Edith Sitwell* (1966). Parker, D. *Sacheverell Sitwell* (1979). Pearson, J. *Sitwells: A Family's Biography* (1978). Salter, E. *Edith Sitwell* (1979). Singleton, G. *Edith Sitwell: The Hymn to Life* (1960). Villa, J., ed. *A Celebration for Edith Sitwell* (1948, rept. 1972).

For articles in reference works, see: *CA. CLC. DLB. MBL & SUP. TCA.*

Other references: *America* (28 February 1981). *American Benedictine Review* (1976). *British Museum Quarterly* (1965). *Bulletin of Bibliography* (1954, 1974). *Catholic World* (1956). *Chicago Review* (Summer 1961). *Cithara* (Fall 1972). *College English* (1952). *Commonweal* (1959, 1965). *CL* (1971). *Contemporary Review* (1959). *Criticism* (1967). *Encounter* (May 1966, November 1981). *Geneologists' Magazine* (1967). *MLN* (1959). *The Month* (1960). *NYRB* (17 December 1981). *New Yorker* (9 November 1981). *The Personalist* (1965). *Poetry* (June 1945). *Poetry Review* (1965). *Renascence* (1951, 1974). *St. Louis Quarterly* (1965). *TLS* (29 April 1965). *TCL* (October 1970).

Marilynn J. Smith

Charlotte Turner Smith

BORN: 4 May 1749, Sussex.
DIED: 28 October 1806, Surrey.
DAUGHTER OF: Nicholas Turner and Anna Towers Turner.
MARRIED: Benjamin Smith, 1765.

S. was one of England's most popular writers in a period when literary tastes mirrored the revolutionary changes taking place in the political and economic spheres of life in the Western world. Her four volumes of poetry, ten novels, translations, and moralistic children's books made her one of the most prolific writers of the last years of the eighteenth century, and readers of the day

were usually quite ready to support both critically and financially this woman who dared on the one hand to question the social structures under which she lived while on the other she challenged the already crumbling literary standards of a rationally prejudiced age.

S.'s first and most enduring literary success was a small volume, *Elegiac Sonnets and Other Essays* (1784), that she published at her own expense, hoping to earn a profit. Her financial motivation was both genuine and psychological, for her wastrel husband had been put in debtors' prison and it was legally impossible for her to collect either his inheritance or her own. Writing seemed the only career open to a woman who wished to support many children (she bore twelve) and still retain a semblance of rural gentility. *Elegiac Sonnets* was a novelty for an audience unaccustomed to Romantic poetry and to a form that had been, with a few random exceptions, out of style for nearly a century, and it was only after S.'s death that the market for the book began to dwindle. By that time Coleridge and Wordsworth's "experimental" *Lyrical Ballads* had been published, with their careful perfection of the technique of transmitting a "true feeling for rural Nature" finally overshadowing S.'s tentative explorations of the revolutionary mode.

The *Emigrants* (1793), a two-volume narrative poem, presents much of the same tone of melancholy that the sonnets do within the context of a politically liberal depiction of the French Revolution. The power of S.'s literary innovations and her sympathies, however, is weakened by descents into domestic and legal complaints, which were real enough but hardly suited to the grandeur of her subject. *Beach Head, with Other Poems* (1807) was published posthumously, and although it contains moments of lovely, almost transcendental identification of the self with Nature, it, like *The Emigrants*, was not a popular success.

Although S. hoped her future reputation would rest upon her poetry, it is for her novels that she is best remembered. Her translations had only limited appeal, and she had found accomplishing them tedious if not (as with *Manon Lescaut*) socially dangerous. Novel writing offered her a way to earn a living that was only slightly less refined than poetry, and its domestic content was more appropriate to the concerns that constantly interrupted her. Four years after *Elegiac Sonnets* she published her first novel, *Emmeline*. Within the following nine years she wrote and published eight more novels, making her average annual production one three-, four-, or five-volume novel. Unlike Fanny Burney, Elizabeth Inchbald, and Ann Radcliffe, S. never received more than £50 a volume, and she never at any time found writing novels more artistically rewarding than writing poetry. Despite her resentment at having to write, S. continued with the novels and later with the even-less-satisfying children's books, for each was popular enough when new to enable her to support the ever-increasing demands of her children and grandchildren and to challenge the circumstances that had once made her dependent upon a husband who was at his best unreliable and at his worst physically cruel.

Almost from the beginning S.'s novels have been criticized for their sentimentality and self-indulgent complaining. Often the accusations have been just, for the novels were written in haste and they exploited her carefully cultivated reputation as a "pathetic poetess." In the novels as in the poetry, however, there is evidence of a genuinely innovative mind at work. The romantic mood of the poetry is carried over into the novels, and it often led the contemporary reader into new territories of genre and even feminism. *The Old Manor House* (1793), S.'s best novel, contains carefully structured scenes of Gothic terror and wilderness sublimity. *Desmond* (1792), her most severely criticized, uses the French Revolution not only to advance the plot and define the characters but to serve as a macrocosm of the chaos that arises out of unnatural patriarchal systems. S.'s often-overlooked feminist assertion can best be seen not in her stereotypically melancholy heroines but in her skillfully wrought, individually heroic minor characters, most notably the autobiographical Mrs. Stafford of *Emmeline* and Mrs. Denzil of *The Banished Man* (1794).

Through the sad voice of her poetry and through thinly disguised fictionalizations of her life's hardships, S. encouraged her public to believe in her mournful authorial persona. Her background of solitary leisure was prized for the opportunity it gave to develop a "superior understanding," but quite early in life she lost the right to function in such a refined milieu. She moved in her maturity in a society in which it was rarely respectable for a woman to go out into the world to earn a living, but she was forced by the circumstances of a large and almost completely irresponsible family to do just that. Her only possible solution to the problem offered a synthesis of old and current values and gave her a temporary opportunity for fame. Writing in a melancholy mood perhaps justified her unmerited fall from grace at the same time it saved her family from absolute poverty but daring to attack the conventions of the day from any stronger position would have meant courting economic and social disaster. When other writers, more secure in their economic, social, and literary positions than S. could ever be, arrived upon the scene and expanded her narrow base of literary perspective, she was relegated to the ranks of minor and then forgotten writers. One of her greatest admirers, William Wordsworth, perhaps best described her place in literature when he called her "a lady to whom English verse is under greater obligations than is likely to be either acknowledged or remembered."

WORKS: *Elegiac Sonnets, and Other Essays* (1784; expanded to two volumes in 1797; further expanded through 1811). English translation of Abbe Prevost's *Manon Lescaut* (1786). *The Romance of Real Life* (1787; a translation from Gayot de Pitival's *Causes Celebres*). *Emmeline, The Orphan of the Castle* (1788). *Ethelinde, or the Recluse of the Lake* (1789). *Celestina. A Novel* (1791). *Desmond. A Novel* (1792). *The Old Manor House* (1793). *The Emi-*

grants, a Poem, in Two Books (1793). The Wanderings of Warwick (1794). The Banished Man. A Novel (1794). Rural Walks: in Dialogues; Intended for the Use of Young Persons (1795). Montalbert, A Novel (1795). A Narrative of the Loss of the Catherine, Venus and Piedmont Transports (1796). Rambles Farther: a Continuation of Rural Walks (1796). Marchmont, A Novel (1796). Minor Morals, Interspersed with Sketches of Natural History, Historical Anecdotes and Original Stories (1798). The Young Philosopher: A Novel (1798). The Letters of a Solitary Wanderer: Containing Narratives of Various Description (1802). Conversations Introducing Poetry: Chiefly on Subjects of Natural History. For the Use of Children and Young Persons (1804). History of England, from the Earliest Records to the Peace of Amiens, in a Series of Letters to a Young Lady at School, Vol. I & II (1806). Beach Head: with Other Poems (1807). The Natural History of Birds, Intended Chiefly for Young Persons (1807).

BIBLIOGRAPHY: Bowstead, D. Fetter'd or Free? British Women Novelists, 1670-1815, ed. M.A. Schofield and C. Macheski (1986). Ehrenpreis, A.H. Introductions to modern editions of The Old Manor House (1969) and Emmeline (1971). Foster, R. PMLA (1928). Hilbish, F. Charlotte Smith: Poet and Novelist (1941). Kavanaugh, J. English Women of Letters: Biographical Sketches (1863). Phillips, R. Public Characters (1798-1809). Rogers, K.M., ed. Before Their Time: Six Women Writers of the Eighteenth Century (1979). Scott, W. Lives of the Novelists (1905). Tompkins, J.M.S. The Popular Novel In England 1770-1800 (1932).

Susan Hastings

Stevie Smith
(pseudonym of Florence Margaret Smith)

BORN: 20 September 1902, Hull, Yorkshire.
DIED: 7 March 1971, London.
DAUGHTER OF: Charles and Ethel Spear Smith.

Author of whimsical, deceptively simple verse, S. also wrote three novels, ten short stories, a BBC radio play, and book reviews. She was given the nickname "Stevie," which she used for all her published work, for her resemblance to a small, popular jockey. S. and her older sister were raised by their mother and their aunt and by the aunt alone after the mother's death during S.'s sixteenth year. Throughout her adult life, S. made her home with her aunt in a northern suburb of London, Palmers Green. Disguised under the names "Bottle Green" and "Syler's Green," Palmers Green became the setting for fiction and essays in which S. comments wryly on the community's "fairly harmless snobbery" and describes nostalgically the woods she and her older sister explored as children. She attended Palmers Green High School and North London Collegiate School for Girls, where the subjects she studied were those studied in boys' schools—an unorthodox curriculum that she appreciated. At school, she learned to love the musical rhythms of the poems she memorized, and she often built her own poetry upon quantitative musical measures. For thirty years she worked as a secretary for two London magazine publishers, employment which gave her time to write poetry, fiction, and book reviews. Her literary reputation grew slowly from 1936 until 1957, when the publication of Not Waving but Drowning won her wider critical acclaim. Her lively, humorous letters to other writers, friends, and editors reveal her intelligence as witty, whimsical, serious, philosophical, and not morbid, though in many of her poems she considers death a welcome guest. When she died of a brain tumor in 1971, she had won a popular audience for her poems, which she read on BBC radio programs. The 1975 publication of her Collected Poems was welcomed with appreciative reviews, and a movie, Stevie, based on a play by Hugh Whitemore and starring Glenda Jackson, appeared in 1978.

Placing herself within a cultural tradition and also challenging its values, S. wrote several poems in which she imaginatively recreates the voice of legendary and literary characters. "I Had a Dream I Was Helen of Troy" offers a critique of the simpering, thoughtless, and inconsistent character in Homer's Iliad. "The Last Turn of the Screw" retells Henry James's tale from the perspective of the not-so-innocent child Miles. Other poems revise the characters of Hamlet's mother Gertrude and her new husband Claudius, of Dido, of Persephone, of Antigone, and of Phaedra (in which she criticizes Marcel Proust's interpretation of Jean Racine's tragic heroine).

In metaphysical poems both serious and comic in tone, she questions Christian doctrine. "How Cruel Is the Story of Eve" explores the traditional interpretation of women as seducers, responsible for original sin. Her speaker notes that the legend has been employed to "give blame to women most/And most punishment." In

SMITH

another poem, "How Do You See," she questions the definitions given for the "Holy Spirit," adopting a style that echoes and mocks a catechism. The poem asks, quite seriously, whether Christianity may not have played out its role in human history. After an allusion to the armed nations ready to destroy each other, she concludes grimly "we shall kill everybody."

S.'s novels are set during times of war, espionage, betrayal, and social unease, but she employs a narrator who breezes through these crises with a crooked smile and an acid tongue. Commenting on England's possible response to the Italian invasion of Abyssinia, the narrator in *Over the Frontier* (1936) notes of herself: "we do not so much like the peace-at-any-price people who go about today to apologize for England and to pretend that she hasn't really got so much of the earth's surface, it only looks that way on these jingo maps. . . . For if we are not nowadays the conquerors and pioneers, we are at least the beneficiaries under empire, and at least and basest we have cheap sugar." She deflates the self-righteous polemic of imperialists and pacifists, then knocks out from under herself any pretentious stand of moral superiority. Her novels sparkle with political insights that are human and funny.

Most critics focus on her nonsense verse, her poems built upon odd and charming patterns of sound. Although they share with children's nursery rhymes certain simple aural pleasures, these poems are only superficially simple in tone and attitude. (The doodling drawings which S. attached to her published poems also suggest a simplicity in attitude, but her cartoons work, as James Thurber's do, upon the fantasies and candid dream images of the unconscious.) Like T.S. Eliot, S. could use chiming rhymes for whimsical satire. Her "The Dedicated Water Bull and the Water Maid," written, her subtitle suggests, in response to a performance of Beethoven's Sonata in F, Opus 17, for Horn and Piano, wittily mocks self-important pomposity: "O I am holy, oh I am plump." Her "The Singing Cat" seems at first a transparent description of an amusing, inconsequential incident in a commuter train but develops a mild critique of those who transform others' pain into their own aesthetic pleasure.

S.'s subtitles often suggest that her verses were prompted by a brief experience, but the poems are not lightly occasional. After reading two paragraphs in a newspaper, she wrote "Valuable," which explores the complex moral and psychological situation of young girls who bear illegitimate babies because they lack a sense of their own worth. An unsympathetic speaker begins the poem in a self-righteous and superior tone of voice, but that stance is challenged both by the image of a panther in a cage and by the voice of one of the young girls, who protests that her low self-esteem merely reflects the community's evaluation of her. S.'s poem, hardly sentimental, implies that the illegitimate babies are the mutual responsibility of society and individuals.

By creating a fiercely comic persona for her poems, fiction, and essays, S. gave voice to her serious questions on Christian doctrine, contemporary morality, the abuse of power, and the literary tradition. In her eccentric voice, she ridiculed the perfect idiocy of much human behavior while revealing her compassion for fellow creatures caged in a prison.

WORKS: *Novel on Yellow Paper* (1936; retitled *Work It Out for Yourself,* 1969). *A Good Time Was Had by All* (1937). *Over the Frontier* (1938). *Tender Only to One* (1938). *Mother, What Is Man?* (1942). *The Holiday* (1949). *Harold's Leap* (1950). *Not Waving but Drowning* (1957). *Some Are More Human Than Others: Sketchbook by Stevie Smith* (1958). *Selected Poems* (1962). *The Frog Prince and Other Poems* (1966). *The Best Beast* (1969). *Two in One* (includes *Selected Poems* and *The Frog Prince,* 1971). *Scorpions and Other Poems* (1972). *Collected Poems* (1975). *Me Again: Uncollected Writings of Stevie Smith* (1981).

BIBLIOGRAPHY: Barbera, J., and W. McBrien, "Introduction," *Me Again: Uncollected Writings of Stevie Smith* (1981). Barbera, J., and W. McBrien, *Stevie: A Biography of Stevie Smith* (1987). Dick, K. *Ivy & Stevie: Ivy Compton-Burnett and Stevie Smith: Conversations and Reflections* (1971). Rankin, A.C. *The Poetry of Stevie Smith—"Little Girl Lost"* (1985).

For articles in reference works, see: *CA. CLC. MBL.*

Other references: *Antiquarian Bookman* (24 June 1971). *Books & Bookmen* (June 1971). Enright, D.J. *Man Is an Onion* (1972). *Poetry* (August 1958, March 1965, and December 1976). Sergeant, H., *Poetry Review* (Spring 1967). *TLS* (14 July 1972).

Judith L. Johnston

420

Mary Somerville

BORN: 26 December 1780, Jedburgh Manse, Burntisland, Scotland.
DIED: 29 November 1872, Naples.
DAUGHTER OF: Admiral Sir William Fairfax and Miss Charters.
MARRIED: Captain Samuel Grieg, 1804; Dr. William Somerville, 1812.

A self-taught mathematician, S. wrote books on physical science, mathematics, and astronomy. S.'s youth was spent in Scotland where she received fitful spurts of education in writing, reading, needlework, cooking, drawing, dancing, and playing the piano but was discouraged from pursuing any formal education or even home-study unrelated to domestic concerns. Her love of nature and her scientific curiosity were viewed as inappropriate, eccentric, and dangerous by her family. Her thirst for knowledge therefore prompted surreptitious reading and study; she quietly taught herself Latin and began to learn about astronomy. Upon seeing algebraic symbols in a monthly magazine, she developed a strong ambition to learn higher mathematics. She studied Euclid, other basic texts, and taught herself Greek.

At the age of twenty-four she married a distantly related cousin, Captain Samuel Grieg, who became Russian consul in London. Grieg, like most of S.'s family, disparaged her studies and ambitions, but S. persevered, teaching herself plane and spherical trigonometry, conic sections, and some astronomy. The couple had two children, one of whom died while very young, and three years after they were married Grieg died.

Having solved an algebraic problem in a mathematical journal, S. received a silver medal. Wallace, the editor of the journal and later professor of mathematics of Edinburgh University, encouraged S. and helped her select books for a small library. At the age of thirty-three, with independent means, she had accumulated the sought-after books and was openly able to pursue her interests.

In 1812, she married another cousin, Dr. William Somerville, whose attitude toward her studies was one of admiration and encouragement. A true companion, Somerville was an excellent classicist and shared many of S.'s scientific interests, including minerology and geology, and assisted her studies in many ways. They lived in Edinburgh for the first years of their marriage, Somerville becoming the head of Army Medical Department of Scotland, then moving to Hanover Square, London, when he was appointed a member of the Army Medical Board in 1816. In London, S. attended lectures at the Royal Institution where she met many of the leading thinkers and scientists of the day. On a visit to Paris, the Marquis de la Place, impressed with S.'s erudition, gave her an inscribed copy of the *Système du Monde*. He later said that S. was the only woman who understood his work. Back in London, S. met, among others, Maria Edgeworth, who became a close friend.

In 1826, she presented her paper, "The Magnetic Properties of the Violet Rays of the Solar Spectrum," to the Royal Society. Although the theory presented in this paper was subsequently refuted by researches of Moser and Ries, the work was nonetheless considered original, speculative, and ingenious and brought her recognition.

She was then asked to write a popularized English version of la Place's *Le Mècanique Céleste*. The publication of this book, titled *Celestial Mechanism of the Heavens* (1831), placed her among the first rank of scientific writers. It was immediately adopted as a textbook at Oxford—a university that at that time did not admit women. She was elected honorary member of several British and foreign learned societies, including the Royal Astronomical Society, which elected S. and Caroline Herschel at the same time, and her bust, executed by Chantrey, was placed in the Great Hall of the Royal Society. Her next book, *On The Connexion of the Physical Sciences* (1834), a summary of research into physical phenomena, went through nine editions and several revisions and was translated into German and Italian; a pirated edition was printed in the United States. A sentence in the 1842 edition is credited by John Couch Adams (1767–1848) with sparking the calculations from which he deduced the orbit of Neptune.

S. was elected honorary member of the Royal Academy of Dublin (1834), of the Sociète de Physique et d'Histoire Naturelle (Geneva 1834), and of the British Philosophical Institution (c. 1835). In 1835, she was elected Honorary Member of the Royal Astronomical Society, which honored S. and Caroline Herschel—their first female members— at the same time. Also in that year she wrote a lengthy essay on comets for *Quarterly Review*. In 1836, her paper "Experiments on the Transmission of Chemical Rays of the Solar Spectrum Across Different Media" appeared in *Comptes Rendus Hebdomadaires des Séances de L'Académie des Sciences*. While in London, she was asked by Lady Byron to direct the mathematical studies of her daughter, Ada Byron (later Lady Lovelace). She was further honored by being made recipient of a lifelong pension of £200, later raised to £300.

Although the Somervilles moved to Italy in 1838 because of her husband's failing health, S. continued to write important scientific works and to conduct scientific experiments on the solar spectrum and the juices of plants. Her *Physical Geography*, on which she worked for many years, was published in 1859 and went through seven subsequent editions. A year later, when her husband died, S. remained in Italy. In 1869, when she was 89, she published *Molecular and Microscopic Science*, a summary of the most recent discoveries in chemistry and physics. In that year she was the recipient of the first gold medal awarded by the Italian Geographical Society as well as the Victoria gold medal of the Royal Geographical Society. She returned to pure mathematics late in life, working until her death on *Theory of Differences*. She died within a month of her ninety-second birthday and was buried at the English Campo Santo at Naples.

S. wrote on scientific and astronomical matters with simplicity and power, explaining complicated subjects with an unpretentious and energetic clarity so that even those unfamiliar with the subject could absorb difficult principles. Her prefaces to her works were published separately for the general public, while the actual works were used as textbooks for university students and mathematics scholars. Her *Personal Recollections*, friendly and engaging, resonates with her enthusiasm for experimentation and the excitement of discovery. She also recounts many customs of Scotland during her girlhood as well as good-naturedly detailing her many frustrations at not being allowed to pursue learning. Interested in promoting education for women, her name headed the Women's Suffrage petition of 1868. She was commemorated after her death in the foundation of Somerville College, Oxford, and in the Mary Somerville scholarship for women in mathematics. A crayon portrait of her which James Swinton executed in 1848 hangs in the National Portrait Gallery, and a copy of the bust made by Lawrence Macdonald in 1844 at Rome was presented to the National Portrait Gallery in Scotland. Her bust adorns not only the Great Hall of the Royal Society but also graces a room in the Royal Institution.

WORKS: *The Mechanism of the Heavens* (1831). *A Preliminary Dissertation on the Mechanism of the Heavens* (1832). *On The Connexion of the Physical Sciences* (1834). *Physical Geography* (1848). *Molecular and Microscopic Science* (1869). *Personal Recollections, From Early Life to Old Age of Mary Somerville with Selections from her Correspondence* by her daughter, Martha Charters Somerville (1873).

BIBLIOGRAPHY: Patterson, E.C. *British Journal for the History of Science* (1969). Patterson, E.C. *Bodleian Library Record* (1970). Patterson, E.C. *Mary Somerville and the Cultivation of Science 1815–1840* (1983). Patterson, E.C. *Proceedings of the American Philosophical Society* (1974). *Personal Recollections, From Early Life to Old Age of Mary Somerville with Selections from Her Correspondence* by her daughter, Martha Somerville (1873). Tabor, M.E. *Pioneer Women*, fourth series (1933). Walford, L.B. *Four Biographies from "Blackwood"* (1888). Wilson, M. *Jane Austen and Some Contemporaries* (1938).

For articles in reference works, see: *Dictionary of Men and Women in the Sciences. DNB.*

Gale Sigal

Somerville and Ross (pseudonyms)

Edith Oenone Somerville

BORN: 2 May 1858, Corfu.
DIED: 8 October 1949, Castle Townshend, Ireland.
DAUGHTER OF: Thomas and Adelaide Coghill Somerville.
WROTE UNDER: Geilles Herring, Viva Graham, Edith OE. Somerville.

Violet Florence Martin

BORN: 11 June 1862, Ross House, County Galway, Ireland.
DIED: 21 December 1915, Cork, Ireland.
DAUGHTER OF: James and Anna Selina Fox Martin.
WROTE UNDER: Martin Ross.

Writing during the time of the Irish Literary Revival, S. and R. depicted Ireland not mythically but realistically, evoking the era when changes in the Land Laws brought about the end of the Anglo-Irish Ascendancy.

Second cousins and members of prominent English families that had established themselves in Ireland in the twelfth and sixteenth centuries, S. and R. grew up in "big houses," and S. was to spend much of her energy trying to find money to maintain the Somerville House and her own pack of hounds, even introducing and successfully raising Friesian cattle in Ireland. When R. met her in 1886, S. had already established herself as a professional illustrator, studying art in Paris with Délécluse and Colarossi and sketching Pasteur in his clinic. The two then began a literary collaboration that was so successful that critics have found it almost impossible to separate their styles and that continued even after R.'s death, with S. asserting that she remained in spiritual communication with her partner and signing both their names to the works she published.

Following in the tradition of Maria Edgeworth, a close friend of S. and R.'s great-grandmother, the two were particularly interested in language and dialect, first working together on *The Buddh Dictionary*, a collection of phrases used by S.'s family, and throughout their lives collecting instances of the Irish use of English. Yeats praised the accuracy of the reported Irish speech in their work. These details of Irish life were the most effective aspect of S. and R.'s first novels, *An Irish Cousin* (1889) and *Naboth's Vineyard* (1891), both of which are burdened with gothic and melodramatic plot devices. *The Real Charlotte* (1894) was S. and R.'s most effective novel and was honored as a World Classic by Oxford University Press in 1948. Set against the background of Anglo-Irish society as portrayed through the decaying Dysart family, it focuses particularly on two women, Francie, an uneducated but beautiful lower-class girl, and Charlotte, an unattractive, driven middle-class woman who is successful in her business dealings but fails in her personal relations. The novel, like many of S. and R.'s, is a study in frustrated desire and has been compared favorably with Austen's novels, George Eliot's *Middlemarch*, and Balzac's *Cousine Bette*. S. and R.'s subsequent novel, *The Silver Fox* (1897), was less successful, perhaps because it deals so intensely with Irish mysticism.

In order to support themselves, S. and R. also wrote, at the same time as their novels, a series of comic sketches of their travels through Ireland and Europe, *Through Connemara in a Governess Cart* (1893), *In the Vine Country* (1893), *Beggars on Horse-back* (1895), and *Stray-Aways* (1920). Many of these were first published in periodicals, as were the Irish R.M. stories, which first appeared in the *Badminton Magazine* in October 1898. S. and R.'s agent, J.B. Pinker, who also worked for Henry James and Arnold Bennett, suggested they work on a series of comic stories about hunting which led to the publication of *Some Experiences of an Irish R.M.* (1899). This work, depicting the adventures of a Resident Magistrate, Major Sinclair Yeates, trying to cope with the Irish peasants and his crafty landlord, Flurry Knox, brought its authors international fame. From then until R.'s death, the pair continued to write mainly hunting stories, *All on the Irish Shore* (1903), articles in *Some Irish Yesterdays* (1906), and a hunting novel, *Dan Russel the Fox* (1911).

After R.'s death, with the worsening situation in Ireland, S. wrote a series of novels that dwelt more specifically, though it had always been a concern of theirs, with the social and political problems of Ireland, particularly with how sectarianism was undermining Irish life. In *Mount Music* (1919), S. writes about religious schisms, in *An Enthusiast* (1921) about political ones. And in *The Big House*

at Inver (1925), S. writes a novel, thought to be as effective as *The Real Charlotte*, about the decay and collapse of the "big houses" in Ireland, with the house modeled on Ross House, R.'s ancestral home.

S. and R. are interesting because, as Lord Dunsany said of the Irish R.M. stories, readers can get "more of Ireland from that book than from anything I can tell them" and because of the relation between the two women. As S. puts it, "the outstanding fact . . . among women who live by their brains, is friendship. A profound friendship that extends through every phase and aspect of life, intellectual, social and pecuniary."

WORKS: S. *The Kerry Recruit* (1889). S. as Geilles Herring and R. *An Irish Cousin* (1889). S. and R. *Naboth's Vineyard* (1891). S. and R. *In the Vine Country* (1893). S. and R. *Through Connemara in a Governess Cart* (1893). S. and R. *The Real Charlotte* (1894). R. and S. *Beggars on Horseback* (1895). R. and S. *The Silver Fox* (1898). S. and R. *Some Experiences of an Irish R.M.* (1899). R. and S. *A Patrick's Day Hunt* (1902). S. and R. *All on the Irish Shore* (1903). S. *Slipper's ABC of Fox Hunting* (1903). S. and R. *Some Irish Yesterdays* (1906). S. and R. *Further Experiences of an Irish R.M.* (1908). S. and R. *Dan Russel the Fox* (1911). S. *The Story of the Discontented Little Elephant* (1912). S. and R. *In Mr. Knox's Country* (1915). S. and (nominally) R. *Irish Memories* (1917). S. and (nominally) R. *Mount Music* (1919). S. and R. *Stray-Aways* (1920). S. *An Enthusiast* (1921). S. and (nominally) R. *Wheel-Tracks* (1923). S. and (nominally) R. *The Big House of Inver* (1925). S. and (nominally) R. *French Leave* (1928). S. *The States Through Irish Eyes* (1930). S. and (nominally) R. *An Incorruptible Irishman* (1932). S. and (nominally) R. *The Smile and the Tear* (1933). S. and (nominally) R. *The Sweet Cry of Hounds* (1936). S. and (nominally) R. *Sarah's Youth* (1938). S. and Boyle Townsend Somerville. *Records of the Somerville Family of Castlehaven and Drishane from 1174 to 1940* (1940). S. and (nominally) R. *Motions in Garrison* (1941). S. and (nominally) R. *Happy Days!* (1946). S. and (nominally) R. *Maria and Some Other Dogs* (1949).

BIBLIOGRAPHY: Collis, M. *Somerville and Ross: A Biography* (1968). Cronin, J. *Somerville and Ross* (1972). Cummins, G. *Dr. E. O.E. Somerville: A Biography* (contains R. Vaughan's "The First Editions of Edith Ocnone Somerville and Violet Florence Martin," 1952). Hudson, E. ed. *A Bibliography of the First Editions of the Works of E. OE. Somerville and Martin Ross* (1942). Institute of Irish Studies, The Queen's University, Belfast. *Somerville and Ross: A Symposium* (1969). Lewis, G. *Somerville and Ross: The World of the Irish R.M.* (1985). Lucas, E.V. *Cloud and Silver* (1916). O'Brien, C.C. *Writers and Politics* (1965). Powell, V. *The Irish Cousins* (1970). Pritchett, V.S. *The Living Novel* (1946). Robinson, H. *Somerville and Ross: A Critical Appreciation* (contains bibliography of periodical articles by S. and R., 1980). Williams, O. *Some Great English Novels* (1926).

For articles in reference works, see: *DIL. DNB. NCBEL.*

Other references: *Ariel* (1970, 1972). *CJIS* (1985). *EI* (1967, 1968, 1982). *Hermathena* (1952). *Kenyon* (1966). *NCF* (1951). *QR* (1913).

Elsie B. Michie

Joanna Southcott

BORN: 25 April 1750, Devonshire.
DIED: 27 December 1814, London.
DAUGHTER OF: William and Hannah Southcott.

Prophet, priestess, and mystic, S. wrote and published 65 religious pamphlets from 1792 to 1814 and was the center of a large religious movement known as the Southcottians, which some have estimated as having up to 100,000 members.

Born the fourth daughter of an unsuccessful farmer, S. sought employment as domestic servant; she rejected numerous marriage proposals from farmers' sons, determined to remain single. During the 1790s, she wrote down her prophecies predicting famine that she felt was caused by failure to take her other prophecies seriously. In 1801, she published her first work, *The Strange Effects of Faith*, financed by her own savings. It attracted a small group of followers, mostly women and members of the working class but also included several Anglican ministers and the engraver William Sharp. S. believed that she heard the Lord's voice and received visions that permitted her to distribute a commonplace seal and that the millenium was exclusively available for her followers, "the sealed people." In 1802, S. visited London, and in 1803 she toured the North and West. From 1804 to 1814, S. lived in London in the house of the wealthy Jane Townely who was her patron and secretary. In 1809, the movement began to decline when the witch and murderess Mary Bateman was associated with a Yorkshire congregation, but it achieved a second impetus in 1814, when S., then sixty-four, promised to give birth to the son of God. Of the nine doctors who examined her, six declared that she was pregnant, and she developed all the signs of pregnancy. At the time of the expected birth, she suddenly died; an autopsy performed on her body revealed no pregnancy. After her death, the movement did not die out but persisted until the end of the nineteenth century. In the early twentieth century, Alice Seymour reissued Southcott's writings, and there is still a small body of followers today.

Southcott's work attracted commentators who are either fervent defenders or detractors. Among her contemporaries, Keats referred to her as a nuisance, Southey referred to her as a freak, and Byron alludes to her failure to give birth to the son of God in attacking Wordsworth in *Don Juan*. Her writing was attacked for alleged vulgarity and indecent allusions. Recent criticism has attempted to be more objective, seeing S. and her radical religious fervor as part of Romanticism.

Critics have pointed out that the movement appealed strongly to women since S. believed that just as a woman had been responsible for the Fall, so she would be for the salvation. In *Strange Effects of Faith*, she asks, "Is it a new thing for a Woman to deliver her people? Did not Esther do it? Did not Judith do it?" The movement also appealed to the working classes' adjustments to economic, agricultural, and military upheavals. Critics have pointed out, however, that her prophecies did not provoke her followers toward political action but instead emphasized personal salvation and thus was in the Methodist tradition.

S. expected Methodist support but was rejected by the Exeter Methodist community and grew disillusioned. Critics see *Divine and Spiritual Communications* as one of her rare polemical works in which she accuses the Methodists of being Calvinistic. She was a devout member of the Church of England, and most of her efforts were directed at persuading individual clergymen and bishops to reexamine her prophecies. She believed that all religious sects were to be united with the Church of England. Her purpose was not to form a competing sect, but her followers eventually founded their own chapels and named them after her. Just as S. perceived herself as a mere vehicle of God, so she perceived her writings; they were not intended for any aesthetic purpose but to spread her message. Critics have noted that her style is a mixture of the mystical and the literal in which biblical allusions combine with autobiographical references. Her handwriting is often illegible, giving the sense of being written in a moment of mystical revelation. Later, her pamphlets had to be dictated to her secretary. The pamphlets, however, were not the only way that S. reached her audience; her actions were widely commented on and debated in the press so that even those who never read any of her pamphlets were aware of her beliefs and activities. Ironically, S. never wanted herself to be the focus of the movement but saw herself as a mere intermediary. Although she is often associated with and admired Richard Brothers, a religious leader who declared himself King of the Hebrews and Nephew of God, S. felt that he succumbed to moral pride.

Today, S. is rarely if ever read, but she provides an interesting footnote to the literary, religious, and social history of early nineteenth-century England.

WORKS: *The Strange Effects of Faith* (1801). *A Continuation of the Prophecies* (1802). *Dispute Between the Woman and the Powers of Darkness* (1802). *Answer of the Lord to the Powers of Darkness* (1802). *Books of Sealed Prophecies* (unknown date). *Second Book of Visions* (1803). *A Word in Season* (1803). *A Word to the Wise* (1803). *Divine and Spiritual Communication* (1803). *Sound an Alarm in My Holy Mountain* (1804). *A Warning to the World* (1804). *On the Prayers for the Fast Day* (1804). *Letters on Various Subjects* (1804). *Copies and Parts of Copies* (1804). *Letters and Communications* (1804). *The Trial of Joanna Southcott* (1804). *Answer to Garrett's Book* (1805). *Answer to the Five Charges in the Leeds Mercury* (1805). *True Explanation of the Bible* (1805). *Explanation of the Parables* (1805). *Kingdom of Christ Is at Hand* (date unknown). *Answer to Rev. Foley* (1805). *Controversy with Elias Carpenter* (1805). *An Answer to the World* (1806). *Full Assurance That the Kingdom of Heaven Is at Hand* (1806). *The Long Wished for Revolution* (1806). *Answer to Mr. Brother's Book* (1806). *Caution and Instruction to the Sealed* (1807). *An Account of the Trials on the Bills of Exchange* (1807). *Answer to a Sermon by Mr. Smith* (1808). *Answer to False Doctrines* (1808). *True Explanation of the Bible*, Part VII (1809). *A True Picture of the World* (1809). *Controversy of the Spirit* (1811). *An Answer to Thomas Paine* (1812). *The Books of Wonders* (1813-1814). *Prophecies Announcing the Birth of the Prince of Peace* (1814).

BIBLIOGRAPHY: Harrison, J.F.C. *Quest for a New Moral World* (1969). Hopkins, J.K. *A Woman to Deliver Her People* (1982). Johnson, D.A. *Women in English Religion* (1982). Thompson, E.P. *Rise of the English Working Class* (1966).

For articles in reference works, see: *Catalogue of the Joanna Southcott Collection at the University of Texas*, ed. E.P. Wright (1969). *DNB. Europa.*

Tony Giffone

Muriel Spark

BORN: 1 February 1918, Edinburgh.
DAUGHTER OF: Bernard Camberg and Sarah Elizabeth Maud Uezzell.
MARRIED: S.O. Spark, 1938.

The wit and style of S.'s novels and short stories express vividly the many themes present in her work. The various genres in which she works range from translations of Horace, Catullus, and Guillaume Apollinaire to radio plays (*Voices at Play*, 1961), stage plays (*Doctors of Philosophy*, 1963), essays, literary criticism, children's stories, biography, poetry, short stories, and novels. Her sense of the comic is visible throughout her work although it is used most often to express serious themes. She is a genius at describing the surfaces of social situations in a way that is anything but flippant.

S. was born to a Presbyterian mother and a Jewish father. Educated at James Gillespie's Girls School, a Protestant school in Edinburgh, she started learning classical languages at the age of seven. She completed her schooling in 1936 and left the following year for Africa, living in Rhodesia and South Africa until 1944. While in Africa she married S.O. Spark, an Englishman, but soon after the birth of their son the marriage was dissolved. Returning to wartime London, S. worked in the Political Intelligence Department of the British Foreign Office until the war was over.

Her first writing job was on the staff of the *Argentor*, a jeweler's trade magazine, but she also worked as editor of *The Poetry Review* for two years as well as put out two issues of her own journal, *Forum*, and she also worked as a part-time editor at a publisher. During this time her main literary interests developed in the direction of poetry and criticism; she had been publishing her poetry since 1941 and was on the fringe of London's literary bohemia. Her poems in *The Fanfarlo and Other Verses* (1952) are of many types, the title poem influenced heavily by the Scottish border ballad form.

From 1950 to 1957 her attention was focussed mainly on non-fictional work. She edited *The Brontë Letters* (1954) and, with Derek Stanford—her literary partner until 1957 and friend of many years who wrote a study of her entitled *Muriel Spark: A Biographical and Critical Study* (1963)—edited the *Letters of John Henry Newman* (1957) and those of Mary Wollstonecraft Shelley in *My Best Mary: The Selected Letters of Mary Wollstonecraft Shelley* (1953) as well as *Tribute to Wordsworth: A Miscellany of Opinion for the Centenary of the Poet's Death* (1950). She concentrated at this time on literary criticism, producing such diverse volumes as *Emily Brontë: Her Life and Work* (1953)—she wrote the biographical first section of this work and Stanford the critical second section—*John Masefield* (1953), and *Child of Light: A Reassessment of Mary Wollstonecraft Shelley* (1951).

S. turned seriously to fiction only after winning a short story contest sponsored by *The Observer* in 1951 with her short story "The Seraph and the Zambesi." Macmillan, interested in her work, invited her to try novel-writing, and she responded (with the additional help of a stipend from Graham Greene) with *The Comforters* in 1957, an experimental work, and the first of her many critically well-received novels. Her attitude toward the novel form has always been mistrustful. Commenting on her first novel, Spark explained that she wrote it in order to try out the form: "So I wrote a novel to work out the technique first, to sort of make it all right with myself to write a novel at all—a novel about writing a novel."

A major influence on S.'s life and her work was her conversion to Catholicism in 1954. "All my best work has come since then," reports Spark. Religion, as well as the self-conscious craft of novel-writing itself, is a major theme in her work; in *The Comforters*, for example, she heavily criticizes "professional" Catholics. Her second novel, *Robinson* (1958), is an adventure story and allegory, and her third, *Memento Mori* (1959), was adapted for the London stage in 1964.

The first collection of her short stories, *The Go-Away Bird and Other Stories* (1958), brought together much of the short fiction S. had been placing in a variety of publications. Her further stories and poems were collected in separate volumes in 1967, including many which were first published in the *New Yorker*. Her stories reveal this talented writer's range, which moves easily from comedy and fantasy ("Miss Pinkerton's Apocalypse") to tragic experience ("Bang-Bang You're Dead"), to laying open, as delicately as a fine surgeon, the characteristic hypocrisy of human beings ("The Black Madonna").

Probably her best-known work, *The Prime of Miss Jean Brodie* (1961) is the story of the influence of an unusually romantic teacher on her students in a girls' school in Edinburgh. Like many of S.'s works, this novel has been adapted for the stage (1964) and screen (1967) and even television (1978). Again like most of her early works, this book focuses on a small society described in accurate detail, in a detached satiric tone which is often described by critics as that of a "dandy." Partly because of the success of this novel, S. left London to live first in New York and then Rome, where she now makes her home. Along with this change in place has come a change in the tone of her novels, which are increasingly harsher and more virulent than her early work, although she is still often described as a writer of comedy. *The Abbess of Crewe: A Modern Morality Tale* (1974) is an example of a work combining these two elements. An allegory of Watergate set in a nunnery, it points out the pervasive influence of the mass media on the modern world.

S.'s work has been burdened by the insistence of traditional scholarship on labeling and categorizing any writer considered as a respectable member of the canon. Her changing styles and autobiographical bent have influenced critics who have overlooked her work on the basis of these "faults." Newer critical methods with more inclusive approaches, however, open her work to more extensive study, such as is shown by her inclusion in Judy Little's study *Comedy and the Woman Writer: Woolf, Spark, and Feminism*. Also examined recently in terms of her use of cinematic technique, psychological exploration of characters, and her quasi-detective fiction, S.'s innovative uses of time and form demand further attention.

WORKS: *Child of Light: A Reassessment of Mary Wollstonecraft Shelley* (1951). *The Fanfarlo and Other Verse* (1952). *Emily Brontë: Her Life and Work* (1953). *John Masefield* (1953). *The Comforters* (1957). *The Go-Away Bird and Other Stories* (1958). *Robinson* (1958). *Memento Mori* (1959). *The Bachelors* (1960). *The Ballad of Peckham Rye* (1960). *The Prime of Miss Jean Brodie* (1961). *Voices at Play* (1961). *The Girls of Slender Means* (1963). *Doctors of Philosophy* (1963). *The Mandelbaum Gate* (1965). *Collected Poems I* (1967). *Collected Stories I* (1967). *The Very Fine Clock* (1968). *The Public Image* (1968). *The Driver's Seat* (1970). *Not to Disturb* (1971). *The Hothouse by the East River* (1973). *The Abbess of Crewe: A Modern Morality Tale* (1974). *The Takeover* (1976). *The Only Problem* (1984). *The Stories of Muriel Spark* (1985). *Mary Shelley: A Biography* (1987).

BIBLIOGRAPHY: Bold, A., ed., *Muriel Spark: An Old Capacity for Vision* (1984). Hoyt, C.A. *Muriel Spark: The Surrealist Jane Austen* (1965). Kemp, P. *Muriel Spark* (1974). Little, J. *Comedy and the Woman Writer: Woolf, Spark, and Feminism* (1984). Malkoff, K. *Muriel Spark* (1968). Massie, A. *Muriel Spark* (1979). Richmond, V.B. *Muriel Spark* (1985). Stanford, D. *Muriel Spark: A Biographical and Critical Study* (1963). Stubbs, P. *Muriel Spark* (1973). Whittaker, R. *The Faith and Fiction of Muriel Spark* (1982).

For articles in reference works, see: CA. CB. CLC. CN. CP. DLB. DEL. MBL SUP. TCW. WA.

Other references: Kermode, F. *The House of Fiction: Interviews with Seven Novelists* (1963). Keyser, B. *Arizona Quarterly* (1976). McBrien, W. *Twentieth-Century Women Novelists* (1982), ed. T. Staley. Whittaker, R. *The Contemporary English Novel*, ed. M. Bradbury and D. Palmer (1972).

Jan Calloway

Lucy Hester Stanhope

BORN: 12 March 1776, Chevening, Kent.
DIED: 23 June 1839, Djoun, Lebanon.
DAUGHTER OF: Charles, Viscount Mahon (afterwards third Earl Stanhope) and Hester Pitt.

Noted traveler to the Levant, mystic, and eccentric, S. drew to her mountain convent in Lebanon such visitors as the fabled literary voyagers Alexander Kinglake, Alphonse de Lamartine, and Eliot Warburton. She embodied the essence of that melancholy romanticism, aristocratic disdain, and extravagant temperament that fired the imagination of European writers of the early nineteenth century. Although her reputation today is wrapped in obscurity, in her heyday her forcefulness of character and the seductiveness of her glamor convinced the Arab tribes of Syria and Palestine among whom she lived of the essential truth of her many oracular pronouncements.

As the granddaughter of the first Lord Chatham, whom she resembled, and daughter of the third Earl Stanhope, the radical politician and famed experimental scientist, she possessed a very definite sense of her station in life. She quickly came to the attention of William Pitt the Younger, her uncle, whom she served as trusted confidant and private secretary. So closely did she identify with this role, a drawing room ornament of the first order, that she wished for nothing more than to be known as "Mr. Pitt's niece." Poorly educated by the standards of the day, having no instruction in the classics when such was the norm, her irrepressible wit and acerbic tongue nevertheless left their marks. With the ascension of William Pitt to the office of Prime Minister in 1804, S. assumed enormous social importance, dispensing much patronage and arranging official banquets.

Proud, imperious, restless—a first-rate conversationalist and a fiery haranguer—she quit the Pitt household upon the Prime Minister's death. She retired to the solitude of Wales after the demise of her favorite brother, Major Stanhope, and Sir John Moore, an admirer and one of her uncle's favorite generals. Subject to fierce bouts of dejection and contempt for a society that no longer recognized her worth, she renounced Europe for the Levant in 1810. In what would later become typical for the Victorian age, she traveled in the grand manner, her entourage growing as she moved east, taxing her financial resources to the limit. After entering Jerusalem and Damascus with great style, she struck east to the famed ruins of Palmyra, the first European woman ever to do so. She finally settled in a half-ruined convent in Djoun on the slopes of Mount Lebanon, eight miles from Sidon. Such was her sway over the neighboring Druses that the most fearsome tribal chieftains and their Turkish overlords came to respect her and heed her word. Not only did she make prodigal provision for her entourage but she also provided a haven for fleeing Europeans after the battle of Navarino (1827) and compelled Ibrahim Pasha to solicit her neutrality when he sought to invade Syria. She was known to have given Pasha, the fierce lieutenant of Mehmet Ali, the Viceroy of Egypt, more trouble than all the insurgent tribes of Syria and Palestine combined.

For writers such as Kinglake, her name was almost as familiar as that of Robinson Crusoe; Kinglake, the author of *Eothen*, the most famous of English travelogues to the Near East and a minor masterpiece much beloved by Winston Churchill, wrote "both [Crusoe and S.] were associated with the spirit of adventure; but whilst the imagined life of the castaway mariner never failed to seem glaringly real, the true story of the Englishwoman ruling over the Arabs always sounded to me like a fable." Combining the charm and commanding temper of her aristocratic line and the melancholy of a stubborn recluse going to partial seed in the East, she could not help but fascinate literary travelers. Although many sought interviews with her, she was loath to grant them. Disgruntled with Europe, she barricaded herself against its influence, never consulting its books or newspapers but trusting to astrology alone. As a mimic of savage repute, she could obliterate any target of her choice. Byron, with his many affected airs, was a natural favorite, and she was known to have attributed to the Romantic poet a "curiously coxcombical lisp." Among her other distinguished victims was Lamartine, whom she found overrefined, bearing himself, in her phrase, "like the humbler sort of English dandy."

In the Levant, S. came to be regarded as a seer and was respected as such; even sober westerners, with a healthy dash of skepticism, could not escape the magnetism of her personality. For the voyager with literary ambitions, she was an obligatory sight on a journey east. Kinglake, her most famous English visitor, characterized her religious beliefs as a curious melange of the different religions of the Ottoman empire although he emphasized that she never lost her practical streak and her famed abhorrence for any display of exquisiteness.

Known by such sobriquets as "The Mad Nun of Lebanon" or such self-styled ascriptions as "Queen of the Arabs," S. died alone and abandoned in 1839, walled up in her half-ruined convent. Deeply in debt in her last years, she reacted with fury when Lord Palmerstone approved the appropriation of her pension to settle the insistent claims of her many creditors. Ever the aristocrat, she refused to accept any visitors and declined into hopeless indigence in her proud tower of isolation.

WORKS: *Memoirs of the Lady Hester Stanhope as Related by Herself in Conversations with Her Physician* (1845). *Travels of Lady Hester Stanhope, Forming the Completion of Her Memoirs Narrated by her Physician* (1846).

BIBLIOGRAPHY: Bruce, I. *The Nun of Lebanon* (1951). Haslip, J. *Lady Hester Stanhope* (1934). Kinglake, A. *Eothen* (1844). Newman, A. *The Stanhopes of Chevening* (1969). Roundell, C. *Lady Hester Stanhope* (1910). Warburton, E. *The Crescent and the Cross* (1845).

Michael Skakun

Henrietta Eliza Vaughn Palmer Stannard

BORN: 13 January 1856, York.
DIED: 13 December 1911, Putney (London).
DAUGHTER OF: The Rev. Henry Vaughn Palmer and Emily Catherine Cowling.
MARRIED: Arthur Stannard, 1884.
WROTE UNDER: John Strange Winter, Violet Whyte, H. Palmer.

S. descended from several generations of soldiers; her father had been an officer in the Royal Artillary before taking holy orders. Brought up on contemporary novels, S. was very well read by the time she entered school at age eleven. Her familiarity with army life inspired her at age eighteen to begin writing short stories and novels of military life which were at first contributed to the *Family Herald* and other journals. Her publishers urged her to adopt the masculine *nom de plume* "John Strange Winter" because "her military novels would stand a better chance as the work of a man." The rousing success of stories such as *Cavalry Life* and *Bootles' Baby* (two million copies sold in ten years) led critics such as Ruskin to describe S. as "the author to whom we owe the most finished and faithful rendering ever yet given to the character of the British soldier." Literary critics consistently refer to S. as a man until 1889, when her enormous popularity led the public to discover her true identity. Except for *The Old Love or the New* (1880), *Broken Sixpence* (1881), and *A Wavering Image* (1881), written under the pseudonym "Violet Whyte," and a few articles written under "H. Palmer," S. used John Strange Winter throughout her life.

S. wrote and published over ninety novels, with a majority set in "Blankshire." The protagonists of many novels reappear as minor figures in other novels; S. seems to enjoy cross-referencing to earlier novels. Her works are sensation novels dealing with the aristocracy and higher gentry. Whether dealing with murder (*A Born Solider* [1895]) or a young woman's secret religious crisis (*The Soul of the Bishop* [1894]), S. artfully spins a tale that keeps the reader in suspense until the last page. She frequently fascinates the reader by contrasting a character's outward social conformity with his/her internal psychological turmoil, a conflict that must have been very real to Victorian readers. While dealing with typical Victorian topics such as morality, marriage, and religion, S.'s approaches are frequently not typical of the times. S. exhibits her wide-ranging literary knowledge by beginning every chapter of a work with an appropriate quote from numerous sources, including Euripedes, Shakespeare, and Longfellow. While a moral lesson is generally intended, S.'s high-born characters are incapable of truly evil comportment.

In 1891 S. began publishing a penny weekly magazine, *Golden Gates*, subsequently changed to *Winter's Weekly*. She shows a real sense of humor, however, in her novel *Confessions of a Publisher, Being the Autobiography of Abel Drinkwater* (1892), in which she pokes fun at male publishers and their condescending attitudes toward female novelists.

In addition to her writing and domestic activities—she had one son and three daughters—S. was first President of the Writers Club, president of the Society of Women's Journalists (1901-03), and a Fellow of the Royal Society of Literature.

WORKS: *A Christmas Fairy* (1878). *The Old Love or the New* (1880). *Broken Sixpence* (1881). *Cavalry Life* (1881). *A Wandering Image* (1881). *Nell's Story* (1881). *Koosje—a Study of Dutch Life* (1883). *Regimental Legends* (1883). *A Man's Man* (1884). *Hoop-la* (1885). *In Quarters with the 25th* (1885). *A Man of Honor* (1886). *Army Society* (1886). *Army Tales—Bootles' Baby* (1886). *Mignon's Secret; the Story of a Barrack Bairn* (1886). *On March* (1886). *Pluck* (1886). *Driver Dallas* (1887). *Garrison Gossip* (1887). *Her Johnnie* (1887). *Mignon's Husband* (1887). *Sophy Carmine* (1887). *That Imp* (1887). *Beautiful Jim of the Blankshire Regiment* (1888). *Bootles Children* (1888). *Confessions of a Publisher* (1888). *Princess Sarah* (1888). *A Little Fool* (1889). *Buttons* (1889). *Harvest* (1889). *Mrs. Bob* (1889). *My Poor Dick* (1889). *Dinna Forget* (1890). *Ferrers Count* (1890). *He Went for a Soldier* (1890). *The Other Man's Wife* (1890). *Goodbye* (1891). *In Luck's*

Way (1891). *Lumley the Painter* (1891). *A Soldier's Children* (1892). *Experiences of a Lady Help* (1892). *Mere Luck* (1892). *My Geoff* (1892). *Only Human, or, Justice* (1892). *Those Girls* (1892). *Aunt Johnnie* (1893). *The Soul of the Bishop* (1893). *A Born Soldier* (1894). *A Seventh Child* (1894). *Blameless Woman* (1894). *Every Inch a Soldier* (1894). *The Stranger Woman* (1894). *A Magnificent Young Man* (1895). *I Married a Wife* (1895). *Private Tinker* (1895). *The Major's Favorite* (1895). *Crip* (1896). *Strange Story of My Life* (1896). *The Same Thing with a Difference* (1896). *The Truth Tellers* (1896). *Everybody's Favorite* (1897). *Into an Unknown World* (1897). *Mary Hamilton's Romance* (1898). *Price of a Wife* (1898). *The Placemakers* (1898). *Wedlock* (1898). *A Mother's Holiday* (1899). *A Name to Conjure With* (1899). *A Summer Jaunt*

(1899). *Heart and Sword* (1899). *Binks' Family* (1899). *Just as It Was* (1900). *Little Gervaise* (1900). *The Married Mrs. Binks* (1900). *The Money Sense* (1900). *A Self-Made Countess: Career of a Beauty* (1901). *The Magic Wheel* (1901). *Blaze of Glory* (1902). *The Soul of Honor* (1902). *A Matter of Sentiment* (1903). *Little Joan* (1903). *Marty* (1903). *Cherry's Child* (1904). *Countess of Mountenoy* (1904). *Little Vanities of Mrs. Whittaker* (1904). *Sly-boots* (1904). *That Little French Baby* (1906).

BIBLIOGRAPHY: Black, H. *Notable Women Authors of the Day* (1893).

For articles in reference works, see: *Who Was Who in Literature 1906-1934* (rpt. 1979).

Carole M. Shaffer-Koros

Enid (Mary) Starkie

BORN: 18 August 1897, Killiney, Dublin.
DIED: 21 April 1970, Oxford.
DAUGHTER OF: William Joseph Myles and May Walsh Starkie.

A scholar of French literature, S. wrote more than 15 books on nineteenth and twentieth century writers. After receiving her undergraduate education at Alexandra College in Dublin, S. received her training in French literature at the Sorbonne, University of Paris, where she earned her doctorate in 1928. S. taught French literature at Exeter University, in several American universities on visiting appointments, and, for most of her career, at Oxford University starting in 1929. She described her childhood and college years in her only autobiographical book, *A Lady's Child*, in 1941.

S. used such biographical sources as manuscripts and correspondence to write her critical studies of French writers and was the first outsider allowed to use Arthur Rimbaud's papers for her 1938 study of the writer's life and works. She felt that better understanding of a work comes from knowing the artist's personality. As she wrote in her *Introduction to Baudelaire* (1958), "True, the intrinsic value of a work of art depends, from the artistic point of view, on itself alone, but those who enjoy it, responding to it sympathetically, will always be interested to discover all they can about the nature of the man who could produce it, and wish to come into contact deeply with his personality."

Always the scholar, S.'s studies of Rimbaud, Baudelaire, Pétrus Borel, André Gide, and Flaubert are known for their careful documentation of sources and assimilation of biographical information into a critical analysis. S.'s studies provide

what critics have called a "joy of continuous discovery." Her last book, published posthumously, was the second volume of her two-part study of Gustave Flaubert, a book called by Flaubert scholar and translator Francis Steegmuller "the most sympathetic, best written modern account in English, or in French, of Flaubert's complete later career. It is a worthy monument to the great novelist and to his indomitable biographer."

Honors in S.'s life include her election to the Irish Academy of Letters, being made Commander of the Order of the British Empire in 1967, and being made Chevalier of the French Legion of Honor in 1948. The Faculty of Modern Languages at the University of Oxford conferred on her the Doctorate of Letters in 1939.

S. was remembered for her individualistic personality, and her obituaries even included references to her touches of rebellious dress and behavior. She campaigned for her choices of candidates for Oxford's prestigious Chair of Poetry, a post decided in an election by the Masters of Arts of the university, and through her efforts W.H. Auden was elected to the post in 1956. Among the French writers she knew well and was instrumental in bringing to Oxford for honors and lectures were Jean Cocteau and André Gide; S. also knew British writer Joyce Cary well.

S. spent several months in America teaching at Berkeley and Seattle in 1951. She was, however, so warmly received at Hollins College in Virginia during her term in 1959 that S. bequeathed her fortune to the college.

WORKS: *Les Sources du lyricisme dans la poésie d'Emile Verhaeren* (1927). *Baudelaire* (1933; rewritten 1957). *Arthur Rimbaud in Abyssinia* (1937). *A*

Lady's Child (1941). *Pétrus Borel en Algerie: sa carrière comme inspectateur de la colonisation* (1950). *André Gide* (1953). *Pétrus Borel* (1954). *From Gautier to Eliot: The Influence of France on English Literature, 1851–1939* (1960). *Flaubert: The Making of the Master* (1967). *Flaubert: The Master* (1971).

BIBLIOGRAPHY: Davin, D. *Closing Times* (1975). Richardson, J. *Enid Starkie* (1973).

For articles in reference works, see: *CA. DIB.* (Ed. H. Boylan, 1978). *NYT Biographical Ed.* (2 May 1970). *TCA.*

Other references: *Books Abroad* (Spring 1971). *French Studies* (October 1970). *NYTBR* (by F. Steegmuller, 29 November 1971).

Marilynn J. Smith

Christina (Ellen) Stead

BORN: 17 July 1902, Rockdale, Australia.
DIED: 31 March 1983, Sydney, Australia.
DAUGHTER OF: David George and Ellen Stead.
MARRIED: William Blake (b. William Blech), 1952.

S. trained at the Sydney Teachers College and became a public school teacher, work she later saw herself unfitted for. After studying typing and shorthand for a business career, in 1928 she sailed to England, working in England and France as a grain clerk and a bank clerk. She met and formed an alliance with William Blake, whom she married in 1952. From 1937 to 1946, S. lived in the United States, publishing several novels and writing scripts for MGM in Hollywood. In 1946 she traveled to Europe again with Blake, returning to England to refresh her feel for the English language. S. returned to Australia in 1974.

Although S. is best known for her eleven novels, she began her writing career with a collection of short stories, *The Salzburg Tales*, parables, allegories, and stories of the grotesque. *The Puzzleheaded Girl* is a collection of four novellas, exploring the figure of the young woman in America. In addition, S. wrote reviews and translated novels from French to English, and she edited two anthologies of short stories, one with her husband. In 1974 S. received the Patrick White Award, recognizing her excellence as an Australian novelist.

The Man Who Loved Children is S.'s acknowledged masterpiece. Ignored for twenty-five years, the novel was reissued in 1965 with an afterword by Randall Jarrell, naming the novel great because it does one thing better than any other fiction—makes the reader part of one family's day-to-day intimate existence. The novel depicts three characters of mythic proportions: the father, Sam; the mother, Hetty; and the daughter, a potential artist, Louisa. The fiction portrays basic conflicts between parents and child for power and independence, between man and woman for identity and understanding, between parents for the soul and allegiances of their child. In a virtuoso performance, S. establishes personality through the distinctive languages of the three principal characters with their obsessions and individual blindnesses. The woman's movement solidified the reputation of the novel and procured a new generation of readers for the unsentimental depiction of a family tearing itself apart.

The Man Who Loved Children can also be seen as a portrait of the artist as a young woman with Louie forming herself out of the conflicting force fields of Sam and Hetty, declaring her resistance in a play about tyranny that she wrote in a language she made up for herself. For Louie, school means the opportunity to make a friend and to create an ego ideal, her teacher Miss Aiden, a muse to dedicate her poetry to. Louie's "I will not serve" encompasses her willingness to kill both her parents and ultimately to run away, to go on her walk around the world.

S.'s novel *House of All Nations* won critical acclaim and popular success at the time of its publication. Critics have called this exploration of the workings of banking and international finance S.'s greatest intellectual achievement because of its scope and complexity. The huge novel displays S.'s mature style, charting a world of avarice with people living not just on but for money and money-making.

A third novel of S.'s that is considered great is *Dark Places of the Heart*, also titled *Cotter's England*. In one sense, it is a depiction of the poverty and ugliness of Britain's industrialized north. In another, it is an analysis of another family and of Nellie Cotter Cook's influence on the people around her. A central concern is the relationship between Nellie and her brother Tom. Like Michael and Catherine Baguenault, the brother-sister pair in *Seven Poor Men of Sydney*, Nellie and Tom seem too close to each other, engaged in a battle for power and personal survival. The dark places of Nellie's heart manifest themselves in a fascination with death, a compulsion to manipulate other people, and a dangerous desire to be more than human, to achieve a charismatic destiny. As in all of S.'s strongest fiction, the plot of the novel is subordinate to the drama of character. Her writing here is sparer and more controlled than in other novels.

S. has only two novels set in Australia, her first, *Seven Poor Men of Sydney*, and her fifth, *For Love Alone*. According to Michael Wilding, the first novel is organized to display the lives and interactions of seven poor men connected to each other by friendship, family, and work. The varieties and different effects of poverty give the novel its unity, imperfect because of other important characters and because of romantic and grotesque passages not directly integrated with the theme. *For Love Alone* depicts the poverty of the central character, Teresa Hawkins, and her relationship to her demanding family, but it also portrays her successful flight to England, a place of wider opportunity. The novel raises questions of women's sexuality and of the difficulty of achieving satisfying relationships between men and women. Teresa seeks her fulfillment in her relationship to a man, Quick, a wealthy American, but she retains to some extent her sexual freedom and her right to a separate consciousness.

Although recognition of her achievement has been slow in coming, S. is now acknowledged to be a significant twentieth-century fiction writer, still mainly because of *The Man Who Loved Children*. She continues the tradition of nineteenth-century realistic novelists, especially the French and Russians. A novelist with a modern, post-Freudian sensibility, S. depicts people's social connections with an understanding of the underlying economic forces that shape their lives. She is compared to Dickens for her density of realistic detail, for her comic eye and her ear for exaggerated rhetoric, for her use of the grotesque, and for her commentary on social conditions. S. uses her characters' language to reveal their deceptions and illusions. The characters express this individuating language in dialogues, in interior monologues, and in letters to each other. S. identified herself as a psychological writer, expressing the drama of the person.

WORKS: Seven Poor Men of Sydney (1934). *The Salzburg Tales* (1934). *The Beauties and the Furies* (1936). *House of All Nations* (1938). *The Man Who Loved Children* (1940, 1965). *For Love Alone* (1944). *Letty Fox: Her Luck* (1946). *A Little Tea, A Little Chat* (1948). *The People with the Dogs* (1952). [trans.] *Colour of Asia*, by F. Gigon (1955). [trans.] *The Candid Killer*, by J. Giltene (1956). [trans.] *In Balloon and Bathyscape*, by A. Piccard (1956; also titled *Earth, Sky and Sea*). *Dark Places of the Heart* (1966). *The Puzzleheaded Girl* (1967). *The Little Hotel* (1974). *Miss Herbert: The Suburban Wife* (1976). *The Christina Stead Anthology*, ed. J.B. Read (1979). *Ocean of Story: The Uncollected Stories of Christina Stead*, ed. R.G. Geering (1986). *I'm Dying Laughing: The Humourist* (1987).

BIBLIOGRAPHY: Brydon, D. *Christina Stead* (1987). Geering, R.G. *Christina Stead* (1969). Jarrell, R. in *The Third Book of Criticism* (1969). Lidoff, J. *Christina Stead* (1983). Sturum, T. *Cunning Exiles: Studies of Modern Prose Writers* (1974).

For articles in reference works, see: *CA. CLC.* Other references: *Aphra* (1976). *Nation* (5 April 1965). *NYRB* (June 1965). *Southerly* (1967). *Studies in the Novel* (1979). *Westerly* (March 1976). *WLWE* (1976).

Kate Begnal

Flora Annie Steel

BORN: 2 April 1847, Harrow, Middlesex.
DIED: 12 April 1929, Talgrath, Wales.
DAUGHTER OF: Isabella and George Webster.
MARRIED: Henry Steel, 1867.

The bulk of S.'s work reflected a woman's view of the colonial experience. Altogether 32 of her books were published between 1884 and her death in 1929.

S. had little or no formal education. Instead she was allowed free run of her parents' library and the moors and woods surrounding her childhood home in Scotland. She was known in her family for her strong personality and indefatigable energy; and when she married at age twenty, she left for India with her husband within 24 hours of the ceremony.

She spent the next 22 years as a tireless organizer of community enterprises wherever she or her husband were posted. During these years she acted as medical advisor to the local population, headed health and education committees, designed and sought funding for municipal buildings and improvements, and set up numerous schools for local children. She learned to speak the local language and displayed a genuine if somewhat paternalistic interest in the lives of the people of India, especially the women. S.'s experiences in India gave her a sense of self-sufficiency that encouraged her to take on all kinds of challenges but that also put her at odds with the patriarchal Raj authorities. She supported British rule in India but stated, "My considered opinion is that there is no greater mistake an honest man can make than to hold his tongue regarding error. It stops progress; it is the great curse which underlies democracy." Despite the fact that she was frequently a thorn in the side of the authorities, they appointed her an inspector of schools. Later, in an effort to terminate her tenure, they transferred her husband, but S., stalwart as ever, remained alone in the school district for a further year and a half.

S. began writing short stories reflecting her experiences and collecting Indian folk tales towards the end of her time in India though only one book was published before she left in 1889. She had a long friendship and business association with the publisher William Heinemann. She wrote copiously and was well received by the British public, becoming somewhat of a literary celebrity and gaining equal popularity with Rudyard Kipling in the London publishers' lists.

Of the numerous novels and short stories she wrote, at least half were concerned with Indian or Anglo-Indian life. Her most famous novel, *On The Face of the Waters* (1896), depicted the so-called Indian Mutiny of 1858, which she felt compelled to write in order to clarify the events for the British public. Much of her writing concerning India was an attempt to educate the British about the culture and customs of the East. One of her themes was that far from the Eastern culture tainting Westerners, the effect of Western ways on Easterners debilitated their traditional culture. She did try to interpret this very different culture by using its own criteria rather than relying on an ethnocentric world view.

S. was an ardent supporter of the suffragist movement, making numerous speeches on its behalf. Though much of her work seems dated to modern readers, repeatedly depending on her pro-

tagonists' untimely deaths, several of her novels stand out, notably *The Reformer's Wife* (1903) and *Mussamat Kirpo's Doll* (1894). She wrote several novels of British life, plus historical novels and nonfiction works on India, but she was at her best when depicting Indian life and the colonial experience.

WORKS: *Wide Awake Stories* (1884). *From the Five Rivers* (1893). *Miss Stuart's Legacy* (1893). *The Flower of Forgiveness* (1894). *The Potter's Thumb* (1894). *Tales of the Punjab* (1894). *Red Rowans* (1895). *On the Face of the Waters* (1896). *In the Permanent Way and Other Stories* (1897). *In the Tideway* (1897). *The Complete Indian Housekeeper and Cook* (1899). *Voices in the Night* (1900). *The Hosts of the Lord* (1900). *In the Guardianship of God* (1900). *A Book of Mortals* (1905). *India* (1905). *A Sovereign Remedy* (1906). *India Through the Ages* (1908). *A Prince of Dreamers* (1908). *The Gift of the Gods* (1911). *King Errant* (1912). *The Adventures of Akbar* (1913). *The Mercy of the Lord* (1914). *Marmaduke* (1917). *Mistress of Men* (1917). *English Fairy Tales* (1918). *A Tale of Indian Heroes* (1923). *A Tale of the Tides* (1923). *The Law of the Threshold* (1924). *The Builder* (1928). *The Curse of Eve* (1929). *The Garden of Fidelity* (1929). *The Indian Scene* (1933).

BIBLIOGRAPHY: Collins, J.P. *The Bookman* (London) (November 1917). Greenburger, A. *The British Image of India* (1969). Parry, B. *Delusions and Discoveries* (1972). Patwardham, D. *A Star of India* (1963). Powell, V. *Flora Annie Steel* (1981).

For articles in reference works, see: *Chamber's. Longman. NCHEL. OCEL. TCA.*

Other references: *The Bookman* (London) (July 1914, June 1923, May 1924).

Hilary D. Witzeman

Anne Stevenson

BORN: 3 January 1933, Cambridge.
DAUGHTER OF: Charles Leslie and Louise Destler Stevenson.
MARRIED: R.L. Hitchcock, 1955; Mark Elvin, 1962; Michael Farley, 1984.

S. was born in Cambridge, England, in 1933, when her father, the philosopher C.L. Stevenson (*Ethics and Language*), was studying there. Her birthplace appears to have been determinative. Like Henry James, T.S. Eliot, and H.D., she has become an American writer unable to live in America. All of her adult life she has lived in Great Britain—in England, Scotland, and Wales

for a few years each; she is now settled near Durham in an ex-mining village. Her present choice of rural life, trying, as she says, "to keep away from 'fame' and 'personalities,'" manifests values evidently formed in the Vermont of her childhood—appreciation of natural locale and personal reticence. These qualities characterize her poetry from early to late.

S. began writing poetry with Donald Hall when she was a student at the University of Michigan (B.A. 1954, M.A. 1962). Her first book of poems, *Living in America*, appeared in 1965. Tension between domesticity and need for larger scope—analogue of the tension between America and England—is a strong and perennial motif in S.'s work. In her early volume, *Reversals* (1969), which includes poems from *Living in America*, marriage, pregnancy, and motherhood claustrophobically enclose the poet but also force her to get outside "the house." Yet joy often prevails over negativity, as in "The Victory," written after childbirth: "Snail! Scary knot of desires!/ Hungry snarl! Small son./ Why do I have to love you? / How have you won?" In "On Not Being Able to Look at the Moon," she warns herself against pathetic fallacy, "a mania for/stealing moonlight and transforming it into my own pain." Here she is defining her poetic stance: the world is self-existent, to be observed with accuracy and delight, not to be appropriated by ego. Therefore the poem itself, she notes in "Morning," is "not made but discovered."

S.'s great poetic strength lies in this discovery of the poem in the place. She continually finds the natural world a rich "objective correlative" for both her emotions and intelligence. In her poems description and commentary therefore subtly blend, as in "England": "The paths are dry, the ponds dazed with reflections./. . . A pearly contamination strokes the river/ As the cranes ride or dissolve in it." Contrapuntal to "England" is "Sierra Nevada," a poem evoking that western mountain range: "Landscape without regrets whose weakest junipers/ strangle and split granite, whose hard, clean light/ is utterly without restraint." S.'s characteristic adherence to forms— to rhyme, although flexible and slant, to long lines and declarative sentences—reflects her respect for the similarly stringent forms of the world. Her poems are thus tight yet detailed, even explanatory, and honest; she works hard not to mislead or be misunderstood.

In her more recent poetry, the forms have loosened and become more experimental. An ambition to combine prose and poetry produced *Correspondences: A Family History in Letters* (1974), in effect, a novel in a book-length poem-series. Tracing an evolution of attitudes through six generations, these poem-epistles reveal interrelationships between members of the Chandler family of Clearfield, Vermont, a family that resembles S.'s own. Their revelations paint a broad historical portrait of nineteenth-century America's influence on the twentieth century. The ancestors' greed, intolerance, sexual repression, and misplaced religion are seen as having bred broken family ties, anger, frustration, and profound uncertainty in the modern descendents. Although S. echoes each character's voice with historically plausible accents, history perhaps concerns her less than paying tribute to her mother. An obituary of the fictive mother, Ruth Chandler Arbeiter, opens the narrative and frames it. She has died young, of cancer (as S.'s

own mother did at the age of fifty-four), and her daughter, Kay Boyd, a poet living in England, sees her mother's life as unfulfilled, following a pattern of nonfulfillment in her female forebears.

Travelling Behind Glass: Selected Poems 1963-1973 (1974) emphasizes the metaphor of "glass," which is both barrier between self and world and transmitter of light to see that world. The title poem, a version of Jack Kerouac's *On the Road*, also examines the itinerant life, whose fragmented experiences and lonely questionings create disheartened confusion: "I have forgotten what/ home it was I came for./. . .this sun is so dull and/ estranged that I know/ this dark glass as/ the only living possession of the valley." In her final vision glass shatters "into its stars, and the stars/ scatter, flashing like kingfishers,/ into the emptiness." Even this much light, however, is little consolation. Fragmentation and pain prevail.

This grappling with stark landscapes—that is, with harsh experiences—extends on into *Enough of Green* (1977), set in Scotland where rocky coasts smell "of fish and of sewage" and "salt-worried faces" and "an absence of trees" abound. Loneliness and transience are expressed by indicative titles: "Temporarily in Oxford," "Hotel in the City," "Goodbye! Goodbye!" Darkness, ruins, and abandoned houses preoccupy her as objective correlatives of domestic breakdown, and as if to live in greenery and comfort were a suspect luxury her New England-trained psyche must deny itself.

This conflict between "green" and "black" continues, though eased, along with motifs of glass and consciousness of time passing, in *Minute By Glass Minute* (1982), written after the poet had moved to Wales. The thematically-central long poem, "Green Mountain, Black Mountain," is an elegy to her dead parents, to her father particularly, which links memories of her Vermont youth with present-day realities of Welsh life. Because her father, musician as well as philosopher, had made music central to his daughters' lives, it becomes—as does poetry, by extension—almost a kind of religion. Cantata-like in form, the poem resolves in a coda uniting memory and language— the green mountains—with the wind, soil and birdsong of the black mountains: "Swifts twist on the syllables of the wind currents./ Blackbirds are the cellos of the deep farms."

Several poems in *The Fiction-Makers* (1985) are also elegies to the dead, including the especially moving "Red Rock Fault" and "Willow Song," in memory of her poet-friend Frances Horovitz. Although informed by sadness and loss, these poems become celebrations, for wreckage and energy strangely co-exist in them. The poet observes how damaged terrain around old mine-pits now produces a lush growth of wild flowers. The breakdown of her illusions has rejuvenated her psychic landscape. She says of this volume: "*The Fiction-Makers* is an effort to disencumber myself of the illusion of believing in my own 'story.'" Thus in "A Legacy," written on her fiftieth birthday, she gives away to friends the fixed components of her "story" in recognition of temporality and the final dissolution to come.

For S. the external world provides an anchor for the mind, which cannot give birth to this world but can mirror it. To mirror truthfully has been her lasting poetic project. This uncommon integrity, like "the genuine" praised by T.S. Eliot in the work of Marianne Moore, is both formal and personal, making S.'s poetry one of the most solid achievements in contemporary British letters.

WORKS: *Living in America* (1965). *Elizabeth Bishop* (1966). *Reversals* (1969). *Correspondences: A Family History in Letters* (1974). *Traveling Behind Glass: Selected Poems 1963-1973* (1974).

Correspondences (1975). *Child of Adam* (1976). *Enough of Green* (1977). *A Morden Tower Reading 3* (1977). *Cliff Walk* (1977). *Minute by Glass Minute* (1982). *The Fiction-Makers* (1985). *Selected Poems 1956-1986* (1987).

BIBLIOGRAPHY: For articles in reference works, see: *CA* (mistakenly attributing another author's novels to S.). *CLC. CP. International Who's Who in Poetry*, Ed. E. Kay (1972).

Other references: *Encounter* (December 1974). *Lines Review* (September 1974). *The Listener* (28 November 1974). *London Magazine* (October–November 1974). *Michigan Quarterly Review* (Fall 1966, April 1971). *The New Review* (London, October 1974). *Open Places* (Spring/Summer 1976). *Ploughshares* (Autumn 1978). *Poetry* (February 1971, November 1975).

Jane Augustine

Mary (Florence Elinor) Stewart

BORN: 17 September 1916, Sunderland.
DAUGHTER OF: Frederick Albert and Mary Edith (Matthews) Rainbow.
MARRIED: Frederick Henry Stewart, 1945.
WRITES UNDER: Mary Stewart.

Educated at the University of Durham, S. received her B.A. with first class honors in 1938, a teaching diploma in 1939, and her M.A. in 1941. In 1945 she married Frederick H. Stewart, a lecturer in geology, but also continued her own teaching career. She began writing in 1949 but did not give up her university career in favor of full-time writing until 1956, at which time she moved to Edinburgh where her husband became Regius professor in the department of geology at the University of Edinburgh.

Her first book, *Madam, Will You Talk?*, was an instant success at its appearance in 1955. In this work she found her original formula for popular romantic thrillers, which she repeated with variations in her next several novels, all of which exhibit an appealing combination of mystery, adventure, romance, and poetic description. Each novel is narrated by the feminine protagonist, a young woman, independent and self-supporting, usually traveling abroad either on vacation or on business when she finds herself caught up in a dangerous criminal intrigue. Each novel is set in a vividly-depicted locale, often somewhere on the continent. Both *Madam, Will You Talk?* and *Nine Coaches Waiting* (1959) are set in France, the first related by a young widow on vacation, the latter by a governess assuming a post, an orphan whose plight recalls that of Jane Eyre. *My Brother Michael* (1959), winner of the British Crime Writers Association Award, is set in Greece, and *The Moon Spinners* (1962), which was made into a Hollywood film, is set in Crete. *This Rough Magic*, winner of the Mystery Writers of America Award for 1964, is set in Corfu, which functions in the novel as the assumed island setting of Shakespeare's *The Tempest*. S.'s interest in Shakespeare is also reflected in *Touch Not the Cat* (1976) which is sprinkled with subtly relevant references to *Romeo and Juliet*.

In 1970 S. deviated from the Gothic romance format with *The Crystal Cave*, a work of historical fiction with elements of fantasy. This novel was the first of a trilogy based on the life of the legendary medieval wizard Merlin, who also serves as first-person narrator. The second volume, *The Hollow Hills* (1973), continues Merlin's account to the coronation of Arthur, while the final volume, *The Last Enchantment* (1979), completes the wizard's career, ending with his magically induced sleep at the hands of the enchantress Nimue. Throughout the trilogy the emphasis is on an historically accurate depiction of life in fifth-century Roman Britain. The central figure of Merlin is, in effect, demythologized from his traditional role as archetypal wizard to the portrayal of a complex, sympathetic human being, gifted only with skills of prophecy.

S. has also written two children's books, *The Little Broomstick* (1972) and *Ludo and the Star Horse* (1974), which won the Scottish Arts Council Award. Her most recent work is a sequel to the Merlin trilogy, *The Wicked Day* (1983), focused on the Arthurian villain, Mordred.

Almost all of S.'s novels have been best sellers. They have also been serialized, broadcast, and translated into sixteen languages, including Finnish, Portugese, Hebrew, and Icelandic. Distinguished by their literary quality, these highly successful novels elude classification among the popular genres they so skillfully blend.

WORKS: *Madam, Will You Talk?* (1955). *Wildfire at Midnight* (1956). *Thunder on the Right* (1957). *Nine Coaches Waiting* (1958). *My Brother Michael* (1959). *The Ivy Tree* (1961). *This Rough Magic* (1964). *Airs Above the Ground* (1965). *The Gabriel Hounds* (1967). *The Crystal Cave* (1970). *The Little Broomstick* (1971). *The Hollow Hills* (1973). *Ludo and the Star Horse* (1974). *Touch Not the Cat* (1976). *The Last Enchantment* (1979). *The Wicked Day* (1983).

BIBLIOGRAPHY: For articles in reference works, see: *CA. CLC. SATA. TCC&MW. TCRGW. TCW. WA.*

Charlotte Spivack

Jan Struther

BORN: 6 June 1901, London.
DIED: 20 July 1953, New York City.
DAUGHTER OF: Henry Torrens Anstruther and Eva Anstruther.
MARRIED: Anthony Maxtone Graham, 1923; Adolf Kurt Placzek, 1948.
WROTE UNDER: Maxtone Graham, Joyce Anstruther, Jan Struther.

Known almost exclusively as the author of one book, *Mrs. Miniver* (1939), S. was married first to the son of a senior member of an Edinburgh law firm and then, following her move to the United States in 1940 with two of her three children, to a librarian at Columbia University. She lectured extensively in the United States during World War II for the British War Relief fund and appeared on the radio program, "Information Please."

Mrs. Miniver was a phenomenon: a Book-of-the-Month selection, a bestseller, and in 1942 an Academy Award-winning movie. The sketches about English family life just before the onset of World War II that comprise *Mrs. Miniver* were first published in the *Times* of London and remain a charming evocation of country houses, leather engagement books, drawing rooms, and parlor maids, a world largely gone from both the United States and Great Britain. It captured the mundane, day-by-day events in a typical middle-class household in England that included Nannie, Mrs. Adie (a Scots cook), Gladys (the house parlormaid), and, on occasion, Mrs. Burchett (to help with the "washing-up" at dinner parties). Mrs. Miniver herself, though beguiling and charming, lives in a world of appointment books and drawing rooms and a country house named "Starling"; her sons attend Eton, she drives up to Scotland in the summer. Yet her perceptions are as apt today as when the book was published, suggesting that the book has a timeless quality unlike many other bestsellers.

S. was also a poet with a darker, grimmer vision that she displayed effectively in *The Glass Blower* (1941). Stephen Vincent Benét observed that S. preferred to write poetry in possible reaction to the public's inability to distinguish S.'s own life from that of Mrs. Miniver. Indeed, S. grew so "heartily sick" of *Mrs. Miniver* that when a contest was announced for the best parody of the book, she wrote a "cruel" parody, submitted it under a pen-name, and won the prize, subsequently donating the prize money to an organization for "distressed gentlewomen."

S. also wrote essays for *Punch* and *The Spectator* that were collected in *Try Anything Twice* (1938) and several collections of light verse. She never escaped the fame of her best character and best-known work, however, and will always be identified more for *Mrs. Miniver* than for any of her other books.

WORKS: *Betsinda Dances and Other Poems* (1931). *Sycamore Square and Other Verses* (1931). *The Modern Struwwelpeter* (1936). *When Grandmother Was Small* (1937). *Try Anything Twice* (1938). *Mrs. Miniver* (1939). *The Glass Blower and Other Poems* (1940). *Letters from Women of Britain* (1941). *Pocketful of Pebbles* (1946).

BIBLIOGRAPHY: For articles in reference works, see: *Authors' and Writers' Who's Who. CB. Longman. TWA* and *SUP.*

Other references: *Book-of-the Month Club News* (July 1940). *New York Herald-Tribune* (25 July 1940). *NYHTBR* (13 October 1940, 2 August 1953). *NYT* (21 July 1953). *NYTBR* (25 August 1940). *Spectator* (24 July 1953). *Time* (4 August 1940). *Times* (London) (21 July 1953). Van Gelder, R. *Writers and Writing* (1946).

Mickey Pearlman

Lady Louisa Stuart

BORN: 1757, London.
DIED: 1851, London.
DAUGHTER OF: John, third Earl of Bute, and Mary, Countess of Bute.

Born the eleventh child of an embittered and repudiated politician, S. spent a lonely childhood in the isolated country house at Luton, where her father retired from public life to botanize in solitude. As an adult she made regular visits to Scotland to visit friends in the country outside Edinburgh and Glasgow. Her grandmother was the famous (or infamous) bluestocking Lady Mary Wortley Montagu. Although S. never knew this grandmother, she was subjected to cruel remonstrances from her brothers and sisters whenever she displayed any signs of intellectual or literary inclinations; the family decidedly did not wish to foster any real or fancied inherited tendencies. Thus S. learned to read surreptitiously and to write in secret.

Fascinated by the political and literary worlds barred to her by class and gender, S. read widely but willingly adhered to the code of conduct for an aristocratic lady, which prohibited publishing one's work or participating publicly in literary or political controversy. To find an outlet for these interests, she developed a wide correspondence with various men of influence and discussed national affairs with a large group of friends and relatives spanning several generations. Consistent with those loyalties to family and class that she cherished throughout her long life, her political views remained steadfastly Tory although she balanced political conservatism with an instinctive human sympathy for people of all classes so long as they remained well behaved.

Until Lady Bute died in 1794, S. served as companion to her mother. Then she made her home in London, leaving frequently for prolonged visits to various country houses from which she wrote many of her finest letters. Financially secure although far from wealthy, S. never married and lived the leisured life of an independent gentlewoman, enlivened by an extraordinary genius for friendship and an all-embracing intellectual curiosity. She died at the age of ninety-four, afflicted by deafness and rheumatism but otherwise in full possession of her faculties.

S. is best known through her connection with Sir Walter Scott. Their correspondence reveals a friendship founded in mutual esteem and affection and shows her to be a brilliantly perceptive literary critic whose opinions Scott highly regarded. There are also two volumes of letters to Louisa Clinton (written 1817–1834, published 1901–1903), a younger woman whose character and opinions Stuart nurtured. Always conscious of the need for self-discipline, especially in women, she counsels Clinton against reverie and the excesses of self-consciousness and repeatedly urges her pupil to acquaint herself with all sides of a given issue. Although she did not regard herself as a feminist, S. laments woman's "natural dependence" on man and expresses considerable contempt for the male preference for silly women of weak intellect. An earlier collection of letters to her favorite sister (Lady Portarlington) shows her rapid intellectual growth and the strategies she employed to reconcile herself to the limitations imposed on her life by class and gender.

Although her letters are engaging and at times exceedingly funny, S. is at her best as a writer of memoirs. Her *Memoir of John, Duke of Argyll* includes a hilarious portrait of her father's cousin, Lady Mary Coke, whose ridiculous self-dramatizations and imaginary conspiracies rendered her the dread of the entire family and the object of their scorn. Even while deftly sketching Lady Mary's bizarre behavior, however, S.'s sympathy remains active, and the finished character's frailties emerge as both devastatingly funny and frighteningly human. The "Introductory Anecdotes" to *The Correspondence of Lady Mary Wortley Montagu* and the *Memoire of Frances Lady Douglas* further demonstrate S.'s talent to be simultaneously respectful and candid in a memoir. This approach also informs her "Notes" to J.H. Jesse's *George Selwyn and His Contemporaries*, which she drew from her customary sources of personal recollection and remembered anecdote. S.'s letters—which include a large collection of unpublished material at the Bodleian, memoirs and short moral fables—combine incisive analysis of current events, polished literary criticism, and witty social satire. She demands of herself high standards of taste, intellectual honesty, stylistic elegance, and human charity. That the products of this vibrant mind remained unpublished in her own day was a significant loss, one that remains not yet wholly rectified.

WORKS: "Introductory Anecdotes" to *The Letters and Works of Lady Mary Wortley Montague*, ed. Lord Wharncliffe (1837). *Gleanings from an Old Portfolio*, ed. Mrs. Godfrey Clark (1895–1898). *Selections from the Manuscripts of Lady Louisa Stuart*, ed. J.A. Home (1899). *Letters of Lady Louisa Stuart to Miss Louisa Clinton*, ed. J.A. Home (1901–1903). *The Letters of Lady Louisa Stuart*, ed. R.B. Johnson (1926). *Memoire of Frances Lady Douglas*, ed. J. Rubenstein (1985).

BIBLIOGRAPHY: Buchan, K.J. *Some Eighteenth Century Byways* (1908). Buchan, S.C. *Lady Louisa Stuart: Her Memories and Portraits* (1932). Graham, H. *A Group of Scottish Women* (1908). MacCunn F. *Sir Walter Scott's Friends* (1909).

Other references: *Scottish Literary Journal* (1980). *The Wordsworth Circle* (1981).

Jill Rubenstein

Mary Stuart, Queen of Scots

BORN: 1542, Linlithgow Palace, Scotland.
DIED: 8 February 1587, Fotheringay Castle.
DAUGHTER OF: James V of Scotland and Mary of Guise.
MARRIED: Francis, Dauphin of France (later Francis II), 1558; Henry Stuart, Lord Darnley, 1565; James Hepburn, Earl of Bothwell, 1567.

A center of controversy in her lifetime, S. has remained an enigma to later ages. Queen of Scotland from the sixth day of her life, she was, when a young child, sent by her mother, the queen regent, to the French court, where she was raised with the children of Francis I in a scintillating, somewhat corrupt Roman Catholic atmosphere. After the death of her young husband, Francis II, S. elected to return to Scotland, a relatively rude, semi-feudal kingdom which was staunchly Protestant, foregoing the luxury—and the difficult intrigues—of the French court but entering tumultuous waters in Scotland. Her marriage to Darnley, her cousin, strengthened her claim to the English throne and incurred the suspicion of Elizabeth I and her advisers, for in 1565 Elizabeth was still quite insecure on her throne and fearful of sedition by Catholic subjects for whom S. was a rallying point. On the other hand, S. was most unappealing as a ruler to the Scottish reformed church, and her position in Scotland was also undermined by Darnley, from whom she became increasingly alienated. The birth of their son, later James VI of Scotland and James I of England, on 19 June 1566, did not strengthen her position; Darnley refused to attend the child's christening.

It is probably impossible to determine the truth concerning S.'s involvement in the most serious of the crimes attributed to her: the murder of Darnley by the Scottish nobles, led by James Hepburn, Earl of Bothwell, on 10 February 1567. It is also impossible to be certain what her feelings for Bothwell were: whether she feared him or was passionately in love with him. What is known is that she and Bothwell were married, in a Protestant ceremony, on 15 May 1567, that the event followed a supposed kidnapping of the queen by Bothwell's forces, and that it led to open, tumultuous outcries against the queen, who was separated forcibly from Bothwell by alienated noblemen and forced to abdicate her throne in favor of her son,

James, on 24 July 1567. James, also separated from her, was raised by her enemies in the Protestant faith.

Imprisoned by her nobles in Lochleven, S. escaped and raised an army but was defeated at Langside. She then decided to throw herself on the protection of Elizabeth, her cousin and sister-queen, a political blunder that she never overcame. S. was kept in varying conditions of captivity by Elizabeth for nineteen years but finally was recognized by her cousin as a grave threat, tried for various political intrigues in which she had been embroiled, and condemned to death. She was executed in Fotheringay Castle on 8 February 1587 and interred in Petersborough. On 11 October 1612, her body was reinterred in Westminster, by order of her son.

A product of the high Renaissance in France, S. was educated by outstanding French writers. She composed occasional verse and prose at critical moments throughout her life. As George Ballard has noted, her verses have never been accorded serious attention as literature: "the many writers of her history," he states, "have been so full in their accounts of her misfortunes and tragical end, and so warmly engaged either in heightening or depressing her reputation in regard to her conduct in life, that they have almost all forgot to transmit to posterity an account of her education and what part she bore in the republic of letters." Nonetheless, her writings are indeed worthy of attention. S. did not publish them herself, but many of her pieces appeared in works by her contemporaries and others were collected after her death and printed in several collections, the most important of which are noted below.

Of her writings, the so-called "casket letters and sonnets," produced at her first English trial as evidence of her complicity in the murder of Darnley, are the most contested. While the letters do speak of the assassination and may be open, therefore, to the suspicion of having been manufactured as evidence against her, the sonnets, which are truly great poems, do not implicate her in the crime but merely attest to her feelings for Bothwell. On that account, they may be more readily recognized as her own work, and they constitute a unique group of passionate love sonnets in a woman's voice. That they can easily be related to the course of S.'s association with Bothwell adds to their poignancy. Her other poetry ranges from a mourning dirge for Francis II to appeals to Elizabeth and a moving type of poetry of resignation and acceptance.

WORKS: *Collection de Manuscrits, Livres Estampes et Objects d'art relatifs a Marie Stuart, Reine de France et D'Ecrosse* (1931). *Last Letter of Mary Queen of Scotland Addressed to her brother in law Henry III King of France on the night before her execution at Fotheringay Castle 8th February 1587* (1927). *Latin Themes of Mary Stuart*, ed. Anatole de Montaignon (n.d.). *Letters and Poems of Mary, Queen of Scots, supposed author*, ed. and trans. Clifford Bax (1947). *Poems of Mary Queen of Scots*, ed. Julian Sharman (1873). *Poems of Mary Queen of Scots, to the Earl of Bothwell* (1932). *Queen Mary's Book, A Collection of Poems and Essays by Mary Queen of Scots*, ed. Mrs. P. Stewart-Mackenzie-Arbuthnot (1907). *Recueil des Letteres et Memoires de Marie Stuart*, ed. Prince Alexander Labanoff (Lobanov-Rostovski) (1844).

BIBLIOGRAPHY: Ballard, G. *Memoirs of Several Ladies of Great Britain* ... (1752). *DNB* (Thomas Finlayon Henderson, "Mary, Queen of Scots [1542-1587]"), XII, 1258-1275. Fraser, A. *Mary, Queen of Scots* (1969). Hays, M. *Female Biography* ... (1807). Strickland, A. *Life of Mary Stuart, Queen of Scots* (1907). Tannenbaum, S. *Elizabethan Bibliographies*. X. *Marie Stuart* (1946). Thomson, G.M. *The Crime of Mary Stuart* (1967). Travitsky, B. ed. *Paradise of Women* ... (1981). Warnicke, R.M. *Women of the English Renaissance and Reformation* (1983). Williams, J. *Literary Women of England* ... (1861).

Betty Travitsky

Ann and Jane Taylor

Ann. BORN: 30 January 1782, London.
DIED: 17 December 1866, Nottingham.
Jane. BORN: 23 September 1783, London.
DIED: 12 April 1824, Ongar.
DAUGHTERS OF: Isaac and Ann Martin Taylor.
Ann. MARRIED: Joseph Henry Gilbert, 1813.
Jane. WROTE UNDER: Q.Q.

Born into a poor but intellectually active and creative nonconformist family, Ann and Jane T. became known in literary circles in their early twenties for fresh, original, and sprightly verse, tales, short stories, and essays for children and young people. Although their writing was to change the nature of children's literature, their impact was even broader. Iona Opie writes of them: "No two young women aroused more affection in the 19th century through their work," an appreciation emanating from the new middle class and authors now in the literary canon. Sir Walter Scott praised their work; Byron parodied it; and Robert Browning, who read their works as a child, later developed one of Jane's tales into a poem.

Ann's "Meddlesome Matty" as a poem may be dated as is Jane's "Busy Idleness," but, as phrases, they have entered into the language, and in spite of inherent moralizing in all their works, the sisters' influence can be traced in late-nineteenth-century and early-twentieth-century writers such as Robert Browning, Lewis Carroll, Robert Louis Stevenson, and Hilaire Belloc. Kate Greenaway illustrated a selection of the sisters' poems, including "The Cow" and "Meddlesome Matty," in 1883; Edith Sitwell and Amy Lowell read them and owned, as adults, copies of their works.

The T.s' father and grandfather bore the same name, Isaac, and practiced the same profession, engraver and illustrator, the son being ordained later in his career. In 1786 the family moved out of London to Lavenham where they remained for ten years. During these years, Ann and Jane were taught at home and allowed to develop their talents. Ann says of her sister that she lived in "a world entirely of her own creation" and invented her extended imaginative games, verse, and stories while watching her spinning top for hours on end. Precocious and lively, Jane was willingly put on display for family friends both in Lavenham and in Colchester where the family moved in 1796.

When the Napoleonic Wars reduced the volume of engraving work, the teen-aged girls were apprenticed to their father as engravers. The engraving demanded careful attention, and the hours of work were long but not rigidly arduous; the girls' friends came visiting into the workroom, and ideas for poems and tales were scribbled on scraps of paper; there was time for dancing lessons, evening literary reading and discussion parties, and competing for prizes offered by the *Minor's Pocket Book*. After some five years of submitting verses and puzzle solutions, the publisher asked them to write "some easy poetry for young children ...[W]hat would be most likely to please little minds." The sisters produced *Original Poems for Infant Minds* (1805–1806), an instant critical and popular success with reviews in several nonconformist periodicals, the general tenor being that the verse was more poetic than moral, yet very moral.

The same years saw the publication of *Rural Scenes* and *City Scenes*, readers with many engravings, both noticed in *Eclectic Review*. *Original Poems* was followed by *Rhymes for the Nursery* (1806) which contains Jane's "The Star" ("Twinkle, twinkle, little star"), the basis of Lewis Carroll's parody in *Alice in Wonderland*, and their joint "The Cow," later used by R.L. Stevenson. *Limed Twigs* (1808), a reader, Ann's "The Wedding among the Flowers" (1809), and her *Signor Topsy-Turvey's Wonderful Magic Lantern* (1810) did not distract from their more serious joint venture, *Hymns for Infant Minds* (1811) for which Ann also did the engravings and which was nearly as popular as *Original Poems*, winning immediate acceptance in the burgeoning Sunday schools and necessitating 48 editions. Most remembered today is Ann's "I thank the goodness and the grace, / Which on my birth has smiled." Thomas Arnold wrote of Ann: "The knowledge and love of Christ can nowhere be more readily gained by young children than from the hymns of this most admirable woman."

The T.s moved to Ongar in 1811, Isaac being called to the meeting house there, a move which was to be the last for the family. The three oldest children spent more time away from home; Ann and Jane spent the winter of 1811–1812 with Isaac in Cornwall where they were able to pursue the arts unhampered. Ann and Isaac would marry but otherwise the home at Ongar would remain until the death of their parents.

Until the volume of publication proved otherwise, Isaac T. insisted that the two young women regard writing as secondary to the security of engraving as a way of earning their living. When writing proved so successful, Mrs. T. also began to publish, her first work, *Maternal Solicitude*, appearing in 1814. She and Jane collaborated on *Correspondence Between a Mother and Her Daughter at School* (1817). Before Ann's marriage in 1813, she and Jane collaborated heavily on much of their writing for children, with some contributions from younger members of the family.

Ann's marriage to Joseph Henry Gilbert, a Congregationalist minister known for his liberal views, was happy, busy, and successful, leaving little time for writing, given the demands of raising eight children, although she found time for reviewing for the *Eclectic Review*. A somewhat negative review of Hannah More's *Christian Morals* angered More who objected to such a tone being taken by an obscure writer. The intervening years saw little writing, and what was written was often in support of Parliamentary reform, abolition, or disestablishment, with some occasional verse. Ann returned to her pen in the 1860s to write her *Autobiography*, used by Virginia Woolf in her essay "Lives of the Obscure" to evoke forgotten nonconformists who lived lives of such high purpose.

Ann's contribution to children's literature included the poem "My Mother" published in volume one of *Original Poems* (1805), which became one of the most popular, imitated, and parodied poems in the nineteenth century. Inspired by Cowper's poem "My Mary," these sentimental verses were parodied by Byron and by a sixteen-year old Bertrand Russell among many others in the last half of the nineteenth century in reaction to the serious imitations of the first half. "My Mother" was described in the *Athenaeum* (12 May 1866) as "one of the most beautiful lyrics in the English language" except for the final verse: "For God, who lives above the skies, / Would look with vengeance in His eyes, / If ever I should dare despise/ My Mother." This verse should, it was suggested, be replaced with one made by the poet laureate, Alfred Lord Tennyson.

In 1817 Jane began to write for *Youth Magazine* under the pseudonym of Q.Q.; these poems and essays were published posthumously in book form as *Contributions of Q.Q.* (1825), and with demand stimulated by praise from Sarah Hale, in book and tract form in the United States. In this collection is printed "How It Strikes a Stranger," which uses a visitor from a small planet to provide perspective on living for earthlings, and "A Day's Pleasure," which describes a group of young people's adventures as they visit a stately house.

Both sisters were influenced in their literary development by their close-knit family and the religious valuation they placed on the imaginative life. To the adult Jane, lyrical and reflective where Ann was concrete and dramatic, unbridled imagination, however tempting, was worldly and hence unacceptable; the resolution of this matter is detailed in a letter she wrote to a friend on the vexed subject of novel reading, which although coming down triumphantly on the side of the novel as a moral instrument, was insufficiently convincing to move Jane to use her gifts in this way. Choosing instead the tale as her vehicle, she created honest, sound psychological sketches. *Display*, written in Cornwall in 1815, was considered by herself and others her major work. Seeming to echo Jane Austen's *Emma* and *Mansfield Park* (but written independently), the novel is a *Bildungsroman* of Emily and Elizabeth who seek happiness in upward mobility, only to find more modest contentment. Broadly reviewed, *Display* went into three editions in six months. Jane, like Maria Edgeworth, shaped her characters to fit her moral, sacrificing the richness of texture characteristic of the true novel.

Jane once described herself as two people, a morning self, busy, pedestrian in thought, even brusque, and an evening self, imaginative and gay; this latter literary self, fascinated by space, stars, and the night sky—"I used to roam and revel 'mid the stars"—produced her two most enduring works, the children's poem, "The Star," and the short story, "How It Strikes a Stranger," the theme of which Robert Browning used in "Rephan," attributing it to her and perhaps forgiving the strong moralistic tone by which she justified her imagination.

Jane died of cancer in 1824 at home in Ongar, but Ann outlived her husband, traveled in England, and wrote her *Autobiography* (published 1874), dying at the age of 88.

WORKS: (Ann and Jane T.) *Rural Scenes* (1805). *Original Poems for Infant Minds* (1805-06). *Rhymes for the Nursery* (1806). *Hymns for Infant Minds* (1810). *City Scenes* (1809). *Limed Twigs to Catch Young Birds* (1808). (Jane T. as Q.Q.): *The Contributions of Q.Q.* (1824). *Writings* (1832).

Essays in Rhymes (1816). *Display, a Tale* (1815). *Jane Taylor, Prose and Poetry.* ed. F.V. Barry. (1925). (Ann T. as sole author) *The Wedding Among the Flowers* (1808). *Autobiography* (1874).

BIBLIOGRAPHY: Armitage, D.M. *The Taylors of Ongar; Portrait of an English Family of the Eighteenth and Nineteenth Centuries* (1939). Kent, M. English (1935): Opie, I. *Three Centuries of Nursery Rhymes and Poetry for Children* (1973). Stewart, C.D. *The Taylors of Ongar; an Analytical Bio-bibliography* (1975). Stewart, C.D., ed. *Ann Taylor Gilbert's Album* (1978). Taylor, I., Jr. *Memoirs and Poetical Remains of Jane Taylor* (1826). Walford, L. *Four Biographies from "Blackwood's."* (1888). Woolf, V. *The Common Reader* (1925).

Eleanor Langstaff

Elizabeth Taylor

BORN: 3 July 1912, Reading, Berkshire.
DIED: 19 November 1975, Grove's Barn, Penn, Buckinghamshire.
DAUGHTER OF: Oliver and Elsie Fewtrell Coles.
MARRIED: John Kendall Taylor, 1936.

Fine ironies and a polished style, a retiring life and a dedicated readership have caused some critics to mention in the same breath Jane Austen and the modern Englishwoman T.

T. was born Elizabeth Coles in Berkshire in 1912 and worked as a governess and a librarian before her marriage in 1936. Having had two children and started to bring them up, she turned in 1945 to full-time authorship after the success of her first novel, *At Mrs. Lippincote's*. She dedicated herself to the short and not-so-simple annals of the British middle class, which she viewed with a penetrating eye and a gentle but not wholly uncontemptuous amusement.

She was especially good at catching the individuating gesture and in penetrating the often-elaborate disguises that stockbrokers and other middle-class suburbanites put on those actions that they think are beneath them and nevertheless perform for some real or imagined advantage. She was not at all surprised to discover in the group of people who "had advantages"—and were typically anxious always to "take advantage" in order to increase that "superiority"—startling inconsistencies; she was able to render these carefully without ever creating characters who were merely puzzling bundles of contradictions. She was able to get right to the heart of characters who were, deep down, at war with the surfaces they deliberately and ingeniously adopted or unfortunately and uncomfortably were compelled by society to adopt.

She chronicled in novels and exquisite short stories (said to be so subtle as to be an acquired taste) the incongruous situations in which perfectly ordinary middle-class people were to be observed doing the most extraordinary things. Hers was the world of human foibles and contradictions that Logan Pearsall Smith described as inhabited by "meat-eating vegetarians" and similar strange but everyday people.

Eschewing the sensational, T. opted for plots that permitted her sometimes improbable characters to exhibit themselves without attracting undue attention to the machinery of the fiction. At the same time she was completely aware that even a pillar of the middle-class Establishment is, on occasion, liable to appear among the respectable in an outrageously loud tie, or kick over the traces and run away with someone's wife, or do in a rich and elderly relative, or take off with the most unpredictable and "unsuitable" companion to some place impossibly distant or déclassé. Her characters inhabited a world of modulated voices and clichéd emotions, a world in which only a few "advanced" or "artistic" persons were expected to be eccentric in manner or extravagant in speech and gesture. S. made it perfectly credible for the momentous to interrupt the mundane.

In character, plot, and dialogue she added a seasoning of malice, a dash of censure or contempt (but never toward the reader, who was invited to be on the side of the Right). We are shown how in their genteel and fundamentally British hypocrisy the characters sometimes fool even themselves, and we are invited to sit in judgment of what fools such mortals can be.

T.'s work is quintessentially British in its shrewd tolerance and its "superior" correction, in its admixture of snobbery with morality, in its skillful combination of the delicious secret guilt of gossip with the properly public stance of "sorting things out." Along with her feminine intuition and village-scandalmonger cattiness—admittedly frequently leavened by a sincere sympathy for characters one might have thought deserved nothing but condemnation—she has an unflinching dedication not only to *setting* things right but also *getting* things right. Her glance is penetrating. Her work is highly crafted, deliberate in every effect, calculated when it seems the most casual. Telling us all about her subjects, also, she wastes little or nothing, except perhaps some compassion on a few wayward people who ought to have known better. All of her people we recognize. Some of them we ought not to like as much as her kindness and art makes us like them.

T.'s wit is the kind vaguely described as "dry," which is to say that it prompts smiles, not guffaws, even at the outrageous. Margaret Willy (in the best brief estimate of T.'s achievement) notes that T.'s ironies have been compared with Austen's and then cleverly adds:

Another attribute shared by these tolerantly amused, intensely feminine delineators of human foible was a distaste for sensational subject-matter and personal publicity alike. This perhaps in part accounts for the comparatively limited recognition, in favour of flashier fictional attractions, accorded to one of the most quietly distinguished talents of our time.

Arguably the simplest explanation of why a dozen novels from *At Mrs. Lippincote's* to the posthumous *Blaming* (1976) have been so "quietly" received by critics is that most book reviewers over that period were men, and T. writes best about and for women. Men may not be able to feel to the same extent the "shock of recognition" at her economical and precise depiction of a young girl's dreams and embarrassments, at a middle-aged woman's hypocrisies and insecurities, at an old woman's disappointments and forced adjustments. Male critics have to acknowlege T.'s art; female critics keep telling us of her heart.

Her skill is evident in novels such as *Palladian* (1946), *A View of the Harbour* (1947), *A Wreath of Roses* (1949), *A Game of Hide and Seek* (1951), *The Sleeping Beauty* (1953), *Angel* (1957), *In a Summer Season* (1961), *The Soul of Kindness* (1964), *The Wedding Group* (1968), and *Blaming* (1976). Her collections of short stories such as *Hester Lilly* (1954), *The Blush* (1958), *A Dedicated Man* (1965), and *The Devastating Boys* (1972) prove that she is also the mistress of the briefer form, but here the influence of her favorite writer (Jane Austen) is perhaps less.

WORKS: At Mrs. Lippincote's (1945). Palladian (1946). A View of the Harbour (1947). A Wreath of Roses (1949). A Game of Hide-and-Seek (1951). The Sleeping Beauty (1953). Hester Lilly and Other Stories (1954). Angel (1957). The Blush and Other Stories (1958). In a Summer Season (1961). The Soul of Kindness (1964). A Dedicated Man and Other Stories (1965). Mossy Trotter (1967). The Wedding Group (1968). Mrs. Palfrey at the Claremont (1971). The Devastating Boys (1972). Blaming (1976).

BIBLIOGRAPHY: Bailley, P. *New Statesman* (10 August 1973). Liddell, R. *Review of English Literature* (April 1960).

For articles in reference works, see: *CA. CLC. SATA. TCA. TCW. Great Writers of the English Language: Novelists.*

Leonard R.N. Ashley

Emma Alice Margaret Tennant

BORN: 2 February 1864, Peebleshire, Scotland.
DIED: 28 July 1945, London.
DAUGHTER OF: Charles and Emma Tennant.
MARRIED: Herbert Henry Asquith, 1894.
WROTE UNDER: Margot Asquith.

Vivacious, outspoken, and original, T. grew up in the Scottish countryside in a prosperous, lively family. As a child she developed a love of the natural world and cultivated her considerable talents as a rider to hounds. T. was taught by governesses, briefly attended finishing school, and completed her studies in Dresden.

Throughout her life, T. read widely and earnestly, although unsystematically. Her views on literature, like her opinions of her contemporaries, were characteristically pronounced, intelligent, and individual. In the 1880s she became a leading member of the "Souls," a coterie that welcomed Liberals and Conservatives alike and occupied its time in fervent discussions of books, energetic recitations of poetry, and witty pencil games. In 1894 T. married H.H. Asquith (later Earl of Oxford and Asquith), who was to hold office as Liberal Prime Minister from 1908 to 1916. T. had a zealous interest in the political scene and in large part helped to promote her husband's career although polite society frequently considered her behavior shocking, and not everyone found her candor charming.

T.'s distinction as an author rests on the claims of her *Autobiography* (1920). Although she wrote of herself, "my only literary asset is natural directness," the book at its best offers well-dramatized depictions of such events as her sister Laura's death, T.'s tempestuous early love affair with Peter Flower, and her prison visit to a female abortionist. In addition, it contains vivid portraits of notable acquaintances like Alfred Tennyson and Benjamin Jowett and, overall, paints an attractive picture of late Victorian and Edwardian high life that is undisturbed by too deep a concern for the social inequities and disruptions of the times. The virtues of T.'s work include an engaging, epigrammatic style and sensitive assessments of human nature; the *Autobiography* is least successful and most self-serving in its recurrent, unabashed quotations of letters and poems on the subject of T. herself.

Many readers disapproved of the *Autobiography*'s frank descriptions of leading social figures and hitherto taboo subjects like childbirth pains, but this did not prevent T. from writing *More Memories* (1933) and *Off the Record* (1943), further memoirs. She also completed *Places and Persons* (1925), an account of her travels, *Lay Sermons* (1927), a book of essays, and *Octavia* (1928), a novel of politics and hunting.

Although perhaps more memorable as a personality than as an author, T. displayed, in her writing, both verve and insight. Her *Autobiography* offers an entertaining if too complacent view of a vanished world.

WORKS: *Margot Asquith: An Autobiography* (1920). *Places and Persons* (1925). *Lay Sermons* (1927). *Octavia* (1928). *More Memories* (1933). *Off the Record* (1943).

BIBLIOGRAPHY: For articles in reference works, see: *DNB.*

Other references: Cowles, V. *Edward VII and His Circle* (1956). Jenkins, R. *Asquith: Portrait of a Man and an Era* (1964). Leslie, A. *Edwardians in Love* (1972). *Times* (London) (30 July 1945).

Anne B. Simpson

Emma Tennant

BORN: 20 October 1937, London.
DAUGHTER OF: Christopher Grey, 2nd Baron Glenconner, and Elizabeth Lady Glenconner.
MARRIED: Sebastian Yorke, 1957; Mr. Cockburn (n.d.); Mr. Dempsey (n.d.).
WROTE UNDER: Emma Tennant, Catherine Aydy.

Shortly after T. was born, her family moved to Scotland, where she lived for nine years before moving back to London. T. attended a village school in Scotland, St. Paul's Girls' School in London, and a finishing school in Oxford, where she was inspired to learn more about art. At fifteen T. traveled to Paris to study art history at the École de Louvre. When she returned to England, T. became a debutante and was presented at Court in 1956.

In 1961 T. began to contribute occasionally to the *New Statesman*. Two years later she became travel correspondent for *Queen*. Her first novel, *The Colour of Rain*, was published pseudonymously in 1964. In 1966 T. became features editor for *Vogue*. When *The Time of the Crack* (1973) was published, T. became a full-time novelist. Since then she has written nine novels and three children's books, edited two anthologies, and contributed to various publications.

T. was the founding editor of *Bananas*, a literary magazine of the British Arts Council, from 1975 to 1978. In 1978 T. began writing book reviews for the *Guardian*, to which she still contributes. She also became general editor of *In Verse* in 1982 and *Lives of Modern Women* in 1985. T. became a Fellow of the Royal Society of Literature in 1982.

Novelist, critic, and editor, T. cannot be pigeonholed. Three of her novels—*The Time of the Crack* (1973), *The Last of the Country House Murders* (1975), and *Hotel de Dream* (1976)—are science-fiction publications. The rest of her novels contain varying amounts of realism. T. herself does not believe that prose literature has an obligation to be realistic. She has said, "I would like to feel that I can go off in any direction that seems right." Consequently, her novels cannot be categorized. T. does, however, admit that "a lot of my books have actually been a blend of Calvinism and romanticism—having to do with murder and morals. . . ." By some critics she has been called a "woman writer" as opposed to a "writer"; that is, she does treat the feminist viewpoint, examining it and at times exhorting it, in most of her works. Nevertheless, she says about feminism, "the theory must never stand in the way of creativity."

After *The Colour of Rain* (1963), a realistic and critical view of English upper-class society, there was a ten-year hiatus in publishing, mainly because of T.'s loss of confidence resulting from a disparaging remark reportedly made about her book during judging for the Prix Formentor. T. re-entered the publishing market by way of the science-fiction genre, whose writers gave her support and confidence, with *The Time of the Crack* (1973). In this novel a huge crack opens unexpectedly in the Thames, separating the North from the South and throwing into chaos the strict separation between social classes that had existed before. The plot also involves two analysts who attempt to cure their patients by regression; the novel is an early example of T.'s criticism of the theories of "experts" in trying to explain a world that includes myth, imagination, and unexplainable phenomena. The *TLS* called the novel "Lewis Carroll technique applied to H.G. Wells material."

The Last of the Country House Murders (1974) is set in an England with a "Big Brother" government some time in the near future. In this parody of an English murder mystery, the murder of a remaining decadent aristocrat is going to be staged by the government for the entertainment of tourists. His only freedom: Jules Tanner gets to choose his murderer. In *Hotel de Dream* (1976) fantasy and reality intermingle as inhabitants of a boarding-house enter each other's dreams, spending much of their time escaping reality by sleeping. These three novels, which T. has called "political satire-fantasy," received fairly good reviews, noting her skill at describing settings and feelings, her intelligent humor, and her satire of modern society.

In *The Bad Sister* (1978) T. broke away from fantasy and returned to a more realistic mode, using "documents" to make up the novel. The bulk of this murder mystery consists of "The Journal of Jane Wild," sandwiched by comments from the "editor" of this journal. Here T. explores the theme of doubles, coupled with a critical look at both patriarchal tradition in society as well as its confrontation by militant revolutionary movements and militant feminism. As the clergyman Stephen remarks in the novel, "'It's the modern evil, I believe, this jumble of Marxism and Tantrism and anything else thrown in, which is used to persuade people to kill each other.'" This novel is based on James Hogg's *The Private Memoirs and Confessions of a Justified Sinner* (1824).

In her next two novels, *Wild Nights* (1979) and *Alice Fell* (1980), T. was less interested in plot and more in perception. Both novels, she has said, were "intended to be short works of poetic prose." *Wild Nights* is a first-person, "fictional childhood memoir," set in the Tennants' family home in Scotland. T. has described *Alice Fell* as a novel about "the fall of a girl, using the myth of Persephone." These two novels, along with her next, *Queen of Stones* (1982), use the theme of childhood. All three were inspired by her daughters' growing up.

Queen of Stones, a female version of *Lord of the Flies*, uses documents to reconstruct a fictional event. Besides presenting the lives of adolescent girls, the novel also satirizes society's official interpretation of adolescence, particularly Freudian analysis. The narrator pontificates: "Thus, perhaps, will the psychopathology of the developing female be more fully comprehended; as also the mythology sustaining our concept of the feminine in society." The narrator, whom T. has described as "pretty stupid," ends by blaming all the sinister events in the novel on the arrival of the first menstrual period of one of the main characters.

In *Woman Beware Woman* (1983, titled *The Half-Mother* in the United States), T. tried to evoke character more strongly than in her previous novels. Each of the three women in this story must beware of the others after the famous husband of one has been found dead. T. says that the book is about "the horrors of the 'perfect' family, and what in fact goes on underneath, the entrapments and tensions." She emphasizes that the characters do not represent women in our time.

Black Marina (1985), another mystery, brings the left-wing politics and feminism of the Portobello Road area, in London, to St. James, a tiny Caribbean Island. The book is also about the search for identity—not only for Marina, a young girl searching for her "roots," but for the entire island. T.'s evocation of place is superb. She describes the library of the last of the white colonial landowners as a place "where the peeling-off spines of the books hang like moths half out of their cocoons. . . ." This is a perfect metaphor for the entire island, which is stuck halfway between its colonial past and the modern world of resorts and condominiums—not to mention revolutions and invasions.

T.'s later novel, *The Adventures of Robina by Herself*, "edited" by Emma Tennant (1986), is a picaresque, autobiographical novel using eighteenth century idiom but set in the 1950s. It traces the adventures of an incredibly naive young woman from Oxford to Paris to London and is based on the premise that "the ways and manners of a certain section of the society in which we live are virtually unchanged since the early eighteenth century."

T.'s success has been in evoking a sense of place. Although she has said, "I think, in most writers, there's some sort of pattern," her own writing exemplifies another statement of hers: "Every different thing demands its own expression."

WORKS: *The Colour of Rain* (pseud. Catherine Aydy, 1963). *The Time of the Crack* (1973). *The Last* of the Country House Murders (1975). *Hotel de Dream* (1976). *The Bad Sister* (1978). (with M. Rayner) *The Boggart* (1979). *Wild Nights* (1979). *Alice Fell* (1980). *The Search for Treasure Island* (1981). *Queen of Stones* (1982). *Woman Beware Woman* (1983; U.S. ed. *The Half-Mother*). *Black Marina* (1985). *The Ghost Child* (1984). *Adventures of Robina by Herself*, ed. Emma Tennant (1986). *The House of Hospitalities* (1987).

BIBLIOGRAPHY: For articles in reference works, see: *CA. CLC. DLB. Science-Fiction Writers* (1981).

Other references: *NYTBR* (12 May 1985). *New Yorker* (20 May 1985). *TES* (23 February 1986). *TLS* (15 June 1973, 19 November 1982, 21 June 1985, 24 January 1986).

Carol Pulham

Ellen Terry

BORN: 27 February 1847, Coventry.
DIED: 21 July 1928, Smallhythe.
DAUGHTER OF: Ben Terry and Sarah Ballard.
MARRIED: George Frederick Watts, 1864; Charles Wardell, 1877; James Carew, 1907.

T. was born into the second generation of a large theatre family that would include her elder sister Kate, her son Edward Gordon Craig, and her great-nephew Sir John Gielgud. T. made her debut at the age of nine as Prince Mamillius in *The Winter's Tale* with Charles Kean. She continued to play minor roles while her sister Kate took center stage until 1864, when she married George Frederick Watts, a portrait artist thirty years her senior. Attracted by his wealth and sophisticated lifestyle, T. retired from the stage to marry him, but the couple separated ten months later.

The next three bleak years were enlivened for T. by friendship and photo sessions with Charles Dodgson, better known as Lewis Carroll. In one of the one-line but perceptive character sketches that fill her writing, T. described her shy friend: "He was as fond of me as he could be of anyone over the age of ten." In 1867, T. appeared with Henry Irving in a one-act travesty, *Katherine and Petruchio*, an inauspicious beginning to what was to be one of the most influential partnerships in British theatre history. T.'s career was once again interrupted in 1868, when she met Edward Godwin, an architect and designer, and retired to live with him (though still legally married to Watts) and raise their two children, Edith (b. 1869) and Edward Gordon Craig (b. 1872), one of the most important theatrical designers and theorists of the twentieth century.

In desperate need of money by 1875, T. broke with Godwin and was lured back to the stage by Charles Reade, her dearest friend and most dedicated teacher. Under his guidance, T. began to develop her own theory of dramatic style, which is recorded in her memoirs, letters, lectures, and acting notes. Filled with detailed directorial notes,

careful explorations of all aspects of a role, and recollections of emotional memories that might be used to create appropriate moods, T.'s writings at this time show that she was developing independently what would later be systematized by Stanislavsky at the Moscow Art Theatre. Rather than relying on instinct, as many actresses of her day did, T. relied on intellect and technique to produce a more natural acting style, free of bombast or presentational theatricality. Using these techniques, T. had her first major success as Portia in *The Merchant of Venice* and claimed the Shakespearean heroines as her own for the next thirty years.

In 1877, finally divorced from Watts, T. married a fellow actor, Charles Wardell (stage name Charles Kelly), primarily to give her family respectability, and initiated a financially and stylistically profitable twenty-two-year partnership with Irving. Together the two revolutionized Victorian theatrical style, researching the plays they produced to insure historical and psychological verisimilitude.

T.'s writings at this time provide perhaps the most detailed and intelligent records of style from the Victorian period. For her role as Ophelia, T. visited an asylum, but concluded that ". . .it is no good observing life and bringing the result to the stage without selection, without a definite idea. The idea must come first, realism afterward." T.'s acting texts are filled with copious notes on delivery, tone, pace, gesture, and motivation, as well as research about how others had performed or misperformed roles. Although her forte was voice and expressive movement, T. did not ignore other aspects of staging; she advised Irving about set, costume, and, in particular, lighting design.

From 1878–1901, T. and Irving reigned in public and in private as the chief theatrical couple, for T. had by now separated from Wardell. Together the two played almost all of Shakespeare and began to infuse the world of theatre with intellectual and social respectability, for which Irving was rewarded in 1894 with the first knighthood to be granted an actor. While she was busy breaking away from Victorian melodramatic style, however, T. almost missed the significance of the Ibsen invasion. Her 1891 "Stray Memories" in the *New Review* dismissed Nora and Hedda as "silly ladies . . . extraordinarily easy to act," a sentiment that earned her Shaw's severe criticism and which she was intelligent enough to omit from her *Memoirs* in 1908.

T.'s letters, memoirs, and notes preserve brilliant sketches of remarkable people, a fascinating record of the Victorian age, and a priceless historical document about the development of modern acting and staging styles. Of chief interest among the letters is her famous and spirited correspondence with Shaw (1892–1922), whom she counted as her second-best friend, and her letters to her son, in which she is by turns scolding and supportive, lamenting always over Craig's profligacy and infidelity but ever confident that his genius would be recognized. T.'s letters and memoirs also record intimate portraits of and communications from Tennyson, Wilde, Arnold, James, Churchill, Bernhardt, Duse, Woolf, Sitwell, Gladstone, and Sackville-West, among others.

Ironically, one of the greatest actresses of the late nineteenth-century is also one of the greatest theatrical historians and theorists. Her writings allow contemporary historians to reconstruct exactly the performances of yesterday and to eavesdrop at the formation of modern acting style. Before Stanislavsky, before Ibsen, before "Method" acting, before Freud, T. began to set down for herself, her age, and her son the scaffolding upon which contemporary theatrical style would be built.

WORKS: *The Story of My Life* (1908). *The Russian Ballet* (1913). *The Heart of Ellen Terry* (1928). *Ellen Terry and Bernard Shaw: A Correspondence*, ed. C. St. John (1931). *Four Lectures on Shakespeare* (1932). *Memoirs*, with Preface, Notes, and Additional Biographical chapters by E. Craig and C. St. John (1933).

BIBLIOGRAPHY: Adland, E. *Edy, Recollections of Edith Craig* (1949). Auerbach, N. *Ellen Terry: A Player in Her Time* (1987). Craig, E.G. *Ellen Terry and Her Secret Self* (1931). Craig, E.G. *Index to the Story of My Days* (1957). Manvell, R. *Ellen Terry* (1968). Nicoll, A. *A History of Late Nineteenth-century Drama* (1949). Prideaux, T. *Love or Nothing: The Life and Times of Ellen Terry* (1975). Shaw, G.B. (attributed) *Lady Wilt Thou Love Me?* (1980). Steen, M. *A Pride of Terrys* (1962).

Suzanne Westfall

Angela Margaret Thirkell

BORN: 30 January 1890, London.
DIED: 29 January 1961, Bramley, Surrey.
DAUGHTER OF: J.W. Mackail and of Margaret Burne-Jones.
MARRIED: James Campbell McInnes, 1911; George Thirkell, 1918.
WROTE UNDER: Leslie Parker, Angela Thirkell.

Born into a milieu of learning, culture, and creativity, T. was the daughter of the classicist and Oxford Professor of Poetry, J.W. Mackail, and of Margaret Burne-Jones, herself the daughter of the famous painter and Georgiana Macdonald Burne-Jones, an aunt of Rudyard Kipling. The Burne-Jones household, where T. and her sister Clare spent much of their early years, was the haunt of such late nineteenth-century notables as George Eliot, Beatrix Potter, Henry James, John Ruskin, and William Morris, and was the subject of her first book, *Three Houses* (1931). At home there was much reading of Dickens, Trollope, Gaskell, Eliot, Charles and Henry Kingsley, and George Macdonald (no relation), all of whose works are reflected in her work.

In 1911 she married James Campbell McInnes; the novelist Colin McInnes is her son.

After divorcing McInnes in 1917, in 1918 she married George Thirkell, an Australian by whom she had a son, Lance, the prototype of Tony Morland in her writing. The Thirkells left England for Australia in 1920 on board a troop ship, a harrowing adventure which was the subject of *Trooper to the Southern Cross* (1934), written under the name of Leslie Parker. The troop ship was crowded with army prisoners, many deserters, and some hardened criminals who organized a near-mutiny. The mayhem and destruction, the first T. experienced in her sheltered life, may have contributed to her lack of confidence in the lower classes, continually expressed in her novels, at first in Dickensian humor, later in bitterness.

Always homesick for England, T. made a long visit in 1928 and returned permanently in 1929, her marriage having failed. As she had in Australia, T. began to write for magazines on literary topics, drawing on her family contacts and her own interests, and published her first novel, the popular autobiographical *Ankle Deep* (1933). During this time she was also reader for a British publisher, using her French and German to good effect.

The first of the "Barsetshire" novels (although not so planned) was *High Rising* (1933) whose heroine was Laura Morland, a valiant lady novelist who wrote to support her family. This book was dismissed as mere "feminism" by the *London Times* but led to *Demon in the House* (1934) in which Barsetshire (modelled on Trollope) was first mentioned as T.'s imaginary world. After a break in 1935, when she published another autobiographical novel, *O These Men, These Men!*, and a children's book, *The Grateful Sparrow*, the "Barsetshire" novels continued yearly until 1960.

The Barsetshire novels have been called both social history by Elizabeth Bowen and social documentary by Richard Church, and as such have engendered controversy as to whether they are valuable as descriptions of a lost middle class or to be condemned for false values. A good deal of the appreciation of her work is due to her unabashed debt to Trollope, the Kingsleys, Meredith, and Dickens. These nineteenth-century writers gave not only rich allusive texture but plots and parts of plots as well. *Miss Bunting* (1945), for instance, has heroines and a plot very similar to Trollope's *The Two Heroines of Plumpington*, a design for the Thirkell material which worked very well until the last tired novels, which are essentially pastiche. Her point of view, if dated carefully, is almost that of an upper-middle-class observer of a decade or so before her birth and owed much to her early Burne-Jones exposure as well as her academic home. Her perspective, seen by critics as reactionary, was in fact nostalgic; she regretted not knowing a world which had never been hers but through hearsay.

Other writings of note include *The Fortunes of Harriette* (1936) and *Coronation Summer* (1937), which utilized her love of research, the first a biography of Harriette Wilson, the intellec-

tually liberated eighteenth-century courtesan, and the second a fictionalization of the coronation festivities of 1837. During her career she also wrote short stories and novelettes for various magazines which she deprecated and which have never been collected.

WORKS: *Three Houses* (1931). *Ankle Deep* (1933). *High Rising* (1933). *The Demon in the House* (1934). (as Leslie Parker) *Trooper to the Southern Cross* (1935). *Wild Strawberries* (1934). *The Grateful Sparrow and Other Stories* (1935). *O These Men, These Men!* (1935). *August Folly* (1936). *The Fortunes of Harriette* (1936). *Coronation Summer* (1937). *Summer Half* (1937). *Pomfret Towers* (1938). *Before Lunch* (1939). *The Brandons* (1939). *Cheerfulness Breaks In* (1940). *Northbridge Rectory* (1941). *Marling Hall* (1942). *Growing Up* (1943). *The Headmistress* (1944). *Miss Bunting* (1945). *Peace Breaks Out* (1946). *Private Enterprise* (1947). *Love Among the Ruins* (1948). *The Old Bank House* (1949). *County Chronicle* (1950). *The Duke's Daughter* (1951). *Happy Returns* (1952). *Jutland Cottage* (1953). *What Did It Mean?* (1954). *Enter Sir Robert* (1955). *Never Too Late* (1956). *A Double Affair* (1957). *Close Quarters* (1958). *Love at All Ages* (1959). *Three Score and Ten* (1961, with C.A. Lejeune).

BIBLIOGRAPHY: Strickland, J. *Angela Thirkell* (1970). McInnes, G. *The Road To Gundagai* (1965, includes reminiscences of his mother). E. Bowen wrote the introduction to *An Angela Thirkell Omnibus* (1966).

For articles in reference works, see: *CA. MBL. TCA* and *SUP. TCW.*

Eleanor Langstaff

Alice Wandesford Thornton

BORN: 13 February 1627, Kirklington, Richmondshire.
DIED: Winter 1706/7, East Newton.
DAUGHTER OF: Christopher Wandesford and Alice Osborne.
MARRIED: William Thornton, 1651.

The life of T. is worth our attention, but, ironically, it comes down to us because her autobiography was valued in the late nineteenth century as "a kind of family history," a reconstruction of several small manuscript volumes, all written by T. Despite the necessity of reading it at second hand, the autobiography today reveals the conditions of life during mid-seventeenth-century England and the particular circumstances and character of an exceptional woman. T.'s lot is one that

attracts our attention because of the many trials and losses that she endured. It also becomes a testimony to the strength and resilience that T. derived from the memory of her mother and from her faith.

T. memorialized her father, Christopher Wandesford, a man of good estate, domestic virtue, and strict religious principles best known as a statesman. He had accompanied his cousin, the Earl of Strafford, to Ireland, where Wandesford became Lord Deputy with a considerable estate and nobility. He died at an early age, however, leaving his widow with three young children. She settled in Hipswell and raised her children according to those principles instilled in her by her own father and honored by her husband, especially the lessons of piety. It is those lessons that sustained T.

T.'s husband was of the minor gentry of Yorkshire, from a family that had been Roman Catholic until the early seventeenth century. During the few years they were married, Thornton was weak and careless; when he died, he left T. with few resources other than those that were a part of her heritage and her character. She remained alone in their home until her death in 1707. During those years, T. wrote of her youth, a time that she recalled with some contentment, especially the days before her marriage when she lived with her mother.

T.'s autobiography, however, is not a pleasant remembrance of things past; it is, instead, a vindication of her name and her actions. With as much evidence as she could gather, T. reveals, point by point, how she was cheated and slandered and how she was forced to endure extreme poverty from the time she married until her death. She was cheated by her brother, she was humiliated by her husband's limitations, and she was slandered by those who stood to benefit from her struggles. Although T.'s autobiography ends in 1669, additional material about her later years comes from the diary and letters of her son-in-law, Dean Comber, and from her last will and testament. From the first pages, T. recounts her gratitude to God, even while she is describing some awful events, such as for example, when she fell and almost died in 1629. The view that she survives to remember God's mercy becomes one of the forces in T.'s life, infusing her autobiography with its power and purpose.

A number of first-hand accounts of the Civil War—the Wandesfords were Royalists—bring to life the confrontations between the religious and political factions. Her account of the beheading of the king testifies to the despair and righteousness of many in England who suffered at the hands of the Parliamentarians. When the Wandesfords' property was sequestered in 1651 and when her oldest brother died, T. suffered even more, this time, however, at the hands of her younger brother, Christopher, who became the heir. To escape his greed, T.'s mother urged T. to marry. T. writes, however: "I was exceedingly sattisfied in that happie and free condittion, wherein I injoyed my time with delight abundantly in the service of my God, and the obedience I owed to such an excelent parent." She marries, but on her wedding day she is so ill that she fears that God does not want her to wed. She writes: "it highly conserned me to enter into this greatest change of my life with abundance of feare and caution, not lightly, nor unadvisedly, nor, as I may take my God to witnesse that knowes the secretts of hearts, I did it not to fulfill the lusts of the flesh, but in chastity and singleness of heart, as marrieing in the Lord."

The problems with her marriage, childbirth, and her widowhood are rich sources for those who need to know more about the condition of women during the seventeenth century. No richer source exists, despite its being secondhand. T.'s patience, goodness, and endurance endear her to her readers, who admire and learn what it was to be a woman then.

WORKS: *The Autobiography of Mrs. Alice Thornton, of East Newton, Co. York*, ed. C. Jackson (1875).

BIBLIOGRAPHY: In *The Weaker Vessel* (1984), A. Fraser provides commentary on hundreds of women of the seventeenth century, frequently referring to T.

For articles in reference works, see: A.M.W. Stirling's *Odd Lives* (1959).

Sophia B. Blaydes

Gillian Tindall

BORN: 4 May 1938, London.
DAUGHTER OF: Parents' names not known.
MARRIED: R.G. Lansdown.

T. is noted for her fiction, but she has also written books on literary biography (George Gissing) and urban history (Bombay and a London suburb). She received a master's degree with first class honors at Oxford and published her first book when she was twenty-one. She regularly contributes essays and reviews to the London *Times*, the *Sunday Times, New Society, The Guardian, The Observer*, and *The New Statesman*, as well as other publications. T., whose range of interests is wide, has been described as "insatiably curious" about topics that interest her. She has won a number of prizes for her books, including the Mary Elgin Prize (1970) and the Somerset Maugham Prize (1972, for *Fly Away Home*). Though she has been compared to other writers, such as Margaret Drabble, her flat, journalistic style and distinctive approach to her characters make her unlike other women writing in Britain in the 1980s.

Her first book, *No Name in the Street* (1959; published in the U.S. as *When We Had Other Names*, 1960) received respectable reviews, as did the several books that followed: *The Water and the Sound* (1961), *The Edge of the Paper* (1963), and *The Israeli Twins* (1963). Most of her protagonists in these, and her other works, are women who have compromised their own values and independence for the security that comes from stable relationships, until the time comes when these relationships are no longer open to them, as with death, war, or other calamity. Reviewers have noted the frequency with which T.'s central characters seem to accept their lives until such unexpected events occur, after which they move on to evaluate options open to them, whether renewed relationships with others, return to their families, or independence. In most cases, acquiescence to conventionality dilutes their individuality and makes them less interesting, but T. evidently intends to suggest that there are relatively few options open and that some of these options carry a price, namely, conformity and compromise.

T.'s openness with her characters' lives is evident in her first two novels and is frequently illustrated thereafter. Both *No Name in the Street* and *The Water and the Sound* present young, self-consciously "emancipated" women exploring new worlds, not only physically (Paris) but even more the freedom of choice suddenly thrust upon them. Hence their self-conscious sexual initiation and awareness of such related activities as miscarriage, a lover's secret homosexuality, and even incest serve only to make them more determined to find their places in life and to do so with drive and tenacity. *The Water and the Sound* is especially effective in showing how the young Nadia gradually discovers the truth about her wild, bohemian father and mother, both of whom had lived fast, romantic lives and died before Nadia was able to piece together their lives when she too moves to Paris.

These characters' relative impotence in the face of overwhelming forces takes a curious turn, however; when they opt for marriage and conventionality, their determination ceases. The wife in *The Edge of the Paper*, for example, has all that a woman might conventionally desire in a mate, including wealth and good looks. But when her husband's psychotic cruelty is revealed, she increasingly feels trapped and threatened but does nothing. The wife in *Someone Else* (1969) reacts intensely to her husband's death, having sublimated all her inner resources to her husband; all she can do is passively to accept the support and vicarious emotional protection offered by other men.

T. often balances such ordinary, unassuming people as these wives and other characters against forces that seem disproportionate to the effect they have on the characters; her novels are filled with fiery accidents, child murder, abortion, murder, incest, and infant deformity, as if to suggest that the reality her characters experience is somehow thrown into relief by the terrors they encounter. All the stories in *Dances of Death:*

Short Stories on a Theme (1973) deal with death in some way, but even here T.'s concern seems to be the inadequate reaction of respectable middle-class people to death. In this and in some of the novels, characters are dispatched with seeming indifference because, as T. notes in her foreword to *Dances of Death*, "It is not the extra-ordinary possibility of life after death which interests me at the moment but, rather, the ordinariness of death, the awkward mystery, within the context of daily life."

Though T.'s fictions have been dismissed as "Bourgeois Hausfrau" novels, she has shown growth as a writer. Her protagonist in *Fly Away Home* (1971), Antonia Boileau, reflects self-consciously about the changes in her life since adolescence and especially her French husband's inability to grapple with his Jewish origins; only after she goes to Israel to see a former lover does she realize that she cannot restore the past. The same necessary acceptance of what is can be found in *The Traveller and His Child* (1975), about a divorced man's grief for his son.

Her more recent novels have focused on her protagonists' efforts to capture the all-but-forgotten past. *The Intruder* (1979) tells of an English woman's being caught with her son in occupied France during World War II and her attempt in the present to find the truth regarding the past; it has been compared favorably to such novels as Elizabeth Bowen's *The Heat of the Day*. Her 1987 novel, *To the City*, also describes an attempt to recapture the past, in this case in the person of a Holocaust survivor who returns some forty-five years later, as a successful publisher, to the Europe of the war years and to a former mistress. Though this novel was received less favorably (it was called "self-indulgent and turgid" in the *TLS*), it does suggest T.'s continuing fascination with her characters' traumatic pasts.

T. has also written well-received works of non-fiction, notably *The Born Exile: George Gissing* (1974), which has been uniformly praised for its intelligence, sensitivity, and care; it reflects a thorough awareness of conventional scholarship on Gissing and is sufficiently detailed and documented to warrant its being called (in *TLS*) the "best critical study of Gissing yet written." T.'s interest in the development of cities has led to her writing *The Fields Beneath: The History of One London Village* (1977), about Kentish Town, a run-down part of the metropolis that was founded in the eleventh century, and *City of Gold: The Biography of Bombay* (1982), both of which have received acclaim from specialists and general readers alike for their vivid recreation of the cities' lives and for her scholarship.

Though T. has not been accorded the quantity or kind of criticism received by other contemporary writers concerned with middle-class women's struggles to find themselves in a world of change and insecurity, she has established a niche with her fiction for the kind of novel that seems on the surface to be little more than a conventional exploration of the same issues that more exciting writers, such as Lessing or Drabble, have made into metaphysical or psychological territory.

WORKS: *No Name in the Street* (1959; in the U.S. as *When We Had Other Names*, 1960). *The Water and the Sound* (1961). *The Edge of the Paper* (1963). *The Israeli Twins* (1963). *A Handbook on Witches* (1965). *The Youngest* (1967). *Someone Else* (1969). *Fly Away Home* (1971). *Dances of Death: Short Stories on a Theme* (1973). *The Born Exile: George Gissing* (1974). *The Traveller and His Child* (1975). *The Fields Beneath: The History of One English Village* (1977). *The Intruder* (1979). *The China Egg* (1981). *City of Gold: The Biography of Bombay* (1982). *Looking Forward* (1983). *Rosamund Lehmann: An Appreciation* (1985). *To the City* (1987).

BIBLIOGRAPHY:
For articles in reference works, see: *CA*. *CLC*. *CN*. *WD*.

Other references: *Books and Bookmen* (September 1973, March 1974, September 1979, July 1983, February 1984, September 1984, March 1985). *Economist* (2 February 1974, 17 September 1977). *Encounter* (September 1975, July 1975). *History Today* (October 1980). *Listener* (5 July 1973, 19 June 1975, 13 September 1979, 14 May 1981, 11 March 1982). *New Statesman* (17 August 1973, 1 February 1974, 27 June 1975, 16 September 1977, 14 September 1979, 16 April 1982, 8 February 1985). *NYTBR* (8 September 1974, 1 December 1974). *Observer* (8 July 1973, 3 February 1974, 15 June 1975, 11 September 1977, 9 September 1979, 12 April 1981, 4 April 1982, 21 August 1983, 16 October 1983, 3 February 1985). *Partisan Review* (Winter 1976). *Punch* (27 February 1980). *Spectator* (9 February 1974, 21 June 1975, 2 May 1981, 10 April 1982, 2 March 1985). *TES* (19 March 1982, 15 February 1985). *TLS* (20 July 1973, 22 February 1974, 20 June 1975, 23 November 1979, 27 March 1981, 16 April 1982, 15 February 1985, 8 May 1987).

Paul Schlueter

Honor Lilbush Wingfield Tracy

BORN: 19 October, 1913, Bury St. Edmunds, East Anglia. (Some sources use 19 December 1915.)
DAUGHTER OF: Humphrey Wingfield and Christabel May Clare (Miller) Tracy.

T. is the daughter of a British surgeon, Humphrey Wingfield, and it is probably not stretching the analogy to say that she has spent her own career dissecting and eviscerating the natives of Ireland, Spain, and the Caribbean. Most of the unwilling patients die on the table, "hapless victims," according to Terrence A. McVeigh, "[of] totally uneven contests and nasty little stories of victim and victimizer."

Many of T.'s fictional efforts, *The Straight and Narrow Path* (1956), *The Prospects Are Pleasing* (1958), *The First Day of Friday* (1963), *The Quiet End of Evening* (1972), *In a Year of Grace* (1975), *The Man from Next Door* (1977), and *The Battle of Castle Reef* (1979), deal with the foibles and failings of the Irish among whom T. lived for the better part of ten years. Ironically, her name and the Irish settings of these novels have convinced many readers that she is Irish. Her usual retort is that her Norman ancestor, Beau Tracy, lived in Ireland until 1775. When he later attempted to have the family reinstated as citizens of Ireland, he was in the Fleet Prison for debtors

in England and the Irish turned down his petition.

When T. was sent to Ireland in 1950 by the *Sunday Times* (of London) as a special correspondent, she became embroiled in a libel suit filed against her by a country priest who felt insulted by one of her articles; this legal action was her introduction to the convoluted and labyrinthine paths of Irish justice. In *Mind You, I've Said Nothing! Forays in the Irish Republic* (1953) (a collection of essays), she explains how her own solicitor managed to defend and betray her in the same courtroom. A somewhat fictionalized account of this same case was the basis for *The Straight and Narrow Path* in which an English anthropologist, Andrew Butler (who speaks for T.), is sued by a canon. The canon is, of course, represented in court by the same charming and devious Irishman who precipitated the legal battle in the first place.

In typical T. style, this canon is cheated by a plumber who builds him an upstairs bath. Unfortunately for the priest, water does not flow to the second story in Patrickstown, the scene of the novel, but, as T. points out, the priest ordered a tub; he never mentioned water. Like all the Irish plumbing in T.'s novels, it doesn't work and we don't expect it to. The constant reader of her fiction is not surprised when Sabrina Boxham's bathtub in *The Quiet End of Evening* is delivered without faucets or a plug and that the old bathtub has already been removed. T.'s novels are peopled with silly, annoying, and devious types running naked through the gardens and pellmell through the books. They usually serve as counterpoint to one sensible character with whom the reader can identify. In *The Prospects Are Pleasing* (1958), he is Felix Horniman, and in *A Number of Things* (1960), set not in Ireland but in Trinidad, he is Henry Lamb, who is entranced by three Indian women, Mummee, Grannee, and Auntee. He is followed in *A Season of Mists* (1961) by Ninian Latouche, only superficially sane, who is surrounded not by Irishmen but by Siamese cats, Italian servants, and the jarring noise of jet planes. This book is a dissection of life in modern anachronistic England.

The First Day of Friday (1963) is again set in Ireland, but it is a more bitter book replete with madness, tormented souls, and melancholia. As Walter Allen has noted, this novel ". . . verges on the comedy of despair." It was followed by several happier novels (particularly *The Quiet End of Evening*) and in 1977 by *The Man from Next Door*. The reasonable, sensible type surfaces in Caroline Bigge, a schoolfriend of Penelope Butler's around whom the novel revolves. Ms. Butler is a recently rich heroine (courtesy of the "football" pools) who is being victimized by her next-door neighbor, Johnny Cruise, and his Indian cohorts, the Khans; Cruise's motive seems to be one thousand years of his ancestors' Irish anger at the English, represented by Ms. Butler. His character is so shady and shallow, and hers so silly and gullible, that the reader has trouble feeling empathy with either of them.

This is perhaps the most glaring fault in the work of T.; as a reviewer in the *Sunday Times* (London) has noted, "some of the jokes are too hoary" and the caricatures are a bit heavyhanded to be believable. The reader is usually amused because T. is funny, clever, and even devilish. But there is always a sense of laughing *at* the characters, who are immersed in their own smug, nonsensical folly. Tracy doesn't have much patience for the delusions of these people, and she is an ardent enemy of the superstitions and hypocrisy that permeate twentieth-century life. One pictures her pouring from the teapot without the tempest.

In any case, her books have been translated into several languages and she is read and admired from Budapest to New York. The critics have consistently praised her travel books, particularly *Winter in Castile*, and in this genre she is considered to be without peer.

WORKS: (translator) B. deLigt, *The Conquest of Violence* (1937). *Kakemono: A Sketch Book of Post-War Japan* (1950). *Mind You, I've Said Nothing! Forays in the Irish Republic* (1953). *Silk Hats and No Breakfast: Notes on a Spanish Journey* (1957). *The Straight and Narrow Path* (1956). *The Prospects Are Pleasing* (1958). *A Number of Things* (1960). *A Season of Mists* (1961). *The First Day of Friday* (1963). *Men at Work* (1966). *The Beauty of the World* (published in the United States as *Settled in Chambers*, 1967). *De l' Angleterre; or Miss Austen Provides a Footnote; The Sorrows of Ireland* (1967). *The Butterflies of the Province* (1970). *The Quiet End of Evening* (1972). *In a Year of Grace* (1974). *The Man from Next Door* (1977). *The Ballad of Castle Reef* (1979).

BIBLIOGRAPHY: Gindin, J. *Postwar British Fiction*, 1962.

For articles in reference works, see: *CN. DIL. DLB.*

Other references: *Book World* (28 April 1968). *National Observer* (10 August 1968). *NYT* (26 December 1979). *NYTBR* (10 March 1968, 8 May 1977). *Time* (5 April 1980).

Mickey Pearlman

Sarah Kirby Trimmer

BORN: 1741.
DIED: 4 January 1811, Brentford, Middlesex.
DAUGHTER OF: Joshua Kirby.
MARRIED: James Trimmer, 1762.

T. was born into a middle-class family of some limited professional accomplishment—her father later became drawing instructor to the Prince of Wales—and a decidedly religious cast of mind. At age twenty-one she married a prosperous brickmaker in the parish of Brentford, west of London, set about bearing his children (ten of whom lived to adulthood), and by degrees discovered a vocation that linked her nursery to a wider world. With her husband's encouragement, T. began to write stories for the instruction of her own children, introducing them to the world around them and publishing them in 1780 as *An Easy Introduction to the Knowledge of Nature*. Thus was launched the career of one of the earliest and most prolific children's authors in our language.

T. seems instinctively to have been a teacher and to have recognized the efficacy of the narrative form for making important moral points for children. In the 1780s she published lessons and prints to assist children in learning English history, scriptural history, and Roman history, sets that became enduring classics for home instruction of middle-class children; these were re-issued and expanded well into the nineteenth century, and the two volumes on scriptural history (one for each testament) were translated into French. In 1786 she also wrote her most famous work, *Fabulous Histories*, more widely known by its familiar title (and most popular story), *The History of the Robins*. It is this book, dedicated to promoting kindness to animals, on which T.'s enduring fame rests; it was translated into French and German, and new editions were being published as late as 1912.

Buoyed by her success and encouraged by friends and reviewers to turn her attention to the legions of children living in poverty and squalor, she quickly wrote a pair of exemplary tales (*The Servant's Friend* and *The Two Farmers*) intended to show them the way to grow. (Most of the credit for inventing and popularizing this genre has gone to her friend and contemporary, Hannah More, but T. also deserves recognition.) More importantly, she set about establishing Sunday schools in Brentford, modelled upon those of Robert Raikes in Gloucester, since she believed that the poor were most desperately in need of moral regeneration and that it would take the combined efforts of many like herself to effect any change for the better. Consequently, she published in 1787 *The Oeconomy of Charity*, an extensive discourse intended to show English ladies how they could help the poor and help themselves at the same time by starting Sunday schools and schools of industry for children of the poor. Recognizing that poor people taught to read would need something wholesome upon which to practice their skills, T. began in 1788 to publish *The Family Magazine*, a monthly journal issued for a year and a half and filled with discourses, poems, reprinted religious tracts, columns of news from foreign parts, tips on domestic economy, and exemplary tales by the editor herself. These tales were later collected and issued under the title *Instructive Tales* by the Society for Promoting Christian Knowledge. Since T. was the first woman to be published by the Society, it was clear that her way of talking to the poor had found favor with the Anglican establishment.

In the last two decades of her life T. wrote more for her wider audience on social questions than for children; those things she wrote for children were not marked by the generosity of spirit that had characterized her early works and never achieved any reputation. She became much more interested in practical theology than she had been before and wrote several books on the sacraments

and offices of the church. Clearly, however, her energies were being absorbed by the great social crisis in England attendant upon the Revolution of 1789 in France. In common with many reputable churchmen, she believed there was a great anti-Christian conspiracy abroad in Europe of which the Revolution was only the greatest manifestation. Her piety, which had been tolerant if not ecumenical before 1789, became markedly more narrow and intolerant of dissent. Her charity was strained by fear of the unregenerate masses, and her publications in the 1790s are more concerned with controlling the poor than regenerating them.

The final chapter of T.'s public career centers around her second venture into periodical publication, *The Guardian of Education*, which she began in May 1802, and which had as its purpose nothing less than the screening of all publications on education and the censoring of those ideas that did not measure up to a proper Christian standard. Education is quite widely defined here to include anything bearing upon the nurture of children; indeed, one of the most interesting features of the publication is the extended essay on Christian child-raising by T. herself, which was posthumously published by the S.P.C.K. She became embroiled in the famous Lancaster-Bell controversy over monitorial education in 1805, when she published her *Comparative View of the New Plan of Education. . . .* Having come under fire from Sydney Smith in the *Edinburgh Review* for those efforts, she ceased publication of *The Guardian* and retired to her study in 1806. She had served notice, however, of the need for a genuinely national, church-based approach to the education of the poor and has been given credit for inspiring the National Society formed in 1812 to accomplish those ends.

WORKS: *Easy Introduction to the Knowledge of Nature* (1780). *Description of a Set of Prints of English History* (1785). *Description of a Set of Prints of Scripture History* (1786). *Fabulous Histories* (1786). *The Oeconomy of Charity* (1787). *The Servant's Friend* (1787). *The Two Farmers* (1787). *Family Magazine* (1788-89). *Description of a Set of Prints of Ancient History* (1789). *Comment on Dr. Watt's Divine Songs for Children* (1789). *Explanation of the Office of Public Baptism . . . and Confirmation* (1791). *Reflections upon the Education of Children in Charity Schools* (1792). *Charity School Spelling Book* (1799). *An Attempt to Familiarize the Catechism* (1800). *Abridgement of Scripture History* (1804). *Help to the Unlearned in the Study of Holy Scripture* (1804). *The Guardian of Education* (1802-06). *A Comparative View of the New Plan of Education Promulgated by Mr. Joseph Lancaster . . . and of the System of Christian Education Founded by Our Pious Forefathers . . .* (1805).

Concise History of England (1808). *Essay on Christian Education* (1812).

BIBLIOGRAPHY: Anonymous. *Some Account of the Life and Writings of Mrs. Trimmer, with Original Letters and Meditations and Prayers, Selected from Her Journal* (1814). Balfour, C.L. *A Sketch of Mrs. Trimmer* (1854). Meigs, C. *A Critical History of Children's Literature* (1953).

For articles in reference works, see: *CBEL*.

Other references: Silver, H. *The Concept of Popular Education* (1965). Sturt, M. *The Education of the People* (1967).

Robert Bonner

Frances Milton Trollope

BORN: 10 March 1779, Stapleton, near Bristol.
DIED: 6 October 1863, Florence.
DAUGHTER OF: William Milton and Frances Gresley.
MARRIED: Thomas Anthony Trollope, 1809.

Although the author of thirty-four novels, T. has been more widely recognized as the mother of Anthony Trollope and as the author of a popular travel book, *Domestic Manners of the Americans*, than for her fictional achievements. Yet her controversial social-reform novels and her recurring use of a new, strong heroine makes T. a significant pioneer in nineteenth-century fiction. Her use of fiction to advocate legal reform and attack social abuses and her development of complex feminine characters influenced the work of many of her contemporaries.

T. was a Bristol clergyman's daughter who lost her mother early and was educated by her father in languages, the classics, and the arts. When her father remarried, she went to London with her brother and sister for five years, not marrying until she was nearly thirty. T.'s marriage was somewhat of a surprise to those who knew her well, for her husband, by whom she had seven children in eight years, was a serious and retiring barrister. After eighteen years in London and Harrow, where the family built a stately home, the Trollopes found themselves on the brink of bankruptcy.

Faced with destitution, T. decided to join an experiment in utopian living in the United States. But the venture was a disappointment, and T. went on to Cincinnati where she tried to find work. Here her life alternated between plans for grandiose business and cultural schemes and devastating failure. At fifty-two, destitute again, she returned to England and published her first book, *Domestic Manners of the Americans*, an instant and controversial bestseller. Exposing "the lamentable insignificance of the American woman" and attacking many of America's most prized beliefs, the book generated some of the harshest criticism of its time, yet went through many editions in America, England, and the Continent.

Domestic Manners of the Americans, which achieved an almost unheard-of success for a first work, is a chronological account of her experiences during her almost four-year stay in the United States. The book's appeal lies in T.'s brilliant selection of detail and the way she transformed her material into representative and amusing vignettes of nineteenth-century American life. According to Mark Twain, her work was accurate enough to be called "photography." The most original part of the book is T.'s underlying thesis that the sins and flaws of America stem mainly from the exclusion of women from the mainstream of American life, a situation resulting, she believed, from male preference, not economic necessity. Throughout the work she documents a hostility toward women lurking beneath the surface of American life.

Thus at fifty-three T. was launched on a writing career. But even the earnings from her subsequent travel books on Germany and Paris and several popular novels failed to keep the family afloat, and they were forced to abandon their home and flee to Belgium, where Trollope could not be sued by his creditors. For several years the Trollopes lived in rented lodgings in Brussels while T. wrote frantically to support the family. At the same time, she nursed several of her children who were dying of tuberculosis; she often spent her time alternating between the care of the mortally ill and the grinding out of fiction.

She continued to make tours, however, hoping to repeat the success of *Domestic Manners of the Americans*. She soon realized, though, that much of what she earned was spent in transporting herself and her family to the places she needed to see. Thus for economic as well as domestic reasons, T. turned primarily to writing fiction.

Through her concentration on social abuses she became one of the first novelists to bring unpleasant subject matter squarely into what had been aptly called "the fairy land of fiction." Her first social-reform novel, *The Life and Adventures of Jonathan Whitlaw* (1836), grew out of her strong revulsion against American slavery. Telling the story of a cruel overseer, T.'s work anticipated the more famous Harriet Beecher Stowe's *Uncle Tom's Cabin* by fifteen years. T.'s next contribution to social-reform fiction was *The Vicar of Wrexhill* (1837), an attack upon evangelical excesses and their unfortunate effects upon women.

In the course of her literary career T. was twice prompted to write a novel advocating legislative reform. In 1839 she began publishing *Michael Armstrong, the Factory Boy* to dramatize the need for passage of a ten-hours bill, and in 1843 she published *Jessie Phillips: A Tale of the Present Day* to demonstrate the weaknesses of the New Poor Law, particularly the bastardy clauses. Both works met with only mediocre popular success and both were harshly criticized although for different reasons. As far as most critics were concerned, *Michael Armstrong* revealed nothing about child labor that the 1832 republication of John Brown's *A Memoir of Robert Blincoe* and the 1837-1838 publication of Charles Dickens' *Oliver Twist* had not already shown. Yet despite the charge that it all had been said before and that reform was on the way, T.'s novel was very much of its time. She investigated factory conditions herself, finding that while some changes had been made many abuses still existed, but the Ten Hours Bill was not passed until 1847.

Jessie Phillips was also often criticized as a second-rate novel dealing with a topic, the New Poor Law, already portrayed in more finely executed works, particularly *Oliver Twist* and Thomas Carlyle's *Past and Present*. Much of the criticism was leveled at T. for having "sinned grievously against good taste and decorum" by dealing with the bastardy clauses of the New Poor Law; yet precisely because it deals with the bastardy clauses *Jessie Phillips* is unique. T. was by no means a first-rate novelist, but her weakness is in her presentation, not her subject matter. Stereotypical and exaggerated characterization and intrusive narrators are her major weaknesses although significant improvements can be seen when later novels are compared with earlier ones.

After her daughter's death in 1848, T. returned to Florence where she embarked upon her last fictional innovation: a group of novels in which the heroines are triumphant, whose most obvious quality is an aggressive independence, and whose most frequent trials are confrontations with tyrannical fathers or marriages to weak or evil men. In her last novel, *Fashionable Life; or, Paris and London* (1856), T. moves from these dominant ladies to a vision of a community of females living in peace, harmony, and cooperation—happier than they had ever been with the men in their lives.

While never becoming a novelist of special distinction, T. did develop as a writer. Her growing understanding of how the structures of the novel—such as characterization, parallelism, and continuity—work to form a whole made her a popular novelist during her lifetime and an interesting figure for study in light of her influence both on society and on other writers.

WORKS: *Domestic Manners of the Americans* (1832). *The Refugee in America: A Novel* (1832). *The Mother's Manual; or, Illustrations of Matrimonial Economy: An Essay in Verse* (1833). *The Abbess: A Romance* (1833). *Belgium and Western Germany in 1833* (1834). *Tremordyn Cliff* (1835). *Paris and the Parisians in 1835* (1836). *The Life and Adventures of Jonathan Jefferson Whitlaw; or, Scenes on the Mississippi* (1836). *The Vicar of Wrexhill* (1837). *Vienna and the Austrians* (1838). *A Romance of Vienna* (1838). *The Widow Barnaby* (1839). *The Life and Adventures of Michael Armstrong, the Factory Boy* (1839-1840). *The Widow Married: A Sequel to The Widow Barnaby* (1840). *One Fault: A Novel* (1840). *Charles Chesterfield; or, The Adventures of a Youth of Genius* (1841). *The Ward of Thorpe Combe* (1841). *The Blue Belles of England* (1842). *A Visit to Italy* (1842); *Jessie Phillips: A Tale of the Present Day* (1842-1843). *The Barnabys in America; or, Adventures of the Widow Wedded* (1843). *Hargrave; or, The Adventures of a Man of Fashion* (1843). *The Laurringtons; or, Superior People* (1844). *Young Love: A Novel* (1844). *The Attractive Man* (1846). *The Robertses on Their Travels* (1846). *Travels and Travellers: A Series of Sketches* (1846). *Father Eustace: A Tale of the Jesuits* (1847). *The Three Cousins* (1847). *Town and Country: A Novel* (1848). *The Young Countess; or, Love and Jealousy* (1848). *The Lottery of Marriage: A Novel* (1849). *The Old World and the New: A Novel* (1849). *Petticoat Government: A Novel* (1850). *Mrs. Mathews; or, Family Mysteries* (1851). *Second Love; or, Beauty and Intellect: A Novel* (1851). *Uncle Walter: A Novel* (1852). *The Young Heiress: A Novel* (1853). *The Life and Adventures of a Clever Woman. Illustrated with Occasional Extracts from Her Diary* (1854). *Gertrude; or, Family Pride* (1855). *Fashionable Life; or, Paris and London* (1856).

BIBLIOGRAPHY: Pope-Hennessy, U. *Three English Women in America* (1929). Sadleir, M. *Anthony Trollope* (1927, 1945). Stebbins, L.P., and R.P. Stebbins, *The Trollopes* (1946). Trollope, F.E. *Frances Trollope: Her Life and Literary Works from George III to Victoria* (1895). Wilson, M. *These Were Muses* (1924).

For articles in reference works, see: *Allibone. BA19C. DLB. DNB.*

Other references: Chaloner, W.H. *Victorian Studies* (1960). Heinemann, H. *American Quarterly* (1969). Heinemann, H. *International Journal of Women's Studies* (1978). Super, R.H. *MLS* (1986).

Lynn M. Alexander

Katharine Tynan

BORN: 23 January 1861, Dublin.
DIED: 2 April 1931, London.
DAUGHTER OF: Andrew and Elizabeth Reily Tynan.
MARRIED: Henry Albert Hinkson, 1893.

T. was a prolific Irish novelist and poet who published some eighty novels, twenty books of poetry, six books of reminiscences, and edited ten collections of works by other writers.

T. was the fourth of her parents' eleven children; her father was a moderately successful farmer and businessman. In 1867, T.'s eyesight began to fail, and within a short time she became blind. After nearly two years of suffering, the cause of T.'s blindness was found to be ulcers on her eyes; once these were removed, T.'s sight returned, but it was never fully restored.

After attending an infant school in Dublin until 1871, T. was sent to the convent of St. Catherine of Siena at Drogheda, where, as Ann Fallon suggests, her experiences were a major influence on her work:

Tynan found the convent school a place of peace and contentment, and, as a result, developed in three short years a lifelong respect and affection for the life of the convent and the nuns who lived there. This love, and her knowledge of the inner workings of convent life, especially the order and cleanliness, inform many passages in her later novels.

T. left Siena in 1874, after the death of her mother, to care for her father and siblings.

T. published her first poem in 1878. In 1879, she joined the Ladies Land League and became friends with Anna Parnell, sister of the Irish political leader Charles Parnell. The year 1885 was extremely important for T., for she published her successful first volume of poetry, Louise de la Valliere and Other Poems, and she met William Butler Yeats, with whom she remained close, although their friendship cooled somewhat in later years because Yeats disapproved of T.'s determination to write prose and journalism solely for money.

Yeats and T. worked together in 1888 on a project that Marilyn Gaddis Rose calls, along with Yeats' The Wandering of Oisin (1889), "the publishing event inaugurating the Irish Renaissance." T. and other young Irish writers, working out of the home of John O'Leary, the Fenian leader, put together a volume entitled Poems and Ballads of Young Ireland, which included the work of T., Yeats, Douglas Hyde, T.W. Rolleston, John Todhunter, and Rose Kavanagh. Shortly after her marriage in 1893, T. published the first of her "formula" novels, The Way of a Maid (1895). Fallon describes that formula:

. . . a young, inexperienced poor girl from a good family of either a noble line in declining circumstances or an old family line which has suffered because of religious reasons. . . . loves, and is loved by, a young, refined, often wealthy, and high-born young man. The course of this romance does not run smoothly because of the interference . . . of the families and because of misunderstandings on the part of the lovers themselves. . . . These romances invariably end happily with the marriages of the major and minor characters.

After her husband's death in 1919, T. travelled extensively throughout Europe and settled for several years in Cologne, where she wrote a memoir, Life in the Occupied Area (1925), in which she suggests unrealistic ways of returning European society to its pre-war structure.

At the end of her career, T. turned to a more "realistic" form of novel-writing. She realized that her female audience had changed: they came from all social classes and some were career women. T. was sympathetic to the shop girl, the office or factory worker, the single woman, and tried to provide "remedies for [the] harsh reality" of their lives. Though these novels had more realistic characters, they still followed the old formula—they still ended in marriage.

T. died in 1931 in London. She will undoubtedly be remembered far more for the poetry of her early years and for her memoirs, which are of significant literary/historical value (due to T.'s careful recording of her meetings with Yeats, as well as other writers of her era—Christina Rossetti, for example), than for the basically trite romantic novels of her later years. Whatever the quality of her work (and how much its quality may have been diluted by its quantity), T. did manage to publish, and to make money, at a time when such accomplishments were difficult for women.

WORKS: Louise de la Valliere and Other Poems (1885). Shamrocks (1887). Ballads and Lyrics (1891). Irish Love-Songs (1892). The Way of a Maid (1895). The Wind in the Trees (1898). The Golden Lily (1899). Poems (1901). The Handsome Quaker and Other Stories (1902). The French Wife (1904). A Daughter of Kings (1905). Her Ladyship (1907). The Lost Angel (1908). Ireland (1909, 1911). New Poems (1911). A Mid-Summer Rose (1913). Twenty-five Years: Reminiscences (1913). The Honourable Molly (1914). The Curse of Castle Eagle (1915). The Holy War (1916). The Middle Years (1916). The Rattlesnake (1917). The Man from Aus-

tralia (1919). *The Years of the Shadow* (1919). *The Second Wife* (1921). *The Wandering Years* (1922). *Mary Beaudesert* (1923). *The House of Doom* (1924). *Memories* (1924). *Life in the Occupied Area* (1925). *The Moated Grange* (1926; called *The Night of Terror* in later editions). *The Respectable Lady* (1927). *Lover of Women* (1928). *The Rich Man* (1929). *Collected Poems* (1930). *Grayson's Girl* (1930). *The Forbidden Way* (1931). *The Pitiful Lady* (1932). *The Playground* (1932). *An International Marriage* (1933). *A Lad Was Born* (1934).

For a more complete listing see: Fallon (182-185) or Rose (94-96).

BIBLIOGRAPHY: Fallon, A. *Katharine Tynan* (1979). Rose, M. *Katharine Tynan* (1974).

For articles in reference works, see: *DIL.*

Other references: *A Round Table of the Representative Irish and English Catholic Novelists* (1897). Boyd, E. *Ireland's Literary Renaissance* (1916). Brown, S. *Ireland in Fiction: A Guide To Irish Novels, Tales, Romances, and Folklore* (1915). Marcus, P. *Yeats and the Beginning of the Irish Renaissance* (1970). Yeats, W.B. *Letters to Katharine Tynan* (1953).

Kate Beaird Meyers

Evelyn Underhill

BORN: 6 December 1875, Wolverhampton.
DIED: 15 June 1941, Hampstead.
DAUGHTER OF: Sir Arthur Underhill and Alice Lucy Ironmonger.
MARRIED: Hubert Stuart Moore, 1907.
WROTE UNDER: John Cordelier, Evelyn Underhill.

A prolific religious writer, authority on mystical theology, and spiritual director, U. began as an agnostic who turned to theism and ultimately in 1921 to the Church of England. Although she had an explicit conversion to Roman Catholicism in 1907, she never joined that church largely because of its position on modernism. She was educated at King's College for Women, London. And although she received numerous honors—she was a Fellow of King's College, Honorary Doctor of Divinity at the University of Aberdeen, the Upton Lecturer on religion at Manchester College, Oxford, in 1921, the first female retreat leader in the Anglican church—she had no affiliation with an academic institution; for over forty years she wrote from her home. Her marriage, to a childhood friend, a barrister, was affectionate but childless.

U.'s works include poetry, novels, devotional works, editions of mystical writings, book reviews, biography, essays, and major historical and analytical studies. She wrote a book of poetry and three novels before she produced *Mysticism: A Study in the Nature and Development of Man's Spiritual Consciousness* (1911), a pioneering work in which mysticism and its relationship to vitalism, psychology, theology, symbolism, and magic are explored as well as the inner processes of the mystical experience.

Mysticism went through twelve editions and has remained in print continuously. As a result of its publication, U. met Baron Friedrich von Hügel, the lay Catholic theologian to whom she said she owed her whole spiritual life. From 1921-1925 he served as her spiritual director. U. contends that mysticism, an essential element in all religion, is available to everyone. While this is a major theme of her writing, particularly in *Practical Mysticism* (1914), U. does not neglect the great mystics. Through the biographies of John Ruysbroeck and Jacopone di Todi, through translations, editions, and introductions to the writings of Ruysbroeck, Jacob Boehme, Walter Hinton, Richard Rolle, and Nicholas of Cusa, and through numerous essays on the mystics, she introduced the lives and contributions of these "pioneers of humanity" to the English reading public.

U.'s efforts to examine the spiritual life are best realized in her Oxford lectures published as *The Life of the Spirit and the Life of To-day* (1922). In these, she brings the experience of the spiritual life into line with the conclusions of psychology. By the late 1920s U. began to give retreat addresses; *Concerning the Inner Life* (1926), *Fruits of the Spirit* (1942), *The Golden Sequence* (1932), and *Light of Christ* (1944) were all first presented in this form. These devotional writings, as well as *House of the Soul* (1929), *The School of Charity* (1934), *The Mystery of Sacrifice* (1938), *Abba* (1940), and *The Spiritual Life* (1937), were well received, and the last, first delivered as a series of broadcast talks, was the most popular. All of these works are characterized by an elegant simplicity and homeliness which made them particularly appealing to women and to preachers.

U.'s last major book was *Worship*, a study of the human response to the Eternal. In it she examined the basic characteristics of worship—ritual, symbol, sacrifice, and sacrament—and then explored the various traditions of Christian worship. It remains a classic study of the subject.

Although U.'s writing focused on the spiritual life, she construed that topic broadly. Her many lectures and essays, collected in three anthologies—*Mixed Pastures* (1933), *Essentials of*

Mysticism (1920), and *Collected Papers* (1946)—illustrate her breadth. She wrote on topics as far-reaching as the vocation of the teacher, the basis of social reform, and the ideals of the ministry of women. As theological editor of the *Spectator* and as a reviewer for *Time and Tide*, U. kept the literature on the spiritual life before the twentieth-century reader.

While a prodigious writer, the last part of U.'s life was given over increasingly to spiritual direction. Her letters, which were published posthumously, reveal her deep and sensitive care for souls. Never a political partisan, U. in 1938 became a pacifist and subsequently wrote *The Church and War* for the Anglican Pacifist Fellowship. This piece must be understood as the fruit of her deepening incarnational theology. U. believed that pacifism was a corollary of the doctrine of universal charity, a personal vocation to speak truth in dark times and give witness to the power of a loving God. As such, it clearly illustrated U.'s final position that it was not one's mystical experience but one's love which counted most.

WORKS: Mysticism: A Study of the Nature and Development of Man's Spiritual Consciousness (1911). *Immanences, A Book of Verses* (1913). *The Mystic Way, A Psychological Study in Christian Origins* (1913). *Practical Mysticism* (1914). *Ruysbroeck* (1915). *Theophanies, A Book of Verses* (1916). *Jacopone da Todi, Poet and Mystic, 1228-1306. A Spiritual Biography* (1919). *Essentials of Mysticism and Other Essays* (1920). *The Life of the Spirit and the Life of To-day* (1922). *The Mystics of the Church* (1925). *Concerning the Inner Life* (1926). *Man and the Supernatural* (1927). *House of the Soul* (1929). *The Golden Sequence, A Four-Fold Study of the Spiritual Life* (1932). *Mixed Pastures, Twelve Essays and Addresses* (1933). *The School of Charity* (1934). *Worship* (1936). *The Spiritual Life* (1937). *The Mystery of Sacrifice, A Meditation on the Liturgy* (1938). *Eucharistic Prayers from the Ancient Liturgies* (1939). *Abba, Meditations Based on the Lord's Prayer* (1940). *Fruits of the Spirit* (1942). *Letters of Evelyn Underhill*, ed. Charles Williams (1943). *Light of Christ* (1944). *Collected Papers*, ed. L. Menzies (1946). *Meditations and Prayers* (1948). *Shrines and Cities of France and Italy* (1949).

BIBLIOGRAPHY: Allchin, A.M., and M. Ramsey. *Evelyn Underhill: Two Centenary Essays* (1971). Armstrong, C. *Evelyn Underhill* (1975). Cropper, M. *Evelyn Underhill* (1958). Wyon, O. *Desire for God* (1966).

For articles in reference works, see: *Dictionary of Christian Spirituality* (1983). *DNB. Oxford Dictionary of the Christian Church* (1958).

Other references: *America* (August 1976). *Anglican Theological Review* (April 1978). *The Month* (July 1959). *Theology* (October 1953).

Dana Greene

Elizabeth Vesey

BORN: c. 1715, Ireland.
DIED: 1791, London.
DAUGHTER OF: Sir Thomas and Mary Muschamp Vesey.
MARRIED: William Handcock, n.d.; Agmondesham Vesey, before 1746.

V. was born in Ireland about 1715. Sometime before 1746 she married her second husband, Agmondesham Vesey, accountant-general of Ireland, amateur architect, and womanizer. Dividing her time between the family home in Ireland and a house she maintained in London, V. attracted many friends and from 1770 until 1786 was a leading Bluestocking. Of her letters, Lord Lyttleton wrote to David Garrick, "You will be charmed (as I am) with the lively coloring and fine touches in the epistolary style of our sylph, joined to the most perfect ease." V.'s letters reflect the sprightly wit and good humor by which she inspired convivial talk among the continental and British literati, philosophers, and scholars who gathered regularly in her "blue room" during the London winter season.

In 1751, Mary Delany dubbed her "the Sylph." Elizabeth Montagu praised the "musick" of her voice and the "gentle vivacity" of her wit. Horace Walpole asked, "What English heart ever excelled hers?" Her witty sallies were commonly aimed at herself, as when, denouncing second marriages, she seemed to overlook her own, finally exclaiming, "Bless me, my dear! I had quite forgotten it." Even when ill she kept up her self-mockery, once remarking that her only happy moment in fourteen days had been a fainting fit, another time fearing for the loss of "seven or eight" of her senses.

But this fascination with her own illnesses suggests a dark side to V. She herself said she had "a mind formed for doubt." Her friend Elizabeth Carter believed that because V. scarcely ever enjoyed "any one object, from the apprehension that something better may possibly be found in another," she lived in "a perpetual forecast of disappointment." Once, V. told Carter of the sublime thrill of reading the agnostic Abbé Raynal during violent thunderstorms. Carter, who saw in her friend "coral groves and submarine palaces," was alarmed, writing back, "'Tis a dangerous amusement to a mind like yours."

When she was forty-seven years old, V. captivated Laurence Sterne, who for five years sought her out and wrote her love letters. Sterne's appreciation must have been a joy, for Mr. Vesey's peccadillos were unceasing. But when V.'s husband died in 1785, he left her hardly anything out of an income of £4000 except their London house while settling on his mistress a legacy of £1000. Although reportedly the nephew and heir "acted with great kindness and liberality," assuring V. of at least a "competency," this double stroke—her husband's death, and evidence of his neglect of her—blasted her already skeptical and apprehensive mind. From age seventy until her death at seventy-six, she was in a state of decline, from uncontrolled weeping to passivity, violent outbursts, and, finally, childlike vulnerability.

While Bluestocking gatherings derived from French salons, the name seems to have been inspired by V.'s assurances, "Pho, Pho, don't mind dress! Come in your blue stockings!" Through studied informality, V. created a casual atmosphere for her conversations; Fanny Burney noted that "she pushed all the small sofas, as well as chairs, pell-mell about the apartments." Her ability to render her guests "easy with one another" (Burney) was often noted. V.'s aim was to draw together the most exciting thinkers in various realms and to get them talking, sometimes stimulated by a reading from a new work. In this way, ideas were kept in motion. Additionally, such literary arts as letter writing and biography owe much to Bluestocking conversations in which the real social world and the world of ideas met in talk that was at once gossipy, thought-provoking, and artful.

V.'s letters sometimes reveal the excesses of imagination that worried her friends: when ill in 1779, she writes to Montagu, "I find the lamp of the mind sinking in its socket and had I courage to face the World unknown I should wish the flame quite extinct." But this same letter also reveals the value she placed on civilized conversation between friends, for she goes on to create solace for herself through her communication of news events, gossip, and political analysis, ending abruptly and wittily with, "here is Ann come with the dressing basket how I hate to look at my own face when I can talk to you." V.'s letters primarily show her delight in language play. They are full of sharp sensuous detail, often in surprising combinations, as in a series which closes her thanks to Lord Lyttleton for his concern while she was ill: "& since you set any value upon my life I don't regret

the blisters bleedings & the Boluses they cram'd down my throat." And sometimes her bright details are used in a game of self-mockery, as when she teases Lyttleton, in 1768, about his supposed proposition that they elope.

Her language play often involves comic hyperbole, and active verbs keep her reader rushing along. For instance, she creates a picture of ridiculous extravagance in the preparations she and Mr. Vesey are making for a party to be held in Lyttleton's honor: "half a dozen oaks stript of their bark, the bed of the River dug up for rustick Stones the bogs and Heaths uncover'd of their Moss the Labourer taken from Harvest the Housekeeper robb'd of her Bread and barley to tempt the Birds to build their nests in Malvina's Bower—and there they are now—such a flight—whistling and singing the fish leaping the Farmer scolding and I almost crying to give up all hopes of seeing you there till next year which is to me for ever." The "whistling and singing" series, dashing from comedy to pure affection, is typical of V.'s prose style. Through her letters one can appreciate the bright spirit that for fifteen years created conversation and good humor among a richly diverse group of friends.

WORKS: Selected letters in the following: Pennington, M., ed. *A Series of Letters Between Mrs. Elizabeth Carter and Miss Catherine Talbot 1741-70 . . . Letters from Mrs. Elizabeth Carter to Mrs. Vesey 1763-87* (1809). Roberts, W., ed. *Memoirs of the Life and Correspondence of Mrs. Hannah More* (1834). Anson, E., and F. Anson, ed. *Mary Hamilton at Court and at Home, from Letters and Diaries 1756 to 1816* (1925). Johnson, E.B., ed. *Bluestocking Letters* (1926).

BIBLIOGRAPHY: Blunt, R., ed. *Mrs. Montagu, "Queen of the Blues," Her Letters and Friendships from 1762 to 1800* (1923). Huchon, R.L. *Mrs. Montagu and Her Friends, 1720-1800* (1907). Wheeler, E.R. *Famous Bluestockings* (1910).

For articles in reference works, see: *DNB. OCEL.*

Other references: Dobson, A., ed. *The Diary and Letters of Madame d'Arblay* (1904-1905). *Edinburgh Review* (October 1925). Lewis, W.S., ed. *Horace Walpole's Correspondence* (1961). Pennington, M., ed. *Letters from Mrs. Carter to Mrs. Montagu 1755-1800* (1817). Tinker, C. *The Salon and English Letters* (1915). Wheatley, H.B. *The Historical and Posthumous Memoirs of Sir Nathaniel William Wraxall, 1772-1784* (1884).

Carolyn Woodward

Queen Victoria

BORN: 24 May 1819, Kensington Palace, London.

DIED: 22 January 1901, Osborne House, Isle of Wight.

DAUGHTER OF: Edward, Duke of Kent, and Princess Mary Louisa Victoria of Saxe-Coburg.

MARRIED: Prince Albert of Saxe-Coburg-Gotha, 1840.

V., Queen of the United Kingdom of Great Britain and Ireland, Empress of India, was her whole life an indefatigable letter writer, addressing her voluminous correspondence to royal friends and relatives throughout Europe, to the ministers of the realm, and to loyal subjects (like Alfred Tennyson) for whom she developed varying degrees of fondness and respect. John Raymond, editor of *Queen Victoria's Early Letters*, remarked of her writing that "Queen Victoria was no verbal artist, as her journals and diaries show. Yet, in her letters, we can hear her authentic voice—rebuking, consoling, confirming, cajoling, upbraiding—in accents unlike those of any British sovereign (Queen Elizabeth I not excepted)." The letters, as well as her highly descriptive diaries and journals, afford us a remarkably rich record of her daily activities and observations—a record which may be of even greater interest to future historians than it has been to past ones, whose hasty dismissal of the literary interest of V.'s writing and whose strictly factual consideration of her prose mostly overlooks its value as historical evidence of a more subtle sort concerning the Queen's womanly and often unheeded moral stance on a vast number of such pressing social questions as slum clearance, civil discontent, and the responsibilities of empire.

V. of the House of Hanover—conceived expressly to provide her fifty-two-year-old father (Edward, Duke of Kent, fourth son of George III) with an heir to the British throne—was born at Kensington Palace on 24 May 1819 and was reared properly for her royal destiny by a strict and protective mother and a sagacious maternal uncle, Leopold of Coburg (later elected King of Belgium).

Upon learning that she would some day be Queen, V. at age twelve prophetically pronounced, "I will be good." Her remarkably detailed journal—a delightful source of information about her education—dates from that year. In 1837, on the very day of her accession, with amazing political acumen, the eighteen-year-old queen effected a polite but clean break from the nearly total control the Coburgs (mother, uncle, and governess) had held up to that point over her life. The young queen shouldered the responsibilities of her new

position, devoting many hours each morning to state, then to personal correspondence; and as the editors noted in the preface to the first series of *The Letters of Queen Victoria,* "nothing comes out more strongly in those documents than the laborious patience with which the Queen kept herself informed of the minutest details of political and social movements in both her own and other countries." Throughout her life, the Queen sought to influence history through her communications to political rivals like Lord Melbourne (Whig) and Sir Richard Peel (Conservative), Lord Palmerston (Foreign Office), and Lord John Russell (Prime Minister). The personal letters that V. wrote to her daughters and granddaughters reveal, as Richard Hough puts it, "a sharply prophetic eye and highly developed intuition" that permitted her "to perceive the dangers that lay ahead."

Of course, none of V.'s correspondence was published during her lifetime. V.'s contemporaries were acquainted with only two of the many collections of her writings now in print: *Leaves from the Journal of Our Life in the Highlands* celebrates the joys of family life with Prince Albert, the Royal Consort; *More Leaves* poignantly evokes the void that the untimely death of Albert left in the Queen's personal life. Even these popular volumes would not have appeared had Arthur Helps been less persuasive than he was in urging their publication, for the Queen protested "that she had no skill whatever in authorship; that these were, for the most part, mere homely accounts of excursions near home; and that she felt extremely reluctant to publish anything written by herself." Since by her own admission the collection referred "to some of the happiest hours" of the Queen's life, *Leaves from the Journal of Our Life in the Highlands* provides an important key to the complex story of Great Britain's most influential monarch.

Still, she would have enjoyed having even greater influence. Near the end of her sixty-four-year reign and after a lifetime of exerting unceasing epistolary pressures upon the governments of the realm, the Queen avowed in despair to her granddaughter Princess Victoria of Hesse: "I feel very deeply that my opinion & my advice are never listened to & that it is almost useless to give any." Unequivocally honest, V.'s letters provide rare insights into the personal and political motives of thousands of her contemporaries—as well as into her own.

WORKS: The Letters of Queen Victoria (First Series, 1907; Second Series, 1926-1928; Third Series, 1930-1932). *The Girlhood of Queen Victoria: A Selection from Her Majesty's Diaries Between the*

Years 1832 & 1840 (1912). *Leaves from a Journal: A Record of the Visit of the Emperor and Empress of the French to the Queen, & of the Visit of the Queen and H.R.H., the Prince Consort, to the Emperor of the French, 1855* (1961). *Letters of Queen Victoria, from the Archives of the House of Brandenburg-Prussia Between Victoria & Her Foreign & Prime Minister, 1837-1865* (1961). *Early Letters* (1963). *Dearest Child: Letters Between Queen Victoria and the Princess Royal, 1858-1861* (1964). *Dearest Mama: Letters Between Queen Victoria and the Crown Princess of Prussia, 1861-1864* (1968). *Dear and Honoured Lady: The Correspondence Between Queen Victoria & Alfred Tennyson* (1969). *Advice to a Grand-daughter: Letters from Queen Victoria to Princess Victoria of Hesse* (1975). *Darling Child: Private Correspondence of Queen Victoria and The Crown Princess of Prussia, 1871-1878* (1976).

BIBLIOGRAPHY: Benson, E.F. *Queen Victoria* (1935). Besant, W. *The Queen's Reign 1837-1897* (1897). Creston, D. *The Youthful Queen Victoria* (1952). Fulford, R. *Queen Victoria* (1951). Gernsheim, H. *Victoria R.: A Biography with 400 Illus-* *trations* (1959). Hardie, F. *The Political Influence of Queen Victoria 1861-1901* (1935). Longford, E.H. *Victoria R.I.* (1983). May, J. *Victoria Remembered* (1983). Mullen, R. and J. Munson. *Victoria: Portrait of a Queen* (1987). Plowden, A. *The Young Victoria* (1981). Sinclair, A. *The Other Victoria* (1981). Sitwell, E. *Victoria of England* (1936). Strachey, L. *Queen Victoria* (1921). Warner, M. *Queen Victoria's Sketchbook* (1979). Woodham Smith, C. *Queen Victoria: Her Life and Times* (1972).

For articles in reference works, see: *Allibone. DNB. Biographical Dictionary and Synopses of Books Ancient and Modern*, ed. C. Warner (1902). *The Bibliophile Dictionary*, comps. N. Dole, F. Morgan, and C. Tichnor (1904). *Childhood in Poetry*, ed. J.M. Shaw (1967). *Dictionary of English Literature*, ed. W.D. Adams (1966). *Everyman's Dictionary of Literary Biography, English & American*, Comps. J.W. Cousin and D.C. Browning (1960).

Other references: [Gosse, Sir Edmund] "Queen Victoria" in *The Quarterly Review* (1901).

R. Victoria Arana

Helen Jane Waddell

BORN: 31 May 1889, Tokyo.
DIED: 5 March 1965, London.
DAUGHTER OF: the Rev. Hugh Waddell and Jane Martin (never married).

W. was an author, translator, lecturer, and scholar whose numerous books in the 1920s and 30s helped to bring the Latin poetry of the Middle Ages into the mainstream of intellectual life. The daughter of an Irish Presbyterian missionary, W. attended Victoria College and Queen's University, Belfast, from which she received the B.A. degree in 1911 and the M.A. in 1912. For the next seven years she cared for her ailing stepmother in Ulster while writing *Lyrics from the Chinese* (1913), articles, reviews, children's devotional stories, and a play, *The Spoilt Buddha* (1919).

She entered Somerville College, Oxford, in 1920, where she gave a series of lectures on medieval mime. After a brief teaching stint at Bedford (1922-1923), she studied in Paris under a Susette Taylor Travelling Scholarship from Lady Margaret Hall (1923-1925). At Paris she completed the original reading of medieval Latin poets which she had begun at Oxford. The results of this inquiry she published as *The Wandering Scholars* (1927) and *Medieval Latin Lyrics* (1929). In the rush of popularity which followed these publications, W. became a much-loved personality in the social circles of London. She gave frequent lectures and addresses and was awarded a stream of honorary degrees. Her friends included G.E.B. Saintsbury, A.E., Max Beerbohm, G.B. Shaw, Siegfried Sassoon, and W.B. Yeats.

Her best work combines the thorough knowledge of the medieval scholar with the expressive energy of the creative writer. She was significant in raising modern consciousness of the medieval spiritual world. The novel *Peter Abelard* (1933) was the ideal vehicle to combine both her love for the twelfth century and her creative imagination, and it is widely considered her best work. While working on her novel, she also produced *A Book of Medieval Latin for Schools* (1931), an edition of *Cole's Paris Journal* (1931), a translation of *Manon Lescaut* (1931), and a play, *The Abbé Prévost* (1931). A translation of Rosweyd's *Vitae Patrum* (1615) appeared as *The Desert Fathers* (1936).

W. planned and had begun work on a study of John of Salisbury, but the onset of World War II diverted her energies. Fiercely patriotic, she wrote and translated poems relating to Britain's struggle. She assumed greater responsibilities at Constable's (her publisher) and became assistant editor of *The Nineteenth Century*. Her translations from this period have been collected by Felicitas Corrigan in *More Latin Lyrics from Virgil to Milton* (1976). Throughout her life she wrote fascinating letters to her sister, Margaret Waddell, in Kilmacrew, and many of these are quoted in Monica Blackett's *The Mark of the Maker* (1973). After the war W. suffered from intermittent amnesia. Her last achievement was the W.P. Ker Lecture at Glasgow University in 1947, published as *Poetry in the Dark Ages* (1948). She died in London on 5 March 1965.

WORKS: *Lyrics from the Chinese* (1913). *The Spoiled Buddha* (1919). *The Wandering Scholars* (1927). *Medieval Latin Lyrics* (1929). *A Book of Medieval Latin for Schools* (1931). *Cole's Paris Journal* (1931). *Manon Lescaut* (1931). *The Abbé Prévost* (1931). *Peter Abelard* (1933). *The Desert*

Fathers (1936). *Beasts and Saints* (1934). *Poetry in the Dark Ages* (1948).

BIBLIOGRAPHY: Blackett, M. *The Mark of the Maker: A Portrait of Helen Waddell* (1973). Corrigan, F., ed. *More Latin Lyrics from Virgil to Milton* (1976).

For articles in reference works, see: *CA. DNB. Longman. TCA* and *SUP. TCW.*

Richard Poss

Barbara Ward (Jackson)

BORN: 23 May 1914, York.
DIED: 31 May 1981, Lodsworth.
DAUGHTER OF: Walter and Teresa Mary Burge Ward.
MARRIED: Robert G.A. Jackson, 1950.

Internationally known economist, journalist, broadcaster, and writer on international affairs, W. was the author of many books and recipient of many awards, including a Life Peeress of the House of Lords in 1976. Born to a Quaker solicitor and a Roman Catholic mother, W. was raised a Catholic near Ipswich and studied in France (including the Sorbonne) and Germany before entering Somerville College, Oxford, where she graduated with highest honors in politics, philosophy, and economics. She then studied abroad for three years and lectured at Cambridge University and to worker groups. Deeply influenced by a papal encyclical that warned against dividing the world into have and have-not nations, she began an illustrious career as a writer defending this principle and working toward developing Third-World nations.

Throughout her life W. was a noted teacher and administrator, as well as a prolific writer, turning out, for example, an unpublished 200,000-word novel when she was fourteen. She published her first book when she was twenty-six, *The International Share-Out* (1938), then joining *The Economist* the year after and becoming foreign editor in 1940. She was also a governor of the BBC from 1946 to 1950 and regularly served on broadcasts of the "Brains Trust" program as well as American interview programs. She lived for several years in Gold Coast (now Ghana) with her husband, an economist and a former Assistant Secretary General of the United Nations. For seven years she was president of the International Institute for Environment and Development, and also taught for a number of years in the United States at Radcliffe, Harvard, and Columbia.

At the heart of her writing is W.'s conviction that richer nations must aid poorer nations in

order for international peace and the security of the West to be maintained, a concept now accepted as gospel. She wrote for both popular and scholarly audiences and was especially skillful at synthesizing complex ideas for the broadest possible audience. Her ideas, however, were not accepted uniformly, and she was sometimes criticized for alleged oversimplification, as in reviews of *Five Ideas That Change the World* (1959), that claimed that she was blind to the economic realities governing investment and political stability.

A firm believer in international order and cooperation, W. proposed (as in *Nationalism and Ideology*, 1966) that the world economy would be better apportioned through the creation of federations above the level of nation and below the level of the United Nations. The "sense of humanity" and "responsibility of power" she described in this work was necessary, she felt, because of the increased rise of nationalism. Critics here, too, faulted her wishful thinking, and even supporters such as Robert L. Heilbroner saw the inconsistency in her asking for "faith" in poorer nations, on the one hand, and documenting the "terrible actualities facing these countries," on the other hand.

She consistently tried to defend environmental issues as well, though here, too (as in reviews of *Only One Earth*, written with René Dubos, 1972), she predictably received criticism. John Kenneth Galbraith, among others, saw that W.'s last book, *Progress for a Small Planet* (1979), was written out of her conviction that a total cooperative effort among nations was necessary to solve the many problems facing "Spaceship Earth" (as she called it in her 1966 book of the same name) but that her optimism and, as some saw it, her inability to see the reality around her was a welcome antidote to the prevailing cynicism.

W. was a brilliant synthesizer of complex economic and political issues, and her influence was great; for example, she served as adviser to United Nations Secretary General U Thant and U.S. Presidents John F. Kennedy and Lyndon B.

Johnson. With evangelical zeal, she warned prophetically of matters that today are accepted worldwide as true, particularly the necessary interdependence of all nations, rich or poor, and the corresponding close integration of economic and ecological priorities. She moved easily and competently through history for her arguments, and she was equally adept at offering sensitive, humane, well-reasoned solutions to the world's ills. Her reliance on her religious faith served as foundation for her thinking, and her "compelling" vision (as it was called in *TLS*) acted as a form of political conscience for some forty years.

WORKS: *The International Share-Out* (1938). (with others) *Hitler's Route to Bagdad* (1939). *Russian Foreign Policy* (1940). *Italian Foreign Policy* (1941). (with others) *A Christian Basis for the Post War World* (1941). *The Defence of the West* (1942). *Turkey* (1942). *Democracy, East and West* (1947, 1949). *The West at Bay* (1948). *Policy for the West* (1951). *Are Today's Basic Problems Religious?* [and] *Moral Order in an Uncertain World* (1953). *Faith and Freedom* (1954). *Britain's Interest in Atlantic Union* (1954). *The Interplay of East and West: Points of Conflict and Cooperation* (1957, 1962; in the U.K. as *The Interplay of East and West: Elements of Contrast and Co-operation*). *My Brother's Keeper* (1957). *Herbert Lehman at 80: Young Elder Statesman* (1958). *Five Ideas that Change the World* (1959). (with others) *The Legacy of Imperialism: Essays* (1960). *The Unity of the Free World* (1961). *India and the West* (1961, 1964). *The Rich Nations and the Poor Nations* (1961). *The Plan under Pressure: An Observer's View* (1963). (with M. Zinkin) *Why Help India?* (1963). *Women in the New Asia: The Changing Social Roles of Men and Women in South and South-East Asia* (1963). *Spirit of '76— Why Not Now?* (1963). *Towards A World of Plenty* (1964). *The Decade of Development: A Study of Frustration* (1965). (with P.T. Bauer) *Two Views on Aid to Developing Countries* (1966). *Spaceship Earth* (1966). *Nationalism and Ideology* (1966).

World Poverty—Can It Be Solved? (1966). (author of commentary) *Populorum Progressio*, by Pope Paul VI (1967). *The Lopsided World* (1968). *Technological Change and the World Market* (1968). *A New History* (1969). *Urbanization in the Second United Nations Development Decade* (1970). *The Widening Gap: Development in the 1970's, A Report on the Columbia Conference on International Economic Development* (1971). *An Urban Planet* (1971). *The Angry Seventies: The Second Development Decade—A Call to the Church* (1972). (with R. Dubos) *Only One Earth: The Care and Maintenance of a Small Planet* (1972). (with others) *Who Speaks for Earth?*, ed. M.F. Strong (1973). *A New Creation? Reflections on the Environmental Issue* (1973). *The Age of Leisure* (1973). *Human Settlements: Crisis and Opportunity* (1974). *A "People" Strategy of Development* (1974). *Habitat 2000* (1975). (with G. Ward) *The John Ward House* (1976). *The Home of Man* (1976). (with W.R. Ward) *The Andrew-Safford House* (1976). (with G. Ward) *Silver in American Life* (1979). *Progress for a Small Planet* (1979). *Peace and Justice in the World* (1981).

BIBLIOGRAPHY: Lean, G., et al. *Tribute to Barbara Ward, the Lady of Global Concern* (1987).

For articles in reference works, see: *CA. Catholic Authors. CB. TCA SUP.*

Other references: *Atlantic* (April 1959, August 1972). Bellringer, A.W. *Prose Studies* (1986). *Christian Science Monitor* (12 March 1959, 7 June 1972, 1 June 1976, 7 November 1979). *Commonweal* (14 January 1955). *Natural History* (October 1972). *New Statesman* (26 May 1972). *Newsweek* (7 April 1947, 2 March 1959, 15 June 1981). *NR* (13 April 1959, 27 October 1979). *New Yorker* (29 October 1979). *NYT* (1 March 1959, 1 June 1981). *Spectator* (20 March 1959). *SR* (20 November 1954). *Time* (19 May 1947, 15 June 1981). *Times* (London) (1 June 1981). *TLS* (30 June 1966). *Washington Post* (1 June 1981).

Paul Schlueter

Maisie Ward

BORN: 4 January 1889, Isle of Wight.
DIED: 28 January 1975, New York.
DAUGHTER OF: Wilfrid and Josephine Ward.
MARRIED: Francis Joseph Sheed, 1926.

W. was a woman of diverse interests: publisher, biographer, and Roman Catholic activist. One of five siblings, she was raised in a literary family, her father being the biographer of Newman and Wiseman and editor of the *Dublin Review* and her mother a novelist.

During the First World War W. served as a nursing aide in military hospitals. When the war ended she joined the Catholic Evidence Guild, street-corner speakers who lectured on Catholicism, where she met her future husband, Frank Sheed, an Australian. In 1926 they started the publishing house of Sheed and Ward, specializing in Catholic books and with a goal of publishing works of literary as well as religious merit. The enterprise prospered, and in 1933 a branch was opened in New York. From then on they lectured extensively on both sides of the Atlantic. Two children were born, a daughter, Rosemary, and a son, Wilfrid Sheed, the novelist.

When the Second World War began W. went to the United States with her children and worked on her best-known book, *Gilbert Keith Chesterton* (1943); she was asked to write the book about her friend by Chesterton's wife, but, as Graham Greene said, "Mrs. W. is too fond of her subject and too close to it to reduce her material into a portrait for strangers." Nine years later *Return to Chesterton* appeared, presenting his family life. W. assembled all the odds and ends of Chestertoniana she could find by visiting his old haunts and cronies, with the result that this book has an intimacy and immediacy that the biography lacked.

W. also believed that the early years of Newman had been neglected. *The Young Mr. Newman* portrays the childhood and university years of Newman as fully as her father had presented the second half of his life. And *Robert Browning and His World* was written because W. was incensed at a contemporary biography subjecting Browning to Freudian theories. W. stresses his masculinity and denies the allegation that he was seeking a mother rather than a mate. "I ended my research believing more than ever in the idyllic love story of Browning," she claimed, and *The Tragi-Comedy of Pen Browning* is the sad story of the poets' only child, an indulged son forever overshadowed by his famous parents.

Quite different from these nineteenth-century subjects is *Caryll Houselander, That Divine Eccentric*. Houselander, artist, writer, therapist of disturbed children and "mystic," became known to W. as a writer of spiritual books. Sheed and Ward also published *This War Is the Passion*, Houselander's best-known book, written at the time of the London blitz.

Unfinished Business (1964), W.'s autobiography, recalls the life of a remarkably energetic woman. W., christened Mary Josephine, was called Maisie in childhood and wrote under that name. Her family knew many of the leading literary figures of the time; Tennyson, Hilaire Belloc, and Chesterton, among others, were friends. A cradle Catholic, W. remained a faithful daughter of the Church, which did not prevent her criticizing what she believed to be its defects. Her interest in the worker-priest movement in France resulted in a book, *France Pagan*? Despite her conservative upbringing, W. came to espouse radical social views reinforced by her association with Dorothy Day of the *Catholic Worker* and Baroness Catherine de Hueck, founder of Friendship House in Harlem.

A sense of optimism, engendered by her strong religious faith, permeated W.'s life and writing. In *To and Fro on the Earth* (1973), a sequel to her autobiography written in her eighties, W. crisscrossed four continents. She delighted in finding pockets of people performing good works amid the spreading chaos of civilization, for she herself, as a young woman, had been engaged in volunteer work for social causes, and in later years she founded subsidized housing for the needy in England and the United States. For writing books was only one of the many activities of this multi-faceted woman.

WORKS: *Father Maturin* (1920). *The Wilfrid Wards and the Transition* (1934). *The Oxford Group* (1937). *Insurrection versus Resurrection* (1937). *This Burning Heat* (1941). *Gilbert Keith Chesterton* (1943). *The Young Mr. Newman* (1948). *France Pagan* (1949). *St. Jerome* (1950). *St. Francis of Assisi* (1950). *Return to Chesterton* (1952). *Be Not Solicitous* (1953). *They Saw His Glory* (1956). *The Rosary* (1957). *Saints Who Made History* (1960). *Caryll Houselander* (1962). *Unfinished Business* (1964). *Robert Browning and His World* (1967). *The Tragi-Comedy of Pen Browning* (1972). *To and Fro on the Earth* (1973).

BIBLIOGRAPHY: *Unfinished Business* (autobiography) (1964). Sheed, W. *Frank and Maisie: A Memoir with Parents* (1985).

For articles in reference works, see: *CA.*

Other references: *Commonweal* (16 February 1968). Greene, G., *Collected Essays* (1969). *New Yorker* (15 March 1952). *New York Herald-Tribune* (9 March 1952). *TLS* (1 October 1964). *Yale Review* (1968).

Joan Ambrose Cooper

Mary Augusta Arnold Ward

BORN: 11 June 1851, Tasmania, Australia.
DIED: 24 March 1920, London.
DAUGHTER OF: Thomas and Julia Sorell Arnold.
MARRIED: Thomas Humphry Ward, 1872.
WROTE UNDER: Mrs. Humphry Ward.

W.'s life as a novelist, journalist, and philanthropist carried on a family tradition of intellectual inquiry, service, and leadership. The granddaughter of Thomas Arnold of Rugby and Matthew Arnold's niece, W. was motivated by their spirit of conservative reform. She came to grips with the relativism of modern thought but never surrendered her faith in unchanging moral laws and inflexible moral duties.

W.'s most famous novel, *Robert Elsmere* (1888), was shaped in part by her own experience with Victorian religious crisis. Her father, Thomas Arnold's second son, showed no sign of wavering from his father's Broad Church Christianity when he went out to homestead in New Zealand in 1847 and married the staunchly Protestant Julia Sorell in 1850. W. was five when his conversion to Roman Catholicism rocked the family and cost him his job as school inspector in 1856. The family returned to Britain and faced a life of relative privation for the next ten years, despite John Henry Newman's help in getting Thomas Arnold employment in Catholic schools. As was usual with interfaith marriges, the daughters remained Protestant like their mother and the sons were raised as Catholics. When W. was fifteen, her father returned to Anglicanism. His new position as tutor moved the family to Oxford, where W. was able to repair the large gaps left in her girl's school education by concentrated study at the Bodleian Library. She married Thomas Humphry Ward, a fellow of Brasenose, in 1872. The second of their three children had just been born when Thomas Arnold went back to Roman Catholicism in 1876. Despite her lifelong loyalty to her father, she keenly felt the sufferings of her mother, who this time refused to follow her husband to the Catholic University in Dublin.

Although W.'s publishing career began officially when *The Churchman's Companion* accepted "A Westmoreland Story" in 1870, her bent for more serious work came out in the many articles on literature and history that soon followed in such periodicals as *Macmillan's*, the *Saturday Review*, the *Oxford Spectator*, the *Times*, the *Fortnightly*, and the *Pall Mall Gazette*. In 1877 she began to contribute entries based on her early studies in Spanish history to *The Dictionary of Christian Biography*. She published a children's story, "Milly and Olly," in 1881, *Miss Bretherton*, her first novel, in 1884, and a translation of Frederic Henri Amiel's *Journal Intime* in 1885. Long devoted to the Brontës' novels, she wrote a series of introductions to the Haworth edition of their works between 1899–1900.

When W. began work on *Robert Elsmere* in 1885, she had already been thinking for many years about the religious issues it raised. Her own historical studies had convinced her to see the Bible as a fallible cultural record. She was confirmed in a liberal, antidogmatic theology by such Oxford intellectuals as Benjamin Jowett, Mark Pattison, and T.H. Green. When she heard the Rev. John Wordsworth attack such liberal theology as sinful in 1881, she responded with "Unbelief and Sin," a pamphlet arguing that intellectual honesty, not weak morality, led men to question dogmatic faith. *Robert Elsmere* recounts the "deconversion" of just such an intellectual. An Oxford philosopher modeled on T.H. Green introduces the first doubts about Christian dogma into the mind of its eponymous hero, a young Anglican clergyman, and reading *The Origin of Species* and contradictory Church histories further erodes his orthodoxy. Skeptical continental scholarship completes the task, and Elsmere, causing much pain to his strictly evangelical wife, leaves the ministry. He continues to serve his fellow man as a social worker and teacher, however, carrying a secularized Christianity into the London slums where he ultimately dies of tuberculosis.

The tremendous success of *Robert Elsmere*, which by 1889 had sold over 300,000 copies in England and 200,000 in the United States, suggests how topical the issues it raised were. Its combination of serious intellectual questions, didactic uplift, and human interest was typical of W.'s later fiction. The strains of religious doubt were again her subject in *The History of David Grieve* (1892) and *Elsmere*'s sequel, *The Case of Richard Meynell* (1911). The Roman Catholic hero of *Helbeck of Bannisdale* (1898), torn between his faith and the nonbeliever he loves, offers the closest analogies with W.'s own family. W.'s essential conservatism where both liberalism and feminism were concerned comes out in her social and political novels, in which the most effective form of social conscience is always allied with a respect for wealth and tradition. She found her ideals in women who fulfilled themselves through subordination to duty, like the self-sacrificing heroine of *Eleanor* (1900), and in reform-minded aristocrats like Aldous Raeburn of *Marcella* (1894) and the title character of its sequel, *Sir George Tressady* (1896). Women who transgressed the bounds of traditional wifely duty, no matter what the provocation, were routinely punished in W.'s novels; Lady Rose in *Lady Rose's Daughter* (1903), Kitty Ashe in *The Marriage of William Ashe* (1905), and Daphne in *Marriage à la Mode* (1909) are cases in point. Believing that direct involvement in political life would "blunt the special moral qualities of women," W. steadfastly opposed the vote for women. In 1908 she organized the Women's Anti-Suffrage League, dedicated to "bringing the views of women to bear on the legislature without the aid of the vote." The subversive potential W. feared in feminism is made clear in *Delia Blanchflower* (1915), where the suffragette is a neurasthenic fanatic who burns down a country home to dramatize her cause. Notwithstanding W.'s skill in combining sensation and melodrama with bracing moral lessons, her attempts to adapt works like *Eleanor* and *The Marriage of William Ashe* for the stage were neither financially nor artistically successful.

W. herself was a tireless if traditional worker for social reform. She was involved in the earliest efforts to open higher education to women in Oxford. After she and her family moved to London in 1881, she became active in planning the Passmore Edwards Settlement; the Settlement House later named after her opened in 1897 to serve the poor of the Bloomsbury community. In later years she was instrumental in gaining government support for child-care centers and schools for handicapped children. In 1908 she toured Canada and the U.S., where she was entertained by President Theodore Roosevelt. At his request, she first undertook several works dramatizing the British war effort for American audiences: *England's Effort* (1916), *Towards the Goal* (1917), and *Fields of Victory* (1919). As a tribute to both her patriotism and her journalistic skill, the British War Ministry allowed her to visit the front and other military installations as a war correspondent. In 1920 she was awarded an honorary degree by Edinburgh University and was selected as one of the first women magistrates of England. Her unfinished autobiography, *A Writer's Recollections*, appeared in 1918.

Although updated with twentieth-century concerns, W.'s writing remains quintessentially Victorian in its peculiar blend of moral seriousness and sentimentality. If bounded by Victorian conceptions of woman's sphere, her life and work were animated by high standards of intellectual and social responsibility that gave both a far-reaching effect.

WORKS: *Milly and Olly*, or *A Holiday among the Mountains* (1881). *Miss Bretherton* (1884). *Robert Elsmere* (1888). *The History of David Grieve* (1892). *Marcella* (1894). *The Story of Bessie Costrell* (1895). *Sir George Tressady* (1896). *Helbeck of Bannisdale* (1898). *Eleanor* (1900). *Lady Rose's Daughter* (1903). *The Marriage of William Ashe* (1905). *Fenwick's Career* (1906). *The Testing of Diana Mallory* (1908). *Daphne*, or *Marriage à la Mode* (1909). *Canadian Born* (1910). *The Case of Richard Meynell* (1911). *The Mating of Lydia* (1913). *The Coryston Family* (1913). *Delia Blanchflower* (1915). *Eltham House* (1915). *A Great Success* (1916). *England's Effort* (1916). *Lady Connie* (1916). *Towards the Goal* (1917). *Missing* (1917). *A Writer's Recollections* (1918). *The War and Elizabeth* (1918). *Fields of Victory* (1919). *Cousin Philip* (1919). *Harvest* (1920).

BIBLIOGRAPHY: Colby, V. *The Singular Anomaly* (1970). Gwynn, S. *Mrs. Humphry Ward* (Writers of the Day, 1917). Huws Jones, E. *Mrs. Humphry Ward* (1973). Peterson, W. *Victorian Heretic* (1976). Phelps, W.L. *Essays on Modern Novelists* (1921). Smith, E.M. *Mrs. Humphry Ward* (1980). Trevelyan, J.P. *The Life of Mrs. Humphry Ward* (1923). Walters, J.S. *Mrs. Humphry Ward, Her Work and Influence* (1912).

For articles in reference works, see: *DLB. DNB.* Platt, V. *Men and Women of the Day* (1917).

Other references: Bellringer, A.W. *Prose Studies* (1986). *Living Age* (January 1902). *Nation* (3 April 1920). *New Statesman and Nation* (19 August 1947). *Nineteenth Century Fiction* (1951). *North American Review* (April 1903). *QR* (July 1920). *TLS* (15 June 1951). *Victorian Studies* (1960).

Rosemary Jann

Sylvia Townsend Warner

BORN: 6 December 1893, Harrow, Middlesex.
DIED: 1 May 1978, Maiden Newton, Dorset.
DAUGHTER OF: George Townsend and Eleanor Mary Warner.

W. was the daughter of a schoolmaster at Harrow but was educated privately, first by her mother and then by a governess and tutors. Given free run of her father's library, she read widely on her own and can thus be considered largely self-educated. She originally aspired to a career in music and at one point intended to study composition with Arnold Schönberg, but the intervention of World War I turned her to musicology. As a young woman, she was the only female editor of the monumental *Tudor Church Music* (10 vols., 1925–1930); however, the encouragement of David Garnett and T.F. Powys helped her decide in favor of literature. In a career spanning more than fifty years, she produced poems, novels, short stories, biographies, and translations. For these accomplishments she was elected a fellow of the Royal Society of Literature and an honorary member of the American Academy of Arts and Letters.

From an early age, W. showed an interest in the supernatural, which is evident in works throughout her career. Her first novel, *Lolly Willowes* (1926), the first book selected by the Book-of-the-Month Club, chronicles the life of a woman who rejects traditional roles and turns to witchcraft. Stories written over many years deal in various ways with supernatural themes, while her novel *The Corner That Held Them* (1948) shows an intimate knowledge of the occult and herbal medicinal lore in its portrayal of life in a fourteenth-century convent. *The Kingdoms of Elfin* (1977) is a collection of *New Yorker* stories, all of which treat the world of elves, fairies, werewolves, and other such creatures as ordinary inhabitants of the planet that mortals think of as exclusively their own. W. never exploits the supernatural for its own sake or for cheap effects. Her interest is primarily in extending the limits of vision or in using the extraordinary as a means of exploring human psychology.

In her novels, W. is less interested in social and political themes than in the interior struggles of her characters. Lolly Willowes chooses witchcraft after a lifetime of searching for a fulfilling alternative to the sterile and boring life that Victorian society permits her; even so, witchcraft is more a symbol of individual freedom than an indictment of social policies. *Mr. Fortune's Maggot* (1927) takes its main character, an innocent missionary, to the tropical island of Fuana where he is sorely tempted by the delights of the pagans he is sent to convert. Far more complex, and often considered W.'s masterpiece, is *The Corner That Held Them*. Its roguish and picaresque central character, Ralph Kello, enters Oby convent during the Black Death, claiming to be a priest, and spends the rest of his life wrestling with the moral consequences and complications of this sin. Others at Oby are similarly torn between worldly temptations and the demands of the church. Complex, detailed, learned, and spirited, this novel has been called a "sustained delight." Similar in theme though Victorian in setting is *The Flint Anchor* (1954), in which John Barnard is moved by experiences as a student to strive for moral perfection only to find that the everyday concerns of business and family life frustrate his lofty ideals. Moreover, idolatry toward his daughter Mary leads to neglect of other family members, each of whom is warped by his tyranny and inability to love. *Summer Will Show* (1936) resembles *The Flint Anchor* in period, but the struggles of its heroine are for identity and purpose in a male-dominated culture which permits little scope or assertiveness for its women.

W. is best known and most highly regarded for her short stories, which range broadly over the British cultural scene but focus mainly on the middle classes. The majority of her characters are women. Often written in the "plotless" vein pioneered by Chekhov, her stories range from brief impressionistic sketches to novella-length studies and, like the novels, focus on character and situation, frequently exploring with wit and irony the follies and foibles of ordinary people. A master of technique and storycraft, W. never settled into a pattern or formula. "The Phoenix" can be construed as a sophisticated joke or as an allegory; "A Garland of Straw" is a disturbing excursion into madness and thwarted love; "The Museum of Cheats" requires only forty pages to satirize the greed and vanity of two and a half centuries;

"Winter in the Air" is a realistic portrayal of a woman whose husband has rejected her for another; "The One and the Other" intertwines the "material world with the immaterial" in a tale at once fantastic and realistic.

In all her fiction, W. is an acute observer of manners, morals, the minutiae of daily existence, and the secret ways of the human heart. Her concern with appearance and reality is humane and liberal; she seldom condemns, preferring to look instead for the secret beneath the surface which enlivens and even ennobles her humblest characters.

W. belongs to the broad mainstream of British fiction and has often been compared with Jane Austen and Katherine Mansfield. Her style exhibits clarity, restraint, precision, and simplicity in both poetry and prose. Wit, grace, humor, subtlety, and charm are frequently noted characteristics, but her special quality resides in a precise yet original use of language. She has a genius for metaphor, drawing on art, music, and nature as the sources of her imagery. Although sometimes criticized for writing with more attention to style than substance, W. is never boring or trite. Readers are required to look carefully, for her effects are often subtle and demand an alert and sensitive audience. These qualities will probably deny her a large following, but critical appreciation of her work is growing and a place for her in twentieth-century letters is assured.

WORKS: *The Espalier* (1925). *Lolly Willowes* (1926). *Mr. Fortune's Maggot* (1927). *Time Importuned* (1928). *The True Heart* (1929). *Some World Far from Ours* and *Stay, Corydon, Thou Swain* (1929). *Elinor Barley* (1930). *A Moral Ending and Other Stories* (1931). *Opus 7: A Poem* (1931). *Rainbow* (1932). *The Salutation* (1932). *Whether a Dove or a Seagull* (with Valentine Ackland, 1933). *More Joy in Heaven and Other Stories* (1935). *Summer Will Show* (1936). *Twenty-four Stories* (with Graham Greene and James Laver, 1939). *Cat's Cradle Book* (1940). *A Garland of Straw: Twenty-Eight Stories* (1943). *Portrait of a Tortoise: Extracted from the Journals of Gilbert White* (1946). *The Museum of Cheats: Stories* (1947). *The Corner That Held Them* (1948). *Somerset* (1949). *Jane Austen: 1775–1817* (1951; rev. ed. 1957). *The Flint Anchor* (1954). *Winter in the Air and Other Stories* (1955). *Boxwood* (1958; rev. ed. 1960). *A Spirit Rises: Short Stories* (1962). *Sketches from Nature* (1963). *Swans on the Autumn River: Stories* (1966). *A Stranger with a Bag and Other Stories* (1966). *T.H. White: A Biography* (1967). *King Duffus and Other Poems* (1968). *The Innocent and the Guilty* (1971). *The Kingdoms of Elfin* (1977). *Scenes from Childhood and Other Stories* (1982). *Letters*, ed. William Maxwell (1983). *Collected Poems*, ed. Claire Harman (1983).

BIBLIOGRAPHY: Daiches, D. *The Present Age in British Literature* (1958). NCBEL.

For articles in reference works, see: *CA.*

Other references: Allen, W. *The Short Story in English* (1981). *London Magazine* (November 1979). *Magill's Literary Annual* (1983, 1984). NR (5 March 1966). *New Yorker* (27 August 1979). *NYT* (19 May 1978). *PN Review* (1981). *SSF* (Winter 1973). *TLS* (23 May 1980). Updike, J. *Hugging the Shore* (1983).

Dean R. Baldwin

Beatrice Potter Webb

BORN: 22 January 1858, Standish House, Gloucestershire.
DIED: 30 April 1943, Passfield Corner, Hampshire.
DAUGHTER OF: Richard and Laurencina Heyworth Potter.
MARRIED: Sidney James Webb, 1892.

W., reformer, researcher, and Fabian Socialist, was the seventh of eight daughters born to Richard Potter, a wealthy and cultivated merchant. Although frequent childhood illness limited her formal education, her father encouraged all his daughters to read widely and independently. She had frequent contact with such free-thinking family friends as T.H. Huxley, John Tyndall, and James Martineau and developed a close relationship with Herbert Spencer.

Intensely introspective, W. grew up haunted by her lack of a meaningful faith and a useful purpose in life. The socialism that finally provided her with alternatives to both religion and profession opposed Spencer's laissez-faire philosophies, but his scientific investigation of social institutions exercised a lasting influence upon her. Her early involvement with the Charity Organisation Society and the Octavia Hill housing projects in London left her dissatisfied that such philanthropic efforts did nothing to reach the roots of poverty. She welcomed the opportunity to investigate working-class labor for Charles Booth's *Inquiry into the Life and Labour of the People of London*, and her essay on "Dock Life in the East End of London" first appeared in *The Nineteenth Century* in 1887. She disguised herself as a seamstress to gather data on the East End tailoring trade later that same year. The articles based on her experiences resulted in her being called to testify before a House of Lords Committee on the Sweating System in 1888. There she made clear her growing conviction that such exploitation was endemic in capitalism itself.

In an effort to develop a more systematic criticism of capitalism, she turned her attention in 1889 to co-operative societies and trade unionism. Research for *The Co-operative Movement in Great Britain* (1891) first introduced her to Sidney Webb, the Fabian Socialist she married, over the objections of friends and family, in 1892. For the next fifty years they formed an intellectual, political, and emotional partnership devoted to furthering Fabian policies of gradual reform, collectivism, and administration by an intellectual elite. Their home at 41 Grosvenor Road became the salon of Fabian thinkers and the workshop for the methodical and meticulously researched studies of social phenomena that were their trademark. Their first joint effort was *The History of Trade Unionism* (1894), followed by *Industrial Democracy* in 1897. In 1894 they used a £10,000 bequest to the Fabian Society to found an institution for the study of political economy that later became the London School of Economics.

In 1905 W. was appointed to a Royal Commission on the Poor Law, which she induced to sponsor many investigations into the impact of government policies on the poor. Although she was unsuccessful in moving the Commission toward changes that might prevent rather than cure poverty, as outlined in her Minority Report of 1909, she had the satisfaction in later years of seeing many of her recommendations adopted. The Webbs' hopes of organizing an Independent Socialist Party in the years before World War I were disappointed by infighting among those who disagreed with their gradualist and collectivist policies and resented their domineering personalities. A project of more lasting effect was their founding of *The New Statesman* in 1913, dedicated to the furthering of Fabian Socialism and the scientific study of social problems.

During and after the war, W. served on the McLean Committee on the reform of local government, the Reconstruction Committee, and the War Cabinet Committee on Women in Industry. Her defense of equality in *The Wages of Men and Women—Should They Be Equal?* (1919) suggests a sensitivity to sexual discrimination missing in her attitudes toward female suffrage and protective factory legislation. She was highly successful with the Seaham Harbour constituency that her husband represented in Parliament from 1919 to 1928, promoting a regular series of educational activities for its members and writing a monthly "News Letter to the Women of Seaham." The useful activities of the Half-Circle Club that she organized in London to bring together the wives of other Labour Party M.P.s were somewhat undercut by members' resentment about W.'s often unsubtle attempts to make them more socially presentable. During the twenties she and Sidney published *English Prisons* (1922), *Statutory Authorities* (1922), revised studies of trade unionism and the co-operative movement, and *English Poor Law History* (1927-29). *The Decay of Capitalist Civilisation* (1923) presented their strongest indictment of the economic and moral bankruptcy of the prevailing system, and *A Constitution for the Socialist Commonwealth of Great Britain* (1920) their impracticably utopian alternatives. In 1929 she gave a series of talks for the B.B.C. on their research techniques, which appeared in 1932 as *Methods of Social Study*. Between 1924 and 1926 W. composed *My Apprenticeship*, her autobiography up to her marriage. Like the diaries it is based upon, this work gives compelling testimony to her own literary gifts. Its projected two-volume sequel, *Our Partnership*, was begun in the late twenties; the only completed volume (1892-1911) appeared after her death in 1948.

In 1929 the Webbs moved from London to Passfield Corner in Hampshire. Sidney chose the title "Baron Passfield" when granted a peerage in 1929, although W. herself steadfastly refused to share the title with him. Despite their earlier skepticism about Soviet Russia and their continued awareness of its many repressive policies, a visit in 1932 made them "fall in love" with this society that seemed to embody so many of their most cherished ideals: production for use rather than for profit, centralized planning and collective ownership, party support for "the vocation of leadership," an intense spiritual commitment to political ideals. They recorded their views in *Soviet Communism: A New Civilisation* (1935) and remained staunch defenders of Russia to the ends of their lives. W. resigned from the Executive Committee of the Fabian Society in 1933 and published her farewell address to it in the *Fabian News* for 1941. Before her death from kidney disease in 1943, she had received honorary degrees from the Universities of Manchester, Edinburgh, and Munich and had become the first woman ever elected to the British Academy. After her husband's death in 1947, their ashes were moved to Westminster Abbey.

W. found her vocation in social science and public service. What struck some observers as arrogance resulted from her confidence in her own vision of the social good and her urgency about making it a reality. She dedicated her life to defining and promoting a society in which economic justice would foster moral and social progress.

WORKS (most written with Sidney Webb): *The Co-operative Movement in Great Britain* (1891). *The History of Trade Unionism* (1894). *Industrial Democracy* (1897). *The Webbs' Australian Diary* (1898). *The Problems of Modern Industry* (1902). *The History of Liquor Licensing in England* (1903). *London Education* (1904). *The Parish and the County* (1906). *The Manor and the Borough* (1908). *Minority Report to the Royal Commission on the Poor Law* (1909). *The State and the Doctor* (1910). *English Poor Law Policy* (1910). *The Prevention of Destitution* (1911). *Grants in Aid* (1911). *The Story of the King's Highway* (1913). *An Appeal to Women* (1917). *The Wages of Men and Women—Should They Be Equal?* (1919). *A Constitution for the Socialist Commonwealth of Great Britain* (1920). *The Consumer's Co-operative Movement* (1921). *English Prisons Under Local Government* (1922). *Statutory Authorities for Special Purposes* (1922). *The Decay of Capitalist Civilisation* (1923). *My Apprenticeship* (1926). *English Poor Law History: The Old Poor Law* (1927). *English Poor Law History: The Last Hundred Years* (1929). *Methods of Social Study* (1932). *Soviet Communism, A New Civilisation* (1935). *Our Partnership* (1948). *Diaries, 1912-24* (1952). *Diaries, 1924-32* (1956) *American Diary, 1898* (1963). *The Diaries of Beatrice Webb, Vol. I, 1873-1892,* ed. Norman and Jeanne MacKenzie (1982). *The Diaries of Beatrice Webb, Vol. II, 1892-1905,* ed. Norman and Jeanne MacKenzie (1983).

BIBLIOGRAPHY: Cole, M. *Beatrice Webb* (1945). Cole, M. *The Story of Fabian Socialism* (1961). Cole, M. (ed.). *The Webbs and Their Work* (1949). Hamilton, M.A. *Sidney and Beatrice Webb* (1933). Hynes, S. *The Edwardian Turn of Mind* (1968). Letwin, S. *The Pursuit of Certainty* (1965). MacKenzie, J. *A Victorian Courtship: The Story of Beatrice Potter and Sidney Webb* (1979). MacKenzie, N. (ed.). *The Letters of Sidney and Beatrice Webb* (1978). Muggeridge, K. and Adam, R. *Beatrice Webb: A Life, 1858-1943* (1967). Nord, D. *The Apprenticeship of Beatrice Webb* (1985).

For articles in reference works, see: *DNB. Longman. TCA* and *SUP.*

Other references: *Proceedings of the British Academy* (1943). *Scrutiny* (1949). *The Times* (London) (1 May 1943). *TLS* (20 October 1940).

Rosemary Jann

(Gladys) Mary Webb

BORN: 25 March 1881, Leighton, Shropshire.
DIED: 8 October 1927, St. Leonards-on-Sea, Sussex.
DAUGHTER OF: George Edward and Sarah Alice Scott Meredith.
MARRIED: Henry Bertram Law Webb, 1912.

A transitional novelist between Victorianism and Modernism, W. lived most of her life in her native county of Shropshire, whose nature she apotheosized in her writings. Eldest of six children born to a Welsh schoolmaster and a distant relative of Sir Walter Scott, W. was educated at home by her governess and lifelong friend, Miss E.M. Lory. W. also attended a finishing school in Southport, Lancashire, for three years. Upon returning from school, she was expected to supervise the education of her younger siblings. At age twenty, W. suffered a collapse from Graves' Disease, which left her with a disfiguring goiter. During her long convalescence she devoted herself to writing essays and poems.

From the beginning, nature was W.'s central subject. As her brother recalled: "Her God was Nature." W.'s first completed work was a collection of nature essays, written between the time of her father's illness and death in 1909 and her marriage in 1912 to Henry Webb, a Shropshire schoolmaster. First published in 1917 as *The Spring of Joy*, these essays, though rather old-fashioned in tone, contain the core of W.'s pantheistic nature mysticism and reveal her precise, minute observation of natural phenomena. They express her faith that health and divine vitality are to be found in "the spiritual ties between man and nature."

At the time of her marriage, W. received a substantial allowance from her mother. With this, W. and her husband were able to establish a modest home near Shrewsbury. For several years they worked as market gardeners, an activity that provided more material for W.'s future novels than income. In the spring of 1915, in three weeks' time, W. wrote her first novel, *The Golden Arrow* (1916). Spasmodic and rapid writing was typical of her manner of composition, and she seldom revised her work.

All six of W.'s novels are love stories; all but one end happily for the lovers. Yet it is nature that seems to be the true hero and heroine of her novels. W.'s nature mysticism acts as a vital, transforming force in her characters' lives. Deborah in *The Golden Arrow* experiences this force in her "apocalypse of love" as a presence "behind light and shadow, under pain and joy . . . —too intangible for materialization into words, too mighty to be expressed by any name of man's." Prue Sarn in

Precious Bane experiences the mystical union as "a most powerful sweetness that had never come to me afore. It was not religious, like the goodness of a text heard at a preaching. It was beyond that." W. may be described as a "transcendental realist," portraying human characters and the natural world with the vision of a poet and the eye of a naturalist.

W.'s most pantheistic work is her memorable tragic novel, *Gone to Earth* (1917), which also marks an impressive technical advance over her earlier writing. Rebecca West, in her review of this work, declared it the novel of the year and pronounced its author "a genius." Here the landscape and its myriad lives are active presences, taking sides in the drama surrounding Hazel Woodus, a wild and graceful child of nature who "can never adjust herself to the strait orbit of human life." Like Catherine in Emily Brontë's *Wuthering Heights*, Hazel "did not want heaven; she wanted earth and the green ways of earth." The fate of the girl who wants only to "be her own" is determined by the conflict between her two lovers, the cruel sensualist Reddin and the tormented idealist Marston. Hazel, more truly spiritual and attuned to the spirit of nature than the conventionally religious world that condemns her, is literally hounded to death by hunters as she chooses to die with her pet fox rather than sacrifice it to the "death pack." Written in the dark days of World War I, the novel echoes "the keening—wild and universal—of life for the perishing matter that it inhabits."

In 1917 W. and her husband moved into "Spring Cottage," a small bungalow they had built according to W.'s own design. Her next novel, *The House in Dormer Forest* (1920), takes for its theme the destructive influence of lifeless tradition on the inheritors of an entailed estate. W. often pits her visionary characters against those whose lives and souls have been stifled by rigid codes of behavior.

The success of *Gone to Earth* had paved the way for greater recognition of W.'s gifts and she began to receive advance royalties for her novels. In 1921, W. and her husband moved to London. Though ultimately disappointed in the literary life there, W. met writers and editors, wrote reviews for the *Bookman* and the *Spectator*, and had several short stories published in the *English Review*. She made the acquaintance of Walter de la Mare, who published three of her poems in his anthology *Come Hither*. In London, W. wrote *Seven for a Secret* (1922), for which Thomas Hardy's novels served as model. She asked and received permission from Hardy to dedicate the book to him.

Precious Bane (1924), her last completed

work, was the novel W. and many of her critics considered her best work. Here nature mysticism is offset by dominant Christian symbolism. Set in England at the end of the Napoleonic wars, *Precious Bane* is a first-person retrospective narrative of the life of a "hare-shotten" young woman. Prue Sarn's harelip is viewed as a sign of witchcraft, the "devil's mark," by the highly superstitious villagers. At the end of the novel, an angry mob nearly drowns Prue on a ducking stool, but she is rescued by the ideal man and her ideal lover, the weaver Kester Woodseaves. W.'s knowledge of the dark side of human nature is balanced here by her passionate faith in the healing power of love. Her portrayal of female sexual feeling is surprisingly bold rather than sentimental. As in her other novels, W.'s prose style reaches heights of lyrical intensity, especially in her descriptions of the landscape. *Precious Bane* was awarded the Prix Femina for the best English novel of 1924-25.

W.'s last novel, *Armour Wherein He Trusted* (1928), remained a fragment and was first published posthumously in a collection of her short stories. Her essays were reissued posthumously, together with some of her poems, as *Poems and the Spring of Joy* (1928), for which Walter de la Mare wrote the introduction, and a final collection of *Fifty-One Poems* was published posthumously in 1946.

W.'s genius as a novelist remains obscure. Her use of dialect, local traditions, and folklore has led to her being classified as a regional or rural writer by some critics, while others have regarded her as a "hierophant" of the "cult of the primitive." Charles Sanders, who compiled an excellent annotated bibliography on W., finds that in spite of her rhapsodic treatment of nature, her novels are essentially modern in their probing of the fear and insecurities of twentieth-century humanity and in their analysis of the "herd instinct" of conventional society.

WORKS: The Golden Arrow (1916). The Spring of Joy (1917; reissued as Poems and the Spring of Joy, 1928). Gone to Earth (1917). The House in Dormer Forest (1920). Seven for a Secret (1922). Precious Bane (1924). Armour Wherein He Trusted (an unfinished novel, together with ten short stories, 1928). Fifty-One Poems (1946). Collected Prose and Poems, ed. G.M. Coles (1977).

BIBLIOGRAPHY: Addison, H. *Mary Webb* (1931). Armstrong, M. "Introduction." *The Essential Mary Webb* (1949). Barale, M.A. *Daughters and Lovers: The Life and Writing of Mary Webb* (1986). Byford-Jones, W. *The Shropshire Haunts of Mary Webb* (1948). Cavaliero, G. *The Rural Tradition in the English Novel, 1900-1939* (1977). Coles, G.M. *The Flower of Light: A Biography of Mary Webb* (1978). de la Mare, W. "Introduction." *Poems and the Spring of Joy* (1928). Duncan, E. "Introduction," *Gone to Earth* (1979). Hannah, B. *Striving Toward Wholeness* (1971). Moult, T. *Mary Webb: Her Life and Works* (1932). Wandor, M. "Preface." *Precious Bane* (1978). Wrenn, D.P.H., *Goodbye to Morning* (1964).

For articles in reference works, see: *DLB. TCA.*
Other references: Davis, W.E. *ELT* (1968). Sanders, C. *ELT* (1966). Sanders, C. *ELT* (1967).

Jean Pearson

Augusta Davies Webster

BORN: 30 January 1837, Poole, Dorset.
DIED: 5 September 1894, Kew.
DAUGHTER OF: George Davies and Julia Hume.
MARRIED: Thomas Webster, 1863.
WROTE UNDER: Augusta Webster, Cecil Home.

W. was the daughter of Vice-Admiral George Davies, who held several coast-guard commands; as a consequence she spent her girlhood on various islands and ships. In her youth she studied classical authors, particularly the Greek dramatists, and in her twenties, she published translations of Aeschylus and Euripides. At the age of twenty-six, she married Thomas Webster, Fellow of Trinity College, Cambridge, and a practicing solicitor. From 1860 until her death, W. wrote plays, poems, and essays on both contemporary and classical themes.

In *A Housewife's Opinions* (1878), she collected her essays on issues related to the lives of married women like herself. For example, she considered seriously the consequences of expecting housewives to do their own housework, anticipating that women's time for study, art, or music would be drastically curtailed thereby as would their time with their husbands. Cooperative housekeeping she ruled out, because of the English ideal of private home life. An ardent feminist, W. believed that gaining suffrage for women was only a matter of time despite the six Parliamentary defeats she personally witnessed in her lifetime. She had a strong commitment to advancing women's educational opportunities and was twice elected to the London School Board, in 1879 and 1885.

W.'s dramas—*The Auspicious Day* (1872), *Disguises* (1879), *In a Day* (1882), and *The Sentence* (1887)—were praised by contemporaries for their "concentrated strength." William Michael Rossetti pronounced *The Sentence* (about Caligula) to be "one of the masterpieces of European drama." *In a Day* was produced at a matinee in 1890, with W.'s adult daughter appearing as the heroine; it was the only one of her dramas to be staged. Also in the dramatic vein, W. composed numerous studies of Christian saints, addressing the glory and the difficulty of asceticism and submission to God, e.g., "Jeanne d'Arc" and "Sister Annunciata" (1866). In 1864, she published a three-volume novel, *Lesley's Guardians*, under the pseudonym Cecil Home.

W.'s most lasting work, however, is her poetry, beginning with the 1866 volume *Dramatic Studies*, which included the widely admired poem "Snow-Waste" and culminating in the unfinished sonnet sequence, *Mother and Daughter*, published the year after her death. Showing the influence of her acknowledged mentor, Robert Browning, W. wrote dramatic monologues in blank verse, often on sociological themes pertaining particularly to women. These pieces are especially interesting for their rendering of female consciousness and are much more psychologically convincing than most contemporary poems on similar subjects. Outstanding examples include "By the Looking-Glass" (1866), about spinsterhood; "The Heiress's Wooer" and "A Mother's Cry" (1867), about the marriage market and parental matchmaking; and "A Castaway" (1870), about a "fallen woman." "A Castaway," a 600-line poem ranging widely over the whole complicated issue of prostitution in the nineteenth century, compares favorably with Dante Gabriel Rossetti's "Jenny," which appeared in the same year. The poem went into three editions and was greatly admired by both Browning and Rossetti, although some contemporary critics complained that the subject matter was unsuitable for a woman poet.

"Circe" (1870) is a psychological character study of the mythological figure; it is notable for its sexual imagery and erotic tone and for its persuasive representation of the heroine's inner life. In *A Book of Rhyme* (1881), W. introduced into English poetry an Italian form of peasant song known as "rispetti" or "stornelli." Her last volume of poetry, *Mother and Daughter* (1895), is at once a personal expression of maternal love and a commentary on the varying moods and experiences of motherhood in the nineteenth century.

W.'s moral leadership was widely recognized in her lifetime. In 1880 Theodore Watts placed W. in the company of George Eliot and Frances Power Cobbe, "who, in virtue of lofty purpose, purity of soul, and deep sympathy with suffering humanity, are just now ahead of the men." Yet Victorian commentators were often made uneasy by the realism and directness of W.'s poetry. Some complained of W.'s eccentricity in printing her blank verse without capitals at the beginning of the lines; others found her diction inadmissibly vulgar, particularly for a woman writer. Mackenzie Bell, while comparing W. favorably with Elizabeth Barrett Browning, Christina Rossetti, and Jean Ingelow, nevertheless remarked, "the other women poets of England must yield to her [W.] in that quality which, as it is generally deemed the specially masculine quality, is called virility." However ambivalent contemporary critics may have been about the characteristic strength and force of W.'s poetry, these are the very qualities that make her work readable today.

WORKS: *Blanche Lisle, and Other Poems* (1860). *Lilian Gray* (1864). *Lesley's Guardians* (1864). *Dramatic Studies* (1866). *A Woman Sold, and Other Poems* (1867). *Portraits* (1870, enlarged 1893). *The Auspicious Day* (1872). *Yu-Pe-Ya's Lute* (1874). *A Housewife's Opinions* (1878). *Disguises* (1879). *A Book of Rhyme* (1881). *In a Day* (1882). *Daffodil and the Croäxaxicans: A Romance from History* (1884). *The Sentence* (1887). *Selections from the Verse of Augusta Webster* (1893). *Mother and Daughter*, ed. William Michael Rossetti (1895).

BIBLIOGRAPHY: For articles in reference works, see: *BA19C*. *English Poetesses*, ed. E.S. Robertson (1883). Evans, B. I. *English Poetry in the Later Nineteenth Century* (1933). Forman, H.B. *Our Living Poets* (1871). Bell, M. "Augusta Webster." *The Poets and the Poetry of the Century*, ed. Alfred H. Miles, vol. 7 (1892).

Other references: Hickok, K. *Representations of Women: Nineteenth-Century British Women's Poetry* (1984). Sackville-West, V. *The Eighteen Seventies*, ed. H. Granville-Barker (1929). Watts, T. *Athenaeum* (15 September 1894).

Kathleen Hickok

Fay Weldon

BORN: 22 September 1933, Alvechurch, Worcestershire.
DAUGHTER OF: Frank T. and Margaret Jepson Birkinshaw.
MARRIED: Ron Weldon, 1960.

"It took me a long time to believe that men were actually human beings," W. writes. Brought up in New Zealand and raised by her mother and sister after her parents' divorce, she attended convent school. In the 1950s she completed her M.A. in economics and psychology at St. Andrews University and was an unmarried mother—"a solitary experience," as she has written. The result of her early life was a unique perspective on the world: "I believed the world was female, whereas men have always believed the world is male. It's unusual for women to suffer from my delusion." W.'s subject has largely been the generation of women that grew up after World War II; her theme is how these women survive being human.

To read a W. novel is to encounter a densely truthful depiction of the claims people make on one another. Each of W.'s novels traces the complex interweavings of human relations and how these inevitably constrain women. *Down among the Women* (1971) follows a group of women of W.'s "generation" as they variously fight, deny, and fail to transcend the label of "woman." In *Praxis* (1978), the expectations forced on women figure in the fate of Praxis Duveen, in prison for infanticide. *Puffball* (1980) is part supernatural parody, part autobiography—about Liffey, going through a pregnancy separated from the father, who has a full and busy life in London while Liffey comes to term amid witches and hauntings in Somerset. *Female Friends* (1975), one of W.'s best novels, records how the concatenation of personal failings and male exploitation defeat even the most modest dreams.

W. has both claimed and disclaimed the feminist viewpoint. She has written that she belongs to the last pre-feminist generation: women without power, without theory, often aware of their impotence and oppression, often angry, frustrated, and despairing but also trying to make a life of it. Thus the last words of *Down among the Women* are "We are the last of the women." One feels that the last two words might be enclosed in their own quotation marks.

W.'s best work is less didactic than it is moral; it seeks less to draw a lesson than to depict the truth. Readers have sensed a distance between W.'s fictional practice and the strident moralism that mars other feminist writing. W. has acknowledged the strong, even lopsided, moral intention in her fiction. She has admitted that she intention-

ally rounds out her female characters more fully than her male characters: "I just make [male characters] behave, talk, and I don't add any justification for their behaviour. Whereas my women characters are all explained." Male behavior is so well established that it hardly needs explication; male domination is such an accomplished fact that it hardly needs mention. Fiction becomes a way of "redressing a balance so far tilted as to be all but unworkable."

Though W. accords her women a fuller explanation, she does not idealize them. Throughout her fiction and drama there is a refusal to invest women characters with unusual courage, resources, or integrity. Lily of *Remember Me* (1976), Chloe of *Female Friends*, Ruth of *Life and Loves of a She-Devil* (1983)—all are women with failings, all dole out their share of hurt and disappointment, and all contribute to their respective fates. All we have is what happens: the ironies of relationships with men; the successes and failures of friendships between women; the demands of motherhood; the coming to terms with menstruation, pregnancy, the physical aspects of being a woman; the lack of an alternative to male-defined roles; and always, isolation. W.'s women often end neither better nor wiser than before. In place of great expectations, they have a clearer view of themselves and of their chances for happiness. Indeed, this final clarity verging on optimism rescues W.'s work from what some readers find is a tragic pessimism relieved only by black humor. Chloe of *Female Friends* searches for some parting wisdom to give the reader, and her conclusions are characteristically concrete: "Take family snaps, unashamed. Dress up for weddings, all weddings. Rejoice at births, all births. For days can be happy—whole futures cannot."

W. may be an even better writer for the stage than she is a novelist; much of her best fiction has been adapted from her dramatic works. Her best single piece of writing, "Polaris," has succeeded equally well as drama, radio play, and short story. Dramatic technique often surfaces in the experimental aspects of her fiction: staccato sentences, short paragraphs, jagged alternations between chronologies and points of view. A novel like *Female Friends* may be rendered largely in stage dialogue, exploiting the inherent irony of the dramatic situation. Her best work delivers what good drama delivers: the impression of voiceless objectivity combined with that of an unmistakable voice.

W. writes about a sharply delimited, not to say claustrophobic, world, which may lead some readers to the impression of sameness from work to work. In the 1980s, a productive period for this very productive writer, she has sought to widen her scope, with her adaptation of and reflections on Jane Austen (1980 and 1984), her book on Rebecca West (1985), and novels such as *The Hearts and Lives of Men* (1987) and *The Rules of Life* (1987). Of the novels, the former is a mock fairy tale and the latter a vicious satire on religion. *The Shrapnel Academy* (1986) explores a theme that has always been in her work: the obsolescence and brutality of war. In these as in all of her other writings, W. struggles against the sermonizing impulse, the desire to bash the reader over the head with the moral import of the tale. She sometimes gives in to this impulse. On the other hand, she has produced a great number of truly good plays, dramas, and pieces of fiction; she is a much better writer than many better-known writers.

WORKS: *Wife in a Blonde Wig* (1966). *The Fat Woman's Tale* (1966). *The Fat Woman's Joke* (1967; in the U.S. as *... And the Wife Ran Away,* (1968). *What About Me* (1967). *Dr. De Waldon's Therapy* (1967). *Goodnight, Mrs. Dill* (1967). *The 45th Unmarried Mother* (1967). *Fall of the Goat* (1967). *Ruined Houses* (1968). *Venus Rising* (1968). *The Three Wives of Felix Hull* (1968). *Hippy Hippy Who Cares* (1968). *£ 13038* (1968). *The Loophole* (1969). *Smokescreen* (1969). *Poor Mother* (1970). *Office Party* (1970). *Permanence* (1970). *Upstairs Downstairs* (1971). *On Trial* (1971). *Down among the Women* (1971). *Old Man's Hat* (1972). *A Splinter of Ice* (1972). *Hands* (1972). *The Lament of an Unmarried Father* (1972). *A Nice Rest* (1972). *Time Hurries On.* In *Scene Scripts,* ed. M. Marland (1972). *Spider* (1973). *Comfortable Words* (1973). *Housebreaker* (1973). *Desirous of Change* (1973). *In Memoriam* (1974). *Mr. Fox and Mr. First* (1974). *Words of Advice* (1974). *The Doctor's Wife* (1975). *Poor Baby* (1975). *Friends* (1975). *Female Friends* (1975). *The Terrible Tale of Timothy Bagshott* (1975). *Aunt Tatty* (1975; from the story by E. Bowen). *Moving House* (1976). *Remember Me* (1976). *Words of Advice* (1977; in the U.K. as *Little*

Sisters, 1978). *Act of Rape* (1977). *Married Love* (1977). *Act of Hypocrisy* (1977). *Chickabiddy* (1978). *Mr. Director* (1978). *Polaris* (radio and stage drama, 1978). *Praxis* (1978). *Weekend* (1979). *All the Bells of Paradise* (1979). (with P. Anderson and M. Stott). *Simple Steps to Public Life* (1980). *Action Replay* (1980). *Puffball* (1980). *Pride and Prejudice* (1980, from the novel by J. Austen). *Honey Ann* (1980). *Life for Christine* (1980). *Watching Me, Watching You* (television drama, 1980; novel, 1981). *I Love My Love* (radio drama, 1981; stage play, 1984). *After the Prize* (1981). *Woodworm* (1981). *The President's Child* (1982). *Little Mrs. Perkins* (1982, from the story by P. Mortimer). *Redundant! or, The Wife's Revenge* (1983). *Life and Loves of a She-Devil* (novel, 1983; television serial, 1986). *Letters to Alice: On First Reading Jane Austen* (1984). *The Western Women* (1984). *Bright Smiler* (1985). *Rebecca West* (1985). *Polaris and Other Stories* (1985). *Jane Eyre* (drama, from the novel by C. Brontë, 1986). *Face at the Window* (1986). *A Dangerous Kind of Love* (1986). *The Shrapnel Academy* (1986). *The Heart of the Country* (television serial and novel, 1987). *The Hole in the Top of the World* (1987). *The Good Woman of Setzuan* (1987, adapted from Brecht). *Scaling Down* (1987). *The Hearts and Lives of Men* (1987). *The Rules of Life* (1987).

BIBLIOGRAPHY: For articles in reference works, see: *CA. CD. CLC. CN. DB. Writer's Directory.*

Other references: *Critique* (1978). *Manchester Guardian* (20 February 1979). *Moderna Sprak* (1979). *NYTBR* (2 October 1977, 26 April 1987). *Observer* (18 February 1979). *Telegraph Sunday Magazine* (London) (16 December 1979). *Time* (22 February 1973). *Times* (London) (17 February 1980). *TLS* (22 February 1980, 13 February 1987, 11 September 1987). Wandor, M., ed. *On Gender and Writing* (1983). Zeman, A. *Presumptuous Girls; Women and Their World in the Serious Woman's Novel* (1977).

John Timpane

Jane West

BORN: 30 April 1758, London.
DIED: 25 March 1852, Little Bowden, Northamptonshire.
DAUGHTER OF: John and Jane Iliffe.
MARRIED: Thomas West, c. 1780.
WROTE UNDER: Jane West, Prudentia Homespun.

W.'s conservative educational tracts and didactic novels were well received by late eighteenth- and early nineteenth-century readers. She was ninety-four when she died, and her writing

covers a period of fifty-three years. During this time she was active as a writer, wife, mother, property owner, and spokeswoman for the Anglican Church.

W. was self-taught and began writing early in her life. Some of her youthful compositions appeared in her first work, *Miscellaneous Poetry,* published in 1786. Around 1780 she married Thomas West, a yeoman farmer, and moved to Little Bowden where she was to live for the rest of her life and where she raised her three sons. During this time W. published poetry, plays, and her first novel, *The Advantages of Education*, an attempt to capitalize on the craze for novels.

W. hoped to advance her family through her novels. In 1800 she wrote to Bishop Percy, "Though a sentiment inherent in my character will ever preserve me from any degrading meanness, yet a just sense of the wants and claims of a rising family inspires me with an anxious wish to procure these emoluments which have sometimes resulted from literary efforts." Her very popular novels and conduct books for young men and women brought her some measure of celebrity.

W. always presented herself first and foremost as a wife and mother. In a letter published in *Gentleman's Magazine* in January 1802, one of her admirers praised her because she "pays the greatest care and attention to her farm, manages her dairy, and even carries her butter to market." The next month, another of her admirers in rebuttal pointed out that W. was too much of a gentlewoman ever to carry her goods to market. Rather, she supervised the sending of the cheeses to market "while knitting stockings for her husband and sons."

W.'s *A Gossip's Story* has often been seen as a source or starting point for Austen's *Sense and Sensibility*. Her early novels are narrated by Prudentia Homespun, an elderly spinster whose observations are as much ironic and humorous as instructive. However, in the introduction to *The Refusal*, published in 1810, W., through another narrator, announces the "demise of that inimitable author." W. explained in an 1811 letter to Bishop Percy that "the wings of my gaiety have been clipped, the history of the times I date in, and the moral purposes of my work, preclude jocularity . . . Mrs. Prudentia Homespun . . . is dead and buried."

At this time W. turned her attention to historical fiction. Her historical romance *Alicia de Lacey* begins with a justification not only of developing fictions around historical characters but also of "making past heroes and heroines talk in the language of common life," perhaps setting a direction for Scott's historical fiction.

She outlived her celebrity, her husband, and all her sons. In her later years she suffered from a growing feeling of isolation and described herself as "an old Q in a corner whom the rest of the world has forgotten." The last image of herself that she left is of a lonely woman who saved all the letters from her sons and her friends, "valuable Scripts . . . reserved as bon bons to gratify" her old age, but "failing eyesight" denied her even this enjoyment.

Although W.'s didacticism eventually overwhelmed her fiction, she explored new issues and fictional forms in her work. She was an early advocate of education for women, and her early works recognized the role that an educated mother could play in a daughter's life. She believed that the past determined the present, and, as a result, her fiction attempted to capture women's lives lived over decades rather than weeks. It is a disappointment that in her fiction these women's lives had to become more circumscribed in order for them to survive.

WORKS: *Miscellaneous Poetry* (1786). *The Humours of Brighthelmstone: A Poem* (1788). *Miscellaneous Poems and a Tragedy* (1791). *The Advantages of Education* (1793). *The Gossip's Story* (1796). *Elegy on Edmund Burke* (1797). *Poems and Plays, Volumes I and II* (1799). *A Tale of the Times* (1799). *Letters To a Young Man* (1801). *The Infidel Father* (1802). *The Sorrows of Selfishness* (1802). *Poems and Plays, Volumes III and IV* (1805). *Letters To a Young Lady* (1806). *The Mother: A Poem in Five Books* (1809). *The Refusal: A Novel* (1810). *The Loyalists: An Historical Novel* (1812). *Select Translations of the Beauties of Massillon* (1812). *Alicia de Lacey: an Historical Romance* (1814). *Scriptural Essays adapted to the Holy Days of the Church of England* (1816). *Ringrove; or Old Fashioned Notions* (1827).

BIBLIOGRAPHY: Butler, M. *Jane Austen and the War of Ideas* (1975). Moler, K. *Jane Austen's Art of Allusion* (1968).

Other references: *N&Q* (December 1984). *RES* (January 1940).

Pamela Lloyd

Rebecca West (pseudonym of Cicily Isabel Fairfield)

BORN: 25 December 1892, London.
DIED: 15 March 1983, London.
DAUGHTER OF: Charles and Isabella MacKenzie Fairfield.
MARRIED: Henry Andrews, 1930.
WROTE UNDER: Rebecca West, Corinne Andrews.

By voicing her ideas memorably in prose that could be raucous, elegant, and precise and by remaining an active writer for more than seventy years, W. earned for herself a unique position in twentieth-century British letters. Working as a novelist, literary and political journalist, biographer, historian, and commentator on the morality of her time, W. repeatedly demonstrated a brilliant fusion of rational analysis and spirited engagement.

Throughout her career, W. published under the pseudonym "Rebecca West," chosen for Henrik Ibsen's defiant character in *Rosmersholm*, and she proclaimed herself a radical feminist not only in her political essays but also in her fictional characters and plots, in her biography of St. Augustine, in her historical analyses, and in her literary criticism. Her imaginative grasp of abstract theories—whether Hegel's dialectic or Jung's unconscious or the Manichean myth of good and evil—enabled her to create characters and narrative structures embodying those concepts she believed essential to understanding twentieth-century history. That she could command a forceful rhetoric to connect disparate concepts and events is evident in *Black Lamb and Grey Falcon* (1941) as she wryly comments on d'Annunzio's seizure of Fiume: "All this is embittering history for a woman to contemplate. I will believe that the battle of feminism is over, and that the female has reached a position of equality with the male, when I hear that a country has allowed itself to be turned upside-down and led to the brink of war by its passion for a totally bald woman writer." Her satire of individual or cultural imbecility combined ruthlessness and wit.

As a literary critic, W. praised the achievements and deplored the inadequacies of her fellow authors. Her literary judgment in *Henry James* (1916) is both irreverent and astute, for, without idolizing the master of psychological insights, she acknowledges his class-conscious aversion to vulgarity and his limited imaginative grasp of women's characters; hers is the first feminist study of James's fiction. She admired James Joyce's "Marion Bloom, the great mother who . . . lies in a bed yeasty with her warmth and her sweat," and she compared Molly's monologue to the "unified beauty" of Beethoven's Fifth Symphony, but she also noted that Joyce "pushes his pen about noisily and aimlessly as if it were a carpet-sweeper, whose technique is a tin can tied to the tail of the dog of his genius." W. wrote a sensitive, appreciative sketch of D.H. Lawrence but brazenly called his genius eccentric.

As a fiction writer, W. chose to adopt a different pattern with each book, but she always created characters in conflict, wrestling with ideas that symbolize real forces in history. W.'s most radical fiction was a short story, "Indissoluble Marriage," published in the first issue (June 1914) of *Blast* (and reprinted in 1982 in *The Young Rebecca*). W. draws upon Jungian symbolism to explore the sexual politics of a marriage. The dramatic tale, narrated by an unsympathetic husband, depicts his wife's powerful sensuality, evident in her body and her voice, and her self-

determined spirit, evident in her advocacy of woman's suffrage. She is indestructible; she nearly drowns. W., affirming the power of female sexuality, undermines the aggressive, misogynist assumptions of Vorticist and Futurist theory.

Her two novels about World War I are unequal in literary quality. *The Return of the Soldier* (1918) imaginatively fleshes out a Freudian interpretation of neurosis, in this case shell shock induced by war. The fictional love triangle contrasts the natural, passionate, lusty, erotic drives with the repressive, materialistic and tyrannical, death-loving drives, both competing for the psyche of the soldier. The shell-shocked soldier, suffering amnesia, remembers only his pre-war lover, a common woman whom his family would never have accepted into their class; he has forgotten his family obligations, his proper, cold wife, and his dutiful participation in the war. W. in her exposition of the story links war's aggression with society's class-consciousness, both exemplary of patriarchal tyranny over the individual. Prompted by the memory of his young son who had died, the soldier regains his memory and returns to his wife and to the war. By contrast with this brilliant fiction, her anonymous fictional memoir, *War Nurse: The True Story of a Woman Who Lived, Loved and Suffered on the Western Front* (1930), ostensibly written by "Corinne Andrews," seems an attempt to earn easy money quickly by competing with the war novels and films of the time.

The Judge (1922) explores the familial triangle of an independent, self-determined woman, her weakling husband, and his domineering, tyrannical mother. The power struggle between daughter-in-law and mother reveals aspects of W.'s rebellion against and respect for her own mother. *Harriet Hume: A London Fantasy* (1929) oddly combines a moral parable with a romantic comedy in an episodic plot that turns on the artistic heroine's ability to read the thoughts of her beloved, an ambitious politician. At the end, the lovers unite, as if two halves of a personality are finally reconciled.

Of the four short novels published under the title *The Harsh Voice* (1935), the most impressive creates a memorable character, Alice Pemberton, who is *The Salt of the Earth*. Alice carefully controls her life, repressing her own and her husband's desires, smothering her family's love for her, and expecting incompetence, carelessness, and inconsiderateness from all around her. As she rubs salt into wounds, she believes herself to be acting sensibly and selflessly in the best interests of her victim. The husband's decision to poison Alice provides a satisfying fictional conclusion.

A partial definition of the happy marriage between female and male power occurs in *The Thinking Reed* (1936) in a dialogue where each spouse admits admiring the other as superior.

Isabella, the rational heroine, widowed at the beginning of the novel, rejects an aristocratic French lover because he is a tyrant (she compares him to the Arc de Triomphe, embodying male patriotic glory), then marries a kind-hearted, intuitive Frenchman who has peasant ancestors but who now owns profitable automobile factories. He can behave like an ass, and she can behave like a maenad, but together they are morally superior to both the imbecilic ruling class and the envious, mean-spirited politicians. She saves her husband's career from disaster, but her action destroys their child she is carrying; Isabella and her husband heal their estrangement, but W. clearly signals the loss of their wealth in the stock market crash.

During World War II, W. published a short, propagandistic novel, *The Second Commandment* (1942), depicting the courage of a Danish actress during the Nazi occupation of Copenhagen, but her next major novel was not published until 1956: *The Fountain Overflows*. W.'s childhood is partially represented in this fictional account of a poor, intellectual family of three sisters, one brother, and a mother who manages their affairs despite periodic financial reverses caused by their impractically idealistic journalist father. Their overflowing love for each other gives them the strength not only to suffer genteel poverty but to offer shelter and support to others.

In *The Birds Fall Down* (1966), W. creates a fiction about expatriate Russians before the 1917 Revolution, pairing a young woman, daughter of an English aristocrat and a Russian emigrée, with a double agent for the Czar and the Revolutionaries. Each character is formed by two antithetical forces at work within: political forces for the double agent, cultural forces for the young woman. The death of the young woman's czarist grandfather provides the crisis which brings these two characters in contact. The double agent passionately explains to the Russian-English woman Hegel's "theory of the dialectic," combining thesis and contradictory antithesis into a new synthesis, so that the reader realizes, as the young woman does not, that he loves her. In her eyes, the double agent threatens her life, and she arranges for his assassination.

W.'s fascination with the mind divided against itself, with the formation of nationalist loyalty and the betrayal of that loyalty, may also be seen in her collected essays on the Nuremburg trials, on the trial of a British Fascist, on the Profumo affair, and on other "sordid and undignified" crimes: *The Meaning of Treason* (1947) and *The New Meaning of Treason* (1964).

The most famous of W.'s books is her *Black Lamb and Grey Falcon* (1941), a two-volume narrative of her travels in Yugoslavia in the spring of 1937. She mixes travelogue, history, fiction, autobiography, and political analysis in a compelling,

entertaining, informative work explaining the cultural differences among the Slavic peoples, narrating a history of violent insurrection against tyranny exposing the origins of a passionate, cruel nationalism. She wrote down her evaluations of Yugoslavian, Austrian, and German motives, "convinced of the inevitability of the second Anglo-German war." Of all her works, *Black Lamb and Grey Falcon* best exemplifies her intellectual range, her ability to move and inform, her imaginative grasp of philosophical, political, and historical movements, her brilliant rhetorical style, and her self-assured judgment.

WORKS: *Henry James* (1916). *The Return of the Soldier* (1918). *The Judge* (1922). *The Strange Necessity* (1928). *Harriet Hume* (1929). *War Nurse: The True Story of a Woman Who Lived, Loved and Suffered on the Western Front* (Anon., as by "Corinne Andrews," 1930). *D.H. Lawrence: An Elegy* (1930). *A Letter to a Grandfather* (1930). *Ending in Earnest: A Literary Log* (1931). *St. Augustine* (1933). *The Harsh Voice: Four Short Novels* (1935). *The Thinking Reed* (1936). *Black Lamb and Grey Falcon: A Journey through Yugoslavia* (1941). *The Meaning of Treason* (1947). *A Train of Powder* (1955). *The Fountain Overflows* (1956). *The Court and the Castle* (1957). *The New Meaning of Treason* (1964; English ed., *The Meaning of Treason, Revised Edition*, 1965). *The Birds Fall Down* (1966). *1900* (1981). *The Young Rebecca: Writings of Rebecca West, 1911-1917*, ed. J. Marcus (1982). *This Real Night* (1985). *Sunflower* (1986). *Family Memories*, ed. F. Evans (1987).

BIBLIOGRAPHY: Deakin, M. *Rebecca West* (1980). Glendinning, V. *Rebecca West: A Life* (1987). Hutchinson, G. *A Preliminary List of the Writings of Rebecca West, 1912-1951* (1957). Hynes, S. "Introduction: In Communion with Reality." *Rebecca West: A Celebration*, ed. S. Hynes (1977). Marcus, J. "Introductions." *The Young Rebecca: Writings of Rebecca West, 1911-1917*, ed. J. Marcus (1982). Orel, H. *The Literary Achievement of Rebecca West* (1986). Ray, G. *H.G. Wells and Rebecca West* (1974). Weldon, F. *Rebecca West* (1986). Wolfe, P. *Rebecca West: Artist and Thinker* (1971).

For articles in reference works, see: *CA. CLC. CN. DLB. MBL. TCA* and *SUP.*

Other references: Adcock, St. J. *The Bookman* (September 1958). Chamberlain, L. *Contemporary Review* (1986). Colquitt, C. *SAR* (1986). Davies, A.P. *NR* (8 June 1953). Davis, H. *Canadian Forum* (June 1931). Dinnage, R. *NYRB* (12 August 1982). Ellmann, M. *Atlantic* (December 1966). Enright, D.J. *New Statesman* (4 November 1966). Feld, R.C. *NYTBR* (11 November 1923). Ferguson, M. *Minnesota Review* (1980). Haley, W. *American Scholar* (Winter 1978). Halper, N. *Partisan Review* (1949). Kalb, B. *SR* (19 March 1955). Kobler, T.S.

Critique: Studies in Modern Fiction (1971). Marcus, J. *Women Writers and the City: Essays in Feminist Literary Criticism*, ed. S.M. Squier (1984). Panter-Downes, M. *New Yorker* (3 December 1977). Pritchett, V.S. *New Yorker* (19 July 1982, 3 December 1966). Rainer, D. *Commonweal* (10 May 1968). Thompson, C.P. *New York Herald-Tribune Magazine* (7 February 1932). Walpole, H. *The Bookman* (May 1925). Webster, H.C. *SR* (8 December 1956).

Judith L. Johnston

Anne Lee Wharton

BORN: June 1659, Spelsbury.
DIED: 29 October 1685, Adderbury.
DAUGHTER OF: Sir Henry Lee and Anne Danvers Lee.
MARRIED: Thomas Wharton, 1673.

Author of only seventeen identifiable poems and a blank verse heroic tragedy that exists only in manuscript, W. was among the most highly praised woman poets of the Restoration.

Orphaned at birth, W. was co-heiress with her sister Eleanora to the estates of their ancestors Sir Henry Lee, Queen Elizabeth's champion, and Sir John Danvers, stepfather of the poets Lord Herbert of Cherbury and George Herbert. She was raised by her grandmother, Anne St. John Lee Wilmot, mother of the poet John Wilmot, Earl of Rochester. At fourteen she married the future Whig leader and established rake, Thomas Wharton. From her letters to her husband, it appears that the early years of her marriage were happy ones, with her actively engaged in helping him to attain his political goals. Wharton on his part seems to have been genuinely considerate of her literary interests, although contemporary reports would have him finding her "Person not so agreeable to him as was necessary to secure his constancy." In addition to one long stay in Paris, W. was involved in the literary and social life of London's court and theater, and she maintained friendships with at least two other women poets, Aphra Behn and Rochester's wife, Elizabeth. Rochester's death, mourned in W.'s most celebrated poem, "An Elegy on the Earl of Rochester," seems to have provided the literary establishment with the justification it needed to admit her to its ranks: as her uncle's "sole Executrix in Wit" she was in a position to redeem his reputation with her pious and melancholy poems, many of which appear to have circulated in manuscript in the months following Rochester's death. By 1682, according to the letters of her spiritual advisor Bishop Gilbert Burnet, W. was indeed ill and unhappy, living in retirement in the country; it is probably between this time and her death that most of her existing poems were written. W. died in 1685, possibly of a "pox" contracted from her husband, at her uncle's Adderbury estate. As was the case with Rochester, many of her poems were printed only after her death. Among her editors were some of the most influential poets of the era, John Dryden, Nahum Tate, and Aphra Behn; one "Song" was set to music by Henry Purcell. Her play, "Love's Martyr, or Witt Above Crowns," was entered in the Stationers' Register for Feb. 1686, but attached to the entry is a caveat against publication.

Despite evidence that much of what she wrote was either carefully edited or completely suppressed, W.'s remaining poetry bears the marks of a conscientious poet who rejected both the prevailing fashion of the erotic pastoral and a doctrinal adherence to the scriptural texts she paraphrased. Her personal unhappiness may have partially accounted for the chaste melancholy of her love lyrics and her Ovidian epistle, "Penelope to Ulysses," but it seems more likely that her wariness in regard to changing attitudes to women writers during the last years of the Restoration caused W. to shy away from any sort of "false affected fondness." In her poem, "To Mrs. A. Behn, On what she Writ of the Earl of Rochester," W. warns Behn to "Scorn meaner Theams, declining low desire,/And bid your Muse maintain a Vestal Fire./If you do this, what Glory will insue,/To all our Sex, to Poesie and you." In her religious poetry, too, she seems to have taken great pains to present a publicly acceptable persona, yet her language indicates that she was familiar with contemporary arguments against the revealed religion she had been primed to preserve; at least once Bishop Burnet felt himself compelled to counsel her against "conceits tending to Atheism." Her single political poem, "Upon the Duke of Buckingham's Retirement, 1683," is her most open testimony to the value of compromise.

Constantly allied to Rochester, W.'s fame declined long before his. The themes of her poetry—disillusionment with love and society, loneliness, health, education, and the very tedium of life—are his, too, but in the dignified poise of her presentations she lacks the light and seemingly easy grace that have made his poems accessible for so many generations.

WORKS: *Poems by Several Hands, and on Several Occasions. Collected by N. Tate* (1685). *Vinculum Societatis* (1687). *The Idea of Christian Love* (1688). *Lycidus: Or the Lover in Fashion* (1688). *Miscellany Poems on Several Occasions* (1692). *The Gentleman's Journal: Or the Monthly Miscellany* (July 1692). *A Collection of Poems by Several Hands Most of them Written by Persons of Eminent Quality* (1693). *The Temple of Death* (1695, 1701, 1702, 1716). *Examen Miscellaneum* (1702). *Ovid's Epistles, Translated by Several Hands, The Eighth Edition* (1712, 1716, 1725). *Whartoniana, or Miscellanies in Verse and Prose by the Wharton Family and Several Other Persons* (1727, 1731, 1740). *The Gentleman's Magazine* (June 1815). "Love's Martyr, or Witt above Crowns," B.M. Add. MS 28693.

BIBLIOGRAPHY: anon. *The Life of Thomas, Marquess of Wharton* (1716). Carswell, J. *The Old Cause: Three Biographical Studies in Whiggism* (1954). Farley-Hills, D., Ed. *Rochester: The Critical Heritage* (1972). Malcolm, J.P., Ed. *Letters of the Reverend James Granger* (1805).

For articles in reference works, see: *DNB, G.E.C. Complete Peerage.*

Susan Hastings

Antonia White

BORN: 31 March 1899, London.
DIED: 10 April 1980, London.
DAUGHTER OF: Cecil George and Christine Julia (White) Botting.
MARRIED: 1921; 1929; H. Tom Hopkinson, 1930. (First two marriages annulled; husbands' names not known.)

Though perhaps best known as a translator from the French of works by Colette and others, W. also wrote a number of well-received novels. Her central concern in much of her fiction is Roman Catholicism, to which faith she was twice converted: first, at the age of seven, when her father converted and brought her mother and W. with him, and, second, during World War II, after a number of lapsed years. Her first novel, *Frost in May* (1933), closely parallels her own experiences as a child. She was a boarding student at a convent school but never felt wholly accepted because she was, as she says, a "middle-class convert among aristocratic 'born' Catholics." When she was fifteen, she planned to write a novel, thinking its emphasis on Catholicism would appeal to her father. With only five chapters written and with forbidden behavior hinted at, the manuscript was confiscated by the nuns and W. was expelled. W.'s sense of guilt, occasioned by her father's shock, made it impossible for her to write fiction for almost twenty years.

After completing her schooling, W. attended the Royal Academy of Dramatic Art (1919–1920) and acted for a year with a touring company. She also worked as a governess, a teacher at a boys' school, and a civil servant. Finally, she began writing again, this time as a free-lance magazine and advertising copy writer. In her thirties she was variously a theatre critic, fashion editor, copywriter for an advertising agency, and teacher at an acting studio; when World War II started, she worked first for the BBC and then for British intelligence in the French section of the British Foreign Office.

W.'s first two marriages were annulled and her third ended in divorce. Following a breakdown during the first (described in *Beyond the Glass*, 1954), she spent nine months in an asylum. During her third marriage, to Tom Hopkinson, also a journalist, she discovered the partial manuscript of her schoolgirl novel and gradually completed it; between 1933, when *Frost in May* was published, and 1950, W. wrote no novels, and a gap of fifteen years exists between the beginning and ending of *The Lost Traveller* (1950).

W. had recurrent spells of mental illness and breakdown, ultimately recovering, she says, through a "remarkably successful" Freudian analysis. Her reconversion to Catholicism in 1940 is reflected in *The Hound and the Falcon* (1965), a series of letters written to a fellow Roman Catholic. Following the war, she translated two or three works a year from the French and found that she could again write fiction; her initial endeavor was the "Clara Batchelor" trilogy—*The Lost Traveller*, *The Sugar House* (1952), and *Beyond the Glass*—based on her life after the convent school. Even though the heroine's name is changed from Nanda Grey in *Frost in May*, the trilogy is clearly a sequel to W.'s first book.

Hence W.'s major writing, four novels, is centered on her life from childhood to her mid-twenties. The central focus in *Frost in May* is on W.'s attempt to answer such questions as why people become Catholic and how one can subjugate one's will to God's. The trilogy, by contrast, explores successively W.'s traumatic childhood, her marital failures, and her mental illness. Samuel Hynes has noted that these four novels "came out of urgent psychic needs rather than out of a strict creative impulse," out of a need to "testify" so as to free herself from the past.

Frost in May covers W.'s heroine's life from

nine through thirteen and is, as Elizabeth Bowen has noted, characterized by an objective quality that allows all events, whether emotionally disturbing ones or the mundane activities of school, to be given relatively similar emphasis. The girls learn that every action in the closed atmosphere of the convent school fits into a structured belief system that they only slowly accept as the standard by which they must live. Though that system equates individual achievement with pride, as with Nanda's writing or with another girl's acting in a school play, the girls nonetheless strive to develop their talents, personalities, values, and friendships.

In *The Lost Traveller*, adolescence with all its bewildering traumas is explored. Clara's confusion about sex and love receives special attention: her parents hold opposing viewpoints about such volatile matters, and although Clara deeply loves her father, it is her mother who understands Clara's approaching womanhood. When Clara considers marriage, it is her mother, not her religious and strict father, who can best advise her. *The Sugar House* tells of Clara's unfortunate relationship with an actor and an unhappy marriage to the man she considered marrying in the previous novel; Clara and her alcoholic husband gradually grow apart and the marriage ends. *Beyond the Glass*, generally acknowledged as the best of the three, focuses on a more "perfect" match, as Clara and Richard communicate telepathically; even so, Clara suffers a breakdown, with all aspects of her psychic trauma offered in the barest but most vivid terms. Clara's Catholicism, like W.'s, underlies her visions, perceptions, memory lapses, fears, and reactions, and her recovery is simply stated.

Novel writing was continually a problem for W., as she seemed unable to separate life from art. Her Catholicism was undoubtedly the single greatest influence on her work, as her work is often therapeutic. W. once observed that "'Creative joy' is something I haven't felt since I was fourteen and don't expect to feel again," suggesting that her attempts to purge herself of her youthful traumas through writing were compulsive, not liberating. Yet her books remain fascinating accounts of the impact of religious obsession on a woman in a constant but unsuccessful struggle to free herself from that obsession.

WORKS: *Frost in May* (1933). *Three in a Room* (1947). [trans.] *A Woman's Life*, by G. de Maupassant (1949). *The Lost Traveller* (1950). *The Sugar House* (1952). [trans.] *A Pathway to Heaven*, by H. Bordeaux (1952). [trans.] *Reflections on Life*, by A. Carrel (1952). [trans.] *Gigi and The Cat*, by Colette (former work trans. by R. Senhouse, latter by W.) (1953). [trans.] *A Sea of Troubles*, by M. Duras (1953). *Strangers* (1954). [trans.] *A German Officer*, by S. Groussard (1955). [trans.] *The Wind Bloweth Where It Listeth*, by P.A. Lesort (1955). [trans.] *Claudine at School*, by Colette (1956). [trans.] *I Am Fifteen and I Do Not Want to Die*, by C. Arnothy (1956). [trans.] *God Is Late*, by C. Arnothy (1957). *Minka and Curdy* (1957). [trans.] *The Branding Iron*, by P.A. Lesort (1958). [trans.] *Claudine in Paris*, by Colette (1958). [trans.] *It Is Not So Easy to Live*, by C. Arnothy (1958). [trans.] *The Stories of Colette* (1958). [trans.] *The Swing*, by F. Rouget (1958). [trans.] *Thou Shalt Love*, by J.M. Langlois-Berthelot (1958). [trans.] *The Charlatan*, by C. Arnothy (1959). [trans.] *Children in Love*, by C. France (1959). [trans.] *I Will Not Serve*, by E. Mahyere (1959). [trans.] *The Tortoises*, by L. Masson (1959). [trans.] *Claudine Married*, by Colette (1960). [trans.] *Till the Shadow Passes*, by J. Storm (1960). [trans.] *The Serpent's Bite*, by C. Arnothy (1961). [trans.] *Claudine and Annie*, by Colette (1962). [trans.] *The Trial of Charles de Gaulle*, by A. Fabre-Luce (1963). [trans.] *Advocate of the Isle*, by L. Masson (1963). [trans.] *The Captive Cardinal*, by C. Arnothy (1964). [trans.] *St. Michel and the Dragon*, by P. Laulliette (1964). [trans.] *The Shackle*, by Colette (1964). *The Hound and the Falcon: The Story of a Reconversion to the Catholic Faith* (1965). [trans.] *The Candle*, by T. de Sainte Phalle (1968). [trans.] *The Innocent Libertine*, by Colette (1968). *Living with Minka and Curdu: A Marmalade Cat and His Siamese Wife* (1970). [trans.] *Memoirs of the Chevalier d'Eon*, by F. Gaillardet (1970). [trans.] *The Glass Cage*, by G. Simenon (1973). [trans.] *The Novels of Smollett*, by P.-G. Boucé (1975). [trans.] *The Complete Claudine*, by Colette (1976). [trans.] *The History of Charles XII, King of Sweden*, by Voltaire (1976). [trans., with others] *The Collected Stories of Colette*, ed. R. Phelps (1983). *As Once in May: The Early Autobiography of Antonia White and Other Writings*, ed. S. Chitty (1984).

BIBLIOGRAPHY: Bowen, E. "Introduction." *Frost in May* (1948). Callil, C. "Introduction." Virago reprint of *The Lost Traveller, The Sugar House,* and *Beyond the Glass* (1979). Flood, J.A. *Critique* (Spring 1983). Hynes, S. *TLS* (3 July 1969).

For articles in reference works, see: *Book of Catholic Authors. CA. CN. Catholic Authors. WA.*

Other references: *Books and Bookmen* (January 1984). *Critique* (Spring 1983). *Economist* (17 December 1983). *Harper's* (April 1981, December 1982). *New Statesman* (27 April 1984). *Newsweek* (26 January 1981). *NYTBR* (5 October 1980). *Observer* (23 July 1978). *TES* (23 January 1981, 7 May 1982, 25 November 1983). *Time* (13 July 1981). *Village Voice* (17 May 1983).

Paul Schlueter

Anna Wickham

BORN: 1884, Wimbledon, Surrey.
DIED: April 1947, Hempstead.
DAUGHTER OF: Geoffrey and Alice (Whelan) Harper.
MARRIED: Patrick Hepburn, 1906.
WROTE UNDER: Edith Harper, John Oland, Anna Wickham.

Born Edith Alice Mary Harper, W.—English poet and vocalist—was not yet a teenager when she adopted her *nom de plume* (and stage name) after Wickham Terrace, Brisbane, where her father on a momentous day in her tenth year had made her promise to be a poet. She had begun writing verse when she was six—to the delight of her self-cultivated, misogynous father and to hoots of derision from her gypsy-like mother. Not surprisingly, W. kept her passion for writing quite to herself—that is, until she was well into adulthood. According to her friend and editor R.D. Smith, W. "wrote compulsively, producing over 1400 poems in her lifetime." The greater part of these, unpublished during the poet's life, remain unpublished still, although many have been preserved in her own typescript. Smith added approximately a hundred previously unpublished poems to the works in print (and his Virago Press edition includes *Fragment of an Autobiography* as well as selected prose pieces). So private is much of W.'s poetry that its publication, given the circumstances, is almost a miracle, and the delay, therefore, unavoidable.

W. had been writing verse for twenty-eight years before the public saw any of it. Even after her marriage in 1906, W. did not "for years" tell her husband that she wrote poetry. In fact, when she published her first volume in 1911, it bore not her "singing name" but a male pseudonym, John Oland. While Patrick Hepburn, a lawyer and an astronomer, was apparently not opposed to his wife's musical activity, he considered public shows of private emotion contemptible. He had, in fact, known of, and himself secretly subsidized, Anna's brief career as an opera singer in Paris. Discovering his anonymous generosity, W. had dropped another lover and married Patrick—a form of passionate impulsiveness that had flattered the young husband. But W.'s poetry was something else: powerful, erotic, searing in its radical anti-domesticity. It seemed especially objectionable to Patrick and his strait-laced family, and it is no wonder that W. poured her intense and wayward emotions into essentially private poems, meant in the beginning primarily as personal release. Smith reports that a jealous Patrick, when he finally did read her work, strenuously opposed its publication, angry to learn the nature of what had been

diverting W.'s attention from him: "their bitterest clash" was caused by W.'s insistent will to write herself out of her intolerable feelings of oppression and to publish her feelings. Her poems "Woman and Artist" and "Genius" best express her sentiments concerning the risks she took and the risks she did not take.

Before Harold Monro and Alida Klemantaski (the renowned owners of the Poetry Bookshop) printed nine of W.'s poems in their collection *Poetry and Drama* (1914), her work received virtually no public acclaim. Two early dramatic pieces, *The Seasons* and *Wonder Eyes*, were printed privately in Sydney when she was seventeen; and *Songs of John Oland*, first published by a feminist vanity press in 1911, had not even been associated with W.'s (or Mrs. Patrick Hepburn's) name until they were reprinted some time later. The Poetry Bookshop published W.'s second volume of verse, *The Contemplative Quarry*, in 1915; Grant Richards published *The Man with a Hammer* in 1916; and, in 1921, these two volumes were published together, through Louis Untermeyer's intervention, in New York. Suddenly, W. had a name; but 1921 (the year of her son Richard's death) marked for a time the end of her efforts to publish although she did not cease to write. On Christmas Day, 1929, Patrick died in a mountaineering accident eerily like one his wife had previsioned in the poem "The Homecoming" (written in 1921). It took W. several years to wind up her husband's law practice. By then, her reputation as a poet was well established.

Untermeyer early identified W.'s originality, associating the poet's artistic probity with that of novelists May Sinclair, Virginia Woolf, Rebecca West, Willa Cather, and Dorothy Richardson, praising W.'s "vigorous self-examination," and finding her "in many ways the best of these seekers and singers." By 1932, Humbert Wolfe had written of her poetry in the *Encyclopaedia Britannica*, 14th Edition; she was in *International Who's Who*; she had joined P.E.N. and was giving readings regularly. Through her close friendship in the 1920s and 1930s with Natalie Barney, the Sapphic American expatriate in Paris, W. was moving in the same literary circles as Rilke, Valéry, d'Annunzio, Colette, Pound, Proust, and Stein. John Gawsworth included her work in his two now-famous collections, *Edwardian Poetry* and *Neo-Georgian Poetry* (both 1937). Malcolm Lowry and Dylan Thomas were friends. Along with seven feminist activists (on 16 June 1938), W. founded *The League for the Protection of the Imagination of Women. Slogan: World's Management by Entertainment.* Among its supporters were Olivia Manning, J.B.S. Haldane, and Gwen le Gallienne.

Not surprisingly, the League's manifesto and program were consistent with the tenor of W.'s life and verse.

Through most of W.'s best poetry runs the obsessive concern to achieve utter freedom of expression and so to create, spontaneously, a poetry as perfect as that for which others labored. That spontaneity seems fully achieved in satirical pieces like "The Housemaid," in lyrics like "The Little Love," in caustic verses like "The Tigress" and "The Sick Assailant," and in strong poems like "The Mill." In "Examination," W. wrote, "If my work is to be good,/ I must transcend skill, I must master mood./ For the expression of the rare thing in me/ Is not in *do*, but deeper, in *to be*." What she in fact had managed to achieve she phrased another way: "The tumult of my fretted mind/ Gives me expression of a find; but it is faulty, harsh, not plain—/ My work has the incompetence of pain." Humbert Wolfe nevertheless admired it, saying that her poems "should be lived with like a great picture rather than caught like the colour of flowers." In 1947, lonely and tired, W. committed suicide by hanging herself. She was survived by three grown sons, to whose morale she had been ministering all through their active service in the war.

We do not know whether or not W. meant her autobiography to be published. Candid, socially and psychologically insightful, and concise—her *Fragment of An Autobiography: Prelude to a Spring Clean* (written in 1935) served the poet as a repository for family history, self-revealing anecdotes, and Lawrentian vignettes about the volatile relations among the members of her family: the dramatic Whelans on her mother's side, the bookish Harpers on her father's side, the snobbish Hepburns into whose bosom she was never taken when she married Patrick, and their respective circles. From the fast-paced narrative emerges the self-portrait of a moody, untidy, often violent woman who at times wrestled mightily with her wild impulses and frequently lost to them. The self-deprecating, slapdash, critical tone of *Fragments* is counterbalanced by R.D. Smith's objective account of W.'s reputation and artistic accomplishments and by his fine critical essay on the poems themselves, in his introduction to the 1984 collection of the poet's writings.

WORKS: *The Seasons—Speaking Tableaux for Girls (100 Performers)* (1901?). *Wonder Eyes—A Journey to Slumbertown (For 80 Little People)* (1901?). *Songs of John Oland* (1911). *The Contemplative Quarry* (1915). *The Man with a Hammer* (1915). *The Contemplative Quarry & The Man With a Hammer*, Intro. by L. Untermeyer (1921). *The Little Old House* (1921). *Thirty-Six New Poems*, ed. J. Gawsworth (1936). *Selected Poems*, Intro. by D. Garnett (1971). *The Writings of Anna Wickham: Free Woman and Poet*, ed. and Intro. by R.D. Smith (1984).

BIBLIOGRAPHY: Untermeyer, L. *Lives of the Poets* (1959).

For articles in reference works, see: *TCA. Who Was Who Among English and European Authors.*

Other references: Wolfe, H. "Modern Developments in British Poetry." *Encyclopaedia Britannica* (1956 ed.) Vol. 18. *Bookman* (December 1921). *NR* (27 April 1921). *Picture Post* (27 April 1946).

R. Victoria Arana

Catherine Winkworth

BORN: 13 September 1827, London.
DIED: 1 July 1878, Monnetier, Savoy, France.
DAUGHTER OF: Henry and Susanna Dickenson Winkworth.

The daughter of a well-to-do silk manufacturer, W. devoted her life to reform: in various social causes, especially having to do with education and careers for women, and above all in English hymnody. Most of her writings were translations from German; her hymns enjoyed great popularity and made a lasting impact.

On her early life there were strong and varied religious and literary influences. One grandfather was for fifty years a deacon in a nonconformist chapel in Tunbridge Wells, the other, William Winkworth, a prominent Evangelical minister in the Church of England. Educated at home in Manchester, she had as tutors successively two scholarly Unitarian clergymen, William Gaskell and James Martineau. Family friends included the novelists Charlotte Brontë and Elizabeth Gaskell, her tutor's wife. Through the latter in 1849 Catherine and her elder sister Susanna met the Prussian ambassador, Baron von Bunsen, a man of many connections and many projects. The association with Bunsen was to shape both sisters' careers.

Already well versed in German language and culture through study and a year's residence in Dresden (1845-1846), W. did some translating to help Susanna with the three-volume biography of B.G. Niebuhr that Bunsen had urged her to undertake. After its appearance in 1852 W. turned to translating hymns from Bunsen's 1833 collection, *Versuch eines allgemeinen evangelischen Gesang-*

und Gebet-buchs. One hundred two of these, carefully chosen to connect with the scripture readings assigned throughout the church year in the English liturgy, were published in 1855 under the title *Lyra Germanica* as an aid to private devotion. The book sold out within two months; by Christmas there was a second edition, with revisions; soon W.'s translations were appearing in anthologies on both sides of the Atlantic, and there was a demand both for more translations and for versions suitable for singing. In 1858 W. published a "second series" of 121 hymns, including some from sources other than Bunsen. She then secured the services of William Sterndale Bennett and Otto Goldschmidt, husband of the singer Jenny Lind, as musical editors and in 1863 published *The Chorale Book for England,* containing 72 new translations in addition to revised versions of 130 from the two *Lyra Germanica* volumes. In 1869 appeared her only original published work, *The Christian Singers of Germany,* an historical survey of the German religious lyric from the eighth century to the nineteenth, with some 130 examples including nearly 100 newly translated by W. for the purpose.

In a busy age of translation—there were some 20 Victorian collections of German hymns, three fourths of them by women—W.'s work was remarkable for both quantity and quality. In volume and range (more than 170 authors representing all schools—Minnesingers, Luther and his followers, Hussites, Pietists, Moravians, Catholics, etc.), it far surpassed that of other translators. Many of her hymns—among them "Now thank we all our God," "Praise to the Lord, the Almighty," and "Lift up your heads, ye mighty gates"—remain in modern hymnals. Routley writes that she "gave a very strong impetus towards raising the standards of translation." She combined accuracy and respect for the spirit of her originals, even to the point of reproducing such devices as alliteration, with sensitivity to English idiom and graceful expression. Many of her early translations involved slight metrical adaptation for the sake of a smoother English rendering; later, however, when producing singing versions for the *Chorale Book,* she retranslated to fit the German tunes. In a few cases she would omit or alter stanzas she considered offensive in doctrine or taste; however, she disapproved of editorial habits of free alteration which resulted in "correct and tiresome flatness."

As her personal religious views developed, W. became critical of both liberal Christianity and Tractarianism and returned to a position closer to her Evangelical heritage. Her *Chorale Book,* especially with its 1865 supplement of English hymns, may have been an effort to compete with the influential Anglo-Catholic *Hymns Ancient and Modern* (1861)). On the other hand, her hymn-writing had an avowed ecumenical purpose, "to make us feel afresh what a deep and true Communion of Saints exists among all the children of God in different churches and lands" (Preface, 1855).

W. was also active in various religious and social causes. Before the age of twelve she was teaching in the church school; on returning from a trip to Switzerland in 1853, she added duties in the District Visiting Society. After the family moved in 1862 to Clifton, a suburb of Bristol, her activities reflect a growing interest in social work and especially in promoting both the welfare of women and the role of women in social ministry. She was the authorized translator from German of biographies of Amelia Wilhelmina Sieveking (1863), founder of the Female Society for the Care of the Sick and Poor in Hamburg, and Theodore Fliedner (1867), who founded a lunatic asylum for women, a normal school for training infant school mistresses, and an order of deaconesses, with houses in several countries, called to the care of the sick, the poor, and the young. Following the example of such reformers, W. assumed a host of responsibilities, such as helping organize in 1868 the Committee to Promote Higher Education of Women, of which in 1870 she became secretary. This group helped women prepare for university entrance examinations and led the way in establishing England's first coeducational institution, University College, Bristol. W. was also a delegate in 1872 to a conference on women's work in Darmstadt, Germany, a promoter of the Clifton High School for Girls, and a board member of the Red Maids' School, Bristol, and Cheltenham Ladies College.

Troubled from youth by periods of ill health, W. died of heart disease at fifty while on a trip to France. In her memory scholarships were endowed at University College, Bristol, and a tablet erected in Bristol Cathedral praising her "clear and harmonious intellect" and "gift of true poetic insight and expression."

WORKS: *Lyra Germanica: Hymns for the Sundays and Chief Festivals of the Christian Year* (translated by Winkworth, 1855; 2nd ed. 1855; 20+ other ed., some with alternate title *Songs for the Household* or *Songs, Sacred and Devotional*). *Lyra Germanica, Second Series: The Christian Life* (translated by Winkworth, 1858; 10+ other ed.). Combined ed. (1879+). *A Selection of Hymns from the Lyra Germanica of Catherine Winkworth,* ed. A. Ewing (1859). *The Chorale Book for England* (assembled and translated by Winkworth, 1863). (Editor) *Supplement to the Chorale Book for England Containing English Hymns with Appropriate Tunes* (1865). *Life of Amelia Wilhelmina Sieveking* (translated by Winkworth, 1863). *Life of Pastor Fliedner of Kaiserswerth* (translated by Winkworth, 1867).

The Christian Singers of Germany (1869, rpt. 1972). *Prayers from the Collection of the Late Baron Bunsen* (translated by Winkworth, 1871). *Letters and Memorials of Catherine Winkworth*, ed. S. Winkworth (1883; incorporated in Shaen, 1908).

BIBLIOGRAPHY: Leaver, R.A. *Catherine Winkworth: The Influence of Her Translations on English Hymnody* (1978). Routley, E. *The Hymn Society of Great Britain and Ireland Bulletin* (1958, 1963). Shaen, M.J., ed. *Memorials of Two Sisters: Susanna and Catherine Winkworth* (1908).

For articles in reference works, see: *Allibone*. *BA19C. DNB.* Julian, J. *A Dictionary of Hymnology* (1891). Routley, E. *An English-Speaking Hymnal Guide* (1979). Routley, E. *A Panorama of English Hymnody* (1979).

Other references: Frost, M., ed. *Historical Companion to Hymns Ancient & Modern* (1962). London *Times* (16 July 1878). Miles, A.H. *The Poets and Poetry of the Century*, vol. 10 (1892). Miles, A.H. *Sacred, Moral, and Religious Verse* (1897).

Charles A. Huttar

Mary Wollstonecraft (Godwin)

BORN: 27 April 1759, London.
DIED: 10 September 1797, London.
DAUGHTER OF: Elizabeth Dickson and Edward Wollstonecraft.
MARRIED: William Godwin, 1797.

W. was the second child and first daughter of seven children born to Edward Wollstonecraft, an unsuccessful farmer and brutal, drunken father. In 1775 W. met Fanny Blood, a painter two years older, who became a powerful influence and friend and who later died in childbirth in W.'s arms. *Mary, A Fiction* (1787), W.'s only complete novel, depicts Blood's situation and conveys W.'s literary and life theme of distrust of marriage.

W. wrote *Thoughts on the Education of Daughters* in 1786 following the failure of a school at Islington that had been established by her, her sister Eliza, and Fanny Blood. In *Thoughts . . .* W. counseled women to seek tranquility through reason and self-discipline; she questioned the underlying purposes of education and concludes: "In a comfortable situation, a cultivated mind is necessary to render a woman contented; and in a miserable one, it is her only consolation."

Following her dismissal as governess to the daughters of Lord and Lady Kingsborough, she became involved in the radical publication, *Analytical Review*, edited by Joseph Johnson. Johnson published her *The Cave of Fancy, or Sagesta, Original Stories from Real Life* (1788) and *The Female Reader* (1789). At Johnson's home she met Thomas Holcroft, Henry Fuseli, William Blake, Anna Laetitia Barbauld, Thomas Paine, and William Godwin, and she wrote translations and reviews revealing her increasing awareness of women's secondary status.

In answer to Edmund Burke, W. wrote *A Vindication of the Rights of Man* (1790), first published anonymously and in her name in a second edition. In this she set herself up as the voice of reason (although she argues emotionally) and spoke out for the rights of the poor, the op-

pressed, and the degraded of either sex.

A Vindication of the Rights of Women, W.'s best known work, was published in 1792. W. has been called the first major feminist because of this work, in which she discussed all aspects of women's education, status, and position in society and dramatically argues that true freedom necessitates equality of men and women.

Following the uproar caused by this publication, W. left for Paris, traveling first with the Fuselis, then alone. There she met Gilbert Imlay, observed the French Revolution, conceived her first child (fathered by Imlay), and wrote *An Historical and Moral View of the Origin and Progress of the French Revolution, and the Effect it Has Produced in Europe* (1794). Her daughter Fanny was born 14 May 1795. Imlay's subsequent indifference led to two suicide attempts, the first in May, the second in October. To rid himself of her, Imlay sent W. on a business trip to Scandinavia, resulting in *Letters Written during a Short Residence in Sweden, Norway, and Denmark* (1796).

Her parting from Imlay was softened by the renewal of her acquaintance with William Godwin, then at the height of his fame as a philosopher and writer; they proved to be a match politically, intellectually, and emotionally. Pregnant since December 1796, W. married Godwin 29 March 1797, despite both having been opposed to marriage. While pregnant, she wrote *The Wrongs of Woman* (1798) and led an unconventionally separate marriage.

W.'s daughter, Mary Godwin (who married Percy Bysshe Shelley), was born 30 August 1797. On 10 September, W. died of septicaemia, the result of the placenta remaining in her for several days and becoming gangrenous. Her death, then, reflected her life: the constraints that held her sex won her final struggle.

WORKS: *Female Reader* (1787). *Cave of Fancy: Sagesta* (1787). *Thoughts on the Education of Daughters; with Reflections on Female Conduct, in the*

PR 5841. W8 267'84
68

More Important Duties of Life (1787). *Mary, a Fiction* (1788). *Original Stories from Real Life; with Conversations, Calculated to Regulate the Affections, and Form the Mind to Truth and Goodness* (1788). (trans.) *On the Importance of Religious Opinions*, by J. Necker (1789). *The Female Reader; or Miscellaneous-Pieces, in Prose and Verse; Selected from the Best Writers, and Disposed Under Proper Heads; for the Improvement of Young Women* (1789). *A Vindication of the Rights of Men, in a Letter to the Right Honourable Edmund Burke* (1790). (trans.) *Young Grandison*, by Mme. de Cambon (1790). (trans.) *Elements of Morality for the Use of Children*, by C.G. Salzmann (1790). *A Vindication of the Rights of Woman with Strictures on Political and Moral Subjects* (1792). *An Historical and Moral View of the Origin and Progress of the French Revolution, and the Effect it Has Produced in Europe* (1794). *Letters Written During a Short Residence in Sweden, Norway, and Denmark* (1796). *The Wrongs of Woman* (1798). *Posthumous Works of the Author of "A Vindication of the Rights of Woman"* (1798). *Mary Wollstonecraft's Original Stories with Five Illustrations by William Blake*, ed. E.V. Lucas (1906). *The Love Letters of Mary Wollstonecraft to Gilbert Imlay, with a Prefatory Memoir*, ed. R. Ingpen (1908). *Memoirs of Mary Wollstonecraft*, ed. W.C. Durant (1927). *Four New Letters of Mary Wollstonecraft and Helen Maria Williams*, ed. B.P. Kurtz and C.C. Autrey (1937). *Letters*, ed. F.L. Jones (1944). *Journal*, ed. F.L. Jones (1947). *Godwin and Mary: Letters of William Godwin and Mary Wollstonecraft*, ed. R.M. *Maria, or The Wrongs of Woman* (1975; as *The Wrongs of Woman; or Maria* (part of *Posthumous Works*, 1978). *Collected Letters of Mary Wollstonecraft*, ed. R.M. Wardle (1979).

BIBLIOGRAPHY: Anon. *A Defence of the Character and Conduct of the Late Mary Wollstonecraft Godwin, Founded on Principles of Nature and Reason, as Applied to the Peculiar Circumstances of Her Case, in a Series of Letters to a Lady* (1803). Detre, J. *A Most Extraordinary Pair: Mary Wollstonecraft and William Godwin* (1975). Ferguson, M., and J. Todd. *Mary Wollstonecraft* (1984). Flexner, E. *Mary Wollstonecraft: A Biography* (1972). George, M. *One Woman's "Situation": A Study of Mary Wollstonecraft* (1970). Godwin, W. *Memoirs of Mary Wollstonecraft*, ed. W.C. Durant (1927). Grylls, R.G. *William Godwin and His World* (1953). James, H.R. *Mary Wollstonecraft: A Sketch* (1932). Jebb, C. *Mary Wollstonecraft* (1912). Linford, M. *Mary Wollstonecraft (1759-1797)* (1924). Nixon, E. *Mary Wollstonecraft: Her Life and Times* (1971). Pennell, E.R. *Mary Wollstonecraft Godwin* (1885). Preedy, G.R. [pseud. for Gabrielle C. Long], *This Shining Woman: Mary Wollstonecraft Godwin* (1937). Rauschenbusch-Clough, E. *A Study of Mary Wollstonecraft and the Rights of Woman* (1898). Robinson, V. *William Godwin and Mary Wollstonecraft* (1907). Sunstein, E.W. *A Different Face: The Life of Mary Wollstonecraft* (1975). Taylor, G.R.S. *Mary Wollstonecraft: A Study in Economics and Romance* (1911). Tomalin, C. *The Life and Death of Mary Wollstonecraft* (1974). Wardle, R. *Mary Wollstonecraft: A Critical Biography* (1966).

For articles in reference works, see: *Allibone. BAB1800. Cassell. Chambers. DLB. DNB. NCHEL. BCEL.*

Other references: Boulton, J.T. *The Language of Politics in the Age of Wilkes and Burke* (1963). Bouten, J. *Mary Wollstonecraft and the Beginnings of Female Emancipation in France and England* (1922). Butler, M. *Women and Literature* (1980). Cameron, K.N., ed. *Shelley and His Circle, 1773-1822* (1961). Cobb, R. *TLS* (6 September 1974). Detre, J. *Ms* (December 1972). Dowden, E. *The French Revolution and English Literature* (1897). Fawcett, M.G. *The Case for Woman's Suffrage*, ed. B. Villiers (1907). Ferguson, M. *Signs* (1978). George, M. *One Woman's Situation: A Study of Mary Wollstonecraft* (1970). Hickey, D.D. *English Language Notes* (1975). Janes, R.M. *Journal of the History of Ideas* (1978). Moers, E. *NYRB* (19 February 1976). Myers, M. *Children's Literature* (1986). Myers, M. *Studies in Eighteenth Century Culture* (1982). Pettingill, P. *New Leader* (19 March 1973). Poovey, M. *Novel* (1982). Sage, L. *Encounter* (December 1974). Shurbutt, S.B. *Kenyon Review* (1982). *TLS* (15 April 1926, 23 June 1927, 4 August 1932, 20 February 1937, 11 September 1953, 25 December 1970). Todd, J. *Frontiers* (Fall 1980). Vlasopolos, A. *Dalhousie Review* (1980). Wardle, R. *PMLA* (1947).

Anne-Marie Ray

Ellen Price Wood

BORN: 17 January 1814, Worcester.
DIED: 10 February 1887, London.
DAUGHTER OF: Thomas and Elizabeth Evans Price.
MARRIED: Henry Wood, 1836.
WROTE UNDER: Mrs. Henry Wood.

W. was the author of the Victorian best-seller *East Lynne* (1861) and more than fifty other works of fiction. From 1865 until her death, she owned and edited the periodical *Argosy*, which serialized the novels of popular writers like Anthony Trollope and Charles Kingsley as well as many of her own works. The daughter of a glove manufacturer, W. was a lifelong invalid who wrote in a reclining chair. Yet she demonstrated the resilience and devotion to work and family characteristic of other well-known women novelists such as Frances Trollope and Dinah Mulock Craik.

W. became an author fairly late in life, her first fictional work, a tale called *Danesbury House* which had won a £100 prize offered by a temperance society, appearing anonymously in *New Monthly Magazine* in 1860. The W. family had been prosperous; her husband, whom she married in 1836, was a member of a banking and shipping firm who had consular duties which required him and his wife to settle in France, where they lived for twenty years. Yet there is speculation that by 1856, when her husband retired and the W.'s and their children returned to London, she had to supplement their income and turned to writing.

East Lynne, W.'s first full-length novel, was enormously successful, selling 500,000 copies by the end of the century. It was paid the dubious compliment of being pirated by American publishers and was adapted numerous times for the stage although W. received no royalties. The book was a quintessential sensation novel (a form popular in the 1860s that featured mysterious and shocking deeds, guilty family secrets, and, often, unconventional feminine behavior). *East Lynne* told the story of Isabel Vane, who marries from duty, mistakenly suspects her husband of infidelity, runs off with a rake, and is punished by disfigurement and the loss of her illegitimate child. Crushed by life, she returns disguised as a governess to do penance and be near her children. Her husband has by this time divorced her and married her bitter rival, and Isabel learns too late the wages of abandoning home and children.

East Lynne was a novel whose anti-heroine was, in the popular phrase of the day, more to be pitied than scorned. Misunderstood, treated as an invalid (a cause for identification on her creator's part?), and shut out from running her own home by her spiteful sister-in-law, Isabel Vane must have earned sympathy from the feminine domestic readership that provided a large part of W.'s market. Indeed, much of the novel's appeal issued from its rather subversive sympathy for an adulteress, even though W. ultimately applauds middle-class virtues and punishes her "fallen woman."

W.'s other popular novels include *The Channings* (1862), a work with a wealth of detail about the lives of the professional classes of a middle-class rural English town. It was the story of a solid, loyal family shaken by accusations about a favorite son. "How God was trying them!" exclaims the aptly named sister Constance. Like most of W.'s work, it combined realistic rendering of middle-class life with suspense and mystery. Particularly notable for their mystery elements were

Lord Oakburn's Daughters (1864), *Elster's Folly* (1866), and *Roland Yorke* (1869).

For *Mr. Halliburton's Troubles* (1862) and *A Life's Secret* (1867) W. drew on memories of her Worcester birthplace and the labor disputes which as a manufacturer's daughter she witnessed there. Both works are unsympathetic to strikers. *Mildred Arkell* (1865) explores another source of uneasiness for W., the vulgar infusion of "new money" into the quiet serenity of genteel provincial life.

W. was compared favorably to Wilkie Collins in her 1860s heyday, but by the time of her death in 1887 her reputation had declined. One critic lamented that she had gone from being "overpraised" to "unduly depreciated." There is justice in this: her work, while melodramatic and didactic, is cleverly plotted and immensely readable. Equally important, it remains an index to prevailing attitudes about marriage and gentility—and to its Victorian readership's fantasies of rebellion and flight.

WORKS: *Danesbury House* (1860). *East Lynne* (1861). *The Golden Casket* (1861). *Mrs. Halliburton's Troubles* (1862). *The Channings* (1862). *The Shadow of Ashlydyat* (1863). *The Foggy Night at Offord* (1863). *Verner's Pride* (1863). *William Allair: or Running Away to Sea* (1864). *Lord Oakburn's Daughters* (1864). *Oswald Cray* (1864). *Trevlyn Hold: or Squire Trevlyn's Heir* (1864). *Mildred Arkell* (1865). *St. Martin's Eve* (1866). *Elster's Folly* (1866). *Lady Adelaide's Oath* (1867). *A Life's Secret* (1867). *Orville College* (1867). *Mixed Sweets from Routledge's Annual* (1867). *Castle Wafer: or the Plain Gold Ring* (1868). *The Red Court Farm* (1868). *Anne Hereford* (1868). *Roland Yorke* (1869). *Bessy Rane* (1870). *George Canterbury's Will* (1870). *Dene Hollow* (1871). *Within the Maze* (1872). *The Master of Greylands* (1873). *Johnny Ludlow* (1874-1889). *Told in the Twilight* (1875). *Bessy Wells* (1875). *Adam Grainger* (1876). *Edina* (1876). *Parkwater* (1876). *Our Children* (1876). *Pomeroy Abbey* (1878). *Court Netherleigh* (1881). *About Ourselves* (1883). *Lady Grace and Other Stories* (1887). *The Story of Charles Strange* (1888). *Featherston's Story* (1889). *The Unholy Wish and Other Stories* (1890). *Edward Burton* (1890). *Summer Stories from the Argosy* (1890). *The House of Halliwell* (1890). *Ashley and Other Stories* (1897).

BIBLIOGRAPHY: Elwin. M. *Victorian Wallflowers* (1934). Hughes, W. *The Maniac in the Cellar: Sensation Novels of the 1860's* (1980). Sergeant, A. *Women Novelists of Queen Victoria's Reign*. Showalter, E. *A Literature of Their Own* (1977). Wood, C.W. *Mrs. Henry Wood* (1894).

For articles in reference works, see: *CBEL. DLB. DNB.*

Other references: Auerbach, N. *Woman and the Demon* (1982). Mitchell, S. Introduction. *East Lynne* (1984). Mitchell, S. *VS* (1976).

Laura Hapke

Virginia Woolf

BORN: 25 January 1882, London.
DIED: 28 March 1941, Monk's House, Rodmell.
DAUGHTER OF: Sir Leslie Stephen and Julia Jackson Duckworth Stephen.
MARRIED: Leonard Woolf, 1912.
WROTE UNDER: Virginia Stephen, Virginia Woolf.

W. survives as several distinct and familiar voices. Her most public voice during her lifetime, the voice in her book reviews and essays on literature, is calm, witty, rational, candid. The voice in her letters to friends and family is sometimes defensive, sometimes caustic, but nearly always clever, charming, and warm. In her diaries, though, the voice seems stricken cold with terror—dread of potential public and critical rejection of her work and fear of the physical and emotional collapses that recurred throughout her life, finally driving her to suicide. Widely read as all these voices have been, however, W. earned her fame with her artist's voice, the voice that speaks in her stories and novels.

From childhood W. knew that she would become a novelist. Her heritage certainly suggested a literary career: her father, Sir Leslie Stephen, literary critic, frustrated philosopher, and original editor of the *Dictionary of National Biography*, was married to one of Thackeray's daughters before he married W.'s mother, and the Stephenses' friends included Henry James, George Meredith, Robert Lowell, and Edward Burne-Jones. W. has preserved an evocative though fictionalized version of her family's life in *To the Lighthouse*. W. modelled the characters of Mr. and Mrs. Ramsay in this novel so closely on her own late parents' personalities that her sister Vanessa, in reading the novel, felt her mother had been "raised from the dead" and said she was shattered to find herself "face to face with those two again."

As a child in London and in Cornwall, W. read voraciously, studied languages, and wrote articles for a weekly family newspaper. When her mother died of influenza in 1895, it was, as W. later remarked, "the greatest disaster that could happen," and a few months later W. had her first breakdown, hearing voices, avoiding food, and suffering from the physical symptoms of extreme anxiety. Her grief over her mother's loss may have been exacerbated by the sexual fondlings of her half-brother, George Duckworth, which certainly upset her during her adolescence and may have contributed to her lifelong inability to respond sexually to men.

Her father's death marked a change in the children's lives; emerging from under his depressed and inhibiting influence, W. and her siblings began "a voyage out" from their eminently Victorian background. Resisting George Duckworth's attempts to introduce them into polite society, they began associating with her brother Thoby's Cambridge friends, the Apostles, a group greatly influenced by the rationalist philosopher G.E. Moore. Clive Bell (later Vanessa's husband), Saxon Sidney-Turner, Lytton Strachey, Desmond MacCarthy, and Leonard Woolf became frequent visitors, first at the Stephens' Gordon Square home and then at the house in Bloomsbury which W. and her brother Adrian rented in 1907. Though the group was diminished by Thoby's death in 1906, it later expanded to include John Maynard Keynes, Duncan Grant, Roger Fry, and —more peripherally—Bertrand Russell, E.M. Forster, and T.S. Eliot. The Bloomsbury Group, bound by no particular philosophy or discipline, came to represent a high level of intellectual discourse; an intense interest in current literary, philosophical, historical, and artistic issues; and a commitment to destroying "all barriers of reticence and reserve."

Associated with new ideas, artistic experimentation, homosexuality, and a certain degree of class snobbery, Bloomsbury was a controversial but nevertheless fertile atmosphere for W.'s writing. In 1907, during that autumn when Bloomsbury began meeting in Fitzroy Square, W. started *Melymbrosia*, which was to become her first novel, *The Voyage Out*, accepted for publication in 1913 after extensive revisions. The six years of labor indicate the difficulties that novel writing always presented to W. Her habitual reaction to stress persisted in her professional life: upon completing each of her major novels, she would collapse in more or less serious breakdowns and, after recovering, would pursue less demanding writing projects to build her strength toward the next important novel.

W.'s most serious breakdown—and her first attempt at suicide—came after her marriage to Leonard Woolf in 1912. Six months after their marriage W.'s condition deteriorated from severe headaches into the violent ravings that her friends and biographers have called "madness" and she tried to overdose on sleeping pills. One of Leonard Woolf's inspirations was to found and operate the Hogarth Press at their London home. W. worked as a reader and typesetter for the press from 1917 until 1937, when she sold her half of the concern to John Lehmann. W.'s first Hogarth publication, "The Mark on the Wall" (1917), is a miniaturized model of her experiments in fiction. Having no action, it can hardly be called a "story," but at the same time, it is too fanciful to be called an "essay."

It is a highly controlled, brief "stream of consciousness," tracing a narrator's thoughts as she observes a spot on the wall across the room from her chair. When in the end her companion makes a complaint about the world war, remarking in passing that there is a snail on the wall, the narrator reacts only to the dissolution of her reverie and the mention of the snail. The relative unimportance of the war typifies W.'s characteristic treatment of the world of politics and events. She criticized the "materialist" novelists of the previous generation—Wells, Galsworthy, and Bennett—for focusing too exclusively on externalities of setting, costume, and behavior; her fiction depicts instead her characters' inner realities, or that "life" which W. calls in her essay "Modern Fiction" (1925) "a luminous halo, a semi-transparent envelope surrounding us from the beginning of consciousness to the end."

Each of W.'s novels takes a different approach in depicting that reality through those "moments of being" when her characters become fleetingly conscious of their memories, their emotions, their perceptions, their constantly shifting selves. Her experiments in narrative technique seldom involve a literal "stream of consciousness" but venture instead into forms of free indirect discourse, following the thoughts of various characters from an external point of view and shifting frequently from observing one character's mind to another's. In *Mrs. Dalloway* (1925), the narrator depicts the inner lives of two very different Londoners: Clarissa Dalloway, a lovely, unhappy, successful socialite whom W. had originally created in *The Voyage Out*, and Septimus Warren Smith, a mad, miserable, "seedy" man who—the novel's structure suggests—has much more in common with Clarissa than is immediately obvious. Touching upon shared public experiences (for instance, watching a sky-writer over London), W. makes transitions among the overtly separate external worlds in the novel.

To the Lighthouse (1927) takes the experiment a step further, ranging among the consciousnesses of many characters but focusing especially on Mr. and Mrs. Ramsay, W.'s portraits of her parents. The novel explores their modes of thinking: Mr. Ramsay's egocentric, intellectual, self-pitying and ambitious grapplings with philosophy; Mrs. Ramsay's maternal, emotional, manipulative, and affectionate attempts to achieve connections among the members of her extended family circle. We observe them from their own points of view as well as through the eyes of their children and friends, especially Lily Briscoe, an unmarried painter who tries simultaneously to come to terms with the Ramsays' relationship and with the frustrations of being a woman artist.

The novel is rich with symbolic significances, though W. herself claimed she couldn't "manage Symbolism except in this vague, generalised way. . . . directly I'm told what a thing means, it becomes hateful to me." Though some early critics, particularly those of the *Scrutiny* school under the influence of F. R. Leavis, condemned W.'s novels as too ethereal, rarified, and amoral, sympathetic readers have found that her symbolism and narrative structure are not at all vague but rather poetically suggestive.

W.'s most ambitious and unconventional novel, *The Waves* (1931), is still more poetic than *To the Lighthouse*. Following the internal lives of a group of friends from schooldays to adulthood as they come to terms individually and collectively with one friend's death, the novel alternates articulations of each character's thoughts with passages describing a seascape in meticulous, almost impersonally observed, densely symbolic detail. Inspired by a recurring mental image of a shark's fin emerging from beneath a wave, this novel most graphically explores the darker corners of consciousness that were such a perpetual source of terror, as well as inspiration, for W.

Self-consciously experimental, W. is also very emphatically a *woman* writer. In essays and lectures like *A Room of One's Own* (1929) or "Professions for Women" (published posthumously, 1942), W. enunciates the difficulties of any woman who wishes to overcome cultural expectations; to throttle the specter of "the Angel in the House" who insists that she maintain charming, unassertive domesticity; and to write. Highly amusing and influential, *A Room* explores the traditional barriers to women artists—from family expectations to educational segregation to self-doubt—and concludes that women can write if they can achieve certain conditions: privacy (represented by their own rooms), independence (represented by a minimum annual income), and an ability to use "the androgynous mind." A crux in W.'s feminism, the androgynous mind would—like Shakespeare's—draw on both its "masculine" and "feminine" creative powers while writing without any self-consciousness of gender or any sense of grievance against the opposite sex. If a woman writer were to achieve this, she would be free to write her vision of life whole and undistorted, finding "a woman's sentence" and new fictional forms in which to express herself. Whether or not the argument is theoretically consistent, it certainly provides insight into W.'s view of the uncharted literary ground that she was to explore so courageously and at so high a cost to her emotional equilibrium.

In March 1941, discouraged by the ominous progress of World War II and its implications for her pacifist Jewish husband, dreading the critical reception of her last novel, *Between the Acts*, and faced with yet another emotional collapse, W. gave in to her despair and drowned herself in the

River Ouse near her home. As an artist, critic, diarist, and literary theoretician, it is unlikely that she could possibly have made a greater contribution than in fact she made to English literature and to women's literature at large.

WORKS: *The Voyage Out* (1915). *The Mark on the Wall* (1917). *Kew Gardens* (1919). *Night and Day* (1919). *Monday or Tuesday* (1921). *Jacob's Room* (1922). *Mr. Bennett and Mrs. Brown* (1924). *The Common Reader* (1925). *Mrs. Dalloway* (1925). *To the Lighthouse* (1927). *Orlando: A Biography* (1928). *A Room of One's Own* (1929). *The Waves* (1931). *Letter to a Young Poet* (1932). *The Common Reader: Second Series* (1932). *Flush: A Biography* (1933). *Walter Sickert: A Conversation* (1934). *The Years* (1937). *Three Guineas* (1938). *Roger Fry: A Biography* (1940). *Between the Acts* (1941).

Posthumously published works and collections: *The Death of the Moth and Other Essays* (1942). *A Haunted House and Other Short Stories* (1943). *The Moment and Other Essays* (1947). *The Captain's Death Bed and Other Essays* (1950). *Granite and Rainbow* (1958). *Contemporary Writers* (1965). *Collected Essays* (4 vols., 1966-1967). *Mrs. Dalloway's Party: A Short Story Sequence by Virginia Woolf* (edited by S. McNichol, 1973). *The Waves: The Two Holograph Drafts* (edited by J.W. Graham, 1976). *Freshwater: A Comedy* (edited by L.P. Ruotolo, 1976). *Books and Portraits: Some Further Selections from the Literary and Biographical Writings of Virginia Woolf* (edited by M. Lyon, 1978). "Virginia Woolf's *The Journal of Mistress Joan Martyn*" (edited by S.M. Squier and L. DeSalvo, *TCL*, 1979). *The Complete Shorter Fiction of Virginia Woolf*, ed. S. Dick (1985). *Essays*, ed. A. McNeillie, vol. 1 (1986), vol. 2 (1987).

Letters and diaries: *A Writer's Diary* (edited by L. Woolf, 1953). *Virginia Woolf and Lytton Strachey: Letters* (edited by L. Woolf and J. Strachey, 1956). *The Letters of Virginia Woolf* (edited by N. Nicolson and J. Trautmann, 6 vols., 1975). *The Diary of Virginia Woolf* (edited by A. Olivier Bell, 1977).

Note: For a complete bibliography of Virginia Woolf's writings, including reviews, see B.J. Kirkpatrick, *A Bibliography of Virginia Woolf* (1980).

BIBLIOGRAPHY: Note: This list includes most books in English about Virginia Woolf through 1987. For a more complete bibliography of early criticism, see R. Majumdar, *Virginia Woolf: An Annotated Bibliography of Criticism, 1915-1974* (1976).

Biography: Bell, Q. *Virginia Woolf: A Biography* (1972), Johnstone, J.K. *The Bloomsbury Group: A Study of E.M. Forster, Lytton Strachey, Virginia Woolf, and Their Circle* (1954). Lehmann, J. *Virginia Woolf and Her World* (1975). Meyers, J. *Married to Genius* (1977). Noble, J.R., ed. *Recollections of Virginia Woolf by her Contemporaries* (1972). Pippett, A. *The Moth and the Star: A Biography of Virginia Woolf* (1955). Poole, R. *The Unknown Virginia Woolf* (1978). Rantavaara, I. *Virginia Woolf and Bloomsbury* (1953). Rillo, L.E. *Katherine Mansfield and Virginia Woolf* (1944). Rose, P. *Woman of Letters: A Life of Virginia Woolf* (1978). Spater, G. and I. Parsons. *A Marriage of True Minds: An Intimate Portrait of Leonard and Virginia Woolf* (1977). Trautmann, J. *The Jessamy Brides: The Friendship of Virginia Woolf and Victoria Sackville-West* (1974). Trombley, S. *All that Summer She Was Mad: Virginia Woolf: Female Victim of Male Medicine* (1982). *The Essays of Virginia Woolf*, vol. 2, ed. A. McNellie (1987).

Criticism: Alexander, J. *The Venture of Form in the Novels of Virginia Woolf* (1974). Bazin, N.T. *Virginia Woolf and the Androgynous Vision* (1973). Beja, M., ed. *Virginia Woolf: To the Lighthouse: A Case Book* (1970). Bennett, J. *Virginia Woolf: Her Art as a Novelist* (1945). Blackstone, B. *Virginia Woolf: A Commentary* (1949). Brewster, D. *Virginia Woolf* (1963). Chambers, R.L. *The Novels of Virginia Woolf* (1947). Collins, R.G. *Virginia Woolf's Black Arrows of Sensation: The Waves* (1962). Daiches, D. *Virginia Woolf* (1945). Davenport, W.A. *To the Lighthouse* (1969). DiBattista, M. *Virginia Woolf's Major Novels: The Fables of Anon.* (1980). Fleischman, A. *Virginia Woolf: A Critical Reading* (1975). Forster, E.M. *Virginia Woolf* (1942). Goldman, M. *The Reader's Art: Virginia Woolf as Literary Critic* (1976). Gruber, R. *Virginia Woolf: A Study* (1935). Guiguet, J. *Virginia Woolf and Her Works* (1965). Hafley, J. *The Glass Roof: Virginia Woolf as Novelist* (1954). Hawthorn, J. *Virginia Woolf's Mrs. Dalloway: A Study in Alienation* (1975). Holtby, W. *Virginia Woolf: A Critical Memoir* (1932). Hungerford, E.A. *The Narrow Bridge of Art: Virginia Woolf's Early Criticism, 1905-1925* (1965). Johnson, M. *Virginia Woolf* (1973). Kapur, V. *Virginia Woolf's Vision of Life and Her Search for Significant Form: A Study in the Shaping Vision* (1981). Kelley, A.V.B. *The Novels of Virginia Woolf: Fact and Vision* (1973). Kettle, A. *Mrs. Dalloway* (1973). Latham, J.E., ed., *Critics on Virginia Woolf* (1970). Leaska, M.A. *The Novels of Virginia Woolf: From Beginning to End* (1978). Lee, H. *The Novels of Virginia Woolf* (1977). Lewis, T.S.W., ed. *Virginia Woolf* (1977). Love, J.O. *Worlds in Consciousness: Mythopoetic Thought in the Novels of Virginia Woolf* (1970). Majumdar, R., and A. McLaurin, eds. *Virginia Woolf: The Critical Heritage* (1975). Marcus, J., ed. *New Feminist Essays on Virginia Woolf* (1981). Marcus, J., ed. *Virginia Woolf: A Feminist Slant* (1983). Marder, H. *Feminism and Art: A Study of Virginia Woolf* (1968). McLaurin, A. *Virginia Woolf: The Echoes Enslaved* (1973). Minow-Pinkney, M. *Virginia Woolf and The Problem of the Subject: Feminine Writing in the Major Novels* (1987). Morris, J. *Time and Timelessness in Virginia Woolf* (1977). Moody, A.D. *Virginia Woolf* (1968). Naremore, J. *The*

World Without a Self: Virginia Woolf and the Novel (1974). Novak, J. *The Razor Edge of Balance: A Study of Virginia Woolf* (1978). Paul, J.M. *The Victorian Heritage of Virginia Woolf: The External World in Her Novels* (1987). Poresky, L.A. *The Elusive Self: Psyche and Spirit in Virginia Woolf's Novels* (1981). Radin, G. *Virginia Woolf's The Years: The Evolution of a Novel* (1981). Richter, H. *Virginia Woolf: The Inward Voyage* (1970). Rosenthal, M. *Virginia Woolf* (1979). Ruddick, L. *The Seen and the Unseen: Virginia Woolf's* To the Lighthouse (1977). Schaefer, J. O. *The Three-Fold Nature of Reality in the Novels of Virginia Woolf* (1965). Schlack, B.A. *Continuing Presences: Virginia Woolf's Use of Literary Allusion* (1979). Spilka, M. *Virginia Woolf's Quarrel with Grieving* (1980). Sprague, C., ed. *Virginia Woolf: A Collection of Critical Essays* (1971). Squier, S.M. *Virginia Woolf and London: The Sexual Politics of the City* (1985). Sugiyama, Y. *Rainbow and Granite: A Study of Virginia Woolf* (1973). Thakur, N.C. *The Symbolism of Virginia Woolf* (1965). Verga, I. *Virginia Woolf's Novels and Their Analogy to Music* (1945). Vogler, T.A. *Twentieth-Century Interpretations of* To the Lighthouse: *A Collection of Critical Essays* (1970). Woodring, C. *Virginia Woolf* (1966).

For articles in reference works, see: *CA. CLC. Longman. MBL* and *SUP. TCA* and *SUP. TCW.*

Other references: Cecil, D. *Poets and Story Tellers* (1949). Dahl, L. *Linguistic Features of the Stream-of-Consciousness Techniques of James Joyce, Virginia Woolf, and Eugene O'Neill* (1970). Daiches, D. *The Novel and the Modern World* (1939). Elert, K. *Portraits of Women in Selected Novels by Virginia Woolf and E.M. Forster* (1979). Fleischman, A. *The English Historical Novel: Walter Scott to Virginia Woolf* (1971). Gill, R. *The English Country House and the Literary Imagination* (1972). Heilbrun, C.G., and M.R. Higgonet, eds. *The Representation of Women in Fiction* (1983). Kaplan, S. J. *Feminine Consciousness in the Modern British Novel* (1975). Little, J. *Comedy and the Woman Writer: Woolf, Spark, and Feminism* (1983).

Robyn R. Warhol

Dorothy Wordsworth

BORN: 25 December 1771, Cockermouth, Cumberland.
DIED: 25 January 1855, Rydal Mount.
DAUGHTER OF: John Wordsworth and Anne Cookson.

The early loss of both parents bound W. closely to her brothers John and especially to William. In 1795 W. and William took up residence together at Racedown in Dorset, and two years later they moved to Alfoxden to be near Coleridge at Nether Stowey. After the publication of *Lyrical Ballads*, W. and William spent a winter in Germany, after which they settled at Dove Cottage in Grasmere. When William married Mary Hutchinson, W.'s long-time and intimate friend, in 1802, W. lived on with her brother and his wife, taking an active interest in their domestic life and their children. The last twenty years of W.'s life were spent as an invalid, afflicted in both body and mind. She survived William by five years.

Despite her literary gifts, W. never became an author in her own right during her lifetime. Yet family and friends, including some of the finest literary minds of the period, recognized her abilities. In one journal entry, W. speaks of a scene making her "more than half a poet," but elsewhere she insists, "I should detest the idea of setting myself up as an Author." She wrote fewer than twenty poems, only five of which were published during her lifetime, and these were incorporated into her brother William's work, as were short extracts from her journals and letters. And although her *Narrative Concerning George and Sarah Green* was meant to be part of the public record of Grasmere Vale, she refused to have it published. Only her *Recollections of a Tour in Scotland*, although actually published posthumously in 1874, was ever intended for publication.

It is for her journal-writing that W. is now praised, especially for the journals kept at Alfoxden (January–May 1798) and Grasmere (May 1800–January 1803); she also kept a journal during her stay in Germany (1798) before her residence at Grasmere. After Grasmere, the intimate record of daily life stops, but W. continues to keep a number of journals about various expeditions: a Scotland tour in 1803; excursions on the banks of Ullswater and up Scawfell Pike in 1805 and 1818, respectively; an 1820 tour of the continent; a second tour of Scotland in 1822; and an 1828 tour of the Isle of Man.

The Alfoxden and Grasmere journals are characterized by a naturalness and spontaneity that seem to bridge the prosaic and poetic details of everyday life with effortlessness and ease. Throughout her writing there is evident what Coleridge described as "her eye watchful in minutest observation of nature" and what De Quincey called her quick and ready "sympathy with either joy or sorrow, with laughter or with tears, with the realities of life or the larger realities of the poets." In her journals, W. tells of making shoes, weeding the garden, copying her brother's poems, packing mattresses, reading Shakespeare, gathering firewood, walking with Coleridge, ironing linen. The poetic and the prosaic, the ready sympathy for the unfortunate, and the keen observation of nature are all brought together in her 18 May 1800 entry. In this representative entry, W. begins by a passing mention of church-going and the weather, moves on to an appreciation of the surrounding valley and mountains with their bare ashes and emerging corn, and follows with a tale of a beggar girl turned out of doors overnight by her stepmother.

W. clearly influenced and inspired some of her brother's poetry. She continued her journal at Grasmere "because I shall give Wm Pleasure by it," and he sometimes had her read aloud journal passages to revive his memory. His poems "I wandered lonely as a cloud," "Beggars," and "Resolution and Independence," among others, all owe a profound debt to W.'s prose descriptions. Not only did her journals give William poetic inspiration but her daily attention to the responsibilities of domestic life (as her journal readily attests) freed him to pursue his poetry. Her ready concern in her brother's labors, illnesses, and achievements provided an important source of emotional support, for which he remembers her in *The Prelude*: "She, in the midst of all, preserved me still/ A Poet" (Book XI). For W., in her modesty, it

seems to have been enough to have inspired her brother as a poet rather than to have emerged as one herself.

WORKS: *George and Sarah Green: A Narrative* (1808, under title *A Narrative Concerning George and Sarah Green of the Parish of Grasmere Addressed to a Friend*, ed. E. de Selincourt, 1936). *Recollections of a Tour in Scotland* (1874). *The Journals of Dorothy Wordsworth* (ed. E. de Selincourt, 1941). *The Early Letters of William and Dorothy Wordsworth* (ed. E. de Selincourt, 1935). *The Letters of William and Dorothy Wordsworth: The Middle Years (1806-1820)* (ed. E. de Selincourt, 1937). *The Letters of William and Dorothy Wordsworth: The Later Years (1821-1850)* (ed. E. de Selincourt, 1939). *The Grasmere Journal*, rev. text (ed. J. Wordsworth, 1987).

BIBLIOGRAPHY: de Selincourt, E. *Dorothy Wordsworth: A Biography* (1933). Homans, M. *Women Writers and Poetic Identity: Dorothy Wordsworth, Emily Brontë, and Emily Dickinson* (1980). Levin, S.M. *Dorothy Wordsworth and Romanticism* (1987). MacLean, C.M. *Dorothy and William Wordsworth* (1927). Willy, M. *Three Diarists* (1964).

For articles in reference works, see: *BA19C.*

Other references: Bawer, B. *New Criterion* (January 1986). Freeman, N. *TLS* (28 June 1985). Huftel, S. *Contemporary Review* (1986). Woof, P. *Wordsworth Circle* (1986).

Eileen Finan

Frances Wright

BORN: 6 September 1795, Dundee, Scotland.
DIED: 13 December 1852, Cincinnati, Ohio.
DAUGHTER OF: James and Camilla Campbell Wright.
MARRIED: Guillaume Phiquepal D'Arusmont, 1831.
WROTE UNDER: Madam D'Arusmont, Frances Wright D'Arusmont, Frances Wright.

A radical woman espousing racial integration, free love (i.e., state-sanctioned marriage vows are unnecessary), working-class rights, birth control, and opposition to the stranglehold of organized religion on human freedom and thought, W. remains one of the most unusual and enigmatic of early feminists. Throughout her life she advocated complete universal suffrage—for blacks, for women, for the working class—and education as the means of achieving equality between male and female, black and white, rich and poor. She was more democratic in her beliefs than any feminist for the following hundred years.

Charismatic leader, orator, and writer, her life and writings reflect her concerns. From an early age

she demonstrated her facility with the English language, the influences of the Enlightenment, and the egalitarian rhetoric of the American and French revolutions. Born in Scotland, W. was daughter to a devotee of Thomas Paine but was orphaned at the age of two. She speaks in her third-person autobiography (*Biography, Notes, and Political Letters of Frances Wright D'Arusmont*, 1844) of being immediately entranced as a young woman with the democratic experiment in the United States. In 1818, at age 23, she and her sister sailed to New York. The letters she wrote home for the next two years to her friend Mrs. Rabina Millar, accounts of her travels, meetings, and observations on American character, institutions, and morals, were published in 1821 as *Views of Society and Manners in America*. This volume, a sensation in England and in France, brought W. to the attention of the aging Marquis de Lafayette, hero of the American Revolution. The essays show a vivid sense of detail and enthusiasm for America as well as insight into such institutions as education, the position of women, and slavery, areas that were to occupy W. for the rest of her life.

Her youthful passions for drama and Byronic

verse found outlet in *Altorf*, a verse drama about Swiss independence, first performed and printed in Philadelphia (1819), and interest in the example of Greece as the first democracy led to her writing a Socratic dialogue, *A Few Days in Athens* (1822). Thereafter most of W.'s work was written not primarily for book publication but as lectures and journalism. Her greatest influence was as an orator and lecturer, and all her charisma and leadership were vented in the persuasive arts.

When she returned to the United States, she quickly modified her earlier enthusiasms. In particular she began worrying over the institution of slavery, having seen a slave ship and auction in Virginia and the wretched condition of freed blacks. She advocated a scheme of gradual emancipation whereby slaves would work off their freedom on productive farms (the land set aside by Congress), participate equally in the affairs of the farm with whites, be educated, and eventually earn their freedom. The idea, she felt, would not pose an economic hardship to southern land owners because they would be given the profits of the blacks' labor for several years. W. published this utopian scheme in 1825 as *A Plan for the Gradual Abolition of Slavery in the United States Without Danger of Loss to the Citizens of the South*; various leaders were encouraging, including Thomas Jefferson and Robert Owen, who had just purchased the Rappite community of New Harmony for his own communal experiment. In December 1825, W. purchased 640 acres east of Memphis, Tenn., bought a number of slaves, and set out to carve a utopia from the mosquito lowlands and pine forests on the Wolf River, calling the community "Nashoba," Chickasaw for "wolf." Nashoba ultimately failed after four years when an abolitionist paper published the community's views on intermarriage and miscegenation. W. published a manifesto in the Memphis *Advocate* restating her compensated-emancipation plan and went on to attack segregation in education and sexual relations, organized religion, and marriage itself, which led to attacks by both dedicated abolitionists and southern slave owners.

W. returned to New York where she had begun work in education and agitation for the working class by publishing and editing the *Free Enquirer*, founding the Workingmen's Institute in an old church on the Bowery, and continuing her lecture circuit. Some of the lectures were collected and published in *Course of Popular Lectures* (1829, 1836). In these, "Of Free Enquiry" for example, W. is much more critical of America than she was in *Views of Society and Manners*. She sees education as the key to equality for all and advocates a system of collective cooperation with a Kantian view of individual rights bounded only by other human beings. She considers children to be human beings and advocates the development of all their faculties. She holds that it is in the interest of all to enlighten females more than males; society can never be perfected with half the population remaining uneducated. She is one of the first to equate women with other subjected classes (blacks, working class), and her use of the term "humankind" predates twentieth-century nonsexist language by 150 years.

W. was so influential in the nascent working-class political movement that the election of 1829 won her group a seat in the New York legislature and the nickname "the Fanny Wright party." Soon, though, she returned to Europe with her dangerously ill sister, this time settling in Paris near Phiquepal D'Arusmont, French doctor and teacher W. had known in New Harmony and New York and whom W. married in 1831. By 1835 W. was again lecturing in America, her family sometimes with her and sometimes remaining in Paris.

After W. inherited the family fortune in Scotland, she and her husband were divorced while she continued lecturing and writing. Her last work, *England the Civilizer* (1848), presents an apocalyptic vision of a new egalitarian society, the instigators being science, industry, and women. At the same time, she had become disenchanted with much of the American "experiment"—critical of attitudes toward women, blacks, and working class, and particularly hostile toward the hold that evangelical religion had on the Midwest and South.

Called "The Priestess of Beelzebub" and her followers dubbed "Fanny Wright Free Lovers," W.'s influence waned after her death from a fall in 1852 at the age of fifty-seven. Although Elizabeth Cady Stanton paid tribute to her in *The History of Woman Suffrage* (1881), most other contemporary works on nineteenth-century women (such as Phoebe A. Hanaford's *Daughters of America or, Women of the Century* [1883]) failed to mention W. For over a century her life and works were essentially forgotten until the second wave of feminism began in the 1960s.

WORKS: *Altorf, a Tragedy* (1819). *Views of Society and Manners in America* (1821). *A Few Days in Athens* (1822). *Course of Popular Lectures* (1829; 1836). *Biography, Notes, and Political Letters of Frances Wright D'Arusmont* (1844). *England the Civilizer* (1848).

BIBLIOGRAPHY: Boyer, P.S. *Notable American Women*, ed. E.T. James *et al.* (1971). Eckhardt, C. *F.W.: Rebel in America* (1984). Ferguson, M. *Eighteenth Century* (1986). Lane, M. *F.W. and the Great Experiment* (1972). Perkins, A.J.G., and T. Wolfson. *F.W.: Free Enquirer* (1939). Stiller, R. *Commune on the Frontier: The Story of F.W.* (1972). Waterman, W. *F.W.* (1924).

Margaret McFadden

Lady Mary Wroth

BORN: 1586 or 1587.
DIED: 1651 or 1653.
DAUGHTER OF: Robert Sidney and Barbara Gamage.
MARRIED: Sir Robert Wroth, 1604.

W. was the eldest daughter of Barbara Gamage, a Welsh heiress, and of Robert Sidney, Earl of Leicester, the younger brother of Sir Philip Sidney and Mary Sidney, Countess of Pembroke. Robert Sidney's letters frequently mention "my daughter Wroth" with particular affection, and he often visited her after her marriage in 1604. In that year W. became part of the court and acted in masques, including Ben Jonson's *The Masque of Blackness*. Her poetry was circulated in manuscript and was praised by such contemporary writers as Nathaniel Baxter, Joshua Sylvester, George Chapman, and Ben Jonson, who said that he had become "a better lover and much better Poet" after reading her sonnets. Jonson dedicated *The Alchemist* to her and praised her as "a Sydney" who incorporated the virtues of all the goddesses; in "To Sir Robert Wroth" Jonson praised W.'s husband and estate much as he had praised her parents in "To Penshurst."

Her extravagant husband died in 1614, leaving the young widow with an infant son and a staggering debt of some £23,000. She undertook to pay off the debt herself and was in financial difficulties throughout the rest of her life. She never remarried, but she bore two illegitimate children to her cousin, William Herbert, third Earl of Pembroke.

Although she wrote a pastoral tragicomedy, *Love's Victorie*, only one of her works was published, *Urania* (1621), an intricate romance patterned on her uncle's *Arcadia*. The first full-length work of fiction by an Englishwoman, its central tale concerns the love of Queen Pamphilia, the image of Constancy, for Amphilanthus ("Lover-of-two"). The female protagonist is condemned to passive suffering more often than active redress, reflecting contemporary gender roles. Love is usually false and the romance has a disillusioned, even cynical, tone; inconstancy appears an almost inevitable male attribute, which is sometimes presented comically: "being a man, it was necessary for him to exceed a woman in all things, so much as inconstancie was found fit for him to excell her in, hee left her for a new." Eventually Pamphilia, like Queen Elizabeth, chose to marry only her kingdom; however, in the unpublished second part, she and Amphilanthus each marry someone else. *Urania* caused a scandal since it supposedly satirized various court intrigues. W. apologized and withdrew the book from sale; it has never been reprinted.

In addition to poems scattered through the text in the manner of Sidney's *Arcadia*, a series of 19 songs and 83 sonnets entitled *Pamphilia to Amphilanthus* is appended to the text, presenting the Petrarchan courtly love traditions from a female perspective. Significantly, W. wrote in an Elizabethan mode like her father's *Rosis and Lysa* and her uncle's *Astrophil and Stella*. The poems have a melancholy tone; Pamphilia is constant in her love to the faithless Amphilanthus. Much of the imagery is Petrarchan, but the tone of suffering seems from the heart. Pamphilia finally turns from love of Amphilanthus to the love of God. The concluding poem speaks of Venus' praise as proper to "young beeginers"; Pamphilia vows to progress now to "truth, which shall eternall goodnes prove;/Injoying of true joye, the most . . . The endles gaine which never will remove."

W. was the first English woman to write a full-length work of prose fiction and the first to write a significant body of secular poetry, but she was castigated for that achievement. Lord Denny admonished her to imitate her "vertuous & learned Aunt, who translated so many godly bookes, & especially the holy Psalms of David" rather than creating "lascivious tales & amarous toyes"; translation, not creation, was the province of a learned woman. W. gave a spirited reply to Denny, but she apparently was forced to learn the womanly virtue of silence; if she did write more after she withdrew her *Urania*, it has not survived.

WORKS: *Love's Victoria* (n.d.). *Urania* (1621, including *Pamphilia to Amphilanthus*, a series of 19 songs and 83 sonnets; although *Urania* has not yet been reprinted, *Pamphilia to Amphilanthus* is available in two modern editions: *Pamphilia to Amphilanthus*, ed. G. Waller [1977] and *The Poems of Lady Mary Wroth*, ed. J.A. Roberts [1983]). A critical edition of *Love's Victoria* is planned.

BIBLIOGRAPHY: Beilin, E.V. *Spenser Studies* (1981). Parry, G. *Proceedings of the Leeds Philosophical and Literary Society* (1975). Paulissen, M.N. *The Love Sonnets of Lady Mary Wroth: A Critical Introduction* (1982). Paulissen, M.N. *Publications of the Missouri Philological Association* (1978). Roberts, J.A. *N&Q* (1977). Roberts, J.A. *Journal of Women's Studies in Literature* (1979). Salzman, P. *RES* (1978).

Margaret Hannay

Ann Cromartie Yearsley

BORN: 1752, Clifton, near Bristol.
DIED: 1806, Melksham, Wiltshire.
WROTE UNDER: Lactilla.

Born to working-class parents, Y. was only minimally educated. Like her mother, she delivered milk from door to door, thus gaining membership in the society of "heaven-taught" poets as "Lactilla," or the poetical milkwoman.

In 1784 Hannah More's cook, one of Y.'s customers, told her employer about this remarkably gifted poet victimized by dire poverty and grinding toil. More attempted to fill in some of the gaps in Y.'s education and then set about editing her poetry and seeking subscriptions for its publication. The first published volume, *Poems on Several Occasions*, earned some £600. More and Elizabeth Montagu took charge of the profits as trustees for the author. Y. strenuously objected to this arrangement, quarreled publicly with her two patronesses, and demanded editorial and financial control of her work. Using the money earned by the first volume, she opened a circulating library at Bristol Hot Wells, but it soon failed. She subsequently published three more volumes of poetry, an unfinished historical novel, an unsuccessful tragedy, and several occasional poems.

Perhaps because of her sporadic education, Y.'s poetry is highly derivative in both form and content. She relished the role of untutored poetess deprived by the cruelty of circumstances, and her poetry is infused by a tone of woe, self-pity, and general lamentation. Most of Y.'s poems are occasional, commemorative, or meditative lyrics, liberally endowed with the formulae and conventions of eighteenth-century verse. At her best, she employed simple metrical and stanzaic forms within a structured narrative whose chronological sequence countered her tendency toward expansiveness.

Given the deplorable conditions of the earlier parts of her life, it is not surprising that Y. cultivated melancholy and meditated frequently upon death. She sought resignation to God's will and wrote elegies that proffered the traditional consolation of the soul's union with loved ones in a better and happier afterlife. Although Y. yearned for the spiritual tranquility of untroubled faith, her speculative nature disturbed the serenity of her religious contemplations.

Y. found consolation in friendship, which she glorified as the highest earthly value; she tries in many poems to distinguish it from self-serving hypocrisy, a concern which probably originated in the quarrel with More. Friendship must be kept uncontaminated by the relationship between dependent and superior, which will destroy both friendship and poetic inspiration. Y. protested in verse More's charges of ingratitude and retaliated with her own accusations of "guilty blandishment."

Y. held a conventional concept of woman's proper role: while men fight the world's battles and do the world's work, the mother should stay home to nurse her child and satisfy its intellectual needs. In the persona of a parent, she expresses her strongest emotions; a successful example is the poem entitled "On Jephtha's Vow," wherein she mixes revulsion and sympathy for the father who exchanged his daughter's life for a promise of victory in battle. Y.'s fondness for parenthood was not accompanied by a similarly conventional view of marriage. In "Lucy, A Tale for the Ladies" she suggests that worldly interests often preclude marriage for love. Women thus become victims of cruel and unloving husbands, but men, too, suffer from the wiles of silly and flirtatious women.

In writing about public events, Y. combined conservative political views with humanitarian sympathies. Her "Ode to the Genius of England," for example, extols the virtues of the social order, while the "Bristol Elegy" mourns the slaughter of a group of demonstrators (whose numbers she grossly exaggerates) protesting unjust bridge tolls. Even while lamenting the murder of innocent victims, however, the poet advises their families to set aside the desire for vengeance and to find solace in "contemplation." Y.'s "Poem on the Inhumanity of the Slave Trade" has a more convincing effect because she replaces abstract morality with humanized narrative, focusing on the disruption of social and domestic bonds as the primary evil of slavery. The poet places her faith in the power of the sympathetic imagination to make us respond to the misery of our fellow creatures.

Y. was delighted to play "Lactilla," and thus many of her poems praise the power of "Nature" as source of the most intense emotions and the finest sensibility. Despite the derivative nature of her verse, she purported to reject both "Rule" and "Education" as trammels upon natural inspiration. In her elegy on Chatterton, the spirit of the dead poet disdains the praise of the traditional Muses but values the tribute of "some rustic Muse, in Nature drest," who bears a singular resemblance to herself. She thought of herself as "unadorned by art, unaccomplished by science" and proudly acknowledged writing "in the short intervals of a life of labour, and under every disadvantage which can possibly result from a confined education." A woman very much of her time, Y. entered into the spirit of Lactilla with considerable enthusiasm and absolutely no discernible sense of irony.

WORKS: *Poems on Several Occasions* (1784). *Poems on Various Subjects* (1787). *Earl Goodwin* (performed 1789, published 1791). *Stanzas of Woe* (1790). *The Royal Captives* (4 vols., 1795). *The Rural Lyre* (1796).

BIBLIOGRAPHY: For articles in reference works, see: *Allibone. DNB.*
     Other references: Cottle, J. *Early Recollections.*

Ferguson, M. *Eighteenth Century* (1986). *Horace Walpole's Correspondence*, ed. W.S. Lewis *et al.* (1937+). *Memoirs of the Life and Correspondence of Mrs. Hannah More*, ed. W. Roberts (1834). Southey, R. *The Lives and Works of the Uneducated Poets* (1836). Tompkins, J.M.S. *The Polite Marriage* (1938).

Jill Rubenstein

Charlotte Mary Yonge

BORN: 11 August 1823, Otterbourne, Hampshire.
DIED: 20 March 1901, Otterbourne, Hampshire.
DAUGHTER OF: William Crawley and Frances Bargus Yonge.

Born the oldest of two children to High Church, upper middle-class parents, Y. passed her entire life in Otterbourne, the village where she taught Sunday school for seventy of her seventy-eight years. Beloved by school girls and the Victorian reading public alike, she published over two hundred works, including nearly one hundred novels and over thirty histories, as well as stories of village life, biographies, books of religious instruction, natural histories, editions, and translations. *The Heir of Redclyff* (1853), an enormous success in its day, has proved to be the most enduring of her novels. Y. created several fictional families, and the sagas of the Mays, in *The Daisy Chain* (1856) and *The Trial* (1864), and the Underwoods, in *The Pillars of the House* (1873), were among her most popular. In her last novel, *Modern Broods* (1900), various Mays, Underwoods, Mohuns, and Merrifields make their final appearances. Over the course of fifty years, Y. also edited and contributed to three journals: the *Monthly Packet* (1851-1894), the *Monthly Paper of Sunday Teaching* (1860-1875), and the *Mothers in Council* (1890-1900). Y. perceived of herself as an "instrument for popularizing Church views," views that were molded by her parents and, more significantly, by John Keble, one of the founders of the Oxford Movement and vicar of the neighboring parish of Hursley. Hers is certainly edifying fiction; nonetheless, her best novels offer lively portraits of Victorian family life, well-delineated characters, and skillful dialogue.

While her upbringing strikes the modern reader as unduly harsh, Y. spoke of her childhood as a happy one and remained devoted to her parents, particularly to her father. Fearful lest they spoil their spirited, pretty, intelligent daughter, the Yonges imposed strict controls on the child.

She was given a diet of dry bread and milk for both breakfast and supper, and her mother discouraged vanity and selfishness by minimizing Charlotte's attractiveness and by chastising her for selfish, though typically childish, desires. Her home education, supervised entirely by her father, was a rigorous affair. From the time she was seven, she rose for an hour of math before breakfast, followed by lessons in Greek, science, and history. Evenings were devoted to an hour of Bible reading, followed by an hour of history. Y.'s many "romantic" histories were written as by a teacher attempting to provide adequate texts for young people.

The absolute necessity of submission and self-sacrifice is both the theme that informs her novels as well as the precept by which she lives her life. In Y.'s world, moral obligation is clear: children must submit to the wisdom of their parents; women must submit to the superior judgment of men; mankind must submit to the will of God. Y. drew support for her belief in the inferiority of women from the biblical account of the fall of man. When her maternal grandmother objected to writing as a suspicious and unfeminine occupation and nearly prevented the publication of *Abbey Church*, Y. agreed to donate the profits from her works to the missions. She submitted her writing for criticism to her father and to Keble; Keble read to assure that "delicacy and reverence" were observed. Not unexpectedly, then, characters in her novels are judged and dealt with according to the degree to which they submit to and obey those wiser than themselves, and female characters who act independently are often made to suffer quite severely.

The life of the shy, socially awkward, spinster "Aunt Charlotte," who is said to have remained fixed in adolescence, was possibly uneventful; nonetheless, the sheer volume and variety of her writing bespeak a rich and active imaginative life. Her first novel, *Abbey Church* (1844), was a frankly Tractarian work. Over the following decade, she published several works; however, it was *The Heir of Redclyff* (1853) that earned her a wide and devoted audience. The tale of Sir Guy Morville, heir to Redclyff and to an ancestral curse that blights the happiness of all the Morvilles, was admired by Dante Gabriel Rossetti, William Morris, and Henry James, who praised the novel and called Yonge a writer with "a force of genius." By 1868, *Heir* was in its seventeenth edition. Even Jo, in *Little Women*, wept over Sir Guy's death. The novel centers on Guy's struggle to subdue his self-destructive temper and to suffer patiently the false attacks of his cousin, Philip. Though Guy is vindicated by the truth and wed to his beloved Amy, his is the ultimate self-sacrifice, for on their honeymoon he nurses the intolerable Philip through a terrible fever which he then catches and dies. Amy later gives birth to a daughter, whereupon Redclyff is passed on to Philip, now a grief-stricken, guilt-ridden man.

As is often noted, Y.'s characters are punished for their transgressions of the moral code as Y. herself perceived it. In *The Clever Woman of the Family* (1865), Rachel Curtis tries to ameliorate the working conditions of girls in the lace-making trade, but, by ignoring the advice of others, she ends up placing the girls in homes where they are mistreated and loses the money she has collected for them to an embezzler. In *Magnum Bonum* (1879), Janet Brownlow studies medicine in order to continue her father's discoveries, but her carelessness and poor judgment bring about the deaths of several people, including her child. Her own death, a result of her work to control an epidemic, serves as a penitential act of self-sacrifice, a pattern reflecting Y.'s deeply-held religious convictions, convictions apparently shared by many of her readers. Yet her novels offered those readers more than a series of didactic plots, for much of her appeal lay in her characters and depictions of life in the Victorian hearth and home.

After 1875, Y. wrote fewer novels and a greater number of children's books and school texts. In her lifetime she was much admired, and devoted readers would make pilgrimages to her home, to her dismay. In the 1940s, her novels enjoyed a revival in England, but today her novels are discussed chiefly in terms of their religious sentiments and their conservative response to the Victorian crisis of faith, of the patterns and concerns characteristic of the fiction of nineteenth-century women novelists, and of their domestic realism.

WORKS: *Le Château de Melville* (1838). *Abbey Church* (1844). *Scenes and Characters* (1847). *Kings of England* (1848). *Henrietta's Wish* (1850). *Kenneth* (1850). *Langley School* (1850). *Landmarks of History* (1852-1857). *The Two Guardians* (1852). *The Heir of Redclyff* (1853). *The Herb of the Field* (1853). *The Castle Builders* (1854). *Heartsease* (1854). *The Little Duke* (1854). *The History of the Life and Death of the Good Knight Sir Thomas Thumb* (1855). *The Lances of Lynwood* (1855). *The Railroad Children* (1855). *Ben Sylvester's Word* (1856). *The Daisy Chain* (1856). *Harriet and her Sister* (1856?). *Leonard the Lionheart* (1856). *Dynevor Terrace* (1857). *The Instructive Picture Book* (1857). *The Christmas Mummers* (1858). *Friarswood Post Office* (1860). *Hopes and Fears* (1860). *The Mice at Play* (1860). *The Strayed Falcon* (1860). *Pigeon Pie* (1860). *The Stokesley Secret* (1861). *The Young Stepmother* (1861). *Biographies of Good Women*, 2 sers. (1862-5). *The Chosen People* (1862). *Countess Kate* (1862). *Sea Spleenwort and Other Stories* (1862). *A History of Christian Names* (1863). *The Apple of Discord* (1864). *A Book of Golden Deeds of All Times and All Lands* (1864). *Historical Dramas* (1864). *Readings from Standard Authors* (1864). *The Trial* (1864). *The Wars of Wapsburgh* (1864). *The Clever Woman of the Family* (1865). *The Dove in the Eagle's Nest* (1866). *The Prince and the Page* (1866). *The Danvers Papers* (1867). *A Shilling's Book of Golden Deeds* (1867). *The Six Cushions* (1867). *Cameos from English History*, 9 vols. (1868-99). *The Chaplet of Pearls* (1868). *Historical Selections* (1868-1870). *New Ground* (1868). *The Pupils of St. John the Divine* (1868). *A Book of Worthies* (1869). *Keynotes of the First Lessons for Every Day in the Year* (1869). *The Seal* (1869). *The Caged Lion* (1870). *A Storehouse of Stories*, 2 sers. (1870-1872). *Little Lucy's Wonderful Glove* (1871). *Musings over the Christian Year and Lyra Innocentium* (1871). *A Parallel History of France and England* (1871). *Pioneers and Founders* (1871). *Scripture Readings for Schools* (1871-1879). *A History of France* (1872). *In Memoriam Bishop Patterson* (1872). *P's and Q's* (1872). *Questions on the Prayer-book* (1872). *Aunt Charlotte's Stories of English History for the Little Ones* (1873). *Life of John Coleridge Paterson* (1873). *The Pillars of the House* (1873). *Aunt Charlotte's Stories of French History for the Little Ones* (1874). *Lady Hester* (1874). *Questions on the Collects* (1874). *Questions on the Epistles* (1874). *Questions on the Gospels* (1874). *Aunt Charlotte's Stories of Bible History for the Little Ones* (1875). *My Young Alcides* (1875). *Aunt Charlotte's Stories of Greek History for the Little Ones* (1875). *Eighteen Centuries of Beginnings of Church History* (1876). *The Three Brides* (1876). *Aunt Charlotte's Stories of German History for the Little Ones* (1877). *Aunt Charlotte's Stories of Roman History for the Little Ones* (1877). *The Disturbing Element* (1878). *A History of France* (1878). *The Story of the Christians and Moors of Spain* (1878). *Burnt Out* (1879). *Magnum Bonum* (1879). *Short English Grammar for Use in Schools* (1879). *Byewords* (1880). *Love and Life* (1880). *Nelly and Margaret* (1880?). *Verses on the Gospel for Sundays and Holy Days* (1880). *Aunt Charlotte's Evenings at*

Home with the Poets (1881). *Cheap Jack* (1881). *Frank's Debt* (1881). *How to Teach the New Testament* (1881). *Lads and Lasses of Langley* (1881). *Practical Work in Sunday Schools* (1881). *Questions on the Psalms* (1881). *Wolf* (1881). *Given to Hospitality* (1882). *Historical Ballads* (1882). *Langley Little Ones* (1882). *Pickle and his Page Boy* (1882). *Sowing and Sewing* (1882). *Talks about the Laws We Live Under* (1882). *Unknown to History* (1882). *Aunt Charlotte's Stories of American History* (1883). *English Church History* (1883). *Landmarks of Recent History 1770-1883* (1883). *Langley Adventures* (1883). *The Miz Maze*, with F. Awdry, M. Bramston, C.R. Coleridge, F.M. Peard et al. (1883). *Shakespeare's Plays for School* (1883). *Stray Pearls* (1883). *The Armourer's 'Prentices* (1884). *The Daisy Chain Birthday Book* (1885). *Higher Reading-book for Schools, Colleges and General Use* (1885). *Nuttie's Father* (1885). *Pixie Lawn* (1885). *The Two Sides of the Shield* (1885). *Astray*, with M. Bramston, C. Coleridge and E. Stuart (1886). *Chantry House* (1886). *Just One Tale More*, with Others (1886). *The Little Rick-burners* (1886). *A Modern Telemachus* (1886). *Teachings on the Catechism* (1886). *Victorian Half-century* (1886). *Under the Storm* (1887). *What Books to Lend and What to Give* (1887). *Womankind* (1887). *Beechcroft at Rochstone* (1887). *Conversations on the Prayer Book* (1888). *Deacon's Book of Dates* (1888). *Hannah More* (1888). *Nurse's Memories* (1888). *Our New Mistress* (1888). *Preparation of Prayer-book Lessons* (1888). *The Cunning Woman's Grandson* (1889). *Neighbor's Fare* (1889). *The Parent's Power* (1889). *A Reputed Changeling* (1889). *Life of HRH the Prince Consort* (1890). *More Bywords* (1890). *The Slaves of Sabinns* (1890). *The Constable's Tower* (1891). *Old Times at Otterbourne* (1891). *Seven Heroines of Christendom* (1891). *Simple Stories Relating to English History* (1891). *Twelve Stories from Early English History* (1891).

Twenty Stories and Biographies from 1066 to 1485 (1891). *Two Penniless Princesses* (1891). *Westminster Historical Reading Books* (1891-1892). *The Cross Roads* (1892). *The Hanoverian Period* (1892). *The Stuart Period* (1892). *That Stick* (1892). *The Tudor Period* (1892). *Chimes for the Mothers* (1893). *The Girl's Little Book* (1893). *Grisly Grisell* (1893). *The Strolling Players*, with C. Coleridge (1893). *The Treasure in the Marches* (1893). *The Cook and the Captive* (1894). *The Rubies of St. Lo* (1894). *The Story of Easter* (1894). *The Carbonels* (1895). *The Long Vacation* (1895). *The Release* (1896). *The Wardship of Steepcombe* (1896). *The Pilgrimage of the Ben Beriah* (1897). *Founded on Paper* (1898). *John Keble's Parishes* (1898). *The Patriots of Palestine* (1898). *Scenes with Kenneth* (1899). *The Herd Boy and His Hermit* (1900). *The Making of a Missionary* (1900). *Modern Broods* (1900). *Reasons Why I Am a Catholic, and Not a Roman Catholic* (1901).

BIBLIOGRAPHY: Avery, G. *Nineteenth-Century Children* (1965). Battiscombe, G. *Charlotte Mary Yonge: The Story of an Uneventful Life* (1943). Battiscombe, G., and M. Laski, eds. *A Chaplet for Charlotte Mary Yonge* (1965). Brownell, D. *The Worlds of Victorian Fiction*, ed. J. Buckley (1975). Colby, V. *Yesterday's Woman: Domestic Realism in the English Novel* (1974). Coleridge, C.R. *Charlotte Mary Yonge: Her Life and Letters* (1903). Mare, M., and A.C. Percival. *Victorian Best-Seller: The World of Charlotte M. Yonge* (1947). Romanes, E. *Charlotte Mary Yonge: An Appreciation* (1908). Showalter, E. *A Literature of Their Own* (1977). Tillotson, K. *Mid-Victorian Studies* (1965).

Other references: *Durham University Journal* (March 1973, December 1900). *Etudes Anglaises* (1980). *Mary Wollstonecraft Journal* (May 1974). *Scrutiny* (Summer 1944).

Patricia A. O'Hara

CONTRIBUTORS AND THEIR ENTRIES

Timothy Dow
Adams

Ruth Fainlight

Lynn Alexander

Jane Austen
Anne Brontë
Charlotte Brontë
Emily Brontë
Maria Edgeworth
George Eliot
Elizabeth Gaskell
Frances Trollope

Katherine Allison

Maureen Duffy
Florida Scott-Maxwell

Victoria Arana

Esther Johnson
Naomi Mitchison
Queen Victoria
Anne Wickham

L. R. N. Ashley

Charlotte Brooke
Charlotte Charke
Agatha Christie
Clemence Dane
Daphne DuMaurier
Pamela H. Johnson
Ngaio Marsh
Nancy Mitford
Elizabeth Taylor

Jane Augustine

Annie Bryher
Mina Loy
Charlotte Mew
Anne Stevenson

Brett Averitt

Penelope Mortimer

Dean R. Baldwin

Sylvia Townsend-
Warner

Carol L. Barash

Vera Brittain
Eliza Haywood
Olive Schreiner
May Sinclair

Kate Begnal

Ivy Compton-Burnett
Christina Stead

Kathleen Collins
Beyer

Eliza Fay

Sophia Blaydes

Robert Bonner

Philip Bordinat

Jan Calloway

Kitti Eastman
Carriker

Miriam Cheikin

Carol Colatrella

Mary Comfort

Paula Connolly

Joan Cooper

Nancy Cotton

Joanne Creighton

Margaret Cruik-
shank

Mary R. Davidson

Marcia Davis

Dolores DeLuise

Sarah Churchill
Anne Murray Halkett
Frances Freke Norton
Mary Boyle Rich
Dorothy O. Temple
Alice Thornton

Sarah Trimmer

Mary Berry
Elizabeth Burnet
Hannah Cowley
Susanna Hopton
Henrietta H. Howard

Storm Jameson
Muriel Spark

Stella Benson

Monica Dickens

Jean Rhys

Jean Adam
Mary Delaney
Hannah Glasse
Mary W. Montagu
Hester Piozzi

Georgette Heyer

Phyllis Bentley
Maisie Ward

Aphra Behn
Elizabeth Cary
Susanna Centlivre
Mary Pix

Margaret Drabble

Barbara Bodichon

Caryl Churchill
Pam Gems

Dorothy Leigh

Adelaide Kemble

Judith Kohl	Mary Bateson Christine Brooke-Rose Frieda Lawrence May McKisack	Elsie Michie	Mathilde Blind Vernon Lee Somerville & Ross
Gail Kraidman	Grace Aguilar Amy Levy Margaret Oliphant	Catherine Milsum	Vita Sackville-West
		JoAnna S. Mink	Barbara Hardy
Eleanor Langstaff	Lucy Lane Clifford Alicia Cockburn Mary V. Cowden- Clarke Mary K. Harrison Geraldine Jewsbury Maria Jane Jewsbury Julia Kavanagh Ann & Jane Taylor Angela Thirkell	Paul Nelsen	Shelegh Delaney Nell Dunn Ann Jellicoe
		Laura Niesen de Abruña	Maud Bodkin Una Ellis-Fermor Helen Gardner
		Patricia O'Hara	Elizabeth B. Browning Mary Cholmondeley Mary Lavin Charlotte Yonge
Ellen Laun	Margaret Forster Ruth Prawer Jhabvala	Alice Lorraine Painter	Antonia Fraser P. D. James Marghanita Laski Ruth Rendell
John E. Lavin, Jr.	Eva Gore-Booth		
Pamela Lloyd	Jane West	Louis J. Parascandola	Anne Beresford Mary E. Coleridge Radclyffe Hall Molly Holden
Marie E. McAllister	Margaret Calderwood Anna Maria Falcon- bridge Elizabeth Percy (Duchess of Northum- berland) Janet Schaw	Susan Pavloska	Laetitia Pilkington
		Mickey Pearlman	Rumer Godden Margery Sharp Jan Struther Honor Tracy
Margaret McFadden	Harriet Taylor Mill Frances Wright		
Loralee MacPike	Isabella Beeton Emily Eden Stella Gibbons	Jean Pearson	Christina Rossetti Anna Sewell Mary Webb
Susan Garland Mann and David D. Mann	Grace N. Gethin	Mary Ferguson Pharr	Hannah More Anna Seward
Carol A. Martin	Mary B. Howitt	Marjorie Podolsky	Molly Keane
Cynthia Merrill	Catherine Gore	Richard Poss	Elizabeth of York Helen Waddell
Kate Beaird Meyers	Susanna Blamire Phyllis Bottome Nancy Cunard Elinor Glyn Anne Killigrew Bathsua Makin Kate O'Brien Mary Robinson Katherine Tynan	Anne Prescott	Mary Astell
		Zelda Provenzano	Barbara Cartland Anne Fanshawe Pamela Frankau Caroline Glyn Jane Porter
Karen Michalson	Charlotte Guest	Carol Pulham	Sarah Grand Emma Tennant

Alan Rauch	Jane Carlyle Beatrix Potter Anne T. Ritchie	*Gale Sigal*	Amelia A. B. Edwards Octavia Hill Liza Lynn Linton Mary Somerville
Anne-Marie Ray	Emmaline Pankhurst Mary Shelley Mary Wollstonecraft	*Anne B. Simpson* *Michael Skakun*	Margaret Tennant Brigid Brophy Lucie Duff-Gordon
Jill Rubenstein	Louisa Stuart Ann Yearsley		Q. D. Leavis Amelia E. Opie Hester Lucy Stanhope
Phyllis Scherle	Isabella Banks Anna Bray Rosa Carey Frances Cobbe Jessie Fothergill Anna Hall Margaret Hungerford	*Marilynn J. Smith*	A. L. Barker Taylor Caldwell Kate Greenaway Caroline Lamb Mary Lamb Edith Sitwell Enid Starkie
Paul Schlueter	Beryl Bainbridge Sybille Bedford Anne Cluysenaar Elaine Feinstein Elizabeth Goudge Winifred Holtby Elizabeth Jennings Jennifer Johnston Sheila Kaye-Smith Margaret Kennedy Doris Lessing Olivia Manning Iris Murdoch Kathleen Nott Ruth Pitter Kathleen Raine Gillian Tindall Barbara Ward Antonia White	*Charlotte Spivack* *Robert Spoo* *Frances Teague* *John Timpane*	Vera Chapman Edith Nesbit Mary Stewart Rose Macauley Anne Cooke Bacon Anne Clifford Elizabeth M. Colville Elizabeth Grymeston Elizabeth Joceline Grace Mildmay Elizabeth Craven Anne Finch Edna O'Brien Anne Radcliffe Fay Weldon
Barbara Schnorrenberg	Elizabeth Bonhote	*Betty Travitsky*	Anne Askew Elizabeth Clinton Joanna (Jane) Lumley Catherine Parr Mary Stuart
Carole Shaffer-Koros	Ada Ellen Bayle Annie French Hector Mary Renault Charlotte Riddell Henrietta Stannard	*Linda Troost* *Rita Verbrugge* *Elizabeth Wahl*	Mary Chandler Hester Chapone Margaret More Roper Jane Barker
Robin Sheets	Angela Carter Catherine Crowe Emily Davies Sarah Ellis Felicia Hemens Anna Jameson Anne Marsh Florence Nightingale	*Glenda Wall* *Robyn Warhol*	Jane Auger Lady Augusta Gregory Katherine Mansfield Constance Garnett Violet Hunt Susanna Rowson Virginia Woolf

Jane Weiss	*Nina Bawden*	*Sharon Winn*	*Ann R. Coleman*
	Lynne Reid Banks		*Jane Lead*
			Mary Leapor
Suzanne Westfall	*Enid Bagnold*		*Caroline Nairne*
	Mrs. Patrick Campbell	*Hilary Witzeman*	*Flora Annie Steel*
	Ellen Terry		
		Carolyn Woodward	*Sarah Fielding*
Katharina M.	*Katherine of Sutton*		*Elizabeth Montagu*
Wilson	*Margery Kempe*		*Sarah Scott*
	Julian of Norwich		*Frances Sheridan*
	Marie de France		*Elizabeth Vesey*

INDEX

This index is necessarily selective. Names of persons and subjects merely mentioned briefly in passing are excluded, except that all references to authors who are the subjects of entries (names and page numbers for which are given in **bold face**) are included. Pseudonyms and variant names used for publication (e.g., titles, birth names, significant marriage names) are followed by *See* and the name for the main entry. We have excluded "Anonymous" from this index, though such by-lines as "Author of . . ." are included since they clearly refer to a single writer and in some cases were used for a number of publications by such a writer.

Excluded from this index, therefore, are names and other information found in headnotes; titles or names of authors given in works or bibliographies; titles of works given in the entries, whether by the subject author or others; names of publishers, theaters, and newspapers and other publications; cities, towns, and estates or other homes; countries or regions; abbeys, cathedrals, or churches; schools, colleges, and universites; kings and queens except for those individuals who were also authors and who are therefore subjects of entries; and literary characters.

One point immediately clear is that no single pattern of usage of names can be used for main entries. In some cases (e.g., George Eliot), authors are entered according to the name by which they are usually catalogued, even if these are pseudonyms; in others, an author's given or married name is used for the main entry, with a possibly more familiar pseudonym (e.g., Josephine Tey, Mrs. Humphry Ward) given as an alternate. But since all such variations are to be found in this index, it is easy to determine if any particular author is the subject of an entry. Indeed, a quick glance at the index will turn up curious, quaint, and intriguing names (e.g., Aunt Belinda, Exploralibus, Galesia, The Great Enchantress, Justicia, Lactilla, The Mad Nun of Lebanon, The Matchless Orinda, An Old Acquaintance of the Public, Perdita, The Queen of the Arabs, The Swan of Lichfield) attributed to some authors that might lead a curious reader to look further among the entries.

Specific topics about which various authors have written are cross-referenced with related topics; thus, for example, a reader looking up "slavery" will be directed to "*See also* abolitionism," and vice versa. Pertinent categories (such as professions) in which a number of authors are represented (actresses, for instance, or journalists) are indexed as well. Consequently, a reader can here also ascertain at a glance those writers falling within such categories.

Major literary genres and other inclusive categories are subdivided, so all references to epistolary novels, for example, will be found under "fiction, epistolary," and most references to women and/or feminism are found under "women," again cross-referenced as needed.